The Bristol and Gloucestershire Archaeological Society
Gloucestershire Record Series

Hon. General Editor
C. R. Elrington, M.A., F.S.A., F.R.Hist.S.

Volume 22

Summary Convictions at Petty Sessions
1781–1837

CALENDAR
OF SUMMARY CONVICTIONS
AT PETTY SESSIONS
1781–1837

Edited by Irene Wyatt

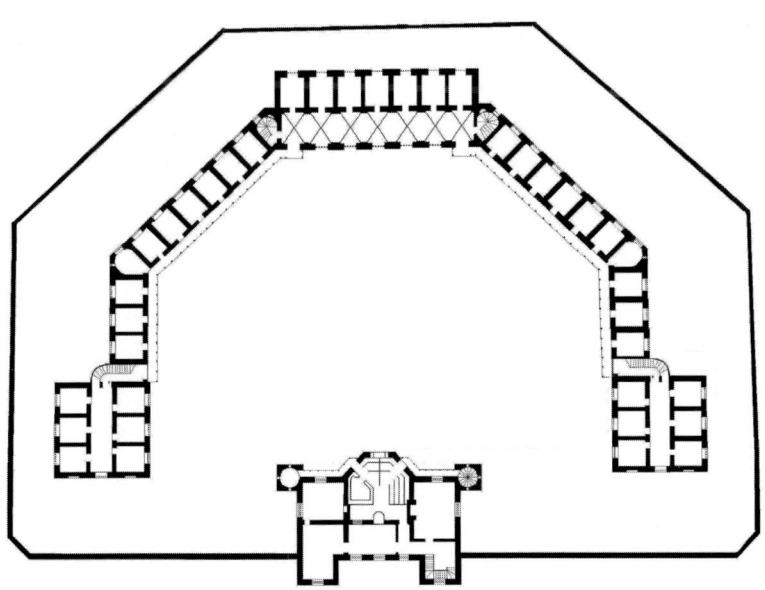

The Bristol and Gloucestershire Archaeological Society

2008

The Bristol and Gloucestershire Archaeological Society
Gloucestershire Record Series

© The Bristol and Gloucestershire Archaeological Society, 2008

ISBN 978 0 900197 71 0

British Library Cataloguing in Publication Data
A catalogue entry for this book is available from the British Library

Printed in Great Britain by 4word Ltd., Bristol

CONTENTS

The illustration on the title-page is of the ground-plan of Northleach house of correction. It is redrawn, by permission, from Gloucestershire Archives, Q/A5.

LIST OF ABBREVIATIONS

D.C.P.	Deputy Clerk of the Peace
JP	Justice of the Peace
Q.S.	Quarter Sessions

GLOSSARY

abb yarn:	the yarn for the woof or weft of a web
etherings:	the bindings for a fence or hedge
forrel:	edging of cloth
higgler:	a huckster or itinerant dealer
kibble:	a large hooked piece of timber
lees dropper	perhaps a muck-spreader or a piece of equipment used in brewing
sharps:	the finer husks and the coarser flour of wheat
shuting:	woollen yarn
sloper:	a maker or seller of loose outer clothing
thrum:	an end or piece of waste thread

ACKNOWLEDGEMENTS

The documents calendared below are among the records of Quarter Sessions in Gloucestershire Archives. Gloucestershire County Council is thanked for permission to publish them and to include the illustration on the title-page and the jacket.

I am very grateful, first, to David J. H. Smith, former County Archivist, who initiated this project and among other things offered useful comments on the Introduction; to Christopher Elrington for his patience and forbearance during my recent domestic problems and for expanding what I had written for the Introduction; and to Brian Frith, whose wealth of knowledge was always available. I owe many thanks also to the staff past and present of Gloucestershire Archives (formerly the Gloucestershire Record Office) who have helped me over the many years which it has taken me to complete this project, particularly Paul Evans, Averil Kear, Victoria Thorpe, Shirley Williams and the late, much lamented Kate Haslem. My daughter Susan and my son Robert have encouraged and supported me in many ways, practical and otherwise. My gratitude to them is unending.

October 2007   Irene Wyatt

TABLE I: PETTY SESSIONS DIVISIONS, FROM 1828

BERKELEY: Upper Berkeley hundred, excluding Arlingham and Ashleworth*.

BIBURY: Brightwells Barrow hundred.

BISLEY or STROUD: Bisley hundred and part of Rapsgate hundred (Brimpsfield and sometimes Cranham).

CHELTENHAM: Cheltenham hundred and parts of the hundreds of Cleeve (sometimes Bishop's Cleeve and Gotherington), Deerhurst (Boddington, Staverton, Uckington, and sometimes Elmstone Hardwicke and Leigh), Dudstone and King's Barton (Badgeworth, Brockworth, Shurdington and Great Witcombe), Rapsgate (Coberley, Cowley, and sometimes Cranham).

CIRENCESTER: Crowthorne and Minety hundred, and sometimes part of Rapsgate hundred (Rendcomb).

FORD or WINCHCOMBE: Lower Kiftsgate hundred (except Dumbleton).

FOREST: Bledisloe, St. Briavels and Westbury hundreds, and Longhope and Huntley in Duchy of Lancaster hundred.

GLOUCESTER: Gloucester city and Dudstone and King's Barton hundred, including Ashleworth* but excluding Badgeworth, Brockworth, Shurdington and Great Witcombe.

GRUMBALDS ASH: Upper and Lower Grumbalds Ash hundred, Pucklechurch hundred, and Marshfield; possibly also Doynton.

KIFTSGATE: Upper Kiftsgate hundred, upper divisions of Tewkesbury and Westminster hundreds, part of upper division of Deerhurst hundred, viz. Preston on Stour, Welford.

LAWFORDS GATE (called variously Barton Regis district, Bristol division and part of Berkeley division), Barton Regis hundred and parishes north and east of Bristol, including Cold Ashton, Bitton, Bristol St. George, Bristol St. James (and St. Paul), Bristol St. Philip and St. Jacob, Clifton, Filton, Frampton Cotterell, Henbury, Horfield, Mangotsfield, Redwick and Northwick, Stapleton, Stoke Gifford, Westbury on Trym and Winterbourne.

LONGTREE: Longtree hundred (which Moir gives as two divisions, Horsley and Tetbury).

NEWENT or BOTLOE: Botloe hundred, and Bulley and Tibberton in Duchy of Lancaster hundred.

NORTHLEACH: Bradley hundred and part of Rapsgate hundred, viz. Chedworth and sometimes Rendcomb]

STOW: Upper and Lower Slaughter hundred.

TEWKESBURY: Tewkesbury and Tibblestone hundreds, part of Deerhurst hundred (Deerhurst and sometimes Elmstone Hardwicke and Leigh) and of Lower Kiftsgate hundred (Dumbleton), and sometimes part of Cleeve hundred.

THORNBURY: Lower Thornbury hundred, Lower Langley and Swinehead hundred excluding Frampton Cotterell and Winterbourne, and part of Henbury hundred (Aust).

WHITSTONE or WHITMINSTER: Whitstone hundred, including Arlingham.

* No conviction for an offence committed in Ashleworth later than 1813 is recorded, but in the early 19th century Ashleworth, a detached part of Berkeley hundred, was in the Gloucester division.

INTRODUCTION

SUMMARY JURISDICTION ADMINISTERED BY JUSTICES OF THE PEACE

By the late 18th century the local magistracy had a long tradition of administering justice. In 1361 a statute had given to justices of the peace, as the local magistates were by then called, the power to try people charged with minor offences. The Crown appointed for each county, and for some boroughs, a group of magistrates chosen from among the principal landowners and leading inhabitants; they were unpaid and subject to the control, lightly exercised, of the court of King's Bench.[1] In the 16th century the powers of the justices of the peace had been greatly extended, and from 1590 the justices met regularly four times a year at quarter sessions to conduct a wide range of business. Between quarter sessions minor offences were tried summarily by a single justice or by two or more, holding what were called petty sessions. Such petty sessions are known to have been held in Gloucestershire in the 17th century but no records of them earlier than the 18th century have been found. Before 1788 a single justice frequently presided, but thereafter proceedings became more formal and petty sessions were usually held by two or more justices.[2] They could convict offenders and punish them, usually with a fine or with a term of imprisonment in the local house of correction, and those who could not or would not pay a fine were sent to the house of correction. The petty sessions were held in various places, at the home of one of the justices, at an inn, at an attorney's office, at the local house of correction or at a sessions house or room provided for the purpose.

DIVISION OF THE COUNTY

The cities of Bristol and Gloucester had each its own quarter sessions: the records edited below relate to Bristol only in so far as parts of some Bristol parishes were in the county of Gloucester, and most of the hundred of Dudstone and King's Barton was in the Gloucester division and subject to the Gloucester quarter sessions. The records include, however, a few notes of convictions by Gloucester JPs, for what reason is not clear. Tewkesbury borough also had its own quarter sessions: the only offence recorded below as committed in Tewkesbury may have been committed outside the borough.[3] There are also notes of a few convictions by JPs sitting outside the county, in Herefordshire and Worcestershire, for offences committed in Gloucestershire or by Gloucestershire residents.[4]

For petty sessions the magistrates were grouped in geographical divisions of the county. An order in council of 1605 had assigned JPs to divisions within the county. The four early divisions of Gloucestershire, Berkeley, the Forest of Dean, Kiftsgate and the Seven Hundreds of Cirencester, came to be found too unwieldy and were subdivided. In the late 18th century Gloucestershire contained more than twenty divisions, the boundaries of which were based on those of the ancient hundreds but appear not to have been firmly fixed. Under an Act of 1828[5] the JPs in quarter sessions revised the arrangement, reducing the number of divisions of Gloucestershire to eighteen.[6] The new divisions remained based

---

[1] See, e.g., Douglas Hay, 'Dread of the Crown: the English magistracy and the King's Bench, 1740–1800,' in *Law, Crime and Society, 1660–1830*, ed. Norma Landau (2002), 19–45.

[2] Cf. I. E. Gray and A. T. Gaydon, *Gloucestershire Quarter Sessions Archives* (1958), 70–1.

[3] Below, no. 54/C/16.

[4] Below, nos. 41/D/27–8; 42/D/14; 45/C/18–19; 48/B/50; 52/A/75; 53/B/195–196; 53/D/159; 55/A/2; 55/B/1; 55/C/41; 56/A/73–5 (Herefs.); 37/C/8; 48/B/2; 52/D/85; 54/A/146; 54/C/17; 56/A/1 (Worcs.).

[5] Division of Counties Act, 9 Geo. IV, c. 43.

[6] E. Moir, *Local Government in Glos. 1775–1800* (1969), 116, where the number of divisions is given as 19; the list on p. 118 (n. 53) includes both Horsley and Tetbury divisions, which together appear to be the division called Longtree in the records of convictions calendared here.

TABLE II: NUMBER OF CERTIFICATES RETURNED BY YEAR AND TERM

Year	Ref.	Epiphany	Easter	Trinity	Michaelmas	Total for year
1782	1	12	20	16	18	66
1783	2	19	36	19	18	92
1784	3	12	21	27	16	76
1785	4	30	23	18	16	87
1786	5	10	34	16	12	72
1787	6	26	9	13	14	62
1788	7	13	24	32	13	82
1789	8	20	7	19	16	62
1790	9	15	14	8	11	48
1791	10	8	10	11	25	54
1792	11	15	21	14	14	64
1793	12	26	23	5	11	65
1794	13	24	16	8	14	62
1795	14	5	3	7	1	16
1796	15	7	14	7	3	31
1797	16	1	20	3	1	25
1798	17	6	5	5	6	22
1799	18	15	1	4	8	28
1800	19	11	7	1	3	22
1801	20	10	12	3	11	36
1802	21	7	11	2	9	29
1803	22	21	9	1	2	33
1804	23	2	6	6	4	18
1805	24	18	8	6	4	36
1806	25	7	8	6	3	24
1807	26	5	2	4	5	16
1808	27	8	12	3	11	34
1809	28	13	1	7	6	27
1810	29	20	11	9	16	56
1811	30	17	23	15	9	64
1812	31	15	19	8	9	51
1813	32	165	5	21	6	197
1814	33	32	22	1	3	58
1815	34	9	14	16	37	76
1816	35	38	75	50	15	178
1817	36	6	4	72	15	97
1818	37	10	7	8	18	43
1819	38	20	23	5	18	66
1820	39	12	77	7	13	109
1821	40	17	14	50	(missing)	(81)
1822	41	13	11	10	28	62
1823	42	55	44	19	15	133
1824	43	30	19	8	8	65
1825	44	18	8	16	15	57
1826	45	19	13	27	38	97
1827	46	27	25	24	43	119
1828	47	37	29	28	65	159
1829	48	72	57	61	99	289
1830	49	80	56	86	46	268
1831	50	88	63	59	111	321
1832	51	96	103	75	107	381
1833	52	88	80	84	86	338
1834	53	132	205	137	159	633
1835	54	297	51	95	84	527
1836	55	93	104	45	120	362
1837	56	78	37	62	108	285

largely on the hundreds, and the records calendared below often refer to petty sessions being held, or to JPs acting, for a hundred rather than for a division or district.[1]

An undated list of divisions, probably from before 1781, has 24 divisions, in which those called Fairford and Sodbury evidently represented Bibury and Grumbalds Ash divisions respectively, those called Campden and Moreton in Marsh were later combined as Kiftsgate division, those called Dursley and Wotton were joined to Berkeley division, and those called Coleford, Lydney, and Newnham were merged in an enlarged Forest division.

The boundaries of the divisions seem to have remained uncertain and subject to alteration: in Cleeve and Deerhurst hundreds, for example, offences committed in Bishop's Cleeve, Elmstone Hardwicke and Leigh were heard usually by the magistrates for Cheltenham division at Cheltenham but occasionally by the magistrates for Tewkesbury division, while in Rapsgate hundred offences committed in Rendcomb were heard variously by the magistrates for Cirencester and for Northleach divisions.

THE RECORDS OF CONVICTIONS AT PETTY SESSIONS

By the 17th century it was the practice for the clerk of each petty sessional division to send notes of convictions, term by term, to the Clerk of the Peace of the county, and two consolidating Acts of 1827 required a JP to send a return of any conviction which he made for an offence under the Acts to the next quarter sessions. The returns survive in two groups of files now held in the Gloucestershire Archives among the records of Quarter Sessions. The first group (Q/PC 1) comprises 15 files for the years 1728–81, classified according to the nature of the offence. The second group (Q/PC 2), the documents which are calendared below, are for the years 1781–1837. A third group, for the period from 1837–8 to 1889, was destroyed.

The group of returns for 1781–1837 consists of 223 files, each inscribed for the law term of the quarter sessions to which the returns were made. The four terms were called after the Christian festivals preceding the opening of the term, Michaelmas (29 Sept.), Epiphany (6 Jan.) and the movable feasts Easter and Trinity. Thus the returns made at each sessions relate to convictions made mainly in the previous three or four months, thus

file for Epiphany: convictions made mainly October to December
          Easter: January to March or April
          Trinity: March or April to June
          Michaelmas: June to September

The files for each year have been given a serial number, and within each year the files for each term are distinguished by letters, thus

Epiphany   A   Trinity   C
Easter   B   Michaelmas   D

One file, for Michaelmas 1821, is missing; it would have been 40/D. Within each file the documents have been numbered consecutively and while they are in no particular order there is often a rough grouping by petty sessional division and sometimes convictions for a particular type of offence within a division come together.

The number of returns in each file varies widely, from as few as one to as many as 297, as shown in Table II. There are several reasons or possible reasons for the variation. The files may be far from complete, either through the failure of magistrates or their clerks to

---

[1] The records name as divisions Berkeley, Bibury, Bisley, Bristol, Cheltenham, Cirencester, Ford, Forest, Kiftsgate, Longtree and Thornbury, and as districts Grumbalds Ash, Slaughter (i.e. Stow), Tewkesbury and Whitstone. They do not name Gloucester, Newent or Northleach as either divisions or districts.

submit certificates or through the loss of certificates after they had been submitted. In the early years of the period, when offences in the Forest of Dean form a very high proportion of the total, there are no returns from the north-east of the county: the Kiftsgate division is not represented until 1784, the Stow division until 1785, and the Tewkesbury division until 1787. One whole file, for Michaelmas term 1821, is completely missing, and some convictions recorded as being for a second or subsequent offence are not matched by a record of an earlier offence. The number of convictions in some files, notably those for Epiphany 1813 (32/A) and Epiphany 1835 (54/A), is unusually high because of the many minor offences relating to weights and measures. The general increase over the whole period reflects the rapid rise in population, and from the later 1820s legislation gave new responsibilities to the magistrates in petty sessions and created new offences, as discussed below, at a time when the crime-rate was rising, the years of the Swing Riots.

With the exception of returns of convictions for defective weights and measures (which are mentioned below) and a very few other convictions,[1] each case was recorded on a separate piece of parchment. In each file the pieces are tied by a cord strung through a hole made in the top left-hand corner. The documents vary in size and shape, ranging from approximately 5 inches by 3 (13 × 8 cm) to 27 inches by 35 (69 × 89 cm). The larger ones usually contained details of poaching offences, frequently with verbatim evidence giving a vivid picture of the event.

The returns are signed by the magistrates concerned[2] and sealed with a small seal. The earlier returns are entirely hand-written, with variation in the wording of common form, but with the returns for Epiphany 1812 printed forms (which are also on parchment) began to be used. Before 1812 convictions for using defective weights and measures were recorded on long sheets of parchment,[3] but with the introduction of printed forms such convictions were usually noted each on a separate form. At first the use of printed forms was confined to a few divisions but it gradually spread, as shown in Table III (below, pages xiv–xv). Eventually by 1830 more than half of the convictions were recorded on printed forms. The earliest forms were printed by Coles & Galpin, stationers at 21 Fleet Street, London; others were produced by Shaw & Son, law publishers, of Fetter Lane, off Fleet Street, London. Later some were printed locally, at Tetbury, Tewkesbury and Stroud. Many bore no printer's name. Towards the end of the period printed forms became more specific to the nature of the offence being recorded. Those for poaching had 'Game' printed in the bottom left-hand corner. Forms for breaches of alehouse licences and for using defective weights or measures were similarly specified. Sometimes forms were adapted by crossing out words relevant to another offence and substituting others more appropriate. It may be noted the neither the Northleach division (for which there are relatively few returns) nor the Newent or Botloe division made any returns on printed forms.

Some files include certificates of convictions made well before the term to which the file relates,[4] either because they were returned significantly late or because they were wrongly filed. A few certificates are of convictions made after the beginning of the term in which they were returned to quarter sessions, suggesting that there was a gap between the end of the term and the convictions being submitted.

The essential information in the notes of convictions is the date of the hearing, the offender's name, the nature of the offence and the name or names of the magistrate or magistrates. Most of the records also give the offender's place of residence, but the numerous notes of convictions for assault often give only the offender's name. Over the period covered

---

[1] e.g. below, nos. 8/D/11–12.

[2] In a few instances where there was more than one magistrate one of them did not sign.

[3] The convictions below at nos. 16/B/1–18 are an exception.

[4] The index of subjects s.v. 'late return' gives references to them.

by the records, the information tends to become fuller, with the offender's occupation in addition to place of residence, the place where the offence was committed and that where the hearing was held, the names, occupations and places of residence of victims, complainants and witnesses, the penalty imposed and the date when the offence was committed. Some records of convictions for offences against the game laws rehearse the evidence presented.

A few notes are not directly of convictions but are notes of fines transmitted or of recognizances related to the convictions or to cases going to quarter sessions. The file for Michaelmas 1782 contains depositions apparently unrelated to convictions; those depositions are not included in the edition below.

OFFENDERS, OFFENCES, MAGISTRATES AND PENALTIES

A detailed analysis of the offences, the men and women who committed them, the magistrates who convicted them, the penalties imposed, and the variations over time and between different parts of the county is beyond the scope of this introduction. A few comments must suffice.

Offenders

The occupations given for many of those convicted show them to have come from a wide social and economic range. As is to be expected, the convictions from the Forest of Dean, which form a high proportion in the earlier years of the period, are often of men concerned with the mining of coal and iron.[1] Similarly the woollen industry of the Stroud valley and the area of Wotton under Edge is reflected in the large number of clothworkers convicted of petty pilfering and possessing stolen goods. The magistrates' concern with weights and measures resulted in the very large numbers of shopkeepers and other retailers among those convicted. Convictions of members of the gentry and the professional classes are largely for trespassing in pursuit of game or for taking game without a licence.

Offences

A wide range of offences is recorded, and an attempt to classify them has been made in the selective index of subjects. A large proportion fall into one of a few main groups: assault, petty theft and damage to property, selling or possessing stolen goods, using defective weights and measures, breaching the conditions of a licence to sell alcoholic drinks, selling such drinks without a licence, taking game illegally (poaching, trespass) and swearing and cursing. Less numerous but nevertheless frequent offences are obstructing or endangering highways, evading turnpike tolls, ill-treating animals, drunkenness and disorderly behaviour, causing dependents to become chargeable to the poor-rate, illegal monetary transactions, vagrancy and lurking with felonious intent.

Assault is much the most frequently recorded offence, though with the exception of three cases of assault on collectors of turnpike tolls[2] no convictions for assault were made at petty sessions until the passing of the Offences against the Person Act, 1828.[3] The Act empowered two JPs acting together to impose a fine and costs for common assault of not more than £5, to be paid to an officer of the parish or place where the assault was committed, and to imprison an offender for up to two months for non-payment. The notes of convictions for assault are usually uninformative, seldom giving details of the occupation or place of residence of either the assailant or the victim or the circumstances of the assault.

---

[1] It may be noted that many of the numerous offenders described as of St. Briavels are probably of the hundred rather than the parish of St. Briavels, as suggested by 31/D/3 and 5.

[2] Below, nos. 27/A/5; 39/C/7; 47/B/24. In no. 46/D/32 the conviction was not for assault but of a constable for failing to arrest the assailants.

[3] Offence against the Person Act, 1828, 9 Geo. IV, c. 31, s. 25.

TABLE III: CONVICTIONS RETURNED

32/A/1–126	Stroud	49/C/5–10	Forest
151–2	Forest	28–37	Lawfords Gate
34/D/2–32	Stroud	38–65	Stroud
35/B/1–67	Kiftsgate	69–72	Kiftsgate
35/C/6–12, 48–9	Stroud	74–83	Cheltenham
36/C/57–64	Stroud	49/D/3, 5	Kiftsgate
36/D/10–11, 15	Stroud	9–15	Cheltenham
37/D/8	Stroud	16–20	Forest
39/A/6	Stroud	21–4, 42–5	Lawfords Gate
39/B/3–71	Stroud	50/A/1–6	Forest
40/C/2–42	Forest	13–17	Lawfords Gate
41/D/27–8	Herefs.	35–6, 42–8	Cheltenham
42/A/2–31	Stroud	55	Kiftsgate
42/B/11–34	Stroud	56–65, 67–83, 88	Stroud
42/C/8	Stroud	50/B/3–5, 9–13	Lawfords Gate
42/D/14	Herefs.	14–15, 17–27	Cheltenham
43/A/15	Lawfords Gate	38–46, 48–51	Stroud
43/B/8–13	Lawfords Gate	55	Kiftsgate
43/C/3–7	Lawfords Gate	50/C/7, 40–52	Cheltenham
44/B/6	Lawfords Gate	8–14, 31–8, 57–9	Stroud
45/C/5–11, 13–17	Stroud	15–30	Lawfords Gate
45/D/26–9	Stroud	53	Kiftsgate
31–3	Lawfords Gate	50/D/19–30, 35–43	Stroud
46/A/13–15	Stroud	55, 57–8	Tewkesbury
19	Lawfords Gate	64–75, 91–106	Cheltenham
46/B/3, 9–17	Lawfords Gate	76–7, 79–86	Lawfords Gate
4–5	Stroud	107–8	Kiftsgate
22	Kiftsgate	51/A/10	Forest
46/C/1–3	Stroud	21–34, 36–9	Cheltenham
7, 15, 19–21	Lawfords Gate	55–63, 65–7	Lawfords Gate
46/D/6	Lawfords Gate	70–80, 85–8	Stroud
16–28	Stroud	51/B/1–3	Kiftsgate
47/A/16–17	Lawfords Gate	14–55	Stroud
47/B/5–8	Lawfords Gate	59–62, 65–6, 69	Lawfords Gate
10–15	Stroud	71	Tewkesbury
47/C/17–19	Lawfords Gate	74–5, 77–83, 85–91, 94–8	Cheltenham
47/D/11–33	Lawfords Gate	51/C/8, 50–69	Cheltenham
34–42	Stroud	9, 20–4	Lawfords Gate
64–5	Kiftsgate	10–14	Forest
48/A/19–26, 72	Stroud	27–30	Kiftsgate
39–50	Lawfords Gate	40	Tewkesbury
48/B/25–6	Kiftsgate	41–8	Stroud
37–9, 41, 43–6	Stroud	51/D/4–5, 8, 64–75, 77–92,	Cheltenham
48/C/17–30, 32–3, 36–8	Stroud	94–106	
48/D/28, 67–85	Stroud	13–19, 21–8	Lawfords Gate
36–7	Cheltenham	33	Tewkesbury
65–6	Kiftsgate	38–48, 51–7	Stroud
49/A/22–3	Kiftsgate	58–63	Kiftsgate
30	Cheltenham	52/A/1, 4–6	Kiftsgate
59–67, 69, 71–80	Stroud	13–16, 20–2, 31	Forest
49/B/1–5	Kiftsgate	35, 37–61	Cheltenham
6–28	Lawfords Gate	62–3, 68, 74	Lawfords Gate
33–8, 40–6	Stroud	52/A/64–7	Stroud
49/B/49–52	Cheltenham	75	Herefs.

USING STANDARD PRINTED FORMS

52/A/76	Tewkesbury
79–82	Stow
52/B/4–6, 8–21, 23–4, 26–8, 50–1, 53, 56–68	Cheltenham
29–35	Kiftsgate
37–47	Stroud
48–9	Tewkesbury
52/C/1–27	Lawfords Gate
28–9, 56–82	Cheltenham
30–9	Forest
41–6	Kiftsgate
47–51	Stroud
53–5	Tewkesbury
52/D/1–12	Stroud
21–31	Lawfords Gate
81	Grumbalds Ash
41–2, 85	Tewkesbury
46–62, 64–72	Cheltenham
73–9	Kiftsgate
53/A/17–19, 21–4, 26–7	Forest
32–45	Berkeley
48–53	Kiftsgate
56–60, 62–4, 69, 76–7	Stroud
79–85, 88, 90–101, 103–5, 107, 109–15	Cheltenham
127, 130–1	Tewkesbury
53/B/15–130	Stroud
137–41	Tewkesbury
142–8, 154–64, 166–85	Cheltenham
186–90, 192–4	Kiftsgate
195–6	Herefs.
53/C/1, 26–44, 46–67	Lawfords Gate
8–15	Forest
73–7, 79–99	Cheltenham
103, 105–11	Kiftsgate
113–17, 119–22, 126–32	Stroud
53/D/2, 15–17, 20–4, 34–51, 66–9, 71–9	Stroud
10–14, 83–90, 92–100, 102–3, 105–13	Cheltenham
80–2	Kiftsgate
114–56	Lawfords Gate
54/A/1, 3–26	Berkeley
33–52, 54–6,	Lawfords Gate
62–4	Forest
69–137	Thornbury
146	Worcs.
154–5	Kiftsgate
150–3	Tewkesbury
157–63, 165–8, 170–5	Stroud
176–247	Berkeley
248–64, 266–73	Cheltenham
54/B/1	Kiftsgate
10–11, 14–20, 22–6	Stroud
54/B/12	Tewkesbury
27–43	Cheltenham
54/C/1–15	Lawfords Gate
17	Worcs.
20–52	Thornbury
53–6	Forest
58–9	Tewkesbury
64–6, 68–70, 72–3	Stroud
77–85, 87–91	Cheltenham
54/D/1–3	Kiftsgate
15–34	Lawfords Gate
36–8, 42, 44–57	Cheltenham
40–1	Tewkesbury
63–4, 67–72, 76	Stroud
55/A/2	Herefs.
3–25, 27–32	Lawfords Gate
33–4, 36–8, 41	Stroud
66–77	Cheltenham
84	Stow
86	Tewkesbury
55/B/23–6, 28–31, 33–4	Stroud
38–41, 43–8, 51–9	Lawfords Gate
66–86	Cheltenham
87–93	Bibury
55/C/17	Tewkesbury
18, 21, 24–6	Stroud
27–38	Cheltenham
39–40	Kiftsgate
41	Herefs.
55/D/3, 5–10, 12–28	Cheltenham
29–39	Kiftsgate
40–63, 65–76	Stroud
112–14	Tewkesbury
56/A/1	Tewkesbury
6	Grumbalds Ash
9–21, 23–6, 28	Stroud
29–31	Kiftsgate
36–55	Cheltenham
59–61	Tewkesbury
56/B/1–14	Cheltenham
15–17	Forest
22	Tewkesbury
23–8, 31–4	Stroud
35–7	Kiftsgate
56/C/1–8	Forest
15–23, 25–8	Stroud
29–39	Cheltenham
43	Tewkesbury
56/D/1–20, 99–104	Cheltenham
22–6	Forest
41–5	Tewkesbury
50–61	Kiftsgate
62–70, 72–85, 89–90, 95–7	Stroud

Some of the assaults are described as violent, but since in law an assault necessarily involved violence the description was redundant. A relatively small number of the assaults were recorded as being with battery or beating, and in a very few instances the nature of the assault (indecent, throwing stones and soil, with a bill-hook, whip or sword, with kicking, with riding on horseback over the victim) is specified. Some of the convictions were for assaulting officials in the execution of their duty; assault on a peace officer was punishable with imprisonment for up to two years, but in all such cases calendared below the penalty in the first instance was a fine, often the maximum of £5 but sometimes relatively small ones. In the index of subjects an attempt has been made to classify the assaults by the gender and number of the assailants and their victims, but the records do not make it clear whether separate convictions relate to separate incidents. Many of the assaults recorded were in Cheltenham, with a high number also in the suburbs of Bristol. Some people, for example Henry Holland and Thomas Wasley, were frequent victims: it is not clear whether they invited attack, perhaps through their behaviour or as easy targets or in the hope of compensation, or were simply unfortunate.

The numerous convictions of shopkeepers and other retailers for possessing defective weights and measures begin in 1797 following an Act of 1795.[1] The Act required that all weights and measures should be marked and sealed by inspectors, and it is likely that many of those that were found not to conform to the standard were defective only in being unmarked or unsealed. Bread was sold either as 'assized bread' by price (penny loaves, twopenny loaves etc.), the price varying according to the price of corn, or as 'prized bread' by weight (quartern, half-peck and peck loaves), the price varying similarly. Only one method could be used at any time in a district. The magistrates decided which it was to be,[2] and fined those who used the wrong method.[3]

Innkeepers and alehouse-keepers were fined for allowing drinking outside permitted hours, drunkenness, illegal games, fighting and quarrelling, meetings of persons of bad character and drinking on Sundays during the hours of church services.

Before the passing of the Game Act, 1831,[4] convictions under the game laws, both the numerous ones for taking game illegally and the small number for selling hares, partridges and pheasants without a licence, can be difficult to assess.[5] Tudor statutes against taking game were still in force, and in the fifty-six years from 1760 no fewer than thirty-three Acts relating to poaching were passed, mostly tightening the law and increasing penalties.[6] Acts of 1770 and 1773 prescribed penalties for taking game at night or on a Sunday.[7] Poachers, using guns, dogs, ferrets, nets or snares, or a combination of more than one means, might be offending either by trespassing or by taking game when not qualified by rank and income[8] or by paying for a licence. The Assessed Taxes Act, 1808, consolidated by a further Act of 1812,[9] imposed a range of taxes on the relatively wealthy, requiring them to pay for certificates or licences for taking game, so that those who heard cases of taking

---

[1] 35 Geo. III, c. 102.

[2] G. Hutcheson, *Treatise on the Offices of Justice of the Peace* etc. (1809), ii. 126–7.

[3] Below, nos. 21/D/8, 33/B/6, 35/B/1, 32, 37, 39, 45, 49, 36/C/51, 65–7.

[4] 1 & 2 Wm. IV, c. 32, which repealed 27 earlier statutes.

[5] Cf. R. Burn, *Justice of the Peace and Parish Officer* (1797 edn.), ii. 359, s.v. Game: 'The statutes relating to this title are very numerous and the sense sometimes a little precarious.'

[6] Charles Chenevix Trench, *The Poacher and the Squire* (1967), 124.

[7] Game Act, 1770, 10 Geo. III, c. 19; Game Act, 1773, 13 Geo. III, c. 80.

[8] Under various statutes only a person of the rank of esquire or higher and qualified by an income of £100 a year from freehold estates (or £150 from long leaseholds) was allowed to use a gun, dog, net etc. to take game: Burn, *Justice of the Peace* (1797 edn.), ii. 384.

[9] 48 Geo. III, c. 55; 52 Geo. III, c. 93.

game without a licence are often named as commissioners for assessed taxes instead of, or as well as, JPs. It is not always clear whether a conviction for killing game or trying to do so is for failing to have a game licence (or a qualification by rank) or for encroaching on the rights of the owner.[1] In some instances, however, an offender was convicted on two separate charges, one for pursuing game without having a game certificate, the other for killing game.[2] From 1831 convictions for trespassing in pursuit or search of game become frequent, perhaps reflecting the passing not only of the Game Act, 1831, but also of the Malicious Injuries to Property Act, 1827.[3]

Swearing and cursing were punishable under the Profane Oaths Act, 1746,[4] which prescribed a penalty of 1s. for labourers and common soldiers and sailors, of 2s. for others below the degree of gentleman and of 5s. for gentlemen and higher ranks. It is not clear whether there was a legal difference between cursing and swearing: presumably cursing was distinguished from swearing in that it was directed against other persons. In only two cases is a victim of cursing named and in each the offender was cursing his wife.[5] There seem to have been outbreaks of swearing, or of charges for swearing, notably from August to November 1788.[6] With a single exception in 1804[7] none of the convictions for swearing or cursing record the penalty imposed. It may be that it was assumed that there was a standard fine of 1s., but the occupation of the offender was not recorded in every instance. The Act of 1746 also ruled that it was to be read publicly after morning or evening prayers on the first Sunday after each quarter day in every church or public chapel, imposing a fine of £5 for failure by the minister to do so;[8] it may be noted that the solitary conviction for such failure[9] occurred in a period when convictions for swearing or cursing were relatively few.

Offences that endangered highways included driving carelessly and carrying too many passengers in a stage-coach. A stage-coach was licensed to carry a certain number of passengers inside and out, and the Stage Carriages Acts imposed fines on both the licensee and the driver for carrying more than the licensed number. It was also an offence to use on a highway a vehicle with wheels of a width thought to damage the road-surface. Besides the convictions for evading turnpike tolls there are several of tollgate keepers for charging excessive tolls: between 23 November 1811 and 4 January 1812 William Nicholls the keeper of the gate at Littleworth suffered 23 convictions for the offence, and if each offence incurred a fine of £5, as at least four did, he paid the large total of £115.[10]

Convictions for the ill-treatment of horses and other animals were evidently based on an Act of 1822, which prescribed fines of from 10s. to £5, with imprisonment for up to three months in default of payment.[11] A conviction in 1826 for what seems to have been bull-baiting[12] was presumably made under that Act, though bull-baiting was adjudged to be not within the Act[13] and was first made illegal by the Cruelty to Animals Act, 1835.[14]

When a man was convicted of leaving his wife or children, the offence was not so much

---

[1] The index of subjects, below, makes only a limited attempt at the distinction.
[2] e.g. below, nos. 21/A/5–6, 21/B/6–7, 22/B/6–7, 33/B/1–4.
[3] 7 & 8 Geo. IV, c. 30.
[4] 19 Geo. II, c. 21.
[5] Below, nos. 17/C/3, 23/C/4.
[6] Below, nos. 7/D/1–11, 8/A/1–11.
[7] Below, no. 23/C/3.
[8] 19 Geo. II, c. 21, s. 13.
[9] Below, no. 39/C/3.
[10] Below, nos. 31/A/6–10, 31/B/2–19.
[11] Cruel Treatment of Cattle Act, 3 Geo. IV, c. 71.
[12] Below, no. 45/D/30.
[13] Burn, *Justice of the Peace* (1837 edn.), i. 590 n.
[14] 5 & 6 Wm. IV, c. 59.

deserting those who should be his responsibility but rather making them chargeable to the parish. Several women were punished for making children so chargeable, in two instances the mothers of bastards.[1]

Most of the illegal monetary transactions resulting in convictions were the payment of wages in other than legal coinage. Others were charging more than the statutory interest on loans, issuing a 10*s.* note illegally and offering Bank of England tokens.

The Magistrates

The records calendared below record the names of 343 magistrates,[2] of whom nearly a quarter were clergymen. To some extent the magistracy seems to have been hereditary: the Horlock family provided five JPs for the Grumbalds Ash district, and the Hicks family eight, mostly for the Bisley division. Four JPs came from each of the families of Cave, Harford, Hayward and Somerset (three being dukes of Beaufort), and several other surnames were represented by two or three JPs, so that the total number of surnames shared by JPs in the records is only 245. Some JPs were concerned in very many convictions, Henry Burgh in about 815 over 35 years, Robert Bransby Cooper in 450 over 27 years. Thirteen others appear in the records more than a hundred times; at the other extreme 47 are named only once.

The time that elapsed between an offence being committed and the subsequent conviction varied widely. The interval could be less than a day[3] or as much as one or two years,[4] even excluding convictions for leaving wife and family chargeable to the parish, when the offender appeared at petty sessions only once he had returned home.

Penalties

The power of JPs to convict was given by Act of parliament.[5] In most instances the Act specified the penalty for an offence, usually a fine of a fixed amount or with a maximum and minimum. JPs could impose a term of imprisonment as an alternative if an offender could not or would not pay the fine. Where an Act made imprisonment the penalty it usually indicated a maximum length.

Most of the penalties imposed at petty sessions were in the first instance fines. Where an alternative of a period in a house of correction was added it was presumably because it was thought that the offender might be unable or unwilling to pay the fine. Fines could be as low as 2*d.* or 3*d.* or even ½*d.* but coupled with costs many times the amount of the fine.[6] Fines as high as £50 were relatively few. The largest was of £400, on a maltster for failing to notify the excise officer of his intention to make malt[7] and so, presumably to avoid payment of tax. An unusually large fine of £85 was laid on each of two men, a labourer and a tailor, for possession of 17 hares which each exposed for sale, £5 for each hare.[8]

Where the fines were variable, it is not known whether the variation reflected the severity of the offence or the ability of the offender to pay. There was no variation in fines for failure to serve in the militia: a surgeon, servants and labourers each paid £20,[9] though the

---

[1] Below, nos. 51/B/47, 52/C/48.

[2] Including two, John Eddy and Joseph Swayne, who are not described there as JP but as commissioner of assessed taxes. The total also includes five JPs for the Gloucester division.

[3] e.g. below, nos. 9/B/11, 18/D/4, 24/D/1, 47/D/38, 51/A/61

[4] e.g. below, nos. 21/B/4, 38/B/13.

[5] Burn, *Justice of the Peace* (1837 edn.), i. 859.

[6] e.g. below, nos. 48/D/77 and 79, 56/A/16.

[7] Below, no. 35/C/50.

[8] Below, nos. 35/C/48–9.

[9] Below, nos. 27/A/2, 27/B/2–6.

fine prescribed by the Militia Act, 1803, was only £10.[1] Occasionally the magistrates mitigated a fine, though no explanation was recorded; often the fine was reduced to half, but occasionally the fine was reduced much further.[2] A sudden rise in the fine for selling ale, beer or cider without licence is evident in the summer of 1797; whereas the usual fine had previously been £2 for a first offence (£4 for the second, £6 for the third) it rose to £10 for a first offence, the offenders being employed in woollen manufacture.[3] The Sale of Beer Act, 1795, had in fact raised the penalty to £20 but gave JPs the power of mitigating it to £10 for a first offence.[4]

Offenders had usually to pay their fines immediately, but the records show that the magistrates often allowed time for payment, the time usually between a day and four weeks but sometimes even longer.[5] Where two or more people were jointly charged, and the fine, costs and damages imposed were not said to be payable by each offender, it may be that they were to be paid jointly, but it is more likely that they were to be paid by each.

The fines were normally payable to the overseers of the poor, or other officers, of the parish in which the offence was committed, but they were sometimes directed to a charitable institution such as the Stroud dispensary or the Gloucester infirmary or to the county treasurer. For some offences the fine or a proportion of it was payable to the Crown. The magistrates sometimes awarded damages to the complainants, and often awarded costs which went to the constable attending the court or to the complainant.

A sentence to a term in a house of correction imposed at petty sessions, whether as an alternative to a fine or as the only penalty, could be as short as a week[6] or as long as six months.[7] Where it was alternative to a fine, the length of the term in the house of correction was in general, but by no means precisely, proportionate to the amount of the fine. From 1828 the magistrates frequently stipulated that poachers, having served a term in the house of correction, should find sureties against re-offending or serve a further, longer term. The county's old houses of correction were replaced in the 1780s, on the initiative of Sir George Onesiphorus Paul, by four new ones[8] to serve areas corresponding roughly to the four earlier petty sessional divisions: that at Northleach, designed as a prototype to hold 37 prisoners, served the divisions of Bibury, Cheltenham, Cirencester, Ford, Kiftsgate, Northleach, Stow and Tewkesbury, that at Horsley, for 46 prisoners, served the divisions of Berkeley, Grumbalds Ash, Longtree, Stroud and Whitstone, that at Littledean, for 24 prisoners, served the Forest and Newent divisions, and that at Lawfords Gate, for 32 prisoners, served the Lawfords Gate and Thornbury divisions. There are isolated instances of offenders being sent to the house of correction at Gloucester from divisions as far distant as Kiftsgate and Lawfords Gate, but the Gloucester house was largely for offenders from the Gloucester division. There are seven instances of offenders from the

[1] 42 Geo. III, c. 90, s. 45. It may be that the offenders were fined doubly, once for failing to serve and again for failing to find a substitute.

[2] In a group of convictions for cutting down trees in the Forest of Dean fines of £20 were reduced to sums between £5 and £1 11s. 6d.: below, nos. 18/D/1–6. It is surprising that the fines of poachers who refused to attend were mitigated: below, 39/A/3–5.

[3] Below, nos. 16/C/1, 17/A/2–4 and later.

[4] 35 Geo. III, c. 113, ss. 1, 14; cf. below, no. 16/D/1.

[5] e.g. below, nos. 50/D/1, 52/A/18, 53/D/65.

[6] A sentence of one day and two sentences of three days in Lawfords Gate house of correction, as an alternative to a small fine and costs (below, nos. 50/A/16, 51/A/58, 55/A/21), were exceptional, as were those of three days and a whipping, mentioned below.

[7] Two sentences of twelve months are recorded, one, at 39/C/4, as an alternative to a fine of £20 for cutting down 100 young trees, the other, at 51/C/16, for a second offence.

[8] J. R. S. Whiting, *A House of Correction* (1979), 19–20.

Longtree division sentenced to hard labour where the record has Horsley house of correction deleted and Littledean substituted, presumably because the Horsley house was full.[1] In one case Gloucestershire JPs sentenced an offender from Warwickshire, should he fail to pay his fine for trespassing in Shenington, which lay detached from the county between Oxfordshire and Warwickshire, to the house of correction at Warwick;[2] in two others men from Kemerton and Ashchurch, on the boundary with Worcestershire, were convicted for assaults in those parishes and sentenced at Pershore to a fine or a month in the Worcester house of correction.[3]

For certain specified offences the justices could sentence an offender who did not pay the fine imposed not merely to a period in the house of correction but to hard labour there. The first such sentence recorded in the documents below was in June 1790,[4] and offenders were frequently sentenced to hard labour from 1809.[5] In eight cases offenders convicted of theft or receiving were sentenced to be whipped, the usual punishment for those found to be rogues and vagabonds:[6] in three of those eight the whipping, with three days in the house of correction, was an alternative to a fine,[7] and in another three it was for refusing or being unable to pay the fine imposed.[8] Offenders were also committed to imprisonment to await trial at quarter sessions.

HISTORICAL VALUE OF THE RECORDS

The notes of convictions clearly provide useful evidence for social and economic history, as touched on above in the discussion of the occupations of offenders, the nature of their offences and the composition and activity of the magistrates. They also provide miscellaneous information on topography and genealogy, among a variety of topics. While the occupations mentioned in the records are mostly typical of the economy of the part of the county concerned, a few are unexpected, such as that of clock-maker in Avening,[9] and the large numbers of shopkeepers and other retailers in rural parishes is evidence of the economic activity and social structure in the villages. The cordwainer of Painswick convicted, twice, of publishing and distributing a printed book not bearing the printer's name and address[10] may have been either diversifying (to use a modern term) or pursuing political ends of a radical nature. It is to be hoped that the material which this edition offers will prove a rich seam to be worked by others.

A point of perhaps minor interest is the range of forenames in use at the time. Unusual classical names that occur include, for example, Xenophon, borne perhaps characteristically by a schoolmaster. Old Testament names, besides those brought into common use in the modern period and long remaining widespread, such as Daniel, Hannah, Joseph and Sarah, range alphabetically from Aaron to Zebulon. They include names now largely restricted to Jewish people and surprising choices like Nebuchadnezzar and, in three separate families,

---

[1] Below, nos. 50/D/39–41; 51/D/41, 54 and 55; 53/C/128. Only in the last of the seven was the sentence of imprisonment an alternative to the payment of a fine. Two Painswick labourers together sentenced each to two months' hard labour were to go one to Horsley and the other to Littledean house of correction: below, no. 49/A/63.

[2] Below, no. 52/A/6.

[3] Below, nos. 54/C/17, 56/A/1.

[4] Below, no. 9/C/1.

[5] Below, no. 28/C/3 and later.

[6] G. Hutcheson, *Treatise on the Offices of Justice of the Peace* etc. (1809), ii. 81–2.

[7] Below, nos. 15/C/4 and 7, 21/C/1.

[8] Below, nos. 3/A/4, 9/C/1, 39/B/1. The other two cases are nos. 5/B/13, 49/A/27.

[9] Below, no. 10/B/6.

[10] Below, nos. 45/D/11–12.

Shadrach, Meshach and Abednego. Also noticeable is an increase over the period covered by the records in the number of people with two forenames among those of apparently low social status.

EDITORIAL METHOD

From each of the original returns the calendar extracts the reference number of the document, the name or names of the offender or offenders, with occupation or status and place of residence if the record includes them, the offence committed, the names of the justices and, if the record includes them, the place of the hearing, the names of complainants and witnesses and any significant information about their evidence, the penalty imposed, and the date of the offence.

The form of words in the documents has been followed where appropriate, so that, for example, in the description of a person the edition has his occupation sometimes before and sometimes after his place of residence.

Words supplied editorially are in square brackets, with editorial comments in italic.

The spelling other than of personal names has been modernised. Where the MS. form of a place-name is significantly different from the modern form it is given in square brackets after the modern form. Where a document uses more than one spelling of a surname it is indicated either in round brackets or by a comment in square brackets.

The forenames of justices are abbreviated to initials except at the first occurrence, and minor variations in their surnames (e.g. in double-barrelled surnames the use of a hyphen) have been ignored.

The JPs described in the documents in various ways as members of the clergy are in the edition simply given the prefix 'Rev.', except that the prefix is omitted when a JP's name has the suffix 'D.D.'

Sums of money which are in pounds, shillings and pence or in pence alone are given with £ *s. d.* but those in shillings and pence or shillings alone are given with an oblique, e.g. 7/6, 10/-.

Where the date of conviction indicates that the return was made significantly late, the edition adds after the date '[*late return*]', but not when the return appears to belong to the term immediately before that of the file in which the return is included, as at 3/B/1 and 3 or 4/A/3 and 6–7. It is possible, as mentioned above, that convictions said to be 'late returns' were in fact not late but wrongly filed.

Many of the repetitive entries have been abbreviated .Where there is a long list of entries, as with convictions for defective weights and measures, a heading has been added.

The punctuation and the use of initial capitals has been standardised.

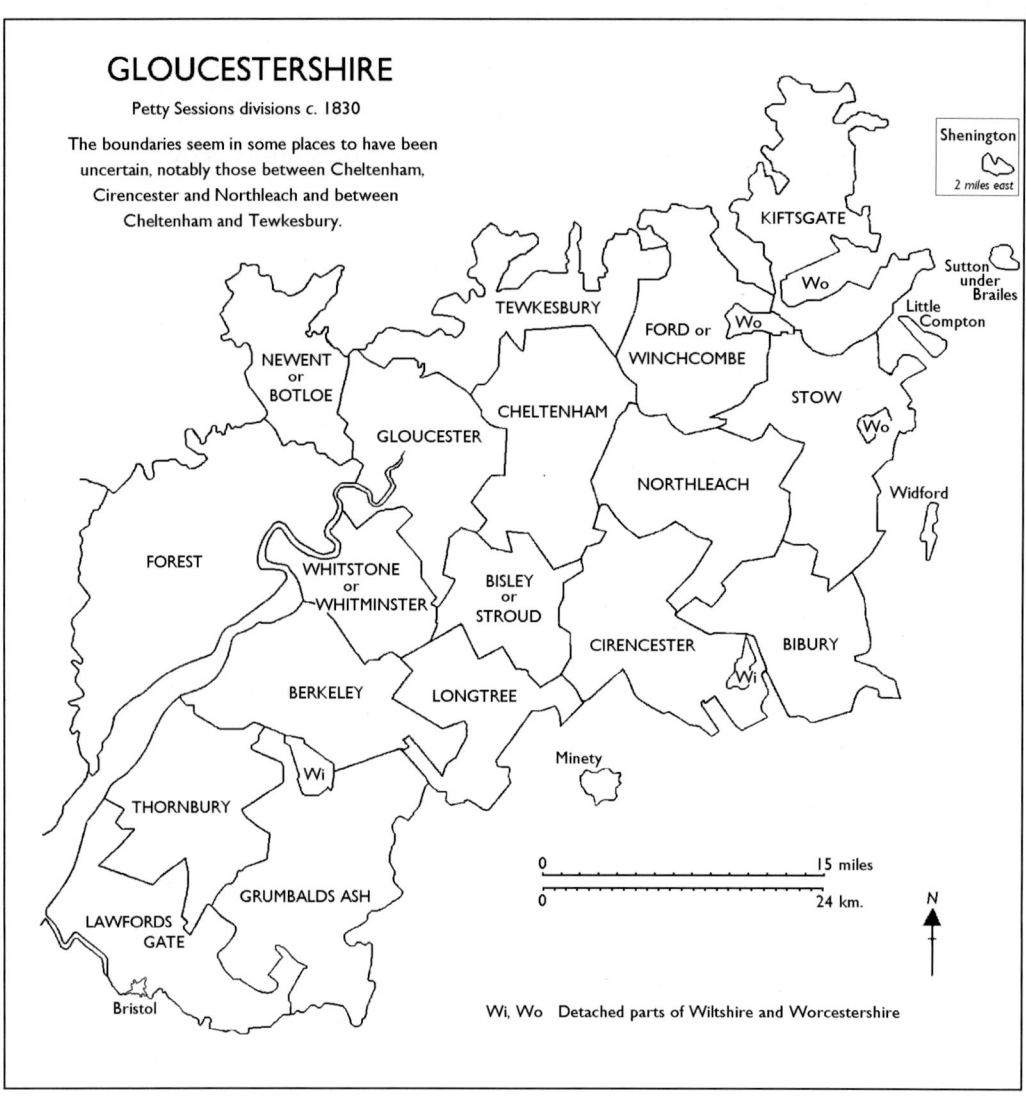

GLOUCESTERSHIRE

Petty Sessions divisions *c.* 1830

The boundaries seem in some places to have been
uncertain, notably those between Cheltenham,
Cirencester and Northleach and between
Cheltenham and Tewkesbury.

Shenington

2 *miles east*

KIFTSGATE

Wo

Sutton
under
Brailes

TEWKESBURY

FORD or
WINCHCOMBE

Wo

Little
Compton

NEWENT
or
BOTLOE

CHELTENHAM

STOW

Wo

GLOUCESTER

NORTHLEACH

Widford

FOREST

WHITSTONE
or
WHITMINSTER

BISLEY
or
STROUD

CIRENCESTER

BIBURY

Wi

BERKELEY

LONGTREE

Minety

Wi

THORNBURY

0 ——————————————— 15 miles
0 ——————————————— 24 km.

N

GRUMBALDS ASH

LAWFORDS
GATE

Bristol

Wi, Wo Detached parts of Wiltshire and Worcestershire

Division	Hundred(s) or area
Berkeley	Berkeley
Bibury	Brightwells Barrow
Bisley or Stroud	Bisley, Bradley (pt), Rapsgate (pt)
Cheltenham	Cheltenham
Cirencester	Crowthorne and Minety
Ford or Winchcombe	Lower Kiftsgate
Forest	Bledisloe, St. Briavels, Westbury, Duchy of Lancaster (pt)
Gloucester	Dudstone and King's Barton
Grumbalds Ash	Upper & Lower Grumbalds Ash
Kiftsgate	Upper Kiftsgate

Division	Hundred(s) or area
Lawfords Gate	parishes north and east of Bristol
Longtree	Longtree
Newent or Botloe	Botloe, Duchy of Lancaster (pt)
Northleach	Bradley (pt), Rapsgate (pt)
Stow	Upper and Lower Slaughter
Tewkesbury	Tewkesbury, Tibblestone, Deerhurst (pt), Cleeve (pt)
Thornbury	Lower Thornbury, Lower Langley & Swinehead (pt)
Whitstone or Whitminster	Whitstone (and Arlingham parish)

For more detail see above, p. viii.

CALENDAR OF
SUMMARY CONVICTIONS AT PETTY SESSIONS
Gloucestershire Archives, Q/PC 2

1/A/1 13 Oct. 1781. William Wilkins of Westbury [on Severn], labourer. Swearing. Samuel Hayward JP.

1/A/2 27 Nov. 1781. John Bowley *alias* Goodman the younger of Down Ampney, labourer. Setting a snare. William Sanford JP. Fine £5 levied by distress. Robert Golding, labourer, witness.

1/A/3 30 Nov. 1781. Thomas May of Horton, baker. Killing game (hares) at Little Sodbury. George Hardwicke JP. Fine £10. First offence. Samuel Arthurs, gamekeeper, witness.

1/A/4 6 Dec. 1781. Thomas Russell the younger of Alveston. Killing game (hares) at Little Sodbury. G. Hardwicke JP. Fine £10. First offence. Samuel Arthurs, gamekeeper, witness.

1/A/5 2 Nov. 1781. Edward Hall of Horton and Richard Limbrick of Charfield. Killing game (hares) at Little Sodbury. G. Hardwicke JP and Isaac Webb Horlock JP. Fine £10 each. First offence. Samuel Arthurs, gamekeeper, and his son Charles, witnesses.

1/A/6 27 Nov. 1781. William Clapton of Latton, Wilts., shepherd (to Lawrence Burgess, yeoman, of Down Ampney). Taking a hare and a snare at Down Ampney. William Sanford JP. Fine £5 by distress. Robert Golding, labourer, witness.

1/A/7 12 Dec. 1781. David Jones of Bream, servant (to William Cook, husbandman). Taking an oak tree (for timber) from the Forest of Dean. S. Hayward JP. Thomas Stephens, forest keeper, complainant.

1/A/8 8 Nov. 1781. Thomas Smith of Weston [under Penyard], Herefs., carpenter. Taking a beech (for timber) from the Forest of Dean. S. Hayward JP. Thomas Blunt, deputy surveyor of the Forest of Dean, complainant.

1/A/9 17 Nov. 1781. Samuel Baker of St. Briavels hundred, collier. Taking a tree (for timber) from the Forest of Dean. S. Hayward JP. Edward Bevan, forest keeper, complainant.

1/A/10 29 Dec. 1781. Thomas Hatton of Ruardean, coalminer. Cutting and taking part of an oak tree from the Forest of Dean. S. Hayward JP. Richard Bradley, forest keeper, complainant.

1/A/11 22 Dec. 1781. James Edwards of Awre, husbandman. Taking an oak tree from the Forest of Dean. S. Hayward JP. William Moiles of Mitcheldean, labourer, complainant.

1/A/12 29 Dec. 1781. William Harris of Ruardean, wood-collier, and James Yearsley, son of Stephen Yearsley of Ruardean, yeoman. Taking an oak tree from the Forest of Dean. S. Hayward JP. Miles Hartland of Mitcheldean, yeoman, complainant.

1/B/1 16 Feb. 1782. William Haviland of Winstone. Avoiding tolls on 100 sheep at Birdlip by taking them across field owned by John Holtham. S. Hayward JP. Samuel Cowley of Wotton, victualler, informant. William Barrow, toll-collector, witness. Fine 40/-. Offence committed 19 Jan. 1782.

1/B/2 18 Feb. 1782. Alice Greenwood, widow. Selling ale without a licence in St. James parish, Bristol. Rowles Scudamore JP. Fine 40/- and 5/- expenses. First offence.

1/B/3 7 Feb. 1782. John Brown, chaise driver. Selling ale without a licence at Clifton. R. Scudamore JP. Fine 40/- and 5/- expenses. First offence.

1

1/B/4   9 March 1782. Christopher Denning of Cromhall. Possessing three crabtree stocks without satisfactory explanation. Peter Hawker JP. Thomas Morgan, steward to Lord Ducie, complainant.

1/B/5   22 Feb. 1782. William Dobbs of Sandhurst, blacksmith. Swearing and cursing at Longford St. Catherines. S. Hayward JP.

1/B/6   19 Jan. 1782. Thomas Mountjoy of Littledean, coalminer. Swearing. S. Hayward JP.

1/B/7   9 Feb. 1782. William Dobson of Weston [under Penyard], Herefs., husbandman. Taking an oak timber tree from the Forest of Dean. S. Hayward JP. John Ennis of the Lea Bailiwick, labourer, complainant.

1/B/8   19 Feb. 1782. Samuel Morse, collier, and James Hughes, collier, both of St. Briavels hundred. Cutting down and taking oak timber in the Forest of Dean. S. Hayward JP. John Hampton, forest keeper, complainant.

1/B/9   7 March 1782. Samuel Robins, coalminer, and Reece Jones, carpenter, both of St. Briavels hundred. Sawing up part of an oak timber tree which they were suspected of cutting down in the Forest of Dean. S. Hayward JP. John Jordan of Speech House Lodge, complainant.

1/B/10   9 Feb. 1782. John Bradley of Lea Bailey in the Forest of Dean, labourer. Cutting down several young oaks and store oak trees in the Forest of Dean. S. Hayward JP. John Ennis of the Lea Bailiwick, labourer, complainant.

1/B/11   9 March 1782. Thomas Meridith, coalminer, and John Steel, coalminer, both of St. Briavels hundred. Cleaving, spoiling or defacing a kibble or a large piece or part of an oak timber tree in the Forest of Dean. S. Hayward JP. John Jordan of Speech House Lodge, complainant.

1/B/12   9 Feb. 1782. John Prichard of Weston [under Penyard], labourer. Cutting down an oak timber tree in the Forest of Dean. S. Hayward JP. John Ennis of the Lea Bailiwick, complainant.

1/B/13   19 Jan. 1782. John Winter of Lydney, yeoman. Taking a large oak timber tree from the Forest of Dean. S. Hayward JP and Thomas Crawley Boevey JP. Thomas Stephens, forest keeper, complainant.

1/B/14   9 Feb. 1782. Henry Howell, labourer, and James Fawkes, labourer, both of Newland. Cutting down and making into stakes an oak tree from the Forest of Dean. S. Hayward JP. William Harvey of St. Briavels hundred, yeoman, complainant.

1/B/15   19 Jan. 1782. Thomas Mountjoy of Littledean, coalminer. Cutting down a holly tree in the Forest of Dean. S. Hayward JP. John Bradley, forest keeper, complainant.

1/B/16   9 Feb. 1782. William Price of Weston [under Penyard], servant to George Morefield, wagoner, of Weston. Felling an oak timber tree in the Forest of Morgan. S. Hayward JP. John Ennis of the Lea Bailiwick, labourer, complainant.

1/B/17   19 Jan. 1782. James Bennett, son of James Bennett of St. Briavels hundred, labourer. Lopping a beech tree in the Forest of Dean. S. Hayward JP. Richard Bradley, forest keeper, complainant.

1/B/18   29 March 1782. James Tingle of St. Briavels hundred, collier. Cutting down and cleaving into kibbles part of an oak tree in the Forest of Dean. S. Hayward JP. William Warr, servant to Thomas Stephens, forest keeper, complainant.

1/B/19   19 Jan. 1782. James Bennett of Ruardean, coalminer. Cutting down a beech tree and lopping branches in the Forest of Dean. S. Hayward JP. Richard Bradley, forest keeper, complainant.

1/B/20   9 Feb. 1782. George Court of Coleford, husbandman. Hauling away an oak timber tree from the Forest of Dean. S. Hayward JP. Richard Jones of Coleford, timber-squarer, complainant.

1/C/1   22 May 1782. Philip Walker, labourer. Swearing. R. Scudamore JP.

1/C/2   23 April 1782. Mark Terratt of North Nibley, clothworker. Unlawful possession of 3 lb. of ends of woollen yarn. Henry Wyatt JP. William Moore Adey of Wotton under Edge, gentleman, witness.

1/C/3   29 June 1782. William Ridler, broadweaver, and John Coxe, broadweaver, both of Bisley. Plucking a quantity of plants from a garden. H. Wyatt JP and Thomas Gryffin JP. Thomas Mundin of Bisley, complainant.

1/C/4   20 April 1782. John Priest of Bream, coalminer. Cutting down an oak tree and carrying away a kibble of cleft oak timber from the Forest of Dean. S. Hayward JP. Thomas Stephens, forest keeper, complainant.

1/C/5   15 April 1782. William Williams of Mitcheldean, labourer. Cutting down and carrying away a young oak tree from the Forest of Dean. S. Hayward JP. Richard Bradley, forest keeper, complainant.

1/C/6   27 April 1782. Philip Hatton, collier, and Thomas Hales, collier, both of the hundred of St. Briavels. Cutting down an oak tree in the Forest of Dean. S. Hayward JP. Thomas Blunt, gentleman, deputy surveyor, Forest of Dean, informant. William Harvey, son of Thomas Harvey, forest keeper, witness.

1/C/7   8 May 1782. Samuel Baker of St. Briavels, coalminer. Cutting down an oak tree in the Forest of Dean. S. Hayward JP. Edward Bevan, forest keeper, complainant. Second offence. [*Cf.* 1/A/9.]

1/C/8   1 June 1782. James Trigg of Mitcheldean, collier. Carrying away cleft oak timber from the Forest of Dean. S. Hayward JP. John Brett, forest keeper, complainant.

1/C/9   20 April 1782. Philip James, servant to Richard James, of Bream, blacksmith. Cutting down and taking away an oak tree from the Forest of Dean. S. Hayward JP. Thomas Stephens, forest keeper, complainant.

1/C/10   20 April 1782. Robert Gwilliam of Elton, Westbury on Severn, labourer, and John Hooper, Robert Hooper and John Brain, of Littledean, labourers. Rooting up or cutting down large quantities of hazel wood and young oaks in the Forest of Dean. S. Hayward JP. John Brett, forest keeper, complainant.

1/C/11   10 April 1782. Samuel Tippings, servant to William James of Bream, coalminer. Carrying away timber from the Forest of Dean. S. Hayward JP. Thomas Stephens, forest keeper, complainant.

1/C/12   6 June 1782. Edward Knight of St. Briavels, coalminer. Cutting branches from an oak tree in the Forest of Dean. S. Hayward JP. Richard Bradley, forest keeper, complainant.

1/C/13   1 June 1782. John Cannock of Elton, Westbury on Severn, yeoman. Cutting and rooting up underwood from the Forest of Dean. S. Hayward JP. John Brett, forest keeper, complainant.

1/C/14   [*Duplicate of* 1/B/18.]

1/C/15   19 July 1782. Richard Burford of Nympsfield, broadweaver. Unlawful possession of young trees. Thomas Pettat JP. Daniel Parslow, woodward, informant. Thomas Daunt Esq. of Owlpen, complainant.

1/C/16   30 April 1782. William Perrott of North Nibley, clothworker. Unlawfully receiving large quantities of ends of woollen yarn from labourers in the woollen trade. H. Wyatt JP and R. Pettat JP. William Moore Adey, gentleman, of Wotton under Edge, complainant.

1/D/1   27 Sept. 1782. Hester Malpass of Berkeley, spinster. Stealing part of a pair of horse traces. William Holwell JP. George Martin of Berkeley, yeoman, informant. Entered into £40 recognizances to prefer charge at next Q.S.

1/D/2   5 Aug. 1782. Thomas Child of Thornbury, carpenter. Stealing various articles from a house. W. Holwell JP. William Cowley of Thornbury, cartwright, complainant. Includes recognizances of £40 each from above and Samuel Murston and Edward Smith, nailer, and his wife Peggy to give evidence.

1/D/3–7   3 Oct. 1782. [Examination of] Jane Stiles, 28, born in Redcliffe, Bristol, formerly servant, now pedlar. Accessory to theft of articles from house at Roel [*MS.* Rowell]. Reg. Wynniatt JP. Includes examinations of Adam Gleed of Roel, victim of theft, and Henry Wood, John Sadler, both of Guiting, and John Arkill, who apprehended accused.

1/D/8   25 July 1782. Alice Greenwood of St. James, Bristol, widow. Selling ale without a licence. R. Scudamore JP. Fine £4. Second offence. [*Cf.* 1/B/2.]

1/D/9   3 Aug. 1782. John Poulson of Woodchester, clothworker. Attempting to kill hares on Lord Ducie's land near Nympsfield. P. Hawker JP. Fine £10. First offence.

1/D/10   5 Aug. 1782. George French of Oldland, labourer. Selling ale without a licence. Henry Creswicke JP. Fine 40/-, 6/- expenses. First offence.

1/D/11   28 Sept. 1782. Thomas Phelps of Newent, husbandman. Swearing and cursing. S. Hayward JP. Offence committed 13 Sept. 1782.

1/D/12   17 Aug. 1782. — Probert, wife of Richard Probert of Newent, labourer. Stealing a quantity of peas from a field. S. Hayward JP. Property of Edward Hartland, husbandman.

1/D/13   14 Sept. 1782. Elizabeth Dowell of Hucclecote, single woman. Stealing ¼ peck of potatoes from a field at Barnwood. S. Hayward JP. Property of Samuel Bubb, husbandman.

1/D/14   [*Duplicate of* 1/D/12.]

1/D/15   6 Aug. 1782. Thomas Knight, son of Richard Knight of St. Briavels, coalminer. Cutting timber in the Forest of Dean. S. Hayward JP. Richard Bradley, forest keeper, complainant.

1/D/16   8 Oct. 1782. William Jenkins of Clearwell, shoemaker. Cutting down and taking away an oak tree from the Forest of Dean. S. Hayward JP. Miles Hartland of Mitcheldean, yeoman, complainant.

1/D/17   21 Sept. 1782. Anthony Roberts of St. Briavels, coalminer, and Richard James of Bream, coalminer. Cutting down and taking away an oak timber tree in the Forest of Dean. S. Hayward JP. Edward Bevan, servant to Robert East, forest keeper, complainant.

1/D/18   21 Sept. 1782. John Blanch, yeoman, and Richard Blanch, yeoman, both of St. Briavels. Cutting down and taking away an oak tree from the Forest of Dean. S. Hayward JP. Thomas Harvey, forest keeper, complainant.

2/A/1   29 Nov. 1782. Thomas Hibbard. Stealing four poles, the property of Edward Bradshaw of Lechlade. Thomas Bush JP. Recognizance by John Parker of Lechlade, yeoman, to appear to give evidence at next Q.S.

2/A/2   4 Nov. 1782. William Peare. Possessing a snare with intent to kill a hare on ground at Arlington, Bibury, belonging to Estcourt Cresswell, Esq. T. Bush JP. John Gough of Bibury, yeoman, witness. First offence. Fine £20.

2/A/3   23 Dec. 1782. John Loyd of Avening, labourer. Possessing a hare at Avening. Thomas Estcourt JP. Robert Emerson of Shipton Moyne, informant. Robert Rendal of Avening, yeoman, witness. Fine £5. Offence committed 4 Aug. 1782.

2/A/4   14 Dec. 1782. Thomas Nowell of Abenhall, journeyman papermaker. Rooting up young underwood and therewith fencing in a piece of land in the Forest of Dean. S. Hayward JP. John Brett, forest keeper, complainant.

2/A/5   14 Dec. 1782. Joseph Adey of Ruardean, collier. Stealing timber from the Forest of Dean. S. Hayward JP. Richard Bradley, forest keeper, complainant.

2/A/6   19 Oct. 1782. Peter James of Bream, coalminer. Cutting timber in the Forest of Dean. S. Hayward JP. Edward Bevan, servant to Robert East, forest keeper, complainant.

2/A/7   23 Oct. 1782. John Cullis of Newland, labourer. Cutting timber in the Forest of Dean. S. Hayward JP. Edward Bevan, servant to Robert East, forest keeper, complainant.

2/A/8   23 Oct. 1782. Thomas Price of St. Briavels, coalminer. Cutting timber in the Forest of Dean. S. Hayward JP. Edward Bevan, servant to Robert East, forest keeper, complainant.

2/A/9   26 Oct. 1782. William Howell, James Jones and Thomas Smith of Newland, labourers. Cutting timber in the Forest of Dean. S. Hayward JP and T. Crawley Boevey JP. Miles Hartland of Mitcheldean, yeoman, complainant.

2/A/10   2 Nov. 1782. Edward Meek of St. Briavels, collier. Stealing timber from the Forest of Dean. S. Hayward JP. John Brett, forest keeper, complainant.

2/A/11   15 Nov. 1782. James Walden of Littledean or Newland, coalminer. Cutting timber in the Forest of Dean. S. Hayward JP. William Stephens, forest keeper, complainant.

2/A/12   15 Nov. 1782. George Doward of St. Briavels, labourer. Cutting timber in the Forest of Dean. S. Hayward JP. Edward Bevan, servant to Robert East, forest keeper, complainant.

2/A/13   30 Nov. 1782. Richard Baker, son of Samuel Baker, of St. Briavels, coalminer. Stealing timber from the Forest of Dean. S. Hayward JP. Edward Bevan, servant to Robert East, forest keeper, complainant.

2/A/14   23 Nov. 1782. William Thomas of Bream, coalminer. Cutting timber in the Forest of Dean. S. Hayward JP. Robert East, forest keeper complainant.

2/A/15   30 Nov. 1782. Evan James of Bream or Newland, labourer. Cutting timber in the Forest of Dean. S. Hayward JP. William Merideth, servant to Robert East, forest keeper, complainant.

2/A/16   30 Nov. 1782. James Jones, collier and George Court, husbandman, both of St. Briavels. Stealing timber from the Forest of Dean. S. Hayward JP. Thomas Blunt, deputy forest surveyor, complainant.

2/A/17   11 Jan. 1783. Benjamin Trigg of St. Briavels, labourer. Cutting down a holly tree in the Forest of Dean. S. Hayward JP. Miles Hartland of Mitcheldean, yeoman, complainant. Offence committed 30 Jan. 1782.

2/A/18   11 Jan. 1783. Mary Merrick of Weston [under Penyard], single woman. Cutting down and stealing timber in the Forest of Dean. S. Hayward JP. Miles Hartland of Mitcheldean, yeoman, complainant.

2/A/19   11 Jan. 1783. James Trigg the younger, of Littledean, collier. Cutting timber in the Forest of Dean. S. Hayward JP. Thomas Wood, forest keeper, complainant.

2/B/1   28 March 1783. George Whitson of St. Briavels, labourer. Killing and stealing two fallow deer in park belonging to Thomas Bathurst Esq. of Lydney. S. Hayward JP and T. Pettat JP. Henry Stephens, gamekeeper to Thomas Bathurst, complainant.

2/B/2   8 Feb. 1783. Samuel Harrison of Horsley, labourer. Cutting down a maple tree in wood belonging to Thomas Jones, yeoman, of Kingscote. P. Hawker JP. Thomas Jones, yeoman, complainant.

2/B/3   18 April 1783. George Edwards of Wotton under Edge, serge-weaver. Buying and receiving stolen woollen abb yarn. H. Wyatt JP and T. Pettat JP

2/B/4   18 April 1783. Stephen Kinsey of Wotton under Edge, narrow weaver. Stealing woollen abb yarn from his employers. H. Wyatt JP and T. Pettat JP. Robert Harris & Co., clothiers, Wotton under Edge, complainants.

2/B/5   23 Jan. 1783. William Lawrence of Chedworth, labourer. Using a net to kill game at Bibury. Estcourt Cresswell JP. Johnson Embury of Bibury, cordwainer, witness. First offence. Fine £10. Offence committed 19 Jan. 1783.

2/B/6   25 Jan. 1783. George Wilson of Hampnett, labourer. Using a dog to kill game at Bibury. E. Cresswell JP. John Gough, yeoman, of Bibury, witness. Fine. £10. Offence committed 19 Jan. 1783.

2/B/7   23 Jan. 1783. John Lawrence of Northleach, labourer. Using a net to kill game at Bibury. E. Cresswell JP. John Gough, yeoman, of Bibury, witness. Offence committed 19 Jan. 1783.

2/B/8   13 March 1783. Thomas Lewis, labourer. Selling ale without a licence at St. Philip and St. Jacob, Bristol. R. Scudamore JP. First offence. Fine 40/- and 5/- expenses.

2/B/9   25 March 1783. William Morgan of Mitcheldean, labourer. Rooting up young trees in the Forest of Dean. S. Hayward JP. George Jones, deputy forest keeper, complainant. Offence committed 28 Feb. 1783.

2/B/10 31 March 1783. Philip Jones of St. Briavels, labourer. Cutting timber in the Forest of Dean. S. Hayward JP. Edward Bevan, forest keeper, complainant. Offence committed 4 Feb. 1783

2/B/11 22 April 1783. Richard Skinner of St. Briavels, collier. Cutting timber in the Forest of Dean. S. Hayward JP. Thomas Wood, forest keeper, complainant.

2/B/12 4 April 1783. James Craught of St. Briavels. Stealing timber in the Forest of Dean. S. Hayward JP. Thomas Stephens, forest keeper, complainant. Offence committed 31 Nov. [sic] 1782.

2/B/13 3 April 1783. Robert Edwards of Mitcheldean, labourer. Rooting up young trees in the Forest of Dean. S. Hayward JP. Richard Bradley, forest keeper, complainant. Offence committed 9 Jan. 1783.

2/B/14 5 April 1783. Thomas Pitt of St. Briavels, labourer. Clearing and enclosing a piece of ground for his own use in the Forest of Dean. S. Hayward JP. George Jones, deputy forest keeper, complainant. Offence committed 16 March 1783.

2/B/15 5 April 1783. William Williams of Mitcheldean, labourer. Clearing and enclosing a piece of ground for his own use in the Forest of Dean. S. Hayward JP. George Jones, deputy forest keeper, complainant. Offence committed 16 March 1783.

2/B/16 11 April 1783. Henry Morgan of St. Briavels, collier. Stealing timber from the Forest of Dean. S. Hayward JP. Edward Bevan, forest keeper, complainant. Offence committed 3 March 1783.

2/B/17 16 April, 1783. John Stephens of Clearwell. Stealing timber from the Forest of Dean. S. Hayward JP. William Meredith, forest keeper, complainant. Offence committed 30 Dec. 1782.

2/B/18 16 April 1783. Isaac Robbins of St. Briavels, coalminer. Stealing timber from the Forest of Dean. S. Hayward JP. William Meredith, forest keeper, complainant. Offence committed 5 Feb. 1783.

2/B/19 19 April 1783. Thomas Haines of St. Briavels, collier. Cutting timber in the Forest of Dean. S. Hayward JP. Edward Bevan, forest keeper, complainant. Offence committed 4 March 1783.

2/B/20 5 April 1783. John Read of Newland, labourer. Grubbing up underwood in the Forest of Dean with intent to take the land for his own use. S. Hayward JP. John Bradley, forest keeper, complainant. Offence committed 8 Jan. 1783.

2/B/21 22 March 1783. Richard Jones and Joseph Wheeler of Littledean, nailers. Cutting and rooting up about 1½ acres of hazel wood in the Forest of Dean. S. Hayward JP. John Brett, forest keeper, complainant. Offence committed 19 March 1783.

2/B/22 20 Jan. 1783. James Trigg the younger of Littledean, collier. Cutting timber in the Forest of Dean. S. Hayward JP. Thomas Wood, forest keeper, complainant. Offence committed 6 Jan. 1783.

2/B/23 18 Jan. 1783. Helm Steel of Coleford, apothecary and surgeon. Stealing timber from the Forest of Dean with intent to enclose land for his own use. S. Hayward JP. Miles Hartland, yeoman, of Mitcheldean, complainant.

2/B/24 14 Jan. 1783. William Hodges of Hope Mansell, Herefs., husbandman. Stealing timber from the Forest of Dean. S. Hayward JP. John Bradley, forest keeper, complainant.

2/B/25 12 Feb. 1783. John Davis of Bream, wood-collier. Stealing timber from the Forest of Dean. S. Hayward JP. Edward Bevan, forest keeper, complainant.

2/B/26 13 Feb. 1783. Joseph Elsemere of St. Briavels, coalminer. Stealing timber from the Forest of Dean. S. Hayward JP. Thomas Stephens, forest keeper, complainant. Offence committed 6 Jan. 1783.

2/B/27 15 Feb. 1783. John Phelps of Weston under Penyard, Herefs., husbandman. Cutting timber in the Forest of Dean. S. Hayward JP. John Bradley, forest keeper, complainant. Offence committed 6 Jan. 1783.

2/B/28 21 Feb. 1783. Richard Marfield of Hope Mansell, Herefs., husbandman. Cutting timber in the Forest of Dean. S. Hayward JP. George Jones of Weston under Penyard, coalminer, complainant. Offence committed 19 Feb. 1783.

2/B/29 25 Feb. 1783. Richard Kear of Newland, husbandman. Stealing timber from the Forest of Dean. S. Hayward JP. William Harvey, forest keeper, and Miles Hartland, yeoman, of Mitcheldean, complainants. Offence committed 11 Feb. 1783.

2/B/30 22 Feb. 1783. John Hill, sawyer, Richard Bull, sawyer, and Edward Jones, mason, all of Dymock. Cutting down and stealing timber in the Forest of Dean. S. Hayward JP. Richard Price, sawyer, of Ruardean, complainant. Offence committed 2 Aug. 1782.

2/B/31 7 March 1783. Jonathan Marfield of Hope Mansell, Herefs., yeoman. Stealing timber from the Forest of Dean. S. Hayward JP. Richard Bradley, forest keeper, complainant. Offence committed 18 Feb. 1783.

2/B/32 20 March 1783. John Dobbs of St. Briavels, collier. Cutting down timber in the Forest of Dean. S. Hayward JP. Edward Bevan, forest keeper, complainant. Offence committed 14 Feb. 1782.

2/B/33 7 March 1783. George Smith, servant to William Cook, yeoman, of Ruardean. Stealing timber from the Forest of Dean. S. Hayward JP. Richard Bradley, forest keeper, complainant. Offence committed 18 Feb. 1783.

2/B/34   8 March 1783. John Niblet of St. Briavels, labourer. Digging up hazel wood and enclosing therewith ¼ acre of land in the Forest of Dean. S. Hayward JP. John Brett, forest keeper, complainant. Offence committed 22 Feb. 1783.

2/B/35   20 Jan. 1783. Samuel Rudge of St. Briavels, shoemaker. Carrying a gun with intent to kill deer in the Forest of Dean. S. Hayward JP. Richard Bradley, forest keeper, complainant. Fine £10.

2/B/36   25 March 1783. William Gough of Mitcheldean, labourer. Rooting up young trees in the Forest of Dean. S. Hayward JP. Richard Bradley, forest keeper, complainant.

2/C/1   6 June 1783. Mary Jones of Horsley. Stealing underwood from a grove belonging to Robert Kingscote Esq. P. Hawker JP. William Moss of Kingscote, complainant.

2/C/2   23 May 1783. William Kemish of Horsley, sawyer. Illegal possession of a large quantity of wood. T. Pettat JP. William Howell, servant to Henry Stephens Esq., complainant.

2/C/3   10 April 1783. Evan Watkins, labourer. Selling ale without a licence in the parish of St. Philip and St. Jacob, Bristol. R. Scudamore JP. First offence. Fine 40/- and 5/- expenses.

2/C/4   5 July 1783. Thomas Coopey the younger of Cam. Obtaining sixpence by false pretences. W. Holwell JP. Examination of Nicholas Ball, hayward, of Cam, complainant. Offence committed 21 June 1783. Includes recognizances of Nicholas Ball to appear at next Q.S., to prosecute, and of Thomas Coopey senior, broadweaver, and Richard Cowley, yeoman, both of Cam, to ensure appearance of accused.

2/C/5–6   4 May 1783. John Roach of St. George, Bristol, starchmaker. Stealing four quarters of horse flesh and four iron shoes. Richard Bayly JP. Informants, Simon Scrase of St. George, yeoman, Benjamin Franklyn of St. Mary Redcliffe, labourer, and William Hatch the younger of Stapleton, smith.

2/C/7   16 June 1783. Betty Britten of Oldland, widow. Selling ale without a licence. R. Bayly JP. First offence. Fine 40/- and 7/- expenses.

2/C/8   23 May 1783. Ambrose Glead of Gloucester, labourer. Stealing three cabbages from a garden belonging to John Pitcher, victualler, of Gloucester. S. Hayward JP. William Higgs, labourer, of Gloucester, witness.

2/C/9   19 June 1783. William James of Newland, collier. Cutting timber in the Forest of Dean. S. Hayward JP. Edward Bevan, forest keeper, complainant.

2/C/10   21 June 1783. James Price of St. Briavels, coalminer. Stealing timber from the Forest of Dean. S. Hayward JP. William Meredith, forest keeper, complainant. Offence committed 4 March 1783.

2/C/11   26 May 1783. Edward Meek of St. Briavels, labourer. Cutting timber in the Forest of Dean. S. Hayward JP. John Bradley, forest keeper, complainant.

2/C/12   1 July 1783. John Wintle of Mitcheldean, cordwainer. Rooting up a large quantity of young trees from an enclosure taken out of the Forest of Dean. S. Hayward JP. William Williams, labourer, of Mitcheldean, complainant. Offence committed 28 June 1783.

2/C/13   7 June 1783. George Martin of Abenhall, labourer. Enclosing a piece of ground in the Forest of Dean and rooting up trees therein. S. Hayward JP. John Brett, forest keeper, complainant. Offence committed 24 April 1783.

2/C/14   3 April 1783. Richard Jones of Littledean, nailer. Cutting and rooting up 1½ acres of hazel wood in the Forest of Dean. S. Hayward JP. Thomas Blunt of Abenhall, deputy surveyor, complainant. Offence committed 20 March 1783.

2/C/15   12 June 1783. Richard Heath of St. Briavels, collier. Cutting timber in the Forest of Dean. S. Hayward JP. Edward Bevan, forest keeper, complainant. Offence committed 18 April 1783.

2/C/16   [*Duplicate of* 2/B/15.]

2/C/17   12 June 1783. William Kear of St. Briavels, coalminer. Stealing timber from the Forest of Dean. S. Hayward JP. Thomas Wood, forest keeper, complainant. Offence committed 1 May 1783.

2/C/18   3 May 1783. James Hobbs of Littledean, labourer. Cutting a quantity of hazel wood with intent to enclose a piece of ground in the Forest of Dean. S. Hayward JP. Jonathan Strong, servant to Thomas Blunt, deputy surveyor, complainant. Offence committed 11 April 1783.

2/C/19   12 June 1783. Joseph James of St. Briavels, coalminer. Stealing timber from the Forest of Dean. S. Hayward JP. Thomas Stephens, forest keeper, complainant. Offence committed 27 May 1783.

2/D/1   1 Oct. 1783. John Sparrow of Stroud, broadweaver. Possession of 3 lb. of abb yarn and a pair of cards without satisfactory explanation. H. Wyatt JP. Offence committed at Minchinhampton 30 Sept. 1783.

2/D/2   30 Aug. 1783. William Chapman of Stroud, wool-scribbler. Embezzling wool, the property of William Capel, clothier, of Stroud. H. Wyatt JP.

2/D/3   1 Oct. 1783. Thomas Blizard of Hucclecote, labourer. Cursing in the parish of Barton Street St. Michael. Charles Barrow JP.

2/D/4   13 Sept. 1783. William Bailey of Hardwicke, yeoman. Having a gun and dogs with intent to kill game at Longney. Charles Bishop JP. John Bate, informant. William Fryer, yeoman, of Longney, witness. Fine £5. Offence committed 27 Aug. 1783.

2/D/5   30 July 1783. Mary Haines of Westbury on Severn, wife of William, labourer. Stealing a small quantity of peas. S. Hayward JP. William Green, husbandman, of Westbury on Severn, complainant.

2/D/6   23 Aug. 1783. Biby White of Bream, innholder. Stealing timber from the Forest of Dean. S. Hayward JP. Miles Hartland, yeoman, of Mitcheldean, complainant. Offence committed 15 Aug. 1783.

2/D/7   15 July 1783. John Boseley of Abenhall, husbandman. Stealing timber from the Forest of Dean. S. Hayward JP. Miles Hartland, servant to Thomas Blunt, deputy surveyor, complainant. Offence committed 27 May 1783.

2/D/8   2 Aug. 1783. William Tingle of Littledean, collier. Enclosing a piece of ground in the Forest of Dean and rooting up the underwood therein. S. Hayward JP. John Brett, forest keeper, complainant. Offence committed 27 June 1783.

2/D/9   23 Aug. 1783. William Kear the younger of St. Briavels, coalminer. Cutting timber, with his brother Richard Kear, in the Forest of Dean. S. Hayward JP. Thomas Wood, forest keeper, complainant. Offence committed 7 April 1783.

2/D/10   23 Aug. 1783. Thomas Beach of St. Briavels, collier. Stealing timber from the Forest of Dean. S. Hayward JP. Edward Bevan, deputy forest keeper, complainant. Offence committed 3 May 1783.

2/D/11   5 Sept. 1783. Evan James of St. Briavels, labourer. Cutting timber in the Forest of Dean. S. Hayward JP. Thomas Wood, forest keeper, complainant. Offence committed 23 May 1783.

2/D/12   13 Sept. 1783. Richard Heath of St. Briavels, coalminer. Stealing timber from the Forest of Dean. S. Hayward JP. Edward Bevan, deputy forest keeper, complainant.

2/D/13   23 Aug. 1783. Richard Jones of St. Briavels, collier. Possessing stolen timber from the Forest of Dean. S. Hayward JP. Edward Bevan, deputy forest keeper, complainant. Offence committed 5 March 1783.

2/D/14   3 Oct. 1783. Warren James of Newland, collier. Stealing timber from the Forest of Dean. S. Hayward JP. Edward Bevan, deputy forest keeper, complainant. Offence committed 30 April 1783.

2/D/15   28 Aug. 1783. Ann Hooper, wife of Robert, of Lea, labourer. Stealing young trees from the Forest of Dean. S. Hayward JP. George Jones, deputy forest keeper, complainant. Offence committed 15 and 28 July and 2 Aug. 1783.

2/D/16   24 Sept. 1783. Thomas Wallden of Littledean, collier, Stealing timber from the Forest of Dean. S. Hayward JP. Edward Bevan, deputy forest keeper, complainant. Offence committed 8 July 1783.

2/D/17   27 Sept. 1783. John Thomas of St. Briavels, gardener. Rooting up underwood in the Forest of Dean in order to take the land for his own use. S. Hayward JP. Miles Hartland, yeoman, of Mitcheldean, complainant. Offence committed 22 Sept. 1783.

2/D/18   27 Sept. 1783. William Boseley of Flaxley, husbandman. Possessing stolen timber from the Forest of Dean. S. Hayward JP. John Brett, forest keeper, complainant. Offence committed 19 Sept. 1783.

3/A/1   5 Nov. 1783. William Bennett of Wotton under Edge, carpenter. Using a dog and nets with intent to kill game at Oldbury on the Hill. Sir William Codrington JP. First conviction.

3/A/2   8 Dec. 1783. Daniel Stockwell of Dursley, labourer. Stealing timber from a wood at North Nibley. W. Holwell JP. Earl of Berkeley, complainant. First offence. Fine £5 and 5/- expenses. Offence committed 17 Sept. 1783.

3/A/3   8 Dec. 1783. Lucy Haglett of North Nibley, spinster. Possessing a quantity of stolen timber. W. Holwell JP. William Morris, yeoman, complainant. First offence. Fine £1 and 5/- expenses.

3/A/4   5 Nov. 1783. William Russell, William Smith, Uriah White, James Pullen, Richard Wilkins, Peter Watts, William Thomas and William Crew, all of Chipping Sodbury. Cutting and stealing timber at Chipping Sodbury and Yate. G. Hardwicke JP. Thomas Brooke Esq., John Codrington Esq., both of Chipping Sodbury, and Nathan Sturge of Yate, complainants. First offence. Each fined 10/-, but on refusal to pay were ordered to be whipped.

3/A/5   10 Dec. 1783. Elizabeth Jackson, wife of George, of Lea hamlet, labourer. Cutting and stealing underwood in the Forest of Dean. S. Hayward JP. George Jones, deputy forest keeper, complainant. Offence committed 4 Nov. 1783.

3/A/6   29 Nov. 1783. Samuel Steel of Littledean, collier. Cutting and stealing oak timber in the Forest of Dean. S. Hayward JP. Miles Hartland, yeoman, of Mitcheldean, complainant.

3/A/7   12 Jan. 1784. Samuel Brinkworth of Littledean, labourer. Clearing and enclosing a piece of land in the Forest of Dean. S. Hayward JP. John Brett, forest keeper, complainant. Offence committed 11 Dec. 1783.

3/A/8   7 Oct. 1783 William Saysell of St. Briavels. Cutting oak timber in the Forest of Dean. S. Hayward JP. Thomas Blunt Esq., deputy forest surveyor, of Mitcheldean, complainant. Offence committed 26 Sept. 1783.

3/A/9   10 Dec. 1783. Alexander Jones of Lea hamlet, labourer. Stealing 2 young beech trees from the Forest of Dean. S. Hayward JP. George Jones, deputy forest keeper, complainant. Offence committed 4 Nov. 1783.

3/A/10 10 Dec. 1783. Thomas Jones of Mitcheldean, husbandman. Stealing a small oak tree from the Forest of Dean. S. Hayward JP. Philip Hardwick of Welsh Bicknor, complainant. Offence committed 25 Nov. 1783.

3/A/11 12 Jan. 1784. Peter James of Bream, labourer. Stealing timber from the Forest of Dean. S. Hayward JP. William Merideth, deputy forest keeper, complainant. Offence committed 30 Dec. 1783.

3/A/12 10 Jan. 1784. Edward Hudd of Wotton Vill, victualler. Illegally possessing a hare. Howe Hicks JP. John Jeffs, labourer, of Chipping Campden, informant. Daniel Taylor, labourer, of Chipping Campden, witness. Fine £5.

3/B/1 15 Dec. 1783. Betty Britten of Oldland, widow. Selling ale without a licence. R. Bayly JP. First offence [but see 2/C/7]. Fine 40/- and 6/- expenses.

3/B/2 9 Feb. 1784. Betty Britten of Oldland, widow. Selling ale without a licence. R. Bayly JP. First offence [but see 3/B/1]. Fine £4 and 6/- expenses.

3/B/3 15 Dec. 1783. Joseph Peacock of Oldland, wagoner. Selling ale without a licence. R. Bayly JP. First offence. Fine 40/- and 6/- expenses.

3/B/4 26 Feb. 1784. John Vizard of King's Stanley, clothworker. Stealing a quantity of oak wood. P. Hawker JP. Thomas Pettat Esq., complainant.

3/B/5 24 March 1784. Ann Workman, wife of William, of Bisley, broadweaver. Cutting and damaging a tree. T. Gryffin JP. Charles Ballinger, complainant. Offence committed 18 March 1784.

3/B/6 17 Feb. 1784. Richard Hands of Maisemore. Swearing and cursing. S. Hayward JP.

3/B/7 21 Feb. 1784. Thomas Williams of St. Briavels, labourer. Cutting and stealing timber in the Forest of Dean. S. Hayward JP. John Duglas, labourer, of St. Briavels, complainant. Offence committed 4 Feb. 1784.

3/B/8 3 Feb. 1784. James Smith of Newland, labourer. Stealing timber from the Forest of Dean. S. Hayward JP. Miles Hartland, yeoman of Mitcheldean, complainant. Offence committed 23 Jan. 1784.

3/B/9 18 Feb. 1784. John Evans of Ruardean, yeoman. Cutting and stealing timber in the Forest of Dean. S. Hayward JP. John Duglas, labourer, of St. Briavels, complainant. Offence committed 28 Jan. 1784.

3/B/10 3 Feb. 1784. Thomas Smith of Weston under Penyard, carpenter. Possessing oak timber without satisfactory explanation. S. Hayward JP. Miles Hartland, yeoman, of Mitcheldean, complainant.

3/B/11 3 Feb. 1784. John Marshall of Lea hamlet, labourer. Possessing oak timber without satisfactory explanation. S. Hayward JP. Miles Hartland, yeoman, of Mitcheldean, complainant.

3/B/12 19 March 1784. William Yem of St. Briavels, collier. Cutting timber in the Forest of Dean. S. Hayward JP. Thomas Bennett, forest keeper, complainant. Offence committed 5 March 1784.

3/B/13 20 March 1784. John Probert of Elton, Westbury on Severn, labourer. Clearing and enclosing land in the Forest of Dean. S. Hayward JP. John Brett, forest keeper, complainant. Offence committed 8 March 1784.

3/B/14 17 March 1784. George Jones of Hope Mansell, Herefs., yeoman. Stealing timber from the Forest of Dean and conveying it to land belonging to his father John Jones. S. Hayward JP. John Pearce, deputy forest keeper, complainant. Offence committed 12 Feb. 1784.

3/B/15   26 March 1784. Samuel Brinkworth of Littledean, labourer. Clearing and enclosing land in the Forest of Dean. S. Hayward JP. Miles Hartland, yeoman, of Mitcheldean, complainant. Offence committed 20 Dec. 1783.

3/B/16   17 March 1784. John Jones the younger, of Hope Mansell, Herefs., husbandman. Stealing timber [*etc.*, *as* 3/B/14].

3/B/17   13 Jan. 1784. Thomas Wallden of Ruardean, coalminer. Cutting timber in the Forest of Dean. S. Hayward JP. Miles Hartland, yeoman, of Mitcheldean, complainant. Offence committed 6 Jan. 1784.

3/B/18   11 Feb. 1784. Richard Dowle of Newland, carpenter. Carrying a gun in the Forest of Dean. S. Hayward JP. Arrested by William Harvey, forest keeper. Fine £10. Committed to gaol until fine paid.

3/B/19   24 Feb. 1784. Thomas Nott. Using a dog and net to kill hares at Wapley and Codrington. I. W. Horlock JP. Offence committed 23 Feb. 1784.

3/B/20   27 Feb. 1784. John Howles of Longhope. Swearing and cursing. Benjamin Newton JP.

3/B/21   12 March 1784. Mathias Baker, yeoman, Thomas Parker, yeoman, and John Rastall *alias* Baker, miller, all of Bisley. Tracking a hare in the snow at Edgeworth. B. Newton JP. Richard Brereton, clerk, of Wotton, informant. James Blackwell and John Hudd, labourers, of Bisley, witnesses. Fine 20/- each. Offence committed 16 Feb. 1784.

3/C/1   7 June 1784. William Langham, baker. Selling ale without a licence in Bitton. William Hayward Winstone JP. First offence. Fine 40/- and 5/- expenses.

3/C/2   27 March 1784. Mary Reed, widow. Selling ale without a licence in the parish of St. George, Bristol. W. H. Winstone JP and R. Bayly JP. First offence. Fine 40/- and 6/- expenses. Fine given to Mr. Fidoe, collector of excise at Bristol.

3/C/3   14 Feb. 1784. Joseph Harris, labourer. Selling ale without a licence in Bitton. W. H. Winstone JP and R. Bayly JP. First offence. Fine 40/- and 6/- expenses. Fine given to Mr. Fidoe, collector of excise at Bristol.

3/C/4   14 Feb. 1784. Samuel Hemmings, labourer. Selling ale without a licence in Mangotsfield. W. H. Winstone JP and R. Bayly JP. First offence. Fine 40/- and 6/- expenses. Fine given to Mr. Fidoe, collector of excise at Bristol.

3/C/5   7 June. 1784. Samuel Jay, coalminer. Selling ale without a licence in Oldland. R. Bayly JP. First offence. Fine 40/- and 5/- expenses.

3/C/6   7 June 1784. Peter Chipper, thatcher. Selling ale without a licence in Bitton. R. Bayly JP. First offence. Fine 40/- and 5/- expenses.

3/C/7   30 April 1784. Sampson Golding of Mangotsfield. Possessing a bundle of cart rods without satisfactory explanation. Sir W. Codrington JP. William Jennings of Pucklechurch, complainant. First offence.

3/C/8   30 April 1784. Mary Jones of Mangotsfield. Cutting underwood in a wood at Pucklechurch. Sir W. Codrington JP. Edward Hathway of Pucklechurch, complainant.

3/C/9   24 May 1784. William Rolph of Old Sodbury, yeoman. Selling beer without a licence. Sir W. Codrington JP. First offence. Fine 40/- and 10/- expenses.

3/C/10   3 May 1784. George Peglar, William Burford, John Poulton and Edward Poulton of Nympsfield, broadweavers. Cutting and stealing a beech tree from a wood at Coaley, the property of Mr. Rosser. P. Hawker JP. Charles Whithorne, complainant.

3/C/11   27 April 1784. John Wilkins and Abraham Burford of Nympsfield, broadweavers. Cutting and stealing several young beech trees from a wood at Coaley, belonging to the earl of Berkeley. P. Hawker JP. William Day, complainant.

3/C/12 7 June 1784. Samuel Brookes of Minchinhampton, broadweaver. Pulling up shrubs and plants from a garden belonging to Mary and Elizabeth Pinfold. P. Hawker JP. Miss Mary Pinfold of Minchinhampton, complainant.

14 June 1784. Thomas Hathin and Samuel Timbrell *alias* Holdman of Minchinhampton, saddle-tree makers. Pulling up shrubs and plants from a garden belonging to Mary and Elizabeth Pinfold. P. Hawker JP. Miss Mary Pinfold of Minchinhampton, complainant.

3/C/13 1 June 1784. George Griffiths of Bream, coalminer. Stealing oak timber from the Forest of Dean. S. Hayward JP. Thomas Wood, forest keeper, complainant. Offence committed 5 April 1784.

3/C/14 1 June 1784. James Trigg the younger of Littledean, coalminer. Stealing timber from the Forest of Dean. S. Hayward JP. Edward Bevan and Thomas Wood, forest keepers, complainants. Offence committed 16 March 1784.

3/C/15 18 May 1784. James Smith of St. Briavels, carpenter. Cutting and stealing timber from the Forest of Dean. S. Hayward JP. John Pearce, glazier, of Mitcheldean, complainant. Offence committed 28 March 1784.

3/C/16 23 June. 1784. Joseph Beard of Standish, tailor. Cursing. S. Hayward JP. Mary Morris, wife of Charles Morris, labourer, of Hardwicke, witness. Offence committed 19 June 1784.

3/C/17 3 May 1784. William Doward the younger of St. Briavels, coalminer. Stealing bark from freshly cut oak trees in the Forest of Dean. S. Hayward JP. Thomas Stephens and William Meredith, forest keepers, complainants. Offence committed 2 May 1784.

3/C/18 8 May 1784. Richard Young of St. Briavels, forgeman. Clearing and enclosing land for his own use in the Forest of Dean. S. Hayward JP. John Brett, forest keeper, complainant. Offence committed 17 April 1784.

3/C/19 18 May 1784. Joseph Parker of Mitcheldean, gardener. Stealing underwood and taking a piece of land for his own use in the Forest of Dean. S. Hayward JP. John Pearce, glazier, of Mitcheldean, complainant. Offence committed 28 April 1784.

3/C/20 8 May 1784. William Thomas of Bream, coalminer. Cutting timber in the Forest of Dean. S. Hayward JP. Thomas Wood, forest keeper, complainant. Offence committed 19 Nov. 1783.

3/C/21 8 May 1784. Samuel Steel of Littledean, coalminer. Stealing timber from the Forest of Dean. S. Hayward JP. Edward Bevan and Thomas Wood, forest keepers, complainants. Offence committed 16 March 1784.

3/C/22 17 June 1784. Alice James, wife of Peter James of Bream, labourer. Cutting oak timber in the Forest of Dean. S. Hayward JP. Thomas Wood, forest keeper, complainant. Offence committed 5 Dec. 1783.

3/C/23 19 June 1784. Giles Yerrett of Coleford, husbandman. Stealing oak timber from the Forest of Dean. S. Hayward JP. Robert East, forest keeper, complainant. Offence committed 6 Dec. 1783.

3/C/24 1 July 1784. Samuel Robins of St. Briavels, collier. Cutting oak timber in the Forest of Dean. S. Hayward JP. Edward Bevan, forest keeper, complainant. Offence committed 16 April 1784.

3/C/25 17 June 1784. Thomas Price of St. Briavels, collier. Stealing timber from the Forest of Dean. S. Hayward JP. Thomas Wood, forest keeper, complainant. Offence committed 20 April 1784.

3/C/26   19 June 1784. Richard Williams of Clearwell, labourer. Stealing timber from the Forest of Dean with intention of enclosing land for his own use. S. Hayward JP. Robert East, forest keeper, complainant. Offence committed 16 Dec. 1783.

3/C/27   28 May 1784. William Beach of Bream, collier. Cutting timber in the Forest of Dean. S. Hayward JP. Thomas Stephens, forest keeper, complainant. Offence committed 8 May 1784.

3/D/1   4 Sept. 1784. William Lewis of Mitcheldean, barber. Swearing. S. Hayward JP. Second conviction. [Cf. 3/D/3.]

3/D/2   17 July 1784. William Phillips of Hartpury, miller. Swearing. S. Hayward JP.

3/D/3   31 Aug. 1784. William Lewis of Mitcheldean, barber. Swearing and cursing. S. Hayward JP.

3/D/4   29 Sept. 1784. Thomas Grindall of St. Briavels, coalminer. Cutting timber in the Forest of Dean. S. Hayward JP. Thomas Stephens, forest keeper, complainant. Offence committed 24 April 1784.

3/D/5   24 Sept. 1784. George Rosser of Newland, stonecutter. Attempting to steal timber from the Forest of Dean. S. Hayward JP. Edward Bevan, forest keeper, complainant. Offence committed 20 Jan. 1784.

3/D/6   24 July 1784. William Robins of St. Briavels, collier. Cutting oak timber in the Forest of Dean. S. Hayward JP. Thomas Wood, forest keeper, complainant. Offence committed 2 April 1784.

3/D/7   24 July 1784. James Bailey of St. Briavels, coalminer. Cutting oak timber in the Forest of Dean. S. Hayward JP. William Meredith, forest keeper, complainant. Offence committed 17 April 1784.

3/D/8   15 Sept. 1784. James Beach of St. Briavels, coalminer. Cutting oak timber in the Forest of Dean. S. Hayward JP. William Meredith, forest keeper, complainant. Offence committed 18 May 1784.

3/D/9   13 Aug. 1784. John Yem of Lea hamlet, yeoman. Cutting oak timber in the Forest of Dean. S. Hayward JP. Thomas Jones, labourer, of Lea hamlet, complainant. Offence committed 12 July 1784.

3/D/10   24 Sept. 1784. Joseph James of St. Briavels, coalminer. Cutting oak timber in the Forest of Dean. S. Hayward JP. William Meredith, forest keeper, complainant. Offence committed 17 April 1784.

3/D/11   24 Sept. 1784. Peter James of Bream, collier. Cutting oak timber in the Forest of Dean. S. Hayward JP. Edward Bevan, forest keeper, complainant. Offence committed 1 Aug. 1784.

3/D/12   11 Sept. 1784. James Griffiths of St. Briavels, coalminer. Cutting oak timber in the Forest of Dean. S. Hayward JP. William Meredith, forest keeper, complainant. Offence committed 18 May 1784.

3/D/13   1 Oct. 1784. Richard Tindale, clerk, of Charfield. Using dogs to kill hares in Charfield. Sir W. Codrington JP. First offence. Fine £20. Offence committed Sunday 29 Aug. 1784.

3/D/14   30 July 1784. William Rolph of Old Sodbury, yeoman. Selling beer without a licence. Sir W. Codrington JP. Second offence [Cf. 3/C/9.] Fine £4 and 20/- expenses. Offence committed 18 July 1784.

3/D/15   26 July 1784. Richard Humphris of Baunton, blacksmith. Using snares at Bibury with intent to kill game. T. Bush JP. First offence. Fine £10. Offence committed Sunday 25 July 1784.

3/D/16 1 Oct. 1784. Joseph Hill of Charfield, labourer. Using a dog to kill hares. Sir W. Codrington JP and G. Hardwicke JP. Richard Limbrick of Charfield informant. Offence committed 30 Aug. 1784.

4/A/1 30 Oct. 1784. John Eastbury of Blockley, Worcs., labourer. Using a net to kill hares at Bourton on the Hill. John Scott JP. First offence. Fine £20. Offence committed 10/11 Oct. 1784.

4/A/2 [*Duplicate of* 4/A/1.]

4/A/3 6 Aug. 1784. Thomas Watson, wagoner. Selling ale without a licence at Bitton. R. Bayly JP. First offence. Fine 40/- and 6/- expenses. Fine received 7 Oct. 1784.

4/A/4 11 Nov. 1784. Samuel Lacey, yeoman. Selling ale without a licence in the parish of St. Philip and St. Jacob, Bristol. R. Scudamore JP. First offence. Fine 40/- and 5/- expenses.

4/A/5 11 Nov. 1784. William Pain, labourer. Selling ale without a licence in the parish of St. Philip and St. Jacob, Bristol. R. Scudamore JP. First offence. Fine 40/- and 5/- expenses.

4/A/6 7 June 1784. William Rogers. Selling ale without a licence in Frampton Cotterell. W. H. Winstone JP. First offence. Fine 40/- and 6/- expenses. Fine received 17 Dec. 1784.

4/A/7 7 June 1784. Robert Wickham, feltmaker. Selling ale without a licence in Oldland. W. H. Winstone JP. First offence. Fine 40/- and 5/- expenses. Fine paid 7 Oct. 1784.

4/A/8 16 Nov. 1784. Richard Mills of Nympsfield, broadweaver. Embezzling 5 lb. of woollen yarn. Rev. P. Hawker JP. Nathaniel and Daniel Loyd, clothiers, of Uley, complainants.

4/A/9 4 Jan. 1785. Jane Webb of Horsley, single woman. Cutting and stealing young beech trees from a wood at Avening belonging to Sophia Small, gentlewoman. P. Hawker JP. John Chandler, complainant.

4/A/10 7 Jan. 1785. Mary Woodham and her daughter Sarah, of Marshfield. Stealing a copper tea-kettle and a pewter plate from the dwelling house of Mary Jones of Marshfield. Sir W. Codrington JP. Recognizance in the sum of £5 each by Mary Jones and Samuel Abbot of Marshfield to appear at next Q.S. to prefer indictment.

4/A/11 23 Nov. 1784. William Rolph of Old Sodbury. Selling beer without a licence within the previous six weeks. Sir W. Codrington JP. Third offence. [*Cf.* 3/C/9, 3/D/14.] Fine £6 and 5/- expenses.

4/A/12 23 Nov. 1784. William Rolph of Old Sodbury. Selling beer without a licence in the week next after 15 Oct. last. Sir W. Codrington JP. Third offence. Fine £6 and 5/- expenses.

4/A/13 23 Nov. 1784. William Rolph of Old Sodbury. Selling beer without a licence on 15 Oct. last. Sir W. Codrington JP. Third offence. Fine £6 and 6/- expenses.

4/A/14 23 Nov. 1784. William Rolph of Old Sodbury. Selling beer without a licence about three weeks now past. Sir W. Codrington JP. Third offence. Fine £6 and 5/- expenses.

4/A/15 15 Nov. 1784. William Rolph of Old Sodbury. Selling beer without a licence on or about 24 Oct. last. Sir W. Codrington JP. Third offence. Fine £6 and 5/- expenses.

4/A/16 23 Nov. 1784. William Rolph of Old Sodbury. Selling beer without a licence about five or six weeks now past. Sir W. Codrington JP. Third offence. Fine £6 and 5/- expenses.

4/A/17 23 Nov. 1784. William Rolph of Old Sodbury. Selling beer without a licence about Michaelmas last. Sir W. Codrington JP. Third offence. Fine £6 and 5/- expenses.

4/A/18 9 Oct. 1784. Ann Curnock of Cam, widow. Selling ale without a licence. W. Holwell JP. First offence. Fine 40/- and 7/- expenses.

4/A/19 9 Oct. 1784. Chapell Davis of Cam, weaver. Selling ale without a licence. W. Holwell JP. First offence. Fine 40/- and 10/6 expenses.

4/A/20 29 Dec. 1784. Robert Cowley of Uley, shearman. Attempting to kill a hare. W. Holwell JP. First offence. Fine £15. Offence committed 24/25 Dec. 1784.

4/A/21 29 Dec. 1784. William Stephens of Uley, labourer. Using a snare with intent to kill a hare. W. Holwell JP. First offence. Fine £10. Offence committed 24/25 Dec. 1784.

4/A/22 11 Nov. 1784. Thomas Worgan of Coleford, collier. Cutting and stealing timber in an enclosure in the Forest of Dean. S. Hayward JP. Thomas Bennett, forest keeper, complainant.

4/A/23 14 Oct. 1784. Joseph Grindall of Littledean, labourer. Stealing timber from the Forest of Dean. S. Hayward JP. Thomas Bennett, forest keeper, complainant. Offence committed 13 Oct. 1784.

4/A/24 14 Oct. 1784. Thomas Wallden of Littledean, collier. Stealing timber from the Forest of Dean. S. Hayward JP. Thomas Bennett, forest keeper, complainant. Offence committed 13 Oct. 1784.

4/A/25 5 Nov. 1784. Robert Tingle of Bream, labourer. Cutting and stealing timber in the Forest of Dean. S. Hayward JP. William Meredith, forest keeper, complainant. Offence committed 4 Nov. 1784.

4/A/26 4 Dec. 1784. William Vaughan of Ruardean, blacksmith. Cutting down an oak tree in the Forest of Dean. S. Hayward JP. Thomas Bennett, forest keeper, complainant. Offence committed 10 Nov. 1784.

4/A/27 27 Oct. 1784. Edward Meek of Lea hamlet, coalminer. Cutting timber in the Forest of Dean. S. Hayward JP. Richard Hawkins, servant to Mr. Thomas Harvey, forest keeper, complainant.

4/A/28 5 Nov. 1784. Benjamin Mason of St. Briavels, coalminer. Cutting and stealing timber in the Forest of Dean. S. Hayward JP. Richard Hawkins, servant to Mr. Thomas Harvey, forest keeper, complainant. Offence committed 4 Nov. 1784.

4/A/29 2 Nov. 1784. John Stephens of St. Briavels, labourer. Cutting and stealing timber in the Forest of Dean. S. Hayward JP. Thomas Bennett, forest keeper, complainant. Offence committed 31 Oct. 1784.

4/A/30 11 Nov. 1784. John Worgan of Coleford, collier. Cutting and stealing a young beech tree in an enclosure in the Forest of Dean. S. Hayward JP. Thomas Bennett, forest keeper, complainant. Offence committed 3 Nov. 1784.

4/B/1 19 Jan. 1785. Rees Thomas of Minchinhampton. Swearing. Rev. P. Hawker JP.

4/B/2 4 March 1785. Daniel Holbrow of Minchinhampton. Swearing and cursing. Rev. P. Hawker JP.

4/B/3 22 Jan. 1785. Richard Teakle of Horsley. Cutting down trees belonging to Mrs. Elizabeth Castleman. Rev. P. Hawker JP. William Adams, complainant.

4/B/4 13 Oct. 1784. William Langaman, maltster. Selling ale without a licence in Bitton. W. H. Winstone JP. Second offence. Fine £4 and 6/- expenses.

4/B/5 13 Oct. 1784. Thomas Watson, wagoner. Selling ale without a licence in Bitton. W. H. Winstone JP. Second offence. [*Cf.* 4/A/3.] Fine £4 and 6/- expenses.

4/B/6 31 Jan. 1785. Robert Wickham. Selling ale without a licence in Oldland. W. H. Winstone JP. Second offence. [*Cf.* 4/A/7.] Fine £4 and 6/- expenses.

4/B/7 31 Jan. 1785. George French, labourer. Selling ale without a licence in Oldland. W. H. Winstone JP. Second offence. [*Cf.* 1/D/10.] Fine £4 and 6/- expenses.

4/B/8 2 April 1785. Thomas Jones of Clearwell, yeoman. Stealing timber in the Forest of Dean. Rev. C. Bishop JP. Miles Hartland, yeoman, of Mitcheldean, complainant. Offence committed 29 March 1785.

4/B/9 2 April 1785. James Baker of Hewelsfield, yeoman. Cutting and stealing timber in the Forest of Dean. Rev. C. Bishop JP. John Brown, labourer, late of Hewelsfield, complainant. Offence committed on or about 22 Feb. 1785.

4/B/10 4 March 1785. James Wood of Littledean, yeoman. Cutting and stealing timber in the Forest of Dean. Rev. C. Bishop JP. Miles Hartland, yeoman, of Mitcheldean, complainant. Offence committed 18 Feb. 1785.

4/B/11 1 April 1785. Joseph Bruton of Uley, broadweaver. Possessing woollen yarn, the property of a person unknown. Rev. George Hayward JP and Charles Hayward JP.

4/B/12 1 April 1785. Joshua Wilkins of Uley, broadweaver. Possessing ends of yarn and woollen cloth. Rev. G. Hayward JP and C. Hayward JP.

4/B/13 1 April 1785. Philadelphia Hill of Cam, broadweaver. Possessing ends of yarn and woollen cloth. Rev. G. Hayward JP and C. Hayward JP.

4/B/14 1 April 1785. Richard Gabb of Coaley, broadweaver. Possessing ends of yarn and woollen cloth. Rev. G. Hayward JP and C. Hayward JP.

4/B/15 15 March 1785. Robert Teakle of Horsley, broadweaver. Buying a quantity of stolen woollen abb yarn. Rev. G. Hayward JP and T. Pettat JP.

4/B/16 5 March 1785. Daniel Smart of Avening, clothworker. Buying a quantity of stolen woollen abb yarn. Rev. G. Hayward JP and T. Pettat JP.

4/B/17 5 March 1785. James Swain of Minchinhampton, serge-weaver. Selling stolen woollen abb yarn. Rev. G. Hayward JP and T. Pettat JP.

4/B/18 5 March 1785. David Jones of Minchinhampton, broadweaver. Buying a quantity of stolen woollen abb yarn. Rev. G. Hayward JP and T. Pettat JP.

4/B/19 5 March 1785. John Buckingham of Rodborough, broadweaver. Selling stolen woollen abb yarn. Rev. G. Hayward JP and T. Pettat JP.

4/B/20 15 March 1785. James Evans of Horsley, broadweaver. Buying a quantity of stolen woollen yarn. Rev. G. Hayward JP and T. Pettat JP.

4/B/21 20 March 1785. Gabriel French, Hester Mercer and Jacob Heath. Cutting and stealing timber from a wood in North Nibley, the property of the earl of Berkeley. Rev. G. Hayward JP. Daniel Munday, complainant.

4/B/22 12 Jan. 1785. John Morse of Bream, coalminer. Cutting and stealing timber from the Forest of Dean with his son John Morse. S. Hayward JP. William Meredith, forest keeper, complainant. Offence committed 15 Nov. 1784

4/B/23 10 Feb. 1785. Richard Phipps of Clearwell, labourer. Stealing timber from the Forest of Dean. S. Hayward JP. William Meredith, forest keeper, complainant. Offence committed 5 May 1784.

4/C/1 14 May 1785. George James of Newland, yeoman. Stealing timber from the Forest of Dean. Rev. C. Bishop JP. Miles Hartland, yeoman, of Mitcheldean, complainant. Offence committed 24 March 1785.

4/C/2 16 May 1785. Ephraim Smith of Highnam, carpenter. Obstructing the highway at Highnam with quantities of timber. Rev. B. Newton JP. Sir Charles Barrow, informant. Fine 5/-.

4/C/3   14 May 1785. William Hamby of English Bicknor, yeoman. Stealing timber from the Forest of Dean. Rev. C. Bishop JP. Miles Hartland, yeoman, of Mitcheldean, complainant. Offence committed 24 March 1785.

4/C/4   14 May 1785. John Phelps of Newcourt, Herefs., yeoman. Stealing timber from the Forest of Dean. Rev. C. Bishop JP. Miles Hartland, yeoman, of Mitcheldean, complainant. Offence committed 24 March 1785.

4/C/5   14 May 1785. James Fostor of English Bicknor, yeoman. Stealing timber from the Forest of Dean. Rev. C. Bishop JP. Miles Hartland, yeoman, of Mitcheldean, complainant. Offence committed 24 March 1785.

4/C/6   14 May 1785. Richard Golding of St. Briavels, yeoman. Stealing timber from the Forest of Dean. Rev. C. Bishop JP. Miles Hartland, yeoman, of Mitcheldean, complainant. Offence committed 24 March 1785.

4/C/7   5 April 1785. Richard Winfield of Hardwicke, labourer. Using gins and snares to kill game. Rev. C. Bishop JP. Thomas Ellis, labourer, of Hardwicke, informant. Fine £5.

4/C/8   14 June. 1785. Keziah Bullock of Minsterworth, widow. Cutting and stealing timber. T. Crawley Boevey JP. Sir C. Barrow, complainant, and William Phelps the younger, informant, both of Minsterworth.

4/C/9   27 May 1785. George Bick of Wotton Hamlet, blacksmith. Swearing in Frampton Mansell. S. Hayward JP.

4/C/10   29 May 1785. Elizabeth Lander of Gloucester, single woman, and Mary Southern of Gloucester, wife of Thomas, labourer. Cutting and stealing cabbages from the garden of James Holbert, gardener, of Kingsholm. S. Hayward JP. John Smith, labourer, of Kingsholm, informant.

4/C/11   27 April 1785. Biby White of Newland, baker. Stealing timber from the Forest of Dean. S. Hayward JP. Thomas Stephens, forest keeper, complainant. Offence committed 20 April 1785.

4/C/12   27 April 1785. Richard Jones *alias* Firk of St. Briavels, collier. Cutting timber in the Forest of Dean. S. Hayward JP. Thomas Stephens, forest keeper, complainant. Offence committed 27 Feb. 1785.

4/C/13   27 April 1785. William Jones of St. Briavels, labourer. Stealing timber (in company with Biby White, baker, of Newland) from the Forest of Dean. S. Hayward JP. Thomas Stephens, forest keeper, complainant. Offence committed 20 April 1785.

4/C/14   14 May 1785. Thomas Broben of St. Briavels, tailor. Clearing and enclosing land for his own use in the Forest of Dean. S. Hayward JP. Joseph Young, servant to John Brett, forest keeper, complainant.

4/C/15   14 May 1785. Edward Teague of St. Briavels, coalminer. Cutting underwood in an enclosure in the Forest of Dean. S. Hayward JP. Miles Hartland, yeoman, of Mitcheldean, complainant.

4/C/16   28 May 1785. James Reece the younger of Littledean, labourer. Clearing and enclosing land for his own use in the Forest of Dean. S. Hayward JP. John Brett, forest keeper, complainant. Offence committed 10 May 1785.

4/C/17   21 May 1785. Edward Teague of St. Briavels, collier. Clearing and enclosing land for his own use in the Forest of Dean. S. Hayward JP. Joseph Young, servant to John Brett, forest keeper, complainant. Offence committed 28 March 1785.

4/C/18   30 May 1785. William Tippings of Mitcheldean, coalminer. Clearing and enclosing land for his own use in the Forest of Dean. S. Hayward JP. Miles Hartland, yeoman, of Mitcheldean, complainant. Offence committed 16 March 1785.

4/D/1   22 July 1785. William Fisher of Uley, broadweaver. Embezzling 6 lb. of woollen yarn, the property of Thomas Cooper & Co., clothiers, of Rodborough and Woodchester. Rev. P. Hawker JP. John Cooper, informant.

4/D/2   16 July 1785. James Exell of Wotton under Edge, broadweaver. Embezzling 4 lb. of woollen yarn, the property of Thomas Pettat Esq. of King's Stanley. Rev. P. Hawker JP. John Remmington, informant.

4/D/3   23 Aug. 1785. Alice Sweetman of Marshfield. Selling beer without a licence. Sir W. Codrington JP. First offence. Fine 40/- and 10/- expenses.

4/D/4   23 Aug. 1785. Joseph Dyer junior of Marshfield. Selling beer without a licence. Sir W. Codrington JP. First offence. Fine 40/- and 10/- expenses.

4/D/5   23 Aug. 1785. Samuel Abbott of Marshfield. Selling beer without a licence. Sir W. Codrington JP. First offence. Fine 40/- and 10/- expenses.

4/D/6   2 Sept. 1785. Sarah Woodham of Marshfield. Selling beer without a licence. Sir W. Codrington JP. First offence. Fine 40/- and 10/- expenses.

4/D/7   2 Sept. 1785. William Trull of Marshfield. Selling beer without a licence. Sir W. Codrington JP. First offence. Fine 40/- and 10/- expenses.

4/D/8   16 July 1785. Thomas Pitt of St. Briavels, yeoman. Cutting timber in the Forest of Dean. S. Hayward JP. Thomas Lloyd, cordwainer, of Mitcheldean, complainant. Offence committed 15 April 1785.

4/D/9   2 Sept. 1785. George Meredith the elder of St. Briavels, coalminer. Cutting and stealing timber in the Forest of Dean. S. Hayward JP. Richard Bennett, forest keeper, complainant. Offence committed 26 Oct. 1784.

4/D/10   16 Sept. 1785. Thomas Barnfield of Shipton Moyne. Shooting a partridge. T. Estcourt JP. John Wood, informant. Fine £20. Offence committed 1 Sept. 1785.

4/D/11   8 March 1785. John Harvey of Coates, yeoman. Using a dog to kill game. T. Estcourt JP. Robert Boyce, gentleman, of Cirencester, informant. John Longford, yeoman, of Cirencester, witness. Offender did not appear. Offence committed 4 March 1785.

4/D/12 –16   13 Sept. 1785. Henry Stephens of Clapton [on the Hill], yeoman. Using dogs to kill game in Sherborne. J. Scott JP.

4/D/12   Recognizance of offender in the sum of £20 to appear at next Q.S. to appeal against conviction.

4/D/13   [*Copy of* 4/D/16.]

4/D/14   Examination of John Cooper, petty constable of Sherborne.

4/D/15   Examination of Thomas Busby, witness.

4/D/16   Richard Lardner, informant. Thomas Busby, witness. Offender did not appear. Fine £20. Offence committed 6 Sept. 1785.

5/A/1   24 Oct. 1785. John Elliots of Wotton under Edge, weaver. Embezzling 4½ lb. of woollen yarn. Rev. G. Hayward JP. Mr. George Harris, clothier, of Uley, complainant.

5/A/2   7 Nov. 1785. Elizabeth Askins of Painswick, spinster. Stealing ¼ peck of potatoes from a field in Painswick. Robert Campbell JP. William Saunders, gardener, of Painswick, complainant. Offence committed 6 Nov. 1785.

5/A/3   21 Nov. 1785. Sarah Steel, Mary Steel, Martha Steel and Elizabeth Steel of Haresfield. Pulling up, with intent to steal, ½ peck of turnips from a field in Brookthorpe. R. Campbell JP. Thomas Gardner, husbandman, of Painswick, complainant. Fine 10/-. Offence committed 16 Nov. 1785.

5/A/4   24 Oct. 1785. Mary Sollis, wife of John Sollis of Painswick, broadweaver. Stealing ¼ peck of potatoes from a field in Painswick. R. Campbell JP. Timothy Wood, scribbler, of Painswick, informant. John Wood, gardener, of Painswick, complainant.

5/A/5   10 Jan. 1786. Elizabeth Annis, Mary Annis and Elizabeth Slater of Upton St. Leonards. Stealing a quantity of turnips from a field in Upton St. Leonards. R. Campbell JP. Mr. Duegard of Upton St. Leonards, complainant. Fine 5/-. Offence committed 8 Jan. 1786.

5/A/6   30 Dec. 1785. Thomas Williams, labourer, and James Bailey, cordwainer, both of Cooper's Hill, Brockworth. Breaking down and taking away posts and rails from a fence at Brockworth Wood. R. Campbell JP. John Horlick, labourer, of Cranham, informant. John Morris Esq. of the Sheephouse, Upton St. Leonards, complainant. Fine 7/- each. Offence committed 26 Dec. 1785.

5/A/7   24 Dec. 1785. Farmer Bellamy of Barton Street. Hauling his narrow-wheeled wagon with five horses along the turnpike road near Mr. Winfield's house in Upton St. Leonards towards the top of Portway. R. Campbell JP. Joseph Perry, informant. Fine 20/- and 2/6 expenses. Offence committed 23 Dec. 1785.

5/A/8   29 Nov. 1785. Tabitha Evans of Horsley, widow. Possessing part an oak tree without satisfactory explanation. Rev. P. Hawker JP. William Skammell, complainant.

5/A/9   1 Dec. 1785. Joseph Jones of Clifton, alehouse keeper. Selling ale without a licence. R. Scudamore JP. First offence. Fine 40/- and 6/- expenses.

5/A/10   29 Oct. 1785 and 5 Nov. 1785. John Clark of Hasfield, farmer. Using a dog to kill game. Sir John Guise JP. John Parker Esq. of Hasfield, informant. Miles Price, gentleman, of Gloucester, witness. Offender did not appear. Fine £5. Offence committed 18 Oct. 1785.

5/B/1   22 Feb. 1786. Joseph Cole of Horsley. Using nets to kill game in Kingscote. Rev. G. Hayward JP. Thomas Risbey, informant.

5/B/2   13 March 1786. George Cave of Owlpen. Cutting and stealing timber in Kingscote. Rev. G. Hayward JP. Mr. William White of Kingscote, complainant. Daniel Hancock, informant.

5/B/3   22 Feb. 1786. William Cole and Isaac Skurton, both of Horsley. Using nets and gins to kill game in Horsley. Rev. G. Hayward JP. Thomas Risbey, informant.

5/B/4   13 March 1786. Obadiah Dolman, James Holder and William Holder of Owlpen. Using gins to kill game in Kingscote. Rev. G. Hayward JP. Daniel Hancock, informant.

5/B/5   24 April 1786. George James of Newland, labourer. Cutting and stealing timber in the Forest of Dean and conveying it to ground belonging to his mother Sarah James, widow. S. Hayward JP. Thomas Wood, forest keeper, complainant. Offence committed 19 April 1786.

5/B/6   21 April 1786. Nathaniel Dancey of Coaley, clothworker. Buying about 3 lb. of ends of woollen yarn. Rev. G. Hayward JP. Edith Horrell of Coaley, informant. Offence committed 3 April 1786.

5/B/7   21 April 1786. Sarah Smith of Coaley. Buying about 3 lb. of ends of woollen yarn. Rev. G. Hayward JP. Edith Horrell of Coaley, informant. Offence committed 4 April 1786.

5/B/8   21 April 1786. Thomas Burroughs of Cam. Selling ends of woollen yarn to Elizabeth wife of Nathaniel Dancey of Coaley. Rev. G. Hayward JP. Edith Horrell of Coaley, informant.

5/B/9   21 April 1786. Elizabeth Dancey, wife of Nathaniel, of Coaley. Buying ends of woollen yarn from Thomas Burroughs of Cam. Rev. G. Hayward JP. Edith Horrell of Coaley, informant.

5/B/10   15 April 1786. Nebuchadnezzar Williams of Uley. Carrying in a bag a quantity of ends of woollen yarn. Rev. G. Hayward JP. Mr. William Holbrow of Leonard Stanley, informant.

5/B/11   15 March 1786. William Coats and William Organ, both of Brockworth, labourers. Cutting and stealing timber from Upton St. Leonards, the property of John Morris Esq. of the Sheephouse. R. Campbell JP. John Horlick, wood keeper, of Cranham, complainant. Fine 5/-. Offence committed 7 March 1786.

5/B/12   4 April 1786. Thomas son of William Rodway, labourer, and John son of Thomas Higgs, blacksmith, both of Upton St. Leonards. Pulling up, with intent to steal, four stakes from a hedge at Upton St. Leonards, the property of Mr. Richard Chandler, wool stapler, of Gloucester. R. Campbell JP. William Greening, labourer, of Upton St. Leonards, complainant. Fine 2/6 each. Offence committed 1 April 1786.

5/B/13   7 March 1786. Daniel Gardner of Painswick, labourer. Breaking down and stealing a quantity of hedge, the property of Thomas Perrott, baker, of Painswick. R. Campbell JP. Richard Perrott, baker, complainant. Ordered to be whipped. Offence committed 6 March 1786.

5/B/14   26 Jan. 1786. Margaret Barnfield of Cranham. Stealing wood from a wood-pile at Cranham. R. Campbell JP. William Keene of Cranham, complainant. Fine 3/-. Offence committed 21 Jan. 1786.

5/B/15   24 March 1786. Richard Meek of Barton Street, gardener. Failing to clean his ditches adjoining the turnpike road near Barton Street. R. Campbell JP. Nathaniel King, turnpike surveyor, complainant. Offender unwell. Wife appeared instead. Fine 10/-.

5/B/16   3 April 1786. Thomas Griffiths of Ruardean, coalminer. Stealing the lop and crop of an oak tree in the Forest of Dean. S. Hayward JP. John Bradley, deputy forest keeper, complainant. Offence committed 18 Feb. 1786.

5/B/17   1 Feb. 1786. Robert Brazington of Whaddon, labourer. Lopping and cropping an oak tree in Whaddon. S. Hayward JP. John Meek, husbandman, of Whaddon, complainant. Offence committed 30 Jan. 1786.

5/B/18   12 April 1786. Peter Yemm of St. Briavels, labourer. Cutting and stealing timber in the Forest of Dean. S. Hayward JP. Thomas Wood, forest keeper, complainant. Offence committed 31 March 1786.

5/B/19   11 Feb. 1786. Robert Wintle of Lea hamlet, labourer. Clearing and enclosing land for his own use in the Forest of Dean. S. Hayward JP. John Pearce, deputy forest keeper, complainant. Offence committed 26 Dec. 1785.

5/B/20   6 Feb. 1786. Elizabeth Saysell of St. Briavels, single woman. Stealing timber from the Forest of Dean. S. Hayward JP. George Smith, servant to John Bradley the elder, forest keeper, complainant. Offence committed 25 Jan. 1786.

5/B/21   11 Feb. 1786. Philip Palmer of Lea hamlet, labourer. Clearing and enclosing land for his own use in the Forest of Dean. S. Hayward JP. John Pearce, deputy forest keeper, complainant. Offence committed 23 Jan. 1786.

5/B/22   3 April 1786. Henry Rudge junior of Ruardean, cordwainer. Stealing the lop and crop of an oak tree in the Forest of Dean. S. Hayward JP. John Bradley, deputy forest keeper, complainant. Offence committed 14 Feb. 1786.

5/B/23   3 April 1786. Thomas Mayo of Ruardean, cordwainer. Lopping and cropping an oak tree in the Forest of Dean. S. Hayward JP. John Bradley, deputy forest keeper, complainant. Offence committed 14 Feb. 1786.

5/B/24   3 April 1786. Joseph Wilce of Ruardean, quarryman. Stealing the lop and crop of an oak tree in the Forest of Dean and conveying it to land taken and enclosed for his own use. S. Hayward JP. John Bradley, deputy forest keeper, complainant. Offence committed 14 Feb. 1786.

5/B/25   15 April 1786. John Jones of Coleford, butcher. Cutting and stealing timber in the Forest of Dean. S. Hayward JP. Richard Hawkins, deputy forest keeper, complainant. Offence committed 13 April 1786.

5/B/26   6 Feb. 1786. James Davis of St. Briavels, carpenter. Stealing timber from the Forest of Dean. S. Hayward JP. John Bradley junior, forest keeper, complainant. Offence committed 6 Dec. 1785.

5/B/27   14 April 1786. William Hill, bailey to James Yarworth of Coleford, husbandman. Stealing timber in the Forest of Dean. S. Hayward JP. James Gething, labourer, of Coleford, complainant. Offence committed 13 April 1786.

5/B/28   7 Jan. 1786. John Cooke of Corse, labourer. Using dogs to kill a hare. Sir J. Guise JP at the King's Head inn, Gloucester. John Parker Esq. of Hasfield, informant. Benjamin Glover, labourer, of Hasfield, witness. Offender did not appear. Fine £5. Offence committed 26 Dec. 1785.

5/B/29   21 Jan. 1786. Richard Werrett of Pauntley, labourer. Possessing a hare at Pauntley. Sir J. Guise JP at the King's Head inn, Gloucester. Richard Lloyd, yeoman, of Upleadon, informant. Thomas Hall, yeoman, of Compton, witness. Defendant pleaded not guilty but fined £5. Offence committed 27 Dec. 1785.

5/B/30   21 Jan. 1786. Francis Werrett of Pauntley, labourer. Tracing and killing a hare in the snow at Pauntley. Sir J. Guise JP at the King's Head inn, Gloucester. Richard Lloyd, yeoman, of Upleadon, informant. Thomas Hall, yeoman, of Compton, witness. Offender did not appear. Fine £5. Offence committed 27 Dec. 1785.

5/B/31   21 Jan. 1786. John Pethorne of Pauntley, labourer. Tracing and killing a hare at Pauntley [*etc., as* 5/B/30].

5/B/32   31 Jan. 1786. Joseph Wilce of Dymock, labourer. Using snares to kill hares at Dymock. Rev. B. Newton JP at his home in Gloucester. Richard Bull, carpenter, of Dymock, informant and witness. Offender did not appear. Fine £5. Offence committed 29 Jan. 1786.

5/B/33   13 March 1786. Samuel Wintle of Epney, labourer. Using a gun and a dog to kill game in Rodley, Westbury on Severn. Rev. C. Bishop JP at his home in Elmore. George Colwell, yeoman, of Westbury on Severn, informant. George Brasington, labourer, of Westbury on Severn, witness. Fine £5. Offence committed 10 March 1786.

5/B/34   13 March 1786. Samuel Rowles of Epney, fisherman. Using a gun and a dog to kill game in Rodley, Westbury on Severn. Rev. C. Bishop JP at his home in Elmore. George Colwell, yeoman, of Westbury on Severn, informant. George Brasington, labourer, of Westbury on Severn, witness. Fine £5. Offence committed 10 March 1786.

5/C/1   27 May 1786. Samuel Webb. Stealing a silver spoon, the property of Christopher Gardner Esq. of Minchinhampton. Sir George O. Paul JP. Fine 20/-.

5/C/2   2 May 1786. Edith Horrell, wife of James, of Coaley. Buying and receiving 1¼ lb. of ends of woollen yarn from Richard Foords, broadweaver, of Coaley. Rev. P. Hawker JP.

5/C/3   29 May 1786. George Dangerfield of King's Stanley. Buying a quantity of ends of woollen yarn from Dennis Clutterbuck of King's Stanley. Rev. G. Hayward JP. Benjamin Davis of King's Stanley, informant.

5/C/4   3 June 1786. Thomas Kilmister of King's Stanley. Buying a quantity of ends of woollen yarn from Benjamin Davis of King's Stanley. Rev. G. Hayward JP. Benjamin Davis of King's Stanley, informant.

5/C/5   27 May 1786. Isaac Legg. Buying a quantity of ends of woollen yarn from Lydia May of North Nibley. Rev. G. Hayward JP. Lydia May of North Nibley, informant.

5/C/6   27 May 1786. William Lewis of Wotton under Edge. Buying a quantity of ends of woollen yarn [*etc., as* 5/C/5].

5/C/7   29 March 1786. John Jenkins, servant to Israel Constant of Clearwell, husbandman. Stealing freshly cut timber in the Forest of Dean. S. Hayward JP. Richard Godding, servant to Robert East, forest keeper, complainant. Offence committed 28 March 1786.

5/C/8   29 April 1786. John Phelps of St. Briavels, labourer. Cutting and rooting up underwood in the Forest of Dean. S. Hayward JP. Thomas Lloyd, cordwainer, of Mitcheldean, complainant. Offence committed 14 April 1786.

5/C/9   29 April 1786. Samuel James of Weston under Penyard, lime-burner. Cutting and rooting up underwood in the Forest of Dean. S. Hayward JP. Thomas Lloyd, cordwainer, of Mitcheldean, complainant. Offence committed 14 April 1786.

5/C/10   31 May 1786. James Williams of Newland or Littledean, collier. Cutting and rooting up underwood in an enclosure taken out of the Forest of Dean. S. Hayward JP. Thomas Lloyd, cordwainer, of Mitcheldean, complainant. Offence committed 7 Jan. 1786.

5/C/11   31 May 1786. Joseph Jones, servant to James Williams of Newland or Littledean, collier. Cutting and rooting up underwood [*etc., as* 5/C/10].

5/C/12   26 April 1786. John Stevens of Littledean, cordwainer. Cutting off three holly trees in the Forest of Dean. S. Hayward JP. Thomas Lloyd, cordwainer, of Mitcheldean, complainant. Offence committed 17 Feb. 1786.

5/C/13   26 April 1786. John Pearce of Mitcheldean, plumber and glazier. Cutting and rooting up underwood in an enclosure taken out of the Forest of Dean. S. Hayward JP. Thomas Lloyd, cordwainer, of Mitcheldean, complainant. Offence committed 30 Jan. 1786.

5/C/14   10 June 1786. James Baldwin of St. Briavels, labourer. Cutting and rooting up a quantity of underwood in the Forest of Dean. S. Hayward JP. Thomas Lloyd, cordwainer, of Mitcheldean, complainant. Offence committed 27 Jan. 1786.

5/C/15   10 June 1786. John Bosley of Abenhall, husbandman. Cutting and stealing a maple tree in the Forest of Dean. S. Hayward JP. Thomas Lloyd, cordwainer, of Mitcheldean, complainant. Offence committed 28 Jan. 1786.

5/C/16   8 June 1786. John Williams of Ruardean, husbandman. Lopping and cropping a beech tree in the Forest of Dean. S. Hayward JP. John Bradley, deputy forest keeper, complainant. Offence committed 19 March 1786.

5/D/1   3 Aug. 1786. Elisha Humpheris, labourer. Selling ale without a licence in the parish of St. Philip and St. Jacob, Bristol. R. Bayly JP. First offence. Fine 40/- and 5/- expenses.

5/D/2   22 Aug. 1786. Mary wife of Samuel Berry, Mary wife of Daniel Clift and Mary Hopson, single woman, all of Stroud. Stealing a quantity of peas from a field belonging to William Pritchard. Nathaniel Winchcombe JP. William Pritchard, complainant. Offence committed 8 Aug. 1786.

5/D/3   25 Sept. 1786. Nicholas Dunn. Cutting and stealing a burden of small wood from Badgeworth Wood, the property of Benjamin Hyett Esq. of Painswick. R. Campbell JP. William Hughes, complainant. Fine 8/6. Offence committed 14 Sept. 1786.

5/D/4   22 Sept. 1786. Thomas Gabb Fords of Coaley, alehouse keeper. Allowing Simon Savage, labourer, of Coaley, to continue tippling for more than three hours so that he was very intoxicated. Rev. G. Hayward JP. Nathaniel Wilkins, complainant.

5/D/5   11 Sept. 1786. Edward Willey. Digging up and stealing a quantity of potatoes from a field at Painswick. R. Campbell JP. John Wood, gardener, of Painswick, complainant. Fine 5/-. Offence committed 9 Sept. 1786.

5/D/6   2 July 1786. Thomas Matthews of St. Briavels, lime-burner. Lopping and cropping a beech tree in the Forest of Dean. S. Hayward JP. John Pearce, plumber and glazier, of Mitcheldean, complainant. Offence committed 16 March 1786.

5/D/7   26 Aug. 1786. Isaac Kear of Bream, coalminer. Cutting and stealing oak timber in the Forest of Dean. S. Hayward JP. William Meredith, servant to Robert East, forest keeper, complainant. Offence committed 24 Aug. 1786.

5/D/8   12 Aug. 1786. John Parker of Abenhall, gardener. Cutting and rooting up a quantity of underwood in an enclosure taken out of the Forest of Dean. S. Hayward JP. Thomas Lloyd, cordwainer, of Mitcheldean, complainant. Offence committed 10 June 1786.

5/D/9   16 Sept. 1786. John Williams of St. Briavels, butcher. Rooting up a quantity of underwood in an enclosure taken out of the Forest of Dean for his own private use. S. Hayward JP. Thomas Lloyd, cordwainer, of Mitcheldean, complainant. Offence committed 3 Aug. 1786.

5/D/10   30 Sept. 1786. John Rosser of Coleford, quarryman. Cutting timber in the Forest of Dean. S. Hayward JP. Thomas Bennett, forest keeper, complainant. Offence committed 18 March 1786.

5/D/11   22 April 1786. James Dobbins of Hailes, yeoman. Assisting Hannah Feltstead to remove her goods and chattels from premises in Prestbury to prevent them being distrained for arrears of rent. S. Hayward JP and Rev. B. Newton JP. Thomas Parker, apothecary, of Gloucester, complainant.

5/D/12   30 Aug. 1786. James Drew of Littledean, labourer. Cutting underwood in the Forest of Dean. S. Hayward JP. Thomas Lloyd, cordwainer, of Mitcheldean, complainant. Offence committed 20 April 1786.

6/A/1   14 Dec. 1786. John Gill of Stroud, labourer. Swearing. T. Gryffin JP.

6/A/2   18 Dec. 1786. Samuel Jenner of Stroud, labourer. Swearing. N. Winchcombe JP.

6/A/3   1 Jan. 1787. Ruth Beard of Painswick, single woman. Pulling up and destroying a quantity of turnips in a field in Painswick belonging to Mr. Edward Palling. N. Winchcombe JP.

6/A/4   24 Nov. 1786. James Mayor of Stroud, clothworker. Pulling up and destroying a quantity of turnips in a field in Painswick belonging to William Dowell. T. Gryffin JP.

6/A/5   18 Dec. 1786. Daniel Gardner of Painswick, labourer. Stealing a young beech tree likely to become timber, the property of Sir William Jerningham. T. Gryffin JP. Richard Tunley, complainant. Offence committed 9 Dec. 1786.

6/A/6   14 Dec. 1786. Thomas Holbrow of Bisley, labourer. Possessing a quantity of underwood without satisfactory explanation. T. Gryffin JP. Thomas Bowyer, complainant.

6/A/7   1 Jan. 1787. William Monk of Painswick, blacksmith. Possessing a stolen piece of iron and failing to apprehend the person who offered it for sale. T. Gryffin JP and N. Winchcombe JP.

6/A/8   24 Nov. 1786. Daniel Gardner *alias* Walkly of Bisley, clothworker. Selling ale without a licence. T. Gryffin JP and N. Winchcombe JP. First offence. Fine 40/- and 4/- expenses.

6/A/9   24 Nov. 1786. Richard Townsend of Sapperton, labourer. Being an alehouse keeper without a licence. T. Gryffin JP and N. Winchcombe JP. First offence. Fine 40/- and 4/- expenses.

6/A/10   24 Nov. 1786. William Fowler of Sapperton, baker. Selling ale without a licence. T. Gryffin JP and N. Winchcombe JP. First offence. Fine 40/- and 4/- expenses.

6/A/11   3 Nov. 1786. Samuel Tyndale of Minchinhampton, carpenter. Selling ale without a licence. Sir G. O. Paul JP. First offence. Fine 40/- and 4/- expenses.

6/A/12   28 Nov. 1786. Daniel Smart. Cutting down an ash tree in Hucclecote, the property of Mrs. Colchester. R. Campbell JP. Nicholas Dunn, complainant. Fine 5/-. Offence committed 15 Nov. 1786.

6/A/13   1 Jan. 1787. Edward James of Painswick, miller. Hauling his six-inch-wheeled wagon with seven horses along Upton Hill leading from Gloucester to Painswick. R. Campbell JP at the Falcon inn, Painswick. John Marmon, informant. Fine £5. Offence committed 30 Dec. 1786.

6/A/14   1 Jan. 1787. Stephen Dangerfield of Painswick, haulier. Hauling his narrow-wheeled wagon with five horses along Upton Hill leading from Gloucester to Painswick. R. Campbell JP at the Falcon inn, Painswick. John Marmon, informant. Fine £5. Offence committed 30 Dec. 1786.

6/A/15   29 Dec. 1786. James Verender the younger of Broadway, Worcs., labourer. Killing and possessing a hare in Pinnock. J. Scott JP and Powell Snell JP. John Pugh, witness. First offence. Fine £20. Offence committed 25 Dec. 1786.

6/A/16   29 Dec. 1786. James Verender the elder of Cutsdean, Worcs., labourer. Killing and possessing a hare in Pinnock. J. Scott JP and P. Snell JP. John Pugh, witness. First offence. Fine £20. Offence committed 25 Dec. 1786.

6/A/17   7 Oct. 1786. Thomas Smith of St. Briavels, labourer. Cutting and stealing timber in the Forest of Dean. T. Crawley Boevey JP. John Bradley, deputy forest keeper, complainant. Offence committed 30 Sept. 1786.

6/A/18   7 Oct. 1786. Thomas Jones of Ruardean, coalminer. Cutting and stealing timber in the Forest of Dean. T. Crawley Boevey JP. John Bradley, deputy forest keeper, complainant. Offence committed 30 Sept. 1786.

6/A/19   16 Dec. 1786. James and William Huggins, sons of William Huggins, labourer, of Newent. Pulling up and stealing a large quantity of turnips from ground in Newent. S. Hayward JP. William Howells, husbandman, of Pauntley, complainant. Offence committed 29 Nov. 1786.

6/A/20   16 Dec. 1786. Charles Weaver of St. Briavels, stonemason. Cutting and stealing timber in the Forest of Dean. S. Hayward JP. James Bennett, deputy forest keeper, complainant. Offence committed 14 Nov. 1786.

6/A/21   11 Nov. 1786. Henry Powell of Blakeney, husbandman. Cutting and stealing timber in the Forest of Dean. S. Hayward JP. Thomas Wood, deputy forest keeper, complainant. Offence committed 8 Nov. 1786.

6/A/22   17 Nov. 1786. William Coleman of St. Briavels, butcher. Cutting and stealing timber in the Forest of Dean. S. Hayward JP. Thomas Lloyd, cordwainer, of Mitcheldean, complainant. Offence committed 25 Sept. 1786.

6/A/23   8 Oct. 1786. Edward Wilding of Bream, coalminer. Cutting timber in the Forest of Dean. S. Hayward JP. William Meredith, deputy forest keeper, complainant. Offence committed 6 Oct. 1786.

6/A/24   4 Nov. 1786. William son of Richard Mawson of St. Briavels, labourer. Lopping and cropping an oak tree in the Forest of Dean. S. Hayward JP. Thomas Lloyd, cordwainer, of Mitcheldean, complainant. Offence committed 28 Jan. 1786.

6/A/25   9 Dec. 1786. Joseph Cook of Abenhall, labourer. Cutting and stealing underwood in the Forest of Dean. S. Hayward JP. William Morgan, labourer, of Mitcheldean, complainant. Offence committed 23 Oct. 1786.

6/A/26   4 Nov. 1786. Richard Williams of Littledean, carpenter. Cutting and stealing timber in the Forest of Dean. S. Hayward JP. Thomas Lloyd, carpenter [*sic*], of Mitcheldean, complainant. Offence committed 14 Oct. 1786.

6/B/1   23 March 1787. James Elmes of Rodborough, cordwainer. Cursing. N. Winchcombe JP. Offence committed 14 March 1787.

6/B/2   23 March 1787. William Slatter of Rodborough, yeoman. Cursing. N. Winchcombe JP. Offence committed 14 March 1787.

6/B/3   23 March 1787. Thomas Bourn of Stroud, broadweaver. Leaving work unfinished and working for another master while still employed by Mr. Charles Hardwick, clothier, of Painswick. T. Gryffin JP and N. Winchcombe JP.

6/B/4   28 March 1787. Thomas Barnard the elder of Horsley, labourer. Cutting down an ash tree in a wood in Horsley, the property of Sir John Smyth and Henry Goodwin Esq. Rev. P. Hawker JP. Anthony Harvey, complainant.

6/B/5   9 March 1787. John Turner of North Nibley. Embezzling a quantity of abb and chain, the property of Messrs. Austin of Wotton under Edge. Rev. G. Hayward JP.

6/B/6   14 Dec. 1786. Thomas Holbrow of Bisley, sawyer. Possessing a young beech tree without satisfactory explanation. T. Gryffin JP. Thomas Bowyer, complainant.

6/B/7   13 April 1787. Robert Cowley of Uley. Buying 1 lb. of yarn, the refuse of cloth. Rev. G. Hayward JP. John Wilkins of Nympsfield, informant. Offence committed 27 Feb. 1787.

6/B/8   13 Jan. 1787. John Hughes of St. Briavels, labourer. Cutting and rooting up a quantity of stubs of underwood and burning the same in the Forest of Dean. S. Hayward JP. Richard Bennett, forest keeper, complainant. Offence committed 13 Nov. 1786.

6/B/9   13 Jan. 1787. George Hughes of St. Briavels, mole-catcher. Cutting and rooting up a quantity of stubs [*etc., as* 6/B/8].

6/C/1   2 July 1787. Richard Teakle of Horsley. Stealing timber from a wood in Nympsfield, the property of Francis, Lord Ducie. Rev. G. Hayward JP. William Dee, complainant. Offence committed 7 June 1787.

6/C/2   2 July 1787. Richard Bushell of Horsley, weaver. Stealing timber [*etc., as* 6/C/1].

6/C/3   13 June 1787. John Ghostly of Wotton under Edge, victualler. Allowing gaming to take place at his house. Rev. G. Hayward JP. John Cornwell, complainant. Offence committed 9 June 1787.

6/C/4   4 July 1787. John Hill of Cam. Embezzling 3 lb. of abb and chain, the property of Messrs. Austin of Wotton under Edge. Rev. G. Hayward JP.

6/C/5   9 May 1787. James Bourne of Cherington, carpenter. Possessing a quantity of timber without satisfactory explanation. Rev. P. Hawker JP. John George, yeoman, of Cherington complainant.

6/C/6   23 Jan. 1787. Sylvia Palmer. Selling ale without a licence in Bitton. W. H. Winstone JP. Second offence. Fine £4 and 6/- expenses. Fine paid 23 April. 40/- to be paid to the Clerk of the Peace.

6/C/7   5 May 1787. William Tustin of Dymock, husbandman. Swearing. S. Hayward JP. Richard Hodges, labourer, of Dymock,complainant. Offence committed 1 May 1787.

6/C/8   22 May 1787. Samuel James and John Phelps, both of St. Briavels, labourers. Cutting and stealing timber in the Forest of Dean. Rev. C. Bishop JP. Thomas Ravenhill, complainant.

6/C/9   19 May 1787. Henry Pritchard of Newland, coalminer, and Anthony Roberts and John Davis, both of St. Briavels, coalminers. Cutting and stealing timber in the Forest of Dean. Rev. C. Bishop JP. William Meredith, complainant. Offence committed 3 April 1787.

6/C/10   23 June 1787. John Brook of Kempley, husbandman. Swearing and cursing. S. Hayward JP. Mary Baker, single woman, of Kempley, complainant. Offence committed 11 June 1787.

6/C/11   2 May 1787. Jonathan Bryan of Littledean, labourer. Cutting and rooting up underwood in an enclosed piece of ground in the Forest of Dean. Rev. C. Bishop JP. Thomas Lloyd, cordwainer, of Mitcheldean, complainant. Offence committed 10 March 1787.

6/C/12   19 May 1787. Anthony Roberts of St. Briavels, labourer. Cutting timber, with intent to steal, in the Forest of Dean. S. Hayward JP. Thomas Cowmeadow, servant to Richard Bradley, forest keeper, complainant. Offence committed 6 April 1787.

6/C/13   19 May 1787. John Davis of St. Briavels, lime-burner. Cutting timber, with intent to steal, in the Forest of Dean [*etc., as* 6/C/12].

6/D/1   14 Sept. 1787. William Cook of Pitchcombe, yeoman. Selling ale without a licence. N. Winchcombe JP. First offence. Fine 40/- and 4/- expenses.

6/D/2   14 Sept. 1787. Robert Viner of Pitchcombe, labourer. Selling ale without a licence. N. Winchcombe JP. First offence. Fine 40/- and 4/- expenses.

6/D/3   31 July 1787. John Keene of Painswick. Swearing and cursing. N. Winchcombe JP.

6/D/4   11 Aug. 1787. William Strain. Swearing. T. Gryffin JP.

6/D/5   4 July 1787. Samuel Tyndale of Minchinhampton, labourer. Selling ale without a licence. Rev. P. Hawker JP. First offence. Fine 40/- and 4/- expenses.

6/D/6   13 Sept. 1787. Joseph Saunders. Selling beer without a licence in the parish of St. Philip and St. Jacob, Bristol. Joseph Atwell Small JP. First offence. Fine 40/- and 5/- expenses. 20/- sent for Exchequer by bearer.

6/D/7   19 Sept. 1787. Richard Hawkins of Coleford, coal-carrier. Cursing. S. Hayward JP. Edward Scotney, cordwainer, of Coleford, complainant. Offence committed 8 Sept. 1787.

6/D/8   14 July 1787. Elizabeth Matthews, wife of Benjamin Matthews of Forthampton, labourer. Picking and stealing a peck of peas from a field in Forthampton belonging to George Evans, bricklayer. S. Hayward JP. John Clifton, labourer, of Forthampton, complainant. Offence committed 6 July 1787.

6/D/9   18 Aug. 1787. John Craddock of Northleach, husbandman. Hauling with six horses a loaded wagon with wheels narrower than six inches on the turnpike road in Barnwood. S. Hayward JP. John Blizzard, husbandman, of Hucclecote, surveyor of the public highway in Barnwood, informant. Offence committed 9 Aug. 1787.

6/D/10   15 Sept. 1787. Benjamin Howell of Aston Ingham, Herefs., yeoman. Driving his wagon off the road and over a hill at the side of the turnpike gate to avoid payment of toll in Mitcheldean. S. Hayward JP. William Weare, keeper of the turnpike gate in Mitcheldean, informant. Fine 20/-. Offence committed 12 Sept. 1787.

6/D/11   11 Sept. 1787. Thomas Lucas of Newnham. Using dogs and a gun to kill game in Flaxley. T. Crawley Boevey JP at Flaxley Abbey. John Price, informant. Fine £20, mitigated to £10. Offence committed 6 Sept. 1787.

6/D/12   11 Sept. 1787. Edward Ball of Ross, Herefs. Using dogs and a gun [*etc., as* 6/D/11].

6/D/13   7 Sept. 1787. William Pinkcott. Selling ale without a licence in Acton Turville. Richard Haynes JP, Sir W. Codrington JP, I. W. Horlock JP and G. Hardwicke JP. First conviction. Offence committed 5 Aug. 1787.

6/D/14   10 Sept. 1787. Edward Ball of Ross, Herefs. Using dogs and a gun to kill game in Rodley, Westbury on Severn. T. Crawley Boevey JP. George Colwell and William Bennett, informants. Fine £20, mitigated to £10. Offence committed 8 Sept. 1787.

7/A/1   24 Dec. 1787. John Ballenger of Churcham, labourer. Possessing a hare. Rev. C. Bishop JP at Elmore. Richard Jenkins, woodward, of Highnam, informant. Samuel Beard, labourer, of Churcham, witness. Fine £5. Offence committed 6 Dec. 1787.

7/A/2   15 Dec. 1787. William Pritchard of Lowbands, Redmarley, Worcs. Stealing a dog in Pauntley. Sir J. Guise JP and Rev. John Foley JP. Richard Loveridge, yeoman, of Pauntley, and William Brookes Esq. of Bromsberrow, complainants.

7/A/3   23 Dec. 1787. William Mayle of Tetbury, labourer. Using dogs to kill game in Oldbury on the Hill. Henry, duke of Beaufort, JP and T. Estcourt JP at Badminton. Robert Cross of Great Badminton, informant. Edward Cross of Great Badminton, witness. Fine £5. Offence committed 22 Dec. 1787.

7/A/4   23 Dec. 1787. James Webb of Tetbury, labourer. Using dogs [*etc., as* 7/A/3].

7/A/5   2 Jan. 1788. William Bushell of Nympsfield, broadweaver. Embezzling 3 lb. of woollen yarn. Rev. G. Hayward JP. Mr. James Harris of Uley, complainant.

7/A/6   14 Dec. 1787. Richard Bushell of Horsley, broadweaver. Stealing two young beech trees from Bowlass Wood in Nympsfield, the property of Francis, Lord Ducie. Rev. G. Hayward JP. Richard Teakle of Horsley, informant.

7/A/7   22 Oct. 1787. Matthew Smith the younger of Uley. Buying 3¾ lb. of ends of woollen yarn (for 3/6) from Edward Hall of King's Stanley. Rev. G. Hayward JP. Edward Hall, weaver, of King's Stanley, informant.

7/A/8   1 Jan. 1788. William Howell of Horsley. Selling beer without a licence. Rev. P. Hawker JP. First offence. Fine 40/- amd 4/- expenses.

7/A/9   17 Nov. 1787. William Stubbs of Staverton, labourer. Cutting off branches from a pear tree and apple trees in an orchard at Staverton without permission. S. Hayward JP. William Togwells, blacksmith, of Staverton, complainant.

7/A/10   25 Oct. 1787. Isaac Frape of Iron Acton, labourer. Swearing and cursing. W. Holwell JP.

7/A/11   10 Nov. 1787. John Brain of Littledean, nailer. Cutting and rooting up a quantity of underwood in the Forest of Dean. S. Hayward JP. John Brett, forest keeper, complainant. Offence committed 8 Oct. 1787.

7/A/12   11 Dec. 1787. Elizabeth Matthews, lately of St. Catherine's parish, Gloucester, single woman. Picking and stealing about a peck of turnips from a field in Barton Street St. Michael, the property of Edward Elton Esq. of Gloucester. S. Hayward JP. Joseph Barnard, labourer, of Barton Street St. Michael, complainant.

7/A/13   10 Nov. 1787. John Grindall of St. Briavels, labourer. Cutting and rooting up underwood in the Forest of Dean. S. Hayward JP. John Brett, forest keeper, complainant. Offence committed 8 Oct. 1787.

7/B/1   29 Feb. 1788. John Curnock of North Nibley. Possessing 3 lb. of ends of woollen yarn. Rev. G. Hayward JP.

7/B/2   9 Feb. 1788. David Jefferys. Cropping young beech trees [*no place named*]. John Selfe JP. Mr. Nathaniel Rogers, complainant. Offence committed 10 Jan. 1788.

7/B/3   18 March 1788. Thomas Holborough of Bisley, sawyer. Possessing a young beech tree without satisfactory explanation. T. Gryffin JP.

7/B/4   29 Feb. 1788. Robert Curnock the elder of North Nibley. Possessing 3 lb. of ends of woollen yarn. Rev. G. Hayward JP.

7/B/5   7 Feb. 1788. John Hobbs. Lopping trees [*no place named*]. Francis Broughton JP. Robert Collins, complainant.

7/B/6   12 Feb. 1788. John Morgan of St. Briavels, labourer. Hunting and killing a fallow deer with two dogs in the Forest of Dean. S. Hayward JP John Brett, forest keeper, informant. Joseph Young, servant to John Brett, witness. Fine £30, £10 of which to be paid to informant, £10 for use of poor in place where offence was committed and £10 to the owner of the deer.

7/B/7   29 Jan. 1788. Charles White of Coleford, joiner and carpenter. Carrying a loaded gun with intent to kill deer in the Forest of Dean. S. Hayward JP. Thomas Bennett, deputy forest keeper, informant. Fine 10/-, one half of which to be paid to the informer. Offence committed 8 Feb. [*sic, recte Jan.*] 1788.

7/B/8   26 Jan. 1788. William Thomas of St. Briavels, labourer. Stealing a beech tree from the Forest of Dean. S. Hayward JP. Thomas Lloyd, cordwainer, of Mitcheldean, complainant. Offence committed 5 Jan. 1788.

7/B/9   19 Jan. 1788. James Rudge of Newland, carpenter, and John Yem of Weston under Penyard, coal-carrier. Cutting oak timber in the Forest of Dean. S. Hayward JP. Richard Bradley, forest keeper, complainant. Offence committed 20 Dec. 1787.

7/B/10   19 Jan. 1788. Richard Marfield of Hope Mansell, Herefs., husbandman. Stealing oak timber in the Forest of Dean. S. Hayward JP. Richard Bradley, forest keeper, complainant. Offence committed 18 Dec. 1787.

7/B/11   8 Feb. 1788. John Clutterbuck and Samuel Bird, both of Leonard Stanley, labourers. Using snares to kill two hares. S. Hayward JP at his home in Gloucester. Charles Bubb, broker, of Gloucester, informant. Fine £10 each. Offence committed 7 Feb. 1788.

7/B/12   28 Feb. 1788. Richard Williams of Stinchcombe, serge-weaver. Buying 1½ lb. of refuse of cloth from Thomas Burroughs (for 1/6). Rev. G. Hayward JP. Thomas Burroughs, weaver, of Cam, informant.

7/B/13   4 Jan. 1788. Edward Trap of the Tilers' Arms, James Warner of the Horse Shoe, Ann Woodham of the Duke William, all of Chipping Sodbury, John Anstee of the Hat and Feather at Codrington, Robert Andrews of the White Hart at Wickwar, William Higgs of the White Hart at Westerleigh and Michael Jordon of the New Inn at Horton. Selling beer after being disabled to sell the same. Sir W. Codrington JP, G. Hardwicke JP, R. Haynes JP and I. W. Horlock JP. First convictions.

7/B/14   15 March 1788. Robert Gwillam of Elton, Westbury on Severn, nailer. Loppping and cropping a beech tree in the Forest of Dean. C. Hayward JP. Thomas Lloyd, servant to Thomas Blunt Esq., deputy forest surveyor, complainant. Offence committed 18 Feb. 1788.

7/B/15   9 Feb. 1788. Thomas Plaister of Mitcheldean, husbandman. Stealing underwood in the Forest of Dean. S. Hayward JP. Miles Hartland, yeoman, of Mitcheldean, complainant. Offence committed 5 Jan. 1788.

7/B/16   8 Feb. 1788. Richard Weaver of St. Briavels, labourer. Cutting and stealing beech timber in the Forest of Dean. S. Hayward JP. James Bennett, deputy forest keeper, complainant. Offence committed 11 Jan. 1788.

7/B/17   8 Feb. 1788. Stephen Trigg of St. Briavels, lime-burner. Felling an oak tree in the Forest of Dean. S. Hayward JP. Thomas Lloyd, servant to Thomas Blunt, deputy forest surveyor, complainant. Offence committed 7 Feb. 1788.

7/B/18   28 Feb. 1788. Isaac Legg of North Nibley, scribbler. Buying 3 lb. of ends of woollen yarn from Thomas Burroughs (for 2/6). Rev. G. Hayward JP. Thomas Burroughs, weaver, of Cam, informant.

7/B/19   28 March 1788. William Thomas the younger of St. Briavels, coalminer. Cutting oak timber in the Forest of Dean. S. Hayward JP. Robert East, forest keeper, complainant.

7/B/20   11 March 1788. George Morse of St. Briavels, collier. Stealing freshly cut oak timber, in company with Richard Heath, in the Forest of Dean. S. Hayward JP. William Meredith, deputy forest keeper, complainant. Offence committed 10 March 1788.

7/B/21   5 Feb. 1788. Mark Terrett of North Nibley. Buying 7 lb. of ends of Spanish yarn from Edward Evans (for 14/-). Rev. G. Hayward JP. Edward Evans, broadweaver, of Uley, informant.

7/B/22   25 March 1788. Mark Terrett of North Nibley. Buying 15 lb. of ends of Spanish yarn from Thomas Burroughs (for 30/-). Rev. G. Hayward JP. Thomas Burroughs, weaver, of Cam, informant. [*Copy. Original document removed to Court of King's Bench, Epiphany Sessions 1789.*]

7/B/23   28 Feb. 1788. John Bruton the younger of Uley, weaver. Buying a quantity of refuse of cloth from Thomas Burroughs (for 14/-). Rev. G. Hayward JP. Thomas Burroughs, weaver, of Cam, informant.

7/B/24   28 March 1788. Abel Cornock of North Nibley. Buying 5 lb. of ends of yarn from Thomas Burroughs (for 14/-, of which only 3/- was paid). Rev. G. Hayward JP. Thomas Burroughs, informant.

7/C/1   6 June 1788. Daniel Dangerfield of Stroud, labourer. Cursing, N. Winchcombe JP.

7/C/2   29 May 1788. Zachariah Greening of Cam, labourer. Cursing. Rev. P. Hawker JP.

7/C/3   4 April 1788. Sarah Holbrook of Iron Acton, spinster. Swearing. W. Holwell JP.

7/C/4   3 June 1788. Edward Tandy of Dursley, broadweaver. Embezzling 2½ lb. of Spanish woollen yarn. N. Winchcombe JP and Rev. G. Hayward JP. Thomas Tippetts Esq., clothier, of Dursley, complainant.

7/C/5   15 May 1788. Susannah Roan of North Nibley. Stealing ½ lb. of wool from the 6 lb. given her to card and spin. Rev. G. Hayward JP. Messrs. Austin, clothiers, of Wotton under Edge, complainants.

7/C/6   15 May 1788. Betty Brown of Wotton under Edge. Stealing 1 lb. of wool from the 15 lb. given her to pick. Rev. G. Hayward JP. Messrs. Austin, clothiers, of Wotton under Edge, complainants.

7/C/7   30 July 1788. Joseph Terrett of North Nibley. Buying 5 lb. of refuse cloth from Thomas Burroughs (for 15/-, of which only 5/- was paid). Rev. G. Hayward JP. Thomas Burroughs, weaver, of Cam, informant.

7/C/8   30 July 1788. Thomas Smith of Stancombe, Stinchcombe. Buying 1½ lb. of ends of woollen yarn from Joseph Bruton (for 4/6). Rev. G. Hayward JP. Joseph Bruton, broadweaver, of Uley, informant.

7/C/9   16 June 1788. Mary Beard of Painswick. Swearing. N. Winchcombe JP.

8 May 1788. John Hill and Samuel Nicholls, both of Stroud, labourers. Swearing. N. Winchcombe JP.

7/C/10   16 April 1788. Betty Clift of Horsley, widow. Selling beer without a licence. Rev. P. Hawker JP. Fine 40/- and 4/- expenses.

7/C/11   20 June 1788. Elizabeth Goodwin, single woman, Ann Colston, single woman, and Sarah wife of Thomas Dangerfield, labourer, all of Haresfield. Swearing. N. Winchcombe JP

7/C/12   30 July 1788. Thomas Walkley of King's Stanley. Buying 7 lb. of refuse of cloth from Joseph Bruton. Rev. G. Hayward JP. Joseph Bruton, broadweaver, of Uley, informant.

7/C/13   9 June 1788. Thomas Whiting, mason, and William Bucknell, weaver, both of Bisley. Selling ale without a licence. J. Selfe JP. First offence. Fine 40/- and 4/- expenses each.

7/C/14   22 May 1788. Sarah Cother of Tibberton, widow. Selling ale without a licence. Rev. J. Foley JP.

7/C/15   15 July 1788. Thomas Brown of St. Briavels, cooper. Stealing a kibble of oak timber in the Forest of Dean. S. Hayward JP. Richard Jones, labourer, of St. Briavels, complainant. Offence committed 14 July 1788.

7/C/16   19 April 1788. George Roberts of St. Briavels or Ruardean, labourer. Cutting and stealing timber in the Forest of Dean. S. Hayward JP. James Moore, labourer, of St. Briavels, complainant. Offence committed 22 March 1788.

7/C/17   9 May 1788. Betty Woodward of Hillesley, Hawkesbury. Carrying a quantity of warp yarn in Green Lane in Hillesley, contrary to law. Rev. G. Hayward JP. Thomas Young, broadweaver, of Sinwell, Wotton under Edge, informant. Offence committed 8 May 1788.

7/C/18   9 July 1788. James Robbins of St. Briavels, coalminer. Cutting and stealing, with others, parts of a large oak tree in the Forest of Dean. S. Hayward JP. William Meredith, deputy forest keeper, complainant. Offence committed 9 July 1788.

7/C/19   28 June 1788. George Husband, late of Mitcheldean, labourer. Stealing a burden of oak and beech underwood, in company with Thomas Pitt, in the Forest of Dean. S. Hayward JP. Thomas Lloyd, servant to Thomas Blunt Esq., complainant. Offence committed 10 Jan. 1788.

7/C/20   28 June 1788. Thomas Pitt, late of Mitcheldean, labourer. Stealing a burden of oak and beech underwood, in company with George Husband, in the Forest of Dean [etc., as 17/C/19].

7/C/21   25 June 1788. George Roberts of St. Briavels, lime-burner. Cutting up part of a tree, freshly felled in the Forest of Dean, in ground in Weston under Penyard, Herefs., belonging to Pumpin Smith. S. Hayward JP. George Court, forest keeper, and Edward Bevan, deputy forest keeper, complainants. Offence committed 12 June 1788.

7/C/22   25 June 1788. Thomas Matthews of St. Briavels, lime-burner. Cutting and stealing oak timber in the Forest of Dean, in company with Samuel Matthews, lime-burner, of St. Briavels. S. Hayward JP. George Court, forest keeper, and Edward Bevan, deputy forest keeper, complainants. Offence committed 4 June 1788.

7/C/23   10 May 1788. John Morgan of St. Briavels, labourer. Cutting several young birch trees, with intent to steal, in the Forest of Dean. C. Hayward JP. John Phillips, deputy forest keeper, complainant. Offence committed 25 Feb. 1788.

7/C/24   3 May 1788. John Boseley of Abenhall, husbandman. Stealing the top and lop of a beech tree in the Forest of Dean. S. Hayward JP. John Jones, servant to Thomas Blunt, deputy forest surveyor, complainant. Offence committed 14 April 1788.

7/C/25   25 June. 1788. Samuel Matthews of St. Briavels, lime-burner. Cutting oak timber in the Forest of Dean in company with Thomas Matthews, lime-burner, of St. Briavels [*etc.*, *as* 7/C/22].

7/C/26   2 May 1788. James Baynham of St. Briavels, labourer. Cutting down a quantity of young beech trees in the Forest of Dean. S. Hayward JP. James Moore, servant to Richard Bradley, forest keeper, complainant. Offence committed 8 March 1788.

7/C/27   5 April 1788. Thomas Jones of St. Briavels, labourer. Lopping an oak timber tree in the Forest of Dean. S. Hayward JP. John Meek, labourer, of St. Briavels, complainant. Offence committed 13 March 1788.

7/C/28   2 May 1788. William Blanch of Ruardean, labourer. Cutting off the limb of a beech tree in the Forest of Dean. S. Hayward JP. Richard Bradley, forest keeper, complainant. Offence committed 9 Jan. 1788.

7/C/29   2 May 1788. Edward Roberts of St. Briavels, collier. Cutting off the limb of a beech tree in the Forest of Dean. S. Hayward JP. Richard Bradley, forest keeper, complainant. Offence committed 24 Dec. 1787.

7/C/30   19 April 1788. Jonathan Rudge of Weston [under Penyard, Herefs.; *MS.* Weston, Glos.], labourer. Stealing a quantity of oak lop wood in the Forest of Dean. S. Hayward JP. Thomas Lloyd, servant to Thomas Blunt, deputy forest surveyor, complainant. Offence committed 13 March 1788.

7/C/31   2 May 1788. Samuel James of Weston under Penyard, Herefs., lime-burner. Stealing part of an oak timber tree in the Forest of Dean. S. Hayward JP. Richard Bradley, forest keeper, complainant. Offence committed 7 April 1788.

7/C/32   5 June 1788. Sarah wife of Mark Terrett of North Nibley. Buying 7 lb. of ends of yarn from Thomas Young (for 1/5½). Rev. G. Hayward JP. Thomas Young, broadweaver, of Sinwell, Wotton under Edge, informant.

7/D/1   27 Sept. 1788. Daniel Hooke of Stroud, cordwainer. Swearing. N. Winchcombe JP.

7/D/2   19 Aug. 1788. Robert Warren of Bisley, weaver. Cursing. N. Winchcombe JP.

7/D/3   2 Sept. 1788. James Mallett of Stroud, weaver. Cursing. N. Winchcombe JP.

7/D/4   5 Aug. 1788. Thomas Pearce of Randwick, weaver. Cursing. N. Winchcombe JP.

7/D/5   1 Oct. 1788. Samuel Gardner and William Simms, both of Painswick, labourers. Swearing. N. Winchcombe JP.

7/D/6   27 Sept. 1788. John Saunders of Bisley, labourer. Cursing. N. Winchcombe JP.

7/D/7   11 Sept. 1788. Isaac Rowland of Stroud, labourer. Swearing. N. Winchcombe JP.

7/D/8   2 Sept. 1788. Esther Hunt of Stroud. Swearing. N. Winchcombe JP.

7/D/9   1 Sept. 1788. Ann Restal of Stroud, single woman. Cursing. N. Winchcombe JP.

7/D/10   16 July 1788. William Horwood of Stroud, weaver. Cursing. Rev. P. Hawker JP.

7/D/11   18 Aug. 1788. Daniel Fords of Nympsfield, baker. Selling ale without a licence. Rev. G. Hayward JP.

7/D/12   23 Sept. 1788. William Willis, clothworker, Samuel Jacobs, barber, Edward Webb, carpenter, James Cooke, Thomas Chew, labourers, and William Johnson, carpenter, all of Painswick. Swearing and cursing. N. Winchcombe JP.

7/D/13   29 Sept. 1788. Roger Cooper of Littledean, labourer. Cutting up and stealing oak timber which had already been made into hogshead and barrel staves, in the Forest of Dean. S. Hayward JP. Thomas Bright, husbandman, complainant, and John Phillips, deputy forest keeper, witness. Offence committed 15 July 1788.

8/A/1   24 Oct. 1788. Thomas Mills of Rodborough, rug-weaver. Cursing. N. Winchcombe JP.

8/A/2   8 Jan. 1789. Samuel Atkins of Painswick, timber dealer. Cursing. N. Winchcombe JP.

8/A/3   23 Dec. 1788. Thomas White of Pitchcombe, labourer. Cursing. N. Winchcombe JP.

8/A/4   10 Nov. 1788. John Caruthers of Standish. Swearing in Pitchcombe. Rev. G. Hayward JP. Offence committed 5 Nov. 1788.

8/A/5   24 Oct. 1788. Joseph Cook of Painswick, cordwainer. Cursing. N. Winchcombe JP.

8/A/6   10 Nov. 1788. William Page of Pitchcombe, yeoman. Cursing. N. Winchcombe JP.

8/A/7   15 Oct. 1788. Thomas Beard of Stroud, labourer. Cursing. N. Winchcombe JP.

8/A/8   31 Oct. 1788. Michael Chew of Stroud, scribbler. Cursing. N. Winchcombe JP.

8/A/9   17 Nov. 1788. James Rowland of Bisley, carpenter. Swearing. N. Winchcombe JP.

8/A/10   17 Nov. 1788. William Gardner of Stroud, farmer. Cursing. N. Winchcombe JP.

8/A/11   29 Oct. 1788. Samuel Aldridge of Stroud, cordwainer. Cursing. N. Winchcombe JP.

8/A/12   3 Nov. 1788. William Mills of Stroud, clothworker, and James Marman of Rodborough, labourer. Lopping and damaging a walnut tree, the property of Mrs. Mary Brown. N. Winchcombe JP. Mrs. Mary Brown, complainant. Offence committed 13 Oct. 1788.

8/A/13   28 July 1788. Peregrine Martin of Littledean, farmer. Stealing an oak timber tree from the Forest of Dean. Sir J. Guise JP. George Court, yeoman, of Littledean, complainant.

8/A/14   28 July 1788. William Turner of Mitcheldean, labourer. Stealing a wagon-load of lops and tops of timber in the Forest of Dean. Sir J. Guise JP. George Court, yeoman, of New Lodge, St. Briavels hundred, complainant.

8/A/15   28 July 1788. Thomas Prosser of St. Briavels, collier. Cutting and destroying a beech timber tree in the Forest of Dean. Sir J. Guise JP. Edward Bevan of New Lodge, Littledean, complainant.

8/A/16   6 Dec. 1788. Joseph Jones. Lopping a timber tree in the Forest of Dean. S. Hayward JP. John Baldwin, complainant.

8/A/17   11 Oct. 1788. John Morgan of St. Briavels, labourer. Cutting and making into hogshead staves part of an oak timber tree in the Forest of Dean. S. Hayward JP. Joseph Young, deputy forest keeper, complainant. William Meredith, deputy forest keeper, witness. Offence committed 12 Jan. 1788.

8/A/18   11 Oct. 1788. James Matthews of Newland, labourer. Cutting [*etc., as* 8/A/17].

8/A/19   22 Oct. 1788. James Hulbert of Kingsholm, gardener. Using a gun to destroy game, without a certificate. Sir J. Guise JP at Gloucester. William Fendall Esq. of Gloucester, informant. Offence committed 13 Sept. 1788.

8/A/20   12 Dec. 1788. Samuel Kyte of Ebrington, yeoman. Selling ale without a licence. J. Scott JP and Rev. Charles Jasper Selwyn JP. First offence. Fine 40/- and 5/- expenses.

8/B/1   16 April 1789. Sarah Cooke of Painswick, single woman. Cursing. N. Winchcombe JP.

8/B/2   12 Feb. 1789. Thomas Estcourt of Painswick, labourer. Swearing and cursing. N. Winchcombe JP.

8/B/3   12 Feb. 1789. Phoebe wife of William Cooke, clothworker, and Hannah wife of Richard Veriby, sawyer, both of Stroud. Pulling up and destroying turnips. N. Winchcombe JP. Offence committed 31 Jan. 1789.

8/B/4   24 Feb. 1789. William James. Cutting down an oak timber tree in the Forest of Dean. S. Hayward JP. Thomas Wood, informant. Offence committed 23 Feb. 1789.

8/B/5   23 Feb. 1789. Hester Peach of Woodchester, widow. Selling ale without a licence. Rev. P. Hawker JP. First offence. Fine 40/- and 4/- expenses.

8/B/6   17 April 1789. Thomas Flight of Rodborough, clothworker. Selling ale without a licence. Rev. P. Hawker JP. First offence. Fine 40/- and 4/- expenses.

8/B/7   16 April 1789. John Fortune of Bisley, clothworker. Cutting and destroying one ash tree, in Bisley, likely to become timber, the property of Dr. Daniel Lysons, Thomas Baghot Delabere Esq. and John Wade Esq. J. Selfe JP. Mr. William Sevill, complainant. Offence committed 24 Jan. 1789.

8/C/1   11 May 1789. Mary wife of Joseph Organ of Painswick, weaver. Swearing. N. Winchcombe JP.

8/C/2   21 May 1789. Daniel Escott of Pitchcombe, weaver. Swearing and cursing. N. Winchcombe JP.

8/C/3   15 June 1789. William Saunders of Stroud, weaver. Cursing. N. Winchcombe JP.

8/C/4   [*Duplicate of* 8/B/1, *replacing* Cursing *with* Swearing.]

8/C/5   7 May 1789. Mary wife of Samuel Berry of Stroud. Cursing. N. Winchcombe JP.

8/C/6   5 May 1789. Thomas Barnard of Horsley, labourer. Cutting down a young ash tree in a wood in Horsley, the property of Sir John Smyth and Henry Goodwin Esq. Rev. P. Hawker JP. Anthony Harvey, complainant.

8/C/7   29 April 1789. Peter James. Cutting part of an oak timber tree in the Forest of Dean. S. Hayward JP. John Hatton, informant.

8/C/8   26 May 1789. Edward Smith of Horsley, clothdrawer. Selling ale without a licence. Rev. P. Hawker JP. First offence. Fine 40/- and 4/- expenses.

8/C/9   27 April 1789. John Price of Barton Street St. Mary, Gloucester. Swearing. S. Hayward JP.

8/C/10   16 May 1789. John Read. Cutting down and stealing two oak timber trees in the Forest of Dean. S. Hayward JP. Hannah wife of William Baggett and Elizabeth Stevens, informants.

8/C/11   2 June 1789. Francis Read. Cutting down and stealing two oak timber trees [*etc., as* 8/C/10, *adding*] Offence committed 7 April 1789.

8/C/12   19 May 1789. Robert Tingle. Cutting, spoiling and destroying an oak timber tree in the Forest of Dean. S. Hayward JP. John Hatton, informant.

8/C/13   2 July 1789. Thomas Davis of Bisley, labourer. Possessing and conveying a quantity of iron without satisfactory explanation. N. Winchcombe JP and J. Selfe JP.

8/C/14   30 June 1789. Anne wife of John Lockyer of Horsley, weaver. Swearing and cursing. Rev. P. Hawker JP.
            30 June 1789. William Howell the younger of Horsley, miller. Cursing. Rev. P. Hawker JP.

8/C/15   30 April 1789. Christopher Archer of Stow on the Wold. Selling ale without a licence. Rev. John Hippisley JP and Rev. Thomas Leigh JP. First offence. Fine 40/- and 5/- expenses.

8/C/16   30 April 1789. Hugh Horseman of the Hide Mill in Maugersbury, Stow on the Wold. Selling ale [*etc., as* 8/C/15].

8/C/17   30 April 1789. Richard Shayler of Stow on the Wold. Selling ale [*etc.*, *as* 8/C/15].

8/C/18   30 April 1789. Robert Henwood of Stow on the Wold. Selling ale [*etc.*, *as* 8/C/15].

8/C/19   10 July 1789. James Payn of Longborough, cordwainer. Stealing one deer from Longborough Park, the property of John Scott Esq. of Banks Fee [*MS.* Bankfee] House. Rev. C. J. Selwyn JP. William Bennett, gamekeeper to John Scott Esq., complainant. Thomas Mason, witness. Offence committed Friday 3 July 1789.

8/D/1   22 Sept. 1789. James Vines the younger of Randwick, labourer. Cursing. N. Winchcombe JP.

8/D/2   31 Aug. 1789. Thomas Purnell and Thomas Eastington, both of Painswick, clothworkers. Cursing. N. Winchcombe JP.

8/D/3   18 Aug. 1789. Samuel Stratford of Tetbury. Selling ale without a licence. Rev. P. Hawker JP. First offence. Fine 40/- and 4/- expenses.

8/D/4   2 Oct. 1789. James Swain of Painswick, weaver. Pulling up and stealing one beech tree likely to become timber, the property of Sir William Jerningham. N. Winchcombe JP. Mr. John Smith, complainant.

8/D/5   21 Sept. 1789. Martha Churches of Stroud, single woman. Failing to spin 1 lb. of Spanish wool yarn, the property of Mr. William Capel and Mr. John Powell, clothiers, of Stroud. N. Winchcombe JP and Benjamin Hyett JP.

8/D/6   18 July 1789. Stephen Churches of Horsley, broadweaver. Possession of a quantity of various yarns without satisfactory explanation. Sir G. O. Paul JP. Offender allowed time to account for possession of yarn before eventual conviction.

8/D/7   25 July 1789. John Price of Barton Street St. Mary, yeoman. Swearing. S. Hayward JP. Offence committed 24 July 1789.

8/D/8   24 Aug. 1789. Thomas Brown of Norton, yeoman. Cursing. S. Hayward JP.

8/D/9   [*Number of*   3 of last year [8/D/13–15] – not signed till this year by R. Scudamore.
convictions below,   8 convictions J.A.S. [*sc.* J. A. Small, 8/D/11–12]
8/D/10–16:]   5 convictions R.S. [*sc.* R. Scudamore, 8/D/16]
                1 conviction double J.H. [*sc.* Joseph Harford, 8/D/10] – 18.0.0.[1]

Memorandum. Dr. Small returned these convictions in open court at Michaelmas Sessions 1789 but did not deliver any money therewith.

8/D/10   28 Aug. 1789. Henry Webb. Selling ale without a licence in the parish of St. Philip and St. Jacob, Bristol. Joseph Harford JP. Second offence. Fine £4 and 5/- expenses.

8/D/11   29 Aug. 1789. John Rogers. Selling ale without a licence in the parish of St. George, Bristol. J. A. Small JP. Fine 40/- and 7/6 expenses.

29 Aug. 1789. George Rogers. Selling ale [*etc.*, *as above*].

29 Aug. 1789. Sarah Cribb, widow. Selling ale [*etc.*, *as above*].

29 Aug. 1789. Joseph Bird. Selling ale without a licence in the parish of St. Philip and St. Jacob, Bristol. J. A. Small JP. Fine 40/- and 7/6 expenses.

8/D/12   29 Aug. 1789. Samuel Stone. Selling ale without a licence in the parish of St. Philip and St. Jacob, Bristol. J. A. Small JP. Fine 40/- and 7/6 expenses.

29 Aug. 1789. Sarah Johnson. Selling ale [*etc.*, *as above*].

29 Aug. 1789. Richard Morgan. Selling ale [*etc.*, *as above*].

---

[1] It is not clear how the apparent total was reached: the sum of the fines excluding those imposed by Dr. Small is £20.

29 Aug. 1789. Elhana Weaver. Selling ale without a licence in Stapleton. J. A. Small JP. Fine 40/- and 7/6 expenses.

8/D/13   27 Jan. 1788 [*late return*]. John Rogers. Selling ale without a licence in the parish of St. Philip and St. Jacob, Bristol. R. Scudamore JP. First offence. Fine 40/- and 5/- expenses.

8/D/14   22 Jan. 1788 [*late return*]. William Easterbrook. Selling ale [*etc., as* 8/D/13].

8/D/15   20 March 1788 [*late return*]. Henry Webb. Selling ale [*etc., as* 8/D/13].

8/D/16   29 Aug. 1789. Moses Elliott, labourer. Selling ale without a licence in Clifton, Bristol. R. Scudamore JP. Fine 40/- and 7/6 expenses.

29 Aug. 1789. Elizabeth Payne, widow. Selling ale [*etc., as above*].

29 Aug. 1789. Francis Williams. Selling ale [*etc., as above*].

29 Aug. 1789. John West. Selling ale [*etc., as above*].

29 Aug. 1789. Elizabeth Johnson, widow. Selling ale [*etc., as above*].

9/A/1   19 Oct. 1789. Richard Aston of St. Briavels, labourer. Aiding the theft of a fallow deer from a park in Mitcheldean and Abenhall, the property of John Colchester Esq. Sir T. Crawley Boevey JP. William Morgan, laboourer, of Mitcheldean, complainant. Offence committed 1 Oct. 1789.

9/A/2   11 Jan. 1790. John son of John Young and John Gardiner, both of Elton, Westbury on Severn, labourers, and John Wilkins of Stantway, Westbury on Severn, yeoman. Stealing a parcel of etherings from the Forest of Dean. Possessing four or five bundles of the above-mentioned etherings. Sir T. Crawley Boevey JP. John Brett, keeper of Littledean Lodge, complainant. Richard Hunt, servant to John Brett, witness.

9/A/3   17 Oct. 1789. John Marshall of Lea Bailey, mason. Stealing oak timber from the Forest of Dean. Sir J. Guise JP. John Vaughn of Ruardean, complainant.

9/A/4   31 Oct. 1789. Richard Mauson *alias* Mazon of Littledean, labourer. Cutting and stealing timber in the Forest of Dean. Sir J. Guise JP. Edward Bevan, yeoman, of St. Briavels, complainant.

9/A/5   13 Nov. 1789. William Hyde of Horsley, broadweaver. Buying 2 lb. of white yarn from James Evans, broadweaver, of Avening. Sir G. O. Paul JP and Rev. P. Hawker JP. Offence committed 9 Nov. 1789.

9/A/6   12 Nov. 1789. Anne Fords of Uley. Failing to return 13 lb. 6 oz. of wool given her to spin by William Heskyns of Horsley on 24 April 1789, and being unable to account for it. Rev. P. Hawker JP.

9/A/7   23 Nov. 1789. William Ball of Minchinhampton, weaver. Swearing and cursing. Rev. P. Hawker JP. First offence. Offence committed 20 Nov. 1789.

9/A/8   11 Dec. 1789. Mary Stephens of Dursley, single woman. Wilfully damaging 1 lb. of Spanish wool given her to spin by Mr. William Capel and Mr. John Powell, clothiers, of Stroud. N. Winchcombe JP and Rev. G. Hayward JP.

9/A/9   4 Nov. 1789. John Woolley of Rodborough, hostler. Cursing. Rev. P. Hawker JP. First offence.

9/A/10   10 Oct. 1789. Mary wife of James Hodges of Rodborough, clothworker. Cursing. Rev. P. Hawker JP. First offence.

9/A/11   30 Nov. 1789. John Chandler of Avening, labourer. Cursing in Horsley. Rev. P. Hawker JP. First offence. Offence committed 21 Nov. 1789.

9/A/12   8 Jan. 1790. William Haviland of Winstone, farmer. Swearing in Painswick. N. Winchcombe JP. Offence committed 21 Dec. 1789.

9/A/13   9 Jan. 1790. John Robbins of Avening and Jonah Tranter of Horsley. Cutting down timber in Avening, the property of Lord Ducie. Rev. G. Hayward JP. Thomas Pegler, informant.

9/A/14   19 Nov. 1789. Henry Fox of Clearwell, tailor. Possessing the head of a fallow deer unlawfully killed in the Forest of Dean. S. Hayward JP. James Bennett, yeoman, of St. Briavels, complainant.

9/A/15   31 Oct. 1789. John Moorfield of Lea Bailey, yeoman. Cutting and stealing a dray-load of underwood in the Forest of Dean. S. Hayward JP. George Court, complainant. Offence committed 4 June 1789.

9/B/1   25 March 1790. William Hill of Woodchester, butcher. Cursing. Rev. P. Hawker JP.

9/B/2   20 March 1790. John Dean of Minchinhampton, weaver. Swearing. Rev. P. Hawker JP.

9/B/3   9 April 1790. Charles Child of Bisley, corn dealer. Swearing and cursing. J. Selfe JP.

9/B/4   12 Jan. 1790. Joseph Evans of Minchinhampton, weaver. Cursing. Rev. P. Hawker JP.

9/B/5   6 April 1790. Oriana Wright of Stroud. Cursing. N. Winchcombe JP.

9/B/6   30 March 1790. John Apperly of Stroud, cordwainer, and John Price of Stonehouse, tailor. Swearing. N. Winchcombe JP.

9/B/7   19 Jan. 1790. John Herbert of King's Stanley, higgler. Cursing. Rev. P. Hawker JP.

9/B/8   28 Jan. 1790. Thomas Hodges of Woodchester. Selling ale without a licence. Rev. P. Hawker JP. First offence. Fine 40/- and 4/- expenses.

9/B/9   8 Feb. 1790. Ann Close of Minchinhampton, spinster. Embezzling 1 lb. of Spanish wool yarn delivered to her for spinning on 16 and 18 Jan. 1790. Rev. P. Hawker JP. Samuel Dudley Manning, clothier, complainant.

9/B/10   2 Feb. 1790. Thomas Barnard of Horsley, labourer. Cutting down a witch-hazel tree in a wood in Horsley, the property of John Smith Esq. and Henry Goodwin Esq. Rev. P. Hawker JP. Anthony Harvey, complainant

9/B/11   27 Jan. 1790. Thomas Hopkins of Avening, weaver. Cutting down and stealing a beech tree in a wood in Avening, the property of Richard Middlemore. Rev. P. Hawker JP. Richard Middlemore, complainant. Offence committed 27 Jan. 1790.

9/B/12   20 Jan. 1790. Alexander Jones of Lea hamlet, labourer. Stealing part of a beech timber tree in the Forest of Dean. Sir T. Crawley Boevey JP. Thomas Blunt Esq. of Abenhall, complainant.

9/B/13   20 Jan. 1790. Joseph Blanch of St. Briavels, coalminer. Cutting part of a beech timber tree in the Forest of Dean. Sir T. Crawley Boevey JP. T. Blunt Esq. of Abenhall, complainant.

9/B/14   20 Jan. 1790. William Virgo of Blakeney, Awre, husbandman. Stealing part on oak timber tree in the Forest of Dean. Sir T. Crawley Boevey JP. T. Blunt Esq. of Abenhall, complainant.

9/C/1   15 June 1790. David Wood of Painswick, labourer. Possessing several young beech trees without satisfactory explanation. B. Hyett JP. Mr. William Loveday, complainant. First offence. Fine 40/- but being unable to pay immediately sentenced instead to one month's hard labour in the house of correction and once whipped.

9/C/2   28 May 1790. Stephen Dangerfield the elder. Cursing. N. Winchcombe JP.

9/C/3   1 June 1790. Stephen Dangerfield the younger. Cursing. N. Winchcombe JP.

9/C/4   1 June 1790. Thomas Bassett of Stroud, labourer. Pulling up a young beech tree likely to become timber in a wood in Stroud, the property of John Delafield Phelps Esq. N. Winchcombe JP. William Smith, complainant. Offence committed in the night of 27 March 1790.

9/C/5   26 April 1790. Robert Teakle of Horsley, broadweaver. Buying and receiving more than 20 lb. of ends of woollen yarn from several persons at his house in Horsley. Rev. P. Hawker JP and Rev. G. Hayward JP. Convicted on own confession. Offence committed between 11 April and 11 July 1789.

9/C/6   26 April 1790. Joseph Gough of Rodborough, labourer. Cutting down two elm trees in Rodborough, the property of William Halliday Esq. Rev. P. Hawker JP. George Williams, complainant.

9/C/7   14 July 1790. Robert Teakle of Horsley, broadweaver. Buying 6 lb. of ends of woollen yarn in Horsley. Rev. G. Hayward JP at Littleworth. James Harris, clothier, of Uley, informant. Offender pleaded not guilty. Adjudged an incorrigible rogue. Offence committed 24 April 1790.

9/C/8   24 April 1790. Edward Elton Esq. of Gloucester, farmer or renter of the tolls at Over turnpike. Overcharging John Haynes, servant to Ephraim Smith, yeoman, of Highnam, when taking five oxen through the turnpike. Sir J. Guise JP. John Haynes, informant. Fine £5.

9/D/1   30 July 1790. William Lewis. Cursing. Rev. P. Hawker JP.

9/D/2   25 Aug. 1790. Mary wife of Philip Ashton of Stroud, cordwainer. Cursing. N. Winchcombe JP.

9/D/3   20 Sept. 1790. Samuel White of Stroud, weaver. Cursing. N. Winchcombe JP.

9/D/4   31 July 1790. John Bassett of Randwick, wool-scribbler. Cursing in Painswick. N. Winchcombe JP.

9/D/5   20 Sept. 1790. John Smith of Stroud, brazier. Swearing. N. Winchcombe JP.

9/D/6   27 Aug. 1790. Sarah Clift of Bisley, single woman. Failing to spin 3¼ lb. of Spanish wool delivered to her on 18 July 1790. B. Hyett JP and N. Winchcombe JP. Mr. William Capel and Co., clothiers, complainants. Convicted on own confession.

9/D/7   31 July 1790. Susannah Evans of St. Briavels. Selling ale without a licence. Sir J. Guise JP. First offence. Fine 20/- and 17/6 expenses.

9/D/8   31 July 1790. Thomas Roach of St. Briavels. Selling ale without a licence. Sir J. Guise JP. First offence. Fine 20/- and 17/6 expenses.

9/D/9   20 Sept. 1790. Robert Townsend of Cirencester, woolcomber. Using snares with intent to kill hares in Ampney Crucis. John Sheppard JP. Joseph Herbert, witness. First offence. Fine £20. Offence committed Sunday 19 Sept. 1790.

9/D/10   20 Aug. 1790. Michael Gale of Cold Ashton. Shooting a hare. R. Haynes JP at Wick and Abson. Robert Whittington, gentleman, informant. Fine £5. Offence committed 14 Aug. 1790.

9/D/11   20 Aug. 1790. Samuel Manning of Cold Ashton. Possessing a snare. R. Haynes JP at Wick and Abson. William Brewer, informant. Michael Gale, witness. Offender pleaded not guilty. Fine £5.

10/A/1   23 Oct. 1790. Benjamin Lewis of Minchinhampton, labourer. Cursing. Rev. P. Hawker JP.

10/A/2   9 Dec. 1790. Samuel Keyte of Ebrington, yeoman. Selling ale without a licence. Rev. C. J. Selwyn JP. Second offence. [Cf. 8/A/20.] Fine £4 and 4/6 expenses.

10/A/3   15 Oct. 1790. Thomas Browning of Bisley, labourer. Swearing. J. Selfe JP.

10/A/4   3 Nov. 1790. Richard Cork of Kingscote. Selling beer without a licence. Rev. G. Hayward JP. William Wright and Thomas Brookes, witnesses. First conviction.

10/A/5   26 Aug. 1790. Hannah wife of John Mabbett. Swearing. W. Holwell JP.

10/A/6   4 Dec. 1790. Hannah Morgan of St. Briavels, widow. Cutting part of an oak timber tree in the Forest of Dean. Sir T. Crawley Boevey JP. Thomas Blunt, gentleman, of Abenhall, complainant. Offence committed 19 Oct. 1790.

10/A/7   11 Dec. 1790. Edward Knight of St. Briavels, collier. Cutting and defacing the upper part of an oak timber tree in the Forest of Dean. Sir T. Crawley Boevey JP. George Court, forest keeper, complainant. Offence committed 26 Nov. 1790.

10/A/8   2 Nov. 1790. Betty Bittle of Stonehouse. Failing to spin or return 4 lb. of wool delivered to her by Benjamin Cooke, clothier, of Stroud, on 10 Nov. 1789. Elizabeth Coxe of Stroud. Failing to spin or return 2¼ lb. of wool delivered to her by Benjamin Cooke, clothier, of Stroud, on 2 Jan. 1790. Mary Chew of Stroud. Failing to spin or return 2¼ lb. of wool delivered to her by Benjamin Cooke, clothier, of Stroud, on 3 April 1790. N. Winchcombe JP and Rev. G. Hayward JP.

10/B/1   26 Feb. 1791. William Simmonds of St. Briavels, labourer. Cutting and destroying underwood in the Forest of Dean. C. Hayward JP. Thomas Blunt, gentleman, of Abenhall, complainant.

10/B/2   2 April 1791. William Taylor of St. Briavels, tiler and plasterer. Stealing part of an oak timber tree in the Forest of Dean. C. Hayward JP. William Meredith, complainant.

10/B/3   26 Feb. 1791. John Imm of St. Briavels, yeoman. Possessing a quantity of underwood stolen from the Forest of Dean. C. Hayward JP. Thomas Blunt, gentleman, of Abenhall, complainant.

10/B/4   13 April 1791. William Thomas of Stroud, cordwainer. Cursing. N. Winchcombe JP. Offence committed 11 April 1791.

10/B/5   4 March 1791. Thomas Stone of Stroud, mason. Cursing. N. Winchcombe JP. Offence committed 28 Feb. 1791.

10/B/6   16 March 1791. Thomas Wood of Avening, clock-maker. Cursing. Rev. P. Hawker JP.

10/B/7   4 March 1791. John Shewell, late of Stroud, stonemason. Cursing. N. Winchcombe JP. Offence committed 28 Feb. 1791.

10/B/8   16 April 1791. Daniel Walkley of Tetbury, husbandman. Using a greyhound to kill a hare. Rev. P. Hawker JP. First offence. Fine £10.

10/B/9   24 Jan. 1791. Philip Farmiloe of Horsley, pargeter. Selling ale without a licence. Rev. P. Hawker JP. First offence. Fine 40/- and 4/- expenses.

10/B/10   8 April 1791. Thomas Evans of Mitcheldean. Selling in his shop a pair of leather gloves bearing insufficient stamp duty. Joseph Pyrke JP. Offence committed 21 March 1791.

10/C/1   2 April 1791. William Taylor of St. Briavels, tiler and plasterer. Stealing oak timber from the Forest of Dean. C. Hayward JP. Miles Hartland, yeoman, of Mitcheldean, complainant. Offence committed 28 March 1791.

10/C/2   17 May 1791. William Shatford of Stroud, clothworker. Cursing. N. Winchcombe JP.

10/C/3   18 May 1791. Ann wife of Samuel Tyndale of Minchinhampton, victualler. Cursing. Rev. P. Hawker JP. Offence committed 18 April 1791.

10/C/4   28 June 1791. John Bright of Minchinhampton, boat-builder, and John Wall of Stroud, mason. Cursing. N. Winchcombe JP.

10/C/5   29 June 1791. James Weight. Selling beer in Stonehouse without a licence. Rev. G. Hayward JP. Edward Pegler and Daniel Cook, witnesses.

10/C/6   20 June 1791. Aaron Brinkworth. Selling cider without a licence in King's Stanley. Rev. G. Hayward JP. Convicted on own confession. First conviction. Offence committed during previous six weeks.

10/C/7 20 June 1791. Mr. Matthew Howell of Cromhall. Cursing. Rev. G. Hayward JP.

10/C/8 20 June 1791. Mr. Matthew Howell of Cromhall. Refusing to pay William Desborough of Stroud wages owed to him for service rendered before illness prevented him from working. Rev. G. Hayward JP. William Desborough hired as servant in 1786 at 12 guineas a year. Served three months before becoming ill. Mr. M. Howell enabled him to become an in-patient in the [Gloucester] infirmary. Wages, though promised, not paid on recovery. Mr. M. Howell ordered to pay £3 0s. 6d.

10/C/9 [*Duplicate of* 10/B/3, *replacing* stolen from *with* without satisfactory explanation in.]

10/C/10 [*Duplicate of* 10/B/1, *replacing* Simmonds *with* Simmons.]

10/C/11 19 March 1791. John Smith of Weston under Penyard, Herefs., labourer. Stealing part of an oak timber tree in the Forest of Dean. Sir J. Guise JP. George Court, forest keeper, complainant. Offence committed 18 March 1791.

10/D/1 1 Sept. 1791. John Luff. Cutting down and stealing a quantity of growing wood suitable for hoop staves, in James's Grove, Tidenham. Sir T. Crawley Boevey JP. Robert Pidcock Esq., complainant. Fine 40/- mitigated to 20/-.

10/D/2 22 July 1791. Philip Farmiloe of Horsley, yeoman, and Thomas Hodges of Woodchester, yeoman. Selling ale without a licence. Sir G. O. Paul JP and Rev. P. Hawker JP. Second offence. [*Cf.* 9/B/8, 10/B/9.] Fine £4 and 4/- expenses each.

10/D/3 22 July 1791. Aaron Fords of Avening, yeoman, Samuel Woodward of Avening, weaver, John Harris of Avening, yeoman, Isaac Clift of Horsley, cordwainer, George Townsend of Horsley, wool-sorter, Robert Guy of Horsley, rug-weaver, Samuel Holliday of Minchinhampton, shopkeeper, William Jones of Rodborough, glazier, John Leech of Rodborough, labourer, Edward Shipway of Rodborough, cordwainer, James Reeves of Woodchester, scribbler. Selling ale or beer without a licence. Sir G. O. Paul JP and Rev. P. Hawker JP. First offence. Fine 40/- and 4/- expenses each.

10/D/4 17 Sept. 1791. John Pill of Mitcheldean, cordwainer. Possessing a quantity of underwood cut in the Forest of Dean. John Parker JP. Miles Hartland, yeoman, of Mitcheldean, complainant. Offence committed 9 June 1791.

10/D/5 17 Sept. 1791. Thomas Mountjoy the younger of Littledean, labourer. Cutting down a beech timber tree in the Forest of Dean. J. Parker JP. John Brett, forest keeper, complainant. Offence committed 2 Sept. 1791.

10/D/6 17 Sept. 1791. Aaron Hale of Littledean, labourer. Lopping and cropping a beech timber tree in the Forest of Dean. J. Parker JP. John Brett, forest keeper, complainant. Offender voluntarily confessed. Offence committed 7 Sept. 1791.

10/D/7 17 Sept. 1791. William Simmonds of St. Briavels, labourer. Cutting up and destroying a quantity of underwood in the Forest of Dean. J. Parker JP. Thomas Blunt, gentleman, of Abenhall, complainant. Offence committed 9 Sept. 1791.

10/D/8 17 Sept. 1791. James Price of St. Briavels, collier. Cutting and stealing part of a birch timber tree in the Forest of Dean. J. Parker JP. Thomas East, complainant.

10/D/9 17 Sept. 1791. James James of St. Briavels, collier. Cutting and stealing part of a birch timber tree in the Forest of Dean. J. Parker JP. Thomas East, complainant.

10/D/10 26 Aug. 1791. William Davis of Eastcombe, Bisley, baker. Selling ale or beer without a licence. J. Selfe JP. First offence. Fine 40/- and 4/- expenses.

10/D/11 30 July 1791. John Townsend of Longhope, labourer. Cutting a quantity of underwood and green stubs in the Forest of Dean. C. Hayward JP. Miles Hartland, yeoman, of Mitcheldean, complainant. Offence committed 30 May 1791.

10/D/12 6 Aug. 1791. Thomas Stephens of St. Briavels, labourer. Lopping and cropping an oak timber tree in the Forest of Dean. C. Hayward JP. Miles Hartland the younger, carpenter, of Gloucester, complainant.

10/D/13 6 Aug. 1791. John Knight of St. Briavels, collier. Cutting and destroying a quantity of underwood in the Forest of Dean. C. Hayward JP. Miles Hartland, yeoman, of Mitcheldean, complainant. Offence committed 29 July 1791.

10/D/14 23 July 1791. John Clutterbuck of Stroud, scribbler. Cursing. N. Winchcombe JP.

10/D/15 17 Sept. 1791. Nathaniel Walden of Littledean. Cutting a quantity of underwood in the Forest of Dean. J. Parker JP. Thomas Blunt, complainant.

10/D/16 28 Sept. 1791. Aaron Fords of Avening, yeoman, Isaac Clift of Horsley, cordwainer, Robert Guy of Horsley, rug-weaver, James Reeves of Woodchester, scribbler. Selling ale or beer without a licence. Rev. P. Hawker JP. Second offence. [Cf. 10/D/3.] Fine £4 and 4/- expenses each.

10/D/17 21 Sept. 1791. Hester Short of Stroud, single woman. Wilfully damaging a quantity of woollen yarn given her to spin by Mr. Robert Hughes, clothier, of Stroud. N. Winchcombe JP and J. Selfe JP. Offence committed between 1 Aug. and 10 Sept. 1791.

10/D/18 15 Sept. 1791. Samuel Daniels of Randwick, labourer. Cursing. N. Winchcombe JP.

10/D/19 18 Aug. 1791. John Orphin of Stroud, pargeter. Cursing. N. Winchcombe JP.

10/D/20 6 Aug. 1791. Charles Budding of Westrip, Stroud, yeoman. Selling ale or beer without a licence. N. Winchcombe JP. First offence. Fine 40/- and 4/- expenses.

10/D/21 10 Aug. 1791. Daniel Dangerfield of Stroud, labourer. Swearing. N. Winchcombe JP.

10/D/22 22 July 1791. Thomas Barnard. Cutting down several young ash trees in a wood in Horsley, the property of Sir John Smith and Henry Goodwin Esq. Rev. P. Hawker JP. Anthony Harvey, complainant.

10/D/23 28 Sept. 1791. Thomas Hodges of Woodchester, yeoman. Selling ale or beer without a licence. Rev. P. Hawker JP. Third offence. [Cf. 10/D/2.] Fine £6 and 4/- expenses.

10/D/24 26 Sept. 1791. James Jefferis of Siston, son of Thomas Jefferis of Siston, carpenter. Using a greyhound to kill two hares in Siston. Sir W. Codrington JP at Dodington. Edward Hathway, informant. William Carpenter Ray and Francis Tompson, witnesses. Offender pleaded not guilty, but convicted. Offence committed 10 Sept. 1791.

10/D/25 26 Sept. 1791. James Jefferis of Warmley, Siston. Using a greyhound to kill game. Sir W. Codrington JP at Dodington. Edward Hathway, gentleman, of Pucklechurch, informant. William Carpenter Ray and Francis Tompson, both of Pucklechurch, witnesses. Offender pleaded not guilty, but convicted. Offence committed 10 Sept. 1791.

11/A/1 31 Dec. 1791. Samuel Ridler of Stroud, clothworker. Swearing. N. Winchcombe JP.

11/A/2 8 Nov. 1791. Richard Vevars of Minchinhampton, weaver. Cursing. Rev. P. Hawker JP.

11/A/3 12 Nov. 1791. John Leech of Rodborough, labourer. Selling ale or beer without a licence. Rev. P. Hawker JP. Second offence. [Cf. 10/D/3.] Fine £4 and 4/- expenses.

11/A/4 15 Dec. 1791. Joseph Miles of Rodborough, labourer. Selling ale or beer without a licence. Rev. P. Hawker JP. First offence. Fine £2 and 4/- expenses.

11/A/5 5 Nov. 1791. William Hopkins of Cheltenham, labourer. Using a greyhound to kill a hare within the manor of Hunt Court at Badgeworth. C. Hayward JP at Gloucester. Fine £20 mitigated to £10.

11/A/6 20 Aug. 1791. Ann wife of Philip Palmer of St. Briavels. Lopping and topping a beech timber tree in the Forest of Dean. C. Hayward JP. Offence committed 8 Aug. 1791.

11/A/7   26 Nov. 1791. John Burns of St. Briavels, labourer. Stealing two young beech trees in the Forest of Dean. Sir T. Crawley Boevey JP. Thomas Blunt, complainant. Offence committed Sat. 19 Nov. 1791.

11/A/8   26 Nov. 1791. Joseph Rudge of Newland, labourer. Stealing a young beech tree in the Forest of Dean. Sir T. Crawley Boevey JP. Thomas Blunt, complainant. Offence committed Sat. 19 Nov. 1791.

11/A/9   3 Dec. 1791. William Wilks of Maisemore, labourer. Lopping an oak timber tree in Woolridge, Maisemore, the property of the Right Rev. Richard, Lord Bishop of Gloucester. Sir T. Crawley Boevey JP. Henry Curtis, complainant. Offence committed 9 Nov. 1791.

11/A/10   26 Dec. 1791. Thomas Carter of South Cerney, labourer. Stealing one ash timber tree from a field in South Cerney, the property of William Smith. Richard Selfe JP. William Smith, yeoman, of South Cerney, complainant. Offence committed 20 Oct. 1791.

11/A/11   5 Nov. 1791. William Hopkins of Cheltenham, labourer. Using a greyhound to kill game within the manor of Hunt Court at Badgeworth. C. Hayward JP at Gloucester. John Wright, glover, of Badgeworth, informant. Benjamin Reading, witness. Offender pleaded not guilty. Fine £5. Offence committed 26 Oct. 1791.

11/A/12   15 Nov. 1791. Robert Gibbins of Brimpsfield, labourer. Using a snare to kill game in Witcombe. C. Hayward JP at Gloucester. William Pearson, labourer, of Witcombe, informant. Thomas Bevan, witness. Offender pleaded not guilty. Fine £5. Offence committed 15 Nov. 1791.

11/A/13   14 Oct. 1791. Henry Bayliffe of Corsham, Wilts. Using a greyhound to kill game in Acton Turville. Sir W. Codrington JP, Dr. G. Hardwicke JP and I. W. Horlock JP at Old Sodbury. Samuel Arthurs, gamekeeper to the duke of Beaufort, of Great Badminton, informant. Offender confessed guilt but claimed he was son and heir apparent of an esquire. This claim adjudged untrue. Fine £5. Offence committed 26 Sept. 1791.

11/A/14   4 Nov. 1791. William Howe of Colerne, Wilts. Using a greyhound to kill game in Acton Turville. Sir W. Codrington JP, R. Haynes JP, I. W. Horlock JP and Dr. G. Hardwicke JP at Old Sodbury. Samuel Arthurs, gamekeeper to the duke of Beaufort, informant. Offender pleaded that Henry Bayliffe, pretending to be qualified, persuaded him to go coursing. Fine £5. Offence committed 26 Sept. 1791.

11/A/15   4 Nov. 1791. John Bence of Biddestone, Wilts. Using a greyhound [*etc., as* 11/A/14].

11/B/1   31 March 1792. — Blunt *alias* Cooke of Weston under Penyard, Herefs., labourer. Stealing several oak trees in the Forest of Dean. C. Hayward JP. George Court, complainant.

11/B/2   6 March 1792. George Osborn of Dursley, weaver. Neglecting his work for eight successive days. N. Winchcombe JP. Thomas Tippetts, clothier, of Dursley, complainant.

11/B/3   24 March 1792. Ann Sinderly of Weston under Penyard, Herefs., single woman. Cutting down a young oak tree in the Forest of Dean. C. Hayward JP. John Jones, complainant. Offence committed 14 March 1792.

11/B/4   11 Feb. 1792. Johannah wife of George Husbands of Mitcheldean. Stealing an oak tree likely to become timber in the Forest of Dean. C. Hayward JP. Miles Hartland, complainant. Offence committed 24 Dec. 1791.

11/B/5   28 Jan. 1792. Aaron Hale of St. Briavels, coalminer. Lopping a birch timber tree in the Forest of Dean. C. Hayward JP. Miles Hartland, complainant. Offence committed 19 Jan. 1792.

11/B/6   26 March 1792. Willam Davis, late of Kempsford, labourer, a rogue and vagabond. Leaving his wife and children chargeable to the parish of Kempsford. Rev. Charles Coxwell JP and R. Selfe JP. John Iles, an overseer of the poor of Kempsford, informant.

11/B/7   17 March 1792. Hester Hockley of Longhope, single woman. Cutting a quantity of underwood in Hazledean Wood, Blaisdon, the property of Thomas Richardson Esq. and others. C. Hayward JP. John Hart, labourer, of Blaisdon, complainant.

11/B/8   24 March 1792. Sarah Porter of St. Briavels, single woman. Cutting a young beech tree likely to become timber in the Forest of Dean. C. Hayward JP. John Jones, complainant. Offence committed 14 March 1792.

11/B/9   25 Feb. 1792. Elizabeth Trigge of St. Briavels, single woman. Cropping a beech timber tree in the Forest of Dean. C. Hayward JP. Miles Hartland, complainant. Offence committed 15 Feb. 1792.

11/B/10   24 March 1792. William Turner of St. Briavels, coalman. Cutting down a holly tree in the Forest of Dean. C. Hayward JP. John Jones, complainant. Offence committed 17 March 1792.

11/B/11   31 March 1792. James Bowery of Lea, labourer. Cutting underwood in the Forest of Dean. C. Hayward JP. George Court, complainant. Offence committed 15 March 1792.

11/B/12   25 Feb. 1792. William Powell of Mitcheldean, mason. Possessing green stubs in the Forest of Dean. C. Hayward JP. Miles Hartland, complainant. Offence committed 24 Feb. 1792.

11/B/13   24 March 1792. Ann wife of John Saysal of Weston under Penyard, Herefs., labourer. Cutting young oak and beech trees likely to become timber in the Forest of Dean. C. Hayward JP. John Jones, complainant. Offence committed 14 March 1792.

11/B/14   17 March 1792. Thomas Simmonds of St. Briavels, labourer. Cutting and destroying underwood in the Forest of Dean. Sir T. Crawley Boevey JP. Miles Hartland, complainant. Offence committed 6 Feb. 1792.

11/B/15   17 March 1792. James Croat of St. Briavels, labourer. Cutting down two beech timber trees in the Forest of Dean. Sir T. Crawley Boevey JP. Miles Hartland, complainant. Offence committed 7 March 1792.

11/B/16   25 Feb. 1792. John Powell of Mitcheldean, mason. Possessing green stubs in the Forest of Dean. C. Hayward JP. Miles Hartland, complainant. Offence committed 24 Feb. 1792.

11/B/17   24 March 1792. Elizabeth Gough of St. Briavels, widow. Cutting two young beech trees likely to become timber in the Forest of Dean. C. Hayward JP. George Court, complainant. Offence committed 14 March 1792.

11/B/18   31 March 1792. James Jacksons of Mitcheldean, cordwainer. Cutting underwood in the Forest of Dean. C. Hayward JP. George Court, complainant. Offence committed 22 March 1792.

11/B/19   29 Feb. 1792. William Nick of Stroud, broadweaver. Neglecting his work for eight successive days. J. Selfe JP and Rev. G. Hayward JP. William Capel & Co., clothiers, complainants.

11/B/20   8 Feb. 1792. Jacob Teakle of Horsley, weaver. Buying and receiving at his home in Horsley 10 lb. of Raven Grey yarn from Jeremiah Hinton, weaver, of Horsley. Sir G. O. Paul JP and Rev. P. Hawker JP. Mr. Gidley, clothier, complainant. Offence committed 5 Dec. 1791.

11/B/21   26 Jan. 1792. Mary Horseman of the Hide Mill, Maugersbury, Stow on the Wold, widow. Selling ale without a licence. Rev. J. Hippesley JP. First offence. Fine 40/- and 5/- expenses.

11/C/1   19 May 1792. James Smith of Rodborough, weaver. Cursing. Rev. P. Hawker JP.

11/C/2   5 May 1792. William Wiley of Woodchester, scribbler. Cursing. Rev. P. Hawker JP.

11/C/3   4 July 1792. William Neale of [Minchin] Hampton, victualler. Cursing. Rev. P. Hawker JP.

11/C/4   2 July 1792. Thomas Hodges of Woodchester, yeoman. Selling ale or beer without a licence. Rev. P. Hawker JP. Fourth offence. [*Cf.* 9/B/8, 10/D/2, 23.] Fine £6 and 4/- expenses.

11/C/5   16 May 1792. Sarah Cottle of Horsley, spinster. Cutting and damaging two young ash trees in Minchinhampton, the property of Edward Sheppard Esq. Rev. P. Hawker JP. Edward Sheppard Esq., complainant.

11/C/6   2 July 1792. Mary Teakle of Horsley. Selling ale or beer without a licence. Rev. P. Hawker JP. Second offence. Fine £4 and 4/- expenses.

11/C/7   2 July 1792. James Reeves of Woodchester, scribbler. Selling ale or beer without a licence. Rev. P. Hawker JP. Third offence. [*Cf.* 10/D/3, 16.] Fine £6 and 4/- expenses.

11/C/8   19 April 1792. James son of Thomas Jefferys of Siston, carpenter. Using a greyhound to kill game in Siston. I. W. Horlock JP at Marshfield. Fine £20. Offence committed 13 Dec. 1791.

11/C/9   23 June 1792. Sarah wife of John Davis of Widford [*MS.* Witford]. Selling ale without a licence. Rev. J. Hippisley JP. William Jenner, supervisor of excise, informant. First offence. Fine 40/- and 5/- expenses.

11/C/10   17 May 1792. Thomas Gardner of Bourton on the Water. Selling ale [*etc., as* 11/C/9].

11/C/11   17 May 1792. Thomas Tombs of Bourton on the Water. Selling ale [*etc., as* 11/C/9].

11/C/12   17 May 1792. William How of Bourton on the Water. Selling ale [*etc., as* 11/C/9].

11/C/13   17 May 1792. John Palmer of Bourton on the Water. Selling ale [*etc., as* 11/C/9].

11/C/14   17 May 1792. William Lock of Bourton on the Water. Selling ale [*etc., as* 11/C/9].

11/D/1   14 Aug. 1792. William Morgan of Bisley, shopkeeper. Cursing. J. Selfe JP. Offence committed 10 Aug. 1792.

11/D/2   4 Aug. 1792. Mary Allen of Stroud, single woman. Wilfully damaging 20 lb. of woollen yarn given her to spin. C. Hayward JP and N. Winchcombe JP. Robert Hughes, clothier, of Stroud, complainant. Offence committed between 20 June and 4 Aug. 1792.

11/D/3   20 Sept. 1792. Thomas Lawrence of Stonehouse. Selling ale without a licence. Rev. G. Hayward JP.

11/D/4   21 Sept. 1792. Richard Pattern of Stonehouse. Selling ale [*etc., as* 11/D/3].

11/D/5   14 April 1792. William Vaughn of Mitcheldean, cordwainer. Cutting underwood in the Forest of Dean. Sir T. Crawley Boevey JP. Miles Hartland the younger, complainant. Offence committed 1 March 1792.

11/D/6   16 June 1792. Henry Bromley of St. Briavels, labourer. Stealing a quantity of underwood in the Forest of Dean. C. Hayward JP. Miles Hartland, complainant. Offence committed 17 May 1792.

11/D/7   9 July 1792. David Davis of Littledean, labourer. Cutting underwood in the Forest of Dean. C. Hayward JP. George Court, complainant.

11/D/8   1 Sept. 1792. Elizabeth wife of Thomas Gardner of St. Briavels, labourer. Cutting a quantity of young oak trees likely to become timber in the Forest of Dean. C. Hayward JP. Miles Hartland, complainant. Offence committed 11 Aug. 1792.

11/D/9   1 Sept. 1792. Susannah Tullemey of St. Briavels, single woman. Cropping an oak timber tree in the Forest of Dean. C. Hayward JP. Miles Hartland, complainant. Offence committed 24 May 1792.

11/D/10   5 May 1792. Sarah Ravenhill of St. Briavels, single woman. Possessing a quantity of underwood in the Forest of Dean. C. Hayward JP. Miles Hartland, complainant. Offence committed 20 April 1792.

11/D/11   11 Aug. 1792. Robert Wintle of St. Briavels, labourer. Cutting a young oak tree likely to become timber in the Forest of Dean. C. Hayward JP. Thomas Blunt, complainant. Offence committed 20 July 1792.

11/D/12   11 Aug. 1792. Richard Harris of St. Briavels, labourer. Possessing a quantity of underwood in the Forest of Dean. C. Hayward JP. Thomas Blunt, complainant. Offence committed 26 June 1792.

11/D/13   27 July 1792. James Cook the younger of Painswick. Possessing several young beech trees without satisfactory explanation. B. Hyett JP. William Loveday of Painswick, complainant.

11/D/14   1 Oct. 1792. William Bennet, William Nelams, Edward Jones *alias* Dipper, all of Ruardean, labourers. Using a lurcher to kill game in Ruardean. Sir T. Crawley Boevey JP at Flaxley Abbey. John Mason, gamekeeper, of Ruardean, informant. Joseph Wilce, quarryman, of Ruardean, witness. All pleaded not guilty. Fine £5 each. Offence committed Sunday 23 Sept. 1792.

12/A/1   6 Nov. 1792. Joseph Arnold of Minchinhampton, labourer. Driving a wagon drawn by seven horses with wheels less than the statutory measurement along the turnpike road to Avening. Rev. P. Hawker JP at Woodchester. Thomas Griffith, informant. Fine 20/-. Offence committed 27 Oct. 1792.

12/A/2   6 Nov. 1792. John Stafford of Minchinhampton, farmer. Allowing a wagon drawn by seven horses with wheels less than the statutory measurement to be driven along the turnpike road to Avening. Rev. P. Hawker JP at Woodchester. Thomas Griffith, informant. Fine £5. Offence committed 27 Oct. 1792.

12/A/3   22 Aug. 1792. Sarah Evans of Horsley. Possessing several small quantities of different sorts of woollen yarn without satisfactory explanation. N. Winchcombe JP and Rev. G. Hayward JP. Offence committed 20 Aug. 1792.

12/A/4   27 Oct. 1792. William Hopkins of Cheltenham, labourer. Using a greyhound to kill a hare within the manor of Hunt Court, Badgeworth. J. Parker JP at Gloucester. Fine £20. Offence committed 2 Oct. 1792. [*Cf.* 12/A/5 *and* 26; *the relationship is not clear.*]

12/A/5   17 Oct. 1792. William Hopkins of Cheltenham, labourer. Using a greyhound to kill a hare in Badgeworth. Anthony Austin JP at Wotton under Edge. Fine £20, mitigated to £10. Offence committed 2 Oct. 1792. [*Cf.* 12/A/4 *and* 26.]

12/A/6   9 Oct. 1792. Solomon Cratchley of Randwick. Swearing. N. Winchcombe JP.

12/A/7   20 Oct. 1792. John Warren of Stroud, weaver. Cursing. N. Winchcombe JP.

12/A/8   1 Dec. 1792. Ann wife of William Sinderberry of Weston under Penyard, Herefs., labourer. Cutting and stealing underwood in the Forest of Dean. Sir T. Crawley Boevey JP. James Bennett, complainant. Offence committed 29 Oct. 1792.

12/A/9   1 Dec. 1792. Sarah wife of Thomas Harris of Lea Bailey, Newland, labourer. Cutting and stealing underwood in the Forest of Dean [*etc., as* 12/A/8].

12/A/10   14 Nov. 1792. Thomas Hodges of Woodchester, yeoman. Selling ale or beer etc. without a licence. Rev. P. Hawker JP. Fifth offence. [*Cf.* 9/B/8, 10/D/2, 23, 11/C/4.] Fine £6 and 4/- expenses.

12/A/11   8 Oct. 1792. William Heskins of Avening, clothier. Selling ale or beer etc. without a licence. Rev. P. Hawker JP. First offence. Fine 40/- and 4/- expenses.

12/A/12 14 Nov. 1792. Thomas Flight of Rodborough. Selling ale [*etc.*, *as* 12/A/11].

12/A/13 14 Nov. 1792. Francis Farr Pike of Minchinhampton. Selling ale [*etc.*, *as* 12/A/11].

12/A/14 8 Oct. 1792. Richard Horwood of Horsley, labourer. Selling ale [*etc.*, *as* 12/A/11].

12/A/15 15 Nov. 1792. Thomas Barnard of Churcham, labourer. Possessing a store oak pole in a wood in Churcham without satisfactory explanation. C. Hayward JP. Elizabeth wife of Thomas Watkins, complainant.

12/A/16 8 Dec. 1792. Elizabeth Cook *alias* Blunt, wife of — Cook *alias* Blunt of Weston under Penyard, Herefs., collier. Cutting and stealing three young beech trees in the Forest of Dean. C. Hayward JP. George Court, complainant. Offence committed 22 Oct. 1792.

12/A/17 8 Dec. 1792. James Younger of St. Briavels, labourer. Lopping a beech timber tree in the Forest of Dean. C. Hayward JP. Edward Bevan, complainant. Offence committed 14 Nov. 1792.

12/A/18 17 Nov. 1792. Thomas Pitt the younger of St. Briavels, labourer. Stealing a quantity of underwood in the Forest of Dean. C. Hayward JP. Miles Hartland, complainant. Offence committed 20 Sept. 1792.

12/A/19 22 Oct. 1792. Reece Jones of St. Briavels, labourer. Cutting and destroying a quantity of underwood in the Forest of Dean. C. Hayward JP. John Hatton, complainant. Offence committed 29 Sept. 1792.

12/A/20 8 Dec. 1792. Winny Younger of St. Briavels, single woman. Lopping a beech timber tree in the Forest of Dean. C. Hayward JP. Edward Bevan, complainant. Offence committed 14 Nov. 1792.

12/A/21 8 Dec. 1792. Margaret Baker of Weston under Penyard, Herefs., single woman. Cutting and stealing a young beech tree in the Forest of Dean. C. Hayward JP. George Court, complainant. Offence committed 22 Oct. 1792.

12/A/22 15 Dec. 1792. Catherine Harris of St. Briavels, widow. Cutting and stealing a quantity of underwood in the Forest of Dean. Thomas Mee JP. Edward Bevan, complainant. Offence committed 29 Nov. 1792.

12/A/23 15 Dec. 1792. William Tingle of St. Briavels, labourer. Cutting a quantity of underwood [*etc.*, *as* 12/A/22].

12/A/24 8 Dec. 1792. John Johnsons of St. Briavels, labourer. Lopping a beech timber tree in the Forest of Dean. T. Mee JP. James Bennett, complainant. Offence committed 5 Nov. 1792.

12/A/25 15 Dec. 1792. John Read of St. Briavels, labourer. Possessing a quantity of underwood in the Forest of Dean. T. Mee JP. Edward Bevan, complainant. Offence committed 5 Dec. 1792.

12/A/26 17 Oct. 1792. William Hopkins of Cheltenham, labourer. Using a greyhound to kill game in the manor of Hunt Court, Badgeworth. A. Austin JP at Wotton under Edge. Edward Bloxsome the younger, gentleman, of Dursley, informant. Offender pleaded guilty. Fine £5. Offence committed 2 Oct. 1792. [*Cf.* 12/A/4–5.]

12/B/1 2 March 1793. John Wilkins of St. Briavels, labourer. Lopping an oak tree in the Forest of Dean. C. Hayward JP. James Bennett, complainant. Offence committed 24 Dec. 1792.

12/B/2 26 Jan. 1793. Eleanor Voice, wife of — Voice of St. Briavels. Cutting a quantity of underwood in the Forest of Dean. C. Hayward JP. Miles Hartland, complainant. Offence committed 12 Feb. 1792.

12/B/3 30 March 1793. William Baldwin of Mitcheldean, blacksmith. Stealing a quantity of underwood in the Forest of Dean. C. Hayward JP. John Jones, complainant. Offence committed 21 March 1793

12/B/4   30 March 1793. William Williams the elder of Mitcheldean, labourer. Cutting underwood in the Forest of Dean. C. Hayward JP. William Moorefield, complainant. Offence committed 30 Feb. [*sic*] 1793.

12/B/5   30 March 1793. James Manning of Mitcheldean. Stealing a quantity of underwood in the Forest of Dean. C. Hayward JP. William Moorefield, complainant. Offence committed 5 Feb. 1793.

12/B/6   30 March 1793. Richard Jones of St. Briavels, labourer. Stealing a quantity of underwood in the Forest of Dean. C. Hayward JP. William Moorefield, complainant. Offence committed 14 Feb. 1793.

12/B/7   26 Jan. 1793. Mary wife of Samuel Hale of St. Briavels, nailer. Cutting a quantity of underwood in the Forest of Dean. C. Hayward JP. Miles Hartland, complainant. Offence committed 12 Jan. 1793.

12/B/8   30 March 1793. William Stephens, late of Mitcheldean, blacksmith. Cutting a quantity of underwood in the Forest of Dean. C. Hayward JP. John Jones, complainant. Offence committed 20 Feb. 1793.

12/B/9   30 March 1793. Elias Guy of Mitcheldean, hatter. Stealing a quantity of underwood in the Forest of Dean. C. Hayward JP. William Moorefield, complainant. Offence committed 7 Feb. 1793.

12/B/10   30 March 1793. Philip Nicholls of Mitcheldean, labourer. Cutting a quantity of underwood in the Forest of Dean. C. Hayward JP. Offender voluntarily confessed. Offence committed 7 Feb. 1793.

12/B/11   30 March 1793. William Powell of Mitcheldean, stonemason. Cutting a quantity of underwood in the Forest of Dean. C. Hayward JP. William Moorefield, complainant. Offence committed 7 Feb. 1793.

12/B/12   16 March 1793. James Morgan of St. Briavels, labourer. Stealing three young oak timber trees in the Forest of Dean. C. Hayward JP. George Court, complainant. Offence committed 28 Feb. 1793.

12/B/13   9 March 1793. Mary wife of Thomas Morgan of St. Briavels, labourer. Cutting a quantity of underwood in the Forest of Dean. C. Hayward JP. George Court, complainant. Offence committed 19 Feb. 1793.

12/B/14   26 Jan. 1790 [*late return*]. Mary wife of Thomas Hayward of St. Briavels, cordwainer. Cutting a young beech timber tree in the Forest of Dean. C. Hayward JP. Miles Hartland, complainant. Offence committed 12 Jan. 1790.

12/B/15   8 Feb. 1793. Nehemiah Baglin the younger of Uley, dyer. Dyeing one piece of woollen serge or kerseymere without the consent of his employers, Messrs. Sheppard and Hicks, clothiers, of Uley. Rev. G. Hayward JP and Rev. William Lloyd Baker JP. Thomas Kilmister, scribbler, of Uley, informant. First offence. Fine 10/-. Offence committed Sept./Oct. 1792.

12/B/16   8 Feb. 1793. George Spratt of Uley, shearman/servant in dyeing business. Dyeing one piece of woollen serge or kerseymere, the property of Joseph Fisher, shearman, of Uley, without the consent of his employers, [*etc., as* 12/B/15].

12/B/17   8 Feb. 1793. George Spratt of Uley, shearman/servant in dyeing business. Dyeing one piece of woollen cloth, the property of Joseph Fisher, shearman, of Uley, without the consent of his employers, [*etc., as* 12/B/15 *except*] Second offence. Fine 20/-. Offence committed 22 Dec. 1792

12/B/18   8 Feb. 1793. George Spratt of Uley, shearman/servant in dyeing business. Dyeing one piece of woollen cloth, the property of Joseph Fisher, shearman, of Uley, without the consent of his employers, [*etc.*, *as* 12/B/15 *except*] Third offence. Fine 40/-. Offence committed 24 Dec. 1792.

12/B/19   8 Feb. 1793. Joseph Fisher of Uley, shearman. Procuring George Spratt and Nehemiah Baglin the younger, both of Uley, to dye one piece of woollen cloth in the dyehouse of their employers, Messrs. Sheppard and Hicks, clothiers, of Uley. Rev. G. Hayward JP and Rev. W. Lloyd Baker JP. Thomas Kilmister, scribbler, of Uley, informant. First offence. Fine 5/-. Offence committed Sept./Oct. 1792.

12/B/20   8 Feb. 1793. Joseph Fisher of Uley, shearman. Procuring George Spratt of Uley to dye one piece of woollen cloth [*etc.*, *as* 12/B/19 *except omitting* scribbler *and*] Second offence. Fine 20/-. Offence committed 22 Dec. 1792.

12/B/21   8 Feb. 1793. Joseph Fisher of Uley, shearman. Procuring George Spratt of Uley to dye one piece of woollen cloth [*etc.*, *as* 12/B/19 *except omitting* scribbler *and*] Third offence. Fine £4. Offence committed 24 Dec. 1792.

12/B/22   4 Feb. 1793. James Mason of Cirencester, labourer. Killing a hare in a snare in Park Wood, Oldbury on the Hill. G. Hardwicke JP at Sodbury. William White of Great Badminton, woodward to the duke of Beaufort, informant. James Cross, witness. Fine £5. Offence committed 4 Feb. 1793.

12/B/23   26 Feb. 1793. Joseph Williams of Over, collier. Using a gin to kill game in Over, Churcham. Sir T. Crawley Boevey JP. John Jenkins, yeoman, of Highnam, informant. Thomas Trigg, labourer, of the hamlet of Lassington, in the parish of Churcham [*sic*], witness. Offender pleaded not guilty. Fine £5. Offence committed 26 Feb. 1793.

12/C/1   1 June 1793. Thomas Kilmister of King's Stanley. Selling malt liquor without a licence. Rev. G. Hayward JP. Joseph Daniels and Richard Cobb, informants. First conviction. Offence committed 29 May 1793.

12/C/2   1 May 1793. Edward Heaven of Minchinhampton, pig dealer. Cursing. Rev. P. Hawker JP.

12/C/3   28 June 1793. Mary Williams of Rodborough. Cursing. Rev. P. Hawker JP.

12/C/4   28 June 1793. Daniel Evans of Rodborough, baker. Cursing. Rev. P. Hawker JP.

12/C/5   15 April 1793. Richard Paine of Stroud, basket-maker. Selling ale or beer without a licence. N. Winchcombe JP. First offence. Fine 40/- and 4/- expenses.

12/D/1   15 July 1793. Stephen Yem, labourer. Cursing. [*Document not signed but note attached reads*:] Joseph Harford Esq. is ill in the country.

12/D/2   16 Sept. 1793. Daniel Fords the younger. Selling excisable liquor without a licence in Coaley. Rev. G. Hayward JP. Convicted on own confession. First conviction. Offence committed within previous three months.

12/D/3   16 Sept. 1793. William Griffin. Selling excisable liquor [*etc.*, *as* 12/D/2].

12/D/4   16 Sept. 1793. Jonah Smith. Selling excisable liquor [*etc.*, *as* 12/D/2].

12/D/5   17 Aug. 1793. James Cowmeadow the younger of St. Briavels, collier. Lopping a beech timber tree in the Forest of Dean. T. Mee JP. James Bennett, complainant. Offence committed 12 July 1793.

12/D/6   25 Sept. 1793. Thomas Adams of Stroud, labourer. Selling ale etc. without a licence. N. Winchcombe JP. First offence. Fine 40/- and 4/- expenses.

12/D/7   19 Aug. 1793. Isaac Harvey of Horsley, labourer. Selling ale etc. without a licence. Rev. P. Hawker JP. First offence. Fine 40/- and 4/- expenses.

12/D/8   12 Sept. 1793. Joseph Hort, late of Bath. Using a dog and a gun to destroy game. R. Haynes JP at Wick. Henry Milliner, husbandman, informant. Offender voluntarily confessed. Fine £5. Offence committed 2 Sept. 1793.

12/D/9   12 September 1793. Aaron Francombe of Doynton, labourer. Using a dog and a gun to destroy game [*etc., as* 12/D/8].

12/D/10   3 Aug. 1793. John Joy of St. Briavels, wood-collier. Lopping a beech timber tree in the Forest of Dean. T. Mee JP. Edward Bevan, complainant. Offence committed 2 July 1793.

12/D/11   11 May 1793. Joseph Wintle of Ruardean, labourer. Stealing a young oak timber tree in the Forest of Dean. C. Hayward JP. George Court, complainant. Offence committed 23 April 1793.

13/A/1   18 Oct. 1793. Ann Axon of Horsley, 'feme covert'. Swearing and cursing. Rev. P. Hawker JP. Offence committed 17 Oct. 1793.

13/A/2   25 Oct. 1793. William Niblett of Minchinhampton, farmer. Cursing. Rev. P. Hawker JP. Offence committed 23 and 25 Oct. 1793.

13/A/3   5 Nov. 1793. Thomas Ockford of Stroud, carpenter. Swearing. N. Winchcombe JP.

13/A/4   18 Oct. 1793. James Holliday of Stroud, labourer. Cursing. N. Winchcombe JP.

13/A/5   3 Dec. 1793. Thomas Cooke of Standish. Swearing. N. Winchcombe JP.

13/A/6   11 Sept. 1793. Thomas Cockhead of Black Bourton, Oxon., yeoman. Using a dog and nets etc. to kill game in Sherborne. Rev. C. Coxwell JP at Ablington. Thomas Webb of Sherborne, witness. Fine £5. Offence committed 7 Sept. 1793.

13/A/7   16 Nov. 1793. Thomas James of Stroud, labourer. Selling ale or beer etc. without a licence. N. Winchcombe JP. First offence. Fine 40/- and 4/- expenses.

13/A/8   29 Oct. 1793. Richard Paine of Stroud, basket-maker. Selling ale or beer etc. without a licence. N. Winchcombe JP. Second offence. Fine £4 and 4/- expenses.

13/A/9   16 Oct. 1793. Ursula Arundell of Stroud, single woman. Selling ale or beer etc. without a licence. N. Winchcombe JP. First offence. Fine 40/- and 4/- expenses.

13/A/10   30 Nov. 1793. Thomas Hill of Minchinhampton, horse dealer. Selling ale or beer etc. without a licence. Rev. P. Hawker JP. First offence. Fine 40/- and 4/- expenses.

13/A/11   25 Nov. 1793. James Shipway of Rodborough. Selling ale [*etc., as* 13/A/10].

13/A/12   5 Nov. 1793. William Harpur of Rodborough. Selling ale [*etc., as* 13/A/10].

13/A/13   9 Nov. 1793. Thomas Flight of Rodborough. Selling ale or beer etc. without a licence. Rev. P. Hawker JP. Second offence. Fine £4 and – expenses.

13/A/14   25 Nov. 1793. James Franklin of Rodborough. Selling ale or beer etc. without a licence. Rev. P. Hawker JP. First offence. Fine 40/- and 4/- expenses.

13/A/15   19 Oct. 1793. William Meredith of St. Briavels, labourer. Cutting an oak timber tree in the Forest of Dean. C. Hayward JP. Thomas Blunt, gentleman, complainant. Offence committed 1 Oct. 1793.

13/A/16   19 Oct. 1793. William Blanch of St. Briavels, labourer. Cutting an oak timber tree in the Forest of Dean. C. Hayward JP. George Court, complainant. Offence committed 8 Oct. 1793.

13/A/17   19 Oct. 1793. John Thompson of Ruardean, farmer. Stealing an oak timber tree in the Forest of Dean. C. Hayward JP. Thomas Blunt, complainant. Offence committed 10 Oct. 1793.

13/A/18   2 Nov. 1793. Elizabeth Cooke *alias* Blunt, wife of — Cooke *alias* Blunt of St. Briavels, collier. Cutting underwood in the Forest of Dean. C. Hayward JP. George Court, complainant. Offence committed 22 Oct. 1793.

13/A/19   26 Oct. 1793. Sarah Gough of St. Briavels, widow. Cutting underwood in the Forest of Dean. C. Hayward JP. Offence committed 7 Oct. 1793.

13/A/20   20 April 1793. Sarah Grindall of St. Briavels, single woman. Stealing underwood in the Forest of Dean. C. Hayward JP. Miles Hartland the younger, complainant. Offence committed 8 Feb. 1793.

13/A/21   30 Dec. 1793. Joseph Cooper of English Bicknor, labourer. Possessing a fallow deer without satisfactory explanation. T. Mee JP. Joseph Harris, servant to Mrs. Jane Clarke of the Hill, Walford, Herefs., complainant. Fine £30. Offence committed 1 Dec. 1793.

13/A/22   30 Dec. 1793. John Cooper of English Bicknor, labourer. Possessing a fallow deer [*etc.*, *as* 13/A/21].

13/A/23   18 Oct. 1793. Edward Gibbons of Prior Park, Som. Using dogs and a gun to kill game in Tormarton. R. Haynes JP and Dr. G. Hardwicke JP at Old Sodbury. Henry Milliner, husbandman, of Great Badminton, informant. Fine £5. Offence committed 24 Sept. 1793.

13/A/24   29 Nov. 1793. William Smith of Norton Grounds, Weston Subedge. Failing to fulfil his legal duty to repair the highway. William Bateson JP and Rev. Joseph Martin JP. Rev. John Pelly, highway surveyor for Weston Subedge, informant.

13/B/1   18 Feb. 1794. Thomas Cooke of Stroud, clothworker. Cursing. N. Winchcombe JP. Offence committed 14 Feb. 1794.

13/B/2   15 Feb. 1794. Joseph Rice of Stroud, labourer. Being drunk and swearing and cursing. N. Winchcombe JP.

13/B/3   29 March 1794. John Leech of Rodborough. Selling ale etc. without a licence. Rev. P. Hawker JP. Fourth offence. [*Cf.* 10/D/3, 11/A/3.] Fine £6 and 4/- expenses.

13/B/4   4 April 1794. John Fry of Horsley, labourer. Selling ale etc. without a licence. Rev. P. Hawker JP. First offence. Fine 40/- and 4/- expenses.

13/B/5   22 Jan. 1794. William Shipway of Rodborough, labourer. Selling ale [*etc.*, *as* 13/B/4].

13/B/6   20 Jan. 1794. William Buck of Stroud, clothworker. Selling ale etc. without a licence. N. Winchcombe JP. First offence. Fine 40/- and 4/- expenses.

13/B/7   22 March 1794. James Bryan of Littledean, labourer. Lopping a beech timber tree in the Forest of Dean. T. Mee JP. Miles Hartland, complainant. Offence committed 10 March 1794.

13/B/8   22 March 1794. Joseph Eddy of Ruardean, yeoman. Stealing an elm tree in the Forest of Dean. T. Mee JP. Miles Hartland, complainant. Offence committed 10 Feb. 1794.

13/B/9   5 April 1794. John Reece of Hope Mansell, Herefs., labourer. Cutting an oak tree in the Forest of Dean. T. Mee JP. Miles Hartland, complainant. Offence committed 11 March 1794.

13/B/10   5 April 1794. James Williams of St. Briavels, labourer. Cutting a young beech tree in the Forest of Dean. T. Mee JP. Miles Hartland, complainant. Offence committed 10 March 1794.

13/B/11   22 March 1794. William Hale of Littledean, labourer. Cutting underwood in the Forest of Dean. T. Mee JP. Miles Hartland, complainant. Offence committed 27 Feb. 1794.

13/B/12 27 April 1794. William Biddington of St. Briavels, mason. Cutting and stealing underwood in the Forest of Dean. Sir T. Crawley Boevey JP. Miles Hartland the younger, complainant. Offence committed 3 April 1794.

13/B/13 20 April 1794. John Moor of St. Briavels, labourer. Cutting a beech tree in the Forest of Dean. Sir T. Crawley Boevey JP. Offender voluntarily confessed. Offence committed 3 April 1794.

13/B/14 29 April 1794. Rebecca Law, wife of — Law of St. Briavels, sawyer. Stealing underwood in the Forest of Dean. Sir T. Crawley Boevey JP. Miles Hartland, complainant. Offence committed 27 March 1794.

13/B/15 1 April 1794. Paris Bull and Robert Bull, both of West Yatton [in Yatton Keynell, Wilts.]. Using snares to kill game in Hawkesbury. R. Haynes JP at Wick. John White, husbandman, of Didmarton, informant. Offence committed 1 April 1794.

13/B/16 21 April 1794. Joseph Walker of Over, labourer. Using a gin to kill game in Lassington. Sir T. Crawley Boevey JP. John Jenkins, witness. Fine £5. Offence committed 20 April 1794.

13/C/1 [Duplicate of 13/B/9, replacing an oak tree with a young oak tree.]

13/C/2 [Duplicate of 13/B/10, replacing labourer with yeoman.]

13/C/3 19 June 1794. Mary wife of Thomas Niblett, of Miserden. Damping wool, given her to spin, in order to increase its weight. N. Winchcombe JP. Offence committed 18 June 1794.

13/C/4 19 June 1794. William Nicholls of Paganhill, labourer. Selling ale etc. without a licence. N. Winchcombe JP. Second offence. Fine £4 and 4/- expenses.

13/C/5 11 July 1794. Susannah Watkins of Stroud, spinster. Swearing. N. Winchcombe JP.

13/C/6 2 June 1794. Ann Bingle of Minchinhampton, spinster. Cursing. Rev. P. Hawker JP. Offence committed 26 May 1794.

13/C/7 30 June 1794. Hannah Selwyn of Rodborough. Swearing and cursing. Rev. P. Hawker JP. Offence committed 27 June 1794.

13/C/8 4 July 1794. William Smith of Middle Norton, Weston Subedge, yeoman. Failing to fulfil his legal duty to repair the highway. W. Bateson JP and J. Scott JP at Bourton on the Hill. Rev. J. Pelly and William Smith, highway surveyors for Weston Subedge, informants. Fine £9. Offence committed 9 June 1794.

13/D/1 1 Aug. 1794. Daniel Clift the younger of Stroud, labourer. Cursing. N. Winchcombe JP.

13/D/2 9 Aug. 1794. James Trigge of Littledean, labourer. Cutting a beech timber tree in the Forest of Dean. T. Mee JP. George Court, complainant. Offence committed 1 Aug. 1794.

13/D/3 5 Aug. 1794. John Coley of Eastington, clothworker. Damaging 4 yd. of woollen cloth given him to shear, the property of Edward Hill & Co. of Stonehouse. N. Winchcombe JP and Rev. G. Hayward JP. Mr. Edward Hill, clothier, of Stonehouse, complainant. Offence committed during previous six weeks.

13/D/4 28 July 1794. Isaac Smith of King's Stanley. Selling ale or beer without a licence. Rev. G. Hayward JP. First offence. Fine 40/- and 4/- expenses. Offence committed within previous three months.

13/D/5 2 Sept. 1794. Isaac Smith of Coaley, weaver. Selling ale or beer without a licence. Rev. G. Hayward JP. First offence. Fine 40/- and 6/- expenses. Offence committed within previous three months.

13/D/6 2 Sept. 1794. William Smith of Coaley, weaver. Selling ale [etc., as 13/D/5].

13/D/7   2 Sept. 1794. Mary Beard of Eastington, single woman. Selling ale [*etc., as* 13/D/5].

13/D/8   1 Oct. 1794. William Smith of Middle Norton, Weston Subedge. Failing to fulfil his legal duty to repair the highway. J. Scott JP and W. Bateson JP at Banks Fee. Rev. J. Pelly and William Smith, highway surveyors, informants. Fine £9. Offence committed 1 Sept. 1794.

13/D/9   27 Aug. 1794. Richard Clark of Minchinhampton, labourer. Selling ale etc. without a licence. Rev. P. Hawker JP. First offence. Fine 40/- and 4/- expenses.

13/D/10   6 Sept. 1794. Samuel Tyndale of Minchinhampton, labourer. Selling ale etc. without a licence. Rev. P. Hawker JP. Second offence. [*Cf.* 6/D/5.] Fine £4 and 4/- expenses.

13/D/11   20 Sept. 1794. Joseph Mills of Rodborough, rug-weaver. Selling ale etc. without a licence. Rev. P. Hawker JP. Second offence. [*Cf.* 11/A/4]. Fine £4 and 4/- expenses.

13/D/12   11 July 1794. Martha Watkins of Stroud, spinster. Swearing. N. Winchcombe JP.

13/D/13   18 Sept. 1794. John Antill of Rodborough, broadweaver. Stealing woollen yarn from Mr. Samuel Wathen, clothier, of Stroud. B. Hyett JP and N. Winchcombe JP. Offence committed between 5 July and 5 Aug. 1794.

13/D/14   30 Aug. 1794. John Mercer of Horsley, weaver. Selling ale etc. without a licence. Rev. P. Hawker JP. First offence. Fine 40/- and 4/- expenses.

14/A/1   30 Dec. 1794. William Bennett of Banks Fee, Longborough, servant. Selling ale without a licence. Rev. J. Hippisley JP. First offence. Fine 40/- and 5/- expenses.

14/A/2   4 Nov. 1794. William Cratchley of Rodborough, weaver. Cursing. Rev. P. Hawker JP.

14/A/3   7 Nov. 1794. Aaron Batt of Siston. Selling ale or beer without a licence. Dr. G. Hardwicke JP and R. Haynes JP. First offence. Fine 40/- and 14/- expenses.

14/A/4   7 Oct. 1794. Jane Webb of Minchinhampton. Selling ale etc. without a licence. Rev. P. Hawker JP. First offence. Fine 40/- and 4/- expenses.

14/A/5   19 Nov. 1794. William Buck of Stroud. Selling ale etc. without a licence. N. Winchcombe JP. [Second offence. *Cf.* 13/B/6.] Fine £4 and 4/- expenses.

14/B/1   7 Feb. 1795. William Bennett of Banks Fee, Longborough, servant. Selling ale without a licence. Rev. J. Hippisley JP. James Batson and John Iles, witnesses. First offence [*but cf.* 14/A/1; *perhaps a later hearing of the same offence*]. Fine 40/- and 5/- expenses.

14/B/2   5 Feb. 1795. William Bennett of Banks Fee, Longborough, servant. Selling ale without a licence. Thomas Leigh JP. Sarah Bond and Mary French, witnesses. First offence [*but cf.* 14/A/1; *perhaps a later hearing of the same offence*]. Fine 40/- and 5/- expenses.

14/B/3   30 Aug. 1794 [*late return*]. John Shipton of Newington Bagpath [*MS.* Cold Newton, Bagpath]. Ill-treating and abusing John Standford Perrott in the execution of his office. Henry, duke of Beaufort, JP. John Standford Perrott, toll-gatherer of the turnpike gate at Dunkirk, Hawkesbury, complainant. Offence committed 30 Aug. 1794.

14/C/1   11 May 1795. William Kirby of Woodchester, labourer. Cursing. Rev. P. Hawker JP. Offence committed 30 April 1795.

14/C/2   29 April 1795. Francis Pyke of Minchinhampton, maltster. Cursing. Rev. P. Hawker JP. Offence committed 24 April 1795.

14/C/3   9 May 1795. Hester Peach of Woodchester, widow. Selling ale etc. without a licence. Rev. P. Hawker JP. Second offence. [*Cf.* 8/B/5.] Fine £4 and 6/- expenses.

14/C/4   28 May 1795. John Pearce of Stroud, labourer. Selling ale etc. without a licence. N. Winchcombe JP. First offence. Fine 40/- and 4/- expenses. Offence committed 25 May 1795.

14/C/5   28 May 1795. Edward Merrett of Stroud, labourer. Selling ale etc. without a licence. N. Winchcombe JP. First offence. Fine 40/- and 4/- expenses. Offence committed 25 May 1795.

14/C/6   5 June 1795. William Buck of Stroud, clothworker. Selling ale etc. without a licence. N. Winchcombe JP. Third offence. [*Cf.* 13/B/6, 14/A/5.] Fine £6 and 4/- expenses.

14/C/7   2 July 1795. Samuel Worrall Esq. of Clifton. Failing to fulfil his legal duty to repair the highway in Clifton. J. Harford JP at Lawfords Gate prison. Solomon Roach, James Richards and Francis James, highway surveyors, informants. John Moore, labourer, of Clifton, witness. Fine £15 (10/- for each offence). Offence committed between 5 March and 30 April 1795.

14/D/1   10 Sept. 1795. William Smith of Middle Norton, Weston Subedge. Failing to fulfil his legal duty to repair the highway in Weston Subedge. W. Bateson JP at the Unicorn inn, Stow [on the Wold]. Rev. J. Pelly and William Smith, highway surveyors, informants. Fine £9. Offence committed between 22 June and 9 July 1795.

15/A/1   13 Nov. 1795. Joseph Day of Tetbury, glazier. Using a greyhound to kill a hare in Tetbury. Isaac Austin JP. First offence. Fine £20 mitigated to £10 and 5/- expenses. Offence committed Sunday 25 Oct. 1795.

15/A/2   16 Nov. 1795. John Haynes of Woolaston, labourer. Using two dogs and a net with intent to kill a hare in Keynsham, Woolaston. Rev. William Seys JP. First offence. Fine £20. Offence committed Monday 26 Oct. 1795.

15/A/3   16 Nov. 1795. John Tooley of Woolaston, shoemaker. Using [*etc.*, *as* 15/A/2].

15/A/4   22 Dec. 1795. William Haynes of Woolaston, labourer. Using [*etc.*, *as* 15/A/2].

15/A/5   16 Nov. 1795. Joseph Brown of Woolaston, shoemaker. Using [*etc.*, *as* 15/A/2].

15/A/6   11 Jan. 1796. William Davis of Bisley, weaver. Buying and receiving 87½ lb. of abb yarn at 10*d.* per lb. from Thomas Rowles, weaver, of Bisley. Rev. P. Hawker JP and Rev. G. Hayward JP. Paul and Nathaniel Wathen, clothiers, complainants. Offence committed between 1 and 12 Nov. 1795.

15/A/7   11 Jan. 1796. Nathaniel Fry of Bisley, weaver. Buying and receiving 24½ lb. of English yarn for £1 11*s.* 6*d.* from Thomas Rowles, weaver, of Bisley. Rev. P. Hawker JP and Rev. G. Hayward JP. Paul and Nathaniel Wathen, clothiers, complainants. Offence committed 14 Nov. 1795.

15/B/1   11 March 1796. William James of Abenhall, labourer, and John Hayward of Abenhall, yeoman. Driving and allowing to be driven a wagon with wheels less that the statutory measurement, between Westbury and Newnham. George Skipp JP at the Grange. John Gauden, nailer, of Littledean, informant. John Hayward fined £5. Offence committed 7 March 1796.

15/B/2   11 March 1796. William James of Abenhall, labourer. Driving a wagon, the property of John Hayward, yeoman, of Abenhall, with wheels less that the statutory measurement, between Westbury and Newnham. G. Skipp JP. John Gauden, nailer, of Littledean, informant. Fine 20/-. Offence committed 7 March 1796.

15/B/3   14 March 1796. David Gardiner of Bisley, clothmaker or weaver. Buying and receiving 45 ells of woollen broadcloth at 4/- per ell from Samuel Smart, weaver, of Bisley, and his wife Ann. John Hollings JP and Rev. P. Hawker JP. Richard Mason, clothier, of Bisley, informant. First offence. Fine £40, distributed thus: £2 expenses, £10 to informant, £28 to the poor. Offence committed between 10 July and 10 Aug. 1794.

15/B/4   3 March 1796. Isaac Tyler of Bisley, weaver. Buying and receiving about 2 lb. of woollen yarn at 6*d.* per lb. from Ann Herbert, single woman, of Bisley. J. Selfe JP,

J. Hollings JP and Rev. P. Hawker JP. John Jones the younger, clothier, of Bisley, informant. First offence. Fine £40, distributed [*as above*]. Offence committed Jan. 1795.

15/B/5   18 March 1796. John Freeman of Stroud, clothworker. Buying and receiving about 40 ells of woollen broadcloth at 4/- per ell from John Jeackes, weaver, of Bisley. N. Winchcombe JP and J. Hollings JP. Nathaniel Wathen, clothier, of Stroud, informant. Fine £40, distributed [*as above*]. Offence committed between 1 Jan. and 25 March 1794.

15/B/6   1 April 1796. James Gagg of Stroud, lath-render. Stealing eleven pieces of ash wood from a grove in Bisley, the property of Richard Davis, timber merchant. J. Hollings JP. Offence committed 12 March 1796.

15/B/7   11 March 1796. William Niblett of Bisley, Stroud, weaver. Buying and receiving about 6 lb. of woollen yarn at 11*d.* per lb. from John Lewis, weaver. J. Hollings JP and Rev. P. Hawker JP. Offence committed 11 Nov. 1795.

15/B/8   5 March 1796. Moses Smart of Bisley, clothier. Buying and receiving about 4 lb. of woollen yarn at 1/1 per lb. from Samuel Smart of Bisley. J. Hollings JP and Rev. P. Hawker JP. Offence committed 28 Dec. 1795.

15/B/9   14 March 1796. George Davis of Bisley, weaver. Buying and receiving about 6 lb. [of] woollen yarn at 9*d.* per lb. from Thomas Bartlett, clothworker. J. Hollings JP and Rev. P. Hawker JP. Offence committed between 1 and 21 Jan. 1796.

15/B/10   10 Feb. 1796. George Stephens of Avening, weaver. Embezzling about one chain of coarse woollen yarn delivered to him at the warehouse in Rodborough. Rev. P. Hawker JP and J. Hollings JP. Paul and Nathaniel Wathen, clothiers, complainants. Offence committed between 1 July 1795 and 10 Feb. 1796.

15/B/11   7 March 1796. Jacob Bath of Bisley, shopkeeper. Buying and receiving about 3 lb. of woollen yarn at 10*d.* per lb. from Samuel Smart. J. Hollings JP and Rev. P. Hawker JP. Offence committed 20 Feb. 1796.

15/B/12   4 March 1796. Richard Cooke of Randwick, labourer. Possessing a young beech tree without satisfactory explanation. J. Hollings JP. William Clissold, complainant. Offence committed 16 Jan. 1796.

15/B/13   7 March 1796. Richard Chew of Bisley, blacksmith. Buying and receiving about 3 lb. of woollen yarn at 1/- per lb. from Samuel Smart. J. Hollings JP and Rev. P. Hawker JP. Offence committed 19 Nov. 1795.

15/B/14   3 March 1796. William Tyler of Bisley, clothier. Buying and receiving about 7 lb. of woollen yarn from Thomas Hunt, weaver, of Bisley. J. Hollings JP and Rev. P. Hawker JP. Offence committed 24 Dec. 1795.

15/C/1   20 April 1796. Thomas Bannister of Ryton, Dymock, labourer. Stealing hedge-wood and other pieces of timber and taking them to his brother-in-law, carpenter George Barksdale's fold. Rev. Henry Gorges Dobyns Yate JP. Offender brought to court by Thomas Forty, yeoman, constable of the Ryeland division, Dymock. James Brooks, yeoman, of Ketford, complainant. John Steward, cordwainer, of Ryton, witness. Fine 10/- mitigated to 5/- and 5/- expenses to be paid to complainant. Offence committed within previous six weeks.

15/C/2   1 July 1796. William Harford, labourer. Stealing one melon plant in Stapleton worth 5/-. J. Harford JP. Andrew Drummond Esq. of Stapleton, complainant.

15/C/3   24 May 1796. Thomas Teakle or Tekell of Bisley, clothier or clothworker. Buying and receiving about 7 lb. of abb woollen yarn from Nathaniel Twissle, weaver, of Bisley. J. Hollings JP and N. Winchcombe JP. Mr. Richard Mason, clothier, of Bisley, informant.

Fine £40 (£12 to informant and the rest to the poor) or six months' hard labour in Horsley house of correction. Offence committed 30 May 1795.

15/C/4   7 June 1796. John Stephens of Bisley, serge-weaver. Buying and receiving 4 lb. of abb woollen yarn from John Lewis, weaver, of Bisley. J. Hollings JP and Rev. P. Hawker JP. Mr. Richard Mason, clothier, informant. Fine £40 [*distributed as above*] or three days in Gloucester house of correction and once publicly whipped. Offence committed between Christmas 1795 and Easter 1796.

15/C/5   30 May 1796. John Gardner of Bisley, weaver. Embezzling about 8 lb. of woollen yarn, the property of his employer Mr. John Knowles, clothier, of Ham Mill, Stroud. J. Selfe JP and J. Hollings JP. Mr. John Chalk, clothier, of Stroud, informant. Offence committed between 25 March and 23 May 1796.

15/C/6   25 April 1796. John Verinder of Bisley, fell-monger. Buying and receiving 6 lb. of scoured abb woollen yarn from Thomas Rowles, weaver, of Bisley. J. Selfe JP and J. Hollings JP. Mr. Charles Innell, clothier, of Bisley, informant. Fine £40 [*distributed as above*] or six months' hard labour in Horsley house of correction. Offence committed 29 Aug. 1795.

15/C/7   9 April 1796. Isaac Tyler of Bisley, serge-weaver. Buying and receiving 2 lb. of abb woollen yarn and 4 thrums of warp woollen yarn from Ann Herbert, single woman, of Bisley. J. Selfe JP and J. Hollings JP. Mr. Richard Mason, clothier, of Bisley, informant. Fine £40 [*distributed as above*] or three days in the house of correction at Gloucester and once publicly whipped. Offence committed between 22 Sept. and 15 Oct. 1795.

15/D/1   13 Aug. 1796. Thomas Jones of St. Briavels, labourer. Cutting and stealing part of an oak timber tree in the Forest of Dean. T. Mee JP. George Court, complainant. Offence committed 23 June 1796.

15/D/2   4 June 1796. Richard Davis of Hope Mansell, Herefs., carpenter. Cutting and stealing an oak timber tree in the Forest of Dean. Sir T. Crawley Boevey JP. Miles Hartland, complainant. Offence committed 5 May 1796.

15/D/3   7 Sept. 1796. Nathaniel King of King's Stanley, broadweaver. Embezzling a quantity of Spanish abb yarn delivered to him to weave by Mr. Paul Beard of King's Stanley. N. Winchcombe JP and Rev. G. Hayward JP. Mr. William Hopkins Merrick, clothier, of King's Stanley, complainant.

16/A/1   10 Dec. 1796. William Read of Tetbury, labourer. Killing two hares in Horsley. Rev. P. Hawker JP. First offence. Fine £10. Offence committed Sunday 20 Nov. 1796.

16/B/1–   [*Dates and names as below.*] Having weights [*except* 16/B/10, 17] not conforming to
17   standard. J. Hollings JP. Peter Gardner, inspector of weights and balances for Bisley hundred, informant. Fine 5/- [*except* 16/B/11].

16/B/1   31 March 1797. Richard Ireland of Bisley, shopkeeper.

16/B/2   21 April 1797. Elizabeth Bucknall of Bisley, shopkeeper.

16/B/3   31 March 1797. William Davis of Bisley, shopkeeper.

16/B/4   21 April 1797. William Hunt of Bisley, shopkeeper.

16/B/5   25 April 1797. William Carter of Bisley, shopkeeper.

16/B/6   31 March 1797. John Smith of Stroud, shopkeeper.

16/B/7   31 March 1797. John Tanner of Stroud, shopkeeper.

16/B/8   21 April 1797. Arthur Rolph of Bisley, shopkeeper.

16/B/9   31 March 1797. Henry Selwin of Miserden, shopkeeper.

16/B/10   21 April 1797. Ralph Gardner of Bisley, shopkeeper. Having one weight [*etc.*].

16/B/11   21 April 1797. Zachariah Davis of Bisley, shopkeeper. Fine 10/-.

16/B/12   31 March 1797. Edward Chandler of Stroud, shopkeeper.

16/B/13   21 April 1797. John Wood of Painswick, shopkeeper.

16/B/14   31 March 1797. Benjamin Neale of Bisley, shopkeeper.

16/B/15   31 March 1797. William Smith of Stroud, shopkeeper.

16/B/16   31 March 1797. Thomas Ellis of Painswick, shopkeeper.

16/B/17   21 April 1797. Mary Webb of Painswick, shopkeeper. Having one weight [*etc.*].

16/B/18   14 Feb. 1797. Richard Alford of Bromsberrow, labourer. Cursing. Rev. H. G. D. Yate JP.

16/B/19   28 Feb. 1797. Stephen Stephens the younger of Dymock, thatcher. Stealing hedge-wood from Dyck House Farm, Bromsberrow. Rev. H. G. D. Yate JP at Bromsberrow Place. William Moore Gibbs, yeoman, of Redmarley D'Abitot, Worcs., complainant. Offender in custody of George Barksdale, constable of Dymock. Thomas Tiler, labourer, of Bromsberrow, witness. Fine 10/- and expenses. Offence committed 18 Feb. 1797.

16/B/20   17 Feb. 1797. John De la Roche of Thornbury, gentleman. Using a greyhound to kill game in Slimbridge. Rev. W. Lloyd Baker JP at Wotton under Edge. John Fords, labourer, of Coaley, informant. Fine £5. Offence committed 5 Jan. 1797.

16/C/1   3 July 1797. William Ayers of Rodborough, weaver. Selling ale without a licence. J. Hollings JP and Philip Sheppard JP. First offence. Fine £10 and 7/6 expenses.

16/C/2   19 June 1797. William Webb of Avening, weaver. Cursing. Rev. P. Hawker JP. Offence committed 13 June 1797.

16/C/3   28 April 1797. Nathaniel Dean of Bisley, weaver. Buying and receiving 5½ lb. of abb and a quantity of warp woollen yarn from Henry Gardner, weaver, of Bisley. N. Winchcombe JP and J. Hollings JP at Stratford House, Stroud. George Davis, clothier, of Bisley, complainant. Fine £30 or six months' hard labour in Horsley house of correction. Offence committed 30 March 1797.

16/D/1   7 Sept. 1797. James Noad. Selling beer without a licence in Acton Turville. Dr. G. Hardwicke JP. First offence. Fine £20 mitigated to £10 and 10/- expenses. Offence committed 29 and 30 Aug. 1797.

17/A/1   12 Oct. 1797. Mark Jones of Littledean, yeoman. Using snares to kill game in Lydney. Charles Edwin JP. William Coles, yeoman, of Lydney, informant. William Willetts, witness. Fine £5. Offence committed 11 Oct. 1797.

17/A/2   5 Oct. 1797. James Lawrence of Woodchester, wool-scribbler. Selling ale etc. without a licence. Rev. P. Hawker JP. First offence. Fine £10 and 6/- expenses.

17/A/3   5 Oct. 1797. Richard Souls of Woodchester, millman. Selling ale [*etc., as* 17/A/2].

17/A/4   5 Oct. 1797. Samuel Clarke of Woodchester, cordwainer. Selling ale [*etc., as* 17/A/2].

17/A/5   11 Nov. 1797. Joseph Parker of Mitcheldean, gardener. Possessing underwood without satisfactory explanation. T. Mee JP. Thomas Bennett, complainant. Offence committed 26 Oct. 1797.

17/A/6   14 Dec. 1797. Sarah Young of Littledean, single woman. Swearing. Rev. H. G. D. Yate JP.

17/B/1   12 April 1798. Thomas Bannister of Dymock, labourer. Stealing wood in Dymock. Rev. H. G. D. Yate JP. John Hartland, yeoman, of Dymock, complainant. Second offence. [*Cf.* 15/C/1.] One month's hard labour in [Littledean] house of correction.

17/B/2   13 April 1798. William Tandy of Dymock, labourer. Cursing. Rev. H. G. D. Yate JP.

17/B/3   2 April 1798. Thomas Pritchard of Walford [*MS.* Wellford], Herefs., stonemason. Stealing oak timber in the Forest of Dean. T. Mee JP. Miles Hartland, complainant. Offence committed 1 April 1798.

17/B/4   2 April 1798. James Seysil of St. Briavels, labourer. Stealing [*etc., as* 17/B/3].

17/B/5   15 Feb. 1798. George Taylor of Tadwick, Som. Possessing 10 nets for killing game in Badminton. Henry, duke of Beaufort, JP at Badminton. John Slade, gamekeeper to Christopher Codrington Esq. of Dodington, informant. Offender pleaded guilty. Fine £5. Offence committed 14 Feb. 1798.

17/C/1   7 July 1798. Mat[t]hew Penrose. Vagrancy in St. James's parish, Bristol. Thomas Walker JP. John Long, constable of St. George, Bristol, informant. William Prichard, witness.

17/C/2   20 April 1798. James Thomson. Vagrancy in Clifton, Bristol. Richard Nelmes JP. John Hale, constable of Clifton, informant. Thomas Harscott, witness.

17/C/3   5 June 1798. William Davies of Bromsberrow, labourer. Cursing his wife Anne Davies. Rev. H. G. D. Yate JP.

17/C/4   11 April 1798. Thomas Bannister of Dymock, labourer. Cutting and stealing hedge-wood in Dymock. Rev. H. G. D. Yate JP. John Hartland, yeoman, of Dymock, complainant. Second offence. [*Cf.* 15/C/1, 17/B/1.] One month in [Littledean] house of correction.

17/C/5   20 May 1798. Thomas Phillips of St. Briavels, labourer. Stealing beech timber in the Forest of Dean. G. Skipp JP. James Bennett, forest keeper, complainant. Fine 40/- mitigated to 5/- and 7/6 expenses. Offence committed 16 May 1798.

17/D/1   6 Aug. 1798. Samuel Baker of St. Briavels, yeoman. Avoiding payment of tolls in Viney Hill, West Dean. Rev. Charles Sandiford JP. Fine £5. Offence committed 19 July 1798.

17/D/2   4 Sept. 1798. John Gillett of Winchcombe, labourer. Using a gate net with intent to kill game in Didbrook. P. Snell JP. Thomas Dyer, labourer, witness. First offence. Fine £20. Offence committed 1 Sept. 1798.

17/D/3   12 Sept. 1798. John Bendall of Mangotsfield, yeoman. Using a tunnel net to kill game in Frenchay. Edmund Probyn JP at his house in Winterbourne. Joseph Wickwick, yeoman, of Winterbourne, informant. First offence. Fine £20 mitigated to £15 and 15/- expenses. Offence committed 31 Aug. 1798.

17/D/4   12 Sept. 1798. George Croom the younger of Mangotsfield, yeoman. Using a tunnel net to kill game in Frenchay. E. Probyn JP. Joseph Wickwick, yeoman, of Winterbourne, informant. First offence. Fine £20 and 15/- expenses. Offence committed 31 Aug. 1798.

17/D/5   12 Sept. 1798. Edward Russell of Mangotsfield, yeoman. Using a tunnel net to kill game in Frenchay. E. Probyn JP. Joseph Wickwick, informant. First offence. Fine £20 mitigated to £15 and 15/- expenses. Offence committed 31 Aug. 1798.

17/D/6   12 Sept. 1798. Thomas Rickards of Winterbourne, yeoman. Using a tunnel net to kill game in Frenchay [*etc., as* 17/D/5].

18/A/1   20 Dec. 1798. John Hawker of Prestbury, labourer. Using a snare to kill game in Bishop's Cleeve. William Hicks JP at Cheltenham. Cornelius Woolley Esq., informant. William Pulham, witness. Fine £5. Offence committed 13 Dec. 1798.

18/A/2   6 Oct. 1798. Robert *alias* Joseph Kendall. Attempting to take and destroy fish in a pond in Wick and Abson, the property of Richard Haynes Esq. Dr. J. A. Small JP. Fine £5. Offence committed 27 Dec. 1797.

18/A/3   3 Jan. 1799. Elizabeth Masters. Charging more than the statutory rate of interest on a loan of 3/- to James Gillmor in St. Philip and St. Jacob's parish, Bristol. Dr. J. A. Small JP and T. Walker JP. Fine £5. Offence committed 24 Dec. 1798. [*Repeated in the same words except that the loan was to* Richard Powell *of the same parish.*]

18/A/4   3 Jan. 1799. Samuel James the younger. Charging [*etc.*, *as* 18/A/3, *with a similar repetition.*]

18/A/5   3 Jan. 1799. Richard Parsons. Charging more than the statutory rate of interest on a loan of 3/- to Richard Powell in St. Philip and St. Jacob's parish, Bristol. [*JPs and fine as above.*] Offence committed 29 Dec. 1798. [*Repeated twice in the same words except that the offence was committed* 15 Dec. 1798 *and* 21 Dec. 1798.]

18/A/6   3 Jan. 1799. Samuel Ogborn. Charging more than the statutory rate of interest on a loan of 2/7 to Richard Powell in St. Philip and St. Jacob's parish, Bristol. [*JPs and fine as above.*] Offence committed 29 Dec. 1798. [*Repeated twice in the same words except that in the first repetition the loan was 5/3 and in the second of 2/7, and in each repetition the offence was committed* 24 Dec. 1798.]

18/A/7   3 Jan. 1799. Peter Canning. Charging more than the statutory rate of interest on a loan of 2/9 to James Gillmor in St. Philip and St. Jacob's parish, Bristol. [*JPs and fine as above.*] Offence committed 15 Dec. 1798. [*Repeated twice in the same words except that in the first repetition the loan was of 3/- and the offence was committed on* 19 Dec. 1798, *and in the second the loan was of 2/8 to Richard Powell, and the offence was committed on* 29 Dec. 1798.]

18/A/8   3 Jan. 1799. Elizabeth Masters. Charging more than the statutory rate of interest on a loan of 3/- to Richard Powell in St. Philip and St. Jacob's parish, Bristol. [*JPs and fine as above.*] Offence committed 20 Dec. 1798.

Sarah Pitcher [*similarly*] on a loan of 2/7 to John Crossley *alias* Cook in Clifton, Bristol. [*JPs and fine as above.*] Offence committed 25 Dec. 1798.

Hannah Husband [*similarly*] on a loan of 2/7 to James Gillmor in Clifton, Bristol. [*JPs and fine as above.*] Offence committed 29 Dec. 1798.

18/A/9   3 Jan. 1799. Samuel Ogborn. Charging more than the statutory rate of interest on a loan of 5/3 to Richard Powell in St. Philip and St. Jacob's parish, Bristol. [*JPs and fine as above.*] Offence committed 31 Dec. 1798.

James Bryant. Charging more than the statutory rate of interest on a loan of 3/- to James Gillmor in St. Philip and St. Jacob's parish, Bristol. [*JPs and fine as above.*] Offence committed 20 Dec. 1798. [*Repeated twice in the same words except that in each repetition the offence was committed on* 24 Dec.1798.]

18/A/10   3 Jan. 1799. Mary Branson. Charging more than the statutory rate of interest on a loan of 2/7 to James Gillmor in St. Philip and St. Jacob's parish, Bristol. [*JPs and fine as above.*] Offence committed 22 Dec. 1798. [*Repeated twice in the same words except that the loan was of 3/- in each repetition and the offence was committed on* 19 Dec. 1798 *and* 17 Dec. 1798 *respectively.*]

18/A/11   3 Jan. 1799. Samuel James the elder. Charging more than the statutory rate of interest on a loan of 3/- to James Gillmor in St. Philip and St. Jacob's parish, Bristol. [*JPs and fine as above.*] Offence committed 24 Dec. 1798. [*Repeated in the same words except that the loan was to* Richard Powell.]

18/A/12   21 Dec. 1798. Thomas Organ of Painswick. Swearing and cursing. J. Hollings JP. Offence committed 2 July 1798.

18/A/13   27 Oct. 1798. John Morgan of Frampton [Mansell]. Swearing. N. Winchcombe JP. Offence committed 22 Oct. 1798.

18/A/14   9 Nov. 1798. Thomas Twissell of Bisley, weaver. Selling 5 lb. of stolen woollen yarn to Martha Twissell of Bisley. B. Hyett JP and J. Hollings JP at Stroud. David Webb, clothier, of Minchinhampton, informant. Fine £20 (£10 to informant and £10 to

Gloucester infirmary) or three months' hard labour in Horsley house of correction. Offence committed between 5 and 16 Oct. 1798.

18/A/15   9 Aug. 1798. Abraham Perrott of North Nibley. Buying 12 lb. of stolen woollen yarn from Samuel Cook, labourer, of Wotton under Edge, the property of Humphrey Austin and Samuel Yeats, clothiers, of Wotton under Edge. Rev. P. Hawker JP and P. Sheppard JP at Horsley. James Swaine, informant. Fine £40 (£10 to informant, £11 17s. 10d. to complainants and remainder to Gloucester infirmary) or six months' hard labour in Horsley house of correction. Offence committed 14 July 1798.

18/B/1   21 Feb. 1799. William Cockshead of Dymock, carpenter. Cutting hedge-wood in Dymock. Rev. H. G. D. Yate JP. Robert Hartland of Dymock, complainant.

18/C/1   18 May 1799. Moses Roberts of the Morse, St. Briavels, labourer. Cutting down an oak timber tree in the Forest of Dean. G. Skipp JP. Miles Hartland, deputy forest surveyor, complainant. Second offence. Fine £30 mitigated to £15. Offence committed 18 May 1799.

18/C/2   29 June 1799. Richard Alford of Bromsberrow, labourer. Cursing and swearing. Rev. H. G. D. Yate JP. Second offence. [Cf. 16/B/18.]

18/C/3   20 June 1799. Nathaniel Rice of Ebley, jenny spinner. Damaging about 26 lb. of woollen yarn. Sir G. O. Paul JP and J. Hollings JP. James Thomas, clothier, of King's Stanley, complainant. Offence committed during previous ten weeks.

18/C/4   2 July 1799. Mary Roan of Eastington, single woman. Stealing 3 lb. of Spanish wool, the property of Henry Hicks & Co., clothiers, of Eastington. C. Hayward JP and Rev. G. Hayward JP.

18/D/1   14 Aug. 1799. William Meek of Weston under Penyard, Herefs., yeoman. Cutting down 60 beech trees in the Forest of Dean. G. Skipp JP. George Court, forest keeper, complainant. Fine £20 mitigated to £1 11s. 6d. and 7/- expenses. Offence committed 9 Aug. 1799.

18/D/2   30 Aug. 1799. John Read of St. Briavels, labourer. Cutting down two birch trees in the Forest of Dean. G. Skipp JP. Roger Cooper, labourer, of St. Briavels, complainant. Fine £20 mitigated to £1 11s. 6d. and 12/6 expenses. Offence committed 15 Aug. 1799.

18/D/3   14 Aug. 1799. Thomas Meek of Weston under Penyard, Herefs., yeoman. Cutting down [etc., as 18/D/1].

18/D/4   18 May 1799. William Roberts of the Morse, St. Briavels, labourer. Cutting down an oak tree in the Forest of Dean. G. Skipp JP. Miles Hartland, deputy forest surveyor, complainant. Fine £20 mitigated to £5. Offence committed 18 May 1799. [Cf. 18/C/1.]

18/D/5   10 Aug. 1799. Thomas Gagg of St. Briavels, coalminer. Cutting down an oak tree in the Forest of Dean. G. Skipp JP. George Court, forest keeper, complainant. Fine £20 mitigated to £2 2s. and 12/6 expenses. Offence committed 5 Aug. 1799.

18/D/6   30 Aug. 1799. Bridgman Meek of St. Briavels, labourer. Cutting down two birch trees in the Forest of Dean. G. Skipp JP. Roger Cooper, keeper of Staple Edge [MS. Stapleidge] inclosure, complainant. Fine £20 mitigated to £1 11s. 6d. and 12/6 expenses. Offence committed 15 Aug. 1799. [Cf. 18/D/2.]

18/D/7   1 Oct. 1799. Joseph Day of Minchinhampton, glazier. Selling ale etc. without a licence. Rev. P. Hawker JP. First offence. Fine £10 and 4/- expenses.

18/D/8   25 July 1799. Samuel Smith. Stealing 19 cabbages worth 6d. from a garden in Rudgeway, Stapleton, the property of Dr. Archibald Drummond. C. J. Harford JP. Fine 10/- (to be given to the poor). Offence committed 9 July 1799.

19/A/1 26 Dec. 1799. Richard Harbert of Condicote, labourer. Using two dogs and a gun with intent to kill game in Temple Guiting. George Talbot JP. First offence. Fine £20. Offence committed 22 Dec. 1799.

19/A/2 11 Jan. 1800. Thomas Casey of Minchinhampton, clothier. Buying and receiving 5 lb. of Spanish wool and 8 lb. of English wool from James Mason, scribbler, of Minchinhampton, the property of John Cooper and Henry Randall, clothiers, of Minchinhampton. Rev. P. Hawker JP and J. Hollings JP. John Cooper, informant. Fine £40 or six months' hard labour in Horsley house of correction. Offence committed between 1 May and 1 Sept. 1799.

19/A/3 11 Jan. 1800. Ann Casey of Minchinhampton, widow. Selling ale etc. without a licence. Rev. P. Hawker JP and J. Hollings JP. First offence. Fine £10 and 10/- expenses.

19/A/4 27 Dec. 1799. John Window of Horsley, weaver. Failing to return 42 lb. of woollen yarn given him to weave. Rev. P. Hawker JP. John Cooper and Henry Randall, clothiers, of Minchinhampton, complainants. Offence committed between 6 July and 1 Sept. 1799.

19/A/5 3 Jan. 1800. Robert Steed of Wotton under Edge, gentleman. Using a gun to kill game. Rev. Lewis Clutterbuck JP. Fine £20 mitigated to £10 16s. Offence committed 24 Dec. 1799.

19/A/6 3 Jan. 1800. William Sladden of Wotton under Edge, gentleman. Using a dog and a gun to kill game [etc., as 19/A/5].

19/A/7 15 Nov. 1799. Isaac Berry of Malmesbury, Wilts., yeoman. Using a gun to kill a pheasant in Berkeley. Rev. William Dechair Tattersall JP at Wotton under Edge. Fine £20. Offence committed 10 Oct. 1799.

19/A/8 15 Nov. 1799. Isaac Berry of Malmesbury, Wilts., yeoman, and Thomas Tallboys, gentleman, of Tetbury, bound in the sum of £30 each to appear at next Quarter Sessions. Rev. W. D. Tattersall JP. Recognizance of Isaac Berry to appear at next Q.S. to appeal against above conviction.

19/A/9 17 Oct. 1799. Alexander Watts the younger of Hawkesbury, yeoman. Using a gun to kill a hare in Upton, Hawkesbury. Henry, duke of Beaufort, JP and R. Haynes JP at Chipping Sodbury. Fine £20. Offence committed 18 Aug. 1799.

19/A/10 19 Oct. 1799. Alexander Watts the younger of Hawkesbury, yeoman, bound in the sum of £20 to appear at next Quarter Sessions. G. Hardwicke JP. Recognizance to appear at next Q.S. to appeal against above conviction.

19/A/11 23 Dec. 1799. Job Wickes of Minchinhampton, miller and baker. Adulterating wheat at his mill in Woodchester. Rev. P. Hawker JP. George Stephens of Avening, witness. Fine £10. Offence committed 19 Dec. 1799.

19/B/1 6 Feb. 1800. Thomas Brookes of Tetbury, yeoman. Using dogs to kill a hare in Tetbury. Rev. George Hayward junior JP at Beverstone. Fine £20. Offence committed 16 Jan. 1800.

19/B/2 4 Feb. 1800. Joseph Smith of King's Stanley, weaver. Possessing stolen woollen yarn. Rev. G. Hayward JP and Rev. G. Hayward junior JP. Nathaniel Alder, weaver, of King's Stanley, witness.

19/B/3 21 Feb. 1800. Thomas Skerrett of Painswick, clothier. Swearing and cursing. J. Hollings JP.

19/B/4 14 Feb. 1800. William Evans of Westbury on Trym, yeoman. Failing to pay stamp duty on a receipt. T. Walker JP. First offence. Fine £10 mitigated to £5. Offence committed 10 Dec. 1799.

19/B/5 7 March 1800. John Edwards of North Nibley, blacksmith. Possessing a quantity of beech wood without satisfactory explanation. Rev. W. D. Tattersall JP. John Court, gamekeeper, of Wotton under Edge, complainant. First offence. Fine 30/- and 10/- expenses. Offence committed 8 Feb. 1800.

19/B/6   7 Sept. 1799 [*late return*]. John Bennett of Avening, weaver. Buying and receiving stolen yarn at his home in Avening from Daniel Bown, weaver, of Horsley. Rev. P. Hawker JP and P. Sheppard JP. Daniel Bown, witness. Fine £40 or six months' hard labour in Horsley house of correction. Offence committed 17 Aug. 1799.

19/B/7   10 Dec. 1799. John Daniels of Minchinhampton, broadweaver. Buying and receiving stolen woollen yarn from James Ayliff, spinner, of Rodborough. Rev. P. Hawker JP and P. Sheppard JP. Mr. Joseph Lewis, clothier, of Stroud, complainant. James Ayliff, witness. Fine £40 or six months' hard labour in Horsley house of correction. Offence committed 9 Dec. 1799.

19/C/1   1 July 1800. Joseph King of King's Stanley, weaver. Refusing to return a broad loom to his employer. Rev. G. Hayward JP and Rev. G. Hayward junior JP. Mr. Henry Eycott, clothier, of Stonehouse, complainant.

19/D/1   10 Sept. 1800. John Ferris of Newnham, labourer. Driving a wagon with undersized wheels in Littledean. Thomas Cannock of Newnham, yeoman. Allowing his wagon to be driven in Littledean with undersized wheels. G. Skipp JP at Flaxley. Richard Gwilliam, nailer, of Flaxley, informant. Owner fined £5. Offence committed 6 Sept. 1800.

19/D/2   28 Aug. 1800. John Leech of Rodborough. Selling beer without a licence. Rev. P. Hawker JP. William Webb, informant. First offence. Offence committed 14 Aug. 1800.

19/D/3   19 Sept. 1800. Elizabeth Hodges of Rodborough, single woman. Buying and receiving 21 lb. of Spanish wool from Mary wife of William King, labourer, of Rodborough. N. Winchcombe JP and J. Hollings JP. Mr. William Workman, clothier, of Stroud, informant. Fine £40 or six months' hard labour in Horsley house of correction. Offence committed between 4 and 16 September 1800.

20/A/1   14 Oct. 1800. Martin Turner, mason, John Winfield, and Joseph Cook, labourers, all of Burford, Oxon. Using nets with intent to kill hares in Sherborne. Rev. G. Coxwell JP. First offence. Fine £20. Offence committed 5 Oct. 1800.

20/A/2   14 Oct. 1800. James Purbrick of Upton, Oxon., basket-maker. Using a net with intent to kill hares in Sherborne [*etc., as* 20/A/1].

20/A/3   24 Nov. 1800. John Hewer the younger of Meysey Hampton [*MS.* Maisey Hampton], yeoman. Using a gun to kill game in Meysey Hampton. Joseph Cripps JP. First offence. Offence committed 16 Nov. 1800.

20/A/4   21 Oct. 1800. John Rogers of Chavenage, Horsley, yeoman. Using a gun to kill a hare in Horsley. P. Sheppard JP at [Minchin] Hampton. Fine £20. Offence committed 18 Oct. 1800.

20/A/5   6 Dec. 1800. Deborah Brown of Rodborough, single woman. Embezzling about 25 lb. of Spanish wool. N. Winchcombe JP and J. Hollings JP. James Lewis, clothier, of Randwick, complainant. First offence. Three months' hard labour in Horsley house of correction.

20/A/6   14 Oct. 1800. Thomas Oatridge of Uley, tailor. Buying a a piece of superfine cloth from Martha Portlock, clothworker, the property of John and Charles Cook, clothiers, of Wotton under Edge. T. Estcourt JP and John Paul Paul JP. John and Charles Cook, informants. Fine £40 or six months' hard labour in Horsley house of correction.

20/A/7   16 Dec. 1800. Daniel Gardner of Painswick, weaver. Buying and receiving about 4 lb. of stolen woollen yarn from Mary Butt, weaver, of Painswick. N. Winchcombe JP and J. Hollings JP. Edward Parker, clothier, of Painswick, complainant. Charles Horlick, clothier, of Painswick, informant. Fine £20 or three months' hard labour in Horsley house of correction. Offence committed between 1 April and 10 May 1800.

20/A/8   5 Nov. 1800. Sarah wife of Nathaniel Pope of Minchinhampton, weaver. Buying and receiving 12 lb. of Spanish wool from Ann Allaway, single woman, of Rodborough. N. Winchcombe JP and J. Hollings JP. James Nick, clothier, of Painswick, informant. Fine £40 or six months' hard labour in Horsley house of correction. Offence committed between 26 and 30 Aug. 1800.

20/A/9   16 Dec. 1800. John Gardner of Painswick, weaver. Buying and receiving 2 lb. of woollen yarn from Mary Butt, weaver, at her home in Painswick. N. Winchcombe JP and J. Hollings JP. Charles Horlick, clothier, informant. Fine £20 or three months's hard labour in Horsley house of correction.

20/A/10   21 Dec. 1800. Joseph Teakel of Stroud, weaver. Having on his premises a large quantity of materials for woollen manufacture without satisfactory explanation. N. Winchcombe JP and J. Hollings JP. Charles Horlick, clothier, of Painswick, informant. Search warrant executed by the above and William Baylis, John Walker and Edward Parker, clothiers, of Painswick. First offence. Fine £20. Offence committed 6 Dec. 1800.

20/B/1   1 April 1801. Sarah Werrett of Pauntley, widow. Pulling up and stealing hedge-wood on land occupied by Richard Loveridge, yeoman, of Pauntley. Rev. H. G. D. Yate JP.

20/B/2   2 March 1801. William Churn, late of Widford, labourer. Cutting down a beech tree at Widford, the property of Charles Fettiplace Esq. Rev. J. Hippisley JP. John Schollar, complainant. Offence committed 15 Jan. 1801.

20/B/3   2 March 1801. John Triptree, late of Widford, labourer. Cutting down [*etc., as* 20/B/2].

20/B/4   2 March 1801. William Wiggins, late of Widford, labourer. Cutting down [*etc., as* 20/B/2].

20/B/5   18 Feb. 1801. Benjamin Paget. Possessing snares etc. for trapping deer without satisfactory explanation. Thomas Ireland JP. William Maylard, complainant.

20/B/6   23 Jan. 1801. Richard Blandford of Brimpsfield, labourer. Cutting a burden of ash poles in woods at Brimpsfield, the property of the earl of Mount Edgcumbe. William Veel JP. Thomas Winning, yeoman, of Brimpsfield, complainant. First offence. Fine 40/-. Offence committed 19 Jan. 1801.

20/B/7   6 Feb. 1801. John Hunt of Bisley, weaver. Embezzling 20 lb. of woollen yarn given him to weave on 4 Oct. 1799. N. Winchcombe JP and J. Hollings JP. William Toghill, clothier, of Bisley, complainant. First offence. Three months' hard labour in Horsley house of correction.

20/B/8   6 Feb. 1801. Samuel Selwin of Painswick, weaver. Buying and receiving from Mary Butt, widow, of Painswick, about 4 lb. of woollen yarn. N. Winchcombe JP and J. Hollings JP. Charles Horlick, clothier, of Painswick, complainant. Fine £40 or six months' hard labour in Horsley house of correction. Offence committed 2 June 1800.

20/B/9   23 March 1801. Mary wife of John Bennett of Avening. Buying and receiving at her home about 3 lb. of coarse woollen yarn from Abraham Bird the younger, weaver, of Minchinhampton. Rev. P. Hawker JP and P. Sheppard JP. Paul Wathen, clothier, of Rodborough, informant. Abraham Bird the younger, witness. Fine £40 or six months' hard labour in Horsley house of correction. Offence committed between 1 Jan. and 20 March 1801.

20/B/10   12 Jan. 1801. John Green. Killing a hare in Farmington Grove. P. Snell JP at Guiting Grange. Thomas Cook of Farmington, gamekeeper to Rev. Henry Waller, witness. First offence. Offender refused to pay fine of £20. Committed to Northleach bridewell for three months. Offence committed Sunday 4 Jan. 1801.

20/B/11   27 Jan. 1801. Thomas Groves of Childswickham, labourer. Found in possession of a bag containing 2 hares and 15 gins. P. Snell JP. Richard Baysend, gamekeeper for the manor of Buckland, informant. Offender refused to pay fine of £5 and had no goods which could be distressed. Committed to Northleach bridewell for three months. Offence committed 17 Jan. 1801.

20/B/12   14 Feb. 1801. Richard Land of Longney, butcher. Using a snare to kill game in Elmore. J. Parker JP. Thomas Smith, gentleman, of Highnam, informant. Thomas Ellis, yeoman, of Elmore, witness. Offender did not appear. Fine £5. Offence committed 30 Jan. 1801.

20/C/1   26 June 1801. John Walker, weaver, and his wife Elizabeth of Rodborough. Cursing in King's Stanley. Rev. P. Hawker JP. Offence committed 20 June 1801.

20/C/2   20 Feb. 1801. Nathaniel Tranter of Horsley, weaver. Stealing part of a beech tree from a wood in Horsley, the property of John Remmington Esq. Rev. P. Hawker JP. John Remmington Esq., complainant. John Hillier, spinner, of Horsley, witness. Fine £2 or three months in Horsley gaol. Offence committed 10 Feb. 1801.

20/C/3   13 May 1801. Thomas Smith of Marshfield, tailor. Stealing two trout from a stream in Broadmead, Marshfield, the property of Christopher Codrington Esq. I. W. Horlock JP at Marshfield. William Golding, steward to Christopher Codrington, informant. Edward Fidoe, yeoman, of Marshfield, witness. Offender pleaded not guilty. Fine £5. Offence committed 25 April 1801.

20/D/1   7 Aug. 1801. Alexander Watts the younger of Hillesley, yeoman. Using a gun to kill game in Kilcott. Henry, duke of Beaufort, JP, I. W. Horlock JP and R. Haynes JP at Old Sodbury. Thomas Reed of Hillesley, informant. William Wallington the younger of Hillesley, witness. Offender pleaded not guilty. Fine £5. Offence committed 8 July 1801.

20/D/2   8 Sept. 1801. Isaac Smith of Horsley, weaver. Embezzling 1 lb. 5 oz. of woollen yarn delivered to him to weave. C. Hayward JP, N. Winchcombe JP, Rev. G. Hayward JP and Rev. G. Hayward junior JP. Stephen Clissold, clothier, of Stonehouse, complainant. John Webster of King's Stanley, witness.

20/D/3   2 Oct. 1801. William Black of Stancombe, clothworker. Buying and receiving about 1 lb. of stolen woollen yarn from Richard Woodward of Stancombe, weaver. Rev. G. Hayward JP and Rev. G. Hayward junior JP at Frocester. Thomas Tippetts and William Smith, informants. Fine £40 or six months' hard labour in Horsley house of correction. Offence committed 18 May 1801.

20/D/4   2 Oct. 1801. Tabitha *alias* Bathia wife of Thomas Gibbs of Dursley. Selling about 1 lb. of stolen woollen yarn to Elizabeth wife of Nathaniel Dauncey, clothworker, of Coaley. Rev. G. Hayward JP and Rev. G. Hayward junior JP at Frocester. Thomas Tippetts and William Smith, informants. Fine £25 or four months' hard labour in Horsley house of correction. Offence committed 1 Aug. 1801.

20/D/5   26 Aug. 1801. Jane Fisher of Dursley, spooler. Selling about 1 lb. of stolen woolen yarn to John Smith, weaver, of Dursley. Rev. G. Hayward JP and Rev. G. Hayward junior JP at Frocester. Thomas Tippetts and William Smith, informants. Fine £20 or three months' hard labour in Horsley house of correction. Offence committed between 25 Dec. 1800 and 25 March 1801.

20/D/6   2 Oct. 1801. Mark Terrett of North Nibley, clothier. Buying and receiving 10 lb. of stolen woollen yarn from John Longstreeth, weaver, of Dursley. Rev. G. Hayward JP and Rev. G. Hayward junior JP at Frocester. Thomas Tippetts and William Smith, informants. Fine £40 or six months' hard labour in Horsley house of correction. Offence committed 30 June 1801.

20/D/7   2 Oct. 1801. Elizabeth wife of Nathaniel Dauncey of Coaley, clothier. Buying and receiving about 6 lb. of woollen yarn on spools, the property of Thomas Tippetts and William Smith, clothiers, of Dursley, from Rachael wife of Robert Webb, weaver, of Dursley. Rev. G. Hayward JP and Rev. G. Hayward junior JP. Fine £25 or four months' hard labour in Horsley house of correction. Offence committed 24 July 1801.

20/D/8   22 Aug. 1801. James Summers of Dursley, shoemaker. Buying and receiving about 3 lb. of woollen yarn, the property of Thomas Tippetts and William Smith, clothiers, of Dursley, from Samuel Gowen, weaver, of Dursley. Rev. G. Hayward JP and Rev. G. Hayward junior JP. Fine £40 or six months' hard labour in Horsley house of correction. Offence committed 6 Aug. 1801.

20/D/9   19 Sept. 1801. John Jefferiess of Nailsworth, victualler. Buying and receiving about 40 yards of Cashmere cloth made from stolen wool from William Smith, weaver, of Dursley. Rev. G. Hayward JP and Rev. G. Hayward junior JP. Thomas Tippetts and William Smith, clothiers, of Dursley, informants. Fine £40 or six months' hard labour in Horsley house of correction. Offence committed 15 July 1801.

20/D/10   29 July 1801. Thomas Pimbury. Cursing. Rev. P. Hawker JP.

20/D/11   3 Aug. 1801. John Coxe. Cursing. Rev. P. Hawker JP.

21/A/1   11 Dec. 1801. William Weight of Dursley, clothworker. Buying and receiving 1½ lb. of stolen woollen yarn from John Smith, weaver, of Dursley. Rev. G. Hayward JP and Rev. G. Hayward junior JP at Frocester. Thomas Tippetts and William Smith, clothiers, of Dursley, informants. Fine £40 or six months' hard labour in Horsley house of correction. Offence committed 10 May 1800.

21/A/2   16 Oct. 1801. Thomas Oatridge of Uley, tailor. Buying and receiving a piece of stolen woollen cloth from Martha Portlock, clothworker. Rev. W. Lloyd Baker JP and R. Nelmes JP. John, Thomas and Charles Cook, clothiers, of Wotton under Edge, informants. Fine £30 or six months' hard labour in Horsley house of correction. Offence committed 24 Sept. 1800.

21/A/3   1 Jan. 1802. William Hanks of Wotton under Edge, pawnbroker. Buying and receiving 44 yards of woollen cloth from Anthony Mabbett, broadweaver. Rev. W. Lloyd Baker JP and Rev. Richard Jones JP. Nathaniel Lloyd, informant. Fine £40 or six months' hard labour in Horsley house of correction. Offence committed 5 March 1801.

21/A/4   16 Oct. 1801. Samuel Cook of Pucklechurch. Using a dog and a gun to kill game in Siston. R. Haynes JP and I. W. Horlock JP at Old Sodbury. Daniel Thompson of Pucklechurch, informant. Fine £5. Offence committed 1 Sept. 1801.

21/A/5   8 Dec. 1801. John Martin of Falfield, yeoman. Using a dog to kill a hare. Frederick Augustus, earl of Berkeley JP at Berkeley Castle. Fine £20. Offence committed 2 Dec. 1801.

21/A/6   8 Dec. 1801. John Martin of Falfield, yeoman. Using a dog to kill game. Earl of Berkeley JP. Guy Nelmes, yeoman, of Rockhampton, informant. Fine £5. Offence committed 2 Dec. 1801.

21/A/7   16 Oct. 1801. James Pensam of Overbury, Worcs., yeoman. Using a dog to kill game in Ashchurch. William Buckle JP. John Hollands, labourer, of Ashchurch, informant. Edward Smith, labourer, of Bishop's Cleeve, witness. Fine £5. Offence committed 5 Sept. 1801.

21/B/1   5 March 1802. Martha March of Bisley, single woman. Embezzling about 12 lb. of woollen yarn. J. Hollings JP and P. Sheppard JP. John Innell the younger, clothier, of Bisley, informant. First offence. Three months' hard labour in Horsley house of correction. Offence committed between 21 and 28 Feb. 1802.

21/B/2   22 Jan. 1802. Thomas Dalby of Rodborough, shearman. Cutting beech timber in Minchinhampton, the property of Nathaniel William Peach Esq. of Acton Hall, Salop. Rev. P. Hawker JP. Thomas Osman, clothworker, of Minchinhampton, complainant. Fine 40/- or one month in Horsley house of correction. Offence committed 13 Jan. 1802.

21/B/3   5 March 1802. John Davis of Bisley, weaver. Buying about 3 lb. of coarse woollen yarn from Thomas Collins, weaver, of Bisley. J. Hollings JP and P. Sheppard JP. William Winn, clothier, of Bisley, informant. Thomas Collins, witness. Fine £40 or six months' hard labour in Horsley house of correction. Offence committed between Jan. and Oct. 1801.

21/B/4   8 Feb. 1802. Nathaniel Antill of Bisley, weaver. Buying 3 lb. of woollen yarn from Richard Wood , weaver, of Bisley. J. Hollings JP and P. Sheppard JP. William Winn, clothier, of Bisley, informant. Richard Wood, witness. Fine £40 or six months' hard labour in Horsley house of correction. Offence committed between Nov. 1800 and April 1801.

21/B/5   10 April 1802. John Smith of Stroud, brazier. Possessing a large quantity of various metals without satisfactory explanation. Rev. P. Hawker JP and J. Hollings JP. Peter Gardner and George Minett, petty constables of Stroud, informants. First conviction. Fine 40/-. Offence committed 9 April 1802.

21/B/6   9 Feb. 1802. Thomas Knapp of Hinton near Berkeley, yeoman. Using a gun to kill a pheasant in Hinton. Rev. G. Hayward JP at Frocester. Fine £20. Offence committed 11 Nov. 1801.

21/B/7   20 Jan. 1802. Thomas Knapp of Hinton near Berkeley, yeoman. Using a gun to kill game in Hinton. Rev. G. Hayward JP at Frocester. John Pick, yeoman, of Hinton, informant. Thomas Chase, labourer, of Berkeley, witness. Fine £5. Offence committed 11 Nov. 1801.

21/B/8   1 March 1802. George Dunn of Down Ampney, labourer. Cutting wood in Down Ampney, the property of the Right Hon. Lord Eliot. Robert Timbrell JP. John Ruck, yeoman, of Down Ampney, complainant.

21/B/9   19 March 1802. William Hanks of Wotton under Edge, pawnbroker. Buying 28 yards of kerseymere cloth from Anthony Mabbett, broadweaver. George Cooke D.D. JP and Rev. W. Lloyd Baker JP. Nathaniel Lloyd, informant. Fine £40 or six months' hard labour in Horsley house of correction. Offence committed 11 July 1801.

21/B/10   22 Jan. 1802. William Hanks of Wotton under Edge, pawnbroker. Buying one piece of kerseymere cloth from Anthony Mabbett by way of pledge. Rev. W. Lloyd Baker JP. Nathaniel Lloyd, informant. Fine £5. Offence committed 14 July 1801.

21/B/11   22 Jan. 1802. William Hanks of Wotton under Edge, pawnbroker. Advancing money to Anthony Mabbett, on the pledge of a piece of cloth, without properly recording the transaction. Rev. W. Lloyd Baker JP. Nathaniel Lloyd, informant. Fine £10. Offence committed 9 June 1801.

21/C/1   30 April 1802. John Jeackes *alias* Jackes or Jakes of Bisley, weaver. Buying 3½ lb. of coarse woollen yarn from John Hunt, weaver, of Bisley. J. Hollings JP and Henry Burgh JP. William Toghill, clothier, of Bisley, informant. John Hunt, witness. Fine £40 or three days in Gloucester house of correction and once publicly whipped. Offence committed between 25 Dec. 1801 and 6 Feb. 1802.

21/C/2   29 May 1802. William Hawkins of Corse, husbandman. Refusing to honour an agreement to apprentice William Hughes of Hasfield. J. Parker JP and Rev. C. Sandiford JP. William Cother and John Legeyt, overseers of the poor of Hasfield, and William Clark and John Marshall, churchwardens of Hasfield, complainants. Fine £10.

21/D/1   11 July 1802. Richard Clayfield of Stroud, cordwainer. Possessing 37 lb. of Spanish wool without satisfactory explanation. J. Hollings JP and H. Burgh JP. Offence committed 11 July 1802.

21/D/2   1 Aug. 1802. Samuel Smith of Stroud, weaver. Embezzling 5 lb. of woollen yarn. J. Hollings JP and H. Burgh JP. Messrs. Charles Wathen and Britain, clothiers, of Stroud, complainants. John Cooper, servant to the above clothiers, witness. First offence. Offence committed between 9 and 20 July 1802.

21/D/3   27 Sept. 1802. John Restal of Stroud, weaver. Possessing about 7 lb. of ends of woollen yarn without satisfactory explanation. J. Hollings JP and H. Burgh JP. Offence committed 25 Sept. 1802.

21/D/4   24 Sept. 1802. Hester Niblett of Stroud, widow. Embezzling about 2 lb. of Spanish wool. J. Hollings JP and H. Burgh JP. Mary Cooke, clothier, of Stroud, complainant. Offence committed between 20 Aug. and 20 Sept. 1802.

21/D/5   28 Sept. 1802. William Ball of King's Stanley, weaver. Cursing. H. Burgh JP. Offence committed 24 Sept. 1802.

21/D/6   6 Sept. 1802. Abigail wife of Edward Chambers of Minchinhampton, labourer. Embezzling about 1 lb. of Spanish wool. Rev. P. Hawker JP and P. Sheppard JP. Messrs. Smith, Tate & Co., clothiers, of Minchinhampton, complainants. First offence. Offence committed between 20 and 27 Aug. 1802.

21/D/7   16 July 1802. Rebecca Perrin of Stroud, single woman. Possessing about 4½ lb. of woollen yarn without satisfactory explanation. J. Hollings JP and H. Burgh JP. Offence committed 12 July 1802.

21/D/8   15 Sept. 1802. John Haydon of Chipping Campden, baker. Offering bread for sale at 1/- per loaf contrary to Assize. Rev. John Pelly JP. Fine 40/-. Offence committed 15 Sept. 1802.

21/D/9   12 Aug. 1802. Richard Boulton of Old Sodbury, labourer. Using dogs to kill a hare in Dodington. Henry, duke of Beaufort, JP at Badminton. John Slade, gamekeeper to Christopher Codrington, of Dodington, informant. Luke Kethro of Dodington, witness. Fine £5. Offence committed 10 Aug. 1802.

22/A/1   24 Dec. 1802. Elizabeth Denly. Damaging underwood, the property of Lord Chedworth. Rev. Benjamin Grisdale JP. William Hughes, complainant.

22/A/2   20 Dec. 1802. James Excell, late of Wotton under Edge, weaver. Persuading Joshua Vines, clothworker, to leave his employer, Thomas Foxwell, clothier. G. Cooke D.D. JP, R. Nelmes JP and Rev. W. Lloyd Baker JP. Three months in gaol. Offence committed 3 Dec. 1802.

22/A/3   20 Dec. 1802. James Excell, late of Wotton under Edge, weaver. Combining with others against Thomas Foxwell, clothier. G. Cooke D.D. JP, R. Nelmes JP and Rev. W. Lloyd Baker JP. Three months in gaol. Offence committed 3 Dec. 1802.

22/A/4   20 Dec. 1802. Charles Snell of Wotton under Edge, weaver. Combining [etc., as 22/A/3].

22/A/5   20 Dec. 1802. John Ford, late of Wotton under Edge, weaver. Combining [etc., as 22/A/3].

22/A/6   20 Dec. 1802. John Ford, late of Wotton under Edge. Persuading Josha Vines to leave his employer, Thomas Foxwell, clothier [etc., as 22/A/2].

22/A/7   20 Dec. 1802. Charles Snell, late of Wotton under Edge, weaver. Persuading [etc., as 22/A/6].

22/A/8   26 Nov. 1802. John Powell of Wotton under Edge, glazier. Buying quantities of stolen lead from Benjamin Moody and Charles Cousens. R. Nelmes JP. First offence. Fine 20/-. Offence committed 23 Nov. 1802.

22/A/9   30 Sept. 1802. James White, yeoman, of Tirley, and William Clarke, yeoman, of Eldersfield, Worcs. Using dogs and guns to kill game in Forthampton. Thomas Dowdeswell JP. William Beauchamp Esq., complainant. Giles Hawker, witness. Fine £5 each. Fines paid immediately. Offence committed 27 Sept. 1802.

22/A/10   18 Nov. 1802. John Hodges of Kingscote, shopkeeper. Cursing. Rev. P. Hawker JP.

22/A/11   17 Dec. 1802. John Brinkworth of Wanswell Court, Berkeley, dairyman. Stealing a hat-lining from James Burchell, yeoman, of Berkeley, in order to avoid paying duty thereon. Earl of Berkeley JP. Fine £20. Offence committed 5 Dec. 1802.

22/A/12   18 Dec. 1802. Thomas Vines, late of Wotton under Edge. Persuading Edward George, clothworker, to leave his employer, Thomas Symmons, clothier. G. Cooke D.D. JP and Rev. W. Lloyd Baker JP. Three months in gaol. Offence committed 13 Dec. 1802.

22/A/13   18 Dec. 1802. William Tidman the younger, late of Wotton under Edge, weaver. Persuading [etc., as 22/A/12].

22/A/14   18 Dec. 1802. Solomon Watkins, late of Wotton under Edge, weaver. Persuading [etc., as 22/A/12].

22/A/15   18 Dec. 1802. John Bruton, late of Wotton under Edge, weaver. Persuading [etc., as 22/A/12].

22/A/16   20 Dec. 1802. William Tidman the younger, late of Wotton under Edge. Attending an illegal meeting held at the King's Arms, Wotton under Edge (John Till's house), to combine against Thomas Symmons, clothier. G. Cooke D.D. JP and Rev. W. Lloyd Baker JP. Three months in gaol in addition to that imposed for the offence [as above, 22/A/13]. Offence committed 6 Dec. 1802.

22/A/17   20 Dec. 1802. Robert Cousens of Wotton under Edge, weaver. Attending a meeting with William Tidman the younger and others at the King's Arms [etc., as 22/A/16 except not stating that the sentence was additional].

22/A/18   29 Nov. 1802. 29 Nov. 1802. Mary wife of Daniel Millard of Leonard Stanley, weaver. Stealing woollen yarn. Rev. G. Hayward JP and Rev. G. Hayward junior JP. William and Samuel Holbrow, clothiers, of Leonard Stanley, complainants. William Mayo, clothworker, of Leonard Stanley, witness. Offence committed 26 Nov. 1802.

22/A/19   29 Nov. 1802. Jane wife of William Spencer of Coaley, labourer. Buying stolen woollen yarn at Coaley from Daniel Millard, weaver, of Leonard Stanley. Rev. G. Hayward JP and Rev. G. Hayward junior JP.

22/A/20   26 Oct. 1802. Henry Child, late of Shepton Mallet, Som., dealer and chapman. Exposing goods for sale in Stow [on the Wold]. Rev. J. Hippisley JP. Joseph Plant, complainant. Offence committed 25 Oct, 1802.

22/A/21   22 Dec. 1802. Thomas Bull of Church Yatton, Wilts. Possessing a net for taking game in Tormarton. R. Haynes JP at Wick. Henry Milner of Great Badminton, complainant. Thomas Webb, witness. Fine £5. Offence committed 22 Dec. 1802.

22/B/1   25 Jan. 1803. Mary Morse of Horsley. Selling ale without a licence. P. Sheppard JP at Box. First offence. Offence committed 8 Jan. 1803.

22/B/2   29 Jan. 1803. William Avery the elder of Avening, serge-weaver. Possessing about 40 lb. of woollen yarn without satisfactory explanation. P. Sheppard JP and Rev. P. Hawker JP. John Tucker, wool-loft man, informant. Fine £20 or one month in Horsley house of correction. Offence committed 27 Jan. 1803.

22/B/3   29 Jan. 1803. William Knight of Box, Minchinhampton, weaver. Possessing 80 lb. of woollen yarn without satisfactory explanation. P. Sheppard JP and Rev. P. Hawker JP. Peter Playne, clothier, of Minchinhampton, informant. Fine £20 or one month in Horsley house of correction. Offence committed 24 Jan. 1803.

22/B/4   18 March 1803. Richard Player of Newnham. Possessing deerskins without satisfactory explanation. Thomas Williams JP. William Cole, complainant. Fine £10. Offence committed 25 Feb. 1803.

22/B/5   7 April 1803. William Harris of Stroud. Shooting a hare in Berkeley. J. Hollings JP. Fine £5. Offence committed 25 Feb. 1803.

22/B/6   7 April 1803. James Kitcat of Bisley, labourer. Shooting [etc., as 22/B/5].

22/B/7   7 April 1803. James Kitcat. Shooting [etc., as 22/B/5].

22/B/8   24 Jan. 1803. John Matthews of Newent, innkeeper and husbandman. Refusing to honour an agreement to take John Baldwyn of Newent as apprentice. James De Visme JP and Rev. J. Foley JP. Joseph Hankins, overseer of the poor, informant. John Wood, visitor, and Miles Astman, guardian of the poor of Newent, witnesses. Fine £10.

22/B/9   24 Jan. 1803. John Hill of Newent, saddler and husbandman. Refusing to honour an agreement to apprentice Elizabeth Roch to learn housewifery [etc., as 22/B/8].

22/C/1   6 May 1803. Deborah Heaven of King's Court [MS. Kingscourt], Rodborough. Selling ale without a licence. J. Hollings JP. William Hedges, Samuel Holliday, William Denton and Anthony Lane, witnesses. Fine £20 and 10/- expenses. Offence committed 3 April 1803.

22/D/1   17 Sept. 1803. Christopher Birt of Woodchester, labourer. Using a gin to kill game in Woodchester. Rev. P. Hawker JP. John Almond, gamekeeper, of Woodchester, witness. First offence. Fine £5. Offence committed 31 Aug. 1803.

22/D/2   14 Sept. 1803. John Hopkins, John Salcomb and Joseph Broadwell of Tirley. Fishing with a net in the Severn at Deerhurst. Martin Lucas JP and Robert Knight JP. John Long of Tewkesbury, witness. Fine 20/- each and 2/- each for expenses. Offence committed 9 Sept. 1803. [Document directed] To Mr. Bloxam, D.C.P. for Gloucestershire.

23/A/1   6 Jan. 1804. Robert Dowdeswell of Slimbridge, baker. Possession of a hare. H. Burgh JP. James Williams of Slimbridge, witness. Fine £5. Offence committed 10 Dec. 1803.

23/A/2   6 Jan. 1804. Robert Dowdeswell of Slimbridge, baker. Possession of a hare. H. Burgh JP. James Williams of Slimbridge, witness. Fine £5. Offence committed 28 Nov. 1803.

23/B/1   19 Jan. 1804. William Wathen of Minchinhampton, tollgate keeper. Refusing to accept a tollgate pass. Rev. P. Hawker JP. William Mayo, tollgate keeper of Foston's Ash, Minchinhampton, complainant. Fine £6. Offence committed 10 Jan. 1804.

23/B/2   12 March 1804. William Fletcher of Eastington, yeoman. Killing game at Coaley [MS. Cowley] without a certificate. Rev. Caleb Carrington JP. Fine £20. Offence committed 3 Feb. 1804.

23/B/3   10 April 1804. Samuel Selwyn of Westbury on Severn, yeoman. Killing game without a certificate. [Certificate:] £4 12s. 3d., after deductions of expenses, paid to the county sheriff, part of a £10 fine. Francis Lawson JP and J. De Visme JP.

23/B/4   27 March 1804. Samuel Selwyn of Westbury on Severn, yeoman. Killing game without a certificate. F. Lawson JP and J. De Visme JP. Fine £20 mitigated to £10. Offence committed 19 Jan. 1804.

23/B/5   27 Feb. 1804. William Lodge, gamekeeper to Mrs. Colchester for the manors of Lea and Baynham, Herefs. Killing game in the manor of Longhope without a certificate. J. De Visme JP. Fine £10. Offence committed 27 Feb. 1804.

23/B/6   16 Feb. 1804. William Lodge, gamekeeper to Mrs. Colchester. Killing game in the manor of Longhope without a certificate. J. De Visme JP at Newent. Fine £20 mitigated to £10. Offence committed 10 Feb. 1804.

23/C/1   16 April 1804. William Fletcher of Eastington, yeoman. Killing game in Slimbridge without a certificate. Rev. C. Carrington JP at Berkeley. Fine £20. Offence committed 28 Feb. 1804.

23/C/2   27 April 1804. Stephen Woore of Drybrook. Possessing the scalp and horns of a fallow deer without satisfactory explanation. T. Williams JP and Rev. Thomas Birt JP. William Cole, complainant. Fine £20. Offence committed 31 Dec. 1803.

23/C/3   2 May 1804. William Roberts of Deerhurst. Swearing and cursing. M. Lucas JP. William Hughes, constable of Deerhurst, witness. Fine 1/-.

23/C/4   12 June 1804. Jonathan Apperley of Woodend [MS. Woodends], Dymock, labourer. Swearing and cursing against his wife and John Hoskins and his wife Eleanor. F. Lawson JP.

23/C/5   22 June 1804. John Dickinson of Bisley, baker. Killing a hare in Bisley. P. Sheppard JP at Gatcombe Park. Fine £20. Offence committed 7 June 1804.

23/C/6   19 June 1804. John Dickinson of Bisley, baker. Keeping a dog for killing game, without a certificate. P. Sheppard JP. William Harris, yeoman, of Stroud, complainant. George Durram, labourer, of Bisley, witness. Fine £5. Offence committed 7 June 1804.

23/D/1   26 July 1804. William Jefferis. Leaving his wife chargeable to the parish of Mangotsfield. T. Walker JP and Rev. Thomas Broughton JP. Samuel Parker, guardian of the poor of Mangotsfield, complainant.

23/D/2   19 Sept. 1804. Michael Gardner of Bisley, weaver. Keeping a dog for killing game, without a certificate. P. Sheppard JP at Gatcombe Park. Fine £10. Offence committed 8 July 1804.

23/D/3   29 Sept. 1804. John Skerrett of Painswick, labourer. Using a dog to kill game, without a certificate. P. Sheppard JP. Fine £20.

23/D/4   19 Sept. 1804. John Lydia of Bisley, labourer. Using a dog to kill game, without a certificate. P. Sheppard JP. Fine £10. Offence committed 8 July 1804.

24/A/1   17 Nov. 1804. Mary Bick of Hartpury, single woman. Lopping timber in Maisemore. Rev. Joseph Bonner Cheston JP. William Vallender, complainant. Offence committed 6 Nov. 1804.

24/A/2   17 Nov. 1804. Sarah wife of Richard Bick of Hartpury, labourer. Lopping [etc., as 24/A/1].

24/A/3   11 Dec. 1804. William Parr of Newland, woodcutter. Possessing a fallow deer without satisfactory explanation. T. Williams JP. William Cole, complainant. Fine £10. Offence committed 27 Oct. 1804.

24/A/4   9 Nov. 1804. Richard Alwood of Bath, news-carrier. Using nets to take game in Great Badminton. R. Haynes JP at Wick. Fine £5. Offence committed 8 Nov. 1804.

24/A/5   15 Dec. 1804. Thomas Ball of Church Yatton, Wilts. Using nets to take game in Little Sodbury. R. Haynes JP at Wick. Fine £5. Offence committed 14/15 Dec. 1804.

24/A/6   11 Oct. 1804. William Jenkins of Arlingham, yeoman. Cursing. Rev. G. Hayward JP.

24/A/7   27 Dec. 1804. Thomas Howell the younger of the Bourne, Stroud, clothier. Using a gun and dog to take game in Bisley without a certificate. P. Sheppard JP at Gatcombe Park. Fine £20. Offence committed 22 Dec. 1804.

24/A/8   16 April 1804 [late return]. Thomas Meek of Ruardean, coalminer. Possessing oak timber from the Forest of Dean without satisfactory explanation. Rev. Richard Wetherell JP at Newnham. Fine £5. Offence committed 26 March 1804.

24/A/9   23 Nov. 1804. Thomas Meek of Ruardean. Possessing four beech trees from the Forest of Dean without satisfactory explanation. Rev. R. Wetherell JP at Westbury on Severn. Fine 40/-. Offence committed 19 Oct. 1804.

24/A/10   17 Dec. 1804. Elizabeth wife of John Smith of St. Briavels. Cutting beech underwood in the Forest of Dean. Rev. R. Wetherell JP at Westbury on Severn. Fine 10/-. Offence committed 22 Nov. 1804.

24/A/11   26 Dec. 1804. Charles Clarke of Hasfield, labourer. Using a gun and a dog to kill game in Deerhurst. M. Lucas JP. William Barnard of Apperley, informant. Fine £5. Offence committed 26 Dec. 1804.

24/A/12   25 June 1804. John Chadwick of Dymock, bargeman and haulier. Driving a wagon not conforming to statutory requirement, between Mitcheldean and Lea. F. Lawson JP and J. De Visme JP at Newent. Thomas Williams, blacksmith, of Dymock, informant. Simon Chadwick, witness. Fine £5. Offence committed 23 June 1804.

24/A/13   25 June 1804. William Smith of Dymock, farmer. Driving [etc., as 24/A/12].

24/A/14   6 Oct. 1804. William Roberts the younger of Ashleworth, husbandman. Using a gun to kill game in Ashleworth. Rev. J. B. Cheston JP at Messrs. Wilton's office in Gloucester. Jane wife of John Geers, labourer, of Ashleworth, informant. John Geers, witness. Fine £5. Offence committed 12 Sept. 1804.

24/A/15   20 Oct. 1804. Michael Wadley the younger of Maisemore, husbandman. Using a dog to kill game in Lassington. J. Parker JP at Messrs. Wilton's office, St. John's Lane, Gloucester. John Jenkins, yeoman, of Highnam, informant. John Simmons of Lassington, witness. Fine £5. Offence committed 13 Oct. 1804.

24/A/16   20 Oct. 1804. William Cother of Sandhurst, yeoman. Using a gun to kill game in Sandhurst. Rev. J. B. Cheston JP at Messrs. Wilton's office, Gloucester. Charles Hooper, yeoman, of Gloucester, informant. Ellis Taylor Farren, yeoman, of Sandhurst, witness. Fine £5. Offence committed 8 Oct. 1804.

24/A/17   6 Oct. 1804. Giles Roberts of Ashleworth, husbandman. Using [etc., as 24/A/14].

24/A/18   27 Dec. 1804. Thomas Howell the younger of Stroud, clothier. Using a gun to kill game in Bisley. P. Sheppard JP. William Stephens, yeoman and prosecutor for the poor of Bisley, informant. William Harris, yeoman, of Stroud, witness. Fine £5. Offence committed 22 Dec. 1804.

24/B/1   11 March 1805. Ann Hale of Littledean. Cutting yew stakes in Long Green Coppice, St. Briavels. Rev. R. Wetherell JP at Newnham. Sir T. Crawley Boevey, complainant. Fine 20/- and 3/- expenses. Offence committed 20 Feb. 1805.

24/B/2   21 Jan. 1805. William Malson of St. Briavels. Cutting holly wood in the Forest of Dean. Rev. R. Wetherell JP and Rev. C. Sandiford JP. Fine 20/- and 5/- expenses. Offence committed 12 Dec. 1804.

24/B/3   21 Jan. 1805. John Malson of St. Briavels. Cutting [etc., as 24/B/2].

24/B/4 21 Jan. 1805. Thomas Mountjoy of St. Briavels. Topping a beech tree in the Forest of Dean. Rev. C. Sandiford JP and Rev. R. Wetherell JP. Fine £10 and 5/- expenses. Offence committed 15 Dec. 1804.

24/B/5 6 Feb. 1805. George Lusty of Avening, weaver. Possessing a hare. Rev. P. Hawker JP at Woodchester. John Almond, gamekeeper, of Woodchester, witness. Fine £5. Offence committed 3 Feb. 1805.

24/B/6 27 Feb. 1805. James Younger *alias* Jones and George Yemm of St. Briavels, labourers. Killing a fallow deer in the Forest of Dean. Rev. C. Sandiford JP. James Powell, complainant. Fine £30. Offence committed 18 Jan. 1805.

24/B/7 20 Dec. 1804. James Williams, late of Horfield, yeoman. Using dogs to kill game in Horfield. Samuel Webb JP at the sessions room, Lawfords Gate. Thomas Willcox, yeoman, of Horfield, informant. Anthony Johnson, yeoman, of St. Philip and St. Jacob, [Bristol], witness. Fine £5. Offence committed 26 Nov. 1804.

24/B/8 22 April 1805. Joel Chew of Bisley, clothier. Using a gun and a dog to kill game in Bisley. P. Sheppard JP. William Harris, gamekeeper, of Bisley, informant. Michael Gardner, weaver, of Bisley, witness. Fine £5. Offence committed 1 Feb. 1805.

24/C/1 12 June 1805. James Powell of St. Briavels, coalminer. Taking bark from oak trees in the Forest of Dean. Rev. R. Wetherell JP. James Bennett, forest keeper, complainant. John Dobbs, coalminer, of St. Briavels, witness. Fine £5 and 13/- costs. Offence committed 25 May 1805.

24/C/2 25 Jan. 1805. William Griffiths of Awre, labourer. Topping beech trees in Hayes Grove, Awre, the property of Sir T. Crawley Boevey. Rev. C. Sandiford JP and Rev. R. Wetherell JP. John Sowle of Flaxley, complainant. Fine 10/- and 3/- costs. Offence committed 6 Dec. 1804.

24/C/3 18 June 1805. Mary White of Newnham, shopkeeper. Selling underweight bread. Rev. C. Sandiford JP and Rev. R. Wetherell JP. John Headford, labourer, of Newnham, complainant.

24/C/4 19 March 1805. Oliver and Isaac Carter of South Cerney, labourers. Cutting down and stealing a tree in South Cerney, the property of Charles Croome, yeoman. R. Timbrell JP. Robert Sutton, yeoman, of Siddington, complainant. First offence. Offence committed 18 March 1805.

24/C/5 29 June 1805. John Risby. Cursing. Rev. P. Hawker JP.

24/C/6 29 April 1805. [*List of those fined for*] Having weights in their premises not according to standard. T. Dowdeswell JP, M. Lucas JP and Rev. Henry Salmon JP at a Petty Sessions for Tewkesbury. Offences committed between 28 March and 12 April 1805. Fines as follows:

> John Purser, grocer, and Thomas Wright, wool retailer, of Twyning, 10/- each.
>
> Joseph Trowton, grocer, £1, William Wilkes, baker and retailer, £1, Joseph Roberts, baker and grocer, £1, William Veale, butcher, 13/-, William Cole, grocer, 7/6, William Baylis, miller and flour retailer, £1, Dean Stephens, miller and flour retailer, £1, John Wadley, butcher, 15/-, Samuel Smith, blacksmith, 5/-, and Thomas White, flour retailer, 10/-, all of Kemerton.
>
> James Roberts, miller and flour retailer, 10/-, and James Mayall, miller and flour retailer, 10/-, of Northway and Newton.
>
> William Hallings, tobacco retailer, 10/-, and John Osbaldeston, blacksmith, 10/-, both of Aston on Carrant.
>
> Ann Attwood, tobacco retailer, of Pamington, 10/-.

Hannah Sutton, grocer, 10/-, James Cresswell, grocer, 15/-, John Drinkwater, bacon and cheese retailer, 7/6, all of Oxenton.

Robert Meredith, grocer, 10/-, William Eagles, grocer, 15/-, Susannah Baylis, grocer, 15/-, and Hannah Healing, grocer, 7/6, all of Apperley.

Joshua Weaver, flour retailer, 15/-, Mary Pendry, tobacco retailer, 5/-, Mary Oakey, flour retailer, 10/-, and Thomas Chadd, blacksmith, 7/6, of Leigh and Evington.

John Jones, miller and grocer, £1, James Turner, thread retailer, 7/6, Thomas Garne, blacksmith, 10/-, and Isaac Davis, grocer, 7/6, all of Forthampton.

Joseph Sleight, flour retailer, 7/6, George Newman, grocer, 10/-, William Clarke, grocer, 15/-, Samuel Simkins, grocer, 10/-, Richard Jeffs, grocer, 10/-, Thomas Ballinger, grocer and coal retailer, 7/6, and Thomas Salcombe, coal retailer, 10/-, all of Tirley and Haw.

Robert Davis of Hasfield, grocer, 15/-.

Thomas Holder, grocer, £1, William Bradstock, blacksmith and grocer, £1, Ann Edwards, hawker, 10/-, all of Corse.

William Lawrence of Tredington, blacksmith, 10/-.

Samuel Healing, miller, 10/-, and James Cox, tobacco retailer, discharged, of Boddington and Barrow.

Jervis Chambers, flour retailer, £1, William Togwell, blacksmith, 15/-, and John Oakey, flour retailer, 15/-, of Hayden and Withy Bridge.

Joseph Cox of Deerhurst, grocer, 10/-.

Old weights sold for £3 8s. 5d.

24/D/1   4 Oct. 1805. Daniel Phillips of Llantrisant. Vagrancy in Littledean. Rev. R. Wetherell JP. Thomas Braine of Littledean, informant. Offence committed 4 Oct. 1805.

24/D/2   29 July 1805. Catherine Knee of King's Stanley, single woman. Embezzling 3 lb. of Spanish wool. H. Burgh JP and Rev. P. Hawker JP. Thomas Cooper and Joseph Wathen, manufacturers, of King's Stanley, complainants. Offence committed 26 July 1805.

24/D/3   2 Aug. 1805. James Heaven of King's Stanley, cordwainer. Buying 3 lb. of Spanish wool from Hannah wife of Joseph Shurmer, scribbler, of King's Stanley. H. Burgh JP and John Fletcher JP. William Cleavy Brown, informant. Fine £30 or three months in Horsley house of correction. Offence committed between 14 July and 1 Aug. 1805.

24/D/4   26 Sept. 1805. Thomas Smith. Keeping and using a gun to kill game. Richard Ivyleafe JP at the sessions room, Lawfords Gate. Fine £5. Offence committed 5 Sept. 1805.

25/A/1   5 Nov. 1805. Sarah wife of John Blood of Uley, mason. Possessing beechwood without satisfactory explanation in Pen Wood, King's Stanley, the property of Sir George O. Paul. H. Burgh JP. Daniel Kirkby, labourer, of Woodchester, informant. Second offence. Fine £5 and 10/- expenses. Offence committed 4 Nov. 1805.

25/A/2   26 Dec. 1805. George Taylor of Newnham, pig dealer. Evading tolls on hogs at St. White's gate in the Forest of Dean. Rev. R. Wetherell JP. Convicted on own confession. Fine 50/- and 4/6 expenses. Offence committed 12 Dec. 1805.

25/A/3   16 Dec. 1805. Thomas Jackson of Westbury on Severn, dealer. Evading tolls on cattle at St. White's gate and Deans Lane End gate in the Forest of Dean. Rev. R. Wetherell JP. Convicted on own confession. Fine 50/- and 3/- expenses. Offence committed 12 Dec. 1805.

25/A/4   16 Dec. 1805. John Jackson of Westbury on Severn, dealer. Evading tolls [*etc., as* 25/A/3].

25/A/5   [*Duplicate of* 24/D/4, *but omitting* at the sessions room, Lawfords Gate *and adding*] Convicted on own confession.

25/A/6   23 Oct. 1805. Edward Russell. Keeping and using a gun to kill game. Dr. J. A. Small JP. Peter Adams, witness. Fine £5. Offence committed 18 Sept. 1805.

25/A/7   [*Date missing, document damaged.*] William Hawkins. Keeping and using a [gun] to kill game. R. Ivyleafe JP at Lawfords Gate sessions room. Fine £5. Offence committed 14 Nov. 1805.

[*The following eight documents are damaged and some details are missing.*]

25/B/1   11 April 1806. Joseph Robbins [?of Ruardean]. Cutting oak timber in the Forest of Dean. Rev. R. Wetherell JP and Rev. C. Sandiford JP. James Green, forest under-keeper, [?complainant]. Fine £20.

25/B/2   — Feb. 1806. Thomas and James Braine of Littledean, labourers. Cutting timber in the Forest of Dean. Rev. R. Wetherell JP and Rev. C. Sandiford JP at Newnham. Fine 40/-.

25/B/3   3 April 1806. Thomas Jones of Longhope, victualler. Allowing tippling during the time of divine service. Rev. R. Wetherell JP. Thomas Reece, churchwarden of [Longhope], complainant.

25/B/4   23 Jan. 1806. William Hancock of St. Briavels, labourer. Cutting underwood in Abbots Wood, the property of Sir T. Crawley Boevey. Rev. R. Wetherell JP. Emanuel Bennett of St. Briavels, [informant]. Fine 40/- and 6/- expenses.

25/B/5   2 April 1806. William Annetts. Riding in his cart without using reins in Blaisdon. Rev. R. Wetherell JP.

25/B/6   1806 [*day and month illegible*]. Richard Trigge and Richard Trigge the younger. Stealing timber in the Forest of Dean. Rev. C. Sandiford JP. First offence. Fine £5 and 7/6 expenses. Offence committed 16 Jan. 1806.

25/B/7   1806 [*day and month illegible*]. Richard Hands, labourer. Keeping a dog to kill game. W. Kendall JP.

25/B/8   1 March 1806. Richard Hands of Maisemore. Using a dog to kill game in Lassington. W. Kendall JP. Edmund Estcourt, [informant]. William Perton, witness.

25/C/1   20 June 1806. John Avery. Swearing. Thomas Smith JP.

25/C/2   12 June 1806. John Antill of Avening, weaver. Tendering a false testimonial to John Brown & Son, clothiers, of Stonehouse, purporting to be signed by Day, Smith & Alder, clothiers, of Nailsworth. Rev. P. Hawker JP and T. Smith JP.

25/C/3   12 June 1806. George Skidmore. Keeping nets etc. to destroy game. S. Webb JP. John Loveridge, witness. Fine £5. Offence committed 10 Feb. 1806.

25/C/4   24 June 1806. William Lewis of St. Briavels, labourer. Possessing oak bark without satisfactory explanation. Rev. C. Sandiford JP. James Powell, forest keeper, complainant. Fine 20/- and 3/6 expenses. Offence committed 17 June 1806.

25/C/5   24 June 1806. Daniel Yemm of St. Briavels, yeoman. Possessing oak bark [*etc., as* 25/C/4].

25/C/6   25 May 1806. John Cottar, late of Chepstow, labourer. Begging in Awre. Rev. C. Sandiford JP. Elizabeth Barrington, spinster, of Awre, informant. Committed to Littledean bridewell for 22 days.

25/D/1   4 Aug. 1806. Robert Hayward of Newland, shoemaker, and Susannah Steele of Littledean, single woman. Stealing peas from a field at Littledean, the property of Daniel Bennett, husbandman, of Westbury on Severn. Rev. R. Wetherell JP. R. Hayward fined 10/-, and 9*d.* for the value of the peas. S. Steele fined 5/-, and 2*d.* for the value of the peas.

25/D/2   5 Sept. 1806. Edward Bedington of St. Briavels, labourer. Stealing timber in the Forest of Dean. Rev. C. Sandiford JP. James Powell, forest keeper, complainant. Fine 10/- and 3/6 expenses. Offence committed 29 Aug. 1806.

25/D/3   5 Sept. 1806. William Bedington of St. Briavels, labourer. Possessing oak bark without satisfactory explanation. Rev. C. Sandiford JP. James Powell, forest keeper, complainant. Fine 20/- and 3/6 expenses. Offence committed 31 Aug. 1806.

26/A/1   20 Dec. 1806. William Alyeff of Minchinhampton, clothworker. Receiving stolen wool. H. Burgh JP and Henry Cooke JP. Thomas Jones, clothier, of Bisley, complainant. William Toghill, clothworker, of Bisley, informant. First offence. Fine £20 or one month in Horsley house of correction.

26/A/2   24 Oct. 1806. James Drew of St. Briavels. Cutting and stealing oak timber in Abbots Wood, the property of Sir T. Crawley Boevey. Rev. R. Wetherell JP at Westbury on Severn. Emanuel Bennett and George Callogan, complainants. Fine £20 and 7/6 expenses. Offence committed 18 Oct. 1806.

26/A/3   27 Oct. 1806. Thomas Hughes. Cutting and damaging a holly tree in the Forest of Dean. Rev. R. Wetherell JP. George Callogan, complainant. Fine 20/- and 4/6 expenses.

26/A/4   23 Oct. 1806. George Brookshaw. Cutting holly trees in the Forest of Dean. Rev. R. Wetherell JP. George Calloghan, complainant. Fine 40/- and 6/- expenses.

26/A/5   2 Dec. 1806. William Still of Aston Blank, labourer. Using snares to kill game in Sherborne. T. Ireland D.D. JP at Bourton on the Water. William Bunting of Sherborne, informant. John Phelp of Sherborne, witness. Fine £5. Offence committed 7 Oct. 1806.

26/B/1   16 Feb. 1807. John Blewett of Longhope, yeoman. Using a snare to kill game in Longhope. Rev. C. Sandiford JP and Rev. R. Wetherell JP. James Roberts, labourer, of Longhope, informant. First offence. Fine £15 and 8/- expenses. Offence committed 18 Jan. 1807.

26/B/2   16 March 1807. Hannah wife of Dan Rolls, weaver, of Bisley. Receiving 100 lb. of stolen wool. H. Burgh JP and H. Cooke JP. William Toghill, clothier, of Bisley, informant. John Hague, machine-man, of Bisley, witness. First offence. Fine £20 or one month in Horsley house of correction.

26/C/1   27 April 1807. Mary wife of James Deane, mason, of St. Briavels. Cropping a young beech tree in the Forest of Dean. Rev. C. Sandiford JP and Rev. R. Wetherell JP at Newnham. Convicted on own confession. Fine 5/- and 3/- expenses.

26/C/2   27 April 1807. John Morgan of St. Briavels, ship-carpenter. Destroying a hazel tree in the Forest of Dean. Rev. C. Sandiford JP and Rev. R. Wetherell JP at Newnham. John Cook, labourer, of St. Briavels, witness. Fine 15/- and 5/- expenses. Offence committed 11 March 1807.

26/C/3   29 April 1807. Margaret wife of Benjamin Small, carpenter, of Mitcheldean. Selling lace without a licence. Rev. R. Wetherell JP and Rev. C. Sandiford JP at Newnham. Elizabeth Barnard of Mitcheldean, informant. Jane Bevan, witness. Fine £5. Offence committed 6 April 1807.

26/C/4   23 June 1807. William Cockshut of Bisley, labourer. Keeping and using a dog to kill game. P. Sheppard JP at Minchinhampton. William Harris, yeoman and prosecutor for the poor of Bisley, informant. Daniel Whitfield of Bisley, witness. Fine £5. Offence committed 15 April 1807.

26/D/1 10 Sept. 1807. Thomas Morris of Swannington, Leics., pedlar. Selling Queens-ware dishes without a licence in Dursley. Rev. W. Lloyd Baker JP at Stoutshill. Charles Thornhill, hawker and pedlar, of Dursley, informant. Fine £12. Offence committed 9 Sept. 1807.

26/D/2 7 July 1807. John Browning of Eastington, higgler. Selling beer without a licence. W. Veel JP. John, Joseph and Samuel Underwood, James Jenkins junior and William Horwood, all of Eastington, witnesses. First offence. Offence committed 19 May 1807.

26/D/3 6 Sept. 1807. George Evans. Cutting beech timber at Horsley, the property of Lady Smyth and Henry Goodwin Esq. P. Sheppard JP. Anthony Harvey, steward to Lady Smyth and H. Goodwin, complainant.

26/D/4 2 Oct. 1807. Matthew Smith of Uley, weaver. Buying stolen woollen yarn, the property of George Daniel Harris, from James Cole, labourer, of Uley. Rev. W. Lloyd Baker JP and Thomas John Lloyd Baker JP. Fine £30 or four months' and two weeks' hard labour in Horsley house of correction. Offence committed 20 Aug. 1807

26/D/5 6 Aug. 1807. Mark Tripp of Coaley, rug-maker. Receiving stolen woollen yarn. Rev. P. Hawker JP and H. Cooke JP. James Clarke, clothier, of Horsley, informant. John Heskins the younger, clothier, of Horsley, witness. First offence. Fine £20 or one month in Horsley house of correction.

27/A/1 8 Dec. 1807. William Armbury of Gloucester, carter. Failing to keep proper control of his wagon and horses in Salperton. Rev. R. Wetherell JP. Fine 10/- and 2/6 expenses. Offence committed 8 Dec. 1807.

27/A/2 5 Jan. 1808. George Box Drayton of Chipping Sodbury, surgeon. Refusing to serve in the militia or to provide a substitute. Henry, duke of Beaufort, JP, G. Cooke D.D. JP and Rev. R. Jones JP. Fine £20.

27/A/3 8 Dec. 1807. Richard George of Blakeney Woodside, haulier. Possessing oak timber without satisfactory explanation. Rev. T. Birt JP. William Coles, gamekeeper to the Right Hon. Charles Bathurst of Lydney Park, complainant. First offence. Fine 40/- and 4/6 expenses. Offence committed 28 Nov. 1807.

27/A/4 6 Oct. 1807. James Nicholls of Newington Bagpath, labourer. Offering a hare for sale in Leighterton. Rev. L. Clutterbuck JP. Samuel Browning, labourer, of Tetbury, informant. Fine £5.

27/A/5 7 Nov. 1807. William Pride of Horsley, yeoman. Assaulting toll-keeper John Heaven at Lightpill gate. T. Smith JP. George Lusty, witness. Fine £2. Offence committed 12 Oct. 1807.

27/A/6 7 Jan. 1808. Samuel Vail of Churcham, farmer. Turning out his apprentice, Joseph Barnes, and refusing to provide for him. F. Lawson JP and J. De Visme JP at Newent. Joseph Pickering, churchwarden, and Richard Williams, overseer of the poor of Bulley, informants. Indenture in possession of Mr. Olive, attorney, of Newnham. Fine 20/- to be applied as recompense for Joseph Barnes. Offence committed 9 Dec. 1807.

27/A/7 7 Jan. 1808. William Pearce of Long Ashton, gentleman. Keeping and using a gun to kill game in Berkeley. Rev. T. Broughton JP at Lawfords Gate. James Williams, servant, of Long Ashton, informant. Thomas Keedwell, gentleman, of Long Ashton, witness. Fine £5. Offence committed 27 Oct. 1807.

27/A/8 9 Dec. 1807. Thomas Neale of Bisley, yeoman. Shooting a partridge. P. Sheppard JP. William Harris, yeoman and prosecutor for the poor of Bisley, informant. Henry Blackwell, labourer, of Bisley, witness. Offence committed 1 Sept. 1807.

27/B/1   14 Nov. 1807. Edmund Gunning of Marshfield, butcher. Possessing a net for killing game. R. Haynes JP at Wick. Nathan Bushell of Castle Combe, informant. John Slade, witness. Fine £5. Offence committed 10 Nov. 1807.

27/B/2   8 Feb. 1808. James Cross of Woolaston, labourer. Failing to appear to take the oath to serve in the militia or to provide a substitute. Rev. R. Wetherell JP. Fine £20. Offence committed 4 Jan. 1808.

27/B/3   8 Feb. 1808. Charles Williams, late of Tidenham, labourer. Failing [etc., as 27/B/2].

27/B/4   8 Feb. 1808. John Rowley, late of St. Briavels, servant. Failing [etc., as 27/B/2, except] Offence committed 18 Jan. 1808.

27/B/5   8 Feb. 1808. John Syms, late of Minsterworth, servant. Failing [etc., as 27/B/2].

27/B/6   8 Feb. 1808. Samuel Evans, late of Aylburton, servant. Failing [etc., as 27/B/2, except] Offence committed 19 Dec. 1807.

27/B/7   4 April 1808. William Millar of South Cerney. Selling ale and beer without a licence. R. Selfe JP. Convicted on own confession. First offence.

27/B/8   4 April 1808. William Davis of South Cerney. Selling ale [etc., as 27/B/7].

27/B/9   4 April 1808. Mary wife of Joseph Townsend of South Cerney. Selling ale [etc., as 27/B/7].

27/B/10   22 April 1808. Mary Ball of Horton. Cutting underwood in Horton belonging to Thomas Brooke Esq. G. Cooke JP and R. Haynes JP. John Higgs, witness. Fine 40/-.

27/B/11   4 April 1808. Elizabeth Miles of South Cerney. Selling ale and beer without a licence. R. Selfe JP. First offence.

27/B/12   29 Jan. 1808. [List of those fined for] Using defective weights or balances. M. Lucas JP, Thomas Nash D.D. JP and Rev. John Timbrill JP at a Petty Sessions for the county of Gloucester.

> John Purser, grocer, and William Glover, blacksmith, both of Twyning. Fine £1 each. Offence committed 26 Dec. 1807.
>
> William Wilkes, grocer, Joseph Trowton, grocer, Joseph Roberts, grocer, William Etheridge, grocer, William Cole grocer, William Baylis, miller, all of Kemerton. Fine £1 each. Offence committed 26 Dec. 1807.
>
> John Child, grocer, Benjamin Tidmarsh, grocer. Fine £1 each. William Smith, butcher. Fine 10/-. All of Beckford. Offence committed 29 Dec. 1807.
>
> James Hall, grocer, James Marshall, butcher, Robert Steight, grocer and blacksmith, Mary and Elizabeth Dobbins, millers, all of Dumbleton. Fine £1 each. Offence committed 30 Dec. 1807.
>
> Michael Stephens, grocer, Charles Agg, grocer, Richard Okey, grocer, Joseph Warder, flour retailer, Thomas Mansell, butcher, all of Alderton. Fine £1 each. Offence committed 31 Dec. 1807.
>
> Richard Peart, flour retailer, of Beckford. Fine £1. Offence committed 4 Jan. 1808.
>
> Benjamin Smith, miller, of Hinton [on the Green]. Fine £1. Offence committed 4 Jan. 1808.
>
> James Tomms, grocer, James Barnard, grocer, both of Ashton under Hill. Fine £1 each. Offence committed 4 Jan. 1808.
>
> Elizabeth Alsop, flour retailer, James Cresswell, grocer, both of Oxenton. Fine £1 each. Offence committed 5 Jan. 1808.
>
> William Bick, grocer. Fine 15/-. John Okey, flour retailer. Fine £1. Both of Hayden. Offence committed 6 Jan. 1808.
>
> Thomas Guarn, grocer and blacksmith, John Jones, grocer. Fine £1 each. Mary Leymore, grocer. Discharged (pauper). All of Forthampton. Offence committed 7 Jan. 1808.

Thomas Holder, grocer and flour retailer, William Bradstock, grocer and blacksmith. Fine £1 each. Offence committed 7 Jan. 1808. William Dobbins, grocer. Fine 15/-. Offence committed 8 Jan. 1808. All of Corse.

Robert Davis, grocer and flour retailer, of Hasfield. Fine £1. Offence committed 8 Jan. 1808.

Elizabeth Steight, flour retailer, Joseph Steight, flour retailer, George Newman, grocer, Thomas Ballanger, grocer, all of Tirley. Fine £1 each. Offence committed 8 Jan. 1808.

Joseph Cox, grocer and retailer. Fine £1. Mary Hampton, cheese retailer. Discharged (pauper). Both of Deerhurst. Offence committed 9 Jan. 1808.

Hannah Eagles, grocer, Susannah Eagles, grocer, both of Apperley. Fine £1 each. Offence committed 9 Jan. 1808.

William Okey, grocer, Joshua Weaver, grocer, both of Leigh. Fine £1 each. Offence committed 11 Jan. 1808.

27/C/1　8 July 1808. Robert Steight, blacksmith, and James Hall, grocer, both of Dumbleton. Obstructing Thomas Steight of Twyning, inspector of weights and balances, in the execution of his duty. Rev. J. Timbrill JP. Fine 40/- each. Offence committed 6 July 1808.

27/C/2　20 June 1808. John Gwillim of Littledean, nailer. Cutting down a young beech tree in the Forest of Dean. Rev. C. Sandiford JP and Rev. R. Wetherell JP at Newnham. Daniel Croome, informant. William Cook, gamekeeper, of Hay Hill, witness. Fine 40/- and 6/- expenses. Offence committed 11 June 1808.

27/C/3　16 May 1808. Thomas Sallis and George Stollard, late of Great Washbourne [*MS. Washbourn Magna*]. Cutting timber in Dumbleton Wood, the property of John Smith and Joseph Crump of Dumbleton. Rev. J. Timbrill JP. John Smith, complainant. Offence committed 15 May 1808.

27/D/1　27 Sept. 1808. [*List of those fined for*] Using faulty weights. Rt. Hon. Charles Bathurst JP and Rev. T. Birt JP at a Petty Sessions for the Forest division. Offences committed between 13 and 23 Sept. 1808. [*The two amounts against each name are respectively the fine and costs.*]

Thomas Hatton, grocer, 10/- and 5/-, Robert Moxham, ironmonger, 5/- and 5/-, John Dew, grocer, 5/- and 5/-, John Watts, baker, 5/- and 4/-, Elizabeth Smith, grocer, 5/- and 5/-, James Attwood, huckster, 5/- and 5/-, John Rosser, bacon retailer, 10/- and 5/-, William Morris, blacksmith, 15/- and 5/-, John Griffiths, grocer, £1 and 5/-, Matthew Kear, huckster, 5/- and 5/-, Elizabeth Wintle, grocer, 15/- and 5/-, all of Coleford.

William Blanch, grocer, 15/- and 5/-, Elizabeth Worgan, grocer, £1 and 5/-, James Deleaney, grocer, £1 and 5/-, William Davis, blacksmith, £1 and 5/-, James Jones, grocer, 5/- and 5/-, Joseph Hall, grocer, £1 and 5/-, Charles Mayo, grocer, 15/- and 5/-, all of St. Briavels.

James Rogers, tanner, 10/- and 5/-, Thomas Bond, blacksmith, 10/- and 5/-, Philip Richards, grocer, £1 and 5/-, all of Newland.

James Davies & Co., millers, 10/- and 5/-, John Collins, grocer, 10/- and 5/-, Ann Collins, huckster, 10/- and 5/-, all of Redbrook.

James Rosser, grocer, £1 and 5/-, James Williams, grocer, £1 and 5/-, Thomas Jones, grocer, 5/- and 5/-, Elizabeth Powell, grocer, 15/- and 5/-, John Jenkins, grocer, £1 and 5/-, James Hayward, grocer, £1 and 5/-, Thomas Lewis, blacksmith, £1 and 5/-, all of Clearwell.

Richard James, grocer, 15/- and 5/-, Richard James, grocer [?*another*], 15/- and 5/-, Richard Evans, grocer, 15/- and 5/-, all of Bream.

Robert Young, grocer, 5/- and 5/-, James Davis, huckster, 15/- and 5/-, James Morgan, blacksmith, 10/- and 5/-, Sarah Davis, grocer, 10/- and 5/-, James Pick, gingerbread retailer, 10/- and 5/-, Mary Dyer, grocer, £1 and 5/-, all of Lydney.

Samuel Edwards, grocer, £1 and 5/-, William Court, grocer, £1 and 5/-, William Mills, grocer and flour retailer, £1 and 5/-, Joseph Holt, flour retailer, £1 and 5/-, Esther Close, grocer, £1 and 5/-, all of St. Briavels.

Thomas Humfrey & Co., of Lydney, iron retailers, 15/- and 5/-.

Thomas Wilce of St. Briavels, retailer, 5/- and 5/-.

Thomas Davis, retailer, £1 and 5/-, Richard Thorn, retailer, 5/- and 5/-, Charles Butler, retailer, 10/- and 5/-, William Moxley, retailer, 15/- and 5/-, John Prince, retailer, £1 and 5/-, all of Hewelsfield.

Thomas White of Aylburton, miller, 10/- and 5/-.

Charles Watkins, grocer, £1 and 5/-, John Holloway, retailer, 15/- and 5/-, John James, retailer, 5/- and 5/-, Thomas Anslow, retailer, 15/- and 5/-, all of Alvington.

Warren Silcocks, blacksmith, 10/- and 5/-, John Hopkins, retailer, 5/- and 5/-, William Crumb, retailer, 5/- and 5/-, Richard Atkins, £1 and 5/-, all of Woolaston.

Elizabeth Davis, grocer, 5/- and 5/-, Ann Young, grocer, 5/- and 5/-, William Butler, 10/- and 5/-, all of Tidenham.

27/D/2 5 Sept. 1808. [*List of those fined for*] Using faulty weights. Rev. C. Sandiford JP and Rev. R. Wetherell JP at a Petty Sessions for the Forest division. Offences committed between 16 and 19 Aug. 1808. [*The two amounts against each name are respectively the fine and costs.*]

Elizabeth Playsted, grocer, £1 and 4/6, John Morse, butcher, £1 and 4/6, John Hobbs, blacksmith, 5/- and 4/6, Richard Phelps, grocer, £1 and 4/6, John Holder, blacksmith, £1 and 4/6, Sarah Bird, fish retailer, 5/- and 4/6, James Hill, butcher, 10/- and 4/6, William Barnard, grocer, 10/- and 4/6, Leonard Knowles, wool retailer, 5/- and 4/6, William Baynham, iron retailer, 5/- and 4/6, Martha Smith, grocer, £1 and 4/6, Samuel Peglar, grocer, £1 and 4/6, John Knowles, grocer, 15/- and 4/6, Joseph Mayo, tanner, 15/- and 4/6, Thomas Pick, tanner, £1 and 4/6, John Playsted, leather retailer, £1 and 4/6, all of Newnham.

Mary Morgan, grocer, £1 and 4/6, Silvia Morse, grocer, £1 and 4/6, Richard Lewis, grocer, 15/- and 4/6, Mary Abrahall, grocer, £1 and 4/6, William Hallier, grocer, £1 and 4/6, James Hobbs, flour retailer, 15/- and 4/6, William Howell, flour retailer, £1 and 4/6, Thomas Lodge, grocer, £1 and 4/6, Ann Cooper, grocer, £1 and 4/6, James Veare, grocer, £1 and 4/6, Benjamin Bennett, grocer, 15/- and 4/6, Alice Hale, huckster, £1 and 4/6, all of Littledean.

William Parker, grocer, £1 and 6/-, Joseph Harker, miller, 10/- and 6/-, both of Abenhall.

Richard Silley, butcher, 5/- and 4/6, Benjamin Small, grocer, £1 and 4/6, William Parsons, flour retailer, 15/- and 4/6, John Bellamy & Co., grocers, £1 and 4/6, Richard Coleman, grocer, £1 and 4/6, William Dobbs, grocer, 10/- and 4/6, all of Mitcheldean.

Jonathan Preese, flour retailer, £1 and 4/6, Richard Elsmore, currier, 15/- and 4/6, Ann Gaye, grocer, £1 and 4/6, William Coleman, grocer, £1 and 4/6, John Hale, retailer of hops, 5/- and 4/6, William Lewis, grocer, 15/- and 4/6, John Marfell, retailer of hops, 5/- and 4/6, William Jones, currier, £1 and 4/6, John Wintle, grocer, £1 and 4/6, Thomas Bennett, flour retailer, 5/- and 4/6, William Marfell, retailer of hops, 5/- and 4/6, William Baldwin, blacksmith, 15/- and 4/6, all of Mitcheldean.

Joseph Robins of Ruardean, grocer, £1 and 4/6.

27/D/3 6 Sept. 1808. [*List of those fined for*] Using faulty weights. Rev. C. Sandiford JP and Rev. R. Wetherell JP at a Petty Sessions of the Forest division. Offences committed between 18 and 30 Aug. 1808. [*The two amounts against each name are respectively the fine and costs.*]

> Mary Meek, grocer, £1 and 5/-, John Porter, grocer, 5/- and 5/-, John Watkins, huckster, £1 and 5/-, John Rudge, grocer, £1 and 5/-, Ann Meek, grocer, £1 and 5/-, George Marfell, grocer, 15/- and 5/-, Hannah Thompson, grocer, 5/- and 5/-, Philip Watkins, grocer, £1 and 5/-, Mary Rudge, grocer, £1 and 5/-, John Davis, blacksmith, £1 and 5/-, all of Ruardean.

> John Cooke, grocer and miller, £1 and 5/-, Richard Tamplin, grocer, 15/- and 5/-, James Pearce, hops and cheese retailer, 5/- and 5/-, William Jones, grocer, 15/- and 5/-, Richard Jones, grocer, £1 and 5/-, James Young, grocer, £1 and 5/-, all of English Bicknor.

> Richard Sladon, flour retailer, £1 and 6/6, Richard Ward, flour retailer, £1 and 6/6, Thomas Jones, grocer and blacksmith, £1 and 6/6, all of St. Briavels.

> Joseph Hill, blacksmith, £1 and 5/6, John Soule, iron retailer, £1 and 5/6, James Russell, grocer, £1 and 5/6, John Boseley, miller, £1 and 5/6, John Boseley, miller [*again*], for obstruction, £2 and 3/-, all of Flaxley.

> Joseph Roberts, miller, 5/- and 4/-, Thomas Cole, grocer, 10/- and 5/-, Sarah Williams, grocer, 5/- and 5/-, all of Blaisdon.

> Ann Aldridge, grocer, £1 and 6/-, William Green, grocer, 10/- and 5/-, Elizabeth Clinton, grocer, £1 and 6/-, Robert Gardner, grocer, £1 and 5/-, all of Huntley.

> Bridget Badger, miller, 5/- and 4/-, William Roberts, grocer, £1 and 5/6, William Wheeldon, grocer, £1 and 5/-, John Wilce, blacksmith, 5/- and 1/-, Israel Haile, grocer, 17/- and 8/-, Thomas Bright, miller, 5/- and 5/-, all of Westbury on Severn.

> Charles Merry, grocer, £1 and 5/-, Jonas Clutterbuck, grocer, £1 and 5/-, Thomas Gibbons, grocer, 10/- and 5/-, John Baylis, blacksmith, £1 and 5/-, Elizabeth Jeffs, grocer, 10/- and 5/-, Benjamin Hipwood, grocer, 15/- and 5/-, all of Rodley.

> John Hunt, grocer, of Broadoak, 15/- and5/-.

> William Richards, blacksmith, of Lea, £1 and 5/-.

> John Hart, grocer, 10/- and 5/-, John Coleman, grocer, £1 and 5/-, Joseph Rudge, blacksmith, £1 and 5/-, all of Longhope.

> Theophilus Constant, grocer, 15/- and 5/-, Thomas Jones, grocer, 5/- and 5/-, Daniel Young, miller, 5/- and 5/-, Thomas Haile, blacksmith, £1 and 5/-, Ann Williams, grocer, £1 and 5/-, all of Longhope.

> Sarah Hill, grocer, 5/- and 5/-, John Elliot, miller, 10/- and 5/-, Richard Martis, grocer, 10/- and 5/-, Newton White, blacksmith, 10/- and 5/-, James Smallwood, blacksmith, 10/- and 5/-, Joseph Hooper, miller, £1 and 5/-, William Mansel, huckster, £1 and 5/-, James Howley, blacksmith, £1 and 5/-, all of Churcham.

> William Smith, blacksmith, £1 and 5/-, Richard Cole, grocer, £1 and 5/-, William Phelps, grocer, £1 and 5/-, Margaret Harper, flour retailer, 5/- and 5/-, Sarah Pool, salt retailer, 5/- and 5/-, all of Minsterworth.

> James Sparrow, grocer, 10/- and 4/6, Mary and Sarah Baron, grocers, 5/- and 4/6, Daniel White, grocer, £1 and 4/6, Henry Thomas, grocer, 10/- and 4/6, Richard White, butcher, 15/- and 4/6, Thomas Browning, miller, 15/- and 4/6, Joseph Virgoe, retailer, 15/- and 4/6, Thomas Stiff, retailer, 15/- and 4/6, all of Blakeney.

> Mary Jones, grocer, 5/- and 4/6, Sarah Phelps, grocer, £1 and 4/6, both of Awre.

> Richard Newman, grocer, of Huntley, £1 and 7/-.

27/D/4   6 Sept. 1808. George Watkins of Ruardean, blacksmith. Using faulty scales. Rev. C. Sandiford JP and Rev. R. Wetherell JP at a Petty Sessions for the Forest division. Fine 20/- and 5/- costs. Offence committed 19 Aug. 1808.

27/D/5   27 Sept. 1808. William Parry of Tidenham, blacksmith. Using faulty scales. Rt. Hon. C. Bathurst JP and Rev. T. Birt JP at a Petty Sessions for the Forest division. Fine 20/- and 5/- costs. Offence committed 19 Sept. 1808.

27/D/6   19 Sept. 1808. Examination of David Randy *alias* Randall Morgan of St. Nicholas, Bristol, son of Moses and Ann Randy, shopkeepers, formerly of St. James, Bristol. Using a forged certificate to obtain poor relief at Stroud. H. Burgh JP at Stroud.

27/D/7   19 Sept. 1808. Deposition of Charles Newman of Stroud, gentleman. H. Burgh JP at Stroud.

27/D/8   19 Sept. 1808. David Randy *alias* Randall Morgan. Using a forged certificate to obtain poor relief at Stroud. H. Burgh JP. Charles Newman of Stroud, informant. Offence committed 17 Sept. 1808.

27/D/9   20 Aug. 1808. Isaac Smith of King's Stanley, weaver. Buying and receiving stolen woollen yarn from Mary wife of Thomas Smith, weaver, of King's Stanley. H. Burgh JP and H. Cooke JP. Joseph Wathen, clothier, of King's Stanley, complainant. George Fluck, wool-loft man, of King's Stanley, informant. First offence. Fine £20 or one month in Horsley house of correction. Offence committed 19 Aug. 1808.

27/D/10   21 Sept. 1808. Jane Hathaway, Mary Tustin, Mary Fletcher, Sarah Wood, Ann Turner and Sarah Sollis. Swearing. Rev. J. Timbrill JP.

27/D/11   9 Aug. 1808. Hannah Young of Eldersfield, widow. Refusing to pay tolls at Corse and Staunton on numerous occasions, amounting to £3 14*s*. 5*d*. Rev. H. G. D. Yate JP. William Dobbins of Corse, farmer and toll-collector, complainant. Fine 40/-. Offences committed between 15 Jan. and 21 July 1808.

28/A/1   3 Dec. 1808. William Abell the younger and Thomas Abell, both of Washbrook, Winstone, yeomen. Killing hares on land in Cowley Downs belonging to William Lawrence Esq. Edwin Bayntun Sandys JP at Miserden Park. Benjamin Wesson, gamekeeper, of Cowley, informant. William Witts, stonemason, of Cowley, witness. Pleaded not guilty. Declared rogues and vagabonds. Sent to Gloucester house of correction to await trial at Q.S. Offence committed 1 Dec. 1808.

28/A/2   17 Oct. 1808. Richard Bailey of St. Briavels, wiredrawer. Selling cider without a licence. Rev. R. Wetherell JP and Rev. C. Sandiford JP. John Smith, witness. First offence. Fine £19 and £1 expenses. Offence committed 6 Aug. 1808.

28/A/3   11 Dec. 1808. Thomas Lerrigo of Newland, miller. Stealing 4 lb. of wheat corn. Rev. R. Wetherell JP. James Hart, labourer, of Ruardean, complainant. Fine £5 and 8/- expenses. Offence committed 1 Dec. 1808.

28/A/4   21 July 1808. James Martin and Thomas Buck, both of Awre, labourers. Stealing timber in the Forest of Dean. Rev. T. Birt JP. Thomas Lowe, labourer, of St. Briavels, witness. Each fined £10 and 4/6 expenses. Offence committed 28 June 1808.

28/A/5   1 Dec. 1808. Hester Cox, wife of Peter Cox of Avening, labourer. Possessing stolen woollen yarn. H. Burgh JP and H. Cooke JP. First offence. William Chamberlain, yarn-maker, of Horsley, informant. Philip Lock, clothier, of Horsley, witness. Fine £20 or one month in Horsley house of correction.

28/A/6   9 Nov. 1808. George Bishop of Cheltenham, labourer. Having nets and dogs with intent to kill hares in Elkstone. Sir William Hicks JP and John Elwes JP. William Lawrence Esq. of Cowley, informant. Charles Booker, labourer, of Coberley, witness. First offence. Fine £20 or three months in Horsley house of correction. Offence committed 5 Nov. 1808.

28/A/7   2 Dec. 1808. David Wilson of Painswick, weaver. Stealing woollen yarn. H. Burgh JP, H. Cooke JP and Rev. William Mills JP. John Cox, clothier, of Oliver's Mill, Painswick, complainant. Mary wife of Mark Archer, spinner, of Painswick, witness. One month in Horsley house of correction.

28/A/8   22 Dec. 1808. John Rabbitts of Stonehouse, weaver. Stealing woollen yarn. H. Burgh JP. William Clavey Brown and John Brown the younger, clothiers, of Stonehouse, complainants. William Grist, pressman, of Stonehouse, witness. One month in Horsley house of correction.

28/A/9   23 Oct. 1808. James Wathen of Minchinhampton, labourer. Possessing stolen lead. H. Burgh JP and H. Cooke JP. Isaac Adlam, glazier, of Stroud, informant. First offence. Fine £2 or one month in Horsley house of correction.

28/A/10   23 Oct. 1808. Samuel Newman of Minchinhampton, pargeter. Possessing stolen lead [*etc., as* 28/A/9].

28/A/11   23 Oct. 1808. William Brown of Ebley, lath-render. Possessing stolen lead [*etc., as* 28/A/9].

28/A/12   2 Dec. 1808. William Sargent of Yate, farmer. Evading payment of tolls between Chipping Sodbury and Westerleigh. Rev. G. Cooke JP, I. W. Horlock JP and R. Haynes JP at the Cross Hands inn, Old Sodbury. Robert Chadwicke, witness. Fine £2. Offence committed 25 Nov. 1808.

28/A/13   2 Dec. 1808. William Sargent of Yate, farmer. Evading payment of tolls between Chipping Sodbury and Westerleigh [*etc., as* 28/A/12 *except*] Offence committed 12 Nov. 1808.

28/B/1   30 Jan. 1809. James Price of Minchinhampton, hatmaker. Possessing a large quantity of stolen woollen ends. P. Sheppard JP and H. Cooke JP. Edward Davies, clothier, of Minchinhampton, informant. Joseph Brown, clothier, of Minchinhampton, witness. First offence. Fine £20 or one month in Horsley house of correction. Offence committed 16 Jan. 1809.

28/C/1   17 June 1809. John Gay of Frampton on Severn, labourer. Cursing. N. Clifford JP.

28/C/2   17 June 1809. George Evans of Frampton on Severn, labourer. Cursing. N. Clifford JP.

28/C/3   3 May 1809. Solomon Weaver of Ashchurch, labourer. Leaving his wife chargeable to the parish of Ashchurch. Rev. J. Timbrill JP and M. Lucas JP at Beckford. Thomas Cull, yeoman, of Ashchurch, informant. Hard labour for one month in Northleach house of correction.

28/C/4   24 April 1809. Joseph Taylor of Twyning, labourer. Leaving his wife and family chargeable to the parish of Twyning. M. Lucas JP at Tewkesbury. William Phelps, yeoman, of Twyning, informant. Hard labour for one month in Northleach house of correction. Offence committed 20 Feb. 1809.

28/C/5   3 May 1809. Sarah wife of Nathaniel Pope of Minchinhampton, weaver. Buying several pounds of stolen wool, the property of Daniel Gardiner Chance, clothier, of Rodborough. H. Burgh JP and H. Cooke JP. Daniel Gardiner Chance, informant. Sarah wife of Joseph Daniels, dyer, of Rodborough, witness. First offence. Fine £40 or six months in Horsley house of correction. Fine paid. Offence committed 29 April 1809.

28/C/6   19 May 1809. Solomon Bucknall of Minchinhampton, weaver. Possessing stolen cloth. H. Burgh JP and H. Cooke JP. John Lewis, clothier, of Stroud, complainant. Richard Dowell, clothworker, of Minchinhampton, informant. First offence. Fine £20 or one month in Horsley house of correction. Imprisoned. Offence committed 13 May 1809.

28/C/7   13 May 1809. James Williams of Gloucester, baker. Attempting to take fish from a stream in Rudford, the property of Sir Berkeley William Guise. Rev. J. B. Cheston JP. John Jenkins, yeoman, of Highnam, informant. Fine £5. Offence committed 10 April 1809.

28/D/1   6 Sept. 1809. Richard May, excise officer. Cursing. N. Clifford JP.

28/D/2   25 Sept. 1809. Elizabeth wife of Thomas Phillips of Churcham, labourer. Damaging underwood in Churcham, the property of Samuel Jones, brushmaker, of Gloucester. Rev. R. Wetherell JP. Wiliam Hall of Churcham, bailiff to Samuel Jones, complainant. Fine 5/- and 1/- expenses.

28/D/3   25 Sept. 1809. Esther wife of Thomas Evans of Churcham, cordwainer. Damaging underwood [*etc., as* 28/D/2].

28/D/4   19 July 1809. John Butt of Twyning, labourer. Leaving his wife and three children chargeable to the parish of Twyning. T. Nash D.D. JP and Rev. J. Timbrill JP at Tewkesbury. William Phelps, yeoman, of Twyning, informant. Hard labour for one month in Northleach house of correction.

28/D/5   30 Sept. 1809. William Carpenter of Cirencester, watchmaker. Being drunk. J. Cripps JP. Edward Orpin, waiter, of Cirencester, complainant. Fine 5/-. Offence committed Sunday 17 Sept. 1809.

28/D/6   18 Aug. 1809. Joseph Day of Minchinhampton, glazier. Leaving his blind daughter Sophia, aged 10 years, chargeable to the parish to the sum of £11 13*s*. 6*d*. H. Burgh JP at Stroud. Warrant issued on 28 Feb. 1809 by Rt. Hon. Thomas Moreton, Lord Ducie, JP, H. Cooke JP and H. Burgh JP. Matthew Jurley, yeoman, of Minchinhampton, informant. Robert Iles, witness. Committed to Gloucester gaol until next Q.S.

29/A/1   20 Dec. 1809. [*List of those fined for*] Using faulty weights. Rev. J. Timbrill JP and M. Lucas JP at a Petty Sessions held at the office of Henry Hooper Fryer in Tewkesbury. All confesssed. Each fined £1 and 3/- costs. Offences committed between 3 and 24 Nov. 1809.

       John Oakey of Hayden, baker.
       William Turner, shopkeeper, Samuel Healing, miller, Jarvis Chambers, miller, all of Boddington.
       James Healing, blacksmith, William Long, baker, both of Apperley.
       Joshua Weaver, shopkeeper, Lancelot Lambert, shopkeeper, both of Leigh.
       William Glover of Twyning, blacksmith.
       James Mayall of Northway, miller.
       Elizabeth Steight, shopkeeper, Charles Clarke, shopkeeper, both of Tirley.
       William Bradstock of Corse, shopkeeper.
       John Jones of Forthampton, miller.

29/A/2   19 Dec. 1809. [*List of those fined for*] Using faulty weights. Rev. J. Timbrill JP and M. Lucas JP at a Petty Sessions held at the Rev. J. Timbrill's house in Beckford. Convicted on own confession and fined £1 and 3/- costs [*except where indicated*]. Offences committed between 6 and 23 Nov. 1809.

       Charles Tidmarsh, miller, Dane Stephens, miller, both of Kemerton.
       Richard White of Aston on Carrant, miller.
       John Tyler of Gretton, shopkeeper (Samuel Mew, witness).
       John Bliby of Winchcombe, miller (William Hyett, witness).

John Johnson of Winchcombe, shopkeeper. (Fine 5/- and 3/- costs).

Moses Sexty of Greet, shopkeeper.

John Ballinger, shopkeeper, Mary Heath, miller, both of Childswickham.

Sarah Restall, shopkeeper, William Richardson, miller, both of Buckland.

Elizabeth Stowe, shopkeeper, Richard Cheshire, shopkeeper, both of Stanton [*MS.* Staunton].

William Hancock of Church Stanway, shopkeeper.

Charles Grizzell of Didbrook, shopkeeper.

Michael Stephens of Alderton, shopkeeper.

William Drinkwater of Ashton under Hill, baker.

29/A/3 29 Oct. 1809. John Jenkins of St. Briavels, collier. Killing a fallow deer in the Forest of Dean, the property of the Hon. C. Bathurst. Rev. R. Wetherell JP. William Coles, park keeper, of Lydney, complainant. Fine £30. Offence committed 31 Aug./1 Sept. 1809.

29/A/4 2 Dec. 1809. Joseph Smith of Chedworth, mason. Killing a hare. Rev. B. Grisdale JP. First offence. Offence committed 12 Nov. 1809.

29/A/5 2 Dec. 1809. Levi Bridges of Chedworth, labourer. Killing a hare [*etc., as* 29/A/4].

29/A/6 2 Nov. 1809. Edward Copson of Grafton [in Beckford]. Stealing wood from an orchard belonging to William Nind of Grafton. Rev. J. Timbrill JP. William Nind, informant. Offence committed 29 Oct. 1809.

29/A/7 2 Nov. 1809. Joseph Jeynes, late of Deerhurst, servant to William Cox, husbandman. Leaving his master. Rev. R. Knight JP. Warrant issued by M. Lucas JP. Sentenced to one month's hard labour in Northleach house of correction.

29/A/8 15 Nov. 1809. John Cox of Boddington, labourer, servant in the business of stone raising. Failing to carry out work assigned to him by William Hill, yeoman, of Leigh. M. Lucas JP. Sentenced to one month's hard labour in Northleach house of correction.

29/A/9 15 Nov. 1809. William Brown of Boddington, servant in the business of stone raising. Failing to carry out [*etc., as* 29/A/8].

29/A/10 4 Dec. 1809. Edward Young of Bisley, weaver. Stealing [woollen] yarn. H. Burgh JP and H. Cooke JP. Thomas Howell the younger, clothier, of Minchinhampton, informant. First offence. Fine £20 or one month in Horsley house of correction.

29/A/11 6 Jan. 1810. James Daniels of Stroud, weaver. Possessing stolen woollen yarn and other materials. H. Burgh JP and H. Cooke JP. John Restall, rag-gatherer, of Stroud, informant. First offence. Fine £20 or one month in Horsley house of correction.

29/A/12 6 Jan. 1810. Charles Holder of Stroud, weaver. Possessing [*etc., as* 29/A/11 *except*] Fine £20 or be detained in Horsley house of correction [*for how long not stated*].

29/A/13 19 Dec. 1809. William Niblett of Rodborough, weaver. Possessing stolen wool. H. Burgh JP and H. Cooke JP. Thomas Carruthers, clothier, of Stroud, informant. First offence. Fine £20 or three months in Horsley house of correction.

29/A/14 1 Nov. 1809. Thomas Neale of Bisley, yeoman. Shooting partridges. Sir E. B. Sandys JP at Birdlip. William Harris of Bisley, gamekeeper to Paul Wathen Esq., informant. Harry Blackwell, labourer, of Bisley, witness. Offender given 2 hours to produce evidence of qualification to shoot game. Evidence of William Loveday and production of title deeds etc. insufficient. Fine £5. Offence committed 1 Sept. 1809.

29/A/15   1 Nov. 1809. Thomas Neale of Bisley, yeoman. Shooting a partridge. Sir E. B. Sandys JP at Birdlip. William Harris, gamekeeper, informant. Samuel Davis, yeoman, of Bisley, witness. Evidence of William Loveday and production of deeds insufficient. Fine £5. Offence committed 4 Oct. 1809.

29/A/16   1 Nov. 1809. Thomas Neale of Bisley, yeoman. Carrying a gun and keeping a dog with intent to kill game. Sir E. B. Sandys JP. William Harris, gamekeeper, informant. Daniel Woodfield, yeoman, of Bisley, witness. Evidence of William Loveday and production of deeds insufficient. Fine £5. Offence committed 7 Oct. 1809.

29/A/17   1 Nov. 1809. Thomas Neale of Bisley, yeoman. Carrying a gun [*etc., as* 29/A/16 *except*] Offence committed 11 Oct. 1809.

29/A/18   1 Nov. 1809. Thomas Neale of Bisley, yeoman. Shooting a pheasant. Sir E. B. Sandys JP. Robert Dowdeswell, yeoman, of Bisley, informant. William Harris, yeoman, of Bisley, witness. William Loveday, witness for defendant. Fine £5. Offence committed 2 Oct. 1809.

29/A/19   1 Nov. 1809. Thomas Neale of Bisley, yeoman. Carrying a gun and keeping a dog with intent to kill game [*etc., as* 29/A/14 *except*] Offence committed 14 Oct. 1809.

29/A/20   1 Nov. 1809. Thomas Neale of Bisley, yeoman. Shooting a hare [*etc., as* 29/A/14 *except*] Offence committed 7 Sept. 1809.

29/B/1   26 Feb.1810. John King of Newnham, labourer. Being drunk. Rev. R. Wetherell JP at Westbury on Severn. Offence witnessed by above magistrate. Fine 5/-.

29/B/2   3 March 1810. William Champion of Cheltenham, labourer. Keeping dogs and nets for killing game. Sir W. Hicks JP. Thomas Ballinger, yeoman and prosecutor for the poor of Cheltenham, informant. William Webley, perfumer, of Cheltenham, witness. Fine £5. Offence committed 27 Feb. 1810.

29/B/3   9 March 1810. John Barnes of Ashchurch, servant in husbandry. Absconding from service. Rev. R. Knight JP at Tewkesbury. Richard Procter, farmer, of Pamington, informant. One month's hard labour in Northleach house of correction. Offence committed 21 Feb. 1810.

29/B/4   20 April 1810. Benjamin Hulin of St. Briavels, tiler and plasterer. Cutting and stealing ash timber in St. Briavels. Rt. Hon. C. Bathurst JP. Orpheus Hulin, tiler and plasterer, of St. Briavels, complainant.

29/B/5   20 April 1810. Henry son of James Hulin of St. Briavels, tiler and plasterer. Cutting and stealing birch timber [*etc., as* 29/B/4].

29/B/6   12 Feb. 1810. Charles Haycock of Boddington, servant in husbandry. Leaving his master's service. M. Lucas JP at Tewkesbury. John Arkell, farmer, of Boddington, informant. One month's hard labour in Northleach house of correction.

29/B/7   29 Jan. 1810. Joseph Evans the elder of Elton, Westbury on Severn, carpenter. Possessing underwood, the property of Sir T. Crawley Boevey of Flaxley. Rev. C. Sandiford JP and Rev. R. Wetherell JP. First offence. Fine 10/- and 4/- expenses. Offence committed 15 Jan. 1810.

29/B/8   19 Feb. 1810. Richard Brain of Ruardean, coalminer. Cutting down a beech tree near Lime Crant in the Forest of Dean. Rev. C. Sandiford JP and Rev. R. Wetherell JP. Thomas Stephens, woodward, of Lea Bailey Lodge, John Hatton and Mary wife of Walter Ellis, labourer, of Bailey Brook, Newland, witnesses. First offence. Fine £10 and 9/6 expenses. Offence committed 30 Jan. 1810.

29/B/9   16 April 1810. Rachael wife of Richard Worgan of Hewelsfield. Cutting underwood in Caswell Wood, Woolaston, the property of William Cooke, yeoman, of Alvington. Rev. C. Sandiford JP and Rev. R. Wetherell JP. Ebenezer Harris Cooke, complainant. First offence. Fine 10/- and 5/- expenses. Offence committed 29 March 1810.

29/B/10   26 March 1810. John Smith of St. Briavels, labourer. Stealing a walnut tree from the Forest of Dean. Rev. C. Sandiford JP and Rev. R. Wetherell JP. Thomas East, complainant. First offence. Fine £5 and 6/- expenses. Offence committed 10 March 1810.

29/B/11   19 March 1810. Thomas Cooper of St. Briavels, labourer. Cutting and stealing underwood, the property of Sir T. Crawley Boevey, in Abbots Wood, East Dean. Rev. C. Sandiford JP and Rev. R. Wetherell JP. Emanuel Bennett, witness. First offence. Fine £2 and 6/- expenses. Offence committed 27 Feb. 1810.

29/C/1   4 July 1810. Thomas Davis of Eastcombe [*MS.* Estcombs], rag-gatherer. Buying stolen cloth yarn and other materials. H. Cooke JP and Samuel Wathen JP. William Shatford, informant. George Blanch, weaver, of Stroud, witness. First offence. Fine £40 or six months' hard labour in Horsley house of correction. Committed to gaol.

29/C/2   25 June 1810. Edward Close of Woodchester, millman. Buying stolen woollen cloth. H. Burgh JP and S. Wathen JP. Paul Wathen Esq. of Woodchester, informant. Joseph Casey, clothworker, of Stroud, witness. First offence. Fine £20 or one month in Horsley house of correction. Committed to gaol. Offence committed 23 June 1810.

29/C/3   20 March 1810. William Niblett, of Stroud, weaver. Buying stolen woollen yarn from Edward Restall, weaver, of Bisley. H. Burgh JP and S. Wathen JP. Thomas Jones, clothier, of Bisley, informant. Edward Restall, witness. First offence. Fine £40 or one month in Horsley house of correction. Committed to gaol.

29/C/4   19 Feb. 1810. Samuel Holder of Stroud. Leaving his wife and family chargeable to the parish. H. Burgh JP.

29/C/5   1 March 1810. Daniel Rowles of France Lynch, weaver. Possessing wool without satisfactory explanation. H. Burgh JP, H. Cooke JP and S. Wathen JP. Aaron Davies, weaver, of France Lynch, informant. Thomas Bartlett, weaver, of France Lynch, witness. First offence. Fine £20 or one month in Horsley house of correction. Committed to gaol. Offence committed 27 Feb. 1810.

29/C/6   13 March 1810. Jonathan Frankis of Painswick, yeoman. Having snares and nets with intent to kill game. H. Burgh JP and H. Cooke JP. William Capel Esq., informant. Private George Drew of the Royal S. Glos. Regt. of militia, witness. Fine £5 or three months in Horsley house of correction. Fine paid. Offence committed 1 March 1810.

29/C/7   13 March 1810. William Bourne of Painswick, shepherd. Using snares and nets to kill game. H. Burgh JP, H. Cooke JP and S. Wathen JP. William Capel Esq. of Painswick, informant. Private George Drew of the Royal S. Glos. Regt. of militia, witness. Fine £5 or three months in Horsley house of correction. Fine paid. Offence committed 25 Dec. 1809.

29/C/8   19 April 1810. Edward Hitchings *alias* Ritchings of Cranham, labourer. Possessing snares and nets with intent to kill game. Rev. W. Mills JP at Miserden. William Cowle, gamekeeper, of Winstone, informant. Samuel Lock of Cowley, witness. Fine £5. Offence committed 30 March 1810.

29/C/9   19 April 1810. Thomas Hitchings *alias* Ritchings of Cranham, labourer. Possessing a dog and nets with intent [*etc., as* 29/C/8, *omitting* at Miserden].

29/D/1   17 Sept. 1810. Jane Weaving. Fortune-telling. H. Burgh JP. Barnabas Parry, weaver, of Rodborough, witness.

29/D/2   18 Aug. 1810. William Miles of Rodborough, millman. Stealing a quantity of flocks, the property of Jeremiah Stanley, clothier, of Pitchcombe. H. Burgh JP and H. Cooke JP. Jeremiah Stanley and Samuel Wood, clothiers, of Pitchcombe, witnesses. First offence. One month's hard labour in Horsley house of correction.

29/D/3   31 Aug. 1810. Daniel Bown of Stroud, weaver. Buying stolen woollen yarn. H. Cooke JP and S. Wathen JP. James Chew, clothier, of Bisley, informant. Robert Butt, weaver, of Bisley, witness. First offence. Fine £20 or 4 months' hard labour in Horsley house of correction. Committed to gaol.

29/D/4   23 Aug. 1810. Mary wife of Robert Butt, weaver, of Bisley. Buying 6 oz. of stolen woollen yarn. H. Burgh JP and S. Wathen JP. James Chew, clothier, of Bisley, informant. Ann Trinder, single woman, of Bisley, witness. First offence. Fined £20 or three months' hard labour in Horsley house of correction. Committed to gaol. Offence committed 21/22 Aug. 1810.

29/D/5   8 Aug. 1810. William Niblett of Houndscroft, Rodborough, weaver. Buying stolen yarn, the property of Messrs. Paul Wathen & Co. of Woodchester. H. Cooke JP and H. Burgh JP. P. Wathen & Co., informants. Catherine wife of William Beard, sloper, of Woodchester, witness. First offence. Fine £40 or six months' hard labour in Horsley house of correction. Offender absconded. Offence committed 2 Aug. 1810.

29/D/6   3 Sept.1810. Sampson Spender of Stroud, labourer. Using a gin with intent to kill game. S. Wathen JP. William Marment, labourer, of Stroud, informant. First offence. Fine £10 or three months in Horsley house of correction. Committed to gaol. Offence committed 2 Sept. 1810.

29/D/7   30 Aug. 1810. Daniel Bishop of Bisley. Using a gin to kill game. S. Wathen JP. Daniel Woodfield, labourer, of Bisley, informant. William Harris, gamekeeper, of Bisley, witness. Fine £5. Offence committed 28 Aug. 1810.

29/D/8   20 Aug. 1810. Richard Roberts of Blaisdon, miller. Failing to display a list of prices and tolls. Rev. C. Sandiford JP and Rev. R. Wetherell JP. William Black of Blaisdon, parish clerk, complainant. Fine 10/-. Offence committed 7 Aug. 1810.

29/D/9   20 Aug. 1810. William Hall of St. Briavels, labourer. Possessing oak underwood without satisfactory explanation. Rev. C. Sandiford JP and Rev. R. Wetherell JP. James Bennett, forest keeper, complainant. Fine £1 and 6/6 expenses.

29/D/10   19 July 1810. [*Conviction, removal order, examination and deposition.*] Thomas Powell of St. Eval [*MS.* St. Tavell] and Rame, Cornwall. Vagrancy: begging in Twyning. M. Lucas JP. Apprehended by William Mann of Twyning. Served John Pearce, blacksmith, of Rame, for one year in 1778. Sent to house of correction for seven days. Offence committed 12 July 1810.

29/D/11   26 July 1810. Samuel Mansell of Apperley, servant in husbandry. Neglecting his work. Rev. R. Knight JP. William Fluck, farmer, of Apperley, informant. One month's hard labour in Northleach house of correction.

29/D/12   24 July 1810. Charles Blick *alias* Blake of Rodborough. Leaving his wife and family chargeable to the parish. H. Burgh JP. John Wood of Rodborough, overseer of the poor, informant.

29/D/13   30 Aug. 1810. William Beard of Horton, labourer. Having a live hare for sale. Henry Charles, duke of Beaufort, JP and G. Cooke D.D. JP at Badminton. John Higgs, informant. John Reed, labourer, of Horton, witness. Offender pleaded not guilty. Fine £5. Offence committed 27 Aug. 1810.

29/D/14   28 Sept. 1810. William Piff of Cheltenham, yeoman. Helping to steal a fallow deer at Charlton Kings, the property of William Hunt Prinn Esq. James Agg JP and Thomas Welles D.D. JP at Cheltenham. Thomas Ballinger, gamekeeper, of Charlton Kings, complainant. Offence committed 15 Sept. 1810.

29/D/15   18 Sept. 1810. William Taylor of Cheltenham, butcher. Killing a fallow deer at Charlton Kings, the property of William Hunt Prinn Esq. J. Agg JP and T. Welles D.D. JP at Cheltenham. Thomas Ballinger, gamekeeper, of Charlton Kings, complainant. Offence committed 17 Sept. 1810.

29/D/16   29 Sept. 1810. Bartley Davis of Brimpsfield, tailor. Keeping nets for killing game. T. Welles D.D. JP and J. Agg JP at Cheltenham. Thomas Ballinger, yeoman and prosecutor for the poor of Charlton Kings, informant. William Reeks, hairdresser, of Cheltenham, witness. Fine £5. Offence committed 29 Sept. 1810.

30/A/1   8 Jan. 1811. Susan wife of Israel Hale of Elton, Westbury on Severn, baker. Selling underweight bread. Rev. R. Wetherell JP. John Bullock, labourer, of Littledean, witness. Fine 2/7½.

30/A/2   19 Nov. 1810. John Preest of Littledean, labourer. Cutting and stealing underwood in Abbots Wood, East Dean, the property of Sir T. Crawley Boevey. Rev. C. Sandiford JP and Rev. R. Wetherell JP. Emanuel Bennett, yeoman, of Flaxley, witness. First offence. Fine 5/- and 4/- expenses. Offence committed 6 Oct. 1810.

30/A/3   19 Nov. 1810. Samuel Mason of St. Briavels, labourer. Cutting and stealing underwood in Abbots Wood [*etc., as* 30/A/2 *except*] Offence committed 18 Oct. 1810.

30/A/4   22 Oct. 1810. Thomas Smith of Weston under Penyard, Herefs., sawyer. Possessing green oak from the Forest of Dean without satisfactory explanation. Rev. C. Sandiford JP and Rev. R. Wetherell JP. John Hatton, deputy forest keeper, informer. Thomas Stephens of Lea Bailey Lodge, witness. First offence. Fine 40/- and 4/- expenses.

30/A/5   5 Nov. 1810. Henry Yemm of Allaston, labourer. Driving a loaded wagon not conforming to statute between Blakeney and Chepstow. Rev. C. Sandiford JP at Mr. Olive's office, Newnham. Thomas Daniel, labourer, of Blakeney, informer. Thomas Wood, labourer, of St. Briavels, witness. Summons served by William Williams, constable. Offender did not appear. Fine 20/-. Offence committed 21 Oct. 1810.

30/A/6   22 Dec. 1810. William Symmonds of Mitcheldean, labourer. Damaging an oak tree in Flaxley Wood, East Dean, the property of Sir T. Crawley Boevey. Rev. R. Wetherell JP. James Bullock, labourer, and Emanual Bennett, yeoman, of Flaxley, witnesses. First offence. Fine £20 and 8/- expenses.

30/A/7   4 Jan. 1811. James Collett of Twyning, apprentice stocking framework knitter. Neglecting or badly performing his work. M. Lucas JP and Robert Lucas D.D. JP at Tewkesbury. Joseph Kendall, stocking framework knitter, of Twyning, complainant. Offender confessed. One month's hard labour in Northleach house of correction.

30/A/8   5 Dec. 1810. Thomas Hill, late of Bredon, Worcs., servant in husbandry. Neglecting or badly performing his work. Rev. J. Timbrill JP at Tewkesbury. Thomas Greening, farmer, of Ashchurch, complainant. Offender confessed. One month's hard labour in Northleach house of correction.

30/A/9   8 Jan. 1811. James Arkell of Cheltenham, baker. Swearing. W. Hicks JP. Fine 2/-. Offence committed 1 Jan. 1811.

30/A/10   8 Jan. 1811. Samuel Britten of Dyrham and Hinton, yeoman. Using a gun and a dog to kill game. R. Haynes JP at Wick. David Hale of Dyrham and Hinton, informer. Peter Clark, witness. Fine £5.

30/A/11　8 Jan. 1811. Samuel Emley of Dyrham and Hinton, labourer. Using a gun and a dog to kill game. R. Haynes JP at Wick. David Hale of Dyrham and Hinton, informer. Peter Clark, witness. Fine £5.

30/A/12　26 Nov. 1810. John Dee of Bisley, weaver. Possessing a quantity of thrums without satisfactory explanation. H. Burgh JP and S. Wathen JP. John Restall, weaver, of Minchinhampton, informer. John Harris, clothworker, of Stroud, witness. First offence. Fine £20 or one month in Horsley house of correction. Offence committed 26 Nov. 1810.

30/A/13　3 Dec. 1810. John Phelps of Bisley, labourer. Possessing woollen yarn without satisfactory explanation. H. Burgh JP and S. Wathen JP. Paul Wathen Esq. of Lypiatt Park, Stroud, informer. Richard Cooper, clothier, of Stonehouse, witness. First offence. Fine £20 or one month in Horsley house of correction. Offence committed 3 Dec. 1810.

30/A/14　26 Nov. 1810. John Antill of Bisley, weaver. Possessing a quantity of thrums [etc., as 30/A/12].

30/A/15　26 Nov. 1810. Robert Davis of Bisley, weaver. Possessing a quantity of thrums [etc., as 30/A/12].

30/A/16　10 Dec. 1810. Joseph Sadler of Elkstone, yeoman. Keeping or using a gin to kill game. Rev. W. Mills JP. James Holtham of Cowley, informer. Samuel Lock, gamekeeper, of Cowley, witness. First offence. Fine £5 or three months in Horsley house of correction. Offence committed 6 Dec. 1810.

30/A/17　27 Nov. 1810. John Bainge of Painswick, labourer. Keeping or using a gin to kill game. H. Burgh JP. Thomas Walker, servant, of Painswick, informer. First offence. Fine £5 or three months in Horsley house of correction. Offence committed 27 Nov. 1810.

30/B/1　4 April 1811. Thomas Smith. Setting a snare with intent to kill hares in Westbury on Trym. S. Webb JP. Thomas Boulton of Westbury on Trym, witness. First offence. Fine £20. Offence committed Sunday 17 March 1811.

30/B/2　4 April 1811. John Long. Setting a snare [etc., as 30/B/1].

30/B/3　30 March 1811. Samuel Giles. Vagrancy. Begging in Awre. Rev. C. Sandiford JP. Apprehended by Richard Ryder, yeoman, of Awre and high constable for the hundred of Bledisloe. Offender pleaded guilty. Committed to Littledean house of correction to be held until next Q.S. unless discharged earlier. Offence committed 30 March 1811.

30/B/4　3 April 1811. John Bridgman the younger of Twyning, labourer. Swearing and cursing. M. Lucas JP.

30/B/5　23 Jan. 1811. Benjamin Margarett of Deerhurst, yeoman's apprentice. Leaving his master's service. M. Lucas JP and T. Nash D.D. JP. William Bridge, yeoman, of Deerhurst, complainant. Apprenticed by parish. One month's hard labour in Horsley house of correction.

30/B/6　25 Feb. 1811. Edward James of St. Briavels, labourer. Cutting underwood in the Forest of Dean. Rev. C. Sandiford JP and Rev. R. Wetherell JP. William Powell, forest keeper, informer. First offence. Mitigated fine of 10/- and 4/- expenses. Offence committed 1 Jan. 1811.

30/B/7　25 Feb. 1811. James Morgan of St. Briavels, labourer. Cutting [etc., as 30/B/6].

30/B/8　25 Feb. 1811. Philip James of St. Briavels. Cutting [etc., as 30/B/6].

30/B/9　15 April 1811. William Phelps alias Blewett of St. Briavels, lime-burner. Lopping a pollard oak near Plump Hill, Mitcheldean. Rev. R. Wetherell JP. John Hatton, deputy forest keeper, informer. Ann wife of William Baldwin, blacksmith, of Mitcheldean, witness. First offence. Mitigated fine of 10/- and 4/- expenses. Offence committed 1 and 2 March 1811.

30/B/10   25 March 1811. John Cannock of Elton, Westbury on Severn, yeoman. Cutting down an oak tree at the Chestnuts in the Forest of Dean. Rev. C. Sandiford JP and Rev. R. Wetherell JP. John White, forest keeper, informer. John Cooke of St. Briavels, deputy forest keeper, witness. First offence. Mitigated fine of £5 and 9/- expenses. Offence committed 6 Feb. 1811.

30/B/11   25 Feb. 1811. Richard Money of Newnham, wireman. Using nets to catch hares in Newnham. Rev. C. Sandiford JP and Rev. R. Wetherell JP. William Cooke, gamekeeper, of Newnham, informer. Thomas Nichols, servant, of Hay Hill, Newnham, witness. First offence. Fine £20 and 4/- costs. Offence committed Sunday 17 Feb. 1811.

30/B/12   25 Feb. 1811. William Reynolds of St. Briavels, forgeman. Using a net with intent to kill a hare in Newnham [*etc.*, *as* 30/B/11].

30/B/13   15 April 1811. James Drew of Littledean, woodcutter. Cropping a beech tree at Edge Hills in the Forest of Dean. Rev. R. Wetherell JP. John Cooke, deputy forest keeper, informer. John White, forest keeper, of Littledean Lodge, witness. First offence. Mitigated fine of £2 and 4/- costs. Offence committed Feb. 1811.

30/B/14   1 March 1811. Thomas Pincott. Leaving his wife and family chargeable to the parish of Bisley. H. Cooke JP and S. Wathen JP. at Stroud.

30/B/15   4 Jan. 1811. Hannah Mansfield of Minchinhampton. Stealing chain and shuting from Messrs. Paul and Obadiah Paul Wathen, clothiers, of Woodchester. H. Burgh JP and H. Cooke JP. Samuel Williams of Woodchester, clerk to Messrs. Wathen, and James Burford, weaver, of Woodchester, witnesses. First offence. One month's hard labour in Horsley house of correction.

30/B/16   8 March 1811. James Brooks of Miserden, stonemason. Using gins to kill game. Rev. W. Mills JP. Joseph Smith, labourer, of Miserden, informer. William Smith, labourer, of Miserden, witness. First offence. Fine £5 or three months in Horsley house of correction. Offence committed 30 Feb. [*sic*] 1811.

30/B/17   1 March 1811. Thomas Smith of Miserden, carpenter. Keeping or using wires to kill game. Rev. W. Mills JP. James Trapp, blacksmith, of Miserden, informer. First offence. Fine £5 or three months in Horsley house of correction. Offence committed 26 Feb. 1811.

30/B/18   22 April 1811. Josiah Ricketts of Stroud, labourer. Keeping or using a gin to kill game. S. Wathen JP. William Harris, gamekeeper, of Stroud, informer. Charles Glover, clothier, of Stroud, witness. First offence. Fine £5 or three months in Horsley house of correction. Offence committed 20 April 1811.

30/B/19   23 Jan. 1811. Nathaniel Lusty of King's Stanley, weaver. Keeping or using a gin to kill game in Woodchester. H. Burgh JP. George Hill, gamekeeper, of Nympsfield, informer. Charles Horwood, labourer, of Nympsfield, witness. First offence. Fine £5 or three months in Horsley house of correction. Offence committed 14 Jan. 1811.

30/B/20   18 Jan. 1811. Samuel Cox of Cam, labourer. Stealing timber. Robert Bransby Cooper JP. John Vizard, solicitor, of Dursley, complainant.

30/B/21   1 March 1811. James Chambers and Peter Buckle, both of Horton, labourers. Cutting down ash poles in Horton, the property of Thomas Brookes Esq. of Chipping Sodbury. G. Cooke D.D. JP. John Reed, complainant. Fine 40/- each. Offence committed 13 Feb. 1811.

30/B/22   22 Jan. 1811. James Browning of Pucklechurch, labourer. Using four dogs for killing game in Wapley and Codrington. R. Haynes JP at Wick. John Slade of Dodington, informer. William Slade, witness. Fine £5. Offence committed 16 Jan. 1811.

30/B/23   17 April 1811. John Herbert of Leckhampton, farmer. Using a dog to kill game in Coberley. Sir W. Hicks JP at Cheltenham. John Kelly, labourer, of Cheltenham, informer. James Mantell, yeoman, of Coberley, witness. Offender pleaded not guilty. Fine £5. Offence committed 23 Jan. 1811.

30/C/1   20 April 1811. Thomas Foxwell, peace officer and high constable for the upper division of the hundred of Berkeley. Disobedience and neglect of duty. Rev. William Davies JP and Rev. C. Carrington JP at a Petty Sessions in Berkeley. Frederick Augustus Carrington, complainant. Fine 40/-. Offence committed c. 4 April 1811.

30/C/2   23 May 1811. Sarah White of Stroud, single woman. Vagrancy. S. Wathen JP. Richard Smith, tithingman of Stroud, witness.

30/C/3   16 May 1811. Elizabeth Chandler. Vagrancy in Stroud. H. Burgh JP and S. Wathen JP. George Mynett, constable of Stroud, witness.

30/C/4   23 May 1811. Sarah Tuskins of Stroud, single woman. Vagrancy [etc., as 30/C/2].

30/C/5   23 May 1811. Grace Tuskins. Vagrancy in Stroud [etc., as 30/C/2].

30/C/6   27 May 1811. Elizabeth Lewis. Vagrancy in Stroud [etc., as 30/C/2].

30/C/7   15 May 1811. Elizabeth Cook. Vagrancy in Stroud [etc., as 30/C/3].

30/C/8   23 May 1811. Margaret Clarke. Vagrancy in Stroud [etc., as 30/C/2].

30/C/9   17 May 1811. Grace Cox. Vagrancy in Stroud. H. Burgh JP. Richard Smith, tithingman of Stroud, witness.

30/C/10   17 May 1811. Elizabeth Turner. Vagrancy in Stroud [etc., as 30/C/9].

30/C/11   31 May 1811. Samuel Smith of Coaley, broadweaver. Possessing a hare. H. Burgh JP. William Dee, gamekeeper, of Coaley, informer. James Griffin, labourer, of Coaley, witness. First offence. Fine £5 or three months in Horsley house of correction. Offence committed 5 March 1811.

30/C/12   31 May 1811. John Smith of Coaley, broadweaver. Shooting a hare [etc., as 30/C/11 except that William Dee is simply 'of Coaley, informer'].

30/C/13   14 May 1811. John Gardner of Eastcombe, Bisley, weaver. Possessing 30 lb. of woollen yarn and other materials without satisfactory explanation. S. Wathen JP and Rev. P. Hawker JP. Richard Smith, tithingman of Stroud, informer. John Harris, clothier, and John Rogers, tithingman, both of Stroud, witnesses. First offence. Fine £20 or one month in Horsley house of correction. Offence committed 13 May 1811.

30/C/14   1 June 1811. John Woodworth of Thornbury, labourer. Allowing wife and child to become chargeable to the parish. Samuel Peach Peach JP and John Charleton D.D. JP. James Cox, overseer of the poor of Thornbury, complainant. Committed to Lawfords Gate house of correction for one month.

30/C/15   10 May 1811. Thomas Higgins of Hill Farm, Bromsberrow, yeoman. Refusing to honour an agreement to accept Joseph Child, aged 10 years, as an apprentice. Rev. H. G. D. Yate JP and Rev. James Commeline JP. John Webb Esq., churchwarden, and Jacob Vertegans and Thomas Jones, yeomen and overseers of the poor, complainants. Fine £10.

30/D/1   20 Sept. 1811. Richard Cross. Possessing part of a fallow deer at Widford [MS. Whitford]. Hon. John Dutton JP. Robert Kilby, complainant. Offence committed 6 Sept. 1811.

30/D/2   5 Sept. 1811. William Smith of Twyning, servant in husbandry. Wastefully thrashing his master's corn. M. Lucas JP. Richard Rammel, farmer, of Twyning, complainant. Committed to Northleach house of correction for six weeks.

30/D/3   7 Oct. 1811. Philip Hawker of St. Briavels, labourer. Stealing a quantity of thorns from Abbots Wood, East Dean, the property of Sir T. Crawley Boevey. F. Lawson JP and Rev. C. Sandiford JP. George Callaghan, yeoman, of Flaxley, informer. First offence. Mitigated fine of 6/- and 4/6 costs. Offence committed 23 Sept. 1811.

30/D/4   26 Aug. 1811. Thomas Gibbs of Mitcheldean, mason. Cutting down an oak tree at the Chestnuts in the Forest of Dean. F. Lawson JP, Rev. C. Sandiford JP and Rev. R. Wetherell JP. Sarah wife of Richard Jones, woodward, witness. First offence. Mitigated fine of £5 and 9/- costs. Offence committed 29 July 1811.

30/D/5   16 Sept. 1811. John Meeke the elder of Bailey Hill, West Dean, labourer. Possessing underwood without satisfactory explanation. F. Lawson JP, Rev. C. Sandiford JP and Rev. R. Wetherell JP. John Hatton, deputy forest keeper, witness. First offence. Mitigated fine of £1 and 4/- costs. Offence committed 6 Sept. 1811.

30/D/6   1 July 1811. James Harris of Woolaston, miller. Selling cider without a licence. F. Lawson JP and Rev. C. Sandiford JP. John Pritchard, excise officer, of Lydney, witness. First offence. Mitigated penalty of £6 6s. including costs. Offence committed 7 May 1811.

30/D/7   1 July 1811. Ann Baynham of English Bicknor. Selling cider without a licence. F. Lawson JP and Rev. C. Sandiford JP. Sarah wife of Richard Roberts, collier, of St. Briavels, witness. First offence. Mitigated fine of £10. Offence committed 7 Sept. 1811.

30/D/8   16 Sept. 1811 Joseph Willetts of St. Briavels, haulier. Attempting to evade tolls on two of his team of oxen at Viney turnpike gate in the Forest of Dean. F. Lawson JP, Rev. C. Sandiford JP and Rev. R. Wetherell JP. Thomas Roberts of Mitcheldean, witness. First offence. Fine £5 and 6/6 costs. Offence committed 4 Sept. 1811.

30/D/9   8 July 1811. Daniel Jenkins of Stow Farm, Newland, farmer. Evading tolls on his horse, a mare and a colt at Newnham. Rev. R. Wetherell JP, Rev. C. Sandiford JP and F. Lawson JP. John Ferris, toll-collector of Newnham, informer. Giles Clements, blacksmith, of Newnham, witness. First offence. Fine £2 and 4/- costs.

31/A/1   24 Dec. 1811. George Lewis of Tibberton, labourer, servant to Mr. Donovan. Using dogs to kill game. Rev. C. Sandiford JP and Rev. R. Wetherell JP at James Sutton Olive's office at Newnham. Summons issued by F. Lawson JP, who was too ill to attend. John Morse, yeoman, of Newent, prosecutor for the poor of Tibberton, informer. Benjamin Phelps, constable of Tibberton, witness. Fine £5. Offence committed 29 Oct. 1811.

31/A/2   24 Dec. 1811. George Lewis of Tibberton. labourer, servant to Mr. Donovan. Shooting game in Taynton in company with Mr. Cross [etc., as 31/A/1 except] Offence committed 15 Oct. 1811.

31/A/3   13 Jan. 1812. Thomas Lawrence, servant in husbandry to John Willis, gardener, of Cheltenham. Driving a wagon which did not conform to statute, from Tewkesbury. Rev. John Neale JP at Boddington. William Browne, informer. Fine 20/-. Offence committed 14 Dec. 1811.

31/A/4   13 Jan, 1812. John Willis of Cheltenham. Allowing his servant Thomas Lawrence to drive a wagon which did not conform to statute, from Tewkesbury. Rev. J. Neale JP at Boddington. Fine £5. Offence committed 14 Dec. 1811.

31/A/5   6 Jan. 1812. William Watkins of Mitcheldean, pedlar or petty chapman. Having no licence and no visible means of livelihood. Rev. C. Sandiford JP and Rev. R. Wetherell JP. Apprehended by Richard Pearce, constable of Mitcheldean. Committed to Littledean house of correction until next Q.S. unless discharged earlier.

31/A/6   7 Dec. 1811. William Nicholls of Littleworth, toll keeper. Charging excessive tolls (1s. instead of 8d.) on two horses drawing a postchaise. J. B. Cheston JP at Gloucester. James Gosden, servant to Charles Owen Cambridge Esq. of Wheatenhurst, informer. John Phillpotts junior, witness. Fine £5. Offence committed 16 Nov. 1811.

31/A/7   7 Dec. 1811. William Nicholls of Littleworth, toll keeper. Charging excessive tolls on two horses [etc., as 31/A/6 except] Offence committed 23 Nov. 1811.

31/A/8   7 Dec. 1811. William Nicholls of Littleworth, toll keeper. Charging excessive tolls on two horses [etc., as 31/A/6 except] Offence committed 21 Nov. 1811.

31/A/9   7 Dec. 1811. William Nicholls of Littleworth, toll keeper. Charging excessive tolls on two horses [etc., as 31/A/6 except] George Caesar Hopkinson JP [and] Offence committed 30 Nov. 1811.

31/A/10   7 Dec. 1811. William Nicholls. Charging excessive tolls on two horses drawing a postchaise. G. C. Hopkinson JP at Gloucester. Charles Owen Cambridge Esq. of Wheatenhurst, informer. John Phillpotts junior, witness. Offence committed 28 Nov. 1811.

31/A/11   15 Oct. 1811. Charles Chew of Stroud, wool-scourer. Stealing a quantity of wool from Mr. Stephen Clissold, clothier, of Stonehouse. H. Burgh JP, H. Cooke JP and Rev. P. Hawker JP. Frederick Clissold, clothier, of Stonehouse, John Webster of King's Stanley, wool-loft man to Mr. Clissold, and William Vines, wool-washer, of Randwick. witnesses. First offence. One month's hard labour in Horsley house of correction.

31/A/12   18 Oct. 1811. Jane Pearce. Vagrancy. S. Wathen JP at Stroud.

31/A/13   6 Dec. 1811. James Thomason of Painswick, labourer. Using a snare to kill game. H. Cooke JP. William Capel Esq. of Painswick, informer. William Richins, yeoman, of Painswick, witness. First offence. Fine £20 or three months in Horsley house of correction. Offence committed 1 Dec. 1811.

31/A/14   18 Oct. 1811. Grace Cox. Vagrancy. S. Wathen JP at Stroud.

31/A/15   6 Dec. 1811. Josiah Ricketts of Painswick, weaver. Possessing snares for killing game. H. Cooke JP. William Capel Esq. of Painswick, informer. William Frankis, yeoman, of Painswick, witness. First offence. Fine £5 or three months in Horsley house of correction. Offence committed 29 Oct. 1811.

31/B/1   — Jan. 1812. Samuel Cox of Cam, weaver. Stealing wool. Rev. W. Lloyd Baker JP and R. B. Cooper JP. Thomas Collis, weaver, of Cam, witness.

31/B/2   4 Jan. 1812. William Nicholls, tollgate keeper, of Littleworth. Charging excessive tolls on two horses drawing a carriage. Rev. J. B. Cheston JP. Daniel John Niblett Esq., complainant. Offence committed 1 Jan. 1812.

          [31/B/3–19 are similar, and below only the number of horses, the complainant and the date of the offence are noted. In each the hearing is stated as being at Gloucester.]

31/B/3   11 Jan. 1812. . . two horses. Mary Hunt, spinster, complainant. 6 Jan. 1812.

31/B/4   21 Dec. 1811. . . one horse. Rev. Thomas Rudge, complainant. 24 Nov. 1811.

31/B/5   4 Jan. 1812. . . one horse. Rev. Thomas Rudge, complainant. 22 Dec. 1811.

31/B/6   21 Dec. 1811. . . two horses. Rev. Thomas Rudge, complainant. 2 Dec. 1811.

31/B/7   21 Dec. 1811. . . one horse. Rev. Thomas Rudge, complainant. 1 Dec. 1811.

31/B/8   4 Jan. 1812. . . one horse. Rev. Thomas Rudge, complainant. 25 Dec. 1811.

31/B/9   23 Nov. 1811. . . two horses. Charles Owen Cambridge complainant. 7 Nov. 1811.

31/B/10   23 Nov. 1811. . . two horses. Charles Owen Cambridge, complainant. 12 Nov. 1811.

31/B/11   23 Nov. 1811. . . two horses. Charles Owen Cambridge, complainant. 14 Nov. 1811.

31/B/12   21 Dec. 1811. . . one horse. Sir Berkeley William Guise, complainant. 10 Dec. 1811.

31/B/13   21 Dec. 1811. . . one horse. Sir B. W. Guise, complainant. 11 Dec. 1811.

31/B/14   21 Dec. 1811. . . two horses. Charles Owen Cambridge, complainant. 5 Dec. 1811.

31/B/15   21 Dec. 1811. . . two horses. Charles Owen Cambridge, complainant. 7 Dec. 1811.

31/B/16   21 Dec. 1811. . . two horses. Richard Browne Cheston Esq., complainant. 4 Dec. 1811.

31/B/17   27 Dec. 1811. . . two horses. Rev. Charles Sandiford, complainant. 18 Dec. 1811.

31/B/18   23 Nov. 1811. . . two horses. Charles Owen Cambridge, complainant. 16 Nov. 1811.

31/B/19   28 Dec. 1811. . . two horses. John Merrett Stephens, complainant. 18 Dec. 1811.

31/C/1   27 May 1812. Edward Price of Kemerton, labourer. Leaving his four children chargeable to the parish. Rev. J. Timbrill JP and Rev. John Keysall JP at Tewkesbury. William Mumford, overseer of the poor of Kemerton, informer. One month's hard labour in Northleach house of correction.

31/C/2   13 May 1812. Elizabeth Lewis. Vagrancy. S. Wathen JP at Stroud.

31/C/3   30 March 1812. Timothy Day of Minchinhampton, rug-weaver. Possessing 2 lb. of wool without satisfactory explanation. H. Burgh JP and H. Cooke JP. Edward Bliss, clothier, of Nailsworth, informer. James Bingel, clothworker, of Minchinhampton, witness. First offence. Fine £20 or one month in Horsley house of correction. Offence committed 28 March 1812.

31/C/4   18 April 1812. James Webb of Cold Ashton, baker. Selling underweight bread. R. Haynes JP. Fine £2. Offence committed 17 April 1812.

31/C/5   20 May 1812. Samuel Baughan of Arlingham. Cursing. N. Clifford JP. Samuel Roach of Arlingham, witness.

31/C/6   21 April 1812. Elizabeth wife of George Elliotts, labourer, of Dursley. Stealing wool from her employer, Edward Wallington, clothier, of Dursley. R. B. Cooper JP and Rev. W. Lloyd Baker JP. Fourteen days' hard labour in Horsley house of correction.

31/C/7   20 April 1812. Samuel Bennett of Dursley, weaver. Buying 1 lb. 10 oz. of stolen wool from Elizabeth wife of George Elliotts of Dursley. R. B. Cooper JP and Rev. W. Lloyd Baker JP. Edward Wallington, informer. Wool conveyed to offender by Mary wife of John Harold, labourer, of Dursley. Fine £30 or 18 weeks' hard labour in Horsley house of correction. Offence committed 30 March 1812.

31/C/8   21 April 1812. Ann wife of John Williams of Stinchcombe, higgler. Buying stolen wool from Samuel Bennett, weaver, of Dursley. R. B. Cooper JP and Rev. W. Lloyd Baker JP. Edward Wallington, informer. Fine £40 or six months in Horsley house of correction. Offence committed 2 April 1812.

31/D/1   6 Sept. 1812. Elizabeth Seymour, Sarah Mitchell and Sarah Wheeler. Vagrancy in Clifton, Bristol. Gabriel Goldney JP at St. James's parish, Stokes Croft. Henry Read, constable of Clifton, informer. Committed to Gloucester house of correction to await next Q.S. unless discharged earlier by due course of law.

31/D/2   18 Aug. 1812. Thomas Gillett of Todenham, servant in husbandry. Using a snare to kill game. Rev. James Adams JP at Stow [on the Wold]. James Harris, yeoman, of Todenham, informer. John Hicks, gamekeeper, of Todenham, witness. Fine £5. Offence committed 15 Aug. 1812.

31/D/3   3 Aug. 1812. Henry Kear of the hundred of St. Briavels, collier. Possessing two pieces of ash wood without satisfactory explanation. F. Lawson JP, Rev. C. Sandiford JP and Rev. R. Wetherell JP. Thomas Freeman, woodward, of Lydney, complainant. William Cole, keeper to Rt. Hon. Charles Bragge Bathurst of Lydney, witness. Fine 40/- and 7/6 expenses. Offence committed 30 July 1812.

31/D/4   7 Sept. 1812. Jeremiah and Charles Parry, of Longhope, labourers. Cutting and destroying a young oak tree in Longhope, the property of Edmund Probyn Esq. of Newland. F. Lawson JP, Rev. C. Sandiford JP and Rev. R. Wetherell JP. John Blewett, cattle dealer, of Longhope, informer. Thomas Haile of Longhope, servant to John Blewett, witness. First offence. Mitigated fine of £5 and 4/- expenses.

31/D/5   17 Aug. 1812. Richard Mails and William Nelmes of Blakeney, sawyers. Cutting down a beech tree at Under Bradley in the Forest of Dean. F. Lawson JP. James Powell, forest keeper, informer. William James, woodward, of the hundred of St. Briavels, witness. Mitigated fine of £10 and 4/- expenses. Offence committed 17 July 1812.

31/D/6   28 July 1812. Richard Green of Southam, Bishop's Cleeve, labourer. Stealing a quantity of beans from a field in Prestbury. J. Agg JP and T. Welles D.D. JP. Joseph Cotterell, farmer, of Prestbury, complainant. Offence committed Sunday 26 July 1812.

31/D/7   22 July 1812. Richard Williams of Little Washbourne, Overbury, Worcs., innkeeper. Selling beer in Dumbleton without a licence. Rev. J. Keysall JP and Rev. J. Timbrill JP. Willis Dixon and Ann Davis, witnesses. First offence. Fine £20 and 19/- expenses.

31/D/8   4 Sept. 1812. John Millard. Leaving his wife and family chargeable to the parish of Stroud. H. Cooke JP, S. Wathen JP and Rev. Robert Lawrence Townsend JP at Stroud.

31/D/9   31 Aug. 1812. Bartley Davis of Brimpsfield, tailor. Using a net to kill game in Cowley. Rev. W. Mills JP. John Taylor, labourer, of Cowley, informer. Thomas Lock, gamekeeper, of Cowley, witness. First offence. Fine £5 or three months in Horsley house of correction. Offence committed 25 Aug. 1812.

32/A/1–   20 Aug., 8 and 22 Sept. 1812. [*Names as below.*] Having defective weights. Rev. R. L.
105   Townsend JP and Edward Aldridge JP at a Petty Sessions for the hundred of Bisley at the King's Arms inn, Stroud. [*Fines and date offence committed (all 1812) as below.*]

32/A/1   8 Sept. 1812. William Hesseldine of Painswick, shopkeeper. Fine 5/- and 6/- costs. (19 Aug.)

32/A/2   22 Sept. 1812. Stephen Cowley of Stroud, shopkeeper. Fine 5/- and 3/- costs. (12 Sept.)

32/A/3   22 Sept. 1812. Benjamin Fisher of Stroud, shopkeeper. Fine 10/- and 6/- costs. (10 Sept.)

32/A/4   22 Sept. 1812. Thomas Bliss of Stroud, shopkeeper. Fine 5/-. (25 Aug.)

32/A/5   22 Sept. 1812. Edith Jennings of Stroud, shopkeeper. Fine 5/- and 3/- costs. (10 Sept.)

32/A/6   22 Sept. 1812. Hester Hogg of Stroud, shopkeeper. Fine 5/- and 6/- costs. (25 Aug.)

32/A/7   8 Sept. 1812. Thomas Damsel of Painswick, shopkeeper. Fine 5/- and 2/6 costs. (19 Aug.)

32/A/8   22 Sept. 1812. James Neale of Stroud, shopkeeper. Fine 5/-. (25 Aug.)

32/A/9   22 Sept. 1812. Betty Hall of Stroud, shopkeeper. Fine 5/- and 3/- costs. (10 Sept.)

32/A/10   22 Sept. 1812. Richard Ayres of Stroud, shopkeeper. Fine 5/- and 3/- costs. (25 Aug.)

32/A/11   22 Sept. 1812. Samuel Poole of Stroud, shopkeeper. Fine 5/- and 3/- costs. (10 Sept.)

32/A/12   22 Sept. 1812. Jacob West of Stroud, shopkeeper. Fine 5/- and 6/- costs.(25 Aug.)

32/A/13   8 Sept. 1812. Daniel Selwyn of Painswick, shopkeeper. Fine 5/- and 6/- costs. (19 Aug.)

32/A/14   8 Sept. 1812. James Cooper of Painswick, shopkeeper. Fine 5/- and 6/- costs. (19 Aug.)

32/A/15   8 Sept. 1812. Samuel Goddard of Painswick, shopkeeper. Fine 10/- and 5/- costs. (18 Aug.)

32/A/16 8 Sept. 1812. Samuel Goddard junior of Painswick, shopkeeper. Fine 5/- and 6/- costs. (18 Aug.)

32/A/17 22 Sept. 1812. John Clutterbuck of Stroud, shopkeeper. Fine 5/-. (25 Aug.)

32/A/18 8 Sept. 1812. Richard Gardner of Painswick, shopkeeper. Fine 10/- and 6/- costs. (19 Aug.)

32/A/19 8 Sept. 1812. Arthur Christie of Painswick, shopkeeper. Fine 20/- and 6/- costs. (18 Aug.)

32/A/20 22 Sept. 1812. James Rowles of Stroud, shopkeeper. Fine 5/- and 6/- costs. (10 Sept.)

32/A/21 8 Sept. 1812. Thomas Carter of Painswick, shopkeeper. Fine 5/- and 6/- costs. (19 Aug.)

32/A/22 22 Sept. 1812. John Aldridge of Stroud, shopkeeper. Fine 5/- and 2/6 costs.(25 Aug.)

32/A/23 22 Sept. 1812. Samuel Chandler of Stroud, shopkeeper. Fine 10/- and 6/- costs. (25 Aug.)

32/A/24 22 Sept. 1812. Joseph Bird of Stroud, shopkeeper. Fine 10/- and 6/- costs. (25 Aug.)

32/A/25 22 Sept. 1812. Mary Mayo of Stroud, shopkeeper. Fine 10/- and 6/- costs. (10 Sept.)

32/A/26 8 Sept. 1812. John Tunley of Painswick, shopkeeper. Fine 5/- and 6/- costs. (19 Aug.)

32/A/27 22 Sept. 1812. William Hodges of Stroud, shopkeeper. Fine 20/- and 6/- costs. (10 Sept.)

32/A/28 8 Sept. 1812. Josiah Gardner of Painswick, shopkeeper. Fine 5/- and 6/- costs. (19 Aug.)

32/A/29 8 Sept. 1812. Joseph Jones of Painswick, shopkeeper. Fine 20/- and 6/- costs. (19 Aug.)

32/A/30 8 Sept. 1812. Nathaniel Rice of Painswick, shopkeeper. Fine 5/- and 6/- costs. (19 Aug.)

32/A/31 8 Sept. 1812. John Gill of Painswick, shopkeeper. Fine 20/- and 6/- costs. (19 Aug.)

32/A/32 8 Sept. 1812. James Birt of Painswick, shopkeeper. Fine 10/- and 6/- costs. (18 Aug.)

32/A/33 8 Sept. 1812. Betty King of Painswick, shopkeeper. Fine 5/- and 6/- costs. (19 Aug.)

32/A/34 22 Sept. 1812. Isaac Haines of Stroud, shopkeeper. Fine 5/- and 6/- costs. (25 Aug.)

32/A/35 8 Sept. 1812. Ann Weeks of Painswick, shopkeeper. Fine 10/- and 6/- costs. (19 Aug.)

32/A/36 8 Sept. 1812. Henry Richens of Painswick, shopkeeper. Fine 5/- and 6/- costs. (19 Aug.)

32/A/37 8 Sept. 1812. Samuel Jacobs of Painswick, shopkeeper. Fine 5/- and 6/- costs. (18 Aug.)

32/A/38 8 Sept. 1812. William Sims of Painswick, shopkeeper. Fine 5/- and 6/- costs. (18 Aug.)

32/A/39 22 Sept. 1812. Thomas Wood of Stroud, shopkeeper. Fine 5/- and 6/- costs. (10 Sept.)

32/A/40 22 Sept. 1812. Daniel Ellis of Stroud, shopkeeper. Fine 5/- and 6/- costs. (14 Sept.)

32/A/41 8 Sept. 1812. Edward Haines, clerk to the Stroudwater Navigation Co., of Painswick, shopkeeper. Fine 20/- and 6/- costs. (19 Aug.)

32/A/42 8 Sept. 1812. William Hinton of Painswick, shopkeeper. Fine 10/- and 6/- costs. (18 Aug.)

32/A/43 8 Sept. 1812. Samuel Gardner of Painswick, shopkeeper. Fine 20/- and 6/- costs. (18 Aug.)

32/A/44 8 Sept. 1812. Timothy Wood of Painswick, shopkeeper. Fine 10/- and 6/- costs. (18 Aug.)

32/A/45 8 Sept. 1812. John Cox of Painswick, shopkeeper. Fine 20/- and 6/- costs. (19 Aug.)

32/A/46 22 Sept. 1812. Mary Lewis of Stroud, shopkeeper. Fine 10/- and 6/- costs. (12 Sept.)

32/A/47 8 Sept. 1812. Solomon Chandler of Stroud, shopkeeper. Fine 10/- and 6/- costs. (12 Sept.)

32/A/48 8 Sept. 1812. Richard Hewett of Painswick, shopkeeper. Fine 20/- and 6/- costs. (19 Aug.)

32/A/49 22 Sept. 1812. Sarah Ockford of Stroud, shopkeeper. Fine 5/- and 6/- costs. (14 Sept.)

32/A/50 22 Sept. 1812. Susannah Cooke of Stroud, shopkeeper. Fine 5/- and 3/- costs. (14 Sept.)

32/A/51 22 Sept. 1812. Mary Aldridge of Stroud, shopkeeper. Fine 5/- and 3/- costs. (25 Aug.)

32/A/52 22 Sept. 1812. Thomas Nichols of Stroud, shopkeeper. Fine 5/- and 3/- costs. (10 Sept.)

32/A/53 22 Sept. 1812. William Smith of Stroud, shopkeeper. Fine 5/- and 5/- costs. (10 Sept.)

32/A/54 22 Sept. 1812. Sarah Halliday of Stroud, shopkeeper. Fine 5/- and 6/- costs. (25 Aug.)

32/A/55 22 Sept. 1812. John Clarke of Stroud, shopkeeper. Fine 10/- and 6/- costs. (12 Sept.)

32/A/56 22 Sept. 1812. Benjamin Bird of Stroud, shopkeeper. Fine 10/- and 6/- costs. (12 Sept.)

32/A/57 22 Sept. 1812. Sarah Gardner of Stroud, shopkeeper. Fine 10/- and 6/- costs. (14 Sept.)

32/A/58 8 Sept. 1812. Mary Willey of Painswick, shopkeeper. Fine 10/- and 6/- costs. (18 Aug.)

32/A/59 8 Sept. 1812. Judith Tucker of Painswick, shopkeeper. Fine 5/- and 6/- costs. (18 Aug.)

32/A/60	8 Sept. 1812. John Skerrett of Painswick, shopkeeper. Fine 5/- and 6/- costs. (18 Aug.)
32/A/61	22 Sept. 1812. Elizabeth Mills of Stroud, shopkeeper. Fine 5/- and 6/- costs. (10 Sept.)
32/A/62	22 Sept. 1812. Charles Kendrick of Stroud, shopkeeper. Fine 5/- and 6/- costs. (10 Sept.)
32/A/63	22 Sept. 1812. Thomas Cooke of Stroud, shopkeeper. Fine 20/- and 6/- costs. (12 Sept.)
32/A/64	22 Sept. 1812. Daniel Clift of Stroud, shopkeeper. Fine 10/- and 6/- costs. (25 Aug.)
32/A/65	22 Sept. 1812. John Smith of Stroud, shopkeeper. Fine 5/- and 6/- costs. (14 Sept.)
32/A/66	22 Sept. 1812. Samuel Smith of Stroud, shopkeeper. Fine 10/- and 6/- costs. (12 Sept.)
32/A/67	8 Sept. 1812. John Lemon of Painswick, shopkeeper. Fine 5/- and 6/- costs. (18 Aug.)
32/A/68	8 Sept. 1812. John Jones of Painswick, shopkeeper. Fine 10/- and 6/- costs. (18 Aug.)
32/A/69	8 Sept. 1812. Samuel Holder of Painswick, shopkeeper. Fine 5/- and 6/- costs. (18 Aug.)
32/A/70	8 Sept. 1812. William Gardner of Painswick, shopkeeper. Fine 10/- and 6/- costs. (18 Aug.)
32/A/71	8 Sept. 1812. Daniel Merrell of Painswick, shopkeeper. Fine 5/- and 6/- costs. (18 Aug.)
32/A/72	8 Sept. 1812. John Okey of Painswick, shopkeeper. Fine 20/- and 6/- costs. (18 Aug.)
32/A/73	8 Sept. 1812. William Wright of Painswick, shopkeeper. Fine 10/- and 6/- costs. (18 Aug.)
32/A/74	8 Sept. 1812. Thomas Hillman of Painswick, shopkeeper. Fine 5/- and 6/- costs. (18 Aug.)
32/A/75	8 Sept. 1812. Mary Hanks of Painswick, shopkeeper. Fine 5/- and 6/- costs. (18 Aug.)
32/A/76	8 Sept. 1812. Samuel Hogg of Painswick, shopkeeper. Fine 5/- and 6/- costs. (18 Aug.)
32/A/77	20 Aug. 1812. John Lock of Bisley, shopkeeper. Fine 20/- and 6/- costs. (11 Aug.)
32/A/78	20 Aug. 1812. William Davis of Bisley, shopkeeper. Fine 20/- and 6/- costs. (11 Aug.)
32/A/79	20 Aug. 1812. Joseph Beard of Bisley, shopkeeper. Fine 5/- and 6/- costs. (10 Aug.)
32/A/80	20 Aug. 1812. Isaac Tyler of Bisley, shopkeeper. Fine 5/- and 6/- costs. (10 Aug.)
32/A/81	20 Aug. 1812. William Tyler of Bisley, shopkeeper. Fine 20/- and 6/- costs. (10 Aug.)
32/A/82	20 Aug. 1812. James Gawn of Bisley, shopkeeper. Fine 5/- and 6/- costs. (10 Aug.)
32/A/83	20 Aug. 1812. Nathaniel Stockham of Bisley, shopkeeper. Fine 5/- and 6/- costs. (10 Aug.)
32/A/84	20 Aug. 1812. Richard Gilbins of Bisley, shopkeeper. Fine 5/- and 6/- costs. (10 Aug.)
32/A/85	20 Aug. 1812. Sarah Purnell of Bisley, shopkeeper. Fine 5/- and 6/- costs. (11 Aug.)
32/A/86	20 Aug. 1812. Henry Merrell [? or Merrett] of Bisley, shopkeeper. Fine 20/- and 6/- costs. (10 Aug.)
32/A/87	20 Aug. 1812. Joseph Baker of Bisley, shopkeeper. Fine 20/- and 6/- costs. (10 Aug.)
32/A/88	20 Aug. 1812. William Bishop of Bisley, shopkeeper. Fine 5/- and 6/- costs. (10 Aug.)
32/A/89	20 Aug. 1812. William Baker of Bisley, shopkeeper. Fine 20/- and 6/- costs. (10 Aug.)
32/A/90	20 Aug. 1812. William Damsell of Bisley, shopkeeper. Fine 20/- and 6/- costs. (10 Aug.)
32/A/91	22 Sept. 1812. Ann Shewell of Stroud, shopkeeper. Fine 5/- and 2/6 costs. (10 Sept.)
32/A/92	8 Sept. 1812. Mary Taylor of Painswick, shopkeeper. Fine 10/- and 6/- costs. (18 Aug.)
32/A/93	22 Sept. 1812. William Hill of Stroud, shopkeeper. Fine 5/- and 6/- costs. (12 Sept.)
32/A/94	22 Sept. 1812. Elizabeth Brown of Stroud, shopkeeper. Fine 5/- and 3/- costs. (10 Sept.)
32/A/95	22 Sept. 1812. Thomas Wilkes of Stroud, shopkeeper. Fine 5/- and 3/- costs. (10 Sept.)
32/A/96	22 Sept. 1812. Edward Wall of Stroud, shopkeeper. Fine 5/- and 6/- costs. (10 Sept.)
32/A/97	22 Sept. 1812. Thomas Gardner of Stroud, shopkeeper. Fine 20/- and 6/- costs. (10 Sept.)
32/A/98	22 Sept. 1812. William Warner of Stroud, shopkeeper. Fine 5/-. (10 Sept.)
32/A/99	22 Sept. 1812. John Haines of Stroud, shopkeeper. Fine 20/- and 6/- costs. (12 Sept.)
32/A/100	22 Sept. 1812. John Biddle of Stroud, shopkeeper. Fine 10/- and 6/- costs. (12 Sept.)
32/A/101	22 Sept. 1812. Samuel Webb of Stroud, shopkeeper. Fine 5/- and 6/- costs. (10 Sept.)
32/A/102	22 Sept. 1812. Samuel Holder of Stroud, shopkeeper. Fine 5/- and 6/- costs. (12 Sept.)
32/A/103	22 Sept. 1812. John Rudge of Stroud, shopkeeper. Fine 5/-. (10 Sept.)

32/A/104	22 Sept. 1812. Thomas Davis of Stroud, shopkeeper. Fine 20/- and 6/- costs. (25 Aug.)
32/A/105	22 Sept. 1812. Joseph Fisher of Stroud, shopkeeper. Fine 5/- and 6/- costs. (10 Sept.)
32/A/106 –123	20 Aug. 1812. [*Names as below.*] Having defective weights. H. Burgh JP and E. Aldridge JP at a Petty Sessions held at the King's Arms inn, Stroud. [*Fines and date offence committed (all 1812) as below.*]
32/A/106	Thomas Franklin of Bisley, shopkeeper. Fine 20/- and 6/- costs. (13 Aug.)
32/A/107	James Keen of Bisley, shopkeeper. Fine 5/- and 6/- costs. (13 Aug.)
32/A/108	William Davis of Bisley, shopkeeper. Fine 20/- and 6/- costs. (11 Aug.)
32/A/109	Samuel Iddles of Bisley, shopkeeper. Fine 5/- and 6/- costs. (11 Aug.)
32/A/110	Thomas Harper of Bisley, shopkeeper. Fine 5/- and 6/- costs. (11 Aug.)
32/A/111	Henry Hook of Bisley, shopkeeper. Fine 5/- and 6/- costs. (11 Aug.)
32/A/112	John Cooke of Bisley, shopkeeper. Fine 10/- and 6/- costs. (12 Aug.)
32/A/113	Zachariah Davis of Bisley, shopkeeper. Fine 20/- and 6/- costs. (12 Aug.)
32/A/114	John Coxe of Bisley, shopkeeper. Fine 5/- and 6/- costs. (12 Aug.)
32/A/115	Jonathan Morgan of Bisley, shopkeeper. Fine 20/- and 6/- costs. (12 Aug.)
32/A/116	William Long of Bisley, shopkeeper. Fine 5/- and 6/- costs. (12 Aug.)
32/A/117	Daniel Price of Bisley, shopkeeper. Fine 5/- and 6/- costs. (12 Aug.)
32/A/118	Thomas Lewis of Bisley, shopkeeper. Fine 5/- and 6/- costs. (13 Aug.)
32/A/119	William Tayloe of Bisley, shopkeeper. Fine 5/- and 6/- costs. (13 Aug.)
32/A/120	Ralph Gardner of Bisley, shopkeeper. Fine 5/- and 6/- costs. (13 Aug.)
32/A/121	Jacob Bath of Bisley, shopkeeper. Fine 5/- and 6/- costs. (13 Aug.)
32/A/122	William Smart of Bisley, shopkeeper. Fine 5/- and 6/- costs. (13 Aug.)
32/A/123	William Carter of Bisley, shopkeeper. Fine 20/- and 6/- costs. (13 Aug.)
32/A/124	6 Nov. 1812. Edward Hobbs of Framilode, fishmonger. Having defective weights. H. Burgh JP at a Petty Sessions held at the King's Arms inn, Stroud. Fine 5/- and 6/- costs. Offence committed 28 Oct. 1812.
32/A/125	20 Aug. 1812. Moses Gardner of Bisley, shopkeeper. Having defective weights. H. Burgh JP and E. Aldridge JP at a Petty Sessions held at the King's Arms inn, Stroud. Fine 5/- and 6/- costs. Offence committed 13 Aug. 1812.
32/A/126	20 Aug. 1812. Giles Driver of Bisley, shopkeeper. Having [*etc., as* 32/A/125].
32/A/127 –133	11 Jan. 1813. [*Names as below.*] Having defective weights. J. Agg JP and T. Welles D.D. JP at a Petty Sessions for Cheltenham district. Fine 5/- and 5/- costs. [*Date offence committed (all 1812) as below.*]
32/A/127	Charles Williams of Cheltenham, grocer. (26 Dec.)
32/A/128	William Scrivens of Cheltenham, baker. (24 Dec.)
32/A/129	Peter Ryan of Cheltenham, butcher. (24 Dec.)
32/A/130	William Barrett of Cheltenham, baker. (24 Dec.)
32/A/131	Benjamin Buckle of Cheltenham, baker. (28 Dec.)
32/A/132	Ann Cooper of Cheltenham, shopkeeper. (24 Dec.)
32/A/133	James Butt of Cheltenham, grocer. (24 Dec.)
32/A/134 –148	5 Jan. 1813. [*Names as below.*] Having defective weights. Rev. J. Neale JP and J. Agg JP at a Petty Sessions for Cheltenham district. Fine 5/- and 5/- costs. [*Date offence committed (all 1812) as below.*]
32/A/134	Thomas Hewett of Cheltenham, [shopkeeper]. (24 Dec.)
32/A/135	Hannah Haynes, widow, of Cheltenham, shopkeeper. (26 Dec.)
32/A/136	Sarah Kilmister, widow, of Cheltenham, [shopkeeper]. (26 Dec.)

32/A/137   John Matthews of Cheltenham, butcher. (28 Dec.)

32/A/138   John Summerfield of Cheltenham, butcher. (24 Dec.)

32/A/139   John Higgs of Cheltenham, shopkeeper. (26 Dec.)

32/A/140   William Hall of Cheltenham, shopkeeper. (26 Dec.)

32/A/141   William Gore of Cheltenham, baker. (26 Dec.)

32/A/142   Isaac Page of Cheltenham, grocer. (28 Dec.)

32/A/143   James Arkell of Cheltenham, baker. (28 Dec.)

32/A/144   John Hawes of Cheltenham, grocer. (24 Dec.)

32/A/145   Richard Dawes of Cheltenham, grocer. (24 Dec.)

32/A/146   Morris Hale of Cheltenham, grocer. (24 Dec.)

32/A/147   George Yeels of Cheltenham, grocer. (26 Dec.)

32/A/148   Thomas Potter of Cheltenham, shopkeeper. (26 Dec.)

32/A/149   6 Jan. 1813. John Ashenford. Possessing two brass weights without satisfactory explanation. H. Burgh JP and H. Cooke JP.

32/A/150   6 Jan. 1813. Shadrach Deane. Stealing a quantity of turnips from a field in Horsley, the property of Daniel Browning, glazier. H. Burgh JP. Offence committed Sunday morning [4 Jan. 1813].

32/A/151   28 Dec. 1812. John Hiatt of Dymock, gentleman. Using a gun to kill game without the required certificate. Rev. Richard Francis Onslow JP. Mitigated fine of £10.

32/A/152   28 Dec. 1812. George Thurston of Dymock, gentleman. Using a gun to kill game without a certificate. Rev. R. F. Onslow JP. Mitigated fine of £10.

32/A/153   19 Dec. 1812. William Hyde of Wotton under Edge, clothier. Buying about 1 lb. of stolen woollen yarn from Jonathan Smith, weaver, of Wotton under Edge. George Austin JP and W. M. Adey JP. Henry Vizard, informer. Fine of £40 paid immediately. Offence committed April or May 1810.

32/A/154   6 Nov. 1812. Mary Webb, clothworker, wife of Thomas Webb of North Nibley, weaver. Stealing woollen yarn. R. B. Cooper JP and G. Austin JP. One month's hard labour in Horsley house of correction.

32/A/155   1 Jan. 1813. Isaac Perrett of North Nibley, labourer. Buying stolen woollen yarn (thrums and forrel) from Matthew Hancock, clothworker, at Dursley. R. Nelmes JP and W. M. Adey JP. Henry Vizard, informer. Fine £20 or three months' hard labour in Horsley house of correction. Offence committed 1 March 1812.

32/A/156   6 Nov. 1812. John Williams of Stinchcombe, labourer. Buying 24 lb. of woollen yarn from Samuel Bennett, clothworker, at Stinchcombe. R. B. Cooper JP and G. Austin JP. Henry Vizard, informer. Fine £40. Offence committed 1 March 1812.

32/A/157   7 Nov. 1812. Joseph Partridge of Wotton under Edge, clothier. Buying 2 lb. of woollen yarn and ends from Mary Webb, clothworker, wife of Thomas Webb, weaver, the property of her employer Edward Sheppard Esq. R. Nelmes JP and G. Austin JP. Samuel Bennett, informer. Fine £40 or six months' hard labour in Horsley house of correction. Offence committed 16 May 1812.

32/A/158   13 Oct. 1812. Robert Edwards of Westerleigh, pig butcher. Using dogs and a gun to kill game at Pucklechurch. R. Haynes JP at Wick. William Hiorns, gamekeeper, of Siston, informer. Robert Haskins, witness. Fine £5. Offence committed 1 Oct. 1812.

32/A/159   9 Jan. 1813. Samuel Jackson of Lea [hamlet], dealer. Failing to pay tolls at Over, Churcham. Rev. T. Rudge JP at Gloucester. John Sanders, informer. Daniel Smith, witness. Offender pleaded not guilty. Fine 40/-. Offence committed 2 Jan. 1813.

32/A/160   19 Oct. 1812. James Nicholls, late of Miserden, labourer. Leaving his wife and family chargeable to the parish. Rev. J. B. Cheston JP. John Archer, yeoman, of Miserden, witness. Offender admitted guilt. Committed to Horsley house of correction until next Q.S. unless earlier discharged by due course of law.

32/A/161   19 Nov. 1812. Daniel Fowler the younger of Winterbourne. Leaving his child chargeable to the parish. G. Goldney JP at Lawfords Gate, St. Philip and St. Jacob, Bristol. Thomas Lawrence, overseer of the poor of Winterbourne, informer. Offender pleaded guilty. Committed to Lawfords Gate house of correction until next Q.S.

32/A/162   12 Nov. 1812. Daniel Savage of North Nibley, yeoman. Using a gun to kill game. H. Burgh JP. Thomas Ford, gamekeeper, of North Nibley, informer. Thomas Millard, labourer, of North Nibley, witness. First offence. Fine £5 or three months in Horsley house of correction. Offence committed 10 Sept. 1812.

32/A/163   20 Oct. 1812. John Rock. Leaving his wife and children chargeable to the parish of Cirencester. Rev. Henry Anthony Pye JP at Cirencester. Jonathan Flower Baldwyn, informer. Offender admitted guilt. Committed to Northleach house of correction until next Q.S. unless earlier discharged by due course of law. Offence committed between 23 June and 20 Oct. 1812.

32/A/164   10 Jan. 1813. John Champion of Cheltenham, labourer. Using nets in enclosed ground, namely the Hamblins, Coberley, with intent to kill hares, in company with William Drinkwater, shoemaker, of Cheltenham, and another unknown. Sir E. B. Sandys JP at Miserden Park. Henry Baker, huntsman, and Samuel Lock, gamekeeper, both of Cowley, informers. Offender apprehended by above at time of offence. Declared a rogue and vagabond. Committed to the house of correction at Gloucester until the next Q.S. Offence committed 20 Oct. 1812.

32/A/165   24 Dec. 1812. Richard Arnold of Cirencester, labourer. Using snares to kill game at Preston. Rev. H. A. Pye JP at Cirencester. Robert Herbert, gamekeeper, of Cirencester, informer. Thomas Moss, labourer, of Cirencester, witness. Fine £5. Offence committed 21 Dec. 1812.

32/B/1   22 March 1813. Joseph White of Blakeney, Awre, baker. Possessing the skin of a fallow deer at Newnham without satisfactory explanation. F. Lawson JP, Rev. C. Sandiford JP and Rev. R. Wetherell JP. William Aldridge, waterman, of Arlingham, informer. William Cooke of Newnham, gamekeeper to Roynon Jones the younger Esq. of Gloucester, witness. Fine £30 and 7/6 costs. Offence committed 9 March 1813.

32/B/2   13 March 1813. Thomas Vimpany of Arlingham, waterman. Cursing. Henry Clifford Clifford JP.

32/B/3   6 Feb. 1813. Samuel Baughan of Arlingham, labourer. Cursing. H. C. Clifford JP.

32/B/4   10 March 1813. Robert Anstee the younger of Dyrham and Hinton, labourer. Possessing snares for killing game. R. Haynes JP at Wick. Fine £5.

32/B/5   22 Jan. 1813. William Cox and Benjamin Cox of Sheperdine and Mark Biddle of Oldbury [on Severn], labourers. Shooting hares in enclosed ground at Berkeley, the property of William Fitzhardinge Berkeley Esq. S. P. Peach JP at Tockington. William Powell, gamekeeper to W. F. Berkeley Esq., apprehended offenders. William Cox escaped but was recaptured. William Cox, yeoman, of Bevington and William Bennett, labourer of Oldbury, witnesses. Declared rogues and vagabonds and committed to Horsley house of correction until next Q.S. Offence committed 20 Jan. 1813.

32/C/1   6 May 1813. John Alexander Jones of Minchinhampton, weaver. Found, armed with a loaded pistol and a bludgeon and in possession of a quantity of wool, at a mill in Minchinhampton belonging to William Gardiner of Chalford, clothier. H. Burgh JP, H. Cooke JP and Rev. P. Hawker JP at Rodborough. John Gardiner, clothier, of Chalford, Bisley, informer. Apprehended by Josiah Gardiner, constable of Bisley, as a rogue and vagabond. William Gardiner, clothier, of Chalford, Bisley, witness. Committed to Horsley house of correction until next Q.S. Offence committed at night 5/6 May 1813.

32/C/2   15 April 1813. John Antill of Bisley, shopkeeper. Possessing cloth yarn and weavers' ends without satisfactory explanation. S. Wathen JP and E. Aldridge JP. Nathaniel Thornbury, clothier, of Stroud, informer. Richard Smith, weaver, of Stroud, witness. First offence. Fine £20 or one month in Horsley house of correction. Fine paid. Offence committed 15 April 1813.

32/C/3   27 Jan. 1813. Charles Thornton of Stroud. Possessing a hare. S. Wathen JP. William Harris, gamekeeper, of Stroud, informer. Joseph White, labourer, of Stroud, witness. First offence. Fine £5 or three months in Horsley house of correction. Fine paid. Offence committed 31 Dec. 1812.

32/C/4   29 Jan. 1813. Deborah Tocknell of Minchinhampton. Buying a quantity of thrums believed to be stolen. Sir Paul Baghott JP and S. Wathen JP. Nathaniel Thornbury of Stroud, informer. John Wheatley, weaver, of Minchinhampton, witness. Fine £20 or three months in Horsley house of correction. Imprisoned. Offence committed 27 Jan. 1813.

32/C/5   29 Jan. 1813. Thomas Howell of Minchinhampton, clothier. Buying a quantity of thrums believed to be stolen. Sir P. Baghott JP and S. Wathen JP. Nathaniel Thornbury, clothier, of Stroud, informer. Obadiah Golding, labourer, of Minchinhampton, witness. Fine £40 or three months in Horsley house of correction. Fine obtained. Offence committed 26 Jan. 1813.

32/C/6   29 Jan. 1813. Thomas Hill of Rodborough, clothier. Buying a quantity of thrums believed to be stolen. Sir P. Baghott JP and S. Wathen JP. Nathaniel Thornbury, clothier, of Stroud, informer. Hannah Golding, spinner, of Minchinhampton, witness. Fine £40 or three months in Horsley house of correction. Fine obtained. Offence committed 25 Jan. 1813.

32/C/7   5 April 1813. Sarah Bryant and Mary Jeffries of Wick and Abson. Stealing a quantity of wood, the property of Samuel Ashley of Wick and Abson, farmer. R. Haynes JP. Fine 10/- each. Offence committed 31 March 1813.

32/C/8   19 March 1813. John Coates of Marshfield, labourer. Stealing a quantity of wood, the property of James Osborne of Cold Ashton, farmer. R. Haynes JP. Fine 40/-. Offence committed during Feb. 1813.

32/C/9   10 June 1813. James Crook of Bisley, weaver. Stealing 2 lb. of woollen yarn. James Clutterbuck JP and E. Aldridge JP. William Sevill the younger, clothier, of Bisley, witness. First offence. Hard labour for one month in Horsley house of correction. Offence committed 1 April 1813.

32/C/10 10 June 1813. John Clissold of Bisley, clothworker. Wilfully damaging a quantity of wool delivered to him to be scoured. J. Clutterbuck JP and E. Aldridge JP. William Tayloe, clothier, of Bisley, witness. First offence. Fine £10 (double the value of the spoiled wool) or hard labour for one month in Horsley house of correction.

32/C/11   14 June 1813. William Ridler of Bisley, weaver. Possessing about 2 lb. of Spanish abb yarn believed to be stolen. H. Burgh JP and H. Cooke JP. Nathaniel Thornbury, informer. Richard Poulson, mason, of Bisley, witness. First offence. Fine £20 or three months in Horsley house of correction.

32/C/12   14 June 1813. Samuel Ridler of Eastcombe, Bisley, weaver. Possessing [*etc.*, *as* 32/C/11, *adding*] Offence committed 12 April 1813.

32/C/13   6 May 1813. John Alexander Jones of Minchinhampton, weaver. Receiving and possessing about 11 lb. of English wool knowing it to be stolen. H. Burgh JP, H. Cooke JP and Rev. P. Hawker JP at Rodborough. John Gardiner, clothier, of Bisley, informer. William Gardiner, clothier, of Bisley, witness. First offence. Fine £20 or one month in Horsley house of correction. [*Cf.* 32/C/1.]

32/C/14   10 June 1813. Thomas Ridler of Horsley, weaver. Possessing and receiving about 46 lb. of wool knowing it to be stolen. J. Clutterbuck JP and E. Aldridge JP at Bisley. Nathaniel Thornbury, clothier, of Stroud, informer. James Fowler, clothworker, of Stroud, witness. First offence. Fine £20 or one month in Horsley house of correction.

32/C/15   18 May 1813. Giles Brown of Bisley, clothworker. Possessing and receiving a quantity of flocks and a cloth remnant knowing them to be stolen. J. Clutterbuck JP and E. Aldridge JP at Bisley. Daniel Cox, clothier, of Bisley, informer. William Gardiner, clothier, of Bisley, witness. First offence. Fine £20 or one month in Horsley house of correction.

32/C/16   3 June 1813. Samuel Winstone of Bisley, mason. Receiving and possessing about 30 lb. of woollen yarn and a quantity of cloth knowing them to be stolen. J. Clutterbuck JP and E. Aldridge JP at Bisley. Nathaniel Thornbury, clothier, of Stroud, informer. James Fowler, clothworker, of Stroud, witness. First offence. Fine £20 or one month in Horsley house of correction.

32/C/17   18 May 1813. John Jacques of Bisley, weaver. Receiving and possessing 127 lb. of English and Spanish wool knowing it to be stolen. J. Clutterbuck JP and E. Aldridge JP at Bisley. Daniel Cox, clothier, of Bisley, informer. William Gardiner, clothier, of Bisley, witness. Fine £20 or one month in Horsley house of correction.

32/C/18   18 May 1813. William Jeffreys of Bisley, clothworker. Receiving and possessing about 20 yards of woollen cloth knowing it to be stolen. J. Clutterbuck JP and E. Aldridge JP at Bisley. William Gardiner, clothier, of Bisley, informer. Daniel Cox, clothier, of Bisley, witness. First offence. Fine £20 or one month in Horsley house of correction.

32/C/19   3 June 1813. Richard Poulson of Bisley, mason. Receiving and possessing a large quantity of English and Spanish abb yarn knowing it to be stolen. J. Clutterbuck JP and E. Aldridge JP at Bisley. Nathaniel Thornbury, clothier, of Stroud, informer. James Fowler, clothworker, of Stroud, witness. First offence. Fine £20 or one month in Horsley house of correction.

32/C/20   18 May 1813. John Goodship of Bisley, labourer. Receiving and possessing a quantity of woollen cloth remnants knowing them to be stolen. J. Clutterbuck JP and E. Aldridge JP at Bisley. Daniel Cox, clothier, of Bisley, informer. Willliam Gardiner, clothier, of Bisley, witness. First offence. Fine £20 or one month in Horsley house of correction.

32/C/21   15 June 1813. William Bath of Bisley, clothworker. Receiving a large quantity of soap, used for milling cloth, from George Lambert, millman to William Gardiner of Bisley. J. Clutterbuck JP and E. Aldridge JP at Bisley. Daniel Cox, clothier, of Bisley, informer. Convicted on own confession. First offence. Fine £20 or one month in Horsley house of correction.

32/D/1   9 Aug. 1813. William Butler of Horton, carpenter and joiner. Shooting a hare. Henry Charles, duke of Beaufort, JP at Badminton. John Reed, servant, of Horton, informer and prosecutor for the poor. Thomas Andrews, turnpike-gate keeper, witness. Offender pleaded guilty. Fine £5. Offence committed 21 July 1813.

32/D/2   9 Aug. 1813. [*List of those fined for*] Having defective weights. T. Nash JP, Rev. J. Keysall JP and Rev. J. Timbrill JP at a Petty Sessions held at Mr. Fryer's office in Tewkesbury. All convicted on own confession [*except where stated otherwise*]. Offences committed between 14 and 17 July 1813. [*The two amounts against each name are respectively the fine and costs.*]

> Edward Roberts of Aston on Carrant, baker, £1 and 3/-.
>
> Sarah Healing of Boddington, miller, £1 and 3/-.
>
> William Bick of Hayden, shopkeeper, £1 and 3/-.
>
> Joseph Roberts, shopkeeper, 10/- and 3/-, William Etheridge, shopkeeper, 10/- and 3/-, Joseph Troughton, shopkeeper, £1 and 3/-, William Halling, shopkeeper, £1 and 3/-, Thomas Stephens, miller, 10/- and 3/-, William Cole, shopkeeper, £1 and 3/-, Richard Williams, blacksmith, £1 and 3/-, all of Kemerton.
>
> Joseph Ayland of Northway and Newton miller, 10/- and 3/-.
>
> Thomas Didcott of Apperley, shopkeeper, 10/- and 3/-.
>
> William Dobbins, shopkeeper, £1 and 3/-, Charles Allen, shopkeeper, 10/- and 3/-, both of Corse.
>
> Convicted on the oath of Samuel Mew: Robert Davis of Hasfield, shopkeeper, £1 and 3/-, Thomas Ellis of Deerhurst, shopkeeper, £1 and 3/-.
>
> Joseph Cox of Deerhurst, shopkeeper, £1 and 3/-.
>
> Joseph Steight of Tirley, shopkeeper, £1 and 3/-.
>
> Thomas Teale, shopkeeper, 10/- and 3/-, Thomas Laughty, shopkeeper, £1 and 3/-, Mary Griffiths, shopkeeper, 10/- and 3/-, all of Twyning.

32/D/3   16 Aug. 1813. [*List of those fined for*] Having defective weights. T. Nash JP and Rev. J. Timbrill JP at a Petty Sessions held at the New Inn, Beckford. All convicted on own confession [*except where stated*] otherwise. Offences committed between 14 and 30 July 1813. [*The two amounts against each name are respectively the fine and costs.*]

> William Richardson of Buckland, shopkeeper, £1 and 3/-.
>
> John Ballinger, shopkeeper, £1 and 3/-, Thomas Moore, miller, £1 and 3/-, both of Childswickham.
>
> Charles Grissell, shopkeeper, £1 and 3/-, Richard Green, shopkeeper, £1 and 3/-, both of Didbrook.
>
> Mary Dobbins, miller £1 and 3/-, James Hall, shopkeeper, £1 and 3/-, both of Dumbleton.
>
> John Doughty, shopkeeper, £1 and 3/-, John Hathaway, shopkeeper, £1 and 3/-, Ann Griffin, shopkeeper, £1 and 3/-, all of Ford.
>
> John Hewlett, shopkeeper, of Gretton, £1 and 3/-.
>
> George Restall of Upper Guiting, shopkeeper, £1 and 3/-.
>
> Thomas Barnes, shopkeeper, £1 and 3/-, John Farthing, blacksmith, 10/- and 3/-, both of Temple Guiting.
>
> George Herbert, shopkeeper, £1 and 3/-, John Williams, shopkeeper, £1 and 3/-, Thomas Wood, shopkeeper, £1 and 3/-, John Steight, shopkeeper, £1 and 3/-, Thomas Hooper, shopkeeper, £1 and 3/-, John Gillett, shopkeeper, £1 and 3/-, all of Lower Guiting.

William Newman of Hawling, shopkeeper, £1 and 3/-.

Edward Walker, shopkeeper, £1 and 3/-, William Atkins, shopkeeper, 10/- and 3/-, both of Stanton [*MS.* Staunton].

Convicted on the oath of Samuel Mew: Samuel Sharp of Toddington, shopkeeper, £1 and 3/-.

William Mason, shopkeeper, £1 and 3/-, Sarah Hughes, shopkeeper, £1 and 3/-, George Hall, shopkeeper, £1 and 3/-, Charles Johnsons, shopkeeper, £1 and 3/-, William Hughes, shopkeeper, £1 and 3/-, Thomas Ashwood, shopkeeper, 10/- and 3/-, Ferdinando Jones, butcher, 10/- and 3/-, William Dobbins, shopkeeper, £1 and 3/-, Richard Turberville, cooper, 10/- and 3/-, all of Winchcombe.

Robert Franklin of Wormington, baker, £1 and 3/-.

Richard Dee of Snowshill, shopkeeper, £1 and 3/-.

James Roberts, baker, 10/- and 3/-, Michael Stephens, shopkeeper, £1 and 3/-, both of Alderton.

George Collett of Church Stanway, miller, £1 and 3/-.

William Drinkwater of Ashton under Hill, shopkeeper, £1 and 3/-.

Mary Surman, shopkeeper, 10/- and 3/-, Lucy Leaver, draper, 10/- and 3/-, Richard Peart, baker, £1 and 3/-, all of Beckford.

32/D/4   2 Oct. 1813. William Shearman of [North] Nibley, weaver. Using a ferret and a net to kill conies without first obtaining a certificate. W. Lloyd Baker and John Wallington at Dursley, commissioners acting in the execution of the Acts relating to assessed taxes for the district of Upper Berkeley hundred. Fine £15. Offence committed 5 Sept. 1813.

32/D/5   2 Oct. 1813. William Adams of [North] Nibley, weaver. Using a ferret [*etc., as* 32/D/4 *except*] Fine £10.

32/D/6   7 Sept. 1813. William Abell of Winstone, yeoman. Possessing the skins of two fallow deer without satisfactory explanation. Rev. W. Mills JP at Miserden. John Cooke, bailiff in husbandry, complainant. Fine £30.

33/A/1   8 Jan. 1814. William Shepherd of Ashleworth, yeoman. Shooting game. Rev. J. B. Cheston JP at Gloucester. William Leach, yeoman, of Ashleworth, informer and prosecutor for the poor. Mary Leach of Ashleworth, witness. Offender pleaded not guilty. Fine £5. Offence committed 7 Nov. 1813.

33/A/2   8 Jan. 1814. William Shepherd of Ashleworth, yeoman. Using a gin to kill game. Rev. J. B. Cheston JP at Gloucester. William Leach, yeoman, of Ashleworth, informer. Mary Leach of Ashleworth, witness. Offender pleaded not guilty. Fine £5. Offence committed 13 Dec. 1813.

33/A/3   15 Oct. 1813. William Smith of Horsley, weaver. Possessing 8 lb. of stolen woollen yarn, the property of Henry and J. P. Hicks, clothiers. H. Burgh JP and H. Cooke JP. John Phillimore Hicks, clothier, of Eastington, informer. George Cowley, spinner, of Eastington, witness. First offence. Fine £20 or one month in Horsley house of correction. Offence committed 22 Aug. 1813.

33/A/4   13 Jan. 1814. John Penny. Shooting pheasants in enclosed ground at Cromhall in company with John Willcox, cordwainer, of Thornbury and John Pearce. John Merrett Stephens JP at Gloucester gaol. James Smith, complainant. Offender pleaded not guilty. Declared a rogue and vagabond. Committed to Horsley house of correction until next Q.S. or until discharged by due course of law. Offence committed at 3 a.m. on 4 Jan. 1814.

33/A/5 24 Dec. 1813. Benjamin Hill of Gloucester, yeoman. Shooting game in Highnam. Rev. J. B. Cheston JP at Gloucester. John Jenkins, yeoman, of Highnam, informer and prosecutor for the poor. John Clutterbuck, labourer, of Highnam, witness. Offender pleaded not guilty. Fined £5. Offence committed 17 Dec. 1813.

33/A/6 10 Jan. 1814. Joseph Berryman of Stroud, labourer. Obtaining 11/- by fortune-telling. H. Burgh JP and E. Aldridge JP. Elizabeth Fowler of Stroud, witness. Declared a rogue and vagabond. Offence committed 12 Oct. 1813.

33/A/7 3 Jan. 1814. Richard Guess of near Littledean, horse follower. Cutting and damaging a 23-year-old oak tree in South Heywood, Forest of Dean. F. Lawson JP and Rev. R. Wetherell JP. John White, keeper of Littledean Walk, informer. John Hatton, woodman, witness. First offence. Mitigated fine of £5 and 4/6 costs. Offence committed 28 Dec. 1813.

33/A/8 27 Dec. 1813. George Drew of Littledean, horse follower. Cutting down a quantity of hawthorn in the Forest of Dean. F. Lawson JP and R. Wetherell JP. Timothy Jones of the Forest of Dean, informer. Thomas Harvey of the Forest of Dean, witness. First offence. Fine 20/- and 6/6 costs. Offence committed 23 Dec. 1813.

33/A/9 3 Jan. 1814. James Bayley of near Mitcheldean, labourer. Possessing a quantity of hollies and thorns. F. Lawson JP and Rev. R. Wetherell JP. John White, keeper of Littledean Walk, informer. Offender confessed. First offence. Mitigated fine of 10/- and 3/6 costs. Offence committed 30 Dec. 1813.

33/A/10 3 Dec. 1813. Stephen Yeels of Marshfield, victualler. Having three non-standard quart cups in his victualling house. I. W. Horlock JP and Rev. Isaac William Webb Horlock JP at a Petty Sessions for Grumbalds Ash district. Charles Bowsher of Marshfield, informer. Fine 5/- and 3/3 costs. Offence committed Wednesday 1 Dec. 1813.

33/A/11 3 Dec. 1813. Stephen Yeels, victualler, Joseph Crease *alias* Clease, shopkeeper, George Wilton, baker, and Thomas Tipper, shopkeeper, all of Marshfield. Having defective weights. I. W. Horlock JP and Rev. I. W. W. Horlock JP. Fine 5/- each, paid to the county treasurer. Offence committed 1 Dec. 1813.

33/A/12 3 Dec. 1813. Joseph Crease *alias* Clease of Marshfield, shopkeeper and retailer, Having defective weights. I. W. Horlock JP and Rev. I. W. W. Horlock JP at a Petty Sessions for Grumbalds Ash district. Charles Bowsher of Marshfield, informer. Fine 5/- and 3/3 costs. Offence committed 1 Dec. 1813.

33/A/13 3 Dec. 1813. George Wilton, baker, and Thomas Tipper, shopkeeper, both of Marshfield. Having defective weights. I. W. Horlock JP and Rev. I. W. W. Horlock JP. Charles Bowsher of Marshfield, informer. Each fined 5/- and 3/3 costs. Offence committed Wednesday 1 Dec. 1813.

33/A/14 15 Oct. 1813. John Trubody of Wick and Abson. Refusing to accept Ann Kains as an apprentice after indentures had been drawn up. Thomas Jones JP, I. W. Horlock JP and I. W. W. Horlock JP. Harry Hathway, churchwarden, and Joseph Perry, overseers of the poor, complainants. Fine £10.

33/A/15 13 Dec. 1813. John Pearson of Haresfield, labourer. Leaving his wife and child chargeable to the parish. Daniel John Niblett JP and Rev. T. Rudge JP at Haresfield. Richard Chamberlain of Haresfield, parish overseer, informer. Declared a rogue and vagabond. Committed to Horsley house of correction until next Q.S. Offence committed sometime during 1811.

33/A/16   11 Nov. 1813. Ezekiel Wood. Conspiring with Thomas Morgan to defraud Thomas Wheeler of £3 by means of an illegal betting game, namely Pricking in the Garter. Joseph Pitt JP and Edward Wilbraham JP at Cirencester. John Brimble, complainant. Committed to Northleach house of correction until next Q.S. unless discharged earlier by due course of law.

33/A/17   11 Nov. 1813. John Tombs of Cirencester, labourer. Being drunk. E. Wilbraham JP at Cirencester. Henry Foreshew, a high constable of Cirencester, complainant. Offender confessed. Fine 5/-. Offence committed 9 Nov. 1813.

33/A/18   11 Nov. 1813. James Brown. Attending fairs with an illegal dice game, lodging in alehouses etc. J. Pitt JP and E. Wilbraham JP at Cirencester. John Brimble, complainant. Offender confessed. Committed to Northleach house of correction until next Q.S. unless discharged earlier by due course of law.

33/A/19   14 Oct. 1813. Isaac Teakle of Minchinhampton, weaver. Buying 2 lb. of woollen yarn from Hannah Maria Stephens of Horsley, wife of Job Stephens, a private serving in the Royal Tower Hamlets militia. E. Wilbraham JP, E. Aldridge JP and J. Clutterbuck JP. William and Peter Playne, clothiers, of Minchinhampton, complainants. Fine £20 or three months' hard labour in Horsley house of correction. Offence committed 14 June 1813.

33/A/20   14 Oct. 1813. Thomas Ridler of Horsley, weaver. Possessing 3 lb. of stolen woollen yarn. E. Wilbraham JP, E. Aldridge JP and J. Clutterbuck JP at Horsley. Daniel Smith Esq. of Minchinhampton, informer. Joseph Brown, clothier, of Minchinhampton and Nathaniel Thornbury, clothier, of Stroud, witnesses. Previous conviction on 10 June 1813 for possession of 46 lb. of stolen wool [cf. 32/C/14]. Fine £30 or two months in Horsley house of correction. Offence committed 13 Oct. 1813.

33/A/21   15 Oct. 1813. Thomas Jones of Beckford, yeoman. Using dogs and a gun to kill game, without a certificate. G. Talbot JP, Rev. J. Timbrill JP and John Eddy, commissioner for assessed taxes for the district of Ford, at the Red Lion inn, Toddington. Fine £20. Offence committed 14 Sept. 1813.

33/A/22   16 Nov. 1813. John Summerfield. Failing to comply with an order to remove a hogsty from near St. James Street, Cheltenham, issued by Theodore Gwinnett, clerk to the commissioners. T. Welles D.D. JP. Fine £6 10s.

33/A/23   20 Nov. 1813. William Dyer. Leaving his son Benjamin chargeable to the parish of Beckford. Rev. J. Timbrill JP at Beckford. William Izard, complainant. John Baldwyn, witness. When charged, prisoner 'stood mute and made no answer.' Committed to Northleach house of correction until next Q.S. unless discharged earlier by due course of law. Offence committed c. 1 Nov. 1813.

33/A/24   12 Nov. 1813. George Phipps of St. Briavels, haulier. Possessing a quantity of beech timber without permission. Edward Davies JP and Rev. Thomas Thomas JP. James Morrison and John Dudgeon, witnesses. Mitigated fine of 40/- and 12/6 costs. Offence committed c. 1 Sept. 1813.

33/A/25   26 Nov. 1813. James Williams of Hewelsfield, labourer. Possessing an oak tree, believed to belong to the duke of Beaufort, without satisfactory explanation. E. Davies JP and Rev. T. Thomas JP. Henry Edwards of Tidenham, woodward to the duke of Beaufort, complainant. Fine 40/- and 7/6/ costs. Offence committed 19 Nov. 1813.

33/A/26   24 Dec. 1813. Hester Jenkins of St. Briavels, single woman. Possessing twigs of underwood, the property of the duke of Beaufort, without satisfactory explanation. E. Davies JP. Isaac Ellaway of Chapel Hill, Monmouth, woodward to the duke of Beaufort, complainant. First offence. Mitigated fine of 5/- and 7/6 costs. Offence committed 8 Dec. 1813.

33/A/27   15 Oct. 1813. Eleanor wife of James Morgan of St. Briavels. Cutting hazel twigs from a hedge belonging to James Prichard, farmer, of Woolaston. Rev. E. Davies JP and Rev. T. Thomas JP. Offender confessed. First offence. Mitigated fine of 10/- and 7/6 costs. Offence committed 27 Sept. 1813

33/A/28   24 Dec. 1813. George Morgan of Lydney, labourer. Possessing underwood, the property of the Rt. Hon. Charles Bathurst of Lydney Park, without satisfactory explanation. E. Davies JP. John Ducker, steward to Rt. Hon. C. Bathurst, informer. First offence. Fine 40/- and 9/- costs. Offence committed 21 Dec. 1813.

33/A/29   26 Nov. 1813. Joseph Biddington of the hundred of St. Briavels, labourer. Possessing part of an oak tree in the Forest of Dean without satisfactory explanation. Rev. T. Thomas JP. Thomas Miles, woodward, of St. Briavels hundred, informer. Fine 40/- and 7/- costs. Offence committed 15 Nov. 1813.

33/A/30   26 Nov. 1813. William Harris of English Bicknor, farmer. Forcing open the turnpike gate at Coleford and refusing to pay tolls on a cart and three horses. E. Davies JP and Rev. T. Thomas JP. Thomas Godding, turnpike keeper and toll-collector, informer. First offence. Mitigated fine of 40/- and 7/- costs. Offence committed 8 Nov. 1813.

33/A/31   26 Nov. 1813. Richard Knight of Ruardean, coalminer. Possessing a beech tree without satisfactory explanation. Rev. T. Thomas JP. William Court of St. Briavels hundred, informer. Mary Yemm, widow, of St. Briavels hundred, witness. First offence. Mitigated fine of 5/- and 6/6 costs. Offence committed 15 Oct. 1813.

33/A/32   5 Jan. 1814. John Willcox and John Pearce. Found in enclosed ground at Cromhall at 3 a.m., armed, with intent to shoot pheasants in company with John Penny of Littleton [upon Severn]. G. Cooke D.D. JP at Tortworth. James Smith, gamekeeper of the manor of Cromhall Abbots, informer. Committed to Horsley house of correction until next Q.S. or until discharged by due course of law. Offence committed 4 Jan. 1814.

33/B/1   22 Jan. 1814. William White of Maisemore, gentleman. Using a greyhound for taking game at Lassington, without the required certificate. John Turner JP and commissioner for taxes in the hundreds of Dudstone and King's Barton. Fine £20. Offence committed 16 Jan. 1814.

33/B/2   22 Jan. 1814. William White. Using a greyhound to kill a hare at Lassington. Rev. J. B. Cheston JP. First offence. Offence committed Sunday 16 Jan. 1814.

33/B/3   29 Jan. 1814. William Wadley. Using a greyhound to kill a hare in Lassington [*etc.*, *as* 33/B/2].

33/B/4   29 Jan. 1814. William Wadley of Maisemore, gentleman. Using a greyhound for taking game without the required certificate. Rev. J. B. Cheston JP and commissioner for taxes in the hundreds of Dudstone and King's Barton. Fine £20. Offence committed 16 Jan. 1814.

33/B/5   15 April 1814. William Coxhead Hill of Aston Blank, mason. Using a gun with intent to kill a hare at Notgrove. Rev. B. Grisdale JP and John Browne JP. First offence. Mitigated fine of £10. Offence committed between 3 a.m. and 4 a.m. on 3 Feb. 1814.

33/B/6   31 March 1814. Edward Dalby of Bourton on the Water, baker. Exposing four prized wheaten loaves for sale, contrary to notice given by magistrates of Slaughter hundred and the relevant laws. J. Hippisley JP, Francis Edward Witts JP and J. Dolphin JP. Fine 10/- and 5/- costs. Offence committed 15 March 1814.

33/B/7   7 March 1814. Thomas Ockwell of Cricklade St. Sampson, labourer. Using a dog with intent to kill a hare at Down Ampney. J. Cripps JP, E. Wilbraham JP and J. Pitt JP. First offence. Fine £10. Offence committed between 1 a.m. and 2 a.m. on 7 March 1814.

33/B/8   7 March 1814. John Thomas of Cricklade St. Sampson, labourer. Using a dog [etc., as 33/B/7].

33/B/9   7 March 1814. John Hopkins of Cricklade St. Sampson, cooper. Using a dog [etc., as 33/B/7].

33/B/10   4 March 1814. Isaac Teakell of Nailsworth. Buying 5 lb. of stolen woollen yarn from Isaac Taylor, weaver, of Painswick. H. Cooke JP and S. Wathen JP. Mr. Peter Playne, clothier, of Box, Minchinhampton, informer. Isaac Taylor, witness. First offence. Fine £40 or six months in Horsley house of correction. Offence committed 7 Jan. 1814. Conviction quashed on the motion of the prosecutors at the ensuing Easter Sessions.

33/B/11   8 March 1814. William Hopkins of Boddington, yeoman. Assisting William Bridge Esq. in the taking of a hare at Cheltenham, without the required certificate. Sir W. Hicks, Bt., and J. Agg Esq., commissioners for taxes for the district of Cheltenham. Fine £10. Offence committed 15 Feb. 1814. Conviction quashed on appeal at ensuing Easter Sessions.

33/B/12   12 March 1814. Joseph Keavel of Avening, weaver. Buying ends and thrums of stolen woollen yarn from Isaac Taylor, weaver, of Painswick. H. Burgh JP and H. Cooke JP. Mr. William Playne, clothier, of Minchinhampton, informer. Isaac Taylor, witness. Fine £20 or three months in Horsley house of correction. Offence committed early in Feb. 1814.

33/B/13   4 March 1814. Thomas Chandler of Stroud, weaver. Buying 12 lb. of coarse ends of stolen woollen yarn from Isaac Taylor, weaver, of Painswick. H. Cooke JP and S. Wathen JP. Mr. Peter Playne, clothier, of Minchinhampton, informer. Isaac Taylor, witness. Fine £40 or six months in Horsley house of correction. Offence committed c. 22 Feb. 1814.

33/B/14   4 March 1814. James Orpin of Stonehouse, millman. Buying 20 ells of stolen raw cloth from Thomas Chandler, weaver, of Stroud. H. Burgh JP and S. Wathen JP. Mr. Stephen Clissold, clothier, of Stroud, informer. Thomas Chandler, witness. Fine £40 or six months in Horsley house of correction. Offence committed 13 Jan. 1814.

33/B/15   2 March 1814. Thomas Walkley of King's Stanley. Buying 2 lb. of woollen yarn from Edward Clutterbuck, spinner, of Eastington. H. Cooke JP and S. Wathen JP. Mr. Thomas Beard, informer. Edward Clutterbuck, witness. Fine £40 or six months in Horsley house of correction. Offence committed 12 Feb. 1814.

33/B/16   1 March 1814. James Beard of Rodborough, shearman. Buying 2½ lb. of stolen woollen yarn from Edward Tocknell, weaver, of King's Stanley. H. Cooke JP and S. Wathen JP. Mr. Peter Playne, informer. Edward Tocknell, witness. Fine £40 or six months in Horsley house of correction. Offence committed 24 Feb. 1814.

33/B/17   28 Feb. 1814. Thomas Ridler of Horsley, weaver. Buying 8 lb. of stolen Spanish wool from Edward Tocknell, weaver, of King's Stanley. H. Cooke JP and S. Wathen JP. John Clissold Daniell, clothier, of Wellow, Som., informer. Edward Tocknell, witness. Fine £40 or six months in Horsley house of correction. Offence committed 11 Jan. 1814.

33/B/18   26 Jan. 1814. Jabeus Wood of Stroud, weaver. Possessing stolen woollen yarn without satisfactory explanation. H. Burgh JP and S. Wathen JP. William Stanton, clothier, of Stroud, informer. Richard Smith, tithingman of Stroud, witness. First offence. Fine £20 or one month in Horsley house of correction. Offence committed 25 Jan. 1814,

33/B/19   1 April 1814. Joshua Wilkins of Horsley, weaver. Buying 1 lb. of Spanish wool thrums from Joseph Keavill, weaver, of Avening. H. Burgh JP and H. Cooke JP. Peter Playne of Minchinhampton, informer. Abraham son of Joseph Keavill, witness. Fine £20 or three months' hard labour in Horsley house of correction. Offence committed 8 Feb. 1814.

33/B/20   1 April 1814. William Niblett of Minchinhampton, weaver. Buying 4 lb. of Spanish woollen yarn from Joseph Keavill, weaver, of Avening. H. Burgh JP and H. Cooke JP. Peter Playne of Minchinhampton, informer. Ann wife of Joseph Keavill, witness. Fine £20 or three months' hard labour in Horsley house of correction. Offence committed 3 March 1814.

33/B/21   25 Feb. 1814. Henry Organ, Giles Organ and John White. Being in Michael Wood [*MS.* St. Michael Wood], Alkington, carrying an air-gun with intent to shoot pheasants, the property of William Fitzhardinge Berkeley Esq. S. P. Peach JP at Tockington. Mark Cullimore, gamekeeper, informer. Thomas Nelmes, labourer, of Berkeley, witness. Offenders pleaded not guilty. Gun produced as evidence. Committed to Horsley house of correction until next Q.S. or until discharged by due course of law. Offence committed after 10 p.m. on 24 Feb. 1814.

33/B/22   26 March 1814. Richard Painter of Elkstone, labourer. Using a gin to kill game. Sir W. Hicks JP at Cheltenham. Charles Booker, yeoman, of Coberley, prosecutor for the poor of Elkstone, informer. Samuel Lock, yeoman, of Coberley, witness. Fine £5. Offence committed 26 March 1814.

33/C/1   17 June 1814. Elizabeth wife of James Cratchley of King's Stanley, labourer. Selling a piece of woollen cloth, the property of her employer Edward Sheppard, clothier, of Uley. Rev. W. Lloyd Baker JP and Rev. W. Davies JP. Two months' hard labour in Horsley house of correction.

33/D/1   13 Aug. 1814. Mary wife of James Dean of the hundred of St. Briavels, mason. Cutting and damaging a beech tree in the Forest of Dean. Josias Verelst JP, E. Davies JP and Philip John Ducarel JP. John Cooke, woodman, of St. Briavels hundred, complainant. First offence. Fine 40/-, which included 19/- costs. Offence committed 1 Aug. 1814.

33/D/2   18 Aug. 1814. Benjamin Fluck, late of Deerhurst, labourer. Leaving his three daughters and one son chargeable to the parish. Rev. J. Keysall JP. John Stephens of Deerhurst, overseer of the poor, complainant. Offender confessed. Committed to Northleach house of correction until next Q.S. unless discharged earlier by due course of law. Offence committed 24 Dec. 1812.

33/D/3   29 Sept. 1814. Nathaniel Beale of Bourton on the Water. Using a dog to kill game at Upper Slaughter. Hon. and Rev. Edward Rice JP, T. Ireland D.D. JP and Rev. J. Hippisley JP at Stow [on the Wold]. John Dolphin, clerk, of Lower Slaughter, informer. William Butler, labourer, of Upper Slaughter, witness. Fine £5. Offence committed between 10 p.m. and 11 p.m. on 27 Sept. 1814.

34/A/1   6 Oct. 1814. Joseph Cowles of Wheatenhurst, labourer. Cursing. N. Clifford JP. Hannah Proben, widow, of Longney, witness. Offence committed 30 Sept. 1814.

34/A/2   5 Jan. 1815. Morwent Baron of Coleford, Newland, attorney-at-law. Issuing a note for 10/- contrary to law. E. Davies JP. Convicted on own confession. Fine £20 mitigated to £5. Offence committed 16 Dec. 1814.

34/A/3   24 Dec. 1814. Richard Cross of Asthall, Oxon., labourer. Illegal possession of part of a deer at Widford. Hon. and Rev. E. Rice JP. William Eels, deer keeper in Wychwood forest, complainant. Fine £30. Offence committed 28 May 1814.

34/A/4   20 Dec. 1814. James Bryant of Hewelsfield, labourer. Cutting underwood at Tidenham, the property of Rev. T. Thomas. J. Verelst JP [*who did not sign*] and P. J. Ducarel JP. John Phillpotts, labourer, of Tidenham, witness. First offence. Fine 10/- and 5/- costs. Offence committed 18 Nov. 1814.

34/A/5   20 Dec. 1814. Adam Williams of Hewelsfield, labourer. Cutting underwood at Woolaston, the property of James Pritchard, farmer. J. Verelst JP [*who did not sign*] and P. J. Ducarel JP. William Seyner, yeoman, of Hewelsfield, witness. First offence. Fine 10/- and 13/6 costs. Offence committed 3 Dec. 1814.

34/A/6   [*Undated letter from Thomas Lucas to Edward Bloxsome Esq., Deputy Clerk of the Peace, asking that he hand two convictions to Mr. Verelst for his signature before going to court.*]

34/A/7   10 Jan. 1815. [*Letter written by R. (reading uncertain) Knight of Stow on the Wold, by the direction of Rev. Mr. Hurd, to Edward Bloxsome Esq. asking him to file the following conviction at the next Q.S., the relevant fee to be paid at their next meeting.*]

34/A/8   22 Dec. 1814. Richard Herbert, late of Temple Guiting, labourer. Cutting and stealing hazel wood, the property of George Talbot Esq. Rev. John Hurd JP. John Hayward, labourer, of Temple Guiting, witness. Offence committed three weeks previously.

34/A/9   6 Oct. 1814. John Pope. Throwing a quantity of rubbish and filth into the Gloucester and Berkeley canal at the North Hamlet. Rev. J. B. Cheston JP. Offence committed about 10.30 p.m. 1 Oct. 1814.

34/B/1   11 Nov. 1813 [*late return*]. William Perrott of North Nibley, clothworker. Using a ferret and a net to kill conies in Stinchcombe without a certificate. T. J. Lloyd Baker and J. Wallington, tax commissioners, at Dursley. Fine £10. Offence committed 30 Oct. 1813.

34/B/2   11 Nov. 1813 [*late return*]. William Bruton of North Nibley, weaver. Using a ferret [*etc., as* 34/B/1].

34/B/3   11 Nov. 1813 [*late return*]. William Perrott of North Nibley, clothworker. Using a ferret and a net to kill conies in Dursley without a certificate. T. J. Lloyd Baker and J. Wallington, tax commissioners, at Dursley. Fine £10. Offence committed 29 Oct. 1813.

34/B/4   28 Feb. 1815. Joseph Hughes of Wotton under Edge, labourer. Using a ferret and a net to kill conies without a certificate. Rev. W. Lloyd Baker JP and tax commissioner, at Stoutshill. Fine £15 and costs. Offence committed 4 Dec. 1814.

34/B/5   28 Feb. 1815. Joseph Young of Wotton under Edge, labourer. Using a ferret and a net to kill conies without a certificate. Rev. W. Lloyd Baker JP and tax commissioner, at Stoutshill. Fine £20 and costs. Offence committed 4 Dec. 1814.

34/B/6   17 Dec. 1813 [*late return*]. John Fowler of Wotton under Edge, labourer. Using a net for taking and killing conies. W. Lloyd Baker JP and tax commissioner. Fine £10. Offence committed 4 Dec. 1813.

34/B/7   19 Oct. 1814. William Hyde of Wotton under Edge, clothier. Buying and receiving 1 lb. of fine Spanish woollen yarn from Thomas Webb, the property of William Perrin, clothier, of Kingswood, Wotton under Edge. R. Nelmes JP and W. M. Adey JP. Samuel Long, informer. Fine £40 or six months' hard labour in Horsley house of correction. Offence committed 8 Oct. 1814.

34/B/8   22 Feb. 1815. Thomas Chew of King's Stanley, weaver. Stealing a quantity of abb yarn from his employers John Dimock and John Hitch, clothiers, of Stonehouse. H. Burgh JP and H. Cooke JP. Thomas Fox, weaver, of King's Stanley, witness. First offence. Committed to Horsley house of correction for three months.

34/B/9   30 Jan. 1815. John Marshall, mariner, and Sarah his wife of Newnham. Holding a protestant religious meeting in their dwelling house, contrary to law. F. Lawson JP, Rev. C. Sandiford JP and Rev. R. Wetherell JP. John Cooper, yeoman, informer. Clement Chadborn, gentleman, and Elizabeth wife of John Pearce, carpenter, both of Newnham, witnesses. More than 20 persons, apart from immediate family and servants, attended. Mitigated fine of £6. Offence committed 9 Nov. 1814.

34/B/10   13 Feb. 1815. Samuel Cannock *alias* Ferris, labourer, William Deane, labourer, both of Newnham, William Creed, carpenter, of St. Nicholas, Gloucester, and William Mellin the younger, labourer, of Westbury on Severn. Using dogs to kill a hare in Westbury on Severn. F. Lawson JP and Rev. R. Wetherell JP. George Callaghan, yeoman, of Flaxley, informer. William Evans, yeoman, and Anselm Jones, gentleman, both of Westbury on Severn, witnesses. First offence. Fine £20. Offence committed between 9 a.m. and 11 a.m. on Sunday 22 Jan. 1815.

34/B/11   13 Feb. 1815. John Gape of Awre, blacksmith. Using a hay net to kill a hare. F. Lawson JP and Rev. R. Wetherell JP. William Cooke, witness, yeoman, of Newnham, informer. Thomas Sterry, labourer, of Newnham, witness. First offence. Mitigated fine of £10. Offence committed between 3 a.m. and 5 a.m. Sunday 29 Jan. 1815.

34/B/12   27 Feb. 1815. William Clarke of Huntley, labourer. Keeping and using a dog to kill a hare in Longhope. F. Lawson JP and Rev. R. Wetherell JP. James Harris, yeoman, of Longhope, informer. William Sinderby, yeoman, of Huntley, witness. First offence. Fine £20. Offence committed Sunday 22 Jan. 1815.

34/B/13   28 Feb. 1815. William Watkins of Newland, labourer. Using a wire to kill a hare. J. Verelst JP, P. J. Ducarel JP and E. Davies JP. Fine £20. Offence committed Sunday 26 Feb. 1815.

34/B/14   20 Feb. 1815. John Abell of Cirencester, labourer. Keeping and using a dog to kill game at Baunton without being qualified. H. A. Pye JP at Cirencester. John Houlding, butler, of Cirencester, informer. David Whitaker, gamekeeper, of Cirencester, witness. Offender admitted being in the place specified but declared that the dog was not his and was a shepherd's dog, not a lurcher. Fine £5. Offence committed 10 Feb. 1815.

34/C/1   11 May 1815. Charles Bruton of Wotton under Edge, cordwainer. Using a ferret and a net to kill conies without a certificate. Rev. W. Lloyd Baker JP at Stoutshill. Offender absconded from process. Fine £20 and 5/- costs. Offence committed 1 Dec. 1814.

34/C/2   [9 May 1815.] Charles Williams, John Kear, John Cox, William Lea, Edward Jones, Mary Ireland, Charles Campbell, James Butt, Oliver Watts, Sarah Kilmister, all shopkeepers, of Cheltenham. Keeping and using false weights and measures. J. Agg JP and T. Welles D.D. JP. Return of forfeitures. Fine 10/- each. Total of £5 4s. 8d. raised by the sale of false weights. Paid to treasurer of county stock.

34/C/3–13 9 May 1815. [*Names as below.*] Using defective weights. J. Agg JP and T. Welles D.D. JP at a Petty Sessions for Cheltenham division. Fine 10/- and 5/- costs. Offence committed 27 March 1815.

34/C/3   James Butt of Cheltenham, shopkeeper.

34/C/4   Charles Campbell of Cheltenham, shopkeeper.

34/C/5   Oliver Watts of Cheltenham, shopkeeper.

34/C/6   John Kear of Cheltenham, shopkeeper.

34/C/7   Mary Ireland of Cheltenham, shopkeeper.

34/C/8   Charles Williams of Cheltenham, shopkeeper.

34/C/9   William Lea of Cheltenham, shopkeeper.

34/C/10   John Merrett of Cheltenham, shopkeeper [*not named above in* 34/C/2].

34/C/11   John Cox of Cheltenham, shopkeeper.

34/C/12   Sarah Kilmister of Cheltenham, shopkeeper.

34/C/13   Edward Jones of Cheltenham, shopkeeper.

34/C/14   6 June 1815. John Webb of Moreton in Marsh. Knowingly permitting rogues and vagabonds to lodge in his house for one week. Rev. J. Adams JP at Bourton on the Hill. Samuel Purser of Moreton in Marsh, informer. Offender confessed. Fine 40/-. Offence committed 27 May 1815.

34/C/15   13 May 1815. William Jones of Cirencester, mason. Leaving his wife and children chargeable to the parish. J. Cripps JP at Cirencester. Thomas Richardson, a guardian of the poor of Cirencester, informer. Offender pleaded that he had been seeking work in his trade. Committed to Northleach house of correction until next Q.S. unless discharged earlier by due course of law. Offence committed *c.* 9 May 1815.

34/C/16   13 May 1815. William Berriman of Cirencester, carpenter. Leaving his wife and children chargeable to the parish [*etc., as* 34/C/15].

34/D/1   21 Sept. 1815. Sarah Vevers of Horsley, single woman. Being an incorrigible rogue and possessing ends of woollen yarn without satisfactory explanation. E. Wilbraham JP. Richard Sawyer, witness. Committed to Horsley house of correction until next Q.S. to be further dealt with. Offence committed 19 Sept. 1815.

34/D/2–32   4 July 1815. [*Names as below.*] Having defective weights. E. Aldridge JP at a Petty Sessions for Bisley hundred held at the George inn, Stroud [34/D/2 at the King's Arms inn, Stroud; 34/D/3 *omits* for Bisley hundred]. Fine 5/- and 6/6 costs [*except as otherwise stated.*] Offence committed 20 May 1815.

34/D/2   Thomas Mills of Painswick, shopkeeper.

34/D/3   Ann Weeks of Bisley hundred, shopkeeper. [*Fine and date of offence not stated.*]

34/D/4   James Birt of Painswick, shopkeeper. Fine 10/- and 6/6 costs.

34/D/5   Samuel Goddard of Painswick, shopkeeper.

34/D/6   Mary Hanks of Painswick, shopkeeper. Fine 10/- and 6/6 costs.

34/D/7   Nathaniel Rice of Painswick, shopkeeper. Fine 10/- and 6/6 costs.

34/D/8   John Tunley of Painswick, shopkeeper. Fine £1 and 6/6 costs.

34/D/9   James Cooper of Stroud, shopkeeper.

34/D/10   Nathaniel Pierce of Stroud, shopkeeper. Fine 10/- and 6/6 costs.

34/D/11   Edward Merrett of Stroud, shopkeeper. Fine £1 and 6/6 costs.

34/D/12   Robert Adams of Sapperton, shopkeeper. Fine 10/- and 6/6 costs.

34/D/13   Robert Davies of Bisley, shopkeeper.

34/D/14   Samuel Clissold of Bisley, shopkeeper. Fine 10/- and 6/6 costs.

34/D/15   Thomas Lewis of Bisley, shopkeeper. Fine £1 and 6/6 costs.

34/D/16   Mary Lewis of Stroud, shopkeeper. Fine 10/- and 6/6 costs.

34/D/17   William Restall of Bisley, shopkeeper.

34/D/18   Daniel Price of Bisley, shopkeeper. Fine 10/- and 6/6 costs.

34/D/19   Abraham Lewis of Bisley, shopkeeper.

34/D/20	Thomas Stevens of Bisley, shopkeeper.
34/D/21	George Davis of Bisley, shopkeeper.
34/D/22	John Dee of Bisley, shopkeeper.
34/D/23	Mary Lemon of Painswick, shopkeeper. Fine £1 and 6/6 costs.
34/D/24	William Nutley of Painswick, shopkeeper.
34/D/25	William Woodward of Painswick, shopkeeper.
34/D/26	William Gardner of Painswick, shopkeeper.
34/D/27	William Wright of Painswick, shopkeeper.
34/D/28	Mary Holder of Painswick, shopkeeper.
34/D/29	Mary Hitchings of Painswick, shopkeeper. Fine 10/- and 6/6 costs.
34/D/30	James Bethway of Painswick, shopkeeper.
34/D/31	Sarah and Isaac Tyler of Painswick, shopkeepers.
34/D/32	Joseph Beard of Painswick, shopkeeper.

34/D/33   8 Aug. 1815. Richard Taylor of Moreton in Marsh. Opening his shop and exposing fruit for sale on a Sunday. Rev. J. Adams JP. Rev. George Welford, curate of Moreton in Marsh, witness. Fine 5/-. Offence committed Sunday 6 Aug. 1815.

34/D/34   28 Aug. 1815. Samuel Cambridge of Stratton, labourer. Using a net with intent to kill a hare at North Cerney. Rev. H. A. Pye JP and J. Cripps JP. First offence. Fine £20. Offence committed between 9 p.m. and 10 p.m. on 21 Aug. 1815.

34/D/35   18 May 1815. John Nourse of Saul, tin-worker. Cursing. N. Clifford JP. Elizabeth Greening, witness. Offence committed 16 May 1815.

34/D/36   4 Aug. 1815. Richard Constable junior of Tetbury. Refusing to pay a toll of 10/- on 7 cwt. excess weight of coal carried on his narrow-wheeled wagon at the turnpike gate at Dunkirk. Rev. I. W. Horlock JP and Rev. T. Jones JP at a Petty Sessions held at the Cross Hands in Old Sodbury. Information originally given to Henry Charles, duke of Beaufort, by Thomas Andrews, turnpike-gate keeper. Fine 40/-. Offence committed 29 July 1815.

34/D/37   9 Sept. 1815. Hester Niblett of Rodborough, widow. Having about 85 lb. of various woollen yarns and waste in her dwelling house without satisfactory explanation. H. Burgh JP and H. Cooke JP. William Neems, yeoman, of Rodborough, informer. Joseph Neems, witness. Offender pleaded not guilty. First offence. Fine £20 or one month in Horsley house of correction. Offence committed 7 Sept. 1815.

35/A/1   27 Nov. 1815. Nicholas Deane of King's Stanley, weaver. Preventing the arrest of Joseph Lusty and Richard Bird, weavers, of King's Stanley, for stealing wood. [Cf. 35/A/35.] H. Burgh JP. Sir G. O. Paul, complainant. Offender refused to pay £10 fine. Committed to Horsley house of correction to serve six months' hard labour.

35/A/2   2 Dec. 1815. John Brush of Siddington, carpenter. Leaving his wife and family chargeable to the parish. Rev. H. A. Pye JP at Cirencester. Robert Sutton, overseer of the poor, complainant. Offender admitted charge. Committed to Northleach house of correction until next Q.S. unless earlier discharged by due course of law.

35/A/3   30 Oct. 1815. Richard Watts of Lechlade, labourer. Using a snare to kill game at Southrop without a certificate. Rev. John Wolvey Astley JP at Quenington. Richard Baker of Eastleach Turville, informer. Offender admitted charge. Fine £5. Offence committed 14 Oct. 1815.

35/A/4– 26 Oct. 1815. [*Names as below.*] Using defective weights. Rev. C. Sandiford JP and
23 Rev. R. Wetherell JP at a Petty Sessions for the Forest division, held at Newnham. Fine £1 and 6/6 costs [*except* 35/A/12]. Offences committed 19 to 22 Sept. 1815 [*except* 35/A/22].

35/A/4 Elizabeth Clinton of Huntley, shopkeeper.

35/A/5 Anne Williams of Longhope, shopkeeper.

35/A/6 Noah Billingham of Mitcheldean, shopkeeper.

35/A/7 John Gay of Mitcheldean, shopkeeper.

35/A/8 John Wilce of Westbury on Severn, shopkeeper.

35/A/9 William Pegler of Newnham, shopkeeper.

35/A/10 Theophilus Constance of Longhope, shopkeeper.

35/A/11 John Fryer of Newnham, shopkeeper.

35/A/12 John Morse of Newnham, shopkeeper. Fine 5/- and 6/6 costs.

35/A/13 Nathaniel Pensam of Longhope, shopkeeper.

35/A/14 William Gwilliam of Littledean, shopkeeper.

35/A/15 William Price of Lea, shopkeeper.

35/A/16 Martha Gardner of Longhope, shopkeeper.

35/A/17 Elizabeth Plaisted of Newnham, shopkeeper.

35/A/18 Joseph Mountjoy of Littledean, shopkeeper.

35/A/19 Thomas Jones of Longhope, shopkeeper.

35/A/20 William Coleman of Mitcheldean, shopkeeper.

35/A/21 William Howell of Littledean, shopkeeper.

35/A/22 Benjamin Small of Mitcheldean, shopkeeper. Offence committed 20 Nov. last [*sic*].

35/A/23 James Williams of Littledean, shopkeeper.

35/A/24– 26 Oct. 1815. [*Names as below.*] Using non-standard measures. At the above Petty
34 Sessions. Fine 10/- and 6/6 costs. Offences committed 19 to 22 Sept. 1815.

35/A/24 William Nicholls of Westbury on Severn, innkeeper.

35/A/25 George White of Westbury on Severn, innkeeper.

35/A/26 Thomas Gibbons of Westbury on Severn, innkeeper.

35/A/27 William Price of Longhope, innkeeper.

35/A/28 Ann Hall of Westbury on Severn, innkeeper.

35/A/29 Sarah Walters of Westbury on Severn, innkeeper.

35/A/30 John Maddocks of Churcham, innkeeper.

35/A/31 John Morgan of Newnham, innkeper.

35/A/32 Thomas Drinkwater of Huntley, innkeeper.

35/A/33 William Lodge of Lea, innkeeper.

35/A/34 John Hunt of Westbury on Severn, innkeeper.

35/A/35 27 Nov. 1815. Joseph Lusty and Richard Bird of King's Stanley, weavers. Stealing beech wood from trees belonging to Sir G. O. Paul at King's Stanley. H. Burgh JP. Sir G. O. Paul, informer. First offence. J. Lusty fined £5 and R. Bird fined 1/- and 9/3 costs. Offence committed 25 Nov. 1815.

35/A/36 8 Dec. 1815. William Webb of Painswick, nurseryman. Stealing shrubs from a plantation at Steanbridge [*MS*. Steambridge], Painswick, the property of R. L. Townsend D.D. H. Burgh JP. William Darby, gamekeeper, of Painswick, complainant. First offence. Fine £2 [*apparently altered from* £5] and 5/- costs. Offence committed 2 Dec. 1815.

35/A/37   23 Oct. 1815. William James. Cursing and swearing. I. W. Horlock JP.

35/A/38   13 Dec. 1815. Thomas Tombs of Bourton on the Water, labourer. Keeping and using snares with intent to kill game at Farmington. Rev. J. Dolphin JP, commissioner for taxes. Fine £20. Offence committed Sunday 26 Nov. 1815.

35/B/1   13 Feb. 1816. Thomas Spilsbury of Clifford Chambers. Offering prized loaves for sale after prohibition thereof. Rev. John Robert Hall JP. William Horn, yeoman, of Moreton in Marsh, witness. Fine 15/-. Offence committed 28 Jan. 1816.

35/B/2–6   [*Dates and names as below.*] Using defective weights. Rev. J. R. Hall JP. [*Fines as below.*] Offences committed 20 to 28 Jan. 1816

35/B/2   13 Feb. 1816. Michael Stephens of Alderton. Fine 5/-.

35/B/3   30 Jan. 1816. John Bissell of [Chipping] Campden, shopkeeper. Fine 5/-.

35/B/4   30 Jan. 1816. Samuel Rawlins of Moreton in Marsh, shopkeeper. Fine 5/-.

35/B/5   30 Jan. 1816. Mary Downs of [Chipping] Campden, shopkeeper. Fine 15/-.

35/B/6   30 Jan. 1816. Daniel Weston of [Chipping] Campden, shopkeeper. Fine 5/-.

35/B/7–   [*Dates and names as below.*] Using defective measures. Rev. William Boughton JP.
13   [*Fines as below.*] Offence committed 4 to 27 Jan. 1816.

35/B/7   16 Jan. 1816. Henry Proctor of Ebrington, innkeeper. Fine 25/-.

35/B/8   16 Jan. 1816. Ann Horne of Moreton in Marsh, innkeeper. Fine 10/-

35/B/9   16 Jan. 1816. Richard Mealings of Moreton in Marsh, innkeeper. Fine 10/-.

35/B/10   16 Jan. 1816. John Baldwin of [Chipping] Campden, innkeeper. Fine 25/-.

35/B/11   13 Feb. 1816. Ann Washbrook of Shenington, innkeeper. Fine 20/-.

35/B/12   12 March 1816. Thomas Usher of [Chipping] Campden, innkeeper. Fine £1.

35/B/13   16 Jan. 1816. John Jackson of Weston Subedge, innkeeper. Fine 25/-.

35/B/14–   24 Feb. 1816. [*Names as below.*] Using defective weights. Rev. J. R. Hall JP [*except*
20   35/B/15]. Fine 5/-. Offences committed 15, 16 Feb. 1816.

35/B/14   William Osbourne of Welford, blacksmith.

35/B/15   John Barnes of Mickleton, baker. Rev. W. Boughton JP.

35/B/16   John Spencer of Coln St. Dennis, shopkeeper.

35/B/17   William Lea of Welford, shopkeeper.

35/B/18   William Gray of Welford, shopkeeper.

35/B/19   Samuel Hemmings of Mickleton, shopkeeper.

35/B/20   William Fairfax of Mickleton, shopkeeper.

35/B/21–   16 Jan. 1816. [*Names as below.*] Using defective measures. Rev. W. Boughton JP.
2   [*Fines as below.*]

35/B/21   Jeremiah Rush of Clifford Chambers, innkeeper. Fine 20/-. Offence committed 10 Jan. 1816.

35/B/22   Mary Holtom of Pebworth, innkeeper. Fine 15/-. Offence committed 11 Jan. 1816.

35/B/23–   [*Dates and names as below.*] Using defective weights [*except as stated below*]. Rev.
67   J. R. Hall JP. [*Fines as below.*] Offences committed 15 and 16 Feb. 1816 [*except as stated below*].

35/B/23   24 Feb. 1816. John Mills of Welford, blacksmith. Fine 5/-.

35/B/24   24 Feb. 1816. Thomas Edkins of Welford, miller. Fine 5/-.

35/B/25   24 Feb. 1816. John Moore of Pebworth, shopkeeper. Fine 10/-.

35/B/26   24 Feb. 1816. Mary Hathaway of Coln St. Dennis, miller. Fine 5/-.

35/B/27   24 Feb. 1816. Robert Coles of Coln St. Dennis, miller. Fine 5/-.

35/B/28   24 Feb. 1816. Edward Hornsby of Mickleton, blacksmith. Fine 10/-.

35/B/29   13 Feb. 1816. Thomas Adams of Preston [on Stour], baker. Fine 10/-. Offence committed 28 Jan. 1816.

35/B/30   13 Feb. 1816. George Collett of Stanway, baker and miller. Fine 15/-.

35/B/31   24 Feb. 1816. Joseph George of Pebworth, shopkeeper. Fine 10/-. Offence committed 16 Feb. 1816.

35/B/32   13 Feb. 1816. Joseph George of Pebworth, shopkeeper. Offering prized bread for sale after the prohibition thereof. Fine 15/-. Offence committed 28 Jan. 1816

35/B/33   13 Feb. 1816. William Heritage of Preston [on Stour], baker. Fine 5/-.

35/B/34   13 Feb. 1816. Ralph Smith of Clifford Chambers, shopkeeper. Fine 10/-.

35/B/35   13 Feb. 1816. John Garfield of Clifford Chambers, shopkeeper. Fine 5/-.

35/B/36   13 Feb. 1816. Michael Smith of Clifford Chambers, shopkeeper. Fine 5/-.

35/B/37   13 Feb. 1816. Richard Oakley of Alderton, shopkeeper. Offering prized bread for sale after the prohibition thereof. Fine 15/-.

35/B/38   13 Feb. 1816. Edward Nurden of Cutsdean, shopkeeper. Fine 15/-.

35/B/39   13 Feb. 1816. Hannah Beesley of Clifford Chambers, shopkeeper. Offering prized bread for sale after the prohibition thereof. Fine 15/-.

35/B/40   13 Feb. 1816. Richard Wiggett of Cutsdean, shopkeeper. Fine 5/-. Offence committed 26 Jan. 1816.

35/B/41   13 Feb. 1816. Thomas Thornett of Sutton under Brailes, shopkeeper. Fine 10/-. Offence committed 27 Jan. 1816.

35/B/42   13 Feb. 1816. William Goffe of Little Compton [*MS.* Compton Parva], shopkeeper. Fine 5/-. Offence committed 25 Jan. 1816.

35/B/43   13 Feb. 1816. Richard Harris of Sutton under Brailes, miller. Fine 5/-. Offence committed 27 Jan. 1816.

35/B/44   13 Feb. 1816. Edward Nurden of Cutsdean, retailer. Fine 10/-. Offence committed 26 Jan. 1816.

35/B/45   13 Feb. 1816. James Roberts of Alderton, baker. Offering prized bread for sale after the prohibition thereof. Fine 15/-. Offence committed 28 Jan. 1816.

35/B/46   13 Feb. 1816. William Wyatt of Clifford Chambers, shopkeeper. Fine 10/-.

35/B/47   13 Feb. 1816. William Butler of Shenington, butcher. Fine 10/-. Offence committed 27 Jan. 1816.

35/B/48   13 Feb. 1816. Thomas Butler of Preston [on Stour], shopkeeper. Fine 10/-.

35/B/49   13 Feb. 1816. John Garfield of Clifford Chambers, shopkeeper. Offering prized bread for sale after the prohibition thereof. Fine 15/-.

35/B/50   13 Feb. 1816. David Buffery of Shenington, miller.
35/B/51   13 Feb. 1816. Joseph Gunn of Shenington, shopkeeper.
35/B/52   13 Feb. 1816. Richard Upton of Shenington, shopkeeper.   } Fine 5/- each. Offences committed 27 Jan. 1816.
35/B/53   13 Feb. 1816. Joseph Smith of Shenington, baker.
35/B/54   13 Feb. 1816. George Boyce of Shenington, baker.

35/B/55   13 Feb. 1816. Hannah Beesley of Clifford Chambers, shopkeeper. Fine 5/-. Offence committed 28 Jan. 1816.

35/B/56   30 Jan. 1816. Richard Emms of [Chipping] Campden, [butcher].   } Fine 5/- each.
35/B/57   30 Jan. 1816. John Freeman of Todenham, shopkeeper.   } Offences committed
35/B/58   30 Jan. 1816. Mary Clark of Moreton in Marsh, shopkeeper.   } 17 to 23 Jan. 1816.

35/B/59   13 Feb. 1816. Henry Baughan of Little Compton, shopkeeper.   Fine 5/- each.

35/B/60   13 Feb. 1816. Hannah Harris of Little Compton.   Offences committed

35/B/61   13 Feb. 1816. James Mace of Little Compton, shopkeeper.   25 Jan. 1816.

35/B/62   30 Jan. 1816. Joseph James of [Chipping] Campden, shopkeeper. Fine 15/-.   Offences

35/B/63   30 Jan. 1816. Thomas Horn of Moreton in Marsh, shopkeeper. Fine 5/-.   committed

35/B/64   30 Jan. 1816. Charlotte Keyte of [Chipping] Campden, shopkeeper. Fine 5/-   17 to 20

35/B/65   30 Jan. 1816. George Matthews of [Chipping] Campden, shopkeeper. Fine 5/-.   Jan. 1816.

35/B/66   13 Jan. [*sic*] 1816. William Randall of Todenham, shopkeeper. Fine 10/-. Offence committed 23 Jan. 1816

35/B/67   30 Jan. 1816. William Cork of [Chipping] Campden, baker. Fine 5/-. Offence committed 20 Jan. 1816.

35/B/68   26 March 1816. George Andrews the elder. Swearing and cursing. I. W. Horlock JP.

35/B/69   2 Feb. 1816. William Wall of Westerleigh, coal-carrier. Forcibly driving his wagon and three horses through the Isle of Ree turnpike gate in Westerleigh and refusing to pay tolls. Rev. T. Jones JP and I. W. Horlock JP at a Petty Sessions held at the Cross Hands at Old Sodbury. Information given by Daniel Ashmead, toll-collector of Westerleigh, on 27 Jan. 1816 at Wickwar. Fine 40/-. Offence committed 6 Jan. 1816.

35/B/70   2 Feb. 1816. Richard Constable senior of Tetbury. Refusing to pay tolls on a wagon and four horses at the turnpike gate in Dunkirk, Hawkesbury. Rev. T. Jones JP and I. W. Horlock JP at the above Petty Sessions. Information given to duke of Beaufort on 16 Jan. 1816 by Thomas Andrews, turnpike-gate keeper. Fine 40/-. Offence committed 23 Dec. 1815.

35/B/71   15 March 1816. William Axon of Horsley, weaver. Failing to return about 4 lb. of wool given him to weave by Joseph Cam, clothier, of Wotton under Edge on 20 Jan. 1816. W. M. Adey JP. First offence.

35/B/72   1 March 1816. John Partridge the younger of Stroud, dyer. Forcibly riding his horse through the turnpike gate at Bowbridge, Stroud, and refusing to pay tolls. S. Wathen JP. Fine £5.

35/B/73   18 March 1816. Edward Cox(e). Using a snare for killing hares at Little Rissington. Rev. Richard Wilbraham Ford JP. Robert Bu[. . .], yeoman, of Little Rissington, informer. Offence committed Sunday 17 March 1816. [*MS. damaged and incomplete.*]

35/B/74   26 March 1816. Daniel Arnold of Cirencester, slater and plasterer. Leaving his wife and family chargeable to the parish. Rev. H. A. Pye JP. Thomas Richardson, guardian of the poor, complainant. Offender said he was seeking work in his trade. Committed to Northleach house of correction until next Q.S. unless discharged earlier. Offence committed 23 March 1816.

35/B/75   7 Feb. 1816. George Bishop, John Champion, Thomas Pollard, Charles Curtis and Samuel Page of Cheltenham, labourers, and Thomas Ashmead of Charlton Kings, sawyer. Entering enclosed ground in Cowley in order to kill hares. Sir W. Hicks JP. John Cossens, fishmonger, of Cheltenham, informer. John Hawker, witness. Committed to Northleach house of correction until next Q.S. unless discharged earlier. Offence committed 18 Jan. 1816. [*MS. damaged and perhaps incomplete.*]

35/C/1   10 July 1816. John Harper of Stroud, labourer. Stealing timber from Pen Wood, King's Stanley. H. Burgh JP at Stroud. Sir G. O. Paul, complainant. Fine £20 and 12/- costs. Offence committed 4 June 1816

35/C/2   10 July 1816. Richard Leech of Stroud, labourer. Stealing timber [*etc.*, *as* 35/C/1].

35/C/3   10 July 1816. Thomas Barnfield of Stroud, labourer. Stealing timber [*etc.*, *as* 35/C/1].

35/C/4   10 July 1816. William Holmes of Stroud, labourer. Stealing timber [*etc.*, *as* 35/C/1].

35/C/5   5 Feb. 1816. Joseph Brown of Stroud, weaver. Possessing two pieces of broadcloth without satisfactory explanation. H. Burgh JP and H. Cooke JP. Robert Keene, clothworker, of Stroud, informer. Richard Smith, weaver, of Stroud, witness. First offence. Fine £20 or one month in Horsley house of correction.

35/C/6–   21 June 1816. [*Names as below.*] Using defective weights. H. Burgh JP and S. Wathen
12   JP at a Petty Sessions held at Stroud for the hundred of Bisley. Fine 20/- and 8/6 costs [*except* 35/C/7]. Offence committed 11 June 1816.

35/C/6   John Critchley of Stonehouse, shopkeeper. [*MS. gives the year of conviction as* 1812.]

35/C/7   Peter Bourne of Stroud, salt dealer. Using defective weights in Eastington. Fine 5/- and 8/6/ costs.

35/C/8   William Critchley of Whitminster, coal dealer.

35/C/9   Richard Franklin of Stonehouse, coal dealer.

35/C/10   The Company of Proprietors of the Stroudwater Navigation, coal dealer. Using defective weights at Whitminster. [*The MS. is much altered, giving the justices as* H. Burgh JP and E. Aldridge JP at a Petty Sessions for the hundred of Whitstone, *but it is signed by* S. Wathen *instead of* E. Aldridge.]

35/C/11   Ambrose Beard of Whitminster, coal dealer.

35/C/12   Thomas Vezey of Stonehouse, coal dealer.

35/C/13   13 May 1816. William Evans of Horsley, weaver. Possessing woollen yarn without satisfactory explanation. H. C. Clifford JP and Rev. W. Lloyd Baker JP. Mr. George Daniel Harris, informer. Fine £20. Offence committed 10 May 1816.

35/C/14   13 May 1816. Joshua Wilkins of Horsley, weaver. Possessing woollen yarn [*etc.*, *as* 35/C/13].

35/C/15   13 May 1816. Joseph Hyde of Horsley, weaver. Possessing woollen yarn [*etc.*, *as* 35/C/13].

35/C/16–   21 May 1816. [*Names as below.*] Using defective weights. J. Agg JP and Robert Capper
37   JP at a Petty Sessions for Cheltenham division. Each fined 10/- and 5/- costs. Offences committed 2 May 1816.

35/C/16   William Gyde of Cheltenham, grocer.

35/C/17   George Randall of Cheltenham, shopkeeper.

35/C/18   Peter Ryan of Cheltenham, butcher.

35/C/19   John Kear of Cheltenham, shopkeeper.

35/C/20   Robert Merchant of Cheltenham, shopkeeper.

35/C/21   Edward Smith of Cheltenham, baker.

35/C/22   Peter Butt of Cheltenham, grocer.

35/C/23   Susannah Dunscombe of Cheltenham, shopkeeper.

35/C/24   Charles Williams of Cheltenham, shopkeeper.

35/C/25   William Gore of Cheltenham, shopkeeper.

35/C/26   James Barnes of Cheltenham, shopkeeper.

35/C/27   Thomas Bullock of Cheltenham, shopkeeper.

35/C/28   James Brookes of Cheltenham, shopkeeper.

35/C/29   Edward Jones of Alstone, Cheltenham, shopkeeper.

35/C/30   James Hodges of Cheltenham, grocer.

35/C/31   Sarah Cole of Cheltenham, dealer.

35/C/32   James Carroll of Cheltenham, shopkeeper.

35/C/33   William Long of Cheltenham, baker.

35/C/34   Thomas Avery of Cheltenham, shopkeeper.

35/C/35   Thomas Pratt of Cheltenham, shopkeeper.

35/C/36   Thomas Smith of Cheltenham, grocer.

35/C/37   William Kemnett of Cheltenham, shopkeeper.

35/C/38   12 June 1816. Elizabeth Martin of Hewelsfield, spinster. Possessing underwood, the property of the duke of Beaufort, without satisfactory explanation. J. Verelst JP and Rev. T. Thomas JP. Isaac Ellaway of Chapel Hill, Monmouth, woodward to the duke of Beaufort, witness. First offence. Fine 20/-. Offence committed 6 May 1816.

35/C/39   12 June 1816. John Vincent the younger of Hewelsfield, trowman. Possessing underwood [*etc., as* 35/C/38].

35/C/40   19 Feb. 1816. George Workman of North Nibley, farmer. Using three dogs to kill conies, without obtaining the required certificate. H. C. Clifford JP and commissioner for taxes, at Stinchcombe. Fine £10. Offence committed 28 Jan. 1816.

35/C/41   19 Feb. 1816. Elijah Hill of North Nibley, weaver. Using three dogs [*etc., as* 35/C/40].

35/C/42   19 Feb. 1816. Abraham Perrett of North Nibley, clothier. Using three dogs [*etc., as* 35/C/40, *except, apparently in error,*] Offence committed 8 Jan. 1816.

35/C/43   19 Feb. 1816. Matthew Robinson of North Nibley, farmer. Using three dogs [*etc., as* 35/C/40].

35/C/44   29 Jan. 1816. Samuel Bruton of North Nibley, labourer. Using a dog, a ferret and nets for killing conies in Stinchcombe without a certificate. H. C. Clifford JP. Fine £20. Offence committed 9 Dec. 1815.

35/C/45   29 Jan. 1816. Isaac Trotman of North Nibley, labourer. Using a dog [*etc., as* 35/C/44, *except*] Fine £10.

35/C/46   29 Jan. 1816. Christopher Gazard of North Nibley, labourer. Using a dog, a ferret and nets for killing conies in North Nibley without a certificate. H. C. Clifford JP. Fine £10. Offence committed 18 Dec. 1815.

35/C/47   29 Jan. 1816. William Read of North Nibley, labourer. Using a dog, a ferret and nets for killing conies in Stinchcombe without a certificate. H. C. Clifford JP. Fine £10. Offence committed 9 Dec. 1815.

35/C/48   9 Dec. 1815 [*late return*]. John Coats of Cranham, labourer, and Bartley Davis of Brimpsfield, tailor. Possessing and exposing 17 hares for sale in Bisley. E. Aldridge JP at Stroud. William Harris, gamekeeper, of Stroud, informer. Samuel Fowler, witness. John Coats did not appear. Fine £85 (£5 for each hare). Offence committed 7 Dec. 1815.

35/C/49   6 Jan. 1816 [*late return*]. Bartley Davis of Brimpsfield, tailor, and John Coates of Cranham, labourer. Possessing [*etc., as* 35/C/48 *except*] Bartley Davis did not appear.

35/C/50   9 Feb. 1816. Thomas Neale, maltster. Failing to notify the excise officer of his intention to make malt at the parish of St. Philip and St. Jacob, Bristol. Charles Joseph Harford JP and G. Goldney JP at the sessions house, Lawfords Gate, Bristol. Abraham Cutts, excise officer, complainant. Thomas Fisher and Giles T[ur]berville, excise officers, seized 668 bushels of malt and corn being made into malt. Fine £400 also. Offence committed 20 Nov. 1815.

35/D/1   [12] Feb. 1816. William Burgum of the hundred of St. Briavels, labourer. Cutting underwood in Badcocks Bailey. Rev. C. Sandiford JP and Rev. R. Wetherell JP. John White, forest keeper, and Richard Jones, labourer, both of St. Briavels hundred, witnesses. First offence. Fine £2 and 5/6 [*sc.* costs]. Offence committed 22 Dec. 1815.

35/D/2   11 March 1816. Thomas Davis of Westbury on Severn, labourer. Cutting and stealing hazel wood in Chestnuts enclosure. Rev. C. Sandiford JP and Rev. R. Wetherell JP. John White, yeoman, of St. Briavels hundred, witness. First offence. Fine 10/- and 3/6 costs.

35/D/3   7 Oct. 1816. George Smith of St. Briavels hundred, labourer. Possessing one oak limb and several beech sticks without permission. Rev. C. Sandiford JP and Rev. R. Wetherell JP. John White and John Cooke, forest keepers, witnesses. First offence. Fine £1 and 7/- costs. Offence committed 20 Aug. 1816.

35/D/4   12 Feb. 1816. William Webb of Lea Bailey, labourer. Cutting out a beech tree in Lea Bailey. Rev. C. Sandiford JP and Rev. R. Wetherell JP. Elizabeth Smith of St. Briavels hundred, witness. First offence. Fine 10/- and 10/6 costs.

35/D/5   15 Jan. 1816. James Hodges of St. Briavels hundred, labourer. Cutting out several young oak trees in Lea Bailey. Rev. R. Wetherell JP. Letitia Price of St. Briavels hundred, witness. First offence. Fine £2 and 10/- costs.

35/D/6   6 Sept. 1816. John Barnard of Stonehouse, shopkeeper. Exposing underweight bread for sale. H. Burgh JP. Fine 10/-. Offence committed 2 Sept. 1816.

35/D/7   11 Oct. 1816. Edward Brainsford of Painswick. Hiring out one horse to draw a gig 6 miles without recording the ninepence duty thereon. H. Burgh JP at Stroud. Samuel Shipley of Oxford, collector of post-horse duties, witness. Offender pleaded not guilty. Fine £5. Offence committed 23 July 1816.

35/D/8   11 Oct. 1816. Edward Brainsford of Painswick. Hiring out 2 horses to draw a chaise 14 miles without issuing the necessary ticket. [*Fine not specified.*] Offence committed 14 July 1816.

35/D/9   11 Oct. 1816. Edward Brainsford of Painswick. Hiring out a horse to draw a gig 3 miles without recording the four and a half pence duty thereon. Fine £5. Offence committed 20 July 1816.

35/D/10   11 Oct. 1816. Edward Brainsford of Painswick. Hiring out 2 horses to draw a chaise 14 miles and recording only 1/9 duty thereon instead of the required 3/6. Fine £5. Offence committed 14 July 1816.

35/D/11   12 Oct. 1816. William Wilkins of Minchinhampton, labourer. Stealing a piece of coal valued at threepence, the property of Richard Miller, merchant, of Minchinhampton. S. Wathen JP. George Richardson, witness. First offence. Fine 1/- and 5/- costs. Offence committed 11 Oct. 1816.

35/D/12   5 Aug. 1816. Samuel Hall junior of Arlingham. Swearing. Charles Owen Cambridge JP. John Townsend, labourer, of Arlingham, witness. Offence committed 28 July 1816.

35/D/13   7 Sept. 1816. Thomas Freeman. Leaving his wife and child chargeable to the parish of Alderton. Rev. J. Timbrill JP at Beckford. Robert Stephens, overseer of the poor of Alderton, complainant. Offender admitted guilt. Committed to Northleach house of correction until next Q.S. or until sooner discharged by due course of law.

35/D/14   4 Oct. 1816. Samuel Cleavely, late of Coates, labourer. Leaving his wife and children twelve months previously, whereby they became chargeable to the parish. Rev. H. A. Pye JP at Cirencester. Harry Howell, overseer of the poor of Coates, complainant. Offender admitted guilt. Committed to Northleach house of correction to be dealt with at next Q.S. unless earlier discharged by due course of law.

35/D/15 12 Aug. 1816. Thomas Butler of Cirencester, mason. Using a snare to kill game in Baunton. J. Cripps JP at Cirencester. Thomas Neale, labourer, of Cirencester, informer. David Whitaker, gamekeeper, witness. Offender admitted having a snare but declared that he had picked it up in a copse in Baunton. Fine £5. Offence committed 9 p.m. on 5 Aug. 1816.

36/A/1 20 Sept. 1816. Hester Niblett of Rodborough. Possessing firewood believed to be stolen. H. Burgh JP. Fine 10/- and 6/6 costs. Offence committed 1 Sept. 1816.

36/A/2 13 Jan. 1817. Anthony Cooper of Littledean, labourer. Cutting and stealing one store ash pole from Linnegars Wood, Flaxley, the property of Sir T. Crawley Boevey. R. Wetherell JP and C. Sandiford JP. George Callaghan, gamekeeper, of Flaxley, complainant. First offence. Fine £2 and 6/6 costs. Offence committed 4 Jan. 1817.

36/A/3 6 Dec. 1816. Nathaniel Lusty of King's Stanley, weaver. Posssessing about 4½ lb. of various woollen yarns believed to be stolen. H. Cooke JP, S. Wathen JP and E. Aldridge JP at Stroud. James Hogg, clothier, of Ebley, informer. Samuel Antill, weaver, of King's Stanley, witness. Fine £20 or one month in Horsley house of correction. Offence committed 5 Dec. 1816.

36/A/4 Return of fines received by J. Timbrill D.D. JP and Rev. J. Keysall JP, acting for the lower divisions of the hundreds of Deerhurst, Tewkesbury, Westminster and Kiftsgate, from persons convicted of having defective weights.

Received of 14 persons on 30 Oct. 1816 [*cf.* 36/A/5]	£10 15*s*.
Produce of false weights broken and sold	3*s*. 11*d*.
	£10 18*s*. 11*d*.
By amount ordered by us to be paid for expenses to Richard Freeman the inspector	£10 18*s*. 11*d*.

36/A/5 30 Oct. 1816. [*List of those fined for*] Having non-standard weights. J. Timbrill D.D. JP and Rev. J. Keysall JP at a Petty Sessions held at Mr. Fryer's office in Tewkesbury. All convicted on own confession. Offences committed 30 Sept. to 19 Oct. 1816. Fines as indicated. Also charged 4/- each in costs.

Isaac Daves of Apperley, baker, 15/-.

Ann Dobbins of Corse, shopkeeper, 10/-.

William Broadstock of Corse, shopkeeper, £1.

Thomas Garn, £1, and John Seymour, £1, both of Forthampton, shopkeepers.

John Buckle of Hayden and Withy Bridge, miller, 10/-.

George Webb, baker, 10/-, Joseph Roberts, £1, Sarah Wilkes, 10/-, and Joseph Troughton, £1, shopkeepers, all of Kemerton.

Joshua Weaver of the Leigh, shopkeeper, £1.

William Chandler of Oxenton, miller, £1.

Samuel Davis of Pamington, butcher, 10/-.

Richard Rammell of Twyning, shopkeeper, 10/-.

36/A/6 29 Oct. 1816. William Greenaway of Thornbury, labourer. Leaving his wife and child chargeable to the parish. Rev. Richard Slade JP at Thornbury. George Hayward, overseer of the poor, informer. Offender apprehended in Evesham, Worcs. Committed to Gloucester gaol to be brought up at next Q.S. Offence committed *c*. 25 Oct. 1816.

36/B/1 14 April 1817. George Sly of Cheltenham, yeoman. Keeping a snare to kill game in Coberley. J. Agg JP. James Holtham, yeoman and prosecutor for the poor of Coberley, informer. Samuel Lock, yeoman, of Coberley, witness. Fine £5. Offence committed 22 Feb. 1817.

36/B/2   10 April 1817. John Webb of Staverton, labourer. Cutting down and stealing four elm stocks at Staverton or Boddington, the property of Rev. John Neale of Staverton. J. Agg JP. Rev. J. Neale, complainant. Fine £10. Offence committed 23 March 1817.

36/B/3   11 Feb. 1817. Richard Howman of Chipping Campden, labourer. Possessing one hare and several snares in Aston Subedge. Rev. W. Boughton JP and Rev. Charles White JP at Bourton on the Hill. Rev. Morgan Graves of Mickleton, informer. George Dance, witness. Fine £5. Offence committed 26 Jan. 1817.

36/B/4   8 Feb. 1817. Joseph Mills of Rodborough, weaver. Possessing 7 lb. of woollen yarn believed to be stolen. J. Clutterbuck JP and Rev. Henry Campbell JP at Minchinhampton. William Close, clothworker, of Avening, informer. Cornelius Blackwell, clothier, of Avening, witness. Fine £20 or one month in Horsley house of correction. Offence committed 4 Feb. 1817.

36/C/1–   21 June 1817. [*Names as below.*] Having defective weights. H. Burgh JP, J. Clutterbuck
50   JP and H. Campbell JP. William Sinkwell, inspector of weights for Longtree hundred, witness. Each fined 5/- and 8/6 costs [*except as otherwise stated.*] Offences committed 2 and 16 June 1817.

36/C/1   Mary Hopkins of Rodborough, shopkeeper.

36/C/2   William Chapman of Rodborough, shopkeeper.

36/C/3   Sarah Wolford of Rodborough, [shopkeeper].

36/C/4   Elizabeth Creed of Woodchester, shopkeeper.

36/C/5   Sarah Browning of Woodchester, shopkeeper.

36/C/6   William Hill of Woodchester, butcher.

36/C/7   Samuel Clark of Woodchester, shopkeeper.

36/C/8   Solomon Fisher of Woodchester, shopkeeper.

36/C/9   William Horlock of Woodchester, baker.

36/C/10   William Summers of Woodchester, shopkeeper.

36/C/11   William Quarrington of Woodchester, shopkeeper. Fine 10/-.

36/C/12   Susannah Niblett of Rodborough, shopkeeper.

36/C/13   William Antill of Rodborough, maltster.

36/C/14   Benjamin Antill of Rodborough, shopkeeper.

36/C/15   William Cook of Minchinhampton, baker.

36/C/16   Philip Carter of Minchinhampton, coal dealer.

36/C/17   Vilot [*sic*] Hicks of Minchinhampton, shopkeeper. Fine 10/-.

36/C/18   James Horton of Michinhampton, coal dealer. Fine £1.

36/C/19   Robert Iles of Minchinhampton, maltster.

36/C/20   Samuel Tainty of Minchinhampton, shopkeeper.

36/C/21   James Hart of Minchinhampton, coal dealer.

36/C/22   Thomas Dutton of Minchinhampton, shopkeeper.

36/C/23   Susannah Davis of Minchinhampton, shopkeeper.

36/C/24   Isaac Wakefield of Minchinhampton, baker.

36/C/25   George Thomas of Minchinhampton, shopkeeper. Fine 10/-.

36/C/26   John Tanner of Minchinhampton, shopkeeper.

36/C/27   John Baker of Minchinhampton, shopkeeper.

36/C/28   Thomas Clark of Minchinhampton, shopkeeper.

36/C/29   William Edwards of Minchinhampton, shopkeeper. Fine 10/-.

36/C/30   John Chambers of Minchinhampton, shopkeeper.

36/C/31   James Critchley of Minchinhampton, shopkeeper.

36/C/32   Thomas Scrivens of Minchinhampton, shopkeeper.

36/C/33   William Heaven of Minchinhampton, shopkeeper.

36/C/34   Samuel Jenkins of Horsley, baker.

36/C/35   Thomas Alder of Minchinhampton, shopkeeper.

36/C/36   Elizabeth Evans of Minchinhampton, shopkeeper. Fine 10/-.

36/C/37   Thomas Cook the younger of Horsley, mealman.

36/C/38   Benjamin Gillman of Horsley, shopkeeper.

36/C/39   William Hillier of Horsley, shopkeeper.

36/C/40   Cornelius Farmiloe of Horsley, shopkeeper.

36/C/41   John Gillman of Horsley, shopkeeper.

36/C/42   Thomas Cooke the elder of Horsley, shopkeeper.

36/C/43   Isaac Brinkworth of Horsley, shopkeeper.

36/C/44   Joseph Farmiloe of Horsley, shopkeeper.

36/C/45   William Lord the younger of Horsley, shopkeeper.

36/C/46   Thomas Davis of Avening, shopkeeper.

36/C/47   Mary Heiron of Avening, shopkeeper. Fine £1.

36/C/48   Alice Deane of Avening, shopkeeper. Fine 10/-

36/C/49   Abraham Cox of Avening, shopkeeper. Fine 10/-.

36/C/50   Robert Ferley of Avening, shopkeeper.

36/C/51   25 March 1817. Edward Wyatt of Stroud, baker. Selling and exposing for sale a sixpenny loaf contrary to statute. S. Wathen JP. Thomas Hall, labourer, of Stroud (who paid 5½d. for a 6d. loaf), witness. Fine 10/- and 7/6/ costs. Offence committed 19 Feb. 1817.

36/C/52   28 April 1817. William Elton of St. Briavels hundred. Unlawful possession of part of a red or fallow deer. Rev. C. Sandiford JP and Rev. R. Wetherell JP. Rev. Charles Crawley, complainant. George Callaghan, gamekeeper, witness. Fine £30. Offence committed 25 Jan. 1817.

36/C/53   7 Feb. 1817. Thomas Smith of King's Stanley, weaver. Possessing 26¼ lb. of various woollen yarns believed to be stolen. H. Burgh JP and H. Cooke JP. Paul Beard, clothier, of King's Stanley, informer. Thomas Bliss of Stroud, witness. Fine £20 or one month in Horsley house of correction. Offence committed 21 Jan. 1817.

36/C/54   25 Feb. 1817. Joseph Wood of Horsley, weaver. Possessing about two yards of undressed cloth believed to be stolen. H. Burgh JP, H. Cooke JP and Rev. H. Campbell JP. Thomas Bliss, informer. Joseph Hyde, weaver, of Horsley, witness. Fine £20 or one month in Horsley house of correction. Offence committed 22 Feb. 1817.

36/C/55   4 Feb. 1817. Hannah wife of Samuel Antill of King's Stanley, weaver. Buying 5 lb. of woollen yarn, 5 lb. of ends of yarn, from Hannah wife of Thomas Rudder of Stroud, clothworker, knowing it to be the property Samuel Clutterbuck and Henry Eycott of Stroud, clothiers. H. Burgh JP and H. Cooke JP. S. Clutterbuck, informer. Fine £40 or three months' hard labour in Horsley house of correction. Offence committed c. Nov. 1816.

36/C/56   4 Feb. 1817. James Bidmead of Bisley, labourer. Buying 6 lb. of woollen ends and 6 lb. of wool, the property of S. Clutterbuck and H. Eycott, clothiers, of Stroud, knowing it to be stolen. H. Burgh JP and H. Cooke JP. S. Clutterbuck, informer. Hannah wife of Thomas Rudder of Stroud, witness. Fine £40 or three months' hard labour in Horsley house of correction. Offence committed c. Nov. 1816.

36/C/57–64 6 June 1817. [*Names as below.*] Having defective weights. H. Burgh JP [and] H. Campbell JP. George Mynett, inspector of weights for Bisley hundred, witness. [*Fines as below.*] Offences committed 28 April to 3 May 1817.

36/C/57 John Haydon of Painswick, shopkeeper. Fine £1 and 7/6/ costs.

36/C/58 James Aldridge of Stroud, shopkeeper. Fine 17/6 and 7/6 costs.

36/C/59 John Buck of Stroud, shopkeeper. Fine 7/6 and 7/- costs.

36/C/60 William Wright of Painswick, shopkeeper. Fine 2/6 and 7/6/ costs.

36/C/61 Samuel Gardner of Painswick, shopkeeper. Fine 5/- and 7/6 costs.

36/C/62 Richard Gardner of Painswick, shopkeeper. Fine 12/6 and 7/6 costs.

36/C/63 James Cooper of Painswick, shopkeeper. Fine 10/- and 7/6 costs.

36/C/64 Ann Weeks of Painswick, shopkeeper. Fine 5/- and 7/6 costs.

36/C/65 25 March 1817. Thomas Dimmock of Stroud, baker. Selling and exposing for sale a sixpenny loaf, contrary to statute. S. Wathen JP. Thomas Hall, labourer, of Stroud (who paid 5½d. for a 6d. loaf), witness. Fine 10/- and 7/6 costs. Offence committed 19 Feb. 1817.

36/C/66 25 March 1817. William Hawkins of Stroud, baker. Selling and exposing for sale a sixpenny loaf, contrary to statute. S. Wathen JP. Thomas Hall, labourer, of Stroud, witness. Fine 10/- and 7/6 costs.

36/C/67 25 March 1817. William Hawkins of Stroud, baker. Selling and exposing for sale a sixpenny loaf, contrary to statute. S. Wathen JP. John Restall, labourer, of Stroud, witness. Fine 10/- and 7/6 costs.

36/C/68 4 July 1817. William Dead of Bristol, stage-coach driver (from Cirencester to Bristol). Furiously driving against another coach in Old Sodbury, endangering the passengers therein. I. W. Horlock JP [and] Francis Pelly JP at a Petty Sessions held at Old Sodbury. Information given to Fitzherbert Brooke JP at Yate by Rev. Thomas Brooke LL.D. (coach passenger) on 27 June 1817. Isaac Cleeter, witness. Driver refused to give his name at time of offence. Fine 40/-. Offence committed 26 June 1817.

36/C/69 [*Copy of* 36/C/68.]

36/C/70 29 May 1817. William Longney of Arlingham, waterman. Swearing. C. O. Cambridge JP.

36/C/71 26 April 1817. John Lediard of Kingsholm, turnpike-gate keeper and renter of tolls. Charging excessive tolls. Rev. Samuel Commeline JP at Gloucester. John McLaren, complainant. Fine £5. Offence committed 18 April 1817.

36/C/72 26 April 1817. John Lediard of Kingsholm, turnpike-gate keeper. Charging excessive tolls. Rev. S. Commeline JP. John Spencer, complainant. Fine £5. Offence committed 17 April 1817.

36/D/1 15 Jan. 1817 [*late return*]. James Hodges of Lea Bailey, labourer. Cutting several young oak trees in the Forest of Dean. Rev. R. Wetherell JP. Letitia Price, single woman, of St. Briavels hundred, witness. First offence. Fine £2 and 10/- costs. Offence committed 12 Dec. 1816.

36/D/2 12 Feb. 1817 [*late return*]. William Webb of Lea Bailey, labourer. Cutting a beech tree in the Forest of Dean. Rev. C. Sandiford JP and Rev. R. Wetherell JP. Elizabeth Smith, single woman, of Weston [under Penyard], Herefs., witness. First offence. Mitigated fine of 10/- and 7/- costs. Offence committed 16 Jan. 1817.

36/D/3   29 June 1817. William Burgum of St. Briavels hundred, labourer. Cutting hazel underwood in Badcocks Bailey. Rev. C. Sandiford JP and Rev. R. Wetherell JP. Richard Jones, woodward, of St. Briavels hundred, witness. First offence. Fine £2 and 6/6 costs. Offence committed 22 Jan. 1817.

36/D/4   8 Oct. 1817. William Bolton of Bishop's Cleeve, toll-collector. Taking unauthorized toll from Joseph Benedict Tidmarsh on his return from religious worship in Cheltenham. J. Timbrill D.D. JP at Beckford. J. B. Tidmarsh of Beckford, informer. Stephen Farmer, witness. Fine 40/-. Offence committed 21 Sept. 1817.

36/D/5   13 Aug. 1817. Thomas Dickenson of Bisley, labourer. Depasturing one scabby or mangy sheep on Bisley common, contrary to statute. E. Aldridge JP. Joseph Fawkes, labourer, of Bisley, witness. Fine £1.

36/D/6   15 Sept. 1817. Thomas Baldwin of Bisley, yeoman. Depasturing four scabby or mangy sheep on Bisley common. E. Aldridge JP. Joseph Fawkes, labourer, of Bisley, witness. Fine £4.

36/D/7   13 Aug. 1817. Samuel Rogers of Bisley, victualler. Depasturing one scabby or mangy sheep on Bisley common . E. Aldridge JP. Joseph Fawkes, labourer, of Bisley, witness. Fine £5.

36/D/8   13 Aug. 1817. William Restall of Bisley, yeoman. Depasturing three scabby or mangy sheep on Bisley common. E. Aldridge JP. Joseph Fawkes, labourer, of Bisley, witness. Fine £3.

36/D/9   13 Aug. 1817. Samuel Turner of Bisley, yeoman. Depasturing one scabby or mangy sheep on Bisley common. E. Aldridge JP. Joseph Fawkes, labourer, of Bisley, witness. Fine £1.

36/D/10   1 Aug. 1817. John Clutterbuck of Minsterworth, dealer and chapman. Having defective weights. H. Burgh JP and S. Wathen JP. George Mynett, inspector of weights for Bisley hundred, witness. Fine 5/- and 7/6 costs. Offence committed 1 Aug. 1817.

36/D/11   1 Aug. 1817. William Crates of Stroud, shopkeeper. Having defective weights [etc., as 36/D/10].

36/D/12   30 Aug. 1817. William Parker of Stroud, clothworker. Buying from James Cole 3½ lb. of stolen wool, the property of John Parrish, wool-dyer, of Stroud, his employer. H. Burgh JP and H. Cooke JP. J. Parrish, informer. Fine £40 or six months' hard labour in Horsley house of correction. First offence. Offence committed 20 Aug. 1817.

36/D/13   12 Sept. 1817. Mary Herbert, late of Cheltenham. Travelling on foot between Bristol, Gloucester and Cheltenham selling Dutch toys and Tunbridge ware without a licence. R. Capper JP at Cheltenham. John Ellison Poole, surveyor of hawkers and pedlars, of Clayton, Stafford Riding [sic, ? Clayton (Staffs.)], informer. William Lane and William Poole, witnesses. Fine £10. Offence committed 12 Sept. 1817.

36/D/14   14 Aug. 1817. Ann Lewis, late of Cheltenham. Selling silk shawls and gloves from house to house in Cheltenham without a licence. R. Capper JP at Cheltenham. John Cossens, yeoman, of Cheltenham, informer. John Bridgewater, witness. Fine £10. Offence committed 14 Aug. 1817.

36/D/15   22 Feb. 1817 [late return]. Francis Pickard, late of Stroud, labourer. Exposing seven hares for sale. S. Wathen JP at Stroud. William Harris, yeoman, of Bisley, informer. Samuel Pinnell, witness. Fine £5 for each hare. Offence committed 20 Jan. 1817.

37/A/1 9 Jan. 1818. Jonathan Smith of Uley, labourer. Lopping the top of an ash tree in the Finger Ground, the property of John Powell of Uley. Rev. W. Lloyd Baker JP. John Powell, farmer, complainant. James Robins, carpenter, witness. First offence. Fine £20. Offence committed 7 Jan. 1818.

37/A/2 12 Jan. 1818. Miles Harvey of Hawkesbury, labourer. Stealing an ash pole (11 ft. long) from Bodkin Wood, Horton, the property of the duke of Beaufort. Rev. T. Jones JP. John Hooper, bailiff, complainant. Abel Kingston of Didmarton, witness. Fine 10/-. Offence committed 7 Jan. 1818.

37/A/3 7 Nov. 1817. Fream(e) Window Sparks, late of Painswick, labourer. Leaving his wife and family chargeable to the parish. H. Burgh JP and E. Aldridge JP at Stroud. Daniel Spring, overseer of the poor of Painswick, complainant. Offender pleaded not guilty. Committed to Horsley house of correction to be further dealt with at next Q.S. Offence committed 24 July 1816.

37/A/4 8 Nov. 1817. William Niblett of Rodborough, weaver. Possessing 68 lb. of various woollen yarns believed to be stolen. H. Burgh JP and H. Cooke JP. Joseph Eycott *alias* Lewis of Randwick, informer. Richard Smith, weaver, of Stroud, witness. Fine £20 or one month in Horsley house of correction. Offence committed 6 Nov. 1817.

37/A/5 30 Dec. 1817. Thomas Lewis of Lydney, labourer. Pulling up an ash tree, the property of the Rt. Hon. Charles Bathurst. Rev. T. Thomas JP. William Cole, yeoman, of Lydney, witness. First offence. Fine £20 and 5/- costs.

37/A/6 30 Dec. 1817. John Parry of Lydney, labourer. Pulling up an ash tree in Lydney, the property [*etc., as* 37/A/5].

37/A/7 7 Nov. 1817. Thomas Earle of King's Stanley, weaver. Possessing 33½ lb. of various woollen yarns believed to be stolen. H. Burgh JP and S. Wathen JP [*who did not sign*]. Charles Thomas Lewis of Randwick, informer. Richard Smith, weaver, of Stroud, witness. Fine £20 or one month in Horsley house of correction. Offence committed 23 Sept. 1817. (Conviction quashed on appeal at Epiphany Sessions 1818.)

37/A/8 24 Nov. 1817. Moses Munday of North Nibley, labourer. Cutting down and stealing a young beech tree in North Nibley, the property of William Fitzhardinge Berkeley of Berkeley Castle. Edward Jenner JP and Rev. W. Davies JP. George Hancock, gamekeeper, of North Nibley, complainant. John Marms, innkeeper, of Berkeley, witness. First offence. Mitigated fine of £10 and 20/- costs. Offence committed 15 Nov. 1817.

37/A/9 3 Nov. 1817. John Bryant of Westerleigh. Shooting a pheasant in Hinton without a licence. E. Jenner JP and Rev. W. Davies JP at the White Hart inn, Berkeley. Mark Cullimore of Michael Wood, gamekeeper to Colonel Berkeley, informer. Thomas Kerslick of Berkeley, gamekeeper to Col. Berkeley, witness. Offender admitted charge. Fine £5. Offence committed 4 Oct. 1817.

37/A/10 5 Dec. 1817. George Bick of Ham, Berkeley, farmer. Possessing pheasants (one of which was delivered to Susannah Bick at the same residence) shot on his order by his servant in husbandry John Far, though not qualified to do so. E. Jenner JP at the White Hart inn, Berkeley. John Powell of Berkeley, gamekeeper to William Fitzhardinge Berkeley, informer. John Far, witness. Fine £20. Offences committed 28 Oct. and 16 Nov. 1817.

37/B/1   18 March 1818. Information given by Thomas Bush, yeoman, of Toddington, Beds., alleging that John Haines used a cart, not bearing his name and address, which had wheel-rims narrower than the statutory six inches, drawn by six horses through Duntisbourne.

37/B/2   19 Marh 1818. Notice of appeal by John Haines against a conviction for using a cart with too narrow wheel-rims. Directed to Edward Wilbraham Esq. A copy of the above was served on Edward Wilbraham at his home the same day by Timothy Stevens.

37/B/3   18 March 1818. Summons to John Haines to appear before Edward Wilbraham at his home in Cirencester at 11 o'clock on the 19 March 1818 to answer charges arising from information given by Thomas Bush, who was also directed to appear. Addressed to the constable of Bagendon.

37/B/4   19 March 1818. John Haines of Bagendon, gentleman. Using a cart with wheel-rims narrower than six inches, drawn by six horses, in Duntisbourne. E. Wilbraham JP. Thomas Bush, yeoman, of Toddington, Beds., informer. Daniel Young the younger, witness. Offender pleaded not guilty, declaring that the cart was used only on his own land for carrying manure, and at the time of the alleged offence he was returning home with the cart empty except for implements used for unloading. Fine £15. Offence committed 18 March 1818.

37/B/5   26 March 1818. Adam Williams of Hewelsfield, labourer [*erroneously named as James Worgan in part of the document*; *cf.* 37/B/6]. Possessing hazel rods or underwood without satisfactory explanation. P. J. Ducarel JP. Isaac Ellaway of Chapel Hill, Monmouth, woodward to Henry Charles, duke of Beaufort, witness. First offence. Fine £2 and 6/6 costs. Offence committed *c.* 19 Jan. 1818.

37/B/6   24 Feb. 1818. James Worgan of Hewelsfield, waterman. Cutting and stealing underwood from Caswell Wood, Tidenham, the property of the duke of Beaufort. Rev. T. Thomas JP. Isaac Ellaway, woodward, of Chapel Hill, Monmouth, witness. First offence. Fine £2 and 6/6 costs. Offence committed 19 Jan. 1818.

37/B/7   10 March 1818. Thomas Evans of St. Briavels, yeoman. Keeping a dog and a gun to kill game without a licence. P. J. Ducarel JP at Coleford, Newland. James Haffenden Esq. of Clearwell, Newland, informer. Thomas Niblett, labourer, of Hewelsfield, witness. Offender admitted he was unqualified but declared the dog was not his. Fine £5. Offence committed 16 Feb. 1818.

37/C/1   16 June 1818. Alexander Williams of St. Briavels, labourer. Cutting and stealing underwood from Caswell Wood, Tidenham, the property of the duke of Beaufort. Rev. T. Thomas JP. Isaac Ellaway of Chapel Hill, Monmouth, witness. First offence. Fine £2. Offence committed 11 June 1818.

37/C/2   17 April 1818. Henry Clayfield, late of Stroud, weaver. Leaving his wife and family chargeable to the parish. H. Burgh JP and E. Aldridge JP. Daniel Peyton, overseer of the poor, witness. Committed to Horsley house of correction until next Q.S. to be further dealt with. Offence committed 12 Dec. 1817.

37/C/3   13 April 1818. John Owen, late of Painswick, sawyer. Leaving his wife and family chargeable to the parish. H. Burgh JP. Daniel Spring, overseer [*etc., as* 37/C/2 *except*] Offence committed 19 Sept. 1816.

37/C/4   1 June 1818. James Lodge, late of Painswick, labourer. Leaving his wife and family chargeable to the parish. H. Burgh JP and Henry Hicks JP [*who did not sign*]. Daniel Spring, overseer [*etc., as* 37/C/2 *except*] Offence committed 1 June 1812.

37/C/5   2 July 1818. James Gardiner of Cirencester, baker. Selling five underweight loaves. Rev. H. Campbell JP. Sarah Wood, single woman, of Minchinhampton, witness. Fine £3 2*s*. 6*d*. (2/6 per oz.). Offence committed 27 June 1818.

37/C/6   2 July 1818. James Gardiner of Cirencester, baker. Selling ten underweight loaves [*etc*., *as* 37/C/5 *except*] Fine £5 10*s*. (2/6 per oz.) and 3/- costs. Offence committed 1 July 1818.

37/C/7   26 June 1818. Joseph Partridge of Wotton under Edge, clothier. Buying and receiving stolen ends of woollen yarn from Mary wife of George Horwood, spinner, of Wotton under Edge, the property of her employer John Carpenter, clothier, of the same parish. Rev. W. Lloyd Baker JP and Rev. L. Clutterbuck JP. John Partridge, informer. Fine £30. Offence committed 14 March 1818.

37/C/8   7 May 1818. William Pensam of Corse. Keeping and using dogs to kill game in Forthampton. Rev. George Turberville JP at Upton upon Severn, Worcs. Giles Hawker of Chaceley, gamekeeper to the Hon. Mrs. Yorke, of Forthampton, informer. John Willis, labourer, of Forthampton, witness. Fine £5. Offence committed 4 March 1818.

37/D/1   12 Aug. 1816 [*late return*]. Emmanuel Drew of Littledean, labourer. Stealing a quantity of hawthorn and holly from the Forest of Dean. Rev. R. Wetherell JP. Thomas Witts, forest keeper, witness. First offence. Fine £1 10*s*. and 6/6 costs. Offence committed 4 June 1816.

37/D/2   24 Feb. 1817 [*corrected from* 1818; *late return*]. John Phipps of St. Briavels hundred, labourer. Possessing a piece of oak (quarter part of a swing gate) without satisfactory explanation. Rev. C. Sandiford JP. Thomas Miles, forest keeper, and Thomas Virgoe, labourer, witnesses, both of St. Briavels hundred. First offence. Fine 10/- and 5/6 costs. Offence committed 14 Feb. 1817.

37/D/3   20 April 1818. John Wickenden of St. Briavels hundred, labourer. Stealing a limb of beech from the Forest of Dean. C. Sandiford JP, Charles Crawley JP and R. Wetherell JP. William James, labourer, of St. Briavels hundred, witness. First offence. Fine 10/- and 6/6 costs. Offence committed 11 April 1818.

37/D/4   5 May 1817 [*late return*]. James Morgan of St. Briavels hundred, labourer. Stealing a quantity of holly and birch wood from the Forest of Dean. C. Crawley JP and R. Wetherell JP [*signature of C. Sandiford crossed out*]. Thomas Witts, forest keeper, witness. First offence. Fine £1 and 9/- costs. Offence committed 13 March 1817.

37/D/5   29 Dec. 1817 [*late return*]. Joseph Hancock of St. Briavels hundred, labourer. Stealing a quantity of whitethorn from the Forest of Dean. C. Sandiford JP, C. Crawley JP and R. Wetherell JP. James Wood, labourer, of St. Briavels hundred, witness. First offence. Fine 5/- and 6/6 costs. Offence committed 22 Dec. 1817.

37/D/6   15 July 1818. James Ind of Tetbury, dealer. Being drunk. T. Estcourt JP. John Overbury, gentleman, of Tetbury, informer. Offender admitted charge. Fine 5/-. Offence committed 10 June 1818.

37/D/7   15 July 1818. Henry Vizer of Tetbury, farmer. Being drunk [*etc*., *as* 37/D/6].

37/D/8   7 Oct. 1818 [*signed at Horsley 8 Oct. 1818*]. Matthew Pinnell of Newington Bagpath, labourer. Exposing one hare for sale in Kingscote. John Delafield Phelps JP at Tetbury. James York, gamekeeper, of Kingscote, informer. Nathaniel Cornock of Kingscote, witness. Offender did not appear. Fine £5. Offence committed 18 Sept. 1818.

37/D/9   17 July 1818. William Hawkins of Stroud, baker. Selling and exposing for sale an underweight loaf. H. Burgh JP. Edward Giddy, witness. Fine 4/- (1/- per oz.)

37/D/10 20 July 1818. William Hawkins of Stroud, baker. Exposing for sale 70 loaves which were a total of 229 oz. underweight. H. Cooke JP. Thomas Mills, gentleman, of Stroud, informer. George Mynett, innkeeper, of Stroud, witness. Fine 2/6 for each ounce underweight (£28 12s. 6d.). Offence committed 20 July 1818.

37/D/11 11 Aug. 1818. William Llewellin of Stroud, weaver. Possessing 7¾ lb. of various woollen yarns believed to be stolen. H. Burgh JP and H. Cooke JP. Richard Smith, weaver, of Stroud, informer. Benjamin Bassett Fisher, labourer, of Stroud, witness. Fine £20 or one month in Horsley house of correction.

37/D/12 4 Sept. 1818. George Bently of Rodborough, labourer. Attempting to net fish from a stream or river in Stonehouse, the property of Stephen Clissold. H. Burgh JP. James Norton, gentleman, of Stonehouse, witness. Fine £5 or one month in Horsley house of correction (unless the fine is paid in the meantime). Offence committed 30 Aug. 1818.

37/D/13 4 Sept. 1818. George Paul of King's Stanley, cooper. Attempting [etc., as 37/D/12].

37/D/14 17 July 1818. William Hawkins of Stroud, baker. Selling and exposing for sale one loaf 5 oz. under weight. H. Burgh JP. Thomas Smith, witness. Fine 5/-. Offence committed 11 July 1818.

37/D/15 25 Aug. 1818. John Hunt, late of Minchinhampton, labourer. Stealing, and attempting to steal with a flue net, fish from a river or stream, the property of John Lewis, clothier, of Stroud. H. Burgh JP. John Lewis, witness. Fine £5 or one month in Horsley house of correction (unless the fine is paid in the meantime). Offence committed 25 Aug. 1818.

37/D/16 6 Oct. 1818. James Goatley of Colesbourne, yeoman. Using a gun and a dog to kill partridges on a Sunday. J. Agg JP. First offence. Fine £10. Offence committed 7 Sept. 1818.

37/D/17 21 Aug. 1818. John Scotts of Cowley, labourer. Keeping and using gins to kill game, not being qualified. R. Capper JP at Cheltenham. William Lawrence Esq., informer. Samuel Locke, yeoman, of Cowley, witness. Fine £5. Offence committed 21 Aug. 1818.

37/D/18 19 Oct. 1818. George Lawrence of Broadway, Worcs. Failing to pay 2 guineas annual duty when paying 5 guineas at Chipping Campden to enter his horse Jack of All Trades for a race to be run for a prize of 30 guineas on Friday 15 May 1818 at Dover's Hill, Weston Subedge. J. Timbrill D.D. JP at Beckford. Mr. Thomas Chamberlain, book-keeper, informer. Richard Andrews, clerk of the course, witness. Fine £20 mitigated to £10. Offence committed 13 May 1818.

38/A/1–6 30 Oct. 1818. [Names and offences as below.] Rev. T. Jones JP and Rev. F. Pelly at a Petty Sessions held at the Cross Hands inn, Old Sodbury. [Fines as below.] Offences committed 28, 29 and 30 Sept. 1818.

38/A/1 William Gibbs, £3 15s. and 15/-, Joseph Gibbs, £4 15s. and 19/-, Thomas Osborne, £2 15s. and 11/-, Hannah White, £2 10s. and 10/-, victuallers, of Westerleigh. Using defective measures.

38/A/2 Isaac Jefferis, victualler, £8 and £1 12s., and Jane Cox, baker, 15/- and 3/-, both of Siston. Using defective measures or weights.

38/A/3 William Evans, £1 5s. and 5/-, and Richard Young, £2 and 8/-, victuallers, and Thomas Withey, shopkeeper, £2 15s. and 11/-, all of Pucklechurch. Using defective weights or measures.

38/A/4 James Webb of Cold Ashton, baker, 15/- and 3/-. Using defective weights.

38/A/5 Robert Kitch, £1 and 4/-, and Simon Nowell, £1 and 4/-, shopkeepers, of Wick and Abson. Using defective weights.

38/A/6   John Trubody, £2 10*s*. and 10/-, and Richard Gully, £2 5*s*. and 9/-, victuallers, of Wick and Abson. Using defective measures.

38/A/7   18 Nov. 1818. Thomas Kean of Hawkesbury, labourer. Possessing snares to kill game. Rev. Thomas Brooke LL.D. JP at Horton. William Pitt, labourer, of Sopworth, Wilts., informer. Offender admitted charge. Fine £5. Offence committed 18 Nov. 1818.

38/A/8   16 Nov. 1818. William Pitt of Sopworth, Wilts., labourer. Possessing snares to kill game at Oldbury on the Hill. Rev. T. Brooke LL.D. JP at Horton. William Roach, game-keeper, of Oldbury on the Hill, informer. Nathaniel Gason, labourer, of Sopworth, witness. Fine £5. Offence committed 14 Nov. 1818.

38/A/9   30 Oct. 1818. George Evans, of Minchinhampton, weaver. Possessing 896 lb. of various woollen yarns believed to be stolen. H. Burgh JP and H. Cooke JP. John Webb, clothier, of Bisley, informer. Robert Keene, weaver, of Stroud, witness. Fine £20. Offence committed 9 Oct. 1818.

38/A/10   21 Dec. 1818. Thomas Hall and John Hall of Pucklechurch, farmers. Keeping and using dogs to kill game in Westerleigh. Rev. F. Pelly JP at Wick. John Tovey, labourer, of Westerleigh, informer. William Bryant, witness. Fine £5 each. Offence committed 15 Dec. 1818.

38/A/11   6 Nov. 1818. Mostyn Jones of Lyncombe and Widcombe, Som. Keeping and using a gun and dogs to kill game in Siston. Rev. F. Pelly JP at Siston. William Hiorns, gamekeeper, of Siston, informer. Thomas Snailum, witness. Fine £5. Offence committed 17 Oct. 1818.

38/A/12   1 Dec. 1818. Edward Greenwood. Offering one 3/- and four 1/6 Bank of England tokens to William Gore at Charlton Kings. J. Agg JP and R. Capper JP. Fine £10. Offence committed 25 Nov. 1818.

38/A/13   30 Oct. 1818. William Fowler of Woodchester, clothworker. Cutting down a laurel bush in a plantation or garden at Rodborough, the property of Sir G. O. Paul. H. Burgh JP. William Neems, yeoman, of Rodborough, witness. First offence. Fine 5/- and 7/6 costs. Offence committed 23 Oct. 1818.

38/A/14   27 Oct. 1818. Sarah Bloodworth of King's Stanley, widow. Cutting down a tree in Pen Wood, the property of Sir G. O. Paul. H. Burgh JP. William Neems, yeoman, of Rodborough, complainant. Thomas Wilkins, weaver, of King's Stanley, witness. First offence. Fine 10/- and 9/6 costs. Offence committed 15 Oct. 1818.

38/A/15   22 Nov. 1818. John Dauncey of Horsley, millwright. Killing a pheasant. H. Burgh JP. George Hill, gentleman, of Nympsfield, informer and complainant (in writing). William Solomon, labourer, of Nympsfield, witness. Fine £20 and 15/- costs. Offence committed on the night of 21 Nov. 1818.

38/A/16   28 Dec. 1818. Benjamin Crowder of Stroud, labourer. Using snares to kill hares in Painswick. H. Cooke JP. William Bennett, labourer, of Painswick, informer and complainant (in writing). John Arnold and Thomas White, labourers, of Painswick, witnesses. Fine £20 and £1 costs.

38/A/17   21 Nov. 1818. John Poole of King's Stanley, yeoman. Depasturing six unmarked lambs on common land. H. Burgh JP. Samuel Burroughs, blacksmith, of King's Stanley, witness. Fine 12/- (2/- per lamb). Offence committed 17 Nov. 1818.

38/A/18   21 Nov. 1818. Charles Poole, yeoman, of King's Stanley. Pasturing a scabby sheep on common land. H. Burgh JP. Samuel Burroughs, blacksmith, of King's Stanley, witness. Fine £1 and 11/6 costs. Offence committed 17 Nov. 1818.

38/A/19 30 Dec. 1818. Mark Hancock, William Hancock and Robert Cook, all of Henbury, labourers. Using dogs to kill hares on a Sunday. John Scandrett Harford JP. Abraham Pope, witness. Fine £20 and 10/- costs. Offence committed Sunday 6 Dec. 1818.

38/A/20 1 Dec. 1818. Thomas Hayward. Obstructing a footpath in Cheltenham with a quantity of bricks. J. Agg JP, R. Capper JP and W. H. Prinn JP. Fine 10/-. Offence committed 1 Dec. 1818.

38/B/1 13 April 1819. James Scales, late of Tetbury, hatmaker. Stealing 5 hats entrusted to him by his employer William Alfred Glover. Robert Kingscote JP and J. D Phelps JP. Three months' hard labour in Horsley house of correction. Offence committed between 1 and 20 Jan. 1819

38/B/2 12 Feb. 1819. Edmund Hill of Uley, weaver. Unlawfully disposing of 1 lb. of woollen yarn entrusted to him by his employer. Rev. W. Lloyd Baker JP and W. M. Adey JP. Two months' hard labour in Horsley house of correction. Offence committed Dec. 1818.

38/B/3 12 Feb. 1819. Richard Fords of Uley, weaver. Receiving stolen woollen yarn from Edmund Hill. Rev. W. Lloyd Baker JP and W. M. Adey JP. Edward Smith informer. First offence. Fine £30. Offence committed Dec. 1818.

38/B/4 8 March 1819. William Etheridge of Toddington. Selling beer without a licence. J. Timbrill JP. William Grimmett, witness. Offender admitted charge. Offence committed 25 Feb. 1819.

38/B/5 20 March 1819. John William Frith of Clifton, Bristol. Attempting to gain employment as a servant, using a false testimonial. G. Goldney JP and John Cave JP. Harriet Walker, widow, of Redland, Bristol, complainant. Offence committed 2 March 1819.

38/B/6 25 Feb. 1819. William Wathen of Painswick, weaver [*erroneously named as George Evans in part of the document*; *cf.* 38/A/9]. Possessing 22 lb. of various woollen yarns believed to be stolen. H. Burgh JP and E. Aldridge JP. Daniel Spring, timber merchant, of Painwick, informer. William Cox, clothier, of Painswick, witness. Fine £20. Offence committed 20 Feb. 1819.

38/B/7 8 March 1819. William Vines of Stroud, clothworker. Possessing 5 lb. of woollen yarn believed to be stolen. H. Burgh JP and E. Aldridge JP. Robert Keene, weaver, of Stroud, informer. Daniel Peyton, clothier, of Stroud, witness. Fine £20. Offence committed 2 Feb. 1819.

38/B/8 25 Jan. 1819. Joseph Jefferies of Rodborough, weaver. Possessing 11 lb. of woollen yarn believed to be stolen. H. Burgh JP and E. Aldridge JP. Edward Mason, clothier, of Stroud, informer. Richard Smith, weaver, of Stroud, witness. Fine £20. Offence committed 22 Jan. 1819.

38/B/9 25 Jan. 1819. William Flight of Rodborough, weaver. Possessing 30 lb. of various woollen yarn believed to be stolen. H. Burgh JP and E. Aldridge JP. William Helme, clothier, of Stroud, informer, Daniel Peyton, clothier, of Stroud, witness. Fine £20. Offence committed 25 Jan. 1819.

38/B/10 24 Dec. 1818. Isaac Taylor of Painswick, weaver. Possessing at Bisley 8 lb. of woollen yarn and ends believed to be stolen. H. Burgh JP and E. Aldridge JP. John Baker, carpenter, of Bisley, informer. William Sevill, clothier, of Bisley, witness. Fine £20. Offence committed 21 Dec. 1818.

38/B/11   11 March 1819. Peter Aldridge of Horsley, weaver. Burning and destroying 33 lb. of woollen yarn committed to his charge by the owners thereof. W. M. Adey JP and H. C. Clifford JP. Edward Austin the elder, Edward Austin the younger, Anthony Austin and Melicent Austin, clothiers, of Wotton under Edge, complainants. Fine £10 (double the value of the yarn).

38/B/12   5 March 1819. Mary wife of Josiah Malpass, haulier, of Cam. Buying and receiving 1 lb. of stolen woollen yarn from Henry King, the property of his employer Edward Jackson. W. M. Adey JP and H. C. Clifford JP. William Cox Buchanan, informer. First offence. Fine £20. Offence committed 15 Dec. 1818.

38/B/13   19 March 1819. John Higgins the younger of Coaley, weaver. Buying and receiving 2½ lb. of stolen woollen yarn from Thomas Brent. W. M. Adey JP and Henry Winchcombe Dyer JP. William Cox Buchanan, informer. First offence. Fine £30. Offence committed latter end of March 1817.

38/B/14   26 Feb. 1819. William Harris *alias* Higgins of Coaley, weaver. Buying and receiving ½ lb. of stolen woollen yarn from Henry King. W. M. Adey JP and H. C. Clifford JP. John Weight, informer. First offence. Fine £30. Offence committed 21 Nov. 1817.

38/B/15   26 Feb. 1819. William Harris *alias* Higgins of Coaley, weaver. Buying [*etc.*, as 38/B/14 *except*] W. C. Buchanan, informer [*and*] Offence committed 23 Dec. 1817.

38/B/16   1 March 1819. Thomas Higgins of Cam, tailor. Buying and receiving 2½ lb. of stolen woollen yarn from Henry King, the property of Edward Jackson. W. M. Adey JP and H. C. Clifford JP. John Weight, informer. First offence. Fine £40. Offence committed 1 June 1818.

38/B/17   5 March 1819. Daniel Smith of Coaley, weaver. Buying and receiving 3¾ lb. of stolen woollen yarn from Thomas Brent, the property of Edward Jackson. W. M. Adey JP and H. C. Clifford JP. Henry King, informer. First offence. Fine £40. Offence committed 25 April 1818.

38/B/18   23 March 1819. Samuel Hieron of Minchinhampton, labourer. Having 50 lb. of wool and woollen yarn (believed to be stolen) concealed in his barn. R. Kingscote JP and Rev. H. Campbell JP. Edward Drake, victualler, of Minchinhampton, informer. Joseph Browne, clothier, of Minchinhampton, witness. First offence. Fine £20 or one month in Horsley house of correction. Offence committed 20 Feb. 1819.

38/B/19   19 March 1819. Enoch Higgins of North Nibley, clothier. Buying and receiving 2½ lb. of stolen woollen yarn from Henry King. W. M. Adey JP and H. W. Dyer JP. John Weight, informer. First offence. Fine £40 or six months' hard labour in Horsley house of correction (unless the fine is sooner paid). Offence committed 5 Dec. 1818. Conviction quashed on appeal at Easter Sessions.

38/B/20   5 March 1819. Nehemiah Curnock of Uley, clothworker. Buying and receiving 7½ lb. of stolen woollen yarn from William Millard. W. M. Adey JP and H. C. Clifford JP. Henry King, informer. First offence. Fine £40 or six months' hard labour in Horsley house of correction. Offence committed 6 April 1818. Conviction quashed on appeal at Easter Sessions.

38/B/21   26 March 1819. Frances wife of William Harris *alias* Higgins of Coaley, weaver. Buying and receiving ½ lb. of stolen woollen yarn from William Millard. W. M. Adey JP and H. C. Clifford JP. Henry King, informer. First offence. Fine £20 or three months' hard labour in Horsley house of correction. Offence committed 20 Jan. 1818. Conviction quashed on appeal at Easter Sessions.

38/B/22   26 March 1819. Mary wife of Josiah Malpass of Cam, haulier. Buying and receiving ¼ lb. of stolen woollen yarn from Henry King. W. M. Adey JP and H. C. Clifford JP. William Millard, informer. First offence. Fine £40 or six months's hard labour in Horsley house of correction. Offence committed 15 Nov. 1818. Conviction quashed on appeal at Easter Sessions.

38/B/23   5 March 1819. Thomas Higgins of Cam, clothworker. Buying and receiving 2 lb. of stolen woollen yarn from Thomas Brent, the property of Edward Jackson. W. M. Adey JP and H. C. Clifford JP. Henry King, informer. First offence. Fine £40 or six months' hard labour in Horsley house of correction. Offence committed 23 Sept. 1817.

38/C/1   26 March 1819. William Taylor of Peasbrook, Broadway, Worcs. Keeping and using dogs (in company with four others) to kill hares in plantations at Temple Guiting belonging to George Talbot Esq. J. Timbrill D.D. JP at Ford. John Day, informer (at Beckford). James Nash, witness. Offender pleaded not guilty, saying he had been invited by Mr. Averill whom he believed to be qualified. Fine £5. Offence committed 30 Jan. 1819.

38/C/2   24 April 1819. Edward Fox. Cutting down an oak sapling in Oddington without the owner's consent. F. E. Witts JP. John Williams, complainant.

38/C/3   6 May 1819. Francis Rice of Painswick, labourer. Cutting down a young ash tree in Painswick, the property of Thomas Preston Esq. H. Burgh JP. Thomas Baylis, yeoman, of Painswick, informer. Thomas Hiden, woodward, of Painswick, witness. First offence. Fine 40/- and 8/6 costs. Offence committed 6 May 1819.

38/C/4   22 May 1819. John Ireland and John Mitchell. Being rogues and vagabonds of evil repute, believed to be in High Street, Cheltenham, with intent to steal. J. Clutterbuck JP at Cheltenham. Edward Bonner, Thomas Little and John Cossens, witnesses. Committed to the house of correction to be further dealt with at next Q.S. Apprehended 20 May 1819.

38/C/5   10 June 1819. Ann Evans of Cheltenham. Fortune-telling. J. Agg JP and R. Capper JP. William Hastings, tailor, of Cheltenham, informer. Mary Mills (who had lived with the accused for 15 months), witness. Offender pleaded not guilty. Committed to Northleach house of correction until next Q.S. unless discharged earlier by due course of law. Offence committed 10 June 1819.

38/D/1–3   7 Oct. 1819. [Names as below.] Having defective weights. T. Jones JP and William Blathwayt JP at a Petty Sessions held at the Cross Hands inn, Old Sodbury. John Minett, witness. Weights forfeited. [Fines as below.] Offences committed 27 and 29 Sept. 1819.

38/D/1   William Lewis of Little Badminton, shopkeeper. Fine 15/- and 8/1½ costs.

38/D/2   John Cole, fine 10/- and 6/3 costs, Elizabeth Hort, fine 10/- and 6/3 costs, and Mary Williams, fine 5/- and 4/4½ costs, all of Great Badminton, shopkeepers.

38/D/3   Charles Hughes, fine £2 and 17/6 costs, and Charles Humphries, fine 5/- and 4/4 costs, both of Leighterton, shopkeepers.

38/D/4   7 Aug. 1819. Daniel Lawrence, victualler, 10/- and 2/6, and Thomas Withey, shopkeeper, 10/- and 2/6, both of Pucklechurch. Having defective weights and measures. T. Jones JP, F. Pelly JP and W. Blathwayt JP at a Petty Sessions held at the Cross Hands inn, Old Sodbury. John Nichols of Pucklechurch, witness. Weights forfeited. Offences committed 22 June 1819.

38/D/5   7 Oct. 1819. James Collins of Alderley, butcher. Fine £1 10s. and 13/9 costs. Having defective weights. T. Jones JP and W. Blathwayt JP at a Petty Sessions held at the Cross Hands inn, Old Sodbury. John Minett, witness. Weights forfeited. Offence committed 27 Sept. 1819.

38/D/6   6 Aug. 1819. Charles Dolling, victualler, fine £3 10s. and £1 7s. 6d. costs, and James Webb, baker, 10/- and 2/6, both of Cold Ashton. Having defective measures and weights [etc., as 38/D/4 omitting of Pucklechurch after the witness's name].

38/D/7   6 Aug. 1819. Mary Stone, victualler, fine 10/- and 2/6 costs, John Spear, £1 5s. and 6/3, George Potter, 15/- and 3/9, Henry Wilmot, £1 5s. and 6/3, and John Preddy, 10/- and 2/6, shopkeepers, all of Siston. Having defective measures and weights. At a Petty Sessions held at the Cross Hands inn, Old Sodbury. Charles Baber, witness. Measures and weights forfeited. Offence committed 22 June 1819.

38/D/8   6 Aug. 1819. John Oatley, butcher, fine 10/- and 2/6 costs, Stephen Dando, £2 and 10/-, Robert Hook, 10/- and 2/-, Mary Tuck, £1 5s. and 6/3, John Collins, 5/- and 1/3, and Joseph Gibbs junior, £1 10s. and 7/6, shopkeepers, all of Westerleigh. Having defective measures and weights. At a Petty Sessions [as above]. Samuel Hathway, witness. Weights and measures forfeited. Offence committed 21 June 1819.

38/D/9   7 Oct. 1819. William Watts, saddler and collar-maker, fine 5/- and 4/4½ costs, John Grader, £1 and 10/-, and John Townsend, £1 5s. and 11/10½, victuallers, William Haynes, 15/- and 8/1½, Robert Clark, £1 and 10/-, and William Chappell, 15/- and 8/1½, shopkeepers, all of Oldbury on the Hill. Having defective measures and weights. T. Jones JP and W. Blathwayt JP at a Petty Sessions [as above]. John Minett, witness. Weights and measures forfeited. Offence committed 29 Sept. 1819.

38/D/10   7 Oct. 1819. Richard Lemon, fine £4 and £1 12s. 6d. costs, and John Hopkins, £6 and £2 7s. 6d., victuallers, John Davis, butcher, 5/- and 4/4½, Thomas Chapman, 5/- and 4/4½, Thomas Andrews, £1 10s. and 13/9, Charles Pritchard, 10/- and 6/3, William Wimbow, 15/- and 8/1½, John Collins, 5/- and 4/4½, James Dutton, 5/- and 4/4½, Robert Stinchcomb, £1 and 10/-, William Stinchcomb, 15/- and 8/1½, and Susanna Witts, £1 10s. and 13/9, shopkeepers, all of Hawkesbury. Having defective measures and weights. At a Petty Sessions [as above]. John Minett, witness. Weights and measures forfeited. Offences committed 27 and 28 Sept. 1819.

38/D/11   13 Oct. 1819. William Hyde of Badgeworth, farmer. Using three dogs to kill a hare in Boddington. Rev. J. Neale JP. First offence. Fine £20. Offence committed Sunday 12 Sept. 1819.

38/D/12   2 Oct. 1819. Richard Loveridge. Using a dog with intent to kill a hare in Norton. R. B. Cooper JP. First offence. Fine £10. Offence committed night of 6/7 Sept. 1819.

38/D/13   7 May 1819 John March of Bisley, weaver. Possessing woollen yarn believed to be stolen. H. Burgh JP and H. Cooke JP. Richard Smith, weaver, of Stroud, informer. George Daniel Harris, clothier, of King's Stanley, witness. Fine £20 (half to informer and half to Stroud dispensary). Offence committed 26 April 1819.

38/D/14   30 July 1819. Jeffery Amhurst Jefferies of Stow on the Wold, labourer. Lopping a fir tree in Lower Swell, the property of Rev. John Hippisley. Rev. F. E. Witts JP. William Day, bailiff, complainant. Fine £5 and 6/- costs. Offence committed 27 July 1819.

38/D/15   18 Sept. 1819. Daniel Packer of Dyrham and Hinton, husbandman. Riding in his cart without reins, thereby obstructing the highway in Cold Ashton. W. Blathwayt JP. Peter Clark of Dyrham and Hinton, informer. John Kearton, witness. Fine 20/-. Offence committed 11 Sept. 1819.

38/D/16   10 Oct. 1819. Thomas Roberts of Tortworth, fine 15/- and 8/1½ costs, James Butler of Horton, 15/- and 8/1½, John Wiltshire of Tormarton, £1 10s. and 13/9, Daniel Bailey, 5/- and 4/4½, and Benjamin Hobbs, £1 and 10/-, of Charfield, shopkeepers. Having defective weights. F. Pelly JP and W. Blathwayt JP at a Petty Sessions held at the Cross Hands inn, Old Sodbury. Weights forfeited.

38/D/17   10 Oct. 1819. John Chandler, fine £4 5s. and £1 14s. costs, and John Ford, 5/- and 4/4½, victuallers, William Park, shopkeeper, [5/-] and 4/4½, all of Wickwar, John Garraway, shopkeeper, £1 10s. and 13/9, and William Foreman, victualler, 10/- and 6/3, both of Old Sodbury. Having defective measures and weights [etc., as 38/D/16].

38/D/18   10 Oct. 1819. Charles Watkins, baker, fine 5/- and 4/4½ costs, Joseph Fowler, salt-refiner, 10/- and 6/3, George Iles, butcher, 5/- and 4/4½, Thomas Alden, butcher, 5/- and 4/4½, Thomas Dutfield, miller, 10/- and 6/3, and William Higgs, tanner, 5/- and 4/4½, all of Chipping Sodbury. Having defective weights [etc., as 38/D/19, adding] Offence committed 22 Sept. 1819.

39/A/1   21 Dec. 1819. John Paffit of Taynton, Oxon., labourer. Killing a male fallow deer in Wychwood Forest, in Widford parish. Rev. E. Rice JP. Job Prattley, deer keeper, complainant. Six months in Gloucester gaol.

39/A/2   18 Dec. 1819. John Jeackes of Bisley, clothworker. Possessing 155 lb. of various woollen yarns believed to be stolen. H. Burgh JP and H. Cooke JP at Stroud. William Toghill, informer. First offence. Fine £20. Offence committed 15 Dec. 1819.

39/A/3   9 Nov. 1819. Richard Hawkins alias King of St. Briavels hundred, labourer. Using a dog and a hay net to kill a hare. Rev. T. Thomas JP. John Teague and Timothy Jones, yeomen, of St. Briavels hundred, informer and witness. First offence. Accused refused to attend. Mitigated fine of £10. Offence committed night of 1 Nov. 1819.

39/A/4   9 Nov. 1819. Edward Aston of St. Briavels hundred, labourer. Using a dog [etc., as 39/A/3].

39/A/5   9 Nov. 1819. James Howell of St. Briavels hundred, labourer. Using a dog [etc., as 39/A/3].

39/A/6   3 Jan. 1820. Recognizance by Luke Williams of Horsley, in the sum of £10, Thomas Spearing, grocer, and Henry Trollip, yeoman and former licensee, both of Horsley, in the sum of £5 each, in support of the licence granted to the above Luke Williams to keep an inn or alehouse in the premises formerly occupied by Henry Trollip. R. Kingscote JP.

39/A/7   28 Oct. 1819. Sarah wife of William Evans of Horsley, clothier. Buying 2 lb. 4 oz. of stolen woollen yarn from Harriet Lovat and Sarah Bingle, single women, of Minchinhampton. Rev. H. Campbell JP and Obadian Paul Wathen JP. John Hunt, informer. Harriet Lovat, witness. First offence. Fine £40 or six months in Horsley house of correction unless penalty is paid earlier. Offence committed 6 Aug. 1819.

39/A/8   4 Nov. 1819. John Jones of Henbury, yeoman. Shooting a partridge on a Sunday. S. Webb JP. Mark Robins, witness. First offence. Fine £10 and £1 10s. costs. Offence committed 10 Oct. 1819.

39/A/9   17 Dec. 1819. William Pegler of Stroud, butcher. Setting a snare net to kill conies in a wood held by John Watling Esq. H. Burgh JP and E. Aldridge JP. Robert Price, labourer, of Stroud, witness. Ordered to pay 10/6 to J. Watling Esq. and 1/3 to Stroud overseers of the poor. Offence committed 20 Nov. 1819.

39/A/10   17 Dec. 1819. Edward Howell of Stroud, blacksmith. Setting a snare [etc., as 39/A/9].

39/A/11   24 Dec. 1819. William Davis of Horsley, labourer. Using a snare net in enclosed ground, namely Old Leaze, Kingscote, held by William Wight, without permission or obtaining a certificate. W. M. Adey JP and commissioner for taxes, at Wotton under Edge. Fine £20. Offence committed 1 Nov. 1819.

39/A/12   24 Dec. 1819. Isaac Daniels of Horsley, labourer. Using a snare net [*etc.*, *as* 39/A/11].

39/B/1   1 April 1820. Moses Sweet of Bitton, coalminer. Cutting underwood in Bean Wood, Wapley and Codrington. Rev. F. Pelly JP. Francis Evans, witness. Committed to the house of correction and to be once whipped on refusal to pay fine of 40/-. Offence committed 31 March 1820.

39/B/2   17 Jan. 1820. Joseph Peterson of Mangotsfield. Using dogs to kill game at Pucklechurch when unqualified. Rev. F. Pelly JP at Siston. Samuel Swears of Bedminster, Som., informer. William James, witnesss. Fine £5. Offence committed 29 Oct. 1819.

39/B/3–71   25 Feb. 1820. [*Names below.*] Having unequal balances and/or defective weights. H. Burgh and E. Aldridge JP at a Petty Sessions for Bisley hundred. Offences committed between 25 Jan. and 10 Feb. 1820. Fine 5/- and 6/- costs [*except* 39/B/45].

39/B/3   Eunice Wood of Painswick, shopkeeper.

39/B/4   Daniel Merrill of Painswick, shopkeeper.

39/B/5   Daniel Ellis of Stroud, shopkeeper.

39/B/6   William Browning of Painswick, shopkeeper.

39/B/7   Job Hill of Stroud, shopkeeper.

39/B/8   William Hazeldine of Painswick, shopkeeper.

39/B/9   John Dutton of Stroud, shopkeeper.

39/B/10   Anthony Partridge of Painswick, shopkeeper.

39/B/11   Ann Roberts of Stroud, shopkeeper.

39/B/12   Daniel Gyde of Painswick, shopkeeper.

39/B/13   Thomas Clissold of Painswick, shopkeeper.

39/B/14   Jacob Bath of Bisley, shopkeeper.

39/B/15   William Smart of Bisley, shopkeeper.

39/B/16   William Long of Bisley, shopkeeper.

39/B/17   Daniel Gardner of Stroud, shopkeeper.

39/B/18   William Selwyn of Bisley, shopkeeper.

39/B/19   Charles Smart of Bisley, shopkeeper.

39/B/20   Richard Camm of Stroud, shopkeeper.

39/B/21   John Pegler of Stroud, shopkeeper.

39/B/22   William Morgan of Stroud, shopkeeper.

39/B/23   Priscilla Holder of Stroud, shopkeeper.

39/B/24   Thomas Dimmock of Stroud, shopkeeper.

39/B/25   Edward Wyatt of Stroud, shopkeeper.

39/B/26   James Neale of Stroud, shopkeeper.

39/B/27   Isaac Hains of Stroud, shopkeeper.

39/B/28   Henry Partridge of Stroud, shopkeeper.

39/B/29   Jacob West of Stroud, shopkeeper.

39/B/30   Thomas Drew of Stroud, shopkeeper.

39/B/31   Thomas Steele of Stroud, shopkeeper.

39/B/32   Charles Pearce of Stroud, shopkeeper.

39/B/33	John Smith of Stroud, shopkeeper.
39/B/34	Ann Hall of Stroud, shopkeeper.
39/B/35	William Hill of Stroud, shopkeeper.
39/B/36	Charles Hodges of Stroud, shopkeeper.
39/B/37	John Buck of Stroud, shopkeeper.
39/B/38	Elizabeth Miles of Stroud, shopkeeper.
39/B/39	Samuel Williams of Stroud, shopkeeper.
39/B/40	Mary Wood of Stroud, shopkeeper.
39/B/41	William Bright of Stroud, shopkeeper.
39/B/42	Samuel Addams of Painswick, shopkeeper.
39/B/43	Thomas Hazle of Bisley, shopkeeper.
39/B/44	James Cooper of Painswick, shopkeeper.
39/B/45	James Gawen of Bisley, shopkeeper. Fine 10/- and 6/- costs.
39/B/46	John Okey of Painswick, shopkeeper.
39/B/47	John Cook of Painswick, shopkeeper.
39/B/48	Ann Weeks of Painswick, shopkeeper.
39/B/49	Daniel Hewlett of Stroud, shopkeeper.
39/B/50	Thomas Clayfield of Stroud, shopkeeper.
39/B/51	Francis Clevely of Painswick, shopkeeper.
39/B/52	James Millard of Bisley, shopkeeper.
39/B/53	James Bethaway of Stroud, shopkeeper.
39/B/54	Thomas Franklin of Bisley, shopkeeper.
39/B/55	James Birt of Painswick, shopkeeper.
39/B/56	Martha Clissold of Miserden, shopkeeper.
39/B/57	Thomas Perkins of Painswick, shopkeeper.
39/B/58	Ann Holder of Painswick, shopkeeper.
39/B/59	Mary Lewis of Stroud, shopkeeper.
39/B/60	John Hinton of Painswick, shopkeeper.
39/B/61	Richard Gardner of Painswick, shopkeeper.
39/B/62	Thomas Carter of Painswick, shopkeeper.
39/B/63	Thomas Jeffrey of Bisley, shopkeeper.
39/B/64	Charles Kemp of Painswick, shopkeeper.
39/B/65	Nathaniel Stockham of Bisley, shopkeeper.
39/B/66	Thomas Smart of Bisley, shopkeeper.
39/B/67	William Clissold of Miserden, shopkeeper.
39/B/68	James Aldridge of Stroud, shopkeeper.
39/B/69	Moses Moreton of Bisley, shopkeeper.
39/B/70	Ralph Okey of Stroud, [butcher], in his stall in the public shambles.
39/B/71	John Clutterbuck of Stroud, shopkeeper.
39/B/72	4 Feb. 1820. Charles Crook of Bisley, weaver. Possessing 47 lb. 10 oz. of various woollen yarns believed to be stolen. H. Cooke JP and E. Aldridge JP. John Driver, clothier, of Minchinhampton, informer. Thomas Jones, clothier, of Bisley, witness. Fine £20. Offence committed 3 Jan. 1820.

39/B/73   29 March 1820. John Brown of Thornbury. Cutting down and stealing one chestnut tree, the property of John Fewster, surgeon, of Thornbury. Rev. R. Slade JP. Nathaniel Jefferys, complainant.

39/B/74   13 Oct. 1819. Thomas Garn of Forthampton, shopkeeper. Using an unequal measure. T. Nash D.D. JP, J. Timbrill D.D. JP and Rev. J. Keysall JP at a Petty Sessions held at Tewkesbury for the lower division of Tewkesbury hundred. Fine 20/-. Offence committed 17 Sept. 1819.

39/B/75   10 April 1820. Thomas Collins, employee of Mr. Thomas Ashwin, maltster, of Willersey. Wetting grain making into malt, after its removal from the cistern, contrary to law. Rev. J. Timbrill JP. John Parkin, excise officer, complainant. Fine of £50 mitigated to £15. Offence committed 8 April 1820.

39/B/76   17 March 1820. John Sandles of Stow on the Wold. Leaving his wife and family chargeable to the parish. Egerton Leigh junior JP. Apprehended by George Pain of Stow on the Wold. Committed to Northleach house of correction for three weeks. Offence committed 17 Feb. 1820.

39/B/77   13 Oct. 1820. [*Those named below were fined as below for*] Having defective weights. T. Nash D.D. JP, J. Timbrill D.D. JP and J. Keysall JP at a Petty Sessions held at Tewkesbury. Convicted [*except as otherwise stated*] on their own confession. Offences committed 7 to 18 Sept. 1820.

John Mathews of Apperley, butcher, 10/-; William Vernon, shopkeeper, 5/-, William Roberts, baker, 10/-, both of Ashton under Hill; William Leaver of Beckford, shopkeeper, 10/-, convicted on the oath of William Dovey; Joseph Lawrence of Deerhurst Walton, shopkeeper, 10/-; Gabriel Little of Grafton, shopkeeper, 10/-; John Dudfield of Fiddington, baker, 10/-, convicted on the oath of William Dovey; Sarah Wilkes, shopkeeper, 20/-, Thomas Smith, butcher, 10/-, both of Kemerton; William Lawrence of Tredington, shopkeeper, 10/-, convicted on the oath of William Dovey; Richard Ramelly of Twyning, shopkeeper, 10/-; Jeremiah Brotheridge of Tirley, shopkeeper, 10/-; William and John Kendall of the Leigh, coal-merchants, 10/-

39/C/1   4 May 1820. William Oldland of Breadstone, Berkeley, husbandman. Cutting down an oak tree in the Lagger or Roundabouts nursery near Breadstone, the property of James Croome. W. Davies D.D. JP and Robert Fitzhardinge Jenner JP. Daniel Croome Esq. of Berkeley, informer. James Croome, land surveyor, witness. First offence. Mitigated fine of 40/- and 2/6 costs.

39/C/2   23 Feb. 1820. John Tombs of Boddington, labourer. Having a dog and a gun for killing game without a licence. J. Timbrill D.D. JP at Tewkesbury. Fine £10. Offence committed 4 Feb. 1820.

39/C/3   19 Jan. 1820. Rev. John Neale, vicar or curate of Boddington. Failing to read publicly, after morning or evening prayer, an Act for the prevention of profanity, contrary to law. J. Timbrill JP and J. Keysall JP. Fine £5. Offence committed Sunday 2 Jan. 1820.

39/C/4   8 June 1820. Thomas Pinfold. Cutting down 100 young timber trees in a wood in Minchinhampton, the property of William Marsh. Rev. H. Campbell JP and O. P. Wathen JP. William Marsh, complainant. First offence. Fine £20 or twelve months in Horsley house of correction. Offence committed 27 May 1820.

39/C/5   10 July 1820. William Falkner of Buckland. Leaving his wife and four children chargeable to the parish. J. Timbrill D.D. JP at Beckford. — Richardson, overseer of the poor of Buckland, complainant. Offender pleaded guilty. Committed to Gloucester gaol until next Q.S. unless discharged earlier by due course of law.

39/C/6   26 May 1820. Benjamin Cooke of Painswick, weaver. Possessing 40 lb. of woollen yarns and 5¾ yards of woollen cloth believed to be stolen. H. Burgh JP and H. Cooke JP. Peter Hawker, gentleman, of Stroud, informer. Robert Keene, weaver, Thomas Nicholls, basket-maker, and Richard Smith, weaver, all of Stroud, witnesses. Fine £20. Offence committed 25 May 1820.

39/C/7   24 May 1820. William Charles Empson of Cheltenham, gentleman. Assaulting Elizabeth Mayer, toll-collector, wife of Samuel Mayer, tailor, of Cheltenham, while in the execution of her duty. J. Clutterbuck JP. Elizabeth and Samuel Mayer, informers. Offender pleaded not guilty. Fine 40/-. Offence committed 23 May 1820.

39/D/1   5 Oct. 1820. William Davis of Stow on the Wold, labourer. Being drunk. E. Leigh junior JP. Convicted 7 Sept. 1820. Fine 5/- .

39/D/2   17 Aug. 1820. Stephen Ague of Stow on the Wold. Selling ale without a licence. F. E. Witts JP and R. W. Ford JP. First offence.

39/D/3   13 Oct. 1820. William Lawrence of Tetbury, hatmaker. Stealing one hat and a quantity of fur entrusted to him by his employer John Cave. J. P. Paul JP. One calendar month in Horsley house of correction. Offence committed between 1 Sept. and 12 Oct. 1820.

39/D/4   9 Aug. 1820. William Edwards of Minchinhampton, baker. Possessing 7 lb. 2 oz. of woollen yarns believed to be stolen. H. Burgh JP and H. Cooke JP. Robert Keene, weaver, of Stroud, informer. Samuel Sandilands and John Clissold, labourers, of Minchinhampton, and Daniel Peyton, clothier, of Stroud, witnesses. Fine £20. Offence committed 5 Aug. 1820.

39/D/5   21 July 1920. Sarah wife of John Jeackes of Bisley, weaver. Possessing 18 lb. 8 oz. of woollen yarns believed to be stolen. H. Burgh JP and H. Cooke JP. Thomas Jones, clothier, of Bisley, informer. Robert Keene and Richard Smith, weavers, of Stroud, witnesses. Fine £20.

39/D/6   9 Oct. 1820. William Parker of Stanley Pontlarge. Leaving his wife and children chargeable to the parish. J. Timbrill JP at Beckford. James Bullock, overseer of the poor, complainant. Offender pleaded guilty. Committed to Northleach house of correction until next Q.S. unless earlier discharged by due course of law.

39/D/7   4 Feb. 1820. Abraham Perrett of North Nibley, clothier. Using a net for killing conies in Millend Wood without a certificate. H. W. Dyer JP at Wotton under Edge. Fine £20. Offence committed 17 Jan. 1820.

39/D/8   28 Jan. 1820. Thomas Robinson of North Nibley, labourer. Using a net [etc., as 39/D/7 except] Fine £10.

39/D/9   10 Oct. 1820. Richard Yates of Dixton, Monmouth, labourer. Using a snare to kill a hare at Staunton. Edward Machen JP. William Barnard, labourer, of Staunton near Coleford, informer. William Powell, yeoman, of Newland, witness. First offence. Mitigated fine of £10. Offence committed Sunday 1 Oct. 1820.

39/D/10   7 Aug. 1820. Edward Mason of Minchinhampton, weaver. Possessing 42 lb. 14 oz. of various woollen yarns believed to be stolen. H. Burgh JP and H. Cooke JP. Robert Keene, weaver, of Stroud, informer. Daniel Peyton, weaver, of Stroud, witness. Fine £20. Offence committed 5 Aug. 1820.

39/D/11   11 Sept. 1820. William Ingram of Gloucester, silversmith. Using a gun and dogs to kill game in Westbury on Severn when unqualified to do so. Rev. C. Crawley JP at Newnham. Maynard Colchester Esq. of Flaxley, informer. Offender admitted charge. Fine £5. Offence committed 1 Sept. 1820.

39/D/12   11 Sept. 1820. William Cooke of Barton St. Mary, Gloucester, gentleman. Using a gun [*etc.*, *as* 39/D/11].

39/D/13   21 Sept. 1820. Richard Claridge of Oddington, farmer. Using a gun and a dog to kill game in Maugersbury when unqualified to do so. Rev. F. E. Witts JP at Stow on the Wold. William Kempester, bailiff, of Wick Hill, Wick Rissington, informer. Thomas English, labourer, of Stow on the Wold, witness. Offender pleaded not guilty. Fine £5. Offence committed 8 Sept. 1820.

40/A/1   2 Jan. 1821. John Worgan of Hewelsfield, labourer. Possessing a bundle of ash poles believed to be cut from a wood in Tidenham. T. Thomas JP. Isaac Ellaway, woodward, of Chapel Hill, Monmouth, informer. Robert Moxham, farmer, of Woolaston, witness. Second offence. Fine £5 and 7/- costs. Offence committed 16 Sept. 1820.

40/A/2   2 Jan. 1821. Henry Wright of Hewelsfield, labourer. Possessing a bundle of hazel rods believed [*etc.*, *as* 40/A/1 *except*] Offence committed 4 Oct. 1820.

40/A/3   30 Dec. 1820. Thomas Midwinter of Great Rissington, labourer. Using a snare for killing game without a licence. Rev. R. W. Ford JP at Little Rissington. Fine £20.

40/A/4   2 Nov. 1820. Thomas Rayer of Stow on the Wold, gentleman. Using a gun and a dog to kill game in Upper Slaughter when not qualified. Rev. F. E. Witts JP at Stow on the Wold. Richard Prosser, yeoman, and Henry Lindow Lindow, gentleman, both of Lower Slaughter, informer and witness. Pleaded not guilty. Fine £5. Offence committed 31 Oct. 1820.

40/A/5   13 Dec. 1820. William Fryer of Eastington, weaver. Stealing 2 lb. of woollen yarn, the property of Messrs. Henry, John Phillimore and Henry Purnell Hicks, clothiers of Eastington. H. Cooke JP and Rev. P. Hawker JP. John Smith, wool-loft man to Messrs. Hicks, witness.

40/A/6   13 Dec. 1820. John Butcher of Cam, weaver. Stealing [*etc.*, *as* 40/A/5].

40/A/7   5 Dec. 1820. Elizabeth wife of Joseph Willis of Rodborough, shopkeeper. Buying 6 lb. of woollen yarn (thrums), the property of Messrs. Hicks, from Thomas Bendall. H. Cooke JP and Rev. P. Hawker JP. J. P. Hicks, clothier, of Eastington, informer. Thomas Hogg and Thomas Bendall, weavers, of Eastington, witnesses. First offence. Fine £20. Offence committed 30 Nov. 1820.

40/A/8   5 Dec. 1820. Joseph Willis of Rodborough, shopkeeper. Buying 12 oz. of woollen yarn (thrums) from James Chapman of Eastington, weaver. H. Cooke JP and Rev. P. Hawker JP. J. P. Hicks, informer. Thomas Hogg and James Chapman, weavers, of Eastington, witnesses. First offence. Fine £20. Offence committed four or five weeks previously.

40/A/9   13 Dec. 1820. Isaac Earle of King's Stanley, weaver. Buying 1 lb. of woollen waste from Betty wife of James Vick, weaver, of Eastington. Rev. P. Hawker JP and H. Cooke JP. J. P. Hicks, informer. Betty Vick, witness. First offence. Fine £20. Offence committed 13 Oct. 1820.

40/A/10   13 Dec. 1820. Isaac Earle of King's Stanley. Possessing 26½ lb. of various woollen yarns believed to be stolen. Rev. P. Hawker JP and H. Cooke JP. J. P. Hicks, informer. George Daniel Harris, clothier, of King's Stanley, and Robert Keene, weaver, of Stroud, witnesses. First offence. Fine £20. Offence committed 8 Dec. 1820.

40/A/11   5 Dec. 1820. John Hathawey of St. Briavels, labourer. Possessing a bundle of ash poles believed to be cut from a wood in Tidenham. T. Thomas JP. Isaac Ellaway, woodward, of Chapel Hill, Monmouth, informer. William Johnson, cordwainer, of Hewelsfield, witness. Fine 40/- and 7/- costs. Offence committed 16 Sept. 1820.

40/A/12   2 Jan. 1821. James Brown of Hewelsfield, labourer. Possessing a bundle of hazel rods believed to be cut from a wood in Woolaston. T. Thomas JP. Isaac Ellaway, woodward, of Chapel Hill, Monmouth, informer. Robert Moxham, farmer, of Woolaston, witness. Fine 20/- and 7/- costs. Offence committed 4 Oct. 1820.

40/A/13   7 Nov. 1820. John Lewis of Hewelsfield, labourer. Possessing a bundle of ash poles believed to be cut from a wood in Tidenham. T. Thomas JP. Robert Moxham, farmer, of Woolaston, witness. First offence. Fine 40/- and 7/- costs. Offence committed 16 Sept. 1820.

40/A/14   2 Jan. 1821. William Colbourn of Newland, labourer. Using a wire to kill a hare in Staunton. T. Thomas JP. First offence. Fine £20. Offence committed 6 Dec. 1820.

40/A/15   1 Dec. 1820. Edmund Jones of Marshfield, labourer. Keeping and using three greyhounds to destroy game. T. Jones JP and F. Pelly JP at Old Sodbury. Thomas Reed of Tormarton, informer. Thomas Webb of Great Badminton, witness. Pleaded not guilty. Fine £5. Offence committed 17 Nov. 1820.

40/A/16   13 Dec. 1820. William Higgins *alias* Harris of Coaley, labourer. Possessing 23½ lb. of various stolen woollen yarns. H. Cooke JP and Rev. P. Hawker JP. Warrant issued and premises searched on information given by J. P. Hicks, clothier, of Eastington. First offence. Fine £20. Offence committed 8 Dec. 1820.

40/A/17   8 Dec. 1820. John King of Tetbury. Using a wire to kill game in Cherington, not having the required qualification. J. D. Phelps JP at Horsley. Thomas Lane, servant, of Cherington, informer. Daniel Hall, labourer, of Cherington, witness. Pleaded not guilty. Fine £5. Offence committed 7 Dec. 1820.

40/B/1   2 Feb. 1821. James Cole of Old Sodbury, farmer. Shooting a hare caught by his pointer dog, when unqualified. T. Brooke LL.D. JP at a Petty Sessions held at the Cross Hands inn, Old Sodbury. John Morley, labourer, of Little Sodbury, informer. Richard Hall of Little Sodbury, witness. Fine £5. Offence committed 14 Nov. 1820.

40/B/2   2 Jan. 1821. Thomas Hawkins the younger of Frampton on Severn. Using a gun for taking game without obtaining the required certificate. T. J. Lloyd Baker JP and commissioner for assessed taxes, at Wheatenhurst. Fine £20. Offence committed 1 Dec. 1820.

40/B/3   24 March 1821. Aaron Bick of Wotton Hamlet. Using a dog to kill conies in enclosed ground, namely the Coombe, Hucclecote, in the tenure of Giles Arkell. Rev. J. B. Cheston JP and commissioner for assessed taxes. Fine £10. Offence committed 11 March 1821.

40/B/4   17 March 1821. Richard Goulding of Elmore labourer. Using a dog to kill conies in enclosed ground in the tenure of George Carveth, namely the Parks, Elmore. Rev. J. B. Cheston JP and commissioner for assessed taxes. Fine £20. Offence committed 4 March 1821.

40/B/5   17 Feb. 1821. Thomas Wadley of Maisemore, yeoman. Using a dog to kill a hare in Lassington. Rev. J. B. Cheston JP and commissioner for assessed taxes. Fine £10. Offence committed 26 Jan. 1821.

40/B/6   5 Dec. 1820. William Smith. Using a forged testimonial to gain employment as a servant to Charles Ludlow Walker Esq. of Stapleton. Stephen Cave JP and G. Goldney JP. Offender confessed. Fine £20. Offence committed 7 June 1820.

40/B/7   2 Jan. 1821. Charles Reed of Frampton on Severn. Shooting game without obtaining a certificate. T. J. Lloyd Baker JP and commissioner for assessed taxes, at Wheatenhurst. Fine £20. Offence committed 1 Dec. 1820.

40/B/8   2 Jan. 1821. Charles Reed of Frampton on Severn. Shooting conies without obtaining a certificate [*etc.*, *as* 40/B/7 *except*] Offence committed 18 Nov. 1820.

40/B/9   1 Nov. 1820. Mark Cullimore of Berkeley, labourer. Using a ferret to kill a coney in enclosed ground in Alkington (in the tenure of George Ponting) without obtaining a certificate. H. W. Dyer JP and commissioner for assessed taxes, at Wotton under Edge. Fine £10. Offence committed 6 Oct. 1820.

40/B/10   19 Jan. 1821. William Brown of Rodborough, labourer. Possessing stolen napping-mill spindles at Stonehouse. H. Burgh JP and H. Cooke JP. Peter Hawker, gentleman, of Stroud, informer. First offence. Fine 20/-.

40/B/11   23 March 1821. Thomas Chandler of Stroud, weaver. Possessing 16 lb. 14 oz. of various woollen yarns believed to be stolen. H. Burgh JP and H. Cooke JP. Warrant issued and premises searched. Robert Keene, weaver, of Stroud, informer. First offence. Fine £20. Offence committed 21 March 1821.

40/B/12   5 March 1821. Daniel Cook of Kemble, labourer. Using a wire to kill game in Cherington. J. P. Paul JP at Tetbury. Thomas Lane and Edward Nurdin, labourers, of Cherington, informer and witness. Pleaded not guilty. Fine £5. Offence committed 16 Feb. 1821.

40/B/13   7 March 1821. George Golding of Tetbury, labourer. Using a wire to kill game in Cherington. J. P. Paul JP, T. Smith JP and Rev. Daniel Lysons JP. Thomas Lane and Charles Hunt, labourers, of Cherington, informer and witness. Pleaded not guilty. Fine £5. Offence committed 24 Feb. 1821.

40/B/14   7 March 1821. Thomas Williams of Tetbury, labourer. Using a wire [*etc.*, *as* 40/B/13].

40/C/1   5 June 1821. George Harris the younger of Coleford, labourer. Using a wire for killing a hare in Staunton [*MS.* Stanton]. E. Machen JP. William Choules, labourer, of Clearwell, informer. William Powell, labourer, of Newland, witness. Accused refused to attend. First offence. Fine £5. Offence committed 20 April 1821.

40/C/2–   12 May 1821. [*Names as below.*] Using non-standard weights. Maynard Colchester JP
42   and Rev. C. Crawley JP at a Petty Sessions for the Forest division. Fine 20/- and 8/6 costs [*except as otherwise stated*]. Offences committed 3, 4, 5, 7, 8 May 1821.

40/C/2   Daniel White of Awre, shopkeeper.

40/C/3   Thomas Cowles of Awre, miller.

40/C/4   William Baldwin of Mitcheldean, blacksmith. Fine 5/- and 8/6 costs.

40/C/5   John Gay of Mitcheldean, shopkeeper.

40/C/6   John Smallwood of Churcham, shopkeeper. Fine 5/- and 8/6 costs.

40/C/7   John Benfield of Churcham, shopkeeper.

40/C/8   Samuel Taylor of Tibberton, shopkeeper. Fine 5/- and 8/6 costs.

40/C/9   William Wheeldon of Westbury on Severn, shopkeeper.

40/C/10   Joseph Rudge of Longhope, blacksmith. Fine 5/- and 8/6/ costs.

40/C/11   James Blethin of Littledean, shopkeeper.

40/C/12   William Green of Huntley, shopkeeper.

40/C/13   William Roberts of Westbury on Severn, shopkeeper.

40/C/14   William Gwilliam of Littledean, shopkeeper.

40/C/15   William Davies of Mitcheldean, shopkeeper.

40/C/16   Mary Hale of Mitcheldean, shopkeeper.

40/C/17   William Hale of Flaxley, blacksmith. Fine 5/- and 8/6 costs.

40/C/18   Thomas Hobbs of Westbury on Severn, blacksmith. Fine 5/- and 8/6 costs.

40/C/19   James Hill on Newnham, butcher. Fine 5/- and 8/6/ costs.

40/C/20	Absolem Smith of Mitcheldean, shopkeeper.
40/C/21	George Wood of Littledean, shopkeeper.
40/C/22	John Morse of Newnham, butcher. Fine 5/- and 8/6 costs.
40/C/23	James Dancey of Awre, shopkeeper.
40/C/24	Thomas Howell of Awre, butcher.
40/C/25	William Price of Lea, shopkeeper.
40/C/26	Thomas Howley of Churcham, shopkeeper. Fine 5/- and 8/6 costs.
40/C/27	John Sims of Minsterworth, shopkeeper. Fine 10/- and 8/6 costs.
40/C/28	William Phelps of Minsterworth, shopkeeper.
40/C/29	William Cooper of Littledean, shopkeeper.
40/C/30	Samuel Wintle of Westbury on Severn, flour dealer.
40/C/31	Jeremiah Bamford of Littledean, shopkeeper.
40/C/32	John Harper of Huntley, blacksmith. Fine 5/- and 8/6 costs.
40/C/33	Elizabeth Baker of Blaisdon, shopkeeper.
40/C/34	William Parker of Abenhall, shopkeeper.
40/C/35	John Baylis of Westbury on Severn, blacksmith. Fine 5/- and 8/6 costs.
40/C/36	William Coleman of Mitcheldean, shopkeeper.
40/C/37	William Griffiths of Mitcheldean, shopkeeper.
40/C/38	Thomas Wheeldon of Mitcheldean, shopkeeper.
40/C/39	Jonathan Preest of Mitcheldean, shopkeeper.
40/C/40	Richard Newman of Huntley, blacksmith. Fine 5/- and 8/6/ costs.
40/C/41	William Jeynes of Awre, shopkeeper.
40/C/42	James Merriman of Littledean, shopkeeper.
40/C/43	5 June 1821. George Harris the younger of Coleford, labourer. Using a wire to kill a hare in Staunton [*MS.* Stanton]. P. J. Ducarel JP and E. Machen JP. First offence. Fine £5. Offence committed Friday 20 April 1821. [*Cf.* 40/C/1.]
40/C/44	15 June 1821. Joseph Bloodworth of Uley, weaver. Persuading Joseph Austin of Uley to leave his employer Joseph Jeens, cloth manufacturer, of Uley, in order to better his wages. H. C. Clifford JP and Rev. W. Lloyd Baker JP at Wotton under Edge. Committed to the common gaol for two calendar months. Offence committed 13 June 1821.
40/C/45	15 June 1821. Charles Powell *alias* Stephens of Uley, weaver. Persuading Joseph Austin [*etc., as* 40/C/44].
40/C/46	15 June 1821. Joseph Powell of Uley, weaver. Entering into an illegal combination in order to obtain a rise in wages from 1/6 to 1/9 per ell. H. C. Clifford JP and Rev. W. Lloyd Baker JP at Wotton under Edge. Committed to the common gaol for two calendar months. Offence committed 13 June 1821.
40/C/47	15 June 1821. Reuben Smith the younger of Uley, weaver. Entering into an illegal combination [*etc., as* 40/C/46].
40/C/48	15 June 1821. Joseph Smith of Uley, weaver. Entering into an illegal combination [*etc., as* 40/C/46 *except*] Committed . . . for one calendar month.
40/C/49	15 June 1821. Ananias Smith of Uley, weaver. Entering into an illegal combination [*etc., as* 40/C/46 *except*] Committed . . . for one calendar month.
40/C/50	15 June 1821. Samuel Bloodworth of Uley, weaver. Entering into an illegal combination [*etc., as* 40/C/46].
40/D	[*File for Michaelmas Sessions missing.*]

41/A/1 15 Nov. 1821. Thomas Stratford of Little Barrington. Using a wire for killing game without obtaining the required certificate. Rev. R. W. Ford JP and commissioner for taxes, at Little Rissington. Fine £20.

41/A/2 15 Nov. 1821. Joseph Taylor of Great Barrington. Using a wire [etc., as 41/A/1].

41/A/3 31 Oct. 1821. John Williams of Stinchcombe, labourer. Possessing 5 lb. of woollen yarn believed to be stolen. H. Burgh JP and H. Cooke JP. H. P. Hicks, clothier, of Eastington, informer. Robert Keene, weaver, of Stroud, witness. First offence. Fine £20. Offence committed 28 Oct. 1821.

41/A/4 31 Oct. 1821. John Williams of Stinchcombe, labourer. Buying and receiving 1 lb. of stolen woollen yarn from James Chapman, weaver, of Eastington. H. Burgh JP and H. Cooke JP. H. P. Hicks, informer. James Chapman, witness. First offence. Fine £40. Offence committed 5 Oct. 1821.

41/A/5 31 Oct. 1821. John Davis of Eastington, weaver. Selling 1 lb. of woollen yarn believed to be stolen to William Higgins *alias* Harries, labourer, of Coaley. H. Burgh JP and H. Cooke JP. J. P. Hicks, clothier, and James Perkins, labourer, both of Eastington, informer and witness. First offence. Fine £40.

41/A/6 31 Oct. 1821. Thomas Walkley of King's Stanley, labourer. Possessing 4 lb. of woollen yarn believed to be stolen. H. Burgh JP and H. Cooke JP. J. P. Hicks, informer. R. Keene, witness. First offence. Fine £20. Offence committed 30 Oct. 1821.

41/A/7 7 Dec. 1821. Samuel Brinkworth of Mangotsfield, auctioneer. Shooting game at Siston when unqualified. Rev. T. Jones JP and Rev. F. Pelly JP at Wick. William Coules of Siston, informer. Robert Haskins, witness. Fine £5. Offence committed 1 Oct. 1821.

41/A/8 12 Nov. 1821. Charles Lydiat of Batheaston, Som. Using a hare net to kill game in Old Sodbury. Rev. F. Pelly JP and Fiennes Trotman junior JP at Wick. William Dyer of Dodington, informer. William Gowen, witness. Fine £5 and £1 15s. costs. Offence committed night of 10/11 Nov. 1821.

41/A/9 19 Nov. 1821. Robert Nelmes of Awre, tiler. Shooting a hare at Newnham. Rev. C. Crawley JP and M. Colchester JP. John Hall, yeoman, of Newnham, informer. Robert Wood, labourer, of Newnham, witness. First offence. Mitigated fine of £5. Offence committed night of 3 Nov. 1821.

41/A/10 19 Nov. 1821. John Thompson the younger of Ruardean, yeoman. Breaking down part of the fence around Crabtreehill enclosure. Rev. C. Crawley JP and M. Colchester JP. Thomas Witts, forest keeper, of the Speech House, informer. Samuel Mountjoy, woodman, of Dean Forest, witness. Fine £10. Offence committed 15 Oct. 1821.

41/A/11 19 Nov. 1821. John Allen of Ruardean, butcher. Breaking down part [etc., as 41/A/10].

41/A/12 19 Nov. 1821. Thomas Hughes the younger of Marstow, Herefs., farmer. Breaking down part [etc., as 41/A/10].

41/A/13 27 Dec. 1821. Joseph Arkell of Condicote, farmer. Keeping and using a gun and dogs to kill game in Temple Guiting when unqualified. Rev. F. E. Witts JP at Stow on the Wold. John Swan, gamekeeper, of Temple Guiting, informer. John Hayward of Temple Guiting, witness. Fine £5. Offence committed 18 Dec. 1821.

41/B/1 19 Feb. 1822. James Martin of Hewelsfield, waterman. Cutting underwood in Brake Wood, the property of Edward Prior. Rev. T. Thomas JP and E. Machen JP. E. Prior, yeoman, of Tidenham, complainant. Fine 20/- and 5/- costs. Offence committed 28 Dec. 1821.

41/B/2   5 March 1822. Tholerain Harris *alias* Innes of St. Briavels hundred, labourer. Possessing a wire for killing a hare. E. Machen JP. William Choales and William Powell, yeomen, of Newland, informer and witness. First offence. Fine £5. Offence committed 22 Feb. 1822.

41/B/3   2 April 1822. John Young of Newland, labourer. Keeping and using a wire to kill a hare. E. Machen JP. W. Chouls, informer. W. Powell, witness. Accused refused to attend. First offence. Fine £5. Offence committed 21 March 1822.

41/B/4   2 April 1822. William Mansell *alias* Mousell of St. Briavels hundred, labourer. Possessing and using a hay net for killing a hare. E. Machen JP. James Haffenden Esq. and Thomas Ridler, yeoman, of Newland, informer and witness. First offence. Fine £5. Offence committed 25 March 1822.

41/B/5   19 Oct. 1821. John Shipton of Eldersfield, farmer. Shooting a pheasant in Forthampton without obtaining the required certificate. Rev. J. Commeline JP and commissioner for taxes. Fine £10. Offence committed 10 Oct. 1821.

41/B/6   4 March 1822. William Durham of Clapton [on the Hill]. Keeping and using wires to kill game when unqualified. Rev. R. W. Ford JP at Little Rissington. Fine £5. Offence committed 18 Feb. 1822.

41/B/7   1 April 1822. John Cannock, yeoman, of Westbury on Severn. Killing a hen sitting on a clutch of 12 eggs, thereby killing the chicks, the property of Mary Broben, widow, of Westbury on Severn. Rev. C. Crawley JP. Fine £1 1*s*. and 7/6 costs to be paid to the complainant. Offence committed 20 March 1822.

41/B/8   1 Feb. 1822. Rowland Davis of Ross, house-painter. Using a dog to kill game in Newland without obtaining the required certificate. Rev. C. Sandiford JP, Rev. C. Crawley JP and Joseph Swayne Esq., commissioners for taxes, at Newnham. Fine £12. Offence committed 10 Nov. 1821.

41/B/9   1 Feb. 1822. Rowland Davis of Ross, house-painter. Refusing to give his name and address to James Haffenden or to produce the required certificate when discovered in the act of using a dog to kill game in Newland [*etc.*, *as* 41/B/8].

41/B/10   9 March 1822. Charles Crook of Bisley, weaver. Possessing ½ lb. of woollen yarn believed to be stolen. H. Burgh JP and H. Cooke JP. Peter Hawker, gentleman, of Stroud, informer. Sampson Wright and Giles Gardner, weavers, of Bisley, witnesses. Fine £20. Offence committed 8 March 1822.

41/B/11   16 Feb. 1822. John Colwell of Minsterworth, cooper. Keeping and using a snare to kill a hare at Highnam. Rev. J. B. Cheston JP at Mr. Henry Hooper Wilton's office, Gloucester. John Clutterbuck, labourer, of Highnam, informer. Samuel Meadows, labourer, witness. Fine £5. Offence committed 7 Feb. 1822.

41/C/1   9 July 1822. Samuel Luff of St. Briavels, labourer. Grubbing up and stealing 20 young ash trees from a grove in Tidenham, the property of Henry Charles, duke of Beaufort. E. Machen JP. Thomas Hoskins, woodward, of Tidenham, and Isaac Ellaway, woodward, of Chapel Hill, Monmouth, witnesses. First offence. Fine £2 and 7/6 costs. Offence committed 27 Feb. 1822.

41/C/2   26 April 1822. Benjamin Neville, late of Stanway, labourer. Leaving his son Richard (less than four years old) chargeable to the parish after the death of the child's mother, his lawful wife Sarah. J. Timbrill D.D. JP at Beckford. George Cook, yeoman, of Stanway, informer (at Tewkesbury). Warrant issued to all constables, particularly John Prosser, for offender's arrest. Accused voluntarily confessed. Committed to house of correction to be dealt with at next Q.S. Offence committed 31 March 1818.

41/C/3   15 June 1822. John Parker *alias* Evans. Wilfully leaving his wife and two children chargeable to the hamlet of Oldland. G. Goldney JP. Robert Jones, witness. Committed to house of correction to be dealt with at next Q.S. Offence committed 1 May 1822.

41/C/4   27 May 1822. William Collinson, hawker of cutlery and hardware. Trading without a licence in Stroud. H. Burgh JP and H. Cooke JP at Stroud. Robert Keene, weaver, of Stroud, informer. John Pierce Brisley, witness. Accused pleaded not guilty. Fine £10.

41/C/5   27 May 1822. Samuel Thomas, hawker of cutlery and hardware. Trading without a licence in Stroud. H. Burgh JP and H. Cooke JP at Stroud. William Thomas Paris, gentleman, of Stroud, informer. J. P. Brisley, witness. Fine £10.

41/C/6   13 July 1822. John Merrett, late of Stroud, labourer. Possessing lead believed to be stolen. H. Burgh JP and H. Cooke JP.

41/C/7   13 July 1822. Samuel Merrett, late of Stroud, labourer. Possessing lead [*etc.*, *as* 41/C/6].

41/C/8   5 June 1822. John Jeackes of Bisley. Possessing 24 lb. of various woollen yarns believed to be stolen. H. Burgh JP and H. Cooke JP. P. Hawker, gentleman, of Stroud, informer. John Capel, clothier, and R. Keene, weaver, both of Stroud, witnesses. Second offence. [*Cf.* 39/A/2.] Fine £30.

41/C/9   4 July 1822. Samuel Lowndes, pedlar or petty chapman. Selling glass without a licence in Cheltenham. R. Capper JP at Cheltenham. Samuel Oakey, informer. Andrew Hathaway, witness. Fine £10. Offence committed 4 July 1822.

41/C/10   17 June 1822. Solomon Phillips, pedlar or petty chapman. Selling glass without a licence in Cheltenham. R. Capper JP at Cheltenham. John Cossens, informer. Mark Brady, witness. Fine £10. Offence committed 17 June 1822.

41/D/1   11 Oct. 1822. Thomas Churm of Burford, labourer. Attempting to kill a fallow deer at Widford in an enclosure in Wychwood Forest, the property of Lord Churchill. Rev. F. E. Witts JP. Joseph Millin, deer keeper, of Southlawn Lodge, Oxon., complainant. Job Pratley, witness. Accused confessed. Offence committed 6 Oct. 1822.

41/D/2   6 Sept. 1822. James Brookes of Gotherington, farmer. Obstructing the road in Gotherington with his wagon by not keeping to the left and thereby preventing Moses Langston from passing. J. Timbrill D.D. JP and Rev. J. Keysall JP. Fine £2 10*s.* Offence committed 30 Aug. 1822.

41/D/3   2 Oct. 1822. John Cresswell of Gotherington, farmer. Refusing to do his required two days' work with his team in repairing the roads as directed by Richard Tree, road surveyor. J. Timbrill D.D. JP and William Dowdeswell JP. Offence committed 27 and 28 May 1822.

41/D/4   4 Sept. 1822. John Wicksey, labourer. Being too far from his wagon to keep proper control of the two horses, at Prestbury. J. Timbrill D.D. JP and Rev. J. Keysall JP at Tewkesbury. Henry Hooper Fryer the younger, gentleman, of Tewkesbury, informer. Moses Langston, witness. Fine 10/-. Offence committed 30 Aug. 1822.

41/D/5   31 July 1822. John Hale of Littledean, labourer. Possessing part of a fallow or red deer without satisfactory explanation. E. Machen JP. William Coles of Lydney, gamekeeper to Rt. Hon. Charles Bathurst, complainant. Fine £30. Offence committed 31 July 1822.

41/D/6   6 Aug. 1822. John Jenkins of Hewelsfield, labourer. Possessing underwood, the property of Henry Charles [*MS.* Charles Henry], duke of Beaufort, without satisfactory explanation. Rev. T. Thomas JP. Thomas Hoskins, woodward, of Tidenham, informer. Isaac Ellaway, woodward of Chapel Hill, Monmouth, witness. First offence. Fine £1 and 7/- costs. Offence committed 4 July 1822

41/D/7   6 Aug. 1822. Warren Hathaway of Hewelsfield, labourer. Possessing underwood [*etc.*, *as* 41/D/6].

41/D/8   6 Aug. 1822. Aaron Butler of St. Briavels, labourer. Possessing underwood [*etc.*, *as* 41/D/6].

41/D/9   6 Aug. 1822. William Jenkins the elder of Frampton on Severn, constable. Encouraging his son to fight another despite being called on to restore order. John Sayer JP and C. O. Cambridge JP at Wheatenhurst. Hester Haines of Frampton on Severn and Thomas Jones, butcher, of Arlingham, complainants. Offender pleaded not guilty. Fine 40/-. Offence committed 22 July 1822. (Fine paid.)

41/D/10   5 Aug. 1822. John Lloyd. Vagrancy, i.e. performing a certain interlude or entertainment of the stage, in Cheltenham. J. Agg JP and R. Capper JP at Cheltenham. Offence committed 2 Aug. 1822.

41/D/11   1 Aug. 1822. William Edwards of Minchinhampton, labourer. Possessing 15 lb. 4 oz. of woollen yarn believed to be stolen. H. Burgh JP and H. Cooke JP. Peter Hawker, gentleman, informer. Robert Keene, constable, and Daniel Peyton, clothier, both of Stroud, witnesses. Second offence. Fine £30. Offence committed 25 July 1822.

41/D/12   10 Aug. 1822. Isaac Estcott of Stroud, labourer. Possessing three-quarters of a yard of woollen cloth believed to be stolen. H. Burgh JP and H. Cooke JP. P. Hawker, gentleman, of Stroud, informer. Robert Keene, weaver, of Stroud, witness. First offence. Fine £20. Offence committed 8 Aug. 1822.

41/D/13   6 Aug. 1822. John March of Bisley, labourer. Possessing 3½ lb. of woollen yarn believed to be stolen. H. Burgh JP and H. Cooke JP. P. Hawker, gentleman, informer. Robert Keene, weaver, of Stroud, witness. Second offence. [*Cf.* 38/D/13.] Fine £30.

41/D/14   10 Oct. 1822. John Wilkins of Horsley, labourer. Possessing 3½ lb. of woollen yarn believed to be stolen. H. Burgh JP and H. Cooke JP. Josiah Howell, baker, of Stroud, informer. Robert Keene, weaver, of Stroud, witness. First offence. Fine £20. Offence committed 9 Oct. 1822.

41/D/15   9 Aug. 1822. William Higgins *alias* Harris of Coaley, labourer. Possessing 13 lb. of woollen yarn believed to be stolen. H. Burgh JP and H. Cooke JP. P. Hawker, gentleman, informer. Robert Keene, constable of Stroud, witness. Second offence. [*Cf.* 40/A/16.] Fine £30. Offence committed 9 Aug. 1822.

41/D/16   20 Aug. 1822. Samuel Brinkworth of Horsley, labourer. Possessing 1 lb. of woollen waste believed to be stolen. H. Burgh JP and H. Cooke JP. P. Hawker, gentleman, informer. Robert Keene, weaver, of Stroud, witness. First offence. Fine £20. Offence committed 19 Aug. 1822.

41/D/17   21 Aug. Thomas Brinkworth of Horsley, labourer. Possessing 12½ lb. of woollen yarn believed to be stolen. H. Burgh JP and H. Cooke JP. P. Hawker, gentleman, informer. Robert Keene, weaver, of Stroud, and Hannah Jowlings, single woman, of Horsley, witnesses. First offence. Fine £20. Offence committed 19 Aug. 1822.

41/D/18   14 Sept. 1822. Charles Crook of Bisley, labourer. Possessing 79 yards of raw woollen cloth and 298 lb. of various woollen yarns believed to be stolen. H. Burgh JP and E. Aldridge JP. Isaac Woodfield, yeoman, of Bisley, informer. Nathaniel Jones, clothier, of Bisley, witness. Third offence. [*Cf.* 39/B/72, 41/B/10.] Fine £40. Offence committed 12 Sept. 1822.

41/D/19   19 Sept. 1822. William Burgess of Henbury, labourer. Keeping and using a snare. G. Goldney JP at Lawfords Gate sessions room, St. Philip and St. Jacob, Bristol. Thomas Goddard, labourer, informer, and Abraham Pope, labourer, witness, both of Henbury. Offender pleaded not guilty, but had been seen taking a snare from Mrs. Castle's hedge and putting it in his hat. Fine £5. Offence committed 17 Sept. 1822.

41/D/20   10 Oct. 1822. Ralph Miles of Condicote, farmer. Keeping and using a gun and two dogs to kill game in Kineton when not qualified. Rev. F. E. Witts JP at Stow on the Wold. John Hayward, under-gamekeeper, of Temple Guiting, informer. John Swan of Temple Guiting, witness. Offender pleaded not guilty. Fine £5. Offence committed 1 Oct. 1822.

41/D/21   24 July 1822. William Davis. Begging under false pretences – playing unlawful games in Tetbury. J. P. Paul JP and Rev. D. Lysons JP. Alexander Sealy, constable of Tetbury, witness. Offence committed 22 July 1822.

41/D/22   24 July 1822. Mary Conell. Selling peppermint water in Tetbury without a licence [*etc., as* 41/D/21].

41/D/23   24 July 1822. John Conell. Keeping and using a gaming table and allowing unlawful games to be played thereon at Tetbury fair [*etc., as* 41/D/21].

41/D/24   14 Aug. 1822. Richard Duncan. Begging under false pretences in Tetbury. J. P. Paul JP. Alexander Sealy, constable of Tetbury, witness. Offence committed 31 July 1822.

41/D/25   14 Aug. 1822. William Reese. Begging [*etc., as* 41/D/24].

41/D/26   1 Aug. 1822. Anthony McConolty. Hawking goods from door to door without a licence, in Tetbury. J. P. Paul JP. Alexander Sealy, constable of Tetbury, witness. Offence committed 31 July 1822.

41/D/27   8 Oct. 1822. Thomas Forty of Dymock, farmer. Keeping and using a gun to kill game when not qualified. Rev. Reginald Pyndar JP at the upper hall, Ledbury, Herefs. Mark Nutting, servant, of Ledbury, informer. John Bowkett, witness. Offender voluntarily confessed. Fine £5. Offence committed 5 Oct. 1822.

41/D/28   8 Oct. 1822. George Tustin of Dymock, farmer. Keeping and using a gun [*etc., as* 41/D/27].

42/A/1   19 Oct. 1822. Charles Crook of Bisley, labourer. Possessing 70 lb. of various woollen yarns and 30 yards of woollen cloth believed to be stolen. H. Burgh JP and E. Aldridge JP. P. Hawker, gentleman, of Stroud, informer. Isaac Woodfield, witness. Third [*sic, recte* fourth] offence. [*Cf.* 39/B/72, 41/B/10, 41/D/18; *also* 42/A/49.] Fine £40.

42/A/2–   20 Dec. 1822. [*Names as below.*] Having defective weights [*except* 43/A/5–6, 9, 18, 26].
31   H. Burgh JP, H. Cooke JP and E. Aldridge JP at a Petty Sessions for Bisley hundred. [*Fines as below*] and 7/- costs. Offences committed between 4 and 18 Dec. 1822.

42/A/2   Charlotte Webb of Painswick, shopkeeper. Fine 10/-.

42/A/3   Henry Musty of Painswick, shopkeeper. Fine 10/-.

42/A/4   Ann Cooke of Painswick, shopkeeper. Fine 5/-.

42/A/5   William Peacey of Stroud, stallholder. Fine 10/-. Having a defective balance.

42/A/6   Daniel Bown of Stroud, shopkeeper. Fine £1. Having defective weights and balance.

42/A/7   Elizabeth Browne of Stroud, shopkeeper. Fine 7/6.

42/A/8   Thomas Bliss of Stroud, shopkeeper. Fine 5/-.

42/A/9   Thomas Beals of Stroud, stallholder. Fine 5/-. Having a defective balance.

42/A/10   Samuel Goddard the younger of Painswick, shopkeeper. Fine 5/-.

42/A/11   James Wood of Painswick, shopkeeper. Fine 5/-.

42/A/12   Eunice Wood of Painswick, shopkeeper. Fine 10/-.

42/A/13   William Wright of Painswick, shopkeeper. Fine £1.

42/A/14   Thomas Carter of Painswick, shopkeeper. Fine 5/-.

42/A/15   Samuel Goddard of Painswick, shopkeeper. Fine 10/-.

42/A/16   John Driver of Painswick, shopkeeper. Fine 7/6.

42/A/17   Thomas Bridges of Painswick, shopkeeper. Fine 5/-.

42/A/18   Mary Lemon of Painswick, shopkeeper. Fine £1. Having defective weights and balance.

42/A/19   Thomas Stephens of Painswick, shopkeeper. Fine 5/-.

42/A/20   Samuel Holder of Painswick, shopkeeper. Fine 5/-.

42/A/21   William Lodge of Painswick, shopkeeper. Fine 5/-.

42/A/22   William Hinton of Painswick, shopkeeper. Fine 5/-.

42/A/23   Charles Wright of Painswick, shopkeeper. Fine 10/-.

42/A/24   Benjamin Paine of Painswick, shopkeeper. Fine 5/-.

42/A/25   John Okey of Painswick, shopkeeper. Fine £1.

42/A/26   Thomas Carter the younger of Painswick, shopkeeper. Fine £1. Having a defective balance.

42/A/27   James Birt of Painswick, shopkeeper. Fine £1.

42/A/28   John Grafton of Stroud, shopkeeper. Fine £1.

42/A/29   Henry Cooke of Painswick, shopkeeper. Fine 5/-.

42/A/30   Ann Weeks of Painswick, shopkeeper. Fine 10/-.

42/A/31   Ann Holder of Painswick, shopkeeper. Fine 10/-.

42/A/32   25 Oct. 1822. Jacob Whiting of Bisley, innkeeper. Failing to observe the conditions of the recognizance entered into when obtaining a licence. H. Burgh JP and E. Aldridge JP. First offence. Fine 5/- and 5/6 costs.

42/A/33   25 Oct. 1822. James Wakefield of Stroud, innkeeper. Failing [*etc.*, *as* 42/A/32].

42/A/34   15 Nov. 1822. William Merrett of Stroud, innkeeper. Failing [*etc.*, *as* 42/A/32].

42/A/35   23 Dec. 1822. William Bush Parker of St. Paul's [Bristol], solicitor. Using a gun and a dog to kill game at Pucklechurch when not qualified. W. Blathwayt JP and F. Trotman junior JP. Information given to Rev. F. Pelly and F. Trotman junior at Wick by James Vincent of Pucklechurch. William Thompson, witness. Fine £5. Offence committed 17 Oct. 1822.

42/A/36   2 Dec. 1822. Edwin son of Joseph Bendall of Old Sodbury, farmer. Shooting a hare in Horton without obtaining the required certificate. Rev. T. Jones JP, tax commissioner for Grumbalds Ash district. Mitigated fine of £10. Offence committed 22 Oct. 1822.

42/A/37   12 Dec. 1822. James Cole of Old Sodbury, farmer. Using a gun and dogs with intent to kill game in Yate without obtaining the required certificate. Rev. T. Jones JP, tax commissioner. Mitigated fine of £10. Offence committed 18 Nov. 1822.

42/A/38   6 Dec. 1822. Joseph Bendall, farmer, and his son Edwin Bendall, of Old Sodbury. Beating over land in Horton and Yate with guns and dogs in pursuit of game without obtaining the required certificate [*etc.*, *as* 42/A/37, *including*] Fine £10 each.

42/A/39   25 Nov. 1822. Joseph Bennett of Littledean, nailer. Using a dog for killing game in the Forest of Dean without obtaining the required certificate. Rev. C. Sandiford JP, Rev. C. Crawley JP and Rev. J. Sayer JP, commissioners for taxes, and John Wright Guise JP at Newnham. Fine £20. Offence committed 22 Oct. 1822.

42/A/40 21 Nov. 1822. John Lyddon of St. Philip and St. Jacob, [Bristol], pawnbroker. Issuing a pawn ticket not stating the abode and status of the person pawning nor giving a fair and legible description of the goods pawned. Charles Ludlow Walker JP. Fine £2. Offence committed 6 Nov. 1822.

42/A/41 21 Nov. 1822. George May of Winterbourne, labourer. Using nets and a snare to kill game in Stoke Gifford when not qualified. C. L. Walker JP at Lawfords Gate. James Howells, labourer, of Stoke Gifford, informer. William Slade, labourer, of Hambrook, witness. Pleaded not guilty. Fine £5. Offence committed 13 Nov. 1822.

42/A/42 21 Nov. 1822. George Adams of Winterbourne, labourer. Using a dog to kill game in Stoke Gifford [etc., as 42/A/41 adding] When challenged Adams escaped.

42/A/43 30 Nov. 1822. John Leader of St. Philip and St. Jacob, [Bristol], pedlar. Selling glass and other wares from house to house without a licence. C. L. Walker JP at Redland, Westbury on Trym. Simon Pain of St. Philip and St. Jacob, inspector of hawkers' licences, informer. Offender confessed. Fine £10. Offence committed 28 Nov. 1822.

42/A/44 7 Nov. 1822. Joseph Lakin of Clifton, pedlar. Selling earthenware from house to house without a licence. John Haythorne JP at Lawfords Gate. Simon Pain, inspector of hawkers' licences, informer. William Pain, yeoman, of St. Philip and St. Jacob, [Bristol], witness. Offender pleaded not guilty. Fine £10. Offence committed 7 Nov. 1822.

42/A/45 16 Dec. 1822. Thomas Thornhill of Great Barrington, labourer. Using snares to kill game without obtaining the required certificate. R. W. Ford JP at Little Rissington, commissioner for assessed taxes in Slaughter district. Fine £20.

42/A/46 3 Dec. 1822. John Shill the younger of Eastington, labourer. Using a snare with intent to kill game. T. J. Lloyd Baker JP. Fine £10. Offence committed Sunday 24 Nov. 1822.

42/A/47 22 Oct. 1822. Paul Mills of Haresfield. Using dogs and ferrets to kill conies without obtaining the required certificate. T. J. Lloyd Baker JP at Wheatenhurst, commissioner for assessed taxes in Whitstone district. Fine £10 each. Offence committed 28 Sept. 1822.

42/A/48 22 Oct. 1822. Charles Ballenger of Haresfield. Using dogs [etc., as 42/A/47].

42/A/49 19 Oct. 1822. Charles Crooke of Bisley, labourer. Possessing 59 lb. of various woollen yarns and waste and 30 yards of cloth believed to be stolen. H. Burgh JP and E. Aldridge JP. Peter Hawker, gentleman, of Stroud, informer. Robert Keene, weaver, of Stroud, witness. Third offence. [Cf. 41/B/10, 41/D/18, 42/A/1.] Fine £40. Offence committed 14 Oct. 1822.

42/A/50 2 Nov. 1822. Nehemiah Curnock of Uley, labourer. Possessing 7 lb. 4 oz. of woollen yarn believed to be stolen. H. Burgh JP and H. Cooke JP. George Daniel Harris, clothier, of King's Stanley, informer. Robert Keene, weaver, and Daniel Peyton clothier, both of Stroud, witnesses. First offence. Fine £20 each. Offence committed 31 Oct. 1822.

42/A/51 2 Nov. 1822. Mark White of Wotton under Edge, labourer. Possessing 123 lb. of various woollen yarns [etc., as 42/A/50].

42/A/52 2 Nov. 1822. Edward Brown of Wotton under Edge, labourer. Possessing 204 lb. 8 oz. of various woollen yarns and waste believed to be stolen. H. Burgh JP and H. Cooke JP. George Daniel Harris, clothier, of King's Stanley, informer. Josiah Howell, baker, D. Peyton, clothier, and R. Keene, weaver, all of Stroud, witnesses. First offence. Fine £20. Offence committed 31 Oct. 1822.

42/A/53   16 Dec. 1822. William Allen of Wotton under Edge, baker. Possessing 51 yards of cloth and 44 lb. 4 oz. of various woollen yarns believed to be stolen. H. Burgh JP and H. Cooke JP. P. Hawker, gentleman, of Stroud, informer. Samuel Seville, clothier, of Bisley, and Josiah Howell, baker, of Stroud, witnesses. First offence. Fine £20. Offence committed 13 Dec. 1822.

42/A/54   16 Dec. 1822. James Crook of Wotton under Edge, labourer. Possessing 20 lb. 7 oz. of various woollen yarns and waste believed to be stolen. H. Burgh JP and H. Cooke JP. P. Hawker, gentleman, of Stroud, informer. R. Keene, weaver, of Stroud, and S. Seville, clothier, of Bisley, witnesses. First offence. Fine £20. Offence committed 13 Dec. 1822.

42/A/55   6 Dec. 1822. George Fords of Uley, labourer. Possessing 103 lb. of various woollen yarns and waste believed to be stolen. H. Cooke JP and E. Aldridge JP. P. Hawker, gentleman, of Stroud, informer. R. Keene, weaver, and J. Howell, baker, both of Stroud, witnesses. First offence. Fine £20. Offence committed 22 Oct. 1822.

42/B/1   20 Feb. 1823. Charles Davis of Cheltenham, licensed hawker. Failing to display 'Licensed Hawker' on his pack. R. Capper JP at Cheltenham. Simon Hathaway, informer. Edward Bonnor, witness. Fine £10. Offence committed 20 Feb. 1823. [*Note added*:] Received in a letter [. . .] from Pruen and Griffith, 9 Aug. 1823.

42/B/2   7 Aug. 1822 [*late return*]. John Lane Cherry of Kemerton, shopkeeper. Selling ale without a licence and charging 2*d*. instead of 1½*d*. per quart. J. Timbrill D.D. JP and Rev. J. Keysall JP at Tewkesbury. Thomas Griffiths, excise officer, informer. George Webb, labourer, and John Franklin, witnesses. Thomas Alexander Johns, brewer, of Tewkesbury, [supplier] and William Buckle [carrier] also testified. Defendant admitted charge. Fine £50. Offence committed 24 July 1822.

42/B/3   20 March 1823. David Stephens of Minchinhampton, mason. Killing a coney without having obtained the required certificate. Rev. P. Hawker JP, commissioner for assessed taxes, at Rodborough. Fine £10. Offence committed 9 March 1823.

42/B/4   23 Jan. 1823. John Cooper of Horsley, labourer. Using a snare to kill game without [*etc.*, *as* 42/B/3 *except*] Offence committed 13 Jan. 1823

42/B/5   17 Feb. 1823. John Shipton of Woodchester, labourer. Taking two conies from Pie Park, Woodchester, without [*etc.*, *as* 42/B/3 *except*] Fine £20. Offence committed 17 Jan. 1823.

42/B/6   5 Feb. 1823. John Lea of Malmesbury, Wilts., hawker. Selling British thread lace from house to house in Clifton without a licence. Henry Wenman Newman JP at Clifton. Simon Pain of Bristol, inspector of hawkers' licences, informer. William King and Elizabeth Powell, witnesses. Offender pleaded not guilty, declaring that he was the nephew and agent of the manufacturer. Fine £10. Offence committed 4 Feb. 1823.

42/B/7   27 Feb. 1823. Isaac Golding, licensed hawker. Selling silk shawls, veils etc. in Clifton without his name and number being properly displayed on his bag. J. Haythorne JP. Simon Pain of Bristol, inspector of licences, informer. William King, witness. Fine £10. Offence committed 26 Feb. 1823.

42/B/8   27 Feb. 1823. William Woodruffe, late of Winterbourne, hatter. Using two dogs to hunt conies in Cloisters Warren, Winterbourne, when not qualified to do so. J. Haythorne JP at Lawfords Gate sessions room. William Slade, gamekeeper to Thomas Wadham Esq., of Winterbourne, informer. Jason Howes of Winterbourne, witness. Defendant pleaded not guilty. Fine £1 15*s*. (treble damages and costs to be paid to Jason Howes) and three months in prison or until sureties for good behaviour be found. Offence committed between 11 and 12 p.m. on Monday 24 Feb. 1823.

42/B/9   27 Feb. 1823. William Frankcombe, late of Winterbourne, hatter. Using [*etc., as* 42/B/8].

42/B/10   27 March 1823. Charles Vernon of Little Rissington, labourer. Keeping and using a dog to kill game when not qualified. Rev. F. E. Witts JP at Stow on the Wold. Thomas Bayliss of Sherborne, gamekeeper and prosecutor for the poor, informer. Thomas Bunting, labourer, of Sherborne, witness. Fine £5. Offence committed 5 March 1823.

42/B/11–   21 Feb. 1823. [*Names as below.*] Having defective weights and/or balances. H. Burgh
34   JP, H. Cooke JP and E. Aldridge JP at a Petty Sessions for Bisley hundred. [*Fines as below*] and 7/- costs. Offences committed 3–5 Feb. 1823.

42/B/11   Joseph Cox of Stroud, shopkeeper. Fine 5/-.

42/B/12   John Coates of Sapperton, shopkeeper. Fine £1.

42/B/13   Ann Roberts of Stroud, shopkeeper. Fine 5/-.

42/B/14   George Wilson of Stroud, shopkeeper. Fine £1.

42/B/15   Elizabeth Haines of Stroud, shopkeeper. Fine 5/-.

42/B/16   Richard Bird of Stroud, shopkeeper. Fine 5/-.

42/B/17   George Hill of Stroud, shopkeeper. Fine 5/-.

42/B/18   Daniel Denton of Stroud, shopkeeper. Fine 10/-.

42/B/19   Joseph Blackmore of Stroud, shopkeeper. Fine 5/-.

42/B/20   Mary Clift of Stroud, shopkeeper. Fine 10/-.

42/B/21   John Webb of Stroud, shopkeeper. Fine 5/-.

42/B/22   Jonathan Coleman of Stroud, shopkeeper. Fine 10/-.

42/B/23   George Franklin of Stroud, shopkeeper. Fine 5/-.

42/B/24   William Chapman of Stroud, shopkeeper. Fine 5/-.

42/B/25   Thomas Hiles of Stroud, shopkeeper. Fine 10/-.

42/B/26   Joseph Baker of Stroud, shopkeeper. Fine 5/-.

42/B/27   Charles Hodges of Stroud, shopkeeper. Fine 5/-.

42/B/28   George Uzzall of Stroud, shopkeeper. Fine 10/-.

42/B/29   David Chapman of Stroud, shopkeeper. Fine 5/-.

42/B/30   John Gibbons of Stroud, shopkeeper. Fine £1.

42/B/31   Isaac Haines of Stroud, shopkeeper. Fine 5/-.

42/B/32   John Webb of Stroud, shopkeeper. Fine £1.

42/B/33   Robert Adams of Sapperton, shopkeeper. Fine 5/-.

42/B/34   Thomas Gardner of Stroud, coal retailer. Fine 5/-.

42/B/35   21 Dec. 1821 [*late return*]. Charles King the younger of Tetbury, labourer. Using a dog to kill conies in Nim Hay, Beverstone, occupied by William Robbins, without the required certificate. W. M. Adey JP, tax commissioner, at Wotton under Edge. Fine £10. Offence committed 9 Dec. 1821.

42/B/36   30 Nov. 1821 [*late return*]. David Buckley of Dursley, labourer. Using a net to kill conies in Park Wood, North Nibley, the property of Purnell Bransby Purnell Esq., without the required certificate. Rev. W. Lloyd Baker JP, tax commissioner, at Wotton under Edge. Fine £10. Offence committed 18 Nov. 1821.

42/B/37   9 Nov. 1821 [*late return*]. Job Martin of Uley, labourer. Using a net to kill conies in Golden Knoll [*MS*. Goldknowe] Wood, Wotton under Edge, the property of William Fitzhardinge Berkeley Esq. W. M. Adey JP, tax commissioner, at Wotton under Edge. Fine £10. Offence committed 22 Oct. 1821.

42/B/38   9 Nov. 1821 [*late return*]. James Turner of Dursley, labourer. Using a net [*etc., as* 42/B/37].

42/B/39 9 Nov. 1821 [*late return*]. Samuel White the younger of Dursley, labourer. Using a net [*etc., as* 42/B/37].

42/B/40 3 Jan. 1823. Joseph Merrett the younger of Awre, labourer. Shooting game in Hinton, Berkeley, without obtaining the required certificate. W. M. Adey JP, tax commissioner, at Wotton under Edge. Fine £15. Offence committed 6 Nov. 1822.

42/B/41 20 Dec. 1822. James Caddy Hamblin of Wotton under Edge, clothier. Shooting game in Sinwell and Bradley without obtaining the required certificate. H. W. Dyer JP, tax commissioner, at Wotton under Edge. Fine £15. Offence committed 16 Oct. 1822.

42/B/42 11 Oct. 1822. Samuel Thomas of Cromhall, farmer. Shooting game without obtaining the required certificate. W. M. Adey JP, tax commissioner, at Wotton under Edge. Fine £10. Offence committed 2 Oct. 1822.

42/B/43 11 Oct. 1822. Samuel Thomas of Cromhall, farmer. Using a dog to kill game without [*etc., as* 42/B/42 *except*] Offence committed 3 Oct. 1822.

42/B/44 3 Feb. 1823. Thomas Bisco of Ross, baker. Using a gun and two dogs to kill game in Oxenhall without obtaining the required certificate. Thomas Richardson JP at Newent. John Warren, labourer, of Oxenhall, informer. William Jones, woodward, of Oxenhall, witness. Information given on 22 Jan. 1823. Fine £5. Offence committed 6 Dec. 1822.

42/C/1 11 June 1823. Daniel Nelson. Begging at Westbury on Severn. Rev. C. Crawley JP. Offence committed 11 June 1823.

42/C/2 13 May 1823. Henry Worgan of St. Briavels, labourer. Cutting and stealing birch underwood at Tidenham, the property of Henry Charles, duke of Beaufort. E. Machen JP. Isaac Ellaway, woodward, of Chapel Hill, Monmouth, witness. First offence. Fine 10/- and 6/6 costs. Offence committed 2 May 1823.

42/C/3 20 March 1823. Moses May. Using a dog to kill game in Winterbourne. J. Haythorne JP. First offence. Fine £10. Offence committed Sunday 16 March 1823.

42/C/4 20 March 1823. Benjamin Webley. Using a dog [*etc., as* 42/C/3].

42/C/5 8 May 1823. Margaret Thomas. Pawning bedding valued at 5/- at St. Philip and St. Jacob, Bristol, the property of John Smith, seaman, without his permission. G. Goldney JP. Fine 20/- and the value of the goods. Offence committed 5 May 1823.

42/C/6 18 June 1823. James Abbott. Using a net at night with intent to kill game in Henbury. C. L. Walker JP. First offence. Fine £10. Offence committed 17 June 1823.

42/C/7 17 April 1823. Frederick Eyre of St. George, Bristol, labourer. Shooting a red tumbler pigeon, the property of Thomas Phipps, labourer, of St. George, Bristol. Thomas Daniel JP and G. Goldney JP at St. Philip and St. Jacob, Bristol. Thomas Phipps, complainant. Sarah Smith, single woman, of St. George, witness. Charles Eyre also present when the offence occurred. Fine 20/-. Offence committed 7 March 1823.

42/C/8 16 May 1823. Thomas Done of Painswick, retailer. Having a defective weight and balance. H. Burgh JP and E. Aldridge JP at a Petty Sessions for Bisley hundred. Fine 20/- and 7/- costs. Offence committed 25 March 1823.

42/C/9 11 June 1823. Thomas Sketchley of Cheltenham, labourer [*erroneously named as* Thomas Tanser *in part of the document*; *cf.* 42/C/10]. Selling earthenware from house to house without a licence. R. Capper JP at Cheltenham. John Chandler, informer. William Ruck, witness. Defendant pleaded not guilty. Fine £10. Offence committed 4 June 1823.

42/C/10   25 June 1823. Thomas Tanser of Cheltenham, labourer. Selling earthenware from house to house without a licence. R. Capper JP at Cheltenham. Edward Bonnor, informer, Simon Hathaway, witness. Defendant pleaded not guilty. Fine £10. Offence committed 25 June 1823.

42/C/11   26 June 1823. Leman Lyons Leman of Cheltenham, labourer. Selling goods from house to house without a licence. R. Capper JP at Cheltenham. John Chandler, informer. William Ruck, witness. Defendant pleaded not guilty. Fine £10. Offence committed 25 June 1823.

42/C/12   22 April 1823. William Buckingham of Minchinhampton, labourer. Cutting down and stealing an oak tree, the property of Robert Snow Paul Esq. H. Burgh JP. William Ayms, informer. Richard Clark, labourer, of Minchinhampton, witness. First offence. Fine £20 (half to informer, half to plaintiff). Offence committed 9 April 1823.

42/C/13   22 April 1823. Daniel Wood of Minchinhampton, weaver. Possessing oak and larch poles believed to be stolen, the property of R. S. Paul Esq. H. Burgh JP. Richard Clark, labourer, of Woodchester, witness. Defendants admitted charge. Fine 20/-.

42/C/14   22 April 1823. Nathaniel Arnold of Minchinhampton, weaver. Possessing oak and larch poles [*etc.*, *as* 42/C/13].

42/C/15   22 April 1823. William Buckingham of Minchinhampton, labourer. Cutting down a larch tree, the property of R. S. Paul Esq. H. Burgh JP. William Ayms of Woodchester, informer. John Clarke, labourer, of Woodchester, witness. Second offence. [*Cf.* 42/C/12.] Fine £30. Offence committed 16 April 1823.

42/C/16   21 April 1823. Isaac Hillier of Minchinhampton, labourer. Possessing 1 lb. of Spanish wool believed to be stolen. H. Burgh JP and E. Aldridge JP. John Edward Gordon, gentleman, of Stroud, informer. R. Keene, weaver, of Stroud, witness. First offence. Fine £20. Offence committed 19 April 1823.

42/C/17   21 April 1823. Thomas Grange of Minchinhampton, labourer. Possessing 20 lb. of Spanish wool [*etc.*, *as* 42/C/16].

42/C/18   30 May 1823. The Hon. Katherine Monson, spinster, of Cheltenham. Allowing bricks on her property to be burnt, thereby causing smoke and smell to foul the air of North Place and an adjacent footway to the annoyance of James Arkell of Field Lodge. Sir W. Hicks JP, J. Agg JP, J. Clutterbuck JP and R. Capper JP. Fine £5. Offence committed 24 May 1823.

42/C/19   10 May 1823. The Hon. Katherine Monson, spinster, of Cheltenham. Causing bricks on her property to be burnt, thereby fouling the air of North Place with smoke. J. Agg JP, J. Clutterbuck JP and R. Capper JP. Fine 10/-. Offence committed 7 May 1823.

42/D/1   2 Oct. 1823. Thomas Stratford of Little Barrington, labourer. Using snares in Great Barrington with intent to kill game without having obtained the required certificate. Hon. and Rev. E. Rice D.D. JP and tax commissioner, at Stow on the Wold. William Cook, labourer, of Little Barrington, witness. Fine £20. Offence committed 2 Oct. 1823.

42/D/2   1 Sept. 1823. William Sparrow of Stroud, labourer. Cutting down a beech tree in Standish, the property of Edward Page, yeoman, of Stroud. H. Burgh JP. Offence committed 30 Aug. 1823.

42/D/3   27 Sept. 1823. Betty Gregory of Stroud. Pawning thee linen sheets and one coat at Messrs. Jones, pawnbrokers, of Stroud, without the owner's permission. H. Burgh JP. James Neal, cordwainer, of Stroud, complainant. Defendant confessed. Fine 20/-. Offence committed 26 Sept. 1823.

42/D/4 19 Aug. 1823. John Halliday of Minchinhampton, labourer. Possessing 2½ lb. of woollen yarn believed to be stolen. H. Burgh JP and H. Cooke JP. George Wyatt, clothier, of Stroud, informer. Robert Keene, weaver, of Stroud, witness. Defendant's premises searched. First offence. Fine £20. Offence committed 18 Aug. 1823.

42/D/5 8 Aug. 1823. John Davis of Bisley, labourer. Possessing 57½ lb. of woollen yarn and waste believed to be stolen. H. Burgh JP and E. Aldridge JP. Isaac Woodfield, yeoman, of Bisley, witness. First offence. Fine £20.

42/D/6 13 Sept. 1823. John Wait of Mangotsfield, labourer. Keeping and using a gun and a dog to kill game in Church Close, Mangotsfield, when not qualified to do so. J. Haythorne JP. William Nicholls, yeoman, informer, Richard Hall, witness, both of Mangotsfield. Defendant stated that Shadrach Thomas had given him permission. Fine £5. Offence committed 11 Sept. 1823.

42/D/7 26 May 1823. Ann Dowell. Selling lace, veils, aprons, collars, handkerchiefs etc. from house to house in Clifton without a licence. S. Cave JP at Clifton. Simon Pain, informer. Offender declared that she had made the goods. Fine £10. Offence committed 26 May 1823.

42/D/8 17 Sept. 1823. Maria Power, widow. Selling fancy chimneypiece ornaments, watch cases etc. from house to house in Clifton without a licence. G. Goldney JP. Simon Pain, inspector of hawkers' licences, informer. Mary Anderson, witness. Fine £10. Offence committed 16 Sept. 1823.

42/D/9 4 Sept. 1823. Charles Edwards of Westbury on Trym, tailor. Removing possessions valued at £2 10s. from his tenement to prevent distraint for arrears of rent. J. Haythorne JP and H. W. Newman JP. Joseph Tedder on behalf of James Jones, both yeomen of Westbury on Trym, informer. Defendant did not appear. Ordered to pay complainant £5 on 18 Sept. Offence committed 12 Aug. 1823.

42/D/10 18 Sept. 1823. Joseph Olds of Mangotsfield. In company with another (not known) keeping and using a dog and a gun to kill game in Farmer Baber's field. H. W. Newman JP. William Nicholls, labourer, of Mangotsfield, informer. William Knight of Mangotsfield, witness. Defendant did not appear. Fine £5. Offence committed 12 Sept. 1823.

42/D/11 2 Sept. 1823 Benjamin Cheer. Selling rush matting from house to house in Clifton without a licence. H. W. Newman JP at St. James, Bristol. Thomas Shepherd of Worcester, surveyor of hawkers' licences, informer. Simon Pain, witness. Fine £10. Offence committed 29 Aug. 1823.

42/D/12 19 July 1823. Richard Putley of Thornbury, cordwainer. Leaving his children chargeable to the parish. S. P. Peach JP at Thornbury.

42/D/13 23 July 1823. John Atkinson. Running a gambling table at Tetbury fair. J. P. Paul JP at Tetbury. James Coxe, a constable of Tetbury, witness. Offence committed 22 July 1823.

42/D/14 2 Sept. 1823. William Beddoe of Ledbury, Herefs. Keeping and using a gun for killing game in Dymock when not qualified to do so. Rev. R. Pyndar JP at the upper hall, Ledbury. John Skipp, gamekeeper, of Ledbury, informer. Fine £5. Offence committed 1 Sept. 1823.

42/D/15 7 Aug. 1823. Thomas Humphries of Condicote, labourer. Keeping and using a snare with intent to kill game in Condicote. Rev. J. Hurd JP at Stow on the Wold. John Hayward, gamekeeper, of Temple Guiting, informer. John Swann, gamekeeper, of Temple Guiting, witness. Summons issued on 14 April. Defendant absconded. Arrest warrant issued. Apprehended 7 Aug. Fine £5. Offence committed 13 April 1823.

43/A/1   19 Dec. 1823. John Hobbs of Uley, weaver. Possessing 1 lb. 4 oz. of woollen yarn believed to be stolen. H. Burgh JP and E. Aldridge JP. Peter Hawker, gentleman, of Stroud, informer. Daniel Peyton, clothier, and Robert Keene, weaver, both of Stroud, witnesses. Offender's house searched. First offence. Fine £20. Offence committed 29 Nov. 1823.

43/A/2   1 Dec. 1823. Joseph Hyde of Uley, weaver. Possessing 2 lb. 12 oz. of woollen yarn believed to be stolen. H. Burgh JP and Rev. P. Hawker JP. George William Saunders, clothier, of Horsley, informer. D. Peyton and R. Keene, witnesses. House searched. First offence. Fine £20. Offence committed 29 Nov. 1823

43/A/3   1 Dec. 1823. Samuel Gabb of Uley, weaver. Possessing 14 lb. 4 oz. of woollen yarn believed to be stolen [*etc., as* 43/A/2].

43/A/4   5 Nov. 1823. Ebsworth Humphries of Winchcombe, victualler. Failing to observe a condition of the recognizance entered into when obtaining a licence. J. Timbrill D.D. JP and Rev. J. Keysall JP. First offence. Fine £2 10*s*.

43/A/5   5 Nov. 1823. James Parker of Winchcombe, victualler. Failing to observe a condition of the recognizance entered into when obtaining a licence. J. Timbrill D.D. JP and Rev. J. Keysall JP. First offence. Fine 1/-.

43/A/6   19 Nov. 1823. William Jones of Forthampton, victualler. Failing to observe a condition of the recognizance entered into when obtaining a licence. J. Timbrill D.D. JP and Rev. J. Keysall JP. First offence. Fine £2 10*s*.

43/A/7   19 Nov. 1823. Richard Wilkins of the Boot public house, Tetbury, victualler. Failing to observe a condition of the recognizance entered into when obtaining a licence. J. P. Paul JP, George Peter Holford JP and Rev. D. Lysons JP. First offence. Fine £3 and 3/- expenses.

43/A/8   15 Nov. 1823. John Swayne of Thornbury, hawker of hardware and other goods. Selling a comb in Rockhampton without a licence. William Norris Tonge JP. Thomas Lovsey, informer. Josiah Thurston, witness. Offender pleaded not guilty. Fine £10. Offence committed 5 Nov. 1823. [*Pencilled note:*] One moiety after deducting expenses to the use of His Majesty, £4 2*s*. 3½*d*. herewith sent from W. Ely. Received, E.B. [*i.e.* Edward Bloxsome] R[ecepit].

43/A/9   24 Oct. 1823. Benjamin Webley of Winterbourne, labourer. Using a gun and a dog to kill game in Frampton Cotterell without obtaining a licence. Sir Richard Vaughan JP, commissioner for taxes for Barton Regis district, at St. James parish, Bristol. Fine £10 in addition to £3 13*s*. 6*d*. duty. Offence committed 22 Sept. 1823.

43/A/10   2 Dec. 1823. Samuel Merrett of Randwick, labourer. Using dogs with intent to kill game. T. J. Lloyd Baker JP. First offence. Fine £10. Offence committed Sunday 9 Nov. 1823.

43/A/11   2 Dec. 1823. Samuel Chandler of Randwick, labourer. Using dogs [*etc., as* 43/A/10].

43/A/12   2 Dec. 1823. Thomas Halsey of Wheatenhurst, labourer. Using a dog to kill a hare without obtaining a certificate. T. J. Lloyd Baker JP and H. Hicks JP, commissioners for taxes. Fine £10. Offence committed 27 Nov. 1823.

43/A/13   2 Dec. 1823. Thomas Earle of Frampton on Severn, gentleman. Shooting a hare and a pheasant when not qualified. H. Hicks JP. Robert Tovey, labourer, of Frampton on Severn, informer. John Neale, gamekeeper, of the same parish, witness. Offender admitted charge. Fine £5. Offence committed 6 Nov. 1823.

43/A/14   4 Dec. 1823. Peter Hill. Damaging the window of a building in Minchinhampton belonging to David Sutton, weaver. Rev. P. Hawker JP. Ordered to pay forthwith £2 10*s*. to the overseer of the poor. Offence committed 29 Nov. 1823.

43/A/15   23 Dec. 1823. William Baker. Vagrancy, and possessing a piece of lead pipe in Clifton without satisfactory explanation. H. W. Newman JP at St. Philip and St. Jacob, Bristol.

43/A/16   4 Dec. 1823. William Hill. Damaging [*etc.*, *as* 43/A/14].

43/A/17   27 Nov. 1823. Stephen Lawes of Bristol, maltster. Keeping or using a gun to kill game in Westbury on Trym without obtaining a licence. H. W. Newman JP at Lawfords Gate, St. Philip and St. Jacob, [Bristol]. William Baker, gamekeeper, of Westbury on Trym, informer. Offender confessed. Fine £5. Offence committed 11 Nov. 1823.

43/A/18   13 Dec. 1823. Christopher Pain of Stow on the Wold, accountant. Using a gun and dogs to kill a hare in Broadwell. Rev. F. E. Witts JP. Joseph Knight, gentleman, of Stow on the Wold, informer. Offender pleaded guilty. Fine £5. Offence committed 9 Dec. 1823.

43/A/19   15 Nov. 1823. Joseph Hopkins of Didbrook, labourer. Carrying a gun with intent to kill game in Greet Grove, Winchcombe. G. Talbot JP at Temple Guiting. Charles Smith, labourer, and Henry Smith, gamekeeper, both of Toddington, informer and witness. Pleaded not guilty. Fine £20. Offence committed 9 Nov. 1823.

43/A/20   6 Nov. 1823. Augustus Clayfield of Stroud, labourer. Throwing fireworks in the street. H. Burgh JP. Robert Keene, weaver, of Stroud, informer. John Lewis, labourer, and James Withey, druggist, both of Stroud, witnesses. Fine 20/-. Offence committed 5 Nov. 1823.

43/A/21   7 Nov. 1823. William Brown of Stroud, labourer. Throwing fireworks in the street. H. Burgh JP. R. Keene, informer. Joseph Horton, cooper, and Samuel Wheeler, mercer, both of Stroud, witnesses. Fine 20/-. Offence committed 5 Nov. 1823.

43/A/22   7 Nov. 1823. James Alder of Stroud, labourer. Throwing fireworks [*etc.*, *as* 43/A/21].

43/A/23   16 Oct. 1823. Henry Duff. Entering the dwelling house of William Johnson, shopkeeper, in St. George, Bristol. Sir R. Vaughan JP at St. Philip and St. Jacob, Bristol. Convicted as a rogue and vagabond. Offence committed in the night of 15 Oct. 1823.

43/A/24   20 Oct. 1823. William Nicholls. Vagrancy: lying in the open air in St. Philip and St. Jacob. Sir R. Vaughan JP at St. Philip and St. Jacob, Bristol. Offence committed in the night of 19 Oct. 1823.

43/A/25   20 Nov. 1823. William Hobbs of St. Philip and St. Jacob, Bristol, victualler. Failing to observe the conditions of a recognizance entered into on obtaining his licence. S. Cave JP and G. Goldney JP. First offence. Fine £1.

43/A/26   25 Dec. 1823. Robert Saunders of Westbury on Trym, labourer. Shooting game when not qualified. G. Goldney JP at Clifton. Stephen White, labourer, of Henbury, informer. George Webb Hall, gentleman, of Westbury on Trym, witness. Offender pleaded not guilty. Fine £5. Offence committed 25 Dec. 1823.

43/A/27   1 Jan. 1824. Arthur Young of Westbury on Trym, labourer. Using a dog and snares to kill game in Henbury. J. Haythorne JP at Lawfords Gate sessions room, St. Philip and St. Jacob, [Bristol]. Joseph Sims, labourer, of Westbury on Trym, informer. Offender admitted charge. Fine £5. Offence committed 26 Dec. 1823.

43/A/28   29 Dec. 1823. John Worthington. Possessing a quantity of brass in Cheltenham, believed to be stolen. J. Agg JP and J. Clutterbuck JP.

43/A/29   13 Dec. 1823. James Baylis of Longford St. Catherine, yeoman. Using a gun and a dog to kill game in Twigworth without obtaining a licence. William Goodrich JP, commissioner for taxes. Fine £20. Offence committed 19 Nov. 1823.

43/A/30   31 Dec. 1823. William Evans of Pendock, Worcs., labourer. Possessing a hare and offering it for sale when not qualified to do so. Rev. J. Keysall JP and Rev. J. Timbrill JP at Mr. Fryer's office, Tewkesbury. William Beale, yeoman, of Forthampton, informer. George Knight and William Hancock, yeoman, of Forthampton, witnesses, who testified they heard a shot on Knight's father's farm and saw the accused pick up an object.

Giving chase, Knight saw a hare's leg protruding below the offender's coat. Pleaded not guilty. Fine £5. Offence committed 3 Dec. 1823.

43/B/1 21 Feb. 1824. Charles Osborne of Olveston, carpenter. Refusing to give evidence in a complaint brought by John Millard, labourer, against William Lee, victualler and beer retailer, both of Olveston. S. P. Peach JP and W. N. Tonge JP. [*Pencilled note*:] Sent in a letter with £1.

43/B/2 24 April 1824. John Ford of Uley, labourer. Possessing 20 lb. of woollen yarn and waste believed to be stolen. O. P. Wathen JP and Rev. P. Hawker JP. William Fryer, gentleman, of Stroud, informer. Robert Keene, constable of Stroud, witness. House searched. First offence. Fine £20. Offence committed 19 April 1824.

43/B/3 24 April 1824. Mark White of Wotton under Edge, labourer. Possessing 80 lb. of woollen yarn believed to be stolen. O. P. Wathen JP and Rev. P. Hawker JP. W. Fryer, gentleman, of Stroud, informer. R. Keene, constable of Stroud, witness. House searched. Second offence. [*Cf.* 42/A/51.] Fine £30. Offence committed 19 April 1824.

43/B/4 24 April 1824. George Ford of Uley, labourer. Possessing 28 lb. of woollen yarn believed to be stolen [*etc.*, *as* 43/B/3. Cf. 42/A/55.]

43/B/5 20 Feb. 1824. John Brush. Leaving his wife and child chargeable to the parish of Siddington. E. Wilbraham JP at Cirencester. Offence committed 6 Feb. 1824.

43/B/6 6 April 1824. Nicholas Jones of Berkeley, innkeeper. Failing to observe a condition of the recognizance entered into on obtaining his licence. W. Davies D.D. JP and R. F. Jenner JP. First offence. Mitigated fine of £3 and 5/- expenses.

43/B/7 19 March 1824. John Williams. Vagrancy in Pucklechurch. F. Trotman junior JP. Offence committed 18 March 1824.

43/B/8 1 April 1824. George Thompson. Vagrancy, and obtaining relief under false pretences in Clifton. C. L. Walker JP at Lawfords Gate, Bristol. Offence committed 31 March 1824.

43/B/9 13 April 1824. Mary Ann Keefe. Vagrancy in Clifton. H. W. Newman JP at St. James, Bristol. Offence committed 12 April 1824.

43/B/10 13 April 1824. Mary Ann Powell. Vagrancy in Clifton [*etc.*, *as* 43/B/9].

43/B/11 25 March 1824. Mary Morgan. Vagrancy in Clifton. G. Goldney JP at Lawfords Gate, Bristol. Offence committed 24 March 1824.

43/B/12 25 March 1824. Eliza Evans. Vagrancy in Clifton [*etc.*, *as* 43/B/11].

43/B/13 25 March 1824. Harriet Jones. Vagrancy in Clifton [*etc.*, *as* 43/B/11].

43/B/14 6 March 1824. William Driver of Morton, Thornbury. Using a gun and a dog to kill game without obtaining the required certificate. J. Haythorne JP and H. W. Newman JP at St. James, Bristol, commissioners for taxes for Barton Regis district. Fine £10. Offence committed 12 Dec. 1823.

43/B/15 6 March 1824. Ephraim Wilson. Using a dog to kill hares in Thornbury. J. Haythorne JP and H. W. Newman JP. First offence. Fine £10. Offence committed Sunday 29 Feb. 1824.

43/B/16 2 Feb. 1824. William Roach of St. George, Bristol, labourer. Using a gun and two dogs to kill conies in Bitton without obtaining the required certificate. Joseph Parker JP, commissioner for taxes. Fine £10. Offence committed 13 Jan. 1824.

43/B/17 18 March 1824. William Bracey of Almondsbury, labourer. Using snares, thereby killing a hare in a field in the occupation of John Powell at Almondsbury. G. Goldney JP at Lawfords Gate, Bristol. James Wilkins and William Webb, labourers, of Almondsbury, informer and witness. Pleaded not guilty. Fine £5. Offence committed about 6 a.m. 24 Feb. 1824.

43/B/18   29 March 1824. George Frape of Tetbury, victualler. Failing to observe a condition of the recognizance entered into when obtaining his licence. R. Kingscote JP and Rev. P. Hawker JP. First offence. Fine £5 and 14/6 expenses.

43/B/19   27 March 1824. John Thompson. Begging in Tetbury. R. Kingscote JP at Kingscote. James Cox, constable of Tetbury, informer. Offence committed 26 Feb. 1824.

43/C/1   20 Feb. 1824. Thomas Bliss of Stroud, victualler. Failing to observe a condition of the recognizance entered into on obtaining his licence. H. Burgh JP, E. Aldridge JP and William Henry Hyett JP. First offence. Fine £5 and 11/- expenses.

43/C/2   1 July 1824. James Champion. Cursing. J. Haythorne JP and G. Goldney JP.

43/C/3   9 July 1824. George Donald. Begging in Clifton. H. W. Newman JP at Lawfords Gate, Bristol. Offence committed 8 July 1824.

43/C/4   13 May 1824. Richard Schuberg. Begging in Clifton. H. W. Newman JP at Lawfords Gate, Bristol. Offence committed 12 May 1824.

43/C/5   5 June 1824. Thomas Morgan. Possessing stolen property without satisfactory explanation, at Westbury on Trym. Sir R. Vaughan JP at Lawfords Gate, Bristol. Offence committed 31 May 1824.

43/C/6   5 June 1824. Richard Rowe. Possessing stolen property [*etc.*, *as* 43/C/5].

43/C/7   20 May 1824. William Thomson. Indecent exposure in Oldland. J. Cave JP at Lawfords Gate, Bristol. Offence committed 6 May 1824.

43/C/8   14 May 1824. James Dauncey of Coaley, clothier. Paying Elizabeth wife of Thomas Jellyman, weaver, of Coaley, 8/1½ due to her in other than legal coinage. W. M. Adey JP and Purnell Bransby Purnell JP at Wotton under Edge. Fine £20. Offence committed 14 Feb. 1824.

43/D/1   5 Oct. 1824. Richard Clarke the elder of Berkeley, innkeeper. Failing to observe a condition of the recognizance entered into on obtaining his licence. W. Davies D.D. JP and R. F. Jenner JP. First offence. Mitigated fine of £1 5*s*. and 5/- expenses.

43/D/2   22 July 1824. John Welch. Being drunk in Clifton. J. Haythorne JP. Fine 5/-. Offence committed Sat. 17 July 1824.

43/D/3   22 July 1824. Robert Parsons. Ill-treating a horse in Clifton. G. Goldney JP. Offence committed 14 July 1824.

43/D/4   30 Sept. 1824. James Bowden. Shooting a pigeon at Frampton Cotterell. G. Goldney JP. Fine 20/-. Offence committed 28 Sept. 1824.

43/D/5   11 Oct. 1824. Thomas Nichols junior, haulier [*MS.* hallier], and Maria Thomas, single woman, both of Westerleigh. Possessing stolen apples, the property of William Iles, farmer, of Wapley and Codrington, and damaging trees and apples in his orchard. Rev. F. Pelly JP. Maria Thomas deemed to be concerned in trespass and damage. Fine £1 1*s*., to be paid forthwith. Offence committed at night between 5 and 6 Oct. 1824.

43/D/6   6 Sept. 1824. Samuel Davis. Leaving his wife and children chargeable to the parish of Tetbury. J. D. Phelps JP at Chavenage, Horsley. Thomas Horne [*or* Home: *reading uncertain*], overseer of the poor, witness. Six weeks' hard labour in Horsley house of correction. Offence committed 18 June 1824.

43/D/7   7 Sept. 1824. — Watts. Begging in Tetbury. Rev. H. Campbell JP at Tetbury. Captain James Richard Dacres, witness. One month's hard labour in Horsley house of correction. Offence committed 7 Sept. 1824.

43/D/8   29 July 1824. Daniel Neale, James Develyn and John Greening. Entering into a combination and persuading Benjamin Lucas, Henry Cole, James Page the elder and James Page the younger, cordwainers, to leave the employ of William Jessett, cordwainer, of Cheltenham, in order to obtain higher wages. J. Agg JP and J. Clutterbuck JP. Two months' hard labour in Northleach house of correction. Offence committed 19 July 1824.

44/A/1   4 Jan. 1825. Charles Newcomb of Tetbury. Leaving his wife and family chargeable to the parish. J. P. Paul JP at Tetbury. Daniel Cole, assistant overseer of the poor, and Charlotte Newcomb, the offender's wife, witnesses. Six weeks' hard labour in Horsley house of correction. Offence committed 1 Dec. 1824.

44/A/2   1 Nov. 1824. William Taylor of Newent, labourer. Keeping and using a dog to kill a hare in Oxenhall. T. Richardson JP and William Munro JP. William Jones, witness. First offence. Mitigated fine of £10. Offence committed Sunday 31 Oct. 1824.

44/A/3   1 Nov. 1824. Charles Phelps of Pauntley, labourer. Keeping and using [*etc., as* 44/A/2].

44/A/4   1 Nov. 1824. John Jackson of Pauntley, labourer. Keeping and using [*etc., as* 44/A/2].

44/A/5   6 Dec. 1824. Harriet Jones. Pawning a cotton umbrella, the property of Mary Colwill, without her permission, in St. Philip and St. Jacob, Bristol. G. Goldney JP. Fine 22/6. Offence committed 3 Dec. 1824.

44/A/6   2 Dec. 1824. Robert Hall. [Destroying a young tree.[1]] G. Goldney JP. Edward King of Clifton, constable and agent to the Society of Merchant Venturers, Bristol, complainant.

44/A/7   30 Dec. 1824. John James of Hazleton, labourer. Being in pursuit of game in Hazleton and Turkdean without obtaining the required certificate. Rev. F. E. Witts JP and Rev. R. W. Ford JP at Stow on the Wold, commisssioners for taxes. Fine £10. Offence committed Sunday 26 Dec. 1824.

44/A/8   27 Oct. 1824. John Gillett of the Leigh, victualler. Failing to observe a condition of the recognizance entered into on obtaining his licence on 15 Sept. J. Timbrill D.D. JP and Rev. J. Keysall JP. First offence. Fine £5 and 11/6 costs.

44/A/9   Statement of that part of fines imposed by J. Timbrill D.D. JP and Rev. J. Keysall JP due to the king, 10 Jan. 1825:

			£	s.	d.
5 Nov. 1823	Ebsworth Humphries of Winchcombe, victualler	For failing to observe a condition of a recognizance	1	5	0
	James Parker of Winchcombe, victualler	[*as above*]			6
19 Nov. 1823	William Jones of Forthampton, victualler	[*as above*]	1	5	0
27 Oct. 1824	John Gillett of the Leigh	[*as above*]	2	10	0
			5	0	6

44/A/10   10 June 1824. William Verrinder. Ill-treating a horse at Painswick, the property of William Cross. H. Burgh JP. William Cross, complainant.

44/A/11   23 Aug. 1824. Francis Meredith. Frequenting the streets of Stroud with intent to commit a felony. E. Aldridge JP. Committed to Horsley house of correction to serve three months' hard labour. Offence committed 21 Aug. 1824.

---

[1] Cf. Glos. R.O., Q/SG 2, Epiphany Sessions 1825.

44/A/12   20 Aug. 1824. Thomas Saunders. Frequenting the streets of Stroud [*etc., as* 44/A/11 *except*] to serve two months' hard labour. Offence committed 20 Aug. 1824.

44/A/13   23 Aug. 1824. Thomas Lever. Frequenting the streets of Stroud [*etc., as* 44/A/11].

44/A/14   6 Aug. 1824. Charles Gardner of Bisley, ale and beer retailer. Failing to observe a condition of the recognizance entered into on obtaining his licence. H. Burgh JP [*who did not sign*] and E. Aldridge JP. First offence. Fine £5 and 5/- costs.

44/A/15   5 Nov. 1824. Thomas and William Batman of Wick and Abson. Using a dog to kill game in Siston and Wick and Abson. Rev. T. Jones JP and Rev. I. W. W. Horlock JP. Information given to Rev. F. Pelly by Mark Tanner of Siston. William Coules, witness. Fine £5 [each]. Offence committed 31 Oct. 1824.

44/A/16   10 Jan. 1825. Richard Cooke of Stonehouse, baker. Possessing two lengths of cloth totalling 9¼ yards believed to be stolen. H. Burgh JP and E. Aldridge JP. Samuel Evans, informer. Robert Keene and Orlando Halliday, witnesses. Premises searched. First offence. Fine £20. Offence committed 30 Nov. 1824.

44/A/17   10 Jan. 1825. William Perrett of Uley, weaver. Possessing 63 lb. of various woollen yarns and waste believed to be stolen. H. Burgh JP and E. Aldridge JP. Daniel Lloyd informer. R. Keene and O. Halliday, witnesses. Premises searched. First offence. Fine £20. Offence committed 27 Nov. 1824.

44/A/18   13 Nov. 1824. Thomas Evans, coachman. Allowing another person to drive his public coach in Sherborne without the consent of the passengers. Sir Alexander Willson JP at Cheltenham. Richard Critchett, informer. Offender admitted charge. Fine £5. Offence committed 7 Nov. 1824.

44/B/1   3 Feb. 1825. William Boxwell of Coates, labourer. Leaving his wife and family chargeable to the parish. Rev. H. A. Pye JP at Cirencester. Three months' hard labour in Northleach house of correction. Offence committed 1 May 1823.

44/B/2   18 March 1825. Abraham Perrett of North Nibley, labourer. Possessing 138 lb. of woollen yarn and waste believed to be stolen. H. Burgh JP and E. Aldridge JP. Daniel Lloyd, informer. Daniel Heaven, Charles Cogswell and Robert Keene, witnesses. Premises searched. First offence. Fine £20. Offence committed 24 Feb. 1825.

44/B/3   4 March 1825. Lucy Sidway of North Nibley, labourer. Possessing 6 lb. of woollen yarn and waste believed to be stolen. H. Burgh JP and E. Aldridge JP. William Cox Buckanan [*sic*], informer. Daniel Lloyd and Joseph Horton, witnesses. Premises searched. First offence. Fine £20. Offence committed 2 March 1825.

44/B/4   25 Feb. 1825. Thomas Webb of North Nibley, labourer. Possessing 1 lb. 8 oz. of woollen yarn believed to be stolen. H. Burgh JP and E. Aldridge JP. John Daniel Lloyd, informer. Robert Keene, witness. Premises searched. First offence. Fine £20. Offence committed 24 Feb. 1825.

44/B/5   9 Feb. 1825. William Hodges of Stroud, labourer. Possessing 1 lb. 8 oz. of woollen yarn believed to be stolen. H. Burgh JP and E. Aldridge JP. Thomas Nicholls, informer. Robert Keene and George Daniel Harris, witnesses. Premises searched. First offence. Fine £20. Offence committed 7 Feb. 1825.

44/B/6   11 Feb. 1825. Thomas Mee, late of Westbury on Trym, hawker. Selling china and earthenware without a licence. John Savage JP at St. James, Bristol. William King of Bristol, inspector of hawkers' licences, informer. Ann Hands and Edward Whiting, witnesses. Offender did not appear. Fine £10. Offence committed 7 Feb. 1825.

44/B/7   3 Feb. 1825. Edmund Harding of Swinbrook, Oxon., labourer. Using a gun in Widford with intent to kill game. Rev. R. W. Ford JP at Stow on the Wold. Charles Pratley, gamekeeper, of Widford, informer. Job Pratley, gamekeeper, of Cap's Lodge in Wychwood Forest, Oxon., witness. Pleaded not guilty. Fine £5. Offence committed 4 Jan. 1825.

44/B/8   9 Feb. 1825. Henry Perrett of North Nibley, labourer. Possessing 29 lb. of woollen yarn and waste believed to be stolen. H. Burgh JP and E. Aldridge JP. Moran MacClean, informer. Robert Keene and George Daniel Harris, witnesses. Premises searched. First offence. Fine £20. Offence committed c. 7 Feb. 1825.

44/C/1(a)   [Note pinned to 44/C/1(b):] Mr. Cadle paid Mr. Bloxsome 10/-, the amount of the fine imposed on William Bradley for ill-treating a gelding, being the penalty mentioned in the annexed conviction. Signed by Mr. Munro.

44/C/1(b)   22 April 1825. William Bradley of Newent, labourer. Ill-treating a horse, the property of Rev. Richard Francis Onslow. W. Munro JP. Rev. R. F. Onslow, George Hammond, labourer, Henry Stone, mason, and James Merrick, all of Newent, witnesses. Mitigated penalty of 10/-. Offence committed 20 April 1825. [Pencilled note:] Received 10/- penalty and 1/- [fee for] filing. [Signed:] A.J.

44/C/2   2 June 1825. George Hillier of Minchinhampton, labourer. Possessing 159 lb. of woollen yarn and 18 yards of cloth believed to be stolen. H. Burgh JP and Rev. P. Hawker JP. Peter Hawker, informer. John Clissold and Daniel Peyton, witnesses. Premises searched. First offence. Fine £20. Offence committed 30 May 1825.

44/C/3   1 June 1825. Thomas Davis of Minchinhampton, labourer. Possessing 218 lb. of woollen yarn and waste, 10 yards of various cloths and 25 lb. of hair list yarn believed to be stolen. H. Burgh JP and Rev. P. Hawker JP. Robert Keene, informer. John Hinde Pelly and Daniel Peyton, witnesses. Premises searched. First offence. Fine £20. Offence committed 30 May 1825.

44/C/4   13 June 1825. Reuben Smith of Berkeley, carpenter. Being drunk, disorderly and riotous. R. F. Jenner JP at Berkeley. Second offence. Offence committed Sunday 12 June 1825.

44/C/5   17 May 1825. William Stone of the White Hart, Berkeley, alehouse keeper. Allowing drinking to continue during the time of divine service and for five hours thereafter. W. Davis D.D. JP. Fine 20/-. Offence committed Sunday 15 May 1825.

44/C/6   17 May 1825. Richard Bartholomew alias Smith of Tetbury. Leaving his wife and family chargeable to the parish. J. P. Paul JP. Daniel Cole, assistant overseer of Tetbury, witness. Six weeks' hard labour in Horsley house of correction. Offence committed in Aug. 1824.

44/C/7   9 July 1825. George Rosser. Using two dogs with intent to kill game in Almondsbury. J. Haythorne JP. First offence. Offence committed Sunday 6 Sept. 1824.

44/C/8   10 May 1825. John Newell of Winchcombe. Leaving his wife and family chargeable to the parish, his legal place of settlement. Rev. J. Keysall JP at Bredon, Worcs. Hard labour in Northleach house of correction until next Q.S. at Gloucester.

44/C/9   6 June 1825. Benjamin Reeves of Arlingham, innkeeper. Failing to observe a condition of the recognizance entered into on obtaining his licence. Rev. C. Crawley JP, J. W. Guise JP and J. Pyrke JP. First offence. Fine £5 and 7/6 costs.

44/C/10   14 April 1825. Samuel Fruen of Clifton, Bristol, watchmaker. Being drunk. G. Goldney JP at Clifton, who witnessed the offence. Fine 5/-.

44/C/11   2 March 1825. William White and John Powderill, both of Winchcombe, butchers, David Skey and Stephen Stanley, both of Snowshill, shopkeepers. Having non-standard weights. J. Timbrill D.D. JP and Rev. J. Keysall JP at a Petty Sessions held in Mr. Fryer's office in Tewkesbury for the lower division of Kiftsgate hundred. Each fined 20/- and 4/6 costs. Weights forfeited. Offence committed 5 and 8 Feb. 1825.

44/C/12   17 Feb. 1825. Charles Grizzell of Didbrook, shopkeeper; John Fort of Dumbleton, shopkeeper. Having non-standard weights. J. Timbrill D.D. JP and Rev. J. Keysall JP at a Petty Sessions held [as above]. Fine 20/- and 10/- respectively and 4/6 costs. Weights forfeited. Offence committed 13 and 14 Jan. 1825.

44/C/13   2 Feb. 1825. Ann Burrows and James Cunningham, shopkeepers; and John Cull, coal dealer, all of Winchcombe. | Having non-standard weights. Having non-standard weights and balances. | At a Petty Sessions [as above]. Each fined 20/- and 4/6 costs. Weights and balances forfeited. Offence committed 7 and 11 Jan. 1825.

Robert Fluck of Hawling, baker. | Having non-standard weights. |

44/C/14   19 Jan. 1825. Sarah Slatter of Winchcombe, shopkeeper. | Having one non-standard weight. | At a Petty Sessions [as above]. Each fined 20/-, [except as otherwise stated], and 4/6 costs. Weights and balances forfeited. Offence committed 7, 10 and 14 Jan. 1825

William Townsend of Winchcombe, shopkeeper. | Having non-standard balances. Fine 5/-. |

Thomas Bennett of Guiting Power, baker. | Having non-standard weights. |

Thomas Hall of Dumbleton, shopkeeper. | Having non-standard weights. |

44/C/15   13 Oct. 1824. John Porter of Kineton, Temple Guiting, baker. Failing to fix a beam and scales in public view, as required by law. J. Timbrill D.D. JP and Rev. J. Keysall JP. Fine 40/-. Offence committed 2 Oct. 1824.

44/C/16   13 Oct. 1824. [List of those fined for] Having non-standard weights [except as otherwise stated]. J. Timbrill D.D. JP and Rev. J. Keysall JP at a Petty Sessions held at Mr. Fryer's office in Tewkesbury. [Fines as below] and 4/6 costs. Offences committed between 16 Sept. and 2 Oct. 1824.

Mary Agg of Forthampton, shopkeeper. Fine 20/-.

Ann Ainge of Aston Somerville, shopkeeper. Fine 5/-.

Mitchell Belcher of Childswickham, blacksmith. Fine 20/-.

Richard Bayliss of Winchcombe, shopkeeper. Fine 20/-.

John Ballinger of Childswickham, shopkeeper. Fine 20/-. Having non-standard balances.

George Bullock of the Leigh, shopkeeper. Fine 10/-.

William Chandler of Oxenton, miller. Fine 20/-.

John Clarke of the Leigh, shopkeeper. Fine 10/-.

John Cooper of Tirley, shopkeeper. Fine 20/-.

John Lane Cherry of Kemerton, shopkeeper. Fine 20/-.

William Cox of Tirley, shopkeeper. Fine 20/-.

Elizabeth Collett of Church Stanway, miller. Fine 20/-.

Robert Evans of Stanton, butcher. Fine 10/-. Having non-standard balances.

Thomas Eagles of Tredington, baker. Fine 20/-.

Thomas Eveniss of Deerhurst, coal dealer. Fine 20/-. Having non-standard weights and balances.

Thomas Farley of Aston Somerville, shopkeeper. Fine 20/-.

Robert Fluck of Hawling, baker. Fine 20/-.

Charles Grizzell of Didbrook, shopkeeper. Fine 20/-.

Thomas Hall of Dumbleton, baker. Fine 20/-.

George Herbert of Guiting Power, shopkeeper. Fine 20/-.

William Hayes of Deerhurst, shopkeeper. Fine 15/-. Having non-standard balances.

Samuel Harris of Hinton on the Green, miller. Fine 10/-.

James Horlick of Didbrook, baker. Fine 20/-.

William Hawling of Aston on Carrant, miller. Fine 10/-.

William Leach of Pamington, shopkeeper. Fine 20/-.

William Lawrence of Gretton, butcher. Fine 15/-.

William Matthews of Winchcombe, grocer. Fine 20/-.

James Mayall of Ashchurch, miller. Fine 20/-.

Daniel Merrett of Dumbleton, miller. Fine 20/-.

James Morris of the Leigh, miller. Fine 20/-.

John New of Northway, miller. Fine 15/-.

William Newman of Forthampton, shopkeeper. Fine 20/-.

John Peart of Beckford, coal dealer. Fine 5/-.

Benjamin Purser of Apperley, shopkeeper. Fine 20/-.

Joseph Staite of Tirley, baker. Fine 20/-.

Stephen Stanley of Snowshill, shopkeeper. Fine 10/-.

Sarah Slatter of Winchcombe, shopkeeper. Fine 20/-.

Joseph Stallard of Beckford, shopkeeper. Fine 5/-.

William Sadler of Pamington, shopkeeper. Fine 5/-.

William Stephens of Alderton, butcher. Fine 20/-.

Thomas Simmons of Winchcombe, shopkeeper. Fine 15/-.

Thomas Taylor of the Leigh, butcher. Fine 20/-.

Edward Tombs of Winchcombe, butcher. Fine 20/-. Having non-standard balances.

John Washbourne of Woolstone, shopkeeper. Fine 20/-. Having a non-standard weight and balances.

44/D/1   4 Oct. 1825. John Freeman of Beckford, yeoman, high constable for Tibblestone hundred. Neglecting his duty: failing to attend a Petty Sessions held at the Plough inn, Ford, on 27 Sept. 1825, convened for the purpose of receiving lists of jurors. J. Timbrill D.D. JP at Ford. Fine 40/-.

44/D/2   15 Oct. 1825. William Hasell of Cheltenham, victualler. Failing to observe a condition of the recognizance entered into on receiving his licence. J. Clutterbuck JP and R. Capper JP. First offence. Fine £5 and 3/6 costs.

44/D/3   17 Sept. 1825. John Oliver the elder of Alderton, farmer. Using a dog and a gun to kill a partridge without obtaining the required certificate. Rev. Christopher Jeaffreson JP, commissioner for taxes, at Longborough. Paul Martin, farmer, of Alderton, witness. Mitigated fine of £10. Offence committed 2 Sept. 1825.

44/D/4   8 Sept. 1825. John Kearsey of Great Barrington, corn dealer. Using a dog and a gun to kill game without obtaining the required certificate. Rev. R. W. Ford JP, commissioner for taxes, at Stow on the Wold. Mitigated fine of £10. Offence committed 5 Sept. 1825.

44/D/5   6 Oct. 1825. Owen Alger of Stow on the Wold. Beating in pursuit of game with a gun and a dog in Donnington when not qualified to do so. Rev. R. W. Ford JP at Stow on the Wold. James Bolt, labourer, of Donnington, informer. Francis Hamp, yeoman, of Donnington, witness. Pleaded not guilty. Fine £5. Offence committed 1 Oct. 1825.

44/D/6   19 July 1825. William Bright of Coleford, engineer. Paying Alexander Ferguson, labourer, 30/- due to him in other than legal coinage when acting as agent for Benjamin Whitehouse and Company, iron manufacturers. Rt. Hon. C. Bathurst JP and E. Machen JP at Lydney. Fine £10.

44/D/7   1 April 1825 [late return]. Ephraim Wilson of Thornbury, labourer. Using two dogs to kill game without obtaining the required certificate. J. Parker JP, commissioner for taxes, at Lawfords Gate sessions room. Mitigated fine of £10. Offence committed 17 March 1825.

44/D/8   31 Aug. 1825. Isaac Packer of Worcester Row, near Cheltenham. Cruelly beating his horse on the public highway between Tewkesbury and Cheltenham. J. Timbrill JP and J. Keysall JP. Offender admitted charge. Fine 10/-. Offence committed Thursday 25 Aug. 1825.

44/D/9   6 Oct. 1825. James White. Using a gaming device in a game of chance called Gold and Silver Lottery, in Gumstool Street, Tetbury. R. Kingscote JP, E. Wilbraham JP, Rev. H. Campbell JP and Walter Matthews Paul JP at Horsley. Three months' hard labour in Horsley house of correction. Offence committed 5 Oct. 1825.

44/D/10   6 Oct. 1825. Samuel Sansom. Using a gaming device in a game of chance called Hap Hazard, in Gumstool Hill, Tetbury [etc., as 44/D/9].

44/D/11   6 Oct. 1825. Maria Smith , widow. Using a gaming device in a game of chance called Black and White Cock, in Gumstool Street, Tetbury [etc., as 44/D/9].

44/D/12   6 Oct. 1825. William Butcher. Using a gaming device in game of chance called Tetotum, in Gumstool Street, Tetbury [etc., as 44/D/9].

44/D/13   17 Sept. 1825. George Need of Highleadon, Rudford, gentleman. Using a gun to kill game without obtaining the required certificate. W. Goodrich JP [who did not sign], Thomas Jones Howell JP and Rev. J. B. Cheston JP, commissioners for taxes. Offender admitted charge. Fine £10. Offence committed 7 Sept. 1825.

44/D/14   14 Oct. 1825. Roynon Mason of Gloucester, gentleman. Using a gun to kill game in Norton on five separate days without obtaining the required certificate. Rev. J. B. Cheston JP, commissioner for taxes. George Henry Mason the younger, gentleman, of South Hamlet, Gloucester, informer. Pleaded guilty. Fine £25 (£5 on each charge). Offence committed 1, 2, 6, 12 and 16 Sept. 1825.

44/D/15   8 Oct. 1825. Thomas Porter Bamford of Norton, farmer. Unlawfully keeping and using a gun and a dog to kill game. Rev. J. B. Cheston JP. John Jones, gentleman, of Norton, informer. George Ashwin, labourer, of Norton, witness. Pleaded not guilty. Fine £5. Offence committed 1 Oct. 1825.

45/A/1   15 Dec. 1824 [late return]. John Phipps of Stow on the Wold, labourer. Beating and ill-treating a heifer he was driving in Longborough. Rev. F. E. Witts JP. Rev. C. Jeaffreson, witness. Fine 10/-. Offence committed 12 Dec. 1824.

45/A/2   2 Dec. 1825. Isaac Gale of Tormarton, labourer. Possessing a hare in Wapley and Codrington. T. Jones JP, F. Pelly JP and F. Trotman JP at Old Sodbury. William Dyer of Dodington, informer. Joseph Edwards, witness. Fine £5. Offence committed 1 Dec. 1825.

45/A/3   8 Oct. 1825. Samuel Seabourn of Wotton under Edge, victualler. Failing to observe the condition of his recognizance. W. M. Adey JP and H. W. Dyer JP. First offence. Fine £4 15s. and 5/- costs.

45/A/4   22 Dec. 1825. John Hannell of Bourton on the Water. Using snares to kill game without obtaining the required certificate. Rev. R. W. Ford JP and commissioner for taxes, at Stow on the Wold. John Poole, gentleman, of Bourton on the Water, informer. William Kimber, yeoman, of Aston Blank, witness. Fine £20. Offence committed Sunday 25 Sept. 1825.

45/A/5   5 Jan. 1826. John Boulton of Henbury, labourer. Using a snare to kill game in a field adjoining Over Park, Almondsbury. J. Cave JP at the sessions room, Lawfords Gate, Bristol. William Cook, labourer, of Almondsbury, informer. William Webb, gamekeeper, of Almondsbury, witness. Offender pleaded not guilty. Was seen setting a snare in company with Henry Boulton and Samuel Williams. Fine £5. Offence committed 8 Dec. 1825.

45/A/6   15 Dec. 1825. Charles Webb of Winterbourne, labourer. Keeping and using a snare and a gin to kill game in Stoke Gifford. J. Parker JP and James Lewis JP at the sessions room, Lawfords Gate, Bristol. James Howells and Benjamin Webley, gamekeepers, of Stoke Gifford, informer and witness. Offender pleaded not guilty. Fine £5. Offence committed 7 Dec. 1825.

45/A/7   27 Oct. 1825. Joseph Hignell of Horfield, labourer. Keeping and using a gun to kill game. J. Parker JP and J. Lewis JP at the sessions room [as above]. Richard Llewellin the younger, gentleman, of Westbury on Trym, informer. Richard Blake, labourer, of Horfield, witness. Offender pleaded not guilty. Fine £5. Offence committed 16 Sept. 1825.

45/A/8   9 Jan. 1826. Thomas Llewelling [sic] of Newent, labourer. Keeping and using a dog, in company with two others, to kill game in Broad Meadow, Oxenhall. J. Commeline JP and T. Richardson JP at Newent. William Jones, woodward, of Oxenhall, informer. Richard Warne, gamekeeper, of Oxenhall, witness. Offender pleaded not guilty. Fine £5. Offence committed 30 Dec. 1825.

45/A/9   20 Dec. 1825. Thomas Whording. Vagrancy in Stroud. H. Burgh JP. Three months' hard labour in Horsley house of correction. Offence committed 19 Dec. 1825.

45/A/10   20 Dec. 1825. Giles Smith. Vagrancy in Stroud [etc., as 45/A/9].

45/A/11   5 Nov. 1825. Thomas Poulson. Wandering in Stroud with intent to commit a felony: a reputed thief. H. Burgh JP. Two months' hard labour in Horsley house of correction. Offence committed 4 Nov. 1825.

45/A/12   12 Nov. 1825. George Dean[s]. Vagrancy in Stroud. H. Burgh JP. One month's hard labour in Horsley house of correction. Offence committed 11 Nov. 1825

45/A/13   24 Nov. 1825. Henry Corry. Gathering alms under false pretences in Stroud. H. Burgh JP. One month's hard labour in Horsley house of correction. Offence committed 23 Nov. 1825.

45/A/14   28 Nov. 1825. Robert Adams. Gathering alms [etc., as 45/A/13 except] Offence committed 27 Nov. 1825.

45/A/15 14 Nov. 1825. Elizabeth Vick, prostitute. Behaving in a disorderly manner in Stroud. H. Burgh JP. One month's hard labour in Horsley house of correction. Offence committed 13 Nov. 1825.

45/A/16 19 Dec. 1825. Giles Edmonds of Lechlade, yeoman. Keeping and using a gun and a dog to kill game. Rev. John William Peters JP at Quenington. Thomas Hawkins, schoolmaster, of Lechlade, informer. Offender admitted charge. Fine £5. Offence committed 1 Dec. 1825.

45/A/17 26 Dec. 1825. William Longford of Cirencester, labourer. Keeping and using a gin or snare to kill game in Baunton. Rev. H. A. Pye JP. First offence. Fine £20. Offence committed Sunday 4 Dec. 1825.

45/A/18 19 Dec. 1825. Giles Edmonds of Lechlade, yeoman. Keeping [*etc.*, *as* 45/A/16 *except*] Offence committed 28 Nov. 1825.

45/A/19 22 Oct. 1825. John Matthews of Rudford, labourer. Keeping and using a gun to kill a pheasant when not qualified. Rev. J. B. Cheston JP. Samuel Locke, gamekeeper, of Highnam, informer. John Stephens, labourer, of Tibberton, witness. Offender pleaded not guilty. Fine £5. Offence committed 18 Oct. 1825.

45/B/1 6 March 1826. Robert Burdock of Farmington, labourer. Beating for and pursuing game without obtaining the required certificate. Rev. R. W. Ford JP and commissioner for taxes, at Little Rissington. Thomas Cook, gamekeeper to Henry Waller Esq., of Farmington, informer. Richard Guy of Sherborne, witness. Fine £20. Offence committed 3 March 1826.

45/B/2 17 Feb. 1826. Henry Okey of Stroud, victualler. Failing to observe a condition of his recognizance. H. Burgh JP and Rev. H. Campbell JP. First offence. Fine £5 and 10/6 costs.

45/B/3 6 March 1826. John Ridler. Vagrancy in Stroud. H. Burgh JP. Three months' hard labour in Horsley house of correction. Offence committed 5 March 1826.

45/B/4 25 Jan. 1826. William Hooper. Frequenting the streets of Stroud with intent to commit a felony: a reputed thief. H. Burgh JP. Three months' hard labour in Horsley house of correction. Offence committed 24 Jan. 1826.

45/B/5 10 March 1826. Benjamin Fisher. Hiding, with unlawful intent, in John Long's dwelling house in Stroud. H. Burgh JP. Three months' hard labour in Horsley house of correction. Offence committed 9 March 1826.

45/B/6 22 March 1826. Valentine Alexander. Vagrancy in Stroud. H. Burgh JP. Six weeks' hard labour in Horsley house of correction. Offence committed 21 March 1826.

45/B/7 25 Jan. 1826. John Summers. Frequenting the streets of Stroud with intent to commit a felony: a reputed thief. H. Burgh JP. Three months' hard labour in Horsley house of correction. Offence committed 24 Jan. 1826.

45/B/8 6 March 1826. Isaac White. Vagrancy in Stroud. H. Burgh JP. Three months' hard labour in Horsley house of correction. Offence committed 5 March 1826.

45/B/9 23 March 1826. David Jones of Westbury on Trym, victualler. Failing to observe a condition of his recognizance. John Vaughan JP and J. Lewis JP. First offence. Fine £5 and 5/6 costs.

45/B/10 9 March 1826. Nathaniel Wilmot. Using a dog to kill hares in Almondsbury. J. Lewis JP. First offence. Mitigated fine of £10. Offence committed Sunday 26 Feb. 1826.

45/B/11   16 March 1826. Peter Griffin of Almondsbury, labourer. Possessing three wire snares. G. Goldney JP and J. Lewis JP at the sessions room, Lawfords Gate, Bristol. William Harvey, labourer, informed J. Vaughan JP at the sessions room on 6 March. George Sheppard, victualler, of Almondsbury, witnessed informer taking snares from accused's pocket. Pleaded not guilty. Fine £5. Offence committed 4 March 1826.

45/B/12   2 March 1826. Benjamin Neale of Woodchester, weaver. Selling 2 lb. of woollen waste knowing it to be stolen. R. Kingscote JP, Rev. P. Hawker JP and Rev. H. Campbell JP. John Hunt, complainant and informer. William Clissold, weaver, of Minchinhampton, witness. First offence. Mitigated fine of £20 or six months' hard labour in Horsley house of correction. Offences committed 21 and 19 Dec. respectively.

45/B/13   2 March 1826. Robert Bowyer of Avening, weaver. Selling 6 lb. 8 oz. of woollen waste knowing it to be stolen [*etc., as* 45/B/12].

45/C/1   20 April 1826. Joseph Vowles. Cutting down and stealing a quantity of poles in Highwood, Almondsbury. Daniel Cave JP, H. W. Newman JP and J. Parker JP for Barton Regis district. John Randalls, constable of St. Philip and St. Jacob, Bristol, complainant. Offence committed 10 Feb. 1826.

45/C/2   10 July 1826. Henry Gardner of Stroud, labourer. Wilfully breaking a window and shutters in a house belonging to the Thames and Severn Canal Navigation Company. H. Burgh JP. Fine £1 and 8/- costs, to be paid forthwith to John Rudge Denyer of Stroud, agent to the company. Offence committed 8 July 1826.

45/C/3   19 May 1826. Thomas Dalby. Levying unlawful charges under a distress for rent. H. Burgh JP for Bisley division. Ordered to pay the complainant, William Horwood, £1 16*s*. in compensation and 11/- costs.

45/C/4   3 March 1826. Richard Mantle of Cowley, labourer. Stealing a Newfoundland dog at Cowley, the property of Thomas Hitchins, labourer, of Cranham. H. Burgh JP and Rev. H. Campbell JP. Offence committed 24 Jan. 1826.

45/C/5   8 June 1826. Martha Morgan. Vagrancy in Stroud. H. Burgh JP at Stroud. Three months' hard labour in Horsley house of correction. Offence committed 28 May 1826.

45/C/6   6 April 1826. John Cox. Entering Thomas Arkwell's house at Rodmarton with intent to commit a felony. H. Burgh JP at Stroud. Three months' hard labour in Horsley house of correction. Offence committed 29 March 1826.

45/C/7   9 June 1826. John Walker. Vagrancy in Stroud. H. Burgh JP at Stroud. Fourteen days' hard labour in Horsley house of correction. Offence committed 8 June 1826.

45/C/8   9 June 1826. William Hooper. Vagrancy in Stroud [*etc., as* 45/C/7 *except*] six weeks' hard labour.

45/C/9   9 June 1826. John Matthews. Vagrancy in Stroud [*etc., as* 45/C/7 *except*] six weeks' hard labour.

45/C/10   21 June 1826. Elizabeth Clift, spinster. Vagrancy in Stroud. H. Burgh JP and Rev. P. Hawker JP. Six weeks' hard labour in Horsley house of correction. Offence committed 13 June 1826.

45/C/11   21 June 1826. James Okey. Vagrancy in Stroud [*etc., as* 45/C/10 *except*] three months' hard labour.

45/C/12   7 July 1826. Isaac Silk of Miserden, victualler. Failing to observe a condition of his recognizance. H. Burgh JP and Rev. P. Hawker JP [*who did not sign*]. First offence. Fine £5 and 8/6 costs.

45/C/13   17 March 1826. John Wilkins of Horsley, weaver. Possessing 3 yards of stolen woollen cloth. H. Burgh JP and Rev. H. Campbell JP. Peter Hawker, gentleman, of Stroud, informer. Robert Keene, weaver, of Stroud, witness. Fine £20. Offence committed 30 Dec. 1825.

45/C/14   11 April 1826. James Davis of Minchinhampton, labourer. Possessing 2 yards of stolen woollen cloth. H. Burgh JP and Rev. H. Campbell JP. Peter Hawker, gentleman, of Stroud, informer. James Jones, pawnbroker, of Stroud, witness. Fine £20. Offence committed 28 Feb. 1826.

45/C/15   21 Feb. 1826. John Davis of Bisley, weaver. Possessing 3 lb. of various stolen woollen yarns. H. Burgh JP and Rev. H. Campbell JP. Peter Hawker, gentleman, of Stroud, informer. Robert Keene, weaver, of Stroud, witness. Fine £20. Offence committed 21 Jan. 1826.

45/C/16   21 April 1826. James Cratchley of Minchinhampton, weaver. Possessing 20 yards of stolen woollen cloth [*etc.*, *as* 45/C/15 *except*] Offence committed within previous three months.

45/C/17   12 June 1826. Enoch Lee of Minchinhampton, weaver. Possessing 8 yards of stolen woollen cloth. H. Burgh JP and Rev. P. Hawker JP. Peter Hawker, gentleman, of Stroud, informer. Robert Keene, weaver, of Stroud, witness. Second offence. Fine £30. Offence committed 1 May 1826.

45/C/18   24 June 1826. Elizabeth Child of Bromsberrow. Leaving her 12 months old son chargeable to the parish although able to maintain him and herself wholly or in part. Rev. R. Pyndar JP at Ledbury, Herefs. Three months' hard labour in Littledean house of correction. Offence committed 15 May 1826.

45/C/19   30 June 1826. Deborah Burlow of Bromsberrow. Leaving her two children under seven years of age chargeable to the parish although able [*etc.*, *as* 45/C/18 *except*] Offence committed 24 June 1826.

45/C/20   5 June 1826. John Harpur, John Baron, labourers, and William Merrett of Newent, carpenter. Wilfully damaging a fence surrounding a meadow occupied by Henry Parlowe, farmer, of Newent. T. Richardson JP. Fine 15/-, to be paid forthwith. Offence committed 29 May 1826.

45/C/21   10 April 1826. Eleanor Beard of Taynton, widow. Damaging underwood in Cockridge Hill [*MS.* Cuggerhill] Coppice, Newent, the property of Rev. William Andrew Foley. T. Richardson JP. Fine 5/-, to be paid forthwith. Offence committed 1 April 1826.

45/C/22   8 May 1826. William Jackson of Longhope, labourer. Evading a toll of 10*d.* at Newent Wharf by removing two of the horses drawing lime from Bayliss's Corner, Culver Street, to or near the Crown inn and re-attaching them after passing through the gate. T. Richardson JP. Fine 5/-. Offence committed 20 April 1826.

45/C/23   27 March 1826. Robert Mason of Newent, labourer. Ill-treating his employer's horse. T. Richardson JP. Jonathan Apperley, labourer, of Newent, witness. Both witness and offender employed by John Bowkett, yeoman, of Newent. Mitigated fine of 10/-. Offence committed Wednesday 13 March 1826.

45/C/24   10 May 1826. Anne Parker of Winchcombe, victualler. Keeping her alehouse open during late hours for purposes other than the reception of travellers. Rev. J. Keysall JP and Rev. C. White JP. George Chadborn, yeoman, of Winchcombe, prosecutor. Offender admitted charge. First offence. Mitigated fine of 20/-. Offence committed 18 April 1826.

45/C/25 10 May 1826. Richard Jones of Winchcombe. Ill-treating a ewe in Bishop's Cleeve, the property of James Shipway. Rev. J. Keysall JP and Rev. C. White JP. [*Witnesses not named.*] Fine 50/-. Offence committed 20 April 1826.

45/C/26 A return of forfeiture levied by Rev. J. Keysall JP and Rev. C. White JP on Richard Jones of Winchcombe, under an Act to prevent cruel and improper treatment of cattle, 10 May 1826. Received £2 10s. [*Signed:*] A. I.

45/C/27 A return of forfeiture levied by Rev. J. Keysall JP and Rev. C. White JP on Anne Parker of Winchcombe under an Act for . . . regulating the manner of licensing alehouses . . ., 10 May 1826. Received 10/- [*the half due to the Crown*]. [*Signed:*] A. I.

45/D/1 15 June 1826. Henry Gore of Stroud, plumber and glazier. Molesting and obstructing James Withey in the execution of his duty, i.e. directing street paving in Stroud. H. Burgh JP. Fine £5 and 8/- costs. Offence committed 13 May 1826.

45/D/2 31 Aug. 1826. William Smith of Burford, Oxon., labourer. Beating for game in Aldsworth without acquiring a certificate. Rev. R. W. Ford JP and tax commissioner, at Little Rissington. William Guy and Thomas Houlton, gamekeepers, of Sherborne, informer and witness. Fine £20. Offence committed 31 Aug. 1826.

45/D/3 19 Sept. 1826. Nathaniel Pope of Horsley, weaver. Possessing 40 lb. of woollen yarn and 11 yards of various cloths believed to be stolen. E. Wilbraham JP and Rev. H. Campbell JP. Isaac Lockier, informer. — Jellyman, said by informer to be authorized to dispose of the materials, absconded before a summons could be served. First offence. Fine £20 or one month in Horsley house of correction.

45/D/4 22 Aug. 1826. Henry Stiles, former servant to Mr. Clement Banks of Winchcombe. Ill-treating his master's mare, injuring the sight of one eye. J. Timbrill D.D. JP. Fine £1. Offence committed 15 Aug. 1826.

45/D/5 Return of forfeiture levied on Henry Stiles of Winchcombe under an Act to prevent the cruel and impropert treatment of cattle. £1. 22 Aug. 1826. [*Signed:*] J. Timbrill.

45/D/6 5 July 1826. Anne Parker of Winchcombe, victualler. Keeping her house open during late hours for purposes other than the reception of travellers. J. Timbrill D.D. JP and Rev. J. Keysall JP. George Chadborn, yeoman, of Winchcombe, prosecutor. John Rowland and Joanna Berry, witnesses. Second offence. [*Cf.* 45/C/24.] Fine £10. Offence committed 24 June 1826.

45/D/7 Return of forfeiture levied on Anne Parker under an Act for . . . regulating the manner of licensing alehouses. £5 [*the half due to the Crown*]. 5 July 1826. [*Signed:*] J. Timbrill, J. Keysall.

45/D/8 18 Sept. 1826. Elizabeth Cole, late of Tetbury, prostitute. Disorderly behaviour in Tetbury. J. P. Paul JP at Tetbury. One month's hard labour in Horsley house of correction. Offence committed 17 Sept. 1826.

45/D/9 24 Aug. 1826. Robert Street of Tetbury, labourer. Stealing a quantity of apples from an orchard in Tetbury, the property of Jeremiah Fry, yeoman. J. P. Paul JP and W. M. Paul JP at Tetbury. Three months' hard labour in Horsley house of correction. Offence committed 19 Aug. 1826.

45/D/10 10 Aug. 1826. John Snelus of Cheltenham. Neglecting or refusing to pay £5 12s. to Richard Billings, town surveyor, for certificates attesting that local regulations had been complied with in the building of sixteen houses. Sir W. Hicks, Bt., JP, J. Agg JP and R. Capper JP. Ordered to pay the sum owing.

45/D/11 21 July 1826. James Wood of Painswick, cordwainer. Publishing and distributing a printed book not bearing the printer's name and address. H. Burgh JP, Rev. P. Hawker JP and Rev. H. Campbell JP. Fine £20. Offence committed 10 July 1826.

45/D/12 26 July 1826. James Wood of Painswick, cordwainer. Publishing and distributing a printed book not bearing the name and address of the printer. H. Burgh JP, Rev. P. Hawker JP and Rev. H. Campbell JP. Fine £20. Offence committed 24 May 1826.

45/D/13 5 Sept. 1826. Charles Clarke, stage-coach driver. Carrying eleven outside passengers at Cheltenham, one more than allowed by law, on the Gloucester to London coach. J. Clutterbuck JP and R. Capper JP at the public office, Cheltenham. Coach owners John Eames and John Bosley summoned but acquitted. John Biers, informer. William Stringle, witness. Offender did not appear. Fine £5. Offence committed 18 Aug. 1826.

45/D/14 5 Sept. 1826. John Murphy, stage-coach driver. Carrying eleven outside passengers at Cheltenham, one more than allowed by law, on the Gloucester to London coach. J. Clutterbuck JP and R. Capper JP at the public office, Cheltenham. Coach owners Robert Gray and John Spencer summoned but acquitted. John Biers, informer. William Stringle, witness. Offender did not appear. Fine £5. Offence committed 29 Aug. 1826.

45/D/15 7 Sept. 1826. Joseph Pratt of Cheltenham, stage-coach owner and driver. Carrying eight outside passengers in Cheltenham on his Cheltenham to Worcester coach, three more than allowed by law. R. L. Townsend D.D. JP, Rev. William Hicks JP and R. Capper JP at Cheltenham. John Biers of Winchester Street, St. James, Clerkenwell, Middx., inspector of hawkers' licences, informer. William Stringle, witness. Offender did not appear. Fine £30. Offence committed 24 Aug. 1826.

45/D/16 [*Copy of* 45/D/15.]

45/D/17 5 Sept. 1826. William Mason of Cheltenham, stage-coach driver. Carrying nine outside passengers in Cheltenham on the Cheltenham to Bath coach, two more than allowed by law. J. Clutterbuck JP and R. Capper JP at Cheltenham. Thomas Haines junior, coach owner. John Biers, informer. William Stringle, witness. Offender pleaded not guilty. Fine £10. Offence committed 21 Aug. 1826.

45/D/18 23 Sept. 1826. Joseph Verrinder of Cranham, labourer. Selling two partridges to Henry Newman, gentleman, of Stroud. H. Burgh JP. H. Newman, witness. Offender admitted charge. Fine £10. Offence committed 9 Sept. 1826.

45/D/19 23 Sept. 1826. Joseph Verrinder of Cranham, labourer. Selling a hare to Henry Newman, gentleman, of Stroud. H. Burgh JP. H. Newman, witness. Offender admitted charge. Fine £5. Offence committed 15 Sept. 1826.

45/D/20 6 Oct. 1826. William Bliss of Painswick, clothworker. Stealing a quantity of apples from an orchard in Painswick, the property of Henry Gyde, clothier. H. Burgh JP. Six weeks' hard labour in Horsley house of correction. Offence committed 23 Sept. 1826.

45/D/21 6 Oct. 1826. Henry Holder of Rodborough, clothworker. Stealing a quantity of apples from an orchard in Stroud, the property of John Trotman, yeoman. H. Burgh JP. One month's hard labour in Horsley house of correction. Offence committed 21 Sept. 1826.

45/D/22 21 July 1826. William Butt of Stroud, carpenter. Obstructing a road in Stroud by depositing rubbish. H. Burgh JP. Fine 10/- and 7/6, costs to be paid forthwith. Offence committed *c.* 11 July 1826.

45/D/23 21 July 1826. Samuel Underwood of Stroud, labourer. Obstructing a road in Stroud by placing a piece of timber therein. H. Burgh JP. Fine 5/- and 7/6 costs. Offence committed *c.* 11 July 1826.

45/D/24 15 Sept. 1826. John Hopkins of Stonehouse, labourer. Attempting to net fish in the Stroudwater canal without a licence. H. Burgh JP at Stroud. William Hare, labourer, of Stonehouse, and George Hawker, gentleman, of Stroud, witnesses. Fine 10/-, to be paid forthwith for the use of the parish poor. Offence committed 31 Aug. 1826.

45/D/25 15 Sept. 1826. James Verrinder and James Ballinger. Stealing a quantity of nuts from an orchard in Painswick, the property of Elizabeth Baldwin. H. Burgh JP at Stroud. Fine £5 and 20/- respectively, to be paid forthwith, or three months' hard labour in Horsley house of correction. Offence committed 2 Sept. 1826.

45/D/26 16 Sept. 1826. Catherine Hunt, prostitute. Disorderly behaviour in Stroud. H. Burgh JP. One month's hard labour in Horsley house of correction. Offence committed 15 Sept. 1826.

45/D/27 16 Sept. 1826. Jane Morgan, prostitute. Disorderly behaviour [*etc., as* 45/D/26].

45/D/28 22 July 1826. William Weysome. Leaving his wife and family chargeable to Stroud parish. H. Burgh JP. One month's hard labour in Horsley house of correction. Offence committed 21 July 1826

45/D/29 11 Oct. 1826. John Bricker. Leaving his wife and family [*etc., as* 45/D/28].

45/D/30 31 Aug. 1826. Thomas Walker. Ill-treating a bull at St. Philip and St. Jacob, Bristol, the property of Nathaniel Dolman, by encouraging a dog to lacerate its nose. H. W. Newman JP. Fine 40/-, to be paid forthwith, or one month in Lawfords Gate house of correction. Offence committed 3 Aug. 1826.

45/D/31 31 Aug. 1826. Samuel Ford of St. George, Bristol, alehouse keeper. Failing to observe a condition of his recognizance. H. W. Newman JP and J. S. Harford JP. First offence. Fine 40/- and 6/6 costs.

45/D/32 31 Aug. 1826. Benjamin Shillard of St. George, Bristol, alehouse keeper. Failing to observe [*etc., as* 45/D/31 *except*] Fine 20/- and 6/6 costs.

45/D/33 27 July 1826. Robert Brown of St. Philip and St. Jacob, Bristol, alehouse keeper. Failing to observe a condition of his recognizance. H. W. Newman JP and W. Munro JP. First offence. Fine 30/- and 6/6 costs.

45/D/34 14 Sept. 1826. George Nicholls of St. Philip and St. Jacob, Bristol, butcher. Swearing. W. Davies JP.

45/D/35 14 Aug. 1826. James Slip. Trespassing and breaking down hedges on land belonging to Richard Dennis of Bitton. J. Parker JP. John Ashton, labourer, witness. Fine 5/- and costs, to be paid forthwith, or one month in Lawfords Gate house of correction.

45/D/36 31 July 1826. John Iverson of Clifton, employee of the proprietors of Keene's *Bath Journal*. Crying and exposing for sale on a Sunday copies of a weekly newspaper. H. W. Newman JP at Stokes Croft, [Bristol]. Edward Shepherd of St. James, Bristol, informer. Offender admitted charge. Fine 5/-. Offence committed Sunday 23 July 1826.

45/D/37 28 Sept. 1826. Francis Flower of Bitton, farmer. Beating a hedge and attempting to kill a partridge, having sent a boy, William Blinmouth, for his gun. H. W. Newman JP at Lawfords Gate. William Bright and Samuel Silcock, labourers, of Bitton, informer and witness. Fine £5. Offence committed 22 Aug. 1826.

45/D/38 21 Aug. 1826. James Packer of Shilton, Berks., labourer. Possessing 18 snares for killing game in Great Barrington. Rev. F. E. Witts JP at Upper Slaughter. William Lowe and Thomas Cook of Great Barrington, bailiff and gamekeeper respectively to Lord Dynevor, informer and witness. Offender pleaded not guilty. Fine £5. Offence committed 19 Aug. 1826.

46/A/1   16 Feb. 1826. Hester Clarke of Minchinhampton, widow. Concealing about 50 lb. of stolen woollen yarn and waste in her dwelling and about 40 lb. of the same in Abel Pride's house in Minchinhampton. Rev. H. Campbell JP and O. P. Wathen JP at Rodborough. Search warrants issued by Rev. P. Hawker and Rev. H. Campbell on 13 Feb. Daniel Smith, informer. First offence. Offender admitted concealing some of the materials. Fine £20 or one month in Horsley house of correction.

46/A/2   6 Nov. 1826. James Hooper of Pauntley, labourer. Using a dog and a gun to kill game in Hill House Wood, Pauntley, when not qualified. T. Richardson JP at Newent. William Jones, woodward, of Newent, informer. Thomas Jones, labourer, of Newent, witness. Offender did not appear. Fine £5. Offence committed 19 Oct. 1826.

46/A/3   8 Jan. 1827. William Price. Neglecting or refusing to work, thereby becoming chargeable to the parish of Taynton for the past 20 days. Rev. R. F. Onslow JP and T. Richardson JP at Newent. One month's hard labour in Littledean house of correction.

46/A/4   22 Nov. 1826. Gabriel Little the younger of Beckford, labourer. Driving a cart not bearing the owner's name. Rev. J. Keysall JP. Fine 20/-. Offence committed 10 Oct. 1826.

46/A/5   22 Nov. 1826. William Wakeman of Beckford, gentleman. Allowing his cart to be driven on the turnpike road without having his name and address painted thereon. Rev. J. Keysall JP. Fine 50/-. Offence committed 10 Oct. 1826.

46/A/6   1 Dec. 1826. Edwin Baxter of Stonehouse, labourer. Breaking down a hedge, the property of Robert Martin, yeoman, of Stonehouse, with intent to remove it. H. Burgh JP. Offence committed 6 Nov. 1826.

46/A/7   24 Nov. 1826. Henry White and John Rust of Stroud, labourers. Cutting down a beech tree in Stroud, the property of William Capel Esq. of Painswick. H. Burgh JP. Offender admitted charge. Offence committed 21 Nov. 1826.

46/A/8   28 Dec. 1826. Gregory Debeth. Breaking a glass pane in Thomas Gurner's in Stroud. H. Burgh JP. Ordered to pay 2/- forthwith. Offence committed 27 Dec. 1826.

46/A/9   3 Jan. 1827. William Grissell the younger of Upton St. Leonards, butcher. Evading a toll of 2d. when travelling with his horse in Painswick. H. Burgh JP. Fine 5/- and 6/- costs. Offence committed 24 Dec. 1826. [Case heard before three JPs but only H. Burgh signed.]

46/A/10   5 Jan. 1827. William Grissell [as above]. Evading a toll of 2d. [etc., as 46/A/8 except] Offence committed 17 Dec. 1826

46/A/11   5 Jan. 1827. William Grissell [as above]. Evading a toll of 6d. on a horse and cart in Painswick [etc., as 46/A/9 except] Offence committed 13 Dec. 1826.

46/A/12   5 Jan. 1827. Moses Moreton of Bisley, alehouse keeper. Failing to observe a condition of his recognizance. H. Burgh JP, W. H. Hyett JP and Edwin Palling Caruthers JP. First offence. Fine 1 guinea and 9/- costs. [Only H. Burgh signed.]

46/A/13   30 Oct. 1826. Jane Morgan, prostitute. Disorderly behaviour in Stroud. H. Burgh JP at Stroud. One month's hard labour in Horsley house of correction. Offence committed 28 Oct. 1826.

46/A/14   30 Oct. 1826. Elizabeth Vick. Disorderly behaviour in Stroud [etc., as 46/A/13].

46/A/15   28 Oct. 1826. Walter Perkins. Vagrancy in Stroud [etc., as 46/A/13].

46/A/16   8 Nov. 1826. Edward Pym. Stealing apples from an orchard in Painswick, the property of James Withey, druggist, of Stroud. H. Burgh JP at Stroud. Six months' hard labour in Horsley house of correction. Offence committed 17 Sept. 1826.

46/A/17 11 Dec. 1826. George Ball and Eli Fry, late of Acton Turville, servants. Using snares and killing a hare. Rev. T. Jones JP. First offence. Fine £10 each or six months mitigated to three months in the house of correction. Offence committed 10 Dec. 1826.

46/A/18 29 Dec. 1826. William Stephens of Uley, labourer. Violently assaulting Susan Dauncey and knocking her to the ground when they were inmates of the workhouse. Edward Sheppard JP.

46/A/19 2 Nov. 1826. Henry Edwards of St. Philip and St. Jacob, Bristol, [alehouse keeper]. Failing to observe a condition of his recognizance. H. W. Newman JP and J. Lewis JP. First offence. Fine 40/- and 6/6 costs. [*A note records 60/- received.*]

46/A/20 4 Jan. 1827. Joseph Eatwell. Ill-treating an ass in St. Philip and St. Jacob, Bristol. J. Parker JP. Offence committed 3 Jan. 1827. [*A note records the penalty as 10/- and 7/6 costs, and receipt of 2/6.*]

46/A/21 1 Dec. 1826. John Nicholls Hudleston of Bitton, gentleman. Using a gun and two dogs to kill game in Siston. H. W. Newman JP at Lawfords Gate, Bristol. John Nachell Brinkworth, gentleman, of Bitton, gave information to J. Savage JP at Stokes Croft, Bristol, on 29 Dec. 1826. Offender admitted charge. Fine £5. Offence committed 30 Oct. 1826.

46/A/22 27 Oct. 1826. Richard Daubeny Brice of Winterbourne. Using a gun and dogs to kill game in Frampton Cotterell. H. W. Newman JP at Lawfords Gate, Bristol. John Randall, constable, and Anthony Johnson, victualler, both of St. Philip and St. Jacob, Bristol, informer and witness respectively. Offender pleaded not guilty. Fine £5. Offence committed 26 Oct. 1826.

46/A/23 24 Oct. 1826. Thomas Earle of Frampton on Severn, gentleman. Shooting game in Mr. Hawkins's withybed, Wheatenhurst, when not qualified. D. J. Niblett JP and J. Sayer JP at the George inn, Wheatenhurst. John Harmer of Eastington informed H. C. Clifford JP 12 Oct. 1826. Charles Edward Hicks, witness. Offender did not appear. Fine £5. Offence committed 11 Oct. 1826.

46/A/24 24 Oct. 1826. Thomas Earle of Frampton on Severn, gentleman. Beating for game with a dog and a gun in Mr. Knelmes's field in Eastington when not qualified. D. J. Niblett JP and J. Sayer JP at the George inn, Wheatenhurst. John Neale of Frampton on Severn informed H. C. Clifford JP 13 Oct. 1826. John Harmer, witness. Offender did not appear. Fine £5. Offence committed 7 Oct. 1826.

46/A/25 24 Oct. 1826. Thomas Earle of Frampton on Severn, gentleman. Using a gun and two dogs to kill game in the lower field in Frampton on Severn when not qualified. D. J. Niblett JP and J. Sayer JP at the George inn, Wheatenhurst. John Harmer of Eastington informed H. Hicks JP on 16 Oct. 1826. John Neale, witness. Offender did not appear. Fine £5. Offence committed 4 Oct. 1826.

46/A/26 24 Oct. 1826. Thomas Earle of Frampton on Severn, gentleman. Using a gun and a dog to kill game in Mr. Hawkins's field in Frampton on Severn when not qualified. D. J. Niblett JP and J. Sayer JP at the George inn, Wheatenhurst. Information given by John Harmer [*as above*] on 17 Oct. 1826. Levi Burley, witness. Offender did not appear. Fine £5. Offence committed 14 Oct. 1826.

46/A/27 10 Oct. 1826. William Miles of Trelleck, Mon., yeoman. Using a greyhound to kill a hare in enclosed ground in Newland. Rt. Hon. C. Bathurst JP and E. Machen JP at Lydney. William Cole, labourer, of Lydney, informer. William Chouls, labourer, of St. Briavels hundred, witness. Offender denied owning the dog. Fine £5. Offence committed 6 Oct. 1826.

46/B/1   26 March 1827. Thomas Harris of Kilcot, Newent, yeoman. Permitting drunkenness and gaming, and keeping his house open during late hours other than for the reception of travellers. T. Richardson JP. William Gabb, labourer, of Dymock, informer. Fine £1. Offence committed 20 March 1827. [*Note records receipt of* 10/-, 'His Majesty's moiety', *signed*:] E.B. [*i.e.* Edward Bloxsome].

46/B/2   15 Feb. 1827. William Burrows of Leckhampton, victualler. Failing to observe a condition of his recognizance. Sir W. Hicks JP and J. Clutterbuck JP. First offence. Fine £2 and 3/6 costs. [*Note records receipt of* 20/-, 'the king's moiety', *signed*:] E.B. [*i.e.* Edward Bloxsome] April 25 1827.

46/B/3   25 Jan. 1827. William Spray of Henbury. Failing to observe a condition of the recognizance entered into on obtaining his licence to sell ale etc. by retail. J. S. Harford JP and H. W. Newman JP. First offence. Fine 20/- and 6/6 costs.

46/B/4   14 April 1827. Richard Mayor of Bisley, weaver. Possessing 4 lb. of woollen thrums believed to be stolen. H. Burgh JP and Rev. P. Hawker JP. William Hunt, clothier, of Bisley, informer. Handy Davis, clothier, John Lewis, baker, both of Bisley, and Ralph Price, oil merchant, of the city of London, witnesses. Fine £20. Offence committed 11 April 1827.

46/B/5   7 April 1827. John Shurmur. Vagrancy in King's Stanley. H. Burgh JP at Stroud. Three months' hard labour in Horsley house of correction. Offence committed 6 April 1827.

46/B/6   20 Jan. 1827. Robert Thomas of Stroud, labourer. Breaking windows in the dwelling house of the John Williams D.D. in Painswick. H. Burgh JP. Ordered to pay the value of the glass, £1 12*s*., to the complainant forthwith.

46/B/7   28 March 1827. George Taylor of Stroud, labourer. Stealing a quantity of carnation plants from a garden in Stroud, the property of Samuel Webb. H. Burgh JP at Stroud. Six months' hard labour in Horsley house of correction. Offence committed 27 March 1827.

46/B/8   9 April 1827. Thomas Corbett and John Burton of Stroud, labourers. Attempting to fish in private water, the property of William Lewis Esq., without permission. H. Burgh JP. Fine 10/- each. Offence committed 9 April 1827.

46/B/9   29 March 1827. William Stone of Westbury on Trym. Failing to observe a condition of the recognizance entered into on obtaining a licence to sell ale etc. by retail. George Hilhouse JP and H. W. Newman JP. First offence. Fine £5 and 6/6 costs.

46/B/10 29 March 1827. Thomas Burfoot of St. Philip and St. Jacob, Bristol. Failing to observe [*etc., as* 46/B/9].

46/B/11 29 March 1827. Thomas Kithro of St. Philip and St. Jacob, Bristol. Failing to observe [*etc., as* 46/B/9].

46/B/12 22 Feb. 1827. Mary Borobeer of Oldland, Bitton. Failing to observe a condition of the recognizance entered into on obtaining a licence to sell ale etc. by retail. Abraham Grey Harford Battersby JP and H. W. Newman JP. First offence. Fine £5 and 6/6 costs.

46/B/13 14 April 1827. William Sindre of Tockington. Possessing snares to kill game in Almondsbury. J. Savage JP at Lawfords Gate sessions room, Bristol. Fine £5 and 10/- costs. Offence committed 13 April 1827.

46/B/14 12 Feb. 1827. Thomas Young of Patchway, Almondsbury, baker. Possessing ten underweight penny loaves. J. Vaughan JP at Almondsbury. Total deficiency 20 oz. Fine £3 10*s*. and 10/- costs.

46/B/15 12 Feb. 1827. Thomas Young of Patchway, baker. Possessing alum, used to adulterate flour or bread. J. Vaughan JP at Almondsbury. Fine £10 and 10/- costs.

46/B/16 25 Jan. 1827. James Burgess of Henbury. Possessing a hare when not qualified. J. S. Harford JP at Lawfords Gate sessions room. Fine £5 including costs. Offence committed 23 Dec. 1826.

46/B/17 8 March 1827. William Parker of Almondsbury. Keeping and using a gun to kill game when not qualified. H. W. Newman JP at Lawfords Gate sessions room. Fine £5 and 10/- costs. Offence committed 19 Feb. 1827.

46/B/18 17 Feb. 1827. Henry Brittan of Bath city, gentleman. Keeping and using a gun to kill game when not qualified. A. G. H. Battersby JP and H. W. Newman JP at Lawfords Gate sessions room. Information laid before J. Savage JP at St. James, [Bristol], by Edward King, constable of Clifton, on 10 Feb. 1827. Offender admitted charge. Fine £5. Offence committed 23 Dec. 1826.

46/B/19 Return of forfeiture, 10/- [in connection with 46/B/20. Signed:] J. Timbrill, 9 March 1827.

46/B/20 9 March 1827. John Green, servant to Henry Green, of Twyning. Beating a mare, his master's property. Rev. J. Timbrill JP. Offender admitted charge. Fine 10/-. Offence committed 7 March 1827.

46/B/21 14 March 1827. Charles Newcombe of Tetbury, plumber and glazier. Using snares to kill hares at Cherington. Rev. Richard Webster Huntley JP, Thomas Kingscote JP and W. M. Paul JP. First offence. Offence committed Sunday 4 March 1827.

46/B/22 5 Feb. 1827. James Lively, late of Bourton on the Hill, labourer. Using three dogs to kill game when not qualified. Rev. J. R. Hall JP at Bourton on the Hill. John Sadler, yeoman, of Moreton in Marsh, informer. William Slatter, witness. Fine £10. Offence committed Sunday 21 Jan. 1827.

46/B/23 26 Jan. 1827. Samuel Seabourn of Wotton under Edge, victualler. Failing to observe a condition of his recognizance. Rev. W. Lloyd Baker JP, W. M. Adey JP, H. W. Dyer JP and P. B. Purnell JP. Second offence. [Cf. 45/A/3.] Fine £9 and £1 costs.

46/B/24 5 Jan. 1827. Daniel Ford of Walcot, Som. Using a gun to kill game in Dyrham and Hinton when not qualified. Rev. F. Pelly JP, Rev. T. Jones JP and F. Trotman JP at a Petty Sessions held at the Cross Hands inn, Old Sodbury. William Eels of Dyrham and Hinton informed Rev. F. Pelly on 6 Dec. 1826. Thomas Alway of Cold Ashton, witness. Offender did not appear. Fine £5. Offence committed 31 Oct. 1826.

46/B/25 5 Jan. 1827. William Carter of Walcot, Som., butcher. Using a gun [etc., as 46/B/24].

46/C/1 11 May 1827. William Chapman. Vagrancy in Stroud. H. Burgh JP at Stroud. Six weeks' hard labour in Horsley house of correction. Offence committed 10 May 1827.

46/C/2 22 May 1827. Benjamin Bassett Fisher, Edward Wilkins, Charles Wilkins, Thomas Poulson and William Poulson. Frequenting a wharf in Stonehouse with intent to commit a felony. Reputed thieves. H. Burgh JP at Stroud. Three months' hard labour in Horsley house of correction. Offence committed 21 May 1827.

46/C/3 24 April 1827. George Antill, Thomas Wordon and John Polson. Vagrancy in Stroud. H. Burgh JP at Stroud. Six weeks' hard labour in Horsley house of correction.

46/C/4 15 June 1827. William Bird, tailor's apprentice. Absenting himself from his master Samuel Estcourt's service in Stroud without permission. H. Burgh JP. Samuel Estcourt, tailor, of Stroud, witness. No premium paid when offender apprenticed. One month's hard labour in Horsley house of correction.

46/C/5 12 May 1827. Henry Poulson. Cutting down four young ash trees and fourteen young beech trees in Stroud, the property of Charles Freebury Kendrick, gentleman. H. Burgh JP.

46/C/6   19 June 1827. Joseph Haigh of Rodborough, clothier. Paying William Gay, weaver, of Stroud, his wages of £3 6s. 2d. in other than lawful coinage. H. Burgh JP and Rev. P. Hawker JP. Fine £10.

46/C/7   21 June 1827. Matthew Howe of St. Philip and St. Jacob, [Bristol], alehouse keeper. Failing to observe a condition of his recognizance. J. Cave JP and H. W. Newman JP. First offence. Fine £3 and 6/6 costs.

46/C/8   28 June 1827. Mary Phillips. Swearing. H. W. Newman JP.

46/C/9   31 May 1827. Samuel Bennett. Beating an ass in Clifton and compelling it to carry a too heavy load of sand. H. W. Newman JP. James Drew the younger of Clifton, gentleman, witness. Fine 10/-.

46/C/10   17 May 1827. John Smith. Ill-treating an ass in St. George, [Bristol]. H. W. Newman JP. William Parry, grocer, of Bristol city, witness. Fine 10/-. Offence committed 9 May 1827.

46/C/11   27 June 1827. Thomas Knight of Pauntley, labourer. Being found in Joseph Phelps's garden in Pauntley and unable to give a good account of himself. Rev. R. F. Onslow JP at Newent. Three months' hard labour in Littledean house of correction. Offence committed night of 26/27 June 1827.

46/C/12   30 June 1827. William Cox. Possessing skeleton keys with felonious intent at Shipton. W. Hicks JP, J. Clutterbuck JP and Rev. W. Hicks JP at Cheltenham. Three months' hard labour each in Horsley house of correction. Offence committed 25 June 1827.

46/C/13   13 [sic, recte 30] June 1827. Egbert Taylor. Possessing skeleton keys [etc., as 46/C/12].

46/C/14   30 June 1827. John Griffiths. Possessing skeleton keys [etc., as 46/C/12].

46/C/15   7 June 1827. Samuel Cousens of St. Philip and St. Jacob, [Bristol], [alehouse keeper]. Failing to observe the conditions of a recognizance. J. Cave JP and Sir R. Vaughan JP. First offence. Fine 20/- and 6/6 costs.

46/C/16   30 April 1827. Thomas Cole. Selling ale in Westbury on Trym without a licence. R. Vaughan JP. Philip Williams, carpenter of Clifton, witness. First offence. Offence committed 29 April 1827.

46/C/17   30 April 1827. Abraham Littlejohns. Selling ale in Westbury on Trym without a licence. R. Vaughan JP. First offence. Offender confessed. Offence committed 29 April 1827.

46/C/18   30 April 1827. Aaron Batt. Selling ale in Westbury on Trym without a licence. R. Vaughan JP. Philip Williams, carpenter of Clifton, witness. First offence. Offence committed 29 April 1827.

46/C/19   24 May 1827. Francis Yeo of St. Philip and St. Jacob, [Bristol], [alehouse keeper]. Failing to observe the conditions of a recognizance. D. Cave JP and H. W. Newman JP. First offence. Fine 20/- and 6/6 costs.

46/C/20   24 May 1827. James Baker of St. James, [Bristol], [alehouse keeper]. Failing to observe [etc., as 46/C/19].

46/C/21   31 May 1827. Elizabeth Williams of St. James, [Bristol], [alehouse keeper]. Failing to observe the conditions of a recognizance. D. Cave JP and H. W. Newman JP. First offence. Fine £5 and 6/6 costs.

46/C/22   28 May 1827. Samuel Harding of Marshfield. Leaving his wife Margaret and their three children chargeable to the parish. I. W. W. Horlock JP at Ashwick House, [Marshfield]. Three months' hard labour in Horsley house of correction.

46/C/23   21 June 1827. Richard Edgell of Clifton. Issuing a receipt for £5 to Margaret Susanna Maria Jackson, widow, of Richmond Terrace, Clifton, without a stamp. H. W. Newman JP at Lawfords Gate sessions room. William Hawkins, constable of St. James, [Bristol], informer. Offender pleaded not guilty. Fine £5. Offence committed 11 April 1827.

46/C/24   5 Feb. 1827. Amy wife of John Hignall, carpenter, of Ampney Crucis. Possessing five pheasants and exposing them for sale. J. Cripps JP at Cirencester. John Larner, labourer, of Harnhill, informer. Edward Nash, labourer, of Ampney St. Mary, witness, deposed that he saw James Gardner, pig dealer, of Ampney Crucis, sell five pheasants to offender for 10/-. Offender denied having five but admitted to three. Fine £25. Offence committed 15 Jan. 1827.

46/D/1   30 Aug. 1827. Robert and Walter Cross of Bourton on the Water, labourers. Stealing apples from an orchard, the property of Rev. John Croome. Rev. F. E. Witts JP at Stow on the Wold. Fine 2/6 each, to be paid to the overseers of the poor of Bourton within seven days. Offence committed 26 Aug. 1827.

46/D/2   4 Oct. 1827. Job Brain of Temple Guiting. Stealing apples from an orchard in Lower Swell, the property of John Shirley. Rev. F. E. Witts JP at Stow on the Wold. Fine 16/- to be paid to the overseers of the poor at Lower Swell within seven days, and 1/- damages to be paid to the plaintiff. Offence committed 29 Sept. 1827.

46/D/3   27 Sept. 1827. James Simpson and Thomas Taylor of Sherborne. Breaking down part of a stone wall, the property of the Rt. Hon. John, Lord Sherborne. Rev. F. E. Witts JP at Stow on the Wold. Fine 10/- and 2/3 damages each, £1 2s. 3d. of which to be paid to the overseers of the poor within seven days and the remainder to John, Lord Sherborne. Offence committed 15 Sept. 1827.

46/D/4   11 Oct. 1827. Charles Turner of Naunton, labourer. Stealing apples from an orchard in Lower Swell [*etc.*, *as* 46/D/2 *omitting the words* to be paid *on the second occasion*].

46/D/5   6 Sept. 1827. Thomas Day, late of Broadwell, labourer. Stealing pears from an orchard in Broadwell, the property of Robert Beman. Rev. F. E. Witts JP at Stow on the Wold. One month's hard labour in Northleach house of correction. Offence committed 31 Aug. 1827.

46/D/6   23 Aug. 1827. Thomas Norton of St. Philip and St. Jacob, [Bristol], [alehouse keeper]. Failing to observe the conditions of a recognizance. Valentine Jones Graeme JP and H. W. Newman JP. First offence. Fine 15/- and 5/- costs.

46/D/7   4 Dec. 1827. John Hignell of Ampney Crucis, carpenter. Possessing and exposing for sale two pheasants in Ampney Crucis. J. Cripps JP at his house in Cirencester. David Huban, yeoman, of Barnsley, informer. William Bisley, gamekeeper, of Barnsley, witness, who alleged that having heard a shot he saw accused leave Knoll Brake carrying a gun and two pheasants. Chased and found him with pheasants in Isaac Wane's shed. Fine £10. Offence committed between 4 and 5 a.m. on 20 Nov. 1827.

46/D/8   12 Oct. 1827. George Ludlow of Cam, labourer. Stealing a quantity of apples from an orchard in Cam, the property of Daniel Hadley, farmer. W. M. Adey JP at Wotton under Edge. One month's hard labour in Horsley house of correction. Offence committed 16 Sept. 1827.

46/D/9   21 Aug. 1827. Ambrose Gleed. Stealing a large quantity of turnips, the property of John Wigmore, yeoman, of Avening. Rev. H. Campbell JP at Minchinhampton. One month's hard labour in Horsley house of correction. Offence committed 19 Aug. 1827.

46/D/10   30 July 1827. George Bown of Forest Green, Avening. Stealing fourteen cabbages and a quantity of lavender and beans from a garden, the property of Edward Gale, millwright, of Horsley. Rev. H. Campbell JP at Minchinhampton. Three months in Horsley house of correction. Offence committed 22 July 1827.

46/D/11   23 Aug. 1827. Enoch Chandler. Stealing a quantity of apples from a garden in Minchinhampton, the property of Charles Xenophon Frames, schoolmaster. Rev. H. Campbell JP at Minchinhampton. Fourteen days in Horsley house of correction. Offence committed 23 Aug. 1827.

46/D/12   18 Aug. 1827. William Cox. Stealing about one gallon of filberts from a garden in Horsley, the property of Charles Jenkins, baker. Rev. H. Campbell JP at Minchinhampton. Six weeks in Horsley house of correction. Offence committed 12 Aug. 1827.

46/D/13   13 [sic] Aug. 1827. Henry Harris. Stealing [etc., as 46/D/12 except] One month in Horsley house of correction.

46/D/14   18 Aug. 1827. Jacob Harris. Stealing [etc., as 46/D/12].

46/D/15   26 July 1827. Robert Pitman. Altering the date on a pawn ticket for a watch, on which he received 10/-, from 3 to 30 July 1826, and selling it to William Wood, clothworker of Horsley, for a piece of music. Rev. H. Campbell JP. Ticket issued by Andrew Michael Isaacs, pawnbroker, of Stroud. Two months in Horsley house of correction. Offence committed 1 July 1827.

46/D/16   21 Aug. 1827. George Wheeler. Being in Samuel Wilkins's house in Painswick with intent to commit a felony. O. P. Wathen JP at Woodchester. Three months' hard labour in Horsley house of correction. Offence committed 21 July 1827.

46/D/17   23 Aug. 1827. Ann Turner. Frequenting High Street in Stroud with intent to commit a felony. Rev. H. Campbell JP at Stroud. Three months' hard labour in Horsley house of correction. Offence committed 22 Aug. 1827.

46/D/18   23 Aug. 1827. J. G. (refused to give his name). Frequenting a street in Stroud with intent to commit a felony. Rev. H. Campbell JP at Stroud. Three months' hard labour in Horsley house of correction. Offence committed 21 Aug. 1827.

46/D/19   5 Oct. 1827. William Cockshut of Painswick, labourer. Stealing apples from an orchard in Painswick, the property of Thomas Holmes. Rev. P. Hawker JP, H. Burgh JP and Rev. H. Campbell JP at Stroud. Fine 5/-, to be paid to Edward Baylis, overseer of the poor of Painswick, and 7/- to reimburse Thomas Holmes.

46/D/20   5 Oct. 1827. John Webb of Stroud, labourer. Stealing posts and rails from a fence, the property of Rev. John Hawkins. Rev. P. Hawker JP, H. Burgh JP and Rev. H. Campbell JP at Stroud. Fine 5/-, to be paid to James Clutterbuck, an overseer of the poor of Stroud, a further 5/- to reimburse Rev. J. Hawkins and 7/- costs, or six weeks' hard labour in Horsley house of correction. Offence committed 2 Oct. 1827.

46/D/21   7 Sept. 1827. Job Sollars and George Foster of Painswick, labourers. Stealing plums from a garden, the property of Richard Sansum of Painswick. Rev. P. Hawker JP and H. Burgh JP at Stroud. Fine 2/- each, and 6d. (the value of the plums) to be paid to Edward Baylis, an overseer of the poor of Painswick, and 10/6 costs to the complainant. Offence committed 3 Sept. 1827.

46/D/22   31 July 1827. John Ridler of Stonehouse, labourer. Stealing beans from a field, the property of Robert Martin of Stonehouse. H. Burgh JP at Stroud. Fine 1/-, to be paid to Stonehouse overseers of the poor, 6/6 costs and 6d. (the value of the beans) to be paid to the complainant, or one month's hard labour in Horsley house of correction. Offence committed 24 July 1827.

46/D/23   21 Sept. 1827. John Bliss and William Swaine of Painswick, labourers. Stealing nuts from an orchard in Painswick, the property of Elizabeth Bartlett. H. Burgh JP and W. H. Hyett JP at Stroud. Fine 2*d.* each (the value of the nuts) and 8/6 costs to be paid to the complainant. Offence committed 9 Sept. 1827.

46/D/24   17 Sept. 1827. Sarah Roberts. Begging in Stroud. H. Burgh JP at Stroud. One month's hard labour in Horsley house of correction. Offence committed 16 Sept. 1827.

46/D/25   21 Sept. 1827. George Marmont of Stonehouse, labourer. Damaging a wall, the property of Samuel Copner, at Stonehouse. H. Burgh JP at Stroud. Fine 7/- (the amount of the damage) and 7/6 costs to the complainant. Offence committed 10 Aug. 1827.

46/D/26   17 Sept. 1827. William Jones and John Lewis. Begging in Stroud. H. Burgh JP at Stroud. One month's hard labour in Horsley house of correction. Offence committed 15 Sept. 1827.

46/D/27   21 Sept. 1827. John and Sarah Butcher of Rodborough, labourers. Stealing plums from a garden, the property of John King. H. Burgh JP at Stroud. Fine 1/6 each and 10/6 costs, of which 2/- should be paid forthwith to John Wood, overseer of the poor of Rodborough, and the rest to the complainant, or one month's hard labour in Horsley house of correction. Offence committed 11 Sept. 1827.

46/D/28   10 Aug. 1827. Robert Knight of Minchinhampton, labourer. Stealing apples from an orchard in Minchinhampton, the property of William Milsome. H. Burgh JP at Stroud. Six weeks' hard labour in Horsley house of correction. Offence committed 6 Aug. 1827.

46/D/29   3 Sept. 1827, 11 a.m. William Long of Dyrham and Hinton. Using a dog and a gun to kill four partridges on land in the tenure of Thomas Crew and Dorcas Matthews at Dyrham and Hinton without a certificate on 11 Aug. 1827. T. Brooke JP, commissioner for taxes, at the Cross Hands inn, Old Sodbury. Complaint made by William Eels of Dyrham and Hinton, gamekeeper to William Blathwayt Esq. [*Signed:*] W. Eels. [*Cf.* 46/D/39, 42.]

46/D/30   3 Sept. 1827. Edward Britten or Brittan of Dyrham and Hinton. Using a dog [*etc., as* 46/D/29. *Cf.* 46/D/40–1.]

46/D/31   1 Aug. 1827. William Hale. Shooting two pigeons in Twelve Acres Field at Deerhurst Walton. J. Timbrill D.D. JP and Rev. J. Keysall JP at Tewkesbury. Fine 10/-, to be paid to Benjamin Purser, an overseer of the poor of Deerhurst Walton. Offence committed 18 July 1827.

46/D/32   20 July 1827. Daniel Chandler of Painswick, hatter. Neglecting his duty as a constable by refusing to arrest two unknown men who assaulted Joseph Hitchins, watchmaker, of Painswick, and threatened to ride over others. H. Burgh JP and W. H. Hyett JP. Defendant admitted charge. Fine 40/-. Offence committed 24 June 1827.

46/D/33   18 Sept. 1827. George Williams of Cheltenham, [alehouse keeper]. Failing to observe the conditions of his recognizance. R. Capper JP and Robert Mansel JP. First offence. Fine 10/- and 3/6 costs.

46/D/34   9 Aug. 1827. Thomas Bevan of Westbury on Trym, butcher. Using a dog to kill conies without a certificate. H. W. Newman JP, commissioner for taxes, at Lawfords Gate sessions room, Bristol. Mitigated fine of £10. Offence committed 27 July 1827.

46/D/35   2 Oct. 1827. Isaac Cook. Stealing pears worth 5/- from an orchard in Gretton, Winchcombe, the property of William Best. J. Timbrill D.D. JP at Beckford. Fine £10 and 8/9 costs in addition to the value of the pears, to be paid forthwith, or four months' hard labour in Northleach house of correction. Offence committed 29 Sept. 1827.

46/D/36   23 Aug. 1827. Elias Ball Slater of Winterbourne. Using a dog to kill game without a certificate. J. Haythorne JP, commissionner for taxes, at Lawfords Gate sessions room, Bristol. Mitigated fine of £10. Offence committed 30 July 1827.

46/D/37   15 Sept. 1827. Luke Barnett. Injuring and thereby killing a pig, the property of Anne Haskins of Bitton, Bristol. J. Parker JP at Bitton. Fine £1 8s. (the value of the pig), to be paid to the overseer of the poor of St. George, and £1 4s. 6d. costs to be paid to the complainant, forthwith, or two months' hard labour in Lawfords Gate house of correction. Offence committed 6 Sept. 1827.

46/D/38   8 Oct. 1827. Charles Fisher. Stealing apples from an orchard in Bitton, the property of Roger Mayne. J. Parker JP at Bitton. Three months' hard labour in Lawfords Gate house of correction. Offence committed 6 Oct. 1827.

46/D/39   5 Oct. 1827. William Long of Dyrham and Hinton. Keeping and using a dog and a gun for killing game without a certificate. F. Trotman JP and T. Brooke JP, commissioners for taxes. Fine £10 each. Offence committed 11 Aug. 1827. [Cf. 46/D/29, 42.]

46/D/40   5 Oct. 1827. Edward Britten or Brittan of Dyrham and Hinton. Keeping and using [etc., as 46/D/39. Cf. 46/D/30, 41.]

46/D/41   5 Oct. 1827. Edward Britten or Brittan of Dyrham and Hinton. Keeping and using a gun and a dog to kill game on Mrs. Dorcas Matthews's land in Hinton. Rev. T. Brooke JP, F. Trotman JP, Rev. T. Jones JP, Rev. F. Pelly JP and I. W. W. Horlock JP at a Petty Sessions held at the Cross Hands inn, Old Sodbury. William Eels, gamekeeper to William Blathwayt Esq., informed T. Brooke at Horton rectory on 3 Sept. Accused summoned to appear at a Petty Sessions on 7 Sept. His solicitor Mr. Saunders asked for an adjournment. Granted until 28 Sept. when further adjournment granted until 5 Oct. Mr. Saunders appeared for the defendant, who pleaded not guilty, and Mr. Swayne for the prosecution. All witnesses – Edward Williams alias Cox, labouring boy to Farmer Crewe of Dyrham and Hinton, and Thomas Crewe, aged 11, son of the above, for the prosecution, and Hannah Gay, daughter of the landlady of the Star inn, Pucklechurch, William Long, defendant's brother-in-law, and Elias Parker, for the defence – were cross-examined. Long declared he had seen no guns carried. Fine £5. Offence committed 11 Aug. 1827. [Mr. Hockey, farmer, was known to have carried a gun that day. Most of the evidence, particularly Cox's, was recorded verbatim. Cf. 46/D/30, 40.]

46/D/42   5 Oct. 1827. William Long of Dyrham and Hinton. Keeping and using a gun and a dog to kill game [etc. as 46/D/41 except that] Long [here the accused] was supported by his brother-in-law Edward Britten or Brittan. Cox and William Skinstone alleged to have been arrested for bad behaviour on Sunday 12 Aug. by Britten the elder. Cox alleged Edward Britten gave him money when on his way to Farmer Austie's cider mill. Accused pleaded not guilty. Fine £5. Offence committed 11 Aug. 1827. [Cf. 46/D/29, 39.]

46/D/43   13 Oct. 1827. Thomas Leighton of Gloucester, gentleman. Keeping and using a gun and dogs to kill game in Norton when not qualified. W. Goodrich JP and James Wintle JP. George Harris, yeoman, of Sandhurst, informer. William Bartlett, yeoman, of Norton, witness. Accused declined to speak. Fine £5. Offence committed 26 Sept. 1827.

47/A/1   13 Dec. 1827. Robert Freeman of Aston Blank, labourer. Using a snare with intent to kill game. Rev. F. E. Witts JP at Upper Slaughter. — Cook, labourer, and Robert Cook, gamekeeper, both of Aston Blank, informer and witness. Fine £5. Offence committed 13 Dec. 1827.

47/A/2   7 Jan. 1828. Giles Gardner of Down Ampney, labourer. Shooting a hare. Rev. H. A. Pye JP. First offence. Mitigated fine of £10. Offence committed 12 noon, Sunday 2 Dec. 1827.

47/A/3   29 Nov. 1827. Thomas Turner of Oddington. Stealing wooden rails, part of a fence in a field belonging to Robert Beman. Rev. F. E. Witts JP at Stow on the Wold. Fine 1/6 and 3/- costs to be paid to the complainant and 8/6 to go to the poor of Oddington, or two months' hard labour in Northleach house of correction. Offence committed 24 Nov. 1827.

47/A/4   29 Nov. 1827. William Newbury of Oddington, labourer. Stealing wooden rails, part of a fence in a field belonging to Thomas Horne. Rev. F. E. Witts JP at Stow on the Wold. Fine 8/6, to be paid to the overseer of the poor, and 3/- costs and 1/6 to be paid to the plaintiff, or two months' hard labour in Northleach house of correction. Offence committed 24 Nov. 1827.

47/A/5   6 Nov. 1827. Charles Merrett of Gloucester city, pastrycook. Using a gun to kill game in Frocester when not qualified. T. J. Lloyd Baker JP, commissioner for taxes, at Wheatenhurst. Fine £20. Offence committed 18 Oct. 1827.

47/A/6   26 Oct. 1827. Charles Merrett of Gloucester city, pastrycook. Beating for game with a gun and a dog in Frocester when not qualified. T. J. Lloyd Baker JP at the George inn, Wheatenhurst. James Ricketts, carpenter, of Frocester, informer. Accused did not appear. Fine £5. Offence committed 18 Oct. 1827.

47/A/7   13 Nov. 1827. Thomas Knapp of Thornbury, farmer. Keeping and using a gun to kill game in Alvington. Rev. T. Thomas JP at Lydney. Edward Long and John Redkin, labourers, of Alvington, informer and witness. Accused pleaded not guilty. Fine £5. Offence committed 4 Oct. 1827. [*Document signed 8 Jan. 1828.*]

47/A/8   13 Nov. 1827. John Smith of Lydney, surgeon and apothecary. Keeping and using a gun to kill game when not qualified. Rev. T. Thomas JP [*etc.*, as 47/A/7, *replacing* Accused *with* Offender].

47/A/9   13 Nov. 1827. John Wade of Woolaston, farmer. Keeping and using a gun [*etc.*, *as* 47/A/8].

47/A/10   23 Oct. 1827. William Watkins of Gloucester, yeoman and coach driver. Carrying eleven instead of five adult outside passengers on a Gloucester to Cheltenham stage coach. R. Capper JP at Cheltenham. Samuel Collett, informer (3 Oct. 1827). Elisha Castle, witness. Fine £10. Offence committed 2 Oct. 1827.

47/A/11   29 Oct. 1827. Robert Morgan (son of James Morgan, farmer, deceased) of Oldbury on Severn. Killing a pheasant with a stone at Hill. William Fitzhardinge Berkeley JP at Berkeley Castle. William Wozley, labourer, of Oldbury on Severn, witness. First offence. Mitigated fine of £10. Offence committed Sunday 21 Oct. 1827.

47/A/12   22 Oct. 1827. William Wozley of Oldbury on Severn, labourer. Exposing a pheasant for sale in Hill. W. F. Berkeley JP at Berkeley Castle. Thomas Lawley, gardener, of Hill, informer. Andrew Watcham, gamekeeper, of Hill, witness. Accused requested that the case be heard immediately. Fine £5, half to informer and the rest to the poor of Hill. Offence committed 21 Oct. 1827.

47/A/13   2 Jan. 1828. Betty wife of John Judge *alias* Compton. Stealing a quantity of dead fence, the property of Robert Ind, dealer, of Tetbury. W. M. Paul JP at Tetbury. Fine 50/- and 4/- costs, the fine to be paid forthwith to Daniel Cole and the costs to Robert Ind, or one month in Horsley house of correction. Offence committed Monday 31 Dec. 1827.

47/A/14 22 Oct. 1827. Charles Ockford of Minchinhampton, labourer. Stealing a quantity of apples (2 charges) from an orchard, the property of Thomas Evans. Rev. H. Campbell JP. Six months' hard labour in Horsley house of correction. Offences committed 24 Sept. and 21 Oct. 1827.

47/A/15 22 Oct. 1827. Peter Baker of Minchinhampton, labourer. Stealing a quantity of apples from an orchard, the property of Thomas Evans. Rev. H. Campbell JP. Three months' hard labour in Horsley house of correction. Offence committed 24 Sept. 1827.

47/A/16 15 Nov. 1827. James Wetherill of Clifton, Bristol, [alehouse keeper]. Failing to observe a condition of his recognizance. G. Hilhouse JP and H. W. Newman JP. First offence. Fine £5 and 9/- costs.

47/A/17 29 Sept. 1827. John Evans of Clifton, Bristol, [alehouse keeper]. Failing to observe a condition of his recognizance. G. Hilhouse JP and H. W. Newman JP. First offence. Fine £5 including 9/- costs.

47/A/18 6 Dec. 1827. Charles Milsom. Shooting a pigeon at Stapleton, the property of John Brown, stonecutter, of Mangotsfield. H. W. Newman JP at Lawfords Gate sessions room, St. Philip and St. Jacob, Bristol. Fine 40/-, to be paid forthwith, or one month's hard labour in Lawfords Gate house of correction. Offence committed 3 Dec. 1827.

47/A/19 15 Nov. 1827. John Bennett. Beating and ill-treating an ass which had fallen down under its load of sand in St. James, [Bristol]. G. Hilhouse JP. Diana Andrews, single woman, of St. James, Bristol, witness. Offence committed 7 Nov. 1827.

47/A/20 25 Oct. 1827. James Stokes of Bedminster, Som., yeoman. Keeping and using a gun and a dog to kill game in Stoke Gifford when not qualified. H. W. Newman JP at Lawfords Gate sessions room, St. Philip and St. Jacob, [Bristol]. Information given to J. Lewis JP on 15 Oct. 1827 by Henry Webb of Stoke Gifford. William Merrick, witness. Offender pleaded not guilty. Fine £5. Offence committed 1 Oct. 1827.

47/A/21 25 Oct. 1827. William Tilly of Stapleton, yeoman. Keeping and using [*etc., as* 47/A/20].

47/A/22 22 Nov. 1827. Charles Edward Bernard of Clifton, gentleman. Keeping and using a gun to kill game at Westbury on Trym when not qualified. H. W. Newman JP at Lawfords Gate sessions room, Bristol. Edward Tratman of Shirehampton informed J. Savage JP on 16 Oct. 1827. Offender admitted charge. Fine £5. Offence committed 10 Oct. 1827.

47/A/23 22 Nov. 1827. John Elliott the younger of Clifton, carpenter. Shooting a hare in Horfield when not qualified. H. W. Newman JP at Lawfords Gate sessions room, Bristol. Richard Shadwell, gentleman, of Bristol, informed Sir R. Vaughan JP on 14 Nov. 1827. William Smith and Reuben Rosling, labourers, of Horfield, witnesses. Defendant did not appear. Represented by his attorney Robert Saunders. Believed to have inherited freehold property, but refused to produce details. Pleaded not guilty. Fine £5. Offence committed 1 Nov. 1827.

47/A/24 25 Oct. 1827. Frederick Douglas Protheroe of Bristol. Shooting a pheasant in Westbury on Trym when not qualified. H. W. Newman JP at Lawfords Gate sessions room, Bristol. Edward Tratman informed J. Savage JP on 16 Oct. 1827. James Lavis, labourer, of Westbury on Trym gave evidence after defendant had left the room. Robert Saunders, attorney, appeared for defendant but offered no evidence. Fine £5. Offence committed 1 Oct. 1827.

47/A/25 19 Dec. 1827. Thomas Shephard of Grafton. Pretending to be a toll-collector at Grafton turnpike gate and charging Paul Martin, farmer, of Alderton 2*d.* to take a horse through a gate (belonging to Mr. Blackburn) into pasture at Ashton under Hill occupied by Mr. Bernard Baldwyn. J. Timbrill JP and Rev. J. Keysall JP. Fine 40/-. Offence committed 22 Nov. 1827.

47/A/26   19 Oct. 1827. James Goodrich, gentleman, of Wotton Hamlet, Gloucester. Using a gun to kill game in Maisemore without obtaining the required certificate. Rev. J. B. Cheston JP, commissioner for taxes. Fine £10. Offence committed 16 Oct. 1827

47/A/27   19 Oct. 1827. William John Pitt Goodrich, gentleman, of Wotton Hamlet, Gloucester. Using a gun [*etc.*, *as* 47/A/26].

47/A/28   19 Dec. 1827. Thomas Shephard of Grafton. Assaulting Joseph Bayzand, labourer, of Ashton under Hill under pretence of being a toll-collector at Grafton turnpike gate and charging him 6*d.* to take a horse and cart through a gate (which belonged to Mr. Blackburn) into pasture occupied by Mr. Bernard Baldwyn. J. Timbrill JP and Rev. J. Keysall JP. Fine 40/-. Offence committed 22 Nov. 1827.

47/A/29   27 Dec. 1827. John Lewis. Leaving his wife and five children chargeable to Dyrham and Hinton parish. F. Trotman JP at Siston. Samuel Britten, constable of Dyrham and Hinton, complainant. Robert Ansty, churchwarden, and John Long, overseer of the poor of the same parish, witnesses. Committed to Gloucester house of correction until next Q.S. unless discharged earlier.

47/A/30   22 Oct. 1827. Richard Trimnell. Vagrancy in Painswick. Rev. P. Hawker JP at Stroud. Three months' hard labour in Horsley house of correction. Offence committed 20 Oct. 1827.

47/A/31   4 Jan. 1828. Joseph Savory, Benjamin Thomas, Philip Burdock and William Johnson of Painswick, labourers. Damaging the dwelling of John Williams, tinman and brazier, of Painswick. Rev. P. Hawker JP at Stroud. Fine 5/- and 3/- costs each, 5/- of which to be paid to the complainant, or two months' hard labour each in Horsley house of correction. Offence committed 25 Dec. 1827.

47/A/32   19 Oct. 1827. Charles Halliday. Causing his wife and family to become chargeable (since March) to the parish of Stroud. Rev. P. Hawker JP at Stroud. One month's hard labour in Horsley house of correction.

47/A/33   6 Nov. 1827. Charles Walters. Using a dog and nets to kill a hare in Marshfield. Rev. I. W. W. Horlock JP. Second offence. Fine £20. Offence committed 2 Nov. 1827.

47/A/34   18 Oct. 1827. James Batchellor, late of Todenham, labourer. Using gins to kill hares. Rev. W. Boughton JP. Jacob Lewis, informer. First offence. Fine £10. Offence committed Sunday 18 March 1827.

47/A/35   7 Dec. 1827. Samuel Cother of Blockley, Worcs., carpenter. Shooting hares in Sezincote. Rev. W. Boughton JP and Rev. C. Jeaffreson JP. First offence. Fine £10. Offence committed at night 6 Dec. 1827.

47/A/36   26 Nov. 1827. John Court, late of Condicote, labourer. Offering a partridge for sale. Rev. C. Jeaffreson JP at Bourton on the Hill. Joseph Arkell, yeoman, of Condicote, informer. Henry Turner, witness. Offender pleaded not guilty. Fine £5. Offence committed 4 Nov. 1827.

47/A/37   2 Nov. 1827. George Hulbert of West Kington, Wilts., labourer. Taking a hare from a snare in a field in Tormarton in the occupation of Betty Marsh. T. Brooke LL.D. JP and Rev. T. Jones JP at a Petty Sessions held at the Cross Hands inn, Old Sodbury. Thomas Webb junior of Great Badminton, informer. Robert Absworth of Tormarton, witness. Offender pleaded not guilty. Fine £5. Offence committed 9 Oct. 1827.

47/B/1   11 March 1828. Charlotte Thomas of King's Stanley, single woman. Stealing a quantity of rails from a fence in King's Stanley, the property of Henry Burgh Esq. Rev. H. Campbell JP at Stroud. Fine £1, to be paid to the complainant, or one month in Horsley house of correction. Offence committed 4 Feb. 1828.

47/B/2   7 Feb. 1828. John Lloyd. Attempting to obtain charitable contributions under false pretences in Clifton. H. W. Newman JP and G. Hilhouse JP at Lawfords Gate sessions room, Bristol. One month in Lawfords Gate house of correction. Offence committed 26 Dec. 1827.

47/B/3   14 Feb. 1828. Charles Smith. Damaging several beech trees in a wood in King's Stanley, the property of Thomas, Lord Ducie. Rev. P. Hawker JP at Rodborough. Fine 5/- and 8/- costs. All sums to be paid to Lord Ducie by 28 Feb. 1828, or one month in Horsley house of correction. Offence committed 27 Jan. 1828.

47/B/4   14 Feb. 1828. Edmund Alder. Damaging several beech trees [*etc.*, *as* 47/B/3].

47/B/5   14 Feb. 1828. William Hunt of St. James, [Bristol]. Failing to observe the conditions of his recognizance entered into on obtaining a licence to sell ale, beer etc. J. Parker JP and H. W. Newman JP. First offence. Fine 20/- and 7/6 costs.

47/B/6   3 March 1828. John Evans of Clifton, alehouse keeper. Failing to observe the conditions of his recognizance entered into on obtaining a licence to sell ale, beer etc. H. W. Newman JP and A. G. H. Battersby JP. Second offence. [*Cf.* 47/A/17.] Fine £5 and £1 12*s*. 6*d*. costs.

47/B/7   7 Feb. 1828. Francis Yeo of St. Philip and St. Jacob, [Bristol], alehouse keeper. Failing to observe the conditions of a recognizance entered into on obtaining a licence to sell ale, beer etc. H. W. Newman JP and G. Hilhouse JP. First offence [*but cf.* 46/C/19]. Fine £5 and 7/6 costs.

47/B/8   21 Feb. 1828. Thomas Hurn of Clifton, alehouse keeeper. Failing to observe the conditions of a recognizance entered into on obtaining a licence to sell ale, beer etc. J. Vaughan JP and H. W. Newman JP. First offence. Fine £2 and £1 6*s*. costs.

47/B/9   28 Feb. 1828. Robert Taylor of Littleton upon Severn, yeoman. Using a gun to kill a hare in Elberton. H. W. Newman JP and V. J. Graeme JP, commissioners for assessed taxes, at Lawfords Gate sessions room. Mitigated fine of £10.

47/B/10   12 Feb. 1828. Mary Ann Elliott and Ann Clissold, prostitutes. Disorderly behaviour in Stroud. H. Burgh JP at Stroud. One month's hard labour each in Horsley house of correction. Offence committed 9 Feb. 1828.

47/B/11   22 Dec. 1827. William Poulson. Entering the house of Charles White, baker, at Stroud with intent to commit a felony. H. Burgh JP at Stroud. Three months' hard labour in Horsley house of correction. Offence committed 21 Dec. 1827.

47/B/12   4 Feb. 1828. Giles Vines and William Nicholls of Stroud, labourers. Stealing a quantity of turnip greens (being grown for food in a field), the property of Thomas Cook, yeoman, of Stroud. H. Burgh JP at Stroud. One month's hard labour in Horsley house of correction. Offence committed 3 Feb. 1828.

47/B/13   24 March 1828. Ann Evans, prostitute. Riotous behaviour in Stroud. O. P. Wathen JP at Woodchester. One month's hard labour in Horsley house of correction. Offence committed 22 March 1828.

47/B/14   17 Oct. 1827. Benjamin Bassett Fisher. Entering the house of Benjamin Bucknall, bookseller, in Stroud with intent to commit a felony. H. Burgh JP. Three months' hard labour in Horsley house of correction. Offence committed 16 Oct. 1827.

47/B/15   29 Feb. 1828. Thomas Hannis. Causing his wife and family to become chargeable to the parish of Painswick. Rev. P. Hawker JP at Stroud. One month's hard labour in Horsley house of correction. Offence committed 28 Feb. 1828.

47/B/16   29 Jan. 1828. Richard Wright. Rooting up a quantity of underwood in Dowdeswell, the property of Miss Hester Rogers. Rev. W. Hicks JP at Cheltenham. Fine 20/-, to be paid immediately to John Arkell, Dowdeswell's overseer of the poor, 2/6 damages to Miss Rogers and 6/- costs to Richard Buck, or two months' hard labour in Northleach house of correction. Offence committed 28 Jan. 1828.

47/B/17   12 Feb. 1828. John Hyett. Unlawfully possessing a quantity of shrubs valued at 4/- in Coberley. R. Mansel JP at Cheltenham. Fine 13/4 and 4/- damages, to be paid immediately to Coberley's overseer of the poor, and 3/4 costs to the complainant Richard Smith, or two months' hard labour in Northleach house of correction. Offence committed 6 Feb. 1828.

47/B/18   16 Feb. 1828. Joseph Richings. Cutting off a beech tree in Miserden, the property of Sir Edwin Sandys. Rev. W. Hicks at Cheltenham. Fine 20/-, to be paid immediately to Miserden's overseer of the poor, 2/- damages to Sir E. Sandys and 7/6 costs to Richard Barnfield, complainant, or two months' hard labour in Northleach house of correction. Offence committed 12 Feb. 1828.

47/B/19   12 Feb. 1828. Thomas Lowes. Unlawfully possessing shrubs in Coberley, valued at 4/-. R. Mansel JP at Cheltenham. Fine 13/4 and 4/-, to be paid immediately to Coberley's overseer of the poor, and 3/4 costs to the complainant Richard Smith, or two months' hard labour in Northleach house of correction. Offence committed 6 Feb. 1828.

47/B/20   12 Feb. 1828. Isaac Mills. Unlawfully possessing shrubs [*etc.*, as 47/B/19].

47/B/21   24 Jan. 1828. William Locke of Moreton in Marsh, labourer. Breaking down and stealing hedge-wood from a fence in Longborough, the property of Joseph Clifford. Rev. F. E. Witts JP at Stow on the Wold. Fine 10/-, to be paid immediately to Longborough's overseers of the poor, and 5/6 costs to the complainant, or one month in Northleach house of correction. Offence committed 26 Dec. 1828.

47/B/22   24 Jan. 1828. Henry Beesley of Stow on the Wold, labourer. Using a net to trap rabbits in Lower Slaughter without first obtaining a licence. Rev. F. E. Witts JP, commissioner for taxes, at Lower Slaughter. Mitigated fine of £10. Offence committed 8 Dec. 1827.

47/B/23   10 April 1828. Mary Sandalls of Stow on the Wold. Breaking down and taking away part of a fence in Maugersbury, the property of John Pegler. Rev. F. E. Witts JP at Stow on the Wold. Fine 4/- and 3/6 costs, to be paid immediately to Maugersbury's overseer of the poor and the complainant respectively, or fourteen days in Northleach house of correction. Offence committed 5 April 1828.

47/B/24   28 Jan. 1828. Samuel Harding of Evesham, Worcs., carrier. Assaulting toll-collector William Sheppard at Grafton tollgate after passing through with his wagon. J. Timbrill D.D. JP. Fine £6. Offence committed 26 Dec. 1827.

47/B/25   14 April 1828. John Beale. Stealing part of a live fence in St. Briavels hundred, the property of Sir Thomas Crawley Boevey. Rev. C. Crawley JP at Newnham. Fine £2 and 5/6 costs, to be paid within two weeks to Emmanuel Bennett of St. Briavels hundred. Offence committed 20 March 1828.

47/B/26   18 Feb. 1828. Thomas Fryer. Leaving his wife and children chargeable to the parish of Westbury on Severn. Rev. C. Crawley JP at Newnham. Three months' hard labour in Littledean house of correction. Offence committed 6 Nov. 1827.

47/B/27   21 Jan. 1828. Joseph Richards of Newnham, [innkeeper]. Keeping his house, the Anchor, open for purposes other than the reception of travellers. J. Pyrke JP. Fine £5.

47/B/28   3 March 1828. William Price of the Cross public house, Longhope. Failing to observe a condition of his recognizance. M. Colchester JP and J. Pyrke JP. First offence. Fine £5 and 10/- costs.

47/B/29   Return of forfeitures levied within the hundreds of Upper and Lower Tewkesbury etc. for using defective weights, measures and balances. J. Timbrill D.D. JP and Rev. J. Keysall JP. Fine £1 each unless stated otherwise.

1 April 1828. Charles Agg, Charles Grizzell, Henry Hall and John Oakley of Alderton.
        Benjamin Burrows of Buckland.
        Thomas Brain of Northway.
        James Boulton and William Weaver of Boddington.

2 April 1828. George Bullock, James Ballinger, William Brown, Thomas Fletcher, John Hyett, Thomas Taylor, John White (fine 5/-) and Joseph Waltham of the Leigh.
        James Ballinger, William Cox, Richard Hogg, John Hopkins, Richard Jeffs, Joseph Staite, Elizabeth Salcomb and James Wadley of Tirley.

1 April 1828. Ann Child, William Leaver and Thomas Taylor of Beckford.
        Elizabeth Collett and John Slatter of Stanway.
        John Clarke, John Coxhead, Silvester Spruce, John Staite, John Williams and Thomas Wood of Guiting Power.
        Charles Cotton of Aston Somerville.
        Anne Cole, Thomas Stephens, George Webb (fine 10/-), Sarah Wilkes and Thomas Williams of Kemerton.
        William Crook of Hasfield.

2 April 1828. Mary Hill of Hasfield.

1 April 1828. David Drinkwater, James Tombs (fine 10/-) and William Vernon of Ashton under Hill.
        John Doughty and James Nash of Ford.
        Charles Grizzell and James Horlick of Didbrook.
        John Healing and Richard White of Tredington.

2 April 1828. Benjamin Hundy, Richard Ramell and Sarah White of Twyning.

1 April 1828. Henry Izard, Ferdinando Jones, William Tustin, Ambrose Williams and Ann Harvey of Winchcombe.
        Stephen Jeynes and John Gillett of Kineton.
        Thomas Keyte, Stephen Stanley and William Woodward of Snowshill.
        William Leach and John Mason of Pamington.
        Elizabeth Merrell of Dumbleton.
        Elizabeth Newman and Michael Williams of Hawling.

2 April 1828. William Newman and William South of Forthampton.

1 April 1828. Samuel Pigeon and Richard Troughton of Greet.
        John Roberts of Deerhurst.
        Samuel Sharp of Toddington.
        Richard Gibbs and Joseph Troughton of Temple Guiting.
        Henry Stanley of Laverton [*MS*. Laberton].
        William Surman of Aston on Carrant.

11 April 1828. William Hitchman of Winchcombe (fine £2).

        Total fines £80 5*s*. Raised from sale of defective weights etc. £1 18*s*. 10*d*.
        Signed by the above magistrates 11 April 1828.

47/C/1 Return of forfeitures levied within Slaughter hundred between 15 April and 15 July 1828 for using defective weights, measures and balances.

6 May 1828. Rev. F. E. Witts JP and Rev. C. Jeaffreson JP.

John Bullard 5/-, Mary Biddle 10/-, Robert Griffin 5/-, of Naunton.

John Brown Collett of Upper Slaughter 5/-.

William Hemming 15/-, Jonathan Bartlett 5/-, William Agg 5/-, of Great Rissington.

Thomas Betteridge of Wick Rissington 5/-.

Thomas Palmer 15/-, Joseph Ransford 5/-, William Colin 5/-, John Palmer 5/-, of Bourton on the Water.

Richard Saunders of Lower Slaughter 5/-.

Thomas Townsend of Great Barrington 5/-.

George Bowles of Broadwell 5/-.

John Harbert of Oddington 5/-.

John Fifield 5/-, Ann Porter 5/-, Thomas James 10/-, of Great Barrington.

Dyer and Kimber 10/-, William Cook 5/-, of Bourton on the Water.

Edward Reynolds of Maugersbury 10/-.

George Bumpas of Lower Slaughter 10/-.

William Dix 10/- and Thomas Collett 10/-, of Upper Slaughter.

Samuel Parker of Lower Slaughter 10/-.

William Nash of Adlestrop 5/-.

Thomas Harris of Lower Slaughter 5/-.

William Lane of Adlestrop 5/-.

Susannah Lowin of Oddington 5/-.

William Day 5/-, Richard Shepherd 10/-, of Broadwell.

John Meadows of Lower Swell. 5/-

Thomas Trinder of Condicote 10/-.

John Clifford 10/-, Joseph Phipps 5/-, William Pooten 5/-, Stephen Hague 5/-, James Large 10/-, John Townsend Tilsley 15/-, Alfred Tanner £1, William Brookes £1, Mary Forty 5/-, John Edginton 5/-, John Privett 5/-, James Pooten 5/-, Edward Richens 5/-, Robert Blizard 5/-, John Cambray 5/-, Richard Minchin 5/-, John Johnsons 10/-, of Stow on the Wold.

Richard Mason of Oddington, £2. Obstructing the weights and measures inspector in the course of his duty. Rev. F. E. Witts JP, Rev. R. W. Ford JP and Rev. C. Jeaffreson JP.

Amount arising from sale of defective weights etc. £2 3*s.* 2*d.*
Signed by the above magistrates.

47/C/2 20 May 1828. James Bailey and William Heaven of King's Stanley, labourers. Being at night in an outhouse belonging to Abraham Robins of King's Stanley with intent to commit a felony. H. Burgh JP at Stroud. One month's hard labour in Horsley house of correction. Offence committed 16 May 1828.

47/C/3 3 July 1828. Thomas Pauling of Burford, Oxon., labourer. Cutting and stealing underwood in Widford, the property of John Freeman, Lord Redesdale. Rev. F. E. Witts JP at Stow on the Wold. Fine 40/-, to be paid immediately to Widford's overseer of the poor, and 5/- costs to Charles Pratley, the complainant for Lord Redesdale, or two months in Northleach house of correction. Offence committed 12 June 1828.

47/C/4   21 June 1828. Benjamin Bassett Fisher. Frequenting a street in Stonehouse with intent to commit a felony. Rev. P. Hawker JP at Woodchester. Three months' hard labour in Horsley house of correction. Offence committed 20 June 1828.

47/C/5   20 June 1828. Thomas Hannis. Neglecting his wife and family, whereby they became chargeable to the parish of Painswick. W. H. Hyett JP and Rev. H. Campbell JP. One month's hard labour in Horsley house of correction. Offence committed 29 March 1828.

47/C/6   6 May 1828. William Clarke of Minchinhampton, clothworker. Found in possession of 27½ yards of raw Cashmere [MS. Cassimere] cloth in Stonehouse, believed to be stolen. H. Burgh JP and Rev. H. Campbell JP. Daniel Robins of King's Stanley, David Heaven and James Moody of Stonehouse, all clothworkers, Daniel Peyton of Stroud, clothier, and William Weeks of King's Stanley, cloth manufacturer, witnesses. Fine £20, half to be paid to Moira Maclean, gentleman, of King's Stanley, informer, and half to Stroud dispensary. Offence committed 1 May 1828.

47/C/7   6 June 1828. William Tyler of Bisley, labourer. Cutting and stealing 100 beech saplings from a wood in Stroud, the property of William Lewis Esq. H. Burgh JP and W. H. Hyett JP at Stroud. Fine 2/6, to be paid to the overseer of the poor, and 2/6, the value of the saplings, and 8/- costs to be paid immediately to W. Lewis, or two months' hard labour in Horsley house of correction. Offence committed 16 May 1828.

47/C/8   14 June 1828. John Campbell. Begging in Stroud. H. Burgh JP at Stroud. One month's hard labour in Horsley house of correction. Offence committed 13 June 1828.

47/C/9   5 June 1828. Isaac Wilkins of Stroud, carpenter. Cutting down seven ash saplings in a fence at Stroud, the property of Thomas Whiley. H. Burgh JP at Stroud. Fine 2/6, a further 2/6 (the value of the saplings), both sums to be paid to the overseer of the poor, and 8/- costs to the complainant, or two months' hard labour in Horsley house of correction. Offence committed 5 June 1828.

47/C/10   12 May 1828. John Tribe. Frequenting streets in Stroud with intent to commit a felony. H. Burgh JP at Stroud. Three months' hard labour in Horsley house of correction. Offence committed 10 May 1828.

47/C/11   23 May 1828. Charles Stephens of Bisley, labourer. Cutting and stealing 100 beech saplings from a wood in Stroud, the property of William Lewis Esq. H. Burgh JP and Rev. H. Campbell JP at Stroud. Fine 2/6, to be paid to the overseer of the poor, a further 2/6 for the value of the saplings and 8/- to be paid to the complainant, or two months' hard labour in Horsley house of correction. Offence committed 16 May 1828.

47/C/12   10 Feb. 1828. Thomas West of Painswick, stonemason. Stealing an ash sapling valued at 2/6 from a wood in Painswick, the property of Jane Fletcher. H. Burgh JP at Stroud. Ordered to pay 12/6 costs and the value of the tree to the complainant and 2/6 to the overseer of the poor of Painswick, or two months' hard labour in Horsley house of correction. Offence committed 5 Feb. 1828.

47/C/13   4 July 1828. Isaac Wilkins of Stroud, labourer. Stealing a quantity of vegetables from a garden in Stroud, the property of Edward Carpenter and Matthew Wingfield. Rev. H. Campbell JP at Stroud. Three months' hard labour in Horsley house of correction. Offence committed 18 June 1828.

47/C/14   5 July 1828. John Williams of Painswick, tinker. Attempting to take fish from a pond, the private property of William Baylis, clothier, of Painswick. W. H. Hyett JP at Stroud. Fine £5 or two months' hard labour in Horsley house of correction. Offence committed 4 July 1828.

47/C/15   2 April 1828. Henry Bicknell. Damaging three apple trees growing in Hodges Orchard, Shipton Moyne, the property of George Emerson. W. M. Paul JP at Tetbury. Fine £5 or six weeks in Horsley house of correction. Offence committed 25 or 26 March 1828.

47/C/16   6 Feb. 1828. Charles King. Cutting a sycamore tree with intent to steal part thereof, the property of Richard Hathway of Grange Farm, Tetbury. R. Kingscote JP at Tetbury. Fine £5 or two months in Horsley house of correction.

47/C/17   12 June 1828. Thomas Cooper of St. Philip and St. Jacob, Bristol, [alehouse keeper]. Failing to observe a condition of his recognizance. J. Parker JP and H. W. Newman JP. First offence. Fine 14/6 and 5/6 costs.

47/C/18   5 June 1828. William Blanchard of Bitton, [alehouse keeper]. Failing to observe a condition of his recognizance. V. J. Graeme JP and H. W. Newman JP. First offence. Fine 20/- and 6/6 costs.

47/C/19   22 May 1828. William Thomas of Clifton, [alehouse keeper]. Failing to observe a condition of his recognizance. H. W. Newman JP and W. Munro JP. First offence. Fine 10/6 and 9/6 costs.

47/C/20   19 June 1828. Stephen Golding. Cruelly beating a horse harnessed to a cart in St. Philip and St. Jacob, Bristol. J. Parker JP. Offence committed 14 June 1828.

47/C/21   11 July 1828. George Lusty of King's Stanley, weaver. Assaulting Samuel Aldridge, weaver, of Stroud. H. Burgh JP and Rev. H. Campbell JP at Stroud. Fine 10/- and 8/- costs or two months in Horsley house of correction. Offence committed 9 July 1828.

47/C/22   14 July 1828. William Palmer of Stroud, weaver. Assaulting Samuel Aldridge, weaver, of Stroud. H. Burgh JP and W. H. Hyett JP at Stroud [etc., as 47/C/21].

47/C/23   6 May 1828. Richard Sayer of Horsley, clothworker. Possessing 36 lb. approximately of various woollen yarns believed to be stolen. H. Burgh JP and Rev. H. Campbell JP. Moira Maclean, gentleman, of King's Stanley, informer. Josiah Thomas Howell, yeoman, of Stroud, William Weeks, cloth manufacturer, of King's Stanley, Daniel Peyton, clothier, of Stroud, and James Moody, clothworker, of Stonehouse, witnesses. Fine £20, half to be paid to the informer and the remainder to Stroud dispensary. Offence committed 2 May 1828.

47/C/24   4 July 1828. John Gibbs of Apperley and Wightfield, Deerhurst, labourer. Stealing a rail about 9 yards long from a fence surrounding Squires Orchard in Apperley and Wightfield, the property of William Chandler, farmer. J. Timbrill D.D. JP, Rev. J. Keysall JP and Rev. C. White JP. Fine 20/-, to be paid to Thomas Healing, an overseer of the poor of Deerhurst, and 8/- damages and 8/6 costs to be paid to the complainant. Offence committed Sunday 22 June. 1828.

47/C/25   22 May 1828. William Clark of Bledington, labourer. Stealing a wooden rail from a fence, the property of William Wilkes. Rev. F. E. Witts JP at Stow on the Wold. Fine 7/6 and 5/6 costs or one month in Northleach house of correction. Offence committed 21 May 1828.

47/C/26   7 July 1828. Samuel Turley. Breaking 31 glass window-panes in Nathaniel Hieron's house in Box, Minchinhampton. E. Wilbraham JP, T. Kingscote JP and David Ricardo JP at Horsley. Fine £3 10s., to be paid to Charles Iles, an overseer of the poor of Minchinhampton, and 10/- costs to the complainant, or two months' hard labour in Horsley house of correction. Offence committed 5 July 1828.

47/C/27   28 April 1828. Joseph Mountjoy, late of St. Briavels hundred, labourer. Stealing underwood in Beechenhurst enclosure in the Forest of Dean, valued at 1/6. J. Pyrke JP at Newnham. Fine 20/- and 4/- costs to be paid to Thomas Witts, gamekeeper, or two months in Littledean house of correction. Offence committed 21 April 1828.

47/C/28   6 May 1828. James Fox of King's Stanley, weaver. Possessing almost 53 lb. of various woollen yarns believed to be stolen. H. Burgh JP [and] Rev. H. Campbell JP. Moira Maclean, gentleman, of King's Stanley and James Moody of Stonehouse, clothworker, witnesses. Fine £20, half to be paid to Donald Maclean of King's Stanley, the informer, and half to Stroud dispensary. Offence committed 1 May 1828.

47/D/1   5 Sept. 1828. Jonas Norris, toll-collector of Nubbis Ash gate, Cam. Refusing to exempt John Neale, constable of Yate, from the toll of 6d. for a horse and cart conveying a prisoner charged with felony to Gloucester gaol. Rev. T. Jones JP and Rev. F. Pelly JP at a Petty Sessions held at Old Sodbury. Warrant of commital, signed by Rev. T. Jones and Rev. Thomas Brooke, which carried exemption, was ignored by offender. Fine 5/- and 13/- costs. Offence committed 23 July 1828.

47/D/2   26 Sept. 1828. Thomas Wintle. Assaulting George Hayward in Westbury [on Severn]. Rev. C. Crawley JP and Rev. J. Pyrke JP at Newnham. Fine 20/- to be paid to John Lucas of Newnham and 8/- costs to the complainant. Offence committed 16 Sept. 1828.

47/D/3   18 Aug. 1828. Richard Drinkwater. Assaulting Mary Ann Coopey at Churcham. Rev. C. Crawley JP and J. Pyrke JP at Newnham. Fine 5/-, to be paid to John Lucas of Newnham, and 5/- costs to the complainant. Offence committed 16 Aug. 1828.

47/D/4   25 Aug. 1828. George Tingle of St. Briavels hundred, coalminer. Using a snare with intent to take deer in Crabtree Hill enclosure in the Forest of Dean. Rev. C. Crawley JP and J. Pyrke JP at Newnham. Fine £20, to be paid immediately to James Thomas, high constable of St. Briavels hundred, or six months in Littledean house of correction. Offence committed 20 Aug. 1828.

47/D/5   25 Aug. 1828. Robert Tingle of St. Briavels hundred, coalminer. Using a snare [etc., as 47/D/4].

47/D/6   25 Aug. 1828. Joseph Hale of St. Briavels hundred, labourer. Using a snare [etc., as 47/D/4].

47/D/7   13 Oct. 1828. Ann wife of John Beale. Assaulting Sarah Whitson at St. Briavels hundred. Rev. C. Crawley JP and J. Pyrke JP at Newnham. Fine £1 1s., to be paid immediately to John Lucas of Newnham, and 7/- costs to be paid to the complainant, or two months in Littledean house of correction. Offence committed 9 Oct. 1828.

47/D/8   28 July 1828. Elizabeth wife of John Lee, late of Pebworth. Leaving her two children chargeable to the parish of Pebworth. Rev. J. R. Hall JP and Rev. W. Boughton JP at Bourton on the Hill. Two months' hard labour in Northleach house of correction. Offence committed 10 Feb. 1826.

47/D/9   17 July 1828. John Harrod. Leaving his wife and child chargeable to the parish of Chipping Campden. Rev. W. Boughton JP at Bourton on the Hill. Two months' hard labour in Northleach house of correction.

47/D/10   23 July 1828. Frederick Bearcroft and John Baylis of Twyning, labourers. Violently assaulting Edmund Haviland at Twyning. J. Timbrill D.D. JP at Tewkesbury. Fine 5/-, to be paid to Peter Dee, an overseer of the poor of Twyning, and 13/- costs to the complainant. Offence committed 19 July 1828.

47/D/11   25 Sept. 1828. Walter Huxtable. Assaulting Walter Thompson Wilkins at Clifton, Bristol. H. W. Newman JP and W. Munro JP at Lawfords Gate sessions room. Fine 9/6 and 11/6 costs or one month in Lawfords Gate house of correction. Offence committed 20 Sept. 1828.

47/D/12   11 Sept. 1828. Abraham Fisher. Assaulting Heather Dodds at Clifton, Bristol. H. W. Newman JP and W. Munro JP at Lawfords Gate sessions room. Fine 5/- and 6/6 costs or fourteen days in Lawfords Gate house of correction. Offence committed 5 Sept. 1828.

47/D/13 25 Sept. 1828. George Millard. Assaulting James Phillips at Clifton, Bristol. H. W. Newman JP and W. Munro JP at Lawfords Gate sessions room. Fine 1/6 and 8/6 costs or fourteen days in Lawfords Gate house of correction. Offence committed 19 Sept. 1828.

47/D/14 11 Sept. 1828. Joseph Lewis. Assaulting Jemima Lowe at Winterbourne. H. W. Newman JP and J. Lewis JP at Lawfords Gate sessions room. Fine 10/- and 14/6 costs or three weeks in Lawfords Gate house of correction. Offence committed 8 Sept. 1828.

47/D/15 9 Oct. 1828. Mary Hodges. Assaulting Martha Flower at St. Philip and St. Jacob, Bristol. D. Cave JP and H. W. Newman JP at Lawfords Gate sessions room. Fine 1/- and 7/6 costs or one week in Lawfords Gate house of correction. Offence committed 6 Oct. 1828.

47/D/16 9 Oct. 1828. Richard Fisher, John Richards and Henry West. Assaulting William Harley at St. Philip and St. Jacob, Bristol. H. W. Newman JP and D. Cave JP at Lawfords Gate sessions room. Fine £1 10s. and £1 2s. 6d. costs or one month in Lawfords Gate house of correction. Offence committed 4 Oct. 1828.

47/D/17 21 August 1828. Edmund Croker. Assaulting Hannah Croker at Almondsbury. T. Daniel JP and G. Hilhouse JP at Lawfords Gate sessions room. Fine 5/- and 8/- costs or one month in Lawfords Gate house of correction. Offence committed 17 August 1828.

47/D/18 11 Sept. 1828. Edmund Curtis. Assaulting Keziah Andrews at Winterbourne. H. W. Newman JP and J. Lewis JP at Lawfords Gate sessions room. Fine £1 and 8/- costs or one month in Lawfords Gate house of correction. Offence committed 8 Sept. 1828.

47/D/19 18 Sept. 1828. Hannah Tyler. Assaulting Elizabeth Raper at Winterbourne. J. Parker JP and H. W. Newman JP at Lawfords Gate sessions room. Fine 5/- and 15/- costs or fourteen days in Lawfords Gate house of correction. Offence committed 15 Aug. 1828.

47/D/20 4 Sept. 1828. John Harris. Assaulting Mary Merrick at St. Philip and St. Jacob, Bristol. H. W. Newman JP and J. Lewis JP at Lawfords Gate sessions room. Fine 10/- and 6/6 costs or fourteen days in Lawfords Gate house of correction. Offence committed 23 Aug. 1828.

47/D/21 21 Aug. 1828. John Clark. Assaulting Susanna Clark at Horfield. T. Daniel JP and G. Hilhouse JP at Lawfords Gate sessions room. Fine £1 and 9/6 costs or two months in Lawfords Gate house of correction. Offence committed 15 Aug. 1828.

47/D/22 7 Aug. 1828. Thomas Ryan. Assaulting John Gerrish at Bitton. C. L. Walker JP and H. W. Newman JP at Lawfords Gate sessions room. Fine 1/- and 9/- costs. Offence committed 24 July 1828.

47/D/23 31 July 1828. Samuel Bryant, Joseph Burchell, George Rogers, William Millard and John Hawkins. Assaulting William Tanner at Mangotsfield. J. Cave JP and H. W. Newman JP at Lawfords Gate sessions room. Fine £5 and £3 4s. costs or one month in Lawfords Gate house of correction. Offence committed 27 July 1828.

47/D/24 4 Sept. 1828. Mark Perryman. Assaulting William Brain at Hanham. H. W. Newman JP and J. Lewis JP at Lawfords Gate sessions room. Fine 5/- and 8/- costs or seven days in Lawfords Gate house of correction. Offence committed 26 Aug. 1828.

47/D/25 4 Sept. 1828. Mark Perryman. Assaulting Robert Hunter at Hanham [etc., as 47/D/24].

47/D/26 31 July 1828. John Dudbridge. Assaulting Thomas Woods at St. James, [Bristol]. H. W. Newman JP and V. J. Graeme JP at Lawfords Gate sessions room. Fine £1 12s. and 8/- costs or six weeks in Lawfords Gate house of correction. Offence committed 13 July 1828.

47/D/27   31 July 1828. Edward Stone. Assaulting William Williams at St. George, [Bristol]. H. W. Newman JP and V. J. Graeme JP at Lawfords Gate sessions room. Fine £1 and 9/- costs or six weeks in Lawfords Gate house of correction. Offence committed 29 July 1828.

47/D/28   31 July 1828. William Strong. Assaulting John Haberfield at St. Philip and St. Jacob, [Bristol]. H. W. Newman JP and V. J. Graeme JP at Lawfords Gate sessions room. Fine £1 12s. 6d. and 7/6 costs or six weeks in Lawfords Gate house of correction. Offence committed 28 July 1828.

47/D/29   7 Aug. 1828. Sampson Densley. Assaulting Ann Taylor at St. George, [Bristol]. C. L. Walker JP and H. W. Newman JP at Lawfords Gate sessions room. Fine 10/- and 7/6 costs or one month in Lawfords Gate house of correction. Offence committed 1 Aug. 1828.

47/D/30   7 Aug. 1828. John Southwood. Assaulting Margaret Pitt at Stapleton. C. L. Walker JP and H. W. Newman JP at Lawfords Gate sessions room. Fine £2 and 13/- costs or six weeks in Lawfords Gate house of correction. Offence committed 3 Aug. 1828.

47/D/31   7 Aug. 1828. John Jolly. Assaulting Jane Bragg at St. James, [Bristol]. C. L. Walker JP and H. W. Newman JP at Lawfords Gate sessions room. Fine 10/- and 10/6 costs or one month in Lawfords Gate house of correction. Offence committed 1 Aug. 1828.

47/D/32   7 Aug. 1828. Eli Trimlett. Assaulting Martha Guest at St. George, [Bristol]. C. L. Walker JP and H. W. Newman JP at Lawfords Gate sessions room. Fine 10/- and 10/6 costs or one month in Lawfords Gate house of correction. Offence committed 5 Aug. 1828.

47/D/33   4 Sept. 1828. Mary Thorne. Assaulting Mary Ann Hallard at St. James, [Bristol]. H. W. Newman JP and J. Lewis JP at Lawfords Gate sessions room. Fine 5/- and 6/6 costs or one month in Lawfords Gate house of correction. Offence committed 27 Aug. 1828.

47/D/34   13 Oct. 1828. Samuel Cooke of Randwick, labourer. Stealing two fence rails, the property of Edward Hoff Esq. of Randwick. H. Burgh JP at Stroud. Fine 5/6, the value of the rails, and 6/6 costs, or one month's hard labour in Horsley house of correction. Offence committed 11 Oct. 1828.

47/D/35   30 July 1828. Joseph Virrinder of Cranham, earthenware man. Assaulting Ezra Gardner, shoemaker, of Painswick, at Cranham. H. Burgh JP and W. H. Hyett JP at Stroud. Fine £2 1s. and 1/- costs or two months in Horsley house of correction. Offence committed 29 July 1828.

47/D/36   30 July 1828. William Virrinder the younger of Cranham, earthenware man. Assaulting Ezra Gardner [etc., as 47/D/35].

47/D/37   12 July 1828. Thomas Carter of Rodborough, labourer. Wilfully injuring a pig at Rodborough, the property of Edmund Haycroft, gentleman, by throwing a reaphook at it. H. Burgh JP at Stroud. Fine 16/- and 10/6 costs or two months' hard labour in Horsley house of correction. Offence committed 7 July 1828.

47/D/38   23 July 1828. Thomas Wilkins of King's Stanley, weaver. Stealing a gate valued at £1 15s., the property of Thomas, Lord Ducie. H. Burgh JP at Stroud. Fine £2 15s. and 14/- costs or two months' hard labour in Horsley house of correction. Offence committed 23 July 1828.

47/D/39   4 Aug. 1828. Nathaniel Workman of Stroud, labourer. Stealing potatoes growing in a field at Stroud, the property of William Clutterbuck Chambers Esq. H. Burgh JP at Stroud. One month's hard labour in Horsley house of correction. Offence committed 3 Aug. 1828.

47/D/40   20 Aug. 1828. Elizabeth Lewis, prostitute. Disorderly behaviour in Stroud. H. Burgh JP at Stroud. One month's hard labour in Horsley house of correction. Offence committed 11 Aug. 1828.

47/D/41 20 Aug. 1828. Hester Vick, prostitute. Disorderly behaviour in Stroud [*etc.*, *as* 47/D/40].

47/D/42 26 Sept. 1828. James Wall the younger, stonemason, of Rodborough, and George Berry of Stroud, labourer. Assaulting Charles Sutton, high constable of Bisley hundred, while in the execution of his duty at Stroud. H. Burgh JP and W. H. Hyett JP at Stroud. Fine £2 and 9/6 costs or two months in Horsley house of correction. Offence committed 20 Sept. 1828.

47/D/43 21 Aug. 1828. Benjamin Robins of Stonehouse, labourer. Shooting a hare in Frocester. H. Burgh JP. Fine £10. First offence. Offence committed Sunday 17 Aug. 1828.

47/D/44 22 Aug. 1828. Thomas Jones of Bisley, clothier. Paying Charles Davis, weaver, of Bisley, 1/5½ in other than lawful coin of the realm. H. Burgh JP and W. H. Hyett JP at Stroud. Fine £20.

47/D/45 5 Sept. 1828. Charles Hancock of North Nibley, labourer. Using a net to take conies, on land occupied by Joseph Dimery at North Nibley, without obtaining the required certificate. W. M. Adey JP at Wotton under Edge, commissioner for taxes. Fine £10. [*Note*: Offender committed to Horsley gaol.] Offence committed 4 Aug. 1828.

47/D/46 5 Sept. 1828. John Mercer *alias* Heath of North Nibley, labourer. Using a net [*etc.*, *as* 47/D/45 *except note*: Fine paid.]

47/D/47 6 Oct. 1828. William Smith of Thornbury, cordwainer. Damaging an apple tree and stealing a quantity of apples in an orchard belonging to Robert Andrew Cox, farmer. Rev. Maurice Fitzgerald Townsend Stephens JP at Thornbury. First offence. Two months' hard labour in Horsley house of correction. Offence committed previous Saturday night/Sunday morning.

47/D/48 8 Sept. 1828. William Green of Cheltenham, labourer. Using a gun and a dog to kill game in Prestbury. Rev. J. Neale JP at Cheltenham. Rev. Christopher Capel, informant, and Rev. John Edwards, witness, both of Prestbury. Offender pleaded not guilty. Fine £5. Offence committed 4 Sept. 1828.

47/D/49 8 Sept. 1828. William Green of Cheltenham, labourer. Using a gun and a dog to kill game in Prestbury. Rev. R. L. Townsend JP at Cheltenham. Rev. Christopher Capel, informant, and Rev. John Edwards, witness, both of Prestbury. Offender pleaded not guilty. Fine £5. Offence committed 2 Sept. 1828

47/D/50 26 Aug. 1828. Esther Peglar, single woman. Receiving one bushel of onions, stolen from a garden in Minchinhampton, the property of Alexander Townsend Esq. Rev. H. Campell JP at Minchinhampton. Six months in Horsley house of correction. Offence committed 24 Aug. 1828.

47/D/51 26 Sept. 1828. William Antill. Stealing one bushel of onions growing in a garden in Minchinhampton, the property of Alexander Townsend Esq. Rev. H. Campbell JP at Minchinhampton. Six months in Horsley house of correction. Offence committed 23 Aug. 1828.

47/D/52 26 Sept. 1828. Thomas Baker. Stealing one bushel of onions [*etc.*, *as* 47/D/51].

47/D/53 25 Aug. 1828. Charles Ockford. Stealing one quart of strawberries from a garden in Minchinhampton, the property of Alexander Townsend Esq. Rev. H. Campbell JP at Minchinhampton. Four months in Horsley house of correction. Offence committed 1 July 1828.

47/D/54 21 Aug. 1828. Thomas Buckingham. Throwing down a stone wall in Rodborough, the property of Robert Snow Paul Esq. Rev. P. Hawker JP and D. Ricardo JP at Rodborough. R. S. Paul Esq. not examined in proof of the offence. Fine 4/-, to be paid to John Wood, an overseer of the poor, and 4/- costs and 1/- damages, or one month in Horsley house of correction. Offence committed 9 Aug. 1828.

47/D/55 21 Aug. 1828. Emanuel Davis. Throwing down a stone wall [*etc., as* 47/D/54].

47/D/56 19 Aug. 1828. Alick Barret. Setting three wires to catch hares in enclosed ground in Cherington. D. Ricardo JP at Minchinhampton. Fine £2 10*s.*, to be paid to Richard Kilmister, an overseer of the poor, and 11/6 costs to the complainant John Phipps, or one month's hard labour in Horsley house of correction. Offence committed 19 Aug. 1828.

47/D/57 13 Sept. 1828. William Risby. Stealing half a peck of turnips from enclosed ground in Avening, the property of George Blackwell. Rev. H. Campbell JP at Minchinhampton. G. Blackwell not examined in proof of the offence. Fine 4/6, to be paid to George Whitley, an overseer of the poor, 6*d.* (the value of the turnips) and 5/- costs. Given two days to pay. Offence committed 6 Sept. 1828.

47/D/58 13 Sept. 1828. Edward Essex. Stealing half a peck of turnips [*etc., as* 47/D/57].

47/D/59 13 Sept. 1828. John Risby. Stealing half a peck of turnips [*etc., as* 47/D/57].

47/D/60 2 Aug. 1828. Lawford Pullin of Tytherington, farmer. Assaulting William Ford, labourer, of Tytherington. W. Davies D.D. JP and Rev. M. F. T. Stephens JP at Thornbury. Fine 40/- including costs, of which £1 9*s.* 6*d.* must be paid to the overseer of the poor within two weeks and the remainder to W. Ford. [*Note dated*] 27 Sept. 1828: £1 9*s.* 6*d.* paid to the churchwarden of Tytherington. [*Signed:*] J. E.

47/D/61 25 Aug. 1828. William Langdon of Thornbury, stonemason. Assaulting Samuel Small, surgeon, of Thornbury. W. N. Tonge JP and M. F. T. Stephens JP at Thornbury. Fine 40/- including costs or one month in Lawfords Gate house of correction. Warrant of commitment sent out. Offence committed 7 Aug. 1828.

47/D/62 6 Sept. 1828. James Coventry of Rangeworthy, labourer. Assaulting Benjamin Baker, farmer, of Rangeworthy. S. P. Peach JP and M. F. T. Stephens JP at Thornbury. Fine 20/- including costs or one month in Lawfords Gate house of correction. Committed for non-payment. Offence committed 28 Aug. 1828.

47/D/63 6 Oct. 1828. George Provin of Westerleigh, labourer. Stealing pears valued at 3*d.* and upwards from a garden or orchard, the property of Edward Renolds of Westerleigh. Rev. F. Pelly JP as Siston rectory. One month's hard labour in Horsley house of correction. Offence committed Monday 15 Sept. 1828.

47/D/64 28 Aug. 1828. Joseph Boucher of Childswickham. Keeping and using a gun to kill game in Broad Campden when not qualified. Rev. J. Adams JP and Rev. J. R. Hall JP at Bourton on the Hill. Richard Tustin, yeoman, of Blockley, Worcs., informer. Joseph Nobbs, labourer, of Chipping Campden, witness. Fine £5 (half to informer and half to the poor). Offence committed during the night of 22 July 1828.

47/D/65 28 Aug. 1828. William Marsh of Broadway, Worcs., cordwainer. Keeping and using a gun [*etc., as* 47/D/64].

48/A/1 4 Aug. 1828. Moses Teague and William Bishop. Assaulting Edward Hook at the hundred of St. Briavels. Rev. C. Crawley JP and J. Pyrke JP at Newnham. Fine 3/6 and 11/- costs. Offence committed 29 July 1828.

48/A/2 22 Dec. 1828. Richard Dobbs of the hundred of St. Briavels, labourer. Violently assaulting Sophia Bishop. J. Pyrke JP and M. Colchester JP at Newnham. Fine £4 6*s.* and 14/- costs or two calendar months in Littledean house of correction. Offence committed 9 Dec. 1828.

48/A/3 9 Dec. 1828. Maria wife of William Jones of Awre, labourer. Cutting underwood at Lydney, the property of the Rt. Hon. Charles Bathurst. Rev. T. Thomas JP at Lydney. Fine 40/- or one calendar month in Littledean house of correction. Offence committed 3 Dec. 1828.

48/A/4   6 Jan. 1829. William Evans of Tidenham, labourer. Killing a pigeon at Tidenham, the property of Mr. John Cadle. Rev. T. Thomas JP at Lydney. Fine £1 and 8/- costs or two calendar months in Littledean house of correction. Fine paid. Offence committed 22 Nov. 1828.

48/A/5   23 Dec. 1828. Henry Beach the younger of Bream, labourer. Cutting underwood at Bream, the property of the Rt. Hon. Charles Bathurst. E. Machen JP at Coleford. Fine £1 and 5/6 costs or two calendar months in Littledean house of correction. Offence committed 12 Dec. 1828.

48/A/6   23 Dec. 1828. George Beach of Bream, labourer. Cutting underwood [etc., as 48/A/5].

48/A/7   28 Oct. 1828. Ann wife of Thomas Grindoll of Coleford, labourer. Violently assaulting Thomas Arabin, labourer, at Coleford. E. Machen JP and P. J. Ducarel JP at Coleford. Fine 5/- and 11/6 costs or two calendar months in Littledean house of correction. Offence committed 1 Aug. 1828.

48/A/8   23 Dec. 1828. George Nash of Coleford, labourer. Violently assaulting David Morgan, labourer, at Coleford. E. Machen JP and P. J. Ducarel JP at Coleford. Fine £2 or two calendar months in Littledean house of correction. Offence committed 20 Dec. 1828.

48/A/9   28 Oct. 1828. Elizabeth wife of James Robins of Bream, labourer. Violently assaulting Sarah Price, spinster, at Bream. E. Machen JP and P. J. Ducarel JP at Coleford. Fine 2/6 and 7/6 costs or two months in Littledean house of correction. Offence committed 4 Oct. 1828.

48/A/10   2 Sept. 1828. Richard Edwards of Coleford, victualler. Failing to observe the conditions of his recognizance. E. Machen JP and P. J. Ducarel JP at Coleford. Fine £4 and £1 costs. First offence.

48/A/11   24 Nov. 1828. Harriet Okey. Cutting and damaging a live hedge at Northwood, Westbury on Severn, the property of John Cadle of the same parish. Rev. C. Crawley JP at Newnham. Fine 1/- and 7/6 costs or two calendar months in Littledean house of correction. Offence committed 20 Oct. 1828.

48/A/12   1 Dec. 1828. John Wilkins of Westbury on Severn, labourer. Leaving wife and children chargeable to the parish. Rev. C. Crawley JP at Newnham. Three months' hard labour in Littledean house of correction. Offence committed 31 May 1828.

48/A/13   22 Dec. 1828. Richard Dobbs of St. Briavels hundred, labourer. Violently assaulting Maria Johnson. J. Pyrke JP and Rev. C. Crawley JP at Newnham, Fine £4 6s. and 14/- costs or two calendar months in Littledean house of correction. Offence committed 9 Dec. 1828.

48/A/14   24 Nov. 1828. Thomas Vaughan of Lea, labourer. Violently assaulting Anne wife of Edward Ambury. Rev. C. Crawley JP and M. Colchester JP at Newnham. Fine 5/- and 7/6 costs or two calendar months in Littledean house of correction. Offence committed 4 Nov. 1828.

48/A/15   24 Nov. 1828. James Roan of Ruddle, Newnham, farmer. Violently assaulting Patience Roberts. Rev. C. Crawley JP and M. Colchester JP at Newnham. Fine £1 10s. and 7/6 costs or two calendar months in Littledean house of correction. Offence committed 21 Nov. 1828.

48/A/16   27 Oct. 1828. John Sysum of Littledean, labourer. Violently assaulting Samuel Mountjoy. Rev. C. Crawley JP and M. Colchester JP at Newnham. Fine £4 12s. and 8/- costs or two calendar months in Littledean house of correction. Offence committed 7 Oct. 1828.

48/A/17 27 Oct. 1828. Robert Stephens of St. Briavels hundred, coalminer. Violently assaulting Thomas Voice at Mitcheldean. Rev. C. Crawley JP and M. Colchester JP at Newnham. Fine £4 12s. and 8/- costs or two calendar months in Littledean house of correction. Offence committed 10 Oct. 1828.

48/A/18 27 Oct. 1828. John Stephens of St. Briavels hundred, coalminer. Violently assaulting Thomas Voice [etc., as 48/A/17].

48/A/19 25 Nov. 1828. Thomas Arundell. Found in an outhouse or schoolroom in Stroud with intent to commit a felony. Rev. H. Campbell JP at Stroud. Two calendar months in Horsley house of correction. Offence committed 24 Nov. 1828.

48/A/20 5 Jan. 1829. Abraham Nash. Indecently exposing himself to Francis [sic] wife of Thomas Currier, innkeeper, at Stroud. H. Burgh JP at Stroud. Three months' hard labour in Horsley house of correction. Offence committed 2 Jan. 1829.

48/A/21 2 Jan. 1829. Martha Masters, prostitute. Riotous behaviour in Stroud. Rev. P. Hawker JP and W. H. Hyett JP at Stroud. One month's hard labour in Horsley house of correction. Offence committed 1 Jan. 1829.

48/A/22 28 Oct. 1828. Enoch Stephens. Leaving wife and children chargeable to the parish of Bisley. H. Burgh JP at Stroud. One month's hard labour in Horsley house of correction. Offence committed between 14 and 28 Oct. 1828.

48/A/23 20 Oct. 1828. William Webber. Entering the dwelling house at Painswick of Henry Gyde, clothier, with intent to commit a felony. H. Burgh JP at Stroud. Three months' hard labour in Horsley house of correction. Offence committed 18 Oct. 1828.

48/A/24 1 Dec. 1828. Mary Gould, prostitute. Riotous behaviour in Stroud. Rev. P. Hawker JP at Stroud. One month's hard labour in Horsley house of correction. Offence committed 29 Nov. 1828.

48/A/25 2 Jan. 1829. Nathaniel Smith and William Cratchley of Stroud, labourers. Stealing part of a dead fence from a field at Haresfield, the property of John Butcher, gentleman. Rev. P. Hawker JP and W. H. Hyett JP at Stroud. Fine 5/- and 7/- costs or one month's hard labour in Horsley house of correction. Offence committed 24 Nov. 1828.

48/A/26 6 Nov. 1828. Richard Davis of Bisley, weaver. Rooting up and damaging growing underwood in Hawkly Thicket at North Nibley. H. Burgh JP at Stroud. Fine 6d. and 7/- costs or two months' hard labour in Horsley house of correction. Offence committed 29 Nov. [? recte Oct.] 1828.

48/A/27 20 July 1827 [late return]. Joseph and Thomas Iles of Minchinhampton, clothiers. Paying or causing to be paid the sum of 14/7½ due to William Browning, weaver, of Stroud, in other than lawful coin. H. Burgh JP and W. H. Hyett JP at Stroud. Fine £20.

48/A/28 7 Nov. 1828. William Panting of Stroud, butcher. Letting off a firework in a public street. H. Burgh JP and Robert Stephens Davies JP at Stroud. Fine £5 and 9/- costs. Offence committed 5 Nov. 1828.

48/A/29 17 Dec. 1828. James Wood. Stealing a quantity of live and dead fence from a hedge in a field belonging to Samuel Albin Saunders at Upton, Tetbury. Thomas Grimston Bucknall Estcourt JP at Tetbury. Fine 20/- and 4/6 costs or two calendar months in Horsley house of correction. Offence committed 5 Dec. 1828.

48/A/30 17 Dec. 1828. Elizabeth Elliotts. Stealing turnips growing on open land at Charlton, Tetbury, occupied by Richard Barber. T. G. B. Estcourt JP at Tetbury. Fine 10/- and 4/6 costs or one calendar month in the house of correction. Offence committed 4 Dec. 1828.

48/A/31 17 Dec. 1828. Mary Shipton. Stealing turnips [etc., as 48/A/30].

48/A/32　17 Dec. 1828. Catherine Wood. Stealing turnips [*etc.*, *as* 48/A/30 *except*] Fine 20/- and 4/6 costs.

48/A/33　3 Dec. 1828. Ann Cox. Stealing turnips growing on enclosed land at Tetbury, the property of John Allaway. T. G. B. Estcourt JP at Tetbury. Fine 2/6 and 6*d.*, the value of the goods, and 6/- costs or one month's hard labour in the house of correction. Offence committed 3 Oct. 1828.

48/A/34　3 Dec. 1828. Mary Lamb. Stealing turnips [*etc.*, *as* 48/A/33].

48/A/35　19 Nov. 1828. Mark Brown. Breaking and damaging parts of a sycamore tree growing at Church Hayes, Tetbury, with intent to steal. D. Ricardo JP at Tetbury. Fine 10/- and 1/6 costs (costs to be paid to Richard Hathway, farmer of the Grange, Tetbury) or one month at hard labour in Horsley house of correction. Offence committed 17 Nov. 1828.

48/A/36　19 Nov. 1828. Betty Judge. Maliciously destroying turnips growing in Burrell's field, the property of John Charles, labourer. D. Ricardo JP at Tetbury. Fine 10/- and 1/6 costs or one month's hard labour in Horsley house of correction. Offence committed 11 Oct. 1828.

48/A/37　19 Nov. 1828. Worthy Mann. Aiding and abetting Mark Brown in damaging, with intent to steal, parts of a sycamore tree growing in Church Hayes, Tetbury. D. Ricardo JP at Tetbury. Fine 10/- and 1/6 costs to be paid to Richard Hathway, farmer, of the Grange, Tetbury, or one month's hard labour in Horsley house of correction. Offence committed 17 Nov. 1828.

48/A/38　12 Dec. 1828. Elizabeth Judge *alias* Compton. Maliciously damaging a withy tree growing on land belonging to Joseph Brookes of Elmstree, Tetbury. W. M. Paul JP at Tetbury. Second offence (previously convicted as Betty Judge). [*Cf.* 48/A/36.] Fine £5 or two months in Horsley house of correction. Offence committed 25 Nov. 1828.

48/A/39　30 Oct. 1828. Stephen Chilcot. Assaulting Susannah Rider at St. George, Bristol. G. Goldney JP and J. Parker JP at Lawfords Gate sessions room. Fine 1/- and 7/- costs or seven days in Lawfords Gate house of correction. Offence committed 20 Oct. 1828.

48/A/40　30 Oct. 1828. Levi Brain. Assaulting Ann Blanchard at Bitton. G. Goldney JP and J. Parker JP at Lawfords Gate sessions room. Fine 1/- and 7/6 costs or seven days in Lawfords Gate house of correction. Offence committed 23 Oct. 1828.

48/A/41　30 Oct. 1828. Grace Tavender. Assaulting Elizabeth Protheroe at Clifton, Bristol. J. Parker JP and H. W. Newman JP at Lawfords Gate sessions room. Fine 1/- and 6/6 costs or seven days in Lawfords Gate house of correction. Offence committed 17 Oct. 1828.

48/A/42　30 Oct. 1828. Grace Tavender. Assaulting and beating Mary Swash at Clifton, Bristol [*etc.*, *as* 48/A/41 *except*] Offence committed 12 Oct. 1828.

48/A/43　4 Dec. 1828. Henry Fox. Assaulting James Purnell Bailey at St. George, Bristol. H. W. Newman JP and V. J. Graeme JP at Lawfords Gate sessions room. Fine 3/- and 7/- costs or one calendar month in Lawfords Gate house of correction. Offence committed 29 Nov. 1828.

48/A/44　11 Dec. 1828. Thomas Osborne. Assaulting Elizabeth Barratt at St. George, Bristol. G. Goldney JP and H. W. Newman JP at Lawfords Gate sessions room. Fine 1/- and 7/6 costs or seven days in Lawfords Gate house of correction. Offence committed 5 Dec. 1828.

48/A/45　11 Dec. 1828. George Taylor. Assaulting Dinah Close at Almondsbury. G. Goldney JP and H. W. Newman JP at Lawfords Gate sessions room. Fine 2/- and 7/6 costs or one calendar month in Lawfords Gate house of correction. Offence committed 7 Dec. 1828.

48/A/46 1 Jan. 1829. Alexander Shedden. Assaulting Mary Ann Hurley at St. James, Bristol. G. Goldney JP and H. W. Newman JP at Lawfords Gate sessions room. Fine10/- and 6/6 costs or one calendar month in Lawfords Gate house of correction. Offence committed 24 Dec. 1828.

48/A/47 1 Jan. 1829. Francis Church. Assaulting James Manning at Clifton, Bristol. G. Goldney JP and C. L. Walker JP at Lawfords Gate sessions room. Fine 10/- and 6/6 costs or one calendar month in Lawfords Gate house of correction. Offence committed 23 Dec. 1828.

48/A/48 1 Jan. 1829. Mary Buck. Assaulting Ann Welch of St. Philip and St. Jacob, Bristol. G. Goldney JP and C. L. Walker JP at Lawfords Gate sessions room. Fine 2/6 and 6/6 costs or fourteen days in Lawfords Gate house of correction. Offence committed 29 Dec. 1828.

48/A/49 27 Nov. 1828. William Whittaker. Assaulting George Fudge at Stapleton. H. W. Newman JP and V. J. Graeme JP at Lawfords Gate sessions room. Fine £1 and 7/- costs or one calendar month in Lawfords Gate house of correction. 19 Nov. 1828.

48/A/50 27 Nov. 1828. William Dodd. Assaulting Elizabeth Fisher at Clifton, Bristol. H. W. Newman JP and V. J. Graeme JP at Lawfords Gate sessions room. Fine 3/6 and 6/6 costs or one calendar month in Lawfords Gate house of correction. Offence committed 22 Nov. 1828.

48/A/51 16 Oct. 1828. John Dash of Alkington, labourer. Cutting and damaging a holly tree growing in Michael Wood, Alkington, the property of William Fitzhardinge Berkeley of Berkeley Castle. R. F. Jenner JP at Berkeley. Fine 12/6 and 1/6, the value of the tree, together with 6/6 costs or five weeks in Horsley house of correction. Offence committed 2 Oct. 1828.

48/A/52 6 Jan. 1829. John Hart of Stow on the Wold, baker. Unlawfully possessing a quantity of underwood and two posts at Oddington, the property of William Springhall of Stow on the Wold, confectioner. Rev. F. E. Witts JP at Upper Slaughter. Search warrant executed. Fine £2 and 14/- costs or two months in Northleach house of correction. Offence committed 6 Jan. 1829.

48/A/53 1 Jan. 1829. John Lock of Bourton on the Water, labourer. Damaging the church clock at Bourton on the Water by throwing stones. Rev. F. E. Witts JP at Stow on the Wold. Fine 2/- and 2/6 costs or one month's hard labour in Northleach house of correction. Offence committed 26 Oct. 1828.

48/A/54 8 Jan. 1829. Thomas Cambray, John Robinson, Henry Phipps and William Palmer, all of Stow on the Wold. Breaking the door of Joseph Cozier's dwelling house at Stow on the Wold. Rev. F. E. Witts JP at Stow on the Wold. Fine 8d. and 5/6 costs each or one month's hard labour each in Northleach house of correction. Offence committed 6 Jan. 1829.

48/A/55 1 Jan. 1829. Stephen Betteridge, Joseph Betteridge, William Palmer, William Palmer [again, possibly another man] and James Cowly, all of Bourton on the Water. Breaking the windows of Bourton on the Water parish church by throwing stones. Rev. F. E. Witts JP at Stow on the Wold. Fine 2/- and 2/6 costs each or one month's hard labour each in Northleach house of correction. Offence committed 17 Dec. 1828.

48/A/56 17 Nov. 1828. John Daniell of Cromhall, farmer's son. Violently assaulting Giles Barton of Thornbury, labourer, at Thornbury. S. P. Peach JP and Rev. M. F. T. Stephens JP at Thornbury. Fine 4/- and 6/- costs. Offence committed 14 Oct. 1828.

48/A/57 1 Nov. 1828. Samuel Gough of Thornbury, cordwainer. Violently assaulting George Nicholls at Thornbury. W. Davies D.D. JP and Rev. M. F. T. Stephens JP at Thornbury. Fine 14/- and 6/- costs. Offence committed 1 Oct. 1828.

48/A/58 1 Nov. 1828. William Wetmore of Hill, farmer's son. Assaulting Charlotte Jotcham of Hill. W. Davies D.D. JP and Rev. M. F. T. Stephens JP at Thornbury. Fine one halfpenny and 2/- costs. Offence committed 29 Oct. 1828. [*Note*:] one halfpenny fine paid to Thornbury overseer of the poor.

48/A/59 8 Dec. 1828. George Pocock and John Tyler, both of Olveston, servants. Setting a wire to destroy game at Olveston. W. Davies D.D. JP and Rev. M. F. T. Stephens JP at Thornbury. Six weeks' hard labour each in Horsley house of correction, after which sureties of £10 each to be found, conditional on not re-offending within a year. In default, a further six months' hard labour each. Offence committed 7 Dec. 1828.

48/A/60 20 Dec. 1828. James Cook of Olveston, labourer. Unlawfully entering a field in Olveston with an air-gun with intent to kill pheasants. S. P. Peach JP and W. Davies D.D. JP at Thornbury. Three calendar months' hard labour in Horsley house of correction, after which sureties of £10 conditional on not re-offending within one year are to be found. In default, a further six calendar months' hard labour. Offence committed at 5.45 p.m. on 21 Nov. 1828.

48/A/61 20 Dec. 1828. James Wood of North Hamlet, labourer. Assaulting, without provocation, Anna Maria wife of William Nash, blacksmith, of Longford. Richard Harward JP and J. Wintle JP. Fine £3 and 14/- costs or two calendar months in Littledean house of correction.

48/A/62 12 Nov. 1828. William Ford of Owlpen, weaver. Possessing 33 lb. of various woollen yarns and ends believed to be stolen. E. Sheppard JP and H. W. Dyer JP. Fine £20, half to be paid to Daniel Powell, farmer, of Owlpen, the informer, and the rest to the treasurer of the charity, Gloucester infirmary. Offence committed 11 Nov. 1828.

48/A/63 16 Dec. 1828. Michael Bird of North Nibley, labourer. Possessing 91 lb. of fine woollen yarns and ends believed to be stolen. W. M. Adey JP and H. W. Dyer JP. Fine £20, half to be paid to Charles Cogswell, saddler, of Wotton under Edge, the informer, and the rest to the treasurer of the charity, Gloucester infirmary. Offence committed 20 Nov. 1828.

48/A/64 24 Dec. 1828. Richard Partridge of Wotton under Edge, clothier. Possessing 71 yards of various broadcloths and 109 lb. of various woollen yarns without satisfactory explanation. R. Kingscote JP and Rev. P. Hawker JP. James Dutton, clothier, Henry Matthew Heskins, labourer, both of Wotton under Edge, and James Counsel, clothier, of Kingswood, Wilts., witnesses. Charles Cogswell, informer. Fine £20, to be divided [*as above*]. Offence committed 17 Nov. 1828.

48/A/65 5 Jan. 1829. Joseph Partridge of Wotton under Edge, labourer. Possessing 1 lb. of woollen yarn without satisfactory explanation [*etc.*, as 48/A/64].

48/A/66 6 Oct. 1828. John Herbert of Ampney Crucis, labourer (in company with William Davis). Illegally possessing three hares at Barnsley. J. Cripps JP at Cirencester. William Poole, gamekeeper, of Arlington, Bibury, informer. William Beaseley, gamekeeper, of Barnsley, witness. Defendant did not appear. Fine £15. Offence committed 26 Sept. 1828.

48/A/67 30 Sept. 1828. William Davis of Ampney Crucis, labourer. Illegally using a snare at Barnsley to kill game which he gave to John Herbert. J. Cripps JP at Cirencester. Sir James Musgrave, Bt., of Barnsley, informer. William Beaseley, gamekeeper, of Barnsley, witness. Defendant did not appear. Fine £5. Offence committed 26 Sept. 1828.

48/A/68 29 Aug. 1828. Joseph Brummell of Coates, labourer. Illegally possessing a hare taken from a trap set in a wood in Coates belonging to Mr. Wickens. J. Cripps JP at Cirencester. John Martin the elder, gamekeeper, of Oakley, Cirencester, informer. John

Martin the younger of Cirencester, witness. Defendant pleaded not guilty. Fine £5. Offence committed 20 Aug. 1828.

48/A/69   7 Nov. 1828. Henry Liles of Marshfield, labourer. Using a dog and a net to take game on enclosed lands at Marshfield in the occupation of Ann Beaford and George Holbrow. W. Blathwayt JP, Rev. T. Brooke LL.D. JP and Rev. F. Pelly JP at a Petty Sessions held at the Cross Hands inn, Old Sodbury. Joseph Edwards of Marshfield, witness. Three calendar months' hard labour in Horsley house of correction, after which sureties of £10 to be found against re-offending within a year. In default, a further six months' hard labour. Offence committed at 1 a.m. Sunday 19 Oct. 1828.

48/A/70   5 Dec. 1828. James Blunsen of Hawkesbury, labourer. Using a snare to catch a pheasant in Bodkin Wood, Hawkesbury. Rev. T. Brooke JP, I. W. W. Horlock JP and Rev. F. Pelly JP at a Petty Sessions held at the Cross Hands inn, Old Sodbury. Daniel Woodman, labourer, of Great Badminton, informer. Thomas Webb, labourer, of Great Badminton, witness. Defendant pleaded not guilty but later admitted the offence. Fine £5, half to go to the informer and the rest to the poor of Hawkesbury. Offence committed Friday 28 Nov. 1828.

48/A/71   5 Dec. 1828. Robert Howes the younger of Winterbourne, feltmaker and fur-cutter. Illegally using a gun and dogs to take game on land at Ivory Hill, Westerleigh, occupied by Jeffery Matthews, farmer, of Frampton Cotterell. Rev. T. Brooke JP, I. W. W. Horlock JP and Rev. F. Pelly JP at a Petty Sessions held at the Cross Hands inn, Old Sodbury. Job Luton, gamekeeper, of Westerleigh, informer. John Smart, labourer, of Westerleigh, witness. Defendant pleaded guilty. Fine £5, half to go to the informer and the rest to the poor of Hawkesbury. Offence committed 27 Sept. 1828.

48/A/72   10 Nov. 1828. George Gough of Rodborough, journeyman carpenter. Illegally possessing two partridges and exposing them for sale. H. Burgh JP at Stroud. William Capel, gentleman, of Painswick, informer. Isaac Bennett, labourer, of Painswick, witness. William Addis, carpenter and joiner, of Stroud, gave evidence for the defendant. Fine £10, half to the informer and the rest to the poor of Painswick. Offence committed 8 Nov. 1828.

48/B/1   22 April 1829. Samuel Chad of Haw Bridge turnpike gate in Apperley and Wightfield, shoemaker. Assaulting John Paine, servant to John Hopkins, farmer, of Tirley, at Haw Bridge. J. Timbrill D.D. JP and Rev. J. Keysall JP at Tewkesbury. Fine 20/- and 9/6 costs or two months in Northleach house of correction. Offence committed 14 April 1829.

48/B/2   11 March 1829. James Hall. Begging, swearing and causing a disturbance at the Rev. Charles Hill's home in Bromsberrow. Rev. J. Commeline JP at Redmarley d'Abitot, Worcs. Committed to Littledean house of correction until next Q.S.

48/B/3   7 April 1829. William Apperley. Assaulting Mary Yearn, single woman, at Newnham. Rev. C. Crawley JP and J. Pyrke JP at Newnham. Fine £2, to be paid to James Hill, overseer of the poor at Newnham, and 8/- costs, or two months in Littledean house of correction. Offence committed 3 April 1829.

48/B/4   2 March 1829. Alexander Gwilliam. Assaulting Anne wife of Thomas Pitt *alias* Burgum at Littledean Hill in St. Briavels hundred. Rev. C. Crawley JP and J. Pyrke JP at Newnham. Fine £2, to be paid to John Lucas of Newnham, gentleman, and 16/6 costs, or two months in Littledean house of correction. Offence committed 19 Feb. 1829.

48/B/5   2 March 1829. William Saunders. Assaulting Anne wife of Thomas Pitt [*etc.*, *as* 48/B/4].

48/B/6   2 March 1829. John Young. Assaulting Anne wife of Thomas Pitt [*etc.*, *as* 48/B/4].

48/B/7   2 March 1829. Timothy Wadley. Assaulting Andrew Husbands at Mitcheldean. Rev. C. Crawley JP and J. Pyrke JP at Newnham. Fine £2 10s., to be paid to Absolom Smith, overseer of the poor at Mitcheldean, and 7/6 costs, or two months in Littledean house of correction. Offence committed 22 Feb. 1829.

48/B/8   3 March 1829. Henry Worgan. Unlawfully possessing underwood valued at 6/- at St. Briavels. Rt. Hon. C. Bathurst JP and Rev. T. Thomas JP at Lydney. Fine £1 12s., to be paid to William Allen, overseer of the poor of St. Briavels, and 8/- costs to be paid to Samuel Luff, complainant, or one month in Littledean house of correction. Offence committed 16 Jan. 1829.

48/B/9   3 March 1829. Henry Knight. Cutting and stealing wood valued at 1/- in Woolaston Wood, the property of the duke of Beaufort. Rt. Hon. C. Bathurst JP and Rev. T. Thomas JP at Lydney. Fine £2 and 7/6 costs to be paid to Samuel Luff. Given 27 days to pay. In default, two months in Littledean house of correction. Offence committed 17 Feb. 1829.

48/B/10   3 Feb. 1829. Aaron Butler. Cutting underwood valued at 1/- in Tidenham. Rt. Hon. C. Bathurst JP and Rev. T. Thomas JP at Lydney. Fine 1/-, the value of the wood, 12/- as penalty to be paid to William Thurston and 8/- costs to be paid within 14 days to Samuel Luff, complainant, or one month in Littledean house of correction. Offence committed 8 Jan. 1829.

48/B/11   14 April 1829. Richard White the younger. Unlawful possession of part of a deer at Awre. E. Machen JP at Coleford. Fine £18, to be paid to Charles Jennings, an overseer of the poor, and £2 costs to be paid within 14 days to the complainant Samuel Luff, or six months in Littledean house of correction. Offence committed 26 March 1829.

48/B/12   20 Jan. 1829. William Baker. Assaulting James Graham at Lydbrook, Ruardean. P. J. Ducarel JP and E. Machen JP at Coleford. Fine £1, to be paid to John Webb, overseer of the poor, and 5/- costs, or two months in Littledean house of correction. Offence committed 15 Jan. 1829.

48/B/13   17 Feb. 1829. William Young. Assaulting Mary Evans at Coleford. P. J. Ducarel JP and E. Machen JP at Coleford. Fine £1 12s., to be paid to Peter Teague, overseer of the poor of Newland, and 8/- costs, or two months in Littledean house of correction. Offence committed 20 Jan. 1829.

48/B/14   17 March 1829. Richard Hodges. Assaulting Mary Wilce at Lydbrook, Ruardean. P. J. Ducarel JP and E. Machen JP at Coleford. Fine £1 10s., to be paid to John Webb, overseer of the poor of Ruardean, and 17/- costs, or two months in Littledean house of correction. Offence committed 14 March 1829.

48/B/15   17 March 1829. John Hatton. Assaulting Mary Wilce [etc., as 48/B/14].

48/B/16   14 April 1829. Thomas Charles. Cutting a hawthorn tree and taking away a quantity of beech and other wood in the Forest of Dean. P. J. Ducarel JP at Coleford. Fine £1 12s., to be paid to Edward Machen Esq., and 8/- costs to be paid to William Witts, the complainant, or one month in Littledean house of correction. Offence committed 7 April 1829.

48/B/17   27 April 1829. William Weatherly. Wandering abroad and begging in Westbury [on Severn]. Rev. C. Crawley JP and J. Pyrke JP at Newnham. William Charley, tiler and plasterer, of Cheltenham, informer. Committed to Littledean house of correction for one month. Offence committed 26 April 1829.

48/B/18   17 Feb. 1829. William Harris. Turning five mules and one ass into an enclosure in the Forest of Dean, thereby damaging the grass and saplings. P. J. Ducarel JP at Coleford. Fine £1 12s., to be paid to Edward Machen Esq., and 8/- costs to John Thomas, the complainant, to be paid within 14 days, or two months in Littledean house of correction. Offence committed 13 Feb. 1829.

48/B/19 17 March 1829. James Hopkins, yeoman. Removing all his good and chattels, with the assistance of five others unknown, from a messuage in Hewelsfield on which he owed £34 10*s*. rent, to avoid distraint in lieu of arrears by the owner of the property. E. Machen JP and P. J. Ducarel JP at Coleford. Mary Strode of St. Briavels, wife and agent of Nathaniel Nugent Strode (then overseas), complainant. John Smith, labourer, of Blakeney, Awre, put in charge of the goods by his master James Bowyer, witness. (Goods itemised and valued at £25.) Offender pleaded not guilty. Fine £50. Offence committed 4 March 1829.

48/B/20 21 Feb. 1829. Alfred Jenkins. Violently assaulting Daniel Cullimore of Thornbury, farmer. S. P. Peach JP and Rev. M. F. T. Stephens JP at Thornbury. Fine 5/- and 3/6 costs. Offence committed 9 Feb. 1829. [*Note:*] 5/- paid to Thornbury overseers.

48/B/21 21 Feb. 1829. Henry Clutterbuck. Violently assaulting [*etc., as* 48/B/20 *except*] Fine 10/- and 3/6 costs [*and note:*] 10/- paid to Thornbury overseers.

48/B/22 24 Nov. 1828. William Cooper, Job Surman and Richard Smith, all of [Chipping] Campden, labourers. Assaulting James Dunn the elder of Campden. Rev. J. Adams JP and Rev. C. Jeaffreson JP at Bourton on the Hill. Fine 20/-, to be paid to Charles Tidmarsh, overseer of the poor of Campden, and 10/- costs, or two months in Northleach house of correction. Offence committed 8 Nov. 1828.

48/B/23 2 March 1829. Stephen Blakeman. Leaving his infant child chargeable to the parish of [Chipping] Campden. Rev. J. Adams JP and Rev. J. R. Hall JP at Bourton on the Hill. Three months' hard labour in Northleach house of correction. Offence committed on or about 10 Dec. 1828.

48/B/24 13 April 1829. William Boyes of Alkerton, Oxon., farmer. Failing to supply transport and labour (six days' statutory duty) for journeys to the stone-pit at Rough Hill, for mending the highway outside the newly built house of Mr. Claridge, after due notice was given. Rev. J. R. Hall JP, Rev. J. Adams JP, Rev. W. Boughton JP and Rev. C. Jeaffreson JP at Bourton on the Hill. Rev. Robert Edward Hughes and John Deeley, highways surveyors, and John Hancox, witnesses. Fine £7 4*s*. Offender pleaded not guilty. Offence committed 9–14 March 1828.

48/B/25 2 March 1829. Joseph Biddle of Blockley, Worcs., labourer. Setting snares to kill hares. Rev. J. R. Hall JP at Bourton on the Hill. Thomas Watkins, labourer, of Moreton in Marsh, informer. William Slatter, labourer, of Batsford, witness. Defendant did not appear. Fine £5. Offence committed 28 Jan. 1829.

48/B/26 24 Feb. 1829. James Betts of Bourton on the Hill. Setting snares to kill game. Rev. J. R. Hall JP at Batsford. William Hancock, labourer, of Bourton on the Hill, informer. William Fletcher, labourer, of Batsford, witness. Fine £5. Offence committed 5 Feb. 1829.

48/B/27 31 March 1829. Martha Hudson, single woman. Stealing part of a dead wood fence in Woodchester Park, Avening, the property of the Rt. Hon. Thomas, Lord Ducie. Rev. P. Hawker JP at Horsley. Fine £5, to be paid to George Whitley, one of the overseers of the poor of Avening, and 8*d*., the value of the wood, or two months in Horsley house of correction. Lord Ducie not examined. Offence committed 23 March 1829.

48/B/28 31 March 1829. Elizabeth Webb, single woman. Stealing part [*etc., as* 48/B/27].

48/B/29 27 April 1829. John Wigmore the younger of Avening, yeoman. Using a dog to kill game at Horsley. Rev. P. Hawker JP and tax commissioner, at Horsley. James Tilling, witness. Fine £20. Offence committed 16 April 1829.

48/B/30   16 April 1829. Joseph Mayo *alias* Phillips. Stealing part of a dead wood fence at Avening, the property of the Rt. Hon. Thomas, Lord Ducie. Rev. P. Hawker JP at Rodborough. Fine £5, to be paid to George Whitley, one of the overseers of the poor of Avening, and £1 10*s*., the value of the stolen wood, or two months' hard labour in Horsley house of correction. Lord Ducie not examined. Offence committed 24 March 1829.

48/B/31   5 Feb. 1829. James Lovett of Horsley, labourer. Using wires to kill game in Rodborough. Rev. P. Hawker JP at Horsley. Henry Hall, labourer, of Horsley, informer. Hugh Hains, constable of Horsley, and James Box, gamekeeper, of Horsley, witnesses. Defendant did not appear. Fine £5. Offence committed 2 Feb. 1829.

48/B/32   5 Feb. 1829. Thomas Lovett of Horsley, labourer. Using a wire to kill game. Rev. P. Hawker JP at Horsley. James Box, gamekeeper, of Horsley, informer. Henry Hall, labourer, of Horsley, witness. Pleaded not guilty. Fine £5. Offence committed 7 Feb. 1829.

48/B/33   24 Feb. 1829. William Monday of Lechlade, victualler. Permitting drunkenness and disorderly behaviour on his premises. M. Hicks Beach JP, William Price JP and Rev. J. W. Peters JP. First offence. Fine £4 and £1 10*s*. costs. Offence committed 27 Dec. 1828.

48/B/34   28 Jan. 1829. Jacob Musty of Chedworth, labourer. Entering Cow Grove, an enclosed wood in Rendcomb, at about 3 a.m. with intent to take game. E. Wilbraham JP and William Croome JP at Cirencester. Three months' hard labour in Northleach house of correction, after which sureties of £20 against re-offending to be found, or a further six months' hard labour. Offence committed 27 Jan. 1829..

48/B/35   20 Feb. 1829. Giles Gardner of Down Ampney, labourer. Unlawfully keeping a gun to kill game. J. Cripps JP at Cirencester. Thomas Potter, steward, of Down Ampney, informer. Charge admitted. Fine £5. Offence committed 13 Feb. 1829.

48/B/36   3 Feb. 1829. Simon Pash of Barnsley, labourer. Using a snare to kill game. Edward Cripps JP at Cirencester. William Poole, gamekeeper, of Barnsley, informer. Charge admitted. Fine £5. Offence committed 3 Feb. 1829.

48/B/37   28 April 1829. Gustavus Orpin of Stroud, labourer. Damaging hedges belonging to Nathan Driver of Painswick. H. Burgh JP at Stroud. Fine 1/- and 8/- costs. Offence committed 27 April 1829.

48/B/38   24 April 1829. William Gardner of Bisley. Stealing a quantity of turnip greens from a garden, the property of Daniel Cox, clothier. H. Burgh JP at Stroud. Fine 5/- and 9/- costs or 14 days' hard labour in Horsley house of correction. Offence committed 14 April 1829.

48/B/39   28 March 1829. Sarah Ball, prostitute. Riotous behaviour in Stroud. H. Burgh JP at Stroud. One month's hard labour in Horsley house of correction. Offence committed 27 March 1829.

48/B/40   10 March 1829. Thomas *alias* John Mills of Stroud, butcher. Ill-treating a goat, the property of George Gingell, innkeeper, of Stroud. H. Burgh JP at Stroud. Nathaniel Thomas, labourer, and Ann Salisbury, spinster, both of Stroud, witnesses.

48/B/41   5 March 1829. Edward Franklin of Miserden and Edmund Griffin of Painswick, labourers. Rooting up and damaging a beech tree in an enclosed wood, the property of the Robert Lawrence Townsend D.D. H. Burgh JP at Stroud. Fine 5/- and 5/- damages and 10/6 costs or two months' hard labour in Horsley house of correction. Offence committed 6 Feb. 1829.

48/B/42 5 March 1829. Edmund Townsend of Painswick, labourer. Attempting to defraud his master Thomas Creed, mealman, of Painswick, by selling meal (sharps) to James Harris, butcher, of Painswick without recording the transaction. H. Burgh JP at Stroud. Thomas Creed, James Harris, William Pitt, labourer, also of Painswick, and Thomas Davis, auctioneer, of Minchinhampton, witnesses. One month's hard labour in Horsley house of correction.

48/B/43 13 Feb. 1829. John Fowler and George Gould of Stroud, labourers. Damaging trees growing in an enclosed wood at Stroud, the property of William Clutterbuck Chambers Esq. H. Burgh JP at Stroud. Fine 10/- each, 2/- damages and 12/6 costs or two months' hard labour in Horsley house of correction. Offence committed 7 Feb. 1829.

48/B/44 23 Feb. 1829. Patience Ayer, prostitute. Riotous behaviour in Stroud. H. Burgh JP at Stroud. One month's hard labour in Horsley house of correction. Offence committed 20 Feb. 1829.

48/B/45 23 Jan. 1829. Henry Davis of Bisley, labourer. Damaging the stool of a tree in a wood, the property of the feoffees of the charity lands of Bisley. H. Burgh JP at Stroud. Fine 3*d*. damages and 8/6 costs or two months' hard labour in Horsley house of correction. Offence committed 21 Jan. 1829.

48/B/46 23 Jan. 1829. Henry Perrott and Edward Goodship of Bisley, labourers. Damaging the stool of a tree in a wood, the property of the feoffees of the charity lands of Bisley. H. Burgh JP at Stroud. Fine 3*d*. each damages and 9/6 costs or two months' hard labour in Horsley house of correction. Offence committed 7 Jan. 1829.

48/B/47 3 March 1829. Samuel Warner of Acton Turville, timber merchant. Using a gun and a dog to kill game in Hinton. W. Davies D.D. JP, commissioner for taxes, at Berkeley. John Powell, gamekeeper, of Hinton, witness. Fine £20. Offence committed 29 Jan. 1829.

48/B/48 17 Feb. 1829. Thomas Ireland of Winchcombe, alehouse keeper. Permitting drunkenness and gaming on his premises, the White Lion public house, Winchcombe, in breach of his licence. J. Timbrill D.D. JP and Rev. J. Hurd JP. First offence. Fine £2 10*s*. and 16/- costs. Offence committed 28 Jan. 1829.

48/B/49 12 Nov. 1827 [*late return*]. James Hall. Entering the workhouse at Bromsberrow with his wife Ann without an order. Causing a riot during which he verbally abused the governor. Refusing to provide for himself and his wife though able to do so. Rev. J. Commeline JP. Three weeks' hard labour in Littledean house of correction. Offence committed 31 Oct. 1827.

48/B/50 17 March 1829. Philip Edwards. Taking a quantity of stakes from a fence at Bromsberrow, the property of Mrs. Brooke, thereby causing considerable damage. Rev. Joseph Higgins JP at Ledbury, Herefs. Fine 10/- and 7/6 costs, the latter to be paid to Lancelot Burrup, or one month in Gloucester house of correction. Offence committed 16 March 1829.

48/B/51 6 March 1829. Jacob [*also named as* James] Gale and Eli Fry. Assaulting Edward Young, schoolmaster, and his sons Frederick and Charles at Tormarton. Rev. I. W. W. Horlock JP and Rev. F. Pelly JP at a Petty Sessions held at the Cross Hands inn, Old Sodbury. Fine £1 10*s*. and 7/- respectively and 5/- costs each, to be paid immediately. Offence committed Sunday evening 1st March 1829.

48/B/52 30 Jan. 1829. Robert Derrett the younger of Wotton under Edge, clothier. Paying or causing to be paid to James Smith, weaver, of Wotton under Edge £1 wages in other than lawful coin. W. M. Adey JP, P. B. Purnell JP and H. W. Dyer JP at Wotton under Edge. Fine £20.

48/B/53 30 Jan. 1829. Isaac Cooper of Wotton under Edge, weaver. Paying or causing to be paid to Jesse Burford, weaver, of Wotton under Edge £1 5s. wages in other than lawful coin. W. M. Adey JP, P. B. Purnell JP and H. W. Dyer JP at Wotton under Edge. Fine £20.

48/B/54 3 April 1829. William Rowland. Vagrancy. Found at night hidden in an outhouse, the property of Thomas Stephens, baker, of Little Barrington. George Talbot, Lord Dynevor, JP at [Great] Barrington. Offender said he was looking for work and living by asking relief from house to house. One month's hard labour. Offence committed 2 April 1829.

48/B/55 29 Dec. 1828. Robert Saunders of Westbury on Trym, attorney. Using three greyhounds to kill a hare on land in Tormarton in the occupation of Joseph Bennett and John Arnold. Rev. F. Pelly JP, informed at Siston rectory by Thomas Webb, gamekeeper to the duke of Beaufort. Offender summoned to a Petty Sessions before the above JP and Rev. T. Jones JP at the Cross Hands inn, Old Sodbury. Asked for an adjournment which was granted. At a Petty Sessions held at the Swan inn, Chipping Sodbury, before Rev. F. Pelly JP, Rev. T. Brooke JP and W. Blathwayt JP offender offered deeds purporting to show ownership of land in Somerset. Witnesses: George Walters of Acton Turville, under-gamekeeper to the duke of Beaufort, John Pearce Morris, land valuer, and John Norvall of East Brent, Som. Fine £5. Offence committed 28 Oct. 1828.

48/B/56 6 Feb. 1829. Thomas James of Walcot, Som., keeper of livery stables. Shooting a pheasant at Dyrham and Hinton. Rev. F. Pelly JP and Rev. T. Brooke JP at a Petty Sessions held at the Cross Hands inn, Old Sodbury. William Eels of Dyrham and Hinton, informer. Offender admitted charge. Fine £5. Offence committed 6 Dec. 1828.

48/B/57 6 March 1829. Edwin Bendall of Old Sodbury, cattle dealer. Shooting a pheasant at Wapley and Codrington, Rev. F. Pelly JP and Rev. I. W. W. Horlock JP at a Petty Sessions held at the Cross Hands inn, Old Sodbury. George Dyer of Dodington, informer. Francis Evans of Wapley and Codrington, witness. Offender protested that witness could not have seen him as the hedge was too high. Fine £5. Offence committed 14 Jan. 1829.

48/C/1 11 May 1829. Joseph Clarke the younger of Newent. Assaulting Sarah Morgan, spinster, of Newent. Rev. R. F. Onslow JP at Newent. Fine £2 2s., to be paid immediately to Samuel Wood, guardian of the poor of Newent, and 3/- costs to Sarah Morgan. Offence committed 6 May 1829.

48/C/2 15 June 1829. William and Maria Paling. Assaulting Joseph Stevens at Sherborne. Rev. F. E. Witts JP and Rev. R. W. Ford JP at Northleach. William fined £5, Maria fined £1 and £2.50 costs, or two months in Northleach house of correction. Offence committed 10 June 1829.

48/C/3 9 July 1829. Jason Neat. Cutting down three trees at Bitton. H. W. Newman JP and J. S. Harford JP at Lawfords Gate sessions room. Fine 1/6 and 6/-, the value of the trees; 18/6 costs to be paid to the complainants Henry Pedlingham and Aaron Cole. Offence committed 8 April 1829.

48/C/4 21 Jan. 1829. Robert Hayes of Sherston, Wilts., labourer. Keeping and using a gun to kill game at Leighterton and Boxwell. G. P. Holford JP at Tetbury. Information laid before R. Kingscote JP on 7 Jan. by Joseph York. Witness: Charles Emerson, gentleman, of Sherston. Offender did not appear. Fine £5. Offence committed 5 Jan. 1829.

48/C/5 1 July 1829. John Pool the younger. Not having proper control of his horse and cart on the Bath turnpike road in Cirencester. Rev. D. Lysons JP. Fine 10/-. Offence committed 26 June 1829.

48/C/6   1 July 1829. Richard Cox. Evading a toll of 7½d. by removing one horse from his wagon while passing through Dunkirk turnpike gate at Hawkesbury. Rev. D. Lysons JP. Fine 10/- and 15/- costs. Offence committed 11 April 1829.

48/C/7   1 July 1829. Nathaniel Fletcher. Evading a toll of 4½d. by taking his horse and cart off the road and passing over the duke of Beaufort's land near Dunkirk gate at Hawkesbury. Rev. D. Lysons JP. Fine 10/- and 10/- costs. Offence committed 6 June 1829.

48/C/8   18 Feb. 1829. Joseph Earl of Horsley, labourer. Keeping and using a greyhound to kill game. R. Kingscote JP and Rev. D. Lysons JP at Tetbury. Henry Hall, labourer, of Horsley, informer. Defendant declined to speak. Fine £5. Offence committed 1 Feb. 1829.

48/C/9   18 June 1829. Mary Ann King. Receiving from Sarah Martin a quantity of dead fence stolen from Shipton Moyne, the property of George Emerson. W. M. Paul JP at Tetbury. Fine 1/- and 1/6 costs or fourteen days in Horsley house of correction. Offence committed 18 June 1829.

48/C/10   18 June 1829. Mary Parker. Stealing (with others) a quantity of dead fence at Shipton Moyne, the property of George Emerson. W. M. Paul JP at Tetbury. Fine £5 or two months in Horsley house of correction. Offence committed night of 17 June 1829.

48/C/11   18 June 1829. Harriet Parker. Stealing [*etc.*, *as* 48/C/10].

48/C/12   18 June 1829. Sarah Martin [*etc.*, *as* 48/C/10].

48/C/13   18 June 1829. Mary Lamb [*etc.*, *as* 48/C/10].

48/C/14   18 June 1829. George Parker [*etc.*, *as* 48/C/10].

48/C/15   18 Feb. 1829. Thomas Howes. Evading a toll of 10½d. by adding one horse to his cart after passing through Tetbury south turnpike gate. Rev. D. Lysons JP. Fine 30/- and 15/- costs, to be paid within two weeks, or two months in Horsley house of correction. Offence committed Friday 6 Feb. 1829.

48/C/16   2 Feb. 1829. Richard Capner. Assaulting William Dyke, grocer, of Tetbury. G. P. Holford JP and W. M. Paul JP at Westonbirt. Fine £2 2s., to be paid to John Warn, overseer of the poor of Tetbury, and 15/- costs to the complainant, to be paid by the following day, or one month in Horsley house of correction. Offence committed 24 Jan. 1829.

48/C/17   16 June 1829. Richard Nicholls. Failing to support his wife and two children for the previous ten weeks thereby leaving them chargeable to the parish of Stroud. H. Burgh JP at Stroud. One calendar month in Horsley house of correction.

48/C/18   2 Jan. 1829. Samuel Critchley, Mary Critchley, John Carless and Edith Carless, all of Randwick. Assaulting Charles Whittick at Randwick. Rev. P. Hawker JP and W. H. Hyett JP at Stroud. Fine £1 each and 17/6 costs or two months in Horsley house of correction. Offence committed 24 Dec. 1828.

48/C/19   2 Jan. 1829. Thomas Critchley of Randwick, labourer. Assaulting Charles Vick at Randwick. Rev. P. Hawker JP and W. H. Hyett JP. Fine £1 and 8/- costs or two months in Horsley house of correction. Offence committed 24 Dec. 1828.

48/C/20   10 March 1829. James Owen of Stonehouse, bargeman. Assaulting Daniel Robins, clothworker, of King's Stanley at Stonehouse. H. Burgh JP and W. H. Hyett JP at Stroud. Fine 5/- and 7/- costs or two months in Horsley house of correction. Offence committed 6 March 1829.

48/C/21   10 March 1829. John Cratchley, William Cratchley, labourers, and James Owen, bargeman, all of Stonehouse. Assaulting William Park, clothworker, of King's Stanley, at Stonehouse. H. Burgh JP and W. H. Hyett JP at Stroud. John Cratchley fined 10/- and the others 5/- each and 14/- costs or two months' hard labour in Horsley house of correction. Offence committed 6 March 1829.

48/C/22   10 March 1829. William Cratchley of Stonehouse, labourer, and Charles Bick of King's Stanley, clothworker. Assaulting William Robins, clothworker, of King's Stanley at Stonehouse. H. Burgh JP and W. H. Hyett JP at Stroud. Fine 5/- and 2/6 respectively and 10/6 costs, or two months' hard labour in Horsley house of correction. Offence committed 6 March 1829.

48/C/23   8 July 1829. Jesse Bown of Horsley, labourer. Stealing seven fish from a pond adjoining Thomas, Lord Ducie's house in Woodchester. H. Burgh JP at Stroud. Fine £2 and 7/- costs or two calendar months in Horsley house of correction. Offence committed 7 July 1829.

48/C/24   11 July 1829. John Bown of Woodchester, weaver. Stealing a quantity of tree limbs valued at 6d. from a park at Woodchester, the property of Thomas, Lord Ducie. H. Burgh JP at Stroud. Fine 5/- and 7/- costs or two months' hard labour in Horsley house of correction. Offence committed 11 July 1829.

48/C/25   29 April 1829. John Kemish of Minchinhampton, weaver. Breaking and stealing part of two timber trees, the property of Robert Snow Paul Esq. at Minchinhampton. H. Burgh JP at Stroud. Fine 5/-, 2/6 damages and 9/- costs or six weeks' hard labour in Horsley house of correction. Offence committed 24 April 1829.

48/C/26   12 June 1829. Elijah Brampton. Begging in Stroud. H. Burgh JP at Stroud. One calendar month's hard labour in Horsley house of correction. Offence committed 11 June 1829.

48/C/27   22 May 1829. Samuel Turner of Stroud, labourer. Cutting down four beech trees in a plantation at Rodborough, the property Richard Smith, clothier. H. Burgh JP at Stroud. Fine £1 10s., 4/- (the value of the trees) and 10/- costs, or six weeks' hard labour in Horsley house of correction. Offence committed 11 May 1829.

48/C/28   22 May 1829. Samuel Merrett and Charles Chandler of Randwick, labourers. Cutting down two fir trees in a plantation at Randwick, the property of Henry Hogg Esq. H. Burgh JP at Stroud. Fine 2/6 each, an additional 2/- each (the value of the trees) and 12/6 costs, or two calendar months in Horsley house of correction. Offence committed 5 May 1829.

48/C/29   8 May 1829. Thomas Lane of Painswick, labourer. Stealing part of a tree, the property of John Haynes and John Barnard, at Painswick. Rev. P. Hawker JP and W. H. Hyett JP at Stroud. Fine 2/6, 1/- (the value of the wood) and 10/6 costs, or one calendar month's hard labour in Horsley house of correction. Offence committed 28 April 1829.

48/C/30   8 May 1829. Henry Wright of Painswick, labourer. Stealing part [etc., as 48/C/29].

48/C/31   27 March 1829. William Chapman of Rodborough, baker. Delivering and selling six underweight loaves to Thomas Powell, weaver, of Rodborough. H. Burgh JP and W. H. Hyett JP. Fine £4. Offence committed 26 March 1829.

48/C/32   19 June 1829. Thomas Wright of Painswick, labourer. Violently and indecently assaulting Elizabeth, infant daughter of Thomas Horlick, weaver, and Mary his wife of Painswick. H. Burgh JP and W. H. Hyett JP at Stroud. Fine £5 or two calendar months in Horsley house of correction. Offence committed 16 June 1829.

48/C/33   19 June 1829. Christopher Patchett of Stroud, labourer. Assaulting Richard Pegler of Stroud, hairdresser. H. Burgh JP, W. H. Hyett JP and Rev. P. Hawker JP at Stroud. Fine £1 and 9/- costs or two calendar months' hard labour in Horsley house of correction. Offence committed 8 June 1829.

48/C/34   30 April 1829. William Smart of Bisley, clothier. Paying or causing to be paid 2/7 in wages to Robert Butt, weaver, of Bisley in other than lawful coin. H. Burgh JP and W. H. Hyett JP at Stroud. Fine £20.

48/C/35   30 April 1829. Aaron Evans of Bisley, clothier. Paying or causing to be paid 2/1 in wages to Thomas Young, weaver, of Bisley in other than lawful coin. H. Burgh JP and W. H. Hyett at Stroud. Fine £20.

48/C/36   — May 1829. William Swaine of Painswick, labourer. Stealing a tree branch at Painswick, the property of John Haynes and John Barnard. W. H. Hyett JP at Painswick. Fine 1/-, 6d. (the value of the tree) and 7/6 costs, or seven days' hard labour in Horsley house of correction. Offence committed 28 April 1829.

48/C/37   6 July 1829. Isaac Pitt. Neglecting his wife and two children, whereby they became chargeable to Stroud parish. H. Burgh JP at Stroud. One calendar month's hard labour in Horsley house of correction.

48/C/38   7 July 1829. James Pearce of Randwick, labourer. Assaulting Samuel Browning, constable of Randwick, in the performance of his duty. H. Burgh JP and Rev. P. Hawker JP at Stroud. Fine £5 or two months in Horsley house of correction. Offence committed 3 July 1829.

48/C/39   24 June 1829. Mary wife of Richard Jaques. Stealing four cabbages valued at 6d. from a garden in Maugersbury, the property of Thomas Ballinger. E. Leigh JP at Stow on the Wold. Hard labour for three calendar months in Northleach house of correction. Offence committed 23 June 1829.

48/C/40   10 July 1829. Charles Ballinger and George Drinkwater, labourers, of Dumbleton, and George Warner, butcher, of Stanton. Stealing a quantity of cherries from a garden in Dumbleton, the property of James Marshall. J. Timbrill D.D. JP at Ford. Fine 5/- each, to be paid to the overseers of the poor at Dumbleton, and 5/6 each costs to be paid to the complainant. Fines paid. Offence committed 8 June 1829

48/C/41   16 May 1829. John Archer of Cirencester, dyer. Stealing asparagus plants from a garden in Cirencester, the property of William Lawrence Esq. W. Croome JP at Cirencester. Hard labour for three months in Northleach house of correction. Offence committed 16 May 1829.

48/C/42   11 May 1829. William Symonds the younger. Assaulting James Rudge at the hundred of St. Briavels. Rev. C. Crawley JP and J. Pyrke JP at Newnham. Fine £1, to be paid to John Lucas of Newnham, and 7/6 costs, or one month in Littledean house of correction. Offence committed 9 May 1829.

48/C/43   22 June 1829. John Thomas. Assaulting John Martin at Newnham. Rev. C. Crawley JP and J. Pyrke JP at Newnham. Fine 10/-, to be paid to James Hill, and 16/6 costs, or one calendar month in Littledean house of correction. Offence committed 18 June 1829.

48/C/44   25 May 1829. John James junior. Assaulting Hannah James at Minsterworth. Rev. C. Crawley JP and J. Pyrke JP at Newnham. Fine £4 12s., to be paid to Thomas Hobbs, overseer of the poor of Minsterworth, and 8/- costs, or two calendar months in Littledean house of correction. Offence committed 14 May 1829.

48/C/45   23 June 1829. James Davis. Assaulting Rebecca wife of Samuel Saunders at Tidenham. Rt. Hon. C. Bathurst JP and Rev. T. Thomas JP at Lydney. Fine 10/-, to be paid to John Cadle, overseer of the poor of Tidenham, and 5/6 costs, or one month in Littledean house of correction. Offence committed 14 June 1829.

48/C/46   26 May 1829. Joseph Davis of Woolaston. Assaulting James Harris at Woolaston. Rt. Hon. C. Bathurst JP and Rev. T. Thomas JP at Lydney. Fine 12/6, to be paid to Richard Smith, overseer of the poor of Woolaston, and 7/6 costs, or one calendar month in Littledean house of correction. Offence committed 15 April 1829.

48/C/47   23 June 1829. George Nash. Assaulting Sophia Jones at Coleford, Newland. Rt. Hon. C. Bathurst JP and Rev. T. Thomas JP at Lydney. Fine 10/-, to be paid to James Teague, overseer of the poor of Newland, and 9/6 costs, or 14 days in Littledean house of correction. Offence committed 20 June 1829.

48/C/48   26 May 1829. John Dibden. Cutting and stealing a quantity of wood at Tidenham, the property of the duke of Beaufort. Rev. T. Thomas JP at Lydney. Fine 12/6, to be paid to John Cadle, overseer of the poor, 5/- (the value of the wood) and 7/6 costs to be paid to the complainant, Samuel Luff, or one calendar month in Littledean house of correction. Offence committed 17 April 1829.

48/C/49   26 May 1829. Thomas Dibden. Cutting and stealing [*etc.*, *as* 48/C/48].

48/C/50   14 May 1829. Henry Cratchley. Begging at Cheltenham. R. Capper JP at Cheltenham. One month's hard labour in Northleach house of correction. Offence committed 13 May 1829.

48/C/51   10 July 1829. Henry Cratchley. Begging at Cheltenham. R. Capper JP at Cheltenham. Second offence. [*Cf.* 48/C/50.] Three months' hard labour in Northleach house of correction. Offence committed 9 July 1829.

48/C/52   20 June 1829. John Wither Bevan. Assaulting William Nostaw at Thornbury. S. P. Peach JP and W. N. Tonge JP at Thornbury. Fine 2/6 and 2/6 costs. Offence committed 18 June 1829.

48/C/53   6 June 1829. John Phillips. Assaulting William Holloway at Thornbury. S. P. Peach JP and W. N. Tonge JP at Thornbury. Fine 2/6 and 5/6 costs. Offence committed 13 May 1829

48/C/54   6 June 1829. Edward Woodward. Assaulting James Collins at Elberton. S. P. Peach JP and W. N. Tonge JP at Thornbury. Fine £2 10*s*. and 10/- costs. Offence committed 19 May 1829.

48/C/55   6 July 1829. Thomas Cambray of Stow on the Wold, labourer. Assaulting Joseph Biddle, labourer, of Blockley, Worcs., at Weston Subedge. Rev. J. R. Hall JP and Rev. J. Adams JP at Bourton on the Hill. Fine £1 17*s*. 6*d*., to be paid to William Eden, overseer of the poor of Weston Subedge, and 12/6 costs. Offence committed 12 June 1829.

48/C/56   23 June 1829. Joseph Plumb, late of Over Norton, Oxon., labourer. Sleeping while in sole charge of a wagon and horses at Little Compton on the turnpike road from Moreton in Marsh to Chipping Norton. Rev. J. Adams JP. Fine 20/-. Offence committed 12 June 1829.

48/C/57   8 June 1829. David Rymel of Longborough, farmer. Assaulting Sally and Caroline Rose of Longborough. Rev. W. Boughton JP and Rev. J. R. Hall JP at Bourton on the Hill. Fine 10/-, to be paid to David Rymill, overseer of the poor, and 8/6 costs, or one week in Northleach house of correction. Offence committed 3 June 1829.

48/C/58   6 July 1829. Samuel Shorey of Broadway, Worcs., labourer. Assaulting Joseph Biddle, labourer, of Blockley, Worcs., at Weston Subedge. Rev. J. R. Hall JP and Rev. J. Adams JP at Bourton on the Hill. Fine £1 17*s*. 6*d*., to be paid to William Eden, overseer of the poor, and 12/6 costs, to be paid by 3 Aug., or two months in Northleach house of correction. Offence committed 12 June 1829.

48/C/59   7 May 1829. Benjamin Webley of Westbury on Trym. Using two greyhounds to take and kill game. C. L. Walker JP and H. W. Newman JP at Lawfords Gate sessions room, commissioners for assessed taxes. Fine £10 and 9/- costs. Offence committed 22 April 1829.

48/C/60 1 May 1829. John Bishop of Little Badminton, labourer. Committing assault and battery on Robert Morse in Horton. F. Trotman JP and Rev. F. Pelly JP at a Petty Sessions held at the Cross Hands inn, Old Sodbury. Fine 4/6 and 5/6 costs. Offence committed 12 April 1829.

48/C/61 4 July 1829. John Hanwell of Bourton on the Water. Keeping and using a snare to kill game. Rev. F. E. Witts JP at Upper Slaughter. William Kimber, miller, of Bourton on the Water, informer. Richard Abbitts, gardener, of Bourton on the Water, witness. Offender did not appear. Fine £5. Offence committed 2 July 1829.

48/D/1 6 Aug. 1829. William Bateman. Assaulting Charles Lewis, labourer, at Bitton. W. Munro JP and V. J. Graeme JP at Lawfords Gate sessions room. Fine 5/- and 8/- costs or 14 days in Lawfords Gate house of correction. Offence committed 30 July 1829.

48/D/2 6 Aug. 1829. William Hutson. Assaulting Hannah Sutton, single woman, at Bitton. W. Munro JP and V. J. Graeme JP at Lawfords Gate sessions room. Fine 10/- and 8/- costs or three weeks in Lawfords Gate house of correction. Offence committed 4 Aug. 1829.

48/D/3 13 Aug. 1829. Charles Knight of St. Philip and St. Jacob, Bristol, victualler. Failing to keep good order in his house and premises. H. W. Newman JP and V. J. Graeme JP. Fine 10/- and 6/6 costs. Offence committed 1 Aug. 1829.

48/D/4 13 Aug. 1829. Charles Smith of St. Philip and St. Jacob, Bristol, victualler. Failing to keep good order [*etc.*, *as* 48/D/3].

48/D/5 23 July 1829. John Hollister. Assaulting James Fowler of Frampton Cotterell. J. Haythorne JP and J. Vaughan JP at Lawfords Gate sessions room. Fine 20/-, to be paid to an overseer of the poor at Frampton Cotterell, and 8/- costs, or two months in Lawfords Gate house of correction. Offence committed 9 July 1829.

48/D/6 13 Aug. 1829. Henry Edwards of St. Philip and St. Jacob, Bristol, victualler. Failing to keep good order in his house and premises. H. W. Newman JP and V. J. Graeme JP. First offence. Fine 10/- and 6/6 costs. Offence committed 1 Aug. 1829.

48/D/7 17 Sept. 1829. Thomas Gum. Assaulting Ann Wyatt of St. Philip and St. Jacob, [Bristol]. G. Hilhouse JP and H. W. Newman JP at Lawfords Gate sessions room. Fine 1/- and 6/6 costs or seven days in Lawfords Gate house of correction. Offence committed 7 Sept. 1829.

48/D/8 8 Oct. 1829. John Tyler. Assaulting Ann Brock of Shirehampton, single woman. J. Haythorne JP and H. W. Newman JP at Lawfords Gate sessions room. Fine £3 19s. and £1 1s. costs or two calendar months in Lawfords Gate house of correction. Offence committed 5 Oct. 1829.

48/D/9 15 Oct. 1829. James Bennett. Assaulting Thomas Legg of St. Philip and St. Jacob, [Bristol], locksmith. J. Haythorne JP and H. W. Newman JP at Lawfords Gate sessions room. Fine 12/6 and 7/6 costs or one calendar month in Lawfords Gate house of correction. Offence committed 8 Oct. 1829.

48/D/10 15 Oct. 1829. Thomas Ball. Assaulting John Hurley of Clifton, tap keeper. J. Haythorne JP and H. W. Newman JP at Lawfords Gate sessions room. Fine 12/6 and 7/6 costs or one calendar month in Lawfords Gate house of correction. Offence committed 10 Oct. 1829.

48/D/11 15 Oct. 1829. Peregrine Rosling. Assaulting Joseph Naish, gentleman, of St. James, [Bristol], at Horfield. J. Haythorne JP and H. W. Newman JP at Lawfords Gate sessions room. Fine £1 and 9/6 costs or seven days in Lawfords Gate house of correction. Offence committed 12 Oct. 1829.

48/D/12 15 Oct. 1829. Benjamin Wait. Assaulting Mark Flook of St. George, [Bristol], labourer. J. Haythorne JP and H. W. Newman JP at Lawfords Gate sessions room. Fine 10/- and 8/- costs or one calendar month in Lawfords Gate house of correction. Offence committed 12 Oct. 1829.

48/D/13 15 Oct. 1829. Henry Fussell. Assaulting Mark Flook [*etc.*, *as* 48/D/12].

48/D/14 1 Oct. 1829. George Lewis. Assaulting Joseph Lewis of St. Philip and St. Jacob, [Bristol], labourer. J. Haythorne JP and J. Lewis JP at Lawfords Gate sessions room. Fine 5/- and 7/6 costs or one month in Lawfords Gate house of correction. Offence committed 29 Sept. 1829.

48/D/15 26 Aug. 1829. George Brimble. Assaulting James King of Mangotsfield, labourer. J. Haythorne JP and J. Savage JP at Lawfords Gate sessions room. Fine £1 7s. and 9/- costs or one month in Lawfords Gate house of correction. Offence committed 23 Aug. 1829.

48/D/16 1 Oct. 1829. William Wright. Assaulting Joseph Lewis [*etc.*, *as* 48/D/14].

48/D/17 1 Oct. 1829. George Jones. Assaulting Joseph Lewis [*etc.*, *as* 48/D/14].

48/D/18 1 Oct. 1829. Henry Pinker. Assaulting Joseph Lewis [*etc.*, *as* 48/D/14].

48/D/19 1 Oct. 1829. Thomas Jones. Assaulting Joseph Lewis [*etc.*, *as* 48/D/14].

48/D/20 26 Aug. 1829. John Sheppard. Assaulting James King [*etc.*, *as* 48/D/15 *except*] Fine £4 11s. and 9/- costs or two calendar months in Lawfords Gate house of correction.

48/D/21 3 Sept. 1829. Charles Wilks. Assaulting Henry Jones of Mangotsfield, yeoman. G. Goldney JP and G. Hilhouse JP at Lawfords Gate sessions room. Fine 10/- and 8/- costs or one calendar month in Lawfords Gate house of correction. Offence committed 28 Aug. 1829.

48/D/22 24 Sept. 1829. James Brison. Assaulting Mary Ann wife of William Coulstring of St. James, [Bristol]. G. Goldney JP and J. Parker JP at Lawfords Gate sessions room. Fine 5/- and 7/6 costs or seven days in Lawfords Gate house of correction. Offence committed 21 Sept. 1829.

48/D/23 3 Sept. 1829. George Dando. Assaulting Henry Jones of Mangotsfield, yeoman. G. Goldney JP and G. Hilhouse JP at Lawfords Gate sessions room. Fine 10/- and 8/- costs or one calendar month in Lawfords Gate house of correction. Offence committed 28 Aug. 1829.

48/D/24 20 Aug. 1829. Luke Bryant. Assaulting George Bailey of Henbury, labourer. G. Goldney JP and H. W. Newman JP at Lawfords Gate sessions room. Fine £4 12s. and 8/- costs or two calendar months in Lawfords Gate house of correction. Offence committed 31 July 1829.

48/D/25 6 Aug. 1829. John Saunders of St. Philip and St. Jacob, [Bristol], victualler. Failing to keep good order in his house and premises. H. W. Newman JP and W. Munro JP. First offence. Fine 10/- and 5/6 costs. Offence committed 1 Aug. 1829.

48/D/26 6 Aug. 1829. John Kelly of St. Philip and St. Jacob, [Bristol], victualler. Failing [*etc.*, *as* 48/D/25].

48/D/27 10 Sept. 1829. William Price of Bitton, victualler. Keeping his house open during the usual afternoon hours of divine service. H. W. Newman JP and G. Goldney JP. First offence. Fine £1 and 8/- costs. Offence committed 23 Aug. 1829.

48/D/28 16 July 1829. John Morse, John Pegler and Daniel Beard, labourers, of Stroud. Stealing a quantity of currants growing in a garden at Stroud, the property of Thomas Newcombe, clothier. H. Burgh JP at Stroud. Six months' each hard labour in Horsley house of correction. Offence committed 14 July 1829.

48/D/29 8 Oct. 1829. William Lett, stage-coach proprietor and driver. Carrying two more outside passengers than the seven allowed by law between Cheltenham and Gloucester. Joseph Ellis Viner JP and Henry Norwood Trye JP at the public office, Cheltenham. George Martin, yeoman, of Oxford Street, Mile End Old Town, Middx., informer. Charles Digby, witness. Fine £40 mitigated to £20 and 7/- costs to go to the informer. Offence committed 28 Sept. 1829.

48/D/30 8 Oct. 1829. Thomas Evans, stage-coach proprietor and driver. Carrying [etc., as 48/D/29].

48/D/31 13 Aug. 1829. James Morgan of Cheltenham, carpenter. Selling beer, to be drunk on his premises, without a licence. R. Capper JP and J. E. Viner JP. Fine £10 and 6/- costs. Offence committed 7 Aug. 1829.

48/D/32 20 Aug. 1829. James Morgan of Cheltenham, carpenter. Selling beer, to be drunk on his premises, without a licence. J. Clutterbuck JP and R. Capper JP. Fine £5 and 11/- costs. Offence committed 15 Aug. 1829.

48/D/33 15 Sept. 1829. Eliakim Jones of Cheltenham, coal merchant. Selling cider, to be drunk on his premises, without a licence. J. E. Viner JP and R. Capper JP. Fine £5 and £1 9s. costs. Offence committed 5 Aug. 1829.

48/D/34 13 Aug. 1829. John Wilkes of Bishop's Cleeve, yeoman. Selling cider, to be drunk on his premises, without a licence. R. Capper JP and J. E. Viner JP. Fine £5 and 12/- costs. Offence committed 23 July 1829.

48/D/35 19 Aug. 1829. Ann Chandler. Receiving half a peck of apples at Cheltenham, the property of John Yeend. R. Capper JP at Cheltenham. Fine £5, to be paid to Peter Butt, overseer of the poor, and 15/- costs, or three calendar months in Northleach house of correction. Offence committed 18 Aug. 1829.

48/D/36 12 Sept. 1829. Peter Romino, hawker. Exposing baskets for sale at Dowdeswell without a licence. Rev. J. Neale JP at Cheltenham. Joseph Atkins of Worcester, inspector of hawkers' licences, informer. William King, witness. Offender pleaded not guilty. Fine £10. Offence committed 11 Sept. 1829. [Note:] 18/- king's moiety of penalty, 36/- being all [that was] received.

48/D/37 12 Sept. 1829. Peter McLory of Cheltenham, yeoman. Exposing for sale a quantity of tablecloths, brown holland, check dowlas, calico and stockings without a licence at Dowdeswell. Rev. J. Neale JP at Cheltenham. William King of Bristol, inspector of hawkers' licences, informer. Joseph Atkins, witness. Offender pleaded not guilty. Fine £10. Offence committed 11 Sept. 1829. [Note:] £1 king's moiety of penalty.

48/D/38 16 Oct. 1829. Thomas Pierce, James Pierce the younger, Joseph Pierce and Samuel Lewis. Stealing a quantity of potatoes growing in an enclosed field at Moreton Valence, the property of Anne Hawkins. R. S. Davies JP at Stonehouse. Each fined 10/-, 15/- (the value of the potatoes) and 5/- costs; 15/- and all the costs to go to the complainant and the residue £10 5s. [sic, recte £4 5s.] to Henry Hewlett, overseer of the poor, or one month's hard labour in Horsley house of correction. Offence committed 15 Oct. 1829.

48/D/39 6 Oct. 1829. Samuel Ridler. Stealing a fence-post at Standish, the property of Thomas Parker. T. J. Lloyd Baker JP at Hardwicke. Fine £5 and 1/- (the value of the post) or one week's hard labour in Horsley house of correction. Offence committed 3 Oct. 1829.

48/D/40 15 Sept. 1829. William Jenkins. Damaging a door, the property of John Watkins of St. Briavels. Rev. T. Thomas JP at Lydney. Fine £2 and 6/6 (the value of the door), to be paid within 14 days, or two months' hard labour in Littledean house of correction. Offence committed 4 Sept. 1829.

48/D/41 15 Sept. 1829. John Worgan. Stealing underwood at Tidenham, the property of the duke of Beaufort. Rev. T. Thomas JP at Lydney. Fine 10/- costs and 1/6 (the value of the underwood) or two months' hard labour in Littledean house of correction. Offence committed 18 Aug. 1829.

48/D/42 3 Aug. 1829. Joseph Wadley. Assaulting Thomas Painter at Awre, Blakeney. Rev. C. Crawley JP and J. Pyrke JP at Newnham. Fine 5/ and 11/- costs or two months in Littledean house of correction. Offence committed 18 July 1829.

48/D/43 12 Oct. 1829. William Watts. Assaulting Edwin Bowles at Rodley. Rev. C. Crawley JP and J. Pyrke JP at Newnham. Fine £2 and 10/- costs or two months in Littledean house of correction. Offence committed 26 Sept. 1829.

48/D/44 3 Aug. 1829. Richard Jones. Unlawful possession of part of a tree in St. Briavels hundred. Rev. C. Crawley JP at Newnham. Fine £1 10s., to be paid to the overseer of the poor at Littledean, and 10/- costs and 2/- (the value of the the wood) to go to E. Machen Esq., or two months' hard labour in Littledean house of correction. Offence committed 17 July 1829.

48/D/45 17 Sept. 1829. Thomas Hathaway, labourer, of Lower Swell, aided and abetted by William Wilcox, labourer, of the same. Using a snare to kill a rabbit in a field in Lower Swell occupied by John Shirley. Rev. F. E. Witts JP at Stow on the Wold. Fine £10 each. Offence committed 11 Sept. 1829.

48/D/46 15 Oct. 1829. Michael Jownley. Stealing pears from an orchard in Little Barrington, the property of Marmaduke Matthews. Rev F. E. Witts JP at Stow on the Wold. Fine 7/6, 5/6 costs and 6d. (the value of the pears). Offence committed 28 Sept. 1829.

48/D/47 12 Oct. 1829. William Clifford, Daniel Shillam, William Beale and Thomas son of Robert Collett, yeoman, of Bourton on the Water, labourers. Damaging a gate, the property of John Poole and James Ashwin, churchwardens of Bourton on the Water. Rev. F. E. Witts JP and Rev. John Croome JP at Bourton on the Water. Each fined 20/-, to be paid to Thomas Wilkins, constable, and 3/- costs and 3d. damages to go to the complainants. Given four days to pay. Offence committed 8 Oct. 1829.

48/D/48 2 Sept. 1829. Hannah Stratford, toll-collector at Sudeley gate. Charging John Attwood, farmer, of Sudeley Castle, 4/- for eight horses although he was exempt. J. Timbrill D.D. JP, Rev. J. Keysall JP and Rev. C. White JP. Fine 40/-. Offence committed 26 Aug. 1829.

48/D/49 8 Aug. 1829. George Morris. Shooting and killing a pointer bitch in a field, the property of the Rev. David Charles Parry of Kemerton. J. Timbrill D.D. JP at Beckford. Dog valued at £5. Fine £5, to be paid to Charles Tidmarsh, overseer of the poor of Kemerton, or two months in Northleach house of correction. Offence committed 7 Aug. 1829. [*Note on back*:] Offender committed to house of correction.

48/D/50 4 Aug. 1829. William Piffe. Digging up potatoes from Stoke Moor, Elmstone Hardwicke, with intent to steal, the property of George Yeend, farmer. J. Timbrill D.D. JP at Beckford. Fine 10/-, to be paid to James Chadd, overseer of the poor, £1 10s. costs and 1/6 damages to go to the complainant, or two months in Northleach house of correction. Offence committed 7 July 1829.

48/D/51   2 Sept. 1829. William Tomkins the elder, William Tomkins the younger and Richard Tomkins. Stealing a quantity of apples from Cumberwood field in Forthampton in the occupation of John Rayer, farmer. J. Timbrill D.D. JP and Rev. J. Keysall JP at Tewkesbury. Fine 20/-, to be paid to Edward Knight, overseer of the poor, and to pay 13/6 costs and 1/- damages to the complainant. Offence committed Sunday 30 Aug. 1829.

48/D/52   30 Sept. 1829. Betty and Honor Mayall, wife and daughter of Joseph Mayall, labourer, of Forthampton. Stealing a quantity of rails from an enclosure in Forthampton, the property of William Rayer, farmer, of Longdon, Worcs. J. Timbrill D.D. JP and Rev. J. Keysall JP at Tewkesbury. Fine 25/-, to be paid to John Cotterell, overseer of the poor, 14/- costs and 1/- damages to go to the complainant, or two months in Northleach house of correction. Offence committed Tuesday 15 Sept. 1829.

48/D/53   7 August 1829. Thomas Shugar of Lechlade, victualler. Failing to observe the conditions of his recognizance. Hon. J. Dutton JP, John Raymond Barker JP and Rev. Thomas Huntingford JP. First offence. Fine £2 and 10/- costs. [*Note:*] King's moiety £1.

48/D/54   25 Aug. 1829. John Craddock Betteridge of Northleach, victualler. Allowing bagatelle to be played in his house. M. Hicks Beach JP and Rev. William Price JP. First offence. Fine £5 and 10/- costs. Offence committed 17 Aug. 1829.

48/D/55   2 Sept. 1829. George Bowyer. Stealing fifteen apples from an orchard in Avening, the property of Thomas Gardner. Rev. H. Campbell JP at Avening. One month's hard labour in Horsley house of correction. Offence committed 27 Aug. 1829.

48/D/56   2 Sept. 1829. Mary Bowyer. Aiding and abetting George Bowyer to steal fifteen apples [*etc., as* 48/D/55 *except*] Two months' hard labour in Horsley house of correction.

48/D/57   11 Sept. 1829. Henry Morgan. Stealing half a peck of apples from an orchard in Avening, the property of Nathaniel Dyer Esq. Rev. H. Campbell JP at Avening. Fine 19/-, to be paid to George Whitley, overseer of the poor, and 1/- recompense to the complainant, or one month's hard labour in Horsley house of correction. Offence committed 10 Sept. 1829.

48/D/58   11 Sept. 1829. James Chandler. Stealing half a peck of apples [*etc., as* 48/D/57].

48/D/59   14 Sept. 1829. Edward Dorney. Stealing half a peck of apples from an orchard, the property of Peter Playne Esq., in Minchinhampton. Rev. H. Campbell JP at Minchinhampton. Two months' hard labour in Horsley house of correction. Offence committed 12 Sept. 1829.

48/D/60   8 Sept. 1829. William Clark. Stealing apples from an orchard in Avening, the property of Mary Smith, widow. D. Ricardo JP at Horsley. Fine 4/-, to be paid to George Whitley, overseer of the poor, and 1/- recompense to the complainant, or one month's hard labour in Horsley house of correction. Offence committed 20 Aug. 1829.

48/D/61   8 Sept. 1829. Isaac Ind. Stealing apples [*etc., as* 48/D/60].

48/D/62   8 Sept. 1829. Richard Essex. Stealing apples [*etc., as* 48/D/60].

48/D/63   28 Sept. 1829. Robert Viner. Stealing a quantity of filberts from a nursery at Rodborough, the property of Robert Snow Paul Esq. Rev. P. Hawker JP at Rodborough. Fine 5/-, to be paid to James Wall, overseer of the poor, and 1/6 recompense to the complainant, or one month's hard labour in Horsley house of correction. Offence committed 30 Aug. 1829.

48/D/64   28 Sept. 1829. Thomas Niblett. Stealing a quantity of filberts [*etc., as* 48/D/63].

48/D/65 5 Oct. 1829. John Davis. Damaging a fence in Moreton in Marsh, the property of Thomas Ellis. Rev. J. R. Hall JP at Bourton on the Hill. Fine 12/-, to be paid to John Keytley, overseer of the poor, £1 costs and 10/- damages to go to the complainant, or two months' hard labour in the house of correction. Offence committed 19 Sept. 1829.

48/D/66 5 Oct. 1829. John Mason of Bourton on the Hill, labourer. Assaulting Richard and Sarah Waters at Bourton on the Hill. Rev. W. Boughton JP and Rev. J. R. Hall JP at Bourton on the Hill. Fine 3/-, to be paid to William Hanks, overseer of the poor, and 7/- costs. Offence committed 29 Sept. 1829.

48/D/67 11 Sept. 1829. Elizabeth wife of James Parker, Mary wife of Joseph Hill, Martha wife of John Arundell, Elizabeth wife of John Thompson, Harriet Parker, Sarah and Mary Fisher. Causing damage to a cornfield in Sapperton occupied by William Lawrence, yeoman. Rev. P. Hawker JP at Stroud. Each fined 6*d*. damages, to be paid to the overseer of the poor, and 10/6 costs to the complainant, or one week's hard labour in Horsley house of correction. Offence committed 29 Aug. 1829.

48/D/68 31 July 1829. Sarah Cook and Sarah Gwinnell of King's Stanley. Found in possession of underwood, the property of Thomas, Lord Ducie, in a wood in King's Stanley. H. Burgh JP and Rev. P. Hawker JP at Stroud. Fine 2/6 each, 3*d*. (the value of the wood) and 7/- costs, or 14 days' hard labour in Horsley house of correction. Offence committed 21 July 1829.

48/D/69 31 July 1829. James Organ of King's Stanley, labourer. Stealing a quantity of tree limbs from an orchard in King's Stanley, the property of Samuel Raikes, yeoman. H. Burgh JP and Rev. P. Hawker JP at Stroud. Fine 5/6 and 8/- costs or two months' hard labour in Horsley house of correction. Offence committed 27 July 1829.

48/D/70 8 Oct. 1829. Henry Merrett of Stonehouse, labourer. Stealing walnuts from an orchard in Stroud, the property of James Arkwell, yeoman. H. Burgh JP and Rev. P. Hawker JP at Stroud. Three weeks' hard labour in Horsley house of correction. Offence committed 5 Oct. 1829.

48/D/71 28 Sept. 1829. John Phelps of Stroud, labourer. Stealing turnips from enclosed ground in Stroud, the property of Daniel Dangerfield. H. Burgh JP at Stroud. One month's hard labour in Horsley house of correction. Offence committed 20 Sept. 1829.

48/D/72 29 July 1829. George Flight of King's Stanley, labourer. Possessing a side of deer believed to be stolen. H. Burgh JP at Stroud. Fine £20 or one month's hard labour in Horsley house of correction. Offence committed 28 July 1829.

48/D/73 29 July 1829. James Bailey of King's Stanley, labourer. Possessing a side of deer believed to be stolen. H. Burgh JP at Stroud. Fine £20 or six months' hard labour. Offence committed 28 July 1829.

48/D/74 11 July 1829. John Bown of Woodchester, labourer. Stealing tree limbs from a park at Woodchester, the property of Thomas, Lord Ducie. H. Burgh JP at Stroud. Fine 5/-, 7/- costs and 1/- damages, or two months' hard labour in Horsley house of correction. Offence committed 11 July 1829.

48/D/75 12 Aug. 1829. Hezekiah Davis and Charles Workman of Bisley, labourers. Stealing apples from an orchard, the property of Thomas Jones, clothier, of Bisley. H. Burgh JP at Stroud. Two months' hard labour in Horsley house of correction. Offence committed 12 Aug. 1829.

48/D/76   27 July 1829. Elizabeth Drew, Sarah Booker, Elizabeth Simmonds and Harriet Pearce. Stealing three-quarters of a peck of apples from an orchard in Painswick, the property of Henry Loveday, maltster. H. Burgh JP at Stroud. Fine 4/-, 11/- costs and 1/- (the value of the apples), or one month's hard labour in Horsley house of correction. Offence committed 26 July 1829.

48/D/77   10 Aug. 1829. Martha Hudson of Avening, spinster. Damaging a wall, the property of Thomas, Lord Ducie. H. Burgh JP at Stroud. Fine 2d. damages and 7/- costs or one month's hard labour in Horsley house of correction. Offence committed 14 July 1829.

48/D/78   17 July 1829. Mary Hudson of Avening, spinster. Found in possession of tree limbs believed to be stolen, the property of Thomas, Lord Ducie. H. Burgh JP at Stroud. Fine 20/-, 7/- costs and 4d. (the value of the wood), or two months' hard labour in Horsley house of correction. Offence committed 14 July 1829

48/D/79   20 July 1829. Elizabeth Jackson of King's Stanley. Damaging trees in a wood, the property of Thomas, Lord Ducie. H. Burgh JP at Stroud. Fine 3d. damages and 7/- costs or one month's hard labour in Horsley house of correction. Offence committed 16 July 1829.

48/D/80   26 Sept. 1829. Charles Cook of Painswick, labourer. Damaging a hedge, the property of John Moss, labourer. W. H. Hyett JP at Stroud. Fine 6d. damages and 7/6 costs or two months' hard labour in Horsley house of correction. Offence committed 26 Sept. 1829.

48/D/81   21 Sept. 1829. Charles Beard. Causing his wife and four children to become chargeable to the parish of Painswick. H. Burgh JP and W. H. Hyett JP at Stroud. One month's hard labour in Horsley house of correction.

48/D/82   11 Aug. 1829. John Estcott and John Denby of Painswick, labourer. Stealing beans from enclosed ground, the property of Daniel Gyde of Painswick, baker. H. Burgh JP and W. H. Hyett JP at Stroud. One month's hard labour in Horsley house of correction. Offence committed 10 Aug. 1829.

48/D/83   20 July 1829. William Clayfield. Causing his wife and four children to become chargeable to Painswick parish by refusing to work for four days. H. Burgh JP and W. H. Hyett JP at Stroud. One month's hard labour in Horsley house of correction. Offence committed 16–20 July 1829.

48/D/84   20 July 1829. James Niblett. Causing his wife and five children to become chargeable [etc., as 48/D/83].

48/D/85   25 Sept. 1829. John Sisom of Painswick, retailer. Using a defective balance. H. Burgh JP and W. H. Hyett JP at a Petty Sessions for Bisley hundred. Fine 5/- and 7/6 costs. Offence committed 15 Sept. 1829.

48/D/86   4 July 1829. Henry Herbert alias Walker of Thornbury. Violently assaulting Samuel Collings junior, watchmaker, at Thornbury. S. P. Peach JP and Rev. W. Davies JP at Thornbury. Fine 14/- and 6/- costs. Offence committed 18 June 1829.

48/D/87   8 Aug. 1829. Rose Drake, wife of Joseph Drake of Dursley, labourer. Assaulting Hannah Salisbury, wife of James Salisbury of Dursley, carpenter. W. M. Adey JP and H. W. Dyer JP at Wotton under Edge. Fine 10/-, to be paid to Sidney Smith, petty constable of Dursley, and 7/6 costs. Given fourteen day to pay. In default, one week in Horsley house of correction. Offence committed 5 Aug. 1829.

48/D/88   17 Sept. 1829. William Knight of Dursley and George Cowley of Cam, labourers. Stealing two pecks of potatoes from enclosed ground in Cam, the property of Edward Bloxsome the elder. P. B. Purnell JP at Stinchcombe. One month's hard labour in Horsley house of correction. Offence committed 15 Sept. 1829.

48/D/89   11 Sept. 1829. Edwin Ford of Owlpen, labourer. Stealing a quantity of apples from an orchard in Owlpen, the property of Thomas Anthony Stoughton Esq. W. M. Adey JP and H. W. Dyer JP at Wotton under Edge. Three months' hard labour in Horsley house of correction. Offence committed 11 Sept. 1829.

48/D/90   11 Sept. 1829. Robert Ford of Owlpen, labourer. Stealing a quantity of apples [*etc.*, *as* 48/D/89 *except*] One month's hard labour.

48/D/91   11 Sept. 1829. Alfred Ford of Owlpen, labourer. [*etc.*, *as* 48/D/90].

48/D/92   7 Aug. 1829. Elizabeth Wall of Dursley, single woman. Cutting down an ash tree in Dursley with intent to steal, the property of George Vizard Esq. W. M. Adey JP and P. B. Purnell JP at Wotton under Edge. Fine 20/-, to be paid to George Lister, overseer of the poor, 7/- costs and 1/- damages, or six weeks' hard labour in Horsley house of correction. Offence committed 28 July 1829.

48/D/93   7 Aug. 1829. Sophia Dainton of Dursley, single woman. Cutting down [*etc.*, *as* 48/D/92].

48/D/94   31 July 1829. John Riddiford of Uley, tailor. Destroying with intent to steal a quantity of pea plants worth sixpence, at Uley, the property of Samuel Went. P. B. Purnell JP and W. M. Adey JP at Wotton under Edge. Fine £5, to be paid to John Ferebee, churchwarden of Uley, 7/- costs and 6*d.* damages. Given fourteen day to pay. In default, three months' hard labour in Horsley house of correction. Offence committed 14 July 1829.

48/D/95   31 July 1829. Charles Hill of Uley, butcher. Stealing four cabbages worth twopence from a garden in Uley [*etc.*, *as* 48/D/94 *except*] 2*d.* damages.

48/D/96   9 Oct. 1829. Enoch Higgins of North Nibley, labourer. Possessing 32 lb. of various yarns and about 28 yards of various cloths believed to be stolen. W. M. Adey JP and H. W. Dyer JP. John Weight, gentleman, of Dursley, informer. John Bletchly, book-keeper, of Charfield, witness. First offence. Fine £20, half to go to the informer and the rest to Gloucester infirmary. Offence committed 7 Oct. 1829.

48/D/97   9 Oct. 1829. Thomas Darter of North Nibley, labourer. Possessing about 7 lb. 5 oz. of various yarns and about 45 yards of various cloths (some partly woven) believed to be stolen. Rev. W. Lloyd Baker JP and H. W. Dyer JP. John Weight [*etc.*, *as* 48/D/96 *except*] Offence committed 28 Sept. 1829.

48/D/98   9 Oct. 1829. James Crook of Wotton under Edge, labourer. Possessing about 63 lb. 4 oz. of various yarns believed to be stolen. Rev. W. Lloyd Baker JP and H. W. Dyer JP. John Weight, gentleman, of Dursley, informer. John Bletchly, book-keeper, of Charfield, witness. Second offence. [*Cf.* 42/A/54.] Fine £30, half to go to the informer and the rest to Gloucester infirmary. Offence committed 28 and 29 Sept. 1829.

48/D/99   22 Sept. 1829. Joseph Hopkins of Winchcombe, labourer. Shooting game without a licence. J. Clutterbuck JP, R. Capper JP and Rev. J. Neale JP at Cheltenham, commissioners for assessed taxes. Fine £10. Offence committed 18 July 1829.

49/A/1   26 Nov. 1829. William Scott. Assaulting Julius Bates, yeoman, of Stapleton. J. S. Harford JP and J. Parker JP at Lawfords Gate sessions room. Fine 10/- and 7/- costs or one month in Lawfords Gate house of correction. Offence committed 19 Nov. 1829.

49/A/2   12 Nov. 1829. Thomas Lewis. Assaulting Elizabeth Storey of Bitton. J. S. Harford JP and J. Parker JP at Lawfords Gate sessions room. Fine 10/- and 8/- costs [*or later in document* 7/- costs] or fourteen days in Lawfords Gate house of correction. Offence committed 8 Nov. 1829.

49/A/3   5 Nov. 1829. John Screen. Assaulting Ann Roach of Frampton Cotterell. J. Parker JP and J. S. Harford JP at Lawfords Gate sessions room. Fine 2/- and 8/- costs or seven days in Lawfords Gate house of correction. Offence committed 1 Nov. 1829.

49/A/4   7 Jan. 1830. George Greenich. Assaulting George Patfield, labourer, of St. Philip and St. Jacob, [Bristol]. J. Cave JP and W. Munro JP at Lawfords Gate sessions room. Fine 7/- and 6/6 costs or one month in Lawfords Gate house of correction. Offence committed 25 Dec. 1829.

49/A/5   17 Sept. 1829. Nathaniel Shill. Shooting a hare at Kington tithing, Almondsbury, when not qualified. H. W. Newman JP at Lawfords Gate sessions room. Information given to W. Munro JP two days earlier by William Webb. Thomas Gazard, witness. Offender pleaded not guilty. Fine £5. Offence committed 7 Sept. 1829.

49/A/6   17 Sept. 1829. George Browne. Using a gun and a dog to kill game in Stoke Gifford when not qualified. H. W. Newman JP at Lawfords Gate sessions room. James Howell, informer. William Merrick, witness. Pleaded not guilty. Fine £5. Offence committed Thursday 3 Sept. 1829.

49/A/7   11 Jan. 1830. Benjamin Neville [named at the end as Richard Neville]. Causing his son Richard to become chargeable to Stanway parish. J. Timbrill D.D. JP at Beckford. One month's hard labour in Northleach house of correction. Offence committed 9 Jan. 1830.

49/A/8   19 Nov. 1829. William Mason. Assaulting Thomas George, labourer, of St. Philip and St. Jacob, [Bristol]. G. Goldney JP and J. Parker JP at Lawfords Gate sessions room. Fine 2/6 and 7/6 costs or one month in Lawfords Gate house of correction. Offence committed 11 Nov. 1829.

49/A/9   7 Dec. 1829. Giles Coates, watchmaker, of Chedworth. Carrying a gun with intent to shoot game in Yanworth Wood when not qualified. Rev. Cornelius Pitt JP at Cirencester. Robert Simper, informer, George Simper, gamekeeper, witness, both of Chedworth. Pleaded not guilty. Fine £5. Offence committed 2 Dec. 1829.

49/A/10   23 Dec. 1829. James Joy, labourer, of Chedworth. Beating for game with a lurcher in Chittle Grove, Rendcomb, when not qualified. Rev. C. Pitt JP at Chedworth. Edmund and Thomas Burrows, gamekeepers, of Rendcomb, informer and witness. Pleaded not guilty. Fine £5. Offence committed 23 Dec. 1829.

49/A/11   24 Nov. 1829. John Hunt, labourer, of Southrop. Cutting down an ash tree growing in a hedge in Southrop, the property of Michael Hicks Beach Esq. J. R. Barker JP, Rev. W. Price JP and Rev. J. W. Peters JP at Bibury. Fine 10/6, to be paid to John Howes, overseer of the poor, 10/6 damages to be paid to the owner and 5/- costs to John Buttles, yeoman, of Southrop, the complainant, or two calendar months in Northleach house of correction. Offence committed 6 Nov. 1829.

49/A/12   4 Dec. 1829. Jacob Mustoe, labourer, of Chedworth. Using a gin to kill a hare in Chittle Grove, Rendcomb, when not qualified. Rev. C. Pitt JP at Chedworth. Edmund and Thomas Burrows, gamekeepers, of Rendcomb, informer and witness. Offender did not appear. Fine £5. Offence committed 30 Nov. 1829.

49/A/13   14 Nov. 1829. Mary Hudson. Stealing half a peck of turnips growing in enclosed land at Avening, the property of Stephen Blackwell. Rev. H. Campbell JP at Minchinhampton. One month's hard labour in Horsley house of correction. Offence committed 9 Nov. 1829.

49/A/14   14 Nov. 1829. Elizabeth Webb. Stealing half a peck of turnips [etc., as 49/A/13].

49/A/15   4 Jan. 1830. Louisa Jenkins. Stealing an oak and an ash tree growing in Shortwood, Horsley, the property of Benjamin Mills, timber merchant, of Nympsfield. Rev. P. Hawker JP and Rev. H. Campbell JP at Horsley. Fine £5, to be paid to John Harvey, overseer of the poor, 1/- damages and 4/6 costs. Offence committed 1 Jan. 1830.

49/A/16   3 Dec. 1829. Robert Fry, yeoman, of Horsley. Shooting game without a licence. Rev. P. Hawker JP and commissioner for assessed taxes, at Horsley. William Cox, witness. Fine £20. Offence committed 28 Oct. 1829.

49/A/17   17 Dec. 1829. Eliza Crow. Stealing twelve turnips growing in enclosed land at Avening, the property of Daniel Stafford. Rev. P. Hawker JP at Rodborough. Fine 19/6, to be paid to George Simpkins, overseer of the poor, 6/- costs and 6d. damages. Offence committed 13 Dec. 1829.

49/A/18   25 Nov. 1829. Ann Fowles. Stealing apples from Coventry's Close, Deerhurst, the property of John White Stephens, farmer. J. Timbrill D.D. JP and Rev. J. Keysell JP at Tewkesbury. Fine 10/-, to be paid to William Whithorn, overseer of the poor, 6d. damages and 9/6 costs, or one calendar month in Northleach house of correction. Offence committed Thursday 12 Nov. 1829. [Note:] Offender committed to Northleach.

49/A/19   11 Nov. 1829. Josiah Holloway. Stealing apples from Croft Orchard, Leigh, the property of Harriet Pensam, farmer. J. Timbrill D.D. JP, Rev. J. Keysall JP and Rev. C. White JP at Tewkesbury. Fine 40/-, to be paid to James Lea, overseer of the poor, 2/- damages and 15/- costs, or two calendar months in Northleach house of correction. Offence committed Saturday morning 7 Nov. 1829. [Note:] Offender committed to Northleach.

49/A/20   30 Dec. 1829. John Newman and Benjamin Fluck. Stealing fence palings and part of a stile from Coal House Meadow, Apperley, Deerhurst, the property of John Dipper. J. Timbrill D.D. JP, Rev. J. Keysall JP and Rev. C. White JP at Tewkesbury. Fine 10/- each, to be paid to William Whithorne, overseer of the poor, 5/- damages and 9/- costs, or two months in Northleach house of correction. Offence committed 14 Dec. 1829.

49/A/21   2 Jan. 1830. John Leach. Stealing fruit trees growing on the Gaston, Aston on Carrant, Ashchurch, the property of Francis Tombs, farmer. J. Timbrill D.D. JP at Beckford. First offence. Fine 50/-, to be paid to Richard Rimell, overseer of the poor of Ashchurch, and 17/6 damages, or two months' hard labour in Northleach house of correction. Offence committed 15 Dec. 1829. [Note:] Offender committed to Northleach.

49/A/22   17 Nov. 1829. Recognizance in the sum of 40/- each, for William Phillips, farmer, William Higley, labourer, both of Bourton on the Hill, and Joseph Purser, labourer, of Blockley, Worcs., to appear at the next Quarter Sessions in Gloucester to give evidence against Joseph Waters for felony. Rev. W. Boughton JP.

49/A/23   9 Nov. 1829. Thomas Harris, late of Cow Honeybourne, labourer. Assaulting Sarah Harris the elder. Rev. C. Jeaffreson JP and Rev. J. R. Hall JP at Bourton on the Hill. Fine £1 10s., to be paid to Underhill Coldicott, overseer of the poor, and £1 10s. costs, or two months in Northleach house of correction. Offence committed 31 Oct. 1829.

49/A/24   25 Nov. 1829. William Hawkins, landowner in Corse. Unlawfully erecting a wall or fence within 25 feet of the middle of the Ledbury to Cheltenham turnpike road at Staunton Swan. Rev. J. Higgins JP. Fine £2, half to go to the trustees of the Ledbury turnpike roads and the remainder with 13/6 costs to be paid to Thomas Jones, road surveyor.

49/A/25   24 Nov. 1829. William Freeman, clothworker, of Wotton under Edge. Possessing 21½ yards of woollen cloth believed to be woven from stolen yarn. W. M. Adey JP and H. W. Dyer JP. Fine £20, half to be paid to John Weight, gentleman, of Dursley, informer, and the rest to the poor. Offence committed 20 Nov. 1829.

49/A/26 23 Nov. 1829. William Freeman, clothworker, of Wotton under Edge. Receiving one piece of stolen Cashmere [*MS.* Cassimere] woollen cloth from John Davis, weaver, the property of Samuel and William Alexander Long, clothiers. W. M. Adey JP, H. W. Dyer JP and P. B. Purnell JP. Fine £40, to be distributed as follows: £5 to the informer, John Weight, gentleman, of Dursley, £32 to the poor of Wotton under Edge, and £3 costs, or six months' hard labour in Horsley house of correction. Offence committed 16 Nov. 1829.

49/A/27 23 Nov. 1829. John Davis, weaver, of Wotton under Edge. Stealing one piece of Cashmere [*MS.* Cassimere] woollen cloth, the property of Samuel and William Alexander Long, clothiers. W. M. Adey JP, H. W. Dyer JP and P. B. Purnell JP. Three months' hard labour in Horsley house of correction and to be publicly whipped. Offence committed 16 Nov. 1829.

49/A/28 8 Dec. 1829. John Richings [*also* Ritchings], yeoman, of Painswick, coach owner and driver. Failing to display the requisite boards on his coach when plying for hire in Cranham. R. Capper JP at Cheltenham, William Latham, yeoman, of Minchinhampton, informer. William Dyer and Ann Latham, witnesses. Offender pleaded not guilty. Fine £5. Offence committed 7 Sept. 1829.

49/A/29 8 Dec. 1829. William Fletcher, yeoman, of Stroud, coach owner and driver. Failing to display the requisite boards on his coach when plying for hire in Pitchcombe [*etc., as* 49/A/28 *except*] Offence committed 24 Sept. 1829.

49/A/30 5 Dec. 1829. Charles Tanner of Cheltenham. Receiving stolen posts and rails, the property of William Bidmead, plumber and glazier, of Cheltenham. H. N. Trye JP at Cheltenham. Fine £1 and 6/6 costs or two months in Northleach house of correction. Offence committed 5 Dec. 1829.

49/A/31 3 Dec. 1829. John Burnett of Cheltenham, licensed victualler. Knowingly allowing persons of notorious bad character to meet at his premises. R. Capper JP and John Harvey Ollney JP. First offence. Fine 50/- and 5/- costs. Offence committed 27 Nov. 1829.

49/A/32 12 Nov. 1829. Thomas Herbert of the Sherborne Arms, Cheltenham, licensed victualler. Allowing gaming on his premises. R. Capper JP and H. N. Trye JP. First offence. Fine 20/- and 5/- costs. Offence committed 7 Nov. 1829.

49/A/33 22 Dec. 1829. William Day, labourer, of Eastington. Illegally using a snare to kill a hare, R. W. Ford JP at Little Rissington. Fine £20. Offence committed 19 Nov. 1829.

49/A/34 26 Nov. 1829. John Harris, labourer, of Condicote. Illegally using a trap to kill a rabbit on Richard Collett's land in Condicote. Rev. F. E. Witts JP at Stow on the Wold. Fine £10. Offence committed 15 Nov. 1829.

49/A/35 17 Dec. 1829. Jane James *alias* Bolton [*also* Boulton], Jemima Betteridge and Sarah Hardiman. Breaking down a hedge (wood fence) with intent to steal, the property of Congreve Harris, at Maugersbury. Rev. F. E. Witts JP at Stow on the Wold. Each fined 9/- and 4/- costs. Given one week to pay. Offence committed 11 Dec. 1829.

49/A/36 5 Nov. 1829. Jane Williams and Jane Smith. Breaking down a hedge (wood fence) with intent to steal, the property of Mary Collett, at Upper Slaughter. Rev. F. E. Witts JP at Stow on the Wold. Fine 2/6 and 1/6 costs each. Given one week to pay. Offence committed 2 Nov. 1829.

49/A/37 26 Nov. 1829. Joseph Arkell the younger of Condicote. Beating for game in Longborough with a gun and a dog when not qualified. Rev. F. E. Witts JP at Stow on the Wold. Thomas Taylor, gamekeeper, of Adlestrop, informer. John Minchin, labourer, of Longborough, witness. Pleaded not guilty. Fine £5. Offence committed 21 Nov. 1829.

49/A/38   3 Dec. 1829. Charles Walker of Condicote. Beating for game [*etc., as* 49/A/37].

49/A/39   21 Nov. 1829. William Gough of Rockhampton. Assaulting John Weeks of Rockhampton. W. Davies D.D. JP and Rev. M. F. T. Stephens JP at Thornbury. Fine 6/- and 4/- costs. Offence committed 12 Nov. 1829.

49/A/40   5 Dec. 1829. James Rice of Thornbury. Assaulting George Grove, cooper, of Thornbury. S. P. Peach JP and Rev. F. M. T. Stephens JP at Thornbury. Fine 5/- and 5/- costs. Offence committed 21 Nov. 1829.

49/A/41   28 Oct. 1829. Thomas Browning. Stealing apples from an orchard at Lowfield Farm, Tetbury, the property of John Cook. J. D. Phelps JP at Tetbury. Fine 1/-, to be paid to John Cook, and 4/- costs to the complainant Henry Robertson. Offence committed 18 Oct. 1829.

49/A/42   28 Oct. 1829. Charles Bond. Stealing apples [*etc., as* 49/A/41].

49/A/43   28 Oct. 1829. Henry Browning. Stealing apples [*etc., as* 49/A/41].

49/A/44   28 Oct. 1829. John Elliotts. Stealing apples [*etc., as* 49/A/41].

49/A/45   28 Oct. 1829. John Williams. Stealing apples [*etc., as* 49/A/41].

49/A/46   6 Jan. 1830. William Whiting of Rodmarton, mason. Shooting a partridge in Home Field, Rodmarton, when not qualified. W. M. Paul JP at Tetbury. Information given to Rev. D. Lysons JP by John Martin the younger, gamekeeper, of Cirencester. Thomas Martin, gamekeeper, of Rodmarton, witness, said that offender offered a bribe when challenged near Mrs. Day's barn, as he was afraid of losing his job with Mr. Lysons. Offender pleaded not guilty. Witness for defence, Thomas Ockell, declared they had no gun but had heard one go off ten minutes earlier and seen a man near Mr. Kearsey's barley rick but could not say if it was Thomas Martin. Fine £5, half to go to the informer. Offence committed 28 Dec. 1829.

49/A/47   9 Dec. 1829. Henry Cleaver. Damaging an ash tree growing at Elmstree, Tetbury, the property of Joseph Brookes. W. M. Paul JP at Tetbury. Fine 1/- and 3/- costs to go to the complainant. Given fourteen days to pay. Offence committed 2 Dec. 1829.

49/A/48   9 Dec. 1829. George Barnfield. Damaging an ash tree [*etc., as* 49/A/47].

49/A/49   9 Dec. 1829. Mary Shipton. Stealing turnips from an enclosed field in Beverstone, the property of William Robbins. W. M. Paul JP at Tetbury. Fine 5/-, 3/- costs and 1/- damages. Given fourteen days to pay. Offence committed 12 Nov. 1829.

49/A/50   9 Dec. 1829. Ann wife of Samuel Baker, labourer, of Tetbury. Stealing turnips [*etc., as* 49/A/49].

49/A/51   9 Dec. 1829. Maria wife of Isaac Godwin, labourer, of Tetbury. Stealing turnips [*etc., as* 49/A/49].

49/A/52   9 Dec. 1829. Charles Reed. Damaging an ash tree [*etc., as* 49/A/47 *except*] Fine 5/-, 3/- costs and 1/- damages.

49/A/53   6 Aug. 1829. Samuel Russ. Stealing vetches, grown as animal food, from an enclosed field in Charlton, Tetbury. W. M. Paul JP at Tetbury. Hard labour for one calendar month in Horsley house of correction. Offence committed 19 July 1829.

49/A/54   19 Aug. 1829. Eliza wife of Worthy Mann, labourer, of Tetbury. Breaking down and stealing part of a maiden ash tree growing in a field in Tetbury in the occupation of Robert Ind. G. P. Holford JP. Fine 1/- and 6/- costs. Offence committed 4 Aug. 1829.

49/A/55   24 Dec. 1829. James Burt, hotel keeper, of Clifton. Keeping and using dogs to kill game in Henbury when not qualified. G. Goldney JP at Lawfords Gate sessions room. William Smith, lodging-house keeper, of Clifton, informer. Offender freely admitted offence, Fine £5. Offence committed 2 Nov. 1829.

49/A/56   24 Dec. 1829. Nathaniel Poole Leigh of Bristol. Keeping and using a dog to kill game in Henbury when not qualified. H. W. Newman JP at Lawfords Gate sessions room. Henry Poole, gentleman, of Bristol, informer. Offender freely admitted offence. Fine £5. Offence committed 2 Nov. 1829.

49/A/57   24 Dec. 1829. George Bush of Clifton, gentleman. Keeping and using a dog to kill game in Henbury when not qualified. H. W. Newman JP at Lawfords Gate sessions room. Henry Poole, gentleman, of Clifton, informer. Offender admitted charge. Fine £5. Offence committed 2 Nov. 1829.

49/A/58   19 Nov. 1829. William Davis of Henbury, labourer. Using a wire to kill a hare when not qualified. H. W. Newman JP at Lawfords Gate sessions room. Robert Baker, yeoman, of Henbury, informer. William Luton, yeoman, of Henbury, witness. Offender pleaded not guilty. Fine £5. Offence committed 7 Nov. 1829.

49/A/59   19 Dec. 1829. Hester Vick, single woman. Riotous behaviour in Stroud. H. Burgh JP at Stroud. Hard labour for one calendar month in Horsley house of correction. Offence committed 18 Dec. 1829.

49/A/60   20 Nov. 1829. Edwin Clissold and Samuel Pierce of Randwick, labourers. Breaking down, with intent to steal, part of a dead fence, the property of Edward Hogg Esq. of Randwick. H. Burgh JP and Rev. P. Hawker JP at Stroud. Fine 10/- and 10/- damages or hard labour for one calendar month in Horsley house of correction. Offence committed 1 Nov. 1829.

49/A/61   20 Nov. 1829. Richard Smith of Stroud, labourer. Cutting down three beech trees in a wood in Stroud, the property of Rev. Richard Morris of Stratford on Avon, Warws. H. Burgh JP and Rev. P. Hawker JP at Stroud. Fine £5, 8/- costs and 4/- damages or hard labour for two calendar months in Horsley house of correction. Offence committed 18 Nov. 1829.

49/A/62   20 Nov. 1829. Charles Beard of Randwick, labourer. Stealing apples from an orchard, the property of Samuel Lawrence, yeoman, of Randwick. H. Burgh JP and Rev. P. Hawker JP at Stroud. Hard labour for one calendar month in Horsley house of correction. Offence committed 3 Nov. 1829.

49/A/63   4 Dec. 1829. William Woodcock and James Roberts, labourers, of Painswick. Stealing apples from an orchard, the property of Daniel Spring, timber merchant, of Painswick. H. Burgh JP and Rev. P. Hawker JP at Stroud. Each sentenced to two months' hard labour, Roberts in Littledean and Woodcock in Horsley house of correction. Offence committed 29 Nov. 1829.

49/A/64   4 Dec. 1829. John Brown, John Weston, William Close and Henry Birt, labourers, of Painswick. Stealing apples [etc., as 49/A/63 except penalty] Hard labour for one month in Horsley house of correction.

49/A/65   14 Nov. 1829. William Lamburn, labourer, of Stroud. Stealing three young beech trees from a plantation in Rodborough, the property of Richard Smith. H. Burgh JP at Stroud. Fine 2/6, 9/- costs and 1/- damages or hard labour for one month in Horsley house of correction. Offence committed 11 May 1829.

49/A/66   23 Oct. 1829. John Wathen of Stroud, labourer. Stealing apples from an orchard in Stroud, the property of John Sims the younger. H. Burgh JP at Stroud. Three weeks' hard labour in Horsley house of correction. Offence committed 17 Oct. 1829.

49/A/67   8 Jan. 1830. John Berriman, clothworker, of Bisley. Assaulting Charles Copner, butcher, of Stroud, in Bisley. H. Burgh JP and Rev. P. Hawker JP at Stroud. Fine £5 or two months in Horsley house of correction. Offence committed 5 Jan. 1830.

49/A/68   22 Dec. 1829. John Purcell, cabinet-maker, of Stroud. Unlawfully selling a hare to Charles Page Sweeting, surgeon, of Stroud. H. Burgh JP at Stroud. Henry Rudge, gentleman, of Stroud, informer. Witness C. P. Sweeting said that he knew the offender, who sold him the hare for 2/6. Offender pleaded not guilty. Fine £5. Offence committed 21 Dec. 1829.

49/A/69   22 Dec. 1829. William Norris of Rodborough, labourer. Unlawfully selling a hare to William Hawtrey Thornton, surgeon, of Stroud. H. Burgh JP at Stroud. Henry Rudge, gentleman, of Stroud, informer. Witness W. H. Thornton said that he knew the offender and bought the hare for 1/-. Offender pleaded not guilty. Fine £5. Offence committed 21 Dec. 1829.

49/A/70   12 Nov. 1829. Daniel Baldwin, writing clerk, of Stroud. Throwing a firework in a street in Stroud. H. Burgh JP and Rev. P. Hawker JP at Stroud. Fine 5/- and 8/- costs. Offence committed 5 Nov. 1829.

49/A/71   30 Dec. 1829. John Barrett of Stroud, labourer. Unlawfully selling a pheasant to Charles Smith, clothier, of Stroud. Rev. P. Hawker JP at Stroud. Samuel Butler, gentleman, of Minchinhampton, informer. Witness C. Smith said that he bought the pheasant from the offender for 2/6. Offender pleaded guilty. Fine £5. Offence committed 30 Dec. 1829.

49/A/72   28 Dec. 1829. Isaac Fisher of Woodchester, labourer. Keeping and using a wire to kill game when not qualified. H. Burgh JP at Stroud. James Kenyon, gamekeeper, of Nympsfield, informer. Thomas Prout, labourer, of King's Stanley, witness. Offender did not appear. Fine £5. Offence committed 21 Nov. 1829.

49/A/73   18 Dec. 1829. George Coleman of King's Stanley, labourer. Keeping and using a bludgeon to kill game in Woodchester. H. Burgh JP at Stroud. James Kenyon, gamekeeper, of Nympsfield, informer. Thomas Prout, labourer, of King's Stanley, witness. Offender pleaded not guilty. Fine £5. Offence committed 21 Nov. 1829.

49/A/74   18 Dec. 1829. James Coleman of King's Stanley, labourer. Keeping and using a bludgeon [etc., as 49/A/73].

49/A/75   27 Nov. 1829. William Clissold of Stroud, labourer. Keeping and using a wire to kill game in Painswick when not qualified. H. Burgh JP at Stroud. William Capel the younger, gentleman, of Painswick, informer. Isaac Bennett, labourer, of Painswick, witness. Offender pleaded not guilty. Fine £5. Offence committed 22 Nov. 1829.

49/A/76   6 Nov. 1829. Thomas Taunton of Shortwood, labourer. Keeping and using a wire to kill game in Horsley when not qualified. H. Burgh JP at Stroud. James Kenyon, yeoman, of Nympsfield, informer. John Barker, gamekeeper, of Horsley, witness. Offender pleaded not guilty. Fine £5. Offence committed 21 Sept. 1829.

49/A/77   26 Oct. 1829. William Cox of Nympsfield, labourer. Keeping and using a dog to kill game when not qualified. H. Burgh JP at Stroud. John Barker, gamekeeper, of Horsley, informer. John Adams, labourer, of Horsley, witness. Offender pleaded not guilty. Fine £5. Offence committed 9 Oct. 1829.

49/A/78   26 Oct. 1829. John Leach of Nympsfield, labourer. Keeping and using dogs [etc., as 49/A/77].

49/A/79   6 Nov. 1829. James Latham of Horsley, labourer. Keeping and using a dog to kill game in Nympsfield when not qualified [etc., as 49/A/77].

49/A/80   1 Jan. 1830. George Dangerfield of King's Stanley, labourer. Keeping and using a wire to kill game in Woodchester. H. Burgh JP at Stroud. James Kenyon, gamekeeper, of Nympsfield, informer. Thomas Prout, gamekeeper, of King's Stanley, witness. Fine £5. Offence committed 21 Nov. 1829.

49/B/1   15 March 1830. George Brown. Breaking down part of a fence in Moreton in Marsh, the property of Sir Charles Cockerell, Bt. Rev. C. Jeaffreson JP, Rev. W. Boughton JP and Rev. J. R. Hall JP at Bourton on the Hill. First offence. Fine £2, to be paid to John Keytley, overseer of the poor, 2/6 damages and 8/6 costs, or hard labour for two calendar months in the house of correction. Offence committed 6 March 1830.

49/B/2   15 March 1830. George Hine. Breaking down part of a fence [etc., as 49/B/1].

49/B/3   15 March 1830. Jesse Syms. Breaking down part of a fence [etc., as 49/B/1].

49/B/4   15 March 1830. George Bridgwater. Breaking down part of a fence [etc., as 49/B/1 except] 2/6 damages and 6/6 costs, or two months in Northleach house of correction.

49/B/5   15 March 1830. Richard Hardiman. Breaking down part of a fence, the property of Sir Richard Cockerell, Bt., at Moreton in Marsh [etc., as 49/B/1 except omitting calendar].

49/B/6   25 Feb. 1830. Thomas Clark. Assaulting Elizabeth Pople at St. James, [Bristol]. G. Goldney JP and G. Hilhouse JP at Lawfords Gate sessions room. Fine 5/- and 6/6 costs or fourteen days in Lawfords Gate house of correction. Offence committed 17 Feb. 1830.

49/B/7   25 Feb. 1830. James Hurle. Assaulting Absalom Hall at Clifton. G. Goldney JP and H. W. Newman JP at Lawfords Gate sessions room. Fine 1/- and 6/6 costs or seven days in Lawfords Gate house of correction. Offence committed 11 Feb. 1830.

49/B/8   29 March 1830. William Moreton. Assaulting James Bailey at Hanham. J. Parker JP and G. Goldney JP at Lawfords Gate sessions room. Fine 5/- and 5/6 costs or one month in Lawfords Gate house of correction. Offence committed 26 March 1830.

49/B/9   4 Feb. 1830. Thomas Smith. Assaulting Eliza Stone at Mangotsfield. G. Goldney JP and H. W. Newman JP at Lawfords Gate sessions room. Fine 5/- and 6/6 costs or seven days in Lawfords Gate house of correction. Offence committed 25 Jan. 1830.

49/B/10   25 Feb. 1830. William Wilson. Assaulting Absalom Hall at Clifton [etc., as 49/B/7].

49/B/11   28 Jan. 1830. George Gabb. Assaulting Samuel Sheering at St. Philip and St. Jacob, [Bristol]. V. J. Graeme JP and H. W. Newman JP at Lawfords Gate sessions room. Fine 1/- and 6/6 costs or seven days in Lawfords Gate house of correction. Offence committed 26 Jan. 1830.

49/B/12   15 April 1830. Joseph Pratt. Assaulting David Malcom at St. Philip and St. Jacob, [Bristol]. J. Parker JP and H. W. Newman JP at Lawfords Gate sessions room. Fine 10/- and 5/6 costs or fourteen days in Lawfords Gate house of correction. Offence committed 27 March 1830.

49/B/13   18 Jan. 1830. James Williams. Assaulting Henry Amos at Wick and Abson. J. Parker JP and George Worrall JP at Lawfords Gate sessions room. Fine £2 10s. and £2 10s. costs or imprisonment for two calendar months in Lawfords Gate house of correction. Offence committed 12 Jan. 1830.

49/B/14   18 Jan. 1830. James Williams. Assaulting William Amos at Wick and Abson [etc., as 49/B/13].

49/B/15   18 March 1830. Henry Goss. Assaulting Ann Harris at St. George, [Bristol]. H. W. Newman JP and J. Parker JP at Lawfords Gate sessions room. Fine 1/- and 9/- costs or fourteen days in Lawfords Gate house of correction. Offence committed 4 March 1830.

49/B/16 1 April 1830. Elizabeth Thomas. Assaulting Ann Thomas at St. Philip and St. Jacob, [Bristol]. J. S. Harford JP and V. J. Graeme JP at Lawfords Gate sessions room. Fine 10/- and 7/6 costs or one calendar month in Lawfords Gate house of correction. Offence committed 30 March 1830.

49/B/17 30 Jan. 1830. Charles Maggs. Assaulting James Ross at Winterbourne. H. W. Newman JP and G. Worrall JP at Lawfords Gate sessions room. Fine 11/- and 9/- costs or one calendar month in Lawfords Gate house of correction. Offence committed 20 Jan. 1830.

49/B/18 30 Jan. 1830. George Barnes. Assaulting James Ross [etc., as 49/B/17].

49/B/19 28 Jan. 1830. Ann Whittaker. Assaulting Francis Bissicks at Clifton. H. W. Newman JP and V. J. Graeme JP at Lawfords Gate sessions room. Fine 1/- and 6/6 costs or seven days in Lawfords Gate house of correction. Offence committed 25 Jan. 1830.

49/B/20 18 March 1830. William Brain. Assaulting John Cox at Bitton. H. W. Newman JP and V. J. Graeme JP at Lawfords Gate sessions room. Fine 5/- and 9/- costs or fourteen days in Lawfords Gate house of correction. Offence committed 16 March 1830.

49/B/21 18 March 1830. Hugh Brain. Assaulting John Cox [etc., as 49/B/20].

49/B/22 15 April 1830. Robert Apperley. Assaulting Sophia Beard at Henbury. J. Parker JP and H. W. Newman JP at Lawfords Gate sessions room. Fine 2/6 and 8/- costs or fourteen days in Lawfords Gate house of correction. Offence committed 8 April 1830.

49/B/23 18 Feb. 1830. James Fowler. Assaulting Absalom Hall at Clifton. H. W. Newman JP and V. J. Graeme JP at Lawfords Gate [etc., as 49/B/7].

49/B/24 18 Feb. 1830. Joseph Wilson. Assaulting Absalom Hall at Clifton [etc., as 49/B/23].

49/B/25 23 March 1830. Thomas Hendy. Assaulting Jonas Smith at Mangotsfield. J. Savage JP and H. W. Newman JP at Lawfords Gate sessions room. Fine 6d. and 8/- costs or fourteen days in Lawfords Gate house of correction. Offence committed 13 March 1830.

49/B/26 23 March 1830. James Bryant. Assaulting Jonas Smith [etc., as 49/B/25].

49/B/27 23 March 1830. William Bryant. Assaulting Jonas Smith [etc., as 49/B/25].

49/B/28 23 March 1830. Joseph Emerson. Assaulting Jonas Smith [etc., as 49/B/25].

49/B/29 26 Feb. 1830. Henry Smith, labourer, of Dursley. Assaulting Joseph Workman, labourer, of Stinchcombe. W. M. Adey JP and H. W. Dyer JP at Wotton under Edge. Fine £3 4s., to be paid to James White, overseer of the poor of Stinchcombe, and 6/- costs, or six weeks in Horsley house of correction. Offence committed 17 Nov. 1830.

49/B/30 2 March 1830. Edwin Morgan, labourer, of Dursley. Assaulting Joseph Workman [etc., as 49/B/29].

49/B/31 22 Jan. 1830. Charles Hancock of North Nibley, labourer. Stealing a beech tree at North Nibley, the property of Purnell Bransby Purnell Esq. W. M. Adey JP and H. W. Dyer JP at Wotton under Edge. Fine 23/-, to be paid to Harry Randall, an overseer of the poor, 6/- costs and 1/-, the value of the tree, or one month's hard labour in Horsley house of correction. Given fourteen days to pay. Offence committed 16 Jan. 1830.

49/B/32 19 Jan. 1830. Isaac Heath of Dursley, labourer. Stealing an oak tree in Dursley, the property of John Delafield Phelps Esq. W. M. Adey JP and H. W. Dyer JP at Wotton under Edge. Fine 33/-, to be paid to petty constable George Roan, 5/- costs and 2/-, the value of the tree, or one month's hard labour in Horsley house of correction. Given seven days to pay. Offence committed 15 Jan. 1830.

49/B/33 18 Feb. 1830. John Bliss and William Gardner of Painswick, labourers. Cutting up and stealing a quantity of tree stools from a wood in Painswick, the property of Thomas Preston Esq. W. H. Hyett JP and Weston Hicks JP at Painswick. Fine 6d. damages and

8/- costs or fourteen days' hard labour in Horsley house of correction. Offence committed 6 Feb. 1830.

49/B/34   18 Feb. 1830. Benjamin Cooke and Joseph Twining, labourers, of Painswick. Stealing apples from an orchard occupied by Samuel Goddard of Painswick. W. H. Hyett JP and W. Hicks JP at Painswick. Fine 2/6 each, to be paid to the overseer of the poor, 1/- damages and 5/6 costs to go to the complainant, or one month's hard labour in Horsley house of correction. Offence committed 13 Sept. 1829.

49/B/35   12 Jan. 1830. John Bown and William White, labourers, of Avening. Stealing wood from a park in Avening, the property of Thomas, Lord Ducie. H. Burgh JP at Stroud. Fine 4/6 each, to be paid to Lord Ducie, or one month's hard labour in Horsley house of correction. Offence committed 11 Jan. 1830.

49/B/36   3 March 1830. John Abell, chimney-sweeper, of Stroud. Stealing stakes from a fence in Painswick, the property of Elizabeth Loveday, widow. H. Burgh JP at Stroud. Fine 10/-, to be paid to the overseer of the poor, 10/6 costs and 2d. damages to the complainant, or one month's hard labour in Horsley house of correction. Offence committed 2 March 1830.

49/B/37   19 Jan. 1830. James Smart. Causing his wife and family to become chargeable to Stroud parish. H. Burgh JP at Stroud. One month's hard labour in Horsley house of correction. Offence committed at various times before 18 Jan. 1830.

49/B/38   6 March 1830. Thomas Horwood, labourer, of Woodchester. Setting snares to catch conies on Thomas, Lord Ducie's land in Woodchester. H. Burgh JP and Rev. P. Hawker JP at Stroud. Fine £5 or one month's hard labour in Horsley house of correction. Offence committed 26 Feb. 1830.

49/B/39   12 Feb. 1830. Daniel Ferrabee. Entering waste land with intent to shoot game. H. Burgh JP and Rev. P. Hawker JP at Stroud. Three calendar months' hard labour in Horsley house of correction, after which sureties of £10 against re-offending must be found, or a further six months' hard labour to be served. Offence committed 5 Feb. 1830.

49/B/40   6 March 1830. Thomas Baghott Esq. of Woodchester. Setting snares and nets to catch conies on Thomas, Lord Ducie's land [etc., as 49/B/38].

49/B/41   25 Feb. 1830. Samuel Bassett of Painswick, labourer. Stealing turnips in Painswick, the property of William Capel the younger. H. Burgh JP and Rev. P. Hawker JP at Stroud. Hard labour for one month in Horsley house of correction. Offence committed 25 Feb. 1830.

49/B/42   16 March 1830. Charlotte Sheil. Begging in Stroud. H. Burgh JP and Rev. P. Hawker JP at Stroud. One month's hard labour in Horsley house of correction. Offence committed 15 March 1830.

49/B/43   12 March 1830. John Clark of Woodchester, labourer. Damaging underwood in Woodchester, the property of Thomas, Lord Ducie. H. Burgh JP and Rev. P. Hawker JP at Stroud. Fine 3d. and 8/- costs to be paid to Lord Ducie, or hard labour for one month in Horsley house of correction. Offence committed 26 Feb. 1830.

49/B/44   26 March 1830. Mary Ann Wood, spinster, of King's Stanley. Stealing a quantity of wood, the property of Thomas, Lord Ducie. H. Burgh JP and Rev. P. Hawker JP at Stroud. Fine 4d. and 7/- costs to be paid to Lord Ducie, or one month's hard labour in Horsley house of correction. Offence committed 9 March 1830.

49/B/45   26 March 1830. James Chappell of Stroud, baker. Assaulting James Hammonds, weaver, of Painswick without provocation at Stroud. H. Burgh JP and Rev. P. Hawker JP at Stroud. Fine £1 and 9/- costs or two months in Horsley house of correction. Offence committed 14 March 1830.

49/B/46 26 March 1830. James Okey the younger of Stroud, carpenter. Damaging shutters and breaking one pane of window glass in the dwelling house of Henry Okey, gardener, of Stroud. H. Burgh JP and Rev. P. Hawker JP at Stroud. Fine 10/- damages and 9/- costs, or two months in Horsley house of correction. Offence committed 23 March 1830.

49/B/47 3 March 1830. Thomas Allard of the Fleet inn, Twyning, innkeeper. Permitting fighting and disorderly behaviour on his premises. J. Timbrill JP and J. Keysall JP. First offence. Fine 40/- and 10/6 costs. Offence committed Tuesday 3 March 1830.

49/B/48 11 Jan. 1830. Sarah wife of Richard Bridges of Chedworth, mason. Selling fifteen pheasants in the Sheldons hotel in Cheltenham, two to Robert Davis and the remainder to John Arpin *alias* Ackey. Rev. C. Pitt JP, Harry Edmund Waller JP and Rev. W. Price JP at Northleach. Edmund Burrows, gamekeeper, of Rendcomb, informer. Jacob Mustoe, labourer, of Chedworth, witness. Offender did not appear. Fine £25. Offence committed 14 Nov. 1829.

49/B/49 27 March 1830. Anthony Major. Assaulting Thomas Treadgold in Cheltenham. R. Capper JP and H. N. Trye JP at Cheltenham. Fine £5. Offence committed 25 March 1830.

49/B/50 27 Feb. 1830. Samuel Hartell, Matthew Wright and James Gardner. Assaulting Harriet Herbert in Cheltenham. J. Clutterbuck JP and R. Capper JP at Cheltenham. Each fined 10/- and 4/4 costs. Offence committed 24 Feb. 1830.

49/B/51 16 March 1830. Joseph Hall. Assaulting Elizabeth Pearce in Cheltenham. H. N. Trye JP and J. H. Ollney JP at Cheltenham. Fine 5/- and 4/3 costs. Offence committed 13 March 1830.

49/B/52 16 March 1830. William Morgan. Assaulting Elizabeth Pearce [*etc.*, *as* 49/B/51].

49/B/53 9 March 1830. Mary Hands, licensed victualler, of Cheltenham. Permitting illegal games on her premises. R. Capper JP and H. N. Trye JP. Fine £1 and 4/6 costs. First offence. Offence committed 3 March 1830.

49/B/54 9 March 1830. Joseph Rone, licensed victualler, of Cheltenham. Allowing persons of notorious ill repute to congregate on his premises. R. Capper JP and H. N. Trye JP. First offence. Fine £2 and 4/6 costs. Offence committed 3 March 1830.

49/B/55 11 Jan. 1830. Richard Bridges of Chedworth, mason. Possessing and using gins to kill game. Rev. C. Pitt JP, H. E. Waller JP and Rev. W. Price JP at Northleach. Edmund Burrows, gamekeeper, of Rendcomb, informer. Jacob Mustoe, labourer, of Chedworth, witness. Offender did not appear. Fine £5. Offence committed 24 Nov. 1829.

49/B/56 2 April 1830. James Sendall, butcher, of Batheaston, Som. Entering Dyrham Wood with a gun and a dog with intent to kill game. F. Trotman JP and W. G. Davy JP at a Petty Sessions held at the Cross Hands inn, Old Sodbury. William Eels, gamekeeper to William Blathwayt Esq., of Dyrham and Hinton, informer. Stephen Eels, employee of Mr. Blathwayt, and John Marshall, witnesses. Defendant asked for time to prepare defence. Magistrates willing, but time (three months) almost expired. Defendant cross-examined witness. Fine £5. Information given 5 March 1830. Offence committed 11 Jan. 1830.

49/C/1 14 May 1830. John Pittaway. Pursuing deer in Widley Chase, Widford, with intent to kill. Rev. F. E. Witts JP at Upper Slaughter. Mitigated fine of £5 or hard labour for two calendar months in Northleach house of correction. Offence committed 1 May 1830.

49/C/2 24 June 1830. John Boulton. Ill-treating an ass. Rev. P. Hawker JP. Joseph Harrison, witness. Fine £3. Offence committed 28 May 1830.

49/C/3   26 May 1830. George Newman of Winchcombe, glazier. Assaulting and threatening to kill Sarah Washbourne at Winchcombe. J. Timbrill D.D. JP and J. Keysall JP at Tewkesbury. Fine 40/-, to be paid to John Mason, an overseer of the poor of Winchcombe, and 12/- costs to go to the victim. Offence committed 12 May 1830.

49/C/4   19 June 1830. Elizabeth wife of Thomas Niblett of Leckhampton. Presenting herself to Hannah Curtis at Leckhampton as one who could cast out devils. Rev. J. Neale JP at Cheltenham. Six weeks' hard labour in Northleach house of correction. Offence committed 7 Nov. 1829.

49/C/5   22 June 1830. Richard Hughes. Stripping bark from oak trees in Dowles Wood, Hewelsfield, the property of George Rooke Esq. Rt. Hon. C. Bathurst JP and Rev. T. Thomas JP at Lydney. Fine £1 12s., to be paid to William Miles, overseer of the poor of Hewelsfield, 8/- costs and 4/- damages, or one month's hard labour in Littledean house of correction. Given fourteen days to pay. Offence committed 7 May 1830.

49/C/6   6 July 1830. William James alias Thomas. Assaulting Susan Morgan at Tidenham. P. J. Ducarel JP and E. Machen JP at Coleford. Fine 5/-, to be paid to William James, overseer of the poor at Tidenham, and 5/6 costs, or ten days' hard labour in Littledean house of correction. Offence committed 28 June 1830.

49/C/7   27 April 1830. Thomas Townsend. Assaulting Henry Miles at Hewelsfield. Rt. Hon. C. Bathurst JP and Rev. T. Thomas JP at Lydney. Fine 12/6, to be paid to William Watkins, overseer of the poor of Hewelsfield, and 7/6 costs, or one month in Littledean house of correction. Offence committed 8 April 1830.

49/C/8   5 July 1830. Thomas Evans. Shooting a pigeon, the property of Thomas Stephens of Chaxhill, Westbury on Severn. Rev. C. Crawley JP and J. Pyrke JP at Newnham. Fine 3/6, to be paid to Thomas Harvey, overseer of the poor of Westbury on Severn, and 6/6 costs, or one month in Littledean house of correction. Offence committed 28 June 1830.

49/C/9   26 April 1830. Job Watkins. Assaulting Ruth wife of Samuel Slaughter at Churcham. Rev. C. Crawley JP and J. Pyrke JP at Newnham. Fine 5/-, to be paid to Joseph Kitchen, overseer of the poor of Churcham, and 6/- costs, or one month in Littledean house of correction. Offence committed 15 April 1830.

49/C/10   1 March 1830. William Lowe. Assaulting Elizabeth Garnes in St. Briavels hundred. Rev. C. Crawley JP and M. Colchester JP. Fine £4 10s., to be paid to the treasurer of the county of Gloucester, and 10/- costs, or two calendar months in Littledean house of correction. Offence committed 16 April 1829.

49/C/11   30 March 1830. George Brown. Cutting underwood in Copse Wood, Hewelsfield, the property of Samuel Turner. Rt. Hon. C. Bathurst JP and Rev. T. Thomas JP at Lydney. Edward Blunt, witness. Fine 1/- and 6/- costs or one calendar month in Littledean house of correction. Given twenty-eight days to pay. Offence committed 25 March 1830.

49/C/12   30 March 1830. John Martin. Cutting underwood [etc., as 49/C/11 except] Fine 6d. and 6/- costs.

49/C/13   30 March 1830. John Worgan. Cuttting underwood [etc., as 49/C/11 except] Fine 6d. damages and 6/- costs.

49/C/14   30 March 1830. Henry Wright. Cuttting underwood [etc., as 49/C/11 except] Fine 6d. damages and 6/- costs.

49/C/15   30 March 1830. Oliver Worgan. Cutting underwood [etc., as 49/C/11 except] Fine 1/- damages and 6/- costs.

49/C/16   11 May 1830. John Ricketts of Uley, clothworker. Stealing forty young trees, valued at 1/-, growing in Ginvill Wood, Newington Bagpath, the property of Edward Sheppard Esq. W. M. Adey JP and H. W. Dyer JP at Wotton under Edge. Fine £4 13s., 1/- damages, to be paid to an overseer of the poor, and 6/- costs, or two calendar months in Horsley house of correction. Offence committed 8 May 1830.

49/C/17   11 May 1830. William Ferebee of Uley, weaver. Stealing forty young trees [etc., as 49/C/16].

49/C/18   21 May 1830. Nathan Pearce of Wick, Berkeley, weaver. Possessing woollen yarn believed to be stolen. W. M. Adey JP and H. W. Dyer JP at Wotton under Edge. Alexander Ingram, watchmaker, of Wotton under Edge, informer. Ann wife of Benjamin Hayward and Daniel Cook, witnesses. First offence. Fine £20, half to go to the informer and the rest to Gloucester infirmary. Offence committed 29 April 1830.

49/C/19   22 May 1830. William Lusty of Uley, handlestock maker. Stealing two young ash trees, valued at 10/-, growing in Ewe Leaze, Uley, the property of Robert Kingscote Esq. W. M. Adey JP and H. W. Dyer JP at Wotton under Edge. Fine £5, to be paid to John Ferebee, churchwarden of Uley, 10/- damages and 6/6 costs, or two months' hard labour in Horsley house of correction. Offence committed 21 May 1830.

49/C/20   11 June 1830. Lewis Jones of Coaley, blacksmith. Damaging a door and window of the dwelling house of Ann and Hester Hadley, spinsters, of Cam. P. B. Purnell JP and H. W. Dyer JP at Wotton under Edge. Fine 1/6 damages, to be paid to James Holloway, petty constable of Cam, and 5/- costs, or fourteen days' hard labour in Horsley house of correction. Offence committed 2 June 1830.

49/C/21   11 June 1830. John Bick of Coaley, blacksmith. Damaging a door [etc., as 49/C/20].

49/C/22   18 June 1830. Thomas Morgan, weaver, of Dursley. Damaging a beech tree, the property of George Vizard Esq. of Dursley. H. W. Dyer JP and E. Sheppard JP at Wotton under Edge. Fine £4 and 1/6 damages, to be paid to William Henry Williams, an overseer of the poor, and 5/- costs, or six weeks' hard labour in Horsley house of correction. Offence committed 10 June 1830.

49/C/23   18 June 1830. Charles Webb, weaver, of Dursley. Damaging a beech tree [etc., as 49/C/22].

49/C/24   25 June 1830. William Wilkins of Cam, labourer. Stealing two wooden rails from a fence, the property of George Purnell of Coaley, farmer. H. W. Dyer JP and P. B. Purnell JP at Wotton under Edge. Fine 10/8 (the value of the rails), to be paid to the petty constable of Coaley, and 5/- costs, or fourteen days' hard labour in Horsley house of correction. Offence committed 15 June 1830.

49/C/25   9 July 1830. John Howell of Wotton under Edge, labourer. Damaging several fir trees, the property of Lewis Clutterbuck Esq. of Ozleworth. W. M. Adey JP and H. W. Dyer JP at Wotton under Edge. Fine 10/- and 1/- damages, to be paid to an overseer of the poor of Ozleworth, and 5/- costs, or one month's hard labour in Horsley house of correction. Offence committed 2 July 1830.

49/C/26   9 July 1830. Thomas Derrett of Wotton under Edge, labourer. Damaging several fir trees [etc., as 49/C/25].

49/C/27   5 July 1830. John Mainstone of Wotton under Edge, handlestock maker. Stealing an ash tree, the property of Ann Bearpacker, spinster, of Wotton under Edge. W. M. Adey JP and H. W. Dyer JP at Wotton under Edge. Fine £5, 10/- (the value of the tree), to be paid to Isaac James, assistant overseer of the poor, and 10/- costs, or two calendar months' hard labour in Horsley house of correction. Offence committed 2 July 1830.

49/C/28   1 June 1830. George Marsh. Trespassing and treading down mowing grass on land belonging to Francis Flowers of Bitton. J. Parker JP at Lawfords Gate sessions room. Fine 1/- damages, to be paid to the overseer of the poor, and 7/6 costs, or one calendar month's hard labour in Lawfords Gate house of correction. Offence committed 19 May 1830.

49/C/29   21 June 1830. John Field. Assaulting Francis Thomas at Henbury. J. Savage JP and J. Haythorne JP at Lawfords Gate sessions room. Fine £2 8s. and 12/- costs or six weeks in Lawfords Gate house of correction. Offence committed 21 May 1830.

49/C/30   3 July 1830. George Jones. Assaulting Richard Warr at Westbury on Trym. H. W. Newman JP and J. Vaughan JP at Lawfords Gate sessions room. Fine £2 and 8/- costs or one month in Lawfords Gate house of correction. Offence committed 26 June 1830.

49/C/31   6 May 1830. John Davis. Assaulting John Gray at Filton. W. Munro JP and H. W. Newman JP at Lawfords Gate sessions room. Fine 2/6 and 6/6 costs or fourteen days in Lawfords Gate house of correction. Offence committed 3 May 1830.

49/C/32   6 May 1830. Mary Gardener. Assaulting John Gray [etc., as 49/C/31].

49/C/33   6 May 1830. Jonathan Higgins. Assaulting Jane Ridler at Clifton. W. Munro JP and H. W. Newman JP at Lawfords Gate sessions room. Fine 3/6 and 6/6 costs or fourteen days in Lawfords Gate house of correction. Offence committed 3 May 1830.

49/C/34   6 May 1830. Samuel Cottle. Assaulting Thomas Wintle at St. Philip and St. Jacob, [Bristol]. W. Munro JP and H. W. Newman JP at Lawfords Gate sessions room. Fine £2 and 17/- costs or one calendar month in Lawfords Gate house of correction. Offence committed 3 May 1830.

49/C/35   6 May 1830. Joseph Cottle senior. Assaulting Thomas Wintle [etc., as 49/C/34 except] Fine £1 and 17/- costs.

49/C/36   29 April 1830. William Jones. Assaulting John Player at Westbury on Trym. J. Vaughan JP and J. Parker JP at Lawfords Gate sessions room. Fine £1 and 6/6 costs or one calendar month in Lawfords Gate house of correction. Offence committed 17 April 1830.

49/C/37   6 May 1830. John Merrick. Assaulting Hannah Hemers at St. Philip and St. Jacob, [Bristol]. H. W. Newman JP and W. Munro JP at Lawfords Gate sessions room. Fine 2/6 and 6/6 costs or one calendar month in Lawfords Gate house of correction. Offence committed 2 May 1830.

49/C/38   23 April 1830. Thomas Saunders of Avening, labourer. Damaging young beech trees in Avening, the property of Thomas, Lord Ducie. H. Burgh JP and Rev. P. Hawker JP at Stroud. Fine 2/-, to be paid to an overseer of the poor, and 2/- damages and 8/- costs, or hard labour for one week in Horsley house of correction. Offence committed 22 April 1830.

49/C/39   23 April 1830. Susan Webb of Avening, single woman. Damaging young beech trees in Avening, the property of Thomas, Lord Ducie. H. Burgh JP and Rev. P. Hawker JP at Stroud. Fine 2/-, 2/- damages, to be paid to an overseer of the poor, and 8/- costs, or one month's hard labour in Horsley house of correction. Offence committed 22 April 1830.

49/C/40   23 April 1830. Mary Hudson of Avening, single woman. Damaging young beech trees in Avening [etc., as 49/C/39 except] two months' hard labour.

49/C/41   23 April 1830. Thomas Boulton of Avening, labourer. Damaging young beech trees [etc., as 49/C/39].

49/C/42   23 April 1830. Edward Hudson of Avening, labourer. Damaging a fir tree in Avening the property of Thomas, Lord Ducie. H. Burgh JP and Rev. P. Hawker JP at Stroud. Fine 1/- damages, to be paid to an overseer of the poor, and 5/- costs, or one month's hard labour in Horsley house of correction. Offence committed 21 April 1830.

49/C/43   23 April 1830. Thomas Saunders of Avening, labourer. Damaging a fir tree in Avening, the property of Thomas, Lord Ducie. H. Burgh JP and Rev. P. Hawker JP at Stroud. Fine 1/- damages and 5/- costs, both to be paid to Lord Ducie, or one month's hard labour in Horsley house of correction. Offence committed 21 April 1830.

49/C/44   18 June 1830. Thomas Wager of Stroud, labourer. Damaging a plantation wall in Stroud, the property of Richard Sandys Esq. H. Burgh JP and Rev. P. Hawker JP. Fine 10/-, to be paid to an overseer of the poor, 4/- damages and 8/- costs, or two months' hard labour in Horsley house of correction. Offence committed 13 June 1830.

49/C/45   18 June 1830. William Holder of Stroud, labourer. Damaging a plantation wall [*etc., as* 49/C/44 *except*] Fine 10/-, 4/- damages, to be paid to an overseer of the poor, and 8/- costs.

49/C/46   18 June 1830. Benjamin Moss of Stroud, labourer. Damaging a plantation wall [*etc., as* 49/C/45].

49/C/47   4 June 1830. Mary Lusty of King's Stanley, single woman. Stealing wood from a park in Nympsfield, the property of Thomas, Lord Ducie. H. Burgh JP and Rev. P. Hawker JP at Stroud. Fine 4*d.* and 5/3 costs or three weeks' hard labour in Horsley house of correction. Offence committed 28 May 1830.

49/C/48   4 June 1830. Elizabeth Lusty of King's Stanley, single woman. Stealing wood [*etc., as* 49/C/47].

49/C/49   21 May 1830. John Holbird of Cranham, stonemason. Assaulting Charles Savory, sawyer, of Painswick. H. Burgh JP and Rev. P. Hawker JP at Stroud. Fine £5, to be paid to an overseer of the poor of Cranham, or two months' hard labour in Horsley house of correction. Offence committed 16 May 1830.

49/C/50   21 May 1830. Henry Barnfield of Cranham, labourer. Assaulting Charles Savory [*etc., as* 49/C/49].

49/C/51   21 May 1830. Jehu Hunt the younger of Cranham, potter. Assaulting Charles Savory [*etc., as* 49/C/49].

49/C/52   7 May 1830. Ann Lee of King's Stanley, single woman. Stealing wood from a park in Nympsfield, the property of Thomas, Lord Ducie. H. Burgh JP and Rev. P. Hawker JP at Stroud. Fine 4*d.* and 5/2 costs or a fortnight's hard labour in Horsley house of correction. Offence committed 22 April 1830.

49/C/53   7 May 1830. Mary Lusty of King's Stanley, single woman. Stealing wood [*etc., as* 49/C/52].

49/C/54   7 May 1830. Mary wife of Charles Cook, labourer, of King's Stanley. Stealing wood [*etc., as* 49/C/52].

49/C/55   19 May 1830. Richard Nicholls of Stroud, stonemason. Stealing cabbages from a garden, the property of William Wood of Stroud. H. Burgh JP at Stroud. Hard labour for six calendar months in Horsley house of correction. Offence committed 16 May 1830.

49/C/56   24 May 1830. William Edwards. Assaulting Benjamin Chandler, labourer, of Stroud. H. Burgh JP at Stroud. Fine £5, to be paid to an overseer of the poor, or two months' hard labour in Horsley house of correction. Offence committed 21 May 1830.

49/C/57   5 May 1830. John Riddford. Begging in Stroud. H. Burgh JP at Stroud. One month's hard labour in Horsley house of correction. Offence committed 2 May 1830.

49/C/58   15 June 1830. Charles Hall. Begging in Stroud. H. Burgh JP at Stroud. One month's hard labour in Horsley house of correction. Offence committed 15 June 1830.

49/C/59   21 May 1830. Eliza Tranter, prostitute. Disorderly behaviour in Stroud. H. Burgh JP and Rev. P. Hawker at Stroud. One month's hard labour in Horsley house of correction. Offence committed 11 May 1830.

49/C/60   21 May 1830. Sarah Woodman, prostitute. Disorderly behaviour [etc., as 49/C/59].

49/C/61   2 July 1830. Thomas Burrows of Bisley, carpenter. Damaging one square yard of turf on Bisley common, the property of William Lewis Esq., lord of the manor. H. Burgh JP and Rev. P. Hawker JP at Stroud. Fine 1/- damages and 8/6 costs or a fortnight's hard labour in Horsley house of correction. Offence committed 19 May 1830.

49/C/62   2 July 1830. Robert Davis of Bisley, gardener. Damaging one square yard [etc., as 49/C/61 except] Fine 2/6 damages and 8/6 costs or hard labour for a fortnight in Horsley house of correction. Offence committed 18 May 1830.

49/C/63   2 July 1830. William Bassett of Painswick, labourer. Ill-treating a mare, the property of William Capel the younger of Painswick. H. Burgh JP and Rev. P. Hawker JP at Stroud. Fine £1, to be paid to the king, or six weeks, without bail or mainprise, in Horsley house of correction. Offence committed 28 June 1830.

49/C/64   21 June 1830. Isaac White of Randwick, labourer. Damaging ash poles, the property of Rt. Hon. John, Lord Sherborne, at Standish. H. Burgh JP at Stroud. Fine 1/- damages and 10/- costs or hard labour for two months in Horsley house of correction. Offence committed 21 June 1830.

49/C/65   21 June 1830. William Barnes of Randwick, labourer. Damaging ash poles [etc., as 49/C/64].

49/C/66   24 June 1830. Daniel Jones, licensed victualler of the George, Minchinhampton. Keeping his premises open other than for the reception of travellers and allowing disorderly conduct. R. Kingscote JP, T. Kingscote JP, Rev. P. Hawker JP and Rev. H. Campbell JP. First offence. Fine £5 and 6/6 costs. Offence committed 7 June 1830.

49/C/67   4 June 1830. George Gully. Assaulting Thomas Webb junior in Great Badminton. F. Trotman JP, W. G. Davy JP and Henry Bush JP at Old Sodbury. Fine 5/-, to be paid to Thomas Osborne, overseer of the poor, and 10/6 costs, or one month in Horsley house of correction. Given twenty-eight days to pay. Offence committed 5 May 1830.

49/C/68   7 May 1830. Thomas Bedford. Assaulting Isaac Walker with a bill-hook in Marshfield. F. Trotman JP, W. Blathwayt JP, H. Bush JP and W. G. Davy JP at Old Sodbury. Fine £2, to be paid to John Jenkins, overseer of the poor, and 19/6 costs, or two months in Horsley house of correction. Given twenty-eight days to pay. Offence committed at about midnight on 1 May 1830.

49/C/69   26 April 1830. William Rogers of Hailes, farmer. Assaulting John Cooper, labourer, of Moreton in Marsh at Lemington. Rev. W. Boughton JP and Rev. J. R. Hall JP at Bourton on the Hill. Fine 20/-, to be paid to James Dee, farmer, overseer of the poor, and 12/6 costs, or two months in Northleach house of correction. Offence committed 19 April 1830.

49/C/70   10 May 1830. John Tracy of Mickleton, labourer. Assaulting George Harris and Thomas Farley at Mickleton. Rev. W. Boughton JP and Rev. J. R. Hall JP at Bourton on the Hill. Fine 3/-, to be paid to Joseph Price, overseer of the poor, and 13/6 costs, or one month in Northleach house of correction. Offence committed 3 May 1830.

49/C/71   10 May 1830. Daniel Ellis of Bourton on the Hill. Assaulting William Smith at Todenham. Rev. W. Boughton JP and Rev. J. R. Hall JP at Bourton on the Hill. Fine 3/-, to be paid to Joseph Partington, overseer of the poor, and 11/6 costs, or one calendar month in Northleach house of correction. Offence committed 10 April 1830.

49/C/72   21 June 1830. Mary Cox of Hidcote Bartrim [*MS.* Hitcott Barthram], single woman. Assaulting Elizabeth Gough. Rev. W. Boughton JP and Rev. J. Adams JP at Bourton on the Hill. Fine 6/-, to be paid to Richard Careless, overseer of the poor, and 8/6 costs, or one week in Northleach house of correction. Offence committed 7 June 1830.

49/C/73   24 June 1830. Richard Middlemore, licensed victualler of the Trumpet, Minchinhampton. Keeping his premises open other than for the reception of travellers and allowing disorderly behaviour and gaming with skittles. R. Kingscote JP, T. Kingscote JP, Rev. P. Hawker JP and Rev. H. Campbell JP. First offence. Fine £5 and 6/6 costs. Offence committed 7 June 1830.

49/C/74   4 May 1830. Samuel Baldry. Assaulting William Tytherleigh Bown, constable of Cheltenham. Sir W. Hicks, Bt., JP and J. H. Ollney JP at Cheltenham. Fine £2 10*s.* and 5/9 costs. Offence committed 1 May 1830.

49/C/75   4 May 1830. Samuel Taylor. Assaulting William Tytherleigh Bown [*etc., as* 49/C/74 *except*] Fine £1 and 5/9 costs.

49/C/76   10 June 1830. John Watson. Assaulting Jesse Castle, constable of Cheltenham. H. N. Trye JP and George Stevenson JP at Cheltenham. Fine £1 and 3/- costs. Offence committed 9 June 1830.

49/C/77   12 June 1830. Robert Wilson. Assaulting Margaret Taylor in Swindon. H. N. Trye JP and G. Stevenson JP at Cheltenham. Fine £1 and 10/6 costs. Offence committed 5 June 1830.

49/C/78   12 June 1830. Henry Jones. Assaulting Margaret Taylor in Swindon. H. N. Trye JP and G. Stevenson JP at Cheltenham. Fine 2/6. Offence committed 5 June 1830.

49/C/79   12 June 1830. Charles Newman. Assaulting Margaret Taylor [*etc., as* 49/C/78].

49/C/80   12 June 1830. William Abell. Assaulting John Addis in Swindon. H. N. Trye JP and G. Stevenson JP at Cheltenham. Fine 5/- and 3/6 costs. Offence committed 10 June 1830.

49/C/81   12 June 1830. John Abell. Assaulting John Addis [*etc., as* 49/C/80].

49/C/82   12 June 1830. Thomas Abell. Assaulting John Addis [*etc., as* 49/C/80].

49/C/83   10 June 1830. John Keeley [*also* Keetley]. Assaulting Thomas Caudle of Cheltenham, labourer. H. N. Trye JP and G. Stevenson JP at Cheltenham. Fine 10/- and 3/- costs. Offence committed 9 June 1830.

49/C/84   12 June 1830. Mary Hands, licensed victualler, of Cheltenham. Allowing drunkenness and disorderly behaviour on her premises. Rev. J. Neale JP and H. N. Trye JP at Cheltenham. Second offence. [*Cf.* 49/B/53.] Fine £1 and 4/6 costs. Offence committed 10 June 1830.

49/C/85   18 June 1830. Joseph Brinkworth, labourer, of King's Stanley. Keeping and using a gun to kill game when not qualified. H. Burgh JP and Rev. P. Hawker JP at Stroud. George Wilcockson, yeoman, of Woodchester, informer. Thomas Prout, under-gamekeeper, of King's Stanley, witness. Fine £5. Offence committed 18 June 1830.

49/C/86   2 July 1830. Richard Cockle of Nympsfield, labourer. Keeping and using a dog to kill game when not qualified. H. Burgh JP and Rev. P. Hawker JP at Stroud. George Wilcockson, yeoman, of Woodchester, informer. John Parker, under-gamekeeper, of Horsley, witness. Offender did not appear. Fine £5. Information given on 15 June 1830. Offence committed 10 June 1830.

49/D/1   1 Sept. 1830. Henry Telling, labourer, of Avening. Stealing peas from a field in Avening occupied by John Cook. G. P. Holford JP. Fine 6*d*. and 5/6 costs, both sums to be paid to the complainant. Offence committed 17 July 1830.

49/D/2   21 July 1830. William Tanner, innkeeper of the Greyhound, Tetbury. Keeping his premises open during the hours of divine service (11–12 o'clock). J. D. Phelps JP and H. Campbell JP. First offence. Fine £5 and 8/6 costs. Offence committed Sunday 11 July 1830.

49/D/3   16 Aug. 1830. William Chamberlain. Stealing vetches growing in a field in Chipping Campden, the property of William Southam. Rev. W. Boughton JP at Bourton on the Hill. Fine 6/- and 6*d*. damages, to be paid to William Stephens, overseer of the poor, and 8/6 costs to the complainant, or hard labour for one calendar month in Northleach house of correction. Offence committed 2 Aug. 1830.

49/D/4   2 Aug. 1830. Maurice Carney. Begging in Moreton in Marsh. Rev. C. Jeaffreson JP at Bourton on the Hill. Hard labour for one calendar month in Northleach house of correction. Offence committed 31 July 1830.

49/D/5   2 Aug. 1830. Richard Stephens. Assaulting William Lane at Chipping Campden. Rev. C. Jeaffreson JP and Rev. J. R. Hall JP at Bourton on the Hill. Fine 5/-, to be paid to Francis William Weston, an overseer of the poor, and 10/6 costs to the complainant, or one calendar month in Northleach house of correction. Offence committed 27 July 1830.

49/D/6   4 Oct. 1830. George Phipps and William Cockerell. Assaulting Thomas Poole at Bourton on the Hill. Rev. W. Boughton JP and Rev. J. R. Hall JP at Bourton on the Hill. Fine £4 4*s*. 6*d*., to be paid to James Wheatley, an overseer of the poor, and 15/6 costs to go to the complainant, or two calendar months in Northleach house of correction. Offence committed 27 Sept. 1830.

49/D/7   3 Sept. 1830. Miles Harvey, labourer, of Hawkesbury. Causing his wife and seven children to become chargeable to the parish for several months. Duke of Beaufort JP, W. Blathwayt JP, William Gabriel Davy JP and G. Bush JP at Old Sodbury. Hard labour for one calendar month in Horsley house of correction. Offence committed during several previous months.

49/D/8   10 Sept. 1830. William Long. Breaking down, with intent to steal, a dead hedge or fence in Acton Turville, the property of James Goutter. Duke of Beaufort JP, F. Trotman JP, W. G. Davy JP and G. Bush JP at Old Sodbury. Fine 1/- damages and 9/- costs or hard labour for one month in Horsley house of correction. Offence committed 7 Sept. 1830.

49/D/9   14 Oct. 1830. Robert Mustoe. Damaging a beech tree in Cranham, the property of Sir Edwin Sandys. Sir W. Hicks, Bt., JP at Cheltenham. Fine 10/-, to be paid to an overseer of the poor. Offence committed 2 Oct. 1830.

49/D/10   14 Oct. 1830. James Derrett. Damaging a beech tree [*etc*., as 49/D9 *adding*] 4/- damages and 3/6 costs to be paid to Sir Edwin Sandys's agent, Richard Barnfield.

49/D/11   12 Aug. 1830. William Little. Assaulting John Beard at Leckhampton. Rev. J. Neale JP and H. N. Trye JP at Cheltenham. Fine 2/6 and 3/6 costs. Offence committed 8 Aug. 1830.

49/D/12   24 Aug. 1830. Mary Powell. Assaulting Eliza Eagles at Cheltenham. Rev. J. Neale JP and Pearson Thompson JP at Cheltenham. Fine 5/- and 3/6 costs. Offence committed 11 Aug. 1830.

49/D/13   14 Oct. 1830. Charles Derrett. Assaulting Henry Cook at Badgeworth. Sir W. Hicks, Bt., JP and H. N. Trye JP at Cheltenham. Fine 5/- and 5/6 costs. Offence committed 11 Oct. 1830.

49/D/14   14 Oct. 1830. Charles Derrett. Assaulting Thomas Cook at Badgeworth. Sir W. Hicks, Bt., JP and H. N. Trye JP at Cheltenham. Fine 5/- and 2/- costs. Offence committed 11 Oct. 1830.

49/D/15   12 Aug. 1830. John Knight. Damaging a quantity of fruit growing in John Cooke's garden at Cheltenham. Rev. J. Neale JP at Cheltenham. Fine 10/-, 6/6 costs and 6d. damages. Offence committed 19 July 1830.

49/D/16   16 Aug. 1830. Elizabeth and William Court. Damaging a quantity of growing potatoes and grass, the property of William Knight, at St. Briavels hundred. C. Crawley JP and M. Colchester JP at Newnham. One calendar month in Littledean house of correction. Offence committed 4 Aug. 1830.

49/D/17   17 Aug. 1830. Sarah Vine. Assaulting Mary wife of James Harris at Woolaston. C. Bathurst JP and T. Thomas JP at Lydney. Fine 2/6, to be paid to William Tudor, overseer of the poor, and 4/6 costs, or one calendar month's hard labour in Littledean house of correction. Given twenty-eight days to pay. Offence committed 7 Aug. 1830.

49/D/18   13 Sept. 1830. Sarah Hayward. Assaulting Charlotte Niblett at Abenhall [*MS.* Abinghall]. C. Crawley JP and J. Pyrke JP at Newnham. Fine 5/-, to be paid to William Burcher, overseer of the poor, and 6/- costs, or one calendar month's hard labour in Littledean house of correction. Given twelve days to pay. Offence committed 8 Sept. 1830.

49/D/19   14 Sept. 1830. Joseph Evans the younger. Stealing nuts and plums and damaging a nut tree in Alvington, the property of Sarah Lucas. C. Bathurst JP and T. Thomas JP at Lydney. Fine 2/- damages and 4/- costs or hard labour for one calendar month in Littledean house of correction. Given fourteen days to pay. Offence committed 5 Sept. 1830.

49/D/20   14 Sept. 1830. Joseph Evans. Stealing nuts and plums [*etc., as* 49/D/19].

49/D/21   12 Aug. 1830. John Clatworthy. Assaulting Elizabeth Cooke at St. Philip and St. Jacob, [Bristol]. J. Parker JP and W. Munro JP at Lawfords Gate sessions room. Fine 10/- and 6/6 costs or one calendar month in Lawfords Gate house of correction. Offence committed 3 Aug. 1830.

49/D/22   5 Aug. 1830. Thomas Bryant. Assaulting Thomas Morgan at Bitton. J. Parker JP and W. Munro JP at Lawfords Gate sessions room. Fine 6/6 and 13/6 costs or one calendar month in Lawfords Gate house of correction. Offence committed 29 July 1830.

49/D/23   16 Sept. 1830. Hannah Fox. Assaulting Ann Mack at St. Philip and St. Jacob, [Bristol]. W. Munro JP and W. Davies D.D. JP at Lawfords Gate sessions room. Fine 2/6 and 6/6 costs or ten days in Lawfords Gate house of correction. Offence committed 8 Sept. 1830.

49/D/24   16 Sept. 1830. Elizabeth Connell. Assaulting Margaret McCarthy at St. Philip and St. Jacob, [Bristol]. W. Munro JP and W. Davies D.D. JP at Lawfords Gate sessions room. Fine 5/- and 12/- costs or fourteen days in Lawfords Gate house of correction. Offence committed 12 Sept. 1830.

49/D/25   17 Aug. 1830. Lewis Chappell of Wotton under Edge, labourer. Stealing gooseberries from a garden, the property of Daniel Lloyd, gentleman, of Wotton under Edge. W. M. Adey JP and H. W. Dyer JP at Wotton under Edge. Twenty-one days' hard labour in Horsley house of correction. Offence committed 8 Aug. 1830.

49/D/26   9 Aug. 1830. Llewellin Smith of Wotton under Edge, labourer. Stealing gooseberries [*etc., as* 49/D/25 *except*] Hard labour for one calendar month.

49/D/27   6 Aug. 1830. George Cox of Cam, labourer. Stealing a quantity of pea plants growing in enclosed land, the property of William Long, farmer, of Cam. W. M. Adey JP and

H. W. Dyer JP at Wotton under Edge. Hard Labour for one calendar month in Horsley house of correction. Offence committed 5 Aug. 1830.

49/D/28   31 Aug. 1830. Thomas Hatherell of Hillesley, labourer. Stealing potatoes growing on land in Hillesley, the property of Joseph Williams, labourer. W. M. Adey JP at Wotton under Edge. Hard labour for one calendar month in Horsley house of correction. Offence committed 31 Aug. 1830.

49/D/29   14 Sept. 1830. Hester wife of Thomas Fletcher, labourer. Stealing potatoes growing in a close of land occupied by Samuel Goodson Dauncey at Wotton under Edge. W. M. Adey JP at Wotton under Edge. Hard labour for twenty-one days in Horsley house of correction. Offence committed 13 Sept. 1830.

49/D/30   16 Sept. 1830. James Bennett, labourer, of Wotton under Edge. Stealing onions growing in a garden in Ozleworth, the property of William Jones, fuller. W. M. Adey JP at Wotton under Edge. Hard labour for six calendar months in Horsley house of correction. Offence committed c. 15 Sept. 1830.

49/D/31   19 Aug. 1830. William Smith of Coaley, weaver. Stealing a quarter of a peck of potatoes growing in a close of land, the property of Charles Smith the elder of Coaley, farmer. W. M. Adey JP and P. B. Purnell JP at Wotton under Edge. Hard labour for one calendar month in Horsley house of correction. Offence committed 28 July 1830.

49/D/32   16 Oct. 1830. John Sargent, late of Kingswood, labourer. Stealing a peck of turnips from enclosed land in Hawkesbury, the property of William Long of Oldbury on the Hill. H. W. Dyer JP at Wotton under Edge. Twenty-one days' hard labour in Horsley house of correction. Offence committed 13 Oct. 1830.

49/D/33   24 Sept. 1830. William Heath *alias* Mercer and Thomas Phelps, labourers, both of Dursley. Stealing potatoes from a garden in Dursley occupied by James Young. W. M. Adey JP and P. B. Purnell JP at Wotton under Edge. Hard labour for four calendar months in Horsley house of correction. Offence committed on the night of 16 Sept. 1830.

49/D/34   20 Aug. 1830. John Fisher of Uley, labourer. Stealing beans from enclosed land in Uley, the property of Thomas John Lloyd Baker, gentleman. P. B. Purnell JP, W. M. Adey JP and H. W. Dyer JP at Wotton under Edge. Twenty-one days' hard labour in Horsley house of correction. Offence committed 12 Aug. 1830.

49/D/35   20 Sept. 1830. George Hooper *alias* Cornock and George Trotman, both of North Nibley, labourers. Stealing potatoes from a close of land in North Nibley occupied by Thomas Gillman. W. M. Adey JP at Wotton under Edge. Twenty-one days' hard labour in Horsley house of correction. Offence committed 30 Aug. 1830.

49/D/36   1 Oct. 1830. John Martin of Cam, labourer. Stealing apples from an orchard, the property of William Hopton Hadley of Cam. W. M. Adey JP and H. W. Dyer JP at Wotton under Edge. Fine 5/-, to be paid to James Holloway, petty constable of Cam, and 5/- costs, or fourteen days' hard labour in Horsley house of correction. Given seven days to pay. Offence committed 1 Oct. 1830.

49/D/37   8 Oct. 1830. Paul Park of Kingswood, labourer. Stealing rails from a fence at Wotton under Edge, the property of William Fitzhardinge Berkeley. W. M. Adey JP at Wotton under Edge. Fine £2, to be paid to Edward Page, an overseer of the poor, 20/- (the value of the rails) and 8/- costs. Given until noon the next day to pay. In default, two months' hard labour in Horsley house of correction. Offence committed 22 Sept. 1830.

49/D/38   8 Oct. 1830. Thomas Vaisey of Kingswood, labourer. Stealing rails [*etc.*, *as* 49/D/37].

49/D/39   5 Aug. 1830. Robert Humphris. Stealing half a peck of peas, worth 6*d.*, the property of Mary Collett of Upper Slaughter. Rev. F. E. Witts JP at Stow on the Wold. Fourteen days' hard labour in Northleach house of correction. Offence committed 31 Aug. [*sic, ? recte* July] 1830.

49/D/40   12 Aug. 1830. William Harris. Stealing half a peck of peas, worth 6*d.*, in Lower Swell, the property of John Merchant. Rev. F. E. Witts JP at Stow on the Wold. Fine 5/-, 6*d.* damages and 1/6 costs. Offence committed 1 Aug. 1830

49/D/41   19 Aug. 1830. William Cook, Richard Stratford and Richard Townley. Cutting down and stealing several young trees in Great Barrington, valued at 3/-, the property of Lord Dynevor. Rev. F. E. Witts JP at Stow on the Wold. Each fined 5/-, to be paid to Joseph Tombs, an overseer of the poor of Great Barrington, 1/- damages and 1/6 costs, or fourteen days' hard labour in Northleach house of correction. Offence committed 18 Aug. 1830.

49/D/42   30 Sept. 1830. Thomas Rogers. Assaulting Elizabeth Spear at Clifton. H. W. Newman JP and G. Goldney JP at Lawfords Gate sessions room. Fine 1/- and 6/6 costs or seven days in Lawfords Gate house of correction. Offence committed 28 Sept. 1830.

49/D/43   30 Sept. 1830. James Amos. Assaulting Mary Woodington at St. George, [Bristol]. H. W. Newman JP and G. Goldney JP at Lawfords Gate sessions room. Fine 10/- and 6/- costs or fourteen days in Lawfords Gate house of correction. Offence committed 23 Sept. 1830.

49/D/44   18 Sept. 1830. Richard Keefe. Assaulting Thomas Mack at St. Philip and St. Jacob, [Bristol]. J. Haythorne JP and J. Savage JP at Lawfords Gate sessions room. Fine £1 12*s.* 6*d.* and 17/6 costs or six weeks in Lawfords Gate house of correction. Offence committed 17 Sept. 1830.

49/D/45   29 July 1830. John Scuse. Assaulting William Tickbon at Winterbourne. J. Parker JP and D. Cave JP at Lawfords Gate sessions room. Fine 11/- and 9/- costs or one calendar month in Lawfords Gate house of correction. Offence committed 27 July 1830.

49/D/46   14 Oct. 1830. Benjamin Hemborough. Setting a wire to catch hares on land belonging to Lord De Clifford at Westbury on Trym. G. Goldney JP at Lawfords Gate sessions room. William Powell Hartley, gentleman, of Bristol, informer. John Grey of Lawrence Weston, witness. Offender did not appear. Fine £5. Offence committed 2 Sept. 1830.

50/A/1   6 Dec. 1830. James Pickthorne. Assaulting Elizabeth Brown at St. Briavels hundred. M. Colchester JP and C. Crawley JP at Newnham. Fine 5/- and 6/- costs or seven days' hard labour in Littledean house of correction. Offence committed 24 Nov. 1830.

50/A/2   7 Dec. 1830. Henry York. Assaulting Timothy Jones at St. Briavels hundred. C. Bathurst JP and George Ormerod JP at Lydney. Fine £2 13*s.* and 7/- costs or two calendar months' hard labour in Littledean house of correction. Given fourteen days to pay. Offence committed 7 Dec. 1830.

50/A/3   25 Oct. 1830. John Beale. Assaulting Richard Glastonbury the younger at Littledean. C. Crawley JP and J. Pyrke JP at Newnham. Fine 2/6 and 3/6 costs or fourteen days' hard labour in Littledean house of correction. Offence committed 4 Oct. 1830.

50/A/4   20 Dec. 1830. John Brown Syms. Assaulting James Davis at Westbury on Severn. Rev. C. Crawley JP and Rev. J. Sayer JP at Newnham. Fine £1 10*s.* and 15/6 costs or two calendar months' hard labour in Littledean house of correction. Offence committed 24 Nov. 1830.

50/A/5   20 Dec. 1830. James Syms. Assaulting James Davis [*etc., as* 50/A/4].

50/A/6　21 Dec. 1830. John Griffiths. Assaulting Eliza Morgan at Newland. P. J. Ducarel JP and E. Machen JP at Coleford. Fine 10/- and 6/- costs or one calendar month's hard labour in Littledean house of correction. Given twenty-eight days to pay. Offence committed 21 Nov. 1830.

50/A/7　3 Jan. 1831. George Hall of Cirencester, victualler. Allowing disorderly conduct on licensed premises. Henry Cripps JP and W. Croome JP. First offence. Fine 10/- and 2/6 costs. Offence committed 27 Dec. 1830.

50/A/8　3 Jan. 1831. William Payne of Cirencester, victualler. Allowing disorderly conduct [etc., as 50/A/7].

50/A/9　3 Jan. 1831. John Pound of Cirencester, carpenter and beer retailer. Selling beer and allowing drinking on his premises after 10 p.m. H. Cripps JP and W. Croome JP. First offence. Fine 40/- and 3/6 costs. Offence committed 18 Dec. 1830.

50/A/10　13 Dec. 1830. James Gardner of Cirencester, baker and beer retailer. Selling beer and allowing drinking on his premises after 10 p.m. Rev. Edward Andrew Daubeny JP and Rev. H. A. Pye JP. First offence. Fine 40/- and 3/6 costs. Offence committed 27 Nov. 1830.

50/A/11　13 Dec. 1830. George Edwards of Cirencester, carpenter and beer retailer. Selling beer [etc., as 50/A/10].

50/A/12　13 Dec. 1830. John Fox of Cirencester, beer retailer. Selling beer [etc., as 50/A/10].

50/A/13　28 Oct. 1830. Joseph Fowler. Assaulting Hannah Millett at Frampton Cotterell. William Fripp JP and H. W. Newman JP at Lawfords Gate sessions room. Fine 2/- and 8/- costs. Offence committed 18 Oct. 1830.

50/A/14　11 Nov. 1830. John Murren. Assaulting James Maluash at St. Philip and St. Jacob, [Bristol]. W. Fripp JP and H. W. Newman JP at Lawfords Gate sessions room. Fine 4/6 and 5/6 costs or ten days in Lawfords Gate house of correction. Offence committed 1 Nov. 1830.

50/A/15　15 Nov. 1830. Tobias Fox. Assaulting William Locke at St. Philip and St. Jacob, [Bristol]. W. Fripp JP and H. W. Newman JP at Lawfords Gate sessions room. Fine £1 and 5/6 costs or one month in Lawfords Gate house of correction.

50/A/16　18 Nov. 1830. Sarah Guppy. Assaulting Abraham Turner at Clifton. W. Fripp JP and H. W. Newman JP at Lawfords Gate sessions room. Fine 6d. and 6/6 costs or one day in Lawfords Gate house of correction. Offence committed 7 Nov. 1830.

50/A/17　25 Nov. 1830. Ann Davis. Assaulting Hester Bennett at St. Philip and St. Jacob, [Bristol]. H. W. Newman JP and J. Lewis JP at Lawfords Gate sessions room. Fine 2/6 and 7/6 costs or ten days in Lawfords Gate house of correction. Offence committed 22 Nov. 1830.

50/A/18　2 Nov. 1830. John Warner of Eastington. Assisting Charles Clutterbuck in the taking of game without a licence. T. J. Lloyd Baker JP and C. O. Cambridge JP at Wheatenhurst. Fine £20. Offence committed 25 Oct. 1830.

50/A/19　2 Dec. 1830. Thomas Sharp of Minchinhampton, beer retailer. Allowing quarrelling and fighting on licensed premises. Rev. H. Campbell JP and T. Kingscote JP. First offence. Fine 40/- and 6/6 costs. Offence committed 28 Nov. 1830.

50/A/20　16 Dec. 1830. Edward Hudson. Stealing two pecks of turnips from enclosed land called Terretts, the property of William Ratcliffe of Woodchester. Rev. P. Hawker JP at Rodborough. One calendar month's hard labour in Horsley house of correction. Offence committed 26 Nov. 1830.

50/A/21　16 Dec. 1830. George Coaley or Cowley. Stealing two pecks of turnips [etc., as 50/A/20].

50/A/22   16 Dec. 1830. William Risby. Stealing two pecks of turnips from enclosed land in Horsley called Harvey's Grave, the property of Hannah Fry, widow [*etc., as* 50/A/20].

50/A/23   16 Dec. 1830. Daniel Gill. Stealing two pecks of turnips [*etc., as* 50/A/22].

50/A/24   7 Sept. 1830. Benjamin Hodges, victualler of the Fish inn, Lechlade. Allowing disorderly conduct on his premises. Hon. James Dutton JP, Rev. W. Price JP, Rev. T. Huntingford JP and Rev. J. W. Peters JP. First offence. Fine £4 and £1 costs. Offence committed 15 July 1830.

50/A/25   10 Nov. 1830. Job Atkins, beer and cider retailer, of Dumbleton. Allowing drinking on his premises after 10 p.m. J. Timbrill D. D. JP and Rev. J. Keysall JP. First offence. Fine 40/- and 9/- costs. Offence committed 5 Nov. 1830.

50/A/26   17 Dec. 1830. John Strange, keeper of the turnpike gate at Dunkirk, Hawkesbury. Illegally demanding a toll of sixpence from Joseph Bence, constable of Marshfield, for a horse and cart conveying a prisoner from Horsley house of correction to a Petty Sessions held at the Cross Hands inn, Old Sodbury. F. Trotman JP and W. G. Davy JP. Fine 1/- and 8/6 costs. Offence committed Friday 3 Dec. 1830.

50/A/27   3 Dec. 1830. Stephen Bryant the younger of Westerleigh. Assaulting Ann Turner by riding over her on horseback in Westerleigh. W. Blathwayt JP and G. Bush JP at Old Sodbury. Fine £3 3*s.* (to pay for surgical treatment) and 17/- costs, or one month in Horsley house of correction. Given four days to pay. Offence committed 24 Sept. 1830.

50/A/28   3 Dec. 1830. Richard Limbrick of Wickwar. Leaving his wife and family chargeable to the parish. W. G. Davy JP, W. Blathwayt JP and G. Bush JP at Old Sodbury. Two previous convictions for same offence. [*Cf.* 50/A/85.] Sentenced to hard labour in Horsley house of correction until next Q.S. Offence committed 29 Nov. 1830.

50/A/29   12 Nov. 1830. James Bruton of Wotton under Edge, weaver. Stealing turnips growing on enclosed land occupied by William Miller Esq. of Ozleworth. W. M. Adey JP and H. W. Dyer JP at Wotton under Edge. Seven days' hard labour in Horsley house of correction. Offence committed 31 Oct. 1830.

50/A/30   29 Oct. 1830. William Chapman of Cromhall, farmer. Assaulting William Kemp of Cromhall. W. M. Adey JP and H. W. Dyer JP at Wotton under Edge. Fine 5/-, to be paid to William Daniells, overseer of the poor, and 5/6 costs, or seven days in Horsley house of correction. Offence committed 15 Oct. 1830.

50/A/31   5 Nov. 1830. David Hopkins of Hillesley, Hawkesbury. Assaulting Alexander Ingram, watchmaker, of Wotton under Edge. W. M. Adey JP and P. B. Purnell JP at Wotton under Edge. Fine £4, to be paid to Edward Page, overseer of the poor of Wotton under Edge, and 5/- costs, or two calendar months' hard labour in Horsley house of correction. Offence committed 3 Nov. 1830.

50/A/32   2 Nov. 1830. John Dyer of Wotton under Edge, labourer. Stealing turnips growing in enclosed ground in Wotton under Edge, the property of Edward Collins, farmer, of Ozleworth. W. M. Adey JP at Wotton under Edge. Three weeks' hard labour in Horsley house of correction. Offence committed 19 Oct. 1830.

50/A/33   29 Oct. 1830. Elizabeth wife of William Pearce, labourer, of Kingswood, Wilts. Stealing part of a fence at Tresham, Hawkesbury, enclosing ground occupied by Elizabeth Worlock, widow. W. M. Adey JP and H. W. Dyer JP at Wotton under Edge. Fine 20/-, 5/- costs and 3*d.* damages or three weeks' hard labour in Horsley house of correction. Offence committed 18 Oct. 1830.

50/A/34   7 Dec. 1830. Robert Aspinall, coachman. Being drunk in charge of a stage-coach at Northleach, thereby endangering passengers. R. Capper JP at Cheltenham. Jacob Caudle, informer. William Pinniger, witness. Fine 40/-. Offence committed 3 Dec. 1830.

50/A/35   11 Dec. 1830. James Garvey, hawker. Offering silk shawls for sale in Shurdington, without a licence. Rev. W. Hicks JP at Cheltenham. Elisha Castle, yeoman, of Cheltenham, informer. Henry Watkins, witness. Fine £10. Offence committed 11 Dec. 1830.

50/A/36   11 Dec. 1830. Francis Runacan, yeoman. Offering silk shawls [*etc., as* 50/A/35].

50/A/37   11 Dec. 1830. Jonathan Briggs of Leckhampton, beer retailer. Allowing drunkenness and disorderly behaviour on his premises. R. Capper JP and Thomas Newell JP at Cheltenham Petty Sessions. First offence. Fine £2 and 9/- costs. Offence committed 7 Dec. 1830.

50/A/38   23 Dec. 1830. Thomas Fox of Cheltenham, beer retailer. Selling beer out of permitted hours. R. B. Cooper JP and T. Newell JP at Cheltenham Petty Sessions. First offence. Fine 40/- and 6/6 costs. Offence committed 21 Dec. 1830.

50/A/39   23 Nov. 1830. John Shotten of Cheltenham, licensed victualler. Allowing drunkenness and disorderly behaviour on his premises. R. B. Cooper JP and R. Capper JP at Cheltenham. First offence. Fine 20/- and 2/- costs. Offence committed 21 Nov. 1830.

50/A/40   13 Dec. 1830. Mary Sheldon of Cheltenham, licensed victualler. Allowing drunkenness and disorderly behaviour on her premises. R. Capper JP and T. Newell JP at Cheltenham. First offence. Fine 20/- and 2/- costs.

50/A/41   7 Dec. 1830. Thomas Gunnall of Cheltenham, beer retailer. Allowing notoriously bad characters to meet on his premises. Sir W. Hicks JP and R. Capper JP at Cheltenham Petty Sessions. First offence. Fine £3 and 4/6 costs. Offence committed 5 Dec. 1830.

50/A/42   30 Dec. 1830. John Fletcher and George Cooper. Assaulting William Robins at Cheltenham. T. Newell JP and Rev. John Edwards JP at Cheltenham. Fine 12/6 and 6/6 costs. Offence committed 27 Dec. 1830.

50/A/43   21 Dec. 1830. Charles Morgan. Assaulting John Milbank at Cheltenham. Sir W. Hicks JP and R. B. Cooper JP at Cheltenham. Fine £1 and 2/- costs. Offence committed 20 Dec. 1830.

50/A/44   26 Oct. 1830. Samuel Arnold. Assaulting Spaul Thurlow at Cheltenham. R. Capper JP and Rev. W. Hicks JP at Cheltenham. Fine 2/6 and 5/6 costs. Offence committed — Oct. 1830.

50/A/45   11 Nov. 1830. Thomas Masters. Assaulting Richard Winter at Charlton Kings. Sir W. Hicks JP and T. Newell JP at Cheltenham. Fine £2 and 9/- costs. Offence committed 8 Nov. 1830.

50/A/46   14 Dec. 1830. Henry Barnes. Assaulting Charles Mott at Cheltenham. R. Capper JP and T. Newell JP at Cheltenham. Fine 10/- and 5/- costs. Offence committed 11 Dec. 1830.

50/A/47   9 Dec. 1830. William Powell, Frederick Postons and Thomas Mitchell. Assaulting Thomas and John Ballinger at Charlton Kings. R. Capper JP and R. B. Cooper JP at Cheltenham. Fine 15/- and 13/6 costs. Offence committed 6 Dec. 1830.

50/A/48   25 Nov. 1830. Samuel Smith. Assaulting Thomas Cooke at Cheltenham. R. B. Cooper JP and R. Capper JP at Cheltenham. Fine £2 and 5/6 costs. Offence committed 24 Nov. 1830.

50/A/49   22 Nov. 1830. William Betteridge of Sutton under Brailes, labourer. Using a snare to kill hares. Rev. J. Adams JP. First offence. Fine £10, half to be paid to William Randall, the informer, and the rest to Edward Whale, overseer of the poor. Offence committed Sunday 31 Oct. 1830.

50/A/50   22 Nov. 1830. William Bryan of Sutton under Brailes, labourer. Using a snare [*etc.*, *as* 50/A/49].

50/A/51   22 Nov. 1830. John Hiorn of Sutton under Brailes, labourer. Using a snare [*etc.*, *as* 50/A/49].

50/ A/52   22 Oct. 1830. James Harding. Begging in [Chipping] Campden. Rev. W. Boughton JP at Blockley. Hard labour for one calendar month in Northleach house of correction. Offence committed 20 Oct. 1830.

50/A/53   1 Nov. 1830. Thomas Farebrother, late of Bourton on the Hill, labourer. Leaving his wife Linda chargeable to the parish. Rev. J. R. Hall JP and Rev. W. Boughton JP at Bourton on the Hill. Hard labour for one calendar month in Northleach house of correction. Offence committed 2 Oct. 1830.

50/A/54   1 Nov. 1830. Richard Charlott, late of Clifford Chambers, labourer. Leaving his wife Elizabeth chargeable to the parish. Rev. J. R. Hall JP at Bourton on the Hill. Hard labour for one calendar month in Northleach house of correction. Offence committed 18 Oct. 1830.

50/A/55   20 Dec. 1830. Richard Mason. Assaulting Thomas Collett at Longborough. Rev. J. Adams JP and Rev. J. R. Hall JP at Bourton on the Hill. Fine 1/6, to be paid to Thomas Alcock, overseer of the poor, and 11/6 costs, or seven days in Northleach house of correction. Offence committed 24 Nov. 1830.

50/A/56   17 Dec. 1830. William Baker. Causing his recently born child to become chargeable to Bisley parish. H. Burgh JP at Stroud. Hard labour for one calendar month in Horsley house of correction. Offence committed 17 Dec. 1830.

50/A/57   6 Nov. 1830. Elizabeth wife of Thomas Gribble of Stroud, labourer. Stealing turnips growing in a field, the property of William Lewis of Stroud. H. Burgh JP at Stroud. Two weeks in Horsley house of correction. Offence committed 28 Oct. 1830.

50/A/58   17 Dec. 1830. Benjamin Lewis of Rodborough, labourer. Breaking two windows at James Barnfield's house at Rodborough. H. Burgh JP at Stroud. Fine 7/- damages and 9/- costs or hard labour for two calendar months in Horsley house of correction. Offence committed 10 Dec. 1830.

50/A/59   11 Dec. 1830. Samuel Cooke and Henry Cratchley, labourers, of Stroud. Stealing part of a fence, the property of Benjamin Chandler, butcher, of Stroud. H. Burgh JP at Stroud. Fine £1, 6*d.* damages and 8/6 costs or hard labour for one calendar month in Horsley house of correction. Offence committed 10 Dec. 1830.

50/A/60   29 July 1830. Nathaniel Partridge the elder and Nathaniel Partridge the younger of Stroud, dyers. Assaulting William Nicholls of Painswick, toll-collector. H. Burgh JP and Rev. P. Hawker JP at Stroud. Fine 2/6 and 11/6 costs. Offence committed 16 July 1830.

50/A/61   23 July 1830. William Shields of Stroud, mop-maker. Assaulting Richard Clarke of Stroud, cloth-dresser. H. Burgh JP and Rev. P. Hawker JP at Stroud. Fine £2 or one month's hard labour in Horsley house of correction. Offence committed 22 July 1830.

50/A/62   24 Sept. 1830. William Sparrow, labourer, and his wife Maria, of Stroud. Assaulting William Collier of Stroud, carpenter. H. Burgh JP and Rev. P. Hawker JP at Stroud. Fine £1 and 12/6 costs or two calendar months in Horsley house of correction. Offence committed 22 Sept. 1830.

50/A/63   28 Aug. 1830. Thomas Pegler of Stroud, labourer. Stealing pears from a garden, the property of George Gingell of Stroud, innkeeper. H. Burgh JP at Stroud. Hard labour for six calendar months in Horsley house of correction. Offence committed 24 Aug. 1830.

50/A/64   28 Aug. 1830. Aaron Sitlington of Stroud, labourer. Stealing pears [*etc.*, *as* 50/A/63].

50/A/65   30 Aug. 1830. Thomas Dalby of Rodborough, labourer. Stealing potatoes from a garden in Rodborough, the property of Henry Burgh Esq. Rev. P. Hawker JP at Stroud. Hard labour for six calendar months in Horsley house of correction. Offence committed 26 Aug. 1830.

50/A/66   18 Aug. 1830. Samuel Webb, tollgate keeper, of Stroud. Obstructing the footway by placing a wooden building on the side of the turnpike road leading to Cainscross. H. Burgh JP. Fine £5. Offence committed 12 Aug. 1830.

50/A/67   8 Oct. 1830. James Bailey of King's Stanley, labourer. Stealing apples from an orchard, the property of Samuel Raisher, yeoman, of King's Stanley. H. Burgh JP and Rev. P. Hawker JP at Stroud. Hard labour for one calendar month in Horsley house of correction. Offence committed 3 Oct. 1830.

50/A/68   6 Dec. 1830. James Wathen, reputed thief. Loitering in Silver Street, Stroud, with intent to commit a felony. H. Burgh JP at Stroud. Hard labour for three calendar months in Horsley house of correction. Offence committed 23 Nov. 1830.

50/A/69   1 Dec. 1830. Mary Ann Clarke, prostitute. Riotous behaviour in a public street in Stroud. H. Burgh JP at Stroud. Hard labour for one calendar month in Horsley house of correction. Offence committed 30 Nov. 1830.

50/A/70   12 Nov. 1830. Thomas Littlewood. Begging in Stroud. H. Burgh JP at Stroud. Hard labour for one calendar month in Horsley house of correction. Offence committed 11 Nov. 1830.

50/A/71   7 Dec. 1830. Martha Mather. Begging in Stroud. H. Burgh JP at Stroud. Hard labour for one calendar month in Horsley house of correction. Offence committed 7 Dec. 1830.

50/A/72   15 Nov. 1830. John Pratt. Leaving his wife and four children chargeable to Painswick parish. H. Burgh JP at Stroud. Hard labour for one calendar month in Horsley house of correction. Offence committed about five months previously.

50/A/73   27 July 1830. Samuel Samuels. Begging in Brookthorpe. H. Burgh JP at Stroud. Hard labour for one calendar month in Horsley house of correction. Offence committed 25 July 1830.

50/A/74   4 Aug. 1830. Mary Kearsey. Begging in Stroud. H. Burgh JP at Stroud. Hard labour for one calendar month in Horsley house of correction. Offence committed 4 Aug. 1830.

50/A/75   21 Aug. 1830. Richard Alder. Vagrancy in Stroud. H. Burgh JP at Stroud. Hard labour for three calendar months in Horsley house of correction. Offence committed 20 Aug. 1830.

50/A/76   22 Aug. 1830. Thomas Williams. Playing a game of chance called Ringing the Bull in Stroud. H. Burgh JP at Stroud. Hard labour for three calendar months in Horsley house of correction. Offence committed 21 Aug. 1830.

50/A/77   22 Aug. 1830. John Riddiford. Playing a game [*etc.*, *as* 50/A/76].

50/A/78   22 Aug. 1830. Joseph Ledwick, reputed thief. Loitering with intent to commit a felony in Stroud. H. Burgh JP at Stroud. Hard labour for three calendar months in Horsley house of correction. Offence committed 21 Aug. 1830.

50/A/79   8 Oct. 1830. William Morgan. Begging in Stroud. H. Burgh JP and Rev. P. Hawker JP at Stroud. Hard labour for one calendar month in Horsley house of correction. Offence committed 7 Oct. 1830.

50/A/80   22 Aug. 1830. Henry Cratchley. Vagrancy in Standish. H. Burgh JP at Stroud. Six weeks' hard labour in Horsley house of correction. Offence committed 22 Aug. 1830.

50/A/81 30 July 1830. Charles Cole. Causing his wife and family to be chargeable to Painswick parish for the previous twelve months. H. Burgh JP at Stroud. Hard labour for one calendar month in Horsley house of correction. Offence committed *c.* July 1829.

50/A/82 7 Sept. 1830. William Clissold. Leaving his wife and three children chargeable to Painswick parish. H. Burgh JP at Stroud. Three weeks' hard labour in Horsley house of correction. Offence committed ten weeks previously.

50/A/83 4 Sept. 1830. Jacob Fisher. Leaving his wife and two children chargeable to Painswick parish. H. Burgh JP at Stroud. Hard labour for two calendar months in Horsley house of correction. Offence committed about five weeks previously.

50/A/84 31 Dec. 1830. John Rawlins. Stealing potatoes from a field in Cold Ashton, the property of John Powney, yeoman. F. Trotman JP at Pucklechurch. Hard labour for one calendar month in Horsley house of correction. Offence committed 30/31 Dec. 1830.

50/A/85 22 July 1830. Richard Limbrick. Leaving his three children chargeable to Wickwar parish. F. Trotman JP at Pucklechurch. William Neale, overseer of the poor of Wickwar, informer. Hard labour for two calendar months in Horsley house of correction. Offence committed 25 March 1830.

50/A/86 30 Aug. 1830. John Sergeant. Leaving his wife and two children chargeable to Marshfield parish. F. Trotman JP at Pucklechurch. William Huff, overseer of the poor of Marshfield, informer. Hard labour for two calendar months in Horsley house of correction. Offence committed 1 April 1830.

50/A/87 25 Jan. 1831. Isaac Thompson. Assaulting John Winbow [*also* Wimbow] at Hawkesbury Upton, tithingman in the execution of his duty. E. J. Somers JP and —— —— at Badminton. Fine 40/-, to be paid to Daniel Brooks, overseer of the poor of Hawkesbury, and 10/- costs. Given one day to pay. In default, one calendar month in Horsley house of correction. Offence committed Saturday evening 22 Jan. 1831.

50/A/88 16 July 1830. William Weaver of Bisley, wheelwright. Exposing one hare for sale in Stroud without a licence. H. Burgh JP and Rev. P. Hawker JP at Stroud. William Robins, gardener, and John Gay, labourer, both of Stroud, informer and witness. Offender did not appear. Fine £5. Offence committed 8 July 1830.

50/B/1 25 Jan. 1831. William Davison, nailer. Becoming chargeable to the parish by returning to Wotton under Edge with his wife and family, having been removed elsewhere by settlement order the previous October. W. M. Adey JP and H. W. Dyer JP at Wotton under Edge. Hard labour for one month in Horsley house of correction.

50/B/2 19 Jan. 1831. Elisha King. Leaving his wife and children chargeable to Cam parish. H. W. Dyer JP at Wotton under Edge. Three months' hard labour in Horsley house of correction. Offence committed Oct. 1830.

50/B/3 20 Jan. 1831. James Clarke. Assaulting James Bryant in Clifton. J. Parker JP and J. S. Harford JP at Lawfords Gate sessions room. Fine £4 11*s.* 6*d.* and 8/6 costs or two calendar months in Lawfords Gate house of correction. Offence committed 17 Jan. 1831.

50/B/4 17 Feb. 1831. Robert William Meloy. Assaulting Mary Meloy at St. Philip and St. Jacob, [Bristol]. A. G. H. Battersby JP and W. Fripp JP at Lawfords Gate sessions room. Fine £1 and 6/- costs or one month in Lawfords Gate house of correction. Offence committed 14 Feb. 1831.

50/B/5 27 Jan. 1831. William Ross. Assaulting William Bryant at St. Philip and St. Jacob, [Bristol]. J. Parker JP and H. W. Newman JP at Lawfords Gate sessions room. Fine 16/- and 4/- costs or one month in Lawfords Gate house of correction. Offence committed 12 Dec. 1830.

50/B/6   24 March 1831. William Upton of Winterbourne. Using a wire to catch game in Olveston without a licence. C. L. Walker JP and H. W. Newman JP at Lawfords Gate sessions room. Fine £10. Offence committed 17 March 1831.

50/B/7   24 March 1831. Moses May of Mangotsfield. Using a wire [*etc.*, *as* 50/B/6].

50/B/8   24 March 1831. James Cook of Olveston. Using a gun to kill game without a licence. C. L. Walker JP and H. W. Newman JP at Lawfords Gate sessions room. Fine £10. Offence committed 26 Dec. 1830.

50/B/9   27 Jan. 1831. Anthony Gudge of St. Philip and St. Jacob, [Bristol]. Keeping his house open and selling beer after 10 p.m. J. Parker JP and J. S. Harford JP at a Petty Sessions for Bristol division. First offence. Fine £2. Offence committed 15 Jan. 1831.

50/B/10   27 Jan. 1831. John Ware of St. Philip and St. Jacob, [Bristol]. Keeping his house open [*etc.*, *as* 50/B/9].

50/B/11   27 Jan. 1831. Samuel Hodges of St. Philip and St. Jacob, [Bristol]. Keeping his house open [*etc.*, *as* 50/B/9 *omitting* First offence].

50/B/12   27 Jan. 1831. Richard Gillam of St. Philip and St. Jacob, [Bristol]. Keeping his house open [*etc.*, *as* 50/B/9].

50/B/13   13 Jan. 1831. James Bryant of Clifton. Permitting unlawful games on licensed premises. J. Vaughan JP and G. Goldney JP at a Petty Sessions for Bristol division. First offence. Fine £3. Offence committed 28 Dec. 1830.

50/B/14   24 March 1831. John Hunt. Assaulting Margaret Crawley, Catherine Smith and Ann White at Leckhampton. R. B. Cooper JP and R. Capper JP at Cheltenham. Fine £1 or fourteen days in Northleach house of correction. Offence committed 20 March 1831.

50/B/15   5 March 1831. Joseph Seward. Assaulting Henry Watkins at Cheltenham. R. Capper JP and Rev. W. Hicks JP at Cheltenham. Fine £1 and 6/- costs or fourteen days in Northleach house of correction. Offence committed 7 Feb. 1831.

50/B/16   22 Feb. 1831. Jemima Bonnewell of Cheltenham. Permitting persons of bad character to meet in her alehouse. R. B. Cooper JP and R. Capper JP at Cheltenham. First offence. Fine £2 and 5/6 costs. Offence committed 19 Feb. 1831.

50/B/17   22 March 1831. John Hill. Assaulting William Morgan at Cheltenham. R. B. Cooper JP and R. Capper JP at Cheltenham. Fine £1 and 5/- costs or one calendar month in Northleach house of correction. Offence committed 7 March 1831.

50/B/18   3 March 1831. Thomas Hodges of Cheltenham, retail beer dealer. Keeping his house open for the sale of beer after 10 p.m. R. Capper JP and R. B. Cooper JP at Cheltenham district Petty Sessions. First offence. Fine £2 and 5/6 costs. Offence committed 28 Feb. 1831.

50/B/19   10 March 1831. Thomas Fox of Cheltenham, retail beer dealer. Keeping his house open for the sale of beer after 10 p.m. R. Capper JP and Rev. W. Hicks JP at Cheltenham district Petty Sessions. Second offence. [*Cf.* 50/A/38.] Fine £4 and 5/6 costs. Offence committed 7 March 1831.

50/B/20   22 March 1831. James Whitfield and John Barton. Assaulting John Venfield at Cheltenham. R. B. Cooper JP and R. Capper JP at Cheltenham. Fine 10/- and 6/6 costs or fourteen days in Northleach house of correction. Offence committed 19 March 1831.

50/B/21   24 March 1831. Thomas Sheldon. Assaulting Ann White at Leckhampton. R. B. Cooper JP and R. Capper JP at Cheltenham. Fine £3 or two calendar months in Northleach house of correction. Offence committed 20 March 1831.

50/B/22   22 March 1831. John Hill. Assaulting Andrew Hathaway at Cheltenham. R. B. Cooper JP and R. Capper JP at Cheltenham. Fine £5 or two months in Northleach house of correction. Offence committed 21 March 1831.

50/B/23   24 March 1831. Thomas Sheldon. Assaulting Margaret Crawley at Leckhampton [*etc.*, *as* 50/B/21].

50/B/24   29 March 1831. George Flowers of Cheltenham, licensed victualler. Permitting drunkenness and disorderly behaviour on his premises. R. Capper JP and Rev. W. Hicks JP at Cheltenham. Second offence. Fine £6 and 5/6 costs. Offence committed 26 March 1831.

50/B/25   24 March 1831. Thomas Sheldon. Assaulting Catherine Smith at Leckhampton [*etc.*, *as* 50/B/21].

50/B/26   24 Feb. 1831. James Morgan of Cheltenham, beer retailer. Keeping his house open for the sale of beer after 10 p.m. R. Capper JP and Rev. W. Hicks JP at Cheltenham district Petty Sessions. First offence. Fine £2 and 4/6 costs. Offence committed 21 Feb. 1831.

50/B/27   5 March 1831. Thomas Turner. Assaulting Rebecca Turner at Cheltenham. R. B. Cooper JP and Rev. W. Hicks JP at Cheltenham. Fine £2 and 5/6 costs or fourteen days in Northleach house of correction. Offence committed 4 March 1831.

50/B/28   24 March 1831. Samuel Milton of Badgeworth, labourer. Possessing and using one wire, one net and one iron trap for the taking of game when not qualified. R. B. Cooper JP and R. Capper JP at Cheltenham. James Burrows, yeoman, of Witcombe, informer and witness. Implements found in offender's house. Offender (reputed poacher) made no defence against charge. Fine £5. Offence committed 22 March 1831.

50/B/29   7 Feb. 1831. William Newcomb of Cirencester, beer retailer. Keeping his house open and allowing beer to be consumed after 10 p.m. Rev. C. Pitt JP and Rev. H. A. Pye JP at Cirencester district Petty Sessions. First offence. Fine 40/- and 5/- costs. Offence committed 5 Jan. 1831.

50/B/30   19 March 1831. Mary Brewer of Cirencester, single woman. Riotous and indecent behaviour in Cirencester. Rev. H. A. Pye JP at Cirencester. Hard labour for two calendar months in Northleach house of correction. Offence committed 18 March 1831.

50/B/31   7 Feb. 1831. George Hinton of Cirencester, licensed victualler. Allowing disorderly conduct on his premises. Rev. C. Pitt JP and Rev. H. A. Pye JP. First offence. Fine 10/- and 5/- costs. Offence committed 8 Jan. 1831.

50/B/32   8 Feb. 1831. William Damp of Cirencester, beer retailer. Keeping his house open and allowing beer to be consumed after 10 p.m. Hon. C. Bathurst JP and Rev. H. A. Pye JP at Cirencester division Petty Sessions. First offence. Fine 40/- and 5/- costs. Offence committed 15 Jan. 1831.

50/B/33   29 Jan. 1831. Richard Bishop of Bibury, cabinet-maker. Keeping and using a dog to kill game when not qualified. Rev. J. W. Peters JP at Quenington. Thomas Bayliss, gamekeeper, and John Hicks, assistant gamekeeper, both of Bibury, informer and witness. Offender pleaded not guilty. Fine £5. Offence committed 28 Jan. 1831.

50/B/34   29 Jan. 1831. James Lees of Bibury, dealer. Using a gun to kill game in Coln St. Aldwyn when not qualified [*etc.*, *as* 50/B/33, *omitting* Offender pleaded not guilty].

50/B/35   10 March 1831. Joseph Jones of Broadwell. Selling beer without a licence. Rev. F. E. Witts JP. First offence. Fine £10 and 9/- costs. Offence committed 22 Feb. 1831.

50/B/36   10 March 1831. Joseph Jones of Broadwell. Selling spirits without a licence [*etc.*, *as* 50/B/35].

50/B/37   10 Feb. 1831. Thomas Pool of the Red Lion, Stow on the Wold. Harbouring notorious bad characters on his premises. Rev. F. E. Witts JP for Slaughter hundred. First offence. Fine £2 and 5/- costs. Offence committed 8 Feb. 1831.

50/B/38   15 March 1831. Daniel Mutlow. Causing his wife and family to become chargeable to Painswick parish for the previous three weeks. H. Burgh JP at Stroud. Hard labour for one calendar month in Horsley house of correction. Offence committed 22 Feb. 1831.

50/B/39   6 March 1831. David Elliotts of Frocester, labourer. Cutting down and stealing an ash tree in a wood, the property of Thomas, Lord Ducie. H. Burgh JP at Stroud. Fine £5 and 1/6 damages or two months hard labour in Horsley house of correction. Offence committed 14 Dec. 1830.

50/B/40   11 March 1831. Hannah Wager, single woman, of Painswick. Damaging a hedge, the property of Thomas Loveday, yeoman, of Painswick. H. Burgh JP at Stroud. Fine 5/-, 1/- damages and 8/- costs or three weeks' hard labour in Horsley house of correction. Offence committed 17 Feb. 1831

50/B/41   11 Feb. 1831. William Sims. Causing his wife to become chargeable to Rodborough parish for the previous month. H. Burgh JP and W. H. Hyett JP at Stroud. Hard labour for one calendar month in Horsley house of correction. Offence committed 11 Jan. 1831.

50/B/42   11 Feb. 1831. Benjamin Pearce and Richard Nicholls of Stroud, labourers. Stealing about four bushels of turnips from ground occupied by William Capel the younger of Painswick. H. Burgh JP at Stroud. Hard labour for one calendar month in Horsley house of correction. Offence committed 11 Feb. 1831.

50/B/43   4 Feb. 1831. William Baker, labourer, of Stroud. Cutting down and stealing a beech tree from a wood in Stroud, the property of John Lewis and Richard Harris. H. Burgh JP at Stroud. Fine 5/-, 1/- damages and 9/- costs or hard labour for one calendar month in Horsley house of correction. Offence committed 1 Feb. 1831.

50/B/44   26 Jan. 1831. Samuel Cooke of Randwick, labourer. Damaging a dead fence, part of a wood in Standish, the property of John, Lord Sherborne. H. Burgh JP at Stroud. Fine 5/- damages and 15/- costs or two months' hard labour in Horsley house of correction. Offence committed 17 Jan. 1831.

50/B/45   25 Jan. 1831. William Bennett and George White, labourers, of Stroud. Cutting down and damaging a beech tree in a wood in Standish, the property of John, Lord Sherborne. H. Burgh JP at Stroud. Fine £4 and 2/6 damages or hard labour for six weeks in Horsley house of correction. Offence committed 22 Jan. 1831.

50/B/46   15 Jan. 1831. Ellen Johnson. Loitering in Stroud with intent to commit a felony. H. Burgh JP at Stroud. Described as a suspected person. Hard labour for three calendar months in Horsley house of correction. Offence committed 14 Jan. 1831.

50/B/47   5 Feb. 1831. Joseph Bellamy, innkeeper of the Crown and Anchor at Stonehouse. Permitting gaming on his premises. H. Burgh JP and P. Hawker JP at Stroud. First offence. Fine £2 and 6/6 costs. Offence committed 1 Feb. 1831.

50/B/48   11 Feb. 1831. John Stockham of Stroud, carpenter. Possessing and exposing one hare for sale. H. Burgh JP at Stroud. John Gay, gamekeeper, of Stroud, informer. Henry Butcher, labourer, of Leonard Stanley, witness. Offender did not appear. His father George, a cooper, of Stroud, his mother Deborah and brother George Joseph deposed that he was ill at the relevant time and was not in his father's workshop. Fine £5. Offence committed 6 Feb. 1831.

50/B/49   5 Nov. 1830. Mark Somers the younger, labourer, of Stroud. Possessing a hare and exposing it for sale. H. Burgh JP at Stroud. William Robins, labourer, of Stroud, informer (on 28 Aug.). John Gay, gamekeeper, of Stroud, witness. Offender pleaded not guilty, but offered no defence. Fine £5. Offence committed 21 Aug. 1830

50/B/50   23 Dec. 1830. Benjamin Robins of Stonehouse, labourer. Using a wire to kill game in Nympsfield. H. Burgh JP at Stroud. George Wilcockson, gamekeeper, of Nympsfield, informer. John Barker, gamekeeper, of Horsley, witness. Offender pleaded not guilty. Fine £5. Offence committed 21 Dec. 1830.

50/B/51   5 Nov. 1830. Mark Somers the younger of Stroud, labourer. Using a wire to kill game in Stroud. H. Burgh JP at Stroud. William Robins, labourer, of Stroud, informer (on 26 Aug.). John Gay, gamekeeper, of Stroud, witness. Fine £5. Offence committed 21 Aug. 1830.

50/B/52   9 March 1831. William Buckle, beer retailer of the Crown, Kemerton. Allowing drunkenness on his premises. J. Timbrill D.D. JP and Rev. J. Keysall JP at a Petty Sessions. First offence. Fine 40/- and 9/- costs. Offence committed Sunday 27 Feb. 1831.

50/B/53   9 March 1831. Hannah Butler, widow, of Dumbleton. Violently beating Elizabeth Burrows in her mother's house at Dumbleton. J. Timbrill D.D. JP and Rev. J. Keysall JP at Tewkesbury. Fine 10/-, to be paid to Thomas Steight, overseer of the poor, and 16/- costs. Offence committed 5 March 1831.

50/B/54   23 March 1831. John Stockwell and Samuel Taylor, butchers, of Cheltenham. Assaulting Daniel Dibbel, labourer, of Deerhurst, without provocation. J. Timbrill D.D. JP and Rev. J. Keysall JP at Tewkesbury. Fine 35/- each, to be paid to Isaac Bloxham, overseer of the poor of Deerhurst, and 24/6 costs. Offence committed 14 March 1831.

50/B/55   17 Jan. 1831. John Roberts, beer retailer, of Long Marston. Allowing beer to be consumed after 10 p.m. Rev. J. R. Hall JP and Rev. J. Adams JP at a Petty Sessions for Kiftsgate hundred (upper division). First offence. Fine £2, one half of which to be paid to the prosecutor, Charles Cooper of Long Marston, and 6/6 costs. Offence committed 27 Dec. 1830.

50/B/56   14 Feb. 1831. Richard Stephens of Chipping Campden, labourer. Refusing to maintain himself, thereby becoming chargeable to the parish. Rev. J. R. Hall JP at Bourton on the Hill. Hard labour for one calendar month in Northleach house of correction. Offence committed 8 Feb. 1831.

50/B/57   3 Jan. 1831. George Young, labourer, of Ebrington. Breaking down posts and rails standing in a sheep-wash, the property of John Phillips of Ebrington, farmer. Rev. J. R. Hall JP at Bourton on the Hill. Fine 6*d.* and 3/- damages, to be paid to Samuel Keyte, overseer of the poor, and 12/6 costs, or hard labour for one month in Northleach house of correction. Offence committed 11 Dec. 1830.

50/B/58   6 Dec. 1830. Sarah the wife of John Hutchins, labourer, of Todenham. Breaking down a dead mound standing in a field, the property of Thomas Wyatt of Todenham, farmer. Rev. J. R. Hall JP at Bourton on the Hill. Fine 3/- and 1/- damages, to be paid to Thomas Holloway, overseer of the poor, and 6/- costs, or hard labour for one month in Northleach house of correction. Offence committed 20 Nov. 1830.

50/B/59   3 Jan. 1831. Nathaniel and William Unitt, labourers of Long Marston. Assaulting Charles Cooper of Long Marston. Rev. W. Boughton JP and Rev. J. R. Hall JP at Bourton on the Hill. Fine £1 and 18/6 costs or one calendar month in Northleach house of correction. Offence committed 27 Dec. 1830.

50/B/60   31 Jan. 1831. Charles Walker of Condicote. Using a gun and dogs to kill game in Sir Charles Cockerill's plantation in Condicote. Rev. C. Jeaffreson JP at Bourton on the Hill. William Fletcher, gamekeeper, and Robert Bowles, both of Sezincote, informer and witness. Pleaded not guilty, but offered no defence. Fine £5. Offence committed 19 Jan. 1831.

50/B/61   14 Jan. 1831. George Shipton of Oldbury on the Hill, labourer. Using a gun to kill game in Rudge Wood, Oldbury on the Hill, the property of the duke of Beaufort. F. Trotman JP, W. G. Davy JP and W. Blathwayt JP at a Petty Sessions held at the Cross Hands inn, Old Sodbury. William Roach, gamekeeper, of Sopworth, Wilts., informer. Abel Kingston, woodward, of Didmarton, witness, deposed that he saw offender with three other men beating for game. When challenged offender broke gun and put it in his pocket. Changed plea to guilty on hearing evidence and declared he would not thereafter use a gun. Fine £5. Offence committed 18 Dec. 1830.

50/B/62   14 Jan. 1831. William Ball, labourer, of Acton Turville. Having a hare in his possession in a field occupied by Mrs. Betty Marsh of Acton Turville. W. G. Davy JP, F. Trotman JP and W. Blathwayt JP at a Petty Sessions held at the Cross Hands inn, Old Sodbury. George Walters of Acton Turville, under-gamekeeper to the duke of Beaufort, informer. Thomas Webb, gamekeeper to the duke of Beaufort, witness. Jeremiah Isaac, constable of Acton Turville, delivered summons but offender did not appear. Fine £5. Offence committed Sunday 14 Nov. 1830.

50/B/63   14 Jan. 1831. Nathaniel Fielding *alias* Fidler and Emanuel Eastmeade, labourers, of Acton Turville. Setting a snare in a field in the occupation of James Hatherall of Acton Turville. W. G. Davy JP, F. Trotman JP and W. Blathwayt JP at a Petty Sessions held at the Cross Hands inn, Old Sodbury. Thomas Webb, gamekeeper, and George Walters, under-gamekeeper, informer and witness. Both [Fielding and Eastmeade] pleaded not guilty but when asked for their defence said they were unemployed and had nothing else to do. Fine £5. Offence committed 25 Nov. 1830.

50/C/1   8 June 1831. George Bowyer. Stealing a quarter of a peck of potatoes growing in enclosed ground in Horsley belonging to Charles Jenkins. Rev. H. Campbell JP at Minchinhampton. Imprisonment for twenty-one days in Horsley house of correction. Offence committed 5 June 1831.

50/C/2   14 June 1831. Richard Chandler. Aiding and abetting William Rodway to damage a bonnet belonging to Eleanor Lockier, spinster, at Avening. Rev. H. Campbell JP at Minchinhampton. Fine 4/-, to be paid to George Whitley, overseer of the poor of Avening, and 9/- costs, or six weeks in Horsley house of correction. Offence committed 10 June 1831.

50/C/3   14 June 1831. Frederick Fox. Aiding and abetting [*etc.*, *as* 50/C/2 *omitting* or six weeks in Horsley house of correction].

50/C/4   14 June 1831. William Rodway. Damaging a bonnet, the property of Eleanor Lockier, spinster, at Avening. Rev. H. Campbell JP at Minchinhampton. Fine 4/-, to be paid to George Whitley, overseer of the poor of Avening, and 12/- costs, or two months' hard labour in Horsley house of correction. Offence committed 10 June 1831.

50/C/5   27 May 1831. John Smith of Dursley, labourer. Assaulting Reuben Hill, assistant overseer of the poor of Dursley. W. M. Adey JP and H. W. Dyer JP at Wotton under Edge. Fine £3, to be paid to Daniel Dimery, petty constable of Dursley, and 6/6 costs, or six weeks in Horsley house of correction. Offence committed 3 May 1831.

50/C/6   3 June 1831. Henry Smith of Dursley, labourer. Assaulting Reuben Hill [*etc.*, *as* 50/C/5].

50/C/7   12 May 1831. Daniel Hancock. Assaulting William Hutchings at Cheltenham. R. B. Cooper JP and G. Stevenson JP at Cheltenham. Fine 5/- and 5/6 costs. Offence committed 7 May 1831.

50/C/8   3 June 1831. William Prior. Begging in Rodborough. H. Burgh JP at Stroud. Hard labour for fourteen days in Horsley house of correction. Offence committed 2 June 1831.

50/C/9   10 June 1831. Thomas Dalby. Being on premises in Stroud, the property of John Price, machine-maker and timber merchant, with intent to commit a felony. H. Burgh JP at Stroud. Three calendar months' hard labour in Horsley house of correction. Offence committed 10 June 1831.

50/C/10   13 June 1831. Benjamin Lewis of Rodborough, labourer. Cutting down twenty young beech trees and five young ash trees growing in a wood at Rodborough, the property of John Pinfold, yeoman. H. Burgh JP at Stroud. Fine £5, 10/- damages and 8/- costs or hard labour for two months in Horsley house of correction. Offence committed 2 June 1831.

50/C/11   17 June 1831. Thomas Latham of Rodborough, labourer. Cutting down twenty young beech trees in a wood in Rodborough, the property of Benjamin Antill, mealman. H. Burgh JP and Rev. P. Hawker JP at Stroud. Fine £5, 10/- damages and 8/- costs or hard labour for two calendar months in Horsley house of correction. Offence committed 3 June 1831.

50/C/12   17 June 1831. Henry Holder of Rodborough, labourer. Cutting down five young ash trees and twenty young beech trees in a wood in Rodborough, the property of John Pinfold, yeoman. H. Burgh JP and Rev. P. Hawker JP at Stroud.. Fine £5, 10/- damages and 8/- costs or hard labour for two calendar months in Horsley house of correction. Offence committed 2 June 1831.

50/C/13   8 April 1831. John Bliss of Painswick, labourer. Cutting down and stealing a young ash tree growing in a wood in Painswick, the property of Thomas Preston Esq. of Nottingham Place, Middx. H. Burgh JP and Rev. P. Hawker JP at Stroud. Fine £5, 1/- damages and 8/- costs or hard labour for two calendar months in Horsley house of correction. Offence committed 4 March 1831.

50/C/14   6 May 1831. Henry Gardner of Stroud, labourer. Assaulting James Fawkes, yeoman, of Stroud. H. Burgh JP and Rev. P. Hawker JP at Stroud. Fine £2 2s. and 8/- costs or hard labour for two months in Horsley house of correction. Offence committed 12 April 1831.

50/C/15   9 June 1831. Joseph Carey of Bitton, beer retailer. Permitting persons of notorious bad character to meet on his premises. V. J. Graeme JP and J. Lewis JP at a Petty Sessions for Bristol division. First offence. Fine £5. Offence committed 31 May 1831.

50/C/16   16 June 1831. John Ware of St. Philip and St. Jacob, [Bristol]. Allowing beer to be consumed after 10 p.m. V. J. Graeme JP and J. Cave JP at a Petty Sessions for Bristol division. Fine 40/-. Offence committed 13 June 1831.

50/C/17   16 June 1831. Mary Robinson of St. Philip and St. Jacob, [Bristol]. Failure to observe conditions of her licence to sell beer etc. V. J. Graeme JP and G. Goldney JP. First offence. Fine 20/-.

50/C/18   14 April 1831. Richard Nutt. Assaulting Elizabeth Giggs at St. Philip and St. Jacob, [Bristol]. G. Goldney JP and W. Fripp JP at Lawfords Gate sessions room. Fine 10/- and 5/6 costs. Offence committed 4 April 1831.

50/C/19   21 April 1831. James Shawl. Assaulting Thomas Burnett at St. Philip and St. Jacob, [Bristol]. G. Goldney JP and W. Fripp JP at Lawfords Gate sessions room. Fine 3/6 and 6/6 costs or fourteen days in Lawfords Gate house of correction. Offence committed 14 April 1831.

50/C/20   28 April 1831. Price Philips [also Phillips]. Assaulting Samuel Gray at St. Philip and St. Jacob, [Bristol]. J. Parker JP and G. Goldney JP at Lawfords Gate sessions room. Fine £4 11s. 6d. and 8/6 costs or two months in Lawfords Gate house of correction. Offence committed 24 April 1831.

50/C/21   19 May 1831. Henry Wakefield. Assaulting John Brennan at St. Philip and St. Jacob, [Bristol]. D. Cave JP and G. Goldney JP at Lawfords Gate sessions room. Fine 5/- and 5/6 costs or one calendar month in Lawfords Gate house of correction. Offence committed 9 May 1831.

50/C/22   19 May 1831. John Marshall. Assaulting James Rich the younger at St. Philip and St. Jacob, [Bristol]. D. Cave JP and G. Goldney JP at Lawfords Gate sessions room. Fine £1 11s. and 9/- costs or one calendar month in Lawfords Gate house of correction. Offence committed 6 May 1831.

50/C/23   19 May 1831. John Highman. Assaulting Robert Nibbs at Clifton. D. Cave JP and G. Goldney JP at Lawfords Gate sessions room. Fine 4/6 and 5/6 costs or one calendar month in Lawfords Gate house of correction. Offence committed 28 April 1831.

50/C/24   19 May 1831. Thomas Mack. Assaulting Charles Mullier at St. Philip and St. Jacob, [Bristol]. D. Cave JP and J. Parker at Lawfords Gate sessions room. Fine 14/6 and 5/6 costs or one calendar month in Lawfords Gate house of correction. Offence committed 4 May 1831.

50/C/25   9 June 1831. Stephen Bennett. Assaulting Sarah Warren at St. Philip and St. Jacob, [Bristol]. V. J. Graeme JP and J. Lewis JP at Lawfords Gate sessions room. Fine 10/- and 5/6 costs or one calendar month in Lawfords Gate house of correction. Offence committed 7 June 1831.

50/C/26   19 June 1831. John Brown. Assaulting Robert Heaven at Redwick and Northwick. V. J. Graeme JP and D. Cave JP at Lawfords Gate sessions room. Fine £1 and 15/6 costs or one calendar month in Lawfords Gate house of correction. Offence committed 23 May 1831.

50/C/27   16 June 1831. Thomas Palmer. Assaulting George Bull at St. George, [Bristol]. V. J. Graeme JP and G. Goldney JP at Lawfords Gate sessions room. Fine 6d. and 5/6 costs or seven days in Lawfords Gate house of correction. Offence committed 7 June 1831.

50/C/28   16 June 1831. Charles Soreen Tovey. Assaulting Elizabeth Brown at Frampton Cotterell. V. J. Graeme JP and G. Goldney JP at Lawfords Gate sessions room. Fine 5/- and 7/- costs or fourteen days in Lawfords Gate house of correction. Offence committed 6 June 1831.

50/C/29   16 June 1831. Mary Williams. Assaulting Mary Tutton at Westbury on Trym. V. J. Graeme JP and G. Goldney JP at Lawfords Gate sessions room. Fine 6d. and 5/6 costs or fourteen days in Lawfords Gate house of correction. Offence committed 10 June 1831.

50/C/30   2 June 1831. James Baker. Assaulting Sarah Lewis at St. James, [Bristol]. H. W. Newman JP and J. Parker JP at Lawfords Gate sessions room. Fine £2 16s. and £2 4s. costs or two calendar months in Lawfords Gate house of correction. Offence committed 21 May 1831.

50/C/31   15 June 1831. Daniel Jellyman the elder of Coaley. Possessing about 55 oz. of various woollen yarns and 27 yards of raw woollen broadcloth believed to be stolen. H. Burgh JP and Rev. P. Hawker JP. James Hill of Rodborough, informer. Josiah Thomas Howell of Stroud, William Weeks of King's Stanley and John Trollope of Rodborough, witnesses. Fine £20, half to be paid to the informer and the remainder to the Stroud dispensary. Offence committed 14 June 1831.

50/C/32   25 April 1831. William Powell, clothworker, of Stonehouse. Possessing 11 lb. of wool and 15½ yards of narrow woollen cloth believed to be stolen. H. Burgh JP and Rev. P. Hawker JP. Moira Maclean, clothier, of King's Stanley, informer. John Heaven and Charles Stephens, both of Stonehouse, witnesses. Fine £20, half to be paid to the informer and the remainder to the Stroud dispensary. Offence committed 22 April 1831.

50/C/33   2 May 1831. James Crook of Wotton under Edge, clothworker. Possessing 84 lb. of various woollen yarns and 21 yards of cloth believed to be stolen. H. Burgh JP and Rev. P. Hawker JP. Moira Maclean, clothier, of King's Stanley, informer. Charles Cogswell, Charles Collins and William Harris, all of Wotton under Edge, William Weeks of King's Stanley, Nathaniel Samuel Marling of Stroud, John Hyde of Minchinhampton and James Owen of North Nibley, witnesses. Fine £20, half to be paid to the informer and the remainder to the Stroud dispensary. Offence committed 26 April 1831.

50/C/34   28 April 1831. Thomas Vines of Wotton under Edge, clothworker. Possessing 55 lb. of various yarns and 28 yards of raw woollen cloth believed to be stolen. H. Burgh JP and John Phillimore Hicks JP. Moira Maclean, clothier, of King's Stanley, informer. Charles, Cogswell of Wotton under Edge and Edward Davies of Stonehouse, witnesses. Fine £20, half to be paid to the informer and the remainder to the Stroud dispensary. Offence committed 26 April 1831.

50/C/35   28 April 1831. Samuel Hill of Uley, shoemaker. Possessing 3 oz. of woollen waste believed to be stolen [*etc.*, *as* 50/C/34 *except*] half to the informer and half to Stroud dispensary.

50/C/36   28 April 1831. Hannah Hall of Wotton under Edge. Possessing 19½ lb. of woollen yarn, 20 lb. of woollen waste and 4 lb. of wool believed to be stolen [*etc.*, *as* 50/C/35 *except*] Offence committed 27 April 1831.

50/C/37   28 April 1831. William Daniels of Wotton under Edge, weaver. Possessing 13 lb. of warp yarn, 13 lb. of abb waste and 28 yards of raw woollen cloth believed to be stolen [*etc.*, *as* 50/C/35].

50/C/38   16 May 1831. William Blick of Horsley, clothworker. Possessing 5½ lb. of woollen abb yarn and 2 lb. of woollen waste believed to be stolen. H. Burgh JP, W. H. Hyett JP and Rev. P. Hawker JP. Moira Maclean, clothier, of King's Stanley, informer. John Heaven and Edward Davies, both of Stonehouse, and William Weeks of King's Stanley, witnesses. Fine £20, half to the informer and half to Stroud dispensary. Offence committed 23 April 1831.

50/C/39   16 May 1831. Richard Sayer of Horsley, clothier. Possessing 1 chain of woollen yarn, 2 yards of which already woven in Cashmere [*MS.* casimere] cloth, believed to be stolen. H. Burgh JP, W. H. Hyett JP and Rev. P. Hawker JP. Moira Maclean, clothier, of King's Stanley, informer. Francis Pickard, constable, William Fryer and Peter Hawker, gentlemen, all of Stroud, Edward Davies, clothier, of Stonehouse, William Weeks, clothier, of King's Stanley and George Bloxsome, gentleman, of Dursley, witnesses. Second offence. [*Cf.* 47/C/23.] Fine £30, half to the informer and half to Stroud dispensary. Offence committed 23 April 1831.

50/C/40   21 May 1831. Charles Dowle of Cheltenham, licensed victualler. Permitting drunkenness and disorderly behaviour on his premises. R. B. Cooper JP and J. H. Ollney JP. First offence. Fine 20/- and 5/6 costs. Offence committed 2 May 1831.

50/C/41   7 June 1831. Charles Mott. Assaulting Henry Averis at Cheltenham. Sir W. Hicks JP and T. Newell JP at Cheltenham. Fine 2/6 and 5/6 costs or fourteen days in Northleach house of correction. Offence committed 4 June 1831.

50/C/42   21 June 1831. Henry Thatcher. Assaulting Louisa Ballinger at Cheltenham. Sir W. Hicks JP and R. B. Cooper JP at Cheltenham. Fine 10/- and 7/6 costs. Offence committed 21 June 1831.

50/C/43   21 April 1831. Sarah Baylis of Cheltenham, licensed victualler. Permitting drunkenness and disorderly behaviour on her premises. R. B. Cooper JP and J. H. Ollney JP. First offence. Fine £2 10*s.* and 5/6 costs. Offence committed 16 April 1831.

50/C/44   11 June 1831. Henry Taylor. Assaulting John Lewis at Cheltenham. T. Newell JP and Rev. J. Edwards JP at Cheltenham. Fine 5/- and 7/6 costs. Offence committed 7 June 1831.

50/C/45   16 April 1831. James Lewis, Edwin Palmer, William Burrows and John Evans. Assaulting Thomas Robinson the younger at Prestbury. R. B. Cooper JP and Rev. J. Edwards JP at Cheltenham. Fine 5/- each and 9/6 costs or one calendar month in Northleach house of correction. Offence committed 11 April 1831.

50/C/46   4 June 1831. Joseph Rowley. Assaulting William Holtham at Cheltenham. Rev. W. Hicks JP and T. Newell JP at Cheltenham. Fine 10/- and 8/- costs. Offence committed 1 June 1831.

50/C/47   4 June 1831. Stephen Berkeley of Cheltenham, retail beer dealer. Keeping his premises open for the sale of beer between 2 and 3 a.m. Rev. W. Hicks JP and T. Newell JP at a Petty Sessions for Cheltenham district. First offence. Fine £2 and 5/6 costs. Offence committed 3 June 1831.

50/C/48   31 May 1831. Benjamin Deaves. Assaulting Mary Deaves at Cheltenham. Sir W. Hicks JP and Rev. W. Hicks JP at Cheltenham. Fine £5 or two calendar months in Northleach house of correction. Offence committed 30 May 1831.

50/C/49   31 May 1831. John Goode. Assaulting Joseph Liley at Cheltenham. Sir W. Hicks JP and Rev. W. Hicks JP at Cheltenham. Fine 10/- and 7/- costs. Offence committed 28 May 1831.

50/C/50   31 May 1831. Thomas Williams. Assaulting William Hall at Cheltenham. Sir W. Hicks JP and Rev. W. Hicks JP at Cheltenham. Fine 20/- and 8/- costs or one calendar month in Northleach house of correction. Offence committed 26 May 1831.

50/C/51   26 May 1831. John Osbaldeston. Assaulting Jesse Castle at Cheltenham. Rev. W. Hicks JP and J. H. Ollney JP at Cheltenham. Fine 5/- and 6/- costs. Offence committed 19 May 1831.

50/C/52   19 May 1831. Harry Giles. Assaulting Thomas Bradford at Cheltenham. R. B. Cooper JP and Rev. W. Hicks JP at Cheltenham. Fine 10/- and 8/- costs or two calendar months in Northleach house of correction. Offence committed 4 May 1831.

50/C/53   6 June 1831. Robert Walker of Moreton in Marsh, licensed beer seller. Allowing drunkenness and disorderly behaviour after 10 p.m. Rev. J. Adams JP and Rev. J. R. Hall JP at a Petty Sessions for Westminster hundred, upper division. First offence. Fine £4, £1 of which to be paid to the prosecutor Thomas Jeys and the remainder to the county treasurer, and 6/6 costs. Offence committed 31 May 1831.

50/C/54   23 May 1831. William Hooper the younger of Moreton in Marsh, labourer. Using a dog to kill hares in Lemington. Rev. J. Adams JP and Rev. J. R. Hall JP. First offence. Fine £10, half to be paid to the informer John Clark Slatter and the rest to the overseer of the poor. Offence committed Sunday 15 May 1831.

50/C/55   6 June 1831. Lewis Thomas, licensee of the Salutation inn, Cirencester. Failing to maintain good order on his premises. Hon. C. Bathurst JP and Rev. H. Cripps JP. First offence. Fine 10/- and 5/- costs. Offence committed 30 May 1831.

50/C/56   19 April 1831. Richard Pope of Coln St. Aldwyn, licensed beer seller. Keeping his premises open for the consumption of beer after 10 p.m. Hon. J. Dutton JP, J. R. Barker JP and Rev. J. W. Peters JP at a Petty Sessions for Bibury division. First offence. Fine 40/- and 10/- costs. Offence committed 4 April 1831.

50/C/57   20 May 1831. Robert Saunders of Stroud. Using a wire to kill game in Stroud. H. Burgh JP at Stroud. William Robins, gardener, and John Gay, gamekeeper, both of Stroud, informer and witness. Offender did not appear. Fine £5. Offence committed 15 May 1831.

50/C/58　17 June 1831. Thomas Lovett of Horsley, labourer. Using a wire to kill game in Horsley. H. Burgh JP at Stroud. George Wilcockson, gamekeeper, of Nympsfield and John Barker, gamekeeper, of Horsley, informer and witness. Offender pleaded not guilty, but made no defence. Fine £5. Offence committed 11 June 1831.

50/C/59　17 June 1831. Thomas Lovett of Horsley, labourer. Exposing one hare for sale at Horsley. H. Burgh JP at Stroud. George Wilcockson, gamekeeper, of Nympsfield, informer. Offender pleaded guilty. Fine £5. Offence committed 11 June 1831.

50/D/1　30 Aug. 1831. William Bird. Assaulting Eliza Hulin at St. Briavels. P. J. Ducarel JP and E. Machen JP at Coleford. Fine £1 5s., to be paid to an overseer of the poor, and 15/- costs, or hard labour for one month in Littledean house of correction. Given six weeks to pay. Offence committed 7 Aug. 1831.

50/D/2　30 Aug. 1831. Henry Worgan. Stealing wood from a wood called James's Thorns at Tidenham, the property of the duke of Beaufort. P. J. Ducarel JP and E. Machen JP at Coleford. Fine £1, to be paid to an overseer of the poor, and 7/6 costs to be paid to William Thurston for the duke of Beaufort, or one month's hard labour in Littledean house of correction. Offence committed 8 Aug. 1831.

50/D/3　28 March 1831 [*late return*]. Joseph Pepler of Wotton under Edge, haulier [*MS.* hallier]. Assaulting Edward Hathaway of Wotton under Edge, blacksmith. W. M. Adey JP and H. W. Dyer JP. Fine 5/-, to be paid to the overseers of the poor, and 5//6 costs. Fine and costs paid. Offence committed 26 Aug. 1830.

50/D/4　11 Oct. 1831. George Trotter of Newland, farmer. Beating for game with a dog and gun without a licence in Newland. P. J. Ducarel JP, Rev. T. Thomas JP, E. Machen JP and G. Ormerod JP at Lydney. James Haffenden, gentleman, of Clearwell, informer. William Powell, gamekeeper, of Staunton, witness. Offender admitted charge. Fine £5. Offence committed 1 Oct. 1831.

50/D/5　11 Oct. 1831. George Trotter of Newland, yeoman. Possessing one hen pheasant (in his coat pocket) at Newland. P. J. Ducarel JP, Rev. T. Thomas JP, E. Machen JP and G. Ormerod JP at Lydney. Thomas Broomby, butler, of Clearwell, informer. William Powell, gamekeeper, of Staunton, witness. Offender pleaded not guilty. Fine £5. Offence committed 1 Oct. 1831.

50/D/6　3 Sept. 1831. Thomas Lusty and Richard Baker. Stealing a quantity of apples from a garden, the property of Hannah Lusty, at King's Stanley. H. Burgh JP at Stroud. First offence. Six calendar months' hard labour in Horsley house of correction. Offence committed 1 Sept. 1831.

50/D/7　3 Sept. 1831. James and William Price. Stealing a quantity of apples from an orchard in King's Stanley, the property of Thomas Goddard. H. Burgh JP at Stroud. First offence. Six weeks' hard labour in Horsley house of correction. Offence committed 3 Sept. 1831.

50/D/8　5 Sept. 1831. Benjamin Ireland. Stealing a quantity of apples from an orchard in King's Stanley, the property of Thomas Goddard. H. Burgh JP at Stroud. First offence. Six calendar months' hard labour in Horsley house of correction. Offence committed 3 Sept. 1831.

50/D/9　16 Aug. 1831. William Aldridge, blacksmith, of Randwick. Stealing peaches, plums, carrots and onions from a garden in Stonehouse, the property of Edward Davies Esq. R. S. Davies JP at Stonehouse. First offence. Fine £10, 4/- damages to the plaintiff (who was not examined as to proof of the offence) and 4/- costs to Thomas Stephens, or three months' hard labour in Horsley house of correction. Offence committed 14 Aug. 1831.

50/D/10   16 Aug. 1831. John Fletcher of Eastington. Taking conies, the property of Frederick Eycott, from land used for breeding conies at Stonehouse. R. S. Davies JP at Stonehouse. Fine 40/-, to be paid to the plaintiff (who was not examined as to proof of the offence), or two calendar months in Horsley house of correction. Offence committed 14 Aug. 1831.

50/D/11   2 Aug. 1831. Charles Cole of Quedgeley. Allowing unlawful games on his licensed premises. H. C. Clifford JP and D. J. Niblett JP at a Petty Sessions for Whitstone hundred. First offence. Fine 40/- and 5/- costs. Offence committed 20 July 1831.

50/D/12   2 Aug. 1831. Charles Cole of Quedgeley. Allowing the consumption of beer after 10 p.m. [etc., as 50/D/11 except] Fine 40/- and 7/- costs.

50/D/13   1 Feb. 1831 [late return]. George Bartlett of Eastington. Allowing unlawful games on his licensed premises. H. C. Clifford JP and R. S. Davies JP at a Petty Sessions for Whitstone hundred. First offence. Fine £5. Offence committed 18 Jan. 1831.

50/D/14   17 Jan. 1831 [late return]. Matilda Smith. Refusing to work to maintain herself, thereby becoming chargeable to Eastington parish. R. S. Davies JP and J. P. Hicks JP at Eastington. Hard labour for one month in Horsley house of correction. Offence committed 11 Jan. 1831.

50/D/15   5 July 1831. William Morgan of Eastington. Allowing consumption of beer on his premises after 10 p.m. T. J. Lloyd Baker JP and H. C. Clifford JP at a Petty Sessions for Whitstone hundred. First offence. Fine 40/-. Offence committed 25 June 1831.

50/D/16   6 Sept. 1831. William White, labourer, of Stonehouse. Using a net to catch conies at Stonehouse without a licence. T. J. Lloyd Baker JP and H. C. Clifford JP at Wheatenhurst, commissioners for assessed taxes for Whitstone district. Fine £10. Offence committed 3 Aug. 1831.

50/D/17   30 Sept. 1831. William Webb and Llewellin Walker, labourers, of Wotton under Edge. Stealing turnips in Ozleworth, the property of Edward Collins, farmer. W. M. Adey JP at Wotton under Edge. Fourteen days' hard labour in Horsley house of correction. Offence committed 28 Sept. 1831.

50/D/18   8 July 1831. Mary Smith, widow, of Wotton under Edge, licensed beer retailer. Keeping her premises open for the sale of beer after 10 p.m. W. M. Adey JP and H. W. Dyer JP at a Petty Sessions for the upper division of Berkeley hundred. First offence. Fine £2 and 7/6 costs. Offence committed 22 June 1831.

50/D/19   23 Aug. 1831. Michael McKeaver. Rogue and vagabond. Playing an illegal game of chance called Hearts and Spades at a fair in Stroud. H. Burgh JP at Stroud. Hard labour for three calendar months in Horsley house of correction. Offence committed 22 Aug. 1831.

50/D/20   23 Aug. 1831. Luce McKeaver. Rogue and vagabond. Playing [etc., as 50/D/19].

50/D/21   23 Aug. 1831. Daniel Grainger. Rogue and vagabond. Playing a game of chance at a fair in Stroud. H. Burgh JP at Stroud. Three calendar months' hard labour in Horsley house of correction. Offence committed 22 Aug. 1831.

50/D/22   5 Aug. 1831. James Sims of Rodborough, labourer. Stealing a quantity of apples from an orchard in Rodborough, the property of Richard Stump. H. Burgh JP at Stroud. Three calendar months' hard labour in Horsley house of correction. Offence committed 4 Aug. 1831.

50/D/23   1 Sept. 1831. James Hart and James Matthews, labourers, of Minchinhampton. Stealing a quantity of onions from a garden, the property of Benjamin Dudbridge, clothier, of Minchinhampton. H. Burgh JP at Stroud. Six calendar months' hard labour in Horsley house of correction. Offence committed 31 Aug. 1831.

50/D/24   27 Aug. 1831. James Damsell of Stroud, labourer. Stealing a quantity of apples from an orchard in Stroud, the property of William Clutterbuck Chambers. H. Burgh JP at Stroud. Hard labour for six weeks in Horsley house of correction. Offence committed 27 Aug. 1831.

50/D/25   2 Aug. 1831. John Harper of Rodborough, labourer. Stealing twenty-three cabbages from a garden in Rodborough, the property of William Halliday Esq. H. Burgh JP at Stroud. Hard labour for three calendar months in Horsley house of correction. Offence committed 1 Aug. 1831.

50/D/26   1 July 1831. Isaac Hunt. Causing his wife and family to become chargeable to Bisley parish. H. Burgh JP and Rev. P. Hawker JP at Stroud. Hard labour for one calendar month in Horsley house of correction. Offence committed 18 June 1831.

50/D/27   9 Sept. 1831. Thomas and Richard Iddols, labourers, of King's Stanley. Cutting down and stealing a larch tree growing in a wood in King's Stanley, the property of Robert Snow Paul Esq. H. Burgh JP and Rev. P. Hawker JP at Stroud. Fine £1, to be paid to an overseer of the poor, 1/- damages and 5/6 cost to go to the complainant, or hard labour for one calendar month in Horsley house of correction. Offence committed 8 Sept. 1831.

50/D/28   30 July 1831. Edwin Nicholls of Stroud, labourer. Stealing a quantity of apples from an orchard in Painswick, the property of Thomas Holbrow. Rev. P. Hawker JP at Stroud. Hard labour for one calendar month in Horsley house of correction. Offence committed 24 July 1831.

50/D/29   29 July 1831. Charles Hall and George Smith, labourers, of Stroud. Stealing a quantity of apples from an orchard in Painswick, the property of Thomas Holbrow Esq. W. H. Hyett JP and Rev. P. Hawker JP at Stroud. Hard labour for one calendar month in Horsley house of correction. Offence committed 24 July 1831.

50/D/30   26 Aug. 1831. Henry Sims of Rodborough, labourer. Stealing a quantity of pears from an orchard, the property of Samuel Laurence, carpenter, of Rodborough. H. Burgh JP and R. S. Davies JP at Stroud. Hard labour for six weeks in Horsley house of correction. Offence committed 25 Aug. 1831.

50/D/31   19 Aug. 1831. Thomas Hopson, beer retailer, of Stroud. Opening his premises for the sale of beer between 10 a.m. and 1 p.m. on a Sunday. H. Burgh JP and R. S. Davies JP at a Petty Sessions for Bisley hundred. First offence. Fine 40/-. Offence committed Sunday 14 Aug. 1831.

50/D/32   19 Aug. 1831. Thomas Hopson, beer retailer, of Stroud. Allowing a person to be drunk on his premises. H. Burgh JP and R. S. Davies JP at a Petty Sessions for Bisley hundred. Second offence. Fine £5. Offence committed 14 Aug. 1831.

50/D/33   19 Aug. 1831. William Jones, beer retailer, of Stroud. Keeping his premises open for the sale of beer after 10 p.m. H. Burgh JP and R. S. Davies JP at a Petty Sessions for Bisley hundred. First offence. Fine £2. Offence committed 13 Aug. 1831.

50/D/34   26 Aug. 1831. William Jones, beer retailer, of the Star, Stroud. Knowingly permitting gaming on his premises. H. Burgh JP and R. S. Davies JP at a Petty Sessions for Bisley hundred. Second offence. Fine £5. Offence committed 13 Aug. 1831.

50/D/35   30 Sept. 1831. Thomas Twinning of Painswick, labourer. Assaulting Thomas West, labourer, of Painswick. H. Burgh JP and Rev. P. Hawker JP at Stroud. Fine £5 or two calendar months' hard labour in Horsley house of correction. Offence committed 25 Sept. 1831.

50/D/36   23 Sept. 1831. Silas Bryant, Ann Bowley, Eliza Dowell and Maria Burton, clothworkers, of Stroud. Stealing a quantity of apples from an orchard, the property of John Neems, yeoman, of Stroud. H. Burgh JP at Stroud. Fine 1/- each and 15/6 costs or fourteen days' hard labour in Horsley house of correction. Offence committed 17 Sept. 1831.

50/D/37   20 Sept. 1831. Thomas Bennett of Painswick, labourer. Stealing a quantity of apples from an orchard in Painswick, the property of Thomas Holbrow. H. Burgh JP at Stroud. Hard labour for three calendar months in Horsley house of correction. Offence committed 18 Sept. 1831.

50/D/38   26 Sept. 1831. Thomas Barnard of Rodborough, labourer. Stealing a quantity of turnips from a garden, the property of Richard Smith, labourer, of Minchinhampton. H. Burgh JP at Stroud. Hard labour for two calendar months in Horsley house of correction. Offence committed 24 Sept. 1831.

50/D/39   3 Oct. 1831. Charles Beaseley of Rodborough, labourer. Stealing a quantity of pears from an orchard, the property of Frederick Pinfold, yeoman, of Rodborough. H. Burgh JP at Stroud. Hard labour for six calendar months in [Horsley *deleted*, Littledean *substituted*] house of correction. Offence committed 2 Oct. 1831.

50/D/40   12 Oct. 1831. Charles Smart. Begging in Rodborough. H. Burgh JP at Stroud. Hard labour for one calendar month in [Horsley *deleted*, Littledean *substituted*] house of correction. Offence committed 11 Oct. 1831.

50/D/41   12 Oct. 1831. John Stewart, James Gall and Nathaniel Taylor. Begging in Minchinhampton [*etc.*, *as* 50/D/40].

50/D/42   23 Aug. 1831. William Matthews. Rogue and vagabond, playing at a game of chance called Hearts and Spades at a fair in Stroud. H. Burgh JP. Hard labour for three calendar months in Horsley house of correction. Offence committed 22 Aug. 1831.

50/D/43   8 July 1831. William Cooke. Leaving his wife and family chargeable to Painswick parish. H. Burgh JP at Stroud. Six weeks' hard labour in Horsley house of correction. Offence committed 20 June 1831.

50/D/44   26 Sept. 1831. Edward Trayhern, tailor, of Thornbury. Stealing a quantity of apples from an orchard, the property of Thomas Gwynn of Thornbury. W. N. Tonge JP at Alveston. Hard labour for one calendar month in Lawfords Gate house of correction. Offence committed on night of Saturday 24 Sept. 1831.

50/D/45   4 July 1831. James Yearsley, beer retailer, of Brand [MS. Bran] Green, Newent. Keeping his premises open for the consumption of beer after 10 p.m. and allowing illegal gaming. Edward Howell JP and Richard Foley Onslow JP at a Petty Sessions for Botloe hundred. First offence. Fine £2 and 9/6 costs. Offence committed 27 June 1831.

50/D/46   1 Aug. 1831. Mary Pew, beer retailer, of Cirencester. Keeping her premises open for the consumption of beer after 10 p.m. Rev. W. Croome JP and Rev. E. A. Daubeny JP at a Petty Sessions for Cirencester division. First offence. Fine 40/- and 5/- costs. Offence committed 13 June 1831.

50/D/47   4 July 1831. Susannah Niblett, victualler, of the Salutation inn, Stratton, Cirencester. Failing to keep good order on her premises. Hon. and Rev. C. Bathurst JP and George Graham Blackwell JP. First offence. Fine 10/- and 5/- costs. Offence committed 26 June 1831.

50/D/48   3 Oct. 1831. James Richardson of Daglingworth, beer retailer. Keeping his premises open for the consumption of beer after 10 p.m. Rev. E. A. Daubeny JP and G. G. Blackwell JP at a Petty Sessions for Cirencester division. First offence. Fine 10/- and 5/- costs. Offence committed 9 Sept. 1831.

50/D/49   16 Sept. 1831. Thomas Turner of Dursley, labourer. Stealing a quantity of apples from an orchard, the property of John Buston, farmer, of Dursley. W. M. Adey JP and H. W. Dyer JP at Wotton under Edge. Fourteen days' hard labour in Horsley house of correction. Offence committed 4 Sept. 1831.

50/D/50   23 Sept. 1831. William Oldland, clothworker, and Samuel George, weaver, both of Wotton under Edge. Stealing a quantity of apples from an orchard, the property of Rev. Rowland Hill of Wotton under Edge. W. M. Adey JP and H. W. Dyer JP at Wotton under Edge. Hard labour for two calendar months in Horsley house of correction. Offence committed 18 Sept. 1831.

50/D/51   23 Sept. 1831. William Manning and John Shipton, labourers, of Kingswood, Wilts. Stealing half a peck of apples from a garden, the property of Thomas Heaven, farmer, of Cromhall. W. M. Adey JP and H. W. Dyer JP at Wotton under Edge. Hard labour for two calendar months in Horsley house of correction. Offence committed 22 Sept. 1831.

50/D/52   29 Sept. 1831. Daniel Purbrick of Fulbrook, [Oxon.], labourer. Using a snare to kill game and pursuing game at Widford without a licence. Rev. F. E. Witts JP, commissioner for assessed taxes, at Stow on the Wold. Fine £10. Offence committed 26 Sept. 1831.

50/D/53   3 May 1831. Richard Chandler of Haresfield. Keeping his licensed premises open for the sale and consumption of cider between 3 p.m. and 5 p.m. [on a Sunday]. H. C. Clifford JP and P. B. Purnell JP at a Petty Sessions for Whitstone hundred. First offence. Fine 40/- and 12/- costs. Offence committed 17 April 1831.

50/D/54   22 June 1831. James Drew, beer retailer, of Alderton. Permitting drunkenness and allowing the consumption of beer on his premises after 10 p.m. J. Timbrill D.D. JP, Rev. J. Keysall JP and John William Martin JP at a Petty Sessions for the county of Gloucester. First offence. Fine £5 and 12/- costs. Offence committed 1 June 1831.

50/D/55   A certificate dated 18 Oct. 1831 directed to a Quarter Sessions to be held on that date discharging James and Richard Robins, labourers, of Deerhurst, from a recognizance made on 28 Jan. 1831 for the personal appearance of the above James to answer a complaint of the churchwardens and overseers of the poor of having made pregnant Mary Price, single woman, of Deerhurst. A filiation order of the child, since born a bastard, was made on 20 July 1831 by J. Timbrill D.D. JP and Rev. J. Keysall JP.

50/D/56   20 July 1831. James Nightingale, carter to Mr. John Kendrick of Winchcombe. Assaulting John Puddle on several occasions and particularly at Winchcombe. J. Timbrill D.D. JP and Rev. J. Keysall JP at Tewkesbury. Fine 5/-, to be paid to John Mason, an overseer of the poor of Winchcombe, and 15/- costs, or two calendar months in Horsley house of correction. Offence committed 18 July 1831.

50/D/57   5 Oct. 1831. A certificate directed to a Quarter Sessions to be held on 18 Oct. 1831 regarding a recognizance entered into by William Slade, farming bailiff, and John Arkell, farmer, both of Whittington, for the personal appearance of the above William to answer a complaint by the churchwardens and overseers of the poor of Deerhurst for making pregnant Jane Fletcher of Deerhurst. William Long affirmed that the child had not yet been born, therefore the recognizance was respited to the next Quarter Sessions by J. Timbrill D.D. JP.

50/D/58   5 Aug. 1831. A recognizance was entered into by William Slade, farming bailiff, and John Arkell, farmer, both of Whittington, in the sum of £20 each for the appearance of the above William at the next Quarter Sessions in respect of a statement by Jane Fletcher, single woman, of Deerhurst naming him as the father of her unborn child, taken by J. Timbrill D.D. JP.

50/D/59   31 Aug. 1831. Henry Cresswell of Tredington, labourer. Violently assaulting Elizabeth wife of William Cresswell at Tredington. J. Timbrill D.D. JP, Rev. J. Keysall JP and J. W. Martin JP at Tewkesbury. Fine £5 including costs, to be paid to William Nind, an overseer of the poor of Tredington, or two months in Northleach house of correction. Offence committed Sunday 21 Aug. 1831. [*Endorsed with a note that the offender was committed to the house of correction 31 Aug. 1831.*]

50/D/60   23 Sept. 1831. George Dyer of Grafton, Beckford, labourer. Stealing apples from an orchard, the property of Mrs. Elizabeth Moore of Grafton. J. Timbrill D.D. JP at Beckford. Fine £5, 1/6 damages and 4/- costs or hard labour for two calendar months in Northleach house of correction. Offence committed at night, 19 Sept. 1831. [*Endorsed with a note that the offender was committed to the house of correction 23 Sept. 1831.*]

50/D/61   28 Sept. 1831. George Williams, apprentice to John Grizzell, cordwainer, of Kemerton. Stealing apples from an enclosed orchard, the property of Miss Ann Holmes of Kemerton, during the hours of divine service. J. Timbrill D.D. JP, Rev. J. Keysall JP and J. W. Martin JP at Tewkesbury. Fine £5, to be paid to Willliam Mumford, an overseer of the poor, 2/- damages and 6/6 costs, or hard labour for two calendar months in Northleach house of correction. Offence committed 25 Sept. 1831.

50/D/62   28 Sept. 1831. Charles Whoods of Aston on Carrant, Ashchurch, miller. Using a gun to kill a hare at Ashchurch, without a licence. J. Timbrill D.D. JP, Rev. J. Keysall JP and J. W. Martin JP, commissioners for taxes, at Tewkesbury. Fine £10. Offence committed 19 Sept. 1831.

50/D/63   14 Oct. 1831. William Newman of Walton Hill, Deerhurst, farmer. Assaulting and kicking Esther Hope in his house. Rev. J. Keysall JP and J. W. Martin JP at Tewkesbury. Fine 26/-, to be paid to Isaac Bloxham, an overseer of the poor, and 14/- costs to the complainant. Offence committed 7 Oct. 1831.

50/D/64   2 July 1831. Thomas Fox of Cheltenham, retail beer dealer. Keeping his premises open for the sale of beer after 10 p.m. R. B. Cooper JP and Rev. Charles Brandon Trye JP at a Petty Sessions for Cheltenham district. Third offence. [*Cf.* 50/A/38, 50/B/19.] Fine 40/- and 5/6 costs. Offence committed 25 June 1831.

50/D/65   29 Sept. 1831. James Nash. Assaulting Sarah Newman at Cheltenham. R. B. Cooper JP and Rev. W. Hicks JP at Cheltenham. Fine 10/- and 4/- costs or one calendar month in Northleach house of correction. Offence committed 27 Sept. 1831.

50/D/66   6 Aug. 1831. William Clark. Assaulting John Pye at Cheltenham. R. B. Cooper JP and Rev. C. B. Trye JP at Cheltenham. Fine £3 and 9/6 costs or two calendar months in Northleach house of correction. Offence committed 29 July 1831.

50/D/67   1 Oct. 1831. Edward Edwin Bligh. Assaulting Stephen Dawson and William Rutherford at Cheltenham. R. B. Cooper JP and J. E. Viner JP at Cheltenham. Fine 40/- and 6/9 costs or one calendar month in Northleach house of correction. Offence committed 28 Sept. 1831.

50/D/68   1 Oct. 1831. Henry Crockett. Assaulting Mary Crockett at Cheltenham. R. B. Cooper JP and J. E. Viner JP at Cheltenham. Fine 20/- and 6/6 costs or one calendar month in Northleach house of correction. Offence committed 28 Sept. 1831.

50/D/69   1 Oct. 1831. John Arkell. Assaulting Stephen Dawson and William Rutherford [*etc., as* 60/D/67].

50/D/70   28 July 1831. Michael O'Keefe. Assaulting Thomas Read at Cheltenham. T. Newell JP and R. B. Cooper JP at Cheltenham. Fine 40/- and 7/- costs or one month in Northleach house of correction. Offence committed 27 July 1831.

50/D/71   9 July 1831. Betty Green, retail beer dealer, of Cheltenham. Allowing persons of notoriously bad character to meet on her premises. R. B. Cooper JP and T. Newell JP at a Petty Sessions for Cheltenham district. First offence. Fine £5 and 5/6 costs. Offence committed 4 July 1831.

50/D/72   14 July 1831. Samuel Wozencroft. Assaulting John Cooke at Cheltenham. Sir W. Hicks, Bt., JP and R. B. Cooper JP at Cheltenham. Fine 10/- and 9/6 costs. Offence committed 4 July 1831.

50/D/73   30 July 1831. William Bedford. Assaulting James Clark at Cheltenham. R. B. Cooper JP and T. Newell JP at Cheltenham. Fine 20/- and 8/- costs. Offence committed 28 July 1831.

50/D/74   14 July 1831. George Witts. Assaulting Charles Williams at Cheltenham. T. Newell JP and R. B. Cooper JP at Cheltenham. Fine 5/- and 7/- costs or fourteen days in Northleach house of correction. Offence committed 8 July 1831.

50/D/75   7 July 1831. Samuel Barnett, late of Cheltenham, labourer. Hawking for sale one bottle of eau de Cologne and one yard of ribbon without a licence at Cheltenham. Sir W. Hicks, Bt., JP, R. B. Cooper JP, Rev. C. B. Trye JP, Rev. W. Hicks JP and J. E. Viner JP at the public office, Cheltenham. Joseph Atkins, labourer, of Worcester, informer. William Page, George Onslow, Richard Wells and Henry Thomas, witnesses. Pleaded not guilty. Fine £10. Offence committed 6 July 1831.

50/D/76   28 July 1831. William Clarke, [beer retailer], of St. George, [Bristol]. Allowing beer to be consumed after 10 p.m. C. L. Walker JP and G. Goldney JP at a Petty Sessions for Bristol division. Fine 40/-. Offence committed 9 July 1831.

50/D/77   1 Sept. 1831. Luke Hipsley, [beer retailer], of St. Philip and St. Jacob, [Bristol]. Allowing beer to be consumed after 10 p.m. D. Cave JP and J. Parker JP at a Petty Sessions for Bristol division. Fine 40/-. Offence committed 24 Aug. 1831.

50/D/78   19 Sept. 1831. William Bush. Maliciously driving a wagon drawn by four horses against a cart drawn by one horse at Bitton, thereby damaging the cart, the property of George Godfrey of Bitton. J. Parker JP. Fine 20/- including costs and 40/- damages or two calendar months in Lawfords Gate house of correction. Offence committed 14 Sept. 1831.

50/D/79   15 Sept. 1831. William Norton. Assaulting Elizabeth Beanes at St. Philip and St. Jacob, [Bristol]. D. Cave JP and W. Fripp JP at Lawfords Gate sessions room. Fine 1/6 and 6/6 costs or fourteen days in Lawfords Gate house of correction. Offence committed 29 Aug. 1831.

50/D/80   14 July 1831. Thomas Flook. Assaulting Henry Coventry at Mangotsfield. G. Goldney JP and W. Fripp JP at Lawfords Gate sessions room. Fine 1/- and 13/- costs or fourteen days in Lawfords Gate house of correction. Offence committed 2 July 1831.

50/D/81   21 July 1831. William Rowe. Assaulting Samuel Hopkins at St. Philip and St. Jacob, [Bristol]. G. Goldney JP and G. Hilhouse JP at Lawfords Gate sessions room. Fine 5/- and 6/6 costs or fourteen days in Lawfords Gate house of correction. Offence committed 21 July 1831.

50/D/82   7 July 1831. Benjamin Hughes. Assaulting John Franklyn at St. Philip and St. Jacob, [Bristol]. G. Goldney JP and G. Hilhouse JP at Lawfords Gate sessions room. Fine 10/- and 6/6 costs or fourteen days in Lawfords Gate house of correction. Offence committed 23 June 1831.

50/D/83   4 Aug. 1831. Abraham Phipps. Assaulting Ann Milsome at St. George, [Bristol]. J. Haythorne JP and H. W. Newman JP at Lawfords Gate sessions room. Fine £1 and 13/- costs or one calendar month in Lawfords Gate house of correction. Offence committed 22 July 1831.

50/D/84   22 Sept. 1831. Thomas Long. Assaulting George Davis at Stapleton. J. S. Harford JP and G. Goldney JP at Lawfords Gate sessions room. Fine 3/- and 7/- costs or twenty-one days in Lawfords Gate house of correction. Offence committed 19 Sept. 1831.

50/D/85   18 Aug. 1831. James Roach. Assaulting John Rennison at St. James, [Bristol]. H. W. Newman JP and G. Goldney JP at Lawfords Gate sessions room. Fine £1 10s. 6d. and 9/6 costs or one calendar month in Lawfords Gate house of correction. Offence committed 31 July 1831

50/D/86   22 Sept. 1831. Henry Cox. Assaulting Mary Ann Onion at Westbury on Trym. J. S. Harford JP and D. Cave JP at Lawfords Gate sessions room. Fine 12/- and 8/- costs or one month in Lawfords Gate house of correction. Offence committed 13 Sept. 1831.

50/D/87   5 July 1831. James Pearse. Stealing 2 quarts of fruit (currants, gooseberries and strawberries) from a garden, the property of Richard Harris of Horsley. Rev. H. Campbell JP at Minchinhampton. Hard labour for six calendar months in Horsley house of correction. Offence committed 5 July 1831.

50/D/88   27 Sept. 1831. Francis Grange. Stealing half a quartern of potatoes growing in enclosed land at Minchinhampton, the property of Isaac Paine. Rev. H. Campbell JP. One month in Horsley house of correction. Offence committed 27 Sept. 1831.

50/D/89   19 Sept. 1831. Recognizance binding John Hart, labourer, and William Taylor, grocer, both of Stow on the Wold, in the sums of £40 and £20 respectively, to be levied on their goods and chattels, to ensure the appearance of the above John Hart at the the next Quarter Sessions to answer a charge of stealing one cock and three hens, the property of William Roffe, victualler, of Stow on the Wold. Taken before Rev. F. E. Witts JP.

50/D/90   19 Sept. 1831. Recognizance binding William Roffe, victualler, and Henry Minchin, constable, both of Stow on the Wold, in the sums of £20 each, to be levied on their goods and chattels, to ensure their appearance at the next Quarter Sessions, the former to prefer a charge of stealing on 18 Sept. one cock and three hens, his property , against John and George Hart, the constable to give evidence. Taken before Rev. F. E. Witts JP.

50/D/91   11 Oct. 1831. John Neville of Cheltenham, retail beer dealer. Keeping his premises open for the sale of beer after 10 p.m. J. E. Viner JP and T. Newell JP at a Petty Sessions for Cheltenham district. First offence. Fine 40/- and 5/6 costs. Offence committed 6 Oct. 1831.

50/D/92   27 Aug. 1831. Thomas Brain. Assaulting John Cooke at Cheltenham. J. E. Viner JP and Rev. C. B. Trye JP at Cheltenham. Fine 20/- and 3/6 costs or one calendar month in Northleach house of correction. Offence committed 25 Aug. 1831.

50/D/93   27 Aug. 1831. Robert Norman. Assaulting John Cooke [etc., as 50/D/92].

50/D/94   30 June 1831. Thomas Aston. Assaulting John Cooke at Cheltenham. J. E. Viner JP and Rev. Thomas Blackman Newell JP at Cheltenham. Fine 15/-, to be paid to the overseer of the poor, and 4/6 costs to be paid to the prosecutor. Offence committed 27 June 1831.

50/D/95   30 June 1831. James Lippiatt. Assaulting John Cooke at Cheltenham. J. E. Viner JP and Rev. T. B. Newell JP at Cheltenham. Fine 10/-, to be paid to the overseer of the poor, and 3/6 to be paid to the prosecutor. Offence committed 27 June 1831.

50/D/96   27 Sept. 1831. Joseph Steward of Cheltenham, retail beer dealer. Keeping his premises open for the sale of beer after 10 p.m. J. E. Viner JP and Rev. T. B. Newell JP at a Petty Sessions for Cheltenham district. First offence. Fine 40/- and 6/6 costs. Offence committed 19 Sept. 1831.

50/D/97   15 Oct. 1831. Thomas Smith. Assaulting Charles Campbell at Cheltenham. J. E. Viner JP and Rev. T. B. Newell JP at Cheltenham. Fine 10/- and 8/6 costs. Offence committed 11 Oct. 1831.

50/D/98   15 Oct. 1831. John Goodchild. Assaulting Charles Smith Barnett at Cheltenham. J. E. Viner JP and Rev. T. B. Newell JP at Cheltenham. Fine 5/- and 6/6 costs. Offence committed 7 Oct. 1831.

50/D/99   25 Aug. 1831. John Bright. Assaulting Charles Steel at Charlton Kings. J. E. Viner JP and Rev. C. B. Trye JP at Cheltenham. Fine 7/6 and 5/6 costs. Offence committed 21 Aug. 1831.

50/D/100   25 Aug. 1831. Samuel Weaver. Assaulting Henry Price at Swindon. J. E. Viner JP and Rev. C. B. Trye JP at Cheltenham. Fine 5/- and 5/6 costs. Offence committed 23 Aug. 1831.

50/D/101   5 July 1831. George Flowers of Cheltenham, victualler. Keeping his premises open until 2 a.m. on a Sunday. Allowing gaming and tippling and failing to maintain good order. Sir W. Hicks, Bt., JP, R. Cooper JP and Rev. W. Hicks JP at a special sessions for Cheltenham district. Fine £50 and £1 9s. 6d. costs. Offence committed 25 June 1831.

50/D/102   24 Sept. 1831. William Pope. Assaulting Charles Louis Barber at Cheltenham. J. E. Viner JP and T. Newell JP at Cheltenham. Fine 5/- and 5/6 costs. Offence committed 28 Aug. 1831.

50/D/103   20 Sept. 1831. Thomas Leabon. Assaulting James Rothwell at Cheltenham. Sir W. Hicks, Bt., JP and T. Newell JP at Cheltenham. Fine 10/- and 3/- costs. Offence committed 19 Sept. 1831.

50/D/104   9 Sept. 1831. George Maley. Assaulting Thomas Witney at Cheltenham. Sir W. Hicks, Bt., JP and T. Newell JP at Cheltenham. Fine 5/- and 7/6 costs or fourteen days in Northleach house of correction. Offence committed 5 Sept. 1831.

50/D/105   30 Aug. 1831. Mary Freeman. Assaulting Sarah Bastin at Prestbury. J. E. Viner JP and Rev. J. Edwards JP at Cheltenham. Fine 5/- and 10/6 costs or fourteen days in Northleach house of correction. Offence committed — July 1831.

50/D/106   27 Sept. 1831. Thomas Leabon. Assaulting John Russell at Cheltenham. Sir W. Hicks, Bt., JP and T. Newell JP at Cheltenham. Fine 20/- and 4/- costs or six weeks in Northleach house of correction. Offence committed 24 Sept. 1831.

50/D/107   18 July 1831. William Willifer of Longborough, farmer. Assaulting Elizabeth March at Longborough. Hon. and Rev. E. Rice D.D. JP and Rev. J. R. Hall JP at Bourton on the Hill. Fine £2, to be paid to William Meadows, overseer of the poor of Longborough, and 16/6 costs to the complainant, or two calendar months in Northleach house of correction. Offence committed 30 June 1831.

50/D/108   12 Sept. 1831. Edmund Driver. Leaving his wife and family chargeable to Moreton in Marsh parish. Rev. J. R. Hall JP at Bourton on the Hill. Hard labour for one calendar month in Northleach house of correction. Offence committed 1 Aug. 1831.

50/D/109   12 Sept. 1831. John Penket *alias* Pincott of Wapley and Codrington. Selling three pints of beer at Wapley without a licence. F. Trotman JP and W. Blathwayt JP at a Petty Sessions held at the Cross Hands inn, Old Sodbury, for Grumbalds Ash district. First offence. Fine £20 mitigated to £5. Offence committed 6 June 1831.

50/D/110   23 Sept. 1831. William Long of Dyrham and Hinton. Having in his dwelling house a hare and a net for catching game. I. J. Horlock JP, F. Trotman JP, W. G. Davy JP and W. Blathwayt JP at a Petty Sessions held at the Cross Hands inn, Old Sodbury. William Dyer of Wapley and Codrington, gamekeeper to Sir C. B. Codrington, Bt., informer. Henry Dyer of Wapley and Codrington, Jeffrey Matthews of Dyrham and Hinton and Joseph Bence, constable of Marshfield, witnesses. The latter deposed that when he went to search defendant's home he was refused admittance and Long threatened to shoot him.

Returning later with an iron bar he made forcible entry and found a partly burnt hare and a net on the fire. Evidence was given that the house had two outside doors, communication on the upper floor, but none on the ground floor. Occupants were Moses Britten (against whom rates were charged), Samuel and George Britten and Long and his wife. Defendant said he lodged with George Britten. Pleaded not guilty. Fine £5, half to the informer and the rest to the poor of Dyrham and Hinton. Offence committed 13 Dec. 1831.

50/D/111 8 July 1831. Jacob Filpott or Philpott of Marshfield, labourer. Possessing one hare and offering it for sale for 2/6. F. Trotman JP and W. Blathwayt JP at a Petty Sessions held at the Cross Hands inn, Old Sodbury. George Dyer of Marshfield, gamekeeper to Sir C. Bethell Codrington, Bt., informed I. J. Horlock JP on 21 June. John Jenkins, innkeeper, of Marshfield deposed that he agreed to pay 2/- and a pint of beer for the hare. Joseph Bence, constable of Marshfield, affirmed that defendant had been duly summoned but failed to appear. Fine £5, half to the informer and half to the poor of Marshfield. Offence committed 4 June 1831.

51/A/1 27 Dec. 1831. Thomas Brewer of Wheatenhurst, yeoman. Trespassing on land in Longney, occupied by William Longney, in pursuit of game. D. J. Niblett JP at Wheatenhurst. Fine £2, to be paid to Nathaniel Hawkins, an overseer of the poor, and 5/6 costs to the complainant T. J. Lloyd Baker. Offence committed 23 Dec. 1831.

51/A/2 6 Dec. 1831. John William Chase, [beer retailer], of Eastington. Allowing gaming on his premises. T. J. Lloyd Baker JP and R. S. Davies JP at a Petty Sessions for Whitstone hundred. First offence. Fine £5. Offence committed 25 Nov. 1831.

51/A/3 6 Dec. 1831. Daniel Hayward, [beer retailer], of Eastington. Allowing gaming on his premises. T. J. Lloyd Baker JP and R. S. Davies JP at a Petty Sessions for Whitstone hundred. First offence. Fine 40/-. Offence committed 24 Nov. 1831.

51/A/4 6 Dec. 1831. Job Smith of Coaley, labourer. Trespassing in pursuit of game in Frocester on land belonging to John Altham Graham Clarke Esq. T. J. Lloyd Baker JP at Wheatenhurst. Fine £2, to be paid to an overseer of the poor, and 8/6 costs to the complainant Thomas Tenniell [reading uncertain], or two months in Horsley house of correction. Given twenty-one days to pay. Offence committed 19 Nov. 1831.

51/A/5 6 Dec. 1831. Charles Richards of Gloucester, joiner. Trespassing on land in Hardwicke, the property of T. J. Lloyd Baker Esq. R. S. Davies JP at Wheatenhurst. Fine £2, to be paid to an overseer of the poor, and 8/6 costs to the complainant William Smith, or two months in Horsley house of correction. Given twenty-one days to pay. Offence committed 19 Nov. 1831.

51/A/6 5 Dec. 1831. Thomas Preen. Stealing 2½ pecks of turnips growing in a garden, the property of John Poole of King's Stanley. Rev. P. Hawker at Woodchester. Three calendar months' hard labour in Horsley house of correction. Offence committed 3 Dec. 1831.

51/A/7 15 Dec. 1831. John Jennings. Breaking thirty-two panes of glass in William Barnfield's dwelling house in Minchinhampton. Rev. P. Hawker JP at Rodborough. Fine 30/-, to be paid to George Simpkins, an overseer of the poor, and 19/- costs, or hard labour for two calendar months in Horsley house of correction. Offence committed 10 Dec. 1831.

51/A/8 24 Oct. 1831. William Chandler and Richard Hyde. Stealing two ferrets, the property of William Housman of Woodchester, gentleman. R. Kingscote JP and O. P. Wathen JP at Horsley. Fine £10, to be paid to Thomas Powell, an overseer of the poor, 10/- (the value of the ferrets) and 14/6 costs. Offence committed 12 Sept. 1831.

51/A/9   5 Nov. 1831. James Biggers. Assaulting John Bennett, gardener, of Kingscote at Horsley. R. Kingscote JP and Rev. P. Hawker JP at Rodborough. Fine £4 6*s.*, to be paid to Edward Wood Mason, an overseer of the poor, and 14/6 costs, or two calendar months in Horsley house of correction. Offence committed 28 Oct. 1831.

51/A/10   8 Nov. 1831. William Hulin. Stealing chestnuts and damaging the trees with intent to steal the chestnuts at St. Briavels. G. Ormerod JP and Rev. T. Thomas JP at Lydney. One calendar month in Littledean house of correction. Offence committed 3 Oct. 1831.

51/A/11   8 Nov. 1831. Joseph Jenkins the younger. Entering enclosed ground at Tidenham with a net or nets with intent to kill game. Rev. T. Thomas JP and G. Ormerod JP at Lydney. Hard labour for fourteen days in Littledean house of correction, after which two sureties of £10 (one for himself and one other) to be found that he will not offend again within the next year. In default, a further six months' hard labour. Offence committed 14 Oct. 1831.

51/A/12   19 Oct. 1831. Daniel Bury, labourer. Using a gun and two dogs to kill game at Staunton near Coleford, without a licence. Rev. C. Crawley JP and commissioner for assessed taxes, at Newnham. William Chowles, gamekeeper, of St. Briavels hundred, complainant. William Powell, gamekeeper, of Staunton, witness. Fine £20 and £1 7*s.* 6*d.* costs. Offence committed 21 Oct. 1831 [*sic, dates transposed?*].

51/A/13   8 Nov. 1831. John Jones the younger. Entering enclosed ground at Tidenham [*etc., as* 51/A/11 *with insignificant variations*].

51/A/14   5 Dec. 1831. John Downs Howell, yeoman, of St. Briavels. Using a gun and two dogs to kill game at Newland without a licence. Rev. C. Crawley JP, a commissioner for assessed taxes, at Newnham. William Powell, gamekeeper, of Staunton near Coleford, complainant. William Chowles, gamekeeper, of St. Briavels hundred, witness. Fine £10. Offence committed 23 Nov. 1831.

51/A/15   2 Jan. 1832. William Biddington of Newnham, licensed beer retailer. Keeping his premises open for the sale of beer after 10 p.m. and allowing drunkenness and disorderly behaviour. Rev. C. Crawley JP and J. Pyrke JP at a Petty Sessions for the Forest division. First offence. Fine £4 11*s.* and 9/- costs. Offence committed 22 Dec. 1831.

51/A/16   21 Nov. 1831. Richard Johnson. Assaulting John Hill at Westbury on Severn. Rev. C. Crawley JP and J. Pyrke JP at Newnham. Fine 40/6 and £1 14*s.* 6*d.* costs, 5/6 to be paid to Thomas Harvey, overseer of the poor, and £1 14*s.* 6*d.* to the complainant, or hard labour for one calendar month in Littledean house of correction. Offence committed 27 Oct. 1831. [*There is a discrepancy in the sums levied and disbursed.*]

51/A/17   20 Dec. 1831. Thomas Morgan. Erecting a house or cottage within 25 feet of the centre of the turnpike road leading from Coleford to Parkend. P. J. Ducarel JP and E. Machen JP. Fine 40/- or three calendar months in Littledean house of correction.

51/A/18   28 Nov. 1831. Benjamin Taylor of Corse, labourer. Assaulting George Simpkins at Upleadon. Rev. J. Commeline JP and R. F. Onslow JP at Newent. Fine 5/- and 8/6 costs. Offence committed 24 Nov. 1831.

51/A/19   7 Nov. 1831. Richard Skipp of Dymock, licensed beer retailer. Permitting beer to be consumed after 10 p.m. Rev. J. Commeline JP and R. F. Onslow JP at a Petty Sessions for Botloe hundred. First offence. Fine 40/- and 9/- costs. Offence committed 16 Oct. 1831.

51/A/20   5 Dec. 1831. Robert Warren of Newent, labourer. Using a gin to catch game, without a licence. Rev. J. Commeline JP and R. F. Onslow JP at Newent. Richard Colwell, woodward, of Newent, complainant. Fine £1 4*s.* 6*d.* and 15/6 costs. Offence committed 28 Nov. 1831.

51/A/21 14 Dec. 1831. Benjamin Chapman. Damaging a fence, the property of William Piff of Cheltenham, by taking his horse over it. R. B. Cooper JP and J. E. Viner JP at Cheltenham. Fine 5/- and 5/6 costs. Offence committed 6 Dec. 1831.

51/A/22 13 Dec. 1831. John Green of Cheltenham, licensed victualler. Permitting card games on his premises. R. B. Cooper JP and J. E. Viner JP. First offence. Fine 10/- and 5/6 costs. Offence committed 9 Dec. 1831.

51/A/23 13 Dec. 1831. Jemima Bonnewell of Cheltenham, licensed victualler. Permitting card games and allowing notoriously bad characters to meet on her premises. R. B. Cooper JP and J. E. Viner JP at Cheltenham. Second offence. [*Cf.* 50/B/16.] Fine £5 10*s.* and 5/6 costs. Offence committed 9 Dec. 1831.

51/A/24 13 Dec. 1831. Josiah Ballinger. Breaking down part of a fence or hedge at Leckhampton, the property of William Piff. R. B. Cooper JP and J. E. Viner JP at Cheltenham. Fine 10/- and 5/9 costs. Offence committed 6 Dec. 1831.

51/A/25 27 Oct. 1831. Thomas Sheen of Cheltenham, retail beer dealer. Permitting drunkenness and other disorderley conduct on his premises. Sir W. Hicks, Bt., JP and R. B. Cooper JP at a Petty Sessions for Cheltenham district. First offence. Fine £5 and 5/6 costs. Offence committed Sunday 23 Oct. 1831.

51/A/26 15 Nov. 1831. Mary Sheldon of Cheltenham, licensed victualler. Permitting drunkenness and other disorderly behaviour on her premises. J. E. Viner JP and T. Newell JP. First offence. Fine £3 and 4/6 costs. Offence committed 12 Nov. 1831.

51/A/27 25 Oct. 1831. James Nicholson Boustead of Cheltenham, retail beer dealer. Permitting card games on his premises. Sir W. Hicks, Bt., JP and R. B. Cooper JP at a Petty Sessions for Cheltenham district. First offence. Fine £4 and 6/6 costs. Offence committed 13 Oct. 1831.

51/A/28 24 Nov. 1831. John Shotten of Cheltenham, licensed victualler. Failing to keep good order and allowing drinking in his alehouse until 12.30 a.m. Sir W. Hicks, Bt., JP and R. B. Cooper JP. First offence. Fine £5 and 5/6 costs. Offence committed 19 Nov. 1831.

51/A/29 29 Nov. 1831. James Townley of Cheltenham, retail beer dealer. Keeping his premises open for the sale of beer until 11.15 p.m. Sir W. Hicks, Bt., JP and R. B. Cooper at a Petty Sessions for Cheltenham district. First offence. Fine £2 and 5/6 costs. Offence committed 26 Nov. 1831.

51/A/30 29 Nov. 1831. Mary Hartell of Cheltenham, licensed victualler. Permitting drinking in her inn between 1 a.m. and 2 a..m. Sir W. Hicks, Bt., JP and T. Newell JP. First offence. Fine 10/- and 5/6 costs. Offence committed 28 Nov. 1831.

51/A/31 3 Dec. 1831. James Morgan of Cheltenham, retail beer dealer. Keeping his premises open for the sale of beer until 10.30 p.m. Sir W. Hicks, Bt., JP and R. B. Cooper JP at a Petty Sessions for Cheltenham district. First offence. Fine £2 and 5/6 costs. Offence committed 28 Nov. 1831.

51/A/32 29 Nov. 1831. James Townley. Assaulting Thomas Hayward at Cheltenham. Sir W. Hicks, Bt., JP and R. B. Cooper JP at Cheltenham. Fine £1 and 5/6 costs. Offence committed 26 Nov. 1831.

51/A/33 29 Nov. 1831. James Townley. Assaulting Henry Newman at Cheltenham [*etc., as* 51/A/32].

51/A/34 29 Nov. 1831. John Waller of Cheltenham, retail beer dealer. Permitting drinking between 12 noon and 1 p.m. on a Sunday and allowing drunkenness on his premises. Sir W. Hicks, Bt., JP and R. B. Cooper JP at a Petty Sessions for Cheltenham district. First offence. Fine £3 and 5/6 costs. Offence committed 27 Nov. 1831.

51/A/35   26 Dec. 1831. Isaac Wager of Witcombe, labourer. Killing a hare without a licence. J. Clutterbuck JP and T. Newell JP at Cheltenham. James Burrows, gamekeeper, of Witcombe, complainant. Fine £5 and 4/6 costs or three calendar months in Northleach house of correction. Offence committed 26 Dec. 1831.

51/A/36   8 Dec. 1831. Joseph Humphris. Assaulting Edward Brown at Cheltenham. R. B. Cooper JP and J. E. Viner JP at Cheltenham. Fine £5 including 4/6 costs or two calendar months in Northleach house of correction. Offence committed 6 Dec. 1831.

51/A/37   8 Dec. 1831. Alfred Shurmer. Assaulting Edward Brown [*etc., as* 51/A/36].

51/A/38   8 Dec. 1831. Sarah Dale. Assaulting Maria Dodd at Cheltenham. R. B. Cooper JP and J. E. Viner JP at Cheltenham. Fine 10/- and 4/6 costs. Offence committed 6 Dec. 1831.

51/A/39   26 Nov. 1831. John Dudfield of Charlton Kings, licensed victualler. Permitting card games and other disorderly behaviour at his inn. J. E. Viner JP and R. B. Cooper JP. Fine £5 and 5/6 costs. Offence committed 8 Nov. 1831.

51/A/40   8 Dec. 1831. Charles Dowle of Cheltenham, victualler. Failing to maintain good order by permitting drinking until almost 1 a.m. R. B. Cooper JP and J. E. Viner JP. First offence. Fine 20/- and 4/6 costs. Offence committed 6 Dec. 1831.

51/A/41   19 Nov. 1831. Richard Richmond of Cheltenham, retail beer dealer. Permitting card games and allowing persons of bad character to meet on his premises. R. B. Cooper JP and T. Newell JP at a Petty Sessions for Cheltenham district. First offence. Fine £1 and 5/6 costs. Offence committed 12 Nov. 1831.

51/A/42   10 Nov. 1831. James King of Dowdeswell, labourer. Entering a wood in Dowdeswell, in the occupation of Hester Rogers, spinster, in pursuit of game without consent or licence. R. B. Cooper JP and J. E. Viner JP at Cheltenham. Richard Ruck, gamekeeper, of Dowdeswell, complainant. Fine £1 and 2/- costs. Offence committed 9 Nov. 1831.

51/A/43   27 Dec. 1831. Henry Welch of Stoke Orchard, Bishop's Cleeve, labourer. Killing a hare in Stoke Orchard without a licence. J. E. Viner JP and T. Newell JP at Cheltenham. Henry Hone, yeoman, of Stoke Orchard, complainant. Fine £5, to be paid to an overseer of the poor, and 4/6 costs, or three calendar months in Northleach house of correction. Offence committed 18 Dec. 1831.

51/A/44   25 Nov. 1831. Deborah French, single woman, of Dursley. Assaulting Sarah Fletcher, single woman, of Dursley. P. B. Purnell JP and H. W. Dyer JP at Wotton under Edge. Fine 4/6, to be paid to Joseph Edmonds, overseer of the poor of Dursley, and 5/6 costs to the complainant. Given seven days to pay. In default, fourteen days in Horsley house of correction. Offence committed 23 Oct. 1831.

51/A/45   25 Nov. 1831. Isaac Smith of Wotton under Edge, beer retailer. Permitting disorderly conduct on his premises. H. W. Dyer JP and P. B. Purnell JP at a Petty Sessions for the upper division of Berkeley hundred. First offence. Fine £3 and 5/6 costs. Offence committed 12 Nov. 1831. [*Note*:] £1 of the above fine paid to the informer.

51/A/46   2 Dec. 1831. James Kite of Wotton under Edge, labourer. Assaulting William White, petty constable of Wotton under Edge. H. W. Dyer JP and P. B. Purnell JP at Wotton under Edge. Fine £4 13s. 6d., to be paid to Joseph Powell, overseer of the poor, and 6/6 costs. Given fourteen days to pay. In default, two calendar months in Horsley house of correction. Offence committed 12 Nov. 1831.

51/A/47   18 Nov. 1831. Henry Smith, tailor, and Thomas Gardener, blacksmith, both of Wotton under Edge. Assaulting Charles Cogswell and William White, petty constables of Wotton under Edge. H. W. Dyer JP and P. B. Purnell JP at Wotton under Edge. Each fined £2 13s. 6d., to be paid to Joseph Powell, an overseer of the poor, and 6/6 costs. Given seven days to pay. In default, two calendar months in Horsley house of correction. Offence committed 12 Nov. 1831.

51/A/48   28 Oct. 1831. Moses Kendall, carpenter, and Peter White, common carrier, both of Cromhall. Assaulting Samuel Pick, labourer, of Cromhall. H. W. Dyer JP and P. B. Purnell JP at Wotton under Edge. Fine £1 5s. each, to be paid to the churchwardens of Cromhall, and 5/- costs, or one month in Horsley house of correction. Offence committed 12 Oct. 1831.

51/A/49   7 Nov. 1831. William Wilson of Cirencester, retail beer seller. Having his premises open at 12 noon on a Sunday for the sale and consumption of beer. Rev. H. A. Pye JP and Rev. Hon. C. Bathurst JP at a Petty Sessions for Cirencester division. First offence. Fine 40/- and 5/- costs. Offence committed 16 Oct. 1831.

51/A/50   12 Dec. 1831. Mary Witts of Cirencester, retail beer seller. Permitting gaming with cards and allowing person of bad character to meet on her premises. Rev. H. A. Pye JP and Rev. Hon. C. Bathurst JP at a Petty Sessions for Cirencester division. First offence. Fine £5 mitigated to 40/- and 5/- costs. Offence committed 6 Dec. 1831.

51/A/51   7 Nov. 1831. Robert Burrows of Cirencester, retail beer seller. Having his premises open at 12 noon on a Sunday for the sale and consumption of beer [etc., as 51/A/49].

51/A/52   29 Dec. 1831. William Tarran and Joseph Hughes, labourers, of Winchcombe. Entering land at Pen Corner, Winchcombe, in search of conies without the consent of the tenant, William Midwinter. J. Timbrill D.D. JP. Offenders admitted charge. Fine £1 and 10/6 costs each, to be paid before 2 Feb. 1832. In default, one calendar month in Northleach house of correction. Offence committed 29 Dec. 1831.

51/A/53   22 Dec. 1831. Thomas Collett (son of Robert Collett of Bourton Mill, miller) and George Hill, shoemaker, both of Bourton on the Water. Trespassing in Sherborne with guns and a dog in pursuit of game. Rev. F. E. Witts JP and Rev. R. W. Ford JP at Stow on the Wold. Thomas Houlton, complainant. Fine £2 and 5/- costs each. Given seven days to pay. In default, one calendar month in Northleach house of correction. Offence committed Wednesday 14 Dec. 1831.

51/A/54   22 Dec. 1831. Thomas Collett (son of Robert Collett of Bourton Mill, miller) and George Hill, shoemaker, both of Bourton on the Water. Using a dog and gun to kill game in Sherborne without obtaining a game licence. Rev. F. E. Witts JP and Rev. R. W. Ford JP at Stow on the Wold. Fine £2 10s. and 5/- costs each. Given seven days to pay. In default, one calendar month in Northleach house of correction. Offence committed 14 Dec. 1831.

51/A/55   15 Dec. 1831. Thomas Long. Assaulting Benjamin Flook at Stapleton. W. Fripp JP and H. W. Newman JP at Lawfords Gate sessions room. Fine £1 and 7/6 costs or one calendar month in Lawfords Gate house of correction. Offence committed 29 Nov. 1831.

51/A/56   15 Dec. 1831. Isaac Matthews. Assaulting Eunice Whitcombe at St. Philip and St. Jacob, [Bristol]. H. W. Newman JP and W. Fripp JP at Lawfords Gate sessions room. Fine 10/- and 6/6 costs or fourteen days in Lawfords Gate house of correction. Offence committed 12 Dec. 1831.

51/A/57   22 Dec. 1831. William Chamberlain. Assaulting Alfred James at Frampton Cotterell. H. W. Newman JP and V. J. Graeme JP at Lawfords Gate sessions room. Fine £1 5s. and 14/6 costs or one calendar month in Lawfords Gate house of correction. Offence committed 19 Dec. 1831.

51/A/58   1 Dec. 1831. William Watkins. Assaulting Elizabeth Moore at Clifton. H. W. Newman JP and J. Lewis JP at Lawfords Gate sessions room. Fine 1/- and 7/- [*or* 7/6] costs or one day in Lawfords Gate house of correction. Offence committed 19 Nov. 1831.

51/A/59   8 Dec. 1831. Peregrine Rosling. Assaulting William Haynes at Horfield. H. W. Newman JP and G. Goldney JP at Lawfords Gate sessions room. Fine 3/- and 7/- costs or fourteen days in Lawfords Gate house of correction. Offence committed 8 Dec. 1831.

51/A/60   17 Nov. 1831. Samuel Brooks. Assaulting William Ridgway at Clifton. G. Goldney JP and H. W. Newman JP at Lawfords Gate sessions room. Fine £1 and 6/6 costs or one calendar month in Lawfords Gate house of correction. Offence committed 14 Nov. 1831.

51/A/61   1 Dec. 1831. William Rice. Assaulting George Bindon at St. Philip and St. Jacob, [Bristol]. J. Lewis JP and W. Fripp JP at Lawfords Gate sessions room. Fine £1 and 11/- costs or one calendar month in Lawfords Gate house of correction. Offence committed 1 Dec. 1831.

51/A/62   27 Oct. 1831. John Hort. Assaulting William Ogborne at Westbury on Trym. J. Lewis JP and W. Munro JP at Lawfords Gate sessions room. Fine 5/- and 8/- costs or fourteen days in Lawfords Gate house of correction. Offence committed 27 Oct. 1831.

51/A/63   8 Nov. 1831. Thomas Britton. Assaulting Edward Waters at St. George, [Bristol]. H. W. Newman JP and J. Lewis JP at Lawfords Gate sessions room. Fine 9/- and 11/- costs or one calendar month in Lawfords Gate house of correction. Offence committed 31 Oct. 1831.

51/A/64   6 Oct. 1831. John Chambers of Olveston. Using a gun to kill game without a licence. W. Fripp JP, a commissioner for assessed taxes, at Lawfords Gate sessions room. Fine £10. Offence committed 28 Sept. 1831.

51/A/65   15 Dec. 1831. William Clatworthy of St. Philip and St. Jacob, [Bristol]. Breaking a condition of his licence to sell beer etc. H. W. Newman JP and V. J. Graeme JP. First offence. Fine 20/- and 6/6 costs.

51/A/66   29 Dec. 1831. William Clatworthy of St. Philip and St. Jacob, [Bristol]. Offending against the tenor of his licence to sell beer etc. C. L. Walker JP and H. W. Newman JP. Second offence. Fine £5 and 8/6 costs.

51/A/67   29 Dec. 1831. George Shepherd of Almondsbury. Offending against the tenor of his licence to sell beer etc. H. W. Newman JP and C. L. Walker JP. First offence. Fine 20/- and 9/- costs.

51/A/68   9 Nov. 1831. Richard Howells, toll-collector at Tirley gate. Illegally charging Richard Hogg, farmer, 10*d.* for twenty head of cattle being taken to pasture. J. Timbrill D.D. JP and J. Keysall JP. Fine 20/- and 8/10 costs. Offence committed Tuesday 25 Oct. 1831.

51/A/69   9 Nov. 1831. Margaret Russell of Forthampton. Stealing a gate from a field called Holmes Ground at Forthampton, the property of Mrs. Ann Bolton. J. Timbrill D. D. JP and J. Keysall JP at Tewkesbury. Fine 20/-, to be paid to John Jones, an overseer of the poor, 6/- (the value of the gate) and 21/- costs. Offence committed Saturday 22 Oct. 1831.

51/A/70   27 Dec. 1831. Richard Boulton of King's Stanley, labourer. Cutting down and stealing two ash trees in a wood, the property of Thomas, Lord Ducie. H. Burgh JP at Stroud. Fine £5, to be paid to an overseer of the poor, 7/- (the value of the trees) and 11/- costs, or two calendar months' hard labour in Horsley house of correction. Offence committed 28 Feb. 1831.

51/A/71   24 Dec. 1831. Charles Lusty. Being in a mill yard in Rodborough belonging to Thomas Marling, clothier, with intent to commit a felony. H. Burgh JP at Stroud. Hard labour for three calendar months in Horsley house of correction. Offence committed 24 Dec. 1831.

51/A/72   20 Dec. 1831. Refused to give his name. Begging in Stroud. H. Burgh JP at Stroud. One calendar month in Littledean house of correction. Offence committed 19 Dec. 1831.

51/A/73   15 Dec. 1831. Benjamin White, Timothy White and Charles Smith, labourers, of Stroud. Cutting down and stealing a beech tree in a park at Standish, the property of John, Lord Sherborne. H. Burgh JP at Stroud. Fine £5, 2/6 damages and 7/6 costs or two calendar months in Horsley house of correction. Offence committed 14 Dec. 1831.

51/A/74   30 Nov. 1831. John Cox. Being in a yard belonging to George Gingell, innkeeper, of Stroud, with intent to commit a felony. H. Burgh JP at Stroud. Three calendar months' hard labour in Horsley house of correction. Offence committed 27 Nov. 1831.

51/A/75   8 Nov. 1831. Samuel Hogg, greengrocer, of Stroud. Assaulting Benjamin Chandler, constable of Stroud, in the execution of his duty. H. Burgh JP and Rev. P. Hawker JP at Stroud. Fine £5 or two calendar months in Horsley house of correction. Offence committed 5 Nov. 1831.

51/A/76   8 Nov. 1831. Adam Bird and John Elliots of King's Stanley, labourers. Damaging a Spanish walnut tree growing in a park at King's Stanley, the property of H. Burgh Esq. of Rodborough. Rev. P. Hawker JP at Stroud. Fine 6d. damages and 17/- costs or hard labour in Horsley house of correction [no term specified]. Offence committed 7 Nov. 1831.

51/A/77   19 Oct. 1831. Sarah Cooke, single woman, of Rodborough. Damaging a tree in a park at Woodchester, the property of Thomas, Lord Ducie. H. Burgh JP at Stroud. Fine 10/- and 11/- costs or hard labour for two calendar months in Horsley house of correction. Offence committed 13 Oct. 1831.

51/A/78   25 Oct. 1831. William Cox and George Matthews, labourers, of Rodborough. Damaging two ash trees in a plantation in Rodborough, the property of Robert Snow Paul Esq. H. Burgh JP at Stroud. Fine £2 and 3/- damages or hard labour for two calendar months in Horsley house of correction. Offence committed 22 Oct. 1831.

51/A/79   7 Nov. 1831. Thomas Dalby of Stroud, labourer. Stealing turnips growing in a field in Rodborough, the property of Frederick Pinfold, yeoman. H. Burgh JP at Stroud. Hard labour for one calendar month in Horsley house of correction. Offence committed 6 Nov. 1831.

51/A/80   21 Oct. 1831. John Chandler, Ner [sic] Browning and Alfred Browning, labourers, of Stroud. Stealing turnips growing in a field in Stonehouse, the property of Robert Martin, yeoman. H. Burgh JP and Rev. P. Hawker JP at Stroud. Hard labour for one calendar month in Horsley house of correction. Offence committed 17 Oct. 1831.

51/A/81   10 Nov. 1831. David Smith of Stroud, labourer. Assisting in making a bonfire in a street in Stroud. H. Burgh JP and Rev. P. Hawker JP at Stroud. Fine £5, to be paid immediately. Offence committed 5 Nov. 1831.

51/A/82   10 Nov. 1831. William Smith of Stroud, labourer. Letting off a firework (a squib) in a public street in Stroud. H. Burgh JP and Rev. P. Hawker JP at Stroud. Fine £5, to be paid immediately. Offence committed 5 Nov. 1831.

51/A/83   10 Nov. 1831. Charles Young of Stroud, labourer. Letting off a a firework [etc., as 51/A/82].

51/A/84   10 Nov. 1831. Samuel Wathen of Stroud, baker. Letting off a firework [etc., as 51/A/82].

51/A/85   6 Nov. 1831. Stephen Johnson. Begging in Rodborough. H. Burgh JP at Rodborough. Hard labour for one calendar month in Littledean house of correction. Offence committed 6 Nov. 1831.

51/A/86   12 Nov. 1831. George Harris. Begging in Rodborough. H. Burgh JP at Stroud. Hard labour for one month in Horsley house of correction. Offence committed 12 Nov. 1831.

51/A/87   11 Nov. 1831. John Quire and Thomas Clayton. Begging in Stroud. H. Burgh JP at Stroud. Hard labour for fourteen days in Horsley house of correction. Offence committed 10 Nov. 1831.

51/A/88   4 Nov. 1831. John Flight of King's Stanley, labourer. Using a gun to kill game when not qualified. H. Burgh JP and Rev. P. Hawker JP at Stroud. George Wilcockson, gamekeeper, of Nympsfield, gave information on 15 Oct. John Webb, gamekeeper, and Thomas Harrison, stonemason, both of King's Stanley, witnesses. Fine £5. Offence committed 4 Aug. 1831.

51/A/89   22 Dec. 1831. George Hill of Cam, labourer. Using a wire to kill game in Slimbridge without a game certificate. W. Davies D.D. JP and R. F. Jenner JP at Berkeley. William Peglar, assistant gamekeeper, of Coaley, informer. Fine 10/- including costs or one month in Horsley house of correction. Offence committed 17 Dec. 1831.

51/A/90   22 Dec. 1831. John Martin of Cam, labourer. Using a pistol to kill game without a game certificate. R. F. Jenner JP and W. Davies JP at Berkeley. George Greening, labourer, of Stinchcombe, complainant. Fine £1 16s. and 4/- costs or one month in Horsley house of correction. Offence committed 8 Dec. 1831.

51/A/91   22 Dec. 1831. Charles Seaborne, labourer, of Cam. Trespassing in Slimbridge in pursuit of game without a licence. R. F. Jenner JP and W. Davies JP at Berkeley. Charles Everett, labourer, of Breadstone, complainant. Fine 5/- and 4/- costs or three weeks' hard labour in Horsley house of correction. Offence committed 1 Dec. 1831.

51/A/92   22 Dec. 1831. John Alder *alias* Holder and John Goatman, labourers, of Frampton on Severn. Using wires to kill game in Slimbridge without a licence. W. Davies D.D. JP and R. F. Jenner JP. Henry Barrett, assistant gamekeeper, of Slimbridge, complainant. Fine 10/- and 4/- costs each, to be paid to an overseer of the poor. Offence committed 16 Dec. 1831.

51/A/93   22 Dec. 1831. John French, labourer, of Cam. Using a pistol to kill game without a game certificate. R. F. Jenner JP and W. Davies JP at Berkeley. George Greening, labourer, of Stinchcombe, complainant. Fine £1 16s., to be paid within one week to an overseer of the poor, and 4/- costs to the complainant. Offence committed 8 Dec. 1831.

51/A/94   22 Dec. 1831. Thomas Smart, labourer, of Cam. Trespassing in Slimbridge in pursuit of game without a licence. R. F. Jenner JP and W. Davies JP at Berkeley. Charles Everett, labourer, of Breadstone, complainant. Fine 5/- and 4/- costs. Offence committed 1 Dec. 1831.

51/A/95   4 Nov. 1831. William John Dutfield, late of Yate, labourer. Using a gun to kill game on land occupied by Mr. Jonathan Corbett of Yate. W. Blathwayt JP, F. Trotman JP, W. G. Davy JP and Arthur Shakespere [*also* Shakespear] JP at Old Sodbury. Henry Ray, gentleman, of Iron Acton, informant. William White, labourer, and his brother Thomas deposed that they saw a dog pointing at a ditch. Mr. Bush of Chipping Sodbury, attorney, threw something and flushed a pheasant. He and the accused both shot at it and ran to a corner of the field, where James Cole reloaded the accused's gun. Defendant pleaded not guilty but offered no defence. Fine £5, to be divided equally between the informant and the poor of Yate. Information given to W. Blathwayt on 28 Oct. 1831. Offence committed 12 Sept. 1831.

51/A/96   4 Nov. 1831. Robert Harrington Bush, gentleman, late of Yate. Using a setting dog to kill game at Yate. W. Blathwayt JP, F. Trotman JP, W. G. Davy JP and A. Shakespere [*also* Shakespear] JP at the Cross Hands inn, Old Sodbury. Henry Ray, gentleman, of Iron Acton, informant. Labourers William White and his brother Thomas, witnesses. William made note at the time of the accused and companion, William John Dutfield. Both carried guns [*see above*, 51/A/95]. William Taylor, constable, deposed that he had personally delivered the summons. Accused did not appear. Fine £5, to be divided equally between the informant and the poor of Yate. Information given to W. Blathwayt on 30 Sept. 1831. Offence committed 12 Sept. 1831.

51/B/1   12 Dec. 1831. Robert Webb. Breaking down and destroying a live fence at Batsford, the property of Thomas Ellis. Hon. and Rev. E. Rice D.D. JP and Rev. J. R. Hall JP at Bourton on the Hill. First offence. Fine 10/-, 7/- damages and 11/6 costs. Given fourteen days to pay. In default, two months in [Northleach] house of correction. Offence committed 21 Nov. 1831.

51/B/2   21 Feb. 1832. Benjamin Watkins, William Cooper and Joseph Southan. Breaking a door and windows of William Ludgate's dwelling house at Moreton in Marsh. Rev. J. R. Hall JP at Moreton in Marsh. First offence. Fine £1 5*s*., to be paid to David Smith, overseer of the poor, 2/- damages and 13/- costs to the complainant, or hard labour for two calendar in [Northleach] house of correction. Offence committed 10 Feb. 1832.

51/B/3   26 Dec. 1831. Richard Gillett, Ezekiel Harris and Charles Harris. Injuring and destroying fowls on George Beman's farm at Todenham. Hon. and Rev. E. Rice JP and Rev. J. R. Hall JP at Bourton on the Hill. First offence. Fine £1 7*s*., 2/- damages, to be paid to Thomas Holloway, overseer of the poor, and 11/- costs to the complainant, or one calendar month in [Northleach] house of correction. Offence committed 18 Dec. 1831.

51/B/4   3 Feb. 1832. Matthias Miller, beer seller, Henry Gomm, Nathaniel Thompson the younger and William Evans, labourers, all of Sherston Magna, Wilts. Trespassing, in company with others unknown, on land at Leighterton occupied by George Leonard. Henry Charles, duke of Beaufort, JP and W. G. Davy JP at a Petty Sessions held at the Cross Hands inn, Old Sodbury. Thomas Lucas, labourer, of Lasborough, informant. Fine £1 each, to be paid to William Tyndale, overseer of the poor, and 5/- costs each to the complainant. Given twenty-one days to pay. In default, two calendar months' hard labour in Horsley house of correction. Offence committed 20 Jan. 1832.

51/B/5   24 Feb. 1832. Nathaniel Thompson of Sherston, Wilts., labourer. Using a gun to kill game in Westonbirt without a game certificate. H. Burgh JP and Rev. P. Hawker JP at Stroud. William Evans, gamekeeper, of Westonbirt, complainant. Fine £5, to be paid to George Leonard, overseer of the poor, and 7/6 costs, or two calendar months in Horsley house of correction. Offence committed 6 Jan. 1832.

51/B/6   24 Feb. 1832. Matthias Miller of Sherston, Wilts., labourer. Using a gun [*etc.*, *as* 51/B/5].

51/B/7   27 March 1832. George Harvey. Assaulting Jane wife of Daniel Harvey, yeoman, of Avening. R. Kingscote JP, J. D. Phelps JP and Thomas Henry Kingscote JP at Horsley. Fine £1 1*s*., to be paid to George Whitley, an overseer of the poor, and 6/6 costs. Offence committed 8 March 1832.

51/B/8   27 March 1832. John Winn, clothier, of Stroud. Entering into an illegal contract at Stroud with Henry Fisher of Bisley, [spinner], whereby he received part of his wages in goods. R. Kingscote JP, J. D. Phelps JP, W. M. Paul JP, T. H. Kingscote JP and Rev. P. Hawker JP at Horsley. William Taylor, spinner, of Bisley, informer. First offence. Fine

£10, £3 to go to the informer and £7 to the county treasurer towards the rates, and 8/- costs to the informer. Offence committed 21 Jan. 1832.

51/B/9   27 March 1832. William Smart, clothier, of Bisley. Paying Samuel King, [weaver], of Bisley his wages in goods instead of legal currency. R. Kingscote JP, J. D. Phelps JP, W. M. Paul JP, T. H. Kingscote JP and Rev. P. Hawker JP at Horsley. William Taylor, spinner, of Bisley, informer. First offence. Fine £5, half to go to the county treasurer towards the rates, the rest and 7/- costs to the informer. Offence committed 2 March 1832.

51/B/10   27 March 1832. William Smart, clothier, of Bisley. Entering into an illegal contract at Minchinhampton with Samuel King, weaver, of Bisley regarding the place, manner and person with whom payment becomes due. R. Kingscote JP, J. D. Phelps JP, W. M. Paul JP, T. H. Kingscote JP and Rev. P. Hawker JP at Horsley. William Taylor, spinner, of Bisley, informer. First offence. Fine £5, half to go to the county treasurer towards the rates, the rest and 7/-costs to the informer. Offence committed 24 Jan. 1832.

51/B/11   27 March 1832. John Winn, clothier, of Stroud. Paying Henry Fisher, spinner, of Bisley in goods instead of legal currency. R. Kingscote JP, J. D. Phelps JP, T. H. Kingscote JP, W. M. Paul JP and Rev. P. Hawker JP at Horsley. William Taylor, spinner, of Bisley, informer. First offence. Fine £10, £7 to go to the county treasurer towards the rates, £3 and 8/- costs to the informer. Offence committed 28 Feb. 1832.

51/B/12   27 March 1832. Daniel Cox, clothier, of Bisley. Paying Mary Smart, clothworker, of Bisley in goods instead of legal currency. R. Kingscote JP, J. D. Phelps JP, T. H. Kingscote JP, W. M. Paul JP and Rev. P. Hawker JP at Horsley. Henry Fisher, spinner, of Bisley, informer. First offence. Fine £10, £7 to go to the county treasurer towards the rates, £3 and 7/- costs to the informer. Offence committed 22 Feb. 1832.

51/B/13   22 March 1832. Benjamin Webley. Trespassing in pursuit of game on land at Westbury on Trym belonging to John Scandrett Harford Esq. H. W. Newman JP and W. Munro JP at the New Inn, Lawfords Gate. Fine £2 and 10/- costs or six weeks in Horsley house of correction. Offence committed Monday 13 Feb. 1832.

51/B/14   9 March 1832. Robert Harris of Stroud, retailer. Having a non-standard balance in his shop. H. Burgh JP, Rev. P. Hawker JP and Rev. H. Campbell JP at a Petty Sessions for Bisley hundred. Fine 5/- and 7/6 costs. Offence committed 5 March 1832.

51/B/15   9 March 1832. Thomas Ball, retailer, of Stroud. Having in his standing place one non-standard weight. H. Burgh JP, Rev. P. Hawker JP and Rev. H. Campbell JP at a Petty Sessions for Bisley hundred. Fine £1 and 7/6 costs. Offence committed 4 Feb. 1832.

51/B/16   9 March 1832. William Sims, retailer, of Painswick. Having one non-standard balance in his shop. H. Burgh JP, Rev. P. Hawker JP and Rev. H. Campbell JP at a Petty Sessions for Bisley hundred. Fine 5/- and 7/6 costs. Offence committed 2 March 1832.

51/B/17   9 March 1832. Samuel Gardner, retailer, of Painswick. Having three non-standard weights in his shop. H. Burgh JP, Rev. P. Hawker JP and Rev. H. Campbell JP at a Petty Sessions for Bisley hundred. Fine £1 and 7/6 costs. Offence committed 2 March 1832.

51/B/18   9 March 1832. Eli James of Stroud, retailer. Having four non-standard weights in his shop. H. Burgh JP, Rev. P. Hawker JP and Rev. H. Campbell JP at a Petty Sessions for Bisley hundred. Fine £1 and 7/6 costs. Offence committed 3 Feb. 1832.

51/B/19   24 Feb. 1832. [*Names as below.*] Having non-standard weights etc. [*as specified below*].
–43   H. Burgh JP and Rev. P. Hawker JP at a Petty Sessions for Bisley hundred. Fine 10/- [*except as otherwise stated*] and 7/6 costs.

51/B/19   George Beesley of Stroud, retailer. Two non-standard weights and one balance in his stall and standing place. Offence committed 3 Feb. 1832.

51/B/20   William Wood of Stroud, retailer. Six non-standard weights in his shop. Fine £1. Offence committed 9 Feb. 1832.

51/B/21   Henry Gardner of Bisley, retailer. Two non-standard weights in his shop. Offence committed 21 Feb. 1832.

51/B/22   Thomas Moss of Bisley, retailer. Three non-standard weights in his shop. Fine 15/-. Offence committed 21 Feb. 1832.

51/B/23   Thomas Smart of Bisley, retailer. Three non-standard weights in his shop. Offence committed 20 Feb. 1832.

51/B/24   Charles Innell of Bisley, retailer. One non-standard weight in his shop. Fine 5/-. Offence committed 20 Feb. 1832.

51/B/25   Jasper Gardner of Bisley, retailer. Four non-standard weights in his shop. Offence committed 20 Feb. 1832.

51/B/26   Marshal Rowles of Bisley, retailer. Two non-standard weights in his shop. Offence committed 20 Feb. 1832.

51/B/27   John Lewis of Bisley, retailer. Five non-standard weights in his shop. Fine £1. Offence committed 20 Feb. 1832.

51/B/28   Samuel Aldum of Bisley, retailer. Three non-standard weights in his premises. Offence committed 20 Feb. 1832.

51/B/29   Charles Smart of Bisley, retailer. Two non-standard weights in his shop. Fine 5/-. Offence committed 20 Feb. 1832.

51/B/30   George Lambert of Bisley, retailer. Three non-standard weights in his shop. Offence committed 20 Feb. 1832.

51/B/31   Joshua Clegg of Bisley, retailer. Four non-standard weights in his shop. Offence committed 20 Feb. 1832.

51/B/32   Joseph Weer of Bisley, retailer. Two non-standard weights in his standing place. Offence committed 20 Feb. 1832.

51/B/33   Sarah Franklin of Bisley, retailer. Three non-standard weights in her shop. Offence committed 18 Feb. 1832.

51/B/34   Ann Fortune of Bisley, retailer. Four non-standard weights in her shop. Offence committed 18 Feb. 1832.

51/B/35   William Selwyn of Stroud, retailer. Four non-standard weights in his shop. Offence committed 18 Feb. 1832.

51/B/36   Joseph Rowe of Stroud, retailer. Four non-standard weights in his shop. Offence committed 18 Feb. 1832.

51/B/37   Nathaniel Ball of Stroud, retailer. Three non-standard weights in his shop. Offence committed 18 Feb. 1832.

51/B/38   George Copner of Stroud, retailer. Three non-standard weights in his shop. Offence committed 14 Feb. 1832.

51/B/39   Samuel Browning of Stroud, retailer. Two non-standard weights in his shop. Fine 5/-. Offence committed 14 Feb. 1832.

51/B/40   William Hall of Stroud, retailer. Two non-standard weights in his premises. Offence committed 14 Feb. 1832.

51/B/41   Ann Jones of Stroud, retailer. One non-standard weight in her shop. Offence committed 9 Feb. 1832.

51/B/42   William Williams of Stroud, retailer. One non-standard weight in his standing place. Fine 5/-. Offence committed 3 Feb. 1832.

51/B/43   Charles Chandler of Stroud, retailer. Four non-standard weights in his standing place. Fine £1. Offence committed 3 Feb. 1832.

51/B/44   28 Feb. 1832. William Hawkins of Stroud, stonemason. Stealing a quantity of turnip greens growing in a field, the property of William Capel the younger, gentleman, of Painswick. H. Burgh JP at Stroud. Hard labour for one calendar month in Horsley house of correction. Offence committed 22 Feb. 1832.

51/B/45   16 March 1832. William Cox and John Matthews, labourers, of Stroud. Stealing a quantity of turnip greens growing in a field, the property of William Hopson, gentleman, of Stroud. H. Burgh JP at Stroud. Hard labour for one calendar month in Horsley house of correction. Offence committed 15 March 1832.

51/B/46   17 Jan. 1832. Absalom Cox, labourer, of Bisley. Assaulting William Tyler, an overseer of the poor of Bisley. H. Burgh JP and Rev. P. Hawker JP at Stroud. Fine £3, to be paid to an overseer of the poor, and 16/6 costs, or hard labour for one calendar month in Horsley house of correction. Offence committed 14 Jan. 1832.

51/B/47   10 Feb. 1832. Mary Twinning of Painswick, single woman. Causing her recently born female bastard child to become chargeable to the parish. H. Burgh JP, R. S. Davies JP and Rev. P. Hawker JP at Stroud. Twelve calendar months hard labour in Horsley house of correction. Child born 29 Dec. 1831.

51/B/48   10 Feb. 1832. Joseph Hill, Joseph Kelford and Thomas Stephens, labourers, of Rodborough. Assaulting William Shurmur, cordwainer, of Rodborough. H. Burgh JP, R. S. Davies JP and Rev. P. Hawker JP at Stroud. Fine £3 and £1 3s. 6d. or hard labour for two calendar months in Horsley house of correction. Offence committed 9 Feb. 1832.

51/B/49–   10 Feb. 1832. [*Names as below.*] Having non-standard weights etc. H. Burgh JP, R. S.
53   Davies JP and Rev. P. Hawker JP at a Petty Sessions for Bisley hundred. Fine 5/- and 7/6 costs. Offence committed 4 Feb. 1832 [*except* 51/B/49].

51/B/49   John Grafton of Stroud, retailer. A non-standard balance in his shop. Offence committed 2 Feb. 1832.

51/B/50   Benjamin Pearce of Stroud, retailer. Two non-standard weights in his standing place.

51/B/51   Daniel Gardner of Stroud, retailer. Four non-standard weights in his standing place.

51/B/52   Charles Harrison of Stroud, retailer. Four non-standard weights in his shop.

51/B/53   Job Blick of Stroud, retailer. Three non-standard weights in his standing place.

51/B/54   18 Feb. 1832. Thomas Jenkins. Begging in Rodborough. H. Burgh JP at Rodborough. Hard labour for fourteen days in Horsley house of correction. Offence committed 18 Feb. 1832.

51/B/55   1 March 1832. William Brown. Begging in Rodborough. H. Burgh JP at Rodborough. Hard labour for one calendar month in Horsley house of correction. Offence committed 1 March 1832.

51/B/56   7 Feb. 1832. Henry Bruce of Gloucester. Trespassing on land in Hardwicke, the property of Thomas John Lloyd Baker Esq., in pursuit of game. C. O. Cambridge JP and J. Sayer JP at Wheatenhurst. John Woodyatt, complainant. Fine £2, to be paid to Thomas Spier, an overseer of the poor, and 6/6 costs. Given twenty-eight days to pay. In default, two calendar months in Horsley house of correction. Offence committed 10 Jan. 1832.

51/B/57   7 Feb. 1832. Henry Brinkworth. Assaulting Maria Pooler of Arlingham. T. J. Lloyd Baker JP and C. O. Cambridge JP at Wheatenhurst. Fine £4, to be paid to John Vernon, overseer of the poor, and 8/6 costs. Offence committed 21 Dec. 1831.

51/B/58   9 Feb. 1832. William Slade of Winterbourne. Using a gun to kill game without a licence. H. W. Newman JP and W. Fripp JP, commissioners for assessed taxes for the district of Barton Regis, at the New Inn near Lawfords Gate. Fine £10. Offence committed 25 Jan. 1832.

51/B/59   19 Jan. 1832. Moses Short of Bitton, alehouse keeper. Keeping his house open for the sale of beer between 10 a.m. and 1 p.m. on a Sunday. J. S. Harford JP and W. Fripp JP at a Petty Sessions for Bristol division. Fine £2. Offence committed 8 Jan. 1832.

51/B/60   19 Jan. 1832. John Morgan of Bitton, alehouse keeper. Keeping his house open for the sale of beer between 10 a.m. and 1 p.m. on a Sunday. J. Parker JP and W. Fripp JP at a Petty Sessions for Bristol division. Fine £2. Offence committed 8 Jan. 1832.

51/B/61   9 March 1832. William Alonzo Sebrey of St. James, [Bristol], alehouse keeper. Keeping his house open for the sale and consumption of beer etc. after 10 p.m. W. Munro JP and H. W. Newman JP at a Petty Sessions held for Bristol division. Fine £2. Offence committed 29 Feb. 1832.

51/B/62   19 Jan. 1832. George Gay of Bitton, alehouse keeper. Keeping his house open for the sale of beer between 10 a.m. and 1 p.m. [on a Sunday]. J. S. Harford JP and W. Fripp JP at a Petty Sessions for Bristol division. Fine £2. Offence committed 8 Jan. 1832.

51/B/63   15 March 1832. John Thomas. Trespassing on land in Westbury on Trym, the property of John Scandrett Harford Esq., in pursuit of game. H. W. Newman JP and W. Munro JP at the New Inn near Lawfords Gate. Fine £2 and 12/- costs or six weeks in Lawfords Gate house of correction. Offence committed 13 Feb. 1832.

51/B/64   12 Jan. 1832. Michael Wagg of the Black Horse, Stokes Croft, St. James, [Bristol], licensed victualler. Keeping his house open for the sale and consumption of liquor after 9 p.m. J. Lewis JP, W. Munro JP and H. W. Newman JP. First offence. Fine 40/- and 10/6 costs. Offence committed 5 Jan. 1832.

51/B/65   12 Jan. 1832. Henry Wakefield. Assaulting Amey and Mary Isles at St. Philip and St. Jacob, [Bristol]. J. Lewis JP and W. Munro JP at Lawfords Gate sessions room. Fine 15/6 and 6/6 costs on each charge or one calendar month in Lawfords Gate house of correction. Offence committed 2 Jan. 1832.

51/B/66   5 April 1832. Thomas Norris. Assaulting Susan Strange at Stapleton. G. Goldney JP and G. Hilhouse JP at the New Inn near Lawfords Gate. Fine 5/- and 9/6 costs or fourteen days in Horsley house of correction. Offence committed 30 March 1832.

51/B/67   2 March 1832. John Gibbons of Dursley, licensed beer retailer. Permitting disorderly conduct in his house. P. B. Purnell JP and H. W. Dyer JP at a Petty Sessions for the upper division of Berkeley hundred. First offence. Fine £3 10s. and 12/- costs. Offence committed 12 Jan. 1832.

51/B/68   17 Feb. 1832. Cyrus Cowley of Dursley, labourer. Cutting an ash tree with intent to steal it from a hedge in Dursley, the property of John Delafield Phelps Esq. H. W. Dyer JP and P. B. Purnell JP at Wotton under Edge. Fine £4 13s., to be paid to Reuben Hill, assistant overseer of the poor, 2/- damages and 5/- costs, or hard labour for two calendar months in Horsley house of correction. Offence committed 3 Feb. 1832.

51/B/69   2 Feb. 1832. Job Moss. Assaulting Diana Hall at St. George, [Bristol]. J. Parker JP and D. Cave JP at Lawfords Gate sessions room. Fine £1 and 9/- costs or one calendar month in Lawfords Gate house of correction. Offence committed 28 Jan. 1832.

51/B/70   8 Feb. 1832. William Hall, beer retailer, of the Plasterers Arms, Winchcombe. Permitting drunkenness and disorderly behaviour on his premises. J. Timbrill D.D. JP,

Rev. J. Keysall JP and J. W. Martin JP at a Petty Sessions. First offence. Fine £4 and 20/- costs. Offence committed 12 Jan. 1832.

51/B/71 8 Feb. 1832. Thomas Baylis of Twyning, labourer. Assaulting James Barton, bricklayer, of Brockeridge Common, Twyning. J. Timbrill D.D. JP, Rev. J. Keysall JP and J. W. Martin JP at Tewkesbury. Fine 10/-, to be paid to Philip Roberts, an overseer of the poor, and 16/- costs. Offence committed 24 Jan. 1832.

51/B/72 24 Feb. 1832. Henry Gomm, basket-maker, of Sherston, Wilts. Using a gun at Westonbirt without a game certificate. H. Burgh JP and Rev. P. Hawker JP at Stroud. Fine £3, to be paid to George Leonard, an overseer of the poor, and 7/6 costs to the complainant, William Evans, gamekeeper, of Westonbirt, or one calendar month in Horsley house of correction. Offence committed 6 Jan. 1832.

51/B/73 24 Feb. 1832. John Winn, clothier, of Stroud. Paying Henry Fisher, spinner and artificer, 11d. wages in goods instead of legal coin at Stroud. H. Burgh JP and Rev. P. Hawker JP at Stroud. First offence. Fine £5, £1 of which to be paid to the informer, William Taylor, clothworker, of Bisley, the remainder to the county treasurer, and 10/6 costs. Offence committed 25 Jan. 1832.

51/B/74 16 Feb. 1832. Edward Cordingley. Assaulting James Smart at Cheltenham. Sir W. Hicks, Bt., JP and R. B. Cooper JP at Cheltenham. Fine 10/- and 5/6 costs. Offence committed 11 Feb. 1832.

51/B/75 16 Feb. 1832. Thomas Fisher of Cheltenham, beer retailer. Allowing unlawful card games on his premises. Sir W. Hicks, Bt., JP and R. B. Cooper JP at a Petty Sessions for Cheltenham district. Second offence. Fine £5 and 5/6 costs. Offence committed 14 Feb. 1832.

51/B/76 21 Feb. 1832. Daniel Hopkins of Cowley, labourer. Using wires for taking game without a certificate. R. B. Cooper JP and J. E. Viner JP at Cheltenham. James Burrows, yeoman, of Cowley, complainant. Fine £2 and 3/- costs or two calendar months in Northleach house of correction. Offence committed 20 Feb. 1832.

51/B/77 28 Feb. 1832. Henry Smith. Assaulting Thomas Guilfoyle at Cheltenham. Sir W. Hicks, Bt., JP and R. B. Cooper JP at Cheltenham. Fine 5/- and 6/6 costs. Offence committed 28 Feb. 1832.

51/B/78 1 March 1832. William Haines of Cheltenham, retail beer dealer. Opening his premises for the sale of beer between 10 a.m. and 1 p.m. on a Sunday, i.e. at 11.45 a.m. Sir W. Hicks, Bt., JP and R. B. Cooper JP at a Petty Sessions for Cheltenham district. First offence. Fine £2 and 5/6 costs. Offence committed Sunday 26 Feb. 1832.

51/B/79 3 March 1832. John Hitchings. Assaulting William Hobbs at Cheltenham. R. B. Cooper JP and J. E. Viner JP at Cheltenham. Fine 5/- and 2/- costs. Offence committed 2 March 1832.

51/B/80 3 March 1832. James Butt. Assaulting Richard Johnson at Cheltenham. R. B. Cooper JP and J. E. Viner JP at Cheltenham. Fine £2 and 8/- costs or two months in Northleach house of correction. Offence committed 26 Feb. 1832.

51/B/81 20 March 1832. Jonathan Briggs of Leckhampton, retail beer dealer. Allowing persons of notoriously bad character to meet on his premises. Sir W. Hicks, Bt., JP and R. B. Cooper JP at a Petty Sessions for Cheltenham district. First offence. Fine £5 and 7/6 costs. Offence committed 19 March 1832.

51/B/82 22 March 1832. Joseph Woollen of Cheltenham, retail beer dealer. Keeping his premises open for the sale of beer after 10 p.m. (i.e. midnight). R. B. Cooper JP and J. E. Viner JP at a Petty Sessions for Cheltenham district. First offence. Fine £2 and 5/6 costs. Offence committed 19 March 1832.

51/B/83   27 March 1832. James Clifford and Emanuel Coombs. Assaulting John Nash Belcher at Prestbury. Sir W. Hicks, Bt., JP and J. E. Viner JP at Cheltenham. Fine £2 and 10/6 costs or two months in Northleach house of correction. Offence committed 25 March 1832.

51/B/84   27 March 1832. Thomas Garn of Charlton Kings, labourer. Using a wire for taking game in Dowdeswell without a game certificate. Rev. W. Hicks JP and J. E. Viner JP at Cheltenham. John Morse, yeoman, of Dowdeswell, complainant. Fine £5 and 3/- costs or three calendar months in Northleach house of correction. Offence committed 26 March 1832.

51/B/85   14 February 1832. Robert Carey. Assaulting James Castins in Cheltenham. Sir W. Hicks, Bt., JP and R. B. Cooper JP at Cheltenham. Fine £1. Offence committed 6 Feb. 1832.

51/B/86   31 Jan. 1832. Jeremiah Watts. Assaulting John Hobbs at Cheltenham. R. B. Cooper JP and J. E. Viner JP at Cheltenham. Fine 10/- and 3/- costs. Offence committed 30 Jan. 1832.

51/B/87   2 Feb. 1832. John Jackson. Assaulting James Costans at Cheltenham. Sir W. Hicks, Bt., JP and J. E. Viner JP at Cheltenham. Fine £4 14s. 6d. and 5/6 costs or two calendar months in Northleach house of correction. Offence committed 31 Jan. 1832.

51/B/88   7 Feb. 1832. James Allen. Assaulting Richard Gwillim at Cheltenham. R. B. Cooper JP and J. E. Viner JP at Cheltenham. Fine £5 or two calendar months in Northleach house of correction. Offence committed 16 Feb. 1832.

51/B/89   9 Feb. 1832. James Pollard. Assaulting Thomas Jolly at Cheltenham. R. B. Cooper JP and T. Newell JP at Cheltenham. Fine 10/- and 7/- costs. Offence committed 2 Feb. 1832.

51/B/90   14 Feb. 1832. George Carey. Assaulting John Russell at Cheltenham. Sir W. Hicks, Bt., JP and R. B. Cooper JP at Cheltenham. Fine £3. Offence committed 6 Feb. 1832.

51/B/91   14 Feb. 1832. Clarence Horatio Carey. Assaulting John Russell at Cheltenham. Sir W. Hicks, Bt., JP and R. B. Cooper JP at Cheltenham. Fine £1. Offence committed 6 Feb. 1832.

51/B/92   21 Jan. 1832. John Banks. Assaulting Samuel Russell at Cheltenham. R. B. Cooper JP and J. E. Viner JP at Cheltenham. Fine 6/- and 4/- costs. Offence committed 20 Jan. 1832.

51/B/93   26 Jan. 1832. Thomas Smith of Winchcombe, labourer. Using wires to take game in Charlton Abbots without a game licence. Sir W. Hicks, Bt., JP and J. E. Viner JP at Cheltenham. John Prince, gentleman, of Cheltenham, complainant. Fine £5 and 9/6 costs. Given fourteen days to pay. In default, three calendar months in Northleach house of correction. Offence committed 25 Jan. 1832.

51/B/94   19 Jan. 1832. Charles Parker. Assaulting Sarah Day at Prestbury. R. B. Cooper JP and J. E. Viner JP at Cheltenham. Fine £1 and 4/6 costs or two months in Northleach house of correction. Offence committed 17 Jan. 1832.

51/B/95   19 Jan. 1832. Jesse Bliss, John Fisher, Richard Davis and James Langstone. Assaulting Sarah Day at Prestbury. R. B. Cooper JP and J. E. Viner JP at Cheltenham. Fine 2/6 and 4/6 costs each or one month in Northleach house of correction. Offence committed 17 Jan. 1832.

51/B/96   17 Jan. 1832. Walter Buckle and Charles Cook. Breaking down a wall at Cheltenham, the property of Thomas Cook. R. B. Cooper JP and J. E. Viner JP at Cheltenham. Fine £2, £1 damages and 11/- costs. Offence committed 15 Jan. 1832.

51/B/97   7 Jan. 1832. Charles Priestly. Assaulting Isaac Deaves at Cheltenham. J. E. Viner JP and T. Newell JP at Cheltenham. Fine £2 and 7/6 costs. Offence committed 1 Jan. 1832.

51/B/98   9 April 1832. James Clifford. Assaulting Thomas Symmonds at Cheltenham. Sir W. Hicks, Bt., JP and R. B. Cooper JP at Cheltenham. Fine 10/- and 3/- costs or one week in Northleach house of correction. Offence committed 8 April 1832.

51/B/99   21 Feb. 1832. Charles Carter. Leaving his wife and seven children chargeable to the parish of Chipping Sodbury. F. Trotman JP at Pucklechurch. Six weeks' hard labour in Horsley house of correction. Offence committed about twenty weeks previously.

51/B/100   6 Feb. 1832. Joseph Parsons of the Bell inn, Cirencester, victualler. Allowing drunkenness and disorderly behaviour on his premises. Hon. C. Bathurst JP and Rev. H. A. Pye JP at Cirencester. First offence. Fine 25/- and 5/- costs. Offence committed 31 Dec. 1831.

51/B/101   13 Feb. 1832. George Hall of Cirencester, victualler. Allowing an unlawful card game called 'Put' to be played on his premises. Hon. C. Bathurst JP and Rev. H. A. Pye JP at Cirencester. Fine £5 and 10/- costs. Offence committed 6 Feb. 1832.

51/B/102   24 Feb. 1832. George Bennett of Wapley and Codrington, labourer. Using a wire to take game without a game certificate. W. Blathwayt JP and Christopher William Codrington JP at Dodington. Francis Evans, complainant. Fine £2, to be paid to James Higgs, constable of Wapley and Codrington, and 3/6 costs, or two months' hard labour in Horsley house of correction. Offence committed 21 Feb. 1832.

51/B/103   13 Jan. 1832. Thomas Fluck of Stapleton, labourer. Using a gun without a game certificate to kill a pheasant. F. Trotman JP and W. G. Davy JP at a Petty Session held at the Cross Hands inn, Old Sodbury. Francis Evans, gamekeeper to Sir Christopher Bethell Codrington, complainant. John Shipp, servant to Richard Iles, of Wapley and Codrington, testified that he saw Fluck shoot a pheasant at the withy beds near Stapleton. John Evans said he heard a shot, ran towards the spot and saw Fluck pick up a pheasant and continued to pursue him for two miles. Summoned by a warrant issued by Isaac John Horlock JP. Fluck did not appear. (John Carter, constable of Westerleigh, was to read the summons to the accused and leave him a copy.) Fine 5/- and £2 17*s.* costs or hard labour for two months in Horsley house of correction. Offence committed 21 Dec. 1831.

51/C/1   18 May 1832. Isaac Taylor, Thomas Perriman and Jonathan Perriman. Trespassing on land called the Brake near Ashwick House, Marshfield, the property of Knightly William Horlock Esq., with intent to destroy rooks. C. W. Codrington JP at Dodington. Fine 1/- each (compensation for trespass), to be paid to an overseer of the poor, and 4/6 costs to be paid to the constable of Marshfield. Given one week to pay. In default, one calendar month in Horsley house of correction. Offence committed Sunday 6 May 1832.

51/C/2   26 April 1832. John Harford. Trespassing on land in Wapley and Codrington called Elmhay, the property of George Horlock, and climbing a tree with intent to destroy rooks. C. W. Codrington JP at Dodington. Fine 1/- (compensation for trespass), to be paid to an overseer of the poor, and 5/- costs to be paid to the constable of Wapley and Codrington. Given fourteen days to pay. In default, one calendar month's hard labour in Horsley house of correction. Offence committed 16 April 1832.

51/C/3   18 May 1832. Jacob Hinton. Trespassing on land called the Brake near Ashwick House, the property of Knightly William Horlock Esq., with intent to destroy rooks. C. W. Codrington JP at Dodington. Warned off by George Coles and two hours later by Charles Treadwell, servants to K. W. Horlock Esq. Fine 5/- (compensation for trespass) and 5/6 costs, both sums to be paid to the constable of Marshfield, or hard labour for one calendar month in Horsley house of correction. Offence committed 6 May 1832.

51/C/4   18 May 1832. Edward Bence. Trespassing on land called the Brake near Ashwick House, Marshfield, the property of Knightly William Horlock Esq., with intent to destroy rooks. C. W. Codrington JP at Dodington. Warned off by George Coles at midday and two hours later by Charles Treadwell, servants to K. W. Horlock Esq. Bence had rooks in his pockets. Refused to give them up or to give his name. Said he came from Chippenham. Fine 2/- (compensation for the trespass) and 6/6 costs. Both sums to be paid to the constable of Marshfield, or hard labour for two calendar months in Horsley house of correction. Offence committed 6 May 1832.

51/C/5   6 April 1832. Richard Tily of Marshfield, labourer. Assault and battery on Mary Coates at Marshfield. John Horlock JP and Knightly William Horlock JP at Marshfield. Fine £1 and 6/- costs. Given one month to pay. In default, two calendar months in Horsley house of correction. Offence committed Wednesday 21 March 1832.

51/C/6   6 April 1832. Robert Andrews, Robert Williams and William Lewis, labourers, of Marshfield. Assault and battery on Mary Coates at Marshfield. J. Horlock JP and K. W. Horlock JP at Marshfield. Fine 14/- and 6/- costs each. Given one month to pay. In default, one calendar month in Horsley house of correction. Offence committed Wednesday 21 March 1832.

51/C/7   27 April 1832. Edward Fisher. Beating for game with a dog and nets on enclosed land in Marshfield occupied by Worthy Bedford. J. Horlock JP and K. W. Horlock JP at Marshfield. George Hall, under-gamekeeper to Sir C. B. Codrington, Bt., of Dodington, complainant. Two calendar months' hard labour in Horsley house of correction. On expiry of this to find two sureties of £10 as a guarantee against re-offending for one year. In default, a further six calendar months' hard labour. Offence committed (with others) at about 2 a.m. on 26 Nov. 1831

51/C/8   16 June 1832. Esau Hancock. Assaulting Esther Hancock at Cheltenham. Rt. Hon. Edward, Lord Ellenborough, JP and T. Newell JP at Cheltenham. Fine £1 and 5/6 costs or one calendar month in Northleach house of correction. Offence committed 14 June 1832.

51/C/9   29 June 1832. William Jukes. Leaving his three children chargeable to the parish of Chipping Sodbury for the past fourteen months. W. G. Davy JP at Wick and Abson. Two calendar months' hard labour in Horsley house of correction. Offence committed 10 April 1831.

51/C/10   10 April 1832. Milson Harris. Assaulting Thomas Dogood at Newland, Coleford. P. J. Ducarel JP and Charles Henry Morgan JP at Coleford. Fine 5/-, to be paid to an overseer of the poor of Newland, and 12/- costs, or hard labour for one calendar month in Littledean house of correction. Offence committed 26 March 1832.

51/C/11   19 June 1832. Sarah Cook. Assaulting Jemima Cook at Alvington. G. Ormerod JP and C. H. Morgan JP at Lydney. Fine 2/6, to be paid to John James, overseer of the poor of Alvington, and 6/- costs, or seven days' hard labour in Littledean house of correction. Offence committed 3 June 1832.

51/C/12   19 June 1832. John Martin. Assaulting William Hazard at Lydney. G. Ormerod JP and Rev. C. H. Morgan JP at Lydney. Fine 2/6, to be paid to James Kelsey, overseer of the poor of Lydney, and 5/6 costs, or seven days' hard labour in Littledean house of correction. Offence committed 24 May 1832.

51/C/13   28 Feb. 1832. James Baldwyn. Assaulting Edward Thompson at English Bicknor. Rev. T. Thomas JP and Rev. C. H. Morgan JP at Lydney. Fine £1, to be paid to an overseer of the poor, and 7/6 costs, or one calendar month in Littledean house of correction. Offence committed 4 Feb. 1832.

51/C/14 27 March 1832. John Harris. Assaulting James Lewis at St. Briavels hundred. Rev. T. Thomas JP and Rev. C. H. Morgan JP at Lydney. Fine £4 9s. 6d., to be paid to the county treasurer, and 10/6 costs, or three calendar months' hard labour in Littledean house of correction. Offence committed 18 Sept. 1831.

51/C/15 27 March 1832. John Powell of Aylburton, Lydney, licensed beer retailer. Allowing card gaming and tippling on his premises. Rev. T. Thomas JP and Rev. C. H. Morgan JP at a Petty Sessions for the Forest division. First offence. Fine £1 12s. and 8/- costs. Offence committed 7 Feb. 1832.

51/C/16 22 May 1832. Henry Worgan. Stealing underwood from Caswell Wood at Tidenham, the property of the duke of Beaufort. G. Ormerod JP and Rev. C. H. Morgan JP at Lydney. Previously convicted of stealing wood from a wood called James's Thorns in Tidenham by P. J. Ducarel JP and E. Machen JP on 30 Aug. 1831, for which he was fined £1 and 7/6 costs. [Cf. 50/D/2.] To serve twelve months in Littledean house of correction. Offence committed 3 Sept. 1831.

51/C/17 13 April 1832. John Long of Dursley, labourer. Found to possess part of a beech tree, the property of Edward Sheppard Esq. (After the execution of a search warrant.) P. B. Purnell JP and H. W. Dyer JP at Wotton under Edge. Fine £1 10s., to be paid to Reuben Hill, assistant overseer of the poor, 2/- damages and 6/6 costs. Given fourteen day to pay. In default, six weeks' hard labour in Horsley house of correction. [Date of offence not stated.]

51/C/18 27 April 1832. John Smith of Dursley, licensed beer retailer. Allowing disorderly behaviour on his premises. H. W. Dyer JP and P. B. Purnell JP at a Petty Sessions for Berkeley upper division. First offence. Fine £3 10s. and £1 2s. 6d. costs. Offence committed 11 April 1832.

51/C/19 3 May 1832. John Freeman, Thomas Freeman, Joseph Collett, William Collett and William Mason, labourers, of Kingham, Oxon. Violently assaulting John and Robert Palmer, pig dealers, of Stow on the Wold. Rev. F. E. Witts JP and Rev. R. W. Ford JP at Stow on the Wold. Fine 30/- each, to be paid to an overseer of the poor, and 23/- each for costs to the complainants. Offence committed 29 April 1832.

51/C/20 19 April 1832. Thomas Fry. Assaulting Harriet Fuller at Westbury on Trym. G. Goldney JP and G. Worrall JP at Lawfords Gate sessions room. Fine 20/- and 7/6 costs or fourteen days in Horsley house of correction. Offence committed 15 April 1832.

51/C/21 19 April 1832. Joseph Miller [also Millar]. Assaulting Margaret Rowclift at St. James, [Bristol]. G. Goldney JP and G. Worrall JP at Lawfords Gate sessions room. Fine £2 10s. and 7/6 costs or one calendar month in Horsley house of correction. Offence committed 17 April 1832.

51/C/22 31 May 1832. George Mauler. Assaulting William Aubery at Stapleton. J. Lewis JP and G. Worrall JP at Lawfords Gate sessions room. Fine £1 and 7/- costs or three weeks in Lawfords Gate house of correction. Offence committed 24 May 1832.

51/C/23 14 June 1832. Francis Bryant the elder and Francis Bryant the younger. Assaulting Martha Guest at St. George, [Bristol]. D. Cave JP and G. Goldney JP at Lawfords Gate sessions room. Fine 10/- each (8/6 to go to an overseer of the poor and 11/6 to the complainant) or one calendar month in Horsley house of correction. Offence committed 12 June 1832.

51/C/24 17 May 1832. William Walker. Assaulting Samuel Long at St. George, [Bristol]. H. W. Newman JP and J. Haythorne JP at Lawfords Gate sessions room. Fine 5/- and 6/6 costs or fourteen day in Lawfords Gate house of correction. Offence committed 8 May 1832.

51/C/25   2 May 1832. Tristram Burridge of St. Augustine, Bristol, fishmonger. Seen to be drunk by Gabriel Goldney JP. G. Goldney JP at Clifton. Fine 5/-. Offence committed 2 May 1832.

51/C/26   7 June 1832. John Taylor Bevan. Taking fish from Hanham mill pond, valued at 20/-, the property of Henry Bush Esq. J. P. Parker JP. Fine 5/- and 7/- costs or fourteen days in Lawfords Gate house of correction. Offence committed 25 May 1832.

51/C/27   12 June 1832. Joseph Watkins of Moreton in Marsh, labourer. Assaulting Samuel Hitchman. Rev. J. R. Hall JP and Frederick Colvile JP at Moreton in Marsh. Fine 4/- and 6/- costs or one calendar month in Northleach house of correction. Offence committed 7 June 1832.

51/C/28   29 May 1832. William Glover of Chipping Campden, licensed beer retailer. Allowing beer to be consumed on his premises after 10 p.m. Rev. J. R. Hall JP and F. Colvile JP at a Petty Sessions for the upper division of Kiftsgate hundred. First offence. Fine £2, half to be paid to John Hanley, the prosecutor, and the rest to the county treasurer, and 6/6 costs. Offence committed 19 May 1832.

51/C/29   17 April 1832. Elizabeth wife of William Partlow. Assaulting William Melen at Quinton. Rev. J. R. Hall JP and Rev. C. Jeaffreson JP at Moreton in Marsh. Fine 5/-, to be paid to Lee Davis, overseer of the poor, and £1 costs to the complainant, or fourteen days in Northleach house of correction. Offence committed 16 April 1832.

51/C/30   1 May 1832. George Hawker of Blockley, Worcs. Trespassing in pursuit of game in a close at Sezincote occupied by Thomas Hands. Rev. J. R. Hall JP at Moreton in Marsh. Fine £1 9s. 6d., to be paid to Thomas Hands, overseer of the poor, and 10/6 costs, to be paid to David Gledhill, the complainant, or two calendar months' hard labour in Northleach house of correction. Offence committed 9 April 1832.

51/C/31   19 June 1832. Richard Limbrick. Leaving a child twelve months previously, and another child ten months later, whereby they became chargeable to the parish of Wickwar. F. Trotman JP at Pucklechurch. Six weeks' hard labour in Horsley house of correction.

51/C/32   11 June 1832. Thomas Gordon, clothier, of Painswick. Paying James Llewellin, weaver, of Stroud his wages in goods instead of current coin. Rev. P. Hawker JP and T. H. Kingscote JP at Horsley. First offence. Fine £5, £4 of which to Samuel King, weaver, of Bisley, informer, and the rest to the county treasurer, 8/6 costs to be paid to the informer. Offence committed 15 March 1832.

51/C/33   19 April 1832. William Smart of Bisley, clothier. Paying Sarah Hunt, clothworker, of Bisley her wages in goods instead of current coin. R. Kingscote JP, T. H. Kingscote JP and Rev. P. Hawker JP at Horsley. First offence. Fine £7, £5 of which to go to Henry Fisher, spinner, of Bisley, informer, and the rest to the county treasurer, 8/6 costs to go to the informer. Offence committed 9 March 1832.

51/C/34   19 April 1832. William Smart of Bisley, clothier. Paying Ann Townsend, clothworker, of Bisley her wages in goods [etc., as 51/C/33].

51/C/35   3 May 1832. Daniel Cox of Bisley, clothier. Paying Hester Jenkins, clothworker, of Bisley wages in goods instead of current coin. R. Kingscote JP, T. H. Kingscote JP and Rev. P. Hawker JP at Horsley. Samuel King, weaver, of Bisley, informer. First offence. Fine £10, £9 10s. of which to go to the informer, in addition to 13/- costs, and 10/- to go to the county treasurer. Offence committed 2 Feb. 1832.

51/C/36   19 April 1832. Nathaniel and Joseph Jones, clothiers, of Minchinhampton. Paying Abraham Aldum, clothworker, of Bisley, wages in goods instead of current coin. R. Kingscote JP, Rev. P. Hawker JP and T. H. Kingscote JP at Horsley. Samuel King, weaver, of Bisley, informer. First offence. Fine £5, £3 of which to go to the informer, in addition to 8/6 costs, and £2 to the county treasurer. Offence committed 8 March 1832.

51/C/37   19 April 1832. Nathaniel and Joseph Jones, clothiers, of Minchinhampton. Paying William Lea, weaver, of Bisley, wages in goods [*etc., as* 51/C/36 *except*] Offence committed 13 Feb. 1832.

51/C/38   15 May 1832. Joseph Lusty of Standish, weaver. Paying Charles Holder, weaver, of Painswick, wages in goods instead of current coin. R. Kingscote JP, T. H. Kingscote JP, A. Shakespeare JP and Rev. P. Hawker JP at Horsley. Samuel King, weaver, of Bisley, informer. First offence. Fine £10, £9 of which to go to the informer, in addition to 8/6 costs, and £1 to the county treasurer. Offence committed 10 March 1832.

51/C/39   15 May 1832. Thomas Gordon, clothier, of Painswick. Paying James Llewellin, weaver, of Stroud, in goods instead of current coin. R. Kingscote JP, T. H. Kingscote JP, A. Shakespeare JP and Rev. P. Hawker JP at Horsley. Henry Fisher, spinner, of Bisley, informer. First offence. Fine £5, £4 of which to go to the informer, in addition to 9/6 costs, and £1 to the county treasurer. Offence committed 25 Feb. 1832.

51/C/40   13 June 1832. George Timbrel of Ford, Temple Guiting. Assaulting Honor Tyrrell in Lower Guiting. J. Timbrill D. D. JP and Rev. J. Keysall JP at Tewkesbury. Fine £3 10*s.* and 30/- costs. Offence committed 28 May 1832.

51/C/41   15 June 1832. Elizabeth wife of William Peyton, labourer, of Bisley. Breaking twenty-six panes of window glass in the dwelling house of Elizabeth Alder, widow, of Bisley. H. Burgh JP and Rev. P. Hawker JP at Stroud. Fine 13/- damages, to be paid to Thomas Hazle, overseer of the poor, and 8/6 costs to the complainant, or two months in Horsley house of correction. Offence committed 7 June 1832.

51/C/42   29 June 1832. Robert Lugg of Bisley, labourer. Trespassing on Bisley Common and digging up and stealing about ten square yards of turf and soil, the property of William Lewis Esq., lord of the manor. H. Burgh JP and Rev. P. Hawker JP at Stroud. Fine 10/- and 7/6 costs, to be paid to the complainant, or two calendar months' hard labour in Horsley house of correction. Offence committed 15 May 1832.

51/C/43   29 June 1832. Thomas Burroughs of Bisley, millwright. Taking away manure from Bisley Common, the property of William Lewis Esq., lord of the manor. H. Burgh JP and Rev. P. Hawker JP at Stroud. Fine 6*d.* and 7/6 costs or two calendar months' hard labour in Horsley house of correction. Offence committed 1 June 1832.

51/C/44   21 May 1832. John Matthews and James Powell, labourers, of Stroud. Stealing about fifty cabbages from a garden in Painswick, the property of Samuel Hatton, clothworker. H. Burgh JP at Stroud. Hard labour for six calendar months in Horsley house of correction. Offence committed 19 May 1832.

51/C/45   10 May 1832. George Matthews of Stroud, labourer. Cutting down and stealing several ash poles from a plantation in Eastington, the property of Peter Leversage Esq. H. Burgh JP at Stroud. Hard labour for two calendar months in Horsley house of correction. Offence committed 9 May 1832.

51/C/46   15 June 1832. Richard Bidmead of Stroud, flock merchant. Assaulting William Brunsdon Cox, labourer, of Stroud at Stonehouse. H. Burgh JP and Rev. P. Hawker JP. Fine £5 including 15/6 costs or two calendar months in Horsley house of correction. Offence committed 3 June 1832.

51/C/47   15 June 1832. Richard Franklin. Causing his three children to become chargeable to the parish of Bisley for the previous month. H. Burgh JP and Rev. P. Hawker JP at Stroud. Hard labour for one calendar month in Horsley house of correction. Offence committed *c.* 15 May 1832.

51/C/48 3 May 1832. Daniel McCarty. Begging in Painswick. H. Burgh JP at Stroud. Hard labour for one calendar month in Horsley house of correction. Offence committed 3 May 1832.

51/C/49 11 June 1832. John Rees of Llandovery, Carmarthen, horse dealer. Leading and driving a horse on a foot pavement in Gosditch ward, Cirencester. J. Cripps JP. Fine 40/-. Offence committed 11 June 1832.

51/C/50 26 June 1832. Thomas and Catherine Smith. Assaulting John Conroy at Cheltenham. R. B. Cooper JP and T. Newell JP at Cheltenham. Fine £1 and 5/10 costs each or two calendar months in Northleach house of correction. Offence committed 25 June 1832.

51/C/51 8 May 1832. Joseph Kitchen. Assaulting Joseph Yeend at Bishop's Cleeve. J. H. Ollney JP and T. Newell JP at Cheltenham. Fine 5/- and 4/6 costs. Offence committed 7 May 1832.

51/C/52 17 May 1832. William Williams. Assaulting William Jennings at Cheltenham. R. B. Cooper JP and T. Newell JP at Cheltenham. Fine 15/- and 5/- costs or one calendar month in Northleach house of correction. Offence committed 16 May 1832.

51/C/53 26 June 1832. Ann Smith. Assaulting John Conroy at Cheltenham. R. B. Cooper JP and T. Newell JP at Cheltenham. Fine 5/- and 5/10 costs or seven days in Northleach house of correction. Offence committed 25 June 1832

51/C/54 3 May 1832. George Cratchley, retail beer dealer, of Cheltenham. Keeping his premises open for the sale of beer until 11.15 p.m. J. E. Viner JP and T. Newell JP at a Petty Sessions for Cheltenham division. First offence. Fine £2 and 5/6 costs. Offence committed 30 April 1832.

51/C/55 31 May 1832. William Miles of Cheltenham, licensed victualler. Allowing beer to be taken from his premises during the hours of divine service at the parish church. J. E. Viner JP and T. Newell JP acting for Cheltenham division. First offence. Fine £1 and 5/6 costs. Offence committed 27 May 1832.

51/C/56 31 May 1832. Thomas Shipton of Cheltenham, retail beer dealer. Keeping his premises open for the sale of beer between midnight and 1 a.m. J. E. Viner JP and T. Newell JP at a Petty Sessions for Cheltenham division. First offence. Fine £2 and 5/6 costs. Offence committed 26 May 1832.

51/C/57 26 May 1832. William Allen. Assaulting Henry Holland at Cheltenham. R. B. Cooper JP and T. Newell JP at Cheltenham. Fine 2/6 and 8/- costs. Offence committed 21 May 1832.

51/C/58 26 May 1832. Thomas Apperley. Assaulting William Quarrel at Cheltenham. R. B. Cooper JP and T. Newell JP at Cheltenham. Fine 5/- and 4/6 costs. Offence committed 23 May 1832.

51/C/59 24 May 1832. John Shear. Assaulting John Walls at Cheltenham. Sir W. Hicks, Bt., JP and R. B. Cooper JP at Cheltenham. Fine 5/-. Offence committed 23 May 1832.

51/C/60 26 May 1832. John Willis. Assaulting Henry Holland at Cheltenham. R. B. Cooper JP and T. Newell JP at Cheltenham. Fine £1 and 8/- costs. Offence committed 21 May 1832.

51/C/61 22 May 1832. John Child. Assaulting William Morgan at Cheltenham. Sir W. Hicks, Bt., JP and R. B. Cooper JP at Cheltenham. Fine £1 and 5/- costs or two months in Northleach house of correction. Offence committed 21 May 1832.

51/C/62 24 May 1832. John Mason. Assaulting Simon Harris at Charlton Kings. Sir W. Hicks, Bt., JP and R. B. Cooper JP at Cheltenham. Fine 5/- and 8/- costs or fourteen days in Northleach house of correction. Offence committed 22 May 1832.

51/C/63   24 April 1832. William Hays. Assaulting William Jennings at Cheltenham. Sir W. Hicks, Bt., JP and J. E. Viner JP at Cheltenham. Fine 15/- and 3/- costs or one calendar month in Northleach house of correction. Offence committed 21 April 1832.

51/C/64   22 May 1832. Henry Davis. Assaulting Henry Holland at Cheltenham. Sir W. Hicks, Bt., JP and R. B. Cooper JP at Cheltenham. Fine £1 and 4/- costs or two months in Northleach house of correction. Offence committed 21 May 1832.

51/C/65   28 April 1832. Robert Green of Cheltenham, licensed victualler. Allowing drunkenness and disorderly behaviour on his premises. Sir W. Hicks, Bt., JP and Rev. W. Hicks JP. Fine £2 10*s*. and 6/6 costs. Offence committed 26 April 1832.

51/C/66   17 May 1832. James Wicksey. Assaulting Mary Chew and Ann Slaney at Bishop's Cleeve. R. B. Cooper JP and J. E. Viner JP at Cheltenham. Fine 10/- and 5/- costs. Offence committed 14 May 1832.

51/C/67   22 May 1832. William Archer. Assaulting Henry Holland at Cheltenham. Sir W. Hicks, Bt., JP and R. B. Cooper JP at Cheltenham. Fine £1 and 7/- costs or one calendar month in Northleach house of correction. Offence committed 21 May 1832.

51/C/68   22 May 1832. John Child. Assaulting Henry Holland at Cheltenham. Sir W. Hicks, Bt., JP and R. B. Cooper JP at Cheltenham. Fine £4 and 5/- costs or two months in Northleach house of correction. Offence committed 21 May 1832.

51/C/69   17 May 1832. James Davis. Assaulting William Tytherleigh Bown at Cheltenham. R. B. Cooper JP and T. Newell JP at Cheltenham. Fine 10/- and 6/6 costs or fourteen days in Northleach house of correction. Offence committed 15 May 1832.

51/C/70   21 June 1832. Richard Haines. Assaulting Elizabeth Brown at Cheltenham. R. B. Cooper JP and T. Newell JP at Cheltenham. Fine 2/- and 4/6 costs. Offence committed 18 June 1832.

51/C/71   14 June 1832. Thomas Carpenter. Assaulting James Pettifer at Prestbury. R. B. Cooper JP and T. Newell JP at Cheltenham. Fine 8/- and 3/- costs. Offence committed 13 June 1832.

51/C/72   14 June 1832. James Postins. Assaulting Samuel Crockford at Charlton Kings. R. B. Cooper JP and T. Newell JP at Cheltenham. Fine 2/- and 8/- costs. Offence committed 11 June 1832.

51/C/73   21 June 1832. Joseph Coombs. Assaulting Richard Page at Cheltenham. R. B. Cooper JP and T. Newell JP at Cheltenham. Fine 10/- and 5/6 costs. Offence committed 19 June 1832.

51/C/74   14 April 1832. Edward Jones, yeoman, of Tuffley. Trespassing in pursuit of game on land at Whaddon occupied by John Long. — [*sc*. W.] Goodrich JP and James H. Byles JP at the Shire Hall. John Taylor, complainant. Fine 40/- and 8/6 costs or two calendar months in Littledean house of correction. Offence committed 14 March 1832.

51/C/75   22 May 1832. James Davis, fishmonger, and John Davis, baker, both of Cheltenham. Removing and concealing James Davis's goods and chattels from his premises to prevent distraint for arrears of rent. R. B. Cooper JP, T. Newell JP and J. E. Viner JP at Cheltenham. Written complaint received 15 May. Justices declared no interest in the premises concerned. William Gyde, complainant. Fine £34, double the value of the goods.

51/D/1   22 Sept. 1832. Charles Bruton of Wotton under Edge, shoemaker. Being on enclosed land with nets at night with intent to take game at Ozleworth. A. Shakespear JP and T. Kingscote JP at Dunkirk inn, Hawkesbury. Hard labour for three calendar months in Horsley house of correction, after which to find sureties of a total of £20 to guarantee good behaviour for one year. In default, a further six calendar months' hard labour. Offence committed 14–15 Sept. 1832.

51/D/2   27 March 1832 [*late return*]. William Hall of Winchcombe, retail beer seller. Allowing beer to be drunk on his premises between 3 p.m. and 5 p.m. on a public fast day. G. Talbot JP and J. Timbrill D.D. JP at a Petty Sessions for Ford division. First offence. Fine 40/-. Offence committed 21 March 1832.

51/D/3   27 March 1832 [*late return*]. George Chadborn of Winchcombe, retail beer seller. Allowing beer to be drunk between 10 a.m. and 1 p.m. on a Sunday. G. Talbot JP and J. Timbrill D.D. JP at a Petty Sessions for Ford division. First offence. Fine 40/-. Offence committed 11 March 1832.

51/D/4   26 April 1831 [*late return*]. Henry Collins. Assaulting Thomas Smith at Cheltenham. R. Capper JP and T. Newell JP at Cheltenham. Fine 10/- and 4/6 costs or fourteen days in Northleach house of correction. Offence committed 22 April 1831.

51/D/5   5 May 1831 [*late return*]. Michael Marran. Assaulting Thomas Trigg at Cheltenham. R. Capper JP and T. Newell JP. Fine 10/- and 6/6 costs or fourteen days in Northleach house of correction. Offence committed 4 May 1831.

51/D/6   27 March 1832 [*late return*]. John Marshall of Stanton, retail beer seller. Allowing beer to be drunk on his premises after 10 p.m. and before 4 a.m. G. Talbot JP and J. Timbrill D.D. JP at a Petty Sessions for Ford division. First offence. Fine 40/-. Offence committed 23–4 Feb. 1832.

51/D/7   27 March 1832 [*late return*]. Robert Wisdom of Winchcombe, retail beer seller. Allowing beer to be drunk on his premises between 3 p.m. and 5 p.m. on a Sunday. G. Talbot JP and J. Timbrill D.D. JP at a Petty Sessions for Ford division. First offence. Fine 40/-. Offence committed Sunday 11 March 1832.

51/D/8   16 Aug. 1832. Thomas Freeman of Prestbury, retail beer dealer. Having his premises open for the sale and consumption of beer at 11.30 a.m. on a Sunday. R. B. Cooper JP and T. Newell JP at a Petty Sessions for Cheltenham district. First offence. Fine £2 and 4/6 costs. Offence committed Sunday 12 Aug. 1832.

51/D/9   11 Oct. 1832. John Winning of Cheltenham, labourer. Trespassing in search of game on woodland in Coberley occupied by Walter Lawrence Lawrence Esq. R. B. Cooper JP at Cheltenham. Elisha Castle, yeoman, complainant. Fine £2 and 9/6 costs. Offence committed 4 Oct. 1832 at approximately 11 a.m.

51/D/10   9 Oct. 1832. John Davis of the Swan inn, Woolaston, alehouse keeper. Keeping his premises open for the consumption of beer after midnight. T. Thomas JP and C. H. Morgan JP for the Forest division. First offence. Fine £2 and 9/- costs. Offence committed 10 Sept. 1832.

51/D/11   11 Oct. 1832. John Vaughan, William Jones and Thomas Fletcher, labourers. Stealing potatoes growing in enclosed land at Malswick, Newent, the property of Thomas Vaughan of Malswick, Newent. R. F. Onslow JP. William Travell, labourer, of Newent, complainant. Hard labour for one calendar month in Littledean house of correction. Offence committed 11 Oct. 1832.

51/D/12   1 Oct. 1832. Thomas Leighton the younger, labourer, William Palmer the younger, cordwainer, and Thomas Wells the younger, labourer, all of Pauntley. Being on enclosed land at Pauntley, occupied by Mary Stokes, widow, with nets and a lurcher with intent to take game. Richard Webb JP and R. F. Onslow JP at Newent. William Bullock, gamekeeper, of Oxenhall, complainant. Leighton and Palmer sentenced to hard labour for three calendar months and Wells for six calendar months in Littledean house of correction, after which all to find sureties of a total of £20 each as a guarantee of good behaviour for one year. In default, a further six calendar months' hard labour. Offence committed at about midnight 29 Sept. 1832.

51/D/13   8 Aug. 1832. William Church of St. Philip and St. Jacob, [Bristol]. Keeping his premises open for the sale of beer between 10 a.m. and 1 p.m. on a Sunday. V. J. Graeme JP and G. Goldney JP at a Petty Sessions for Bristol division. Fine £2 including costs. Offence committed 15 July 1832.

51/D/14   2 Aug. 1832. Joseph Hunt of Henbury. Allowing beer etc. to be consumed after 10 p.m. C. L. Walker JP and V. J. Graeme JP at a Petty Sessions for Bristol division. Fine £2 including costs. Offence committed 30 June 1832.

51/D/15   23 Aug. 1832. William Clapp of St. Philip and St. Jacob, [Bristol]. Allowing beer etc. to be consumed after 10 p.m. T. Daniel JP and G. Goldney JP at a Petty Sessions for Bristol division. Fine £2 including costs. Offence committed 4 Aug. 1832.

51/D/16   23 Aug. 1832. John Shorland of St. Philip and St. Jacob, [Bristol]. Allowing beer [*etc., as* 51/D/15].

51/D/17   23 Aug. 1832. Benjamin Jones of St. Philip and St. Jacob, [Bristol]. Allowing beer [*etc., as* 51/D/15].

51/D/18   23 Aug. 1832. Joseph Sidney of St. Philip and St. Jacob, [Bristol]. Allowing beer [*etc., as* 51/D/15].

51/D/19   23 Aug. 1832. James Bryant of Clifton, licensed beer retailer. Refusing to provide Henry Rawson, a private in the 17th Regiment of Lancers, with proper accommodation. G. Goldney JP, C. L. Walker JP and V. J. Graeme JP at a Petty Sessions for part of Berkeley division. Fine 40/- and 11/- costs. Offence committed 13 Aug. 1832.

51/D/20   14 April. 1832. Thomas Mann. Beating and ill-treating a horse at Clifton. J. Lewis JP. Charge made on evidence of two witnesses [*not named*]. Fine 10/-. Offence committed 7 April 1832.

51/D/21   23 Aug. 1832. Isaac Carter. Assaulting Ann Collins at St. Philip and St. Jacob, [Bristol]. V. J. Graeme JP and G. Goldney JP at Lawfords Gate sessions room. Fine 2/6 and 6/6 costs or fourteen days in Lawfords Gate house of correction. Offence committed 10 Aug. 1832.

51/D/22   11 Oct. 1832. Charles Ellis. Assaulting Jane Ellis at St. Philip and St. Jacob, [Bristol]. J. Parker JP and H. W. Newman JP at Lawfords Gate sessions room. Fine 5/- and 12/6 costs or seven days in Lawfords Gate house of correction. Offence committed 6 Oct. 1832.

51/D/23   11 Oct. 1832. George Nicholls. Assaulting William Nicholls at St. Philip and St. Jacob, [Bristol]. J. Parker JP and H. W. Newman JP at Lawfords Gate sessions room. Fine 2/6 and 7/6 costs or seven days in Lawfords Gate house of correction. Offence committed 8 Oct. 1832.

51/D/24   2 Aug. 1832. Philip Nicholls. Assaulting Thomas Gibbons at Clifton. H. W. Newman JP and G. Goldney JP at Lawfords Gate sessions room. Fine 5/- and £1 15*s.* costs or one calendar month in Lawfords Gate house of correction. Offence committed 23 July 1832.

51/D/25   20 Sept. 1832. Joseph Sharpe. Assaulting William Wheeler at Winterbourne. H. W. Newman JP and J. Haythorne JP at Lawfords Gate sessions room. Fine 1/- and 15/10 costs or fourteen days in Lawfords Gate house of correction. Offence committed 16 Sept. 1832.

51/D/26   4 Oct. 1832. John Jossham. Assaulting Ann Wiltshire at St. Philip and St. Jacob, [Bristol]. H. W. Newman JP and J. Parker JP at Lawfords Gate sessions room. [*No indication of fine.*] Fourteen days in Lawfords Gate house of correction. Offence committed 22 Sept. 1832.

51/D/27   2 Aug. 1832. William Henley. Assaulting William Harris at St. Philip and St. Jacob, [Bristol]. C. L. Walker JP and G. Goldney JP at Lawfords Gate sessions room. Fine 1/- and 14/- costs or fourteen days in Lawfords Gate house of correction. Offence committed 30 July 1832.

51/D/28   23 Aug. 1832. Joseph Sharpe. Assaulting Benjamin Williams at Winterbourne. C. L. Walker JP and G. Goldney JP at Lawfords Gate sessions room. Fine £1 and 8/6 costs or one calendar month in Lawfords Gate house of correction. Offence committed 13 Aug. 1832.

51/D/29   19 Sept. 1832. Thomas Bromley of Tetbury, labourer. Stealing apples from a garden in Tetbury, the property of Charles Wickes, gentleman. T. G. B. Estcourt JP and W. M. Paul JP. Fine £2 including costs. Offence committed 3 Aug. 1832

51/D/30   19 Sept. 1832. Charles Bond of Tetbury, cordwainer. Stealing apples [*etc.*, *as* 51/D/29].

51/D/31   27 Sept. 1832. Edwin Fisher, stonemason, of Tetbury. Stealing apples [*etc.*, *as* 51/D/29 *except*] Fine £2 10*s.* including costs.

51/D/32   25 July 1832. Job Rogers, maltster, of Winchcombe. Failing to pay £96 9*s.* 9*d.* duty on 747 bushels of malt made between 5 Jan. and 19 Feb. J. Timbrill D.D. JP and Rev. J. Keysall JP at 11 a.m. at the office of Thomas Phillips White at Tewkesbury. Henry Evans, excise officer, informer. Joseph Chapman, excise officer, of Winchcombe, witness. Tax due 17 July. Written demand made 20 July 1832. Defendant did not appear. Ordered to pay double the amount owing.

51/D/33   8 Aug. 1832. John Wright, labourer, of Kemerton. Stealing apples from an orchard in Kemerton, the property of John Peart. J. Timbrill D.D. JP and Rev. J. Keysall JP at Tewkesbury. Fine 10/-, to be paid to John White, overseer of the poor, 6*d.* damages and 6/6 costs. Offence committed 4 Aug. 1832.

51/D/34   19 Sept. 1832. Charles James of Wotton under Edge. Being in Stirt field at Hawkesbury, occupied by Mary Frankcom, with a dog and net with intent to take two hares. T. Kingscote JP and A. Shakespear JP at Dunkirk inn, Hawkesbury. Peter May and William Hort, witnesses. Hard labour for three calendar months in Horsley house of correction, after which to find sureties of a total of £20 against re-offending for a year. In default, a further six months' hard labour. Offence committed 2 a.m. 19 Sept. 1832.

51/D/35   13 Sept. 1832. Mary Betteridge. Breaking down an ash tree at Wick Rissington with intent to steal, the property of Charles Pole Esq. Rev. F. E. Witts JP at Stow on the Wold. Fine £1, 2/- damages to the complainant and 3/- costs to be paid to Joseph Kempster, or two calendar months in Northleach house of correction. Offence committed 5 Sept. 1832.

51/D/36   23 Aug. 1832. Richard Williams of Oddington. Using a snare to kill a hare without obtaining a licence. Rev. R. W. Ford JP at Stow on the Wold, commissioner for assessed taxes. Fine £10 or three calendar months in Northleach house of correction. Offence committed 17 Aug. 1832.

51/D/37   6 Aug. 1832. William Barson, late of Widford. Using a net to trap and kill deer in Wychwood Forest. Rev. R. W. Ford JP at Little Rissington. Fine £10 or hard labour for six calendar months in Northleach house of correction. Offence committed 6 Aug. 1832.

51/D/38   24 Aug. 1832. Charles Beard. Refusing to work to maintain his wife and family whereby they became chargeable to Painswick parish. H. Burgh JP, R. S. Davies JP and Rev. P. Hawker JP at Stroud. Hard labour for one calendar month in Horsley house of correction. Offence committed 14 Aug. 1832.

51/D/39   24 Aug. 1832. William Cook. Refusing to work to maintain his wife and family [*etc.*, *as* 51/D/38 *except*] Hard labour for two weeks.

51/D/40   16 July 1832. Ann Roberts, prostitute. Disorderly behaviour in Stroud. H. Burgh JP at Stroud. Hard labour for fourteen days in Horsley house of correction. Offence committed 14 July 1832.

51/D/41   2 Oct. 1832. George Arundell. Leaving his wife and family chargeable to Minchinhampton parish. H. Burgh JP at Stroud. Hard labour for three calendar months in [Horsley *deleted*, Littledean *substituted*] house of correction. Offence committed 2 Sept. 1832.

51/D/42   8 Aug. 1832. William Hall. Vagrancy: lodging in outhouses in Stroud. H. Burgh JP at Stroud. Hard labour for two calendar months in Horsley house of correction. Offence committed 7 Aug. 1832.

51/D/43   12 Sept. 1832. James Faulkes and Peter Taylor, labourers, of Stroud. Stealing apples growing in an orchard in Stroud occupied by Edward Darkes, coal merchant. H. Burgh JP at Stroud. Both sentenced to hard labour in Horsley house of correction, Taylor for fourteen days and Faulkes for three calendar months. Offence committed 1 Sept. 1832.

51/D/44   12 Sept. 1832. Ann Andrews of Stroud, single woman. Breaking three glass window-panes in inkeeper Richard Jones's house at Stroud. H. Burgh JP at Stroud. Fine 2/- damages and 9/- costs or hard labour for one calendar month in Horlsey house of correction. Offence committed 11 Sept. 1832.

51/D/45   17 Aug. 1832. Thomas Clissold of Painswick, labourer. Stealing a peck of ears of wheat growing in a field occupied by Samuel Gardner, yeoman. H. Burgh JP at Stroud. Hard labour for one calendar month in Horsley house of correction. Offence committed 16 Aug. 1832.

51/D/46   7 Sept. 1832. William Pearce. Stealing apples from a garden, the property of Nathaniel Davis, weaver, of Bisley. H. Burgh JP and Rev. P. Hawker JP at Stroud. Hard labour for three calendar months in Horsley house of correction. Offence committed 2 Sept. 1832.

51/D/47   27 July 1832. John March of Bisley, weaver. Assaulting Ezra Gardner of Stroud, bailiff. H. Burgh JP and Rev. P. Hawker JP at Stroud. Fine 10/- and 7/- costs or hard labour for one calendar month in Horsley house of correction. Offence committed 19 July 1832.

51/D/48   27 July 1832. John March of Bisley, weaver. Assaulting William Baker of Bisley, carpenter [*etc.*, *as* 51/D/47].

51/D/49   27 July 1832. John Poole of King's Stanley, yeoman. Evading payment of twopence toll at Rodborough in respect of the horse he was riding. H. Burgh JP and Rev. P. Hawker JP. Fine £5 or three calendar months in Horsley house of correction. Offence committed 13 July 1832.

51/D/50   1 Aug. 1832. James Llewellyn of Stroud, weaver. Failing to return cloth, or yarn supplied to weave it, or to give a satisfactory account of its disposal. H. Burgh JP. Thomas Thompson Gordon, clothier, of Painswick, complainant. One calendar month in Horsley house of correction. Offence committed 7 June 1832.

51/D/51   11 July 1832. William Carter the younger of Stroud, labourer. Breaking forty-one panes of two windows in the dwelling-house of William Carter the elder, labourer, of Stroud. H. Burgh JP at Stroud. Fine £1 5*s.* and 10/6 costs or hard labour for two calendar months in Horsley house of correction. Offence committed 10 July 1832.

51/D/52   21 Aug. 1832. Thomas Lusty, Emanuel Lusty, Richard Neale and Robert Alder, labourers, of King's Stanley. Stealing wood from a wood in King's Stanley, the property of Thomas, Lord Ducie. H. Burgh JP at Stroud. Fine £5 and 2/- (the value of the wood) or hard labour for two calendar months in Horsley house of correction. Offence committed 20 Aug. 1832.

51/D/53   22 Aug. 1832. Matthew Paul of Stroud, labourer. Stealing apples from an orchard in Stroud, the property of John Sims, common brewer. H. Burgh JP at Stroud. Hard labour for six calendar months in Horsley house of correction. Offence committed 22 Aug. 1832.

51/D/54   19 Sept. 1832. William Swain of Painswick, labourer. Stealing a quantity of bolls of onion seed growing in a garden in Painswick, the property of Thomas Goddard, gardener. H. Burgh JP at Stroud. Hard labour for six calendar months in [Horsley *deleted*, Littledean *substituted*] house of correction. Offence committed 13 Sept. 1832.

51/D/55   19 Sept. 1832. Daniel Holbrow of Stroud, labourer. Stealing pears from a garden, the property of Thomas Holbrow Esq. of Painswick. H. Burgh JP at Stroud. Hard labour for six calendar months in [Horsley *deleted*, Littledean *substituted*] house of correction. Offence committed 17 Sept. 1832.

51/D/56   25 Sept. 1832. Harriett Tyler of Bisley, single woman. Aiding, abetting and procuring Edwin Tyler, labourer, of Bisley, to steal turnips from a field, the property of William Tyler of Bisley. H. Burgh JP at Stroud. Hard labour for one calendar month in Horsley house of correction. Offence committed 23 Sept. 1832.

51/D/57   28 Sept. 1832. Joel John Tanner of Stroud, beer seller. Refusing to provide proper accommodation for John Wood, a soldier. H. Burgh JP and Rev. P. Hawker JP at Stroud. Fine 40/- or six months in Horsley house of correction. Offence committed 24 Sept. 1832.

51/D/58   21 Aug. 1832. Daniel Stanley. Assaulting Anna Smith at Chipping Campden. Rev. J. R. Hall JP and F. Colvile JP at Moreton in Marsh. Fine 5/-, to be paid to William White, an overseer of the poor, and 12/- costs, or one calendar month in Northleach house of correction. Offence committed 20 Aug. 1832.

51/D/59   7 Aug. 1832. Thomas Terry. Assaulting John Webb at Chipping Campden. Rev. J. R. Hall JP and Rev. C. Jeaffreson JP at Moreton in Marsh. Fine 5/-, to be paid to William Wyatt, an overseer of the poor, and 8/6 costs, or one calendar month in Northleach house of correction. Offence committed 25 July 1832.

51/D/60   7 Aug. 1832. William Price of Chipping Campden, licensed beer retailer. Allowing beer to be consumed at 10.30 p.m. Rev. J. R. Hall JP and F. Colvile JP at a Petty Sessions for Kiftsgate hundred upper division. First offence. Fine £1 8*s.*, one half to be paid to John Webb of Chipping Campden, the prosecutor, and the remainder to the county treasurer, and 12/- costs. Offence committed 23 July 1832.

51/D/61   24 July 1832. William Gillett and Samuel Fletcher. Assaulting Thomas Wilks at Moreton in Marsh. Rev. J. R. Hall JP and F. Colvile JP at Moreton in Marsh. Fine £1, to be paid to Charles Phipps, an overseer of the poor, and 10/6 costs, or one month in Northleach house of correction. Offence committed 28 June 1832.

51/D/62   4 Oct. 1832. John Cooper. Stealing apples, the property of William Lardner of Moreton in Marsh. Rev. J. R. Hall JP at Bourton on the Hill. Fine 10/-, to be paid to James Newman, an overseer of the poor, and 9/- costs, or two months in [Northleach] house of correction. Offence committed 2 Oct. 1832. [*The name William Evans is written where the names of the JPs are usually written regarding penalty.*]

51/D/63 4 Oct. 1832. Richard Charlotte. Leaving his wife chargeable to Clifford Chambers parish. Rev. J. R. Hall JP at Bourton on the Hill. Hard labour for one calendar month in Northleach house of correction. Offence committed 18 Sept. 1832.

51/D/64 2 Oct. 1832. John Willett. Assaulting Thomas Monk at Cheltenham. Sir W. Hicks, Bt., JP and R. B. Cooper JP at Cheltenham. Fine 5/- and 2/- costs. Offence committed 1 Oct. 1832.

51/D/65 9 Oct. 1832. Abraham Cooper. Assaulting George Evans at Cheltenham. R. B. Cooper JP and T. Newell JP at Cheltenham. Fine 2/6 and 5/6 costs or one calendar month in Northleach house of correction. Offence committed 3 Oct. 1832.

51/D/66 9 Oct. 1832. John Morris. Assaulting Lot Organ at Cheltenham. R. B. Cooper JP and T. Newell JP at Cheltenham. Fine 2/6 and 4/3 costs. Offence committed 4 Oct. 1832.

51/D/67 9 Oct. 1832. Benjamin Denley. Assaulting Lot Organ at Shurdington. R. B. Cooper JP and T. Newell JP at Cheltenham. Fine 4/- and 4/3 costs. Offence committed 4 Oct. 1832.

51/D/68 11 Oct. 1832. Charles Beams and William Gardner. Damaging a tree at Cheltenham, the property of the Rev. Spencer William Phillips. R. B. Cooper JP and T. Newell JP at Cheltenham. Fine 5/- each and 9/- costs. Offence committed 8 Oct. 1832.

51/D/69 11 Oct. 1832. William Dawes. Assaulting Richard Cottreall at Cheltenham. R. B. Cooper JP and T. Newell JP at Cheltenham. Fine 5/- and 5/6 costs. Offence committed — Oct. 1832.

51/D/70 11 Oct. 1832. William Dawes. Assaulting John Hill at Cheltenham. R. B. Cooper JP and T. Newell JP at Cheltenham. Fine 10/- and 7/6 costs. Offence committed — Oct. 1832.

51/D/71 11 Oct. 1832. William Gregory of Shurdington, retail beer dealer. Keeping his premises open for the sale of beer until 11.30 p.m. R. B. Cooper JP and T. Newell JP at a Petty Sessions for Cheltenham district. First offence. Fine £2 and 7/- costs. Offence committed 4 Oct. 1832.

51/D/72 15 Sept. 1832. Henry Andrews of Cheltenham, retail beer dealer. Opening his premises for the sale of beer between 10 a.m. and 1 p.m. on a Sunday. R. B. Cooper JP and T. Newell JP at a Petty Sessions for Cheltenham district. First offence. Fine £2 and 5/6 costs. Offence committed 9 Sept. 1832.

51/D/73 15 Sept. 1832. William Little of Cheltenham, retail beer dealer. Keeping his premises open for the sale of beer until 10.35 p.m. R. B. Cooper JP and T. Newell JP at a Petty Sessions for Cheltenham district. First offence. Fine £2 and 5/6 costs. Offence committed 8 Sept. 1832.

51/D/74 15 Sept. 1832. John Thache of Cheltenham, licensed victualler. Allowing beer and other liquors to be conveyed from his premises during the hours of divine service, i.e. at 12.20 p.m. R. B. Cooper JP and T. Newell JP at a Petty Sessions for Cheltenham district. First offence. Fine £2 and 5/6 costs. Offence committed Sunday 9 Sept. 1832.

51/D/75 15 Sept. 1832. Richard Parks. Assaulting John Balton at Cheltenham. R. B. Cooper JP and T. Newell JP at Cheltenham. Fine £1 and 7/6 costs or two calendar months in Northleach house of correction. Offence committed 12 Sept. 1832.

51/D/76 18 Sept. 1832. John Clark of Boddington, labourer. Trespassing in pursuit of game in Boddington on land occupied by the Rev. John Neale. R. B. Cooper JP at Cheltenham. John Blagdon Esq. of Cheltenham, complainant. Fine 20/- and 7/6 costs. Offence committed 11 a.m. 14 Sept. 1832.

51/D/77 20 Sept. 1832. John Green of Cheltenham, licensed victualler. Permitting drinking on his premises during the hours of divine service, i.e. at 12 noon. Sir W. Hicks, Bt., JP and R. B. Cooper JP at Cheltenham. First offence. Fine £2 and 5/6 costs. Offence committed Sunday 16 Sept. 1832.

51/D/78   20 Sept. 1832. Richard Harman. Assaulting Sarah Jones at Cheltenham. Sir W. Hicks, Bt., JP and R. B. Cooper JP at Cheltenham. Fine 2/6 and 5/6 costs or seven days in Northleach house of correction. Offence committed 18 Sept. 1832.

51/D/79   20 Sept. 1832. Hannah Wilson. Assaulting Betty Dobbs at Cheltenham. Sir W. Hicks, Bt., JP and R. B. Cooper JP at Cheltenham. Fine 2/6 and 5/6 costs. Offence committed 18 Sept. 1832.

51/D/80   14 July 1832. Richard Harman of Cheltenham, beer dealer. Keeping his house open for the sale of beer after 11.15 p.m. R. B. Cooper JP and T. Newell JP at a Petty Sessions for Cheltenham district. First offence. Fine £2 and 6/- costs. Offence committed 9 July 1832.

51/D/81   22 Sept. 1832. William Spencer. Assaulting Martha Studham at Cheltenham. R. B. Cooper JP and T. Newell JP at Cheltenham. Fine 5/- and 5/6 costs. Offence committed 19 Sept. 1832.

51/D/82   27 Sept. 1832. Mary Stollard. Assaulting Jane Berkeley at Cheltenham. Sir W. Hicks, Bt., JP and R. B. Cooper JP at Cheltenham. Fine 5/- and 5/6 costs or fourteen days in Northleach house of correction. Offence committed 25 Sept. 1832.

51/D/83   29 Sept. 1832. John Goode. Assaulting William Clarke at Cheltenham. R. B. Cooper JP and J. E. Viner JP at Cheltenham. Fine £1 and 5/6 costs. Offence committed 26 Sept. 1832.

51/D/84   4 Sept. 1832. Charles Dowle of Cheltenham, licensed victualler. Allowing beer and other liquor to be conveyed from his premises during the hours of divine service, i.e. at 12.30 p.m. R. B. Cooper JP and T. Newell JP. First offence. Fine £2 and 5/6 costs. Offence committed Sunday 2 Sept. 1832.

51/D/85   4 Sept. 1832. Mary Sheldon of Cheltenham, licensed victualler. Failing to maintain good order by allowing persons to drink in her taproom between 11 p.m. and midnight. R. B. Cooper JP and T. Newell JP. First offence. Fine £2 10s. and 6/6 costs. Offence committed 24 Aug. 1832.

51/D/86   4 Sept. 1832. John Taylor. Assaulting John Miles at Cheltenham. R. B. Cooper JP and T. Newell JP at Cheltenham. Fine £1 and 7/- costs or one calendar month in Northleach house of correction. Offence committed 1 Sept. 1832.

51/D/87   6 Sept. 1832. Charles Marshall of Cheltenham, licensed victualler. Failing to maintain good order by allowing persons to drink between midnight and 1 a.m. R. B. Cooper JP and T. Newell JP. First offence. Fine £2 and 4/6 costs. Offence committed 2 Sept. 1832.

51/D/88   6 Sept. 1832. John Guy. Assaulting John Falvey at Cheltenham. R. B. Cooper JP and T. Newell JP at Cheltenham. Fine 10/- and 5/6 costs or one month in Northleach house of correction. Offence committed 5 Sept. 1832.

51/D/89   6 Sept. 1832. Jane Backman. Assaulting George Liebenrood at Cheltenham. R. B. Cooper JP and T. Newell JP at Cheltenham. Fine 2/6 and 7/6 costs. Offence committed 30 Aug. 1832.

51/D/90   8 Sept. 1832. John Sheldon of Cheltenham, licensed victualler. Keeping his premises open until almost midnight and allowing disorderly behaviour. R. B. Cooper JP and J. E. Viner JP. First offence. Fine £5 and 5/6 costs. Offence committed 5 Sept. 1832.

51/D/91   10 Sept. 1832. Robert Gibbons. Assaulting John Cooke at Cheltenham. R. B. Cooper JP and T. Newell JP at Cheltenham. Fine £1 and 4/- costs or one calendar month in Northleach house of correction. Offence committed 9 Sept. 1832.

51/D/92   15 Sept. 1832. Richard Sayer. Assaulting George Lynall at Whitminster. R. B. Cooper JP and T. Newell JP at Cheltenham. Fine 10/- and 5/6 costs. Offence committed 13 Sept. 1832.

51/D/93 15 Sept. 1832. William Price of Uckington, Elmstone Hardwicke, labourer. Using a gun and three dogs with intent to take game at Uckington. R. B. Cooper JP and T. Newell JP at Cheltenham. Samuel Herbert, farmer, of Uckington, complainant. Fine £5 and 7/- costs or two calendar months in Northleach house of correction. Offence committed 19 Aug. 1832.

51/D/94 10 July 1832. Sarah Painter. Assaulting Mary Gardner at Charlton Kings. Sir W. Hicks, Bt., JP and R. B. Cooper JP at Cheltenham. Fine 10/- and 5/6 costs or one month in Northleach house of correction. Offence committed 1 July 1832.

51/D/95 14 July 1832. Andrew Girdwood. Assaulting James Turner at Leckhampton. R. B. Cooper JP and T. Newell JP at Cheltenham. Fine £1 and 5/6 costs. Offence committed 9 July 1832.

51/D/96 21 July 1832. Joseph Charlewood. Assaulting Elinor Kent at Cheltenham. R. B. Cooper JP and T. Newell JP at Cheltenham. Fine £1 and 5/6 costs or one month in Northleach house of correction. Offence committed 19 July 1832.

51/D/97 21 July 1832. Henry Smith. Assaulting Robert Clark at Cheltenham. R. B. Cooper JP and T. Newell JP at Cheltenham. Fine £1 and 9/- costs or one month in Northleach house of correction. Offence committed 16 July 1832.

51/D/98 26 July 1832. Martha Sanders of Cheltenham, retail beer dealer. Keeping her premises open for the sale of beer until 11.30 p.m. R. B. Cooper JP and T. Newell JP at a Petty Sessions for Cheltenham district. First offence. Fine £2 and 5/6 costs. Offence committed 14 July 1832.

51/D/99 2 Aug. 1832. James Edmunds of Cheltenham, yeoman. Selling beer to be consumed in a booth at Prestbury without a licence. R. B. Cooper JP and T. Newell JP. First offence. Fine £5 and 4/6 costs. Offence committed 15 July 1832.

51/D/100 2 Aug. 1832. John Arkell. Assaulting Richard Jones at Cheltenham. R. B. Cooper JP and T. Newell JP at Cheltenham. Fine 5/- and 5/6 costs. Offence committed 31 July 1832.

51/D/101 9 Aug. 1832. Joseph Wells. Assaulting George Bentley at Cheltenham. R. B. Cooper JP and T. Newell JP at Cheltenham. Fine 5/- and 8/- costs. Offence committed 7 Aug. 1832.

51/D/102 11 Aug. 1832. Joseph Stroud Drinkwater. Assaulting John Kent at Cheltenham. R. B. Cooper JP and Rev. J. Edwards JP at Cheltenham. Fine 10/- and 4/- costs. Offence committed 9 Aug. 1832.

51/D/103 11 Aug. 1832. John Stroud Drinkwater. Assaulting Barnabas Barton at Cheltenham. R. B. Cooper JP and Rev. J. Edwards JP at Cheltenham. Fine £1 and 3/- costs or one month in Northleach house of correction. Offence committed 9 Aug. 1832.

51/D/104 11 Aug. 1832. John Twining. Assaulting John Kent at Cheltenham. R. B. Cooper JP and Rev. J. Edwards JP at Cheltenham. Fine 5/- and 4/- costs. Offence committed 9 Aug. 1832.

51/D/105 21 Aug. 1832. James Ruddington, Patrick Ruddington and Bridget Ruddington. Assaulting John Hobbs at Cheltenham. R. B. Cooper JP and T. Newell JP at Cheltenham. Each fined 10/- and 4/- costs or two months in Northleach house of correction. Offence committed 20 Aug. 1832.

51/D/106 21 Aug. 1832. John Wanklin, retail beer dealer, of Cheltenham. Opening his premises for the sale of beer at 10.30 a.m. on a Sunday. R. B. Cooper JP and T. Newell JP at a Petty Sessions for Cheltenham district. First offence. Fine £2 and 6/- costs. Offence committed 19 Aug. 1832.

51/D/107   3 Oct. 1832. Thomas Stokes and William Ferley, both of Wotton under Edge, labourers. Beating for game with a dog and nets on land, Stirt field, occupied by Mary Frankcom at Hawkesbury. A. Shakespear JP and T. Kingscote JP at Boxwell. Peter May, witness. Hard labour for three calendar months in Horsley house of correction, after which to find sureties of £10 each that they will not re-offend within one year. In default, a further six months' hard labour. Offence committed about 3 a.m. Tuesday 21 Aug. 1832.

52/A/1   20 Nov. 1832. Joseph Arkell. Assaulting William Fletcher at Longborough. Rev. J. R. Hall JP and F. Colvile JP at Moreton in Marsh. Fine 10/-, to be paid to William Meadows of Longborough, an overseer of the poor, and 14/6 costs, or one month in Northleach house of correction. Offence committed 14 Nov. 1832.

52/A/2   1 Nov. 1832. John Weyman of Olveston. Being with others on land in Tormarton (Nighfield) occupied by John Arnold with a dog and a net, with intent to take hares. J. Horlock JP and K. W. Horlock JP at Rocks House, Marshfield. George Dyer, Henry Dyer and William Edwards, witnesses. Hard labour for two calendar months in Horsley house of correction, after which to find sureties totalling £20 against re-offending within one year. In default, a further six months' hard labour. Offence committed between 11 p.m. and midnight Monday 29 Oct. 1832.

52/A/3   19 Nov. 1832. Stephen Young of Chipping Sodbury, labourer. Setting a snare to kill a hare at Old Sodbury without a game certificate. J. Horlock JP and K. W. Horlock JP at Rocks House, Marshfield. Edward Dyer of Wapley and Codrington, complainant. William Edwards of Dodington, witness. Fine £5, to be paid to Daniel Smith, an overseer of the poor, Old Sodbury, and £1 costs, or hard labour for three calendar months in Horsley house of correction. Offence committed 17 Nov. 1832.

52/A/4   20 Nov. 1832. Joseph Arkell. Assaulting John Bowles at Longborough. Rev. J. R. Hall JP and F. Colvile JP at Moreton in Marsh. Fine 10/-, to be paid to William Meadows, an overseer of the poor of Longborough, and 15/- costs, or one month in Northleach house of correction. Offence committed 14 Nov. 1832.

52/A/5   20 Nov. 1832. Joseph Arkell of Stratford on Avon, Warws. Trespassing in search of game on a plantation at Sezincote [*MS.* Seasoncott], the property of Sir Charles Co[c]kerell, Bt. Rev. J. R. Hall JP at Moreton in Marsh. Fine £1, to be paid to John Ward, an overseer of the poor, and 15/- costs to go to the complainant William Fletcher, or one calendar month in Northleach house of correction. Offence committed 14 Nov. 1832.

52/A/6   23 Nov. 1832. Thomas Ainge of Leamington Priors, [Warws.].Trespassing in search of game in a close occupied by Henry Shelswell at Shenington. F. Colvile JP and Rev. J. R. Hall JP at Moreton in Marsh. Fine £1, to be paid to Daniel Shelswell, an overseer of the poor, and £2 4*s.* costs to the complainant John Brain. Given fourteen days to pay. In default, one calendar month in Warwick house of correction. Offence committed 2 Oct. 1832.

52/A/7   4 Dec. 1832. George Hawker of Blockley, labourer. Trespassing with a gun in pursuit of game in a plantation at Sezincote, the property of Sir Charles Cockerell, Bt. F. Colvile JP and Rev. J. R. Hall JP at Moreton in Marsh. First offence. Hard labour for three calendar months in Northleach house of correction, after which to find sureties of £10 as guarantee against re-offending for one year. In default, a further six months' hard labour. Offence committed 11.30 p.m. 3 Dec. 1832.

52/A/8   3 Dec. 1832. William Phillpotts of Ruardean, labourer. Trespassing in pursuit of game on land occupied by John Thompson at Ruardean. Rev. C. Crawley JP and J. Pyrke JP at Newnham in the Forest division. Joseph Baldwin, yeoman, complainant. Fine £2, to be paid to John Terrett, an overseer of the poor, and 8/6 costs, or hard labour for one calendar month in Littledean house of correction. Offence committed 12 noon 19 Oct. 1832.

52/A/9 3 Dec. 1832. John Allen of Ruardean, butcher. Trespassing in pursuit of game at Ruardean. Rev. C. Crawley JP and J. Pyrke JP at Newnham in the Forest division. Richard Court, yeoman, complainant. Fine £2, to be paid to Edward Machen Esq., deputy surveyor of the Forest, and 9/6 costs, or one calendar month in Littledean house of correction. Offence committed 12 noon 17 Nov. 1832.

52/A/10 3 Dec. 1832. Thomas Mills of Walford [Herefs.], labourer. Trespassing [*etc.*, *as* 52/A/9].

52/A/11 3 Dec. 1832. William Phillpotts of Ruardean, labourer. Trespassing in pursuit of game in Ruardean on land occupied by Thomas Edwards. Rev. C. Crawley JP and J. Pyrke JP at Newnham in the Forest division. William Baldwin, yeoman, of Ruardean, complainant. Fine £2, to be paid to John Terrett, overseer of the poor, and 8/6 costs, or one calendar month in Littledean house of correction. Offence committed 12 noon 19 Oct. 1832.

52/A/12 6 Nov. 1832. Joseph Morris, beerhouse keeper, of Blaisdon. Keeping his premises open and allowing tippling after 10 p.m. Rev. C. Crawley JP and M. Colchester JP at a Petty Sessions for the Forest division. First offence. Fine £2 1*s.* and 9/- costs. Offence committed 29 Oct. 1832.

52/A/13 3 Dec. 1832. Henry Griffiths. Assaulting Henry Morse at Newnham. Rev. C. Crawley JP and M. Colchester JP at Newnham. Fine £1 5*s.* 8*d.* [£1 5*s.* 10*d. later in document*], to be paid to Richard Merrick, overseer of the poor, and £1 1*s.* 10*d.* costs, or hard labour for two calendar months in Littledean house of correction. Offence committed 19 Nov. 1832.

52/A/14 3 Dec. 1832. Thomas Stephens. Assaulting Henry Morse at Newnham [*etc.*, *as* 52/A/13 *without the alternative figure of* £1 5*s.* 10*d.*].

52/A/15 3 Dec. 1832. James Rudge. Assaulting Henry Morse at Newnham [*etc.*, *as* 52/A/14].

52/A/16 23 Oct. 1832. Thomas Garland. Shooting five pigeons at Aylburton, the property of Charles Bathurst Esq. P. J. Ducarel JP and E. Machen JP at Coleford. Fine £1, 10/- damages and 9/- costs or hard labour for one calendar month in Littledean house of correction. Offence committed 27 Sept. 1832.

52/A/17 6 Nov. 1832. William Evans. Setting nets with intent to take game on land occupied by John Williams at Tidenham. Rev. T. Thomas JP and Rev. C. H. Morgan JP at Lydney. George Vaughan, labourer, of Tidenham, complainant. Hard labour for three calendar months in Littledean house of correction, after which to find sureties totalling £20 against re-offending for one year. In default, a further six months' hard labour. Offence committed midnight 15 Sept. 1832.

52/A/18 6 Nov. 1832. John Watts. Shooting a partridge in Woolaston without a game licence. Rev. T. Thomas JP and Rev. C. H. Morgan JP at Lydney in the Forest division. Fine £1 12*s.*, to be paid to William Tudor, an overseer of the poor, and 8/- costs to go to James Ball. Given until 1 Jan. 1833 to pay. In default, one calendar month in Littledean house of correction. Offence committed 5 Oct. 1832.

52/A/19 6 Nov. 1832. Yate Fosbrooke, clerk, of St. Briavels. Trespassing in Hewelsfield in search of game on land occupied by Samuel Edwards. Rev. T. Thomas JP and Rev. C. H. Morgan JP at Lydney. Fine £1, to be paid to the overseer of the poor, and 9/- costs to go to William Yemm, complainant, or one calendar month in Littledean house of correction. Offence committed 12 noon 30 Oct. 1832.

52/A/20 4 Dec. 1832. Richard Williams. Assaulting John Fryer at Tidenham. Rev. C. H. Morgan JP and G. Ormerod JP at Lydney in the Forest division. Fine 10/- and 8/- costs or fourteen days' hard labour in Littledean house of correction. Offence committed 1 Nov. 1832.

52/A/21   6 Nov. 1832. William Evans. Assaulting John Adams at Tidenham. Rev. T. Thomas JP and Rev. C. H. Morgan JP at Lydney. Fine £1 12s., to be paid to the overseer of the poor at Woolaston [? *recte* Tidenham], and 8/- costs. Offence committed 14 Oct. 1832.

52/A/22   4 Dec. 1832. George Vaughan. Stealing wood at Tidenham valued at 10/-, the property of James Madley. Rev. C. H. Morgan JP and G. Ormerod JP at Lydney. Fine 10/- and 6/6 costs or hard labour for one calendar month in Littledean house of correction. Offence committed 12 Nov. 1832.

52/A/23   6 Nov. 1832. 6 Nov. 1832. John Davis, alehouse keeper, of the Swan, Woolaston. Keeping his premises open and allowing tippling all night. Rev. T. Thomas JP and Rev. C. H. Morgan JP. First offence. Fine £4 12s. and 8/- costs. Offence committed 25 Sept. 1832.

52/A/24   20 Nov. 1832. Joseph Anthony Simmonds, labourer. Trespassing in pursuit of game at Newland on land occupied by John Worgan. P. J. Ducarel JP and E. Machen JP at Coleford. William Powell of St. Briavels hundred, complainant. Fine £2, to be paid to John Trotter, an overseer of the poor, costs [*variously given as* 6/- *and* 10/-] to go to the complainant, or one calendar month in Littledean house of correction. Offence committed 12 noon 30 Oct. 1832.

52/A/25   25 Oct. 1832. George Cooper, alehouse keeper, of English Bicknor. Keeping his premises open and allowing tippling after 10 p.m. E. Machen JP and P. J. Ducarel JP at a Petty Session for the Forest division. Second offence. Fine £9 8s. and 12/- costs. Offence committed 24 Sept. 1832.

52/A/26   18 Dec. 1832. Richard Powell, labourer. Using traps in Newland without a game certificate. P. J. Ducarel JP and E. Machen JP at Coleford in the Forest division. Joseph Cox, yeoman, complainant. Fine £4 12s., to be paid to John Trotter, an overseer of the poor, and 8/- costs. Given twenty-eight days to pay. In default, one calendar month in Littledean house of correction. Offence committed 21 Oct. 1832.

52/A/27   18 Dec. 1832. Edward Wilcox of Coleford, labourer. Using wires to kill game in St. Briavels hundred without a game certificate. P. J. Ducarel JP at Coleford. John Thomas, yeoman, complainant. Fine £1 11s., to be paid to Edward Machen Esq., deputy surveyor of the Forest, and 9/- costs, or one calendar month in Littledean house of correction. Offence committed 30 Oct. 1832.

52/A/28   18 Dec. 1832. John Baker. Trespassing in pursuit of game on land in English Bicknor occupied by Mrs. Knight. P. J. Ducarel JP and E. Machen JP at Coleford in the Forest division. John Addis, complainant. Fine £2, to be paid to Miles Bennett, an overseer of the poor, and 9/- costs, or one calendar month in Littledean house of correction. Offence committed midday 31 Oct. 1832.

52/A/29   18 Dec. 1832. Richard Aston, labourer. Trespassing in Newland in pursuit of game on land occupied by William Worgan. P. J. Ducarel JP and E. Machen JP at Coleford. Daniel Howles, yeoman, complainant. Fine 11/-, to be paid to John Trotter, an overseer of the poor, and 9/- costs, or one calendar month in Littledean house of correction. Offence committed 10 Dec. 1832.

52/A/30   20 Nov. 1832. James Moxham, labourer. Trespassing in pursuit of game at Newland on land occupied by Edward Baynton. P. J. Ducarel JP and E. Machen JP at Coleford in the Forest division. William Powell of St. Briavels hundred, complainant. Fine £2, to be paid to John Trotter, an overseer of the poor, and 10/- costs, or one calendar month in Littledean house of correction. Offence committed midday 31 Oct. 1832.

52/A/31 20 Nov. 1832. James Voice. Assaulting John Aston at St. Briavels. E. Machen JP and P. J. Ducarel JP at Coleford. Fine £1 and £1 costs or hard labour for one calendar month in Littledean house of correction. Offence committed 13 Nov. 1832.

52/A/32 4 Dec. 1832. Edward Jones. Trespassing in search of game on land in Hardwicke owned by Thomas John Lloyd Baker Esq. J. Sayer JP at Wheatenhurst. William Bick, complainant. Fine £2, to be paid to Thomas Spire, overseer of the poor, and 6/- costs, or two calendar months in Horsley house of correction. Offence committed 15 Nov. 1832.

52/A/33 29 Dec. 1832. William Curry. Assaulting Thomas Jacobs at Cheltenham. R. B. Cooper JP and T. Newell JP at Cheltenham. Fine 2/6 and 4/6 costs. Offence committed 27 Dec. 1832.

52/A/34 29 Dec. 1832. James Oakey. Assaulting Mary Summers at Cheltenham. R. B. Cooper JP and T. Newell JP at Cheltenham. Fine 2/6 and 9/- costs. Offence committed 17 Dec. 1832.

52/A/35 22 Dec. 1832. John Herbert, licensed victualler, of Cheltenham. Allowing ale to be taken from his premises during the hours of morning service at the parish church. T. Newell JP and Thomas Josephus Baines JP at Cheltenham. First offence. Fine £1 and 5/6 costs. Offence committed Sunday 16 Dec. 1832.

52/A/36 17 Nov. 1832. Thomas Greening. Killing and stealing two carrier pigeons at Boddington, the property of Richard Harman the younger. T. Newell JP at Cheltenham. Fine £1, to be paid to an overseer of the poor, 10/- (the value of the pigeons) to be paid to Richard Harman and 8/6 costs to the complainant. Offence committed 16 Nov. 1832.

52/A/37 22 Nov. 1832. Joseph Bidmead. Assaulting Thomas Husbands at Cheltenham. Rev. W. Hicks JP and T. Newell JP at Cheltenham. Fine £1 and 7/6 costs. Offence committed 17 Nov. 1832.

52/A/38 22 Nov. 1832. John French. Assaulting Sarah Steward at Cheltenham. Rev. W. Hicks JP and T. Newell JP at Cheltenham. Fine 2/6 and 5/6 costs. Offence committed 20 Nov. 1832.

52/A/39 20 Oct. 1832. Mark Sparrow. Assaulting Lydia Tustin at Cheltenham. Sir W. Hicks, Bt., JP and T. Newell JP at Cheltenham. Fine 2/6 and 5/6 costs. Offence committed 13 Oct. 1832.

52/A/40 20 Oct. 1832. James Gardner of Cheltenham, retail beer dealer. Allowing unlawful games and disorderly conduct, i.e. fighting, on his premises. Sir W. Hicks, Bt., JP and T. Newell JP at a Petty Sessions for Cheltenham district. First offence. Fine £2 and 5/6 costs. Offence committed 18 Oct. 1832.

52/A/41 27 Oct. 1832. Thomas Fox. Assaulting John Russell at Cheltenham. R. B. Cooper JP and T. Newell JP at Cheltenham. Fine £1 and 5/6 costs. Offence committed 23 Oct. 1832.

52/A/42 30 Oct. 1832. Alexander Lane of Cheltenham, retail beer dealer. Keeping his premises open for the sale of beer until almost 11 p.m. R. B. Cooper JP and T. Newell JP at a Petty Sessions for Cheltenham district. First offence. Fine £2 and 4/6 costs. Offence committed 27 Oct. 1832.

52/A/43 30 Oct. 1832. William Beard of Cheltenham, retail brewer. Allowing drunkenness and other disorderly behaviour on his premises. R. B. Cooper JP and T. Newell JP at a Petty Sessions for Cheltenham district. First offence. Fine £2 and 6/6 costs. Offence committed Sunday 28 Oct. 1832.

52/A/44 30 Oct. 1832. William Hill of Cheltenham, retail beer dealer. Allowing unlawful games and card playing on his premises. R. B. Cooper JP and T. Newell JP at a Petty Sessions for Cheltenham district. First offence. Fine £2 and 5/6 costs. Offence committed 28 Oct. 1832.

52/A/45   3 Nov. 1832. William Rossiter. Assaulting Charles Marlborough at Cheltenham. Sir W. Hicks, Bt., JP and R. B. Cooper JP at Cheltenham. Fine 2/6 and 5/6 costs. Offence committed 31 Oct. 1832.

52/A/46   1 Nov. 1832. Richard Howell, retail beer dealer, of Cheltenham. Keeping his premises open for the sale of beer until 11.30 p.m. Sir W. Hicks, Bt., JP and R. B. Cooper JP at a Petty Sessions for Cheltenham district. First offence. Fine £2 and 5/6 costs. Offence committed 30 Oct. 1832.

52/A/47   3 Nov. 1832. Thomas Edmunds. Assaulting James Davis at Cheltenham. Sir W. Hicks, Bt., JP and R. B. Cooper JP at Cheltenham. Fine 2/6 and 4/6 costs. Offence committed 27 Oct. 1832.

52/A/48   3 Nov. 1832. Thomas Parker and John Maule, retail beer dealers, of Cheltenham. Allowing card games and other disorderly conduct on their premises. Sir W. Hicks, Bt., JP and R. B. Cooper JP at a Petty Sessions for Cheltenham district. First offence. Fine £5 and 5/6 costs. Offence committed 1 Nov. 1832.

52/A/49   6 Nov. 1832. Elizabeth Bown. Assaulting Mary Page at Prestbury. R. B. Cooper JP and T. Newell JP at Cheltenham. Fine 5/6 and 4/6 costs. Offence committed 4 Nov. 1832.

52/A/50   10 Nov. 1832. William and Thomas Verrinder. Assaulting Samuel Lovegrove at Cranham. Sir W. Hicks, Bt., JP and R. B. Cooper JP at Cheltenham. William fined £1 and 16/3 costs or two months in Northleach house of correction, and Thomas 10/- and 16/3 costs or one month in Northleach house of correction. All costs to go to the complainant, and the rest to an overseer of the poor. Offence committed 8 Nov. 1832.

52/A/51   13 Nov. 1832. Edwin Bird and Charles Gray. Assaulting Daniel Browning at Cheltenham. R. B. Cooper JP and T. Newell JP at Cheltenham. E. Bird fined £1 and 3/- costs, and C. Gray 10/- and 3/- costs. Offence committed 11 Nov. 1832.

52/A/52   20 Nov. 1832. Thomas Tawney. Assaulting Samuel Page at Cheltenham. T. Newell JP and Rev. J. Edwards JP at Cheltenham. Fine /- and 6/- costs. Offence committed 17 Nov. 1832.

52/A/53   24 Nov. 1832. James Nicholls. Assaulting John Bolton at Cheltenham. Sir W. Hicks, Bt., JP and T. Newell JP at Cheltenham. Fine 10/- and 3/- costs. Offence committed 22 Nov. 1832.

52/A/54   27 Nov. 1832. Richard Staite of Charlton Kings, retail beer dealer. Keeping his premises open for the sale of beer until 10.30 p.m. Sir W. Hicks, Bt., JP and T. Newell JP at a Petty Sessions for Cheltenham district. First offence. Fine 5/- and 4/6 costs. Offence committed 13 Nov. 1832.

52/A/55   27 Nov. 1832. William Kear, retail beer dealer, of Charlton Kings. Keeping his premises open for the sale of beer until 10.45 p.m. Sir W. Hicks, Bt., JP and T. Newell JP at a Petty Sessions for Cheltenham district. First offence. Fine 5/- and 7/6 costs. Offence committed 21 Nov. 1832.

52/A/56   27 Nov. 1832. Thomas Smith. Assaulting Henry Hollands at Cheltenham. Sir W. Hicks, Bt., JP and T. Newell JP at Cheltenham. Fine 10/- and 3/- costs or fourteen days in Northleach house of correction. Offence committed 25 Nov. 1832.

52/A/57   29 Nov. 1832. William Charles Porter, retail beer dealer, of Cheltenham. Keeping his premises open for the sale of beer until 2 a.m. Sir W. Hicks, Bt., JP and R. B. Cooper JP at a Petty Sessions for Cheltenham district. Fine £2 and 5/6 costs. Offence committed 23 Nov. 1832.

52/A/58 6 Dec. 1832. John Sheldon of Cheltenham, licensed victualler. Allowing drunkenness and disorderly behaviour on his premises. R. B. Cooper JP and T. Newell JP. Second offence. [*Cf.* 51/D/90.] Fine £5 and 5/6 costs. Offence committed Sunday 2 Dec. 1832.

52/A/59 6 Dec. 1832. Thomas Hobbs. Assaulting Daniel Browning at Cheltenham. R. B. Cooper JP and T. Newell JP at Cheltenham. Fine £1 and 5/6 costs. Offence committed 29 Nov. 1832.

52/A/60 17 Dec. 1832. Charles Keene. Assaulting John Herbert at Cheltenham. Sir W. Hicks, Bt., JP and T. J. Baines JP at Cheltenham. Fine £1 and 3/- costs or fourteen days in Northleach house of correction. Offence committed 15 Dec. 1832.

52/A/61 27 Dec. 1832. Abraham Saunders. Assaulting Sarah Palmer Dukes at Cheltenham. Rev. W. Hicks JP and J. E. Viner JP at Cheltenham. Fine £1 and 8/- costs. Offence committed 24 Dec. 1832.

52/A/62 25 Oct. 1832. James Vowles. Assaulting James Weymouth at Filton. D. Cave JP and H. W. Newman JP at Lawfords Gate sessions room. Fine 4/- and 6/- costs. Offence committed 14 Oct. 1832.

52/A/63 2 Nov. 1832. William Rice. Assaulting William Henry Ridler at St. Philip and St. Jacob, [Bristol]. H. W. Newman JP and D. Cave JP at Lawfords Gate sessions room. Fine £3 17*s.* and £1 3*s.* costs or two calendar months in Lawfords Gate house of correction. Offence committed 23 Oct. 1832.

52/A/64 29 Dec. 1932. John Vandeluce. Begging in Stroud. H. Burgh JP at Stroud. Hard labour for one calendar month in Horsley house of correction. Offence committed 28 Dec. 1832.

52/A/65 26 Oct. 1832. James Niblett. Failing to work, thereby causing his wife and family to become chargeable to Painswick parish. H. Burgh JP at Stroud. Hard labour for one calendar month in Horsley house of correction. Offence committed 19 Oct. 1832.

52/A/66 26 Oct. 1832. William Clayfield. Failing to work [*etc., as* 52/A/65].

52/A/67 14 Dec. 1832. Edward Howell of Rodborough, beer seller. Trespassing in search of game on land at Painswick, the property of Thomas Preston Esq. of Nottingham Place, Middlesex. H. Burgh JP at Stroud. Thomas Heyden, complainant. Fine £1 and 8/6 costs or hard labour for one calendar month in Horsley house of correction. Offence committed 23 Nov. 1832.

52/A/68 8 Nov. 1832. Jeremiah Fear of Clifton. Keeping his premises open for the sale of beer between 10 a.m. and 1 p.m. H. W. Newman JP and J. Cave JP at a Petty Sessions for Bristol division. Fine £2 including costs. Offence committed Sunday 21 Oct. 1832.

52/A/69 22 Nov. 1832. Joseph Webley. Trespassing with a double-barrelled gun and two dogs in pursuit of game on land in Filton occupied by Benjamin Bridgman. H. W. Newman JP and J. Cave JP at the King's Arms, Durdham Down, Clifton. Robert Hopton, complainant. Fine 40/- and 8/- costs or hard labour for two calendar months in Lawfords Gate house of correction. Offence committed 7 Nov. 1832.

52/A/70 6 Dec. 1832. William Thomas Hammond. Trespassing in pursuit of game on land in Westbury on Trym, the property of Robert Hopton. H. W. Newman JP and G. Goldney JP at the King's Arms, Durdham Down, Clifton. Fine 20/- and 8/- costs or hard labour for one calendar month in Lawfords Gate house of correction. Offence committed 30 Oct. 1832.

52/A/71 6 Dec. 1832. William Thomas Hammond. Trespassing in pursuit of game on land in Henbury, the property of Edward Sampson Esq. [*etc., as* 52/A/70 *except*] Offence committed 23 Nov. 1832.

52/A/72 8 Nov. 1832. Benjamin Hembrow. Using a wire to kill game in Henbury when not licensed. H. W. Newman JP and J. Cave JP, commissioners for assessed taxes in Barton Regis district, at the King's Arms, Durdham Down, Clifton. Fine £10. Offence committed 20 Oct. 1832.

52/A/73 25 Oct. 1832. Benjamin Hembra *alias* Hember. Trespassing in pursuit of game on land in King's Weston, Henbury, the property of the Rt. Hon. the Lord De Clifford, deceased. D. Cave JP and G. Goldney JP at the King's Arms, Durdham Down, Clifton. Robert Baker, complainant. Fine 40/- and 8/- costs or hard labour for two calendar months in Lawfords Gate house of correction. Offence committed 12 Oct. 1832.

52/A/74 25 Oct. 1832. William Clapp of St. Philip and St. Jacob, [Bristol]. Keeping his premises open for the sale of beer between 10 a.m. and 1 p.m. on a Sunday. G. Goldney JP and H. W. Newman JP at a Petty Sessions for Bristol division. Fine 40/- including costs. Offence committed Sunday 16 Sept. 1832.

52/A/75 21 Nov. 1832. William Lea. Assaulting John Dodd at Dymock. Osman Ricardo JP and Rev. J. Commeline JP, magistrates for Herefordshire and Gloucestershire at Ledbury [Herefs.]. Fine 2/6 and 8/- costs or two calendar months in Littledean house of correction. Offence committed Wednesday 14 Nov. 1832.

52/A/76 19 Dec. 1832. William Mason of Twyning. Assaulting John Berwick, blacksmith, of Twyning without provocation. Rev. J. Keysall JP and J. W. Martin JP at Tewkesbury. Fine 50/-, 38/6 of which to be paid to Samuel Nash, overseer of the poor of Twyning, and 11/6 to the complainant, or two calendar months in Northleach house of correction. Offence committed 11 Dec. 1832. [*Endorsed with a note that the offender was committed to Northleach 19 Dec. 1832.*]

52/A/77 29 Nov. 1832. James Price. Trespassing on Ten Acres at Horsley in search of game. R. Kingscote JP at Horsley. Charles Jacob Adams, complainant. Fine £2, to be paid to Hugh Haines, an overseer of the poor, and 9/- costs. Given five days to pay. In default, two calendar months' hard labour in Horsley house of correction. Offence committed 7 Nov. 1832.

52/A/78 29 Nov. 1832. James Price. Trespassing in search of conies on land occupied by Anthony Stoughton Esq. at Petersnest Wood, Owlpen. R. Kingscote JP at Horsley. Charles Trotman, complainant. Fine £2, to be paid to William Taylor, an overseer of the poor, and 9/- costs. Given five days to pay. In default, two calendar months' hard labour in Horsley house of correction. Offence committed 7 Nov. 1832

52/A/79 20 Dec. 1832. Recognizance binding John Bryan, mercer and draper, of Stow on the Wold in the sum of £20 to give evidence at the next Quarter Sessions at the trial of William Jefferies, labourer, late of the same parish, for stealing two rabbits on 13 Oct. 1832, valued at 10/-. Rev. F. E. Witts JP.

52/A/80 20 Dec. 1832. Recognizance binding John Bryan, mercer and draper, of Stow on the Wold in the sum of £10 to ensure the appearance of his servant Edward Rouse at the next Quarter Sessions to give evidence on a charge preferred by John Bryan against William Jefferies, late of Stow on the Wold, of stealing two rabbits valued at 10/- on 13 Oct. 1832. Rev. F. E. Witts JP.

52/A/81 20 Dec. 1832. Recognizance binding Thomas Sedgley, saddler, of Stow on the Wold in the sum of £10 to ensure the appearance of Robert Douglas, labourer, of the same parish at the next Quarter Sessions, to give evidence on a charge preferred by John Bryan against William Jefferies for stealing two rabbits on 13 Oct. 1832. F. E. Witts JP.

52/A/82 20 Dec. 1832. Recognizance binding Henry Minchin, constable, in the sum of £10 to appear at the next Quarter Sessions to give evidence on a charge preferred against William Jefferies by John Bryan for stealing two rabbits valued at 10/- on 13 Oct. 1832. F. E. Witts JP.

52/A/83 6 Dec. 1832. Joseph Clifford of Bourton on the Water. Trespassing in search of game on enclosed land in Clapton [on the Hill], the property of Vernon Dolphin Esq. Rev. F. E. Witts JP and Rev. R. W. Ford JP at Stow on the Wold. Charles Shepherd, complainant. Fine £2 and 5/- costs or hard labour for two calendar months in Northleach house of correction. Offence committed 28 Nov. 1832.

52/A/84 25 Oct. 1832. Henry Dimmock of Stow on the Wold, beer retailer. Keeping his premises open for the sale of beer until after 11 p.m. Rev. F. E. Witts JP and Rev. R. W. Ford JP at a Petty Sessions for Slaughter hundred. First offence. Fine 40/- and 6/- costs. Offence committed 24 Oct. 1832.

52/A/85 6 Dec. 1832. Joseph Clifford of Bourton on the Water. Using a dog to kill game at Clapton [on the Hill] without a game licence. Rev. F. E. Witts JP and Rev. R. W. Ford JP at Stow on the Wold. Charles Shepherd, complainant. Fine £2 10s. and 5/- costs or hard labour for two calendar months in Northleach house of correction. Offence committed 28 Nov. 1832. [Cf. 52/A/83.]

52/A/86 17 Sept. 1832. John Trinder of Meysey Hampton [MS. Maiseyhampton], beer retailer. Keeping his premises open for the consumption of beer after 10 p.m. Rev. E. A. Daubeny JP and Rev. H. A. Pye JP at a Petty Sessions for Cirencester division. First offence. Fine 40/- and 5/- costs. Offence committed Saturday 1 Sept. 1832.

52/A/87 5 Nov. 1832. Christopher Brown of Cirencester, beer retailer. Keeping his premises open for the consumption of beer after 10 p.m. Rev. H. Cripps JP and Rev. E. A. Daubeny JP at a Petty Sessions for Cirencester division. First offence. Fine 40/- and 5/- costs. Offence committed 29 Oct. 1832.

52/A/88 15 Nov. 1832. Richard Collett of Cirencester, labourer. Trespassing on land at Bagendon [MS. Badgington] at night with gins and other instruments with intent to take game. J. Cripps JP and E. Cripps JP at Cirencester. First offence. Hard labour for three calendar months in Northleach house of correction, after which to find sureties totalling £20 against re-offending for one year. In default, a further six months' hard labour. Offence committed 14 Nov. 1832.

52/B/1 1 April 1833. George Stiff, William Jenkins, William Turner and Charles Townsend, labourers, of Chipping Sodbury. Assaulting Henry Harding, Eleanor his wife and their servant Charles Barker at Chipping Sodbury. F. Trotman JP and W. G. Davy JP at Pucklechurch. Each fined £1 8s. 6d. and 11/6 costs or two calendar months in Horsley house of correction. Offence committed 23 March 1833.

52/B/2 7 Feb. 1833. William Lusty the younger. Trespassing with a gun at night with intent to take game at Pastell's, Newington Bagpath. R. Kingscote JP and T. Kingscote JP at Horsley. Hard labour for three calendar months in Horsley house of correction, after which to find sureties totalling £20 against re-offending for one year. In default, a further six months' hard labour. Offence committed 12 Jan. 1833.

52/B/3 11 March 1833. Alfred Fords. Stealing a gatepost with two iron hooks attached from a field called the Maples occupied by John Norris at Uley. T. Kingscote JP at Kingscote. Complainant examined to prove case. Fine £2 10s., 1/- (the value of the post) and 12/- costs or one calendar month in Horsley house of correction. Offence committed 6 March 1833.

52/B/4 29 Dec. 1832. Robert Green, licensed victualler, of Cheltenham. Allowing disorderly behaviour and keeping his premises open until 4 a.m. for the consumption of liquor. R. B. Cooper JP and T. Newell JP for Cheltenham district. Second offence. [*Cf.* 51/C/65.] Fine £10 and 11/6 costs. Offence committed 6–7 Dec. 1832.

52/B/5 29 Dec. 1832. William Brown of Cheltenham, retail beer dealer. Keeping his premises open for the sale of beer until 10.30 p.m. T. Newell JP and R. B. Cooper JP at a Petty Sessions for Cheltenham district. First offence. Fine £2 and 4/6 costs. Offence committed 15 Dec. 1832.

52/B/6 29 Dec. 1832. William Hill of Cheltenham, retail beer dealer. Keeping his premises open for the sale of beer until 11.30 p.m. T. Newell JP and T. J. Baines JP at a Petty sessions for Cheltenham district. First offence. Fine £2 and 5/6 costs. Offence committed 26 Dec. 1832.

52/B/7 1 Jan. 1833. John Shill of Badgeworth, labourer. Trespassing in search of game on land in Badgeworth occupied by Anthony Bubb. Sir W. Hicks, Bt., JP and T. Newell JP at Cheltenham. George Larner, yeoman, of Badgeworth, complainant. Fine £2 and 5/6 costs or two months in Northleach house of correction. Offence committed 8 a.m. 1 Jan. 1833.

52/B/8 3 Jan. 1833. Charlotte Carpenter. Assaulting Susan Holder at Cheltenham. T. Newell JP and T. J. Baines JP at Cheltenham. Fine 5/- and 5/6 costs. Offence committed 1 Jan. 1833.

52/B/9 10 Jan. 1833. Thomas Jones, retail cider dealer, of Cheltenham. Allowing cider to be drunk on his premises between 3 p.m. and 5 p.m. on a Sunday. Sir W. Hicks, Bt., JP and R. B. Cooper JP at a Petty Sessions for Cheltenham district. First offence. Fine £2 and 5/6 costs. Offence committed 6 Jan. 1833.

52/B/10 10 Jan. 1833. Isaac Heven. Assaulting Isaac Deaves at Cheltenham. Sir W. Hicks, Bt., JP and R. B. Cooper JP at Cheltenham. Fine £1 and 5/6 costs or one month in Northleach house of correction. Offence committed 7 Jan. 1833.

52/B/11 10 Jan. 1833. James Vale of Cheltenham, retail beer dealer. Keeping his premises open for the sale of beer until 10.30 p.m. R. B. Cooper JP and T. Newell JP at a Petty Sessions for Cheltenham district. First offence. Fine £2 and 5/6 costs. Offence committed 4 Jan. 1833.

52/B/12 10 Jan. 1833. Robert Greenwood. Assasulting Isaac Deaves at Cheltenham. Sir W. Hicks, Bt., JP and T. Newell JP at a Petty Sessions for Cheltenham district. Fine 5/- and 5/6 costs. Offence committed 7 Jan. 1833.

52/B/13 10 Jan. 1833. Serina Knight, widow, retail beer dealer, of Cheltenham. Keeping her premises open for the sale of beer until 10.30 p.m. Sir W. Hicks, Bt., JP and Rev. J. Edwards JP at a Petty Sessions for Cheltenham district. First offence. Fine £2 and 3/- costs. Offence committed 4 Jan. 1833.

52/B/14 10 Jan. 1833. James Bevan, retail beer dealer, of Cheltenham. Allowing beer to be consumed on his premises between 3 p.m. and 5 p.m. on a Sunday. T. Newell JP and John Blagdon JP at a Petty Sessions for Cheltenham district. First offence. Fine £2 and 5/6 costs. Offence committed 6 Jan. 1833.

52/B/15 15 Jan. 1833. William Hill of Cheltenham, retail beer dealer. Allowing card games to be played on his premises. T. Newell JP and T. J. Baines JP at a Petty Sessions for Cheltenham district. First offence. Fine £5 and 5/6 costs. Offence committed 11 Jan. 1833.

52/B/16 19 Jan. 1833. Thomas Teale of Cheltenham, retail beer dealer. Allowing violent, quarrelsome and other disorderly conduct on his premises. R. B. Cooper JP and T. Newell JP at a Petty Sessions for Cheltenham district. First offence. Fine £2 and 5/6 costs. Offence committed 16 Jan. 1833.

52/B/17   22 Jan. 1833. William Higgs. Assaulting Thomas Williams at Cheltenham. R. B. Cooper JP and T. J. Baines JP at Cheltenham. Fine £1 and 3/- costs. Offence committed 21 Jan. 1833.

52/B/18   22 Jan. 1833. John Hazeldine, beer retailer, of Cheltenham. Keeping his premises open for the sale of beer until 10.30 p.m. Rev. J. Edwards JP and T. J. Baines JP at a Petty Sessions for Cheltenham district. First offence. Fine £2 and 5/6 costs. Offence committed 18 Jan. 1833.

52/B/19   26 Jan. 1833. Charles Barnett. Assaulting Henry Holland at Cheltenham. T. J. Baines JP and J. Blagdon JP at Cheltenham. Fine £1 and 5/6 costs. Offence committed 19 Jan. 1933.

52/B/20   7 Feb. 1833. William Thomas Newenham. Assaulting Sarah Green at Cheltenham. R. B. Cooper JP and T. Newell JP at Cheltenham. Fine £1 and 6/6 costs. Offence committed 5 Feb. 1833.

52/B/21   7 Feb. 1833. James Vale. Assaulting Stephen Lawes at Cheltenham. R. B. Cooper JP and T. Newell JP at Cheltenham. Fine £2 and 4/- costs. Offence committed 7 Feb. 1833.

52/B/22   9 Feb. 1833. George Chandler and Edwin Palmer of Prestbury. Trespassing in search of game at Prestbury. T. Newell JP and Rev. J. Edwards JP at Cheltenham. Robert Wells, labourer, of Prestbury, complainant. Fine £2 and £1 respectively and 5/6 costs each. Offence committed 10 a.m. 14 Jan. 1833.

52/B/23   9 Feb. 1833. Emanuel Higgs and William Hands. Assaulting Stephen Law at Cheltenham. R. B. Cooper JP and T. Newell JP at Cheltenham. Fine £1 and 7/- costs. Offence committed 5 Feb. 1833.

52/B/24   16 Feb. 1833. James Ballinger. Assaulting Frances Hill and Mary Pearce at Leigh. T. Newell JP and T. J. Baines JP at Cheltenham. Fine £3 and 6/6 [costs] on each charge or two terms of two months in Northleach house of correction. Offence committed 12 Feb. 1833.

52/B/25   16 Feb. 1833. Henry Cook of Cheltenham, labourer. Refusing to be examined on oath regarding a complaint against Richard Page, beer retailer, of Cheltenham for allowing card games on his premises. R. B. Cooper JP and T. Newell JP at a Petty Sessions held at the public office, Cheltenham. Fine £10. Offence committed 11 a.m. Saturday 16 Feb. 1833.

52/B/26   21 Feb. 1833. Joseph Stewart of Cheltenham, retail beer dealer. Permitting drinking on his premises between 3 p.m. and 5 p.m. on a Sunday. Sir W. Hicks, Bt., JP and R. B. Cooper JP at a Petty Sessions for Cheltenham district. First offence. Fine £2 and 5/6 costs. Offence committed 17 Feb. 1833.

52/B/27   23 Feb. 1833. Michael McCarthy. Assaulting John Hobbs at Cheltenham. T. Newell JP and T. J. Baines JP at Cheltenham. Fine 5/- and 5/6 costs. Offence committed 23 Feb. 1833.

52/B/28   28 Feb. 1833. Charles Hobbs. Assaulting Edward Cossens at Cheltenham. R. B. Cooper JP and T. J. Baines JP at Cheltenham. Fine 10/- and 6/6 costs. Offence committed 27 Feb. 1833.

52/B/29   12 Feb. 1833. Richard Jervis of Weston Subedge, seller of ale, beer etc. Permitting the consumption of beer on his premises until 11.30 p.m. Rev. J. R. Hall JP and William Dickins JP at a Petty Sessions for Kiftsgate hundred upper division. First offence. Fine £2, half to be paid to Rev. Charles Edward Henry of Weston Subedge and the remainder to the county treasurer, and 12/6 costs. Offence committed 4 Feb. 1833.

52/B/30   29 Jan. 1833. Robert Hookham of Moreton in Marsh, seller of ale etc. Permitting card games to be played on his premises. Rev. J. R. Hall JP and F. Colvile JP at a Petty Sessions for Westminster hundred upper division. First offence. Fine £2, to be paid to the county treasurer, and 10/6 costs. Offence committed afternoon of 7 Jan. 1833.

52/B/31   29 Jan. 1833. Robert Hookham of Moreton in Marsh, seller of ale, beer etc. Permitting drinking on his premises until 10.30 p.m. Rev. J. R. Hall JP and F. Colvile JP at a Petty Sessions for Westminster hundred upper division. First offence. Fine £2, to be paid to the county treasurer, and 7/6 costs. Offence committed 7 Jan. 1833.

52/B/32   15 Jan. 1833. Thomas Dunn of Chipping Campden, seller of ale, beer etc. Permitting drinking on his premises until 10.30 p.m. Rev. J. R. Hall JP and F. Colvile JP at a Petty Sessions for Kiftsgate hundred upper division. First offence. Fine £2, to be paid to the county treasurer, and 11/6 costs. Offence committed 8 Jan. 1833.

52/B/33   15 Jan. 1833. Thomas Dunn of Chipping Campden, seller of ale, beer etc. Permitting card games to be played on his premises. Rev. J. R. Hall JP and F. Colvile JP at a Petty Sessions for Kiftsgate hundred upper division. First offence. Fine £2, to be paid to the county treasurer, and 7/6 costs. Offence committed between 9 p.m. and 10 p.m. on 8 Jan. 1833.

52/B/34   1 Jan. 1833. Thomas Farebrother of Bourton on the Hill, labourer. Trespassing in search of game in Bourton Wood, the property of Rt. Hon. Lord Redesdale. Rev. J. R. Hall JP and F. Colvile JP at Moreton in Marsh. Fine £2 10s., to be paid to William Phillips, an overseer of the poor, and 10/- costs to go to John Sadler, complainant. Given fourteen days to pay. In default, two months' hard labour in Northleach house of correction. Offence committed 30 Dec. 1832.

52/B/35   1 Jan. 1833. William Cockerell. Assaulting Samuel Fletcher at Bourton on the Hill. Rev. J. R. Hall JP and F. Colvile JP at Moreton in Marsh. Fine 6/-, to be paid to William Phillips, an overseer of the poor, and 9/- costs, or one calendar month in Northleach house of correction. Offence committed 12 Dec. 1832.

52/B/36   22 Feb. 1833. John and Henry Lovesy of Compton Abdale, labourers. Failing to complete a contract agreed with John Humphries, farmer, of Hazleton, to breast-plough one whole field and part of two others between February and harvest 1832. Payment received on completion of first two tasks. Refused to do third. Rev. Thomas Leveson Lane JP and Rev. T. B. Newell JP at Andoversford inn. Complaint by Humphries to the latter JP, 20 Aug. 1832. Defendants summoned on 20 Aug. Pleaded not guilty. Agreement made to complete final task. Defendants failed to honour agreement. Warrant issued. Sentenced to fourteen days' hard labour in Northleach house of correction.

52/B/37   21 March 1833. John Webb of Avening, labourer. Stealing part (i.e. one man's burden) of a load of hedge-wood, the property of Rt. Hon. Thomas, Lord Ducie, at Nympsfield. H. Burgh JP at Stroud. Fine 6d. (the value of the wood) and 9/- costs, or hard labour for two calendar months in Horsley house of correction. Offence committed 18 March 1833.

52/B/38   12 Feb. 1833. William Lewis *alias* Barter and Thomas Pitt of Stroud, labourers. Stealing turnips growing in a field in Painswick, the property of William Capel the younger, gentleman. H. Burgh JP at Stroud. Hard labour for one calendar month in Horsley house of correction. Offence committed 9 Feb. 1833.

52/B/39   9 Feb. 1833. Peter Hall of Stroud, labourer. Stealing turnips growing in a field in Painswick [*etc.*, *as* 52/B/38].

52/B/40   13 Feb. 1833. James Virgo of Woodchester, labourer. Trespassing in search of game on land at Nympsfield, the property of Rt. Hon. Thomas, Lord Ducie. H. Burgh JP at Stroud. Fine £2 and 8/6 costs or hard labour for two calendar months in Horsley house of correction. Offence committed 12 Feb. 1833.

52/B/41   13 Feb. 1833. Richard Cockle of Nympsfield, labourer. Trespassing [*etc.*, *as* 52/B/40].

52/B/42   4 Jan. 1833. Henry Fletcher of Painswick, labourer. Trespassing in search of game on land at Painswick, the property of the devisee [*name illegible*] of the late Edward Wick.

H. Burgh JP at Stroud. Fine £1 and 7/- costs or hard labour for one calendar month in Horsley house of correction. Offence committed 3 Jan. 1833.

52/B/43   8 Feb. 1833. Thomas Smart of Bisley, beer retailer. Having in his dwelling house 120 lb. of various kinds of woollen waste believed to be stolen. H. Burgh JP, R. S. Davies JP and J. P. Hicks JP. Daniel Cox, clothier, of Bisley, informer. Thomas Jones, clothier, of Bisley, witness. Fine £20, half to go to the informer and the rest to Stroud dispensary. Offence committed 4 Nov. 1832.

52/B/44   8 Feb. 1833. Thomas Smart of Bisley, beer retailer. Having in his dwelling house 22½ lb. of various woollen waste believed to be stolen. H. Burgh JP, R. S. Davies JP and J. P. Hicks JP. Thomas Jones, clothier, of Bisley, informer. Jesse Davis, clothier, of Minchinhampton and William Nest, police officer, of Gloucester, witnesses. Second offence. [*Cf.* 52/B/43.] Fine £30, half to go to the informer and the rest to Stroud dispensary. Offence committed 30 Nov. 1832

52/B/45   8 Feb. 1833. John Davis of Bisley, weaver. Having in his dwelling house 126 lb. 8 oz. of various woollen materials believed to be stolen, some made into mops. H. Burgh JP, R. S. Davies JP and J. P. Hicks JP. Daniel Cox, clothier, of Bisley, informer. Thomas Jones, clothier, of Bisley, witness. Fine £20, half to go to the informer and the rest to Stroud dispensary. Offence committed 4 Nov. 1832.

52/B/46   22 March 1833. Henry Wright of Painswick, labourer. Damaging a gate at Painswick, the property of Samuel Gyde, yeoman. H. Burgh JP and R. S. Davies JP at Stroud. Fine 5/-, to be paid to an overseer of the poor, 9/- costs and 1/- damages to be paid to the complainant, or two months' hard labour in Horsley house of correction. Offence committed 5 March 1833.

52/B/47   22 March 1833. Henry Wright of Painswick, labourer. Damaging a wall at Painswick, the property of Thomas Loveday, yeoman. H. Burgh JP and R. S. Davies JP at Stroud. Fine 5/-, to be paid to an overseer of the poor, 9/- costs and 6/- damages to the complainant, or two months' hard labour in Horsley house of correction. Offence committed 5 March 1833.

52/B/48   27 March 1833. John Morton of Evesham, servant. Assaulting George Vallencourt of Twyning. J. Timbrill D.D. JP, Rev. J. Keysall JP and J. W. Martin JP at Tewkesbury. Fine 14/-, to be paid to Samuel Nash, overseer of the poor of Twyning, and 26/- costs to the complainant. Offence committed Tuesday 17 March 1833.

52/B/49   6 Feb. 1833. Thomas Patrick the younger of Mythe Hook, in the parish of Twyning [*sic, recte* Tewkesbury]. Trespassing in search of game without a licence, with a gun and a dog, in an orchard in Twyning, the property of Thomas Tolley. J. Timbrill D.D. JP, Rev. J. Keysall JP and J. W. Martin JP at Tewkesbury. Fine £5, to be paid to Samuel Nash, overseer of the poor, and 11/6 costs to the complainant. Offence committed Thursday 31 Jan. 1833.

52/B/50   14 March 1833. Samuel Newman. Assaulting Richard Cheney, William Mann and Thomas Wasley at Cheltenham. R. B. Cooper JP and T. Newell JP at Cheltenham. Fine £1 10*s.* and 5/- costs or two calendar months in Northleach house of correction. Offence committed 13 March 1833.

52/B/51   21 March 1833. Robert John Davy. Assaulting Thomas Guilfoyle and Richard Gwillym at Cheltenham. R. B. Cooper JP and T. Newell JP at Cheltenham. Fine £1 and 14/- costs. Offence committed 19 March 1833.

52/B/52   14 March 1833. Charles Dawes. Killing a pigeon at Cheltenham valued at 6*d.*, the property of George Long. R. B. Cooper JP and T. Newell JP at Cheltenham. Fine £2, 6*d.* damages and 4/6 costs. Offence committed 9 March 1833.

52/B/53   14 March 1833. William Dunn. Assaulting Richard Cheney and Thomas Wasley at Cheltenham. R. B. Cooper JP and T. Newell JP at Cheltenham. Fine £1 and 5/- costs. Offence committed 13 March 1833.

52/B/54   12 March 1833. Edward Ballinger, yeoman, of Charlton Kings. Killing a partridge at Coberley. Sir W. Hicks, Bt., JP and R. B. Cooper JP at Cheltenham. Henry Norwood Trye Esq. of Leckhampton, complainant. Fine £1, to be paid immediately. Offence committed 1 March 1833.

52/B/55   12 March 1833. Edward Ballinger, yeoman, of Charlton Kings. Trespassing in pursuit of game at Coberley on land belonging to Henry Norwood Trye Esq. Sir W. Hicks, Bt., JP and R. B. Cooper JP at Cheltenham. Fine £2 and 5/6 costs or two calendar months in Northleach house of correction. Offence committed about 12 noon 1 March 1833.

52/B/56   12 March 1833. John Redding. Assaulting John Wilden at Badgeworth. Sir W. Hicks, Bt., JP and R. B. Cooper JP at Cheltenham. Fine 10/- and 8/6 costs or one month in Northleach house of correction. Offence committed 3 March 1833.

52/B/57   12 March 1833. William Gardner. Assaulting Thomas Low at Badgeworth. Sir W. Hicks, Bt., JP and R. B. Cooper JP at Cheltenham. Fine £1 and 3/- costs or one month in Northleach house of correction. Offence committed 3 March 1833.

52/B/58   26 March 1833. Maria Dee of Cheltenham, retail beer dealer. Keeping her house open for the sale of beer until after 11 p.m. R. B. Cooper JP and T. Newell JP at a Petty Sessions. First offence. Fine £2 and 5/6 costs. Offence committed 23 March 1833.

52/B/59   12 March 1833. William Belcher. Assaulting Thomas Low at Badgeworth [etc., as 52/B/57 except] 8/6 costs.

52/B/60   26 March 1833. Thomas Gunnell of Cheltenham, retail beer dealer. Keeping his house open for the sale of beer until almost 11 p.m. R. B. Cooper JP and T. Newell JP at a Petty Sessions for Cheltenham district. First offence. Fine £2 and 5/6 costs. Offence committed 23 March 1833.

52/B/61   26 March 1833. Alexander Lane of Cheltenham, retail beer dealer. Keeping his house open [etc., as 52/B/60].

52/B/62   26 March 1833. James Morgan of Cheltenham, retail beer dealer. Keeping his house open for the sale of beer until 11.30 p.m. [etc., as 52/B/58].

52/B/63   26 March 1833. Richard Page of Cheltenham, retail beer dealer. Keeping his house open for the sale of beer until almost 11 p.m. [etc., as 52/B/60].

52/B/64   7 March 1833. John Hulbert. Assaulting Thomas Smith at Brockworth. R. B. Cooper JP and T. Newell JP at Cheltenham. Fine £1 and 5/6 costs. Offence committed 3 March 1833.

52/B/65   7 March 1833. John Hunt. Assaulting John Powers at Brockworth. R. B. Cooper JP and T. J. Baines JP at Cheltenham. Fine £1 and 5/6 costs. Offence committed 3 March 1833.

52/B/66   2 March 1833. Robert Greenough. Assaulting Richard Lacey at Cheltenham. R. B. Cooper JP and T. Newell JP at Cheltenham. Fine 10/- and 7/- costs or fourteen days in Northleach house of correction. Offence committed 2 March 1833.

52/B/67   2 March 1833. Alexander Trotter. Assaulting Susan Trotter at Cheltenham. R. B. Cooper JP and T. Newell JP at Cheltenham. Fine 10/- and 5/6 costs or fourteen days in Northleach house of correction. Offence committed 28 Feb. 1833.

52/B/68   28 Feb. 1833. James Cole of Cheltenham, retail beer dealer. Allowing beer to be consumed on his premises between one and two o'clock in the morning. R. B. Cooper JP and T. J. Baines JP at a Petty Sessions for Cheltenham district. First offence. Fine £2 and 5/6 costs. Offence committed Sunday 24 Feb. 1833.

52/B/69 1 Feb. 1833. John Joachim of Chedworth, labourer. Trespassing with a gun in search of game at Winson, Bibury. Rev. H. A. Pye JP and E. Cripps JP at Cirencester. First offence. Hard labour for three calendar months in Northleach house of correction, after which to find sureties totalling £20 against re-offending for one year. In default, a further six calendar months' hard labour. Offence committed 9 p.m. 31 Jan. 1833.

52/B/70 4 March 1833. Ann Snell, single woman, of South Cerney, retail beer seller. Keeping her house open for the sale and consumption of beer after 10 p.m. Rev. Hon. C. Bathurst JP and W. Croome JP at a Petty Sessions for Cirencester division. First offence. Fine 40/- and 5/- costs. Offence committed Saturday 26 Jan. 1833.

52/B/71 1 Feb. 1833. Thomas Reames, labourer, of Winson, Bibury. Trespassing with a gun in search of game in Winson [etc., as 52/B/69].

52/B/72 19 Nov. 1832. Aaron Brown of Minety, retail beer seller. Keeping his house open for the sale and consumption of beer after 10 p.m. Rev. Hon. C. Bathurst JP and J. Pitt JP at a Petty Sessions for Cirencester division. First offence. Fine 40/- and 5/- costs. Offence committed 6 Oct. 1832.

52/B/73 12 Jan. 1833. Richard Walker of Compton Abdale, labourer. Trespassing with a gun in search of game. Rev. W. Price JP and Rev. Thomas Pettat JP at Northleach. First offence. Hard labour for three calendar months in Northleach house of correction, after which to find sureties totalling £20 against re-offending for one year. In default, a further six months' hard labour. Offence committed 9 Jan. 1833.

52/B/74 8 March 1833. Harriette Parker, single woman, of Tetbury. Stealing turnip greens from a field, the property of Samuel Albin Saunders Esq. of Upton, Tetbury. W. M. Paul JP and Robert Staynor Holford JP. Second offence. Previously convicted (7 Feb. 1833) for stealing turnips from a field in Long Newnton, Wilts., the property of farmer Richard Leonard. Three calendar months in Horsley house of correction. Offence committed 25 Feb. 1833.

52/B/75 23 Jan. 1833. John Sharp the younger, labourer, of Tetbury. Using lurchers to kill game at Cherington. W. M. Paul JP at Tetbury. Rev. William George, complainant. Fine 1/- and 6/- costs. Given three days to pay. In default, one calendar month's hard labour in Horsley house of correction. Offence committed 20 Jan. 1833.

52/B/76 5 Dec. 1832. James Bishop, plasterer, of Tetbury. Stealing grapes from a garden, the property of Robert Tanner, farmer, of Tetbury. W. M. Paul JP at Tetbury. Fine 5/- and 6/6 costs or hard labour for six calendar months in Horsley house of correction. Offence committed 25 Nov. 1832.

52/B/77 21 Nov. 1832. Richard Essex of Avening, mason. Stealing turnips from a field, the property of Daniel Harvey, farmer, of Avening. R. S. Holford JP. Complainant gave evidence. Fine 6d. and 5/6 costs. Given sixteen days to pay. Offence committed 9 and 12 Nov. 1832.

52/B/78 21 Nov. 1832. Hannah Parker and Charlotte Mann, single women. Stealing turnips from a field in Shipton Moyne, the property of Thomas Grimston Bucknall Estcourt Esq. of Estcourt House. R. S. Holford JP. Each fined 1/- and 3/3 costs. Given nine days to pay. Fines and costs to go to complainant. Offence committed 13 Nov. 1832. [Endorsed: 5 convictions, i.e. 52/B/74–8.]

52/B/79 1 Feb. 1833. George Marsh of Wick and Abson, labourer. Trespassing in pursuit of game at Dyrham and Hinton. Henry Charles, duke of Beaufort, JP and Robert Hale Blagden Hale JP at a Petty Sessions held at the Cross Hands inn, Old Sodbury. Complainant Diana Alway, husbandwoman. Fine £2, to be paid to William Gould, overseer of the poor, and

£1 7s. costs. Given four weeks to pay. In default, two calendar months' hard labour in Horsley house of correction. Offence committed between 8 a.m. and 9 a.m. 26 Jan. 1833.

52/B/80 1 Feb.1833. Emanuel Eastmeade of Acton Turville, labourer. Using a wire to kill a hare on land occupied by Betty Marsh of Acton Turville. F. Trotman JP, W. Blathwayt JP and R. H. B. Hale JP at a Petty Sessions held at the Cross Hands inn, Old Sodbury. Thomas Webb, gamekeeper to the duke of Beaufort, informed A. Shakespear JP, who issued summons which was read to accused by William Light, constable of Great Badminton. Labourer William Watts gave evidence that he saw accused remove a hare and wire. Accused did not appear. Fine £3 3s. and £1 17s. costs or hard labour for two calendar months in Horsley house of correction. Offence committed Saturday and Sunday 26 and 27 Jan. 1833.

52/C/1 14 March 1833. John Jones of St. Philip and St. Jacob, [Bristol]. Permitting beer to be consumed on his premises between 3 p.m. and 5 p.m. [on a Sunday]. J. Parker JP and G. Goldney JP at a Petty Sessions for Bristol division. Fine £2 and 7/6 costs. Offence committed Sunday 3 March 1833.

52/C/2 14 March 1833. Richard Gentle of St. Philip and St. Jacob, [Bristol]. Permitting beer to be consumed on his premises between 10 a.m. and 1 p.m. [on a Sunday]. J. Parker JP and G. Goldney JP at a Petty Sessions for Bristol division. Fine £2 and 7/6 costs. Offence committed Sunday 3 March 1833.

52/C/3 13 March 1833. Benjamin Hill of St. Philip and St. Jacob, [Bristol]. Permitting beer to be consumed on his premises [etc., as 52/C/2 except] Fine £2 including costs.

52/C/4 21 March 1833. Benjamin Hill of St. Philip and St. Jacob, [Bristol]. Permitting beer to be consumed on his premises between 10 a.m. and 1 p.m. [on a Sunday]. G. Goldney JP and H. W. Newman JP at a Petty Sessions for Bristol division. Fine £2 including 9/- costs. Offence committed Sunday 3 March 1833. [The relationship with 52/C/3 is not clear.]

52/C/5 28 March 1833. Sarah Shepherd of St. Philip and St. Jacob, [Bristol]. Permitting beer to be consumed on her premises between 3 p.m. and 5 p.m. [on a Sunday]. D. Cave JP and H. W. Newman JP at a Petty Sessions for Bristol division. Fine £2 including 9/- costs. Offence committed Sunday 17 March 1833.

52/C/6 2 May 1833. Jonathan Dawes of Henbury. Permitting beer to be consumed on his premises after 10 p.m. W. Fripp JP and H. W. Newman JP at a Petty Sessions for Bristol division. Fine £2 and 7/- costs. Offence committed 25 April 1833.

52/C/7 2 May 1833. John Nelson of Westbury on Trym. Permitting beer to be consumed on his premises after 10 p.m. W. Fripp JP and Rev. William Mirehouse JP at a Petty Sessions for Bristol division. Fine £2 and 6/6 costs. Offence committed 13 April 1833.

52/C/8 2 May 1833. William Hale of Westbury on Trym. Permitting beer to be consumed on his premises after 10 p.m. [etc., as 52/C/7].

52/C/9 21 March 1833. James Bryant of Clifton. Permitting beer to be consumed on his premises between 10 a.m. and 1 p.m. [on a Sunday]. J. S. Harford JP and J. Parker JP at a Petty Sessions for Bristol division. Fine £2 and 6/6 costs. Offence committed Sunday 10 March 1833.

52/C/10 21 Feb. 1833. Joseph Carey of Bitton. Permitting beer and/or porter to be consumed after 10 p.m. H. W. Newman JP and V. J. Graeme JP at a Petty Sessions for Bristol division. Fine £2 including costs. Offence committed Sunday 17 Feb. 1833.

52/C/11 21 Feb. 1833. Abraham Fry of Oldland, Bitton. Permitting beer and/or porter to be consumed on his premises after 10 p.m. V. J. Graeme JP and H. W. Newman JP at a Petty Sessions [etc., as 52/C/10 except] Fine £2 including 9/- costs.

52/C/12   24 May 1833. Ann Dunn. Assaulting Pricilla [*sic*] Porter at Clifton. C. L. Walker JP and Rev. W. Mirehouse JP at Lawfords Gate sessions room. Fine 20/- and 4/6 costs or one calendar month in Lawfords Gate house of correction. Offence committed 24 May 1833.

52/C/13   24 May 1833. James Dunn. Assaulting Pricilla [*sic*] Porter at Westbury on Trym. C. L. Walker JP and Rev. W. Mirehouse JP at Lawfords Gate sessions room. Fine £2 and 7/- costs or one calendar month in Lawfords Gate house of correction. Offence committed 1 May 1833.

52/C/14   9 May 1833. John Bailey. Assaulting Hester Bennett at St. Philip and St. Jacob, [Bristol]. C. L. Walker JP and Rev. W. Mirehouse JP at Lawfords Gate sessions room. Fine 10/- and 14/- costs or one calendar month in Lawfords Gate house of correction. Offence committed 7 May 1833.

52/C/15   4 Feb. 1833. Thomas Winstone. Assaulting Sophia Winstone at Winterbourne. J. Savage JP and Rev. W. Mirehouse JP at Lawfords Gate sessions room. Fine 11/- and 11/6 costs or one calendar month in Lawfords Gate house of correction. Offence committed 3 Feb. 1833.

52/C/16   14 Feb. 1833. James Hall. Assaulting John Bunce at St. Philip and St. Jacob, [Bristol]. G. Goldney JP and H. W. Newman JP at Lawfords Gate sessions room. Fine 10/- and 6/6 costs or fourteen days in Lawfords Gate house of correction. Offence committed 11 Feb. 1833.

52/C/17   31 Jan. 1833. Mary and Caroline Hill. Assaulting Rebecca Southcott at St. Philip and St. Jacob, [Bristol]. G. Goldney JP and H. W. Newman JP at Lawfords Gate sessions room. Fine 6*d.* and 13/- costs or one calendar month in Lawfords Gate house of correction. Offence committed 28 Jan. 1833.

52/C/18   14 Jan. 1833. Daniel Daker [*recte* ? Baker] and James Chandler. Assaulting Hannah Bryant at St. George, [Bristol]. Rev. W. Mirehouse JP and H. W. Newman JP at Lawfords Gate sessions room. Fine 6/- and 14/- costs or one calendar month in Lawfords Gate house of correction. Offence committed 14 Jan. 1833.

52/C/19   10 Jan. 1833. George Godfrey. Assaulting John Ashley at Bitton. G. Goldney JP and H. W. Newman JP at Lawfords Gate sessions room. Fine 6*d.* and 7/- costs or seven days in Lawfords Gate house of correction. Offence committed 4 Jan. 1833.

52/C/20   7 Jan. 1833. Mary Edney. Assaulting Ann Robins of St. James, [Bristol]. H. W. Newman JP and Rev. W. Mirehouse JP at Lawfords Gate sessions room. Fine 6*d.* and 4/6 costs or seven days in Lawfords Gate house of correction. Offence committed 5 Jan. 1833.

52/C/21   7 Jan. 1833. William Fowler. Assaulting Daniel Fowler at Winterbourne. H. W. Newman JP and Rev. W. Mirehouse JP at Lawfords Gate sessions room. Fine £2 and 8*s.* costs or one calendar month in Lawfords Gate house of correction. Offence committed 26 Dec. 1832.

52/C/22   7 Jan. 1833. Thomas Bowden and John Narroway. Assaulting Samuel Whiting at St. Philip and St. Jacob, [Bristol]. H. W. Newman JP and Rev. W. Mirehouse JP at Lawfords Gate sessions room. Fine 6*d.* and 11/- costs or fourteen days in Lawfords Gate house of correction. Offence committed 31 Dec. 1832.

52/C/23   23 Feb. 1833. Francis Bryant. Assaulting Isaac Fox at St. George, [Bristol]. H. W. Newman JP and Rev. W. Mirehouse JP at Lawfords Gate sessions room. Fine £1 7*s.* 6*d.* and 8/6 costs or one calendar month in Lawfords Gate house of correction. Offence committed 17 Feb. 1833.

52/C/24   17 Jan. 1833. Moses Baker. Assaulting William Kent at St. Philip and St. Jacob, [Bristol]. J. Parker JP and H. W. Newman JP at Lawfords Gate sessions room. Fine 3/- and 7/- costs or fourteen days in Lawfords Gate house of correction. Offence committed 14 Jan. 1833.

52/C/25   18 April 1833. James Bryant. Wounding John Sterling with a sword at Clifton. W. Munro JP and J. Lewis JP at Lawfords Gate sessions room. Fine £3 11*s*. 6*d*. and £1 8*s*. 6*d*. costs or two calendar months in Lawfords Gate house of correction. Offence committed 26 March 1833.

52/C/26   25 April 1833. William Ashman. Assaulting George Dean at St. George, [Bristol]. W. Munro JP and H. W. Newman JP at Lawfords Gate sessions room. Fine 14/6 and 5/6 costs or one calendar month in Lawfords Gate house of correction. Offence committed 19 April 1833.

52/C/27   18 April 1833. Abraham Phipps, William Phipps and George Smith. Assaulting John Rich at St. Philip and St. Jacob, [Bristol]. A. G. H. Battersby JP and Rev. W. Mirehouse JP at Lawfords Gate sessions room. Fine 5/- and 5/6 costs or fourteen days in Lawfords Gate house of correction. Offence committed 16 April 1833.

52/C/28   1 July 1833. Thomas Bryan. Assaulting Richard Cheney and Henry Hollands at Cheltenham. T. J. Baines JP and T. Newell JP at Cheltenham. Fine £1 and 4/- costs. Offence committed 30 June 1833.

52/C/29   25 June 1833. James Harris. Assaulting Daniel Browning at Cheltenham. Sir W. Hicks, Bt., JP and T. J. Baines JP at Cheltenham. Fine £4 4*s*. and 6/- costs or two calendar months in Northleach house of correction. Offence committed 23 June 1833.

52/C/30   6 May 1833. Benjamin Mason. Assaulting Thomas White at St. Briavels hundred. J. Pyrke JP and C. Crawley JP at Newnham. Fine £4, to be paid to the high constable of St. Briavels hundred, and £1 costs to the complainant, or hard labour for two calendar months in Littledean house of correction. Offence committed 21 April 1833.

52/C/31   6 May 1833. Moses Webb. Assaulting Thomas White [*etc., as* 52/C/30].

52/C/32   20 May 1833. George Williams. Assaulting Sarah White at Newnham. J. Pyrke JP and C. Crawley JP at Newnham. Fine £4, to be paid to an overseer of the poor, and £1 costs to the complainant, or hard labour in Littledean house of correction [*length of sentence not given*]. Offence committed 18 May 1833.

52/C/33   6 May 1833. Elizabeth wife of James Hall. Assaulting her husband at St. Briavels hundred. J. Pyrke JP and C. Crawley JP at Newnham. Fine £2, to be paid to the high constable of St. Briavels, and 10/- costs to the victim, or hard labour for one calendar month in Littledean house of correction. Offence committed 2 May 1833.

52/C/34   3 June 1833. William Selwyn. Assaulting James Smith at Littledean. J. Pyrke JP and C. Crawley JP at Newnham. Fine 12/- and 8/- costs or hard labour for two calendar months in Littledean house of correction. Offence committed 21 May 1833.

52/C/35   3 June 1833. John Bellamy. Trespassing by fishing in a brook in Westbury on Severn, the property of Samuel Bullock. J. Pyrke JP and C. Crawley JP at Newnham. Fine 10/6 and 9/6 costs or hard labour for two calendar months in Littledean house of correction. Offence committed 17 May 1833.

52/C/36   3 June 1833. Daniel Packer. Trespassing by fishing in a brook at Westbury on Severn [*etc., as* 52/C/35 *except*] Fine £4 11*s*. 6*d*. and 8/6 costs [*and omitting* calendar].

52/C/37   24 May 1833. John Bellamy. Assaulting Jonathan Beaman at Westbury on Severn. J. Pyrke JP and C. Crawley JP at Littledean. Fine £3 17*s*. and £1 3*s*. costs or hard labour for two calendar months in Littledean house of correction. Offence committed 23 May 1833.

52/C/38   6 May 1833. John Smith. Assaulting James Bullock at Westbury on Severn. J. Pyrke JP and C. Crawley JP at Newnham. Fine £4 and £1 costs or hard labour for two calendar months in Littledean house of correction. Offence committed 29 April 1833.

52/C/39   24 May 1833. John Bellamy. Assaulting John Davis at Westbury on Severn [*etc.*, *as* 52/C/37 *except*] Fine £1 7*s.* 6*d.* and £1 2*s.* 6*d.* costs.

52/C/40   23 April 1833. Edward Thompson, keeper of the Bell inn, English Bicknor. Keeping a disorderly house: allowing tippling and drunkenness. Rev. T. Thomas JP and Rev. C. H. Morgan JP. First offence. Fine £2 and 8/- costs. Offence committed 30 March 1833.

52/C/41   21 May 1833. William Fincher of Long Marston, alehouse keeper. Allowing Thomas Wainer and others to consume beer and cider until 10.30 p.m. Rev. J. R. Hall JP and W. Dickins JP at Moreton in Marsh for Kiftsgate hundred upper division. First offence. Fine £2, one half and 16/6 costs awarded to Charles Cooper of Long Marston, the prosecutor, and the remainder to the county treasurer. Offence committed 4 May 1833.

52/C/42   23 April 1833. James Wrighton. Assaulting Julia Haines at Chipping Campden. Rev. J. R. Hall JP and Rev. C. Jeaffreson JP at Moreton in Marsh. Fine £1, to be paid to Peter Haynes, an overseer of the poor of Chipping Campden, and 13/6 costs to the complainant. Offence committed 19 April 1833.

52/C/43   23 April 1833. Samuel Lardner. Assaulting Edward Benbow at Moreton in Marsh. Rev. J. R. Hall JP and Rev. C. Jeaffreson JP at Moreton in Marsh. Fine 5/-, to be paid to Ralph Wells, an overseer of the poor, and 7/6 costs to the complainant, or one month in Northleach house of correction. Offence committed 14 April 1833.

52/C/44   23 April 1833. George Terry. Assaulting Sabina Lardner at Moreton in Marsh. Rev. J. R. Hall JP and Rev. C. Jeaffreson JP at Moreton in Marsh. Fine 5/-, to be paid to Ralph Wells, an overseer of the poor, and 7/6 costs to the complainant, or one month in Northleach house of correction. Offence committed 14 April 1833.

52/C/45   4 June 1833. William Drury. Assaulting John Brotheredge at Chipping Campden. Rev. J. R. Hall JP and W. Dickins JP at Moreton in Marsh. Fine 8/6, to be paid to Peter Haynes, an overseer of the poor, and 11/6 costs to the complainant, or one month in Northleach house of correction. Offence committed 31 May 1833.

52/C/46   21 May 1833. Frances Johnes of Chipping Campden, [alehouse keeper]. Allowing beer etc. to be consumed by Richard Harrison and others until 10.15 p.m. Rev. J. R. Hall JP and W. Dickins JP at Moreton in Marsh. First offence. Fine £2, one half and £1 5*s.* 6*d.* costs to be paid to the prosecutor, William Cooper of Chipping Campden, and the remainder to the county treasurer. Offence committed 12 May 1833.

52/C/47   28 June 1833. Charles and Samuel Hall. Vagrancy: having no visible means of subsistence at Painswick. H. Burgh JP at Stroud. Hard labour for three calendar months in Horsley house of correction. Offence committed 26 June 1833.

52/C/48   25 May 1833. Ann Carter. Causing herself and her unborn bastard child to be chargeable to Stroud parish by returning there after being removed by legal order to Bromsberrow [*MS.* Bromsborough] on 6 May 1833. H. Burgh JP at Stroud. Ten days' hard labour in Horsley house of correction. .

52/C/49   10 June 1833. Joseph and William Carter. Vagrancy in Painswick: no visible means of subsistence. H. Burgh JP at Stroud. Hard labour for one calendar month in Horsley house of correction. Offence committed 9 June 1833.

52/C/50   26 April 1833. James Smart. Failing to maintain his wife and two children, thereby causing them to become chargeable to Bisley parish. H. Burgh JP at Stroud. Hard labour for one calendar month in Horsley house of correction. Offence committed two months previously.

52/C/51 2 July 1833. Peter Hall. Vagrancy: lodging in an outhouse in Stroud, and unable to give a good account of himself. H. Burgh JP at Stroud. Hard labour for three calendar months in Horsley house of correction. Offence committed 29 June 1833.

52/C/52 17 April 1833. Thomas Eagles of Apperley, Deerhurst. Allowing drunkenness, gaming and disorderly behaviour on his premises. J. Timbrill D.D. JP, Rev. C. White JP and J. W. Martin JP at a Petty Sessions. First offence. Fine 50/- including costs. Offence committed 4 April 1833.

52/C/53 1 May 1833. William Tarrant of Winchcombe, labourer. Assaulting John Hooper and his wife Elizabeth of Winchcombe and challenging constable William Kitchen and others to fight. J. Timbrill D.D. JP and J. W. Martin JP at Tewkesbury. Fine 1/-, to be paid to John Mason, overseer of the poor of Winchcombe, and 4/- costs. Offence committed about 11 p.m. Sunday 28 April 1833.

52/C/54 1 May 1833. William Wiltshire of Winchcombe, labourer. Assaulting John Hooper [etc., as 52/C/53 except] Fine 10/-, to be paid to John Mason, overseer of the poor, and 15/3 costs.

52/C/55 1 May 1833. John Smith of Winchcombe, labourer. Assaulting John Hooper [etc., as 52/C/54].

52/C/56 1 June 1833. Joseph Sollis. Assaulting Alexander Stevens at Charlton Kings. Sir W. Hicks, Bt., JP and J. E. Viner JP at Cheltenham. Fine 10/- and 5/6 costs. Offence committed 30 May 1833.

52/C/57 4 June 1833. Thomas Shurmer. Assaulting Elizabeth Bunting at Leckhampton. R. B. Cooper JP and J. E. Viner JP at Cheltenham. Fine 2/6 and 5/6 costs. Offence committed 2 June 1833.

52/C/58 6 June 1833. John Wanklin of Cheltenham, retail beer dealer. Keeping his premises open for the sale of beer until 10.45 p.m. J. E. Viner JP and T. J. Baines JP at a Petty Sessions for Cheltenham division. First offence. Fine £2 and 5/6 costs. Offence committed 1 June 1833.

52/C/59 6 June 1833. Alexander Rice. Assaulting Tabitha Knight of Cheltenham. R. B. Cooper JP and T. Newell JP at Cheltenham. Fine 5/- and 4/6 costs. Offence committed 3 June 1833.

52/C/60 8 June 1833. Joel Tanner. Assaulting Samuel Meddins at Cheltenham. Sir W. Hicks, Bt., JP and J. E. Viner JP at Cheltenham. Fine 10/- and 6/6 costs. Offence committed 3 June 1833.

52/C/61 11 June 1833. Richard Parke. Assaulting Henry Holland at Cheltenham. R. B. Cooper JP and T. Newell JP at Cheltenham. Fine 10/- and 4/- costs or one month in Northleach house of correction. Offence committed 10 June 1833.

52/C/62 13 June 1833. Richard Havard. Assaulting John Hitchings at Cheltenham. Sir W. Hicks, Bt., JP and J. E. Viner JP at Cheltenham. Fine 2/6 and 3/6 costs. Offence committed 12 June 1833.

52/C/63 15 June 1833. Daniel Hitchings. Assaulting James Butler at Cheltenham. Sir W. Hicks, Bt., JP and J. E. Viner JP at Cheltenham. Fine 20/- and 7/6 costs or one calendar month in Northleach house of correction. Offence committed 10 June 1833.

52/C/64 20 June 1833. Samuel Hamlet. Assaulting Benjamin James of Charlton Kings. R. B. Cooper JP and T. Newell JP at Cheltenham. Fine 5/- and 8/- costs. Offence committed 17 June 1833.

52/C/65 22 June 1833. Henry Hyett. Assaulting William Barnard at Cheltenham. R. B. Cooper JP and T. Newell JP at Cheltenham. Fine 5/- and 10/6 costs. Offence committed 5 June 1833.

52/C/66 27 June 1833. Joseph Seward. Assaulting Charles Evans and Thomas Hayward at Cheltenham. R. B. Cooper JP and T. Newell JP at Cheltenham. Fine 5/- and 3/- costs on each charge or fourteen days in Northleach house of correction. Offence committed 26 June 1833.

52/C/67 26 June 1833. John McGill. Assaulting Elizabeth Edwards at Cheltenham. R. B. Cooper JP and G. Stevenson JP at Cheltenham. Fine 7/- and 3/6 costs. Offence committed 25 June 1833.

52/C/68 27 June 1833. Alexander Trotter. Assaulting John Poole at Cheltenham. R. B. Cooper JP and T. Newell JP at Cheltenham. Fine 10/- and 7/6 costs. Offence committed 25 June 1833.

52/C/69 29 June 1833. Richard Richmond. Assaulting Esther Ancock at Cheltenham. R. B. Cooper JP and T. Newell JP at Cheltenham. Fine 5/- and 5/6 costs. Offence committed 26 June 1833.

52/C/70 1 July 1833. James Ballinger. Assaulting Mary Ann Wakeman at Leigh [*MS.* Lye]. R. B. Cooper JP and T. J. Baines JP at Cheltenham. Fine £1 and 9/- costs or two months in Northleach house of correction. Offence committed 28 June 1833.

52/C/71 11 April 1833. Joseph Palmer. Assaulting Thomas Randall at Cheltenham. J. E. Viner JP and T. Newell JP at Cheltenham. Fine 20/- or one month in Northleach house of correction. Offence committed 9 April 1833.

52/C/72 13 April 1833. John Barton. Stealing underwood at Charlton Kings, the property of William Troughton. R. B. Cooper JP at Cheltenham. Fine £2, to be paid to an overseer of the poor, 3/- (the value of the underwood) and 5/6 costs, or two months in Northleach house of correction. Offence committed 8 April 1833.

52/C/73 16 April 1833. Richard Harman of Cheltenham, retail beer dealer. Keeping his premises open for the sale of beer until 10.25 p.m. R. B. Cooper JP and T. Newell JP at a Petty Sessions for Cheltenham division. First offence. Fine £2 and 5/6 costs. Offence committed 12 April 1833.

52/C/74 18 April 1833. Richard Liddell of Cheltenham, licensed victualler. Keeping his premises open for the consumption of beer during the usual hours of afternoon divine service at the parish church. R. B. Cooper JP and T. Newell JP for Cheltenham division. First offence. Fine 40/- and 5/6 costs. Offence committed Sunday 14 April 1833.

52/C/75 2 May 1833. John Hays. Stealing three wooden fence poles valued at 2/- at Cheltenham, the property of Edward Cope. J. E. Viner JP and T. J. Baines JP at Cheltenham. Fine 10/- and 5/6 costs. Offence committed 1 May 1833.

52/C/76 7 May 1833. William Cook. Assaulting Mary Ann Hulls at Cheltenham. Sir W. Hicks, Bt., JP and T. Newell JP at Cheltenham. Fine 10/- and 6/6 costs or one month in Northleach house of correction. Offence committed 4 May 1833.

52/C/77 9 May 1833. John Turner of Cheltenham, retail beer dealer. Selling beer on his premises at 12 noon on a Sunday. Sir W. Hicks, Bt., JP and T. J. Baines JP at a Petty Sessions for Cheltenham division. First offence. Fine £2 and 5/6 costs. Offence committed 5 May 1833.

52/C/78 14 May 1833. Robert Green of Cheltenham, licensed victualler. Failing to keep good order on his premises. Sir W. Hicks, Bt., JP and T. J. Baines JP for Cheltenham division. First offence. Fine 40/- and 6/6 costs. Offence committed 11 May 1833.

52/C/79 23 May 1833. John Thomas. Assaulting Thomas Wasley at Cheltenham. Sir W. Hicks, Bt., JP and J. E. Viner JP at Cheltenham. Fine 40/- and 7/6 costs or one calendar month in Northleach house of correction. Offence committed 17 May 1833.

52/C/80   28 May 1833. David North. Breaking off a tree branch with intent to steal, the property of William Jearrad, at Cheltenham. Sir W. Hicks, Bt., JP and T. J. Baines JP at Cheltenham. Fine 20/- and 5/6 costs. Offence committed 28 May 1833.

52/C/81   30 May 1833. Susanna Bolton. Assaulting Sophia Jones at Cheltenham. Sir W. Hicks, Bt., JP and T. J. Baines JP at Cheltenham. Fine 2/6 and 6/6 costs or fourteen days in Northleach house of correction. Offence committed 25 May 1833.

52/C/82   1 June 1833. George Smith. Assaulting John Cook at Cheltenham. T. Newell JP and T. J. Baines JP at Cheltenham. Fine 20/- and 4/- costs or one month in Northleach house of correction. Offence committed 30 May 1833.

52/C/83   27 March 1833. Moses Luton and Thomas England, labourers, of Westerleigh. Using guns to kill game in Shortwood, Pucklechurch. F. Trotman JP, W. G. Davy JP, A. Shakespear JP and R. H. B. Hale JP at a Special Sessions held at Old Sodbury. Benjamin Guy Phillips Esq. of Pucklechurch, complainant. Fine £1 each, to be paid to Daniel Brain, an overseer of the poor of Pucklechurch, and £1 0s. 6d. each for costs, or two calendar months each in Horsley house of correction. Given twenty-one days to pay. Offence committed Sunday 13 Jan. 1833.

52/C/84   9 April 1833. Thomas Hays, William Ricketts and John Bolwell, labourers, of Batheaston, Som. Trespassing in search of game or conies with dogs and nets at Marshfield. K. W. Horlock JP at Marshfield. Charles Dyer, farmer, of Marshfield and Thomas Beaman, farmer, of St. Catherine, Som., complainants. Fine 5/- and 8/- costs each or hard labour for two months in Horsley house of correction. Given fourteen days to pay. Offence committed Sunday 17 March 1833.

52/D/1   25 July 1833. Christopher Mynett of Minchinhampton, apprentice cordwainer. Absconding from serving his master, George Bird. H. Burgh JP at Stroud. Not more than £20 paid on entering apprenticeship. Hard labour for three months in Horsley house of correction. Offence committed 17 July 1833.

52/D/2   26 July 1833. Joseph Lovegrove, John Hunt and George Richings, all of Cranham, potters. Assaulting Thomas Smith, baker, of Cranham. H. Burgh JP, John Mills JP, Donald Maclean JP, Edmund Gilling Hallewell JP and Nathaniel Samuel Marling JP at Stroud. Fine £2 and 4/8 costs each or two months in Horsley house of correction. Offence committed 22 July 1833.

52/D/3   2 Sept. 1833. William Lewis of Bisley, labourer. Stealing a quantity of apples from an orchard, the property of Walter Ridler, yeoman, of Bisley. H. Burgh JP at Stroud. Hard labour for two calendar months in Horsley house of correction. Offence committed 4 Aug. 1833.

52/D/4   25 Sept. 1833. Matthew Paul, Mortimer Grange and Henry Aldridge, labourers, of Stroud. Stealing a quantity of apples from an orchard, the property of John Neems, yeoman, of Stroud. H. Burgh JP, E. G. Hallewell JP and N. S. Marling JP at Stroud. M. Paul sentenced to hard labour for six calendar months, the others to one calendar month in Horsley house of correction. Offence committed 24 Sept. 1833.

52/D/5   23 Aug. 1833. Elizabeth Lawler. Begging in Stroud. H. Burgh JP, J. Mills JP, D. Maclean JP, E. G. Hallewell JP and N. S. Marling JP at Stroud. Hard labour for one calendar month in Horsley house of correction. Offence committed 21 Aug. 1833.

52/D/6   27 Sept. 1833. Cornelius Driscoll. Begging in Painswick. H. Burgh JP, D. Maclean JP, E. G. Hallewell JP and N. S. Marling JP at Stroud. Hard labour for one calendar month in Horsley house of correction. Offence committed 26 Sept. 1833.

52/D/7   20 Sept. 1833. Robert Bird. Causing his wife and four children to become chargeable to Stroud parish by refusing or neglecting to work. H. Burgh JP and E. G. Hallewell JP at Stroud. Hard labour for one calendar month in Horsley house of correction. Offence committed 13 Sept. 1833.

52/D/8   14 Aug. 1833. William Brown, indentured apprentice, of Stonehouse. Absconding from his master, Richard Smith, cordwainer, of Stonehouse. N. S. Marling JP at Stroud. Not more than £15 paid on Brown's binding out. Hard labour for one calendar month in Horsley house of correction. Offence committed 12 Aug. 1833.

52/D/9   27 July 1833. Stephen Howell, Samuel Milsom and William Lodge, labourers, of Painswick. Stealing half a peck of potatoes and a quantity of onions growing in a garden, the property of William Hatton, clothworker, of Painswick. H. Burgh JP at Stroud. Hard labour for three calendar months in Horsley house of correction. Offence committed 22 July 1833.

52/D/10   2 Oct. 1833. William Cox and Joseph Mead, labourers, of Stroud. Stealing a quantity of apples from an orchard in Stroud, the property of Paul Read, schoolmaster. H. Burgh JP and E. G. Hallewell JP at Stroud. Hard labour for one calendar month in Horsley house of correction. Offence committed 1 Oct. 1833.

52/D/11   9 Aug. 1833. Maria Beard, Eliza Birt and Ann Birt, single women, of Painswick. Stealing wood from a field in Painswick occupied by Samuel Gyde, yeoman. H. Burgh JP, J. Mills JP, D. Maclean JP, E. G. Hallewell JP and N. S. Marling JP at Stroud. Each fined 1/- (the value of the wood) and 2/2 costs, or hard labour for two calendar months in Horsley house of correction. Offence committed 6 Aug. 1833.

52/D/12   9 Aug. 1833. Benjamin Berriman and John Workman, labourers, of Bisley. Stealing a quantity of apples growing in an orchard occupied by Thomas Dickenson, yeoman, of Bisley. H. Burgh JP, D. Maclean JP and E. G. Hallewell JP at Stroud. Berriman fined 2/- and Workman 6d., to be paid to an overseer of the poor, and each fined 6d. (the value of the apples) and costs of 3/3, or hard labour for two calendar months in Horsley house of correction. Offence committed 21 July 1833.

52/D/13   12 July 1833. James Miles, beer retailer, of Stroud. Causing annoyance by depositing rubbish on the roadway. H. Burgh JP, J. Mills JP, D. Maclean JP, E. G. Hallewell JP and N. S. Marling JP at Stroud. Fine £1 and 10/6 costs. Offence committed 27 June 1833.

52/D/14   26 March 1833. William Fowles, beer retailer, of Avening. Keeping his house open after 10 p.m. and permitting drunkenness and disorderly behaviour. R. Kingscote JP and Rev. William George JP at a Petty Sessions for Longtree division. First offence. Fine £3 and 10/- costs. Offence committed Saturday 2 March 1833.

52/D/15   11 July 1833 [*MS.* 1823; *possibly a very late return*]. Henry Leonard. Leaving Horsley two years previously, causing his wife Hannah and two children to become chargeable to the parish. O. P. Wathen JP at Woodchester. Hard labour for three calendar months in Horsley house of correction.

52/D/16   18 July 1833. George Heskins. Leaving Horsley six weeks previously, causing his wife Sarah to become chargeable to the parish. D. Ricardo JP and Thomas Reddall Haycock JP at Rodborough. Hard labour for three calendar months in Horsley house of correction.

52/D/17   1 July 1833. Isaiah Horlick of Horsley, beer retailer. Keeping his premises open for the sale of beer until 10.45 p.m. R. Kingscote JP, T. Kingscote JP, D. Ricardo JP and T. R. Haycock JP at a Petty Sessions for Longtree division. First offence. Fine 40/- and 9/6 costs. Offence committed 27 May 1833.

52/D/18   1 July 1833. William Brown the elder of Horsley, beer retailer. Keeping his premises open for the sale of beer between 3 p.m. and 4 p.m. on a Sunday. R. Kingscote JP, T. Kingscote JP, D. Ricardo JP and T. R. Haycock JP at a Petty Sessions for Longtree division. First offence. Fine 40/- and 13/6 costs. Offence committed 26 May 1833.

52/D/19   18 Sept. 1833. Thomas Buckingham, John Judge *alias* Compton and Thomas White *alias* Taylor, labourers, of Tetbury. Using nets to take game without a certificate. T. G. B. Estcourt JP and W. M. Paul JP. Fine £5 each, to be paid to an overseer of the poor after the deduction of costs. Given fourteen days to pay. In default, three calendar months' hard labour in Horsley house of correction. Offence committed Sunday 18 Aug. 1833.

52/D/20   18 Sept. 1833. James Bishop of Tetbury, plasterer. Using wires to kill game without a game certificate. T. G. B. Estcourt JP and William Playne JP. Fine £5, to be paid to an overseer of the poor after the deduction of costs. Given fourteen days to pay. In default, three calendar months' hard labour in Horsley house of correction. Offence committed 9 Sept. 1833.

52/D/21   12 Sept 1833. George Marling of Clifton. Failing to display his name and 'licensed to sell beer by retail' in the appropriate style above the door of his house. C. L. Walker JP and G. Hilhouse JP. Fine £10. Offence committed 6 Sept. 1833.

52/D/22   12 Sept 1833. John Payne and Joseph Sage. Assaulting John Dickenson at St. Philip and St. Jacob, [Bristol]. C. L. Walker JP and G. Hilhouse JP at Lawfords Gate sessions room. Fine 10/- and 6/6 costs or one calendar month in Lawfords Gate house of correction. Offence committed 10 Sept. 1833.

52/D/23   12 Sept 1833. William Jenkins. Assaulting Dennis Murphy at Westbury on Trym. C. L. Walker JP and G. Hilhouse JP at Lawfords Gate sessions room. Fine £2 and 6/6 costs or two calendar months in Lawfords Gate house of correction. Offence committed 27 Aug. 1833.

52/D/24   12 Sept. 1833. Charles Blissett. Assaulting Thomas Tudball at Clifton. C. L. Walker JP and W. Munro JP at Lawfords Gate sessions room. Fine 12/- and 7/6 costs or fourteen days in Lawfords Gate house of correction. Offence committed 29 Aug. 1833.

52/D/25   5 Sept. 1833. Edward Hankins. Assaulting John Milsome at St. George, [Bristol]. G. Goldney JP and Rev. W. Mirehouse JP at Lawfords Gate sessions room. Fine 6*d.* and 9/6 costs or fourteen days in Lawfords Gate house of correction. Offence committed 20 Aug. 1833.

52/D/26   5 Sept. 1833. William Jones. Assaulting David Jones at Westbury on Trym. G. Goldney JP and Rev. W. Mirehouse JP at Lawfords Gate sessions room. Fine 1/- and 7/- costs or twenty-one days in Lawfords Gate house of correction. Offence committed 24 Aug. 1833.

52/D/27   22 Aug. 1833. William Wilkinson. Assaulting James Gwyther at Clifton. H. W. Newman JP and W. Munro JP at Lawfords Gate sessions room. Fine 1/- and 9/- costs or one calendar month in Lawfords Gate house of correction. Offence committed 9 Aug. 1833.

52/D/28   22 Aug. 1833. Solomon Harris. Assaulting Isabella Cox at Bitton. H. W. Newman JP and W. Munro JP at Lawfords Gate sessions room. Fine 1/- and 9/- costs or fourteen days in Lawfords Gate house of correction. Offence committed 4 Aug. 1833.

52/D/29   24 Aug. 1833. Henry Tyley. Assaulting Price Phillips at St. Philip and St. Jacob, [Bristol]. H. W. Newman JP and W. Munro JP at Lawfords Gate sessions room. Fine 5/- and 6/6 costs or fourteen days in Lawfords Gate house of correction. Offence committed 24 Aug. 1833.

52/D/30   3 Oct. 1833. Ellen Sullivan. Assaulting Mary Williams at Clifton. H. W. Newman JP and W. Fripp JP at Lawfords Gate sessions room. Fine 2/6 and 7/6 costs or twenty-one days in Lawfords Gate house of correction. Offence committed 2 Oct. 1833.

52/D/31   29 Aug. 1833. Henry Tyley. Assaulting Michael Wayland at St. Philip and St. Jacob, [Bristol]. H. W. Newman JP and W. Munro JP at Lawfords Gate sessions room. Fine 10/- and 5/6 costs or one calendar month in Lawfords Gate house of correction. Offence committed 24 Aug. 1833.

52/D/32   13 Aug. 1833. Richard Carpenter. Stealing half a peck of potatoes from a garden in Newent, the property of Robert Colwell. Rev. R. F. Onslow JP and R. F. Onslow JP at Newent. Hard labour for five calendar months in Littledean house of correction. Offence committed 10 Aug. 1833.

52/D/33   23 Sept. 1833. Thomas Onions of Dymock, cider retailer. Keeping his premises open for the sale of cider after 10 p.m. Rev. J. Commeline JP and O. Ricardo JP at a Petty Sessions for Botloe hundred. First offence. Fine 40/- (10/- of which awarded to the informer, the rest to the county treasurer) and 11/- costs. Offence committed 20 Sept. 1833.

52/D/34   18 March 1833 [*late return*]. Thomas Jones of Dymock, horse dealer and beer retailer. Keeping his premises open for the sale and consumption of beer between 3 p.m. and 5 p.m. on a Sunday. Rev. R. F. Onslow JP and R. F. Onslow JP at a Petty Sesssions for Botloe hundred. First offence. Fine £2 (4/- of which awarded to the informer Elizabeth wife of James Burton, the rest to the county treasurer) and 10/- costs. Offence committed Sunday 10 March 1833.

52/D/35   7 Oct. 1833. William Barker. Begging in a court at Stardens, Newent. R. F. Onslow JP at Newent. Hard labour for one month in Littledean house of correction. Offence committed Sunday 6 Oct. 1833.

52/D/36   11 March 1833 [*late return*]. Thomas Wilkes of Upleadon, labourer. Using a gun without a game certificate at Newent. Rev. R. F. Onslow JP and R. F. Onslow JP. James Cummins Esq. of Newent, complainant. Fine £1 18*s*. and 12/- costs or two calendar months in Littledean house of correction. Offence committed 23 Feb. 1833.

52/D/37   8 Oct. 1833. Thomas Price. Stealing poles valued at 2/- from Caswell Wood, Tidenham, the property of the duke of Beaufort. Rev. T. Thomas JP at Lydney. Fine £2 and 8/- costs, to be paid to William Thurston, agent for the duke of Beaufort, or six weeks in Littledean house of correction. Offence committed 20 Sept. 1833.

52/D/38   7 Oct. 1833. John White of Kingswood, Wilts., labourer. Stealing apples from an orchard in Charfield, the property of William Champion, farmer. John Burland Harris JP at Wotton under Edge. Hard labour for six weeks in Horsley house of correction. Offence committed 5 Oct. 1833.

52/D/39   11 Oct. 1833. James Howell of Wotton under Edge, beer retailer. Keeping his premises open for the sale of beer between 10 a.m. and 1 p.m. on a Sunday. William Leman JP and J. B. Harris JP at a Petty Sessions for Berkeley hundred. First offence. Fine 40/- Offence committed Sunday 6 Oct. 1833.

52/D/40   11 Oct. 1833. Samuel Seabourne of Wotton under Edge, beer retailer. Keeping his premises open [*etc.*, as 52/D/39 *adding* upper division *after* Berkeley hundred].

52/D/41   7 Aug. 1833. Harry Clarke and James Smith, labourers, of Kemerton. Riotous assembly and breach of the peace with others at Kemerton. J. Timbrill D.D. JP, Rev. J. Keysall JP and J. W. Martin JP at Tewkesbury. Thomas Quarrel, complainant. Fine 10/- each, to be paid to John Bee, overseer of the poor, and 3/6 each for costs. Offence committed 28 July 1833.

52/D/42   25 Sept. 1833. William Allard of Oxenton, labourer. Violently assaulting William Smith, yeoman, of Overbury, Worcs., at Oxenton. J. Timbrill D.D. JP, Rev. J. Keysall JP and J. W. Martin JP at Tewkesbury. Fine £4 5s., to be paid to William Tyler Chandler, an overseer of the poor of Oxenton, and 15/- costs, or two calendar months in Northleach house of correction. Offence committed Wednesday 11 Sept. 1833. [*Endorsed* Allard committed to prison.]

52/D/43   28 Sept. 1833. Thomas Smith of Harescombe. Failing to pay the highway surveyor 10/- composition in lieu of labour etc. W. Goodrich JP and J. H. Byles JP. John Harris, surveyor of the highway within Harescombe, complainant. Fine 20/- and 3/- costs.

52/D/44   2 Oct. 1833. William Dunn of Almondsbury, labourer. Vagrancy: sleeping under a hayrick at Almondsbury and in a lead ore pit at Ridgewood. S. P. Peach JP at Tockington. Hard labour for three months in Lawfords Gate house of correction. Offence committed 23 and 27 Sept. 1833.

52/D/45   26 Aug. 1833. George Hall. Abusing returning churchgoers, particularly women, with obscene language at Cold Ashton. F. Trotman JP at Pucklechurch. Hard labour for one month in Horsley house of correction. Offence committed Sunday 25 Aug. 1833.

52/D/46   22 Aug. 1833. William Coates of Cranham, retail beer seller. Keeping his premises open for the sale and consumption of beer until 10.30 p.m. Sir W. Hicks, Bt., JP and J. Blagdon JP at a Petty Sessions for Cheltenham district. First offence. Fine £2 and 6/6 costs. Offence committed 19 Aug. 1833.

52/D/47   22 Aug. 1833. Thomas and Nancy Verrinder. Assaulting Joseph Horlick at Cranham. Sir W. Hicks, Bt., JP and J. Blagdon JP at Cheltenham. Thomas fined 10/- and 4/3 costs, and Nancy 5/- and 4/- costs. Offence committed 19 Aug. 1833.

52/D/48   15 Aug. 1833. John Wilson. Assaulting James Pocket at Cheltenham. T. J. Baines JP and J. Blagdon JP at Cheltenham. Fine 10/- and 4/6 costs. Offence committed 10 Aug. 1833.

52/D/49   6 Aug. 1833. Sophia Jones. Assaulting William Kellow at Cheltenham. R. B. Cooper JP and T. J. Baines JP at Cheltenham. Fine £5. Offence committed 31 July 1833.

52/D/50   6 Aug. 1833. Edward Charlwood. Stealing pears from a garden, the property of Joseph Moody, at Cheltenham. R. B. Cooper JP at Cheltenham. Fine 10/-, 1/- (the value of the pears) and 2/- costs.Offence committed 2 Aug. 1833.

52/D/51   30 July 1833. Richard Beard. Assaulting William Hatherell at Cheltenham. R. B. Cooper JP and T. J. Baines JP at Cheltenham. Fine 10/- and 4/- costs. Offence committed 29 July 1833.

52/D/52   25 July 1833. Thomas Mullins. Assaulting Henry Collins at Cheltenham. Sir W. Hicks, Bt., JP and R. B. Cooper JP at Cheltenham. Fine £2 and 5/- costs. Offence committed 23 July 1833.

52/D/53   23 July 1833. Thomas Lawrence, James Collins, Samuel Howly and William Craddock. Assaulting John Curtis at Cheltenham. Sir W. Hicks, Bt., JP and R. B. Cooper JP at Cheltenham. Fine 10/- and 4/- costs each. Offence committed 18 July 1833.

52/D/54   23 July 1833. Mary Conolly. Assaulting Esther Workman at Cheltenham. Sir W. Hicks, Bt., JP and R. B. Cooper JP at Cheltenham. Fine £1 and 6/6 costs. Offence committed 20 July 1833.

52/D/55   20 July 1833. Joseph Rone of Cheltenham, licensed victualler. Allowing drunkenness and disorderly behaviour on his premises. R. B. Cooper JP and T. J. Baines JP. First offence. Fine £2 and 9/6 costs. Offence committed 18 July 1833.

52/D/56   20 July 1833. John Packer. Assaulting Richard Payne at Cheltenham. T. Newell JP and T. J. Baines JP at Cheltenham. Fine £2 and 12/6 costs. Offence committed 17 July 1833.

52/D/57   18 July 1833. Michael Lynch. Assaulting James Fletcher at Cheltenham. R. B. Cooper JP and T. J. Baines JP at Cheltenham. Fine 10/- and 3/- costs. Offence committed 17 July 1833.

52/D/58   4 July 1833. Thomas Dyer. Assaulting Mary Collett at Cheltenham. T. Newell JP and T. J. Baines JP at Cheltenham. Fine 10/- and 8/- costs. Offence committed 3 July 1833.

52/D/59   5 Oct. 1833. George Oakey of Bishop's Cleeve, retail beer dealer. Keeping his premises open after 10 p.m. and allowing card playing and other disorderly behaviour. R. B. Cooper JP and T. J. Baines JP at a Petty Sessions for Cheltenham district. First offence. Fine £5 and £2 and 15/6 costs. Offence committed 28 Sept. 1833.

52/D/60   5 Oct. 1833. John Everis. Assaulting Thomas Sparrow at Cheltenham. R. B. Cooper JP and J. Blagdon JP at Cheltenham. Fine 10/- and 6/6 costs. Offence committed 2 Oct. 1833.

52/D/61   5 Oct. 1833. John Sole. Assaulting Stephen Law at Cheltenham. T. J. Baines JP and J. Blagdon JP at Cheltenham. Fine £1 and 3/- costs. Offence committed 3 Oct. 1833.

52/D/62   5 Oct. 1833. Henry Everiss. Assaulting Thomas Sparrow at Cheltenham. J. E. Viner JP and T. J. Baines JP at Cheltenham. Fine £1 and 6/- costs. Offence committed 2 Oct. 1833.

52/D/63   3 Oct. 1833. James Lawrence of Norton, yeoman. Trespassing in pursuit of game on land belonging to Nathaniel Clark Dyer Esq. at Norton. R. B. Cooper JP at Cheltenham. James Stephens, yeoman, of Boddington, complainant. Fine £1 and 12/- costs. Offence committed 26 Sept. 1833.

52/D/64   17 Sept. 1833. Edward Dutton. Assaulting John Collett at Cheltenham. Sir W. Hicks, Bt., JP and T. J. Baines JP at Cheltenham. Fine 2/6 and 7/6 costs. Offence committed 7 Sept. 1833.

52/D/65   12 Sept. 1833. William Morgan, retail beer seller, of Cheltenham. Allowing beer to be consumed on his premises between 3 p.m. and 5 p.m. on a Sunday. R. B. Cooper JP and T. J. Baines JP at a Petty Sessions for Cheltenham district. First offence. Fine £2 and 4/6 costs. Offence committed Sunday 8 Sept. 1833.

52/D/66   7 Sept. 1833. James Butler. Assaulting John Pitt at Cheltenham. Sir W. Hicks, Bt., JP and T. J. Baines JP at Cheltenham. Fine 5/- and 3/6 costs. Offence committed 3 Sept. 1833.

52/D/67   7 Sept. 1833. William Clifford. Assaulting Henry Hollands at Cheltenham. Sir W. Hicks, Bt., JP and T. J. Baines JP at Cheltenham. Fine £1 and 4/- costs. Offence committed 7 Sept. 1833.

52/D/68   5 Sept. 1833. Charles Wootton. Assaulting John Kerton at Cheltenham. R. B. Cooper JP and T. J. Baines JP at Cheltenham. Fine £1 and 6/6 costs. Offence committed 27 Aug. 1833.

52/D/69   31 Aug. 1833. William Verrinder. Assaulting Samuel Lovegrove at Cranham. R. B. Cooper JP and T. J. Baines JP at Cheltenham. Fine £2 and 7/6 costs. Offence committed 24 Aug. 1833.

52/D/70   27 Aug. 1833. William Milsom. Assaulting Stephen Laws at Cheltenham. Sir W. Hicks, Bt., JP and R. B. Cooper JP at Cheltenham. Fine 5/- and 3/- costs. Offence committed 26 Aug. 1833.

52/D/71   27 Aug. 1833. William Gibbins. Assaulting William Dean at Cheltenham. Sir W. Hicks, Bt., JP and R. B. Cooper JP at Cheltenham. Fine 10/- and 3/- costs. Offence committed 26 Aug. 1833.

52/D/72   27 Aug. 1833. William Collins, Henry Jeens and Nathaniel Chandler. Breaking the coping stone on a wall eleven yards long, the property of George Grendan Wall, at Cheltenham. Sir W. Hicks, Bt., JP at Cheltenham. Fine £2 and 2/- damages each and 10/6 costs. Offence committed 25 Aug. 1833.

52/D/73   1 Oct. 1833. John Shelton of Longborough, labourer. Using a ferret to kill rabbits on a Sunday at Sezincote. Rev. C. Jeaffreson JP at Longborough. Robert Bowles, complainant. Fine £2 and £1 costs or hard labour for one month in Northleach house of correction. Offence committed Sunday 18 Aug. 1833.

52/D/74   24 Sept. 1833. John Pulham, Thomas Driver and Richard Gardner. Stealing a quantity of pears from an orchard, the property of Thomas Hemming, at Moreton in Marsh. Rev. J. R. Hall JP at Moreton in Marsh. Fine 4/-, 3/- damages and 11/- costs or hard labour for one month in [Northleach] house of correction. Complainant not examined as to proof of offence. Offence committed 15 Sept. 1833.

52/D/75   20 Aug. 1833. John and George Butler. Assaulting William Lardner at Moreton in Marsh. Rev. J. R. Hall JP and Rev. C. Jeaffreson JP at Moreton in Marsh. Fine 10/-, to be paid to Ralph Wells, an overseer of the poor, and 16/- costs to the complainant, or one month in Northleach house of correction. Offence committed 11 Aug. 1833.

52/D/76   17 Sept. 1833. Sarah Hutchin. Assaulting Sophia Bartlett at Todenham. Rev. C. Jeaffresson JP and Rev. J. R. Hall JP at Moreton in Marsh. Fine 2/6, to be paid to Thomas Solloway, an overseer of the poor, and 11/6 costs to the complainant, or one month in Northleach house of correction. Offence committed 6 Sept. 1833.

52/D/77   3 Sept. 1833. Elizabeth Booker. Assaulting Ann Smith at Ebrington. Rev. J. R. Hall JP and Rev. C. Jeaffreson JP at Moreton in Marsh. Fine 5/-, to be paid to William Keyte, an overseer of the poor, and 15/- costs to the complainant, or one month in Northleach house of correction. Offence committed 27 Aug. 1833.

52/D/78   23 July 1833. Joseph Blotheridge. Assaulting John Terry at Chipping Campden. F. Colvile JP and Rev. J. R. Hall JP at Moreton in Marsh. Fine 1/-, to be paid to Peter Haines, an overseer of the poor, and 14/- costs to the complainant, or one month in Northleach house of correction. Offence committed 10 July 1833.

52/D/79   9 July 1833. William Jarvis of Ebrington, beer retailer. Allowing beer to be consumed after 10 p.m. W. Dickins JP and Rev. C. Jeaffreson JP at Moreton in Marsh. First offence. Fine £1 4s., 12/- of which awarded to Richard Fletcher of Ebrington, prosecutor, and the remainder to the county treasurer, and 16/- costs. Offence committed 17 June 1833.

52/D/80   16 Aug. 1833. John Evans. Leaving his wife and children chargeable to Uley parish. Benjamin Chapman Browne JP at Uley. Hard labour for two calendar months in Horsley house of correction. Offence committed 17 June 1833.

52/D/81   27 Sept. 1833. William Mills. Assault and battery on James Pritchard at Old Sodbury. Duke of Beaufort JP, F. Trotman JP, A. Shakespear JP, W. G. Davy JP, R. H. B. Hale JP and W. Blathwayt JP at Old Sodbury. Fine 10/-, to be paid to Robert Collins, overseer of the poor, and 17/10 to the complainant, or one month in Horsley house of correction. Offence committed Friday 13 Sept. 1833.

52/D/82   19 July 1833. Joseph Simms of Hillesley, Hawkesbury, beer retailer. Keeping his premises open for the sale and consumption of beer until 11 p.m. W. G. Davy JP and R. H. B. Hale JP at a Petty Sessions for Grumbalds Ash district. First offence. Fine 40/- and 19/- costs. Offence committed Saturday 22 June 1833.

52/D/83   21 July 1833. William Phipp, yeoman, of Lechlade, beer retailer [*erroneously named as Thomas Newport in part of the document*; *cf.* 52/D/84]. Keeping his house open for the sale and consumption of beer after 10 p.m. J. R. Barker JP for Bibury division. First offence. Fine 40/- and 5/- costs. Offence committed 10 July 1833.

52/D/84   6 Aug. 1833. Thomas Newport of Eastleach Turville, beer retailer. Keeping his house open for the sale and consumption of beer after 10 p.m. J. R. Barker JP and Rev. W. Price JP at a Petty Sessions for Bibury division. First offence. Fine 40/- and 5/- costs. Offence committed Monday 1 July 1833.

52/D/85   27 Aug. 1833. George Quarrel of Kemerton, yeoman. Using a gun without a game licence at Kemerton. Major General Thomas Marriott JP at the magistrates' office, Pershore, Worcs. Thomas Mumford, complainant. Mitigated fine of £2 10*s.* and 14/- costs or hard labour for two calendar months in the common gaol. Offence committed 16 Aug. 1833.

52/D/86   10 Oct. 1833. George Ball of Acton Turville. Setting a wire to catch hares at Acton Turville without a game certificate. I. J. Horlock JP and C. W. Codrington JP. William Watts of Great Badminton, complainant. Thomas Webb, gamekeeper to the duke of Beaufort, witness. Fine £5, to be paid to James Daw, an overseer of the poor, and £1 15*s.* costs, or hard labour for three calendar months in Horsley house of correction. Offence committed Tuesday 8 Oct. 1833.

53/A/1   11 Nov. 1833. Edward Carpenter of Newent, labourer. Damaging underwood at College Wood, Newent, the property of Miss Elizabeth Foley. O. Ricardo JP and R. F. Onslow JP at Newent. Fine 3*d.* and 10/9 costs, to be paid to the complainant, or hard labour for one calendar month in Littledean house of correction. Offence committed Sunday 13 Oct. 1833.

53/A/2   1 Nov. 1833. William Warren of Newent, labourer. Damaging underwood [*etc., as 53/A/1 except*] hard labour for six weeks [*and omitting* Sunday].

53/A/3   23 Dec. 1833. Thomas Bundy of Newent, beer retailer. Keeping his house open for the sale of beer between 3 p.m. and 5 p.m. on a Sunday. Rev. R. F. Onslow JP and R. F. Onslow JP at a Petty Sessions for Botloe hundred. First offence. Fine 40/-, one moiety of which to be paid to the informer and the remainder to the county treasurer. Offence committed Sunday 1 Dec. 1833.

53/A/4   2 Dec. 1833. William Lewis of Newent, farrier. Assaulting Moses Webley, tailor, of Newent without provocation. Rev. J. Commeline JP and R. F. Onslow JP at Newent. Fine 2/6 and 7/6 costs or fourteen days in Littledean house of correction. Offence committed 18 Nov. 1833.

53/A/5   23 Dec. 1833. Joseph Addis of Newent, labourer. Assaulting Thomas Joy the younger without provocation at Newent. O. Ricardo JP and Thomas Wallis JP at Newent. Fine £3 13*s.* and £1 7*s.* costs or two calendar months in Littledean house of correction. Offence committed 1 Dec. 1833.

53/A/6   23 Dec. 1833. William Ship. Damaging herbage in a field at Bitton, the property of Ann Knapp. J. Parker JP at Bitton. Fine 6*d.* damages and 7/- costs or hard labour for one calendar month in Lawfords Gate house of correction. Offence committed 20 Dec. 1833.

53/A/7   7 May 1833 [*late return*]. Edward Howell. Trespassing in pursuit of game at Wheatenhurst. T. J. Lloyd Baker JP and C. O. Cambridge JP at Wheatenhurst. Fine £2 and 7/6 costs. Given fourteen days to pay. Offence committed 15 Feb. 1833.

53/A/8   9 July 1833. Charles Aldridge. Using a wire to catch game at Frampton on Severn without a licence. Thomas Niblett JP and R. S. Davies JP at Wheatenhurst. Fine £5 and 7/6 costs or hard labour for one calendar month in Horsley house of correction. Offence committed 7 July 1833.

53/A/9   27 Dec. 1833. John White. Assaulting Edwin Jasper at Stonehouse. R. S. Davies JP and
D. Maclean JP at Stonehouse. Fine £2, to be paid to Joachim Cooper Hayward, overseer
of the poor, or one calendar month in Horsley house of correction. Offence committed
26 Dec. 1833.

53/A/10   27 Dec. 1833. Joseph Freeman. Assaulting Edward Sharp at Stonehouse. R. S. Davies JP
and D. Maclean JP at Stonehouse. Fine £2, to be paid to J. C. Hayward, overseer of the
poor, or two months in Horsley house of correction. Offence committed 26 Dec. 1833.

53/A/11   27 Dec. 1833. John Dangerfield and Reuben Owen. Assaulting John Sharp at
Stonehouse. R. S. Davies JP and D. Maclean JP at Stonehouse. Fine £4, to be paid to
J. C. Hayward, overseer of the poor, or two calendar months in Horsley house of
correction. Offence committed 26 Dec. 1833.

53/A/12   3 Dec. 1833. Job Hobbs. Leaving a timber carriage unattended on the turnpike road at
Ebley longer than necessary to unload it. T. J. Lloyd Baker JP and R. S. Davies JP at
Stonehouse. Fine £1, one moiety of which to go to the informer George Basham and the
remainder to the treasurer of the trustees for repairing the road on which the offence
occurred. Offence committed 18 Nov. 1833.

53/A/13   1 Oct. 1833. Drucilla Copner, [beer retailer], of Haresfield. Permitting drunkenness on her
premises. T. J. Lloyd Baker JP and R. S. Davies JP at a Petty Sessions for Whitstone
hundred. First offence. Fine 40/- and 10/- costs. Offence committed 23 Sept. 1833.

53/A/14   1 Oct. 1833. Drucilla Copner, [beer retailer], of Haresfield. Allowing beer to be consumed
on her premises after 10 p.m. [etc., as 53/A/13].

53/A/15   6 Aug. 1833. William Dangerfield. Assaulting constable Benjamin Brewer in the
execution of his duty at Stonehouse. T. J. Lloyd Baker JP and R. S. Davies JP at
Wheatenhurst. Fine £5. Given seven weeks to pay. In default, two months in Horsley
house of correction. Offence committed 19 July 1833.

53/A/16   4 June 1833 [late return]. William Pearce of Randwick. Permitting beer to be consumed
on his premises between 10 a.m. and 1 p.m. on a Sunday. Rev. J. Sayer JP and R. S.
Davies JP at a Petty Sessions for Whitstone hundred. First offence. Fine 40/- and 7/6
costs. Offence committed 26 May 1833.

53/A/17   17 Dec. 1833. Charles Webb and Amos Williams. Damaging a house at Hewelsfield, the
property of James Williams. E. Machen JP and P. J. Ducarel JP at Coleford in the Forest
division. Fine £1 damages and 14/- costs, to be paid to the complainant. Given six weeks
to pay. In default, one month's hard labour in Littledean house of correction. Offence
committed 19 Nov. 1833.

53/A/18   17 Dec. 1833. John Harris. Assaulting William Lewis of English Bicknor. E. Machen JP
and P. J. Ducarel JP at Coleford. Fine 10/-, to be paid to the overseer of the poor, and 8/-
costs to the complainant. Given four weeks to pay. In default, one calendar month in
Littledean house of correction. Offence committed 14 Sept. 1833.

53/A/19   17 Dec. 1833. Isaac Jones. Assaulting Elmes Benfield at Coleford. E. Machen JP and
P. J. Ducarel JP at Coleford. Fine 15/-, to be paid to the overseer of the poor of Newland,
and 7/- costs. Given four weeks to pay. In default, one calendar month in Littledean
house of correction. Offence committed 5 Dec. 1833.

53/A/20   17 Dec. 1833. Thomas Howells of Newland. Keeping and using a gun at Staunton
without a licence. E. Machen JP and P. J. Ducarel JP. Fine £2, to be paid to John Morgan,
an overseer of the poor, and 8/- costs to the complainant Timothy Jones. Given two
weeks to pay. In default, one calendar month in Littledean house of correction. Offence
committed 2 Oct. 1833.

53/A/21 4 Nov. 1833. Matthew Phelps. Assaulting Elizabeth his wife at Awre. C. Crawley JP and J. Pyrke JP at Newnham. Fine £4 10s., to be paid to William Jennings, overseer [of the poor] of Awre, and 10/- costs to Elizabeth Phelps, or hard labour for two calendar months in Littledean house of correction. Offence committed 7 Oct. 1833.

53/A/22 2 Dec. 1833. Benjamin Mason. Assaulting Joseph Bradley at St. Briavels hundred. C. Crawley JP and J. Pyrke JP at Newnham. Fine £4, to be paid to the high constable of St. Briavels hundred, and £1 costs, or hard labour for two calendar months in Littledean house of correction. Offence committed 16 Nov. 1833.

53/A/23 2 Dec. 1833. James Cooksey. Assaulting Joseph Bradley [etc., as 53/A/22].

53/A/24 4 Nov. 1833. William Russell. Damaging a walnut tree and stealing a quantity of walnuts at Westbury on Severn, the property of William Trigg. C. Crawley JP and J. Pyrke JP at Newnham. Fine 30/- damages and 10/- costs or hard labour for two calendar months in Littledean house of correction. Offence committed 6 Oct. 1833.

53/A/25 16 Dec. 1833. John Douglas. Keeping and using a gun at St. Briavels hundred without a game certificate. J. Pyrke JP. Fine £1, to be paid to the high constable of St. Briavels hundred, and £1 8s. costs to William Brooke, complainant, or two months in Littledean house of correction. Offence committed 4 Dec. 1833.

53/A/26 17 Dec. 1833. John Morgan. Assaulting Frederick Hawkins at St. Briavels hundred. P. J. Ducarel JP and E. Machen JP at Coleford. Fine £1, to be paid to the high constable of St. Briavels hundred, and 8/- costs, or hard labour for one calendar month in Littledean house of correction. Offence committed 10 Dec. 1833.

53/A/27 3 Dec. 1833. John Baynham. Assaulting William Hughes at St. Briavels hundred. T. Thomas JP and C. H. Morgan JP at Lydney. Fine 10/-, to be paid to the high constable of St. Briavels hundred, and 8/- costs. Given fourteen days to pay. In default, one calendar month in Littledean house of correction. Offence committed 16 Nov. 1833.

53/A/28 3 Dec. 1833. James Henry Ball of Woolaston, labourer. Keeping and using a dog to kill game at Woolaston without a licence. T. Thomas JP and C. H. Morgan JP. Fine £1 10s., to be paid to John James, an overseer of the poor, and 10/- costs to the complainant Edward Worgan, or one calendar month in Littledean house of correction. Offence committed 24 Nov. 1833.

53/A/29 17 Dec. 1833. Edwin Whitehouse, gentleman, of Newland. Trespassing 'with force and arms' in pursuit of game 'without the licence and consent' of the occupier John Worgan of Staunton near Coleford. E. Machen JP and P. J. Ducarel JP at Coleford. Offender seen with two others and two dogs by witness Timothy Jones, labourer. Offender did not appear. Fine £2, to be paid to John Morgan, overseer of the poor, and 8/- costs to be paid to the witness. In default of payment on demand, one calendar month in Littledean house of correction. Offence committed 2 Oct. 1833.

53/A/30 17 Dec. 1833. Alfred Whitehouse, gentleman, of Monmouth. Trespassing in pursuit of game on land in Staunton near Coleford occupied by John Worgan. E. Machen JP and P. J. Ducarel JP at Coleford. Timothy Jones, labourer, witness. Fine £2, to be paid to John Morgan, overseer of the poor, and 8/- costs to be paid to William Cox, the complainant. In default of payment on demand, one calendar month in Littledean house of correction. Offence committed 17 Oct. 1833.

53/A/31 17 Dec. 1833. Alfred Whitehouse, gentleman, of Monmouth. Trespassing in pursuit of game on land in Staunton near Coleford occupied by John Worgan. E. Machen JP and P. J. Ducarel JP at Coleford. Timothy Jones, labourer, and William Cox, witness and complainant respectively. Fine £2, to be paid to John Morgan, overseer of the poor, and 8/- costs to the complainant. In default of payment on demand, one calendar month in Littledean house of correction. Offence committed 2 Oct. 1833.

53/A/32   19 Dec. 1833. George Richards of Westbury on Trym. Allowing beer to be consumed on his premises between 10 a.m. and 1 p.m. on a Sunday. H. W. Newman JP and W. Munro JP at a Petty Sessions for part of Berkeley division. Fine £2 including costs. Offence committed 8 Dec. 1833.

53/A/33   19 Dec. 1833. Charles Edwards of Westbury on Trym. Allowing beer [etc., as 53/A/32].

53/A/34   7 Nov. 1833. Charles Lovell, [beer retailer], of St. Philip and St. Jacob, [Bristol]. Allowing gaming on his premises. J. Parker JP and H. W. Newman JP at a Petty Sessions for part of Berkeley division. First offence. Fine £2 10s. including costs. Offence committed 30 Oct. 1833.

53/A/35   21 Nov. 1833. Thomas and William Hopes. Assaulting Ann Caple at Bitton. J. Parker JP and G. Goldney JP at Lawfords Gate sessions room. Fine £1 each and 8/- costs or six weeks in Lawfords Gate house of correction. Offence committed 11 Nov. 1833.

53/A/36   14 Nov. 1833. John Haskins. Assaulting Jane Godfrey at Bitton. Rev. W. Mirehouse JP and G. Goldney JP at Lawfords Gate sessions room. Fine 12/- and 8/- costs or one calendar month in Lawfords Gate house of correction. Offence committed 4 Nov. 1833.

53/A/37   7 Nov. 1833. William and Thomas Henley. Assaulting John Henley at St. Philip and St. Jacob, [Bristol]. H. W. Newman JP and J. Parker JP at Lawfords Gate sessions room. Fine 3/- and 7/- costs or one calendar month in Lawfords Gate house of correction. Offence committed 28 Oct. 1833.

53/A/38   14 Nov. 1833. Alfred Wiltshire. Assaulting Joseph Osborne at Frampton Cotterell. Rev. W. Mirehouse JP and J. Parker JP at Lawfords Gate sessions room. Fine 12/- and 8/- costs or one calendar month in Lawfords Gate house of correction. Offence committed 11 Nov. 1833.

53/A/39   31 Oct. 1833. James Bennett. Assaulting John Flower at St. Philip and St. Jacob, [Bristol]. H. W. Newman JP and Rev. W. Mirehouse JP at Lawfords Gate sessions room. Fine 4/- and 6/- costs or ten days in Lawfords Gate house of correction. Offence committed 23 Oct. 1833.

53/A/40   31 Oct. 1833. George Osborne. Assaulting Mary Thomas at St. Philip and St. Jacob, [Bristol]. H. W. Newman JP and Rev. W. Mirehouse JP at Lawfords Gate sessions room. Fine 1/- and 12/- costs or ten days in Lawfords Gate house of correction. Offence committed 28 Oct. 1833.

53/A/41   31 Oct. 1833. Samuel Bishop. Assaulting Eliza Thomas at St. Philip and St. Jacob, [Bristol] [etc., as 53/A40].

53/A/42   24 Oct. 1833. Joseph Brittain and William Phipps. Assaulting James Rogers at Bitton. H. W. Newman JP and W. Fripp JP at Lawfords Gate sessions room. Fine 2/6 and 7/- costs or seven days in Lawfords Gate house of correction. Offence committed 20 Oct. 1833.

53/A/43   19 Dec. 1833. William Evans. Assaulting John Grant at Clifton. W. Munro JP and W. Fripp JP at Lawfords Gate sessions room. Fine 10/- and 5/6 costs or fourteen days in Lawfords Gate house of correction. Offence committed 10 Dec. 1833.

53/A/44   12 Dec. 1833. Charles Tucker. Assaulting Henry Williams at Westbury on Trym. A. G. H. Battersby JP and W. Munro JP at Lawfords Gate sessions room. Fine 5/- and 6/6 costs or one calendar month in Lawfords Gate house of correction. Offence committed 17 [sic, ? recte 7] Dec. 1833.

53/A/45   5 Nov. 1833. William Ferris. Assaulting Daniel and Henry Briggs at St. Philip and St. Jacob, [Bristol]. J. Cave JP and H. W. Newman JP at Lawfords Gate sessions room. Fine 5/- and 6/6 costs or seven days in Lawfords Gate house of correction. Offence committed 29 Oct. 1833.

53/A/46 16 Dec. 1833. Richard Kirk. Stealing turnips at Winterbourne, the property of Thomas Lawrence, yeoman. Rev. W. Mirehouse JP at Winterbourne. Fine 6/- and 7/6 costs or hard labour for one calendar month in Lawfords Gate house of correction. Offence committed 13 Dec. 1833.

53/A/47 21 Oct. 1833. Edward Jones. Stealing a dog valued at £6 from George Adams of Winterbourne. Rev. W. Mirehouse JP at Lawfords Gate sessions room. Fine £14 including costs and £6 (the value of the dog), or six calendar months in Lawfords Gate house of correction. Offence committed 30 Sept. 1833.

53/A/48 3 Nov. 1833. William Herbert of Stourton [*MS*. Stowerton], [Warws.]. Using a gun to kill game at Todenham without a game certificate. W. Dickins JP and F. Colvile JP at Moreton in Marsh. Fine £3, to be paid to Thomas Solloway, overseer of the poor, and 10/- costs to the complainant William Randall, or hard labour for two calendar months in Northleach house of correction. Offence committed 25 Oct. 1833.

53/A/49 25 Nov. 1833. William Bryan of Sutton under Brailes, labourer. Using a gun to kill game in Todenham without a game certificate. W. Dickins JP and F. Colvile JP. Fine £5, to be paid to Thomas Solloway, overseer of the poor, or hard labour for three calendar months in Northleach house of correction. Offence committed 25 Oct. 1833.

53/A/50 19 Nov. 1833. George Gardner of Bourton on the Hill. Assaulting Robert Bowles at Bourton on the Hill. Rev. J. R. Hall JP and F. Colvile JP at Moreton in Marsh. Fine 10/- and 12/6 costs or one month in Northleach house of correction. Offence committed 15 Nov. 1833.

53/A/51 19 Nov. 1833. William Hooper of Moreton in Marsh, labourer. Using snares (or gins) to kill game at Todenham without a game certificate. Rev. J. R. Hall JP and F. Colvile JP at Moreton in Marsh. William Randall, complainant. Fine £5 and 10/- costs or hard labour for two months in Northleach house of correction. Offence committed 18 Nov. 1833.

53/A/52 19 Nov. 1833. William Cook and George Brown of Moreton in Marsh, labourers. Using snares (or gins) [*etc., as* 53/A/51 *except*] Each fined £5 and 10/- costs.

53/A/53 3 Dec. 1833. James Eastbury of Moreton in Marsh, labourer. Using snares to kill game at Lemington [*MS*. Lemingington] without a game certificate. Rev. J. R. Hall JP and F. Colvile JP at Moreton in Marsh. George Fletcher, complainant. Fine £5 and 10/- costs or hard labour for two months in Northleach house of correction. Offence committed 17 Nov. 1833.

53/A/54 10 Dec. 1833. Thomas Cinders and Thomas Lambert. Damaging underwood at Rook Wood, occupied by Samuel Ashley of Wick and Abson. F. Trotman JP and W. G. Davy JP at Pucklechurch. Fine 10/- each, to be paid to Emmerson Gerrish, overseer of the poor, and £1 8*s*. 6*d*. [costs] and 3/- damages to the complainant, or hard labour for one calendar month in Horsley house of correction. Offence committed Friday 29 Nov. 1833.

53/A/55 2 Dec. 1833. Titus Baglin. Leaving his three children chargeable to Uley parish for almost five months. B. C. Browne JP at Uley. Hard labour for six weeks in Horsley house of correction. Offence committed 17 July 1833.

53/A/56 14 Nov. 1833. James Cole of Horsley, labourer. Assaulting Henry Horn, sawyer, of Nympsfield at Avening. H. Burgh JP and Henry Wyatt JP at Stroud. Fine £5 or two calendar months in Horsley house of correction. Offence committed 28 Oct. 1833.

53/A/57 15 Nov. 1833. Charles Hall, Samuel Hall, Daniel Holbrow and William Lodge. Vagrancy: lodging in an outhouse in Stroud; no visible means of subsistence. H. Burgh JP, D. Maclean JP, H. Wyatt JP, William Henry Stanton JP, E. G. Hallewell JP and Peter Leversage JP at Stroud. Hard labour for three calendar months in Horsley house of correction. Offence committed 14 Nov. 1833.

53/A/58   18 Nov. 1833. Samuel Deane of Stroud, labourer. Cutting down and stealing three ash trees and one maple tree growing in a wood in Stroud, the property of John Lewis Esq. and the representatives of the late Richard Harris. H. Burgh JP at Stroud. Fine £5, to be paid to an overseer of the poor, and 4/- damages to the complainants, or hard labour for two calendar months in Horsley house of correction. Offence committed 16 Nov. 1833.

53/A/59   29 Nov. 1833. Thomas Blanch of Stroud, labourer. Assaulting John Shipway, constable of Stroud, in the execution of his duty. H. Burgh JP, J. Mills JP, H. Wyatt JP and E. G. Hallewell JP at Stroud. Fine £2 and 10/- costs or two calendar months in Horsley house of correction. Offence committed 16 Nov. 1833.

53/A/60   27 Nov. 1833. Isaac Smith of Bisley, labourer. Assaulting Ezra Gardner of Stroud, bailiff, at Bisley. H. Burgh JP, J. Mills JP, H. Wyatt JP and E. G. Hallewell JP at Stroud. Fine 10/- and 9/- costs or two calendar months in Horsley house of correction. Offence committed 19 Nov. 1833.

53/A/61   2 Dec. 1833. John Hill of Nympsfield, labourer. Using a net to kill game at Nympsfield without a game certificate. H. Burgh JP and E. G. Hallewell JP at Stroud. Fine £5 or hard labour for three calendar months in Horsley house of correction. Offence committed 30 Nov. 1833.

53/A/62   9 Dec. 1833. George Lacey. Vagrancy: wandering abroad; no visible means of subsistence, at Stroud. H. Burgh JP at Stroud. Hard labour for fourteen days in Horsley house of correction. Offence committed 6 Dec. 1833.

53/A/63   13 Dec. 1833. Thomas Chandler of Stroud, weaver. Possessing almost 30 lb. of various woollen yarns and waste and one yard of woollen cloth believed to be stolen. H. Burgh JP, J. Mills JP, D. Maclean JP, H. Wyatt JP, E. G. Hallewell JP, N. S. Marling JP and P. Leversage JP. Francis Pickard, constable of Stroud, and Thomas Jones, clothier, of Bisley, witnesses. Fine £20, half to be paid to George Holmes, clothworker, of Minchinhampton, the informer, and the remainder to Stroud dispensary. Offence committed 25 Oct. 1833.

53/A/64   13 Dec. 1833. John Rogers. Failing to maintain his wife and child in Stroud whereby they became chargeable to the parish. H. Burgh JP at Stroud. Hard labour for one calendar month in Horsley house of correction. Offence committed 5 Dec. 1833.

53/A/65   31 Oct. 1833. Elizabeth Elliot. Stealing turnips at Avening, the property of Daniel Harvey. D. Ricardo JP at Horsley. Fine 6d., to be paid to George Whitley, overseer of the poor, 4/6 costs and 6d. damages to the complainant. Given nine days to pay. Offence committed 29 Oct. 1833.

53/A/66   31 Oct. 1833. Mary Hopes, Hannah Hopes and Ann Woods. Stealing parts of trees at Avening, the property of Wiliam Playne Esq. R. Kingscote JP and T. Kingscote JP at Horsley. Fine 1/-, to be paid to George Whitley, an overseer of the poor, 8/- costs and 2/- damages to the complainant, or fourteen days in Horsley house of correction. Offence committed 15 Oct. 1833.

53/A/67   31 Oct. 1833. Charlotte Mann. Stealing half a bushel of turnips growing on land belonging to Daniel Harvey at Avening. T. R. Haycock JP at Horsley. Fine 6d., to be paid to George Whitley, an overseer of the poor, 6d. damages and 4/6 costs to the complainant. Given nine days to pay. Offence committed 29 Oct. 1833.

53/A/68   22 Aug. 1833. William Walkley of Horsley, beer retailer. Keeping his premises open for the sale of beer between 3 p.m. and 5 p.m. on a Sunday. Rev. H. Campbell JP, D. Ricardo

JP, T. Kingscote JP and W. Playne JP at a Petty Sessions for Longtree division. First offence. Fine 40/- and 9/6 costs. Offence committed 28 July 1833.

53/A/69 23 Dec. 1833. William Smith of Stroud, labourer. Assaulting Mary Davis of Stroud. H. Burgh JP, H. Wyatt JP and E. G. Hallewell JP at Stroud. Fine £5 or two calendar months in Horsley house of correction. Offence committed 21 Dec. 1833.

53/A/70 24 Dec. 1833. Abednego Clifford of Avening, labourer. Trespassing in search of game on the property of Thomas, Lord Ducie, at Avening. H. Burgh JP at Stroud. Gamekeeper John Webb, complainant. Fine £2, to be paid to George Whitley, an overseer of the poor, and 9/- costs to the complainant, or hard labour for two calendar months in Horsley house of correction. Offence committed 1 Nov. 1833.

53/A/71 25 Oct. 1833. William Cockshut of Stroud, labourer. Using a trap to kill game at Stroud without a certificate. H. Burgh JP, J. Mills JP, D. Maclean JP, W. H. Stanton JP, E. G. Hallewell JP, N. S. Marling JP and P. Leversage JP at Stroud. Fine £5, to be paid to George Whitley, an overseer of the poor, and 8/- costs to gamekeeper John Gay, the complainant, or two calendar months' hard labour in Horsley house of correction. Offence committed 5 Oct. 1833.

53/A/72 1 Nov. 1833. John Gibbins of Minchinhampton, labourer. Using a gun to kill game at Avening without a game certificate. H. Burgh JP, D. Maclean JP, W. H. Stanton JP, E. G. Hallewell JP, N. S. Marling JP and P. Leversage JP. Fine £5, to be paid to George Whitley, overseer of the poor, and 6/- costs to the complainant Samuel Baker of Avening, gamekeeper, or hard labour for two calendar months in Horsley house of correction. Offence committed 20 Oct. 1833.

53/A/73 1 Nov. 1833. John Gibbins of Minchinhampton, labourer. Using a gun to kill game at Avening on a Sunday. H. Burgh JP, D. Maclean JP, H. Wyatt JP, W. H. Stanton JP, N. S. Marling JP and P. Leversage JP at Stroud. Fine £5, to be paid to George Whitley, an overseer of the poor, and 6/- costs to the complainant Samuel Baker, gamekeeper, of Avening, or hard labour for two calendar months in Horsley house of correction. Offence committed 20 Oct. 1833.

53/A/74 1 Nov. 1833. Charles Pilsworth of Minchinhampton, cordwainer. Using a gun to kill game at Avening without a game certificate. H. Burgh JP, D. Maclean JP, H. Wyatt JP, W. H. Stanton JP, N. S. Marling JP and P. Leversage JP at Stroud. Fine £5, to be paid to George Whitley, an overseer of the poor, and 6/- costs to the complainant Samuel Baker, gamekeeper, of Avening, or hard labour for two calendar months in Horsley house of correction. Offence committed 20 Oct. 1833.

53/A/75 1 Nov. 1833. Charles Pilsworth of Minchinhampton, cordwainer. Using a gun to kill game at Avening on a Sunday [etc., as 53/A/74].

53/A/76 31 Oct. 1833. Simeon Tainton of Avening, labourer. Assaulting constable Thomas Cordy of Nympsfield in the execution of his duty at Avening. H. Burgh JP and N. S. Marling JP at Stroud. Fine £5 or two calendar months in Horsley house of correction. Offence committed 28 Oct. 1833.

53/A/77 1 Nov. 1833. James Walkley of Woodchester, labourer. Assaulting constable Thomas Cordy of Nympsfield in the execution of his duty at Avening. H. Burgh JP, D. Maclean JP, H. Wyatt JP, N. S. Marling JP and P. Leversage JP at Stroud. Fine £5 or two calendar months in Horsley house of correction. Offence committed 28 Oct. 1833.

53/A/78 2 Nov. 1833. Elijah Clifford, labourer, of Avening. Trespassing in search of game in Avening on land belonging to Thomas, Lord Ducie. H. Burgh JP. Gamekeeper George Wilcockson of Nympsfield, complainant. Fine £2, to be paid to George Whitley, an overseer of the poor, and 6/- costs, or hard labour for two calendar months in Horsley house of correction. Offence committed 1 Nov. 1833.

53/A/79 5 Dec. 1833. Charles and Elizabeth Wilkinson. Committing an assault at Cheltenham [*victim not named*]. R. B. Cooper JP and J. E. Viner JP at Cheltenham. Each fined 5/6 costs, to be paid to an overseer of the poor. Offence committed — Dec. 1833.

53/A/80 3 Dec. 1833. William Coleman. Assaulting John James at Dowdeswell. R. B. Cooper JP and J. E. Viner JP at Cheltenham. Fine 10/- and 5/6 costs. [*Date of offence not given.*]

53/A/81 26 Nov. 1833. Isaac Gregory. Assaulting Thomas Wasley at Cheltenham. R. B. Cooper JP and T. J. Baines JP at Cheltenham. Fine 10/- and 3/- costs. Offence committed 23 Nov. 1833.

53/A/82 21 Nov. 1833. John Bethel. Assaulting Sarah Addis at Cheltenham. R. B. Cooper JP and J. E. Viner JP at Cheltenham. Fine 2/- and 8/- costs. Offence committed 14 Nov. 1833.

53/A/83 19 Nov. 1833. John Tanner. Assaulting Joseph Symonds at Cheltenham. R. B. Cooper JP and J. E. Viner JP at Cheltenham. Fine 5/- and 3/- costs. Offence committed 17 Nov. 1833.

53/A/84 16 Nov. 1833. William Holder. Assaulting Eliza Craddock at Cheltenham. R. B. Cooper JP and T. J. Baines JP at Cheltenham. Fine 10/- and 3/- costs. Offence committed 13 Nov. 1833.

53/A/85 7 Nov. 1833. Sarah Weston. Assaulting Mary Stump at Cheltenham. R. B. Cooper JP and J. E. Viner JP at Cheltenham. Fine 10/- and 5/6 costs. Offence committed 2 Nov. 1833.

53/A/86 9 Nov. 1833. James Dodwell of Cheltenham, labourer. Trespassing in pursuit of game on the property of John Gardner Esq. at Cheltenham. Sir W. Hicks, Bt., JP and R. B. Cooper JP at Cheltenham. George Russell of Cheltenham, complainant. Fine £2, to be paid to William Allen, overseer of the poor, and 5/6 costs, or two months in Northleach house of correction. Offence committed at about 2 p.m. 29 Oct. 1833.

53/A/87 9 Nov. 1833. William Green of Cheltenham, yeoman. Using a gun without a game licence at Cheltenham. Sir W. Hicks, Bt., JP and R. B. Cooper JP at Cheltenham. George Russell, complainant. Fine £5, to be paid to William Allen, an overseer of the poor, and 5/6 costs, or three calendar months in Northleach house of correction. Offence committed 29 Oct. 1833.

53/A/88 9 Nov. 1833. Mary Sevell. Assaulting Joanna Kench at Cheltenham. Sir W. Hicks, Bt., JP and R. B. Cooper JP at Cheltenham. Fine 2/6 and 6/6 costs. Offence committed 6 Nov. 1833.

53/A/89 7 Nov. 1833. John Peart of Bishop's Cleeve, yeoman. Trespassing in pursuit of game on the property of the Hon. Berkeley Craven in Bishop's Cleeve. R. B. Cooper JP. John Barnes, labourer, of Bishop's Cleeve, complainant. Fine £2 and 7/- costs. Offence committed about noon 2 Nov. 1833.

53/A/90 5 Nov. 1833. Thomas Everill. Assaulting William Jackson at Cheltenham. R. B. Cooper JP and T. J. Baines JP at Cheltenham. Fine £1 and 7/6 costs. Offence committed 1 Nov. 1833.

53/A/91 10 Dec. 1833. John Moody. Assaulting Sarah Hunt at Cheltenham. J. E. Viner JP and T. J. Baines JP at Cheltenham. Fine £2 and 4/- costs. Offence committed 7 Dec. 1833.

53/A/92 10 Dec. 1833. Edward Brainsford of Cheltenham, licensed beer retailer. Having his premises open for the sale of beer at 4 p.m. on a Sunday. J. E. Viner JP and T. J. Baines JP. First offence. Fine £2 and 6/6 costs. Offence committed 8 Dec. 1833.

53/A/93 10 Dec. 1833. Samuel Bullock of Cheltenham, licensed retail beer dealer. Having his premises open for the sale of beer [*etc.*, *as* 53/A/92 *except*] 5/6 costs.

53/A/94 10 Dec. 1833. Thomas Day of Cheltenham. Licensed retail beer dealer. Permitting illegal games, i.e. card-playing, and other disorderly conduct on his premises. J. E. Viner JP and T. J. Baines JP. First offence. Fine £3 and 5/6 costs. Offence committed 7 Dec. 1833.

53/A/95 10 Dec. 1833. Charles Dawes. Assaulting William Pimble at Cheltenham. J. E. Viner JP and T. J. Baines JP at Cheltenham. Fine 5/- and 5/6 costs. Offence committed — Dec. 1833.

53/A/96 24 Oct. 1833. James Ridler of Cheltenham, licensed retail beer dealer. Keeping his premises open for the sale of beer until 11 p.m. R. B. Cooper JP and T. J. Baines JP. First offence. Fine £2 and 5/6 costs. Offence committed 20 Oct. 1833.

53/A/97 22 Oct. 1833. John Trickey. Assaulting Mary Parker Butt at Cheltenham. J. E. Viner JP and T. J. Baines JP at Cheltenham. Fine 10/- and 3/- costs. Offence committed 20 Oct. 1833.

53/A/98 19 Oct. 1833. John Gwinnett. Assaulting Thomas Tarling at Bishop's Cleeve. J. E. Viner JP and T. J. Baines JP at Cheltenham. Fine £1 and 9/6 costs. Offence committed 17 Oct. 1833.

53/A/99 19 Oct. 1833. Samuel Davidson. Assaulting Stephen Lewis at Cheltenham. J. E. Viner JP and T. J. Baines JP at Cheltenham. Fine £1 and 3/- costs. Offence committed 17 Oct. 1833.

53/A/100 3 Dec. 1833. James Bevan of Cheltenham, licensed beer retailer. Keeping his premises open for the sale of beer until 1 a.m. R. B. Cooper JP and J. E. Viner JP. First offence. Fine £2 and 6/6 costs. Offence committed night of 1 Dec. 1833.

53/A/101 22 Oct. 1833. Charles Turk. Assaulting William Dean at Cheltenham. R. B. Cooper JP and T. J. Baines JP at Cheltenham. Fine 10/- and 3/- costs. Offence committed 20 Oct. 1833.

53/A/102 19 Oct. 1833. Charles Wood of Bishop's Cleeve, labourer. Trespassing in pursuit of game on the property of the Hon. Augustus Berkeley Craven at Bishop's Cleeve. J. E. Viner JP at Cheltenham. Offender admitted charge. Fine £2 and 5/6 costs. Offence committed about noon 7 Oct. 1833.

53/A/103 21 Dec. 1833. Richard Harman of Cheltenham, licensed retail beer dealer. Having his premises open for the sale of beer at 4 p.m. on a Sunday. R. B. Cooper JP and T. J. Baines JP. First offence [*but cf.* 51/D/80, 52/C/73]. Fine £2 and 5/6 costs. Offence committed 15 Dec. 1833.

53/A/104 21 Dec. 1833. Henry Gore of Cheltenham, licensed retail beer dealer. Permitting illegal games on his premises. R. B. Cooper JP and T. J. Baines JP. First offence. Fine £3 and 5/6 costs. Offence committed 14 Dec. 1833.

53/A/105 19 Dec. 1833. Henry Field and John Hayward. Assaulting Thomas Hayward at Cheltenham. R. B. Cooper JP and T. J. Baines JP at Cheltenham. Fine 10/- and 3/- costs each. Offence committed 18 Dec. 1833.

53/A/106 5 Dec. 1833. Berther Herbert of Prestbury, yeoman. Trespassing in pursuit of game at Prestbury on the property of Thomas Edwards Esq. R. B. Cooper JP at Cheltenham. John Robinson, yeoman, of Prestbury, complainant. Fine £2 and 5/6 costs. Offence committed 5 Dec. 1833.

53/A/107 12 Dec. 1833. George Lucas of Cheltenham, licensed retail beer dealer. Keeping his premises open for the sale and consumption of beer until 10.30 p.m. R. B. Cooper JP and T. J. Baines JP. First offence. Fine £2 and 5/6 costs. Offence committed 7 Dec. 1833.

53/A/108 10 Dec. 1833. John Shill of Witcombe, yeoman. Trespassing in pursuit of game at Cowley on the property of Dr. Lawrence. T. J. Baines JP at Cheltenham. James Burrows, yeoman, of Witcombe, complainant. Fine £2 and 6/- costs. Offence committed about 1 p.m. 29 Nov. 1833.

53/A/109 31 Oct. 1833. James Robinson of Cheltenham, licensed retail beer dealer. Permitting illegal card games on his premises. R. B. Cooper JP and T. J. Baines JP. First offence. Fine £5 and 6/6 cost. Offence committed 27 Oct. 1833.

53/A/110 31 Oct. 1833. John Hill. Assaulting Henry Holland at Cheltenham. R. B. Cooper JP and T. J. Baines JP. Fine 10/- and 3/- costs. Offence committed 29 Oct. 1833.

53/A/111 29 Oct. 1833. John Matthews. Stealing four plants from a garden, the property of William Halford of Cheltenham. R. B. Cooper JP and J. E. Viner JP at Cheltenham. Fine 5/- and 5/6 costs. Offence committed 20 Oct. 1833.

53/A/112 29 Oct. 1833. William Cotton. Assaulting Jesse Castle at Cheltenham. R. B. Cooper JP and J. E. Viner JP at Cheltenham. Fine £1 and 3/- costs. Offence committed 28 Oct. 1833.

53/A/113 24 Oct. 1833. George Nash. Assaulting John Cook at Leckhampton. R. B. Cooper JP and T. J. Baines JP at Cheltenham. Fine £1 and 7/- costs. Offence committed 10 Oct. 1833.

53/A/114 24 Oct. 1833. James Hill and Samuel Cherrington. Assaulting John Matthews at Leckhampton. R. B. Cooper JP and T. J. Baines JP at Cheltenham. Each fined £1 and 7/- costs. Offence committed 10 Oct. 1833.

53/A/115 22 Oct. 1833. John Baylis. Assaulting Joseph Symonds at Cheltenham. R. B. Cooper JP and T. J. Baines JP at Cheltenham. Fine £1 and 3/- costs. Offence committed 20 Oct. 1833.

53/A/116 22 Oct. 1833. Richard Jones of Bishop's Cleeve, yeoman. Trespassing in pursuit of game on the property of the Hon. Augustus Berkeley Craven at Bishop's Cleeve. R. B. Cooper JP. Fine £2 and 6/- costs. Offender admitted charge. Offence committed 3 Oct. 1833.

53/A/117 18 Nov. 1833. James Stephens of Batheaston, Som., labourer. Trespassing with others with a spaniel, a ferret and nets in search of game on land at Combs in Marshfield occupied by Robert Grainger. C. W. Codrington JP and I. J. Horlock JP at Dodington. Fine £1, to be paid to James Barton, overseer of the poor of Marshfield, and 11/- costs to the complainant Thomas Fletcher. Given fourteen days to pay. In default, two calendar months' hard labour in Horsley house of correction. Offence committed 10 Nov. 1833.

53/A/118 18 Nov. 1833. Edward Trotman of Batheaston, Som., labourer. Trespassing [etc., as 53/A/117].

53/A/119 18 Nov. 1833. Henry Wiltshire of Batheaston, Som. labourer. Trespassing with others with a spaniel, a ferret and nets in search of game on land at Combs in Marshfield occupied by Robert Grainger. C. W. Codrington JP and I. J. Horlock JP at Dodington. Fine 5/-, to be paid to James Barton, an overseer of the poor, and 11/- costs to the complainant Thomas Fletcher. Given seven days to pay. In default, one calendar month's hard labour in Horsley house of correction. Offence committed 10 Nov. 1833.

53/A/120 18 Nov. 1833. George Shill of Batheaston, Som., labourer. Trespassing [etc., as 53/A/119].

53/A/121 6 Dec. 1833. Edwin Page, gentleman, of Pucklechurch. Trespassing in search of game at Shortwood on land occupied by John Haskins. F. Trotman JP, A. Shakespear JP and R. H. B. Hale JP at a Petty Sessions held at the Old Cross Hands inn, Old Sodbury. Information given by John Haskins on 28 Oct. Offender did not appear. Benjamin Guy Philips Esq., witness, said he saw his pheasants were disturbed. On investigation found three dogs hunting and two men, one he recognized as William Tompson, a neighbour.

The other carried a gun and produced a certificate showing him to be Edwin Page. Asked if his intention was to kill witness's pheasants, said that he would if he saw them. Fine 10/-, to be paid to Joel Baber, overseer of the poor, and £1 9s. 9d. costs to John Haskins, or one calendar month in Horsley house of correction. Offence committed 4 Oct. 1833.

53/A/122 6 Dec. 1833. William Tompson of Pucklechurch, tiler and plasterer. Trespassing in pursuit of game at Shortwood Hill, Pucklechurch, on land occupied by John Haskins, farmer. F. Trotman JP, A. Shakespear JP and R. H. B. Hale JP at a Petty Sessions held at the Old Cross Hands inn, Old Sodbury, at 11 a.m. Information given three days earlier by John Haskins, and summons issued. Defendant did not appear. Circumstantial evidence given [see 53/A/121] by Benjamin Guy Philips. Witness George Martin, labourer, of Pucklechurch, said that accused had told him of having shot a pheasant in Haskins's little paddock and another in Farmer Tiler's field. Witness thought this incident to be that now under consideration. Fine 5/-, to be paid to Joel Baber, an overseer of the poor, and £1 9s. 9d. costs to the complainant, or one month in Horsley house of correction. Offence committed 4 Oct. 1833.

53/A/123 27 Dec. 1833. Richard Lapper of Hazleton, toll-collector at Puesdown Gate. Demanding 1/4 toll from Francis Martindale, driver of a public stage-coach drawn by four horses, although he was exempt having paid the toll when passing through from Northleach to Cheltenham earlier the same day. Rev. T. B. Newell JP and Rev. T. L. Lane JP. Fine 50/-. Offence committed 9 Dec. 1833.

53/A/124 20 Nov. 1833. George Pettiford. Using nets for taking game at Rodmarton. T. G. B. Estcourt JP and W. M. Paul JP at Tetbury. Fine £2, to be paid to an overseer of the poor, and 12/6 costs to the complainant Michael Shipton. Given fourteen days to pay. In default, two calendar months' hard labour in Horsley house of correction. Offence committed Sunday 10 Nov. 1833.

53/A/125 20 Nov. 1833. Job Welsh. Using nets to take game at Rodmarton T. G. B. Estcourt JP and W. M. Paul JP at Tetbury. Fine £2, to be paid to an overseer of the poor, and 10/- costs to the complainant Michael Shipton, or two months in Horsley house of correction. Offence committed Sunday 10 Nov. 1833.

53/A/126 20 Nov. 1833. Robert Harrington Bush and Charles Bush. Trespassing on Lord Ducie's land in search of game. T. G. B. Estcourt JP at Tetbury. Fine £2 each, to be paid to an overseer of the poor, and 6/6 costs each to the complainant William Evans. Offence committed 1 Oct. 1833.

53/A/127 23 Oct. 1833. Thomas Smith and Richard Pugh, labourers, of Kemerton. Riotous assembly, with others, breaking the peace with fighting and other disorderly conduct at Kemerton. J. Timbrill D.D. JP and Rev. J. Keysall at Tewkesbury. Fine 10/-, to be paid to John Bee, an overseer of the poor, and 7/6 each costs to Thomas Quarrel, the complainant. Offence committed Sunday 28 July 1833. [Note on document:] Received of White 5s.

53/A/128 20 Nov. 1833. George Quarrell the younger of Kemerton. Using a gun to kill game without first obtaining a licence. J. Timbrill D.D. JP and Rev. J. Keysall JP at Tewkesbury, commissioners for assessed taxes for lower Tewkesbury district. Fine £10. Offence committed 15 Aug. 1833.

53/A/129 4 Dec. 1833. Thomas Allard of the Fleet public house, Twyning. Permitting beer to be consumed between 10 [a.m.] and 1 [p.m.] on a Sunday. J. Timbrill D.D. JP, Rev. J. Keysall JP and J. W. Martin JP. First offence. Fine 20/- and 8/6 costs. Offence committed 24 Nov. 1833.

53/A/130 18 Dec. 1833. John Howes of Forthampton, cowman. Assaulting Philip Redding, labourer, of Forthampton without provocation. J. Timbrill D.D. JP, Rev. J. Keysall JP and J. W. Martin JP at Tewkesbury. Fine 20/-, to be paid to Edward Knight, an overseer of the poor, and 11/10 costs to the complainant. Offence committed Monday 2 Dec. 1833.

53/A/131 18 Dec. 1833. James Hochkins and Collingwood Price, both of Twyning. Assaulting John Strawford without provocation. J. Timbrill D.D. JP, Rev. J. Keysall JP and J. W. Martin JP at Tewkesbury. Fine 5/- each, to be paid to Peter Dee, an overseer of the poor, and 3/10 each costs to the complainant. Offence committed 15 Dec. 1833.

53/A/132 17 Dec. 1833. Edwin Whitehouse, gentleman, of Newland. Trespassing 'with force and arms' in pursuit of game at Staunton on land occupied by John Worgan. E. Machen JP and P. J. Ducarel JP at Coleford. Defendant did not appear. Complainant Timothy Jones, labourer, of Staunton gave evidence that he heard the report of a gun and on investigation saw defendant on Worgan's land. Fine £2, to be paid to John Morgan, an overseer of the poor, and 8/6 costs to the complainant. In default of payment on demand, one calendar month in Littledean house of correction. Offence committed 17 Oct. 1833.

53/B/1 25 March 1834. Joseph Savage. Trespassing in pursuit of game on land at Frampton on Severn, the property of Henry Clifford Clifford Esq. T. J. Lloyd Baker JP and D. Maclean JP at Wheatenhurst. Fine £2 and 6/6 costs or two calendar months in Horsley house of correction. Offence committed 11 Feb. 1834.

53/B/2 25 March 1834. Benjamin Jones. Trespassing in pursuit of game [etc., as 53/B/1].

53/B/3 25 Feb. 1834. John Cook. Trespassing in pursuit of game on land at Standish, the property of John Niblett Esq. T. J. Lloyd Baker JP, Henry Clifford Clifford JP, D. Maclean JP, Thomas Barwick Lloyd Baker JP and P. Leversage JP at Wheatenhurst. Fine £2 and 6/6 costs. Given four weeks to pay. In default, two calendar months in Horsley house of correction. Offence committed 10 Feb. 1834.

53/B/4 25 Feb. 1834. John Jones. Trespassing in pursuit of game on land in Longney occupied by William Longney. H. C. Clifford JP, D. Maclean JP, T. B. Lloyd Baker JP and P. Leversage JP at Wheatenhurst. Fine £2 and 6/6 costs, or two calendar months in Horsley house of correction. Offence committed 1 Feb. 1834.

53/B/5 25 Feb. 1834. Charles Daniels. Trespassing in pursuit of game at Frampton on Severn on the property of Samuel Peach Peach. T. J. Lloyd Baker JP, D. Maclean JP, T. B. Lloyd Baker JP and P. Leversage JP at Wheatenhurst. Fine £2 and 6/6 costs. Given four weeks to pay. In default, two calendar months in Horsley house of correction. Offence committed 12 Feb. 1834.

53/B/6 7 Jan. 1834. George Carveth, usher, of Wotton under Edge. Using a gun to kill game at Hardwicke without a licence. H. C. Clifford JP, R. S. Davies JP, D. Maclean JP and P. Leversage JP at Wheatenhurst. Fine £10. Offence committed 27 Dec. 1833.

53/B/7 25 Feb. 1834. Mark Summers. Trespassing in pursuit of game at Standish on land occupied by Samuel Butcher. T. J. Lloyd Baker JP, H. C. Clifford JP, D. Maclean JP, T. B. Lloyd Baker JP and P. Leversage JP at Wheatenhurst. Fine £2 and 6/6 costs. Given until 29 April to pay. In default, two calendar months in Horsley house of correction. Offence committed 16 Feb. 1834.

53/B/8 25 Feb. 1834. William Collyer. Trespassing in pursuit of game at Standish [etc., as 53/B/7].

53/B/9 7 Jan. 1834. Joseph Hale. Trespassing in pursuit of conies on the property of Mary Sly at Longney. H. C. Clifford JP, R. S. Davies JP, D. Maclean JP and P. Leversage JP at Wheatenhurst. Fine £2 and 6/6 costs. Given until 7 Feb. to pay. In default, two calendar months in Horsley house of correction. Offence committed 24 Dec. 1833.

53/B/10   7 Jan. 1834. William Gooding. Trespassing in pursuit of game on the property of Mary Sly at Longney. H. C. Clifford JP, D. Maclean JP, R. S. Davies JP and P. Leversage JP at Wheatenhurst. Fine £2, to be paid to William Sims, overseer of the poor, and 7/6 costs to the complainant. Offence committed 24 Dec. 1833.

53/B/11   7 Jan. 1834. Jane Barnes. Assaulting Edwin Cook at Randwick. T. J. Lloyd Baker, H. C. Clifford JP, D. Maclean JP, R. S. Davies JP and P. Leversage JP at Wheatenhurst. Fine £1 and 6/- costs or one month in Horsley house of correction. Offence committed 23 Dec. 1833.

53/B/12   7 Jan. 1834. Charles Cook. Assaulting Edwin Cook at Randwick. T. J. Lloyd Baker, H. C. Clifford JP, D. Maclean JP, R. S. Davies JP and P. Leversage JP at Wheatenhurst. Fine £1 and 6/- costs, to be paid by 7 Feb. In default, one calendar month in Horsley house of correction. Offence committed 23 Dec. 1833.

53/B/13   6 Feb. 1834. Charles Jackson. Assaulting Daniel Jones at Eastington. R. S. Davies JP and P. Leversage JP at Eastington. Fine 4/-, to be paid to Thomas Mitchell, assistant overseer of the poor. Offence committed 4 Feb. 1834.

53/B/14   25 Feb. 1834. Samuel Ravenhill. Assaulting James Marment at Stonehouse. T. J. Lloyd Baker JP, H. C. Clifford JP, D. Maclean JP, T. B. Lloyd Baker JP and P. Leversage JP at Wheatenhurst. Fine £1 and 5/- costs. Given four weeks to pay. In default, one calendar month in Horsley house of correction. Offence committed 15 Feb. 1834.

53/B/15– 66   10 March 1834. [*Names as below.*] Possessing defective weights. R. Kingscote JP, T. Kingscote JP and T. R. Haycock JP at a Petty Sessions held at Horsley. Cornelius Bown [*except 53/B/26–31, 39–40 and 56, when it was* William Clements], inspector of weights and balances, complainant. Weights forfeited. [*Fines as below*] and 14/6 costs [*except 53/B/35*]. [*Date offence committed (all 1834) as below.*]

53/B/15   Henry Hayward of Rodborough, retail pig butcher. Three defective weights. Fine 10/-. (25 Feb.)

53/B/16   William Keen of Rodborough, baker. Three defective weights. Fine 10/-. (25 Feb.)

53/B/17   Stiles Rich of Tetbury, worsted maker. Six defective weights. Fine 20/-. (14 Feb.)

53/B/18   Ebenezer Lloyd of Tetbury, hatter and worsted maker. Three defective weights. Fine 10/-. (14 Feb.)

53/B/19   William Hayes [*also* Haynes] of Tetbury, dairyman. Two defective weights. Fine 10/-. (14 Feb.)

53/B/20   James Heart of Tetbury, shopkeeper. Three defective weights. Fine 5/-. (13 Feb.)

53/B/21   John Wall of Tetbury, baker. Two defective weights. Fine 10/-. (13 Feb.)

53/B/22   Maurice Butler of Tetbury, butcher. Two defective weights. Fine 10/-. (13 Feb.)

53/B/23   William Walker of Tetbury, grocer. Two defective weights. Fine 5/-. (13 Feb.)

53/B/24   Sarah Mills of Tetbury, shopkeeper. Six defective weights. Fine 5/-. (13 Feb.)

53/B/25   William Holliday of Shipton Moyne, dairyman. Three defective weights. Fine 20/-. (13 Feb.)

53/B/26   William Benjamin of Horsley, grocer. Five defective weights. Fine 20/-. (25 Jan.)

53/B/27   John Welch of Horsley, shopkeeper. Three defective weights. Fine 10/-. (25 Jan.)

53/B/28   John Hand of Horsley, shopkeeper. Six defective weights. Fine 5/-. (25 Jan.)

53/B/29   James Gale of Horsley, shopkeeper. Two defective weights. Fine 5/-. (24 Jan.)

53/B/30   James Weight of Horsley, shopkeeper. Five defective weights. Fine 5/-. (24 Jan.)

53/B/31   William Brinkworth of Horsley, baker. Six defective weights. Fine 10/-. (24 Jan.)

53/B/32   Daniel Holloway of Rodborough, retail pig butcher. Four defective weights. Fine 5/-. (25 Feb.)

53/B/33   Charles Longford of Rodborough, shopkeeper. Two defective weights. Fine 5/-. (25 Feb.)

53/B/34   Richard Burford of Horsley, shopkeeper. Five defective weights. Fine 10/-. (17 Feb.)

53/B/35   George Pearce of Minchinhampton, shopkeeper. Two defective weights. Fine 5/- [*no costs*]. (11 Feb.)

53/B/36   Thomas Ellis of Minchinhampton, baker. Two defective weights. Fine 10/-. (11 Feb.)

53/B/37   Ann Woodward of Minchinhampton, grocer. Two defective weights. Fine 5/-. (11 Feb.)

53/B/38   Robert Pinnell of Minchinhampton, retail pig butcher. Six defective weights. Fine 5/-. (11 Feb.)

53/B/39   Thomas Edge of Avening, shopkeeper. Five defective weights. Fine 10/-. (25 Jan.)

53/B/40   William Gould of Avening, retailer. Three defective weights. Fine 10/-. (25 Jan.)

53/B/41   Charles Millard of Horsley, leather-cutter. Five defective weights. Fine 5/-. (18 Feb.)

53/B/42   Jeremiah Hewitt of Horsley, baker. Six defective weights. Fine 10/-. (18 Feb.)

53/B/43   Jacob Browning of Horsley, shopkeeper. Four defective weights. Fine 20/-. (18 Feb.)

53/B/44   John Fewster of Minchinhampton, mealman. Five defective weights. Fine 20/-. (17 Feb.)

53/B/45   Thomas Burford of Minchinhampton, shopkeeper. Six defective weights. Fine 20/-. (17 Feb.)

53/B/46   John George of Minchinhampton, grocer. Three defective weights. Fine 5/-. (11 Feb.)

53/B/47   Mark Hampton of Horsley, smith and shopkeeper. Three defective weights. Fine 5/-. (19 Feb.)

53/B/48   Luke Day of Avening, dairyman. Four defective weights. Fine 10/-. (17 Feb.)

53/B/49   William Webber of Rodmarton, shopkeeper. Four defective weights. Fine 10/-. (14 Feb.)

53/B/50   John Cook of Tetbury, maltster and common brewer. Eight defective weights. Fine 20/-. (13 Feb.)

53/B/51   John King of Rodborough, retail pig butcher. Six defective weights. Fine 20/-. (25 Feb.)

53/B/52   Henry White of Rodborough, dairyman. Two defective weights. Fine 10/-. (25 Feb.)

53/B/53   Peter King of Rodborough, mealman. Three defective weights. Fine 20/-. (25 Feb.]

53/B/54   William Minty of Avening, retail pig butcher. Three defective weights. Fine 5/-. (18 Feb.)

53/B/55   James Hillman of Rodborough, mealman. Three defective weights. Fine 20/- (25 Feb.)

53/B/56   William Walkley of Horsley, baker. Seven defective weights. Fine 20/-. (24 Jan.)

53/B/57   James Pincott of Shipton Moyne, shopkeeper. Six defective weights. Fine 20/-. (12 Feb.)

53/B/58   Simon Stephens of Shipton Moyne, shopkeeper. Two defective weights. Fine 10/-. (12 Feb.)

53/B/59   Thomas Moss of Shipton Moyne, grocer. Seven defective weights. Fine 20/-. (12 Feb.)

53/B/60   Sarah Tugwell of Shipton Moyne, dairywoman. Two defective weights. Fine 10/-. (12 Feb.)

53/B/61   Zebulon Harewell of Cherington, innkeeper and pig butcher. Three defective weights. Fine 10/-. (14 Feb.)

53/B/62   Daniel and Robert Tanner of Shipton Moyne, dairymen and co-partners. Two defective weights. Fine 20/-. (13 Feb.)

53/B/63   John Neale of Minchinhampton, maltster. Six defective weights. Fine 20/-. (11 Feb.)

53/B/64   John Ashby of Westonbirt, shopkeeper. Four defective weights. Fine 20/-. (12 Feb.)

53/B/65   William Tiley of Woodchester, butcher. Two defective weights. Fine 5/-. (17 Feb.)

53/B/66   Thomas Hillier of Shipton Moyne, dairyman. Four defective weights. Fine 20/-. (12 Feb.)

53/B/67– 74   27 March 1834. [*Names as below.*] Possessing defective weights. R. Kingscote JP, T. Kingscote JP and T. R. Haycock JP at a Petty Sessions held at Horsley. William Clements, inspector of weights and balances, complainant. Weights forfeited. [*Fines as below*] and 14/6 costs. [*Date offence committed (all 1834) as below.*]

53/B/67   John Nicholls of Avening, mealman. Three defective weights. Fine 5/-. (17 March.)

53/B/68   William Fowler of Rodborough, shopkeeper. Four defective weights. Fine 5/-. (13 March.)

53/B/69   Samuel Weight of Rodborough, shopkeeper. Three defective weights. Fine 20/-. (13 March.)

53/B/70   Mary Birt of Rodborough, shopkeeper. Two defective weights. Fine 5/-. (13 March.)

53/B/71   John Bennett of Rodborough, shopkeeper. Five defective weights. Fine 20/-. (13 March.)

53/B/72   Jasper Hewer of Avening, dairyman. Four defective weights. Fine 20/-. (7 March.)

53/B/73   Mary Stafford of Avening, coal-seller and dairywoman. Three defective weights. Fine 10/-. (11 March.)

53/B/74   John Fowles of Avening, baker. Two defective weights. Fine 5/-. (17 March.)

53/B/75   7 April 1834. Matthew Saunders of Avening, dairyman. Possessing five defective weights. T. Kingscote JP, W. Playne JP and Rev. W. George JP at a Petty Sessions held at Horsley. William Clements, inspector of weights and balances, complainant. Weights forfeited. Fine 20/- and 14/6 costs. Offence committed 17 March 1834.

53/B/76– 130   6 Feb. 1834. [*Names as below.*] Possessing defective weights. R. Kingscote JP, T. Kingscote JP and T. R. Haycock JP at a Petty Sessions held at Horsley. Cornelius Bown [*except 53/B/108–9 and 111–28, when it was* William Clements], inspector of weights and balances, complainant. Weights forfeited. [*Fines as below*] and 14/6 costs [*except 53/B/117*]. [*Date offence committed (all 1834 except 53/B/108–28) as below.*].

53/B/76   Elizabeth Latham of Rodborough, shopkeeper. Three defective weights. Fine 5/-. (7 Jan.)

53/B/77   Samuel Morse of Rodborough, shopkeeper. Five defective weights. Fine 20/-. (7 Jan.)

53/B/78   Humphrey Hooper of Rodborough, butcher. Three defective weights. Fine 10/-. (6 Jan.)

53/B/79   William Antill of Rodborough, butcher. Six defective weights. Fine 20/-. (6 Jan.)

53/B/80   Benjamin Antill of Rodborough, grocer and maltster. Three defective weights. Fine 20/-. (6 Jan.)

53/B/81   Thomas Faulkes of Rodborough, grocer. Eight defective weights. Fine 20/-. (6 Jan.)

53/B/82   William Simmonds of Rodborough, shopkeeper. One defective weight. Fine 5/-. (6 Jan.)

53/B/83   Giles Pearce of Rodborough, retail pig butcher. Six defective weights. Fine 20/-. (6 Jan.)

53/B/84   William Flight of Rodborough, shopkeeper. Six defective weights. Fine 20/-. (6 Jan.)

53/B/85   Joseph Harris of Rodborough, shopkeeper. Eight defective weights. Fine 5/-. (6 Jan.)

53/B/86   Sarah Barnfield, of Avening, shopkeeper. Four defective weights. Fine 10/-. (3 Jan.)

53/B/87   William Evans of Minchinhampton, shopkeeper. Five defective weights. Fine 20/-. (1 Jan.)

53/B/88   Charles Jones of Minchinhampton, shopkeeper. Seven defective weights. Fine 20/-. (1 Jan.)

53/B/89   John Packer of Minchinhampton, shopkeeper. One defective weight. Fine 5/-. (1 Jan.)

53/B/90   William Horwood of Minchinhampton, shopkeeper. One defective weight. 5/-. (1 Jan.)

53/B/91   William Wathen of Rodborough, shopkeeper. Nine defective weights. Fine 20/-. (7 Jan.)

53/B/92   Daniel Evans of Minchinhampton, shopkeeper and beer retailer. Two defective weights. Fine 10/-. (7 Jan.)

53/B/93   Thomas Davis of Rodborough, meat seller. Six defective weights. Fine 20/-. (7 Jan.)

53/B/94   Richard Ball Smart of Rodborough, victualler. Six defective weights. Fine 20/-. (7 Jan.)

53/B/95   Richard Hicks of Minchinhampton, shopkeeper. Three defective weights. Fine 10/-. (2 Jan.)

53/B/96   William Nichols of Minchinhampton, shopkeeper. Five defective weights. Fine 20/-. (2 Jan.)

53/B/97   William Cook of Minchinhampton, shopkeeper. Two defective weights. Fine 20/-. (1 Jan.)

53/B/98   Edwin Taylor of Minchinhampton, grocer. Six defective weights. Fine 20/-. (2 Jan.)

53/B/99   William Heaven of Minchinhampton, shopkeeper. Two defective weights. Fine 5/-. (2 Jan.)

53/B/100   Nathaniel Dancey of Minchinhampton, grocer. Six defective weights. Fine 20/-. (2 Jan.)

53/B/101   William Davis of Minchinhampton, grocer. One defective weight. Fine 5/-. (2 Jan.)

53/B/102   Priscilla Webber of Minchinhampton, meat seller. Five defective weights. Fine 20/-. (2 Jan.)

53/B/103   Nathan Leighton of Minchinhampton, seedsman. One defective weight. Fine 5/-. (2 Jan.)

53/B/104   Joseph Lewis of Minchinhampton, butcher. Two defective weights. Fine 20/-. (2 Jan.)

53/B/105   Joseph Franklin of Rodborough, shopkeeper. Three defective weights. Fine 10/-. (6 Jan.)

53/B/106   Daniel Hill of Minchinhampton, shopkeeper. Two defective weights. Fine 10/-. (2 Jan.)

53/B/107   Frederick Evill of Minchinhampton, grocer and druggist. Two defective weights. Fine 20/-. (2 Jan.)

53/B/108   William Avery of Avening, shopkeeper. Six defective weights. Fine 20/-. (18 Dec. 1833.)

53/B/109   William Fowles of Avening, shopkeeper. Three defective weights. Fine 20/-. (18 Dec. 1833.)

53/B/110   Elizabeth Clark, widow, of Avening, retailer. Nine defective weights. Fine 20/-. (27 Dec. 1833.)

53/B/111   Christopher Keen of Rodmarton, shopkeeper. Ten defective weights. Fine 20/-. (19 Dec. 1833.)

53/B/112   William Holbrow of Avening, baker. Five defective weights. Fine 20/-. (19 Dec. 1833.)

53/B/113   Sampson Thomas of Avening, shopkeeper. Two defective weights. Fine 5/-. (18 Dec. 1833.)

53/B/114   Charles Lediard of Rodborough, shopkeeper. Five defective weights. Fine 20/-. (23 Dec. 1833.)

53/B/115   Isaac Chapman of Rodborough, shopkeeper. Five defective weights. Fine 20/-. (23 Dec. 1833.)

53/B/116   Rachel Jennings, widow, of Rodborough, [retailer]. Six defective weights. Fine 5/-. (23 Dec. 1833.)

53/B/117   Thomas May of Avening, meat seller. Four defective weights. Fine 5/- [*no costs*]. (19 Dec. 1833.)

53/B/118   Richard Parker of Avening, shopkeeper. Four defective weights. Fine 20/-. (19 Dec. 1833.)

53/B/119   George Thomas of Minchinhampton, grocer. Six defective weights. Fine 20/-. (27 Dec. 1833.)

53/B/120   Peter Cox of Avening, shopkeeper. Four defective weights. Fine 20/-. (18 Dec. 1833.)

53/B/121 Henry Fisher of Avening, grocer. Four defective weights. Fine 20/-. (27 Dec. 1833.)

53/B/122 Mary Hooper, spinster, of Avening, [retailer]. Eight defective weights. Fine 20/-. (18 Dec. 1833.)

53/B/123 Anselm Cook of Rodborough, shopkeeper. Five defective weights. Fine 20/-. (23 Dec. 1833.)

53/B/124 John Pride of Rodborough, shopkeeper. Seven defective weights. Fine 20/-. (23 Dec. 1833.)

53/B/125 Solomon Cox of Avening, shopkeeper. Four defective weights. Fine 20/-. (19 Dec. 1833.)

53/B/126 William Weight of Avening, baker. Two defective weights. Fine 10/-. (19 Dec. 1833.)

53/B/127 Charles White of Avening, shopkeeper. Five defective weights. Fine 20/-. (18 Dec. 1833.)

53/B/128 Thomas Hall of Cherington, shopkeeper. Six defective weights. Fine 20/-. (19 Dec. 1833.)

53/B/129 James Haynes of Avening, shopkeeper. Six defective weights. Fine 20/-. (3 Jan.)

53/B/130 George Bown of Avening, shopkeeper. Nine defective weights. Fine 20/-. (3 Jan.)

53/B/131 6 Feb. 1834. Edmund Roberts. Assaulting James Clutterbuck at Woodchester. W. Playne JP and T. R. Haycock JP at Horsley. Fine 1/-, to be paid to Thomas Powell, an overseer of the poor, and 6/- costs to the complainant, or two calendar months in Horsley house of correction. Offence committed 4 Feb. 1834.

53/B/132 6 Feb. 1834. Thomas Roberts. Assaulting James Clutterbuck [*etc.*, *as* 53/B/131].

53/B/133 6 Feb. 1834. William Tyler. Assaulting James Clutterbuck [*etc.*, *as* 53/B/131].

53/B/134 6 Feb. 1834. Nathaniel Roberts. Assaulting James Clutterbuck [*etc.*, *as* 53/B/131].

53/B/135 6 Feb. 1834. James Clutterbuck. Assaulting and beating Ann Roberts at Woodchester. W. Playne JP and T. R. Haycock JP at Horsley. Fine £1, to be paid to Thomas Powell, an overseer of the poor, and 7/- costs to the complainant, or two calendar months in Horsley house of correction. Offence committed 4 Feb. 1834.

53/B/136 6 March 1834. Thomas Jones Freebury, beer retailer, of Rodborough. Allowing five persons to play an illegal card game on his premises, contrary to the terms of his licence. T. Kingscote JP and W. Playne JP at a Petty Sessions for Longtree division. First offence. Fine £5 and 8/- costs. Offence committed 13 Jan. 1834.

53/B/137 18 Dec. 1833. John Baylis of Twyning. Assaulting John Strawford, pig dealer, of Twyning. J. Timbrill D.D. JP and Rev. J. Keysall JP at Tewkesbury. Fine 5/-, to be paid to Peter Dee, an overseer of the poor, and 3/6 costs. Offence committed 15 Dec. 1833.

53/B/138 22 Jan. 1834. William Wilson, labourer, and William Barnes, gardener, both of Ashchurch. Assaulting William Allsop of Ashchurch. J. Timbrill D.D. JP and Rev. J. Keysall JP at Tewkesbury. Each fined 10/-, to be paid to Thomas Greening, an overseer of the poor, and 10/6 costs. Offence committed Tuesday 14 Jan. 1834.

53/B/139 5 Feb. 1834. William James of Tewkesbury, labourer. Assaulting John Baylis of Forthampton, labourer. J. Timbrill D.D. JP and Rev. J. Keysall JP at Tewkesbury. Fine 10/-, to be paid to John White, an overseer of the poor of Forthampton, and 12/- costs. Offence committed Sunday 5 Jan. 1834.

53/B/140 19 Feb. 1834. Thomas Smith of Apperley, Deerhurst, waterman. Trespassing in pursuit of game in an enclosed plantation, the property of Miss Juliana Sabrina Strickland, at Apperley. J. Timbrill D.D. JP, Rev. J. Keysall JP and J. W. Martin JP at Tewkesbury. Fine 40/-, to be paid to Thomas Bomford, an overseer of the poor of Deerhurst, and 10/- costs to Richard Lawson, the complainant, or hard labour for one calendar month in Northleach house of correction. Offence committed 22 Jan. 1834.

53/B/141 19 Feb. 1834. Samuel Dunn of Tirley, waterman. Trespassing [*etc.*, *as* 53/B/140. *Endorsed*] Samuel Dunn committed to the house of correction 19 Feb. 1834.

53/B/142 2 April 1834. Charles Webster. Assaulting Henry Holland at Cheltenham. T. J. Baines JP and J. Blagdon JP at Cheltenham. Fine 5/- and 5/- costs. Offence committed 2 April 1834.

53/B/143 21 Jan. 1834. James Hignell of Cheltenham, retail beer dealer. Keeping his premises open for the sale of beer until 10.45 p.m. T. J. Baines JP and J. Blagdon JP at Cheltenham. First offence. Fine £2 and 5/6 costs. Offence committed 17 Jan. 1834.

53/B/144 21 Jan. 1834. John Mann of Charlton Kings, innkeeper. Failing to keep good order and keeping his premises open for the consumption of beer until midnight. T. J. Baines JP and J. Blagdon JP. First offence. Fine £2 and 6/6 costs. Offence committed 16 Jan. 1834.

53/B/145 18 Jan. 1834. William Martin of Cheltenham, retail beer dealer. Keeping his premises open for the sale of beer until almost 11 p.m. T. J. Baines JP and J. Blagdon JP at Cheltenham. First offence. Fine £2 and 5/6 costs. Offence committed 13 Jan. 1834.

53/B/146 18 Jan. 1834. George Stoyle of Cheltenham, licensed victualler. Keeping his alehouse open and allowing drinking therein until 2 p.m. T. J. Baines JP and J. Blagdon JP. First offence. Fine £2 and 5/6 costs. Offence committed 15 Jan. 1834.

53/B/147 27 Jan. 1834. James Kent. Damaging two trees at Cheltenham, the property of Robert Jearrad. R. B. Cooper JP at Cheltenham. Fine 10/-, to be paid to an overseer of the poor, 5/- costs and 2/- damages to the complainant. Offence committed 26 Jan. 1834.

53/B/148 30 Jan. 1834. William Smith. Damaging two trees [*etc.*, *as* 53/B/147 *except*] Fine 10/- and 7/6 costs [*omitting payment to an overseer and with no damages*].

53/B/149 3 April 1834. Henry Rogers of Cowley, yeoman. Using a wire to kill game in Cowley without a game licence. J. E. Viner JP and T. J. Baines JP at Cheltenham. Robert Archer, yeoman, of Witcombe, complainant. Fine £1 and 5/6 costs or one month in Northleach house of correction. Offence committed 23 March 1834.

53/B/150 6 Feb. 1834. John Russell of Cheltenham, gentleman. Trespassing in pursuit of game on land at Hazleton, the property of Harry Edmund Waller Esq. R. B. Cooper JP at Cheltenham. John Cook, yeoman, of Cheltenham, complainant. Fine £2 and 9/6 costs. Offence committed 2 Jan. 1834.

53/B/151 6 Feb. 1834. John Russell of Cheltenham, gentleman. Trespassing in pursuit of game on land at Hampnett, the property of Henry Thomas Hope Esq. R. B. Cooper JP at Cheltenham. John Cook, yeoman, of Cheltenham, complainant. Fine £2 and 9/6 costs. Offence committed about 12 noon 19 Dec. 1833.

53/B/152 28 Jan. 1834. Henry Insall of Tewkesbury, yeoman. Trespassing in pursuit of game on land at Bishop's Cleeve, the property of the Rev. William Lawrence Townsend. R. B. Cooper JP at Cheltenham. James Barnes, yeoman, of Bishop's Cleeve, complainant. Fine £2 and 10/6 costs. Offence committed about 12 noon 18 Jan. 1834

53/B/153 8 Feb. 1834. John Shill of Witcombe, labourer. Trespassing in pursuit of game on land at Great Witcombe, the property of Sir William Hicks, Bt. R. B. Cooper JP at Cheltenham. James Burrows, yeoman, of Witcombe, complainant. Fine £2 and 8/- costs. Offence committed about 10 a.m. 4 Feb. 1834.

53/B/154 6 Feb. 1834. Thomas Sheldon. Assaulting Nathaniel Dean at Cheltenham. R. B. Cooper JP and J. E. Viner JP at Cheltenham. Fine 5/- and 8/- costs. Offence committed 1 Dec. 1833.

53/B/155 15 Feb. 1834. James Morgan of Cheltenham, retail beer dealer. Keeping his premises open for the sale of beer until 11 p.m. R. B. Cooper JP and T. J. Baines JP. First offence. Fine £2 and 5/6 costs. Offence committed 8 Feb. 1834.

53/B/156 15 March 1834. John Phillips. Assaulting Maria Hodges at Cheltenham. R. B. Cooper JP and T. J. Baines JP at Cheltenham. Fine 10/- and 6/6 costs or fourteen days in Northleach house of correction. Offence committed 9 March 1834.

53/B/157 1 Feb. 1834. James Townley of Cheltenham, retail beer dealer. Keeping his premises open for the sale of beer until 2 a.m. and permitting unlawful games. R. B. Cooper JP and T. J. Baines JP. First offence. Fine £5 and 6/6 costs. Offence committed 29 Jan. 1834.

53/B/158 5 April 1834. Charles Grant. Assaulting James Stevens at Cheltenham. R. B. Cooper JP and T. J. Baines JP at Cheltenham. Fine 10/- and 7/6 costs. Offence committed 6 March 1834.

53/B/159 8 Feb. 1834. James Hale. Assaulting Nathaniel Dean at Cheltenham. R. B. Cooper JP and T. J. Baines JP at Cheltenham. Fine 10/6 and 9/6 costs. Offence committed 1 Dec. 1833.

53/B/160 27 March 1834. John Doxsey. Assaulting Charles Watts at Cheltenham. R. B. Cooper JP and T. J. Baines JP at Cheltenham. Fine 10/- and 5/6 costs. Offence committed 24 March 1834.

53/B/161 27 March 1834. Benjamin Bubb. Assaulting Susan Jones at Cheltenham. R. B. Cooper JP and T. J. Baines JP at Cheltenham. Fine 10/- and 3/- costs. Offence committed 25 Jan. 1834.

53/B/162 27 Feb. 1834. Samuel Greenall. Assaulting Charles Watts at Cheltenham. R. B. Cooper JP and T. J. Baines JP at Cheltenham. Fine 10/- and 5/6 costs. Offence committed 24 Feb. 1834.

53/B/163 30 Jan. 1834. George Barnett. Assaulting John Artus at Cheltenham. R. B. Cooper JP and T. J. Baines JP at Cheltenham. Fine £1 and 10/6 costs. Offence committed 25 Jan. 1834.

53/B/164 15 March 1834. Thomas Clements of Staverton, retail beer dealer. Permitting illegal card games on his premises. R. B. Cooper JP and T. J. Baines JP. First offence. Fine £2 and 5/6 costs. Offence committed 26 Feb. 1834.

53/B/165 4 Jan. 1834. Benjamin Abbot. Assaulting Samuel Francis at Cheltenham. R. B. Cooper JP and T. J. Baines JP at Cheltenham. Fine 5/- and 4/- costs. Offence committed 2 Jan. 1834

53/B/166 13 March 1834. William Hill of Cheltenham, retail beer dealer. Permitting unlawful games and keeping his premises open until 11 p.m. R. B. Cooper JP and T. J. Baines JP. First offence. Fine £2 and 5/6 costs. Offence committed 10 March 1834.

53/B/167 15 Feb. 1834. William Saxton of Cheltenham, retail beer dealer. Having his premises open for the sale of beer at 11 p.m. R. B. Cooper JP and T. J. Baines JP. First offence. Fine £2 and 5/6 costs. Offence committed 9 Feb. 1834.

53/B/168 1 March 1834. William Beard of Cheltenham, retail beer dealer. Permitting drunkenness and other disorderly behaviour in his premises. R. B. Cooper JP and T. J. Baines JP. First offence. Fine £2 and 7/6 costs. Offence committed 23 Feb. 1834.

53/B/169 4 Jan. 1834. Benjamin Bullock of Cheltenham, retail beer dealer. Permitting card games to be played in his premises. R. B. Cooper JP and T. J. Baines JP. First offence. Fine £4 and 5/6 costs. Offence committed 28 Dec. 1833.

53/B/170 4 Feb. 1834. Richard Johnson. Assaulting Charlotte Lloyd at Cheltenham. J. E. Viner JP and T. J. Baines JP at Cheltenham. Fine 5/- and 5/6 costs. Offence committed 1 Feb. 1834.

53/B/171   4 Jan. 1834. Selina Knight of Cheltenham, beer retailer. Permitting unlawful games in her alehouse. R. B. Cooper JP and T. J. Baines JP. First offence. Fine £2 and 5/6 costs. Offence committed 28 Dec. 1833.

53/B/172   9 Jan. 1834. John Addis. Assaulting William Jones at Cheltenham. R. B. Cooper JP and T. J. Baines JP. Fine 10/- and 7/6 costs. Offence committed 7 Jan. 1834.

53/B/173   6 Feb. 1834. James Edmunds of Cheltenham, retail beer and cider dealer. Selling cider at 4.03 p.m. on a Sunday. R. B. Cooper JP and J. E.Viner JP. First offence. Fine £2 and 5/6 costs. Offence committed 2 Feb. 1834

53/B/174   7 Jan. 1834. Joseph Limbrick of Charlton Kings, retail beer dealer. Keeping his premises open until 11 p.m. and permitting drunkenness and other disorderly conduct. R. B. Cooper JP and J. E. Viner JP. First offence. Fine £5 and 7/- costs. Offence committed 30 Nov. 1833.

53/B/175   18 Feb. 1834. Henry Humphris. Assaulting Joseph Pound at Charlton Kings. R. B. Cooper JP and J. E. Viner JP at Cheltenham. Fine 5/- and 8/6 costs. Offence committed 15 Feb. 1834

53/B/176   25 Feb. 1834. Thomas Turner. Assaulting William Jackson at Cheltenham. R. B. Cooper JP and J. E. Viner JP at Cheltenham. Fine 10/- and 7/6 costss. Offence committed 22 Feb. 1834.

53/B/177   20 Feb. 1834. Edmund Gore. Assaulting Thomas Bliss at Cheltenham. R. B. Cooper JP and J. E. Viner JP at Cheltenham. Fine 5/- and 6/6 costs. Offence committed 18 Feb. 1834.

53/B/178   11 Jan. 1834. George Lucas of Cheltenham, retail beer dealer. Keeping his premises open for the sale of beer until almost midnight. R. B. Cooper JP and T. J. Baines JP. First offence. Fine £2 and 6/6 costs. Offence committed 8 Jan. 1834.

53/B/179   4 March 1834. Michael Bryan. Assaulting Thomas Hayward at Cheltenham. R. B. Cooper JP and J. E. Viner JP at Cheltenham. Fine 7/6 and 3/- costs. Offence committed 3 March 1834.

53/B/180   13 March 1834. George Harker. Assaulting Joseph Simmonds at Cheltenham. R. B. Cooper JP and J. E. Viner JP at Cheltenham. Fine £1 and 5/- costs. Offence committed 8 March 1834.

53/B/181   20 Feb. 1834. William Lovesy. Assaulting James Geeves at Cheltenham. R. B. Cooper JP and J. E. Viner JP at Cheltenham. Fine 10/- and 9/6 costs. Offence committed 17 Feb. 1834.

53/B/182   18 Feb. 1834. Charles Dawes. Assaulting Joseph Compton at Cheltenham. R. B. Cooper JP and J. E. Viner JP at Cheltenham. Fine £2 and 9/6 costs. Offence committed 8 Feb. 1834.

53/B/183   7 Jan. 1834. Robert Tarling of Charlton Kings, retail beer dealer. Keeping his premises open for the sale of beer until 11.30 p.m. R. B. Cooper JP and J. E. Viner JP. First offence. Fine £2 and 8/- costs. Offence committed 24 Dec. 1833.

53/B/184   16 Jan. 1834. Giles Giles of Cheltenham, licensed victualler. Keeping his alehouse open until 2 a.m. and permitting drinking therein. R. B. Cooper JP and J. E. Viner JP. First offence. Fine £2 and 5/6 costs. Offence committed 15 Jan. 1834.

53/B/185   11 Feb. 1834. William Baldwin. Assaulting John Venfield at Cheltenham. R. B. Cooper JP and J. E. Viner JP at Cheltenham. Fine £1 and 6/6 costs. Offence committed 6 Feb. 1834.

53/B/186 25 March 1834. William Keeley and George Goodson. Breaking and taking away part of a holly tree growing in the garden of Thomas Franklin and John Mander, the property of James Roberts West Esq. of Newcomb, Saintbury. W. Dickins JP at Moreton in Marsh. First offence. Fine 2/- and 5/- damages or hard labour for one calendar month in [Northleach] house of correction. Offence committed 22 Dec. 1833.

53/B/187 25 March 1834. Joseph Parker of Tidmington, [Warws.], labourer. Using a snare (or gin) to take game at Todenham without a game certificate. W. Dickins JP and F. Colvile JP at Moreton in Marsh. William Randall, complainant. Fine £1 6s. 6d., to be paid to John Timms, an overseer of the poor, and 13/6 costs, or two calendar months in Northleach house of correction. Offence committed 17 Feb. 1834.

53/B/188 25 Feb. 1834. John Lane of Chipping Campden, [alehouse keeper]. Allowing tippling and card games in his house. Rev. J. R. Hall JP and W. Dickins JP at Moreton in Marsh for the upper division of Kiftsgate. First offence. Fine £2 10s., half to be paid to William Wilson of Chipping Campden and the remainder to the county treasurer, and £1 10s. 6d. costs. Offence committed 29 Jan. 1834.

53/B/189 21 Jan. 1834. George Hawker, late of Blockley, [Worcs.], labourer. Using a gun to kill game at Sezincote [MS. Seasoncott]. Rev. J. R. Hall JP and F. Colvile JP at Moreton in Marsh. Fine £5, to be paid to George Crossley, an overseer of the poor, and £1 12s. 6d. costs to Charles Sanders, or three calendar months' hard labour in Northleach house of correction. Offence committed Sunday 19 Jan. 1834.

53/B/190 7 Jan. 1834. John Terry, Thomas Cox, James Skey, Thomas Terry and George Luckett. Assaulting William Wilson at Chipping Campden. Rev. J. R. Hall JP and W. Dickins JP at Moreton in Marsh. John Terry, Thomas Cox and James Skey each fined 8/- and 4/- costs. Thomas Terry and George Luckett each fined 17/- and 5/- costs. All costs to go to William Wilson. The remainder to be paid to Peter Haines, overseer of the poor, or one calendar month in Northleach house of correction. Offence committed 25 Dec. 1833.

53/B/191 7 Jan. 1834. Richard Smith of Chipping Campden, [alehouse keeper]. Permitting tippling and card playing on his premises. Rev. J. R. Hall JP and W. Dickins JP. First offence. Fine £5, half of which to be paid to William Wilson, informer, and 10/- costs. Offence committed 13 Dec. 1833.

53/B/192 22 Oct. 1833. Richard Court and Thomas Cooke. Breaking the dwelling house windows of John Gardner at Aston Subedge. Rev. J. R. Hall JP at Moreton in Marsh. First offence. Fine 14/10, to be paid to an overseer of the poor, 18/6 costs and 6/8 damages to the complainant, or two calendar months' hard labour in [Northleach] house of correction. Offence committed 12 Oct. 1833.

53/B/193 25 March 1834. Ann Andrews. Behaving in an indecent manner in the presence of the magistrate at Moreton in Marsh and admitting to begging. Rev. J. R. Hall JP at Moreton in Marsh. Hard labour for one calendar month in Northleach house of correction. Offence committed 25 March 1834.

53/B/194 26 March 1834. William Walton the younger and George [also named as Charles] Cockerell, both of Bourton on the Hill. Trespassing in search of game at Bourton on the Hill on land occupied by William Phillips. Rev. J. R. Hall JP at Moreton in Marsh. Peter Brookes, complainant. Fine 12/6 each, to be paid to an overseer of the poor, and 7/6 each costs to the complainant, or hard labour for one calendar month in Northleach house of correction. Offence committed 9 March 1834.

53/B/195 22 Jan. 1834. Thomas and James Symonds. Assaulting Richard Nash and damaging the door of his house at Dymock. Rev. J. Higgins JP and R. Webb JP at Ledbury, magistrates for Herefs. and Glos. Fine 17/- and 13/- costs or one calendar month in Littledean house of correction. Fines paid. Offence committed 5 Jan. 1834.

53/B/196   5 March 1834. Hannah Hodges. Wilfully damaging a hedge and palings in the garden and premises of John Williams at Kempley. Rev. J. Higgins JP at Ledbury. Fine 6*d.* damages and 7/6 costs or one calendar month in Littledean house of correction. Fine not paid: imprisoned. Offence committed 28 Jan. 1834.

53/B/197   1 March 1834. George Thomas, beer and cider retailer of the White Bear, Thornbury. Selling cider between 10 a.m. and 1 p.m. on a Sunday. Robert John Charleton D.D. JP and W. Davies D.D. JP at a Petty Sessions for Thornbury division. Second offence. [*Cf.* 53/B/198.] Fine £5 and 7/- costs. Offence committed Sunday 23 Feb. 1834.

53/B/198   7 Dec. 1833. George Thomas, beer and cider retailer of the White Bear, Thornbury. Allowing cider to be consumed on his premises between 10 p.m. and 4 a.m. W. Davies D.D. JP and Rev. M. F. T. Stephens JP at a Petty Sessions for Thornbury division. First offence. Fine 40/- and 5/- costs. Offence committed 18 Nov. 1833.

53/B/199   21 Jan. 1834. Thomas Newport of Eastleach Turville, beer retailer. Keeping his house open for the sale and consumption of beer after 10 p.m. Rev. W. Price JP and Rev. Edward Leigh Bennett JP at a Petty Sessions for Bibury division. Second offence. [*Cf.* 53/B/200.] Fine £5 and 10/- costs. Offence committed Monday 16 Dec. 1833.

53/B/200   6 Aug. 1833 [*late return*]. Thomas Newport of Eastleach Turville, beer retailer. Keeping his premises open for the sale and consumption of beer after 10 p.m. J. R. Barker JP and Rev. W. Price JP at a Petty Sessions for Bibury division. First offence. Fine 40/- and 5/- costs. Offence committed Monday 1 July 1833.

53/B/201   21 Jan. 1834. John Green of Arlington, Bibury, beer retailer. Keeping his house open for the sale and consumption of beer at 4 p.m. on a Sunday. Rev. T. Pettat JP and Rev. E. L. Bennett JP at a Petty Sessions for Bibury division. First offence. Fine 40/- and 5/- costs. Offence committed Sunday 8 Dec. 1833.

53/B/202   3 March 1834. George Hinton, victualler, of the Ship inn, Cirencester. Allowing drunkenness and other disorderly behaviour on his premises. Rev. H. A. Pye JP and Rev. H. Cripps JP. First offence. Fine 15/- and 5/- costs. Offence committed 11 Feb. 1834.

53/B/203   3 March 1834. George Evans, victualler, of the Pack Horse inn, Cirencester. Allowing an illegal game, All Fours, to be played in his premises and failing to maintain good order. Rev. H. A. Pye JP and Rev. H. Cripps JP. First offence. Fine 15/- and 5/- costs. Offence committed 14 Feb. 1834.

53/B/204   14 Jan. 1834. Thomas Bruton of Uley, labourer. Leaving his wife and children chargeable to the parish. B. C. Browne JP at Uley. Hard labour for six weeks in Horsley house of correction. Offence committed 4 Dec. 1833.

53/B/205   7 Feb. 1834. Daniel Ford of Uley, beer retailer. Allowing unlawful games and gaming in his house. P. B. Purnell JP and Rev. James Harley Dunsford JP at a Petty Sessions for the upper division of Berkeley. First offence. Fine 40/- and 3/6 costs. Offence committed Friday 31 Jan. 1834.

53/C/1   17 June 1834. Isaac Willcox, yeoman, of Stoke Gifford, Barton Regis. Using a dog to kill game without obtaining the required certificate. J. Parker JP and H. W. Newman JP at Lawfords Gate sessions room, commissioners for assessed taxes. Fine £10. [*Date of offence not given.*]

53/C/2   24 June 1834. Henry White. Stealing apples growing in an orchard at Stonehouse belonging to Reuben Hyde. D. Maclean JP and R. S. Davies JP at Wheatenhurst. Fine 5/-

and 7/6 costs, all to be paid to the complainant, or one month in Horsley house of correction. Offence committed 17 June 1834.

53/C/3 24 June 1834. Henry Critchley. Assaulting Ann Paine at Stonehouse. D. Maclean JP and R. S. Davies JP at Wheatenhurst. Fine £2, to be paid to William John Wood, an overseer of the poor, and 7/6 costs, or one month in Horsley house of correction. Offence committed 22 June 1834.

53/C/4 27 May 1834. Samuel Phelps. Assaulting Charles Millington at Quedgeley. H. C. Clifford JP and D. Maclean JP at Wheatenhurst. Fine 1/- and 6/6 costs. Offence committed 16 May 1834.

53/C/5 28 April 1834. William Kitchen. Assaulting William Batewell at Eastington. J. P. Hicks JP and P. Leversage JP at Eastington. Fine 5/-, to be paid to Thomas Mitchell, assistant overseer of the poor, and 5/- costs. Offence committed 23 April 1834.

53/C/6 15 May 1834. William Bennett and William Redman. Cutting and stealing part of a tree at King's Stanley, the property of Henry Lewis and others. D. Maclean JP at King's Stanley. Fine 3/- and 5/- costs or one month in Horsley house of correction. Offence committed 13 May 1834.

53/C/7 27 May 1834. Isaac Vines. Assaulting Hannah Vick Pearce at Randwick. H. C. Clifford JP and D. Maclean JP at Wheatenhurst. Fine 5/-, to be paid to Samuel Browning, assistant overseer of the poor, and 6/6 costs, or one month in Horsley house of correction. Offence committed 29 April 1834.

53/C/8 16 June 1834. Thomas Carpenter. Assaulting John Simmonds at Longhope. C. Crawley JP and J. Pyrke JP at Newnham. Fine £2 and 8/- costs or two calendar months in Littledean house of correction. Offence committed 23 May 1834.

53/C/9 16 June 1834. William Dawe. Assaulting John Simmonds [etc., as 53/C/8].

53/C/10 3 June 1833 [late return]. William Matthews. Shooting at a shutter, the property of James Ruck, at St. Briavels hundred, causing £1 4s. damage. E. Machen JP and P. J. Ducarel JP at Coleford in the Forest division. Fine £1 4s. amd 16/- costs or hard labour for two calendar months in Littledean house of correction. Offence committed 11 March 1833.

53/C/11 2 June 1834. James Cowmeadow. Assaulting James Wilson at St. Briavels hundred. C. Crawley JP and J. Pyrke JP at Newnham. Fine £1, to be paid to the high constable of St. Briavels hundred, and 8/- costs. Given fourteen days to pay. In default, two calendar months in Littledean house of correction. Offence committed 17 May 1834

53/C/12 2 June 1834. Sarah wife of John Palmer. Assaulting Mary Baynham at Newnham. C. Crawley JP and J. Pyrke JP at Newnham. Fine 10/- and 8/- costs or fourteen days in Littledean house of correction. Offence committed 17 May 1834.

53/C/13 2 June 1834. Ann Cowmeadow. Assaulting James Wilson [etc., as 53/C/11].

53/C/14 25 Feb. 1834. Edward Goold. Assaulting William Jones at Aylburton. G. Ormerod JP and T. Thomas JP at Lydney. Fine 5/- and 9/- costs or hard labour for one month in Littledean house of correction. Offence committed 11 Feb. 1834.

53/C/15 25 Feb. 1834. Charles Vaughan. Assaulting Jeremiah Brettel at Tidenham. G. Ormerod JP and T. Thomas JP at Lydney. Fine £1 and 14/6 costs or hard labour for one month in Littledean house of correction. Offence committed 18 Jan. 1834.

53/C/16 20 June 1834. John Hawkins. Cruelly beating an ass at St. Briavels hundred, the property of George Kear. C. Crawley JP and J. Pyrke JP. Henry Sanders, witness. Fine £2 and £1 5s. 6d. costs or three calendar months in Littledean house of correction. Offence committed 11 June 1834.

53/C/17   7 May 1834. John Palmer of Bourton on the Water, licensed beer retailer. Permitting disorderly conduct in his premises. Rev. F. E. Witts JP and Rev. R. W. Ford JP at a Petty Sessions for Slaughter hundred. First offence. Fine 40/- and 10/- costs. Offence committed 2 May 1834.

53/C/18   7 May 1834. John Gibbs of Bourton on the Water, licensed beer retailer. Permitting disorderly conduct in his premises. Rev. F. E. Witts JP and Rev. R. W. Ford JP at a Petty Sessions for Slaughter hundred. First offence. Fine 40/- and 10/- costs. Offence committed 2 May 1834.

53/C/19   25 Nov. 1833 [*late return*]. John Handman of Kempley, licensed cider retailer. Keeping his house open for the sale of cider after 10 p.m. E. Howell JP and R. F. Onslow JP at a Petty Sessions for Botloe hundred. First offence. Fine 40/-, of which 5/- to be paid to the informer, the remainder to the county treasurer, and 8/- costs. Offence committed 14 Nov. 1833.

53/C/20   25 Nov. 1833 [*late return*]. Edward Eaton of Oxenhall, carpenter. Assaulting John Fishpool of Newent, haulier, without provocation. E. Howell JP and R. F. Onslow JP at Newent. Fine 1/- and 13/6 costs or fourteen days in Littledean house of correction. Offence committed 8 Oct. 1833.

53/C/21   24 Feb. 1834. John Partridge, a pauper in the poorhouse. Drunkenness in the public poorhouse at Newent. Rev. R. F. Onslow JP. [*Sentence not recorded.*] Offence committed 21 Feb. 1834.

53/C/22   17 Feb. 1834. Thomas Wilkes of Upleadon, labourer. Assaulting Thomas Patrick, labourer, at Upleadon without provocation. Rev. R. F. Onslow JP and Rev. J. Commeline JP at Newent. Fine 11/6 and 8/6 costs or fourteen days in Littledean house of correction. Offence committed 10 Feb. 1834.

53/C/23   13 Jan. 1834. Philip Jenkins the younger, horse dealer, and Charles Davis, labourer, both of Newent. Assaulting William Taylor of Newent, labourer. Rev. R. F. Onslow JP and Rev. J. Commeline JP at Newent. Fine 2/- and 9/- costs or seven days in Littledean house of correction. Offence committed 7 Jan. 1834.

53/C/24   14 April 1834. John Bourne of Pauntley, labourer. Assaulting Elizabeth wife of Samuel Wiggle, labourer, of Pauntley without provocation. Rev. R. F. Onslow JP and Rev. J. Commeline JP at Newent. Fine 5/- and 8/6 costs or fourteen days in Littledean house of correction. Offence committed 7 April 1834.

53/C/25   10 March 1834. Thomas Harris of Lea Bailey in St. Briavels hundred. Assaulting Christopher Tranter, brickmaker, of Gorsley at Newent without provocation. Rev. R. F. Onslow JP and R. F. Onslow JP at Newent. Fine 15/- and 13/6 costs or fourteen days in Littledean house of correction. Offence committed 2 March 1834.

53/C/26   19 June 1834. Elijah Thomas. Assaulting William Clark at Stapleton. G. Goldney JP and W. Fripp JP at Lawfords Gate sessions room. Fine 2/6 and 8/- costs or fourteen days in Lawfords Gate house of correction. Offence committed 9 June 1834.

53/C/27   13 March 1834. William Hibbs. Assaulting Leah Skidmore at Frampton Cotterell. H. W. Newman JP and W. Fripp JP at Lawfords Gate sessions room. Fine 1/- and 8/- costs or seven days in Lawfords Gate house of correction. Offence committed 3 March 1834.

53/C/28   9 Jan. 1834. James Peacock. Assaulting Levi Brain at Bitton. A. G. H. Battersby JP and W. Munro JP at Lawfords Gate sessions room. Fine 2/- and 8/- costs or seven days in Lawfords Gate house of correction. Offence committed 26 Dec. 1833.

53/C/29 16 Jan. 1834. Richard Wren. Assaulting James Huggins at St. Philip and St. Jacob, [Bristol]. J. Cave JP and W. Munro JP at Lawfords Gate sessions room. Fine 12/- and 8/- costs or two months in Lawfords Gate house of correction. Offence committed 14 Jan. 1834.

53/C/30 6 Feb. 1834. Abraham Watson and John Bartlett. Assaulting Charles Watson at Bitton. G. Goldney JP and G. Hilhouse JP at Lawfords Gate sessions room. Fine 7/6 each, including costs, or ten days in Lawfords Gate house of correction. Offence committed 23 Jan. 1834.

53/C/31 6 Feb. 1834. John Thomas Luff, [innkeeper]. Keeping his house open for purposes other than the reception of travellers during the hours of afternoon divine service. G. Goldney JP and W. Mirehouse JP at Lawfords Gate sessions room. First offence. Fine £1 12s. and 8/- costs. Offence committed Sunday 29 Dec. 1833. [Location not given.]

53/C/32 13 Feb. 1834. James Edwin Carver. Displaying a printed paper in his shop window at Clifton, which contrary to law did not bear the number and address of the printer. H. W. Newman JP and W. Mirehouse JP at Lawfords Gate sessions room. Fine £5, and 16/- costs awarded to Frederick Nelson Watkins. Offence committed 23 Jan. 1834.

53/C/33 16 Jan. 1834. Thomas Wren. Assaulting William Harris at St. Philip and St. Jacob, [Bristol]. J. Cave JP and W. Munro JP at Lawfords Gate sessions room. Fine 2/- and 8/- costs or one month in Lawfords Gate house of correction. Offence committed 14 Jan. 1834.

53/C/34 29 Jan. 1834. Thomas Iles. Assaulting William Cross at St. James, [Bristol]. A. G. H. Battersby JP and J. Savage JP at Lawfords Gate sessions room. Fine £2 and 6/6 costs or one calendar month in Lawfords Gate house of correction. Offence committed 23 Jan. 1834.

53/C/35 20 Jan. 1834. Jonathan Pendock. Assaulting Hannah Edwards at Winterbourne. A. G. H. Battersby JP and W. Munro JP at Lawfords Gate sessions room. Fine 5/- and 8/- costs or fourteen days in Lawfords Gate house of correction. Offence committed 22 Jan. 1834.

53/C/36 20 Feb. 1834. James Thomas. Assaulting Elizabeth Scapens at St. Philip and St. Jacob, [Bristol]. G. Goldney JP and H. W. Newman JP at Lawfords Gate sessions room. Fine 1/- and 6/6 costs or ten days in Lawfords Gate house of correction. Offence committed 17 Feb. 1834.

53/C/37 20 Feb. 1834. Edward Colston Stroud. Assaulting Mary Spokes at St. Philip and St. Jacob, [Bristol]. H. W. Newman JP and Rev. W. Mirehouse JP at Lawfords Gate sessions room. Fine 40/- and 6/6 costs or six weeks in Lawfords Gate house of correction. Offence committed 18 Feb. 1834.

53/C/38 27 Feb. 1834. Jane Thomas. Assaulting Eliza Kimber at Clifton. T. Daniel JP and Rev. W. Mirehouse JP at Lawfords Gate sessions room. Fine 1/- and 7/- costs. Offence committed 20 Feb. 1834.

53/C/39 27 Feb. 1834. Samuel Fussell. Assaulting Hannah Stone at Bitton. H. W. Newman JP and Rev. W. Mirehouse JP at Lawfords Gate sessions room. Fine 1/- and £1 0s. 6d. costs or fourteen days in Lawfords Gate house of correction. Offence committed 21 Feb. 1834.

53/C/40 13 March 1834. Moses May. Trespassing in search of game on the property of Sir William Holt, Bt., at Almondsbury. H. W. Newman JP and Rev. W. Mirehouse JP at Lawfords Gate sessions room. Fine £2. Offence committed 12 Feb. 1834.

53/C/41 20 March 1834. Nathaniel Bryant. Assaulting Hannah Harrington at Bitton. H. W. Newman JP and W. Fripp JP at Lawfords Gate sessions room. Fine 12/- and 8/- costs or one month in Lawfords Gate house of correction. Offence committed 15 March 1834.

53/C/42 22 March 1834. Benjamin Webley. Assaulting John Kelson at Winterbourne. H. W. Newman JP and Rev. W. Mirehouse JP at Lawfords Gate sessions room. Fine 40/- and 13/- costs or one month in Lawfords Gate house of correction. Offence committed 19 March 1834.

53/C/43 27 March 1834. John Delve of St. Philip and St. Jacob, [Bristol]. Keeping his house open for the sale of beer after 10 p.m. H. W. Newman JP and Andrew Carrick JP at a Petty Sessions for Bristol division. Fine 40/- including costs. Offence committed 11 March 1834.

53/C/44 27 March 1834. Elizabeth Hughes of St. James, [Bristol]. Keeping her house open for the sale and consumption of beer between 3 p.m. and 4 p.m. on a Sunday. H. W. Newman JP and A. Carrick JP at a Petty Sessions for part of Berkeley division. Fine 40/- including costs. Offence committed 16 March 1834.

53/C/45 27 March 1834. Henry Fox. Assaulting Mary Greenaway at St. George, [Bristol]. H. W. Newman JP and A. Carrick JP at Lawfords Gate sessions room. Fine 1/- and 8/- costs or seven days in Lawfords Gate house of correction. Offence committed 19 March 1834.

53/C/46 27 March 1834. Richard Matthews. Assaulting Stephen Monks at Clifton. H. W. Newman JP and A. Carrick JP at Lawfords Gate sessions room. Fine 4/6 and 15/6 costs or one month in Lawfords Gate house of correction. Offence committed 27 March 1834.

53/C/47 7 April 1834. Daniel Rodman of Frampton Cotterell. Keeping his house open for the sale of beer between 3 p.m. and 5 p.m. on a Sunday. H. W. Newman JP and J. Parker JP at a Petty Sessions for part of Berkeley division. Fine 40/- including costs. Offence committed 30 March 1834.

53/C/48 7 April 1834. Joseph Millett of Frampton Cotterell. Permitting unlawful games to be played within his licensed premises. H. W. Newman JP and D. Cave JP at a Petty Sessions for part of Berkeley division. Fine 40/- including costs. Offence committed 28 March 1834.

53/C/49 17 April 1834. Samuel Iles, Samuel Nott, William Shepherd and Robert Demery. Assaulting Henry Fussell at Bitton. J. S. Harford JP and D. Cave JP at Lawfords Gate sessions room. Fine 5/- each and £1 1s. 6d. costs or one calendar month in Lawfords Gate house of correction. Offence committed 28 March 1834.

53/C/50 17 April 1834. Samuel Nott. Assaulting Robert Jones at Bitton. J. S. Harford JP and D. Cave JP at Lawfords Gate sessions room. Fine 10/- and 8/- costs or one calendar month in Lawfords Gate house of correction. Offence committed 28 March 1834.

53/C/51 17 April 1834. Joseph Hunt of St. James, [Bristol]. Permitting drunkenness or disorderly conduct on his premises. H. W. Newman JP and D. Cave JP at a Petty Sessions for part of Berkeley division. Fine 40/- including costs. Offence committed 31 March 1834.

53/C/52 1 May 1834. John Moth. Assaulting Sarah Bush at Bitton. W. Munro JP and A. G. H. Battersbury JP at Lawfords Gate sessions room. Fine 5/- and 8/- costs or fourteen days in Lawfords Gate house of correction. Offence committed 27 April 1834.

53/C/53 1 May 1834. William Ferris. Assaulting William Owen and his wife Martha at St. Philip and St. Jacob, [Bristol]. W. Munro JP and A. G. H. Battersbury JP at Lawfords Gate sessions room. Fine 10/- and 5/- costs. Offence committed 22 April 1834.

53/C/54 22 May 1834. John Savage. Assaulting William Carpenter at St. George, [Bristol]. A. G. H. Battersby JP and H. W. Newman JP at Lawfords Gate sessions room. Fine 12/- and 8/- costs or fourteen days in Lawfords Gate house of correction. Offence committed 14 May 1834.

53/C/55 22 May 1834. William Perry. Assaulting James Thomas at St. Philip and St. Jacob, [Bristol]. H. W. Newman JP and A. G. H. Battersby JP at Lawfords Gate sessions room. Fine 13/6 and 6/6 costs or one calendar month in Lawfords Gate house of correction. Offence committed 13 May 1834.

53/C/56 22 May 1834. Michael Redhead. Assaulting William Clarke at Clifton. H. W. Newman JP and A. G. H. Battersby JP at Lawfords Gate sessions room. Fine 10/- and 13/- costs or one calendar month in Lawfords Gate house of correction. Offence committed 7 May 1834.

53/C/57 22 May 1834. Thomas Lawrence West of St. Philip and St. Jacob, [Bristol]. Keeping his house open for the sale of beer after 10 p.m. A. G. H. Battersby JP and H. W. Newman JP at a Petty Sessions for part of Berkeley division. Fine 40/- including costs. Offence committed 3 May 1834.

53/C/58 22 May 1834. James Wilkins of St. Philip and St. Jacob, [Bristol]. Keeping his house open [*etc., as* 53/C/57].

53/C/59 22 May 1834. John Cook of St. Philip and St. Jacob, [Bristol]. Keeping his house open [*etc., as* 53/C/57].

53/C/60 22 May 1834. Samuel Sweet of St. Philip and St. Jacob, [Bristol]. Keeping his house open [*etc., as* 53/C/57 *except*] Offence committed 5 May 1834.

53/C/61 26 May 1834. George Sharpe. Assaulting William Webb at Winterbourne. Rev. W. Mirehouse JP and H. W. Newman JP at Lawfords Gate sessions room. Fine 5/- and 14/6 costs or twenty-one days in Lawfords Gate house of correction. Offence committed 3 May 1834.

53/C/62 29 May 1834. Aaron Golding of Winterbourne. Keeping his house open for the sale of beer after 10 p.m. J. Cave JP and G. Goldney JP at a Petty Sessions for part of Berkeley division. Fine 40/- including costs. Offence committed 17 May 1834.

53/C/63 29 May 1834. John Williamson. Assaulting John Skreen at Frampton Cotterell. Rev. W. Mirehouse JP and A. Carrick JP at Lawfords Gate sessions room. Fine 10/- or fourteen days in Lawfords Gate house of correction. [*Costs not stated.*] Offence committed 24 April 1834.

53/C/64 19 June 1834. William Hopes. Attempting to steal ten perch, valued at 1/-, from a pond in a close at Bitton belonging to the dwelling house of William Henderson, who had the right to fish there. G. Goldney JP at Lawfords Gate sessions room. Fine 10/- and 8/- costs or hard labour for twenty-one days in Lawfords Gate house of correction. Offence committed between 6 p.m. and 7 p.m. 6 June 1834.

53/C/65 19 June 1834. Daniel Manners. Attempting to steal perch from a pond [*etc., as* 53/C/64 *except*] Offence committed between 6 p.m. and 7 p.m. 9 June 1834.

53/C/66 19 June 1834. Ann Leonard. Damaging William Bull's window at St. George, [Bristol]. G. Goldney JP at Lawfords Gate sessions room. Fine 7/6 as compensation to the complainant. [*Costs not stated.*] Given fourteen days to pay. In default, hard labour for ten days in Lawfords Gate house of correction. Offence committed — June 1834.

53/C/67 19 June 1834. George Short. Attempting to steal ten perch from a pond [*etc., as* 53/C/65].

53/C/68 25 June 1834. Richard Bunting *alias* Barnfield. Damaging a quantity of potatoes growing in a field at Tetbury by cutting their stalks down to earth, the property of William Crew, plasterer. W. M. Paul JP at Tetbury. Hard labour for one calendar month in Horsley house of correction. Offence committed 21 June 1834.

53/C/69   23 Jan. 1834. Luke Cox. Entering a field at night in Horsley and taking a rabbit. T. G. B. Estcourt JP and W. M. Paul JP at Tetbury. Hard labour for three calendar months in Horsley house of correction, after which to find £10 surety himself and two other sureties of £5 each or one of £10 against offending within the ensuing year. In default, a further six months' hard labour. Offence committed 4 Nov. 1834. Offence committed 4 Nov. 1834.

53/C/70   30 Jan. 1834. William Cleaver *alias* Bowman, Richard Bunting *alias* Barnfield and Jeremiah Cox, labourers, of Tetbury. Stealing part of a dead fence from a rick barton in Tetbury, the property of Robert Tanner, farmer. W. M. Paul JP at Highgrove, Tetbury. Fine £2 and 2/- costs each or hard labour for two calendar months in Horsley house of correction. Offence committed 30 Jan. 1834.

53/C/71   7 April 1834. Robert Crew, victualler, of the Three Tuns inn, Chesterton, Cirencester. Permitting drunkenness and other disorderly conduct in his premises. Rev. H. Cripps JP and Rev. H. A. Pye JP. First offence. Fine £5 and 10/- costs. Offence committed 30 March 1834.

53/C/72   8 May 1834. Richard Halliday, licensed beer retailer of Minchinhampton. Permitting unlawful card games to be played in his premises, contrary to his licence. W. Playne JP and T. R. Haycock JP at a Petty Sessions for Longtree hundred. First offence. Fine £4 11s. 6d. and 8/6 costs. Offence committed Saturday 5 April 1834.

53/C/73   26 June 1834. William White. Assaulting Elizabeth Haines at Cheltenham. R. B. Cooper JP and T. J. Baines JP at Cheltenham. Fine £2 and 5/6 costs. Offence committed 24 June 1834.

53/C/74   19 April 1834. Thomas Clark. Assaulting William Workman at Cheltenham. T. J. Baines JP and J. Blagdon JP at Cheltenham. Fine 10/- and 3/6 costs. Offence committed 16 April 1834.

53/C/75   26 June 1834. James Cooper. Assaulting Mary Ann Maile at Cheltenham. R. B. Cooper JP and T. J. Baines JP at Cheltenham. Fine 10/- and 5/6 costs. Offence committed 23 June 1834.

53/C/76   15 April 1834. Henry Giles. Assaulting Henry Holland at Cheltenham. T. J. Baines JP and J. Blagdon JP at Cheltenham. Fine £1 and 3/- costs. Offence committed 10 April 1834.

53/C/77   20 May 1834. Robert Tombs. Assaulting Charles Watts at Cheltenham. T. J. Baines JP and J. Blagdon JP at Cheltenham. Fine £1 and 5/- costs. Offence committed 19 May 1834.

53/C/78   3 May 1834. Jacob Tombs. Assaulting William Herbert at Cheltenham. T. J. Baines JP and J. Blagdon JP at Cheltenham. Fine £1 and 3/- costs. Offence committed 2 May 1834.

53/C/79   3 May 1834. Richard Mantell of Cheltenham, innkeeper. Allowing illegal games to be played in his premises. T. J. Baines JP and J. Blagdon JP. First offence. Fine £1 and 5/6 costs. Offence committed 1 May 1834.

53/C/80   27 May 1834. William Gwinnell. Assaulting William Kent at Cheltenham. J. E. Viner JP and J. Blagdon JP at Cheltenham. Fine 10/- and 6/6 costs. Offence committed 22 May 1834.

53/C/81   22 May 1834. George Lucas of Cheltenham, retail beer dealer. Keeping his house open for the sale of beer after 10 p.m. J. E. Viner JP and J. Blagdon JP. First offence. Fine £2 and 5/6 costs. Offence committed 17 May 1834.

53/C/82   19 April 1834. William Sadler. Assaulting William Workman at Cheltenham. T. J. Baines JP and J. Blagdon JP at Cheltenham. Fine £1 and 3/6 costs. Offence committed 16 April 1834.

53/C/83 17 May 1834. Daniel Ward. Assaulting Ephraim Sperring at Cheltenham. T. J. Baines JP and J. Blagdon JP at Cheltenham. Fine £1 and 6/6 costs. Offence committed 14 May 1834.

53/C/84 21 June 1834. James Gardner of Cheltenham, retail beer dealer. Keeping his house open for the sale of beer until almost midnight. T. J. Baines JP and J. Blagdon JP. First offence. Fine £2 and 8/6 costs. Offence committed 20 June 1834.

53/C/85 7 April 1834. Henry Watkins. Assaulting James Smith at Cheltenham. J. E. Viner JP and T. J. Baines JP at Cheltenham. Fine 10/- and 6/6 costs. Offence committed 27 March 1834.

53/C/86 3 June 1834. Charles Cook. Assaulting John Flavell at Prestbury. J. E. Viner JP and T. J. Baines JP at Cheltenham. Fine 10/- and 6/6 costs. Offence committed 1 June 1834.

53/C/87 3 June 1834. James Jenkins. Assaulting Henry Card at Cheltenham. J. E. Viner JP and T. J. Baines JP at Cheltenham. Fine 10/- and 8/6 costs. Offence committed 29 May 1834.

53/C/88 31 May 1834. John Clifford. Assaulting Charles Jenk at Cheltenham. J. E. Viner JP and T. J. Baines JP at Cheltenham. Fine £1 and 3/- costs. Offence committed 30 May 1834.

53/C/89 24 April 1834. John Mason. Assaulting John Didcote at Cheltenham. R. B. Cooper JP and T. J. Baines JP at Cheltenham. Fine £1 and 4/6 costs. Offence committed 22 April 1834.

53/C/90 7 June 1834. John Wicks. Assaulting Thomas Leveson Lane at Cheltenham. J. E. Viner JP and T. J. Baines JP at Cheltenham. Fine 10/- and 6/6 costs. Offence committed 2 June 1834.

53/C/91 11 June 1834. James Brown of Cheltenham, retail beer dealer. Keeping his house open for the sale of beer after 10 p.m. J. E. Viner JP and T. J. Baines JP. First offence. Fine £2 and 5/6 costs. Offence committed 4 June 1834.

53/C/92 12 June 1834. Thomas Phipps of Cheltenham, retail beer dealer. Keeping his house open for the sale of beer after 10 p.m. J. E. Viner JP and David Latimer St. Clair JP. First offence. Fine £2 and 5/6 costs. Offence committed 7 June 1834.

53/C/93 8 May 1834. John Haines. Assaulting Thomas Hayward at Cheltenham. T. J. Baines JP and D. L. St. Clair JP at Cheltenham. Fine 5/- and 3/- costs. Offence committed 7 May 1834.

53/C/94 15 June 1834. Louisa Bourne of Cheltenham, retail beer dealer. Keeping her house open for the sale of beer after 10 p.m. T. J. Baines JP and D. L. St. Clair JP. First offence. Fine £2 and 5/6 costs. Offence committed 10 May 1834.

53/C/95 8 May 1834. John Turner of Cheltenham, retail beer dealer. Keeping his house open for the sale of beer after 10 p.m. T. J. Baines JP and D. L. St. Clair JP. First offence. Fine £2 and 5/6 costs. Offence committed 3 May 1834.

53/C/96 8 May 1834. John Bennett. Assaulting William Mills at Cheltenham. T. J. Baines JP and D. L. St. Clair JP at Cheltenham. Fine 10/- and 5/6 costs. Offence committed 23 April 1834.

53/C/97 24 June 1834. James Hignell of Cheltenham, retail beer dealer. Keeping his house open for the sale of beer after 10 p.m. R. B. Cooper JP and T. J. Baines JP. First offence. Fine £2 and 5/6 costs. Offence committed 22 June 1834.

53/C/98 24 June 1834. James Bevan of Cheltenham, retail beer dealer. Keeping his house open for the sale of beer until 10.30 p.m. R. B. Cooper JP and T. J. Baines JP. First offence. Fine £2 and 5/6 costs. Offence committed 21 June 1834.

53/C/99 5 June 1834. James Lane. Assaulting William Overton at Cheltenham. T. J. Baines JP and J. Blagdon JP at Cheltenham. Fine £1 and 6/6 costs. Offence committed 3 June 1834.

53/C/100 29 April 1834. Henry Barrow of Cheltenham, yeoman. Trespassing in pursuit of game on land belonging to Walter Lawrence Lawrence Esq. J. E. Viner JP at Cheltenham. Fine £2 and 7/6 costs. Offence committed about noon 15 April 1834.

53/C/101 13 May 1834. William Clarke of Wotton under Edge, labourer. Stealing a quantity of birchwood from a plantation at Wotton under Edge, the property of Robert Hale Blagdon Hale Esq. J. B. Harris JP at Wotton under Edge. Fine £5, to be paid to petty constable Charles Cogswell of the same parish, 1/- for the wood and 7/6 costs, or hard labour for two calendar months in Horsley house of correction. Offence committed 20 Nov. 1833.

53/C/102 21 March 1834. Stephen Young of Chipping Sodbury, labourer. Trespassing with a gun in pursuit of game on land at Dodington occupied by John Sherborne. F. Trotman JP, R. H. B. Hale JP and A. Shakespear JP. James Harrison, gamekeeper to Sir C. B. Codrington, Bt., complainant. Fine £1 and 18/6 costs. Given twenty-one days to pay. In default, six weeks' hard labour in Horsley house of correction. Offence committed Friday 28 Feb. 1834.

53/C/103 17 June 1834. James Gardner of Moreton in Marsh, labourer. Maliciously damaging a 'lees dropper' at Longborough, the property of Mary Bennett. Rev. J. R. Hall JP at Moreton in Marsh. First offence. Fine 10/-, to be paid to — Jayes of Moreton for the overseers of the poor of Longborough, 3/- damages and 13/- costs. Given four weeks to pay. In default, two calendar months' hard labour in Northleach house of correction. Offence committed 4 June 1834.

53/C/104 18 April 1834. William Davis, late of Chipping Campden, labourer. Attempting to impose on James Hemming by practising palmistry at Chipping Campden. Rev. J. R. Hall JP at Moreton in Marsh. Three calendar months in Northleach house of correction. Offence committed 14 April 1834.

53/C/105 17 June 1834. Benjamin Watkins of Moreton in Marsh, labourer. Assaulting George Kench at Longborough. Rev. J. R. Hall JP and W. Dickins JP at Moreton in Marsh. Fine 10/-, to be paid to — Jayes of Moreton for the overseers of the poor of Longborough, and 8/- costs. Given twenty-eight days to pay. In default, two calendar months in Northleach house of correction. Offence committed 4 June 1834.

53/C/106 17 June 1834. Benjamin Watkins. Damaging the ornamental part of a bridge at Sezincote, the property of Sir Charles Cockerell, Bt. Rev. J. R. Hall JP at Moreton in Marsh. Fine £1, to be paid to — Jayes for the overseers of the poor of Sezincote, 5/- damages to Sir Charles Cockerell and 14/6 costs to James Balass, the complainant. Given one week to pay. In default, two calendar months in Northleach house of correction. Offence committed 25 May 1834.

53/C/107 17 June 1834. William Gardner. Maliciously damaging the roof of a privy in Longborough [on land] occupied by William Bennett, the property of Chandos Lee Esq. Rev. J. R. Hall JP at Moreton. First offence. Fine 10/-, to be paid to — Jayes, constable of Moreton, for the poor of Longborough, 10/- costs and 3/- damages. Given twenty-eight days to pay. In default, two calendar months' hard labour in Northeach house of correction. Offence committed 4 June 1834.

53/C/108 17 June 1834. James Gardner of Moreton in Marsh, labourer. Assaulting William Partington at Longborough. Rev. J. R. Hall JP and W. Dickins JP at Moreton in Marsh. Fine 10/-, to be paid to — Jayes, constable of Moreton, for the overseers of the poor of Longborough, and 13/- costs. Given twenty-eight days to pay. In default, two calendar months in Northleach house of correction. Offence committed 4 June 1834.

53/C/109 17 June 1834. John Gillett of [Chipping] Campden. Assaulting Hannah Smith at Campden. Rev. J. R. Hall JP and W. Dickins JP at Moreton in Marsh. Fine £1, to be paid to Peter Kaines, overseer of the poor, and 15/- costs. Given twenty-eight days to pay. In default, one calendar month in Northleach house of correction. Offence committed 14 June 1834.

53/C/110 17 June 1834. William Gardner of Moreton in Marsh. Assaulting William Marnes at Longborough. Rev. J. R. Hall JP and W. Dickins JP at Moreton in Marsh. Fine £1, to be paid to — Jayes, constable of Moreton, for the overseers of the poor of Longborough, and 12/6 costs. Given twenty-eight days to pay. In default, two calendar months in Northleach house of correction. Offence committed 4 June 1834.

53/C/111 26 May 1834. Recognizance binding William Gillett, tailor, and James Cooper, labourer, both of Chipping Campden, in sureties of £10 each that George Sears, rag dealer, would appear at the next Quarter Sessions to be held at Gloucester to answer an indictment against him for a misdemeanour to be preferred by John Cotterill, constable of Chipping Campden. Acknowledged before Rev. J. R. Hall JP.

53/C/112 29 May 1834. William Colin of Bourton on the Water, beer shop keeper. Allowing drunkenness and disorderly conduct on his premises. Rev. F. E. Witts JP and Rev. C. Jeaffreson JP at a Petty Sessions for Slaughter hundred. First offence. Fine 40/- and 7/6 costs. Offence committed 4 May 1834.

53/C/113 22 May 1834. William Hale of Winstone, labourer. Breaking one panel of looking-glass on a cabinet in a house at Winstone occupied by Rev. Sir Windsor Bayntun Sandys, Kt., the property of Sir Edwin Bayntun Sandys, Bt. H. Burgh JP at Stroud. Fine £4 10s. damages and 10/- costs, to go to Sir E. B. Sandys, or hard labour for two calendar months in Horsley house of correction. Offence committed 20 May 1834.

53/C/114 5 May 1834. William Lodge. Begging in Rodborough. H. Burgh JP at Stroud. Hard labour for one calendar month in Horsley house of correction. Offence committed 5 May 1834.

53/C/115 11 April 1834. John Saunders of Leonard Stanley, labourer. Assaulting William White of Stroud, cordwainer. H. Burgh JP and J. Mills JP at Stroud. Fine £3 4s. and 16/- costs or two calendar months in Horsley house of correction. Offence committed 29 March 1834.

53/C/116 17 Jan. 1834. Thomas Smart of Bisley, weaver. Possessing almost 25 lb. of various yarns and waste believed to be stolen. H. Burgh JP, J. Mills JP, D. Maclean JP, H. Wyatt JP, W. H. Stanton JP, E. G. Hallewell JP, N. S. Marling JP and P. Leversage JP. Fine £40, half of which to be paid to Henry Jones, clothier, of Bisley, informer, and the remainder to Stroud dispensary. Witnesses Francis Pickard, constable of Stroud, and others. Offence committed 7 Dec. 1833.

53/C/117 19 March 1834. Matthew Furley of Sapperton, labourer. Breaking eleven panes of glass in John Hieron's dwelling house at Sapperton. H. Burgh JP and E. G. Hallewell JP at Stroud. Fine £1 18s. 6d. damages and 10/- costs, to be paid to the complainant, or hard labour for two calendar months in Horsley house of correction. Offence committed 19 March 1834.

53/C/118 14 March 1834. John Abel of Miserden, labourer. Using a gun without a game certificate. H. Burgh JP, J. Mills JP, D. Maclean JP, H. Wyatt JP, W. H. Stanton JP and E. G. Hallewell JP at Stroud. Fine £2, to be paid to Robert Tuffley, overseer of the poor of Miserden, and 10/- costs to the complainant William Mills the younger of Miserden, or hard labour for one calendar month in Horsley house of correction. Offence committed 7 Feb. 1834.

53/C/119   15 March 1834. William Butt of Bisley, labourer. Stealing ten stakes of dead fence, the property of Thomas Hazle of Bisley, yeoman. H. Burgh JP at Stroud. Thomas Hazle examined as to proof of the offence. Fine £1 and 2/- damages, to be paid to the overseer of the poor of Bisley, and 8/- costs to the complainant, or hard labour for two calendar months in Horsley house of correction. Offence committed 22 Feb. 1834.

53/C/120   14 Feb. 1834. William Henry Guy of Stroud, tailor. Assaulting John Bown, weaver, of Bisley at Bisley. H. Burgh JP, D. Maclean JP and J. Mills JP at Stroud. Fine £2 and 10/- costs or two months in Horsley house of correction. Offence committed 6 Feb. 1834.

53/C/121   14 March 1834. William Short of Sapperton, labourer. Cutting and stealing underwood, the property of John Tanner, weaver, of Bisley. H. Burgh JP, J. Mills JP, D. Maclean JP, H. Wyatt JP, W. H. Stanton JP and E. G. Hallewell JP at Stroud. Complainant examined as to proof of the offence. Fine £1 and 2/- costs (the value of the underwood) or hard labour for one calendar month in Horsley house of correction. Offence committed 10 March 1834.

53/C/122   28 Feb. 1834. Isaiah Weight of Stroud, blacksmith. Assaulting James Cooper, yeoman, of Painswick at Stroud. D. Maclean JP and J. Mills JP at Stroud. Fine 10/- and 5/6 costs or one calendar month in Horsley house of correction. Offence committed 14 Feb. 1834.

53/C/123   28 Feb. 1834. Thomas Strong of Bisley, labourer. Setting a trap for game without authorisation. D. Maclean JP and J. Mills JP at Stroud. Fine £2, to be paid to George Young, an overseer of the poor of Bisley, or hard labour for two calendar months in Horsley house of correction. Offence committed 17 Jan. 1834.

53/C/124   28 Feb. 1834. Isaac and John Berry of Stroud, labourers. Trespassing in search of conies in Painswick on land occupied by Thomas Holmes, mealman. D. Maclean JP and J. Mills JP at Stroud. Fine 10/-, to be paid to Henry Partridge, an overseer of the poor, and 9/- costs to the complainant, or fourteen days in Horsley house of correction. Offence committed 16 Feb. 1834.

53/C/125   31 Jan. 1834. James Hill of Painswick, beer retailer. Allowing beer to be sold and consumed on his premises after 10 p.m. H. Burgh JP, J. Mills JP and D. Maclean JP at a Petty Sessions for Bisley hundred. First offence. Fine £5. Offence committed 24 Dec. 1833.

53/C/126   6 Sept. 1833 [*late return*]. Samuel Smart of Bisley, labourer. Possessing almost 18¾ lb. of various woollen yarns believed to be stolen. H. Burgh JP, H. Daubeny JP, J. Mills JP, D. Maclean JP, N. S. Marling JP and E. G. Hallewell JP. Witnesses William Taylor, gentleman, and Joseph Jones, clothier, both of Bisley. Fine £20, half to go to the informer Daniel Cox, clothier, of Bisley and the remainder to the treasurer of Stroud dispensary. Offence committed 27 June 1833.

53/C/127   27 Sept. 1833 [*late return*]. William Wathen, Henry Nicholls and Richard Face, reputed thieves. Frequenting a street in Stroud with intent to commit a felony. H. Burgh JP, H. Daubeny JP, D. Maclean JP, E. G. Hallewell JP and N. S. Marling JP at Stroud. Hard labour for three calendar months in Horsley house of correction. Offence committed 26 Sept. 1833.

53/C/128   24 June 1834. Daniel Holbrow of Stroud, labourer. Breaking a pane of glass in a dwelling-house window, the property of John Gallop, book-keeper, of Stroud. H. Burgh JP at Stroud. Fine 2/6 damages and 8/6 costs or hard labour for two calendar months in [Horsley *deleted*, Littledean *substituted*] house of correction. Offence committed 18 June 1834.

53/C/129   24 June 1834. George Damant of Stroud, labourer. Assaulting John Thornton of Stroud, innkeeper. H. Burgh JP and E. G. Hallewell JP at Stroud. Fine £1 and 8/6 costs or two calendar months in Horsley house of correction. Offence committed 23 June 1834.

53/C/130   16 June 1834. Henry Nurden of King's Stanley, labourer. Stealing a terrier dog, the property of Robert Gardner of King's Stanley, maltster. H. Burgh JP at Stroud. Fine £5, to be paid to an overseer of the poor, £1 (the value of the dog) and 8/6 costs, or hard labour for two calendar months in Horsley house of correction. Offence committed 2 June 1834.

53/C/131   12 June 1834. Joseph Gadon. Begging in Stroud. H. Burgh JP at Stroud. Hard labour for one calendar month in Horsley house of correction. Offence committed 10 June 1834.

53/C/132   4 June 1834. William Ansloe, William Dutton the younger and Daniel Lewis, labourers, of Bisley. Cutting and stealing underwood, the property of William Clift, innkeeper, of Bisley. H. Burgh JP at Stroud. Fine 7/6, 5/- damages and 12/6 costs or hard labour for two calendar months in Horsley house of correction. Offence committed 28 May 1834.

53/C/133   27 Sept. 1833 [*late return*]. Henry Barrett of Stroud, labourer. Using a net for taking and killing game. H. Burgh JP, H. Daubeny JP, D. Maclean JP, E. G. Hallewell JP and N. S. Marling JP at Stroud. Fine £5, to be paid to Thomas Essington, an overseer of the poor of Stroud, and 10/6 costs to the complainant John Gay, or hard labour for three calendar months in Horsley house of correction. Offence committed Sunday 22 Sept. 1833.

53/C/134   27 Sept. 1833 [*late return*]. Thomas Dunning of Stroud, clothworker. Using a net for taking and killing game without a game certificate at Stroud [*etc., as* 53/C/133 *omitting of Stroud after Essington's name and omitting* Sunday].

53/C/135   27 Sept. 1833 [*late return*]. Thomas Dunning of Stroud, clothworker. Using a net for taking and killing game [*etc., as* 53/C/133, *a near duplicate of* 53/C134, *omitting* without a game certificate at Stroud, *including* of Stroud *after Essington's name and including* Sunday].

53/C/136   27 Sept. 1833 [*late return*]. Henry Barrett of Stroud, labourer. Using a net for taking and killing game without a game certificate at Stroud [*etc., as* 53/C/134, *a near duplicate of* 53/C/133].

53/C/137   8 May 1834. William Cousins of Wotton under Edge, clothier. Buying and receiving 24 lb. 8 oz. of woollen abb yarn, the property of co-partners Peter Playne and Daniel Smith, clothiers, at Wotton under Edge. O. P. Wathen JP and T. R. Haycock JP. Samuel Williams the elder and Samuel Williams the younger, witnesses. Yarn entrusted to Thomas Williams to weave into cloth. Yarn bought from Simon Smith. First offence. Fine £40, to be distributed as follows, £12 14*s*. 6*d*. costs to Peter Playne, £7 7*s*. damages to Peter Playne and Daniel Smith, £9 12*s*. 6*d*. to the informer Daniel Smith and the remaining £10 6*s*. to the treasurer of Stroud dispensary, or hard labour for six months in Horsley house of correction. Offence committed 17 Jan. 1834.

53/D/1   30 Sept. 1834. James Davis of Marshfield, labourer. Using snares with intent to kill game in an enclosed field called the Middle Tining occupied by Robert Granger at Marshfield. C. W. Codrington JP and I. J. Horlock JP at Dodington House. Hard labour for three calendar months in Horsley house of correction, after which to find sureties totalling £20 against re-offending for one year. In default, a further six months' hard labour. Offence committed Monday 15 Sept. 1834, between 8 p.m. and 9 p.m.

53/D/2   24 July 1834. Thomas Chapman of Rodborough, retail beer seller. Possessing two defective one-quart measures. D. Ricardo JP and T. R. Haycock JP at a Petty Sessions for Longtree division at Horsley. Cornelius Bown, inspector of measures, witness. Measures forfeited. Fine 10/- and 14/6 costs. Offence committed 7 July 1834.

53/D/3   18 Aug. 1834. James Fishpool the younger of Taynton, farmer. Assaulting Richard Moody, butcher, of Newent without provocation. Rev. R. F. Onslow JP and R. F. Onslow

JP at Newent. Fine 2/6, to be paid to an overseer of the poor of Newent, and 9/- costs, or one week in Littledean house of correction. Offence committed 28 July 1834.

53/D/4 28 July 1834. Thomas Payne of Newent, labourer. Assaulting George Trigge, labourer, of Lea Bailey, St. Briavels hundred, without provocation at Newent. Rev. R. F. Onslow JP and R. F. Onslow JP at Newent. Fine £4 8*s.*, to be paid to an overseer of the poor, and 12/- costs, or two calendar months in Littledean house of correction. Offence committed 22 July 1834.

53/D/5 14 July 1834. Thomas Apperley the younger of Pauntley, mason. Using a gun to kill game at Pauntley. Rev. R. F. Onslow JP and O. Ricardo JP at Newent. Fine 2/-, to be paid to an overseer of the poor, and 8/- costs to the complainant William Bullock, gamekeeper, of Oxenhall, or one week in Littledean house of correction. Offence committed Sunday 29 June 1834.

53/D/6 29 Aug. 1834. John Gurney of Newent, labourer. Assaulting Benjamin Priday, labourer, of Tibberton without provocation at Newent. Rev. R. F. Onslow JP and T. Wallis JP at Newent. Fine £1 10*s.* 6*d.* and 11/6 costs or two calendar months in Littledean house of correction. Offence committed 17 Aug. 1834.

53/D/7 29 Aug. 1834. Thomas Murrell of Newent, labourer. Assaulting Benjamin Priday [*etc.*, *as* 53/D/6 *except*] Fine £1 2*s.* and £1 costs.

53/D/8 25 Aug. 1834. Thomas Probyn the younger of Newent, labourer. Assaulting Charles Lodge, gardener, of Tibberton at Newent. Rev. R. F. Onslow JP and T. Wallis JP at Newent. Fine £1 7*s.* 6*d.* and 14/6 costs or two calendar months in Littledean house of correction. Offence committed 17 Aug. 1834.

53/D/9 28 July 1834. James Phelps of Newent, labourer. Assaulting George Trigge, labourer, of Lea Bailey at Newent without provocation. Rev. R. F. Onslow JP and Rev. J. Commeline JP at Newent. Fine £4 7*s.* 6*d.* and 12/6 costs or two calendar months in Littledean house of correction. Offence committed 22 July 1834.

53/D/10 17 July 1834. John Busan. Assaulting Robert Burnell at Cheltenham. J. E. Viner JP and T. J. Baines JP at Cheltenham. Fine 5/- and 3/- costs. Offence committed 16 July 1834.

53/D/11 23 Sep. 1834. John Green of Cheltenham, licensed victualler. Keeping his premises open and allowing drinking until 1 a.m. J. E. Viner JP and T. Newell JP at Cheltenham. First offence. Fine £2 and 5/6 costs. Offence committed 20 Sept. 1834.

53/D/12 29 July 1834. James Kitchen. Assaulting George Townsend and Samuel Roberts at Bishop's Cleeve. J. E. Viner JP and T. Newell JP at Cheltenham. Fine £1 and 13/6 costs. Offence committed 27 July 1834.

53/D/13 4 Sept. 1834. Elizabeth James. Assaulting Charlotte Tanner at Cheltenham. R. B. Cooper JP and J. E. Viner JP at Cheltenham. Fine 10/- and 8/- costs. Offence committed 1 Sept. 1834.

53/D/14 17 July 1834. Arthur Parker the younger. Assaulting John Bryant at Cheltenham. J. E. Viner JP and T. J. Baines JP at Cheltenham. Fine 10/- and 6/6 costs. Offence committed 14 July 1834.

53/D/15– 24 July 1834. [*Names as below.*] Possessing defective measures or weights. D. Ricardo 31, 34–51 JP and T. R. Haycock JP at a Petty Sessions held at Horsley for Longtree division. [*Witnesses as below*, William Clements *and* Cornelius Bown, *each described variously as* inspector of measures, inspector of weights and measures *or* inspector of weights and balances; *in* 53/D/29 *they are not witnesses but complainants.*] Measures forfeited [*except* 53/D/29–31]. [*Fines as below*] and 14/6 costs [*except* 53/D/29–31, *where the offence was not simply the possession of a defective measure. Date offence committed (all 1834) as below.*]

53/D/15   Richard Middlemor of Minchinhampton, victualler. One defective 1-quart measure. Witness Clements. Fine 5/-. (2 June).

53/D/16   Philip Tainton of Horsley, beer seller. A defective 1-quart measure. Witness Bown. Fine 5/-. (20 June).

53/D/17   John Weight of Avening, beer seller. A defective 1-pint measure. Witness Bown. Fine 5/-. (20 June).

53/D/18   William Peacey of Woodchester, victualler. Four defective 1-quart measures. Witness Bown. Fine 20/-. (7 July).

53/D/19   John Pool of Rodborough, beer seller. Two defective 1-quart measures. Witness Bown. Fine 10/-. (8 July).

53/D/20   James Mortimer of Minchinhampton, meat seller. One defective ½-lb. weight. Witness Clements. Fine 5/-. (27 May).

53/D/21   Timothy Barnard of Minchinhampton, baker. One defective 2-lb. weight. Witness Clements. Fine 5/-. (27 May).

53/D/22   Rachel Jennings of Rodborough, shopkeeper. One defective ¼-lb. weight. Witness Bown. Fine 20/-. (5 July).

53/D/23   William Essex of Avening, beer retailer. One defective 1-pint measure. Witness Clements. Fine 5/-. (12 June).

53/D/24   Mary Saunders of Avening, beer seller. One defective 1-quart measure. Witness Bown. Fine 5/-. (20 June).

53/D/25   Edward Edwards of Tetbury, victualler. Two defective measures, 1-quart and 1-pint. Witness Bown. Fine 10/-. (17 June).

53/D/26   Richard Draper of Tetbury, victualler. One defective 1-quart measure. Witness Clements. Fine 5/-. (17 June).

53/D/27   James Wall of Rodborough, beer seller. Two defective 1-pint measures. Witness Bown. Fine 10/-. (7 July).

53/D/28   John Charles of Tetbury, beer retailer. One defective 1-quart measure. Witness Clements. Fine 5/-. (17 June).

53/D/29   James Heaven Oliver of Wotton under Edge, confectioner. Two defective weights and obstructing and preventing the inspectors from removing them from his stall. Complainants Clements and Bown. Fine 5/- and 12/- costs. (27 May).

53/D/30   Peter Cox of Avening, shopkeeper. Refusing to produce his weights and balances for inspection. Witnesses Clements and Bown. Fine £2 and 12/- costs. (12 June)

53/D/31   Thomas Hiatt the elder of Minchinhampton, victualler. Preventing his measures being inspected by allowing his wife to lock the door of the bar. Witnesses Clements and Bown. Fine £3 and 12/- costs. (2 June).

53/D/32   26 July 1834. William Workman. Trespassing in search of game with a dog and a net on Tresham Down, the property of Robert Blagdon Hale Esq. at Hawkesbury. T. Kingscote JP. Fine £2, to be paid to Isaac James, an overseer of the poor, and 7/- costs to the complainant Daniel Hardwick, or hard labour for two calendar months in Horsley house of correction. Offence committed 26 July 1834.

53/D/33   5 Aug. 1834. Benjamin Carpenter. Trespassing in search of game with a dog on Tresham Down [*etc., as* 54/D/32].

53/D/34–51   24 July 1834. [*Continued from* 53/D/15–31: *see above.*]

53/D/34   Henry Hayward of Rodborough, beer seller. One defective 1-quart measure. Witness Bown. Fine 5/-. (5 July).

53/D/35   Richard King of Minchinhampton, victualler. Two defective 1-quart measures. Witness Clements. Fine 10/-. (30 May).

53/D/36   Thomas Lusty of Rodborough, beer seller. Four defective 1-quart measures. Witness Bown. Fine 20/-. (7 July).

53/D/37   James Davis of Minchinhampton, victualler. Defective measures, three 1-quart and one 1-pint. Witness Clements. Fine 20/-. (2 June).

53/D/38   Matthew Bayton of Minchinhampton, beer retailer. One defective 1-quart measure. Witness Clements. Fine 5/-. (30 May).

53/D/39   George Gardner of Minchinhampton, victualler. One defective 1-quart measure. Witness Clements. Fine 5/-. (19 June). [*The hearing is dated* 25 July, *evidently in error.*]

53/D/40   Thomas Hill of Minchinhampton, victualler. One defective 1-quart measure. Witness Clements. Fine 5/-. (2 June).

53/D/41   Joshua Matthews of Rodborough, beer seller. Two defective 1-quart measures. Witness Bown. Fine 10/-. (7 July).

53/D/42   Charles Chandler of Horsley, victualler. One defective ½-pint measure. Witness Bown. Fine 5/-. (21 June).

53/D/43   Zebulon Harewell of Cherington, victualler. One defective 1-quart measure. Witness Bown. Fine 5/-. (3 July).

53/D/44   John Viner of Minchinhampton, victualler. One defective 1-pint measure. Witness Clements. Fine 5/-. (30 May).

53/D/45   Edward Josiah Howell of Minchinhampton, victualler. Two defective 1-quart measures. Witness Bown. Fine 10/-. (25 June).

53/D/46   James Mason of Minchinhampton, beer seller. One defective 1-quart measure. Witness Bown. Fine 5/-. (11 July).

53/D/47   Joseph Hyde of Minchinhampton, shopkeeper. Four defective weights, one 1-lb., one ½-lb., one ¼-lb. and one 1-oz. Witness Clements. Fine 10/-. (27 May).

53/D/48   William Clark of Minchinhampton, shopkeeper. Seven defective weights, two 2-lb., two 1-lb., one ½-lb. and two 2-oz. Witness Clements. Fine 10/. (27 May).

53/D/49   William Croker of Minchinhampton, beer seller. Three defective weights, one ½-lb., one ¼-lb. and one 2-oz. Witness Clements. Fine 10/-. (27 May).

53/D/50   Thomas Rowland of Avening, shopkeeper. Three defective weights, one 1-lb., one ¼-lb. and one 1-oz.. Witness Clements. Fine 20/-. (12 July).

53/D/51   Daniel Darke of Avening, beer seller. Four defective measures, one 1-quart and three 1-pint. Witness Bown. Fine 20/-. (8 July).

53/D/52   9 Oct. 1834. Thomas Martin of Siston, labourer. Breaking down nut boughs in Shortwood, Pucklechurch. F. Trotman JP at Pucklechurch. Two charges. Fine 1/-, to be paid to Henry Smith, an overseer of the poor, 1/- damages and 7/6 costs to Benjamin Guy Phillips Esq., or one month in Horsley house of correction. Offences committed about 1 p.m. on Saturday and 12 noon on Sunday 23 and 24 Aug. 1834.

53/D/53   2 Aug. 1834. Charles Bruton and John Howard of Wotton under Edge, labourers. Vagrancy: being in an enclosed garden at Wotton under Edge with intent to steal vegetables. W. Leman JP at Wotton under Edge. Hard labour for two calendar months in Horsley house of correction. Offence committed 11 p.m. 1 Aug. 1834.

53/D/54   25 July 1834. William Curtis of Dursley, labourer. Stealing seven ferrets usually kept confined, the property of James White of Stinchcombe. P. B. Purnell JP, B. C. Browne JP, and W. Leman JP at Wotton under Edge. Fine £12, to be paid to Samuel Cam, churchwarden of Stinchcombe, 30/- (the value of the ferrets) and 9/6 costs to James

White, or six months' hard labour in Horsley house of correction. Offence committed at night 20 July 1834.

53/D/55   26 Sept. 1834. George Cross and Charles Grubb, labourers, of Pucklechurch. Damaging underwood and breaking boughs of nut bushes at Shortwood, Pucklechurch, and stealing nuts valued at more than 1/-. Henry Charles, duke of Beaufort, JP, F. Trotman JP, R. H. B. Hale JP and A. Shakespear JP at Old Sodbury. Fine 1/- and 11/6 costs each. Given twelve days to pay. In default, one calendar month's hard labour in Horsley house of correction. Cross committed offence on Sunday 24 Aug. and Grubb on Sunday 7 Sept. 1834.

53/D/56   29 July 1834. William Browning. Assaulting Sarah Mynett at Frampton on Severn. R. S. Davies JP and D. Maclean JP at Wheatenhurst. Fine 5/- and 6/- costs or one month in Horsley house of correction. Offence committed 6 June 1834.

53/D/57   29 July 1834. Daniel Fryer. Assaulting Christian Hawkins at Eastington. R. S. Davies JP and D. Maclean JP at Wheatenhurst. Fine 1/- and 6/- costs. Given four weeks to pay. In default, fourteen days in Horsley house of correction. Offence committed 16 July 1834.

53/D/58   29 July 1834. Stephen Taylor. Assaulting Joseph Sadler of King's Stanley. R. S. Davies JP and D. Maclean JP at Wheatenhurst. Fine 20/- and 6/- costs, to be paid within one month. In default, one month in Horsley house of correction. Offence committed 14 July 1834.

53/D/59   26 Aug. 1834. William Lewis and William Baldwin. Assaulting John and Joseph Page at Saul. R. S. Davies JP and D. Maclean JP at Wheatenhurst. Fine 10/- and 5/- costs each, or fourteen days in Horsley house of correction. Offence committed 4 July 1834.

53/D/60   26 Aug. 1834. James Bennett. Assaulting Eliza Etheridge at King's Stanley. R. S. Davies JP and D. Maclean JP at Wheatenhurst. Fine 5/- and 6/6 costs or one month in Horsley house of correction. Offence committed 12 Aug. 1834.

53/D/61   26 Aug. 1834. Joseph Evans Dickman of King's Stanley, victualler. Knowingly allowing unlawful games and gaming on his premises. R. S. Davies JP and D. Maclean JP acting in and for Whitstone hundred. Fine £1, of which 10/- to be paid to the prosecutor and the remainder to the county treasurer. Offence committed 14 July 1834.

53/D/62   30 Sept. 1834. William Summers of Harescombe, [beer retailer]. Allowing beer to be consumed on his premises after 10 p.m. C. O. Cambridge JP and D. Maclean JP at a Petty Sessions for Whitstone hundred. First offence. Fine £2, of which 6/10 to be paid to the prosecutor and the remainder to the county treasurer. Offence committed 11 Aug. 1834.

53/D/63   10 Sept. 1834. John Wood. Stealing turnips growing in a field at King's Stanley, the property of Samuel Raisher. D. Maclean JP at King's Stanley. Hard labour for fourteen days in Horsley house of correction. Offence committed 7 Sept. 1834.

53/D/64   30 Sept. 1834. Edward Jones. Trespassing in Hardwicke in pursuit of game on land occupied by Lemuel Jenner. C. O. Cambridge JP and D. Maclean JP at Wheatenhurst. Fine £2, to be paid to an overseer of the poor, and 6/6 costs to John Woodyatt, the complainant. Given three weeks to pay. In default, two months' hard labour in Horsley house of correction. Offence committed 18 Sept. 1834.

53/D/65   30 Sept. 1834. Edward Jones. Using a wire to kill game in Hardwicke when not possessing a game certificate. C. O. Cambridge JP and D. Maclean JP at Wheatenhurst. Fine £3 and 6/6 costs. Given eight weeks to pay. In default, two calendar months' hard labour in Horsley house of correction. Offence committed 18 Sept. 1834.

53/D/66   4 July 1834. William Bendall and Joseph Wood, labourers, of Stroud. Violently assaulting Frances Aldridge, single woman, at Stroud. H. Burgh JP and D. Maclean JP at Stroud. Fine £2 and 8/- costs each. In default, two calendar months in Horsley house of correction. Offence committed 22 June 1834.

53/D/67   3 Oct. 1834. Samuel Abel. Violently assaulting Richard Jones, confectioner, of Stroud. H. Burgh JP and J. Mills JP at Stroud. Fine £2 and 6/6 costs or two calendar months in Horsley house of correction. Offence committed 27 Sept. 1834.

53/D/68   25 Sept. 1834. John Smith. Begging in Painswick. H. Burgh JP at Stroud. Hard labour for one calendar month. Offence committed 24 Sept. 1834.

53/D/69   29 Sept. 1834. Benjamin Jefferies, labourer, of Rodborough. Stealing apples from an orchard in Rodborough, the property of Frederick Pinfold, gentleman. H. Burgh JP at Stroud. Hard labour for three calendar months in Horsley house of correction. Offence committed 27 Sept. 1834.

53/D/70   23 Aug. 1834. Edward Hudson, labourer, of Avening. Using a wire to kill game at Horsley when not possessing a game certificate. H. Burgh JP and W. H. Stanton JP at Stroud. Fine £5, to be paid to John Harvey, an overseer of the poor of Horsley, and 13/6 costs to the complainant, John Adams, labourer, of Horsley, or hard labour for three calendar months in Horsley house of correction. Offence committed 11 Aug. 1834.

53/D/71   22 Sept. 1834. Charles Elliott of Stroud, labourer. Stealing apples from an orchard, the property of John Hopson, butcher, of Stroud. H. Burgh JP at Stroud. Hard labour for three calendar months in Horsley house of correction. Offence committed 20 Sept. 1834.

53/D/72   3 Oct. 1834. William Burdock of Painswick, labourer. Assaulting Abigail Mitchell, spinster, of Painswick. H. Burgh JP and J. Mills JP at Stroud. Fine £5 or two calendar months in Horsley house of correction. Offence committed 30 Sept. 1834.

53/D/73   3 Oct. 1834. William Walden of Winstone, labourer. Assaulting William Ludlow, labourer, of Brimpsfield at Winstone. H. Burgh JP and J. Mills JP at Stroud. Fine £5 or two calendar months in Horsley house of correction. Offence committed 20 Sept. 1834.

53/D/74   16 Sept. 1834. Henry Restall and Edward Taylor, labourers, of Stroud. Stealing a quantity of apples growing in a garden, the property of Edward Darke, coal merchant, of Stroud. H. Burgh JP at Stroud. Hard labour for six weeks in Horsley house of correction. Offence committed 16 Sept. 1834.

53/D/75   16 Sept. 1834. James Fox and William Cox, labourers, of Stroud. Stealing a quantity of apples [etc., as 53/D/74 except] Offence committed 8 Aug. 1834.

53/D/76   7 Oct. 1834. Henry Gardner of Stroud, labourer. Assaulting Edith wife of John Hamlett, stonecutter, of Stroud. H. Burgh JP and H. Wyatt JP at Stroud. Fine £1 and 9/- costs or two calendar months in Horsley house of correction. Offence committed 19 Sept. 1834.

53/D/77   7 Oct. 1834. John Hayward. Failing to maintain his wife and child for three years, causing them to become chargeable to Stroud parish. H. Burgh JP at Stroud. Hard labour for one calendar month in Horsley house of correction.

53/D/78   14 Aug. 1834. John Young and Edward Davis. Begging in Stroud. H. Wyatt JP at Stroud. Hard labour for one calendar month in Horsley house of correction. Offence committed 13 Aug. 1834.

53/D/79   9 Oct. 1834. Thomas Waldin of Stroud, labourer. Stealing potatoes growing on land occupied by William Capel the younger, gentleman, of Painswick. H. Burgh JP at Stroud. Hard labour for one calendar month in Horsley house of correction. Offence committed 9 Oct. 1834.

53/D/80   9 Sept. 1834. James Stanley and Charles Steel. Stealing a quantity of fruit growing in Weston Subedge, the property of Thomas Rimell. F. Colvile JP at Moreton in Marsh. Fine 4/6 and 6d. (the value of the fruit), to be paid to Thomas Beman, an overseer of the poor, and 15/- costs to the complainant Thomas Rimell, who was examined in proof of the offence, or hard labour for fourteen days in Northleach house of correction. Offence committed 4 Aug. 1834.

53/D/81   9 Sept. 1834. James Ward of Preston on Stour, farmer. Assaulting and beating William Thompson at Preston on Stour. F. Colvile JP and Rev. C. Jeaffreson JP at Moreton in Marsh. Fine £1 and 20/- costs or one month in Northleach house of correction. Offence committed 12 Aug. 1834.

53/D/82   23 Sept. 1834. Robert Breakspear and Benjamin Watkins of Moreton in Marsh, labourers. Using snares to take game at Sezincote without a licence. Rev. J. R. Hall JP and Rev. C. Jeaffreson JP at Moreton in Marsh. Fine £5 each, to be paid to an overseer of the poor, and 15/- each for costs to William Fletcher, the complainant, or hard labour for three calendar months in Northleach house of correction. Offence committed 16 Sept. 1834.

53/D/83   26 Aug. 1834. Thomas Herbert of Cheltenham, licensed victualler. Keeping his premises open and selling beer and other liquors during the usual hours of divine service at the parish church. R. B. Cooper JP and T. J. Baines JP. First offence. Fine £1 and 5/6 costs. Offence committed Sunday 24 Aug. 1834.

53/D/84   14 July 1834. John Baugh. Assaulting Henry Holland at Cheltenham. R. B. Cooper JP and T. J. Baines JP at Cheltenham. Fine 20/- and 3/- costs. Offence committed 13 July 1834.

53/D/85   8 July 1834. Thomas Allen. Assaulting John Didcote at Cheltenham. R. B. Cooper JP and T. J. Baines JP at Cheltenham. Fine 10/- and 3/- costs. Offence committed 7 July 1834.

53/D/86   11 Oct. 1834. Esau Hancock. Assaulting Samuel Russell at Cheltenham. R. B. Cooper JP and T. J. Baines JP at Cheltenham. Fine 12/6 and 4/6 costs or fourteen days in Northleach house of correction. Offence committed — Oct. 1834.

53/D/87   26 July 1834. William Burrows. Assaulting James Dawson at Cheltenham. R. B. Cooper JP and J. Blagdon JP at Cheltenham. Fine £2 and 10/6 costs. Offence committed 21 July 1834.

53/D/88   5 July 1834. George Crowder. Assaulting Elizabeth Kemys at Cheltenham. R. B. Cooper JP and T. Newell JP at Cheltenham. Fine 10/- and 5/6 costs. Offence committed 3 July 1834.

53/D/89   6 Sept. 1834. James Doogan. Assaulting John Baker at Cheltenham. R. B. Cooper JP and T. Newell JP at Cheltenham. Fine 10/- and 5/6 costs. Offence committed 3 Sept. 1834.

53/D/90   6 Sept. 1834. William Powell. Assaulting Sarah Herbert at Cheltenham. R. B. Cooper JP and T. Newell JP at Cheltenham. Fine 10/- and 4/- costs. Offence committed 4 Sept. 1834.

53/D/91   23 Sept. 1834. Charles White, yeoman, of Kemerton. Trespassing in pursuit of game at Bishop's Cleeve on land belonging to the Hon. Berkeley Craven. T. Newell JP at Cheltenham. Fine £2, to be paid to an overseer of the poor, and 10/- costs to the complainant, Rev. William Lawrence Townsend. Offence committed 12 Sept. 1834.

53/D/92   9 Oct. 1834. Mary Taylor. Assaulting and beating John Martin at Cheltenham. T. Newell JP and T. J. Baines JP at Cheltenham. Fine £5 or two months in Northleach house of correction. Offence committed — Oct. 1834.

53/D/93   9 Oct. 1834. Richard Twinbro of Cheltenham, retail beer dealer. Keeping his premises open for the sale of beer at late hours in the evening. T. Newell JP and T. J. Baines JP. First offence. Fine £2 and 5/6 costs. Offence committed 6 Oct. 1834.

53/D/94   2 Oct. 1834. James Smith. Assaulting Thomas Wasley at Cheltenham. T. Newell JP and T. J. Baines JP at Cheltenham. Fine 5/- and 4/6 costs. Offence committed 1 Oct. 1834.

53/D/95   5 July 1834. James Castle. Assaulting John Timbrell at Cheltenham. R. B. Cooper JP and T. Newell JP at Cheltenham. Fine 20/- and 6/6 costs. Offence committed 4 July 1834.

53/D/96   19 Aug. 1834. John Champion. Assaulting William Jones at Cheltenham. R. B. Cooper JP and T. Newell JP at Cheltenham. Fine 10/- and 6/6 costs. Offence committed 17 Aug. 1834.

53/D/97   22 July 1834. Samuel Hill of Cheltenham, retail beer dealer. Permitting drunkenness and other disorderly behaviour in his premises. R. B. Cooper JP and T. Newell JP. First offence. Fine £2 and 8/6 costs. Offence committed 17 July 1834.

53/D/98   22 July 1834. Edwin Ford of Gloucester, yeoman. Selling beer and other excisable liquors in a booth at Prestbury without a licence. R. B. Cooper JP and T. Newell JP. Fine £10 and 9/6 costs. Offence committed 13 July 1834.

53/D/99   21 Aug. 1834. James Croney. Assaulting Richard Forrest at Cheltenham. R. B. Cooper JP and T. Newell JP at Cheltenham. Fine 5/- and 5/6 costs. Offence committed 19 Aug. 1834.

53/D/100   17 July 1834. James Garn. Damaging a fence enclosing a garden occupied by James Protherough at Charlton Kings, the property of Richard Pruen, gentleman. R. B. Cooper JP and T. J. Baines JP at Cheltenham. Fine 40/-, 2/6 damages and 9/6 costs or one month in Northleach house of correction. Offence committed 3 June 1834.

53/D/101   27 Sept. 1834. Richard Yarnell, yeoman, of Tewkesbury. Trespassing in pursuit of game on land at Bishop's Cleeve, the property of Rogers Coxwell Esq. R. B. Cooper JP at Cheltenham. George Turner, servant, of Stoke Orchard, complainant. Fine £2 and 10/6 costs. Offence committed 20 Sept. 1834.

53/D/102   13 Sept. 1834. Frederick Donovan. Assaulting Thomas Sparrow at Cheltenham. R. B. Cooper JP and T. J. Baines JP at Cheltenham. Fine 10/- and 5/6 costs. Offence committed 10 Sept. 1834.

53/D/103   7 Oct. 1834. John Carver of Cheltenham, retail beer dealer. Keeping his premises open for the sale of beer until 10.30 p.m. R. B. Cooper JP and T. J. Baines JP. First offence. Fine £2 and 5/6 costs. Offence committed 3 Oct. 1834.

53/D/104   9 Sept. 1834. James Churn of Coberley [*MS*. Cubberley], labourer. Trespassing in pursuit of game at Coberley on land belonging to — Lawrence Esq. T. J. Baines JP at Cheltenham. Robert Archer, yeoman, of Coberley, complainant. Fine £1 and 6/6 costs. Offence committed about 6 a.m. 9 Sept. 1834.

53/D/105   22 July 1834. William Nicholls of Cheltenham, yeoman, Selling beer and other excisable liquors in a booth at Prestbury without a licence. R. B. Cooper JP and T. Newell JP. Fine £10 and 6/6 costs. Offence committed 13 July 1834.

53/D/106   27 Sept. 1834. Sarah Holland. Assaulting Mary Lapping at Cheltenham. R. B. Cooper JP and T. J. Baines JP at Cheltenham. Fine £2 and 6/6 costs, or two months in Northleach house of correction. Offence committed 11 Sept. 1834.

53/D/107   16 Sept. 1834. George Griffiths. Assaulting William Herbert at Cheltenham. R. B. Cooper JP and T. J. Baines JP at Cheltenham. Fine 10/- and 3/- costs or imprisonment in Northleach house of correction. [*Length of sentence not specified*.] Offence committed 15 Sept. 1834.

53/D/108   2 Aug. 1834. William Gould. Assaulting Charles Watts at Cheltenham. R. B. Cooper JP and T. J. Baines JP at Cheltenham. Fine £1 and 6/- costs. Offence committed 1 Aug. 1834.

53/D/109   27 Aug. 1834. John Wills. Assaulting George Reins at Cheltenham. R. B. Cooper JP and T. J. Baines JP at Cheltenham. Fine 5/- and 3/- costs. Offence committed 26 Aug. 1834.

53/D/110   30 Aug. 1834. John Pearson. Assaulting Mary Roberts and Mary Pinchin at Woolstone. R. B. Cooper JP and T. J. Baines JP at Cheltenham. Fine 3/6 and 12/- costs. Offence committed 26 Aug. 1834.

53/D/111   24 July 1834. James Heven. Assaulting William Clark at Cheltenham. R. B. Cooper JP and T. J. Baines JP at Cheltenham. Fine £1 1s. and 6/6 costs. Offence committed 22 July 1834.

53/D/112   7 Aug. 1834. Thomas Pates. Assaulting Edward Ballinger at Charlton Kings. T. J. Baines JP and J. Blagdon JP at Cheltenham. Fine 5/- and 8/6 costs. Offence committed 4 Aug. 1834.

53/D/113   6 Aug. 1834. Benjamin Taylor. Assaulting Richard Smith at Cheltenham. T. J. Baines JP and J. Blagdon JP at Cheltenham. Fine 5/- and 2/- costs. Offence committed 5 Aug. 1834.

53/D/114   2 Oct. 1834. Thomas Emery. Stealing a dog (by finding) at Clifton, the property of Francis Thomas New. H. W. Newman JP at Lawfords Gate sessions room. Fine 4/- and 16/- [damages] (the value of the dog) or hard labour for one calendar month in Lawfords Gate house of correction. Offence committed 25 Sept. 1834.

53/D/115   24 July 1834. George Adams. Stealing a dog (by finding) at Winterbourne, the property of Benjamin Webley. H. W. Newman JP at Lawfords Gate sessions room. Fine £5 and 17/6 costs, and 40/- (the value of the dog), or hard labour for three calendar months in Lawfords Gate house of correction. Offence committed 8 July 1834.

53/D/116   25 Sept. 1834. Nathaniel Bryant. Assaulting George Godfrey the younger at Bitton. H. W. Newman JP and W. Munro JP [who did not sign] at Lawfords Gate sessions room. Fine 1/- and 15/6 costs or fourteen days in Lawfords Gate house of correction. Offence committed 11 Sept. 1834.

53/D/117   7 Aug. 1834. James Tanner the elder. Assaulting Henry Watkins at Henbury. J. S. Harford JP [who did not sign] and H. W. Newman JP at Lawfords Gate sessions room. Fine 13/- and 7/- costs or one calendar month in Lawfords Gate house of correction. Offence committed 2 Aug. 1834.

53/D/118   24 July 1834. Sarah Cribb. Assaulting Hannah Powell at Oldland. H. W. Newman JP and G. Goldney JP [who did not sign] at Lawfords Gate sessions room. Fine 1/- and 16/6 costs or fourteen days in Lawfords Gate house of correction. Offence committed 14 July 1834.

53/D/119   10 July 1834. Joseph Henley. Assaulting John Nicholls at St. George, [Bristol]. H. W. Newman JP and G. Goldney JP [who did not sign] at Lawfords Gate sessions room. Fine 9/- and 11/- costs or one calendar month in Lawfords Gate house of correction. Offence committed 5 July 1834.

53/D/120   7 Aug. 1834. Henry Tiley. Assaulting Benjamin Solomon at St. Philip and St. Jacob, [Bristol]. H. W. Newman JP and J. S. Harford JP [who did not sign] at Lawfords Gate sessions room. Fine 3/6 and 6/6 costs or imprisonment in Lawfords Gate house of correction. [Length of sentence not specified.] Offence committed 29 July 1834.

53/D/121   24 July 1834. Edward Gingell. Assaulting John Wright at Frampton Cotterell. H. W. Newman JP and J. S. Harford JP at Lawfords Gate sessions room. Fine £1 and 7/- costs or two calendar months in Lawfords Gate house of correction. Offence committed 14 July 1834.

53/D/122   7 Aug. 1834. George Ross. Assaulting Elizabeth Wade at St. Philip and St. Jacob, [Bristol]. J. S. Harford JP and H. W. Newman JP Lawfords Gate sessions room. Fine 4/6 and 5/6 costs or ten days in Lawfords Gate house of correction. Offence committed 29 July 1834.

53/D/123   28 Aug. 1834. James Rogers [*also* Rodgers] of the General Draper inn, Clifton. Keeping his premises open for purposes other than the reception of travellers during the hours of afternoon divine service and failing to maintain good order. J. S. Harford JP and H. W. Newman JP at Lawfords Gate sessions room. First offence. Fine 40/- and 5/6 costs. Offence committed Sunday 24 Aug. 1834.

53/D/124   28 Aug. 1834. James Burtt, licensee of the Clifton hotel, Clifton. Keeping his premises open [*etc., as* 53/D/123 *except that the magistrates are*] J. Haythorne JP and H. W. Newman JP.

53/D/125   24 July 1834. Daniel Johnson. Assaulting William Stadden at St. Philip and St. Jacob, [Bristol]. H. W. Newman JP and A. Carrick JP [*who did not sign*] at Lawfords Gate sessions room. Fine £1 and 6/6 costs or seven days in Lawfords Gate house of correction. Offence committed 18 July 1834.

53/D/126   24 July 1834. Stephen Rossiter. Assaulting Mary Smith at St. George, [Bristol]. H. W. Newman JP and A. Carrick JP [*who did not sign*] at Lawfords Gate sessions room. Fine 1/- and 15/6 costs or ten days in Lawfords Gate house of correction. Offence committed 15 June 1834.

53/D/127   4 Sept. 1834. William Shaffcote. Assaulting William Jefferies at St. Philip and St. Jacob, [Bristol]. W. Munro JP and A. Carrick JP [*who did not sign*] at Lawfords Gate sessions room. Fine 12/6 and 7/6 costs or twenty-one days in Lawfords Gate house of correction. Offence committed 31 Aug. 1834.

53/D/128   5 July 1834. Henry Worlock. Stealing potatoes from a garden in St. Philip and St. Jacob, [Bristol], the property of John Andrews. J. Savage JP at Lawfords Gate sessions room. Fine 10/6 and costs [*amount not specified*] and 1/6 (the value of the potatoes), or hard labour for fourteen days in Lawfords Gate house of correction. Offence committed 2 July 1834.

53/D/129   22 July 1834. John Bryant. Stealing potatoes valued at 6*d.* growing in Westbury on Trym, the property of Lady Hartopp. J. Savage JP at Lawfords Gate sessions room. Hard labour for fourteen day in Lawfords Gate house of correction. Offence committed 2 July 1834.

53/D/130   29 July 1834. John Battle. Exposing himself with intent to insult a female, Milbro Wilcox, at Westbury on Trym. J. Savage JP at Lawfords Gate sessions room. Hard labour for three calendar months in Lawfords Gate house of correction. Offence committed 28 July 1834.

53/D/131   17 Sept. 1834. Lewis Merrick. Refusing to maintain his wife, thereby causing her to become chargeable to Clifton parish. J. Savage JP at Lawfords Gate sessions room. Hard labour for one calendar month in Lawfords Gate house of correction. Offence committed on or about 5 July 1834.

53/D/132   18 Sept. 1834. Charles Johnson. Refusing to maintain his wife [*etc., as* 53/D/131 *except*] Offence committed 10 Sept. 1834.

53/D/133   11 Sept. 1834. Peter Edwards. Stealing apples from an orchard at Henbury, the property of George Hilhouse. W. Munro JP at Lawfords Gate sessions room. Fine 10/6, 6*d.* (the value of the apples) and 6/- costs, or hard labour for one calendar month in Lawfords Gate house of correction. Offence committed 31 Aug. 1834.

53/D/134 10 July 1834. William Caines. Being drunk in Westbury on Trym. G. Goldney JP at Lawfords Gate sessions room. Fine 5/-, to be paid to the churchwardens within one week. Offence committed 6 July 1834.

53/D/135 10 July 1834. George Newbury. Being drunk [*etc.*, *as* 53/D/134].

53/D/136 21 Aug. 1834. William Bryant. Being drunk at Clifton. J. Parker JP at Lawfords Gate sessions room. Fine 5/-, to be paid to the churchwardens within one week. Offence committed 10 Aug. 1834.

53/D/137 21 Aug. 1834. Jacob Green. Being drunk in Clifton [*etc.*, *as* 53/D/136 *except*] Offence committed 8 Aug. 1834.

53/D/138 11 Sept. 1834. John Morris. Running away and leaving his wife chargeable to St. Philip and St. Jacob's parish, [Bristol]. H. W. Newman JP at Lawfords Gate sessions room. Hard labour for three calendar months in Lawfords Gate house of correction. Offence committed 10 Sept. 1834.

53/D/139 7 Aug. 1834. John Ball of Stapleton. Keeping his house open for the sale of beer after 10 p.m. G. Goldney JP and D. Cave JP at Lawfords Gate sessions room. Fine 40/-. Offence committed 21 July 1834.

53/D/140 7 Aug. 1834. James Daniel of Stapleton. Keeping his house open [*etc.*, *as* 153/D/139].

53/D/141 28 Aug. 1834. Thomas Kayes of Clifton. Keeping his house open for the sale of beer between 3 p.m. and 5 p.m. on a Sunday. J. Parker JP and H. W. Newman JP at Lawfords Gate sessions room. Fine 40/-. Offence committed Sunday 24 Aug. 1834.

53/D/142 18 Sept. 1834. Benjamin Neale. Vagrancy: being on dwelling-house premises with unlawful intent at Bitton. H. W. Newman JP at Lawfords Gate sessions room. Hard labour for three calendar months in Lawfords Gate house of correction. Offence committed 17 Sept. 1834.

53/D/143 17 July 1834. Thomas Jenkins. Causing his children to become chargeable to St. Philip and St. Jacob's parish, [Bristol]. H. W. Newman JP at Lawfords Gate sessions room. Hard labour for one calendar month in Lawfords Gate house of correction. [*Date of offence not given.*]

53/D/144 18 Sept. 1834. Samuel Cox of St. Philip and St. Jacob, [Bristol], [alehouse keeper]. Keeping his house open for the sale of beer between 3 p.m. and 5 p.m. on a Sunday. W. Munro JP and H. W. Newman JP at Lawfords Gate sessions room. Fine 40/-. Offence committed Sunday 14 Sept. 1834.

53/D/145 18 Sept. 1834. Henry [*also named as* William] Fedder of Westbury on Trym, [alehouse keeper]. Keeping his house open for the sale of beer after 10 p.m. W. Munro JP and H. W. Newman JP at Lawfords Gate sessions room. Fine 40/-. Offence committed 6 Sept. 1834.

53/D/146 28 Aug. 1834. William Dawes of Clifton, [alehouse keeper]. Keeping his house open for the sale of beer between 10 a.m. and 1 p.m. on a Sunday. H. W. Newman JP at Lawfords Gate sessions room. Fine 40/-. Offence committed Sunday 24 Aug. 1834.

53/D/147 24 July 1834. William Dawes of Clifton, [alehouse keeper]. Keeping his house open for the sale of beer between 3 p.m. and 5 p.m. on a Sunday. G. Goldney JP and H. W. Newman JP at Lawfords Gate sessions room. Fine 40/-. Offence committed Sunday 20 July 1834.

53/D/148 24 July 1834. Benjamin Collins of St. George, [Bristol]. Keeping his house open for the sale of beer after 10 p.m. G. Goldney JP and H. W. Newman JP at Lawfords Gate sessions room. Fine 40/-. Offence committed 14 July 1834.

53/D/149   17 July 1834. John Hedges. Assaulting George Boyd Falconbridge at St. Philip and St. Jacob, [Bristol]. H. W. Newman JP and G. Hilhouse JP at Lawfords Gate sessions room. Fine 5/- and 5/- costs or fourteen days in Lawfords Gate house of correction. Offence committed 11 July 1834.

53/D/150   26 Sept. 1834. George Watkins. Assaulting Edward Edwards at St. Philip and St. Jacob, [Bristol]. Rev. W. Mirehouse JP and G. Goldney JP at Lawfords Gate sessions room. Fine £1 13s. and 7/- costs or one calendar month in Lawfords Gate house of correction. Offence committed 26 Sept. 1834.

53/D/151   9 Oct. 1834. Daniel Tucker. Assaulting Thomas Sheppard at Bitton. G. Goldney JP and G. Hilhouse JP at Lawfords Gate sessions room. Fine 5/- and 7/- costs or seven days in Lawfords Gate house of correction. Offence committed 28 Sept. 1834.

53/D/152   4 Sept. 1834. William Ferris. Assaulting John Franklin at St. Philip and St. Jacob, [Bristol]. W. Munro JP and H. W. Newman JP at Lawfords Gate sessions room. Fine £1 13s. and 7/- costs or one calendar month in Lawfords Gate house of correction. Offence committed 27 Aug. 1834.

53/D/153   21 Aug. 1834. John Ellis. Assaulting William Barrell at St. Philip and St. Jacob, [Bristol]. J. Parker JP and D. Cave JP at Lawfords Gate sessions room. Fine £3 15s. 6d. and £1 14s. 6d. costs or two calendar months in Lawfords Gate house of correction. Offence committed 20 Aug. 1834.

53/D/154   17 July 1834. Ann Roberts. Assaulting Mary Ann Bennett at St. George, [Bristol]. G. Goldney JP and H. W. Newman JP at Lawfords Gate sessions room. Fine 1/- and 7/- costs or one week in Lawfords Gate house of correction. Offence committed 8 July 1834.

53/D/155   2 Oct. 1834. Sarah Haynes, licensed victualler of St. George, [Bristol]. Keeping her house open for purposes other than the reception of travellers during the hours of afternoon divine service. G. Goldney JP and H. W. Newman JP at Lawfords Gate sessions room. Fine 10/-. Offence committed Sunday 21 Sept. 1834.

53/D/156   17 Oct. 1834. Moses Bruton. Killing two fowls, the property of John Wathen of Bitton. J. Parker JP at Bitton. Fine 2/- (the value of the fowls) and 7/- costs, or hard labour for one calendar month in Lawfords Gate house of correction. Offence committed 5 Oct. 1834.

53/D/157   31 July 1834. John Chappell of Hotwell Road, Clifton. Selling a newspaper on which stamp duty had not been paid. G. Goldney JP and Rev. W. Mirehouse JP at Lawfords Gate sessions room. Fine £20 mitigated to £10. Offence committed 15 July 1834.

53/D/158   4 Sept. 1834. George Cann of Winterbourne. Using a gun to kill a pheasant on land belonging to Mr. Daubeny Brice at Winterbourne without a licence. H. W. Newman JP and commissioner for assessed taxes, at Lawfords Gate sessions room. Information given at St. James and St. Paul, Barton Regis, on 29 Aug. by Charles Cottell. Offender did not appear. In evidence, William Fowler said he met accused walking with William Bell. A pheasant rose and accused shot it. Thomas Upton, labourer, of Hambrook and John Cuss of Mangotsfield gave similar evidence. Fine £20 mitigated to £10. Offence committed 27 Aug. 1834.

53/D/159   10 Sept. 1834. Thomas Jones of Dymock, horse dealer. Removing household goods worth £10 6s. 3d. from his dwelling to prevent distraint for rent arrears of more than £30 owing to Mr. Richard Hiatt, farmer, of Dymock. Rev. J. Higgins JP and O. Ricardo JP at Ledbury, [Herefs.], magistrates for Hereford and Gloucester counties. Francis Higgins, gentleman, of Ledbury, informer and witness, acting for solicitors J. and R. Higgins, agents for R. Hiatt. Mary Phillips, widow, Robert Jones, constable, and Joseph Bird, auctioneer, witnesses, all of Ledbury. Charles Woodyatt, coal dealer, of Ledbury helped offender and another man to remove goods between midnight and 1 a.m. on 7 Aug. Goods thought to be hidden on Noah Jones's premises. A dresser retrieved from Mary Philips, who had lived until recently with Thomas Jones. Offender did not appear. Fine £20 12s. 6d. (double the value of the goods), to be paid by 24 Sept. 1834.

54/A/1, 3–26   11 Nov. 1834. [*Names as below.*] Possessing non-standard weights. W. Davies D.D. JP and Rev. J. H. Dunsford JP at a Petty Sessions held at Berkeley for the upper division of Berkeley hundred. [*Fines as below*] and 5/- costs [*except 54/A/1; 3–5, 7, 9, 25–6. Date offence committed (all 1834) as below.*]

54/A/1   William Day of Berkeley, salt seller. Four non-standard weights. Fine 9/- and 5/6 costs. (22 Oct.)

54/A/2   2 Jan. 1835. David Dauncey of Dursley, beer and cider retailer. Selling cider after 10 p.m. and allowing unlawful games on his premises. Rev. J. H. Dunsford JP and P. B. Purnell JP. First offence. Fine £2 and 8/- costs. Offence committed 29 Dec. 1834.

54/A/3–26   11 Nov. 1834. [*Continued from A54/A/1: see above.*]

54/A/3   Henry Luce of Berkeley, butcher. Three non-standard weights. Fine 8/- and 5/6 costs. (22 Oct.)

54/A/4   Robert Ruther of Berkeley, shopkeeper. Two non-standard weights. Fine 8/- and 5/6 costs. (22 Oct.)

54/A/5   Betty Kingscott of Berkeley, shopkeeper. Two non-standard weights. Fine and 5/6 costs. (22 Oct.)

54/A/6   James Taylor of Stone, Berkeley, flour dealer and mealman. Two non-standard weights. Fine 8/-. (8 Oct.)

54/A/7   Esau Lewis of Berkeley, flour seller. Five non-standard weights. Fine 9/6 and 5/6 costs. (22 Oct.)

54/A/8   Daniel Smith of Newport, Alkington, Berkeley, shopkeeper. Seven non-standard weights. Fine 10/6. (7 Oct.)

54/A/9   William Clarke of Berkeley, butcher. Two non-standard weights. Fine 8/- and 5/6 costs. (22 Oct.)

54/A/10   Stephen Alpass of Berkeley, butcher. Three non-standard weights. Fine 8/6. (22 Oct.)

54/A/11   Thomas Pegler of Halmore, Berkeley, butcher. Two non-standard weights. Fine 8/-. (27 Oct.)

54/A/12   William Sheppard of Stone, Berkeley, baker, shopkeeper and beer retailer. Three non-standard weights. Fine 8/6. (8 Oct.)

54/A/13   John Shipway of Alkington, Berkeley, shopkeeper and beer retailer. Two non-standard weights. Fine 7/6. (7 Oct.)

54/A/14   William Fowler of Alkington, Berkeley, shopkeeper. Three non-standard weights. Fine 8/6. (7 Oct.)

54/A/15   Sarah Grafton of Alkington, Berkeley, shopkeeper and beer retailer. Five non-standard weights. Fine 9/6. (7 Oct.)

54/A/16   Charles Edmonds of Newport, Alkington, Berkeley, shopkeeper and saddler. Four non-standard weights. Fine 8/6. (7 Oct.)

54/A/17   Philip Creese of Halmore, Berkeley, shopkeeper. Five non-standard weights. Fine 9/6. (27 Oct.)

54/A/18   Samuel Harris of Newport, Alkington, Berkeley, shopkeeper. Four non-standard weights. Fine 9/-. (7 Oct.)

54/A/19   William Croome of Stone, Berkeley, pig butcher and farmer. Three non-standard weights. Fine 8/-. (8 Oct.)

54/A/20   Thomas Merrett of Purton [*MS.* Pyrton], Berkeley, shopkeeper. Four non-standard weights. Fine 9/-. (27 Oct.)

54/A/21   Abraham Tanner of Stone, Berkeley, tailor and shopkeeper. Five non-standard weights. Fine 9/6. (8 Oct.)

54/A/22   John Dash of Woodford, Alkington, Berkeley, shopkeeper. Four non-standard weights. Fine 9/-. (7 Oct.)

54/A/23   James Fowler of Woodford, Alkington, Berkeley, shopkeeper. Two non-standard weights. Fine 8/-. (7 Oct.)

54/A/24   Elizabeth Mason of Alkington, Berkeley, shopkeeper. Eight non-standard weights. Fine 11/-. (7 Oct.)

54/A/25   Rebecca Dowell of Berkeley, shopkeeper. Two non-standard weights. Fine 8/- and 5/6 costs. (22 Oct.)

54/A/26   Robert Pearce of Berkeley, salt seller and maltster. Two non-standard weights. Fine 8/- and 5/6 costs. (22 Oct.)

54/A/27   25 Nov. 1834. Thomas Jones. Assaulting James Hopton at Arlingham. D. Maclean JP and P. Leversage JP at Wheatenhurst. Fine 1/-, to be paid to an overseer of the poor, and 6/6 costs, or imprisonment in Horsley house of correction. [*Length of sentence not specified.*] Offence committed 23 Nov. 1834.

54/A/28   21 Oct. 1834. Samuel Wheeler. Assaulting Hester Coleman at King's Stanley. T. J. Lloyd Baker JP and D. Maclean JP at Wheatenhurst. Fine 2/6, to be paid to an overseer of the poor, and 5/6 costs, or imprisonment in Horsley house of correction. [*Length of sentence not specified.*] Offence committed 3 Oct. 1834.

54/A/29   21 Oct. 1834. Thomas Smith. Trespassing during the day time in pursuit of game on land at Eastington [occupied by] Robert Carefield. T. J. Lloyd Baker JP and D. Maclean JP at Wheatenhurst. George Dangerfield, complainant. Fine £2 and 6/6 costs. Given one week to pay. In default, two months' hard labour in Horsley house of correction. Offence committed 27 Sept. 1834.

54/A/30   21 Oct. 1834. Thomas Vick. Trespassing during the day time in pursuit of game on land at Eastington occupied by Robert Carefield [*etc., as* 54/A/29 *except*] two calendar months' hard labour.

54/A/31   30 Dec. 1834. William Pearce. Breaking down and stealing two wooden rails, part of a fence, at Randwick, the property of John Butcher. R. S. Davies JP at Stonehouse. Fine £1 12s. including 8/- costs or one calendar month in Horsley house of correction. Offence committed 18 Dec. 1834.

54/A/32   15 Dec. 1834. Jesse King. Breaking down a fence rail, the property of John Lusty of King's Stanley, with intent to steal it. R. S. Davies JP and D. Maclean JP at King's Stanley. Fine £1 including 6/- costs, to be paid within three weeks, or hard labour for one month in Horsley house of correction. Offence committed 15 Dec. 1834.

54/A/33   18 Dec. 1834. George Davis, [alehouse keeper], of St. James and St. Paul, [Bristol]. Keeping his house open for the sale of beer after 10 p.m. D. Cave JP and H. W. Newman JP at a Petty Sessions for part of Berkeley division. First offence. Fine £1 9s. 6d. and 10/6 costs. Offence committed 12 Dec. 1834.

54/A/34   24 Nov. 1834. William Griffiths, [alehouse keeper], of St. Philip and St. Jacob, [Bristol]. Keeping his house open for the the sale of beer after 10 p.m. W. Fripp JP and

J. Haythorne JP at a Petty Sessions for part of Berkeley division. First offence. Fine £1 12*s*. 6*d*. and 7/6 costs. Offence committed 10 Nov. 1834.

54/A/35 20 Nov. 1834. George Theodore Harper, [alehouse keeper], of St. Philip and St. Jacob, [Bristol]. Keeping his house open for the sale of beer after 10 p.m. W. Fripp JP and Rev. W. Mirehouse JP at a Petty Sessions for part of Berkeley division. Fine £1 12*s*. 6*d*. and 7/6 costs. Offence committed 10 Nov. 1834.

54/A/36 20 Nov. 1834. William Davey, victualler, of the Crown and Anchor, St. Philip and St. Jacob, [Bristol]. Failing to maintain good order in his house. W. Fripp JP and J. Haythorne JP at Lawfords Gate sessions room. First offence. Fine £5 and 7/6 costs. Offence committed 10 Nov. 1834

54/A/37 20 Nov. 1834. Robert Everson, victualler, of St. Philip and St. Jacob, [Bristol]. Failing to maintain good order in his house. W. Fripp JP and Rev. W. Mirehouse JP at Lawfords Gate sessions room. First offence. Fine £2 and 7/6 costs. Offence committed 10 Nov. 1834.

54/A/38 1 Jan. 1835. William Richards. Assaulting Mary Bryant at St. Philip and St. Jacob, [Bristol]. G. Goldney JP and J. S. Harford JP at Lawfords Gate sessions room. Fine 5/- and 8/6 costs or twenty-one days in Lawfords Gate house of correction. Offence committed 26 Dec. 1834.

54/A/39 30 Oct. 1834. Ann Scales. Assaulting Sarah White at St. Philip and St. Jacob, [Bristol]. G. Goldney JP and A. G. H. Battersby JP at Lawfords Gate sessions room. Fine 14/6 and 5/6 costs or one calendar month in Lawfords Gate house of correction. Offence committed 2 Oct. 1834.

54/A/40 15 Dec. 1834. James Pickford. Assaulting Frederick Watkins at Clifton. J. Savage JP and H. W. Newman JP at Lawfords Gate sessions room. Fine 13/- and 7/- costs or six weeks in Lawfords Gate house of correction. Offence committed 13 Dec. 1834.

54/A/41 18 Dec. 1834. Samuel Davis. Assaulting Fanny Burchell at Bitton. H. W. Newman JP and D. Cave JP at Lawfords Gate sessions room. Fine 10/- and 7/- costs or one calendar month in Lawfords Gate house of correction. Offence committed 13 Dec. 1834.

54/A/42 18 Dec. 1834. John Crates. Assaulting Henry Tiley at St. James, [Bristol]. D. Cave JP and H. W. Newman JP at Lawfords Gate sessions room. Fine 1/- and 6/6 costs or fourteen days in Lawfords Gate house of correction. Offence committed 6 Dec. 1834.

54/A/43 18 Dec. 1834. Samuel Spokes. Assaulting Philip Nutt at St. Philip and St. Jacob, [Bristol]. D. Cave JP and H. W. Newman JP at Lawfords Gate sessions room. Fine 9/6 and 10/6 costs or one calendar month in Lawfords Gate house of correction. Offence committed 5 Dec. 1834.

54/A/44 18 Dec. 1834. Richard Fowler. Assaulting John Higgs at St. Philip and St. Jacob, [Bristol]. D. Cave JP and H. W. Newman JP at Lawfords Gate sessions room. Fine 1/- and 16/6 costs or one calendar month in Lawfords Gate house of correction. Offence committed 2 Dec. 1834.

54/A/45 27 Nov. 1834. George Briggs. Assaulting Joseph Scales at St. Philip and St. Jacob, [Bristol]. W. Fripp JP and H. W. Newman JP at Lawfords Gate sessions room. Fine £1 and 8/6 costs or one calendar month in Lawfords Gate house of correction. Offence committed 8 Oct. 1834.

54/A/46 20 Nov. 1834. William Edmunds. Assaulting Elizabeth Palmer at Westbury on Trym. W. Fripp JP and Rev. W. Mirehouse JP at Lawfords Gate sessions room. Fine 12/- and 8/- costs or fourteen [days] in Lawfords Gate house of correction. Offence committed 14 Nov. 1834.

54/A/47   20 Nov. 1834. Thomas Sutton. Assaulting Edward Russell at Mangotsfield. W. Fripp JP and G. Worrall JP at Lawfords Gate sessions room. Fine £2 and 16/- costs or one calendar month in Lawfords Gate house of correction. Offence committed 5 Nov. 1834.

54/A/48   13 Nov. 1834. James Barnett. Assaulting William Wiltshire at St. Philip and St. Jacob, [Bristol]. G. Goldney JP and Rev. W. Davies JP at Lawfords Gate sessions room. Fine 3/6 and 6/6 costs or fourteen days in Lawfords Gate house of correction. Offence committed 10 Nov. 1834.

54/A/49   6 Nov. 1834. Joseph Wilson. Assaulting Jemima Jones at Westbury [on Trym]. W. Fripp JP and J. Haythorne JP at Lawfords Gate sessions room. Fine £4 15s. and 5/- costs or two calendar months in Lawfords Gate house of correction. Offence committed 6 Nov. 1834.

54/A/50   6 Nov. 1834. William Upton. Assaulting John Nichols at Winterbourne. W. Fripp JP and G. Goldney JP at Lawfords Gate sessions room. Fine £2 10s. and 14/6 costs or two calendar months in Lawfords Gate house of correction. Offence committed 5 Oct. 1834.

54/A/ 51   6 Nov. 1834. Jeremiah Williams. Assaulting Hester Williams at Clifton. W. Fripp JP and J. S. Harford JP at Lawfords Gate sessions room. Fine £1 11s. and 9/- costs or one calendar month in Lawfords Gate house of correction. Offence committed 22 Oct. 1834.

54/A/52   30 Oct. 1834. James Lanning. Assaulting Mary Robins at St. Philip and St. Jacob, [Bristol]. G. Goldney JP and A. G. H. Battersby JP at Lawfords Gate sessions room. Fine 4/6 and 5/6 costs or fourteen days in Lawfords Gate house of correction. Offence committed 23 Oct. 1834.

54/A/53   23 Oct. 1834. William Caines. Assaulting Samuel Gingell at Bitton. G. Goldney JP and G. Hilhouse JP at Lawfords Gate sessions room. Fine £1 12s. and 8/- costs [*later in the document given as* 7/-] or one calendar month in Lawfords Gate house of correction. Offence committed 12 July 1834.

54/A/54   23 Oct. 1834. Nathaniel Bryant. Assaulting Samuel Gingell [*etc., as* 54/A/53, *including the discrepancy about costs*].

54/A/55   23 Oct. 1834. William Clark. Assaulting Samuel Gingell [*etc., as* 54/A/53, *including the discrepancy about costs, except*] Fine £4 12s. .

54/A/56   23 Oct. 1834. Thomas Wilkins. Assaulting Thomas Morgan at Clifton. G. Goldney JP and H. W. Newman JP at Lawfords Gate sessions room. Fine 10/- and 5/6 costs or one calendar month in Lawfords Gate house of correction. Offence committed 17 Oct. 1834.

54/A/57   22 Dec. 1834. John Morgan, Ann Morgan and Thomas Finch. Assaulting John Gurney the younger, constable, at Bulley without provocation. O. Ricardo JP and R. F. Onslow JP at Newent. Fine 1/- and 12/- costs or fourteen days in Littledean house of correction. Offence committed 6 Dec. 1834.

54/A/58   3 Nov. 1834. James Walker. Begging in Newent. Rev. J. Commeline JP and R. F. Onslow JP at Newent. Hard labour for one calendar month in Littledean house of correction. Offence committed 2 Nov. 1834.

54/A/59   27 Oct. 1834. William Nash *alias* Ashwin. Stealing half a peck of pears growing in a nursery at Tibberton, the property of Thomas Humpidge. O. Ricardo JP at Newent. Fine 3/- and 6d. (the value of the pears), to be paid to an overseer of the poor, and 8/6 costs. Complainant examined as to proof of offence. Offence committed 12 Oct. 1834.

54/A/60   1 Dec. 1834. Joseph Mason. Begging in Newent. O. Ricardo JP and R. F. Onslow JP at Newent. Hard labour for fourteen days in Littledean house of correction. Offence committed 1 Dec. 1834.

54/A/61   22 Dec. 1834. Elizabeth Gatfield. Assaulting Harriet wife of William Gatfield of Aston Ingham, Herefs., at Newent. O. Ricardo JP and R. F. Onslow JP at Newent. Fine 1/6 and 10/6 costs or fourteen days in Littledean house of correction. Offence committed 24 Nov. 1834.

54/A/62   20 Oct. 1834. Edward Jones. Assaulting Samuel Wood at Awre. C. Crawley JP and J. Pyrke JP at Newnham in the Forest division. Fine £2 10*s.* and 8/- costs or two calendar months in Littledean house of correction. Offence committed 4 Oct. 1834.

54/A/63   15 Dec. 1834. Cornelius Baldwin. Assaulting Richard Court at St. Briavels hundred. C. Crawley JP and J. Pyrke JP at Newnham in the Forest division. Fine 50/- and 8/- costs. Given four weeks to pay. In default, two calendar months in Littledean house of correction. Offence committed 25 Nov. 1834.

54/A/64   20 Oct. 1834. Elmes Edward Harrison. Assaulting John Needs at Blakeney. C. Crawley JP and J. Pyrke JP at Newnham in the Forest division. Fine £1 and 8/- costs or fourteen days in Littledean house of correction. Offence committed 9 Oct. 1834.

54/A/65   16 Dec. 1834 Edward James of Bream, labourer. Trespassing in pursuit of game on land at Newland occupied by Edward Machen Esq. P. J. Ducarel JP at Coleford. James James, yeoman, of Bream, complainant. Fine £2. E. Machen to receive 8/- costs. Given four weeks to pay. In default, two calendar months in Littledean house of correction. Offence committed about 10 a.m. 25 Nov. 1834.

54/A/66   18 Nov. 1834. John Preece of Whitchurch, Herefs., innkeeper. Trespassing in pursuit of game on His Majesty's land at St. Briavels hundred. P. J. Ducarel JP at Coleford. George Brammer, yeoman, of St. Briavels hundred, complainant. Fine £2, to be paid to the high constable of St. Briavels hundred, or two calendar months in Littledean house of correction. Offence committed about 10 a.m. 3 Oct. 1834.

54/A/67   18 Nov. 1834. John Corles, gentleman, and William Corles, both of Ross, Herefs. Trespassing on His Majesty's land in Staunton in pursuit of game. P. J. Ducarel JP at Coleford. George Brammer, yeoman, of St. Briavels hundred, complainant. Fine 10/- each, to be paid to the high constable of St. Briavels hundred, and 6/6 costs each to the complainant, or two calendar months in Littledean house of correction. Offence committed about 10 a.m. 12 Nov. 1834.

54/A/68   19 Nov. 1834. Thomas Davis of Ruardean, labourer. Using a wire to kill game in Ruardean. J. Pyrke JP and M. Colchester JP at Littledean. William Yemm, yeoman, of Ruardean, complainant. Fine £5, to be paid to an overseer of the poor, or two months in Littledean house of correction. Offence committed 6 Oct. 1834.

54/A/69–   22 Dec. 1834. [*Names as below.*] Possessing defective weights. W. N. Tonge JP and
137   W. Davies D.D. JP at a Petty Sessions held at the Swan inn, Thornbury, for Thornbury division. William Clements, inspector of weights and balances, complainant. Weights forfeited. [*Fines and date Offence committed (all 1834) as below.*]

54/A/69   Elizabeth Knapp, blacksmith, of Thornbury. Four defective weights in her shop. Fine 5/- and 8/- costs. (11 Dec.)

54/A/70   William Mill Mawley of Thornbury, grocer. Five defective weights. Fine 7/6 and 8/- costs. (10 Dec.)

54/A/71   Messrs. Councell Jennings and Company of Thornbury, grocers. Three defective weights. Fine 5/- and 8/- costs. (10 Dec.)

54/A/72   Aaron Marsh of Thornbury, tinman. Five defective weights in his shop. Fine 5/- and 8/- costs. (10 Dec.)

54/A/73   Abraham Thomas of Olveston, shopkeeper. Four defective weights. Fine 5/- and 8/6 costs. (12 Dec.)

54/A/74   John Millard of Olveston, shopkeeper. Five defective weights. Fine 5/- and 8/6 costs. (12 Dec.)

54/A/75   John Taylor of Olveston, baker. Three defective weights in his bakehouse. Fine 5/- and 8/6 costs. (12 Dec.)

54/A/76   George Williams of Olveston, shopkeeper. Four defective weights. Fine 10/- and 8/6 costs. (12 Dec.)

54/A/77   James Millard of Olveston, shopkeeper. Four defective weights. Fine 5/- and 8/6 costs. (12 Dec.)

54/A/78   Thomas Williams Peters of Olveston, grocer. Four defective weights. Fine 7/6 and 8/6 costs. (12 Dec.)

54/A/79   Mary Williams of Olveston, shopkeeper. Four defective weights. Fine 7/6 and 8/6 costs. (12 Dec.)

54/A/80   Ann Reed of Thornbury, shopkeeper. Four defective weights. Fine 5/- and 8/- costs. (11 Dec.)

54/A/81   Thomas Nelmes of Thornbury, butcher. Ten defective weights. Fine 10/- and 8/- costs. (11 Dec.)

54/A/82   Joseph Walker of Thornbury, butcher. Five defective weights. Fine 7/6 and 8/- costs. (11 Dec.)

54/A/83   John Williams of Thornbury, grocer. Five defective weights. Fine 5/- and 8/- costs. (11 Dec.)

54/A/84   William Trotman of Thornbury, retailer. Two defective weights in his house. Fine 7/6 and 8/- costs. (15 Dec.)

54/A/85   Thomas Wicks of Thornbury, shopkeeper. Five defective weights. Fine 5/- and 8/6 costs. (15 Dec.)

54/A/86   Samuel Trotman of Thornbury, retailer. Four defective weights in his house. Fine 5/- and 8/6 costs. (15 Dec.)

54/A/87   John Rugman of Thornbury, butcher. Four defective weights. Fine 7/6 and 8/6 costs. (15 Dec.)

54/A/88   Sarah Olive of Alveston, shopkeeper. Five defective weights. Fine 10/- and 8/6 costs. (13 Dec.)

54/A/89   Mary Wilks of Thornbury, shopkeeper. Four defective weights. Fine 5/- and 8/6 costs. (13 Dec.)

54/A/90   Thomas Watkins of Thornbury, pig butcher. Eight defective weights. Fine 15/- and 8/6 costs. (13 Dec.)

54/A/91   Thomas Pritchard of Thornbury, pig butcher. Three defective weights. Fine 5/- and 8/6 costs. (13 Dec.)

54/A/92   Jonah Whitfield of Thornbury, baker. Two defective weights in his mill. Fine 5/- and 8/6 costs. (13 Dec.)

54/A/93   George Thomas of Thornbury, baker. Three defective weights in his house. Fine 5/- and 8/6 costs. (13 Dec.)

54/A/94   Mark Williams of Thornbury, blacksmith. Two defective weights. Fine 5/- and 8/- costs. (10 Dec.)

54/A/95   Thomas Smith of Thornbury, tea dealer. Two defective weights. Fine 5/- and 8/- costs. (10 Dec.)

54/A/96   George Shepherd of Thornbury, grocer. Three defective weights. Fine 5/- and 8/- costs. (10 Dec.)

54/A/97   Hannah Parkhouse of Thornbury, grocer. Three defective weights. Fine 10/- and 8/- costs. (10 Dec.)

54/A/98   William Radford Wilcox of Thornbury, grocer. Six defective weights. Fine 5/- and 8/- costs. (10 Dec.)

54/A/99   James Smart of Thornbury, butcher. Two defective weights. Fine 5/- and 8/6 costs. (15 Dec.)

54/A/100   Mary Sharp of Thornbury, fishwoman. Three defective weights in her house. Fine 5/- and 8/6 costs. (15 Dec.)

54/A/101   Robert Allen of Thornbury, fisherman. One defective weight in his shop. Fine 5/- and 8/6 costs. (15 Dec.)

54/A/102   Frederick White of Thornbury, fisherman. Three defective weights in his house. Fine 5/- and 8/6 costs. (15 Dec.)

54/A/103   William and Hannah Greenwood of Thornbury, maltsters. One defective weight. Fine 5/- and 8/- costs. (10 Dec.)

54/A/104   Daniel Isles of Thornbury, rope-maker. Two defective weights. Fine 5/- and 8/- costs. (10 Dec.)

54/A/105   Jesse Cossham of Thornbury, grocer. Two defective weights. Fine 5/- and 8/- costs. (10 Dec.)

54/A/106   Charles White of Thornbury, glazier. Two defective weights. Fine 6/- and 8/- costs. (10 Dec.)

54/A/107   George Cossham of Thornbury, grocer. Seven defective weights. Fine 10/- and 8/- costs. (10 Dec.)

54/A/108   John Carwardine of Thornbury, tallow chandler. Six defective weights. Fine 10/- and 8/- costs. (10 Dec.)

54/A/109   Daniel Pitcher of Thornbury, saddler. Three defective weights. Fine 5/- and 8/- costs. (10 Dec.)

54/A/110   Daniel Palser of Thornbury, tinman. Four defective weights. Fine 5/- and 8/- costs. (11 Dec.)

54/A/111   George Nichols of Thornbury, butcher. Three defective weights. Fine 5/- and 8/- costs. (11 Dec.)

54/A/112   George Rice of Thornbury, butcher. Three defective weights. Fine 5/- and 8/- costs. (11 Dec.)

54/A/113   George Motley of Thornbury, grocer. Four defective weights. Fine 10/- and 8/- costs. (11 Dec.)

54/A/114   William Hartnell of Thornbury, baker. Four defective weights. Fine 5/- and 8/- costs. (11 Dec.)

54/A/115   Thomas Evans of Thornbury, baker. Six defective weights. Fine 20/- and 8/- costs. (10 Dec.)

54/A/116   Hester Pitcher of Thornbury, shopkeeper. Five defective weights. Fine 7/6 and 8/6 costs. (9 Dec.)

54/A/117   Martha Eley of Thornbury, spinster. Four defective weights. Fine 6/- and 8/- costs. (10 Dec.)

54/A/118   Hannah Lucas of Thornbury, spinster. Eight defective weights. Fine 10/- and 8/- costs. (10 Dec.)

54/A/119   Joseph Laver of Thornbury, tea dealer. Five defective weights. Fine 5/- and 8/- costs. (10 Dec.)

54/A/120   George Laver of Thornbury, confectioner. Four defective weights. Fine 5/- and 8/- costs. (10 Dec.)

54/A/121   James Smith of Thornbury, shopkeeper. Four defective weights. Fine 7/6 and 8/6 costs. (13 Dec.)

54/A/122   Thomas Hitchings of Thornbury, shopkeeper. Four defective weights in his house. Fine 5/- and 8/6 costs. (13 Dec.)

54/A/123   Robert Howard of Thornbury, shopkeeper. Six defective weights. Fine 10/- and 8/6 costs. (15 Dec.)

54/A/124   George Gazard of Thornbury, baker. Three defective weights. Fine 5/- and 8/6 costs. (13 Dec.)

54/A/125   Frederick Biddle of Thornbury, shopkeeper. Four defective weights. Fine 10/- and 8/6 costs. (15 Dec.)

54/A/126   John Taylor of Thornbury, fisherman. One defective weight in his house. Fine 5/- and 8/6 costs. (15 Dec.)

54/A/127   Nicholas King of Thornbury, baker. Two defective weights in his house. Fine 5/- amd 8/6 costs. (16 Dec.)

54/A/128   Joseph Williams of Thornbury, blacksmith. Three defective weights. Fine 5/- and 8/- costs. (11 Dec.)

54/A/129   Thomas Facey of Thornbury, grocer. Two defective weights. Fine 5/- and 8/- costs. (11 Dec.)

54/A/130   James Bennett of Thornbury, retailer. Five defective weights in his house. Fine 5/- and 8/6 costs. (9 Dec.)

54/A/131   George Walker of Thornbury, baker. Four defective weights. Fine 7/6 and 8/- costs. (11 Dec.)

54/A/132   William Churchus of Olveston, shopkeeper. Three defective weights. Fine 5/- and 8/6 costs. (12 Dec.)

54/A/133   Samuel Gazard of Thornbury, retailer. Four defective weights. Fine 5/- and 8/6 costs. (13 Dec.)

54/A/134   Mary Cossham and Elizabeth Taylor of Thornbury, shopkeepers. Three defective weights. Fine 5/- and 8/- costs. (11 Dec.)

54/A/135   Mary Meachin of Thornbury, fishwoman. Two defective weights in her house. Fine 5/- and 8/6 costs. (15 Dec.)

54/A/136   William Davis of Thornbury, baker. Two defective weights in his house. Fine 5/- and 8/6 costs. (16 Dec.)

54/A/137   Abraham Cole of Thornbury, butcher. Two defective weights. Fine 5/- and 8/- costs. (10 Dec.)

54/A/138   15 Nov. 1834. Robert Knapp Barrow of Thornbury, gentleman. Trespassing in search and pursuit of game, the property of Samuel Cruger Peach and Danvers Ward Esqs. of Tockington, on land at Olveston occupied by Charles Neate, yeoman. W. N. Tonge JP, W. Davies D.D. JP and Rev. M. F. T. Stephens JP at Thornbury. Thomas Fry, labourer, of Olveston, agent for the owners of the game and the occupier of the land, complainant. Fine 5/-, to be paid to Thomas Williams Peters, overseer of the poor of Olveston, and 12/- costs to the complainant, or one calendar month in Lawfords Gate house of correction. Offence committed at 12 noon Saturday 1 Nov. 1834.

54/A/139   6 Dec. 1834. Nathaniel Shield of Thornbury, yeoman. Trespassing in search and pursuit of game at Littleton upon Severn on land occupied by Mapson Taylor. W. N. Tonge JP, W. Davies D.D. JP and Rev. M. F. T. Stephens JP at Thornbury. William Harvey, labourer, of Elberton, complainant and agent for Samuel Cruger Peach Esq. of Tockington, owner of the game. Fine £1, to be paid to Benjamin Collins, overseer of the poor of Littleton upon Severn, and 10/- costs to the complainant, or one calendar month in Lawfords Gate house of correction. Offence committed about 9 a.m. Saturday 15 Nov. 1834.

54/A/140   6 Dec. 1834. Robert Knapp Barrow, gentleman, of Thornbury. Trespassing in pursuit of game at Thornbury on land occupied by James Cullimore the elder. W. N. Tonge JP, W. Davies D.D. JP and Rev. M. F. T. Stephens JP at Thornbury. William Harvey, labourer, of Elberton, agent for Samuel Cruger Peach Esq. of Tockington, owner of the game, complainant. Fine £1, to be paid to Thomas Nelmes, assistant overseer of the poor of Thornbury, and 10/- to the complainant, or one calendar month in Lawfords Gate house of correction. Offence committed about 9 a.m. 15 Nov. 1834.

54/A/141   20 Dec. 1834. Robert Jones, gentleman, of Olveston. Trespassing in pursuit and search of game on land at Olveston occupied by William Millard. [*Two charges.*] Dr. A. Carrick M.D. JP, W. Davies D.D. JP and Rev. M. F. T. Stephens JP at Thornbury. Thomas Fry, labourer, of Olveston, complainant and agent for Samuel Cruger Peach Esq. of Tockington, owner of the game. Fine £1 on each charge, to be paid to Thomas Williams Peters, overseer of the poor of Olveston, and 7/6 costs to go to the complainant, or one calendar month in Lawfords Gate house of correction on each charge. Offence committed Wednesday 12 Nov. 1834 at about 2 p.m. and Friday 14 Nov. 1834 at 9 a.m.

54/A/142   4 Oct. 1834. William Bush Parker, gentleman, of Henbury. Trespassing in pursuit of game 'with force and arms' on land at Olveston belonging to William Lane, gentleman, and occupied by James Williams the younger, yeoman. R. J. Charleton D.D. JP, W. Davies D.D. JP and W. N. Tonge JP at the Swan inn, Thornbury. Thomas Fry, labourer, agent for Samuel Cruger Peach Esq., owner of the game, William Lane, gentleman, and James Williams the younger informed the first-mentioned magistrate of the offence on 29 Sept. Offender summoned but did not appear. Thomas Fry deposed that he saw the offender with another person, unknown, beating for game, with a gun, two greyhounds and a pointer. When challenged, offender declared he had Farmer Williams's permission. James Williams said this was not so. Fine £2, to be paid to Thomas Wilcox [*sic*] Peters, an overseer of the poor, and 14/- costs to Thomas Fry within two weeks. In default, one calendar month in Lawfords Gate house of correction. Offence committed Friday 26 Sept. at about 5 p.m.

54/A/143   18 Oct. 1834. Robert Jones, gentleman, of Olveston. Trespassing in search and pursuit of game at Littleton upon Severn on land occupied by Samuel Keen. W. N. Tonge JP, W. Davies D.D. JP and Rev. M. F. T. Stephens JP at Thornbury. William Harvey of Elberton, labourer, agent for Samuel Cruger Peach Esq. of Tockington, owner of the game, complainant. Fine £1, to be paid to Benjamin Collins, an overseer of the poor, and 12/- costs to the complainant, before 1 Nov. In default, one calendar month in Lawfords Gate house of correction. Offence committed about noon Tuesday 7 Oct. 1834.

54/A/144   1 Nov. 1834. Benjamin Webley, late of Henbury, with four others unknown. Trespassing on land at Almondsbury belonging to William Chester Master Esq., occupied by William Young, in search of game, with two greyhounds, a pointer and a spaniel, and coursing and killing a hare. W. N. Tonge JP, W. Davies D.D. JP and Rev. M. F. T. Stephens JP at the Swan inn, Thornbury. George Lippiatt, labourer and agent for W. C. Master Esq., informer (on 10 Oct.) and witness. Offender summoned but did not appear. Fine £5, to be paid to Benjamin Smith, overseer of the poor, and 17/6 costs to G. Lippiatt, or hard labour for three calendar months in Lawfords Gate house of correction. Offence committed Tuesday 30 Sept. 1834.

54/A/145 27 Nov. 1834. Timothy Guest of Sherston, Wilts. Damaging by cutting several times with a hookett the tilt or cover of a cart, the property of William Higgs, carver, of Chipping Sodbury, standing in the street at Hawkesbury Upton. F. Trotman JP. Fine £1 8*s.* costs, to be paid to John Winbow, constable of Hawkesbury Upton, for expenses incurred and necessary assistants during three days, and 3/- damages to William Higgs, or one calendar month in Horsley house of correction. Offence committed 8 Nov. 1834.

54/A/146 30 Dec. 1834. William Gilders, late of Willersey. Killing a hare at Willersey without possessing a game certificate. N. W. Marriott JP and C. E. Hanford JP at a Petty Sessions held at the magistrates' office, Pershore, Worcs. Fine £5, to be paid to an overseer of the poor, and £1 8*s.* 6*d.* [costs] to William Shepherd, the complainant, or hard labour for two calendar months in Gloucester house of correction. Offence committed 8 Dec. 1834.

54/A/147 17 Dec. 1834. Thoms Darby. Trespassing in pursuit of game or conies at Rodmarton without a game certificate. W. M. Paul JP at Tetbury. Fine £2, to be paid to an overseer of the poor, and 8/6 costs to the complainant Michael Shipton, or hard labour for two calendar months in Horsley house of correction. Offence committed 17 Nov. 1834.

54/A/148 31 Dec. 1834. Edward James Howell. Using a gun to kill game at Rodmarton without a game certificate. T. G. B. Estcourt JP and W. M. Paul JP at Tetbury. Fine £5, to be paid to an overseer of the poor, and 14/6 costs to the complainant Michael Shipton, or hard labour for three calendar months in Horsley house of correction. Offence committed 17 Nov. 1834.

54/A/149 30 Dec. 1834. Edward Griffin of Eastington, labourer. Assaulting Caroline Morgan at Eastington. D. J. Niblett JP and P. Leversage JP at Wheatenhurst. Fine £2 and 6/- costs or one month in Horsley house of correction. Offence committed 9 Nov. 1834.

54/A/150 22 Oct. 1834. Charles New of Beckford, yeoman. Assaulting and challenging to fight Joseph Dyer, labourer, of Beckford without provocation. Rev. C. White JP and J. Timbrill D.D. JP at Tewkesbury. Fine 20/-, to be paid to Joseph Freeman, overseer of the poor of Beckford, and 14/- costs to the complainant. Offence committed 7 Oct. 1834.

54/A/151 5 Nov. 1834. George Bailey of Forthampton, labourer. Cutting and stealing a branch of a pear tree growing in an orchard called the Croft, occupied by John Cotterell, farmer, the property of Joseph Yorke Esq. of Forthampton. J. Timbrill D.D. JP and Rev. J. Keysall JP at Tewkesbury. Fine 5/-, to be paid to an overseer of the poor, and 12/- costs to the complainant J. Cotterell. Offence committed 26 Oct. 1834.

54/A/152 5 Nov. 1834. George Drinkwater of Beckford, labourer. Trespassing by climbing over iron rails into the garden of Nathan Cotton at Beckford and violently assaulting and threatening him. J. Timbrill D.D. JP and Rev. J. Keysall JP at Tewkesbury. Fine £2 6*s.* 6*d.*, to be paid to Joseph Freeman, overseer of the poor, and 13/6 costs to the complainant. Offence committed 13 Oct. 1834.

54/A/153 31 Dec. 1834. Captain George Younghusband of Twyning. Killing a hare, in shrubbery in his own occupation, without a game certificate. J. Timbrill D.D. JP, Rev. J. Keysall JP and J. W. Martin JP at Tewkesbury. Fine £5, to be paid to Peter Dee, an overseer of the poor of Twyning, and 7/6 costs to the complainant William Hale. Offence committed 10 Nov. 1834.

54/A/154 16 Dec. 1834. John Phipps of Longborough, labourer. Assaulting Eliza Shelton. Rev. C. Jeaffreson JP and Rev. J. R. Hall JP at Moreton in Marsh. Fine £2, to be paid to Richard Edgington, an overseer of the poor of Longborough, and 13/6 costs, or two calendar months in Northleach house of correction. Offence committed 13 Dec. 1834.

54/A/155 4 Nov. 1834. Joseph Newman of Todenham, labourer. Using a snare for taking game at Todenham without a game certificate. Rev. J. R. Hall JP and Rev. C. Jeaffreson JP at Moreton in Marsh. Fine £5, to be paid to an overseer of the poor, and 10/- costs to William Randall, complainant, or hard labour for three calendar months in Northleach house of correction. Offence committed 4 Nov. 1834.

54/A/156 2 Jan. 1835. William King of Bisley, licensed beer retailer. Allowing beer to be consumed within his premises after 10 p.m. H. Burgh JP and H. Wyatt JP at a Petty Sessions for Bisley hundred. First offence. Fine £2 including 9/- costs. Offence committed 11 Dec. 1834.

54/A/157 31 Dec. 1834. Henry Nickolls, Thomas Pitt and Thomas Papps, labourers, of Stroud. Stealing part of a dead fence, the property of Robert May, beer seller, of Stroud. H. Burgh JP at Stroud. Fine £3, to be paid to an overseer of the poor. Also fined 2/- each (the value of the fence), to be paid to an overseer of the poor, and 6/- each costs, or hard labour for two calendar months in Horsley house of correction. Complainant examined as to proof of offence. Offence committed 30 Dec. 1834.

54/A/158 20 Dec. 1834. James Hatton of Painswick, labourer. Violently assaulting James Cooper, yeoman, of Painswick. H. Burgh JP and N. S. Marling JP at Stroud. Fine £4 12s. and 8/- costs or two calendar months in Horsley house of correction. Offence committed 13 Dec. 1834.

54/A/159 19 Dec. 1834. Henry Hawkins of Painswick, gentleman. Violently assaulting George Partridge of Painswick, labourer. H. Burgh JP and N. S. Marling JP at Stroud. Fine 6d., to be paid to an overseer of the poor, and 7/6 costs to the complainant, or two calendar months in Horsley house of correction. Offence committed 8 Dec. 1834.

54/A/160 19 Dec. 1834. Henry Hawkins of Painswick, gentleman. Violently assaulting Samuel Holliday of Painswick, labourer [etc., as 54/A/159].

54/A/161 19 Dec. 1834. Henry Hawkins of Painswick, gentleman. Violently assaulting Richard Partridge of Painswick, labourer [etc., as 54/A/159].

54/A/162 16 Dec. 1834. William Adey of Randwick, labourer. Stealing turnips growing on land in Randwick occupied by John Butcher, yeoman. H. Burgh JP at Stroud. Hard labour for one calendar month in Horsley house of correction. Offence committed 15 Dec. 1834.

54/A/163 5 Dec. 1834. Samuel Cooke and Thomas White, labourers, of Randwick. Cutting and stealing underwood at Randwick, the property of Rt. Hon. John, Lord Sherborne. H. Burgh JP and D. Maclean JP at Stroud. Fine £2, to be paid to an overseer of the poor, 12/- costs and 1/6 damages to Lord Sherborne, or hard labour for one calendar month in Horsley house of correction. Offence committed 27 Nov. 1834.

54/A/164 21 Nov. 1834. Thomas West of Painswick, labourer. Using a wire to kill game without a game certificate. H. Burgh JP and N. S. Marling JP at Stroud. Fine 10/-, to be paid to Richard Bishop Constable, an overseer of the poor, and 10/- costs to William Cooke of Painswick, complainant, or hard labour for two calendar months in Horsley house of correction. Offence committed 7 Nov. 1834.

54/A/165 11 Nov. 1834. George Waldon of Winstone, labourer. Violently assaulting William Ludlow, labourer, of Winstone. H. Burgh JP and J. Mills JP at Stroud. Fine £4 3s. 6d., to be paid to an overseer of the poor, and 16/6 costs to the complainant, or two calendar months in Horsley house of correction. Offence committed 24 Sept. 1834.

54/A/166 11 Nov. 1834. Henry Nickolls and Thomas Papps, labourers, of Painswick. Stealing a quantity of potatoes growing on land occupied by Seth Sims, yeoman, of Painswick. H. Burgh JP at Stroud. Hard labour for one calendar month in Horsley house of correction. Offence committed 22 Oct. 1834.

54/A/167   2 Nov. 1834. Samuel Kirby and Joseph Webb of Minchinhampton, labourers. Violently assaulting William Humphris, labourer, of Minchinhampton. H. Burgh JP and D. Maclean JP at Stroud. Fine £4 12*s.* and 8/- costs or two calendar months in Horsley house of correction. Offence committed 27 Oct. 1834.

54/A/168   4 Nov. 1834. William Biggers of Rodborough, labourer. Violently assaulting James Hyett, labourer, of Stroud. H. Burgh JP and N. S. Marling JP at Stroud. Fine £4 12*s.* and 8/- costs or two calendar months in Horsley house of correction. Offence committed 3 Nov. 1834.

54/A/169   3 Nov. 1834. James Virgo of Woodchester, labourer. Trespassing in search of conies at Avening on land belonging to the Rt. Hon. Thomas, Lord Ducie. H. Burgh JP at Stroud. David Bushell of Avening, complainant. Fine £2 and 10/- costs or hard labour for two calendar months in Horsley house of correction. Offence committed 25 Sept. 1834.

54/A/170   14 Oct. 1834. Peter Hall and Richard Face. Rogues and vagabonds: being in an enclosed yard at Stroud with intent to commit a felony. H. Burgh JP at Stroud. Hard labour for three calendar months in Horsley house of correction. Offence committed 13 Oct. 1834.

54/A/171   3 Oct. 1834. William Waldon of Winstone, labourer. Violently assaulting William Ludlow of Winstone, labourer. H. Burgh JP and J. Mills JP at Stroud. Fine £4 9*s.* and 11/- costs or two calendar months in Horsley house of correction. Offence committed 24 Sept. 1834.

54/A/172   1 Dec. 1834. Jeremiah Bryant of Stroud, labourer. Violently assaulting John Bird, butcher, of Stroud, a tithingman executing his duty. H. Burgh JP and H. Wyatt JP at Stroud. Fine £4 12*s.* and 8/- costs or two calendar months in Horsley house of correction. Offence committed 30 Nov. 1834.

54/A/173   1 Aug. 1834. Charles Russell of Bisley, labourer. Maliciously injuring a sheep, the property of John Ballinger Esq. of Bisley. J. Mills JP and E. G. Hallewell JP at Stroud. Fine 10/- damages and 10/6 costs, both sums to be paid to the complainant, or hard labour for one calendar month in Horsley house of correction. Offence committed 21 May 1834.

54/A/174   1 Aug. 1834. Thomas Abel of Winstone, labourer. Attempting to take fish from [a stretch of] water, the private property of William Penn Gaskell Esq. at Winstone. J. Mills JP, E. G. Hallewell JP and N. S. Marling JP at Stroud. Fine 10/-, to be paid to an overseer of the poor, and 10/- costs, or hard labour for one calendar month in Horsley house of correction. Offence committed 2 July 1834.

54/A/175   18 July 1834. George Waldon of Winstone, labourer. Attempting to take fish from [a stretch of] water, the private property of William Penn Gaskell Esq. at Winstone. E. G. Hallewell JP and N. S. Marling JP at Stroud. Fine 10/-, to be paid to an overseer of the poor, and 10/- costs, or hard labour for one month in Horsley house of correction. Offence committed 3 July 1834.

54/A/176 –247   19 Dec. 1834. [*Names as below.*] Possessing defective weights. P. B. Purnell JP, B. C. Browne JP and Rev. J. H. Dunsford JP at a Petty Sessions held at Dursley town hall for the upper division of Berkeley hundred. William Clements, inspector of weights and balances, complainant. Weights forfeited. [*Fines as below*] and 5/- costs. [*Date offence committed (all 1834) as below.*]

54/A/176   Harriet Gardener of Dursley, shopkeeper. Four defective weights. Fine 5/-. (30 Sept.)

54/A/177   Charles King of Dursley, butcher. Two defective weights. Fine 5/-. (30 Sept.)

54/A/178   James Stagg or Dursley, shopkeeper. Four defective weights. Fine 8/-. (30 Sept.)

54/A/179   Elizabeth Moore of Dursley, grocer. One defective weight. Fine 5/-. (30 Sept.)

54/A/180   William Gunter of Dursley, shopkeeper. Seven defective weights. Fine 10/-. (29 Sept.)

54/A/181   John Harding of Dursley, grocer. Five defective weights. Fine 9/-. (29 Sept.)

54/A/182   Humphrey Austin of Dursley, seedsman. Two defective weights. Fine 5/-. (30 Sept.)

54/A/183   Abraham Austin of Uley, shopkeeper. Three defective weights. Fine 7/-. (26 Sept.)

54/A/184   Mary Higgs of Dursley, shopkeeper. One defective weight. Fine 5/-. (30 Sept.)

54/A/185   George Organ of Dursley, pig butcher. Five defective weights. Fine 9/-. (29 Sept.)

54/A/186   Samuel Bendall of Dursley, shopkeeper. Thirteen defective weights. Fine 20/-. (29 Sept.)

54/A/187   John Smith of Dursley, shopkeeper. Five defective weights. Fine 9/-. (29 Sept.)

54/A/188   George Harvey of Dursley, pig butcher. Seven defective weights. Fine 10/-. (29 Sept.)

54/A/189   Samuel Price of Uley, grocer. Two defective weights. Fine 5/-. (27 Sept.)

54/A/190   Eli Jakeway of Dursley, flour seller. Three defective weights. Fine 7/-. (29 Sept.)

54/A/191   Timothy Player of Dursley, shopkeeper. Three defective weights. Fine 7/-. (29 Sept.)

54/A/192   John Heath of Dursley, shopkeeper. Two defective weights in his house. Fine 5/-. (6 Oct.)

54/A/193   Ann Harris of Dursley, grocer. Three defective weights. Fine 7/-. (30 Sept.)

54/A/194   William Roberts of Dursley, shopkeeper. Seven defective weights. Fine 11/-. (30 Sept.)

54/A/195   John Davis of Dursley, bacon seller. Four defective weights in his bacon house. Fine 8/-. (30 Sept.)

54/A/196   William Clarke of Dursley, cheese seller. Four defective weights in his house. Fine 10/-. (30 Sept.)

54/A/197   Mary Ann Cook of Dursley, grocer. Three defective weights. Fine 7/-. (29 Sept.)

54/A/198   William Robinson of Dursley, baker. Two defective weights. Fine 5/-. (29 Sept.)

54/A/199   Meshach Dauncey of Dursley, pig butcher. Three defective weights. Fine 7/-. (29 Sept.)

54/A/200   Richard Tyndall of Dursley, grocer. Two defective weights. Fine 5/-. (29 Sept.)

54/A/201   James Smith of Dursley, shopkeeper. Five defective weights. Fine 10/-. (29 Sept.)

54/A/202   Cornelius Window of Uley, shopkeeper. Two defective weights. Fine 5/-. (27 Sept.)

54/A/203   Richard Souls of Uley, pig butcher. Four defective weights. Fine 8/-. (27 Sept.)

54/A/204   David Dauncey of Dursley, shopkeeper. Three defective weights in his house. Fine 7/-. (29 Sept.)

54/A/205   Thomas Perrin of Kingscote, shopkeeper. One defective weight. Fine 5/-. (26 Sept.)

54/A/206   Thomas White of Cam, shopkeeper. Five defective weights in his house. Fine 9/-. (1 Oct.)

54/A/207   Samuel Lord of Slimbridge, butcher. Four defective weights. Fine 8/-. (3 Oct.)

54/A/208   Samuel Pearce of Cam, mealman. One defective weight. Fine 5/-. (1 Oct.)

54/A/209   William Cave of Cam, butcher. Three defective weights. Fine 7/-. (1 Oct.)

54/A/210   Joseph Nicholls of Cam, butcher. Five defective weights. Fine 9/-. (1 Oct.)

54/A/211   Jonathan Gabb of Cam, butcher. Four defective weights. Fine 10/-. (12 Nov.)

54/A/212   Jonathan Gabb of Cam, butcher. Two defective weights. Fine 8/-. (1 Oct.) [*Cf.* 54/A/211, *which appears to result from a later visit by the inspector.*]

54/A/213   Richard Smart of Cam, shopkeeper. Two defective weights. Fine 5/-. (1 Oct.)

54/A/214   Samuel Holloway of Cam, shopkeeper. One defective weight. Fine 5/-. (1 Oct.)

54/A/215   Daniel Freem of Cam, shopkeeper. Two defective weights. Fine 5/-. (1 Oct.)

54/A/216   William Gunter of Cam, shopkeeper. Two defective weights. Fine 5/-. (1 Oct.)

54/A/217   Charles Goulding of Cam, baker. Three defective weights in his bakehouse. Fine 7/-. (1 Oct.)

54/A/218   Thomas Bendall of Cam, shopkeeper. Two defective weights. Fine 5/-. (1 Oct.)

54/A/219   James Peglar of Coaley, butcher. Four defective weights. Fine 8/-. (2 Oct.)

54/A/220   William Kearslake of Slimbridge, shopkeeper. Two defective weights. Fine 5/-. (3 Oct.)

54/A/221   William Tanner of Slimbridge, shopkeeper. Four defective weights. Fine 8/-. (3 Oct.)

54/A/222   William Mallett of Slimbridge, shopkeeper. Four defective weights. Fine 8/-. (3 Oct.)

54/A/223   Ann Hathaway of Slimbridge, shopkeeper. One defective weight. Fine 5/-. (3 Oct.)

54/A/224   William Huntley of Slimbridge, shopkeeper. Seven defective weights. Fine 11/-. (3 Oct.)

54/A/225   William Savage of Coaley, pig butcher. Three defective weights in his house. Fine 8/-. (2 Oct.)

54/A/226   Ira Smith of Coaley, shopkeeper. Three defective weights in his house. Fine 8/-. (2 Oct.)

54/A/227   Edward Underwood of Coaley, grocer. Three defective weights. Fine 7/-. (2 Oct.)

54/A/228   Daniel Frape of Coaley, shopkeeper. One defective weight. Fine 5/-. (2 Oct.)

54/A/229   Ralph Ashman of Uley, shopkeeper. Two defective weights. Fine 5/-. (27 Sept.)

54/A/230   Nathaniel French of Uley, shopkeeper. Six defective weights in his house. Fine 12/-. (27 Sept.)

54/A/231   Joseph King of Uley, shopkeeper. Two defective weights. Fine 5/-. (4 Oct.)

54/A/232   John Farr of Coaley, baker. Four defective weights in his house. Fine 8/-. (2 Oct.)

54/A/233   Joseph Fords of Coaley, shopkeeper. Three defective weights. Fine 7/-. (2 Oct.)

54/A/234   William Lord of Coaley, shopkeeper. Three defective weights. Fine 7/-. (2 Oct.)

54/A/235   Henry Edmonds of Coaley, shopkeeper. Two defective weights in his house. Fine 5/-. (2 Oct.)

54/A/236   Levi Smith of Coaley, shopkeeper. Five defective weights. Fine 9/-. (2 Oct.)

54/A/237   Mary Humphris of Uley, shopkeeper. Two defective weights. Fine 5/-. (27 Sept.)

54/A/238   Charles Hill of Uley, butcher. Five defective weights. Fine 9/-. (26 Sept.)

54/A/239   George Howell of Uley, baker. One defective weight. Fine 5/-. (27 Sept.)

54/A/240   Daniel Neale of Uley, dairyman and beer seller. Two defective weights in his dairy. Fine 5/-. (26 Sept.)

54/A/241   Charles Smith of Uley, shopkeeper. Two defective weights. Fine 5/-. (26 Sept.)

54/A/242   John Wight of Kingscote, maltster. Two defective weights in his house. Fine 5/-. (26 Sept.)

54/A/243   Charles Jackson of Uley, butcher. Two defective weights. Fine 5/-. (26 Sept.)

54/A/244   Benjamin Allen Weaver of Dursley, shopkeeper. Four defective weights. Fine 8/-. (30 Sept.)

54/A/245   Abraham Cole of Uley, shopkeeper. Four defective weights. Fine 8/-. (27 Sept.)

54/A/246   George Dangerfield of Uley, grocer. Four defective weights. Fine 8/-. (26 Sept.)

54/A/247   David Elliott of Owlpen, shopkeeper. Six defective weights. Fine 10/-. (26 Sept.)

54/A/248   16 Oct. 1834. Thomas Barnett. Assaulting Peter Simon at Cheltenham. J. E. Viner JP and J. Blagdon JP at Cheltenham. Fine 20/-, to be paid to an overseer of the poor, and 6/6 costs to the complainant. Offence committed 16 Oct. 1834.

54/A/249 18 Oct. 1834. Thomas Hanbury, clerk. Assaulting William Franklin at Cheltenham. R. B. Cooper JP and T. J. Baines JP at Cheltenham. Fine £4 15s. and 5/- costs. Offence committed 17 Oct. 1834.

54/A/250 23 Oct. 1834. Edward Ayliffe. Assaulting James Kitchen at Bishop's Cleeve. T. J. Baines JP and D. L. St. Clair at Cheltenham. Fine 10/- and 7/- costs. Offence committed 22 Oct. 1834.

54/A/251 25 Oct. 1834. James Garrett of Cheltenham, retail beer dealer. Permitting unlawful games in his premises. R. B. Cooper JP and T. J. Baines JP. First offence. Fine 40/- and 5/6 costs. Offence committed 18 Oct. 1834.

54/A/252 25 Oct. 1834. John Williams. Assaulting Josiah Mee at Cheltenham. R. B. Cooper JP and T. J. Baines JP at Cheltenham. Fine 10/- and 5/6 costs. Offence committed 18 Oct. 1834.

54/A/253 1 Nov. 1834. William Tuffley. Assaulting Mary Piff at Cheltenham. R. B. Cooper JP and T. J. Baines JP at Cheltenham. Fine 2/6 and 5/6 costs. Offence committed 29 Oct. 1834.

54/A/254 8 Nov. 1834. William Stevens. Assaulting George Bowles at Boddington. R. B. Cooper JP and T. J. Baines JP at Cheltenham. Fine £1 1s. and 7/6 costs. [Date of offence not given.]

54/A/255 11 Nov. 1834. Thomas Rose. Assaulting Jesse Castle at Cheltenham. J. E. Viner JP and J. Blagdon JP at Cheltenham. Fine 5/- and 4/- costs. Offence committed 11 Nov. 1834.

54/A/256 13 Nov. 1834. Joseph Patterson. Assaulting David Browning at Cheltenham. T. J. Baines JP and J. Blagdon JP at Cheltenham. Fine 40/- and 4/- costs. Offence committed 12 Nov. 1834.

54/A/257 15 Nov. 1834. John Mayo. Assaulting Joseph Symonds at [Cheltenham]. R. B. Cooper JP and T. J. Baines JP at Cheltenham. Fine 10/- and 5/- costs. Offence committed 13 Nov. 1834.

54/A/258 15 Nov. 1834. Sarah Smith. Assaulting Margaret Webb at Cheltenham. R. B. Cooper JP and T. J. Baines JP at Cheltenham. Fine 15/- and 6/6 costs. Offence committed 10 Nov. 1834.

54/A/259 18 Nov. 1834. Charles Craddock. Assaulting John Venfield at Cheltenham. R. B. Cooper JP and D. L. St. Clair JP at Cheltenham. Fine 20/- and 6/6 costs. Offence committed 28 Oct. 1834.

54/A/260 20 Nov. 1834. Edward Kemings, Richard Staite and George Wilson. Assaulting William Quarrell and others at Charlton Kings. R. B. Cooper JP and J. Blagdon JP at Cheltenham. Fine 20/- each, to be paid to an overseer of the poor of Cheltenham, and 5/6 each for costs. Offence committed 16 Nov. 1834.

54/A/261 20 Nov. 1834. William Postans. Assaulting William Quarrell at Charlton Kings. R. B. Cooper JP and J. Blagdon JP at Cheltenham. Fine 10/-, to be paid to an overseer of the poor of Charlton Kings, and 6/6 costs. Offence committed 16 Nov. 1834.

54/A/262 22 Nov. 1834. Henry Hobbs of Cheltenham, retail beer dealer. Allowing drunkenness and disorderly conduct in his alehouse. R. B. Cooper JP and T. J. Baines JP. First offence. Fine £1 and 6/6 costs. Offence committed 20 Nov. 1834.

54/A/263 25 Nov. 1834. William Browning. Assaulting Thomas Wasley at Cheltenham. J. E. Viner JP and J. Blagdon JP at Cheltenham. Fine 2/6 and 4/- costs. Offence committed 24 Nov. 1834.

54/A/264 25 Nov. 1834. Robert Apperley. Assaulting Thomas Wasley at Cheltenham. J. E. Viner JP and J. Blagdon JP at Cheltenham. Fine 10/- and 4/- costs. Offence committed 24 Nov. 1834.

54/A/265   27 Nov. 1834. Henry Merrett of Cheltenham. licensed game dealer. Buying four hares from an unlicensed source, Richard Pinchin, at Cheltenham. T. J. Baines JP and J. Blagdon JP at Cheltenham. Henry Fern, servant, of Cheltenham, complainant. Fine £5 and 3/- costs. Offence committed 27 Nov. 1834.

54/A/266   27 Nov. 1834. John Godfrey. Assaulting Ann Griffiths and Maria Wright at Cheltenham. T. J. Baines JP and D. L. St. Clair JP at Cheltenham. Fine £1 and 8/- costs. Offence committed 25 Nov. 1834.

54/A/267   27 Nov. 1834. Thomas and William Ayres. Assaulting Charles Edwards at Cheltenham. T. J. Baines JP and D. L. St. Clair JP at Cheltenham. Fine £1 and 6/6 costs. Offence committed 24 Nov. 1834.

54/A/268   4 Dec. 1834. Thomas Packer. Assaulting Thomas Sparrow at Cheltenham. R. B. Cooper JP and T. J. Baines JP at Cheltenham. Fine 16/- and 5/6 costs. Offence committed 29 Nov. 1834.

54/A/269   6 Dec. 1834. John Togwell. Assaulting Esther Shurmer at Boddington. R. B. Cooper JP and T. J. Baines JP at Cheltenham. Fine £3 and 9/- costs. Offence committed 4 Dec. 1834.

54/A/270   16 Dec. 1834. Sophia Townsend. Assaulting Joseph Hunt at Cheltenham. R. B. Cooper JP and T. J. Baines JP at Cheltenham. Fine 10/- and 7/6 costs. Offence committed 13 Dec. 1834.

54/A/271   18 Dec. 1834. William Smith and John Allen. Assaulting and beating Priscilla Gillett at Leigh. R. B. Cooper JP and J. E. Viner JP at Cheltenham. Smith fined 20/- and 7/6 costs, and Allen 5/- and 6/6 costs. Offence committed 15 Dec. 1834.

54/A/272   20 Dec. 1834. Thomas Oakey. Assaulting Thomas Wasley at Cheltenham. R. B. Cooper JP and T. J. Baines JP at Cheltenham. Fine 20/- and 4/- costs. Offence committed 18 Dec. 1834.

54/A/273   23 Dec. 1834. John Hughes. Assaulting and beating Hannah Mitchell at Cheltenham. R. B. Cooper JP and T. J. Baines JP at Cheltenham. Fine 20/- and 4/- costs. Offence committed 21 Dec. 1834.

54/A/274   5 Jan. 1835. Nathan Hunt. Being on enclosed land at Hawkesbury at night with six nets with intent to kill game. T. Kingscote JP and A. Shakespear JP at Horsley. Hard labour for three calendar months in Horsley house of correction, after which to find sureties totalling £20 against re-offending for one year. In default, a further six calendar months' hard labour. Offence committed the night of 22 Sept. 1834.

54/A/275   5 Jan. 1835. John Sellwood. Being on enclosed land [etc., as 54/A/274].

54/A/276   5 Jan. 1835. Isaac Hopkins. Being on enclosed land [etc., as 54/A/274].

54/A/277   5 Jan. 1835. John Chappell. Being on enclosed land [etc., as 54/A/274].

54/A/278   13 Dec. 1834. William Tandy. Being on enclosed land called Forty Acres at Beverstone at night with two gate nets with intent to kill game [etc., as 54/A/274 except] Offence committed 13 Dec. 1834.

54/A/279   23 Dec. 1834. Charles Bruton. Being on enclosed land at Bowldown Wood, Lasborough, with two nets at night with intent to kill game. T. Kingscote JP and A. Shakespear JP at Horsley. Previous conviction for similar offence at Ozleworth before the same magistrates on 22 Sept. 1832. [Cf. 51/D/1.] Hard labour for six calendar months in Horsley house of correction, after which to find sureties totalling £40 against re-offending within two years. In default, a further one year's hard labour. Offence committed 4 Nov. 1834.

54/A/280   17 Dec. 1834. Benjamin Carpenter. Being on enclosed land at Bowldown Wood, Lasborough, with two nets at night with intent to kill game [*etc., as* 54/A/274 *except*] Offence committed 18 Nov. 1834.

54/A/281   27 Dec. 1834. John Leonard. Being on enclosed land at Boxwell with a net at night with intent to kill game [*etc., as* 54/A/274 *except*] Offence committed 4 Dec. 1834 [*but cf.* 54/D/79, *where the offence is said to have been committed* 13 Nov. 1834].

54/A/282   19 Dec. 1834. John Shipton. Being on enclosed land called Forty Acres at Beverstone with two nets at night with intent to kill game. R. Kingscote JP and T. Kingscote JP at Kingscote [*etc., as* 54/A/274 *except omitting* calendar *and*] Offence committed 13 Dec. 1834.

54/A/283   19 Nov. 1834. Samuel Farr. Being in Bowldown Wood at Lasborough with two nets at night with intent to kill game. R. Kingscote JP and T. Kingscote JP at Kinsgscote [*etc., as* 54/A/274 *except omitting* calendar *and*] Offence committed 18 Nov. 1834.

54/A/284   23 Dec. 1834. John Bird. Stealing about four bushels of turnips valued at 3/- growing on land at Wotton under Edge, the property of John Mills. T. Kingscote JP and A. Shakespear JP at Horsley. One calendar month in Horsley house of correction. Offence committed 23 Dec. 1834.

54/A/285   31 Dec. 1834. Frederick White. Being on enclosed land adjoining Bodkin Wood, Horton, with four nets at night with intent to kill game [*etc., as* 54/A/274 *except omitting* calendar *and*] Offence committed 10 Dec. 1834.

54/A/286   31 Dec. 1834. Moses Manning. Being on enclosed land adjoining Bowldown Wood at Lasborough with four nets at night with intent to kill game [*etc., as* 54/A/274 *except omitting* calendar *and*] Offence committed 11 Nov. 1834.

54/A/287   31 Dec. 1834. William Workman. Being on enclosed land at Oldbury on the Hill with two nets at night and killing two hares [*etc., as* 54/A/274 *except omitting* calendar *and*] Offence committed 25 July 1834.

54/A/288   31 Dec. 1834. Absalom White. Being on enclosed land adjoining Bodkin Wood at Horton with two nets at night with intent to kill game [*etc., as* 54/A/274 *except omitting* calendar *and*] Offence committed 10 Dec. 1834.

54/A/289   31 Dec. 1834. George Alexander Anderson. Being on enclosed land at Ozleworth with two nets at night with intent to kill game [*etc., as* 54/A/274 *except omitting* calendar *and*] Offence committed 12 Dec. 1834.

54/A/290   27 Nov. 1834. John Organ. Trespassing on enclosed land at Sherborne at night armed with a gun and shooting eleven pheasants; land occupied by Lord Sherborne. Rev. F. E. Witts JP and Charles Pole JP at Stow on the Wold. Hard labour for three calendar months in Northleach house of correction, after which to find sureties totalling £20 against re-offending for one year. In default, a further six months' hard labour. Offence committed 26 Nov. 1834.

54/A/291   4 Dec. 1834. Hannah Cosier and Mary Fisher. Stealing wood from a fence at Lower Swell, the property of William Phillips. Rev. F. E. Witts JP and Rev. C. Jeaffreson JP at Stow on the Wold. Fine 10/-, to be paid to John Tysoe, an overseer of the poor, and 7/- costs to the complainant. Given one week to pay. Offence committed 22 Nov. 1834.

54/A/292   30 Oct. 1834. Mary Betteridge. Damaging a board in her dwelling house at Wick Rissington, the property of Charles Pole Esq. Rev. F. E. Witts JP and Rev. C. Jeaffreson JP at Stow on the Wold. Fine £1, to be paid to William Mace, an overseer of the poor, and 7/- costs to the complainant, or hard labour for two calendar months in Northleach house of correction. Offence committed 23 Oct. 1834.

54/A/293   19 Dec. 1834. Daniel Gazzard of Chipping Sodbury, labourer. Shooting a hare at Tormarton when not in possession of a game certificate. F. Trotman JP, W. G. Davy JP and A. Shakespear JP at Old Sodbury. Edmund Webb, under-gamekeeper, and Thomas Webb, gamekeeper, both of Badminton, complainant and witness. Fine £1, to be paid to John Arnold, an overseer of the poor, and 10/3 costs to the complainant. Given two weeks to pay. In default, one calendar month's hard labour in Horsley house of correction. Offence committed 3 Dec. 1834.

54/A/294   19 Dec. 1834. Stephen Young of Chipping Sodbury, labourer. Trespassing with a gun in search and pursuit of game at Tormarton on land occupied by William Arnold. F. Trotman JP, W. G. Davy JP and A. Shakespear JP at Old Sodbury. Edmund Webb, under-gamekeeper, of Badminton, complainant, and Thomas Webb, gamekeeper to the duke of Beaufort, of Badminton, witness. Fine £1, to be paid to John Arnold, an overseer of the poor, and 10/3 costs to the complainant. Given two weeks to pay. In default, one calendar month's hard labour in Horsley house of correction. Offence committed 3 Dec. 1834 between 12 noon and 1 p.m.

54/A/295   17 Dec. 1834. William Smith of Rangeworthy. Using wires to kill hares at Dodington without a game certificate. I. J. Horlock JP and K. W. Horlock JP. William Lewis of Dodington, under-gamekeeper to Sir C. B. Codrington, Bt., complainant, and William Edwards, labourer, of Dodington, witness. Fine £5, to be paid to an overseer of the poor, and 15/- costs to the complainant, or hard labour for three calendar months in Horsley house of correction. Offence committed 16 Dec. 1834.

54/A/296   3 Nov. 1834. George Peck of Yate, labourer. Shooting a pheasant in or near Hazel Wood at Horton. Henry Charles, duke of Beaufort, JP and Henry Somerset, marquess of Worcester, JP at Badminton. George Limbrick of Horton, complainant, and John Watt of Hawkesbury, witness. Fine £5, to be paid to William Beard, an overseer of the poor, and 12/- costs to the complainant, or three calendar months in Horsley house of correction. Offence committed Sunday 2 Nov. 1834.

54/A/297   24 Oct. 1834. Samuel Wickham of Chipping Sodbury, butcher. Trespassing in search of game on land occupied by Mrs. Jane Bennett of New House, Tormarton. W. Blathwayt JP, F. Trotman JP, W. G. Davy JP, H. Bush JP and R. H. B. Hale JP at the Cross Hands, Old Sodbury, at 11 a.m. Information given to first-named JP by Edmund Webb, under-gamekeeper to the duke of Beaufort, on 15 Oct. 1834. Summons delivered by William Carradine, constable of Chipping Sodbury. Offender did not appear. Jane Bennett confirmed that no permission had been given. Thomas Webb, gamekeeper to the duke of Beaufort, deposed that he heard two shots while in a field belonging to William Minett, ran across road to a bank from which he saw offender put a hare into his pocket. Another man ran to a third person and got in his gig calling to offender to drop hare and run away. Witness caught offender who, when asked for the hare, denied there was one. Witness took the pocket and saw the hare. Offender gave name as George Falking. Not satisfied, witness asked a thresher in Mrs. Bennett's barn, George Farr of Acton Turville, if he knew the offender. Farr identified him as Samuel Wickham, butcher, of Chipping Sodbury. Fine £1, to be paid to John Bennett, overseer of the poor of Tormarton, and £1 costs to the informer. Given seven days to pay. In default, one calendar month in Horsley house of correction. Offence committed about 4 p.m. 15 Oct. 1834.

54/B/1   10 Feb. 1835. Thomas Blackford of Aston Subedge. Assaulting John Gardner at Aston Subedge. Rev. J. R. Hall JP and F. Colvile JP at Moreton in Marsh. Fine 10/- and 10/- costs or one month in Northleach house of correction. Offence committed 29 Jan. 1835.

54/B/2   24 Feb. 1835. Benjamin Webley, gentleman, of Hambrook, Winterbourne. Trespassing in pursuit of game at Alkington, Berkeley, on land called Arling Grove, occupied by Charles Biss Esq. W. Davies D.D. JP and Rev. J. H. Dunsford JP at Berkeley. James Barrett, gamekeeper, of Alkington, informer. Fine £2, to be paid to John Bendall, overseer of the poor of Alkington, and 19/- costs to the informer. Offence committed at 12.30 p.m. 27 Dec. 1834.

54/B/3   19 Feb. 1835. William Green. Stealing wood valued at sixpence from a fence at Naunton, the property of John Bullock. Rev. F. E. Witts JP and Rev. R. W. Ford JP at Stow on the Wold. Fine 6/-, to be paid immediately to John Hanks, overseer of the poor, and 4/- costs to the complainant. Offence committed 16 Feb. 1835.

54/B/4   19 Feb. 1835. Henry and William Jefferies. Stealing wood valued at sixpence from a fence at Upper Slaughter, the property of Edward Lea. Rev. F. E. Witts JP and Rev. R. W. Ford JP at Stow on the Wold. Fine 10/- each, to be paid immediately to William Gregory, overseer of the poor, and 6/- each costs, to be paid immediately to the complainant. Offence committed 13 Feb. 1835.

54/B/5   12 Jan. 1835. Stephen Summerill. Leaving his wife and family in Feb. 1834, thereby causing them to become chargeable to Wick and Abson parish. F. Trotman JP at Pucklechurch. Hard labour for six weeks in Horsley house of correction.

54/B/6   30 Jan. 1835. Thomas Wood. Trespassing in Hunting Orchard, Berkeley, with a gun at night and killing two pheasants. R. Kingscote JP and T. Kingscote JP at Kingscote. Hard labour for three calendar months in Horsley house of correction, after which to find sureties totalling £20 against re-offending in the ensuing year. In default, a further six months' hard labour. Offence committed 15 Nov. 1834..

54/B/7   27 March 1835. James Wall of the Mason's Arms, Stroud, licensed beer retailer. Allowing gaming on his premises. H. Burgh JP and H. Wyatt JP at a Petty Sessions for Bisley hundred. First offence. Fine £5 and 10/- costs. Offence committed 17 March 1835.

54/B/8   27 March 1835. Thomas Moss of Bisley, licensed beer retailer. Keeping his house open for the sale of beer after 10 p.m. H. Burgh JP and H. Wyatt JP at a Petty Sessions for Bisley hundred. First offence. Fine £2 and 10/- costs. Offence committed 14 March 1835.

54/B/9   27 March 1835. Henry Gardner of Bisley, licensed beer retailer. Keeping his house open for the sale of beer after 10 p.m. H. Burgh JP and H. Wyatt JP at a Petty Sessions for Bisley hundred. First offence. Fine £2 and 10/- costs. Offence committed 17 Jan. 1835.

54/B/10   31 March 1835. John Lewis of Stroud, labourer. Navigating a vessel on the Thames and Stroudwater canal[1] at Stroud without the required three men able to work the vessel. H. Burgh JP at Stroud. Fine £1, to be paid to the treasurer of the monies raised by virtue of the Canal Act, and 10/- costs to John Rudge Denyer, the complainant, or three months in Horsley house of correction. Offence committed 29 March 1835.

54/B/11   31 March 1835. John Lewis of Stroud, labourer. Hauling a vessel along the Thames and Stroudwater canal at Stroud without a helmsman to navigate [*etc., as* 54/B/10].

54/B/12   25 Feb. 1835. William Greenhall of Buckland, labourer. Violently assaulting David Stanford at Buckland without provocation. J. Timbrill D.D. JP, Rev. J. Keysall JP and J. W. Martin JP at Tewkesbury. Fine 10/-, to be paid to John Taylor, overseer of the poor, and 26/- costs. Offence committed Sunday 11 Jan. 1835. [*Endorsed with a note that the offender was committed to Northleach house of correction on 25 Feb. for two calendar months for not paying the 10/- fine.*]

---

[1] The Thames and Severn canal met the Stroudwater canal at Wallbridge, in Stroud. The Canal Act referred to is presumably the Thames and Severn Canal Act, 53 Geo. III, c. 181 (Local and Personal).

54/B/13   27 March 1835. Charles Chandler of the Red Lion, Stroud, licensed beer retailer. Allowing gaming on his premises. H. Burgh JP and H. Wyatt JP at a Petty Sessions for Bisley hundred. First offence. Fine £5 and 10/- costs. Offence committed 17 March 1835.

54/B/14   10 Jan. 1835. Benjamin Sims of Stroud, labourer. Assaulting Lt. Col. Charles Richard Fox at Stroud. H. Burgh JP and H. Wyatt JP at Stroud. Fine £5 or two calendar months in Horsley house of correction. Offence committed 9 Jan. 1835.

54/B/15   30 Jan. 1835. Thomas Cooke of Randwick, labourer. Stealing a tree at Standish, the property of John, Lord Sherborne. H. Burgh JP and J. Mills JP at Stroud. Fine £3 and 1/- damages or hard labour for two calendar months in Horsley house of correction. Offence committed 15 Jan. 1835.

54/B/16   30 Jan. 1835. William Blackwell of Stroud, stonemason. Cutting and stealing a tree at Stroud, the property of Elizabeth Cox. H. Burgh JP and J. Mills JP at Stroud. Fine 10/-, 1/- damages and 8/- costs or hard labour for two calendar months in Horsley house of correction. Offence committed 22 Jan. 1835.

54/B/17   28 Jan. 1835. Charles Cooke of Randwick, labourer. Stealing a tree at Standish, the property of John, Lord Sherborne. H. Burgh JP at Stroud. Fine £4 and 2/- damages or hard labour for two calendar months in Horsley house of correction. Offence committed 20 Jan. 1835.

54/B/18   3 Feb. 1835. Joseph Freeman of Stonehouse, labourer. Assaulting Thomas Cooke, labourer, of Stroud at Stroud. H. Burgh JP and E. G. Hallewell JP at Stroud. Fine £1 and 8/- costs or two calendar months in Horsley house of correction. Offence committed 24 Dec. 1834.

54/B/19   13 Feb. 1835. William Lewis of Bisley, labourer. Assaulting Abraham Lewis, labourer, of Bisley. H. Burgh JP and J. Mills JP at Stroud. Fine £4 10s. 6d. and 9/6 costs or two calendar months in Horsley house of correction. Offence committed 4 Feb. 1835.

54/B/20   19 Feb. 1835. George Cratchley. Being in an enclosed yard at Stroud with intent to commit a felony. H. Burgh JP at Stroud. Hard labour for three calendar months in Horsley house of correction. Offence committed 19 Feb. 1835.

54/B/21   27 Feb. 1835. Walter Knee of Stroud, labourer. Causing a nuisance by burning an effigy in a public road. H. Burgh JP and W. H. Hyett JP at Stroud. Fine £2 and 8/- costs. Offence committed 21 Jan. 1835.

54/B/22   27 Feb. 1835. Richard Clarke and John Phillpott, labourers, of Minchinhampton. Stealing a rail from a garden fence, the property of George Taylor, clothworker, at Stroud. H. Burgh JP and W. H. Hyett JP at Stroud. Complainant examined as to proof of offence. Fine £1 and 6d. damages or hard labour for one calendar month in Horsley house of correction. Offence committed 15 Feb. 1835.

54/B/23   5 March 1835. John Parsons and Thomas Papps, labourers, of Stroud. Stealing turnip greens from a field occupied by William Iles, yeoman, of Painswick. N. S. Marling JP at Stroud. One calendar month in Horsley house of correction. Offence committed 5 March 1835.

54/B/24   10 March 1835. John Bliss of Painswick, labourer. Damaging a field wall, the property of Thomas Loveday, yeoman, of Painswick. H. Burgh JP at Stroud. Fine 10/- for damages and 10/- for costs, or hard labour for two calendar months in Horsley house of correction. Offence committed 5 March 1835.

54/B/25   13 March 1835. Thomas Poulson of Bisley, labourer. Stealing part of a dead fence from a field at Bisley, the property of John Ballinger Esq. H. Burgh JP and E. G. Hallewell JP at Stroud. Fine 10/-, 8/- costs and 4*d*. damages or hard labour for fourteen days in Horsley house of correction. Offence committed 9 March 1835.

54/B/26 19 March 1835. John Davis of Stroud, labourer. Stealing turnip greens from a garden, the property of Thomas King, labourer, of Bisley. H. Burgh JP at Stroud. Hard labour for three calendar months in Horsley house of correction. Offence committed 8 March 1835.

54/B/27 29 Jan. 1835. Richard Wright. Assaulting Richard Cheney at Cheltenham. R. B. Cooper JP and William Pitt JP at Cheltenham. Fine 20/- and 2/- costs. Offence committed 28 Jan. 1835.

54/B/28 29 Jan. 1835. Joseph Grivel, John Biggs and Levi Mustoe. Assaulting Richard Cheney at Cheltenham [*etc., as* 54/B/27 *except*] Each fined 5/- and 3/- costs.

54/B/29 21 Feb. 1835. Thomas Smith. Assaulting William Thomson at Cheltenham. R. B. Cooper JP and J. Blagdon JP at Cheltenham. Fine 5/- and 5/6 costs. Offence committed 19 Feb. 1835.

54/B/30 10 Feb. 1835. John Jones. Assaulting William Yates at Cheltenham. R. B. Cooper JP and W. Pitt JP at Cheltenham. Fine 2/6 and 7/6 costs. Offence committed 8 Feb. 1835.

54/B/31 12 March 1835. Alexander Rose. Assaulting James Bevan at Cheltenham. R. B. Cooper JP and J. Blagdon JP at Cheltenham. Fine 20/- and 4/- costs. Offence committed 11 March 1835.

54/B/32 24 Jan. 1835. Thomas Roberts. Assaulting Hannah Peart at Cheltenham. R. B. Cooper JP and J. Blagdon JP at Cheltenham. Fine 2/6 and 9/6 costs. Offence committed 17 Jan. 1835.

54/B/33 24 Jan. 1835. Thomas Davison. Assaulting Maria Higgs at Cheltenham. R. B. Cooper JP and J. Blagdon JP at Cheltenham. Fine 10/- and 6/6 costs. Offence committed 24 Jan. 1835.

54/B/34 15 Jan. 1835. John Cakebread. Assaulting Thomas Curtis at Cheltenham. R. B. Cooper JP and J. Blagdon JP at Cheltenham. Fine 20/- and 5/- costs. Offence committed 13 Jan. 1835.

54/B/35 24 March 1835. William Luker. Assaulting Ann Beasley at Charlton Kings. R. B. Cooper JP and J. Blagdon JP at Cheltenham. Fine 20/- and 9/6 costs. Offence committed 21 March 1835.

54/B/36 12 Feb. 1835. William Fluke and John Greening. Assaulting John Mann at Cheltenham. R. B. Cooper JP and J. Blagdon JP at Cheltenham. Each fined 5/- and 7/6 costs. Offence committed 10 Feb. 1835.

54/B/37 26 Feb. 1835. Jeremiah Taylor, licensed retail beer dealer of Cheltenham. Keeping his house open for the sale of beer until 10.30 p.m. R. B. Cooper JP and J. Blagdon JP at Cheltenham. First offence. Fine 40/- and 5/6 costs. Offence committed 24 Feb. 1835.

54/B/38 10 March 1835. William Phelps. Assaulting Joseph Simmonds at Cheltenham. R. B. Cooper JP and J. Blagdon JP at Cheltenham. Fine 10/- and 3/- costs. Offence committed 7 March 1935.

54/B/39 17 Feb. 1835. Edward Letton. Assaulting William Rodway at Cheltenham. J. Blagdon JP and W. Pitt JP at Cheltenham. Fine 10/- and 4/- costs. Offence committed 14 Feb. 1835.

54/B/40 7 April 1835. John Jones. Assaulting Ann Smart at Shurdington. J. Blagdon JP and W. Pitt JP at Cheltenham. Fine 7/- and 5/6 costs. Offence committed 5 April 1835.

54/B/41 10 Feb. 1835. Timothy Sweeney. Assaulting Ann Hanley at Cheltenham. R. B. Cooper JP and J. Blagdon JP at Cheltenham. Fine 10/- and 4/- costs. Offence committed 9 Feb. 1835.

54/B/42   1 Jan. 1835. William Fluck. Assaulting Charles Harse at Cheltenham. J. E. Viner JP and Rev. C. B. Trye JP [*who did not sign, but document signed by* J. Blagdon] at Cheltenham. Fine 2/6 and 5/6 costs. Offence committed 27 Dec. 1834.

54/B/43   5 March 1835. James County. Assaulting John Byrne at Cheltenham. J. E. Viner JP and J. Blagdon JP at Cheltenham. Fine 40/- and 7/6 costs. Offence committed 4 March 1835.

54/B/44   14 Feb. 1835. George Gale. Trespassing in search of game on land at Acton Turville occupied by William Minett. T. Kingscote JP at Kingscote. Thomas Webb informer. Fine £2, to be paid to an overseer of the poor, and 14/- costs to the informer, or hard labour for two calendar months in Horsley house of correction. Offence committed 16 Nov. 1834.

54/B/45   13 March 1835. William Fry of Tormarton. Assaulting John Webb at Marshfield. F. Trotman JP, R. H. B. Hale JP and A. Shakespear JP at the Cross Hands inn, Old Sodbury. Fine 6/- and 11/6 costs or one calendar month in Horsley house of correction. Offence committed 22 Feb. 1835.

54/B/46   6 Feb. 1835. William Sendall of Dyrham and Hinton, labourer. Trespassing in search of game in Dyrham Wood with a ferret and nets. F. Trotman JP, W. G. Davy JP, A. Shakespear JP and C. W. Codrington JP. Lord of the manor William Blathwayt, complainant. William Long, labourer, of Dyrham and Hinton, witness. Fine £2 and 14/- costs or two calendar months in Horsley house of correction. Offence committed between 11 a.m. and noon 14 Dec. 1834.

54/B/47   6 Feb. 1835. William Moss of Dyrham and Hinton, labourer. Trespassing and picking up a shot hare and running away with it at Four Acres, land at Wapley and Codrington occupied by John Wickham jnr. F. Trotman JP, W. G. Davy JP, A. Shakespear JP, W. Blathwayt JP and R. H. B. Hale JP. Complainant Francis Evans, under-gamekeeper to Sir Christopher Bethell Codrington, Bt., of Dodington. Witnesses William and Frederick Watts of Wapley and Codrington, farmers. Fine £1 and 10/- costs. Given fourteen days to pay. In default, one calendar month in Horsley house of correction. Offence committed between 2 p.m. and 3 p.m. Friday 16 Jan. 1835. [*Cf.* 54/B/50.]

54/B/48   20 Feb. 1835. John and William Gribble of Old Sodbury, labourers. Trespassing in search of game or conies at Coles Brake, Old Sodbury, occupied by Sir C. B. Codrington, Bt., F. Trotman JP and R. H. B. Hale JP at Old Sodbury. Henry Martin, gamekeeper to Sir C. B. Codrington, Bt., complainant. William White, labourer, of Old Sodbury, witness. Each fined 10/- and 6/3 costs. Given fourteen days to pay. In default, one calendar month in Horsley house of correction. Offence committed between 1 p.m. and 2 p.m. Thursday 22 Jan. 1835.

54/B/49   13 March 1835. Joel Baber of Mangotsfield, yeoman. Trespassing with two greyhounds and a lurcher in search of game and conies at Goldings Home Ground at Wapley and Codrington, occupied by William Iles. A. Shakespear JP, F. Trotman JP and R. H. B. Hale JP at a Petty Sessions held at the Cross Hands inn, Old Sodbury, at 11 a.m. Information given to A. Shakespear JP at Boxwell Court, Boxwell and Leighterton, 14 Feb. 1835 by Henry Martin, gamekeeper to Sir C. B. Codrington, Bt., of Dodington. Summons issued. Francis Evans, labourer, of Wapley and Codrington, witness. Offender did not appear. Fine £2 and 19/6 costs or one calendar month in Horsley house of correction. Offence committed between 11 a.m. and 3 p.m. Wednesday 28 Jan. 1835.

54/B/50   6 Feb. 1835. John Baker of Dyrham and Hinton, labourer. Trespassing in search of game with a gun at Four Acres, Wapley and Codrington, land occupied by John Wickham jnr. W. Blathwayt JP, F. Trotman JP, W. G. Davy JP, A. Shakespear JP and R. H. B. Hales JP at a Petty Sessions held at the Cross Hands in, Old Sodbury, at 11 a.m. Information given to W. Blathwayt JP at Dyrham House on 20 Jan. 1835 by Francis Evans, under-gamekeeper to Sir C. B. Codrington, Bt., of Dodington. Summons issued. Offender did not appear. Frederick Watts, farmer, stated that he saw offender shoot a hare which was then picked up and taken away by William Morse. [*Cf.* 54/B/47.] Evidence corroborated by his brother William Watts. Fine £2 and 11/- costs. Given fourteen days to pay. In default, one calendar month in Horsley house of correction. Offence committed between 2 p.m. and 3 p.m. Friday 16 Jan. 1835.

54/B/51   13 March 1835. Joel Baber of Mangotsfield, yeoman. Trespassing with dogs in search of game at the Tyning, Wapley and Codrington, land occupied by John Wickham. F. Trotman JP and R. H. B. Hale JP at a Petty Sessions held at the Cross Hands inn, Old Sodbury, at 11 a.m. Offence reported to W. Blathwayt JP at Dyrham House on 30 Jan. by Francis Evans, under-gamekeeper to Sir C. B. Codrington, Bt. Summons issued. Offender did not appear. John Pincott, labourer, of Wapley and Codrington gave evidence that he had seen offender, with others, beating for game with dogs. Fine £2 and £1 0*s*. 6*d*. costs or one calendar month in Horsley house of correction. Offence committed between 12 noon and 1 p.m. or 2 p.m. 26 Jan. 1835.

54/C/1   25 June 1835. William Paling of Clifton. Keeping his house open for the sale of beer after 10 p.m. Rev. W. Davies JP and G. Worrall JP at a Petty Sessions for part of Berkeley division. Fine £1 12*s*. 6*d*. and 7/6 costs. Offence committed 10 June 1835.

54/C/2   25 June 1835. John Sprague of Clifton. Keeping his house open [*etc., as* 54/C/1 *except*] Offence committed 19 June 1835.

54/C/3   25 June 1835. Robert Neale of Clifton. Keeping his house open [*etc., as* 54/C/1 *except*] Offence committed 19 June 1835.

54/C/4   30 April 1835. Richard Fowler. Assaulting Henry Tiley at Winterbourne. J. Cave JP and W. Munro JP at Lawfords Gate sessions room. Fine £2 and 16/- costs or six weeks in Lawfords Gate house of correction. Offence committed 22 April 1835.

54/C/5   23 April 1835. Henry Thomas. Assaulting James Wilkins at St. Philip and St. Jacob, [Bristol]. J. Cave JP and Rev. W. Mirehouse JP at Lawfords Gate sessions room. Fine 2/6 and 7/6 costs or seven days in Lawfords Gate house of correction. Offence committed 20 April 1835.

54/C/6   23 April 1835. William Perry. Assaulting James Wilkins [*etc., as* 54/C/5].

54/C/7   7 May 1835. William Britton. Assaulting Elizabeth Britton at Bitton. C. L. Walker JP and Rev. W. Mirehouse JP at Lawfords Gate sessions room. Fine 6*d*. and 6/- costs or fourteen days in Lawfords Gate house of correction. Offence committed 2 May 1835.

54/C/8   28 May 1835. William Kingdon. Assaulting Thomas Pearce at Clifton. Rev. W. Mirehouse JP and G. Goldney JP at Lawfords Gate sessions room. Fine £2 10*s*. and 13/- costs or six weeks in Lawfords Gate house of correction. Offence committed 14 May 1835.

54/C/9   23 April 1835. Francis Jones. Assaulting Henry Thomas Watts at Clifton. G. Goldney JP and A. H. G. Battersby JP at Lawfords Gate sessions room. Fine £1 13*s*. and 7/- costs or six weeks in Lawfords Gate house of correction. Offence committed 19 April 1835.

54/C/10   23 April 1835. George Jefferies. Assaulting Henry Thomas Watts [*etc., as* 54/C/9].

54/C/11   11 June 1835. Joseph Scales. Assaulting John Hall at St. Philip and St. Jacob, [Bristol]. W. Fripp JP and G. Goldney JP at Lawfords Gate sessions room. Fine £1 and 17/- costs or one calendar month in Lawfords Gate house of correction. Offence committed 9 June 1835.

54/C/12   21 May 1835. Charlotte Young. Assaulting Sophia Davis at St. Philip and St. Jacob, [Bristol]. W. Fripp JP and Rev. W. Mirehouse JP at Lawfords Gate sessions room. Fine £1 and 7/6 costs or one calendar month in Lawfords Gate house of correction. Offence committed 10 May 1835.

54/C/13   11 June 1835. James Olds. Assaulting Job Thomas at Bitton. W. Fripp JP and G. Goldney JP at Lawfords Gate sessions room. Fine 12/- and 8/- costs or twenty-one days in Lawfords Gate house of correction. Offence committed 4 June 1835.

54/C/14   11 June 1835. Sarah Orchard. Assaulting Susannah Corbett at St. Philip and St. Jacob, [Bristol]. W. Fripp JP and Rev. W. Mirehouse JP at Lawfords Gate sessions room. Fine 6d. and 7/6 costs or fourteen days in Lawfords Gate house of correction. Offence committed 8 June 1835.

54/C/15   9 May 1835. Edward Wright. Assaulting Jane Ponchard at St. Philip and St. Jacob, [Bristol]. J. Haythorne JP and Rev. W. Mirehouse JP at Lawfords Gate sessions room. Fine 1/- and 16/- costs or fourteen days in Lawfords Gate house of correction. Offence committed 20 April 1835.

54/C/16   27 June 1835. William Finch of Cheltenham, stage-coach man. Found to be carrying more outside passengers at Tewkesbury, on his Worcester to Gloucester stage-coach, than his licence allowed. R. B. Cooper JP at Cheltenham. Elisha Castle, informer and prosecutor. Fine £5 and 5/6 costs. Offence committed 11 June 1835.

54/C/17   28 April 1835. George Webb the younger of Kemerton. Assaulting Joseph Sherwood at Kemerton. C. E. Hanford JP and T. Marriot JP at a Petty Sessions held in the magistrates' office, Pershore, [Worcs.]. Fine 3/6 and 5/6 costs or one calendar month in the house of correction at Worcester. Offence committed 17 April 1835.

54/C/18   23 March 1835. John Stephens of Tibberton, thatcher. Maliciously breaking a glass lamp, the property of John Matthews, innkeeper, of Rudford. Rev. R. F. Onslow JP and R. F. Onslow JP at Newent. Ordered to pay 8/- and 9/6 costs to the complainant, or one calendar month in Littledean house of correction. Offence committed 18 March 1835.

54/C/19   20 Jan. 1835. Edward Daw of Taynton, labourer. Damaging underwood growing at Cockridge [MS. Cuggeridge] Hill Coppice at Newent, the property of Miss Elizabeth Foley. Rev. R. F. Onslow JP at Newent. Ordered to pay 6d. and 9/6 cost to the complainant, or hard labour for one calendar month in Littledean house of correction. Offence committed 3 Jan. 1835.

54/C/20–52   9 May 1835. [Names as below.] Possessing defective weights and measures [except 54/C/33 and 36]. Dr. A. Carrick M.D. JP and W. Davies D.D. JP at a Petty Sessions held at the Swan inn, Thornbury, for the Thornbury division. William Clements, inspector of weights, measures and balances, complainant [his office variously described]. Weights, measures etc. forfeited [except 54/C/36]. Fine 5/- and 8/6 costs [except 54/C/20, 33, 36, 38 and 50]. [Date offence committed (all 1835) as below.]

54/C/20   Mary Meredith of Alveston, shopkeeper. Five defective weights in her shop. Fine 7/6 and 8/6 costs. (8 April).

54/C/21   Jonathan Blanch of Iron Acton, innkeeper. Four defective measures in his house. (8 April).

54/C/22   Thomas Daniels of Tytherington, shopkeeper. One defective measure. (8 April).

54/C/23   Luke Lewis of Iron Acton, shopkeeper. A defective pair of scales in his shop. (9 April).

54/C/24   Francis Fussell of Iron Acton, innkeeper. Four defective measures in his house. (9 April).

54/C/25 Thomas Bush of Rangeworthy, shopkeeper. Two defective measures in his shop. (10 April).

54/C/26 James Packer of Rangeworthy, beer seller. Three defective measures in his house. (10 April).

54/C/27 Nathaniel Hale of Rangeworthy, beer retailer and shopkeeper. Two defective weights and a defective pair of scales in his shop. (10 April).

54/C/28 Edward Mills of Rangeworthy, beer retailer. Four defective measures in his house. (10 April).

54/C/29 Mary Britton of Iron Acton, shopkeeper. One defective weight in her shop. (10 April).

54/C/30 William Linard of Iron Acton, beer retailer. Three defective measures in his house. (10 April).

54/C/31 Charles Jones of Thornbury, innkeeper. Three defective measures in his bar. (17 April).

54/C/32 Thomas Hudson of Thornbury, beer retailer. Three defective measures in his bar. (17 April).

54/C/33 Augustus Cullimore of Thornbuy, beer retailer. Refusing to produce measures for examination. Fine 5/- and 6/- costs. (17 April).

54/C/34 William Birt of Thornbury, beer retailer. Four defective measures in his house. (20 April).

54/C/35 George Gazard of Thornbury, baker. A defective pair of scales in his bakehouse. (20 April).

54/C/36 Thomas Pritchard of Thornbury, pig butcher. Refusing to produce his weights and scales for examination. Fine 5/- and 6/- costs. (20 April).

54/C/37 John Alpasss of Thornbury, beer retailer. Four defective measures in his house. (20 April).

54/C/38 Charles Jones of Thornbury, innkeeper. Three defective measures in his house. Fine 5/- and 8/- costs. (21 April).

54/C/39 Edward Doward of Alveston, innkeeper. Two defective measures in his house. (21 April).

54/C/40 John Williams of Alveston, beer retailer. Three defective measures in his house. (21 April).

54/C/41 James Russell of Olveston, beer retailer. Three defective measures in his house. (21 April).

54/C/42 John Taylor of Olveston, innkeeper. Two defective measures in his house. (21 April).

54/C/43 Joseph Hancock of Olveston, beer retailer. Three defective measures in his house. (21 April).

54/C/44 Joseph Pole of Thornbury, innkeeper. Five defective measures in his house. (22 April).

54/C/45 William Hulance of Tytherington, shopkeeper. A defective pair of scales in his shop. (23 April).

54/C/46 Elizabeth Browne of Almondsbury, shopkeeper. One defective weight in her shop. (28 April).

54/C/47 Martha Sidway and Mary Bell of Almondsbury, shopkeepers. One defective weight and one defective measure in their shop. (24 April).

54/C/48 Thomas Young of Almondsbury, innkeeper. Four defective measures in his house. (24 April).

54/C/49 Sarah Shepherd of Almondsbury, innkeeper. Three defective measures in her house. (24 April).

54/C/50 William Cooke of Almondsbury, shopkeeper. One defective weight and one defective measure. Fine 10/- and 8/6 costs. (24 April).

54/C/51   John Taylor of Almondsbury, beer retailer. Four defective measures in his house. (24 April).

54/C/52   John Francis Always of Aust, shopkeeper. A defective pair of scales. (25 April).

54/C/53   15 June 1835. Samuel Bick. Assaulting Benjamin Harris at Huntley. C. Crawley JP and J. Pyrke JP at Newnham. Fine £2 and £3 costs. Offence committed 7 June 1835.

54/C/54   6 April 1835. Matthew Stevens. Assaulting Emanuel Sterry at Huntley. C. Crawley JP and J. Pyrke JP at Newnham. Fine £1 and £1 12s. [costs] or hard labour for two calendar months in Littledean house of correction. Offence committed 28 March 1835.

54/C/55   15 June 1835. Charles Bodenham. Assaulting Benjamin Harris at Huntley. C. Crawley JP and J. Pyrke JP at Newnham. Fine £2 and £3 costs or hard labour for two calendar months in Littledean house of correction. Offence committed 7 June 1835.

54/C/56   6 April 1835. Matthew Stevens. Assaulting Samuel Sterry at Huntley [etc., as 54/C/54].

54/C/57   15 June 1835. Jonathan Parry of Longhope, cider retailer. Selling cider and permitting tippling in his house after 9.30 p.m. Rev. C. Crawley JP and J. Pyrke JP at a Petty Sessions for the Forest division. First offence. Fine £4 and £1 costs. Offence committed 29 May 1835.

54/C/58   17 June 1835. Charles Merrick, son of Luke Merrick of Tewkesbury, schoolmaster. Assaulting John Attwood and John Fisher, labourers, of Twyning at the Fleet inn, Twyning. J. Timbrill D.D. JP, Rev. J. Keysall JP and J. W. Martin JP at Tewkesbury. Fine £2 16s., to be paid to Peter Dee, overseer of the poor, and £2 4s. costs to the complainants. Offence committed Monday 15 June 1835.

54/C/59   22 April 1835. John Clarke of Postlip, Winchcombe, servant to Mr. Richard Lacey. Killing and stealing a dove or pigeon in the foldyard at Dry Field farm at Winchcombe, the property of Mr. Richard Lacey. J. Timbrill D.D. JP, Rev. C. White JP and J. W. Martin JP at Tewkesbury. Fine 10/-, to be paid to John Mason, an overseer of the poor, 12/- costs and 1/- damages to George Hone, the complainant. Offence committed Sunday 12 April 1835.

54/C/60   3 June 1835. Thomas Allard of Twyning, innkeeper. Keeping his house open for the sale and consumption of beer during the hours of afternoon divine service at the parish church. J. Timbrill D.D. JP and Rev. J. Keysall JP. Second offence. [Cf. 53/A/129.] Fine £2 and 6/6 costs. Offence committed Sunday 17 May 1835.

54/C/61   29 Jan. 1835. Peter Fisher. Cutting a growing tree with intent to steal, the property of Edward Sheppard Esq., at Uley. T. Kingscote JP and W. Playne JP at Horsley. Fine £2 9s., to be paid to an overseer of the poor, 1/- damages to Edward Sheppard and 9/- costs to Benjamin Tilley, the complainant, or hard labour for two calendar months in Horsley house of correction. Offence committed 16 Jan. 1835.

54/C/62   2 April 1835. Anselm Cook of Rodborough, beer retailer. Permitting drunkenness and disorderly conduct in his premises. T. Kingscote JP , W. Playne JP and T. R. Haycock JP at a Petty Sessions for Longtree hundred. First offence. Fine £4 10s. 6d. and 9/6 costs. Offence committed 17 March 1835.

54/C/63   7 May 1835. James Ricketts, late of Dursley, labourer. Leaving his wife and children chargeable to Dursley parish. Edward Weight JP at Dursley. Hard labour for one calendar month in Horsley house of correction. Offence committed 7 Feb. 1835.

54/C/64   8 May 1835. Thomas Taylor, servant and labourer in husbandry to Isaac Pinchin, yeoman, of Cranham. Absenting himself from his master's service without permission. H. Burgh JP and E. G. Hallewell JP at Stroud. Hard labour for six weeks in Horsley house of correction. Offence committed 5 May 1835.

54/C/65   8 May 1835. James Hatton of Stroud, clothworker. Violently assaulting James Cooper, yeoman, of Painswick. H. Burgh JP and E. G. Hallewell JP at Stroud. Fine £5, to be paid to an overseer of the poor of Painswick, or two calendar months in Horsley house of correction. Offence committed 23 April 1835.

54/C/66   8 May 1835. Lewellin Brunsden of Painswick, labourer. Obliterating the letters PP marked on a wheelbarrow, the property of the overseers of the poor of Painswick. H. Burgh JP and E. G. Hallewell JP at Stroud. [*Sentence not given.*] Offence committed within previous four months.

54/C/67   8 May 1835. Richard Ayers. Evading paying a toll of 3*d.* when driving three beasts through a tollgate at Painswick on the Lightpill to Birdlip turnpike road. H. Burgh JP. Fine 10/-. Offence committed 25 Feb. 1835.

54/C/68   11 May 1835. Stephen Hayes of Stroud, labourer. Violently assaulting Mary wife of Daniel Coleman of Stroud, labourer. H. Burgh JP and H. Wyatt JP at Stroud. Fine £2, to be paid to an overseer of the poor, or two calendar months in Horsley house of correction. Offence committed 22 April 1835.

54/C/69   11 May 1835. William Cooke of Stroud, labourer. Assaulting John Chew of Stroud, street-keeper. H. Burgh JP and H. Wyatt JP at Stroud. Fine £2, to be paid to an overseer of the poor, or two calendar months in Horsley house of correction. Offence committed 23 April 1835.

54/C/70   15 June 1835. John Hinton of Painswick, labourer. Violently and indecently assaulting Lydia Leech, milliner, of Painswick. H. Burgh JP and N. S. Marling JP at Stroud. Fine £5, to be paid to an overseer of the poor, or two calendar months in Horsley house of correction. Offence committed 11 June 1835.

54/C/71   19 June 1835. Paul Mills of Stroud, licensed beer seller. Keeping his house open for the sale of beer after 10 p.m. H. Burgh JP and E. G. Hallewell JP at a Petty Sessions for Bisley hundred. First offence. Fine £2 including costs of 10/-. Offence committed 11 June 1835.

54/C/72   19 June 1835. Giles Smith of Stroud, yeoman. Violently assaulting Joseph Swainson, yeoman, of Stroud. H. Burgh JP and E. G. Hallewell JP at Stroud. Fine 1/-, to be paid to an overseer of the poor, and 8/- costs, or two weeks in Horsley house of correction. Offence committed 16 June 1835.

54/C/73   19 June 1835. Henry Wood of Painswick, labourer. Violently assaulting William Wood, labourer, of Painswick. H. Burgh JP and E. G. Hallewell JP at Stroud. Fine 10/-, to be paid to an overseer of the poor, and 8/- costs, or two calendar months in Horsley house of correction. Offence committed 7 June 1835.

54/C/74   7 May 1835. John Flight. Using a wire for taking and killing game at Frocester without a game licence. H. Burgh JP and N. S. Marling JP at Stroud. Fine £5, to be paid to an overseer of the poor, and 8/- costs to the complainant William Baker, or hard labour for three calendar months in Horsley house of correction. Offence committed 7 May 1835.

54/C/75   24 April 1835. Maurice Fawkes of Bisley, licensed beer seller. Keeping his house open for the sale of beer after 10 p.m. H. Burgh JP and E. G. Hallewell JP at a Petty Sessions for Bisley hundred. First offence. Fine £2 and 8/- costs. Offence committed 12 April 1835.

54/C/76   21 May 1835. George Skey, Thomas Clark, Joseph Baker and William Gardner, labourers, of Cheltenham. Trespassing in search and pursuit of game at Prestbury on land belonging to William John Agg Esq. J. E. Viner JP and Rev. J. Edwards JP at Cheltenham. Thomas Williams, yeoman, of Prestbury, complainant. Fine £1 each, to be paid to an overseer of the poor, and 4/6 each costs. [*Total cost given as* 14/-, *perhaps a clerical error.*] Offence committed 17 May 1835.

54/C/77   23 April 1835. William Lusty. Assaulting Joseph Preston at Cheltenham. J. Blagdon JP and W. Pitt JP at Cheltenham. Fine 5/- and 7/- costs. Offence committed 18 April 1835.

54/C/78   28 April 1835. Absalom Holland. Assaulting Sarah Holland at Cheltenham. W. Pitt JP and William John Agg JP at Cheltenham. Fine 5/- and 5/6 costs. Offence committed 24 April 1835.

54/C/79   28 April 1835. Amelia Wiltshire. Assaulting Mary Richards at Cheltenham. W. Pitt JP and W. J. Agg JP at Cheltenham. Fine 2/6 and 5/6 costs. Offence committed 25 April 1835.

54/C/80   30 April 1835. Michael Madden. Assaulting James Theyers at Cheltenham. R. B. Cooper JP and J. E. Viner JP at Cheltenham. Fine 10/- and 7/- costs. Offence committed 21 April 1835.

54/C/81   14 May 1835. William Streather of Cheltenham, retail beer dealer. Keeping his premises open for the sale of beer until 10.30 p.m. and permitting disorderly behaviour. J. E. Viner JP and W. Pitt JP. First offence. Fine 40/- and 7/6 costs. Offence committed 9 May 1835.

54/C/82   14 May 1835. Thomas Jones. Assaulting Samuel Taylor at Cheltenham. J. E. Viner JP and W. Pitt JP. Fine 5/- and 5/- costs. Offence committed 12 May 1835.

54/C/83   23 May 1835. Paul Davis. Damaging a wheelbarrow at Cheltenham, the property of James Harper. J. E. Viner JP at Cheltenham. Fine 5/- and 5/6 costs. Offence committed 18 May 1835.

54/C/84   26 May 1835. Richard Clark. Damaging a holly tree in Puckham Wood, Sevenhampton. W. Pitt JP at Cheltenham. Fine £1, to be paid to an overseer of the poor, 5/- damages and 3/- costs, or two months in Northleach house of correction. Offence committed 24 May 1835.

54/C/85   26 May 1835. William Johnson. Assaulting William Pear at Cheltenham. J. E. Viner JP and W. Pitt JP at Cheltenham. Fine 5/- and 8/6 costs. Offence committed 21 May 1835.

54/C/86   26 May 1835. Edward Martin of Cheltenham, labourer. Trespassing in search and pursuit of game on land in Prestbury, the property of William John Agg Esq. J. E. Viner JP and W. Pitt JP at Cheltenham. Thomas Williams, yeoman, of Prestbury, complainant. Fine £1 and 9/6 costs. Offence committed 17 May 1835.

54/C/87   6 June 1835. William Davison and William Kemmis. Assaulting William Smart at Brockworth. Rev. W. Hicks JP and J. E. Viner JP at Cheltenham. Fine 5/- and 5/6 costs each. Offence committed 3 June 1835.

54/C/88   11 June 1835. John Cunningham. Assaulting William Herbert at Cheltenham. R. B. Cooper JP and J. Blagdon JP at Cheltenham. Fine 16/- and 4/- costs. Offence committed 9 June 1835.

54/C/89   11 June 1835. Thomas Taylor. Assaulting John Townsend at Cheltenham. R. B. Cooper JP and J. Blagdon JP at Cheltenham. Fine 5/- and 5/6 costs. Offence committed 10 June 1835.

54/C/90   11 June 1835. Charles Meek. Assaulting Mary and George Bentley at Cheltenham. R. B. Cooper JP and J. Blagdon JP at Cheltenham. Fine 7/6 and 9/- costs. Offence committed 8 June 1835.

54/C/91   16 June 1835. James Lane. Assaulting Thomas Baynton at Cheltenham. R. B. Cooper JP and T. Newell JP at Cheltenham. Fine 10/- and 7/6 costs. Offence committed 13 June 1835.

54/C/92   5 June 1835. Stephen Young of Chipping Sodbury, labourer. Cutting down and taking away underwood valued at 3/- at Haynes Grove, Wapley and Codrington, the property of Sir C. B. Codrington, Bt. W. G. Davy JP and A. Shakespear JP at Old Sodbury. Francis Evans, on behalf of Sir C. B. Codrington, complainant. Fine £1 10s., to be paid to the overseer of the poor for the use of the general rate of the county, and 14/- costs. In default of payment before 18 June, two calendar months in Horsley house of correction. Offence committed between 2 p.m. and 3 p.m. Saturday 23 May 1835.

54/C/93   22 May 1835. Isaac Sampson of Hawkesbury, mason. Assaulting Nathaniel Watts of Hawkesbury by throwing stones and soil in his face. W. Blathwayt JP, W. G. Davy JP, A. Shakespear JP and H. Bush JP at the Cross Hands inn, Old Sodbury. George Hyde of Hawkesbury, witness. Fine £1 and 11/- costs, to be paid within two weeks, or one calendar month in Horsley house of correction. Offence committed Saturday 16 May 1835.

54/C/94   22 May 1835. George Walters of Ram Hill [*MS*. Ran Hill], Westerleigh, retail beer seller. Keeping his house open for the sale and consumption of beer between 11 p.m. and midnight. W. Blathwayt JP [*who did not sign*], W. G. Davy JP, A. Shakespear JP and H. Bush JP [*who did not sign*] at a Petty Sessions for Grumbalds Ash district. First offence. Fine 20/- and 16/6 costs. Offence committed Saturday 2 May 1835.

54/C/95   8 May 1835. Benjamin Shellard of Wick and Abson, innkeeper. Assaulting and beating Esther Sandy of Wick and Abson. W. Blathwayt JP, W. G. Davy JP, A. Shakespear JP, H. Bush JP and R. H. B. Hale JP at the Cross Hands inn at Old Sodbury. Fine £3, to be paid to George Williams, overseer [of the poor] of Wick and Abson, and £1 8*s*. costs, to be paid within twelve days. In default, one calendar month in Horsley house of correction. Offence committed between 1 a.m. and 2 a.m. Wednesday 29 April 1835.

54/D/1   6 Oct. 1835. Samuel Gough, late of Long Marston [*MS*. Marston Sicca], labourer. Leaving his wife and family chargeable to the parish. Rev. J. R. Hall JP at Moreton in Marsh. William Hodges, overseer of the poor, witness. Offender admitted offence. Hard labour for one calendar month in Northleach house of correction. Offence committed 1 Aug. 1835.

54/D/2   29 Sept. 1835. Thomas Ward of Clifford Chambers. Assaulting and beating Daniel Wakefield at Clifford Chambers. Rev. J. R. Hall JP and Rev. C. Jeaffreson JP [*who did not sign*] at Moreton in Marsh. Fine £1 and £1 1*s*. costs or one month in Northleach house of correction. Offence committed 26 Sept. 1835.

54/D/3   4 July 1835. George Hawker of Blockley, [Worcs.], labourer. Using a snare to kill game at Bourton on the Hill. Rev. C. Jeaffreson JP and Rev. J. R. Hall JP at Moreton in Marsh. Fine £5 and 18/- costs or hard labour for three months in Northleach house of correction. Offence committed 3 July 1835.

54/D/4   11 Feb. 1835 [*late return*]. Henry Heaven. Assaulting Thomas Dowdeswell at Eastington. C. O. Cambridge JP and P. Leversage JP at Eastington. Fine 5/- and 7/- costs or one calendar month in Horsley house of correction. Offence committed 29 Jan. 1835.

54/D/5   29 Feb. 1835 [*late return*]. Thomas Walkley. Assaulting Abraham Haines at King's Stanley. T. J. Lloyd Baker JP and C. O. Cambridge JP at Wheatenhurst. Fine 2/6 and 7/- costs or fourteen days in Horsley house of correction. Offence committed 4 Feb. 1835.

54/D/6   28 April 1835. Thomas Hopkins. Stealing fish from private water, the property of Sir Paul Baghott, knight, at Stonehouse. D. Maclean JP at Wheatenhurst. Fine 5/- and 6/- costs, to be paid to an overseer of the poor within fourteen days, or imprisonment in Horsley house of correction. [*Length of sentence not stated.*] Offence committed 13 April 1835.

54/D/7   28 April 1835. William Butcher. Stealing fish from private water [*etc.*, as 54/D/6 *except*] Fine 6/- costs.

54/D/8   8 Sept. 1835. Joseph Harding. Stealing a quantity of apples growing in an orchard at Randwick, the property of Henry Lewis. D. Maclean JP at King's Stanley. Hard labour for fourteen days in Horsley house of correction. Offence committed 6 Sept. 1835.

54/D/9   16 Sept. 1835. Henry Merrett. Attempting to steal fish from private water at Stonehouse, the property of Henry Lewis of Randwick. D. Maclean JP at King's Stanley. Fine £2 and 7/6 costs, to be paid within fourteen days. In default, fourteen days' hard labour in Horsley house of correction. Offence committed 6 Sept. 1835.

54/D/10   1 Sept. 1835. William Redman and Frederick Deane. Stealing a ferret from its place of confinement at Frocester, the property of Charles Townsend. D. Maclean JP at King's Stanley. Each fined £9 9s., 3/6 (the value of the ferret) and 7/6 costs, or hard labour for four months in Horsley house of correction. Offence committed 19 Aug. 1835.

54/D/11   16 Sept. 1835. Edwin Saunders. Attempting to steal fish from a stretch of water at Stonehouse, the private fishery of Henry Lewis. D. Maclean JP at King's Stanley. Fine £1, to be paid to an overseer of the poor, and 7/6 costs to the complainant, within fourteen days, or hard labour for fourteen days in Horsley house of correction. Offence committed 6 Sept. 1835.

54/D/12   24 July 1835. William Hopson. Assaulting George Walkley at King's Stanley. D. Maclean JP and P. Leversage JP at King's Stanley. Fine £1 and 12/- costs or fourteen days in Horsley house of correction. Offence committed 22 July 1835.

54/D/13   26 May 1835. Ruth Collier. Assaulting Harriett Grimes at Fretherne. D. J. Niblett JP and D. Maclean JP at Wheatenhurst. Fine 6d. and 6/6 costs. Given four weeks to pay. In default, one week in Horsley house of correction. Offence committed 18 May 1835. [MS. mistakenly gives the costs as awarded to the offender instead of to the complainant.]

54/D/14   23 June 1835. Onosiphorus [sic] Palmer. Breaking part of a plantation fence at Eastington, the property of Frederick Eycott. D. J. Niblett JP and D. Maclean JP at Wheatenhurst. Fine 5/-, 6d. damages and 6/- costs or one month in Horsley house of correction. Offence committed 2 June 1835.

54/D/15   3 Sept. 1835. John Weldon of Clifton. Keeping his house open for the sale of beer after 10 p.m. Rev. W. Mirehouse JP and G. Goldney JP at a Petty Sessions for part of Berkeley division. Fine £1 12s. 6d. and 7/6 costs. Offence committed 30 Aug. 1835.

54/D/16   17 Sept. 1835. Samuel Verender of Clifton. Keeping his house open for the sale of beer between 3 p.m. and 5 p.m. [on a Sunday]. G. Goldney JP and C. L. Walker JP at a Petty Sessions for part of Berekeley division. Fine £1 11s. 6d. and 8/6 costs. Offence committed Sunday 13 Sept. 1835.

54/D/17   17 Sept. 1835. John Sprague of Clifton. Keeping his house open for the sale of beer [etc., as 54/D/16 except] Fine £1 12s. 6d. and 7/6 costs.

54/D/18   19 Aug. 1835 William Hook. Assaulting Mary Wathen at Bitton. G. Goldney JP and J. Haythorne JP at Lawfords Gate sessions room. Fine £1 and £1 8s. costs, or one calendar month in Lawfords Gate house of correction. Offence committed 8 Aug. 1835.

54/D/19   28 Sept. 1835. George Gardner. Assaulting and beating John Eacott at Winterbourne. Rev. W. Mirehouse JP and C. L. Walker JP at Lawfords Gate sessions room. Fine £2 and 13/- costs or one calendar month in Lawfords Gate house of correction. Offence committed 25 Sept. 1835.

54/D/20   28 Sept. 1835. James Hopkins. Assaulting Ann Griffiths at St. Philip and St. Jacob, [Bristol]. C. L. Walker JP and Rev. W. Mirehouse JP at Lawfords Gate sessions room. Fine 5/- and 15/- costs or fourteen days in Lawfords Gate house of correction. Offence committed 21 Aug. 1835.

54/D/21   10 Sept. 1835. William Fussell. Assaulting Ann Fussell at Stapleton. Rev. W. Mirehouse JP and W. Fripp JP at Lawfords Gate sessions room. Fine 10/- and 9/- costs or fourteen days in Lawfords Gate house of correction. Offence committed 6 Sept. 1835.

54/D/22 10 Sept. 1835. Alfred Wiltshire. Assaulting Joseph Fowler at Frampton Cotterell. C. L. Walker JP and G. Goldney JP at Lawfords Gate sessions room. Fine 1/6 and 16/6 costs or fourteen days in Lawfords Gate house of correction. Offence committed 5 Sept. 1835.

54/D/23 17 Sept. 1835. Thomas Peachey. Assaulting Ann Mullins at St. Philip and St. Jacob, [Bristol]. G. Goldney JP and C. L. Walker JP at Lawfords Gate sessions room. Fine 5/- and 16/- costs or twenty-one days in Lawfords Gate house of correction. Offence committed 4 Sept. 1835.

54/D/24 24 Sept. 1835. William Pullen. Assaulting John Hill at Oldland. C. L. Walker JP and G. Goldney JP at Lawfords Gate sessions room. Fine 5/- and 9/- costs or fourteen days in Lawfords Gate house of correction. Offence committed 20 Sept. 1835.

54/D/25 17 Sept. 1835. Moses Collins. Assaulting Sarah West at Henbury. C. L. Walker JP and G. Goldney JP at Lawfords Gate sessions room. Fine 10/6 and 9/6 costs or six weeks in Lawfords Gate house of correction. Offence committed 16 Sept. 1835.

54/D/26 17 Sept. 1835. Sally McGill. Assaulting Lucy Royal at St. Philip and St. Jacob, [Bristol]. C. L. Walker JP and G. Goldney JP at Lawfords Gate sessions room. Fine 5/- and 6/6 costs or ten days in Lawfords Gate house of correction. Offence committed 3 Sept. 1835.

54/D/27 8 Oct. 1835. Samuel Holland. Assaulting Joseph Monks at St. George, [Bristol]. C. L. Walker JP and Rev. W. Mirehouse JP at Lawfords Gate sessions room. Fine 5/- and 6/6 costs or fourteen days in Lawfords Gate house of correction. Offence committed 3 Oct. 1835.

54/D/28 23 July 1835. Cicely Baker. Assaulting William Card at St. Philip and St. Jacob, [Bristol]. Rev. W. Mirehouse JP and C. L. Walker JP at Lawfords Gate sessions room. Fine 5/- and 6/6 costs or seven days in Lawfords Gate house of correction. Offence committed 21 July 1835.

54/D/29 8 Oct. 1835. George Holland. Assaulting Joseph Monks [*etc., as* 54/D/27].

54/D/30 24 Sept. 1835. John Seaward. Assaulting Mary Ann Gallop at St. Philip and St. Jacob, [Bristol]. C. L. Walker JP and Rev. W. Mirehouse JP at Lawfords Gate sessions room. Fine £2 and 9/6 costs or one calendar month in Lawfords Gate house of correction. Offence committed 19 Sept. 1835.

54/D/31 8 Oct. 1835. Daniel Crease. Assaulting William Treble at St. Philip and St. Jacob, [Bristol]. Rev. W. Mirehouse JP and C. L. Walker JP at Lawfords Gate sessions room. Fine £1 and 9/6 costs or twenty-one days in Lawfords Gate house of correction. Offence committed 3 Oct. 1835.

54/D/32 23 July 1835. Cicely Baker. Assaulting Sarah Phipps at St. Philip and St. Jacob, [Bristol]. Rev. W. Mirehouse JP and C. L. Walker JP at Lawfords Gate sessions room. Fine 1/- and 6/6 costs or seven days in Lawfords Gate house of correction. Offence committed 21 July 1835.

54/D/33 24 Sept. 1835. James Caines. Assaulting John Hill at Oldland. C. L. Walker JP and G. Goldney JP at Lawfords Gate sessions room. Fine 5/- and 9/- costs or fourteen days in Lawfords Gate house of correction. Offence committed 20 Sept. 1835.

54/D/34 10 Sept. 1835. William Hill. Assaulting Amelia Leonard at St. George, [Bristol]. Rev. W. Mirehouse JP and W. Fripp JP at Lawfords Gate sessions room. Fine £1 and 8/- costs or one calendar month in Lawfords Gate house of correction. Offence committed 6 Sept. 1835.

54/D/35 30 Sept. 1835. George Golding, toll-collector at the Tetbury south turnpike gate. Demanding ninepence toll from Thomas Hughes of Cirencester, cornet of Cirencester troop of Gloucester Yeomanry Cavalry, for his carriage, which was exempt as it carried stores for H. M. Forces from Bristol to Cirencester. T. Kingscote JP. Fine £5. Offence committed 12 Sept. 1835.

54/D/36   10 Sept. 1835. James Wasley. Assaulting Richard Newman at Elmstone Hardwicke. T. Newell JP and D. L. St. Clair JP at Cheltenham. Fine 9/- and 5/- costs. Offence committed 3 Sept. 1835.

54/D/37   16 July 1835. John Hawkins. Assaulting James Lane at Prestbury. R. B. Cooper JP and J. Blagdon JP at Cheltenham. Fine 5/- and 5/- costs or fourteen days in Northleach house of correction. Offence committed 15 July 1835.

54/D/38   10 Oct. 1835. Edwin Cooper. Assaulting Henry Charles Knightley at Cheltenham. R. B. Cooper JP and J. Blagdon JP at Cheltenham. Fine £2 and 8/- costs or two months in Northleach house of correction. Offence committed 10 Oct. 1835.

54/D/39   2 Sept. 1835. George Whithorn of Alderton, labourer. Trespassing with a gun in search of conies on land called Anikeers at Stanley Pontlarge. J. Timbrill D.D. JP and Rev. J. Keysall JP at Tewkesbury. Fine 5/-, to be paid to Arthur Heavens, overseer of the poor, and 13/- costs to Elijah James, the complainant. Offence committed 30 Aug. 1835.

54/D/40   5 Aug. 1835. William Taylor of Coombe Hill, the Leigh, labourer. Killing a hare in Lowlands field at the Leigh on land occupied by Mr. Thomas Trinder, without a game licence. Rev. J. Keysall JP and Rev. C. White JP at Tewkesbury. Fine 50/-, to be paid to Henry Trinder, overseer of the poor, and 13/- costs to James Hopkins, the complainant, on or before 1 Sept. In default, one calendar month in Northleach house of correction. Offence committed 18 June 1835.

54/D/41   19 Aug. 1835. William Weaver, son of Peter Weaver, farmer, of Stub Hill, Twyning. Assaulting William Thomas, baker, of St. Martin's, [Worcester], without provocation at Stub Hill, Twyning. Rev. J. Keysall JP, Rev. C. White JP and J. W. Martin JP at Tewkesbury. Fine £1 14s., to be paid to William Dee, an overseer of the poor, and 16/- costs to the complainant. Offence committed Tuesday 11 Aug. 1835.

54/D/42   7 July 1835. William Berry. Assaulting Edward Lediard at Cheltenham. Rev. W. Hicks JP and J. Blagdon JP at Cheltenham. Fine 5/- or fourteen days in Northleach house of correction. Offence committed 3 July 1835.

54/D/43   21 July 1835. Absalom Holland. Failing to support his wife, thereby causing her to become chargeable to Cheltenham parish. R. B. Cooper JP at Cheltenham. Hard labour for one month in Northleach house of correction. Offence committed 13 July 1835.

54/D/44   29 Sept. 1835. John White. Trespassing in pursuit of game on land belonging to Edward Coxwell Rogers Esq. at Bishop's Cleeve. R. B. Cooper JP at Cheltenham. Fine 20/- and 9/- costs. Offence committed 21 Sept. 1835.

54/D/45   18 July 1835. James Chew. Assaulting Thomas Williams at Prestbury. R. B. Cooper JP and T. Newell JP at Cheltenham. Fine 20/- and 6/- costs or one month in Northleach house of correction. Offence committed 15 July 1835.

54/D/46   23 July 1835. Thomas Boodle of Cheltenham, innkeeper. Selling excisable liquors to be consumed in a booth on the racecourse at Cheltenham without a licence, his innkeeper's licence covering only the inn and no other premises. R. B. Cooper JP and T. Newell JP at Cheltenham. Fine £5 and 5/6 costs. Offence committed Sunday 12 July 1835.

54/D/47   3 Oct. 1835. William Lineham of Cheltenham, beerhouse keeper. Keeping his house open for the sale of beer after 10 p.m. R. B. Cooper JP and T. Newell JP at Cheltenham. First offence. Fine £2 and 4/6 costs. Offence committed 29 Sept. 1835.

54/D/48   15 Aug. 1835. Thomas Bryant. Assaulting Eliza Lane at Cheltenham. R. B. Cooper JP and T. Newell JP at Cheltenham. Fine £2 and 7/6 costs. Offence committed 12 Aug. 1835.

54/D/49 24 Sept. 1835. Hannah Shepherd. Assaulting Mary Ann Watts at Cheltenham. R. B. Cooper JP and T. Newell JP at Cheltenham. Fine 2/6 and 5/6 costs. Offence committed 21 Sept. 1835.

54/D/50 25 July 1835. Peter Day. Assaulting Charles Okey at Cheltenham. R. B. Cooper JP and T. Newell JP at Cheltenham. Fine 10/- and 3/- costs or fourteen days in Northleach house of correction. Offence committed 21 July 1835.

54/D/51 30 July 1835. William Haines. Stealing a dog, the property of John James, in Cheltenham. R. B. Cooper JP. First offence. Fine £20. Offence committed 11 July 1835.

54/D/52 24 Sept. 1835. Charles Buckingham. Trespassing in pursuit of game on land belonging to John Gregory Welch Esq. at Cheltenham. R. B. Cooper JP. Fine £2 and 5/6 costs. Offence committed 22 Sept. 1835.

54/D/53 6 Aug. 1835. John Price. Trespassing in pursuit of game on land belonging to Conway Whithorn Lovesy Esq. at Charlton Kings. J. E. Viner JP at Cheltenham. Fine 10/- and 5/6 costs. Offence committed 13 July 1835.

54/D/54 20 Aug. 1835. Joseph Clarke. Assaulting Susan Wood at Bishop's Cleeve. T. Newell JP and W. Pitt JP at Cheltenham. Fine 5/- and 8/6 costs. Offence committed 17 Aug. 1835.

54/D/55 22 Sept. 1835. John Hill of Cheltenham, beerhouse keeper. Opening his house for the sale of beer before 1 p.m. on a Sunday. T. Newell JP and J. E. Viner JP at Cheltenham. First offence. Fine £2 and 4/6 costs. Offence committed 20 Sept. 1835.

54/D/56 16 July 1835. Thomas Dix. Assaulting WilliamWilkes at Bishop's Cleeve. R. B. Cooper JP and J. Blagdon JP at Cheltenham. Fine 20/- and 4/6 costs or one month in Northleach house of correction. Offence committed 15 July 1835.

54/D/57 9 July 1835. John Lewis of Cheltenham, beerhouse keeper. Keeping his house open for the sale of beer after 11 p.m. R. B. Cooper JP and J. Blagdon JP at Cheltenham. First offence. Fine £2 and 5/6 costs. Offence committed 6 July 1835.

54/D/58 13 July 1835. Sidney Liddiard of Rodborough, labourer. Using a gun to kill conies on land occupied by tenant Edward Taylor at Rodborough, without obtaining a licence. O. P. Wathen JP and W. Playne JP at Rodborough in Longtree district, commissioners for assessed taxes. Information given to O. P. Wathen JP. Thomas Weaving and Edward Taylor, witnesses. Fine £10. Offence committed 16 May 1835.

54/D/59 29 Sept. 1835. Walter Harris. Stealing a quantity of pears growing in a garden at Wheatenhurst, the property of James Brewer. T. J. Lloyd Baker JP and P. Leversage JP at Wheatenhurst. Hard labour for two calendar months in Horsley house of correction. Offence committed 27 Aug. 1835.

54/D/60 25 Aug. 1835. William Gower. Assaulting Hannah Grimes at Eastington. T. J. Lloyd Baker JP and P. Leversage JP at Wheatenhurst. Fine 10/- and 6/6 costs or fourteen day in Horsley house of correction. Offence committed 27 July 1835.

54/D/61 22 July 1835. John Davis and John Harris. Playing an unlawful game with a pea and thimbles at Hempsted. T. J. Lloyd Baker JP at Hardwicke. Hard labour for three months in Horsley house of correction. Offence committed 22 July 1835.

54/D/62 14 Sept. 1835. William Hunt of Stow on the Wold, innkeeper. Permitting drunkenness in his house. [Rev.] F. E. Witts JP and [Rev.] C. Jeaffreson JP. First offence. Fine £2 5s. and 5/- costs. Offence committed Sunday 13 Sept. 1835.

54/D/63 9 Oct. 1835. Mary and Elizabeth Ireland of Bisley, spinsters. Stealing turnips growing in a field at Painswick, the property of John Silk, yeoman, of Cranham. H. Burgh JP and

H. Wyatt JP at Stroud. Hard labour for fourteen days in Horsley house of correction. Offence committed 2 Oct. 1835.

54/D/64   23 Sept. 1835. Henry Harris, Henry Leech, Henry Ireland and Joseph Smart, labourers, of Stroud. Stealing a quantity of pears growing in an orchard at Stroud, the property of John Neems, yeoman. H. Burgh JP at Stroud. Harris sentenced to hard labour for one calendar month, the others to hard labour for fourteen days, in Horsley house of correction. Offence committed 22 Sept. 1835.

54/D/65   11 Sept. 1835. Richard Clarke of Stroud, labourer. Trespassing in search of game on land at Stroud, the property of William Lewis Esq. H. Burgh JP and N. S. Marling JP at Stroud. Fine £2, to be paid to John Elliott, overseer of the poor, and 9/- costs to Daniel Woodfield, the complainant, or hard labour for two calendar months in Horsley house of correction. Offence committed 30 Aug. 1835.

54/D/66   11 Sept. 1835. Thomas Blackwell of Stroud, labourer. Trespassing in search of game [etc., as 54/D/65].

54/D/67   11 Sept. 1835. Thomas Aldridge of Stroud, labourer. Assaulting Hannah wife of John Heaven, clothworker, of Stroud. H. Burgh JP and J. Mills JP at Stroud. Fine £5 or two calendar months in Horsley house of correction. Offence committed 9 Aug. 1835.

54/D/68   28 Aug. 1835. William Lander of Stroud, labourer. Assaulting Charles Wheeler, constable of Stroud. H. Burgh JP and J. Mills JP at Stroud. Fine £5 or two calendar months in Horsley house of correction. Offence committed 27 Aug. 1835.

54/D/69   6 Oct. 1835. James Kirby, William Young and Thomas Poulson, labourers, of Bisley. Stealing a quantity of pears growing in an orchard at Stroud, the property of Thomas Shill, yeoman. H. Burgh JP at Stroud. Hard labour for two calendar months in Horsley house of correction. Offence committed 2 Sept. 1835.

54/D/70   11 Aug. 1835. John Jones of Stroud, tailor. Maliciously pulling up and destroying a quantity of potatoes growing in a garden, the property of Walter Watkins, gentleman, of Stroud. H. Burgh JP at Stroud. Fine 3/- damages and 9/- costs, to be paid to the complainant, or hard labour for two calendar months in Horsley house of correction. Offence committed 8 July 1835.

54/D/71   31 July 1835. Edwin Hind of Rodborough, labourer. Cutting and stealing trees from a wood, the property of Edward Hogg Esq. of Randwick. H. Burgh JP and J. Mills JP at Stroud. Fine £5, to be paid to an overseer of the poor, 1/- damages and 8/- costs, or hard labour for one calendar month in Horsley house of correction. Offence committed 20 July 1835.

54/D/72   21 July 1835. John Davis of Bisley, labourer. Stealing a quantity of apples growing in an orchard at Bisley, the property of Richard Baughan of Bisley, yeoman. H. Burgh JP at Stroud. Hard labour for two calendar months in Horsley house of correction. Offence committed 21 July 1835.

54/D/73   17 July 1835. Robert Spire of Bisley, innkeeper of the Duke of York. Allowing gaming on his premises. H. Burgh JP and E. G. Hallewell JP. First offence. Fine 5/- and 7/6 costs. Offence committed 6 July 1835.

54/D/74   3 July 1835. Thomas Jones, clothier, of Bisley. Employing a person under eighteen year of age in his woollen mill beyond the permitted hours. H. Burgh JP. Thomas Jones Howells Esq., inspector of factories, complainant. Offender admitted charge. George Holmes, aged fifteen, was employed from 7 a.m. until 10 p.m. on 22 June 1835. [Penalty not recorded.]

54/D/75   3 July 1835. Thomas Jones, clothier, of Bisley. Employing a person under eighteen year of age [etc., as 54/D/74 except] between 8.30 p.m. and 5.30 a.m. on 22–3 June 1835. [The document presumably should have named a different boy and repeated the name George Holmes in error.]

54/D/76   3 July 1835. James Crook of Bisley, labourer. Assaulting Elizabeth Whiting, spinster, of Bisley. H. Burgh JP and H. Wyatt JP at Stroud. Fine £5 or two calendar months in Horsley house of correction. Offence committed 11 June 1835.

54/D/77   19 June 1835. Jane Wood. Leaving her two children (both under sixteen years of age) chargeable to Horsley parish. W. Playne JP at Horsley. Hard labour for three calendar months in Horsley house of correction. Offence committed 20 May 1835.

54/D/78   3 Sept. 1835. John Woodman, licensed beer retailer, of Horsley. Keeping his house open for the sale of beer between 11 p.m. and midnight. O. P. Wathen JP, T. Kingscote JP, W. Playne JP and T. R. Haycock JP at a Petty Sessions held at Horsley for Longtree division. First offence. Fine 40/- and 10/- costs. Offence committed 29 Aug. 1835.

54/D/79   22 Jan. 1835 [*late return*]. John Leonard. Trespassing at night at Tortworth and taking three pheasants. T. Kingscote JP, A. Shakespear JP and B. C. Browne JP at Horsley. Previous conviction for similar offence on 13 Nov. 1834 at Boxwell and sentenced on 27 Dec. 1834 to hard labour for three calendar months, after which to find sureties of £20 against re-offending for one year or serve a further six months' hard labour. [*Cf.* 54/A/281, *where the first offence is said to have been committed* 4 Dec. 1834.] For this second offence to serve hard labour for six calendar months in Horsley house of correction, after which to find sureties totalling £40 against re-offending, or hard labour for one year in Horsley house of correction. Offence committed 4 Dec. 1834.

54/D/80   8 July 1835. Anselm Cook of Rodborough, beer retailer. Using a gun without a licence to kill conies on land occupied by tenant Thomas Boulton at Rodborough. O. P. Wathen JP, commissioner for assessed taxes, at Rodborough. Fine £10. Offence committed 13 May 1835.

54/D/81   28 Sept. 1835. John Flight. Trespassing with a gun at night in search of game in King's Stanley wood. T. Kingscote JP and A. Shakespear JP at Kingscote. Hard labour for three calendar months in Horsley house of correction, after which to find sureties of £20 against re-offending for one year. In default, a further six months' hard labour. Offence committed 27 Sept. 1835.

54/D/82   23 July 1835. Joseph Clark, clothworker, of Horsley. Possessing 102 lb. of various woollen yarns and waste believed to be stolen. O. P. Wathen JP, T. Kingscote JP, B. C. Browne JP, D. Ricardo JP and T. R. Haycock JP. Information given by John Hyde to first- and last-named JPs on 11 July. Premises searched. Offender given time to provide proof of purchase and delivery. No evidence produced. First offence. Fine £20, half to be paid to the informer and the rest to the treasurer of Gloucester infirmary. Offence committed 11 July 1835.

54/D/83   15 Oct. 1835. George Peck. Trespassing at night with nets and dogs in search of game at Tormarton. T. Kingscote JP and B. C. Browne JP at Horsley. Hard labour for three calendar months in Horsley house of correction, after which to find sureties of £20 against re-offending for one year. In default, a further six months' hard labour. Offence committed 14 Oct. 1835.

54/D/84   25 Sept. 1835. James Flower of Walcot, Som. Trespassing on land called the Moore at Dodington, occupied by John Sherborne, and taking a hare from a snare. W. Blathwayt JP, W. G. Davy JP, A. Shakespear JP and R. H. B. Hale JP at Old Sodbury. Henry Martin, gamekeeper to Sir C. B. Codrington, Bt., complainant. David Bennett, witness. Fine £1, half of which to be paid to the overseer of the poor and half to the complainant in addition to £1 9s. costs, or one month in Horsley house of correction. Offence committed Saturday 22 Aug. 1835 between 3 p.m. and 4 p.m.

55/A/1   18 Jan. 1836. Thomas Brown of Littleton Drew, Wilts., labourer. Using a wire to take game at Acton Turville [MS. Acton Turnville], without a licence. W. C. Codrington M.P. JP at Dodington House. Fine £2, to be paid to William Minett, overseer of the poor, and 7/6 to the complainant William Watts, or hard labour for two calendar months in Horsley house of correction. Offence committed 18 Jan. 1836.

55/A/2 16 Dec. 1835. William Sheppard. Leaving his two children chargeable to Bromsberrow parish. Rev. J. Higgins JP at Ledbury, Herefs. Hard labour for one calendar month in Littledean house of correction.

55/A/3 19 Nov. 1835. Richard Dickenson of Bitton. Keeping his house open for the sale of beer after 10 p.m. D. Cave JP and A. G. H. Battersby JP at a Petty Sessions for part of Berkeley division. Fine £1 11s. and 9/- costs. Offence committed 7 Nov. 1835.

55/A/4 19 Nov. 1835. Robert Worlock of Bitton. Keeping his house open [etc., as 55/A/3].

55/A/5 19 Nov. 1835. John White of Bitton. Keeping his house open [etc., as 55/A/3].

55/A/6 19 Nov. 1835. Hannah Harvey of Bitton. Keeping her house open [etc., as 55/A/3].

55/A/7 19 Nov. 1835. Thomas Howes of Winterbourne. Keeping his house open for the sale of beer after 10 p.m. D. Cave JP and A. G. H. Battersby JP at a Petty Sessions for part of Berkeley division. Fine £1 12s. and 8/- costs. Offence committed 9 Nov. 1835.

55/A/8 19 Nov. 1835. William French of Bitton. Keeping his house open for the sale of beer after 10 p.m. D. Cave JP and A. G. H. Battersby JP at a Petty Sessions for part of Berkeley division. Fine £1 9s. and 11/- costs. Offence committed 14 Nov. 1835.

55/A/9 19 Nov. 1835. Henry Fussell of Bitton. Keeping his house open for the sale of beer after 10 p.m. D. Cave JP and A. G. H. Battersby JP at a Petty Sessions for part of Berkeley division. Fine £1 11s. and 9/- costs. Offence committed 14 Nov. 1835.

55/A/10 19 Nov. 1835. Richard Sweet of Bitton. Keeping his house open for the sale of beer after 10 p.m. D. Cave JP and A. G. H. Battersby JP at a Petty Sessions for part of Berkeley division. Fine £1 12s. and 8/- costs. Offence committed 14 Nov. 1835.

55/A/11 19 Nov. 1835. Moses Davis of Bitton. Keeping his house open for the sale of beer after 10 p.m. D. Cave JP and A. G. H. Battersby JP at a Petty Sessions for part of Berkeley division. Fine £1 12s. and 8/- costs. Offence committed 7 Nov. 1835.

55/A/12 21 May 1835 [late return]. John Pain of Clifton. Keeping his house open for the sale of beer after 10 p.m. Rev. W. Mirehouse JP and T. Daniel JP at a Petty Sessions for part of Berkeley division. Fine £1 12s. 6d. and 7/6 costs. Offence committed 2 May 1835.

55/A/13 17 Dec. 1835. George Smith of St. George, [Bristol]. Keeping his house open for the sale of beer after 10 p.m. W. Munro JP and J. Cave JP at a Petty Sessions for part of Berkeley division. Fine £1 10s. and 10/- costs. Offence committed 5 Dec. 1835.

55/A/14 26 Nov. 1835. Benjamin Bracey of Mangotsfield. Keeping his house open for the sale of beer after 10 p.m. D. Cave JP and G. Worrall JP at a Petty Sessions for part of Berkeley division. Fine £1 10s. and 10/- costs. Offence committed 14 Nov. 1835.

55/A/15 26 Nov. 1835. Enos Howes of St. George, [Bristol]. Keeping his house open for the sale of beer after 10 p.m. D. Cave JP and G. Worrall JP at a Petty Sessions for part of Berkeley division. Fine £1 10s. and 10/- costs. Offence committed 16 Nov. 1835.

55/A/16 26 Nov. 1835. Thomas Shepherd of Mangotsfield. Keeping his house open for the sale of beer after 10 p.m. D. Cave JP and G. Worrall JP at a Petty Sessions for part of Berkeley division. Fine £1 11s. and 9/- costs. Offence committed 14 Nov. 1835.

55/A/17 12 Nov. 1835. Mary Ward of Stapleton. Keeping her house open for the sale of beer after 10 p.m. D. Cave JP and G. Goldney JP at a Petty Sessions for part of Berkeley division. Fine £2 and 10/6 costs. Offence committed 8 Oct. 1835.

55/A/18 19 Nov. 1835. Joseph Fryer, licensed beer retailer, of the Crown, Mangotsfield. Allowing illegal games to be played in his premises. D. Cave JP and A. G. H. Battersby JP at Lawfords Gate sessions room. First offence. Fine 5/- and 10/- costs. Offence committed Saturday 14 Nov. 1835.

55/A/19 12 Nov. 1835. William Hathway *alias* Belcher. Assaulting James Goodsir at St. George, [Bristol]. G. Goldney JP and T. Daniel JP at Lawfords Gate sessions room. Fine 4/6 and 15/6 costs or fourteen days in Lawfords Gate house of correction. Offence committed 3 Nov. 1835.

55/A/20 3 Dec. 1835. Ann Wiltshire. Assaulting Elizabeth Iles at Bitton. W. Munro JP and A. G. H. Battersby JP at Lawfords Gate sessions room. Fine 5/- and 8/- costs or fourteen days in Lawfords Gate house of correction. Offence committed 8 Nov. 1835.

55/A/21 5 Nov. 1835. Peter Gerrish. Assaulting Charles Taylor at Bitton. C. L. Walker JP and D. Cave JP at Lawfords Gate sessions room. Fine 1/- and 10/6 costs or three days in Lawfords Gate house of correction. Offence committed 8 Oct. 1835.

55/A/22 13 Aug. 1835. Thomas Ham [? Hain]. Assaulting Robert Reeves at St. James, [Bristol]. W. Munro JP and J. Cave JP at Lawfords Gate sessions room. Fine 5/- and 9/6 costs or one calendar month in Lawfords Gate house of correction. Offence committed 8 Aug. 1835.

55/A/23 13 Aug. 1835. William Lacy. Assaulting John Randell at St. Philip and St. Jacob [Bristol]. W. Munro JP and J. Cave JP at Lawfords Gate sessions room. Fine 1/- and 13/6 costs or one calendar month in Lawfords Gate house of correction. Offence committed 8 Aug. 1835.

55/A/24 6 Aug. 1835. Edward Thomas. Assaulting George Fudge at St. Philip and St. Jacob, [Bristol]. J. Cave JP and W. Munro JP at Lawfords Gate sessions room. Fine 2/- and 14/- costs or one calendar month in Lawfords Gate house of correction. Offence committed 26 July 1835.

55/A/25 17 Sept. 1835. Ann Hanks. Assaulting Catherine Agnes Sargent at St. James and St. Paul, [Bristol]. Rev. W. Mirehouse JP and T. Daniel JP at Lawfords Gate sessions room. Fine 5/- and 7/6 costs or fourteen days in Lawfords Gate house of correction. Offence committed 20 Aug. 1835.

55/A/26 1 Oct. 1835. Samuel Newman. Assaulting Abraham Roberts at St. George, [Bristol]. G. Worrall JP and G. Goldney JP at Lawfords Gate sessions room. Fine £3 and 7/- costs or six weeks in Lawfords Gate house of correction. Offence committed 25 Sept. 1835.

55/A/27 15 Oct. 1835. Edward Cole. Assaulting Philip Nutt at St. Philip and St. Jacob, [Bristol]. G. Goldney JP and W. Fripp JP at Lawfords Gate sessions room. Fine 10/- and 8/6 costs or twenty-one days in Lawfords Gate house of correction. Offence committed 8 Oct. 1835.

55/A/28 1 Oct. 1835. Charles Gough. Assaulting John Bird at St. Philip and St. Jacob, [Bristol]. G. Goldney JP and G. Worrall JP at Lawfords Gate sessions room. Fine £2 10*s.* and 15/- costs or six weeks in Lawfords Gate house of correction. Offence committed 26 Sept. 1835.

55/A/29 6 Aug. 1835. William Butt. Assaulting Joseph Tilly at Horfield. A. G. H. Battersby JP and G. Worrall JP at Lawfords Gate sessions room. Fine 2/6 and 7/6 costs or seven days in Lawfords Gate house of correction. Offence committed 1 Aug. 1835.

55/A/30 6 Aug. 1835. William Butt. Assaulting Joseph Tilly the younger at Horfield. A. G. H. Battersby JP and G. Worrall JP at Lawfords Gate sessions room. Fine 2/6 and 7/6 costs or seven days in Lawfords Gate house of correction. Offence committed 1 Aug. 1835.

55/A/31   27 Aug. 1835. William Cox. Assaulting Henry Tiley at St. Philip and St. Jacob, [Bristol]. A. G. H. Battersby JP and G. Worrall JP at Lawfords Gate sessions room. Fine 5/- and 6/6 costs or one calendar month in Lawfords Gate house of correction. Offence committed 17 Aug. 1835.

55/A/32   23 July 1835. Joseph Coombs. Assaulting Elizabeth Connell at St. Philip and St. Jacob, [Bristol]. J. S. Harford JP and D. Cave JP at Lawfords Gate sessions room. Fine 1/6 and 8/6 costs or fifteen days in Lawfords Gate house of correction. Offence committed 16 July 1835.

55/A/33   2 Jan. 1836. John Basons of Bisley, labourer. Violently assaulting Susan Whiting, single woman, of Bisley. H. Wyatt JP and N. S. Marling JP at Stroud. Fine £4 12s. and 8/- costs or two calendar months in Horsley house of correction. Offence committed 11 June 1835.

55/A/34   5 Dec. 1835. Charles Smart and William Wicks, labourers, of Nympsfield. Stealing turnips growing on land occupied by William Rasher, yeoman, of Nympsfield. H. Burgh JP at Stroud. Hard labour for one calendar month in Horsley house of correction. Offence committed 4 Dec. 1835.

55/A/35   2 Dec. 1835. William Cockshut the younger, labourer, of Stroud. Trespassing in pursuit of conies on land at Painswick, the property of William Capel Esq. H. Burgh JP at Stroud. Fine £2, to be paid to William Iles, overseer of the poor, and 11/6 costs to Charles Capel, the complainant, or hard labour for two calendar months in Horsley house of correction. Offence committed 28 Nov. 1835.

55/A/36   27 Nov. 1835. James Brinkworth. Violently assaulting Thomas Ball the younger, waterman, of Stourport, Worcs., at Stroud. H. Burgh JP and H. Wyatt at Stroud. Fine 10/- and 8/- costs or two calendar months in Horsley house of correction. Offence committed 26 Nov. 1835.

55/A/37   20 Nov. 1835. John Weaving of Winstone, labourer. Violently assaulting Stephen Price, yeoman, of Nympsfield, at Winstone. H. Burgh JP and J. Mills JP at Stroud. Fine £1 and 11/- costs or two calendar months in Horsley house of correction. Offence committed 13 Oct. 1835.

55/A/38   20 Nov. 1835. John Dutton the younger and Obed Herbert, labourers, of Bisley. Violently assaulting John Rodway, innkeeper, of Bisley. H. Burgh JP and J. Mills JP at Stroud. Fine £1 and 13/- costs or two calendar months in Horsley house of correction. Offence committed 13 Nov. 1835.

55/A/39   30 Nov. 1835. Jesse King. Trespassing in search of game on land at King's Stanley, the property of the Rt. Hon. Thomas, Lord Ducie. H. Burgh JP and H. Wyatt JP at Stroud. Fine £2, to be paid to William Hobbs, an overseer of the poor of King's Stanley, and 7/- costs to William Baker of King's Stanley, complainant, or hard labour for two calendar months in Horsley house of correction. Offence committed 28 Nov. 1835.

55/A/40   30 Nov. 1835. John Blood. Using a gun to kill game in King's Stanley without a game certificate. H. Burgh JP and H. Wyatt JP at Stroud. Fine £5, to be paid to William Hobbs, an overseer of the poor of King's Stanley, and 5/- costs to William Baker of the same parish, complainant, or hard labour for three calendar months in Horsley house of correction. Offence committed 28 Nov. 1835.

55/A/41   12 Nov. 1835. Joseph Collier. Violently and indecently assaulting Charlotte Baker, spinster, of Stroud. H. Burgh JP and H. Wyatt JP at Stroud. Fine £5 or two calendar months in Horsley house of correction. Offence committed 4 Aug. 1835.

55/A/42   24 Dec. 1835. Charles Daniels, pig butcher and retail beer seller, of Horsley. Using ferrets and a net to take and kill five conies at Wickley Wood, Horsley. W. Playne JP and commissioner for assessed taxes, at Horsley. Fine £10. Offence committed 7 Dec. 1835.

55/A/43   24 Nov. 1835. Thomas Whitehead. Wilfully damaging a tollgate at the Cainscross division of roads at Standish. D. Maclean JP and P. Leversage JP at Wheatenhurst. Fine £1 and 2/6 costs. Offence committed 6 Oct. 1835.

55/A/44   24 Nov. 1835. Thomas Whitehead. Passing through a tollgate at the Cainscross division of roads at Standish with four horses drawing, without paying the appropriate toll. D. Maclean JP and P. Leversage JP at Wheatenhurst. Fine £1 and 2/6 costs. Offence committed 6 Oct. 1835.

55/A/45   25 Nov. 1835. Robert Pool. Assaulting Sarah Curtis at King's Stanley. D. Maclean JP and P. Leversage JP at King's Stanley. Fine 14/- and 16/- costs or one calendar month in Horsley house of correction. Offence committed 10 Nov. 1835.

55/A/46   24 Nov. 1835. John Park, Mark Harris, Peter Harris and James Freeman. Assaulting Charles Walter at Haresfield. D. Maclean JP and P. Leversage at Wheatenhurst. Each fined 6d. and 7/6 costs or fourteen days in Horsley house of correction. Offence committed 31 Oct. 1835.

55/A/47   29 Dec. 1835. Henry Whitmore. Assaulting Joseph Adlum at Eastington. T. J. Lloyd Baker JP and H. C. Clifford JP at Wheatenhurst. Fine 2/- and 7/6 costs, to be paid within one month, or fourteen days in Horsley house of correction. Offence committed 6 Dec. 1835.

55/A/48   29 Dec. 1835. Thomas Baghott, gentleman, late of Moreton Valence. Trespassing in pursuit of game on land belonging to Thomas Skipp Esq. at Moreton Valence. T. J. Lloyd Baker JP and H. C. Clifford JP at Wheatenhurst. Frederick Eycott and John Heaven, witnesses. Fine £2, to be paid to an overseer of the poor of Moreton Valence, and 8/6 costs to Frederick Eycott, or two calendar months in Horsley house of correction. Offence committed 26 Nov. 1835.

55/A/49   29 Dec. 1835. Thomas Baghott, gentleman, late of Stonehouse. Trespassing in pursuit of game at Stonehouse on land belonging to Edward Palling Caruthers Esq. T. J. Lloyd Baker JP and H. C. Clifford JP at Wheatenhurst. William White and John Heaven, witnesses. Fine £2, to be paid to an overseer of the poor of Stonehouse, and 8/6 costs to William White, or two calendar months in Horsley house of correction. Offence committed 26 Nov. 1835.

55/A/50   24 Aug. 1835. John Davis of Tibberton, labourer. Assaulting Hester Phelps at Tibberton. O. Ricardo JP and R. F. Onslow JP at Newent. Fine 10/- and 9/6 costs or one calendar month in Littledean house of correction. Offence committed 15 Aug. 1835.

55/A/51   9 Feb. 1835 [late return]. Joseph Winter of Aston Ingham, Herefs., labourer. Using a gin to take and kill game at Oxenhall. Rev. R. F. Onslow JP and O. Ricardo JP. John Warren, broomstail maker, of Oxenhall, complainant. Fine £4 7s. and 13/- costs or two calendar months in Littledean house of correction. Offence committed 15 Nov. 1834.

55/A/52   5 Jan. 1835 [late return]. Edward Cooper. Negligently driving a wagon drawn by several horses on the turnpike road at Churcham thereby interrupting the free passage of a carriage belonging to James Money Esq. Rev. R. F. Onslow JP and O. Ricardo JP. Charles Freeman, witness. Fine 20/-. Offence committed 31 Dec. 1834.

55/A/53   12 Jan. 1835 [late return]. Thomas Prosser. Negligently driving a wagon drawn by several horses on the turnpike road at Churcham thereby [etc., as 55/A/52 except] Fine 40/-.

55/A/54   28 Sept. 1835. Thomas Wilkes of Upleadon, labourer. Assaulting Betty wife of Younger Jones, labourer, at Upleadon without provocation. O. Ricardo JP and R. F. Onslow JP at

Newent. Fine 7/6 and 7/- costs or fourteen days in Littledean house of correction. Offence committed 29 July 1835.

55/A/55   28 Sept. 1835. Thomas Wilkes of Upleadon, labourer. Assaulting Younger Jones, labourer, of Upleadon, without provocation [*etc.*, *as* 55/A/54 *except*] or twenty-one days in Littledean house of correction.

55/A/56   24 Aug. 1835. Sarah wife of William Daw, labourer, of Newent. Assaulting Margaret, wife of James Davis, labourer, of Newent, without provocation. Rev. J. Commeline JP and R. F. Onslow JP at Newent. Fine 6*d.* and 7/6 costs or seven days in Littledean house of correction. Offence committed 18 Aug. 1835.

55/A/57   19 Oct. 1835. Ann, wife of John Markey, labourer, of Taynton. Assaulting Hester Clarke, single woman, of Huntley at Taynton. Rev. J. Commeline JP and R. F. Onslow JP at Newent. Fine 1/- and 8/6 costs or seven days in Littledean house of correction. Offence committed 11 Oct. 1835.

55/A/58   14 Sept. 1835. Thomas Lyes of Newent, labourer. Assaulting John Thurston, shopkeeper, of Newent, without provocation. Rev. J. Commeline JP and O. Ricardo JP at Newent. Fine 10/- and 5/- costs or one calendar month in Littledean house of correction. Offence committed 12 Sept. 1835.

55/A/59   20 July 1835. Robert Miles of Ashleworth, boatman. Assaulting William Meredith, boatman, of Newent, without provocation at Newent. O. Ricardo JP and R. F. Onslow JP at Newent. Fine 6*d.* and 7/- costs or seven days in Littledean house of correction. Offence committed 17 July 1835.

55/A/60   19 Oct. 1835. Charles Cotterell, labourer, of Ledbury, Herefs. Using a gin to kill game at Bromsberrow. Rev. J. Commeline JP and R. F. Onslow JP at Newent. William Cook, gamekeeper, of Bromsberrow, complainant. Fine £5, half to be paid to an overseer of the poor of Bromsberrow and the remainder, together with 10/- costs, to the complainant, or three calendar months in Littledean house of correction. Offence committed 18 Oct. 1835.

55/A/61   23 Nov. 1835. John Probyn of Newent, labourer. Assaulting Esther Dobbins without provocation at Newent. O. Ricardo JP and R. F. Onslow JP at Newent. Fine 2/6 and 9/6 costs or seven days in Littledean house of correction. Offence committed 18 Nov. 1835.

55/A/62   14 Dec. 1835. John Probyn of Newent, labourer. Cutting and breaking up part of a fence growing on land belonging to Paul Apperley at Newent. O. Ricardo JP and R. F. Onslow JP at Newent. Fine 10/-, 9/- costs and 6*d.* damages or hard labour for one calendar month in Littledean house of correction. Complainant not examined as to proof of offence. Offence committed 11 Dec. 1835.

55/A/63   2 Nov. 1835. Charles Richards of Gloucester, carpenter. Using a gun, without a game certificate, in search of game at Pauntley. Rev. J. Commeline JP and Rev. Thomas Hill JP. William Bullock, gamekeeper, of Oxenhall, complainant. Fine £5, half to be paid to an overseer of the poor of Pauntley and the remainder, together with 17/- costs, to the complainant, or hard labour for three calendar months in Littledean house of correction. Offence committed 19 Oct. 1835.

55/A/64   26 Oct. 1835. David Lane, cordwainer, of Gloucester. Trespassing in pursuit of game in woodland at Pauntley belonging to Osman Ricardo Esq., and when challenged refusing to give his real name and parish. Rev. J. Commeline JP and Rev. T. Hill JP at Newent. William Bullock of Oxenhall, gamekeeper to O. Ricardo Esq., complainant. Fine £2 10*s.*, half to be paid to an overseer of the poor and the remainder, together with 6/6 costs, to the complainant, or two calendar months in Littledean house of correction. Offence committed at 5 p.m. 16 Oct. 1835.

55/A/65   26 Oct. 1835. Charles Chesterton, labourer, of Gloucester. Trespassing in pursuit of game in woodland at Collin Park, Pauntley, occupied by Osman Ricardo Esq. Rev. J. Commeline JP and Rev. T. Hill JP at Newent. William Bullock, gamekeeper, complainant, of Oxenhall. Fine 20/-, half to be paid to an overseer of the poor and the remainder, together with 6/6 costs, to the complainant, or one calendar month in Littledean house of correction. Offence committed at 5 p.m. 16 Oct. 1835.

55/A/66   29 Oct. 1835. William Dawes. Assaulting James Brown at Cheltenham. R. B. Cooper JP and J. Blagdon JP at Cheltenham. Fine 2/6 and 6/6 costs. Offence committed 26 Oct. 1835.

55/A/67   24 Nov. 1835. William Baylis. Assaulting Harriett Purnell at Cheltenham. R. B. Cooper JP and J. Blagdon JP at Cheltenham. Fine 10/- and 5/6 costs. Offence committed 22 Nov. 1835.

55/A/68   24 Nov. 1835. James Ballinger. Assaulting Harriet Purnell [*etc.*, *as* 55/A/67].

55/A/69   17 Nov. 1835. Isaac Higgs, licensed beer retailer, of Cheltenham. Allowing drinking on his premises after midnight. R. B. Cooper JP and J. Blagdon JP at Cheltenham. First offence. Fine 40/- and 6/6 costs. Offence committed 12 Nov. 1835.

55/A/70   14 Nov. 1835. Sarah Martin. Assaulting John Gain [? Garn] at Cheltenham. R. B. Cooper JP and J. Blagdon JP at Cheltenham. Fine 2/6 and 2/- costs. Offence committed 13 Nov. 1835.

55/A/71   7 Nov. 1835. Thomas Boodle of Cheltenham, licensed retailer of excisable liquors. Permitting drinking on his premises at 3 a.m. R. B. Cooper JP and J. Blagdon JP at Cheltenham. Fine 40/- and 5/6 costs. Offence committed 4 Nov. 1835.

55/A/72   7 Nov. 1835. William Parker. Trespassing in pursuit of game on land at Bishop's Cleeve belonging to the Rev. William Lawrence Townsend. R. B. Cooper JP at Cheltenham. Fine 40/- and 13/- costs. Offence committed 2 Nov. 1835.

55/A/73   29 Dec. 1835. John Hobbs. Buying two hares at Cheltenham from a person not licensed to sell game. T. Newell JP and Fulwar Craven JP at Cheltenham. Fine £5 and 5/6 costs. Offence committed 12 Nov. 1835.

55/A/74   24 Dec. 1835. John Abel. Assaulting Thomas Parry at Cheltenham. R. B. Cooper JP and F. Craven JP at Cheltenham. Fine 1/- and 6/6 costs. Offence committed 21 Dec. 1835.

55/A/75   29 Dec. 1835. William Mathews. Buying three hares at Cheltenham from a person not licensed to sell game. T. Newell JP and F. Craven JP at Cheltenham. Fine £3 and 5/6 costs. Offence committed 14 Oct. 1835.

55/A/76   31 Oct. 1835. John James. Assaulting Benjamin Bullock at Cheltenham. R. B. Cooper JP and J. Blagdon JP. Fine 2/6 and 4/6 costs. Offence committed 27 Oct. 1835.

55/A/77   1 Jan. 1836. John Griffin. Using a gin to kill game at Shipton Oliffe without a game certificate. The Hon. and Rev. George Gustavus [*MS.* George Augustus] Chetwynd Talbot JP and Walter Lawrence Lawrence JP at Cheltenham. Fine £5 and 4/6 costs. Offence committed 8 Nov. 1835.

55/A/78   10 Dec. 1835. Robert Ireland. Assaulting Mary Ireland at Syreford [*MS.* Sierford], Whittington. Rev. W. Hicks JP, Rev. T. B. Newell JP and W. L. Lawrence JP at Andoversford. Fine £2, to be paid to Mr. John Arkell, overseer [of the poor] of Whittington, and 4/6 costs to the complainant, or one calendar month in Northleach house of correction. Offence committed 5 Dec. 1835.

55/A/79   2 Dec. 1835. William Griffin, labourer, of Shipton Solers. Using a gin to kill game at Shipton Oliffe without a game certificate. The Hon. and Rev. George Gustavus [*MS.* George Gustaous] Chetwynd Talbot JP and W. L. Lawrence JP. James Kitchener, gamekeeper, of Salperton, complainant. Fine £5, to be paid to an overseer of the poor of Sevenhampton, and 4/6 costs to the complainant, or hard labour for three calendar months in Northleach house of correction. Offence committed 8 Nov. 1835.

55/A/80 30 Nov. 1835. Thomas Perry of Hawling [*MS.* Halling], labourer. Using a gin to kill game at Shipton Oliffe without a game certificate [*etc., as* 55/A/79].

55/A/81 4 Dec. 1835. Reuben Coombs of Acton Turville, labourer. Trespassing in pursuit of game on land at Great Badminton occupied by the duke of Beaufort, called Gossy Ground. W. Blathwayt JP at Old Sodbury. Thomas Webb, gamekeeper to the duke of Beaufort, complainant, Edmund Webb, witness, both of Great Badminton. Fine £1, half to be paid to the overseer of the poor, to go to the general rate of the county, and the remainder, together with 9/- costs, to the complainant, or one month in Horsley house of correction. Offence committed at about 4.15 p.m. Saturday 28 Nov. 1835.

55/A/82 5 Dec. 1835. Thomas Sutton of Chipping Sodbury, labourer. Trespassing with a gun at night and killing two pheasants on land called the Lawn at Dodington, occupied by Sir Christopher Bethell Codrington, Bt. W. Blathwayt JP and K. W. Horlock JP at Marshfield. Henry Martin and William Dance, witnesses. Hard labour for three calendar months in Horsley house of correction, after which to find sureties totalling £20 against re-offending for one year. In default, a further six calendar months' hard labour. Offence committed at about 3 a.m. or 4 a.m. Friday 4 Dec. 1835.

55/A/83 30 Oct. 1835. Sargeant Morse of Doynton [*MS.* Doyton], shoemaker. Trespassing with a gate net at night on land at Dyrham and Hinton occupied by George Matthens, with intent to take hares. A. Shakespear JP and C. W. Codrington JP at Old Sodbury. Peter Clark and Thomas Edwards, witnesses. Hard labour for three calendar months in Horsley house of correction, after which to find sureties totalling £20 against re-offending for one year. In default, a further six months' hard labour. Offence committed between 1 a.m. and 2 a.m. Sunday 27 Sept. 1835.

55/A/84 4 Jan. 1836. Thomas Woodman and Thomas Parker, labourers, of Burford, Oxon. Using an engine to take and kill one hare at Little Barrington without acquiring a game certificate. R. W. Ford JP and commissioner for assessed taxes for Slaughter district, at Little Rissington. Fine £10. Offence committed 30 Dec. 1835.

55/A/85 11 Nov. 1835. Thomas Archer, carpenter, and William Wood, labourer, both of Dumbleton. Trespassing on enclosed land at night, belonging to Charles Hanbury Tracy Esq., in Toddington and killing one hen pheasant. J. Timbrill D.D. JP, J. W. Martin JP and John Surman JP at Tewkesbury. Hard labour for three calendar months in Northleach house of correction, after which to find sureties totalling £20 each against re-offending for one year. In default, a further six months' hard labour. Offence committed between 1 a.m. and 2 a.m. 7 Nov. 1835.

55/A/86 9 Dec. 1835. William Clarke of Forthampton, labourer. Violently assaulting Thomas Clift of Forthampton by striking him on the chest without provocation. J. Timbrill D.D. JP, J. W. Martin JP and J. Surman JP at Tewkesbury. Fine 10/-, to be paid to William Jones, overseer of the poor of Forthampton, and 10/6 costs to the complainant. Offence committed Monday 16 Nov. 1835.

55/A/87 1 Dec. 1835. John Harvey of Fairford, retail beer seller. Keeping his house open for the sale and consumption of beer after 8 p.m. Sir M. H. Hicks Beach, Bt., JP and J. R. Barker JP at a Petty Sessions for Bibury division held at Fairford. Second offence. [*Cf.* 55/A/92]. Fine 40/- and 5/- costs. Offence committed 9 p.m 14 Nov. 1835.

55/A/88 1 Dec. 1835. Jeremiah Hewer of Fairford, retail beer seller. Keeping his house open for the sale and consumption of beer after 8 p.m. J. R. Barker JP and Sir M. H. Hicks Beach, Bt., JP, at a Petty Sessions for Bibury division held at Fairford. First offence. Fine 40/- and 5/- costs. Offence committed 10.15 p.m. 28 Nov. 1835.

55/A/89   1 Dec. 1835. James Giles of Fairford, retail beer seller. Keeping his house open [*etc.*, *as* 55/A/88 *except*] Offence committed 9 p.m. 19 Nov. 1835.

55/A/90   1 Dec. 1835. William Tackley of Fairford, retail beer seller. Keeping his house open [*etc.*, *as* 55/A/88 *except*] Offence committed 9–9.45 p.m. 13 Nov. 1835.

55/A/91   1 Dec. 1835. Charles Staples of Kempsford, retail beer seller. Keeping his house open [*etc.*, *as* 55/A/88 *except*] Offence committed 8–8.45 p.m. 2 Nov. 1835.

55/A/92   1 Dec. 1835. John Harvey of Fairford, retail beer seller. Keeping his house open [*etc.*, *as* 55/A/88 *except*] Offence committed 9.30 p.m. 13 Nov. 1835.

55/A/93   5 Dec. 1835. Stephen Bennett, late of Olveston, yeoman. Trespassing with a gun and two dogs in pursuit of game on land at Olveston occupied by Samuel Cruger Peach Esq. of Tockington. Rev. M. F. T. Stephens JP and W. Davies D.D. JP at the Swan inn, Thornbury. Witness Thomas Fry, labourer, of Olveston, agent for S. C. Peach Esq., informed first-named JP on 13 Nov. Offender summoned but did not appear. Fine £2, to be paid to William Price, overseer of the poor of Olveston, and 15/- costs to the complainant within thirteen days, or hard labour for one calendar month in Lawfords Gate house of correction. Offence committed at 1 p.m. Friday 6 Nov. 1835.

55/B/1   24 Feb. 1836. George Baylis the elder. Assaulting James Jines at Dymock. Rev. J. Higgins JP and R. Webb JP at Ledbury for the counties of Gloucester and Hereford. Fine 5/-, to be paid to an overseer of the poor, to go to the general rate of Gloucestershire, and 7/6 costs to the complainant, or one calendar month in Littledean house of correction. Offence committed 22 Feb. 1836. [*Sum at end of document shows total amount. Note that E. B. paid the fine to Mr. Rea 16 April.*]

55/B/2   13 Jan. 1836. George and Robert Hodges. Damaging a parlour door and a chair in the dwelling house of William Lane, beer retailer, of Dymock. Rev. J. Higgins JP for Herefordshire and Gloucestershire. Fine 15/-, to be paid to an overseer of the poor, and 10/- damages and 10/- costs to the complainant, by the following day, or one calendar month in Littledean house of correction. Offence committed 10 Jan. 1836. [*Sum at end of document shows total amount. Note that the fine was paid to Mr. Rea on 16 April and that costs and damages were also paid.*]

55/B/3   31 March 1836. James Longstreeth of Dursley, weaver. Leaving his four children chargeable to the parish. B. C. Browne JP at Uley. Hard labour for twenty-one days in Horsley house of correction. Offence committed 14 March 1836.

55/B/4–21   24 March 1836. [*Names as below.*] Possessing defective weights, measures or scales [*as below.*] O. P. Wathen JP, T. Kingscote JP, W. Playne JP and T. R. Haycock JP at a Petty Sessions held at Horsley for Longtree division. William Clements, inspector of weights and balances [*or weights, measures and balances*], complainant. Weights [*or measures, scales*] forfeited. Fine 20/- and 18/- costs. [*Date offence committed (all 1836) as below.*]

55/B/4   William Benjamin of Horsley, shopkeeper. Three defective weights. (2 Feb.)

55/B/5   William Hill of Minchinhampton, retailer. One defective weight. (3 March.)

55/B/6   Edward Goodrich of Horsley, shopkeeper. Three defective weights. (3 Feb.)

55/B/7   William Smith of Avening, retailer. One defective weight. (24 Feb.)

55/B/8   Job Wilkins of Minchinhampton, retailer. One defective weight. (22 Feb.)

55/B/9   James Bubb of Woodchester, baker. Two defective weights. (10 Feb.)

55/B/10   Isaac Shipton of Horsley, baker and flour-seller. Five defective weights. (8 Feb.)

55/B/11   William Fry of Horsley, retailer. Seven defective measures. (2 Feb.)

55/B/12   Thomas Cook of Minchinhampton, retailer. Two defective measures. (17 Feb.)

55/B/13   Richard Burford of Minchinhampton, retailer. Two defective measures. (22 Feb.)

55/B/14   Joseph Dangerfield of Horsley, bacon retailer. Four defective weights. (1 Feb.)

55/B/15   John Parsons of Minchinhampton, retailer. One defective measure. (22 Feb.)

55/B/16   William Harding of Woodchester, retailer. Three defective measures. (2 March.)

55/B/17   Abraham Cox of Rodborough, retailer. One defective weight. (3 March.)

55/B/18   Richard Smith of Minchinhampton, retailer. Two defective weights. (3 March.)

55/B/19   James Buck of Rodborough, retailer. Defective scales. (3 March.)

55/B/20   Robert Cox of Horsley, retailer. Four defective measures. (1 Feb.)

55/B/21   Francis Hyde of Woodchester, pig butcher. Defective scales. (10 Feb.)

55/B/22   8 April 1836. Henry Smith. Using a gun to kill game at Painswick without a game certificate. H. Burgh JP and H. Wyatt JP at Stroud. Fine £2, to be paid to Richard Bishop Constable, an overseer of the poor, and 11/- costs to gamekeeper John Gay of Painswick, complainant, or hard labour for two calendar months in Horsley house of correction. Offence committed 30 March 1836.

55/B/23   7 April 1836. Emanuel Lusty of King's Stanley, weaver. Cutting down and stealing a tree from a wood, the property of Thomas, Lord Ducie. H. Burgh JP and H. Wyatt JP at Stroud. Fine £5, to be paid to an overseer of the poor, and 1/- to the complainant Thomas, Lord Ducie, or two calendar months in Horsley house of correction. Offence committed 1 April 1836.

55/B/24   18 March 1836. John Brown. Causing his wife and family to be chargeable to Bisley parish for one month. H. Burgh JP and E. G. Hallewell JP at Stroud. Hard labour for one calendar month in Horsley house of correction. Offence committed 27 Feb. 1836.

55/B/25   18 March 1836. Thomas Poulson of Bisley, labourer. Stealing a bushel of turnips growing on land occupied by Marshall Rowles, yeoman, of Bisley. H. Burgh JP and E. G. Hallewell JP at Stroud. Hard labour for one calendar month in Horsley house of correction. Offence committed 14 March 1836.

55/B/26   11 March 1836. Thomas West of Painswick, labourer. Assaulting and beating Mary wife of John Skerrett, beer seller, of Painswick. H. Burgh JP and E. G. Hallewell JP at Stroud. Fine £5 or two calendar months in Horsley house of correction. Offence committed 12 Feb. 1836.

55/B/27   11 March 1836. Peter Blackwell of Bisley, labourer. Trespassing in search of conies on land in Painswick, the property of Edward Palling Caruthers Esq. H. Burgh JP at Stroud. Fine £2, to be paid to William Iles, an overseer of the poor, and 10/- costs to gamekeeper John Gay, complainant, or hard labour for two calendar months in Horsley house of correction. Offence committed 29 Feb. 1836.

55/B/28   29 Feb. 1836. Samuel Kirby of Stroud, labourer. Violently assaulting Lucy Workman of Stroud, widow. H. Burgh JP and H. Wyatt JP at Stroud. Fine £5 or two calendar months in Horsley house of correction. Offence committed 26 Feb. 1836.

55/B/29   10 Feb. 1836. Charles Beard of Stroud, weaver. Stealing a quantity of apples growing in an orchard, the property of John Phipps, yeoman, of Stroud. H. Burgh JP at Stroud. Hard labour for six months in Horsley house of correction. Offence committed 20 Oct. 1835.

55/B/30   8 Feb. 1836. Samuel Smith of Stonehouse, labourer. Stealing twelve pecks of turnips growing on land at Stonehouse occupied by John Butcher, gentleman, of Randwick. H. Burgh JP at Stroud. Hard labour for one calendar month in Horsley house of correction. Offence committed 6 Feb. 1836.

55/B/31   29 Feb. 1836. Samuel King of Rodborough, clothworker. Violently assaulting William Ridler, labourer, of Bisley at Stroud. N. S. Marling JP, H. Wyatt JP and E. G. Hallewell JP, at Stroud. Fine £5 or two calendar months in Horsley house of correction. Offence committed 20 Oct. 1835.

55/B/32   15 Jan. 1836. James Cooke of Painswick, labourer. Using a wire to take and kill game at Painswick without a game certificate. H. Wyatt JP and E. G. Hallewell JP at Stroud. Fine 10/-, to be paid to William Iles, an overseer of the poor, and 8/- costs to James Cripps, cordwainer, of Painswick, complainant, or hard labour for two calendar months in Horsley house of correction. Offence committed 24 Dec. 1835.

55/B/33   15 Jan. 1836. Charlotte Woodard of Cranham, single woman. Violently assaulting Elizabeth Turner, single woman, of Cranham. H. Wyatt JP and E. G. Hallewell JP at Stroud. Fine 10/- and 8/- costs or one calendar month in Horsley house of correction. Offence committed 11 Nov. 1835.

55/B/34   15 Jan. 1836. Harriett wife of Henry Gibbins, labourer, of Cranham. Violently assaulting Elizabeth Turner [*etc., as* 55/B/33].

55/B/35   22 Feb. 1836. William White of Taynton, labourer. Assaulting John Tyrrell, labourer, of Taynton without just cause or provocation. Rev. R. F. Onslow JP and R. Webb JP at Newent. Fine 1/- and 8/6 costs or two calendar months in Littledean house of correction. Offence committed 15 Feb. 1836.

55/B/36   22 Feb. 1836. William Stock of Taynton, labourer. Assaulting John Tyrrell, labourer, of Taynton without just cause or provocation. Rev. R. F. Onslow JP and R. Webb JP at Newent. Fine 1/- and 8/6 costs or two calendar months in Littledean house of correction. Offence committed 10 Feb. 1836.

55/B/37   6 Feb. 1836. Charles Hopton, licensed beer and cider retailer of the Red Lion inn, Thornbury. Permitting gaming on his premises. W. Davies D.D. JP and Rev. M. F. T. Stephens JP at a Petty Sessions held at Thornbury for Thornbury division. First offence. Fine 40/- including costs. Offence committed 28 Jan. 1836.

55/B/38   10 March 1836. Robert Worlock of Bitton. Keeping his licensed house open for the sale of beer after 10 p.m. H. W. Newman JP and Rev. W. Mirehouse JP at a Petty Sessions for part of Berkeley division. Fine £1 8*s.* and 12/- costs. Offence committed 20 Feb. 1836.

55/B/39   4 Feb. 1836. George Phillips of Frampton Cotterell. Keeping his licensed house open for the sale of beer after 10 p.m. A. G. H. Battersby JP and A. Hilhouse JP at a Petty Sessions for part of Berkeley division. Fine £2 and 9/- costs. Offence committed 23 Feb. 1836.

55/B/40   4 Feb. 1836. Thomas Robottom of Winterbourne. Keeping his licensed house open for the sale of beer after 10 p.m. A. G. H. Battersby JP and Abraham Hilhouse JP at a Petty Sessions for part of Berkeley division. Fine £1 10*s.* and 10/- costs. Offence committed 16 Jan. 1836.

55/B/41   4 Feb. 1836. Joseph Norgrove of Winterbourne. Keeping his licensed house open for the sale of beer after 10 p.m. A. G. H. Battersby JP and A. Hilhouse JP at a Petty Sessions for part of Berkeley division. Fine £1 12*s.* and 8/- costs. Offence committed 16 Jan. 1836.

55/B/42   10 Dec. 1835. Charles Edwards of Westbury on Trym. Keeping his licensed house open for the sale of beer after 10 p.m. W. Munro JP and G. Worrall JP at a Petty Sessions for part of Berkeley division. Fine £1 11*s.* 6*d.* and 8/6 costs. Offence committed 28 Nov. 1835.

55/B/43   25 Feb. 1836. John Powell of Stapleton. Keeping his licensed house open for the sale of beer after 10 p.m. H. W. Newman JP and Rev. W. Mirehouse JP at a Petty Sessions for part of Berkeley division. Fine £1 10*s.* and 10/- costs. Offence committed 20 Feb. 1836.

55/B/44   25 Feb. 1836. Henry Milsom of Mangotsfield. Keeping his licensed house open for the sale of beer after 10 p.m. H. W. Newman JP and Rev. W. Mirehouse JP at a Petty Sessions for part of Berkeley division. Fine £1 11s. and 9/- costs. Offence committed 22 Feb. 1836.

55/B/45   18 Feb. 1836. Thomas Jones of St. George, [Bristol]. Keeping his licensed house open for the sale of beer after 10 p.m. Rev. W. Mirehouse JP and H. W. Newman JP at a Petty Sessions for part of Berkeley division. Fine £1 10s. and 10/- costs. Offence committed 15 Feb. 1836.

55/B/46   25 Feb. 1836. Henry Ball of Mangotsfield. Keeping his licensed house open for the sale of beer after 10 p.m. H. W. Newman JP and Rev. W. Mirehouse JP at a Petty Sessions for part of Berkeley division. Fine £1 8s. and 12/- costs. Offence committed 30 Jan. 1836.

55/B/47   4 Feb. 1836. William Long of Bitton. Keeping his licensed house open for the sale of beer after 10 p.m. Rev. W. Mirehouse JP and A. Hilhouse JP at a Petty Sessions for part of Berkeley division. Fine £1 10s. and 10/- costs. Offence committed 26 Dec. 1835.

55/B/48   25 Feb. 1836. William Pow. Assaulting John Harris at Oldland. H. W. Newman JP and Rev. W. Mirehouse JP at Lawfords Gate sessions room. Fine 5/- and 10/6 costs or fourteen days in Lawfords Gate house of correction. Offence committed 20 Feb. 1836.

55/B/49   1 April 1836. Samuel Fussell. Assaulting Hannah Stone, at Bitton. A. G. H. Battersby JP and H. W. Newman JP at Lawfords Gate sessions room. Fine 10/- and 9/- costs or three weeks in Lawfords Gate house of correction. Offence committed 29 March 1836.

55/B/50   18 Feb. 1836. George Powell. Assaulting John Harris at St. George, [Bristol]. H. W. Newman JP and Rev. W. Mirehouse JP at Lawfords Gate sessions room. Fine 7/- and 7/- costs or one week in Lawfords Gate house of correction. Offence committed 15 Feb. 1836.

55/B/51   10 March 1836. James Rodway. Assaulting and beating Hannah Maggs at Winterbourne. H. W. Newman JP and G. Goldney JP at Lawfords Gate sessions room. Fine 1/- and 8/- costs or one week in Lawfords Gate house of correction. Offence committed 14 Feb. 1836.

55/B/52   14 Jan. 1836. Robert Maggs. Assaulting and beating Thomas Cooke at Winterbourne. Rev. W. Mirehouse JP and A. G. H. Battersby JP at Lawfords Gate sessions room. Fine 5/6 and 14/6 costs or fourteen days in Lawfords Gate house of correction. Offence committed 11 Jan. 1836.

55/B/53   28 Jan. 1836. James Brain. Assaulting Patience Sheppard at Stapleton. A. G. H. Battersby JP and Rev. W. Mirehouse JP at Lawfords Gate sessions room. Fine £4 11s. and 9/- costs or two calendar months in Lawfords Gate house of correction. Offence committed 20 Jan. 1836.

55/B/54   28 Jan. 1836. Henry Rodman. Assaulting and beating Eliza Osborne at Frampton Cotterell. A. G. H. Battersby JP and Rev. W. Mirehouse JP at Lawfords Gate sessions room. Fine £2 and 8/- costs or one calendar month in Lawfords Gate house of correction. Offence committed 23 Jan. 1836.

55/B/55   31 Dec. 1835. Stephen Rossiter. Assaulting and beating George May Tanner at St. George, [Bristol]. A. G. H. Battersby JP and G. Worrall JP at Lawfords Gate sessions room. Fine £1 and 8/- costs or one calendar month in Lawfords Gate house of correction. Offence committed 26 Dec. 1835.

55/B/56   4 Feb. 1836. Joseph Britton. Assaulting and beating George Burchell at Bitton. Rev. W. Mirehouse JP and A. Hilhouse JP at Lawfords Gate sessions room. Fine £2 and 11/- costs or one calendar month in Lawfords Gate house of correction. Offence committed 30 Jan. 1836.

55/B/57   11 Feb. 1836. William Jenkins. Assaulting and beating Philip Tyler at Westbury on Trym. Rev. W. Mirehouse JP and G. Hilhouse JP at Lawfords Gate sessions room. Fine 13/6 and 16/6 costs or twenty-one days in Lawfords Gate house of correction. Offence committed 24 Jan. 1836.

55/B/58   11 Feb. 1836. James Peach. Assaulting and beating Michael Frost at Westbury on Trym [*etc., as* 55/B/57].

55/B/59   4 Feb. 1836. George Osborne. Assaulting and beating Thomas Stanmore at Bitton. Rev. W. Mirehouse JP and A. Hilhouse JP at Lawfords Gate sessions room. Fine £1 and 11/- costs or twenty-one days in Lawfords Gate house of correction. Offence committed 30 Jan. 1836.

55/B/60   11 Feb. 1836. Thomas Sutton of Deerhurst, licensed cider retailer. Keeping his house open for the sale and consumption of cider after 9 p.m. J. Timbrill D.D. JP, J. W. Martin JP and Charles Edward Harford JP at a Petty Sessions for the county of Gloucester. Fine 40/- and 8/6 costs. Offence committed 25 Jan. 1836.

55/B/61   11 Feb. 1836. Thomas Sutton of Deerhurst, licensed cider retailer. Keeping his house open [*etc., as* 55/B/60 *except*] 10/6 costs. Offence committed 24 Jan. 1836.

55/B/62   24 March 1836. Thomas James of Dumbleton. Selling one pint of beer to be consumed on his premises when not licensed. J. Timbrill D.D. JP, J. W. Martin JP, Rev. C. White JP, C. E. Harford JP and J. Surman JP. Fine £5 and £2 costs. Offence committed 18 Dec. 1835.

55/B/63   24 March 1836. William Weley of Twyning, labourer. Violently assaulting Sarah Hathaway, servant to Mr. Peter Weaver, farmer, of Stub Hill, Twyning, without just cause. J. Timbrill D.D. JP and J. W. Martin JP at Tewkesbury. Fine 2/6, to be paid to Peter Dee, overseer of the poor of Twyning, and 8/6 costs to the complainant. Offence committed Tuesday 22 March 1836.

55/B/64   29 Feb. 1836. Samuel Cox and William Lapper. Stealing seven wooden fence rails at Bledington, valued at 2/-, the property of John Tysoe. Rev. R. W. Ford JP at Stow on the Wold. Each fined £1 18*s.* 3*d.*, to be paid to William Stow, an overseer of the poor of Bledington, and 11/9 costs to the complainant, over and above the value of the rails, or hard labour for two calendar months in Northleach house of correction. Offence committed 27 Feb. 1836.

55/B/65   10 March 1836. John Smart of Stow on the Wold, innkeeper. Permitting drunkenness and disorderly behaviour on his premises. Rev. R. W. Ford JP and Rev. C. Jeaffreson JP for Slaughter hundred. First offence. Fine 40/- and 10/6 costs. Offence committed Sunday 6 March 1836.

55/B/66   2 April 1836. James Bowstead. Assaulting Mary Price at Cheltenham. T. Newell JP and W. Pitt JP at Cheltenham. Fine 2/6 and 4/6 costs. Offence committed 2 April 1836.

55/B/67   30 March 1836. Owen Grant. Assaulting John Macvoy at Cheltenham. D. L. St. Clair JP and W. Pitt JP at Cheltenham. Fine 20/- and 8/9 costs. Offence committed 28 March 1836.

55/B/68   16 Feb. 1836. Thomas Musty. Assaulting Thomas Masters at Cheltenham. R. B. Cooper JP and F. Craven JP at Cheltenham. Fine 5/- and 5/6 costs. Offence committed 15 Feb. 1836.

55/B/69   27 Feb. 1836. William Burrows. Assaulting William Cakeburn at Cheltenham. R. B. Cooper JP and D. L. St. Clair JP at Cheltenham. Fine 5/- and 5/6 costs. Offence committed 24 Feb. 1836.

55/B/70   12 March 1836. Neighbour Higgins. Shooting a partridge on a Sunday at Bishop's Cleeve. R. B. Cooper JP and D. L. St. Clair JP at Cheltenham. Fine 40/- and 7/6 costs. Offence committed Sunday 21 Feb. 1836.

55/B/71   10 March 1836. Thomas Boodle of Cheltenham, licensed victualler. Keeping his house open for the sale of beer during the usual hours of divine service. R. B. Cooper JP and

D. L. St. Clair JP at Cheltenham. First offence. Fine £2 and 5/6 costs. Offence committed Sunday 6 March 1836.

55/B/72 20 Feb. 1836. George Hawkins of Cheltenham, licensed victualler. Permitting gaming in his house. R. B. Cooper JP and D. L. St. Clair JP at Cheltenham. First offence. Fine 10/- and 4/6 costs. Offence committed 16 Feb. 1836.

55/B/73 13 Feb. 1836. James Baker. Assaulting Charles Pope at Cheltenham. R. B. Cooper JP and D. L. St. Clair JP at Cheltenham. Fine 20/- and 4/6 costs. Offence committed 9 Feb. 1836.

55/B/74 29 Jan. 1836. Thomas Shurmer. Assaulting and kicking Priscilla Packer at Sevenhampton. W. L. Lawrence JP and Rev. T. B. Newell JP at Andoversford. Fine £1 and 4/6 costs or twenty-one days in Northleach house of correction. Offence committed 26 Jan. 1836.

55/B/75 29 Jan. 1836. Hannah Humphries. Pulling up and carrying away a burden of underwood from Shipton Oliffe. W. L. Lawrence JP and Rev. T. B. Newell JP at Andoversford. Fine 20/- and 1/- (the value of the underwood) or one month in Northleach house of correction. Offence committed 5 Dec. 1835.

55/B/76 22 March 1836. William Christie of Cheltenham, licensed victualler. Failing to maintain good order in his house. R. B. Cooper JP and D. L. St. Clair JP. First offence. Fine £2 and 5/6 costs. Offence committed 19 March 1836.

55/B/77 23 Feb. 1836. Thomas Williams. Assaulting John Osbaldeston at Prestbury. F. Craven JP and D. L. St. Clair JP at Cheltenham. Fine 5/- and 9/6 costs. Offence committed 16 Oct. 1835.

55/B/78 18 Feb. 1836. Robert Emerson. Assaulting Edward MacClean at Cheltenham. R. B. Cooper JP and D. L. St. Clair JP. Fine 5/- and 3/- costs. Offence committed 16 Feb. 1836.

55/B/79 28 Jan. 1836. Richard Liddell of Cheltenham, licensed victualler. Permitting gaming in his house. R. B. Cooper JP and F. Craven JP. First offence. Fine £1 and 6/6 costs. Offence committed 25 Jan. 1836.

55/B/80 4 Feb. 1836. Henry Newman. Assaulting Richard Fryer at Cheltenham. R. B. Cooper JP and D. L. St. Clair JP at Cheltenham. Fine 10/- and 4/6 costs. Offence committed 2 Feb. 1836.

55/B/81 6 Feb. 1836. Isaac Belcher. Assaulting John Stroud at Cheltenham. D. L. St. Clair JP and F. Craven JP at Cheltenham. Fine 10/- and 4/6 costs. Offence committed 5 Feb. 1836.

55/B/82 28 Jan. 1836. John Harris of Cheltenham, licensed beer retailer. Keeping his house open for the sale of beer during the hours of divine service. R. B. Cooper JP and F. Craven JP. First offence. Fine 10/- and 6/- costs. Offence committed Sunday 24 Jan. 1836.

55/B/83 7 April 1836. Thomas Hyett. Assaulting William Christie at Cheltenham. R. B. Cooper JP and D. L. St. Clair JP at Cheltenham. Fine 40/- and 7/- costs. Offence committed 3 April 1836.

55/B/84 19 March 1836. James Goode. Assaulting an infant named Margaret at Cheltenham. R. B. Cooper JP and D. L. St. Clair JP at Cheltenham. Fine 20/- and 6/6 costs. Offence committed 14 March 1836.

55/B/85 13 Feb. 1836. Joseph Humphris of Cheltenham, licensed beer retailer. Keeping his house open for the sale of beer until 2 a.m. and permitting gaming. R. B. Cooper JP and D. L. St. Clair JP at Cheltenham. First offence. [*Fine not stated*] 6/6 costs. Offence committed 9 Feb. 1836.

55/B/86 16 Feb. 1836. George Clutterbuck, Samuel Richards, Thomas Wells and John Harward. Maliciously breaking down fences enclosing a meadow occupied by James Arkell at Cheltenham. R. B. Cooper JP and F. Craven JP at Cheltenham. Each fined 7/-, to be paid to an overseer of the poor of Cheltenham, and 6*d*. damages and 3/- costs to the complainant, or one calendar month in Northleach house of correction. Offence committed 13 Feb. 1836.

55/B/87   8 March 1836. Samuel Jarvis. Maliciously breaking a chaff-cutting machine at Charingworth, Ebrington, the property of John Milward. Rev. J. R. Hall JP at Moreton in Marsh. Fine 16/- costs and 3/- damages or hard labour for two calendar months in [Northleach] house of correction. Offence committed 25 Feb. 1836.

55/B/88   8 March 1836. William Cother of Chipping Campden, labourer. Using a gun and a dog to kill and take game at Aston Subedge. Rev. J. R. Hall JP and Rev. C. Jeaffreson JP at Moreton in Marsh. Fine £4 4s., one moiety of which and 16/- costs to be paid to William Gardiner, farmer, of Aston Subedge, informant, and the remainder to an overseer of the poor. Given fourteen days to pay. In default, two calendar months' hard labour in Northleach house of correction. Offence committed Sunday 31 Jan. 1836.

55/B/89   23 Feb. 1836. Benjamin James of Chipping Campden, labourer. Using a gun and a dog to kill and take game at Aston Subedge [etc., as 55/B/88 except omitting Given fourteen days to pay].

55/B/90   26 Jan. 1836. James Newman, licensed victualler of the Black Bear, Moreton in Marsh. Keeping his house open during the usual hours of morning divine service. Rev. C. Jeaffreson JP and Rev. J. R. Hall JP at Moreton in Marsh for the upper division of Westminster hundred. First offence. Fine £4 5s., half of which and 15/- costs to be paid to Henry Fifield, labourer, of Moreton in Marsh, prosecutor, and the remainder to the county treasurer. Offence committed Sunday 10 Jan. 1836.

55/B/91   15 Dec. 1835. John Dee, John Harwood and John Ashfield. Stealing three rails valued at 1/6 from a dead fence at Chipping Campden, the property of William Stevens. J. R. Hall JP at Moreton in Marsh. Complainant examined as to proof of offence. First offence. Fine 5/6 and 1/6 damages, to be paid to Henry Grove, an overseer of the poor of Chipping Campden, and 15/- costs to the complainant, or hard labour for one month in Northleach house of correction. Offence committed 28 Nov. 1835.

55/B/92   15 Dec. 1835. Thomas Dunn of Chipping Campden. Trespassing in search of game on enclosed land occupied by Robert Canning Esq. at Lark Stoke. J. R. Hall JP at Moreton in Marsh. William Blackford Rose, complainant. Fine £1, half to be paid to an overseer of the poor and the remainder and £1 costs to the complainant, or two calendar months in Northleach house of correction. Offence committed 5 Dec. 1835.

55/B/93   10 Dec. 1835. George Hawker of Blockley, Worcs. Using a gun to kill game at Sezincote without a game certificate. Rev. J. R. Hall JP and F. Colvile JP at Moreton in Marsh. Francis Groom, complainant. Fine £4 10s., to be paid to George Crossley, overseer of the poor of Sezincote, and 10/- costs to the complainant, or hard labour for three calendar months in Northleach house of correction. Offence committed 9 Dec. 1835.

55/B/94   24 Sept. 1835. William Walkley, licensed beer retailer, of Horsley. Keeping his house open for the sale of beer after 10 p.m. O. P. Wathen JP, T. Kingscote JP, B. C. Browne JP, W. Playne JP and T. R. Haycock JP at a Petty Sessions for Longtree division. First offence. Fine 40/- and 7/6 costs. Offence committed between 11 p.m. and midnight 8 Aug. 1835.

55/B/95   24 Sept. 1835. Harriet Lord, widow, of Horsley, licensed beer retailer. Keeping her house open for the sale of beer after 10 p.m. O. P. Wathen JP, T. Kingscote JP, W. Playne JP and T. R. Haycock JP at a Petty Sessions for Longtree division. First offence. Fine 40/-. [Costs not specified.] Offence committed between 11 p.m. and midnight 31 Aug. 1835.

55/B/96   24 Dec. 1835. Thomas Browning of Minchinhampton, licensed beer retailer. Keeping his house open for the sale of beer between 3 p.m. and 5 p.m. [on a Sunday]. T. Kingscote JP, D. Ricardo JP, B. C. Browne JP and W. Playne JP at a Petty Sessions for Longtree division. Fine 40/- and 6/6 costs. Offence committed 4 p.m. 13 Dec. 1835.

55/B/97   24 Dec. 1835. Thomas Browning of Minchinhampton, licensed beer retailer. Keeping his house open for the sale of beer before 1 p.m. [on a Sunday]. T. Kingscote JP, D. Ricardo JP, B. C. Browne JP and W. Playne JP at a Petty Sessions for Longtree division. First offence. Fine 40/- and 6/6 costs. Offence committed 10 a.m. Sunday 13 Dec. 1835.

55/B/98   24 Dec. 1835. William Cosburn of Minchinhampton, licensed beer retailer. Keeping his house open for the sale of beer between 3 p.m. and 5 p.m. [on a Sunday] [*etc., as* 55/B/97 *except*] Offence committed 4 p.m. Sunday 13 Dec. 1835.

55/B/99   24 Dec. 1835. William Cosburn, beer retailer, of Minchinhampton. Permitting card gaming and disorderly conduct in his house. T. Kingscote JP, D. Ricardo JP, B. C. Browne JP and W. Playne JP at a Petty Sessions for Longtree division. First offence. Fine £5 and 6/6 costs. Offence committed 3 Dec. 1835.

55/B/100   24 Dec. 1835. Richard Burford of Horsley, licensed beer retailer. Keeping his house open for the sale of beer between 3 p.m. and 5 p.m. [on a Sunday]. T. Kingscote JP, D. Ricardo JP, B. C. Browne JP and W. Playne JP at a Petty Sessions for Longtree division. First offence. Fine 40/- and 8/6 costs. Offence committed 3.30 p.m. Sunday 29 Nov. 1835.

55/B/101   24 Dec. 1835. Thomas Stockham of Minchinhampton, licensed beer retailer. Permitting card gaming and disorderly conduct in his house. T. Kingscote JP, D. Ricardo JP, B. C. Browne JP and W. Playne JP at a Petty Sessions for Longtree division. First offence. Fine £5 and 6/6 costs. Offence committed 5 Dec. 1835.

55/B/102   5 Jan. 1836. William Parsons of Pucklechurch. Trespassing with two greyhounds and several other dogs in pursuit of game and conies on a close of land called Crows Burbarrow occupied by John Sargeant in Wapley and Codrington, without consent or licence. W. Blathwayt JP and A. Shakespear JP at a Petty Sessions held at the Cross Hands inn, Old Sodbury. John Sargeant and Paul Pincott of Wapley and Codrington, witnesses. Fine £2, one moiety to be paid to an overseer of the poor and the remainder to Sir Christopher Bethell Codrington, informer, or two months in Horsley house of correction. Offence committed between 1 p.m. and 3 p.m. Saturday 14 Nov. 1835.

55/B/103   5 Feb. 1836. George Deacon of Hawkesbury, labourer. Trespassing in pursuit of game without consent in company with William Coates in the Long Plantation at Hawkesbury, a preserve for game, occupied by the duke of Beaufort. Coates was carrying a gun and shot at a hare. W. Blathwayt JP, R. H. B. Hale JP and A. Shakespear JP at a Petty Sessions held at the Cross Hands inn, Old Sodbury. Peter May, gamekeeper to the duke of Beaufort, complainant. Alexander Watts of Hawkesbury, witness. Fine £1. One moiety to be paid to an overseer of the poor and the remainder with 10/6 costs to the complainant, or one calendar month in Horsley house of correction. Offence committed at 5 p.m. Monday 14 Dec. 1835.

55/B/104   11 Jan. 1836. At Dyrham House, Dyrham and Hinton. Henry Martin, gamekeeper to Sir C. B. Codrington, informed W. Blathwayt JP in the presence of one credible witness on oath that William Bush Parker, attorney at law of Downend, Mangotsfield, trespassed in pursuit of game and conies with two greyhounds and several other dogs on land at Wapley and Codrington occupied by John Sargeant. Parker was summoned to appear before W. Blathwayt JP and others at a Petty Session to be held at the Cross Hands inn on Friday 15 Jan. 1836 at 11 a.m. Joseph Tomkins, the defendant's clerk, appeared and asked that the hearing be deferred because of his master's ill health. Adjournment granted.
Friday 5 Feb. 1836. W. Blathwayt JP, A. Shakespear JP and R. H. B. Hale JP at the Cross Hands inn, Old Sodbury. Joseph Tomkins pleaded guilty on his master's behalf. Fine £2, one moiety to be paid to gamekeeper Henry Martin, the informant, with 16/- costs and the remainder to an overseer of the poor, or two calendar months in Horsley

house of correction. Offence committed between 1 p.m. and 3 p.m. Saturday 14 Nov. 1835.

55/C/1   16 April 1836. Thomas Peters, late of Cam, labourer. Leaving his wife about two years ago to become, and still remains, chargeable to Cam parish. J. Wallington JP at Dursley. Hard labour for two calendar months in Horsley house of correction.

55/C/2   27 June 1836. John Stephens of Bromsberrow, labourer. Killing three conies in a warren used for breeding, the property of William Cook at Bromsberrow. Rev. R. F. Onslow JP and R. F. Onslow JP at Newent. Fine 5/- and 10/- costs or fourteen days in Littledean house of correction. Offence committed 26 June 1836.

55/C/3   2 May 1836. John Gardner of Cirencester, licensed beer retailer. Keeping his house open for the sale and consumption of beer until 11 p.m. Rev. John Price Jones JP and Rev. H. Cripps JP at a Petty Sessions for Cirencester division. First offence. Fine 40/- and 5/- costs. Offence committed 30 April 1836.

55/C/4   26 April 1836. John James. Selling one gallon of beer by retail without a licence at Moreton Valence. C. O. Cambridge JP and P. Leversage JP at Wheatenhurst. Fine £2 10s., to be paid to Henry Evans, supervisor of Excise. Offence committed 18 Jan. 1836.

55/C/5   29 March 1836. James Cook, licensed beer retailer, of King's Stanley. Allowing gaming in his house. C. O. Cambridge JP and P. Leversage JP at Wheatenhurst. Fine £2 and 7/6 costs. Offence committed 7 March 1836.

55/C/6   29 March 1836. John Pegler licensed beer retailer. Keeping his house open for the sale and consumption of beer after midnight. C. O. Cambridge JP and P. Leversage JP at Wheatenhurst. Fine £5, £1 2s. of which to be paid to Nestor Hudd, the prosecutor, and the remainder to the treasurer of the county stock. Costs assessed at 7/6. Offence committed 6 March 1836.

55/C/7   29 March 1836. John Pegler, licensed beer retailer of King's Stanley. Allowing gaming in his house. C. O. Cambridge JP and P. Leversage JP at Wheatenhurst. Fine £2, 10/- of which to be paid to Rhoda Bishop, the prosecutor. The remainder to be paid to the treasurer of the county stock. Costs assessed at 7/6. Offence committed 7 March 1836.

55/C/8   23 Feb. 1836. William Hopson. Assaulting George Sillington at Stonehouse. T. J. Lloyd Baker JP and P. Leversage JP at Wheatenhurst. Fine 5/- and 7/6 costs or a fortnight in Horsley house of correction. Offence committed 9 Feb. 1836.

55/C/9   23 Feb. 1836. Thomas Lusty. Assaulting Mary Cowley at King's Stanley. T. J. Lloyd Baker JP and P. Leversage JP at Wheatenhurst. Fine 1/- and 6/6 costs or imprisonment in Horsley house of correction [*length of sentence not stated*]. Offence committed 23 Jan. 1836.

55/C/10   11 June 1836. John Bendall. Destroying a carp in a stretch of the Stroudwater at Eastington, the property of George Hawker, clerk to Stroudwater Navigation Company. P. Leversage JP at Eastington. Fine 10/- and 6/- costs or hard labour for fourteen days in Horsley house of correction. Offence committed 28 May 1836.

55/C/11   8 April 1836. William Organ. Cutting and damaging a tree at Frocester, the property of J. A. G. Clarke Esq. P. Leversage JP at Eastington. Fine 1/-, 2/- damages and 7/- costs or hard labour for one calendar month in Horsley house of correction. Offence committed 7 April 1836.

55/C/12   8 March 1836. Frederick Deane. Cutting and damaging a tree, the property of Thomas Fowler of Leonard Stanley. D. Maclean JP at King's Stanley. Fine £5 and 6/6 costs, or hard labour for two calendar months in Horsley house of correction. Offence committed 6 Feb. 1836.

55/C/13   26 Jan. 1836. John Arkell. Trespassing in pursuit of game on land at Hardwicke, the property of John Curtis Hayward Esq. D. Maclean JP and P. Leversage JP at Wheatenhurst. Fine £2, to be paid to an overseer of the poor, and 8/6 costs to John Woodyatt, or one calendar month in Horsley house of correction. Offence committed 15 Jan. 1836.

55/C/14   9 Jan. 1836. Joseph Stevens. Stealing a fence pole valued at 1/- at King's Stanley, the property of William Leach. D. Maclean JP at King's Stanley. Fine £2 10*s.*, 1/- damages and 8/6 costs or two calendar months in Horsley house of correction. Offence committed 13 Dec. 1835.

55/C/15   31 May 1836. Alfred Stephens, Elijah Sparks, Henry Martin, William Powell, Thomas Venn, Joseph Harris, Henry Moseley, William White, Charles Pearce and William King. Assaulting John Miller of Stonehouse, weaver. C. O. Cambridge JP and P. Leversage JP at Wheatenhurst. Fine 1/- and 7/6 costs, to be paid within one month. In default, fourteen days' hard labour in Horsley house of correction. Offence committed 24 May 1836.

55/C/16   31 May 1836. Owen Osborne and Samuel White. Assaulting John Miller of Stonehouse, weaver. C. O. Cambridge JP and P. Leversage JP at Wheatenhurst. Each fined 5/- and 7/6 costs, to be paid within one month. In default, one calendar month in Horsley house of correction. Offence committed 24 May 1836.

55/C/17   21 April 1836. Alfred Newman, son of Mr William Ireland Newman of Deerhurst Walton. Violently assaulting James Hartland, servant in husbandry to Mr John Lane of Deerhurst Walton. J. Timbrill D.D. JP and J. W. Martin JP at Tewkesbury. Fine 5/-, to be paid to Isaac Bloxham, overseer of the poor of Deerhurst, and 14/10 costs to the complainant. Offence committed Saturday 2 April 1836.

55/C/18   21 June 1836. Peter Herbert. Rogue and vagabond: lodging in an outhouse in the occupation of John Neems, yeoman, of Stroud. H. Burgh JP and H. Wyatt JP at Stroud. Hard labour for two weeks in Horsley house of correction. Offence committed 12 June 1836.

55/C/19   20 May 1836. John Elliott of Stroud, labourer. Furiously driving a carriage loaded with timber along Great George Street in Stroud, endangering other persons there. H. Burgh JP and H. Wyatt JP at Stroud. Fine £2 10*s.*, to be paid forthwith. Offence committed 14 May 1836.

55/C/20   22 April 1836. Henry White of Stroud, labourer. Using a gun for killing game without possessing a game certificate. H. Burgh JP and H. Wyatt JP at Stroud. John Ashmead, complainant. Fine £1 7*s.*, to be paid to Charles Halliday, overseer of the poor of Stroud, and 7/- costs to the complainant. Offence committed 18 April 1836.

55/C/21   19 April 1836. Joseph Wathen of Stroud, labourer. Assaulting and beating Joseph Ponting, innkeeper, at Stroud. H. Burgh JP and N. S. Marling JP at Stroud. Fine £4 14*s.* and 6/- costs or two calendar months in Horsley house of correction. Offence committed 18 April 1836.

55/C/22   15 April 1836. John Bliss. Using a wire for taking and killing game at Painswick without possessing a game certificate. H. Burgh JP and J. Mills JP at Stroud. Fine £4 9*s.* 6*d.*, to be paid to an overseer of the poor; and 10/6 costs to Edwin Davis, the complainant, or hard labour for two calendar months in Horsley house of correction. Offence committed 6 Oct. 1835.

55/C/23   15 April 1836. John Bliss of Painswick, labourer. Using a wire for taking and killing game at Miserden without possessing a game certificate. H. Burgh JP and J. Mills JP at Stroud. Fine £4 9*s.* 6*d.*, to be paid to an overseer of the poor, and 10/6 costs to Thomas Birt of Painswick, the complainant, or hard labour for two calendar months in Horsley house of correction. Offence committed Sunday 4 Oct. 1836.

55/C/24   14 April 1836. George Hodges, Michael Vick and George Vick, labourers, of Stroud. Stealing 200 heads of broccoli from a garden at Stroud, the property of Richard Chew, blacksmith. H. Burgh JP at Stroud. All sentenced to hard labour, Hodges for six months, Michael Vick six weeks and George Vick for fourteen days, in Horsley house of correction. Offence committed 13 April 1836.

55/C/25   13 April 1836. John Moss and John Merchant of Painswick, labourers. Damaging a live fence, the property of Daniel Smith, innkeeper, at Stroud. E. G. Hallewell JP at Stroud. Fine 2/6 damages, to be paid to an overseer of the poor, and 8/6 costs to the complainant, who was examined as to proof of offence, or hard labour for one calendar month in Horsley house of correction. Offence committed 3 April 1836.

55/C/26   21 April 1834 [*late return*]. Joseph Smith of Minchinhampton, labourer. Possessing a quantity of woollen yarn believed to be stolen. H. Burgh JP, E. G. Hallewell JP and N. S. Marling JP. Fine £20, half of which to be paid to Jesse Davis, clothier, of Minchinhampton, and the remainder to Stroud dispensary. George Holmes, clothworker, of Minchinhampton, witness. Offence committed 2 April 1834.

55/C/27   27 June 1836. Thomas Mills and John Troughton. Damaging with intent to steal strawberry plants growing in a garden at Prestbury, the property of George Overton. John Carrington Smith JP at Cheltenham. Each fined 5/6, to be paid to an overseer of the poor, and 2/6 damages and 5/3 costs to the complainant. Offence committed 26 June 1836.

55/C/28   18 June 1836. William Singleton of Cheltenham, licensed beer and cider retailer. Keeping his house open for the sale and consumption of beer and cider until 2 a.m. T. Newell JP and J. C. Smith JP. First offence. Fine 40/- and 6/6 costs. Offence committed 15 June 1836.

55/C/29   14 June 1836. William Lines. Assaulting and beating Joseph White at Cheltenham. J. C. Smith JP and T. Newell JP at Cheltenham. Fine 2/6 and 6/6 costs. Offence committed 9 June 1836.

55/C/30   14 June 1836. Thomas Foil. Assaulting William Stephens, journeyman cabinet-maker, of Cheltenham. J. C. Smith JP and T. Newell JP. Fine 20/- and 7/6 costs or one month in Northleach house of correction. Offence committed 13 June 1836.

55/C/31   14 June 1836. Charles Green. Assaulting and beating Richard Durham at Cheltenham. J. C. Smith JP and T. Newell JP at Cheltenham. Fine 2/6 and 6/6 costs or fourteen days in Northleach house of correction. Offence committed 7 June 1836.

55/C/32   2 June 1836. Benjamin Mayer, licensed beer and cider retailer, of Cheltenham. Keeping his house open for the sale of beer and cider until a late hour at night. T. Newell JP and J. C. Smith JP at Cheltenham. First offence. Fine 40/- and 4/6 costs. Offence committed 28 May 1836.

55/C/33   28 May 1836. Christopher Garrett, licensed beer and cider retailer, of Cheltenham. Keeping his house open for the sale of beer and cider until a late hour at night. J. C. Smith JP and J. E. Viner JP at Cheltenham. First offence. Fine 40/- and 5/6 costs. Offence committed 24 May 1836.

55/C/34   12 May 1836. Edward Saunders, licensed beer and cider retailer, of Cheltenham. Keeping his house open for the sale of beer and cider until past 12 o'clock. R. B. Cooper JP and T. Newell JP. First offence. Fine 40/- and 5/6 costs. Offence committed 9 May 1836.

55/C/35   21 April 1836. John Moss. Trespassing in search of conies, the property of Henry Skelton at Charlton Kings. T. Newell JP and R. B. Cooper JP. Fine 4/- and 6/6 costs. Offence committed 17 April 1836.

55/C/36   19 April 1836. John Sheldon of Cheltenham, licensed retailer of excisable liquors. Failing to maintain good order in his licensed public house. William Seale Evans JP and R. B. Cooper JP. First offence. Fine 40/- and 5/6 costs. Offence committed 12 April 1836.

55/C/37   16 April 1836. William Phipps of Cheltenham, licensed beer and cider retailer. Keeping his house open for the sale of beer and cider until a late hour at night. R. B. Cooper JP and T. Newell JP. First offence. Fine 40/- and 5/6 costs. Offence committed 12 April 1836.

55/C/38   14 April 1836. James Patch. Assaulting and beating William Allen, innkeeper, of Cheltenham. J. C. Smith JP and T. Newell JP at Cheltenham. Fine 5/- and 8/6 costs. Offence committed 26 Dec. 1835.

55/C/39   3 May 1836. Thomas George of Saintbury. Stealing a rail, part of a dead fence, the property of Daniel Elly, at Saintbury. Rev. J. R. Hall JP at Moreton in Marsh. Fine 5/6, to be paid to an overseer of the poor, and 15/- costs and 6*d.* damages to the complainant, who was not examined as to proof of offence, or hard labour for one calendar month in [Northleach] house of correction. Offence committed 11 April 1836.

55/C/40   8 March 1836. William Reeve of Blockley, Worcs. Using a snare to kill game at Bourton on the Hill without possessing a game certificate. Rev. J. R. Hall JP and Rev. C. Jeaffreson JP at Moreton in Marsh. Fine £1 4*s.*, to be paid to an overseer of the poor, and 16/- costs to John Keyte of Blockley, informer, or hard labour for two calendar months in Northleach house of correction. Offence committed 5 March 1836.

55/C/41   23 June 1836. James Meredith. Stealing a rail valued at 2/6, the property of Nathaniel Hemming of Dymock. O. Ricardo JP at Ledbury, Herefs. Anthony Parsons, witness. Fine 10/-, to be paid to an overseer of the poor, and 2/6 damages and 7/6 costs to the complainant, or one calendar month in Littledean house of correction. Offence committed 31 May 1836.

55/C/42   8 June 1836. Thomas Perriman and Charles Dyer, labourers, of Marshfield. Using guns to kill game in Marshfield Wood without a game certificate. K. W. Horlock JP and R. H. B. Hale JP at Ashwick. John Gunning, complainant. John Webb, witness. Fine £5 each, one moiety of which to be paid to the complainant, together with 9/- each costs. The remainder to go to the overseer of the poor, Charles James Dowding, or three calendar months' hard labour in Horsley house of correction. Offence committed 29 May 1836.

55/C/43   20 May 1836. William Priece of Pucklechurch, licensed beer retailer. Keeping his house open for the sale and consumption of beer during the hours of morning divine service and later in the evening. R. H. B. Hale JP and K. W. Horlock JP at a Petty Sessions for Grumbalds Ash district. First offence. Fine 40/-, one moiety of which to be paid to constable William Green, the informer. Costs assessed at 13/-. Offence committed between 10 a.m. and 1 p.m. and at 10.15 p.m. Sunday 1 May 1836.

55/C/44   3 June 1836. Henry Dyer in company with Edward Dyer, labourers, of Marshfield. Trespassing in Marshfield Wood, a game preserve occupied by Sir C. B. Codrington, Bt., and firing a double-barrelled gun without permission. W. Blathwayt JP, R. H. B. Hale JP, A. Shakespear JP, H. Bush JP and K. W. Horlock JP at Old Sodbury. Henry fined £2 and Edward 10/-, half of which total to be paid to an overseer of the poor, and 6/6 costs each to John Gunning of Marshfield, complainant. Given thirteen days to pay. In default, one calendar month in Horsley house of correction. John Webb of West Kington [*MS.* West Kingston], Wilts., witness. Offence committed 8.30 p.m. Saturday 28 May 1836.

55/C/45   7 March 1836. William Drew, overseer of the poor of Preston. Non-payment of poor-rate collected by him, totalling £9 5*s.*, due to be paid to the board of guardians of Newent poor law union. O. Ricardo JP and Robert Canning JP at the magistrates' court, Newent. Offender appointed overseer of the poor of Preston, Dymock, on 30 March 1835 until

25 March 1836. Demand issued by Abraham Lauder, clerk to the board of guardians, Rev. John Simons, Thomas Hankins Esq. and Joseph Stallard Esq. on 12 Oct. 1835 requesting payment to William Russell Skey, banker of Gloucester, or his agent John Matthews at Newent. Order delivered to Henry Bruton, relieving officer for Preston, Dymock, by Thomas Cadle Esq., clerk to the magistrates. Several demands were made, under different hands, J. G. S. Lefevre and George Nicholls, gentleman, poor law commissioners. Witnesses: W. R. Skey, J. Matthews, H. Bruton, T. Cadle and John Thurston, constable of Newent. Fine £5.

55/D/1   4 Aug. 1836. Thomas Grimes. Trespassing in pursuit of game on land at Owlpen Wood, the property of Edward Sheppard the younger Esq. T. Kingscote JP and B. C. Browne JP at Horsley. Henry Sherwood, complainant. Fine £2, one moiety of which to be paid to William Taylor, an overseer of the poor, and the remainder and 10/- costs to the complainant, or hard labour for two calendar months in Horsley house of correction. Offence committed 17 July 1836.

55/D/2   4 Aug. 1836. Charles Tainton. Trespassing in pursuit of game [*etc.*, *as* 55/D/1].

55/D/3   30 Sept. 1836. Edward Dangerfield of Cheltenham, coach proprietor. Carrying eleven outside passengers on his stage-coach driven by Butler between Cheltenham and Gloucester when licensed to carry only eight. J. C. Smith JP at Cheltenham. Fine £15 (three penalties of £5) mitigated to £3 15s., half of which to be paid to the Clerk of the Peace. The remainder with 5/- cost to be paid to the informer Charles Wootton. Offence committed 22 Sept. 1836.

55/D/4   Gloucestershire Michaelmas Sessions 1836. Cheltenham Division. Account of fines imposed under the Stage Coach Act [2 & 3 Wm. IV, c. 120, s. 34] with the last quarter.
     1836 Sept. 30. Parties fined: Edward Dangerfield.
              For what offence: Against the Stage Coach Act.
              Amount of fine: 3-15-0.
              King's Moiety thereof: 1-17-6.
              Amount paid to informer: 1-17-6.

1836 Michaelmas Sessions. Rec[d]. the above sum of £1 17s. 6d. and gave receipt to Messrs. Straford and Cox's clerk.   E. B.   J. C. Straford, clerk to the magistrates.

55/D/5   8 Aug. 1836. Henry Robinson. Assaulting and beating Richard Smith at Cheltenham. R. B. Cooper JP and W. S. Evans JP at Cheltenham. Fine 10/-, to be paid to an overseer of the poor, and 4/- costs. Offence committed 7 Aug. 1836.

55/D/6   3 Aug. 1836. John Andrews of Staverton. Assaulting and beating Isaac Withers, labourer, of Staverton. J. C. Smith JP and W. S. Evans JP at Cheltenham. Fine 20/-, to be paid to an overseer of the poor, and 6/6 costs. Offence committed 2 Aug. 1836.

55/D/7   18 July 1836. Henry Mead of Cheltenham. Assaulting and beating Thomas Chick at Cheltenham. J. C. Smith JP and W. S. Evans JP at Cheltenham. Fine 5/-, to be paid to an overseer of the poor, and 5/- costs. Offence committed 16 July 1836.

55/D/8   3 Aug. 1836. Benjamin Brawn, licensed beer and cider retailer, of Cheltenham. Keeping his house open for the sale of beer after 10 p.m. J. C. Smith JP and W. S. Evans JP at Cheltenham. First offence. Fine 40/-, one moiety of which to be paid to Thomas Trigg, the informer, and the remainder to the county treasurer. Costs 4/6. Offence committed 30 July 1836.

55/D/9   12 Oct. 1836. William Hodges, licensed beer retailer of the Carpenter's Arms, Cheltenham. Refusing admittance to Daniel Browning, a police officer, after his application and request to enter. R. B. Cooper JP and J. C. Smith JP. First offence. Fine £5, one moiety of which to be paid to the informer and the remainder to the county treasurer. Costs 7/-. Offence committed 9 Oct. 1836.

55/D/10   9 Oct. 1836. William Rose. Assaulting and beating Thomas Woodard at Cheltenham. R. B. Cooper JP and Samuel Gale JP at Cheltenham. Fine 20/-, to be paid to an overseer of the poor, and 4/6 costs. Offence committed 8 Oct. 1836.

55/D/11   5 Oct. 1836. David Ray of Cheltenham, licensed retailer of excisable liquors. Keeping his house open at an improper time of night. R. B. Cooper JP and J. C. Smith JP. First offence. Fine 40/-, one moiety of which to be paid to Stephen Lawes, the informer, and the remainder to the county treasurer. Costs 4/-. Offence committed 1 Oct. 1836.

55/D/12   3 Oct. 1836. Thomas Bowyer. Assaulting Daniel Hall at Shurdington. R. B. Cooper JP and S. Gale JP at Cheltenham. Fine 20/-, to be paid to an overseer of the poor, and 7/- costs. Offence committed 24 Sept., 1836.

55/D/13   30 Sept. 1836. Joseph Phillips. Assaulting and beating Benjamin Johnson at Cheltenham. R. B. Cooper JP and J. C. Smith JP at Cheltenham. Fine £4 10s., to be paid to an overseer of the poor, and 10/- costs to the complainant, or hard labour for six weeks in Northleach house of correction. Offence committed 28 Sept. 1836.

55/D/14   30 Sept. 1836. John Phillips. Assaulting and beating Benjamin Johnson [etc., as 55/D/13].

55/D/15   28 Sept. 1836. William Oakley. Assaulting and beating William Arundell at Cheltenham. R. B. Cooper JP and S. Gale JP at Cheltenham. Fine 2/6, to be paid to an overseer of the poor, and 6/- costs. Offence committed 26 Sept. 1836.

55/D/16   28 Sept. 1836. Thomas Fletcher. Assaulting Daniel Browning at Cheltenham. R. B. Cooper JP and S. Gale JP at Cheltenham. Fine 5/-, to be paid to an overseer of the poor, and 3/- costs. Offence committed 27 Sept. 1836.

55/D/17   26 Sept. 1836. John Minett. Assaulting Charlotte Constable at Cheltenham. R. B. Cooper JP and J. C. Smith JP at Cheltenham. Fine 10/-, to be paid to an overseer of the poor, and 5/- costs. Offence committed 2 Sept. 1836.

55/D/18   21 Sept. 1836. John Crawford. Assaulting and beating Esther Hooper at Cheltenham. R. B. Cooper JP and S. Gale JP at Cheltenham. Fine 10/-, to be paid to an overseer of the poor, and 3/- costs. Offence committed 20 Sept. 1836.

55/D/19   21 Sept. 1836. Thomas Bowyer. Assaulting and beating James Bowstead at Cheltenham. R. B. Cooper JP and S. Gale JP at Cheltenham. Fine 5/-, to be paid to an overseer of the poor, and 4/- costs. Offence committed 20 Sept. 1836.

55/D/20   16 Sept. 1836. William Cook. Assaulting and beating Thomas Cook at Cheltenham. R. B. Cooper JP and J. C. Smith JP at Cheltenham. Fine 5/-, to be paid to an overseer of the poor, and 6/- costs. Offence committed 9 Sept. 1836.

55/D/21   9 Sept. 1836. William Blakeney. Assaulting and beating Thomas Silley at Cheltenham. R. B. Cooper JP and W. Pitt JP at Cheltenham. Fine 20/-, to be paid to an overseer of the poor, and 3/- costs. Offence committed 7 Sept. 1836.

55/D/22   7 Sept. 1836. Jabez Jackson of Cheltenham, dyer. Assaulting and beating Emma Gale at Cheltenham. J. C. Smith JP and S. Gale JP at Cheltenham. Fine 10/-, to be paid to an overseer of the poor, and 4/- costs. Offence committed 4 Sept. 1836.

55/D/23   7 Sept. 1836. Jabez Jackson of Cheltenham, dyer. Assaulting and beating John Parkinson at Cheltenham [etc., as 55/D/22 except] Offence committed 27 Aug. 1836.

55/D/24   7 Sept. 1836. George Hawkins of Cheltenham, licensed retailer of excisable liquors. Keeping his house open during the usual hours of afternoon divine service at the parish church or chapel. J. C. Smith JP and S. Gale JP at Cheltenham. First offence. Fine 40/-, one moiety of which to be paid to Thomas Sparrow, the informer, and the remainder to the county treasurer, and 6/- costs. Offence committed 4 Sept. 1836.

55/D/25   5 Sept. 1836. George Williams. Assaulting and beating Thomas Williams at Cheltenham. R. B. Cooper JP and J. C. Smith JP at Cheltenham. Fine 40/-, to be paid to an overseer of the poor, and 7/- costs. Offence committed 31 Aug. 1836.

55/D/26   2 Sept. 1836. John Sims, licensed beer and cider retailer, of Cheltenham. Keeping his house open for the sale of beer after 10 p.m. R. B. Cooper JP and J. C. Smith JP at Cheltenham. First offence. Fine 40/-, the moiety of which to be paid to Thomas Trigg, the informer, and the remainder to the county treasurer, and 5/- costs. Offence committed 29 Aug. 1836.

55/D/27   29 Aug. 1836. Thomas Smith. Assaulting and beating Joseph Bailey at Cheltenham. R. B. Cooper JP and J. C. Smith JP at Cheltenham. Fine 20/-, to be paid to an overseer of the poor, and 6/- costs. Offence committed 27 Aug. 1836.

55/D/28   19 Aug. 1836. Richard Tale. Assaulting and beating John Bradshaw. R. B. Cooper JP and J. C. Smith JP at Cheltenham. Fine 2/6, to be paid to an overseer of the poor, and 4/6 costs. Offence committed 16 Aug. 1836.

55/D/29   26 July 1836. Robert Doyly, gentleman, of Moreton in Marsh. Assaulting and beating William Fletcher Roberts at Moreton in Marsh. Rev. J. R. Hall JP and F. Colvile JP at Moreton in Marsh. Fine £1, to be paid to Thomas Horne, overseer of the poor, and 12/- costs to the complainant, or one calendar month in Northleach house of correction. Offence committed 22 July 1836.

55/D/30   20 Sept. 1836. Francis Franklin, licensed retailer of beer, cider etc., of Moreton in Marsh. Permitting disorderly conduct in his premises. W. Dickins JP and F. Colvile JP at Moreton in Marsh at a Petty Sessions for the upper division of Westminster hundred. First offence. Fine 40/-, one moiety of which to be paid to George Millington, the prosecutor, and the remainder to the county treasurer. Costs 11/-. Offence committed 1 Sept. 1836.

55/D/31   20 Sept. 1836. James Lively late of Bourton on the Hill, labourer. Using a gun to take and kill game at Bourton on the Hill. W. Dickins JP and F. Colvile JP at Moreton in Marsh. Fine £4 10s., one moiety of which to be paid to Peter Brookes, of Batsford, informer and prosecutor, with 10/- costs, and the remainder to John Gardner, overseer of the poor, or hard labour for two calendar months in Northleach house of correction. Offence committed Sunday 11 Sept. 1836.

55/D/32   20 Sept. 1836. Edward Baldwin, late of Bourton on the Hill, labourer. Using a gun to take and kill game at Bourton on the Hill [etc., as 55/D/31].

55/D/33   23 Aug. 1836. William Walton of Bourton on the Hill. Trespassing in search of game on enclosed land at Sezincote [MS. Seasoncote] occupied by Sir Charles Cockerell, Bt. W. Dickins JP at Moreton in Marsh. Fine £1 10s. [later given as 50/-], one moiety of which to be paid to Francis Groom, complainant, with 10/- costs, and the remainder to an overseer of the poor, or hard labour for two calendar months in Northleach house of correction. Offence committed 31 March 1836.

55/D/34   23 Aug. 1836. Thomas Parker. Stealing a quantity of apples growing in an orchard at Moreton in Marsh, the property of Thomas Horne. W. Dickins JP at Moreton in Marsh. Fine £1 10s., to be paid to an overseer of the poor, and 10/- costs to Richard Pitman, the complainant, or hard labour for two calendar months in Northleach house of correction. Offence committed 14 Aug. 1836.

55/D/35   23 Aug. 1836. Joseph Miles. Stealing a quantity of apples from a field at Moreton in Marsh, the property of Thomas Horne. W. Dickins JP at Moreton in Marsh. Fine 10/-, to be paid to an overseer of the poor and 10/- costs to Richard Pitman, the complainant, or hard labour for one calendar month in Northleach house of correction. Offence committed 31 July 1836.

55/D/36   12 July 1836. John Boseley of Ebrington, labourer. Assaulting and beating William Seymour Booker at Ebrington. Rev. J. R. Hall JP and Rev. C. Jeaffreson JP at Moreton in Marsh. Fine 10/-, to be paid to Samuel Keyte, overseer of the poor, and 9/- costs to the complainant, or two calendar months in Northleach house of correction. Offence committed 9 July 1836.

55/D/37   12 July 1836. Joseph Russell of Ebrington, labourer. Assaulting and beating William Seymour Booker [etc., as 55/D/36].

55/D/38   23 May 1836. Thomas Booker. Breaking a chaff-cutting machine at Charingworth, Ebrington, the property of John Milward. Rev. J. R. Hall JP at Batsford. Fine 3/- and 16/- costs, to be paid to the complainant, or hard labour for two calendar months in [Northleach] house of correction. Offence committed 25 Feb. 1836.

55/D/39   20 Sept. 1836. Benjamin Watkins of Moreton in Marsh. Assaulting Richard Clifford at Moreton in Marsh. W. Dickins JP and F. Colvile JP at Moreton in Marsh. Fine 10/-, to be paid to Thomas Foster, overseer of the poor, and 10/- costs to the complainant, or one calendar month in Northleach house of correction. Offence committed 6 Sept. 1836.

55/D/40   2 Sept. 1836. William Cox of Stroud, labourer. Assaulting Samuel Stables of Stroud, labourer. H. Burgh JP and H. Wyatt JP at Stroud. Fine £5, to be paid to an overseer of the poor, or two calendar months in Horsley house of correction. Offence committed 12 Aug. 1836.

55/D/41   24 Sept. 1836. Solomon Chapman and Nathaniel Stephens, labourers, of King's Stanley. Cutting down and stealing part of a fir tree at King's Stanley, the property of Henry Burgh Esq. of Rodborough. H. Wyatt JP at Stroud. Fine £5, to be paid to John Pegler, overseer of the poor, and 2/- damages to the complainant, or hard labour for two calendar months in Horsley house of correction. Offence committed 19 Sept. 1836.

55/D/42   2 Sept. 1836. George Hewlett, blacksmith, of Stroud. Assaulting Samuel Stables, labourer, of Stroud. H. Burgh JP and H. Wyatt JP at Stroud. Fine £4 4s., to be paid to an overseer of the poor, and 16/- costs to the complainant, or two calendar months in Horsley house of correction. Offence committed 12 Aug. 1836.

55/D/43   2 Sept. 1836. William Hewlett, blacksmith, of Stroud. Assaulting Samuel Stables [etc., as 55/D/42].

55/D/44   19 Sept. 1836. William Latham of Stroud, labourer. Assaulting and beating Ann wife of John Hawks, blacksmith, of Stroud. H. Burgh JP and H. Wyatt JP at Stroud. Fine £4 16s., to be paid to an overseer of the poor, and 10/- costs to the complainant, or two calendar months in Horsley house of correction. Offence committed 17 Sept. 1836.

55/D/45   21 Sept. 1836. Thomas Hill of Stroud, nailmaker. Violently assaulting John Bird, butcher, of Stroud. H. Burgh JP and H. Wyatt JP at Stroud. Fine £4 15s., to be paid to an overseer of the poor, and 5/- costs to the complainant, or two calendar months in Horsley house of correction. Offence committed 17 Sept. 1836.

55/D/46   21 Sept. 1836. Thomas Huggins of Stroud, nailmaker. Violently assaulting John Bird [etc., as 55/D/45].

55/D/47   21 Sept. 1836. John Comeley of Stroud, nailmaker. Violently assaulting John Bird [etc., as 55/D/45].

55/D/48   8 Oct. 1836. Charles Gwinnell of King's Stanley, labourer. Cutting down and stealing a tree growing in a wood at King's Stanley, the property of the Rt. Hon. Thomas, Lord Ducie. H. Burgh JP at Stroud. Fine £4 10s., to be paid to John Pegler, overseer of the poor, and 2/6 damages and 10/- costs to the complainant, or hard labour for two calendar months in Horsley house of correction. Offence committed 1 April 1836.

55/D/49   31 Aug. 1836. William Nutt of Stroud, labourer. Causing an obstruction in a public street in Stroud. H. Burgh JP at Stroud. Fine £5. Offence committed 31 Aug. 1836.

55/D/50   4 Sept. 1836. George Cratchley of Stroud, labourer. Stealing a quantity of potatoes growing in a garden in Stroud, the property of George Hooper. H. Burgh JP at Stroud. Hard labour for three calendar months in Horsley house of correction. Offence committed 3 Sept. 1836.

55/D/51   20 Sept. 1836. William Ridler of Bisley, labourer. Cutting down and stealing a sycamore tree at Bisley, the property of Ann Walling, spinster. H. Burgh JP at Stroud. Fine £5, to be paid to an overseer of the poor, and 7/6 costs and 1/- damages to the complainant, or hard labour for two calendar months in Horsley house of correction. Offence committed 15 Aug. 1836.

55/D/52   19 Aug. 1836. William Rowles. Neglecting his wife and child, causing them to become chargeable to Bisley parish. H. Burgh JP and J. Mills JP at Stroud. Hard Labour for one calendar month in Horsley house of correction.

55/D/53   27 June 1836. Joseph Collier of Stroud, labourer. Cutting down and destroying trees in a wood at Stroud, the property of Samuel Copner. H. Burgh JP at Stroud. Fine £4, to be paid to an overseer of the poor, and 8/- costs and 1/- damages to the complainant, or hard labour for two calendar months in Horsley house of correction. Offence committed 13 May 1836.

55/D/54   19 Aug. 1836. Nathaniel Witts, wool-sorter, of Bisley. Assaulting Samuel Wheeler, linen-draper, of Stroud at Bisley. H. Burgh JP and J. Mills JP at Stroud. Fine 11/-, to be paid to an overseer of the poor, and 9/- costs to the complainant, or hard labour for two calendar months in Horsley house of correction. Offence committed 15 Aug. 1836.

55/D/55   16 Aug. 1836. John Chandler. Neglecting his wife and child, causing them to become chargeable to Painswick parish. H. Burgh JP at Stroud. Hard labour for one calendar month in Horsley house of correction. Offence committed 2 Aug. 1836.

55/D/56   26 Aug. 1836. Enoch Gill of Painswick, labourer. Stealing a quantity of apples growing in an orchard at Painswick, the property of John Weeks, baker. H. Burgh JP and J. Mills JP at Stroud. Hard labour for two calendar months in Horsley house of correction. Offence committed 17 Aug. 1836.

55/D/57   5 Aug. 1836. George Cole of Randwick, yeoman. Violently assaulting Mary Ann wife of James Lee, labourer, of Stroud at Standish. E. P. Caruthers JP and H. Wyatt JP at Stroud. Fine 10/-, to be paid to an overseer of the poor, and 8/6 costs to the complainant, or hard labour for one calendar month in Horsley house of correction. Offence committed 2 Aug. 1836.

55/D/58   5 Aug. 1836. Ann Wilkins, widow, Mary Ann wife of James Lee, labourer, and Harriett wife of Edward Aldridge, labourer, all of Stroud. Rooting up the stools of trees in a wood at Standish, the property of the Rt. Hon. John, Lord Sherborne. E. P. Caruthers JP and H. Wyatt JP at Stroud. Fine 1/- damages and 11/6 costs, or hard labour for one week in Horsley house of correction. Offence committed 1 Aug. 1836.

55/D/59   19 Aug. 1836. George Bedford of Stroud, cordwainer. Assaulting Henry Fletcher, labourer, of Stroud. H. Burgh JP and J. Mills JP at Stroud. Fine 2/6, to be paid to an overseer of the poor, and 7/6 costs to the complainant, or hard labour for one calendar month in Horsley house of correction. Offence committed 16 Aug. 1836.

55/D/60   15 Oct. 1836. Ann Vines of Stroud, spinster. Stealing half a peck of apples from an orchard at Randwick occupied by Robert Martin, yeoman, of Stonehouse. H. Burgh JP at Stroud. Hard labour for three calendar months in Horsley house of correction. Offence committed 11 Oct. 1836.

55/D/61   17 Oct. 1836. William Ireland of Stroud, labourer. Stealing a quantity of walnuts from an orchard at Stroud, the property of Charles Jones, baker. H. Burgh JP. Hard labour for three calendar months in Horsley house of correction. Offence committed 17 Oct. 1836.

55/D/62   1 July 1836. John Gay of Painswick, labourer. Violently assaulting William Henry Swayne, labourer, of Painswick. H. Burgh JP and E. G. Hallewell JP at Stroud. Fine 1/-, to be paid to an overseer of the poor, and 6/6 costs to the complainant, or two calendar months in Horsley house of correction. Offence committed 28 June 1836.

55/D/63   23 Sept. 1836. Joseph Taylor of Stroud, labourer. Assaulting and beating Soloman Ind, labourer, of Rodborough at Stroud. H. Burgh JP, J. Mills JP and E. G. Hallewell JP at Stroud. Fine £4 12s. 6d., to be paid to Charles Halliday, overseer of the poor, and 7/6 costs to the complainant, or two calendar months in Horsley house of correction. Offence committed 17 Sept. 1836.

55/D/64   23 Sept. 1836. John Clarke of Nympsfield, labourer. Trespassing in search of game on land at King's Stanley, the property of the Rt. Hon Thomas, Lord Ducie. H. Burgh JP, J. Mills JP and E. G. Hallewell JP at Stroud. Fine £1 10s., to be paid to John Pegler, overseer of the poor, and 10/- costs to William Baker, gamekeeper, of King's Stanley, complainant, or hard labour for two calendar months in Horsley house of correction. Offence committed 1 Sept. 1836.

55/D/65   23 Sept. 1836. John Clutterbuck the younger of King's Stanley, gentleman. Trespassing in pursuit of game on land at King's Stanley occupied by Mary Claister, widow. H. Burgh JP, J. Mills JP and E. G. Hallewell JP at Stroud. Fine £1 10s., to be paid to John Pegler, overseer of the poor, and 10/- costs to William Baker, gamekeeper, of King's Stanley, complainant, or hard labour for two calendar months in Horsley house of correction. Offence committed 1 Sept. 1836.

55/D/66   23 Sept. 1836. Nathaniel Lusty of King's Stanley, labourer. Trespassing in pursuit of game [etc., as 55/D/64].

55/D/67   23 Sept. 1836. Eliza wife of Samuel Trotman, labourer, and Mary wife of William Workman, labourer, all of Bisley. Stealing a quantity of potatoes from a field occupied by Isaac Woodfield, yeoman, at Bisley. H. Burgh JP and J. Mills JP at Stroud. Hard labour for one calendar month in Horsley house of correction. Offence committed 22 Sept. 1836.

55/D/68   1 July 1836. Joseph Wright of Painswick, labourer. Violently assaulting William Henry Swayne, labourer, of Painswick. H. Burgh JP and E. G. Hallewell JP at Stroud. Fine 1/-, to be paid to an overseer of the poor, and 6/6 costs to the complainant, or two calendar months in Horsley house of correction. Offence committed 28 June 1836.

55/D/69   19 Aug. 1836. Edward Birt of Painswick, weaver. Assaulting Jabez Wood, weaver, of Painswick. H. Burgh JP and E. G. Hallewell JP at Stroud. Fine 9/-, to be paid to an overseer of the poor, and 11/- costs to Samuel Wheeler, or hard labour for two calendar months in Horsley house of correction. Offence committed 15 Aug. 1836.

55/D/70   29 June 1836. John Niblett and William West, labourers, of Painswick. Stealing a quantity of fruit growing in a garden at Painswick, the property of John Clarke Wallop, yeoman. H. Burgh JP and E. G. Hallewell JP at Stroud. Hard labour for one calendar month in Horsley house of correction. Offence committed 25 June 1836.

55/D/71   29 June 1836. William Cooke of Painswick, weaver. Pulling down and damaging the wall of the garden and destroying trees of Charles Savory, sawyer, at Painswick. H. Burgh JP and E. G. Hallewell JP at Stroud. Fine £4 damages, to be paid to an overseer of the poor, or hard labour for two calendar months in Horsley house of correction. Offence committed 28 June 1836.

55/D/72   18 July 1836. John Cook of Painswick, cordwainer. Assaulting and beating his wife. J. Mills JP and E. G. Hallewell JP at Stroud. Fine £5, to be paid to an overseer of the poor, or two calendar months in Horsley house of correction. Offence committed 16 July 1836.

55/D/73   13 Aug. 1836. Mortimer Grange of Painswick. Stealing a quantity of apples growing in an orchard, the property of widow Elizabeth Phillips. H. Burgh JP and E. G. Hallewell JP, at Stroud. Hard labour for fourteen days in Horsley house of correction. Offence committed 9 Aug. 1836.

55/D/74   19 Aug. 1836. Jacob Fawkes the younger and Jacob Davis, yeomen, of Bisley. Violently assaulting Thomas Hazle of Bisley, yeoman. H. Burgh JP and E. G. Hallewell JP at Stroud. Fine 1/- each, to be paid to an overseer of the poor, and 13/- costs to the complainant, or fourteen days in Horsley house of correction. Offence committed 4 Aug. 1836.

55/D/75   1 July 1836. James Cripps of Painswick, labourer. Violently assaulting William Henry Swayne of Painswick [*etc.*, *as* 55/D/68].

55/D/76   23 Aug. 1836. William Cooke of Painswick, weaver. Assaulting Jabez Wood of Painswick, weaver. H. Burgh JP and E. G. Hallewell JP at Stroud. Fine £1, to be paid to an overseer of the poor, and 9/- costs to the complainant, or one calendar month in Horsley house of correction. Offence committed 21 Aug. 1836.

55/D/77   29 Aug. 1836. Hannah Burlow, single woman, maintained in Newent union workhouse. Refusing to do work suited to her age, strength and capacity. O. Ricardo JP and R. F. Onslow JP at Newent. Hard labour for fourteen days in Littledean house of correction. Offence committed 26 Aug. 1836.

55/D/78   29 Aug. 1836. Sarah Ingram, widow, maintained in Newent union workhouse. Refusing to do work suited to her age [*etc.*, *as* 55/D/77].

55/D/79   29 Aug. 1836. Elizabeth Burton, single woman, maintained in Newent union workhouse. Refusing to do work suited to her age [*etc.*, *as* 55/D/77].

55/D/80   29 Aug. 1836. Ann Stone, single woman, maintained in Newent union workhouse. Refusing to do work suited to her age [*etc.*, *as* 55/D/77].

55/D/81   28 Sept. 1836. William Dobbs. Stealing three pecks of potatoes growing on enclosed land at Newent, the property of Thomas Keyse. R. F. Onslow JP at Newent. Fine 1/- (the value of the potatoes) and 10/-, to be paid to an overseer of the poor, and 10/- costs to the complainant, who was examined as to proof of offence. All to be paid by 3 Oct. In default, one calendar month in Littledean house of correction. Offence committed 10 Sept. 1836.

55/D/82   2 Aug. 1836. John Dadge. Neglecting to maintain his wife and her two children by her former husband (both aged less than sixteen), thereby causing them to become chargeable to Newent parish. Rev. R. F. Onslow JP at Newent. Hard labour for one calendar month in Littledean house of correction. Offence committed 21 May 1836.

55/D/83   22 Aug. 1836. Robert Pitt of Pauntley, carpenter. Killing a coney at Caps Grove in Newent, kept for breeding of conies, occupied by Mr. John Hill. O. Ricardo JP and R. F. Onslow JP at Newent. Fine £4 1*s.*, to be paid to an overseer of the poor, and 19/- costs to

John Rudge the complainant, or two calendar months in Littledean house of correction. Offence committed 9 Aug. 1836.

55/D/84   21 June 1836. Henry Brinkworth, of Framilode. Selling one pint of beer by retail, to be consumed in his house, without having an excise licence. C. O. Cambridge JP and P. Leversage JP at Wheatenhurst. Fine £20. Offence committed 10 May 1836.

55/D/85   21 June 1836. Jesse Wright of Leonard Stanley. Selling two pints of beer by retail, to be consumed in his house, without having an excise licence. C. O. Cambridge JP and P. Leversage JP at Wheatenhurst. Fine £5. Offence committed 3 May 1836.

55/D/86   21 June 1836. Giles Edwards of Leonard Stanley. Opening his house and selling two pints of beer by retail, to be consumed on the premises, without [*etc., as* 55/D/85].

55/D/87   21 June 1836. John Hemming of Leonard Stanley. Selling two pints of beer by retail, to be consumed in his house, without [*etc., as* 55/D/85].

55/D/88   21 June 1836. John King. Assaulting Richard Whittard at Leonard Stanley. C. O. Cambridge JP and P. Leversage JP at Wheatenhurst. Fine one halfpenny, to be paid to an overseer of the poor, and 6/6 costs to the complainant. Offence committed 5 June 1836.

55/D/89   21 June 1836. Samuel Dowdeswell. Breaking a quart cup and a bench at Epney, the property of Benjamin Jones. C. O. Cambridge JP and P. Leversage JP at Wheatenhurst. Fine 7/9, to be paid to an overseer of the poor of Moreton Valence, and 7/6 costs to the complainant. Offence committed 16 June 1836.

55/D/90   21 June 1836. Joseph Gwinnell. Assaulting John Cook at King's Stanley. C. O. Cambridge JP and P. Leversage JP at Wheatenhurst. Fine 5/-, to be paid to an overseer of the poor, and 8/6 costs to the complainant, or fourteen days in Horsley house of correction. Offence committed 17 June 1836.

55/D/91   25 June 1836. Miles Pool. Turning out and keeping eleven sheep to depasture on Selsley Hill common when they were infected with scab. D. Maclean JP at King's Stanley. Fine £6, to be distributed as the law directs. Offence committed 21 June 1836.

55/D/92   26 July 1836. Charles Teakle. Causing his wife and family to become chargeable to Standish parish. H. C. Clifford JP and P. Leversage JP at Wheatenhurst. Hard labour for one calendar month in Horsley house of correction.

55/D/93   30 Aug. 1836. Samuel Phelps. Assaulting John Greenaway at Quedgeley. H. C. Clifford JP and P. Leversage JP at Wheatenhurst. Fine £2, to be paid to an overseer of the poor, and 6/6 costs to the complainant. Offence committed 23 July 1836.

55/D/94   30 Aug. 1836. Frederick Deane. Assaulting Ruth Clarke at Leonard Stanley. H. C. Clifford JP and P. Leversage JP at Wheatenhurst. Fine 10/-, to be paid to an overseer of the poor, and 7/6 costs to the complainant, or one calendar month in Horsley house of correction. Offence committed 13 Aug. 1836.

55/D/95   27 Sept. 1836. William Silvey. Assaulting George Hayward at Eastington. H. C. Clifford JP and C. O. Cambridge JP at Wheatenhurst. Fine 5/-, to be paid to an overseer of the poor, and 5/- costs to the complainant, or one calendar month in Horsley house of correction. 17 Sept. 1836.

55/D/96   27 Sept. 1836. Joseph Gwinnell. Assaulting William Hooper at Leonard Stanley. H. C. Clifford JP and C. O. Cambridge JP at Wheatenhurst. Fine £5 or two calendar months in Horsley house of correction. Offence committed 28 Aug. 1836.

55/D/97   2 Aug. 1836. John Williams. Causing two of his children to become chargeable to Stonehouse parish. R. S. Davies JP at Stonehouse. Hard labour for one calendar month in Horsley house of correction.

55/D/98   28 July 1836. John Smart of Stow on the Wold, innkeeper. Permitting persons of notorious bad character to assemble and meet in his house. Rev. R. W. Ford JP and Rev. C. Jeaffreson JP. Second offence. [*Cf.* 55/B/65.] Fine £7 10*s.* and 10/- costs. Offence committed 25 July 1836.

55/D/99–   23 June 1836. [*Names as below.*] Using measures or scales [*except* 55/D/100] found to
110   be unjust by Cornelius Bown, inspector of weights and measures for Longtree hundred. T. Kingscote JP and W. Playne JP. William Clements, patten woodcutter, of Horsley, informer [*Clements is not given an address in* 55/D/100]. Fine 5/- [*except* 55/D/106 and 109]. [*Date offence committed* (*all 1836*) *as below.*]

55/D/99   Stephen Smith of Tetbury. Using two one-quart measures. (24 May.)

55/D/100   James Davis of Minchinhampton, victualler. Refusing to allow William Clements, patten woodcutter, and Cornelius Bown, inspectors of weights and measures, into a room in his dwelling house to examine his weights and measures. T. Kingscote JP and W. Playne JP. Informer William Clements. Fine 5/-. (16 May.)

55/D/101   James Hooper of Rodborough. Two one-quart and one pint measure. (29 April.)

55/D/102   Hannah Dickes of Cherington. One one-quart and one noggin or gill measure. (6 June.)

55/D/103   Robert Emerson of Shipton Moyne. One half-pint and one half-noggin or gill measure. (20 May.)

55/D/104   Charlotte Walkley of Minchinhampton. Three one-quart and one pint measure. (3 June.)

55/D/105   Ambrose Fisher of Minchinhampton. One one-quart and four one-pint measures. (16 May.)

55/D/106   Richard King of Minchinhampton. One noggin or gill and one half-noggin measure. Fine £1. (30 April.)

55/D/107   Daniel Sweeting of Tetbury. A pair of scales. (31 May.)

55/D/108   George Tainty of Minchinhampton. One one-quart and one pint measure. (30 April.)

55/D/109   Simon Stephens of Shipton Moyne. Three one-quart measures. Fine £1. (20 May.)

55/D/110   Robert Taylor of Tetbury. Four one-quart measures. (24 May.)

55/D/111   Michaelmas Sessions 1836. T. P. White in a/c with Edward Bloxham Esq.
Fees for returning the following convictions   £ *s. d.*

		£	s.	d.
viz. William Glover		1	–	
James Hale		1	–	
Henry Lyes,				
George Hall and	}	1	–	
Richard Pugh				
		3	–	Received E. B.

55/D/112   8 Sept. 1836. William Glover of Twyning, farmer. Violently assaulting Elizabeth wife of Benjamin Glover, labourer, at the Little Grove field, Twyning, without provocation. J. Timbrill D.D. JP and J. Surman JP at Tewkesbury. Fine £1 10*s.*, to be paid to Thomas Allard, overseer of the poor of Twyning, and 13/- costs to the complainant. Offence committed Saturday 3 Sept. 1836.

55/D/113   29 Sept. 1836. James Hale of Twyning, bricklayer. Violently assaulting Charles Aston on the highway outside the Fountain beershop at Twyning without provocation. J. Timbrill D.D. JP and J. W. Martin JP at Tewkesbury. Fine £1, to be paid to Thomas Allard, overseer of the poor, and 17/6 costs to the complainant. Offence committed Friday 23 Sept. 1836.

55/D/114   13 Oct. 1836. Henry Lyes and George Hall of Overbury and Richard Pugh of Kemerton, labourers. Bursting into George Webb's house at Kemerton and threatening him and his companions, William Franklin and Thomas Williams, with murder. J. Timbrill D.D. JP,

J. W. Martin JP and J. Surman JP at Tewkesbury. Fine £4 12*s.* each, to Richard Baldwin, overseer of the poor of Kemerton, and 8/- each costs to the complainant. Offence committed 9 p.m. 7 Oct. 1836. [*Endorsed*:] In default of immediate payment of fines all were committed to Northleach house of correction for two calendar months.

55/D/115 1 July 1836. Thomas Harding of Hawkesbury, labourer. Trespassing in pursuit of game at Walk Wood, a game preserve, the property of the Court of Chancery, at Horton, in company with John Blaken of Hawkesbury, who had a gun (which he fired) and a dog. R. H. B. Hale JP, W. Blathwayt JP, A. Shakespear JP and H. Bush JP at a Petty Sessions held at the Cross Hands inn, Old Sodbury at 11 a.m. Offender summoned but did not appear. George Limbrick, deputed to look after the Chancery property at Horton, informer. John Watts of Hawkesbury deposed that he heard a gunshot and ran towards the sound and saw them passing nearby. He called to them not to run as he knew them well. Fine £2, one moiety of which to be paid to an overseer of the poor and the remainder with 10/- costs to the informer, or two calendar months in Horsley house of correction. Offence committed between 8 p.m. and 9 p.m. Friday 17 June 1836.

55/D/116 22 July 1836. George Hall of Tormarton, labourer. Trespassing at Twelve Acres, enclosed land belonging to Thomas Brookman, at Tormarton in pursuit of game and taking a hare from a gin which was set up without the required licence. W. Blathwayt JP, R. H. B. Hale JP and A. Shakespear JP. Henry Martin, complainant. James Bennett of Dodington, witness. Fine £2, one moiety of which to be paid to an overseer of the poor and the remainder, with 8/6 costs, to the complainant, or one calendar month in Horsley house of correction. Offence committed between 4 p.m. and 5 p.m. 15 July 1836.

55/D/117 19 Aug. 1836. Charles Sealey of Old Sodbury, licensed beer and cider retailer. Keeping his house open for the sale and consumption of beer until almost 11 p.m. W. Blathwayt JP, A. Shakespear JP and H. Bush JP at a Petty Sessions for Grumbalds Ash district at the Cross Hands inn, Old Sodbury. First offence. Fine 40/-. Costs of 6/6 deducted from the penalty, to be paid to the informer Charles Light. Offence committed Monday 4 July 1836.

55/D/118 9 Sept. 1836. William Sneylome of Siston. Using a gun to kill conies at Siston Warren without having the required certificate. W. Blathwayt JP and commissioner for assessed taxes, at Old Sodbury. Fine £10 and £1 4*s.* costs. Offence committed on Tuesday morning 2 Aug. 1836.

55/D/119 1 July 1836. John Blaken of Hawkesbury. Trespassing in pursuit of game at Walk Wood, a game preserve, with a gun (which he fired) and a dog. R. H. B. Hale JP, W. Blathwayt JP, A. Shakespear JP and H. Bush JP at a Petty Sessions held at the Cross Hands inn, Old Sodbury, at 11 a.m. Offender summoned but did not appear. George Limbrick of Horton, complainant. John Watts, gamekeeper of Horton manor, deposed that he heard a gunshot, ran towards the sound and saw offender with Thomas Harding. He called to them not to run because he knew them well. Fine £5, one moiety of which to be paid to an overseer of the poor, and the remainder, with 10/- costs, to the complainant, or three calendar months in Horsley house of correction. Offence committed between 8 p.m. and 9 p.m. 17 June 1836.

55/D/120 30 Sept. 1836. Edmund Dutfield of Old Sodbury, inmate. Trespassing in search of game with two dogs and a gun, and chasing and shooting a hare in Nineteen Acres at Old Sodbury, land occupied by William Arnold, yeoman. W. Blathwayt JP, H. Bush JP and A. Shakespear JP. William Arnold, complainant. James Bennett of Dodington, witness. Fine £2, one moiety of which to be paid to an overseer of the poor, and the remainder, with 8/6 costs, to the complainant, or one calendar month in Horsley house of correction. Offence committed Thursday 1 Sept. 1836 between 6 a.m. and 7 a.m.

56/A/1   17 June 1834 [*late return*]. Aaron Pike the younger of Ashchurch. Assaulting George Newman, labourer, of Kinsham, Worcs., without just cause at Ashchurch. T. Marriott JP and C. E. Harford JP at a Petty Sessions held at the magistrates' office, Pershore, Worcs. Fine 3/6 and 5/- costs or one calendar month in Worcester house of correction. Offence committed Monday 26 May 1834.

56/A/2   17 Jan. 1834 [*late return*]. Thomas Butler of Iron Acton, labourer. Using a gun and a dog to kill game at Yate without the required certificate. F. Trotman JP, commissioner for assessed taxes, at Old Sodbury. Fine £10. Offence committed 18 Nov. 1833.

56/A/3   17 Jan. 1834 [*late return*]. Mark Dyer of Iron Acton, labourer. Using two dogs for killing game at Yate without the required certificate [*etc., as* 56/A/2].

56/A/4   27 Dec. 1833 [*late return*]. Edwin E. Page of Wick and Abson, attorney-at-law. Trespassing with dogs and a gun in search of game in Bean Wood, land occupied by Sir C. B. and Captain Codrington at Wapley and Codrington. F. Trotman JP, W. Blathwayt JP and A. Shakespear JP at a Petty Sessions held at the Cross Hands inn, Old Sodbury, at 11 a.m. James Harrison, gamekeeper for Sir C. B. Codrington, informer. Offender summoned, but did not appear. Constable John Fussell of Wick and Abson deposed that he had handed a copy of the summons to accused. Labourer John Evans of Wapley and Codrington deposed that he saw Mr. Edwin Page with a gun and three dogs and two men beating for game in the Withy preserve. The beaters ran when they saw him and accused came out of the wood. Witness told accused he was trespassing and put his hand on offender's chest and advised him to go back to his (Evans's) father. Accused said 'don't thee do that no more or I'll shoot thee.' Witness cried 'For God's sake don't shoot me.' Accused then went with witness to Francis Evans, labourer. When questioned, above-named said Page gave his name as Charles Slade of Westgate Buildings, Bath, but that he was certain that he had made no mistake in the name as he made a note inside his hat, which he later copied into his memorandum book. Fine £1, to be paid to Richard Iles, an overseer of the poor of Wapley and Codrington, and £1 6s. costs to the informer. Given until Monday 13 Jan. 1834 to pay. In default, to serve one calendar month in Horsley house of correction. Offence committed between 2 p.m. and 3 p.m. Monday 7 Oct. 1833.

56/A/5   14 Dec. 1836. Edward and William Barnard of Nailsworth, clothiers trading as Edward Barnard and Son. Employing Philip Essex, aged nine, in Nailsworth Upper Mill without a certificate from a physician to affirm that the boy was of ordinary strength and appearance of a child that age or a ticket from a schoolmaster attesting that Philip had attended school for two hours at least for six out of seven days of the preceding week. Thomas Jones Howell, inspector of factories. Offence confessed by William Barnard. Fine 40/-. to be paid to the benefit of Nailsworth British School. Offence committed 14 Dec. 1836. Memorandum: The penalty of 40/- was paid on 17 [Dec.] 1836 to Mr. Anthony Fewster of Horsley, treasurer of the Nailsworth British School.

56/A/6   16 Aug. 1836. William King of Chipping Sodbury, labourer. Stealing a quantity of apples from an orchard at Chipping Sodbury, the property of John Watts. W. Blathwayt JP at Dodington. Hard labour for six calendar months in Horsley house of correction. Offence committed between 8 p.m. and 9 p.m. Monday 15 Aug. 1836.

56/A/7   15 Nov. 1836. George Gardner, Isaac Reeves and George Ames, labourers, of Iron Acton. Throwing stones and breaking a window and a door of labourer Samuel Organ's dwelling house at Iron Acton and endangering him and his family. Rev. M. F. T. Stephens JP at Thornbury. Fine 30/- and £1 12s. 3d. costs, all to be paid to the complainant, or hard labour for two calendar months in Lawfords Gate house of correction. Offence committed 12 Nov. 1836.

56/A/8   19 Nov. 1836. George Gardner of Iron Acton. Assaulting William Wain of Iron Acton, labourer. A. Carrick JP and M. F. T. Stephens JP at Thornbury. Fine £5, to be paid to Charles Gibbs, an overseer of the poor of Iron Acton, or two calendar months in Lawfords Gate house of correction. Offence committed 16 Nov. 1836.

56/A/9   3 Jan. 1837. William Cratchley of Stroud, labourer. Cutting down and stealing two beech trees at Stroud, valued at 10/-, the property of Samuel Copner, mealman, of Stonehouse. H. Burgh JP at Stroud. Fine £4 12s. 6d., to be paid to Charles Halliday, an overseer of the poor of Stroud, and 7/6 costs and 10/- damages to the complainant, or hard labour for two calendar months in Horsley house of correction. Offence committed 16 Dec. 1836.

56/A/10   30 Dec. 1836. Joseph Taylor of Stroud, labourer. Assaulting and beating Thomas Okey, cordwainer, of Stroud. H. Burgh JP and J. Mills JP at Stroud. Fine 10/-, to be paid to Charles Halliday, an overseer of the poor of Stroud, and 7/6 costs to the complainant, or two calendar months in Horsley house of correction. Offence committed 26 Dec. 1836.

56/A/11   30 Dec. 1836. William Williams of Stroud, labourer. Assaulting and beating Charles Gay, baker, of Stroud. H. Burgh JP and E. P. Caruthers JP at Stroud. Fine 10/-, to be paid to Charles Halliday, an overseer of the poor of Stroud, and 7/6 costs to the complainant, or one calendar month in Horsley house of correction. Offence committed 26 Dec. 1836.

56/A/12   30 Dec. 1836. Samuel Bassett, cordwainer, of Stroud. Refusing to maintain his wife and family, by means of labour and an annual pension, thereby causing them to become chargeable to Stroud parish. H. Burgh JP and J. Mills JP at Stroud. Hard labour for one calendar month in Horsley house of correction.

56/A/13   22 Dec. 1836. William Freeman of Bisley, labourer. Stealing a post, part of a bridge fence at Stroud, valued at 6d., the property of William Lewis Esq. H. Burgh JP at Stroud. Fine £1, to be paid to Charles Halliday, an overseer of the poor of Stroud, and 5/6 costs and 6d. damages to the complainant, or hard labour for three weeks in Horsley house of correction. Offence committed 22 Dec. 1836.

56/A/14   22 Dec. 1836. Charles Smith of Stroud, labourer. Cutting and stealing two beech trees at Stroud, the property of Samuel Copner, mealman, of Stonehouse. H. Burgh JP at Stroud. Fine £4 12s. 6d., to be paid to Charles Halliday, an overseer of the poor of Stroud, and 10/- damages and 7/6 costs to the complainant, or hard labour for two calendar months in Horsley house of correction. Offence committed 16 Dec. 1836.

56/A/15   23 Dec. 1836. John Aldridge and Reuben Davis, labourers, of Stroud. Damaging two trees at Stroud, the property of William and John Lewis Esqs. H. Burgh JP and E. G. Hallewell JP at Stroud. Fine 2d. damages and 11/- costs to be paid to the complainants, or hard labour for fourteen days in Horsley house of correction. Offence committed 20 Dec. 1836.

56/A/16   23 Dec. 1836. James Clift of Stroud, labourer. Damaging a wall on land occupied by Robert Keene, yeoman, at Stroud. H. Burgh JP at Stroud. Fine 6d., to be paid to Charles Halliday, an overseer of the poor of Stroud, and 2/- damages and 7/6 costs to the complainant, or hard labour for fourteen days in Horsley house of correction. Offence committed 18 Dec. 1836.

56/A/17   23 Dec. 1836. William Hill of Rodborough, clothworker. Stealing a rail from a garden fence, the property of John Webb, clothier, at Stroud. H. Burgh JP at Stroud. Fine 1/-, to be paid to Charles Halliday, an overseer of the poor of Stroud, and 6d. damages and 9/- costs to the complainant, or hard labour for one calendar month in Horsley house of correction. Offence committed 19 Dec. 1836.

56/A/18   2 Nov. 1836. William Heaven of King's Stanley, labourer. Stealing a bushel of apples growing in an orchard, the property of Thomas Thompson Gordon, yeoman, at King's

Stanley. H. Burgh JP at Stroud. Hard labour for six calendar months in Horsley house of correction. Offence committed 2 Nov. 1836.

56/A/19 4 Nov. 1836. John Rudge of Painswick labourer. Assaulting Mary [*surname not given*] at Painswick. H. Burgh JP and E. G. Hallewell JP at Stroud. Fine 12/6, to be paid to Nathaniel Iles Butler, an overseer of the poor of Painswick, and 7/6 costs, or one calendar month in Horsley house of correction. Offence committed 19 Oct. 1836.

56/A/20 4 Nov. 1836. Henry Smith, Henry Wood, William Proverbs, Samuel Beard and Charles Musty, labourers, of Painswick. Assaulting and beating Daniel Birt, labourer, of Painswick. H. Burgh JP and E. G. Hallewell JP at Stroud. Fine 5/-, to be paid to Nathaniel Iles Butler, an overseer of the poor of Painswick, and 20/- costs to the complainant, or one calendar month in Horsley house of correction. Offence committed 18 Oct. 1836.

56/A/21 4 Nov. 1836. Joseph Fawlkes and George Fawlkes of Bisley, yeomen. Assaulting and beating John Soul(e), yeoman, of Bisley. H. Burgh JP and H. Wyatt JP at Stroud. Fine 5/-, to be paid to Daniel Cox, an overseer of the poor of Bisley, and 11/- costs to the complainant, or one calendar month in Horsley house of correction. Offence committed 27 Oct. 1836.

56/A/22 18 Nov. 1836. William Munden, labourer, and Rebecca Munden, spinster, both of Bisley. Stealing half a peck of turnips growing in a close of land occupied by George Ridler, yeoman, at Stroud. H. Burgh JP and J. Mills JP at Stroud. Hard labour for one calendar month in Horsley house of correction. Offence committed 29 Oct. 1836.

56/A/23 25 Nov. 1836. Isaac Tanner of Bisley, labourer. Trespassing in search of conies on land occupied by Thomas and William Baker, gentlemen, at Bisley. H. Burgh JP and H. Wyatt JP at Stroud. Fine £1 8*s*. 6*d*., to be paid to Thomas Dickerson, an overseer of the poor of Bisley, and 11/6 costs to the complainants, or hard labour for two calendar months in Horsley house of correction. Offence committed 29 Oct. 1836.

56/A/24 25 Nov. 1836. George Butt of Bisley, labourer. Trespassing in search of conies [*etc., as* 56/A/23].

56/A/25 23 Sept. 1836. Thomas Smith. Rogue and vagabond, being in the dwelling house of William Dangerfield, coal dealer, at Stroud with intent to commit a felony. H. Burgh JP and J. Mills JP at Stroud. Hard labour for one calendar month in Horsley house of correction. Offence committed 22 Sept. 1836.

56/A/26 2 Dec. 1836. Philip Burdock of Painswick, labourer. Assaulting and beating Robert Whitcombe Constable, grocer, of Painswick. H. Burgh JP and E. P. Caruthers JP at Stroud. Fine 10/-, to be paid to William Rogers Poulton, an overseer of the poor of Painswick, and 7/6 costs to the complainant, or two calendar months in Horsley house of correction. Offence committed 5 Nov. 1836.

56/A/27 6 Dec. 1836. Daniel Baker of Bisley, labourer. Returning to Bisley without a certificate from churchwardens or overseers of the poor of any other parish, having been legally removed from there to Woodchester on the 1 Aug. 1836, that being his last place of settlement. H. Burgh JP at Stroud. Hard labour for one calendar month in Horsley house of correction.

57/A/28 23 Nov. 1836. John Stockwell of Stroud, labourer. Assaulting and beating Thomas Cratchley at Stroud. H. Burgh JP and P. Leversage JP at Stroud. Fine £5, to be paid to Charles Halliday, an overseer of the poor of Stroud, or two calendar months in Horsley house of correction. Offence committed 19 June 1836.

56/A/29   13 Dec. 1836. William Hall of Moreton in Marsh. Trespassing in search of game on Batsford land belonging to John, Lord Redesdale. Rev. J. R. Hall JP at Moreton in Marsh. Fine £1 7s., one moiety of which to be paid to Peter Brookes, gamekeeper, of Batsford, informer, and 13/- costs. The remainder to go to Thomas Horne, overseer of the poor of Batsford, or hard labour for two calendar months in Northleach house of correction. Offence committed 7 Dec. 1836.

56/A/30   13 Dec. 1836. John Hopkins of Moreton in Marsh, labourer. Assaulting James Careless at Moreton in Marsh. Rev. J. R. Hall JP and F. Colvile JP at Moreton in Marsh. Fine 5/-, to be paid to Thomas Horne, overseer of the poor, and 11/- costs to the complainant, or one calendar month in Gloucester house of correction. Offence committed 29 Nov. 1836.

56/A/31   13 Dec. 1836. William Parker of Moreton in Marsh. Using a gun for killing game without obtaining a game certificate, at Bourton on the Hill. Rev. J. R. Hall JP and F. Colvile JP at Moreton in Marsh. Fine £5, one moiety to go to Peter Brookes, gamekeeper, of Batsford, informer, in addition to 15/- costs, and the remainder to Thomas Horne, overseer of the poor, or hard labour for three calendar months in Gloucester house of correction. Offence committed 29 Nov. 1836.

56/A/32   19 Nov. 1836. John Corson and William Haiden. Using a snare to kill game at Coberley without a game certificate. Henry Elwes JP and Rev. W. Hicks JP at Coberley. Fine £5 or hard labour for six weeks in Northleach house of correction. Offence committed 19 Nov. 1836.

56/A/33   22 Oct. 1836. George Latham of Great Barrington, labourer. Using a certain engine to kill a hare without obtaining the required certificate. R. W. Ford JP at Bourton-on-the-Water. Fine £20. [*Endorsed*:] Registered this 21 Nov. 1836 pursuant to 52 Geo. III, cap. 93.

56/A/34   22 Oct. 1836. James Parker of Great Barrington. Using a certain engine to kill a hare [*etc., as* 56/A/33, *including endorsement*].

56/A/35   22 Oct. 1836. Henry Parker of Great Barrington, labourer. Using a certain engine to kill a hare [*etc., as* 56/A/33, *including endorsement*].

56/A/36   26 Nov. 1836. William Richardson of Cheltenham, alehouse keeper. Permitting gaming and other disorderly conduct in his house. Rev. W. Hicks JP and W. S. Evans JP. First offence. Fine 20/-, one moiety to go to Robert Green, the prosecutor, with 6/- costs, and the remainder to the county treasurer. Offence committed 23 Nov. 1836.

56/A/37   5 Dec. 1836. John Cowmeadow. Assaulting and beating Ann Jones at Cheltenham. J. C. Smith JP and S. Gale JP at Cheltenham. Fine 5/-, to be paid to an overseer of the poor, and 5/- costs to the complainant. Offence committed 4 Dec. 1836.

56/A/38   10 Dec. 1836. Susan Hopkins. Assaulting and beating Margaretta Sutton at Cheltenham. D. L. St. Clair JP and S. Gale JP at Cheltenham. Fine 5/-, to be paid to an overseer of the poor, and 8/- costs to the complainant. Offence committed 6 Dec. 1836.

56/A/39   12 Dec. 1836. Isaac Packwood. Assaulting and beating Enoch Dyer at Cheltenham. R. B. Cooper JP and S. Gale JP at Cheltenham. Fine 20/-, to be paid to an overseer of the poor, and 4/- costs to the complainant. Offence committed 10 Dec. 1836.

56/A/40   15 Dec. 1836. Samuel Davison. Trespassing in search of game in a close at Arle possessed by Thomas Freeman. R. B. Cooper JP and J. C. Smith JP at Cheltenham. Fine 40/-, to be paid to an overseer of the poor, and 6/- costs to the complainant. Offence committed 12 Dec. 1836.

56/A/41   19 Dec. 1836. John Wilson. Assaulting and beating Edmund Langley at Cheltenham. R. B. Cooper JP and J. C. Smith JP at Cheltenham. Fine 2/-, to be paid to an overseer of the poor, and 7/- costs to the complainant. Offence committed 8 Dec. 1836.

56/A/42   19 Dec. 1836. Edward Maclean. Assaulting and beating Charles Maclean at Cheltenham. R. B. Cooper JP and D. L. St. Clair JP at Cheltenham. Fine 5/-, to be paid to an overseer of the poor, and 7/- costs to the complainant. Offence committed 17 Dec. 1836.

56/A/43   24 Dec. 1836. Christopher Walter, alehouse keeper, of Prestbury. Permitting disorderly conduct in his house. R. B. Cooper JP and S. Gale JP at Cheltenham. First offence. Fine 40/-, one moiety to be paid Samuel Tarling, the prosecutor, and the other moiety to the county treasurer. Costs assessed at 7/-. Offence committed 18 Dec. 1836.

56/A/44   24 Dec. 1836. William Johnson. Assaulting and beating Edward Matthews at Cheltenham. R. B. Cooper JP and S. Gale JP at Cheltenham. Fine 20/- and 6/- costs or one calendar month in house Northleach of correction. Offence committed 22 Dec. 1836.

56/A/45   24 Dec. 1836. William Johnson. Assaulting and beating Eliza Davis at Cheltenham. R. B. Cooper JP and S. Gale JP at Cheltenham. Fine 20/- and 4/- costs or two calendar months in Northleach house of correction. Offence committed 22 Dec. 1836.

56/A/46   31 Oct. 1836. George Mullis. Trespassing in search of game at Prestbury in a close of land possessed by Richard Thornton. R. B. Cooper JP and S. Gale JP at Cheltenham. Fine 10/-, to be paid to an overseer of the poor of Prestbury, and 11/- costs to the complainant. Offence committed 24 Oct. 1836.

56/A/47   31 Oct. 1836. James Langston. Trespassing in search of game at Prestbury in a close of land possessed by Richard Thornton. R. B. Cooper JP and S. Gale JP at Cheltenham. Fine 10/-, to be paid to an overseer of the poor of Prestbury, and 11/- costs to the complainant. Offence committed 24 Oct. 1836.

56/A/48   2 Jan. 1837. George Hawker. Assaulting and beating Deborah Webb at Bishop's Cleeve. R. B. Cooper JP and J. C. Smith JP at Cheltenham. Fine 5/-, to be paid to an overseer of the poor, and 9/6 costs to the complainant. Offence committed 30 Dec. 1836.

56/A/49   24 Oct. 1836. Samuel Smith of Charlton Kings, hurdle maker. Assaulting and beating Harriett Banbury at Cheltenham. R. B. Cooper JP and S. Gale JP at Cheltenham. Fine 10/-, to be paid to an overseer of the poor, and 5/- costs to the complainant. Offence committed 17 Oct. 1836.

56/A/50   2 Nov. 1836. George Golding, licensed beer and cider retailer, of Cheltenham. Permitting disorderly conduct within his house. R. B. Cooper JP and S. Gale JP at Cheltenham. First offence. Fine 40/-; one moiety to be paid to William Woolley, the prosecutor, and the other moiety to the county treasurer. Costs assessed at 7/-. Offence committed 29 Oct. 1836.

56/A/51   7 Nov. 1836. William Arkell. Assaulting and beating Priscilla Smith at Cheltenham. R. B. Cooper JP and J. C. Smith JP at Cheltenham. Fine 10/-, to be paid to an overseer of the poor, and 7/- costs to the complainant. Offence committed 4 Nov. 1836.

56/A/52   10 Nov. 1836. Thomas Mitchell. Assaulting and beating Henry Pates at Charlton Kings. R. B. Cooper JP and S. Gale JP at Cheltenham. Fine 5/-, to be paid to an overseer of the poor, and 5/- costs to the complainant. Offence committed 5 Nov. 1836.

56/A/53   10 Nov. 1836. Thomas Powis. Assaulting and beating Henry Pates at Charlton Kings [etc., as 56/A/52].

56/A/54   12 Nov. 1836. William Johnson. Assaulting and beating Martha Merrett at Cheltenham. R. B. Cooper JP and D. L. St. Clair JP at Cheltenham. Fine 5/-, to be paid to an overseer of the poor, and 7/- costs to the complainant. Offence committed 8 Nov. 1836.

56/A/55   24 Nov. 1836. William Onion. Assaulting and beating John Ricketts at Cowley. W. S. Evans JP and S. Gale JP at Cheltenham. Fine 10/-, to be paid to an overseer of the poor, and 11/- costs to the complainant. Offence committed 15 Nov. 1836.

56/A/56 10 Nov. 1836. William Quarrington. Stealing a fence stake from a fir plantation at Woodchester, the property of Thomas Reddall Haycock Esq. T. Kingscote JP and D. Ricardo JP at Horsley. Fine £2 10s., to be paid to William Tiley, an overseer of the poor, 4/6 costs to William Beard, labourer, of Woodchester, and 1/- damages to T. R. Haycock Esq., or hard labour for one calendar month in Horsley house of correction. Offence committed 6 Nov. 1836.

56/A/57 10 Nov. 1836. Thomas Fords. Stealing a fence stake from a fir plantation at Woodchester [etc., as 56/A/56 except] Fine £4 10s. [and] hard labour for two calendar months.

56/A/58 23 Nov. 1836. Benjamin Jones. Stealing a fence stake from a fir plantation at Woodchester, the property of Thomas Reddall Haycock Esq. O. P. Wathen JP at Woodchester. Fine £2 10s., to be paid to William Tiley [etc., as 56/A/56].

56/A/59 13 Oct. 1836. Henry Lyes and George Hall of Overbury, Worcs., and Richard Pugh of Kemerton, labourers. Bursting into George Webb's house at Kemerton and assaulting him and William Franklin and Thomas Williams, and threatening to murder them. J. Timbrill D.D. JP and J. W. Martin JP at Tewkesbury. Fine £4 12s. each, to be paid to John Lucas Cox, overseer of the poor of Kemerton, and 8/- each costs to the complainants. Offence committed 9 p.m. Friday 7 Oct. 1836. [Endorsed:] 13 Oct. 1836, offenders committed to Northleach house of correction for two calendar months in default of payment of fines.

56/A/60 27 Oct. 1836. William Crisp of Aston on Carrant, Ashchurch, labourer. Assaulting and beating with a whip Anna Halling and her mother Matilda in the courtyard of the premises occupied by her father John Halling at Aston on Carrant. J. Timbrill D.D. JP, and J. W. Martin JP at Tewkesbury. Fine 1/-, to be paid to William Edwards, an overseer of the poor of Ashchurch, and 8/- costs to Anna Halling. Offence committed 25 Oct., 1836. [Endorsed:] Offender committed to Northleach house of correction 27 Oct. 1836 for two calendar months in default of payment of fines.

56/A/61 10 Nov. 1836. Richard Robbins of Walton Hill, Deerhurst, labourer. Stealing a quantity of wooden railing, the property of John Allis Hartland of Tewkesbury, tanner, from a field called the Gaston at Deerhurst occupied by Simeon Warder, farmer. J. Timbrill D.D. JP and J. W. Martin JP at Tewkesbury. Fine 10/-, to be paid to Isaac Bloxham, an overseer of the poor of Deerhurst, and 12/4 costs to the complainant. Offence committed Monday 7 Nov. 1836.

56/A/62 1 Dec. 1836. John Lewis. Stealing a quantity of apples growing in a garden at Painswick, the property of Robert Lawrence Townsend Esq. H. Burgh JP at Stroud. Hard labour for fourteen days in Horsley house of correction. Offence committed 27 Nov. 1836.

56/A/63 2 Nov. 1836. Sarah Cook. Stealing a quantity of potatoes growing on enclosed land at Stonehouse, the property of Samuel Lawrence. R. S. Davies JP at Stonehouse. Fine 5/-, to be paid to an overseer of the poor, and 7/6 costs and 3d. damages to the complainant, or hard labour for one calendar month in Horsley house of correction. Offence committed 18 Oct. 1836.

56/A/64 29 Oct. 1836. William Smith. Stealing a quantity of potatoes growing on enclosed land at Stonehouse, the property of Henry Harrison. R. S. Davies JP at Stonehouse. Fine £1 and 1/- damages, to be paid to an overseer of the poor, and 6/- costs to the complainant, or hard labour for one calendar month in Horsley house of correction. Offence committed 19 Oct. 1836.

56/A/65 29 Oct. 1836. William Smith. Cutting and damaging apple trees in an orchard at Stonehouse, the property of Reuben Hyde. R. S. Davies JP at Stonehouse. Fine £2 and 10/- damages, to be paid to an overseer of the poor, and 6/- costs to the complainant, or hard labour for two calendar months in Horsley house of correction. Offence committed 28 July 1836.

56/A/66   29 Nov. 1836. John White. Trespassing in search of game on land occupied by William Trotman Wherrett, the property of Frederick Eycott, called Dudbridge Close, at Stonehouse. T. J. Lloyd Baker JP and H. C. Clifford JP at Wheatenhurst. Fine £2, to be paid to an overseer of the poor, and 8/4 costs to the complainant, or two calendar months in Horsley house of correction. Offence committed 7 Nov. 1836.

56/A/67   25 Oct. 1836. George Lander. Trespassing in search of game on land at Frampton on Severn called Lower Lord's Meadow occupied by Susannah Browning, the property of Henry Clifford Clifford Esq. T. J. Lloyd Baker JP and P. Leversage JP at Wheatenhurst. Fine £1 and 7/10 costs or one calendar month in Horsley house of correction. Offence committed 3 Oct. 1836.

56/A/68   25 Oct. 1836. George Lander. Trespassing in search of game on land at Frampton on Severn called the Lower Town Fields occupied by Joseph Barrett, the property of Samuel Peach Peach Esq. T. J. Lloyd Baker JP and P. Leversage JP at Wheatenhurst. Fine £1 and 9/10 costs or one calendar month in Horsley house of correction. Offence committed 3 Oct. 1836.

56/A/69   25 Oct. 1836. George Long. Attempting to take fish from a stretch of the Stroudwater canal at Frampton [on Severn], the private property of George Hawker, clerk to the Stroudwater Canal Navigation Company. T. J. Lloyd Baker JP and P. Leversage JP at Wheatenhurst. Fine 1/- and 8/10 costs. Offence committed 21 Sept. 1836.

56/A/70   21 June 1836. John Harrison, stonemason, of King's Stanley. Refusing to pay wages owing to John Garns, journeyman stonemason. T. J. Lloyd Baker JP and R. S. Davies JP at Wheatenhurst. Amount of wages owed, £3 12s. 9d. (at a rate of 2/6 per day), and 7/6 costs. No goods or chattels on which to raise money. Two calendar months in county gaol.

56/A/71   27 Dec. 1836. John Hardwick of Alvington, farmer. Being drunk. C. Bathurst JP at Lydney. Fine 5/-.

56/A/72   20 Dec. 1836. Samuel Mann of Tetbury, mason. Trespassing at night with a dog and three nets with intent to take and kill game on enclosed land at Beverstone occupied by Mr Jacob Hayward. T. G. B. Estcourt JP and W. M. Paul JP. Hard labour for one calendar month in Horsley house of correction, after which to find sureties totalling £20 against re-offending for one year. In default, a further six calendar months' hard labour. Offence committed 13 Dec. 1836.

56/A/73   12 Oct. 1836. Henry Jones. Assaulting Joseph Harbour at Bromsberrow. Rev. J. Higgins JP and O. Ricardo JP at Ledbury, Herefs. Fine 5/- and 10/- costs or one calendar month in Littledean house of correction. Fine paid. Offence committed 3 Oct. 1836.

56/A/74   6 July 1836. Daniel Pincham. Assaulting William Hartland at Preston. Rev. J. Higgins JP and O. Ricardo JP at Ledbury, Herefs. Fine 12/- and 8/- costs or one calendar month in Littledean house of correction. Fine paid. Offence committed 4 July 1836.

56/A/75   21 Dec. 1836. John Hodges. Trespassing in a garden at Dymock and cutting and damaging cabbages and other greens, the property of Joseph Daw. Rev. J. Higgins JP at Ledbury, Herefs. Fine 10/- and 7/6 costs or two calendar months in Littledean house of correction. Fine paid. Offence committed 22 Oct. 1836.

56/A/76   18 Nov. 1836. William Brooks of Hawkesbury, labourer. Trespassing on a field called the First Slait adjoining Bodkin Wood at Horton, occupied by Edward Sidney, and setting up a wire for killing game. C. W. [*reading uncertain*] Codrington JP and W. Blathwayt JP. Peter May, gamekeeper to the duke of Beaufort at Badminton, informer. John Green of

Hawkesbury, witness. Offender admitted charge. Fine £1, one moiety of which to be paid to the overseer of the poor of Horton, and the remainder with 12/6 costs to the informer, to be paid before 1 Dec. 1836, or one calendar month in Horsley house of correction. Offence committed about 7 p.m. 4 Oct. 1836.

56/A/77   5 Dec. 1836. George Marsh of Wick and Abson, labourer. Using a gun and a dog in a game preserve at Wapley and Codrington, firing the gun and having a pheasant in his pocket without possessing a game certificate. Henry, duke of Beaufort, JP and Lord Robert Edward Henry Somerset JP at Badminton. Edmund Webb of Badminton, complainant. William Dance, gamekeeper to Sir C B Codrington, Bt., of Dodington, witness. Fine £5, one moiety of which to be paid to an overseer of the poor, and the remainder with 14/- costs to the complainant, or three calendar months in Horsley house of correction. Offence committed at about 1 o'clock, 5 Dec. 1836.

56/A/78   2 Dec. 1836. John Wait of Chipping Sodbury, licensed beer and cider retailer. Keeping his premises open until almost 11 p.m. and allowing seven persons, two of whom were prostitutes, to play illegal card games such as All Fours. W. Blathwayt JP and R. H. B. Hale JP at a Petty Sessions for Grumbalds Ash district. First offence. George Rice, constable, and Henry Watts, labourer, both of Chipping Sodbury, prosecutor and witness. First offence. Fine £2 10*s.*, one moiety of which to be paid to the prosecutor and the remainder to the county treasurer. Costs assessed at 7/-. Offence committed Monday 21 Nov. 1836.

56/B/1   2 Jan. 1837. George Hawker. Assaulting and beating Deborah Webb at Bishop's Cleeve. R. B. Cooper JP and J. C. Smith JP at Cheltenham. Fine 5/- and 9/6 costs. Offence committed 30 Dec. 1836.

56/B/2   12 Jan. 1837. Edward Marden. Assaulting and beating James Tarling at Cheltenham. R. B. Cooper JP and D. L. St. Clair JP at Cheltenham. Fine 5/- and 6/- costs. Offence committed 10 Jan. 1837.

56/B/3   14 Jan. 1837. Thomas Matty. Assaulting Mary Lawrence at Cheltenham. J. C. Smith JP and Joseph Overbury JP at Cheltenham. Fine 40/- and 9/- costs or one calendar month in Northleach house of correction. Offence committed 10 Jan. 1837.

56/B/4   23 Jan. 1837. James Martin, licensed ale retailer, of Cheltenham. Keeping his house open at unlawful hours. R. B. Cooper JP and D. L. St. Clair JP. First offence. Fine 10/-, one moiety to be paid to the county treasurer and the remainder to John Russell, the informer. Offence committed 16 Jan. 1837.

56/B/5   28 Jan. 1837. William Baker. Assaulting and beating Anthony Gardner at Cheltenham. J. C. Smith JP and D. L. St. Clair JP at Cheltenham. Fine £4 and £1 costs. Offence committed 11 Jan. 1837.

56/B/6   13 Feb. 1837. Robert Roff. Assaulting John Russell at Cheltenham. R. B. Cooper JP and J. C. Smith JP at Cheltenham. Fine 10/- and 5/6 costs or two calendar months in Northleach house of correction. Offence committed 11 Feb. 1837.

56/B/7   18 Feb. 1837. John Carey of Cheltenham, licensed beer and cider retailer. Permitting disorderly conduct in his house. R. B. Cooper JP and D. L. St. Clair JP. First offence. Fine 40/-, half of which to be paid to the county treasurer and the remainder to John Russell, informer. Costs assessed at 7/-. Offence committed 13 Jan. 1837. [*Signed by* J. Overbury *instead of* D. L. St. Clair.]

56/B/8   25 Feb. 1837. Thomas Davison. Assaulting and beating William Shaw at Cheltenham. R. B. Cooper JP and J. Overbury JP at Cheltenham. Fine 2 guineas and 7/6 costs or two calendar months in Northleach house of correction. Offence committed 23 Feb. 1837.

56/B/9   25 Feb. 1837. William Sewell [*reading uncertain*, ? Jewell]. Assaulting and beating William Shaw at Cheltenham. R. B. Cooper JP and J. Overbury JP at Cheltenham. Fine £4 and £1 costs or two calendar months in Northleach house of correction. Offence committed 23 Feb. 1837.

56/B/10   25 Feb. 1837. James Wood. Assaulting and beating William Shaw [*etc.*, *as* 56/B/9].

56/B/11   4 March 1837. John Mann. Assaulting and beating Sophia Ingram at Charlton Kings. R. B. Cooper JP and J. C. Smith JP at Cheltenham. Fine 20/- and 11/- costs. Offence committed 27 Feb. 1837.

56/B/12   4 March 1837. George Mann. Assaulting and beating Sophia Ingram [*etc.*, *as* 56/B/11 *except*]. Fine 40/- and 11/- costs.

56/B/13   13 March 1837. William Pratt licensed beer and cider retailer of Cheltenham. Permitting gambling in his house. R. B. Cooper JP and J. C. Smith JP. First offence. Fine 40/-; half to be paid to the county treasurer and half to John Scott, witness. Costs assessed at 7/-. Offence committed 10 March 1837.

56/B/14   2 March 1837. Samuel Molton of Cheltenham, coach driver. Neglecting to account for a 2/- fare from Cheltenham to Cirencester. J. Overbury JP at Cheltenham. Thomas Haines his employer, complainant. Fine £5, mitigated to £2 10*s*., half of which to be paid to the Clerk of the Peace, and the remainder with 12/6 costs to the complainant. Offence committed 21 Feb. 1837.

56/B/15   24 Jan. 1837. James Dowle of Aylburton. Assaulting John Harris of Aylburton. C. Bathurst JP and G. Ormerod JP at Lydney in the Forest division. Fine 1/- and 7/6 costs or seven days in Littledean house of correction. Offence committed 21 Jan. 1837.

56/B/16   24 Jan. 1837. William Cooke of Alvington. Violently assaulting Henry Hardwicke of Alvington. C. Bathurst JP and Rev. C. H. Morgan JP at Lydney in the Forest division. Fine 2/6 and 7/6 costs or fourteen days in Littledean house of correction. Offence committed 14 Jan. 1837.

56/B/17   24 Jan. 1837. Sarah Williams of Alvington. Stealing a quantity of turnips, the property of Thomas Dowle of Alvington. C. Bathurst JP and G. Ormerod JP at Lydney in the Forest division. Fine 20/-, 1/- (the value of the turnips) and 9/- costs or one calendar month in Littledean house of correction. Offence committed 8 Jan. 1837.

56/B/18   7 Jan. 1837. William Werrett, innkeeper, of Frampton Cotterell. Trespassing in pursuit of game at Olveston, on land the property of Samuel Peach Peach Esq. of Tockington. Dr. A. Carrick JP and Rev. M. F. T. Stephens JP at Thornbury. James Wright, gamekeeper, agent for S. P. Peach Esq., complainant. Fine 10/-, to be paid to Richard Russell, an overseer of the poor of Olveston, and 7/- costs to the complainant, or fourteen days in Lawfords Gate house of correction. Offence committed about 3 p.m. Wednesday 14 Dec. 1836.

56/B/19   7 Jan. 1837. William Werrett, innkeeper, of Frampton Cotterell. Trespassing in pursuit of game at Olveston [*etc.*, *as* 56/B/18 *except*] Offence committed at about 2.30 pm. Wednesday 21 Dec. 1836.

56/B/20   4 Feb. 1837. John Smith the younger, licensed beer and cider retailer, of Thornbury. Opening his beerhouse before 1 p.m. on a Sunday, i.e. between 11 a.m. and noon, and allowing drunkenness. Dr. A. Carrick JP and Rev. M. F. T. Stephens JP at a Petty Sessions for Thornbury division. First offence. Fine 40/- and 6/6 costs. Offence committed Sunday 1 Jan. 1837.

56/B/21   1 April 1837. John Wilcox, innkeeper, of the Bowl inn, Almondsbury. Keeping his premises open other than for the reception of travellers and allowing drunkenness, i.e.

during the hours of divine service at the parish church, 11 a.m. – 1 p.m. Dr. A. Carrick JP and Rev. M. F. T. Stephens JP. First offence. Fine 20/- and 10/10 costs. Offence committed Sunday 12 Feb. 1837.

56/B/22 12 Jan. 1837. David Lockhart of Twyning, labourer. Assaulting John Scudder, labourer, of Twyning at Brockeridge Common without provocation. J. Timbrill D.D. JP and J. W. Martin JP at Tewkesbury. Fine 10/-, to be paid to Thomas Allard, overseer of the poor of Twyning, and 15/- costs to the complainant. Offence committed Thursday 5 Jan. 1837. [*Note*:] Received of Mr. White. E.B. [*i.e.* Edward Bloxsome].

56/B/23 27 Feb. 1837. John Butler of Bisley, labourer. Stealing about four yards of fence or hedge, the property of George Ridler, yeoman, of Stroud. H. Burgh JP and E. P. Caruthers JP at Stroud. Fine 10/-, to be paid to William Fisher, overseer of the poor; and 9/- costs and 1/6 damages to the complainant, or hard labour for one calendar month in Horsley house of correction. Offence committed 22 Feb. 1837.

56/B/24 13 March 1837. Eli Butler and William Smith of Bisley, labourers. Stealing about four yards of fence or hedge, the property of George Ridler, yeoman, of Stroud. H. Burgh JP at Stroud [*etc., as* 56/B/23 *except*] 7/6 costs.

56/B/25 13 March 1837. Samuel Smith of Stroud, labourer. Cutting down and stealing three trees growing in a wood at Standish, the property of the Rt. Hon. John, Lord Sherborne. H. Burgh JP at Stroud. Fine 10/-, 7/6 costs and 1/6 damages or hard labour for two calendar months in Horsley house of correction. Offence committed 28 Jan. 1837.

56/B/26 27 Feb. 1837. Joseph Gardner of Bisley, labourer. Stealing two yards of fence or hedge, the property of Jeremiah Restall, timber merchant, of Bisley. H. Burgh JP and E. P. Caruthers JP at Stroud. Fine 10/-, to be paid to Thomas Dickerson, overseer of the poor, and 9/- costs and 1/- damages to the complainant, or hard labour for one calendar month in Horsley house of correction. Complainant examined on oath as to proof of offence. Offence committed 17 Feb. 1837.

56/B/27 17 Feb. 1837. Enoch Deane of Bisley, labourer. Cutting and stealing underwood at Bisley, the property of Edmund Clutterbuck, gentleman, of Avening. H. Burgh JP and E. P. Caruthers JP at Stroud. Fine £1, to be paid to Thomas Dickerson, overseer of the poor, and 9/- costs and 1/- damages to the complainant, or hard labour for one calendar month in Horsley house of correction. Offence committed 17 Feb. 1837.

56/B/28 3 Feb. 1837 [*MS.* 1836]. Eli and Miles Daniels of Stroud, labourers. Assaulting and beating Joseph Hunt, labourer, of Minchinhampton at Stroud. H. Burgh JP and E. G. Hallewell JP at Stroud. Fine £4, to be paid to William Fisher, overseer of the poor, or two calendar months in Horsley house of correction. Offence committed 26 Jan. 1837.

56/B/29 6 Jan. 1837. Peter Arkwell of Stroud, millwright. Trespassing in pursuit of game in enclosed land occupied by William Capel Esq. at Painswick. H. Burgh JP and E. G. Hallewell JP at Stroud. Fine £2, to be paid to Nathaniel Iles Butler, overseer of the poor, and 12/6 costs to the complainants, or hard labour for two months in Horsley house of correction. Offence committed 25 Dec. 1836.

56/B/30 7 Feb. 1837. Eliza wife of Samuel Trotman, labourer, William Ansloe, labourer, Rachel Davis, single woman, Sarah Baker, single woman, and Elizabeth Liddiatt, single woman, all of Bisley. Stealing three bushels of turnips growing in a field at Bisley, the property of Thomas Blanch, yeoman. H. Burgh JP at Stroud. Hard labour for one calendar month in Horsley house of correction. Offence committed 5 Feb. 1837.

56/B/31 27 Jan. 1837. Thomas Parsons of Stroud, accountant [*MS.* accomptant]. Assaulting and beating Nathaniel Partridge, dyer, of Stroud. H. Burgh JP, E. P. Caruthers JP and E. G.

Hallewell JP at Stroud. Fine 2/6, to be paid to William Fisher, overseer of the poor, and 11/6 cost, or fourteen days in Horsley house of correction. Offence committed 18 Jan. 1837.

56/B/32 28 Feb. 1837. William Horton of Minchinhampton, labourer. Cutting down and stealing a tree growing in a plantation at Minchinhampton, the property of Robert Snow Paul Esq. H. Burgh JP at Stroud. Fine 5/-, 1/- damages and 7/6 costs or hard labour for five weeks in Horsley house of correction. Offence committed 24 Feb. 1837.

56/B/33 3 Feb. 1837. James Pearce the younger of Randwick, labourer. Stealing two yards of dead fence from enclosed arable land at Standish, the property of yeoman Edward Page. H. Burgh JP and E. G. Hallewell JP at Stroud. Fine £2, 1/- damages and 7/6 costs or hard labour for two calendar months in Horsley house of correction. Offence committed 23 Jan. 1837.

56/B/34 10 April 1837. William Cratchley of Stroud, labourer. Assaulting and beating William Pitt, labourer, of Stroud. H. Burgh JP and H. Wyatt JP at Stroud. Fine £4 12s. 6d., to be paid to William Ponting, overseer of the poor and 7/6 costs, or two calendar months in Horsley house of correction. Offence committed 7 April 1837.

56/B/35 23 Dec. 1836. William Hall. Trespassing in an enclosure at Sezincote and killing a pheasant. Rev. J. R. Hall JP and Rev. C. Jeaffreson JP at Moreton in Marsh. Hard labour for three calendar months in Northleach house of correction, after which to find sureties totalling £20 against re-offending for one year. In default, a further six calendar months' hard labour. Offence committed at about 2 a.m. 23 Dec. 1836.

56/B/36 24 Jan. 1837. John Pullam of Moreton in Marsh, labourer. Assaulting and beating George Millington at Moreton in Marsh. Rev. J. R. Hall JP and Rev. C. Jeaffreson JP at Moreton in Marsh. Fine £1, to be paid to Thomas Horne, an overseer of the poor, and 10/- costs to the complainant, or one calendar month in Northleach house of correction. Offence committed 23 Jan. 1837.

56/B/37 24 Jan. 1837. Robert Coles of Bourton on the Hill. Assaulting and beating Charles Bennett at Bourton on the Hill. Rev. J. R. Hall JP and Rev. C. Jeaffreson JP at Moreton in Marsh. Fine 17/-, to be paid to John Gardner, overseer of the poor, and 11/- costs to the complainant, or one calendar month in Northleach house of correction. Offence committed 3 Jan. 1837.

56/C/1 18 April 1837. Richard James. Assaulting Thomas Jolly at Lydney. C. Bathurst JP and Rev. C. H. Morgan JP at Lydney in the Forest division. Fine 5/- and 7/- costs or fourteen days in Littledean house of correction. Offence committed 12 April 1837.

56/C/2 18 April 1837. John Hardwick. Assaulting Mary Ward at Alvington. C. Bathurst JP and Rev. C. H. Morgan JP at Lydney in the Forest division. Fine 5/- and 7/- costs or fourteen days in Littledean house of correction. Offence committed 1 April 1837.

56/C/3 18 April 1837. Thomas Prosser. Assaulting William Ellway at Alvington. C. Bathurst JP and Rev. C. H. Morgan JP at Lydney in the Forest division. Fine 5/- and 10/- costs or fourteen days in Littledean house of correction. Offence committed 26 March 1837.

56/C/4 30 May 1837. William Chivers. Assaulting Decima Hamblin at Coleford. E. Machen JP and P. J. Ducarel JP at Coleford in the Forest division. Fine 7/6 and 7/- costs or hard labour for fourteen days in Littledean house of correction. Offence committed 17 May 1837.

56/C/5 30 May 1837. Thomas Lewis. Assaulting John White at Lydney. E. Machen JP and P. J. Ducarel JP at Coleford in the Forest division. Fine 1/- and 7/6 costs or hard labour for seven days in Littledean house of correction. Offence committed 18 May 1837.

56/C/6   12 June 1837. Robert Hathaway. Stealing a quantity of vetches at Churcham, the property of Elizabeth Elliott. Rev. C. Crawley JP and J. Pyrke JP at Newnham in the Forest division. Fine 10/- and 7/6 costs or hard labour for fourteen days in Littledean house of correction. Offence committed 1 June 1837.

56/C/7   12 June 1837. William Lloyd. Assaulting constable Philip Glastonbury while in the execution of his duty at Littledean. Rev. C. Crawley JP and J. Pyrke JP at Newnham in the Forest division. Fine 20/- and 7/6 costs or hard labour for one month in Littledean house of correction. Offence committed 6 June 1837.

56/C/8   16 May 1837. Thomas Ward. Assaulting Sarah Cooke at Alvington. C. Bathurst JP and Rev. C. H. Morgan JP at Lydney. Fine 2/6 and 7/- costs or one week in Littledean house of correction. Offence committed 26 April 1837.

56/C/9   16 May 1837. William Williams. Assaulting John Stidder at Alvington. C. Bathurst JP and Rev. C. H. Morgan JP at Lydney. Fine 5/- and 7/- costs or fourteen days in Littledean house of correction. Offence committed 26 April 1837.

56/C/10 5 Dec. 1836. Joseph Smith *alias* Thurston. Stealing turnips growing on enclosed land, the property of James Fishpool, at Taynton. R. F. Onslow JP at Newent. Fine 5/- and 3*d.* (the value of the turnips), to be paid to an overseer of the poor, and 8/- costs to the complainant, who was examined as to proof of the offence, or fourteen days in Littledean house of correction. Offence committed 25 Nov. 1836.

56/C/11 17 Oct. 1836. Thomas [*later in the document named as* John] Underwood, labourer, of Dymock. Damaging a gate leading to common pound at Dymock, the property of Thomas Barnes at Dymock. R. F. Onslow JP at Newent. Fine £1, to be paid to the overseer of the poor, £1 costs and 1/6 damages to the complainant, who was not examined as to proof of offence, or one calendar month's hard labour in Littledean house of correction. Offence committed 16 Oct. 1836.

56/C/12 5 May 1837. Stephen Young of Chipping Sodbury, labourer. Trespassing with a gun in search of game on land called the Upper Three Acres, the Long Ground and Broad Marsh at Dodington, occupied by Richard Hobbs. W. Blathwayt JP and A. Shakespear JP. Henry Martin, gamekeeper, of Dodington, complainant. James Neale, witness. Offender admitted charge. Fine £2, one moiety of which to be paid to the overseer of the poor and the remainder with 12/6 costs to be paid to the complainant within three weeks. In default, two calendar months in Horsley house of correction. Offence committed between 4 p.m. and 5 p.m. Tuesday 14 March 1837.

56/C/13 20 May 1837. Edmund Green, labourer, of Withington. Assaulting Mary Slade at Withington. G. G. C. Talbot JP and W. L. Lawrence JP at Andoversford. Fine £2, to be paid to John Field, overseer of the poor of Withington, and 7/6 costs to the complainant within seven days, or two calendar months in Northleach house of correction. Offence committed Wednesday 17 May 1837. [*Note on back*:] Offender absconded and fine not paid.

56/C/14 5 May 1837. George Kendle of Chipping Sodbury, labourer. Trespassing with a gun, in company with Stephen Young, on land at Dodington called the Upper Three Acres, Broad Marsh and the Long Ground, occupied by Richard Hobbs. W. Blathwayt JP and A. Shakespear JP at Chipping Sodbury. Henry Martin, gamekeeper, of Dodington, complainant. James Neale, witness. Offender admitted charge. Fine 10/- and 12/6 costs, to be paid within three weeks, or one calendar month in Horsley house of correction. Offence committed between 4 p.m. and 5 p.m. Tuesday 14 March 1837.

56/C/15 27 May 1837. Elizabeth Mayer. Failing to maintain herself and two children by work, thereby becoming chargeable to Bisley parish. H. Burgh JP and H. Wyatt JP. Hard labour for one calendar month in Horsley house of correction. Offence committed within the previous three months.

56/C/16 11 April 1837. James Eddles. Being in an outhouse belonging to James Clutterbuck Esq. at Minchinhampton with intent to commit a felony. H. Burgh JP at Rodborough. Hard labour for three calendar months in Horsley house of correction. Offence committed 11 April 1837.

56/C/17 8 May 1837. Robert Brown. Begging in Stroud. E. P. Caruthers JP and H. Wyatt JP at Stroud. Hard labour for one calendar month in Horsley house of correction. Offence committed 7 May 1837.

56/C/18 2 June 1837. Deborah wife of Samuel Butler, labourer, and Jemima Warren, single woman, all of Bisley. Damaging a tree growing in a wood at Stroud, the property of John and William Lewis. H. Burgh JP, E. P. Caruthers JP and E. G. Hallewell JP at Stroud. Fine 10/6 and 6d. damages to be paid to the complainants, or hard labour for one calendar month in Horsley house of correction. Offence committed 26 May 1837.

56/C/19 2 June 1837. Mary wife of Alfred March, labourer, and Emma Mason, single woman, all of Bisley. Stealing part of a fence from a field at Bisley, the property of yeoman John Stafford. H. Burgh JP, E. P. Caruthers JP and E. G. Hallewell JP at Stroud. Fine 6d., to be paid to William Long, overseer of the poor, and 6d. damages and 10/6 costs to the complainant, or hard labour for one calendar month in Horsley house of correction. Offence committed 20 May 1837.

56/C/20 21 June 1837. William Stephens of Rodborough, labourer. Cutting down and stealing sixty trees growing in a wood at Woodchester, the property of the Rt. Hon. Thomas, earl of Ducie. H. Burgh JP, E. P. Caruthers JP and E. G. Hallewell JP at Stroud. Fine £2, to be paid to the overseer of the poor, and 1/6 damages and 7/6 costs to Lord Ducie, or hard labour for six weeks in Horsley house of correction. Offence committed 17 June 1837.

56/C/21 17 June 1837. John Merchant and Daniel Gardner, labourers, of Painswick. Damaging a tree growing in a wood at Miserden, the property of Robert Lawrence Townsend Esq. H. Burgh JP and E. G. Hallewell JP at Stroud. Fine 3d. damages and 5/6 costs to be paid to the complainant, or hard labour for fourteen days in Horsley house of correction. Offence committed 17 June 1837.

56/C/22 10 June 1837. Samuel Vines of Stroud, labourer. Stealing half a peck of onions growing in a garden at Stroud, the property of Richard Gay, labourer. H. Burgh JP at Stroud. Hard labour for six calendar months in Horsley house of correction. Offence committed 9 June 1837.

56/C/23 12 May 1837. Thomas Peyton of Stroud, weaver. Assaulting and beating Thomas Shipway, beer seller, of Stroud. E. P. Caruthers JP, H. Wyatt JP and E. G. Hallewell JP at Stroud. Fine 5/-, to be paid to William Augustus Baylis, an overseer of the poor, and 8/6 costs to the complainant, or one calendar month in Horsley house of correction. Offence committed 10 May 1837.

56/C/24 9 June 1837. Richard Webb, licensed beer retailer, of Bisley. Opening his house for the sale and consumption of beer between 10 a.m. and 1 p.m. on a Sunday. H. Burgh JP, E. P. Caruthers JP, H. Wyatt JP and E. G. Hallewell JP at a Petty Sessions. First offence. Fine £2 and 10/6 costs. Offence committed Sunday 9 April 1837.

56/C/25 12 May 1837. John Elliott labourer of Rodborough. Injuring an ass, the property of Charles Mayer, labourer, of Stroud. E. P. Caruthers JP, H. Wyatt JP and E. G. Hallewell JP at Stroud. Fine £1 for the amount of injury caused and 9/6 costs, all to be paid to the complainant, or hard labour for two calendar months in Horsley house of correction. Offence committed 18 April 1837.

56/C/26   19 April 1837. William Williams of Stroud, labourer. Stealing two bushels of turnip tops growing on enclosed land at Painswick, the property of William Capel the younger, gentleman. H. Burgh JP at Rodborough. Hard labour for one calendar month in Horsley house of correction. Offence committed 18 April 1837.

56/C/27   15 April 1837. Ann Elliott, Elizabeth Lewis and Hester Vick, spinsters, of Stroud. Assaulting and beating Samuel Smith, butcher, of Minchinhampton at Stroud. H. Burgh JP and H. Wyatt JP at Stroud. Fine £5 each, to be paid to William Ponting, overseer of the poor, or two calendar months in Horsley house of correction. Offence committed 14 April 1837.

56/C/28   10 March 1837. John Wood of King's Stanley, labourer. Stealing one peck of turnips growing in a field at Nympsfield, the property of Henry, Lord Moreton. H. Burgh JP and E. G. Hallewell JP at Stroud. Hard labour for fourteen days in Horsley house of correction. Offence committed 25 Feb. 1837.

56/C/29   18 May 1837. William Ayers. Assaulting and kicking Esther Avery the younger at Cheltenham. J. C. Smith JP and W. S. Evans JP at Cheltenham. Fine 5/-, to be paid to an overseer of the poor, and 5/- costs to the complainant. Offence committed 15 May 1837.

56/C/30   22 May 1837. James Clemens [*also* Clements] of Cheltenham, licensed retailer of excisable liquors. Allowing card-playing in his house. J. C. Smith JP and W. S. Evans JP at Cheltenham. First offence. Fine £5. Costs 40/- to be divided equally between the county treasurer and the informer, Ephraim Ireland. Offence committed 18 May 1837.

56/C/31   15 April 1837. Mary Hands, licensed retailer of excisable liquors, of Cheltenham. Failing to maintain good order in her house. R. B. Cooper JP and W. S. Evans JP. First offence. Fine £5. Costs 40/- to be divided equally between the county treasurer and the informer, Stephen Lawes. Offence committed 13 April 1837.

56/C/32   20 April 1837. William Dawes. Assaulting and striking Thomas Sparrow and John Bishop, peace officers, in the execution of their duty at Cheltenham. J. C. Smith JP and W. S. Evans JP at Cheltenham. Fine 20/-, to be paid to an overseer of the poor, and 4/- costs, to be shared equally between the complainants. Offence committed 15 April 1837.

56/C/33   13 April 1837. James Heast, licensed retailer of beer and cider, of Cheltenham. Keeping his house open for the sale of beer and cider until 10.45 p.m. J. C. Smith JP and W. S. Evans JP at Cheltenham. First offence. Fine 40/-, half of which to be paid to the county treasurer and the remainder to the informer, Charles Palmer. Costs 7/-. Offence committed 8 April 1837.

56/C/34   13 April 1837. James Meek of Cheltenham, licensed retailer of excisable liquors. Keeping his house open for the sale of such liquors during the hours of divine service. J. C. Smith JP and W. S. Evans JP at Cheltenham. First offence. Fine £5. Costs 10/- to be divided equally between the county treasurer and the informer, Ephraim Ireland. Offence committed Sunday 9 April 1837.

56/C/35   29 April 1837. John Llewellin. Assaulting and kicking Thomas Pash at Cheltenham. R. B. Cooper JP and W. S. Evans JP at Cheltenham. Fine 5/-, to be paid to an overseer of the poor, and 4/- costs to the complainant. Offence committed 28 April 1837.

56/C/36   1 June 1837. Jonathan Smith, peace officer. Assaulting and striking William Cole, peace officer, in the execution of his duty at Cheltenham. J. Overbury JP and J. C. Smith JP at Cheltenham. Fine £3, to be paid to an overseer of the poor, and 4/- costs to the complainant. Offence committed 28 May 1837.

56/C/37   1 June 1837. Thomas Smith. Assaulting and striking John Osborne, peace officer, in the execution of his duty at Cheltenham. J. Overbury JP and J. C. Smith JP at Cheltenham.

Fine £1, to be paid to an overseer of the poor, and 4/- costs to the complainant. Offence committed 28 May 1837.

56/C/38   1 June 1837. Amos Holder. Assaulting and striking John Osborne, peace officer [*etc., as* 56/C/37].

56/C/39   22 June 1837. John Jackson. Stealing a quantity of cabbages growing in a garden occupied by Isaac Wood at Cheltenham. R. B. Cooper JP and W. S. Evans JP at Cheltenham. Fine 10/-, to be paid to an overseer of the poor, 1/- damages and 5/6 costs. Offence committed 18 June 1837.

56/C/40   15 June 1837. Charlotte Mann of Tetbury, single woman. Stealing part of a live fence in a field at Tetbury occupied by Mr. Joseph Hughes. W. M. Paul JP. Fine 3*d.* damages, to be paid to an overseer of the poor, and 2/9 costs to the complainant, who was examined as to proof of the offence. Given one week to pay. In default, one calendar month's hard labour in Horsley house of correction. Offence committed 26 May 1837.

56/C/41   15 June 1837. Hannah Cox of Tetbury, single woman. Stealing part of a live fence in a field at Tetbury [*etc., as* 56/C/40].

56/C/42   15 June 1837. Eliza Mann of Tetbury. Trespassing in a field occupied by Mr. Martin Tanner at Horsley, and throwing down or damaging part of a fence. W. M. Paul JP. Fine 6*d.* and 4/6 costs or hard labour for one calendar month in Horsley house of correction. Offence committed 6 June 1837.

56/C/43   20 April 1837. John Price of Twyning, labourer. Violently assaulting William Clifford, labourer, of Twyning without just cause. J. Timbrill D.D. JP and Rev. C. White JP at Tewkesbury. Fine 10/-, to be paid to Richard Castle, overseer of the poor, and 9/6 costs to the complainant. Offence committed Wednesday 5 April 1837.

56/C/44   1 June 1837. Nancy widow of Thomas Eagles of the Maypole inn, Apperley, Deerhurst, innkeeper. Keeping her house open for the sale and consumption of beer and cider after 9 p.m. J. Timbrill D.D. JP and J. W. Martin JP at a Petty Sessions for Gloucester county. Fine 40/- and 17/- costs. Offence committed Monday 15 May 1837.

56/C/45   15 June 1837. William Smith of Chipping Campden. Using a gun to kill game at Stanway without a game certificate. J. Timbrill D.D. JP and Rev. C. White JP at Tewkesbury. Fine £2 10*s.*, to be paid to the overseer of the poor, and £3 12*s.* 3*d.* costs to the complainant, Anthony Allington, or hard labour for two calendar months in Northleach house of correction. Offence committed 24 Dec. 1836. [*Endorsed with a note that the offender was immediately imprisoned.*]

56/C/46   15 June 1837. Charles Lacey of Alderton. Assaulting and threatening John Gorton of Alderton. J. Timbrill D.D. JP and Rev. C. White JP at Tewkesbury. Fine £1, to be paid to an overseer of the poor, and £1 5*s.* 10*d.* costs to the complainant. Offence committed 19 April 1837. [*Endorsed with a note that the offender was immediately imprisoned for two calendar months in Northleach house of correction.*]

56/C/47   26 Jan. 1837. Ambrose Fisher, licensed victualler, of the Salutation inn, Minchinhampton. Keeping his house open other than for the reception of travellers between 11 a.m. and 12 noon, the hours of divine service. T. Kingscote JP and D. Ricardo JP at a Petty Sessions for Longtree hundred. First offence. Fine £4 13*s.* and 7/- costs. Offence committed Sunday 25 Dec. 1836.

56/C/48   12 Jan. 1837. William Essex, licensed victualler, of the New Inn, Avening. Permitting drunkenness and disorderly behaviour in his house at about half-past midnight. T. Kingscote JP and D. Ricardo JP at a Petty Sessions for Longtree hundred. First offence. Fine £4 13*s.* and 7/- costs. Offence committed 29 Dec. 1836.

56/C/49   30 March 1837. Jehu Dee of Rodborough, licensed beer retailer. Keeping his house open for the sale of beer at about 4.20 p.m. on a Sunday in violation of an order made on 6 Sept. 1836 by justices at Horsley. T. Kingscote JP and Joseph Hort JP at a Petty Sessions for Longtree hundred. First offence. Fine 40/- and 7/- costs. Offence committed 19 March 1837.

56/C/50   30 March 1837. James Barter of Rodborough, licensed beer retailer. Keeping his house open for the sale of beer at about 10.45 p.m. in violation of an order made on 6 Sept. 1836 by justices at Horsley. T. Kingscote JP and J. Hort JP at a Petty Sessions for Longtree hundred. First offence. Fine £1 and 7/- costs. Offence committed 18 March 1837.

56/C/51   22 Dec. 1836 [*late return*]. John Sansum of Minchinhampton, licensed beer retailer. Keeping his house open for the sale of beer at about 10.50 p.m. in violation of an order made on 6 Sept. 1836 by justices at Horsley. T. Kingscote JP and D. Ricardo JP at a Petty Sessions for Longtree hundred. First offence. Fine £1 13*s*. and 7/- costs. Offence committed 5 Dec. 1836.

56/C/52   12 Jan. 1837. James Fowles of Minchinhampton, licensed beer retailer. Keeping his house open for the sale of beer after 8.30 p.m. in violation of an order [*etc., as* 56/C/51 *except*] Offence committed Sunday 4 Dec. 1836.

56/C/53   12 Jan. 1837. William Newman of Minchinhampton, licensed beer retailer. Keeping his house open for the sale of beer at about 11 a.m. during the hours of divine service. T. Kingscote JP and D. Ricardo JP at a Petty Sessions for Longtree hundred. First offence. Fine 40/- and 7/- costs. Offence committed Sunday 25 Dec. 1836.

56/C/54   12 Jan. 1837. Clement Hunt of Minchinhampton, licensed beer retailer. Keeping his house open for the sale of beer after 8.30 p.m. in violation of an order [*etc., as* 56/C/51 *except*] Offence committed Sunday 11 Dec. 1836.

56/C/55   12 Jan. 1837. William Holbrow of Avening, licensed beer retailer. Keeping his house open for the sale of beer at 10.30 p.m. in violation of an order [*etc., as* 56/C/51 *except*] Fine 40/- and 7/- costs. Offence committed 8 Dec. 1836.

56/C/56   26 Jan. 1837. Thomas Blackwell of Avening, licensed beer retailer. Keeping his house open for the sale of beer at 11.30 a.m. on a Sunday in violation of an order [*etc., as* 56/C/51 *except*] Fine 40/- and 7/- costs. Offence committed 15 Jan. 1837.

56/C/57   23 Feb. 1837. Richard Burford of Horsley, licensed beer retailer. Keeping his house open for the sale of beer between 12 noon and 1 p.m. on a Sunday. T. Kingscote JP and W. Playne JP at a Petty Sessions for Longtree hundred. First offence. Fine 40/- and 7/- costs. Offence committed 5 Feb. 1837.

56/C/58   27 April 1837. George Gardner of Minchinhampton, licensee of the Reform tavern. Keeping his tavern open other than for the reception of travellers at 11.30 a.m. during the hours of divine service. T. Kingscote JP and J. Hort JP at Petty Sessions for Longtree hundred. First offence. Fine £2 10*s*. and 7/- costs. Offence committed Sunday 9 April 1837.

56/C/59   8 June 1837. Joseph Shearman, licensed game dealer. Possessing a pheasant more than forty days after 1 Feb. 1837. T. Kingscote JP and J. Hort JP. Fine £1, one moiety to be paid to George Hancock, informer, with costs [*unspecified*], and the remainder to an overseer of the poor, or hard labour for two calendar months in Horsley house of correction. Offence committed 25 May 1837.

56/C/60   8 June 1837. Joseph Shearman. Stealing an egg from a pheasant's nest on land occupied by — Randle at North Nibley. T. Kingscote JP and J. Hort JP. Fine 5/-, one moiety of which to be paid to George Hancock, the informer, in addition to costs [*unspecified*], the remainder to be paid to an overseer of the poor, or hard labour for one calendar month in Horsley house of correction. Offence committed 25 May 1837.

56/C/61   27 April 1837. John Rowland of Avening, licensed beer retailer. Keeping his house open for the sale and consumption of beer between 10 a.m. and 12 noon on a Sunday in violation of an order made by justices for the county on 6 Sept. 1836. T. Kingscote JP and J. Hort JP at a Petty Sessions for Longtree hundred. First offence. Fine 1/- and 7/- costs. Offence committed Sunday 2 April 1837.

56/C/62   26 Jan. 1837. Daniel Parsons of Avening, licensee of the Star inn. Keeping his house open other than for the reception of travellers between 11 a.m. and 12 noon, the hours of divine service. T. Kingscote JP and D. Ricardo JP at a Petty Sessions for Longtree hundred. First offence. Fine £4 13*s.* and 7/- costs. Offence committed 15 Jan. 1837.

56/D/1   26 June 1837. Jacob Vaughan. Assaulting and beating John Taylor [*also* Tailor] at Cheltenham. W. S. Evans JP and J. Overbury JP at Cheltenham. Fine 20/- and 4/- costs or two calendar months in Northleach house of correction. Offence committed 25 June 1837.

56/D/2   26 June 1837. — Elliston. Assaulting and beating Richard French at Cheltenham. W. S. Evans JP and J. Overbury JP at Cheltenham. Fine 5/- and 3/6 costs. Offence committed 25 June 1837.

56/D/3   26 June 1837. — Elliston. Assaulting and beating Thomas Trigg at Cheltenham. W. S. Evans JP and J. Overbury JP at Cheltenham. Fine 5/- and 3/6 costs. Offence committed 25 June 1837.

56/D/4   1 July 1837. Thomas Poulson. Assaulting and beating Thomas Trigg at Cheltenham. J. C. Smith JP and Thomas Henney JP at Cheltenham. Fine £2 and 6/- costs or six weeks in Northleach house of correction. Offence committed 30 June 1837.

56/D/5   10 July 1837. John Gray. Assaulting and beating Charles Wilkins at Cheltenham. R. B. Cooper JP and J. C. Smith JP at Cheltenham. Fine 5/-, to be paid to an overseer of the poor, and 5/- costs to the complainant. Offence committed 9 July 1837.

56/D/6   10 July 1837. Daniel Murphy. Assaulting Joseph Simmonds at Cheltenham. R. B. Cooper JP and J. C. Smith JP at Cheltenham. Fine 5/- and 5/- costs or ten days in Northleach house of correction. Offence committed 8 July 1837.

56/D/7   13 July 1837. William Giles. Assaulting John Osborne at Cheltenham. R. B. Cooper JP and J. C. Smith JP at Cheltenham. Fine 10/-, to be paid to an overseer of the poor, and 4/- costs to the complainant. Offence committed 12 July 1837.

56/D/8   13 July 1837. William Arkell of Cheltenham, licensed beer retailer. Keeping his house open for the sale of beer at 3.55 p.m. on a Sunday. R. B. Cooper JP and J. C. Smith JP at Cheltenham. First offence. Fine 40/-, half of which to be paid to the county treasurer and the remainder to Thomas Sparrow, the informer. Costs assessed at 7/-. Offence committed 9 July 1837.

56/D/9   13 July 1837. Richard Goodrich of Leckhampton, licensed beer retailer. Keeping his house open for the sale of beer at 3.40 p.m. on a Sunday [*etc., as* 56/D/8].

56/D/10   20 July 1837. Joseph Hawker. Assaulting and beating Ephraim Ireland at Cheltenham. R. B. Cooper JP and J. C. Smith JP at Cheltenham. Fine 20/- and 7/- costs or two calendar months in Northleach house of correction. Offence committed 19 July 1837.

56/D/11   10 Aug. 1837. John Davis. Assaulting Benjamin Barnes at Cheltenham. J. Overbury JP and T. Henney JP at Cheltenham. Fine 10/-, to be paid to an overseer of the poor, and 14/- costs to the complainant. Offence committed 8 Aug. 1837.

56/D/12   7 Sept. 1837. Sarah Baylis of Cheltenham, licensed retailer of excisable liquors. Keeping her house open for the sale of excisable liquors at 4 p.m. on a Sunday. J. C. Smith JP and Rev. W. Hicks JP at Cheltenham. First offence. Fine £5, mitigated to 40/-, half of which to be paid to John Osborne, the prosecutor, and the remainder to the county treasurer. Costs assessed at 5/6. Offence committed 3 Sept. 1837.

56/D/13   11 Sept. 1837. Thomas Bailey. Assaulting and beating Rachael Rooke at Cheltenham. R. B. Cooper JP and J. Overbury JP at Cheltenham. Fine 5/-, to be paid to an overseer of the poor, and 6/6 costs to the complainant. Offence committed 8 Sept. 1837.

56/D/14   23 Sept. 1837. Charles Scott of Cheltenham, licensed retailer of excisable liquors. Keeping his house open for the sale of excisable liquors until 1.30 a.m. R. B. Cooper JP and J. C. Smith JP. First offence. Fine £5, mitigated to 40/-, half of which to be paid to John Osborne, the prosecutor, and the remainder to the county treasurer. Costs assessed at 7/-. Offence committed 19 Sept. 1837.

56/D/15   28 Sept. 1837. Robert Dyer of Cheltenham, licensed beer retailer. Keeping his house open for the sale of beer at 4 p.m. on a Sunday. R. B. Cooper JP and J. C. Smith JP. First offence. Fine 40/-, half of which to be paid to John Russell, the prosecutor, and the remainder to the county treasurer. Costs assessed at 7/-. Offence committed 24 Sept. 1837.

56/D/16   28 Sept. 1837. Richard Wright of Cheltenham, licensed retailer of excisable liquors. Keeping his house open for the sale of excisable liquors and allowing disorderly behaviour until midnight. R. B. Cooper JP and J. C. Smith JP. First offence. Fine £5 mitigated to 40/-, half of which to be paid to Thomas Sanders, the prosecutor, and the remainder to the county treasurer. Costs assessed at 7/-. Offence committed 23 Sept. 1837.

56/D/17   5 Oct. 1837. Thomas Alderson of Cheltenham, licensed beer retailer. Keeping his house open for the sale of beer until 11.15 p.m. R. B. Cooper JP and J. C. Smith JP. First offence. Fine 40/-, half of which to be paid to Ethelbert Smith, the prosecutor, and the remainder to the county treasurer. Costs assessed at 7/-. Offence committed 30 Sept. 1837.

56/D/18   5 Oct. 1837. Thomas Brooks. Assaulting John Dempsey at Charlton Kings. R. B. Cooper JP and J. C. Smith JP at Cheltenham. Fine 5/- and 3/- costs or one calendar month in Northleach house of correction. Offence committed 4 Oct. 1837.

56/D/19   5 Oct. 1837. Edwin Chapman. Assaulting John Dempsey at Charlton Kings. R. B. Cooper JP and J. C. Smith JP at Cheltenham. Fine 20/- and 3/- costs [*said in error to be awarded to offender*], or one calendar month in Northleach house of correction. Offence committed 4 Oct. 1837.

56/D/20   7 Oct. 1837. Thomas Ebbles. Assaulting and beating William Seabright at Cheltenham. J. C. Smith JP and J. Overbury JP at Cheltenham. Fine 20/-, to be paid to an overseer of the poor, and 5/- costs to the complainant. Offence committed 6 Oct. 1837.

56/D/21   13 June 1837. William Phillips of Lydney, beerhouse keeper. Allowing gambling in his house. C. Bathurst JP and Rev. C. H. Morgan JP at a Petty Sessions for the Forest division. First offence. Fine 40/- and 7/6 costs. Offence committed 18 May 1837. [*Note:*] Received of Mr. Lucas 8*s*.

56/D/22   5 Sept. 1837. Thomas Prosser. Assaulting Joseph Evans at Woolaston. G. Ormerod JP and Rev. C. H. Morgan JP at a Petty Sessions at Lydney for the Forest division. Fine 20/- and 7/6 costs or one calendar month in Littledean house of correction. Offence committed 5 Aug. 1837.

56/D/23   5 Sept. 1837. William Willetts. Using a gun to kill game at Oakenhill Enclosure in the Forest of Dean without a game certificate. G. Ormerod JP and Thomas Thatcher JP at Lydney in the Forest division. Fine 20/-, and 7/6 costs to be paid to Richard Hatton, ranger of the Forest of Dean, or one calendar month in Littledean house of correction. Offence committed 2 Aug. 1837.

56/D/24   5 Sept. 1837. James Cradock. Assaulting Elizabeth Willetts at Lydney. G. Ormerod JP and Rev. C. H. Morgan JP at Lydney in the Forest division. Fine 6d. and 7/6 costs or seven days in Littledean house of correction. Offence committed 26 Aug. 1837.

56/D/25   5 Sept. 1837. Alice Cooper. Assaulting Sarah wife of Philip Jones at St. Briavels hundred. G. Ormerod JP and Thomas Thatcher JP at Lydney in the Forest division. Fine 1/-, to be paid to the overseer of the poor of Newland, the nearest parish to where the offence took place, and 8/- costs, or seven days in Littledean house of correction. Offence committed 12 Aug. 1837.

56/D/26   5 Sept. 1837. William Williams. Assaulting James Williams at Alvington. Rev. C. H. Morgan JP and T. Thatcher[1] JP at Lydney in the Forest division. Fine 40/- and 7/6 costs or fourteen days in Littledean house of correction. Offence committed 21 Aug. 1837.

56/D/27   5 Sept. 1837. Joseph Harris of English Bicknor, beerhouse keeper. Allowing tippling in his house on a Sunday. G. Ormerod JP and T. Thatcher JP at a Petty Sessions for the Forest division. First offence. Fine 40/- and 6/- costs. Offence committed 27 Aug. 1837.

56/D/28   5 Sept. 1837. Joseph Harris of English Bicknor, beerhouse keeper. Allowing disorderly conduct in his house. G. Ormerod JP and T. Thatcher JP at a Petty Sessions for the Forest division. Second offence. Fine 40/- and 6/- costs. Offence committed Sunday 27 Aug. 1837.

56/D/29   12 Dec. 1836 [late return]. Jonathan Wood of Newent, labourer. Trespassing with a gun in search of game at Newent in a close of land occupied by John Balding. O. Ricardo JP at Newent. Fine £1 10s., one moiety of which to be paid to John Warren, the complainant, with 10/- costs, and the remainder to an overseer of the poor, or two calendar months in Littledean house of correction. Offence committed 3 Dec. 1836.

56/D/30   25 Sept. 1837. William Chamberlain of Longhope, labourer. Using a gun without a game certificate to kill game at Longhope. R. F. Onslow JP and John Probyn JP at Newent. James Turner, woodward, of Longhope, complainant. Fine £2, half to be paid to James Turner with 11/- costs and the remainder to the overseers of the poor of Longhope, or hard labour for two calendar months in Littledean house of correction. Offence committed 10 Sept. 1837.

56/D/31   25 Sept. 1837. William Trigg of Huntley, labourer. Trespassing in pursuit of game at Longhope on land at Huntley Hill occupied by John Watkins. R. F. Onslow JP at Newent. Fine £2, half of which to be paid to William Edwards, complainant, with 13/- costs, and the remainder to an overseer of the poor, or hard labour for two calendar months in Littledean house of correction. Offence committed 10 Sept. 1837.

56/D/32   25 Sept. 1837. Thomas Sinderbury of Longhope, labourer. Using a gun without a game certificate to take game at Longhope. R. F. Onslow JP and J. Probyn JP at Newent. Fine £2, one moiety of which to be paid to the complainant, James Turner of Longhope, woodward, together with 11/- costs, and the remainder to an overseer of the poor, or hard labour for two calendar months in Littledean house of correction. Offence committed 10 Sept. 1837.

---

[1] The title 'Colonel' before his name has been erased, and Thatcher initialled the amendment.

56/D/33   25 Sept. 1837. Mary Turner. Stealing seven cabbages growing on enclosed land at Newent, the property of Samuel Aston. R. F. Onslow JP. Fine 20/-, to be paid to an overseer of the poor, 2/6 damages to Samuel Aston, who was not examined as to proof of offence, and 13/- costs to Thomas Selwyn, the complainant. Given fourteen days to pay. In default, one calendar month in Littledean house of correction. Offence committed 24 Sept. 1837.

56/D/34   25 Jan. 1836 [*late return*]. Henry Smith of Oxenhall, lath ripper. Using two gins without a game certificate to kill game at Oxenhall. O. Ricardo JP and R. Webb JP at Newent. Fine £5, one moiety of which, together with 11/- costs, to be paid to William Bullock, gamekeeper, of Oxenhall, complainant, and the remainder to an overseer of the poor, or hard labour for two calendar months in Littledean house of correction. Offence committed 22 Jan. 1836.

56/D/35   5 Dec. 1836 [*late return*]. Joseph Winter of Newent, labourer. Using a gin without a game certificate for taking game at Oxenhall. O. Ricardo JP and R. Webb JP at Newent. Fine £5, one moiety of which, together with 8/- costs, to be paid to the complainant, William Jones, wood turner, and the remainder to an overseer of the poor, or three calendar months in Littledean house of correction. Offence committed 2 Dec. 1836.

56/D/36   18 Sept. 1837. Edward Cooper. Breaking a hedge-fence at Newent, the property of Thomas Bailey. O. Ricardo JP at Newent. Fine 1/6 and 6*d*. damages, to be paid to an overseer of the poor, and 8/- costs to the complainant, who was examined as to proof of offence, or hard labour for one calendar month in Littledean house of correction. Offence committed 4 Sept. 1837.

56/D/37   14 Aug. 1837. Thomas Andrews of Taynton, labourer. Cutting and damaging a tree growing on land at Newent occupied by Elizabeth Foley. R. F. Onslow JP at Newent. Fine 10/-, to be paid to an overseer of the poor, 1/- damages to Elizabeth Foley, who was not examined as to proof of offence, and 9/- costs to Joseph Colwell, the complainant, or hard labour for six weeks in Littledean house of correction. Offence committed 3 June 1837.

56/D/38   26 Sept. 1837. Abraham Golding of Lechlade, licensed beer retailer. Keeping his house open for the sale and consumption of beer at 11 a.m. on a Sunday. Rev. E. L. Bennett JP and Rev. T. Pettat JP at a Petty Sessions for Bibury division. First offence. Fine 40/- and 10/- costs. Offence committed 17 Sept. 1837.

56/D/39   13 Sept. 1837. James Yarnold of Tewkesbury, stocking framework knitter. Stealing a quantity of apples and pears valued at 2/6 growing in a garden called Sling occupied by Emanuel Taylor at Twyning. J. Surman JP at Tewkesbury. Hard labour for three calendar months in Northleach house of correction. Offence committed Monday 11 Sept. 1837.

56/D/40   13 Sept. 1837. William Yarnold of Tewkesbury, stocking framework knitter. Stealing a quantity of apples and pears [*etc., as* 56/D/39 *except*] One calendar month in Northleach house of correction.

[*Note pinned to* 56/D/40:] T. P. White in account with Edward Bloxham Esq. D.C.P., Michaelmas Sessions 1837. Fees on returning the under-mentioned convictions. Vizt.

James Dudfield	1*s*.	William Taylor	1*s*.
Thomas Fletcher	1*s*.	James Yarnold	1*s*.
William Aston	1*s*.	William Yarnold	1*s*.
William Derrett	1*s*.		
		[*total*]	7*s*.

1837 Michaelmas Sessions

Received E. B.

56/D/41   6 July 1837. James Dudfield of Twyning, farmer. Violently assaulting Ann wife of John Arch, labourer, of Twyning without provocation. J. Timbrill D.D. JP, Rev. C. White JP, J. W. Martin JP and J. Surman JP at Tewkesbury. Fine £3 1*s*. 6*d*., to be paid to Richard Castle, overseer of the poor, and £1 18*s*. 6*d*. costs to the complainant. Offence committed Wednesday 14 June 1837.

56/D/42   13 July 1837. Thomas Fletcher the younger of the Leigh, waterman. Violently assaulting John Humble, labourer, of Deerhurst near the Swan inn, the Leigh. J. Timbrill D.D. JP, Rev. C. White JP, J. W. Martin JP and J. Surman JP at Tewkesbury. Fine 1/-, to be paid to Joseph Brown, overseer of the poor, and £1 15*s*. 6*d*. costs to the complainant. Offence committed Wednesday 21 June 1837.

56/D/43   4 Aug. 1837. William Aston of Gloucester, waterman. Trespassing in search of conies at Cherry Hill, Apperley, Deerhurst, land occupied by Miss Juliana Sabina Strickland. Rev. C. White JP at Tewkesbury. Fine 1/-, to be paid to Joseph Overton, overseer of the poor, and 7/- costs to Richard Lawson, bailiff to Miss Strickland, complainant. Offence committed Thursday 3 Aug. 1837.

56/D/44   24 Aug. 1837. William Derrett of Apperley, Deerhurst labourer. Violently assaulting William Barnard, farmer, of Deerhurst at Wightfield [*MS*. Whitefield], Deerhurst. J. Timbrill D.D. JP and J. Surman JP at Tewkesbury. Fine £2, to be paid to Joseph Overton, overseer of the poor, and 10/6 costs to the complainant. Offence committed Monday 14 Aug. 1837.

56/D/45   24 Aug. 1837. William Taylor of Evington, the Leigh, labourer. Violently assaulting George Featherstone of St. Clement's, Worcester, boat owner, at Evington, without provocation. J. Timbrill D.D. JP and J. Surman JP at Tewkesbury. Fine 1/-, to be paid to Joseph Brown, overseer of the poor of the Leigh, and £3 15s. 6*d*. costs to the complainant. Offence committed Friday 21 July 1837.

56/D/46   27 June 1837. Charles Wiles. Assaulting and beating James Trotman, labourer, of Woodford, Alkington, at Berkeley. Rev. J. H. Dunsford JP and E. Weight JP at Berkeley. Fine 5/-, to be paid to the overseer of the poor of Alkington, and 10/4 costs to the complainant, or seven days in Horsley house of correction. Offence committed 8 June 1837.

56/D/47   15 Sept. 1837. James Rickards, keeper of the turnpike gate at Wotton under Edge. Using a cart drawn by one horse on the turnpike road at Charfield without having his full name and address painted on it. W. Blathwayt JP and H. Bush JP. Fine £2 and 10/- costs or one month in Horsley house of correction. Offence committed 26 Aug. 1837.

56/D/48   15 Sept. 1837. William Mills of Hillesley, Hawkesbury, weaver. Pulling up ten or a dozen rows of potatoes growing in a garden at Hillesley occupied by Elizabeth Dean. W. Blathwayt JP and H. Bush JP at Old Sodbury. Elizabeth Dean and Hugh Watts of Hillesley, witnesses. Fine 5/-, to be paid to an overseer of the poor, and 10/6 costs to the complainant. In default of payment by 13 Oct., one calendar month in Horsley house of correction. Offence committed Thursday night or following morning 31 Aug. 1837.

56/D/49   29 Sept. 1837. John Nicholls, labourer, and Charles Liles, mason, both of Doynton. Trespassing with guns in search of game without a game certificate on land at Dyrham and Hinton called Horse Lease and Wood Lease. H. Bush JP and A. Shakespear JP at Old Sodbury. Peter Clark, gamekeeper, of Dyrham and Hinton, informer. John Rawlings of the same parish, witness. Fine £2 10*s*. each, one moiety of which to be paid to the overseer of the poor, and the remainder, together with 11/- costs each, to the informer. Given one month to pay. In default, two calendar months in Horsley house of correction. Offence committed Saturday 2 Sept. 1837.

56/D/50   26 Sept. 1837. George Halford of Moreton in Marsh. Trespassing in search of game on enclosed land occupied by Thomas Horne at Moreton in Marsh. Rev. J. R. Hall JP at Moreton in Marsh. Fine £1 6s., one moiety of which to be paid to Francis Groom of Sezincote, informer, together with 14/- costs, and the remainder to George Franklin, an overseer of the poor, or hard labour for one calendar month in Northleach house of correction. Offence committed 6 Sept. 1837.

56/D/51   26 Sept. 1837. George Fletcher of Moreton in Marsh. Trespassing in search of game [etc., as 56/D/50 except] overseer of the poor of Moreton [etc.].

56/D/52   26 Sept. 1837. James Brown of Moreton in Marsh, labourer. Assaulting and beating Charles Bennett at Moreton in Marsh. Rev. J. R. Hall JP and Rev. C. Jeaffreson JP at Moreton in Marsh. Fine 10/-, to be paid to George Franklin, overseer of the poor, and 10/- costs to the complainant, or one calendar month in Northleach house of correction. Offence committed 2 June 1837.

56/D/53   26 Sept. 1837. James Williams late of Bourton on the Hill. Assaulting and beating Martha Watkins at Bourton on the Hill. Rev. J. R. Hall JP and Rev. C. Jeaffreson JP at Moreton in Marsh. Fine 5/-, to be paid to John Gardner, overseer of the poor, and 19/- costs to the complainant, or one calendar month in Northleach house of correction. Offence committed 2 Sept. 1837.

56/D/54   5 Sept. 1837. William Walton, late of Bourton on the Hill. Assaulting and beating Martha Watkins at Bourton on the Hill. Rev. J. R. Hall JP and F. Colvile JP at Moreton in Marsh. Fine 10/-, to be paid to John Gardner overseer of the poor of Bourton on the Hill, and 10/- costs to the complainant, or one calendar month in Northleach house of correction. Offence committed 2 Sept. 1837.

56/D/55   5 Sept. 1837. Henry Hawker of Chipping Campden. Assaulting and beating Mary Cooper at Weston Subedge. Rev. J. R. Hall JP and F. Colvile JP at Moreton in Marsh. Fine 4/-, to be paid to William Gardner, overseer of the poor of Weston Subedge, and 16/- costs to the complainant, or one calendar month in Northleach house of correction. Offence committed 28 Aug. 1837.

56/D/56   5 Sept. 1837. Thomas Butler of Moreton in Marsh. Assaulting and beating Jane Powers at Moreton in Marsh. Rev. J. R. Hall JP and F. Colvile JP at Moreton in Marsh. Fine 9/-, to be paid to George Franklin, overseer of the poor, and 11/- costs to the complainant, or one calendar month in Northleach house of correction. Offence committed 3 Aug. 1837.

56/D/57   5 Sept. 1837. George Cockerell, late of Bourton on the Hill. Assaulting and beating Martha Watkins [etc., as 56/D/54].

56/D/58   22 Aug. 1837. Lucy Smith and Ann Dee, prostitutes. Wandering the public streets and behaving in a riotous manner at Chipping Campden. Rev. J. R. Hall JP at Moreton in Marsh. Hard labour for one calendar month in Northleach house of correction. Offence committed 21 Aug. 1837.

56/D/59   16 Aug. 1837. James Eastbury of Moreton in Marsh, labourer. Assaulting and beating Richard Phipps at Lemington. Rev. J. R. Hall JP and F. Colvile JP at Moreton in Marsh. Fine 10/-, to be paid to George Franklin, an overseer of the poor, and 10/- costs to the complainant, or one calendar month in Northleach house of correction. Offence committed 15 Aug. 1837.

56/D/60   8 Aug. 1837. Thomas Butler of Moreton in Marsh, labourer. Assaulting and beating Jane wife of William Powers at Moreton in Marsh. Rev. J. R. Hall JP and at F. Colvile JP, at Moreton in Marsh. Fine 8/- and 12/- costs or one calendar month in Northleach house of correction. Offence committed 3 Aug. 1837. [The relationship with 56/D/56 is not clear.]

56/D/61   25 July 1837. George Pain. Wilfully and lewdly insulting a female at Moreton in Marsh. Rev. J. R. Hall JP at Moreton in Marsh. One calendar month in Northleach house of correction. Offence committed 11 July 1837.

56/D/62   25 Aug. 1837. Samuel Hallowell. Leaving his wife and four children chargeable to Stroud parish. H. Burgh JP, J. Mills JP and E. G. Hallewell JP at Stroud. Hard labour for two calendar months in Horsley house of correction. Offence committed about March 1836.

56/D/63   19 July 1837. Edward Birt. Leaving his wife and children chargeable to Painswick parish. H. Burgh JP at Stroud. Hard labour for three calendar months in Horsley house of correction. Offence committed about 1 June 1837.

56/D/64   2 June 1837. Charles Davis. Leaving his two children chargeable to Bisley parish. H. Wyatt JP at Stroud. Hard labour for one calendar month in Horsley house of correction. Offence committed in Feb. 1837.

56/D/65   12 Sept. 1837. William Brown. Begging in a public street in Stroud. H. Burgh JP, E P. Caruthers JP and E. G. Hallewell JP at Stroud. Hard labour for fourteen days in Horsley house of correction. Offence committed 11 Sept. 1837.

56/D/66   5 Sept. 1837. Edward Fluck. Neglecting to maintain his wife by work as a labourer, thereby causing her to become chargeable to Stroud parish. H. Burgh JP at Stroud. Hard labour for one calendar month in Horsley house of correction. Offence committed about two months previously.

56/D/67   19 Aug. 1837. Richard Baker. Vagrancy: wandering abroad and lodging in the open air at Stroud, with no visible sign of subsistence. H. Burgh JP at Stroud. Hard labour for three calendar months in Horsley house of correction. Offence committed 19 Aug. 1837.

56/D/68   9 Sept. 1837. Charles Pearce, George Dowell and Charles Woodfield, clothworkers, of Stroud. Stealing a quantity of apples growing in an orchard at Stroud, the property of George Stockham. H. Burgh JP at Stroud. Hard labour for one calendar month in Horsley house of correction. Offence committed 7 Sept. 1837.

56/D/69   12 Sept. 1837. Joseph Mayer of Bisley, labourer. Stealing a quantity of apples growing in an orchard in Bisley, the property of Edward Restall, timber merchant. H. Burgh JP, E. P. Caruthers JP and E. G. Hallewell JP at Stroud. Hard labour for three calendar months in Horsley house of correction. Offence committed 9 Sept. 1837.

56/D/70   20 July 1837. Mary Cratchley of Rodborough. Stealing a quantity of cabbage plants from a garden at Rodborough, the property of James Wall, stonemason. H. Burgh JP at Stroud. Hard labour for five calendar months in Horsley house of correction. Offence committed 20 July 1837.

56/D/71   1 Sept. 1837. Isaac Buck, licensed beer retailer, of Stroud. Keeping his house open for the sale and consumption of beer between 3 p.m. and 5 p.m. on a Sunday. H. Burgh JP, E. P. Caruthers JP, J. Mills JP and E. G. Hallewell JP at a Petty Sessions for Bisley hundred. First offence. Fine £1 12s. 6d. and 7/6 costs. Offence committed 27 Aug. 1837.

56/D/72   7 April 1837. Thomas Darby of Minchinhampton, labourer. Cutting down and stealing a tree valued at 3/- from a wood at Minchinhampton, the property of William Ireland, cloth factor, of Painswick. H. Burgh JP, E. P. Caruthers JP and J. Mills JP at Stroud. Fine 10/-, 3/- damages and 10/- costs or hard labour for six weeks in Horsley house of correction. Offence committed 6 April 1837.

56/D/73   18 Aug. 1837. Edward White of Stroud, labourer. Assaulting and beating Henry Harris of Stroud, clothworker. H. Burgh JP and J. Mills JP at Stroud. Fine 6*d*., to be paid to William Ponting, an overseer of the poor, and 11/6 costs to the complainant. Given seven days to pay. In default, fourteen days in Horsley house of correction. Offence committed 15 Aug. 1837.

56/D/74   7 April 1837. Nathaniel Smith of Stroud, labourer. Cutting down and stealing three trees, valued at 1/6, at Standish, the property of the Rt. Hon. John, Lord Sherborne. H. Burgh JP, E. P. Caruthers JP and J. Mills JP. Fine 10/-, 1/6 damages and 11/6 costs or hard labour for two calendar months in Horsley house of correction. [Offence committed] 28 Jan. 1837.

56/D/75   7 July 1837. William Smith of Stroud, labourer. Cutting down and stealing from a wood in Stroud, owned by John and William Lewis, gentlemen, a quantity of underwood valued at 1/-, their property. H. Burgh JP, E. P. Caruthers JP and J. Mills JP. Fine 4/-, to be paid to William Ponting, an overseer of the poor, and 1/- damages and 6/6 costs to the complainants, or hard labour for two calendar months in Horsley house of correction. Offence committed 9 May 1837.

56/D/76   14 Aug. 1837. Matilda wife of Edwin Seymour, painter, of Stroud. Wilfully breaking seven panes of glass valued at 4/8 in a window of a dwelling house occupied by Jane Cooper, widow, at Stroud. H. Burgh JP at Stroud. Fine 4/8 damages and 9/- costs or hard labour for two calendar months in Horsley house of correction. Offence committed 12 Aug. 1837.

56/D/77   12 Aug. 1837. Thomas Skinner the younger of Stroud, labourer. Stealing a quantity of apples from an orchard at Stroud, the property of Richard Sandys, gentleman. H. Burgh JP at Stroud. Hard labour for three calendar months in Horsley house of correction. Offence committed 11 Aug. 1837.

56/D/78   20 July 1837. Mary Cratchley of Rodborough. Stealing a quantity of potatoes from a close of land at Rodborough, the property of George Hooper, yeoman. H. Burgh JP at Stroud. Hard labour for one calendar month in Horsley house of correction. Offence committed 20 July 1837.

56/D/79   21 July 1837. Daniel Brown and Philip Gardner, labourers, of Bisley. Cutting down and stealing underwood from a wood in Bisley, the property of and occupied by Thomas Baker, gentleman. H. Burgh JP, E. P. Caruthers JP and H. Wyatt JP at Stroud. Fine 4/-, to be paid to Richard Gibbins, overseer of the poor, and 1/- damages and 12/6 costs to the complainant, or hard labour for one calendar month in Horsley house of correction. Offence committed 13 July 1837.

56/D/80   23 June 1837. Elizabeth wife of Daniel Scott, yeoman, and John and Samuel Scott, labourers, all of Painswick. Assaulting and beating George White, labourer, of Painswick. H. Burgh JP, E. P. Caruthers JP and H. Wyatt JP at Stroud. Fine 6*d*., to be paid to Charles Gardner, overseer of the poor, and 14/6 costs to the complainant, or fourteen days in Horsley house of correction. Offence committed 14 June 1837.

56/D/81   16 June 1837. Jesse Bishop of Bisley, yeoman. Assaulting and beating Daniel Lewis, of Bisley, labourer. H. Burgh JP, E. P. Caruthers JP, H. Wyatt JP, and E. G. Hallewell JP at Stroud. Fine 12/6, to be paid to Richard Gibbins, overseer of the poor, and 7/6 costs to the complainant, or one calendar month in Horsley house of correction. Offence committed 14 June 1837.

56/D/82   29 Aug. 1837. Joseph Shipway of Stroud, labourer. Wilfully destroying a pint cup, the property of John Burnett of Stroud, innkeeper. H. Burgh JP at Stroud. Fine 3*d*., the value of the cup, to be paid to William Ponting, overseer of the poor, and 7/6 costs to the complainant, or hard labour for one calendar month in Horsley house of correction. Complainant examined as to proof of offence. Offence committed 28 Aug. 1837.

56/D/83   28 Aug. 1837. William Ireland of Stroud, labourer. Stealing a quantity of pears from an orchard at Stroud, the property of William Hopson, gentleman. H. Burgh JP at Stroud. Hard labour for three calendar months in Horsley house of correction. Offence committed 27 Aug. 1837.

56/D/84   28 Aug. 1837. James Clift of Stroud, labourer. Stealing a quantity of apples from an orchard in Stroud, the property of William Hopson, gentleman [*etc., as* 56/D/83].

56/D/85   9 June 1837. George Davis of Bisley, labourer. Damaging a tree in a wood at Stroud, the property of John and William Lewis, gentlemen. H. Burgh JP, E. P. Caruthers JP and E. G. Hallewell JP at Stroud. Fine 6*d*. damages and 10/6 costs to be paid to the complainants, or hard labour for one calendar month in Horsley house of correction. Offence committed 25 May 1837.

56/D/86   15 Sept. 1837. Edward Howell. Trespassing in pursuit of game on enclosed land at Stroud, the property of William Clutterbuck Chambers Esq. H. Burgh JP, E. P. Caruthers JP and E. G. Hallewell JP at Stroud. Fine £2, to be paid to William Ponting, overseer of the poor, and 12/6 costs to the complainant, or hard labour for two calendar months in Horsley house of correction. Offence committed 2 Sept. 1837.

56/D/87   15 Sept. 1837. James Hodges. Trespassing in pursuit of game on enclosed land at Stroud, [*etc., as* 56/D/86].

56/D/88   23 Sept. 1837. John Flight of King's Stanley, weaver. Using an engine for killing game at King's Stanley without possessing a game certificate. H. Burgh JP and P. Leversage JP at Stroud. Fine £5, to be paid to an overseer of the poor, and 10/- costs to the complainant, William Baker, gamekeeper, or hard labour for three calendar months in Horsley house of correction. Offence committed 22 Sept. 1837.

56/D/89   22 Sept. 1837. William Bingle, labourer of Bisley. Stealing a quarter of a peck of potatoes growing in a close of land at Bisley, the property of John Ridler, clothworker. H. Burgh JP and E. G. Hallewell JP at Stroud. Hard labour for one calendar month in Horsley house of correction. Offence committed 16 Sept. 1837.

56/D/90   22 Sept. 1837. William Bingle, labourer, of Bisley. Stealing three quarters of a peck of potatoes from a close of land at Bisley, the property of Abraham Davis, yeoman. H. Burgh JP and E. G. Hallewell JP at Stroud. Hard labour for one calendar month in Horsley house of correction. Offence committed 17 Sept. 1837.

56/D/91   22 Sept. 1837. John Cratchley, licensed beer retailer of Stroud. Keeping his house open for the sale and consumption of beer after 10 p.m. H. Burgh JP and E. G. Hallewell JP at a Petty Sessions for Bisley hundred. First offence. Fine £1 12*s*. and 8/- costs. Offence committed 16 Sept. 1837.

56/D/92   22 Sept. 1837. Charles Bingle, licensed beer retailer, of Stroud. Keeping his house open for the sale and consumption of beer between 10 a.m. and 1 p.m. on a Sunday. H. Burgh JP and E. G. Hallewell JP at a Petty Sessions for Bisley hundred. First offence. Fine £1 12*s*. and 8/- costs. Offence committed 17 Sept. 1837.

56/D/93 8 Sept. 1837. Thomas Stephens, labourer of King's Stanley. Causing an obstruction in High Street and preventing free passage-way on the foot pavement at Stroud. H. Burgh JP, E. P. Caruthers JP and E. G. Hallewell JP. Fine 5/- and 7/6 costs. Offence committed 2 Sept. 1837.

56/D/94 8 Sept. 1837. Charles Wager, labourer, of Stroud. Causing an obstruction in High Street [*etc., as* 56/D/93].

56/D/95 20 Sept. 1837. Stephen Briant. Begging in Stroud. H. Burgh JP and E. G. Hallewell JP at Stroud. Hard labour for one calendar month in Horsley house of correction. Offence committed 19 Sept. 1837.

56/D/96 18 Sept. 1837. Ann Cooke, prostitute. Wandering in a public street in Stroud and behaving in an indecent manner. H. Burgh JP at Stroud. Hard labour for one calendar month in Horsley house of correction. Offence committed 16 Sept. 1837.

56/D/97 18 Sept. 1837. Joseph Shipway. Wandering abroad and lodging in an outhouse at Stroud with no visible means of subsistence and not giving a good account of himself. H. Burgh JP at Stroud. Hard labour for one calendar month in Horsley house of correction. Offence committed 17 Sept. 1837.

56/D/98 5 May 1837. Jonathan Freeman, licensed beer retailer, of Painswick. Keeping his house open for the sale and consumption of beer between 3 p.m. and 5 p.m. on a Sunday. E. P. Caruthers JP, J. Mills JP, H. Wyatt JP and E. G. Hallewell JP, at a Petty Sessions for Bisley hundred. First offence. Fine £2 and 9/- costs. Offence committed 9 April 1837.

56/D/99 26 Sept. 1837. John Harding of Cranham. Using gins or wires to kill game at Dowdeswell when not in possession of a game certificate. F. Craven JP and W. L. Lawrence JP at Andoversford. Fine £5, one moiety of which to be paid to Edward Williams, gamekeeper, of Dowdeswell, informer and prosecutor, with 5/- costs, the remainder to be paid to Edward Arkell, overseer of the poor, or hard labour for three calendar months in Northleach house of correction. Offence committed 26 Sept. 1837.

56/D/100 26 Sept. 1837. John Heyden of Cranham. Using gins or wires to kill game at Dowdeswell [*etc., as* 56/D/99].

56/D/101 29 Aug. 1837. Thomas Smith of Winchcombe. Using gins or wires to kill game at Sevenhampton when not in possession of a game certificate. W. L. Lawrence JP and G. G. C. Talbot JP at Andoversford. Fine £5, one moiety of which to be paid to William Tombs, gamekeeper, of Winchcombe, informer and prosecutor, with 11/6 costs, and the remainder to Charles Cook, overseer of the poor, or hard labour for three calendar months in Northleach house of correction. Offence committed 27 Aug. 1837.

56/D/102 29 Aug. 1837. John Smith of Winchcombe. Using gins or wires to kill game at Sevenhampton [*etc., as* 56/D/101].

56/D/103 16 Aug. 1837. Charles Stratford of Withington. Using gins to kill game at Withington when not in possession of a game certificate. H. E. Waller JP and Rev. W. Price JP at Northleach. Fine £5, one moiety of which to be paid to John Humphris, yeoman, of Withington, informer and prosecutor, with 11/6 costs, and the remainder to John Field, overseer of the poor, or hard labour for three calendar months in Northleach house of correction. Offence committed 15 Aug. 1837.

56/D/104 27 Sept. 1837. John Festus Fegan [*also* Fagan] of Charlton Kings. Trespassing in search of game at Phelps Hill, Withington, land occupied by — Craddock, tenant of the Hon. and Rev. G. G. C. Talbot. H. E. Waller JP and Rev. W. Price JP at Northleach. Fine 7/-, one moiety of which to be paid to John Humphris, yeoman, of Withington, informer and prosecutor, with 13/- costs, and the remainder to John Field, overseer of the poor. Offence committed 15 Sept. 1837.

56/D/105 13 Sept. 1837. Joseph Hooper of Northleach. Stealing ten apples valued at one penny from an orchard at Windrush, the property of William Smith. H. E. Waller JP at Northleach. Fourteen days in Northleach house of correction. Offence committed 3 Sept. 1837.

56/D/106 6 Sept. 1837. Thomas Soul. Breaking down a stile, part of a fence, the property of Samuel Walker, at Turkdean. H. E. Waller JP, Rev. W. Price JP and Rev. G. G. C. Talbot JP at Northleach. Fine 6/6 and 5/- damages, to be paid to William Hewer, overseer of the poor, and 8/6 costs to the complainant, who was examined as to proof of the offence. Given three days to pay. In default, one calendar month in Northleach house of correction. Offence committed 2 July 1837.

56/D/107 23 Sept. 1837. Robert Watkins of Olveston, labourer. Trespassing in search of conies on land at Olveston occupied by Robert Fry Esq., the property of Samuel Peach Peach Esq. of Tockington. Rev. M. F. T. Stephens JP and Adrian Stokes JP at Thornbury. Fine £2, of which 12/2 is to be paid to James Wright, gamekeeper and agent for S. P. Peach Esq., the complainant, and 7/10 to Thomas Theobald, overseer of the poor, or seven days in Lawfords Gate house of correction. Offence committed Thursday 31 Aug. at 6.30 p.m.

56/D/108 2 Sept. 1837. William Cox of Thornbury, yeoman. Trespassing in search of game on land at Thornbury occupied by William Vizard Foxwell, tenant of Hector Maclaine Esq. Rev. M. F. T. Stephens JP and A. Stokes JP at Thornbury. Fine 10/-, to be paid to John Carwardine, overseer of the poor, and 10/- costs to John Boulton, labourer, agent for Hector Maclaine Esq., complainant, or seven days in Lawfords Gate house of correction. Offence committed 5.30 a.m. Thursday 24 Aug. 1837.

INDEX OF PERSONS AND PLACES

An asterisk * indicates that a name occurs more than once on the page. Roman lower-case numerals refer to the pages of the introduction. Places are in Gloucestershire unless otherwise indicated. The index includes the titles 'Dr.', 'Rev.' and 'Sir' prefixed to names, but not 'Esq.', 'Mr.' or 'Mrs.'. References to JPs are distinguished from those to other men of the same name or to the same men in other capacities. References to places do not distinguish those of residence, those where offences were committed, those for which officers acted and those to or from which roads ran.

Persons and places are indexed when they are implied by '*etc., as . . .*' though not actually named in the text (with the page-number in brackets if the page does not contain the name), but occurrences implied by '*Duplicate*' are not indexed.

455

SELECTIVE INDEX OF SUBJECTS

A large proportion the entries relate to the less common occupations of offenders, of complainants or victims and of informers and others, which are grouped under those three headings, and to the offences resulting in conviction, which are distributed, with cross-references from the heading 'OFFENCES'. An asterisk * indicates that a subject is mentioned more than once on the page, whether directly or by implication; if the subject is mentioned on a page only by implication the page-number in the index is in square brackets. Roman lower-case numerals refer to the pages of the introduction, in which the subjects are not comprehensively indexed.

515